Theories of Personality: *Primary Sources and Research*

Theories of Personality:

Primary Sources and Research

EDITED BY

Gardner Lindzey
University of Texas

Calvin S. Hall
Institute of Dream Research

JOHN WILEY & SONS, INC., NEW YORK · LONDON · SYDNEY

Library of Congress Catalog Card Number: 65-16416
Printed in the United States of America

THIRD CORRECTED PRINTING, AUGUST, 1968

Preface

It is now roughly seven years since we prepared a book (*Theories of Personality*) intended to provide a sympathetic and yet objective coverage of the major influential personality theories then existing. In the intervening years there have been changes both in the details of these theories and in the existing research that relates to them. The present volume is intended to provide a reasonable representation of contemporary theoretical contributions and at the same time to give a sample of the most interesting and pertinent empirical studies available. In addition, it seeks to enrich the original book by placing the reader in direct contact with the thinking and writing of many of the major personality theorists.

A systematic summary of the major ideas of important intellectual figures serves an essential didactic role, especially in view of the fact that the most creative and influential theorists have seldom devoted much of their energy to summarizing and systematizing their ideas; but it remains a matter of first importance that students be exposed directly to the original writings of these contributors. This is particularly necessary in an area where there is relatively little in the way of formal elegance and where much of the impact of any theory is indirect, heuristic, and mediated by complex processes that do not involve formal deductions and specific hypothesis testing.

Although the various theories showed considerable difference in the quantity of material that was available for inclusion, all offered many alternatives. Consequently, it was necessary to establish criteria for selection that would provide a rational basis for eliminating all but the few items that space permitted us to include.

In the selection of material written by the originator of the theory, that is, *primary sources*, we were guided by the following considerations:

1. The material included should be representative of the theorist both in regard to the content of his ideas and his usual style of thinking and writing.

2. The content of the paper should deal with one or more issues that are central to the position of the theorist.

3. If possible the paper should include not only theoretical statement and supporting reasoning but also empirical data of the sort that the theorist often used in developing or defending his conceptual position.

4. It should be relatively self-contained so that the reader can appreciate its message without exposure to other related papers.

5. It should be comprehensible to an advanced undergraduate or graduate student who has not had specialized training in this area of psychology.

6. Where feasible it should provide insight into changes that have been introduced by the theorist since the time that *Theories of Personality* was prepared.

v

The major considerations that influenced our selection of empirical studies were:

1. Where possible the article should provide clear evidence relevant to a hypothesis explicitly derived from the relevant theory. Just as our original book was focused on a statement of the positive aspects of the various theories, so here we were less interested in studies that provided negative results than those that provided confirmatory findings.

2. Where possible the research should be contemporary, objective, and quantitative.

3. Preferably the study should not have been discussed in *Theories of Personality*.

4. Reasonable diversity should be achieved so that as many varieties of different types of derivative research as possible could be represented.

5. Where possible we selected studies that deal with research topics that possess theoretical relevance and at the same time are of some intrinsic interest to persons interested in human behavior.

6. The paper should be comprehensible to an advanced undergraduate student or graduate student who has not had previous training in this area of psychology.

It is our conviction that these papers will be read with more comprehension and interest when they are coupled with the chapters contained in *Theories of Personality*. However, we do not consider them dependent on the other book so that they can be used independently.

March 1, 1965

GARDNER LINDZEY
CALVIN S. HALL

Acknowledgments

We wish to acknowledge helpful advice and assistance received from the following persons: Gordon W. Allport, H. L. Ansbacher, Raymond B. Cattell, Max Dertke, J. H. Eysenck, I. E. Farber, James Hillman, Richard M. Jones, A. H. Maslow, Gardner Murphy, Henry A. Murray, Morris B. Parloff, Julie Reventos, Pauline S. Sears, M. Brewster Smith, Otto Allen Will, Jr., Ruth C. Wylie. Calvin Hall wishes to acknowledge the assistance he received from Robert L. Van de Castle in making selections for this volume. He was aided by Dr. Van de Castle from the inception of the project in combing the literature for appropriate articles and in screening them. The final choices represent, therefore, a joint undertaking of search, screening, and selection by Hall and Van de Castle. Gardner Lindzey was in residence at The Center for Advanced Study in the Behavioral Sciences while preparing this book and is deeply grateful to Ralph Tyler and his staff for facilitating his work.

G.L.
C.S.H.

Contents

SECTION XII MURPHY'S BIOSOCIAL THEORY

Freud's Psychoanalytic Theory

In selecting articles to represent Freud's theory and the research which it has generated, one is confronted by a profusion of riches. For not only are there the twenty-three volumes of Freud's psychological writings which constitute the primary source but there are also a multitude of volumes written by his fellow workers which, in many cases, are substantial additions to the theoretical fountainhead. As for the research, even if we limit ourselves only to that which is in accord with the positivistic tradition of American psychology, there is so much to choose from that the final selection becomes very difficult. Many papers that we would like to include have had to be omitted for lack of space.

When one surveys this empirical literature, it hardly seems possible that Sears' rather bleak overview of psychoanalytically oriented research was published less than twenty-five years ago. The situation is far from bleak today. The sophistication of investigators with respect both to methodology and to derivation of relevant hypotheses from Freudian theory has grown greatly in the last ten years. No other theory, apart from behaviorism, has stirred up so many first-rate investigations; no other current theory aside from behaviorism and self theory has generated so many hypotheses which have been confirmed. Not the least of one's astonishment over this state of affairs arises from the fact that Freud's theory, which grew out of his observations of patients, is now being confirmed not only by studies using college sophomores as subjects but also by experiments making use of the American psychologists' other favorite animal, the rat—or in the case of the experiment reprinted in this chapter, his diminutive cousin, the mouse.

The selections from the primary sources are restricted to the works of Freud, although as intimated before one could also have made selections from the writings of Abraham, Ferenczi, Roheim, Jones, Melanie Klein, Anna Freud, and a number of others. The first paper, *Instincts and Their Vicissitudes*, represents Freud's metapsychological contributions. By metapsychological Freud meant describing a psychical process in its dynamic,

1

topographical, and economic aspects. *Instincts and Their Vicissitudes* was selected for several reasons. First, it deals with one of the key concepts in classical psychoanalysis, and one of its most controversial ones. Second, unlike some of his other papers, it is not too difficult for the reader who is being introduced to Freud for the first time. Third, it displays the careful, step-by-step analysis which is characteristic of Freud's writings.

The second paper, *Some Psychical Consequences of Anatomical Distinction between the Sexes*, was chosen because it deals with a topic that engaged Freud's attention throughout his life. Libido theory and its applications which were first developed at length in *Three Essays on Sexuality* were topics that Freud returned to again and again. With each return he brought new insights. The ideas set forth in the present paper represent Freud's final views regarding sex differences.

Freud is seen in his work clothes in the third selection. He is writing as a therapist and dream interpreter. The dream of the white wolves is probably the most thoroughly analyzed dream in all of Freud's writings not excepting those in *The Interpretation of Dreams*. For, as our colleague Richard Jones has pointed out to us, no dream in that great volume is carried back to an infantile wish. The one presented here is. It is a magnificent *tour de force* of dream analysis.

The research papers reflect as many dimensions of contemporary investigatory activity as could be accommodated in this volume. They are all quantitative and well-controlled, represent a variety of subject populations, and in all of them the hypotheses under investigation were confirmed.

The first paper by Hall and Van de Castle makes use of dreams in order to test a hypothesis regarding sex differences discussed by Freud in the second of his papers reprinted here.

The second paper by Adelson and Redmond represents a sophisticated extension of the work that has been done on the repression out of consciousness of threatening experiences. The investigators use the Blacky Test which was devised by Gerald Blum in order to assess the relative strengths of the various psychosexual components. By means of this test, Adelson and Redmond identify two contrasting groups, anal retentives and anal expulsives, and find, as they predicted, that anal retentives remember more than anal expulsives.

An outstanding feature of the Zamansky paper is the ingenious technique and excellent controls he devised for assessing homosexual tendencies, in order to test the hypothesis that latent homosexuality is implicated in paranoid delusions. It shows what great strides have been made in methodology since the publication of Sears' survey of psychoanalytically oriented research.

The last paper in this showcase of empirical studies demonstrates that in order to test certain Freudian propositions it is necessary to employ a type of animal whose genetic constitution and environment can be manipulated and controlled more precisely than is possible with human subjects.

1. Instincts and their vicissitudes

SIGMUND FREUD

WE HAVE OFTEN HEARD IT MAINTAINED that sciences should be built up on clear and sharply defined basic concepts. In actual fact no science, not even the most exact, begins with such definitions. The true beginning of scientific activity consists rather in describing phenomena and then in proceeding to group, classify and correlate them. Even at the stage of description it is not possible to avoid applying certain abstract ideas to the material in hand, ideas derived from somewhere or other but certainly not from the new observations alone. Such ideas —which will later become the basic concepts of the science—are still more indispensable as the material is further worked over. They must at first necessarily possess some degree of indefiniteness; there can be no question of any clear delimitation of their content. So long as they remain in this condition, we come to an understanding about their meaning by making repeated references to the material of observation from which they have been imposed. Thus, strictly speaking, they are in the nature of conventions—although everything depends on their not being arbitrarily chosen but determined by their having significant relations to the empirical material, relations that we seem to sense before we can clearly recognize and demonstrate them. It is only after more thorough investigation of the field of observation that we are able to formulate its basic scientific concepts with increased precision, and progressively so to modify them that they become serviceable and consistent over a wide area. Then, indeed, the time may have come to confine them in definitions.

SOURCE. Selection from Sigmund Freud, "Instincts and their vicissitudes" in *The Standard Edition*, Vol. XIV, pp. 117–140. London: The Hogarth Press, 1957 (First published 1915).

The advance of knowledge, however, does not tolerate any rigidity even in definitions. Physics furnishes an excellent illustration of the way in which even "basic concepts" that have been established in the form of definitions are constantly being altered in their content.

A conventional basic concept of this kind, which at the moment is still somewhat obscure but which is indispensable to us in psychology, is that of an "instinct." Let us try to give a content to it by approaching it from different angles.

First, from the angle of *physiology*. This has given us the concept of a "stimulus" and the pattern of the reflex arc, according to which a stimulus applied to living tissue (nervous substance) *from* the outside is discharged by action *to* the outside. This action is expedient in so far as it withdraws the stimulated substance from the influence of the stimulus, removes it out of its range of operation.

What is the relation of "instinct" to "stimulus"? There is nothing to prevent our subsuming the concept of "instinct" under that of "stimulus" and saying that an instinct is a stimulus applied to the mind. But we are immediately set on our guard against *equating* instinct and mental stimulus. There are obviously other stimuli to the mind besides those of an instinctual kind, stimuli which behave far more like physiological ones. For example, when a strong light falls on the eye, it is not an instinctual stimulus; it *is* one, however, when a dryness of the mucous membrane of the pharynx or an irritation of the mucous membrane of the stomach makes itself felt.

We have now obtained the material necessary for distinguishing between instinctual stimuli and other (physiological) stimuli that operate on the mind. In the first place, an instinctual stimulus does not arise from the external world but from within the organism itself. For this reason it operates differently upon the mind and different actions are necessary in order to remove it. Further, all that is essential in a stimulus is covered if we assume that it operates with a single impact, so that it can be disposed of by a single expedient action. A typical instance of this is motor flight from the source of stimulation. These impacts may, of course, be repeated and summated, but that makes no difference to our notion of the process and to the conditions for the removal of the stimulus. An instinct, on the other hand, never operates as a force giving a *momentary* impact but always as a constant one. Moreover, since it impinges not from without but from within the organism, no flight can avail against it. A better term for an instinctual stimulus is a "need." What does away with a need is "satisfaction." This can be attained only by an appropriate ("adequate") alteration of the internal source of stimulation.

Let us imagine ourselves in the situation of an almost entirely helpless living organism, as yet unoriented in the world, which is receiving stimuli in its nervous substance. This organism will very soon be in a position to make a first distinction and a first orientation. On the one hand, it will be aware of stimuli which can be avoided by muscular action (flight); these it ascribes to an external world. On the other hand, it will also be aware of stimuli against which such action is of no avail and whose character of constant pressure persists in spite of it; these stimuli are the signs of an internal world, the evidence of instinctual needs. The perceptual substance of the living organism will thus have found in the efficacy of its muscular activity a basis for distinguishing between an "outside" and an "inside."

We thus arrive at the essential nature of instincts in the first place by considering their main characteristics—their origin in source of stimulation within the organism and their appearance as a constant force—and from this we deduce one of their further features, namely, that no actions of flight avail against them. In the course of this discussion, however, we cannot fail to be struck by something that obliges us to make a further admission. In order to guide us in dealing with the field of psychological phenomena, we do not merely apply certain conventions to our empirical material as basic

concepts: we also make use of a number of complicated *postulates.* We have already alluded to the most important of these, and all we need now do is to state it expressly. This postulate is of a biological nature, and makes use of the concept of "purpose" (or perhaps of expediency) and runs as follows: the nervous system is an apparatus which has the function of getting rid of the stimuli that reach it, or reducing them to the lowest possible level; or which, if it were feasible, would maintain itself in an altogether unstimulated condition. Let us for the present not take exception to the indefiniteness of this idea and let us assign to the nervous system the task—speaking in general terms—of *mastering stimuli.* We then see how greatly the simple pattern of the physiological reflex is complicated by the introduction of instincts. External stimuli impose only the single task of withdrawing from them; this is accomplished by muscular movements, one of which eventually achieves that aim and thereafter, being the expedient movement, becomes a hereditary disposition. Instinctual stimuli, which originate from within the organism, cannot be dealt with by this mechanism. Thus they make far higher demands on the nervous system and cause it to undertake involved and interconnected activities by which the external world is so changed as to afford satisfaction to the internal source of stimulation. Above all, they oblige the nervous system to renounce its ideal intention of keeping off stimuli, for they maintain an incessant and unavoidable afflux of stimulation. We may therefore well conclude that instincts and not external stimuli are the true motive forces behind the advances that have led the nervous system, with its unlimited capacities, to its present high level of development. There is naturally nothing to prevent our supposing that the instincts themselves are, at least in part, precipitates of the effects of external stimulation, which in the course of phylogenesis have brought about modifications in the living substance.

When we further find that the activity of even the most highly developed mental apparatus is subject to the pleasure principle, i.e., is automatically regulated by feelings belonging to the pleasure–unpleasure series, we can hardly reject the further hypothesis that these feelings reflect the manner in which the process of mastering stimuli takes place—certainly in the sense that unpleasurable feelings are connected with an increase and pleasurable feelings with a decrease of stimulus. We will, however, carefully preserve this assumption in its present highly indefinite form, until we succeed, if that is possible, in discovering what sort of relation exists between pleasure and unpleasure, on the one hand, and fluctuations in the amounts of stimulus affecting mental life, on the other. It is certain that many very various relations of this kind, and not very simple ones, are possible.

If now we apply ourselves to considering mental life from a *biological* point of view, an "instinct" appears to us as a concept on the frontier between the mental and the somatic, as the psychical representative of the stimuli originating from within the organism and reaching the mind, as a measure of the demand made upon the mind for work in consequence of its connection with the body.

We are now in a position to discuss certain terms which are used in reference to the concept of an instinct—for example, its "pressure," its "aim," its "object" and its "source."

By the pressure (*Drang*) of an instinct we understand its motor factor, the amount of force or the measure of the demand for work which it represents. The characteristic of exercising pressure is common to all instincts; it is in fact their very essence. Every instinct is a piece of activity; if we speak loosely of passive instincts, we can only mean instincts whose *aim* is passive.

The aim (*Ziel*) of an instinct is in every instance satisfaction, which can only be obtained by removing the state of stimulation at the source of the instinct. But although the ultimate aim of each instinct remains unchangeable, there may yet be different paths leading to the same ultimate aim; so that an instinct may be found to have various nearer or intermediate aims, which are combined or interchanged with one another. Experience permits us to also to speak of instincts which are "inhibited in their aim," in the case of processes which are allowed to make some advance towards instinctual satisfaction but are then inhibited or deflected. We many suppose that even processes of this kind involve a partial satisfaction.

The object (*Objekt*) of an instinct is the thing in regard to which or through which the instinct is able to achieve its aim. It is what is most variable about an instinct and is not originally connected with it, but becomes assigned to it only in consequence of being peculiarly fitted to make satisfaction possible.

The object is not necessarily something extraneous: it may equally well be a part of the subject's own body. It may be changed any number of times in the course of the vicissitudes which the instinct undergoes during its existence; and highly important parts are played by this displacement of instinct. It may happen that the same object serves for the satisfaction of several instincts simultaneously, a phenomenon which Adler has called a "confluence" of instincts (*Triebverschrankung*). A particularly close attachment of the instinct to its object is distinguished by the term "fixation." This frequently occurs at very early periods of the development of an instinct and puts an end to its mobility through its intense opposition to detachment.

By the source (*Quelle*) of an instinct is meant the somatic process which occurs in an organ or part of the body and whose stimulus is represented in mental life by an instinct. We do not know whether this process is invariably of a chemical nature or whether it may also correspond to the release of other, e.g., mechanical, forces. The study of the sources of instincts lies outside the scope of psychology. Although instincts are wholly determined by their origin in a somatic source, in mental life we know them only by their aims. An exact knowledge of the sources of an instinct is not invariably necessary for purposes of psychological investigation; sometimes its source may be inferred from its aim.

Are we to suppose that the different instincts which originate in the body and operate on the mind are also distinguished by different *qualities,* and that that is why they behave in qualitatively different ways in mental life? This supposition does not seem to be justified; we are much more likely to find the simpler assumption sufficient—that the instincts are all qualitatively alike and owe the effect that they make only to the amount of excitation they carry, or perhaps, in addition, to certain functions of that quantity. What distinguishes from one another the mental effects produced by the various instincts may be traced to the difference in their sources. In any event, it is only in a later connection that we shall be able to make plain what the problem of the quality of instincts signifies.

What instincts should we suppose there are, and how many? There is obviously a wide opportunity here for arbitrary choice. No objection can be made to anyone's employing the concept of an instinct of play or of destruction or of gregariousness, when the subject-matter demands it and the limitations of psychological analysis allow of it. Nevertheless, we should not neglect to ask ourselves whether instinctual motives like these, which are so highly specialized on the one hand, do not admit of further dissection in accordance with the *sources* of the instinct, so that only primal instincts—those which cannot be further dissected—can lay claim to importance.

I have proposed that two groups of such primal instincts should be distinguished: the *ego*, or self-preservative instincts, and the *sexual* instincts. But this supposition has not the status of a necessary postulate, as has, for instance, our assumption about the biological purpose of the mental apparatus; it is merely a working hypothesis, to be retained only so long as it proves useful, and it will make little difference to the results of our work of description and classification if it is replaced by another. The occasion for the hypothesis arose in the course of the evolution of psycho-analysis, which was first employed upon the psychoneuroses, or, more precisely, upon the group described as "transference neuroses" (hysteria and obsessional neurosis); these showed that at the root of all such affections there is to be found a conflict between the claims of sexuality and those of the ego. It is always possible that an exhaustive study of the other neurotic affections (especially of the narcissistic psychoneuroses, the schizophrenias) may oblige us to alter this formula and to make a different classification of the primal instincts. But for the present we do not know of any such formula, nor have we met with any argument unfavourable to drawing this contrast between sexual and ego-instincts.

I am altogether doubtful whether any decisive pointers for the differentiation and classification of the instincts can be arrived at on the basis of working over the psychological material. This working-over seems rather itself to call for the application to the material of definite assumptions concerning instinctual life, and it would be a desirable thing if those assumptions could be taken from some other branch of knowledge and carried over to psychology. The contribution which biology has to make here certainly does not run counter to the distinction between sexual and ego-instincts. Biology teaches that sexuality is not to be put on a par with other functions of the individual;

for its purposes go beyond the individual and have as their content the production of new individuals—that is, the preservation of the species. It shows, further, that two views, seemingly equally well-founded, may be taken of the relation between the ego and sexuality. On the one view, the individual is the principal thing, sexuality is one of its activities, and sexual satisfaction one of its needs; while on the other view the individual is a temporary and transient appendage to the quasi-immortal germ-plasm, which is entrusted to him by the process of generation. The hypothesis that the sexual function differs from other bodily processes in virtue of a special chemistry is, I understand, also a postulate of the Ehrlich school of biological research.

Since a study of instinctual life from the direction of consciousness presents almost insuperable difficulties, the principal source of our knowledge remains the psycho-analytic investigation of mental disturbances. Psycho-analysis, however, in consequence of the course taken by its development, has hitherto been able to give us information of a fairly satisfactory nature only about the *sexual* instincts; for it is precisely that group which alone can be observed in isolation, as it were, in the psychoneuroses. With the extension of psycho-analysis to the other neurotic affections, we shall no doubt find a basis for our knowledge of the ego-instincts as well, though it would be rash to expect equally favourable conditions for observation in this further field of research.

This much can be said by way of a general characterization of the sexual instincts. They are numerous, emanate from a great variety of organic sources, act in the first instance independently of one another and only achieve a more or less complete synthesis at a late state. The aim which each of them strives for is the attainment of "organ-pleasure"; only when synthesis is achieved do they enter the service of the reproductive function and thereupon become generally recognizable as sexual instincts. At their first appearance they are attached to the instincts of self-preservation, from which they only gradually become separated; in their choice of object, too, they follow the paths that are indicated to them by the ego-instincts throughout life and furnish them with libidinal components, which in normal functioning easily escape notice and are revealed clearly only by the onset of illness. They are distinguished by possessing the capacity to act vicariously for one another to a wide extent and by being able to change their objects readily. In consequence of the latter properties they are capable of functions which are far removed from their original purposive actions—capable, that is, of "sublimation."

Our inquiry into the various vicissitudes which instincts undergo in the process of development and in the course of life must be confined to the sexual instincts, which are the more familiar to us. Observation shows us that an instinct may undergo the following vicissitudes: reversal into its opposite; turning round upon the subject's own self; repression and sublimation.

Since I do not intend to treat of sublimation here and since repression requires a special chapter to itself, it only remains for us to describe and discuss the two first points. Bearing in mind that there are motive forces which work against an instinct's being carried through in an unmodified form, we may also regard these vicissitudes as modes of *defence* against the instincts.

Reversal of an instinct into its opposite resolves on closer examination into two different processes: a change from activity to passivity, and a reversal of its content. The two processes, being different in their nature, must be treated separately.

Examples of the first process are met with in the two pairs of opposites: sadism—masochism and scopophilia—exhibitionism. The reversal affects only the *aims* of the instincts. The active aim (to torture, to look at) is replaced by the passive aim (to be tortured, to be looked at). Reversal of *content* is found in the single instance of the transformation of love into hate.

The turning round of an instinct upon the subject's own self is made plausible by the reflection that masochism is actually sadism turned round upon the subject's own ego, and that exhibitionism includes looking at his own body. Analytic observation, indeed, leaves us in no doubt that the masochist shares in the enjoyment of the assault upon himself, and that the exhibitionist shares in the enjoyment of (the sight of) his exposure. The essence of the process is thus the change of the *object*, while the aim remains unchanged. We cannot fail to notice, however, that in these examples the turning round upon the subject's self and the transformation from activity to passivity converge or coincide.

To elucidate the situation, a more thorough investigation is essential.

In the case of the pair of opposites sadism—masochism, the process may be represented as follows: (*a*) Sadism consists in the exercise of violence or power upon some other person as object. (*b*) This object is given up and replaced by the subject's self. With the turning round upon the self the change from an active to a passive instinctual aim is also effected. (*c*) An extraneous person is once more sought as object; this person, in consequence of the alteration which has taken place in the instinctual aim, has to take over the role of the subject.

Case (*c*) is what is commonly termed masochism. Here, too, satisfaction follows along the path of the original sadism, the passive ego placing itself back in phantasy in its first role, which has now in fact been taken over by the extraneous subject. Whether there is, besides this, a more direct mashochistic satisfaction is highly doubtful. A primary masochism, not derived from sadism in the manner I have described, seems not to be met with. That it is not superfluous to assume the existence of stage (*b*) is to be seen from the behavior of the sadistic instinct in obsessional neurosis. There is a turning round upon the subject's self *without* an attitude of passivity towards another person: the change has only got as far as stage (*b*). The desire to torture has turned into self-torture and self-punishment, not into masochism. The active voice is changed, not into the passive, but into the reflexive, middle voice.

Our view of sadism is further prejudiced by the circumstance that this instinct, side by side with its general aim (or perhaps, rather, within it), seems to strive towards the accomplishment of a quite special aim—not only to humiliate and master, but, in addition, to inflict pains. Psycho-analysis would appear to show that the infliction of pain plays no part among the original purposive actions of the instinct. A sadistic child takes no account of whether or not he inflicts pains, nor does he intend to do so. But when once the transformation into masochism has taken place, the pains are very well fitted to provide a passive masochistic aim; for we have every reason to believe that sensations of pain, like other unpleasurable sensations, trench upon sexual excitation and produce a pleasurable condition, for the sake of which the subject will even willingly experience the unpleasure of pain. When once feeling pains has become a masochistic aim, the sadistic aim of *causing* pains can arise also, retrogressively; for while these pains are being inflicted on other people, they are enjoyed masochistically by the subject through his identification of himself with the suffering object. In both cases, of course, it is not the pain itself which is enjoyed, but the accompanying sexual excitation—so that this can be done especially conveniently from the sadistic position. The enjoyment of pain would thus be an aim which was originally masochistic, but which can only become an instinctual aim in someone who was originally sadistic.

For the sake of completeness I may add that feelings of pity cannot be described as a result of a transformation of instinct occurring in sadism, but necessitate the notion of a *reaction-formation* against that instinct. (For the difference, see later.)

Rather different and simpler findings are afforded by the investigation of another pair of opposites—the instincts whose respective aim is to look and to display oneself (scopophilia and exhibitionism, in the language of the perversions). Here again we may postulate the same stages as in the previous instance: (*a*) Looking

as an *activity* directed towards an extraneous object. (*b*) Giving up of the object and turning of the scopophilic instinct towards a part of the subject's own body; with this, transformation to passivity and setting up of a new aim —that of being looked at. (*c*) Introduction of a new subject to whom one displays oneself in order to be looked at by him. Here, too, it can hardly be doubted that the active aim appears before the passive, that looking precedes being looked at. But there is an important divergence from what happens in the case of sadism, in that we can recognize in the case of the scopophilic instinct a yet earlier stage than that described as (*a*). For the beginning of its activity the scopophilic instinct is auto-erotic: it has indeed an object, but that object is part of the subject's own body. It is only later that the instinct is led, by a process of comparison, to exchange this object for an analogous part of someone else's body—stage (*a*). This preliminary state is interesting because it is the source of *both* the situations represented in the resulting pair of opposites, the one or the other according to which element in the original situation is changed. The following might serve as a diagrammatic picture of the scopophilic instinct:

(a) Oneself looking at   =   A sexual organ being
       a sexual organ   looked at by oneself
                    | |
(b) Oneself looking at an extraneous object   (c) An object which is oneself or part of
       (active scopophilia)   oneself being looked at by an extraneous person (exhibitionism)

A preliminary stage of this kind is absent in sadism, which from the outset is directed upon an extraneous object, although it might not be altogether unreasonable to construct such a stage out of the child's efforts to gain control over his own limbs.

With regard to both the instincts which we have just taken as examples, it should be remarked that their transformation by a reversal from activity to passivity and by a turning round upon the subject never in fact involves the whole quota of the instinctual impulse. The earlier active direction of the instinct persists to some degree side by side with its later passive direction, even when the process of its transformation has been very extensive. The only correct statement to make about the

scopophilic instinct would be that the stages of its development, its auto-erotic, preliminary stage as well as its final active or passive form, co-exist alongside one another; and the truth of this becomes obvious if we base our opinion, not on the actions to which the instinct leads, but on the mechanism of its satisfaction. Perhaps, however, it is permissible to look at the matter and represent it in yet another way. We can divide the life of each instinct into a series of separate successive waves, each of which is homogeneous during whatever period of time it may last, and whose relation to one another is comparable to that of successive eruptions of lava. We can then perhaps picture the first, original eruption of the instinct as proceeding in an unchanged form and undergoing no development at all. The next wave would be modified from the outset —being turned, for instance from active to passive—and would then with this new characteristic, be added to the earlier wave, and so on. If we were then to take a survey of the instinctual impulse from its beginning up to a given point, the succession of waves which we have described would inevitably present the picture of a definite development of the instinct.

The fact that, at this later period of development of an instinctual impulse, its (passive) opposite may be observed alongside of it deserves to be marked by the very apt term introduced by Bleuler—"ambivalence."

This reference to the developmental history of instincts and the permanence of their intermediate stages should make the development of instincts fairly intelligible to us. Experience shows that the amount of demonstrable ambivalence varies greatly between individuals, groups and races. Marked instinctual ambivalence in a human being living at the present day may be regarded as an archaic inheritance, for we have reason to suppose that the part played in instinctual life by the active impulses in their unmodified form was greater in primaeval times than it is on an average today.

We have become accustomed to call the early phase of the development of the ego, during which its sexual instincts find auto-erotic satisfaction, "narcissism," without at once entering on any discussion of the relation between auto-erotism and narcissism. It follows that the preliminary stage of the scopophilic instinct, in which the subject's own body is the object of the scopophilia, must be classed under narcissism, and that we must describe it as a narcissistic formation. The active scopophilic instinct develops from this, by leaving narcissism behind. The passive scopophilic instinct, on the contrary, holds fast to the narcissistic object. Similarly, the transformation of sadism into masochism implies a return to the narcissistic object. And in both these cases (i.e., in passive scopophilia and masochism) the narcissistic *subject* is, through identification, replaced by another, extraneous ego. If we take into account our constructed preliminary narcissistic stage of sadism, we shall be approaching a more general realization—namely, that the instinctual vicissitudes which consist in the instinct's being turned round upon the subject's own ego and undergoing reversal from activity to passivity are dependent on the narcissistic organization of the ego and bear the stamp of that phase. They perhaps correspond to the attempts at defence which at higher stages of the development of the ego are effected by other means.

At this point we may call to mind that so far we have considered only two pairs of opposite instincts: sadism–masochism and scopophilia–exhibitionism. These are the best known sexual instincts that appear in ambivalent manner. The other components of the later sexual function are not yet sufficiently accessible to analysis for us to be able to discuss them in a similar way. In general we can assert of them that their activities are *auto-erotic;* that is to say, their object is negligible in comparison with the organ which is their source, and as a rule coincides with that organ. The object of the scopophilic instinct, however, though it too is in the first instance a part of the subject's own body, is not the eye itself; and in sadism the organic source, which is probably the muscular apparatus with its capacity for action, points unequivocally at an object other than itself, even though that object is part of the subject's own body. In the auto-erotic instincts, the part played by the organic source is so decisive that, according to a plausible suggestion of Federn and Jekels, the form and function of the organ determine the activity or passivity of the instinctual aim.

The change of the *content* of an instinct into its opposite is observed in a single instance only —the transformation of *love into hate*. Since it is particularly common to find both these directed simultaneously towards the same object, their co-existence furnishes the most important example of ambivalence of feeling.

The case of love and hate acquires a special interest from the circumstance that it refuses to be fitted into our scheme of the instincts. It is impossible to doubt that there is the most intimate relation between these two opposite feelings and sexual life, but we are naturally unwilling to think of love as being some kind of special component instinct of sexuality in the same way as the others we have been discussing. We should prefer to regard loving as the expression of the *whole* sexual current of feeling; but this idea does not clear up our difficulties, and we cannot see what meaning to attach to an opposite content of this current.

Loving admits not merely of one, but of three opposites. In addition to the antithesis "loving–hating," there is the other of "loving–

being loved"; and, in addition to these, loving and hating taken together are the opposite of the condition of unconcern or indifference. The second of these three antitheses, loving–being loved, corresponds exactly to the transformation from activity to passivity and may be traced to an underlying situation in the same way as in the case of the scopophilic instinct. This situation is that of *loving oneself*, which we regard as the characteristic feature of narcissism. Then, according as the object or the subject is replaced by an extraneous one, what results is the active aim of loving or the passive one of being loved—the latter remaining near to narcissism.

Perhaps we shall come to a better understanding of the several opposites of loving if we reflect that our mental life as a whole is governed by *three polarities,* the antitheses:

Subject (ego)–Object (external world),
Pleasure–Unpleasure,
Active–Passive.

The antithesis ego–non-ego (external), i.e., subject–object, is, as we have already said, thrust upon the individual organism at an early stage, by the experience that it can silence *external* stimuli by means of muscular action but is defenceless against *instinctual* stimuli. This antithesis remains, above all, sovereign in our intellectual activity and creates for research the basic situation which no efforts can alter. The polarity of pleasure–unpleasure is attached to a scale of feelings, whose paramount importance in determining our actions (our will) has already been emphasized. The antithesis active–passive must not be confused with the antithesis ego-subject–external world-object. The relation of the ego to the external world is passive in so far as it receives stimuli from it and active when it reacts to these. It is forced by its instincts into a quite special degree of activity towards the external world, so that we might bring out the essential point if we say that the ego-subject is passive in respect of external stimuli but active through its own instincts. The antithesis active–passive coalesces later with the antithesis masculine–feminine, which, until this has taken place, has no psychological meaning. The coupling of activity with masculinity and of passivity with femininity meets us, indeed, as a biological fact; but it is by no means so invariably complete and exclusive as we are inclined to assume.

The three polarities of the mind are connected with one another in various highly significant ways. There is a primal psychical situation in which two of them coincide. Originally, at the very beginning of mental life, the ego is cathected with instincts and is to some extent capable of satisfying them on itself. We call this condition "narcissism" and this way of obtaining satisfaction "auto-erotic." At this time the external world is not cathected with interest (in a general sense) and is indifferent for purposes of satisfaction. During this period, therefore, the ego-subject coincides with what is pleasurable and the external world with what is indifferent (or possibly unpleasurable; as being a source of stimulation). If for the moment we define loving as the relation of the ego to its sources of pleasure, the situation in which the ego loves itself only and is indifferent to the external world illustrates the first of the opposites which we found to "loving."

In so far as the ego is auto-erotic, it has no need of the external world, but, in consequence of experiences undergone by the instincts of self-preservation, it acquires objects from that world, and, in spite of everything, it cannot avoid feeling internal instinctual stimuli for a time as unpleasurable. Under the dominance of the pleasure principle a further development now takes place in the ego. In so far as the objects which are presented to it are sources of pleasure, it takes them into itself, "introjects" them (to use Ferenczi's term); and, on the other hand, it expels whatever within itself becomes a cause of unpleasure.

Thus the original "reality-ego," which distinguished internal and external by means of a sound objective criterion, changes into a purified "pleasure-ego," which places the characteristic of pleasure above all others. For the pleasure-ego the external world is divided into a part that is pleasurable, which it has incorporated into itself, and a remainder that is extraneous to it. It has separated off a part of its own self, which it projects into the external world and feels as hostile. After this new arrangement, the two polarities coincide once more: the ego-subject coincides with pleasure, and the external world with unpleasure (with what was earlier indifference).

When, during the stage of primary narcissism, the object makes its appearance, the second opposite to loving, namely hating, also attains its development.

As we have seen, the object is brought to the ego from the external world in the first instance by the instincts of self-preservation; and it cannot be denied that hating, too, originally characterized the relation of the ego to the alien external world with the stimuli it introduces. Indifference falls into place as a special case of hate or dislike, after having first appeared as their forerunner. At the very beginning, it seems, the external world, objects, and what is hated are identical. If later on an object turns out to be a source of pleasure, it is loved, but it is also incorporated into the ego; so that for the purified pleasure-ego once again objects coincide with what is extraneous and hated.

Now, however, we may note that just as the pair of opposites love–indifference reflects the polarity ego–external world, so the second antithesis love–hate reproduces the polarity pleasure–unpleasure, which is linked to the first polarity. When the purely narcissistic stage has given place to the object-stage, pleasure and unpleasure signify relations of the ego to the object. If the object becomes a source of pleasurable feelings, a motor urge is set up which seeks to bring the object closer to the ego and to incorporate it into the ego. We then speak of the "attraction" exercised by the pleasure-giving object, and say that we "love" that object. Conversely, if the object is a source of unpleasurable feelings, there is an urge which endeavors to increase the distance between the object and the ego and to repeat in relation to the object the original attempt at flight from the external world with its emission of stimuli. We feel the "repulsion" of the object, and hate it; this hate can afterwards be intensified to the point of an aggressive inclination against the object—an intention to destroy it.

We might at a pinch say of an instinct that it "loves" the objects towards which it strives for purposes of satisfaction; but to say that an instinct "hates" an object strikes us as odd. Thus we become aware that the attitudes of love and hate cannot be made use of for the relations of *instincts* to their objects, but are reserved for the relations of the *total ego* to objects. But if we consider linguistic usage, which is certainly not without significance, we shall see that there is a further limitation of the meaning of love and hate. We do not say of objects which serve the interests of self-preservation that we *love* them; we emphasize the fact that we *need* them, and perhaps express an addi-

tional, different kind of relation to them by using words that denote a much reduced degree of love—such as, for example, "being fond of," "liking" or "finding agreeable."

Thus the word "to love" moves further and further into the sphere of the pure pleasure-relation of the ego to the object and finally becomes fixed to sexual objects in the narrower sense and to those which satisfy the needs of sublimated sexual instincts. The distinction between the ego-instincts and the sexual instincts which we have imposed upon our psychology is thus seen to be in conformity with the spirit of our language. The fact that we are not in the habit of saying of a single sexual instinct that it loves its object, but regard the relation of the ego to its sexual object as the most appropriate case in which to employ the word "love"—this fact teaches us that the word can only begin to be applied in this relation after there has been a synthesis of all the component instincts of sexuality under the primacy of the genitals and in the service of the reproductive function.

It is noteworthy that in the use of the word "hate" no such intimate connection with sexual pleasure and the sexual function appears. The relation of *unpleasure* seems to be the sole decisive one. The ego hates, abhors and pursues with intent to destroy all objects which are a source of unpleasurable feeling for it, without taking into account whether they mean a frustration of sexual satisfaction or of the satisfaction of self-preservative needs. Indeed, it may be asserted that the true prototypes of the relation of hate are derived not from sexual life, but from the ego's struggle to preserve and maintain itself.

So we see that love and hate, which present themselves to us as complete opposites in their content, do not after all stand in any simple relation to each other. They did not arise from the cleavage of any originally common entity, but sprang from different sources, and had each its own development before the influence of the pleasure–unpleasure relation made them into opposites.

It now remains for us to put together what we know of the genesis of love and hate. Love is derived from the capacity of the ego to satisfy some of its instinctual impulses auto-erotically by obtaining organ-pleasure. It is originally narcissistic, then passes over on to objects, which have been incorporated into the extended ego, and expresses the motor efforts of the ego towards these objects as sources of pleasure. It becomes intimately linked with the activity of the later sexual instincts and, when these have been completely synthesized, coincides with the sexual impulsion as a whole. Preliminary stages of love emerge as provisional sexual aims while the sexual instincts are passing through their complicated development. As the first of these aims we recognize the phase of incorporating or devouring—a type of love which is consistent with abolishing the object's separate existence and which may therefore be described as ambivalent. At the higher stage of the pregenital sadistic-anal organization, the striving for the object appears in the form of an urge for mastery, to which injury or annihilation of the object is a matter of indifference. Love in this form and at this preliminary stage is hardly to be distinguished from hate in its attitude towards the object. Not until the genital organization is established does love become the opposite of hate.

Hate, as a relation to objects, is older than love. It derives from the narcissistic ego's primordial repudiation of the external world with its outpouring of stimuli. As an expression of the reaction of unpleasure evoked by objects, it always remains in an intimate relation with the self-preservative instincts; so that sexual and ego-instincts can readily develop an antithesis which repeats that of love and hate. When the ego-instincts dominate the sexual function, as is the case at the stage of the sadistic-anal organization, they impart the qualities of hate to the instinctual aim as well.

The history of the origins and relations of love makes us understand how it is that love so frequently manifests itself as "ambivalent"— i.e., as accompanied by impulses of hate against the same object. The hate which is admixed with the love is in part derived from the preliminary stages of loving which have not been wholly surmounted; it is also in part based on reactions of repudiation by the ego-instincts, which, in view of the frequent conflicts between the interests of the ego and those of love, can find grounds in real and contemporary motives. In both cases, therefore, the admixed hate has as its source the self-preservative instincts. If a love-relation with a given object is broken off, hate not infrequently emerges in its place, so that we get the impression of a transformation of love into hate. This account of what happens leads on to the view that the hate, which has its real motives, is here reinforced by a regression of the love to the sadistic preliminary stage; so that the hate acquires an erotic character and the continuity of a love-relation is ensured.

The third antithesis of loving, the transformation of loving into being loved, corresponds to the operation of the polarity of activity and passivity, and is to be judged in the same way as the cases of scopophilia and sadism.

We may sum up by saying that the essential feature in the vicissitudes undergone by instincts lies in *the subjection of the instinctual impulses to the influences of the three great polarities that dominate* mental life. Of these three polarities we might describe that of activity–passivity as the *biological,* that of ego–external world as the *real,* and finally that of pleasure–unpleasure as the *economic* polarity.

2. Some psychical consequences of the anatomical distinction between the sexes

SIGMUND FREUD

IN MY OWN WRITINGS AND IN THOSE OF MY FOL-LOWERS more and more stress is laid on the necessity that the analyses of neurotics shall deal thoroughly with the remotest period of their childhood, the time of the early efflorescence of sexual life. It is only by examining the first manifestations of the patient's innate instinctual constitution and the effects of his earliest experiences that we can accurately gauge the motive forces that have led to his neurosis and can be secure against the errors into which we might be tempted by the degree to which things have become remodelled and overlaid in adult life. This requirement is not only of theoretical but also of practical importance, for it distinguishes our efforts from the work of those physicians whose interests are focused exclusively on therapeutic results and who employ analytic methods, but only up to a certain point. An analysis of early childhood such as we are considering is tedious and laborious and makes demands both upon the physician and upon the patient which cannot always be met. Moreover, it leads us into dark regions where there are as yet no signposts. Indeed, analysts may feel reassured, I think, that there is no risk of their work becoming mechanical, and so of losing its interest, during the next few decades.

In the following pages I bring forward some findings of analytic research which would be of great importance if they could be proved to

SOURCE. Selection from Sigmund Freud, "Some psychical consequences of the anatomical distinction between the sexes" in *The Standard Edition*, Vol. XIX, pp. 248–258. London: The Hogarth Press, 1961 (First published 1925).

apply universally. Why do I not postpone publication of them until further experience has given me the necessary proof, if such proof is obtainable? Because the conditions under which I work have undergone a change, with implications which I cannot disguise. Formerly, I was not one of those who are unable to hold back what seems to be a new discovery until it has been either confirmed or corrected. My *Interpretation of Dreams* and my "Fragment of an Analysis of a Case of Hysteria" (the case of Dora) were suppressed by me—if not for the nine years enjoined by Horace—at all events for four or five years before I allowed them to be published. But in those days I had unlimited time before me—"oceans of time" as an amiable author puts it—and material poured in upon me in such quantities that fresh experiences were hardly to be escaped. Moreover, I was the only worker in a new field, so that my reticence involved no danger to myself and no loss to others.

But now everything has changed. The time before me is limited. The whole of it is no longer spent in working, so that my opportunities for making fresh observations are not so numerous. If I think I see something new, I am uncertain whether I can wait for it to be confirmed. And further, everything that is to be seen upon the surface has already been exhausted; what remains has to be slowly and laboriously dragged up from the depths. Finally, I am no longer alone. An eager crowd of fellow-workers is ready to make use of what is unfinished or doubtful, and I can leave to them that part of the work which I should otherwise have done myself. On this occasion, therefore, I feel justified in publishing something which stands in urgent need of confirmation before its value or lack of value can be decided.

In examining the earliest mental shapes assumed by the sexual life of children we have been in the habit of taking as the subject of our investigations the male child, the little boy. With little girls, so we have supposed, things must be similar, though in some way or other they must nevertheless be different. The point in development at which this difference lay could not be clearly determined.

In boys the situation of the Oedipus complex is the first stage that can be recognized with certainty. It is easy to understand, because at that stage a child retains the same object which he previously cathected with his libido—not as yet a genital one—during the preceding period while he was being suckled and nursed. The fact, too, that in this situation he regards his father as a disturbing rival and would like to get rid of him and take his place is a straightforward consequence of the actual state of affairs. I have shown elsewhere how the Oedipus attitude in little boys belongs to the phallic phase, and how its destruction is brought about by the fear of castration—that is, by narcissistic interest in their genitals. The matter is made more difficult to grasp by the complicating circumstance that even in boys the Oedipus complex has a double orientation, active and passive, in accordance with their bisexual constitution; a boy also wants to take his *mother's* place as the love-object of his *father*—a fact which we describe as the feminine attitude.

As regards the prehistory of the Oedipus complex in boys we are far from complete clarity. We know that the period includes an identification of an affectionate sort with the boy's father, an identification which is still free from any sense of rivalry in regard to his mother. Another element of that stage is invariably, I believe, a masturbatory activity in connection with the genitals, the masturbation of early childhood, the more or less violent suppression of which by those in charge of the child sets the castration complex in action. It is to be assumed that this masturbation is attached to the Oedipus complex and serves as a discharge for the sexual excitation belonging to it. It is, however, uncertain whether the masturbation has this character from the first, or whether on the contrary it makes its first appearance spontaneously as an activity of a bodily organ and is only brought into relation with the Oedipus

complex at some later date; this second possibility is by far the more probable. Another doubtful question is the part played by the bedwetting and by the breaking of that habit through the intervention of training measures. We are inclined to make the simple connection that continued bed-wetting is a result of masturbation and that its suppression is regarded by boys as an inhibition of their genital activity— that is, as having the meaning of a threat of castration; but whether we are always right in supposing this remains to be seen. Finally, analysis shows us in a shadowy way how the fact of a child at a very early age listening to his parents copulating may set up his first sexual excitation, and how that event may, owing to its after-effects, act as a starting-point for the child's whole sexual development. Masturbation, as well as the two attitudes in the Oedipus complex, later on become attached to this early experience, the child having subsequently interpreted its meaning. It is impossible, however, to suppose that these observations of coitus are of universal occurrence, so that at this point we are faced with the problem of "primal phantasies." Thus the prehistory of the Oedipus complex, even in boys, raises all of these questions for sifting and explanation; and there is the further problem of whether we are to suppose that the process invariably follows the same course, or whether a great variety of different preliminary stages may not converge upon the same terminal situation.

In little girls the Oedipus complex raises one problem more than in boys. In both cases the mother is the original object; and there is no cause for surprise that boys retain that object in the Oedipus complex. But how does it happen that girls abandon it and instead take their father as an object? In pursuing this question I have been able to reach some conclusions which may throw light precisely on the prehistory of the Oedipus relation in girls.

Every analyst has come across certain women who cling with especial intensity and tenacity to the bond with their father and to the wish in which it culminates of having a child by him. We have good reason to suppose that the same wishful phantasy was also the motive force of their infantile masturbation, and it is easy to form an impression that at this point we have been brought up against an elementary and unanalysable fact of infantile sexual life. But a thorough analysis of these very cases brings something different to light—namely, that here the Oedipus complex has a long prehistory and is in some respects a secondary formation.

The old paediatrician Lindner once remarked that a child discovers the genital zones (the penis or the clitoris) as a source of pleasure while indulging in sensual sucking (thumb-sucking). I shall leave it an open question whether it is really true that the child takes the newly found source of pleasure in exchange for the recent loss of the mother's nipple—a possibility to which later phantasies (fellatio) seem to point. Be that as it may, the genital zone is discovered at some time or other, and there seems no justification for attributing any psychical content to the first activities in connection with it. But the first step in the phallic phase which begins in this way is not the linking-up of the masturbation with the object-cathexes of the Oedipus complex, but a momentous discovery which little girls are destined to make. They notice the penis of a brother or playmate, strikingly visible and of large proportions, at once recognize it as the superior counterpart of their own small and inconspicuous organ, and from that time forward fall a victim to envy for the penis.

There is an interesting contrast between the behaviour of the two sexes. In the analogous situation, when a little boy first catches sight of a girl's genital region, he begins by showing irresolution and lack of interest; he sees nothing or disavows what he has seen, he softens it down or looks about for expedients for bringing it into line with his expectations. It is not until later, when some threat of castration has obtained a hold upon him, that the observation becomes important to him: if he then recollects or repeats it, it arouses a terrible storm of emotion in him and forces him to believe in the reality of the threat which he has hitherto laughed at. This combination of circumstances leads to two reactions, which may become fixed and will in that case, whether separately or together or in conjunction with other factors, permanently determine the boy's relations to women: horror of the mutilated creature or triumphant contempt for her. These developments, however, belong to the future, though not to a very remote one.

A little girl behaves differently. She makes her judgment and her decision in a flash. She has seen it and knows that she is without it and wants to have it.

Here what has been named the masculinity complex of women branches off. It may put great difficulties in the way of their regular development towards femininity, if it cannot be got over soon enough. The hope of some day obtaining a penis in spite of everything and so of becoming like a man may persist to an incredibly late age and may become a motive for strange and otherwise unaccountable actions. Or again, a process may set in which I should like to call a "disavowal," a process which in the mental life of children seems neither uncommon nor very dangerous but which in an adult would mean the beginning of a psychosis. Thus a girl may refuse to accept the fact of being castrated, may harden herself in the conviction that she *does* possess a penis, and may subsequently be compelled to behave as though she were a man.

The psychical consequences of envy for the penis, in so far as it does not become absorbed in the reaction-formation of the masculinity complex, are various and far-reaching. After a women has become aware of the wound to her narcissism, she develops, like a scar, a sense of inferiority. When she has passed beyond her first attempt at explaining her lack of a penis as being a punishment personal to herself and has realized that the sexual character is a universal one, she begins to share the contempt felt by men for a sex which is the lesser in so important a respect, and, at least in holding that opinion, insists on being like a man.

Even after penis-envy has abandoned its true object, it continues to exist: by an easy displacement it persists in the character-trait of *jealousy*. Of course, jealousy is not limited to one sex and has a wider foundation that this, but I am of opinion that it plays a far larger part in the mental life of women than of men and that that is because it is enormously reinforced from the direction of displaced penis-envy. While I was still unaware of this source of jealousy and was considering the phantasy "a child is being beaten," which occurs so commonly in girls, I constructed a first phase for it in which its meaning was that another child, a rival of whom the subject was jealous, was to be beaten. This phantasy seems to be a relic of the phallic period in girls. The peculiar rigidity which struck me so much in the monotonous formula "a child is being beaten" can probably be interpreted in a special way. The child which is being beaten (or caressed) may ultimately be nothing more nor less than the clitoris itself, so that at its very lowest level the statement will contain a confession of masturbation, which has remained attached to the content of the formula from its beginning in the phallic phase till later life.

A third consequence of penis-envy seems to be a loosening of the girl's relation with her mother as a love-object. The situation as a whole is not very clear, but it can be seen that in the end the girl's mother, who sent her into the world so insufficiently equipped, is almost always held responsible for her lack of a penis. The way in which this comes about historically is often that soon after the girl has discovered that her genitals are unsatisfactory she begins to show jealousy of another child on the ground that her mother is fonder of it than of her, which serves as a reason for her giving up her affectionate relation to her mother. It will fit in with this if the child which has been preferred by her mother is made into the first object of the beating-phantasy which ends in masturbation.

There is yet another surprising effect of penis-envy, or of the discovery of the inferiority of the clitoris, which is undoubtedly the most important of all. In the past I had often formed an impression that in general women tolerate masturbation worse than men, that they more frequently fight against it and that they are unable to make use of it in circumstances in which a man would seize upon it as a way of escape without any hesitation. Experience would no doubt elicit innumerable exceptions to this statement, if we attempted to turn it into a rule. The reactions of human individuals of both sexes are of course made up of masculine and feminine traits. But it appeared to me nevertheless as though masturbation were further removed from the nature of women than of men, and the solution of the problem could be assisted by the reflection that masturbation, at all events of the clitoris, is a masculine activity and that the elimination of clitoridal sexuality is a necessary precondition for the development of femininity. Analyses of the remote phallic period have now taught me that in girls, soon after the first signs of penis-envy, an intense current of feeling against masturbation makes its appearance, which cannot be attributed exclusively to the educational influence of those in charge of the child. This impulse is clearly a forerunner of the wave of repression which at puberty will do away with a large amount of the girl's masculine sexuality in order to make room for the development of her femininity. It may happen that this first opposition to auto-erotic activity fails to attain its end. And this was in fact the case in the instances which I analysed. The conflict continued, and both then and later the girl did everything she could to free herself from the compulsion to masturbate. Many of the later manifestations of sexual life in women remain unintelligible unless this powerful motive is recognized.

I cannot explain the opposition which is raised in this way by little girls to phallic masturbation except by supposing that there is some concurrent factor which turns her violently against that pleasurable activity. Such a factor lies close at hand. It cannot be anything else than her narcissistic sense of humiliation which is bound up with penis-envy, the reminder that after all this is a point on which she cannot compete with boys and that it would therefore be best for her to give up the idea of doing so. Thus the little girl's recognition of the anatomical distinction between the sexes forces her away from masculinity and masculine masturbation on to new lines which lead to the development of femininity.

So far there has been no question of the Oedipus complex, nor has it up to this point played any part. But now the girl's libido slips into a new position along the line—there is no other way of putting it—of the equation "penis-child." She gives up her wish for a penis and puts in place of it a wish for a child: and *with that purpose in view* she takes her father as a love-object. Her mother becomes the object of her jealousy. The girl has turned into a little woman. If I am to credit a single analytic instance, this new situation can give rise to physical sensations which would have to be regarded as a premature awakening of the female genital apparatus. When the girl's attachment to her father comes to grief later on and has to be abandoned, it may give place to an identification with him and the girl may thus return to her masculinity complex and perhaps remain fixated in it.

I have now said the essence of what I had to say: I will stop, therefore, and cast an eye over our findings. We have gained some insight into the prehistory of the Oedipus complex in girls. The corresponding period in boys is more or less unknown. In girls the Oedipus complex is a secondary formation. The operations of the castration complex precede it and prepare for it. As regards the relation between the Oedipus and castration complexes there is a fundamental contrast between the two sexes. *Whereas in boys the Oedipus complex is destroyed by the castration complex, in girls it is made possible and led up to by the castration complex.* This contradiction is cleared up if we reflect that the castration complex always operates in the sense implied in its subject-matter: it inhibits and limits masculinity and encourages femininity. The difference between the sexual development of males and females at the stage we have been considering is an intelligible consequence of the anatomical distinction between their genitals and of the psychical situation involved in it; it corresponds to the difference between a castration that has been carried out and one that has merely been threatened. In their essentials, therefore, our findings are self-evident and it should have been possible to foresee them.

The Oedipus complex, however, is such an important thing that the manner in which one enters and leaves it cannot be without its effects. In boys the complex is not simply repressed, it is literally smashed to pieces by the shock of threatened castration. Its libidinal cathexes are abandoned, desexualized and in part sublimated; its objects are incorporated into the ego, where they form the nucleus of the super-ego and give that new structure its characteristic qualities. In normal, or, it is better to say, in ideal cases, the Oedipus complex exists no longer, even in the unconscious; the super-ego has become its heir. Since the penis (to follow Ferenczi) owes its extraordinarily high narcissistic cathexis to its organic significance for the propagation of the species, the catastrophe to the Oedipus complex (the abandonment of incest and the institution of conscience and morality) may be regarded as a victory of the race over the individual. This is an interesting point of view when one considers that neurosis is based upon a struggle of the ego against the demands of the sexual function. But to leave the standpoint of individual psychology is not of any immediate help in clarifying this complicated situation.

In girls the motive for the demolition of the Oedipus complex is lacking. Castration has already had its effect, which was to force the child into the situation of the Oedipus complex. Thus the Oedipus complex escapes the fate which it meets with in boys: it may be slowly abandoned or dealt with by repression or its effects may persist far into women's normal mental life. I cannot evade the notion (though I hesitate to give it expression) that for women the level of what is ethically normal is different from what it is in men. Their super-ego is never so inexorable, so impersonal, so independent of its emotional origins as we require it to be in men. Character-traits which critics of every epoch have brought up against women—that they show less sense of justice than men, that they are less ready to submit to the great exigencies of life, that they are more often influenced in their judgments by feelings of affection or hostility—all these would be amply accounted for by the modification in the formation of their super-ego which we have inferred above. We must not allow ourselves to be deflected from such conclusions by the denials of the feminists, who are anxious to force us to regard the two sexes as completely equal in position and worth; but we shall, of course, willingly agree that the majority of men are also far behind the masculine ideal and that all human individuals, as a result of their bisexual disposition and of cross-inheritance, combine in themselves both masculine and feminine characteristics, so that pure masculinity and femininity remain theoretical constructions of uncertain content.

I am inclined to set some value on the considerations I have brought forward upon the psychical consequences of the anatomical distinction between the sexes. I am aware, however, that this opinion can only be maintained if my findings, which are based on a handful of cases, turn out to have general validity and to be typical. If not, they would remain no more than a contribution to our knowledge of the different paths along which sexual life develops.

3.   The dream and the primal scene

SIGMUND FREUD

I HAVE ALREADY PUBLISHED THIS DREAM ELSE-
WHERE,[1] on account of the quantity of material
in it which is derived from fairy tales; and I
will begin by repeating what I wrote on that
occasion:

" 'I dreamt that it was night and that I was
lying in my bed. (My bed stood with its foot
toward the window; in front of the window
there was a row of old walnut trees. I know it
was winter when I had the dream, and night-
time.) Suddenly the window opened of its own
accord, and I was terrified to see that some
white wolves were sitting on the big walnut
tree in front of the window. There were six or
seven of them. The wolves were quite white,
and looked more like foxes or sheep-dogs, for
they had big tails like foxes and they had their
ears pricked like dogs when they pay attention
to something. In great terror, evidently of being
eaten up by the wolves, I screamed and woke
up. My nurse hurried to my bed, to see what
had happened to me. It took quite a long while
before I was convinced that it had only been
a dream; I had had such a clear and life-like
picture of the window opening and the wolves
sitting on the tree. At last I grew quieter, felt
as though I had escaped from some danger, and
went to sleep again.

" 'The only piece of action in the dream was
the opening of the window; for the wolves sat
quite still and without making any movement
on the branches of the tree, to the right and
left of the trunk, and looked at me. It seemed

SOURCE. Selection from Sigmund Freud, "The
dream and the primal scene," section from "An
infantile neurosis" in The Standard Edition, Vol.
XVII, pp. 29–47. London: The Hogarth Press,
1955 (First published 1918).

---

[1] The Occurrence in Dreams of Material from
Fairy Tales.

as though they had riveted their whole attention
upon me. I think this was my first anxiety
dream. I was three, four, or at most five years
old at the time. From then until my eleventh or
twelfth year I was always afraid of seeing something terrible in my dreams.'

"He added a drawing of the tree with the
wolves, which confirmed his description. The
analysis of the dream brought the following material to light.

"He had always connected this dream with
the recollection that during these years of his
childhood he was most tremendously afraid of
the picture of a wolf in a book of fairy tales.
His elder sister, who was very much his superior, used to tease him by holding up this
particular picture in front of him on some excuse or other, so that he was terrified and began
to scream. In this picture the wolf was standing upright, striding out with one foot, with its
claws stretched out and its ears pricked. He
thought this picture must have been an illustration to the story of Little Red Riding-Hood.

"Why were the wolves white? This made
him think of the sheep, large flocks of which
were kept in the neighbourhood of the estate.
His father occasionally took him with him to
visit these flocks, and every time this happened
he felt very proud and blissful. Later on—according to inquiries that were made it may
easily have been shortly before the time of the
dream—an epidemic broke out among the sheep.
His father sent for a follower of Pasteur's, who
inoculated the animals, but after the inoculation
even more of them died than before.

"How did the wolves come to be on the tree?
This reminded him of a story that he had heard
his grandfather tell. He could not remember
whether it was before or after the dream, but
its subject is a decisive argument in the favour
of the former view. The story ran as follows.
A tailor was sitting at work in his room, when
the window opened and a wolf leapt in. The
tailor hit after him with his yard—no (he cor-

rected himself), caught him by his tail and pulled it off, so that the wolf ran away in terror. Some time later the tailor went into the forest, and suddenly saw a pack of wolves coming towards him; so he climbed up a tree to escape from them. At first the wolves were in perplexity; but the maimed one, which was among them and wanted to revenge himself on the tailor, proposed that they should climb one upon another till the last one could reach him. He himself—he was a vigorous old fellow—would be the base of the pyramid. The wolves did as he suggested, but the tailor had recognized the visitor whom he had punished, and suddenly called out as he had before: 'Catch the grey one by his tail!' The tailless wolf, terrified by the recollection, ran away, and all the others tumbled down.

"In this story the tree appears, upon which the wolves were sitting in the dream. But it also contains an unmistakable allusion to the castration complex. The *old* wolf was docked of his tail by the tailor. The fox-tails of the wolves in the dream were probably compensations for this taillessness.

"Why were there six or seven wolves? There seemed to be no answer to this question, until I raised a doubt whether the picture that had frightened him could be connected with the story of *Little Red Riding-Hood*. This fairy tale only offers an opportunity for two illustrations —Little Red Riding-Hood's meeting with the wolf in the wood, and the scene in which the wolf lies in bed in the grandmother's night-cap. There must therefore be some other fairy tale behind his recollection of the picture. He soon discovered that it could only be the story of *The Wolf and the Seven Little Goats*. Here the number seven occurs, and also the number six, for the wolf only ate up six of the little goats, while the seventh hid itself in the clockcase. The white, too, comes into this story, for the wolf had his paw made white at the baker's after the little goats had recognized him on his first visit by his grey paw. Moreover, the two fairy tales have much in common. In both there is the eating up, the cutting open of the belly, the taking out of the people who have been eaten and their replacement by heavy stones, and finally in both of them the wicked wolf perishes. Besides all this, in the story of the little goats the tree appears. The wolf lay down under a tree after his meal and snored.

"I shall have, for a special reason, to deal with this dream again elsewhere, and interpret it and consider its significance in greater detail. For it is the earliest anxiety-dream that the dreamer remembered from his childhood, and its content, taken in connection with other

dreams that followed it soon afterwards and with certain events in his earliest years, is of quite peculiar interest. We must confine ourselves here to the relation of the dream to the two fairy tales which have so much in common with each other, *Little Red Riding-Hood* and *The Wolf and the Seven Little Goats*. The effect produced by these stories was shown in the little dreamer by a regular animal phobia. This phobia was only distinguished from other similar cases by the fact that the anxiety-animal was not an object easily accessible to observation (such as a horse or a dog), but was known to him only from stories and picture books.

"I shall discuss on another occasion the explanation of these animal phobias and the significance attaching to them. I will only remark in anticipation that this explanation is in complete harmony with the principal characteristic shown by the neurosis from which the present dreamer suffered later in his life. His fear of his father was the strongest motive for his falling ill, and his ambivalent attitude towards every father-surrogate was the dominating feature of his life as well as of his behaviour during the treatment.

"If in my patient's case the wolf was merely a first father-surrogate, the question arises whether the hidden content in the fairy tales of the wolf that ate up the little goats and of Little Red Riding-Hood may not simply be infantile fear of the father.[2] Moreover, my patient's father had the characteristic, shown by so many people in relation to their children, of indulging in 'affectionate abuse'; and it is possible that during the patient's earlier years his father (though he grew severe later on) may more than once, as he caressed the little boy or played with him, have threatened in fun to 'gobble him up.' One of my patients told me that her two children could never get to be fond of their grandfather, because in the course of his affectionate romping with them he used to frighten them by saying he would cut open their tummies."

Leaving on one side everything in this quotation that anticipates the dream's remoter implications, let us return to its immediate interpretation. I may remark that this interpretation was a task that dragged on over several years. The patient related the dream at a very early stage of the analysis and very soon came to share my conviction that the causes of his in-

---

[2] "Compare the similarity between these two fairy tales and the myth of Kronos, which has been pointed out by Rank."

fantile neurosis lay concealed behind it. In the course of the treatment we often came back to the dream, but it was only during the last months of the analysis that it became possible to understand it completely, and only then thanks to spontaneous work on the patient's part. He had always emphasized the fact that two factors in the dream had made the greatest impression on him: first, the perfect stillness and immobility of the wolves, and secondly, the strained attention with which they all looked at him. The lasting sense of reality, too, which the dream left behind it, seemed to him to deserve notice.

Let us take this last remark as a starting-point. We know from our experience in interpreting dreams that this sense of reality carries a particular significance along with it. It assures us that some part of the latent material of the dream is claiming in the dreamer's memory to possess the quality of reality, that is, that the dream relates to an occurrence that really took place and was not merely imagined. It can naturally only be a question of the reality of something unknown; for instance, the conviction that his grandfather really told him the story of the tailor and the wolf, or that the stories of *Little Red Riding-Hood* and of *The Seven Little Goats* were really read aloud to him, would not be of a nature to be replaced by this sense of reality that outlasted the dream. The dream seemed to point to an occurrence the reality of which was very strongly emphasized as being in marked contrast to the unreality of the fairy tales.

If it was to be assumed that behind the content of the dream there lay some such unknown scene—one, that is, which had already been forgotten at the time of the dream—then it must have taken place very early. The dreamer, it will be recalled, said: "I was three, four, or at most five years old at the time I had the dream." And we can add: "And I was reminded by the dream of something that must have belonged to an even earlier period."

The parts of the manifest content of the dream which were emphasized by the dreamer, the factors of attentive looking and of motionlessness, must lead to the content of this scene. We must naturally expect to find that this material reproduces the unknown material of the scene in some distorted form, perhaps even distorted into its opposite.

There were several conclusions, too, to be drawn from the raw material which had been produced by the patient's first analysis of the dream, and these had to be fitted into the collocation of which we were in search. Behind the mention of the sheep-breeding, evidence was to be expected of his sexual researches, his interest in which he was able to gratify during his visits with his father; but there must also have been allusions to a fear of death, since the greater part of the sheep had died of the epidemic. The most obtrusive thing in the dream, the wolves of the tree, led straight to his grandfathers' story; and what was fascinating about this story and capable of provoking the dream can scarcely have been anything but its connection with the theme of castration.

We also concluded from the first incomplete analysis of the dream that the wolf may have been a father-surrogate; so that, in that case, this first anxiety-dream would have brought to light the fear of his father which from that time forward was to dominate his life. This conclusion, indeed, was in itself not yet binding. But if we put together as the result of the provisional analysis what can be derived from the material produced by the dreamer, we then find before us for reconstruction some such fragments as these:

A real occurrence—dating from a very early period—looking—immobility—sexual problems—castration—his father—something terrible.

One day the patient began to continue with the interpretation of the dream. He thought that the part of the dream which said that "suddenly the window opened of its own accord" was not completely explained by its connection with the window at which the tailor was sitting and through which the wolf came into the room. "It must mean: 'My eyes suddenly opened,' I was asleep, therefore, and suddenly woke up, and as I woke I saw something: the tree with the wolves." No objection could be made to this; but the point could be developed further. He had woken up and had seen something. The attentive looking, which in the dream was ascribed to the wolves, should rather be shifted on to him. At a decisive point, therefore, a transposition has taken place; and moreover this is indicated by another transposition in the manifest content of the dream. For the fact that the wolves were sitting on the tree was also a transposition, since in his grandfather's story they were underneath, and were unable to climb on to the tree.

What, then, if the other factor emphasized by the dreamer were also distorted by means of a transposition or reversal? In that case instead of immobility (the wolves sat there motionless; they looked at him, but did not move) the meaning would have to be: the most violent motion. That is to say, he suddenly woke up, and saw in front of him a scene of violent movement at which he looked with strained attention. In the one case the distortion would consist in an interchange of subject and object, of activity and passivity; being looked at instead of looking. In the other case it would consist in a transformation into the opposite; rest instead of motion.

On another occasion an association which suddenly occurred to him carried us another step forward in our understanding of the dream: "The tree was a Christmas-tree." He now knew that he had dreamt the dream shortly before Christmas and in expectation of it. Since Christmas Day was also his birthday, it now became possible to establish with certainty the date of the dream and of the change in him which proceeded from it. It was immediately before his fourth birthday. He had gone to sleep, then, in tense expectation of the day which ought to bring him a double quantity of presents. We know that in such circumstances a child may easily anticipate the fulfillment of his wishes. So it was already Christmas in his dream; the content of the dream showed him his Christmas box, the presents which were to be his were hanging on the tree. But instead of presents they had turned into—wolves, and the dream ended by his being overcome by fear of being eaten by the wolf (probably his father), and by his flying for refuge to his nurse. Our knowledge of his sexual development before the dream makes it possible for us to fill in the gaps in the dream and to explain the transformation of his satisfaction into anxiety. Of the wishes concerned in the formation of the dream the most powerful must have been the wish for the sexual satisfaction which he was at that time longing to obtain from his father. The strength of this wish made it possible to revive a long-forgotten trace in his memory of a scene which was able to show him what sexual satisfaction from his father was like; and the result was terror, horror of the fulfilment

of the wish, the repression of the impulse which had manifested itself by means of the wish, and consequently a flight from his father to his less dangerous nurse.

The importance of this date of Christmas Day had been preserved in his supposed recollection of having had his first fit of rage because he was dissatisfied with his Christmas presents. The recollection combined elements of truth and of falsehood. It could not be entirely right, since according to the repeated declarations of his parents his naughtiness had already begun on their return in the autumn and it was not a fact that they had not come on till Christmas. But he had preserved the essential connection between his unsatisfied love, his rage and Christmas.

But what picture can the nightly workings of his sexual desire have conjured up that could frighten him away so violently from the fulfillment for which he longed? The material shows that there is one condition which this picture must satisfy. It must have been calculated to create a conviction of the reality of the existence of castration. Fear of castration could then become the motive power for the transformation of the affect.

I have now reached the point at which I must abandon the support I have hitherto had from the course of the analysis. I am afraid it will also be the point at which the reader's belief will abandon me.

What sprang into activity that night out of chaos of the dreamer's unconscious memory-traces was the picture of copulation between his parents, copulation in circumstances which were not entirely usual and were especially favourable for observation. It gradually became possible to find satisfactory answers to all the questions that arose in connection with this scene; for in the course of the treatment the first dream returned in innumerable variations and new editions, in connection with which the analysis produced the information that was required. Thus in the first place the child's age at the date of the observation was established as being about one and a half years.[3] He was suffering at the time from malaria, an attack of which used to come on every day at a particular

---

[3] The age of six months came under consideration as a far less probable, and indeed scarcely tenable, alternative.

hour.[4] From this tenth year onwards he was from time to time subject to moods of depression, which used to come on in the afternoon and reached their height at about five o'clock. This symptom still existed at the time of the analytic treatment. The recurring fits of depression took the place of the earlier attacks of fever or languor; five o'clock was either the time of the highest fever or of the observation of the intercourse, unless the two times coincided.[5] Probably for the very reason of this illness, he was in his parents' bedroom. The illness, the occurrence of which is also corroborated by direct tradition, makes it reasonable to refer the event to the summer, and, since the child was born on Christmas Day, to assume that his age was $n + 1\frac{1}{2}$ years. He had been sleeping in his cot, then, in his parents' bedroom, and woke up, perhaps because of his rising fever, in the afternoon, possibly at five o'clock, the hour which was later marked out by depression. It harmonized with our assumption that it was a hot summers' day, if we suppose that his parents had retired, half undressed,[6] for an afternoon siesta. When he woke up, he witnessed a coitus a tergo (from behind), three times repeated;[7] he was able to see his mother's genitals as well as his father's organ; and he understood the process as well as its significance.[8] Lastly he interrupted his

parents' intercourse in a manner which will be discussed later.

There is at bottom nothing extraordinary, nothing to give the impression of being a product of an extravagant imagination, in the fact that a young couple who had only been married a few years should have ended a siesta on a hot summer's afternoon with a love-scene, and should have disregarded the presence of their little boy of one and a half, asleep in his cot. On the contrary, such an event would, I think, be something entirely commonplace and banal; and even the position in which we have inferred that the coitus took place cannot in the least alter this judgment—especially as the evidence does not require that the intercourse should have been performed from behind each time. A single time would have been enough to give the spectator an opportunity for making observations which would have been rendered difficult or impossible by any other attitude of the lovers. The content of the scene cannot therefore in itself be an argument against its credibility. Doubts as to its probability will turn upon three other points: whether a child at the tender age of one and a half could be in a position to take in the perceptions of such a complicated process and to preserve them so accurately in his unconscious; secondly, whether it is possible at the age of four for a deferred revision of the impression so received to penetrate the understanding; and finally, whether any procedure could succeed in bringing into consciousnes coherently and convincingly the details of a scene of this kind which had been experienced and understood in such circumstances.[9]

Later on I shall carefully examine these and

---

[4] Compare the subsequent metamorphoses of this factor during the obsessional neurosis. In the patient's dreams during the treatment it was replaced by a violent wind. "Aria" = "air." ("Malaria" = "bad air.")

[5] We may remark in this connection that the patient drew only five wolves in his illustration to the dream, although the text mentioned six or seven.

[6] In white underclothes: the white wolves.

[7] Why three times: He suddenly one day produced the statement that I had discovered this detail by interpretation. This was not the case. It was a spontaneous association, exempt from further criticism; in his usual way he passed it off on to me, and by this projection tried to make it seem more trustworthy.

[8] I mean that he understood it at the time of the dream when he was four years old, not at the time of the observation. He received the impressions when he was one and a half; his understanding of them was deferred, but became possible at the time of the dream owing to his development, his sexual excitations, and his sexual researches.

---

[9] The first of these difficulties cannot be reduced by assuming that the child at the time of his observation was after all probably a year older, that is to say two and a half, an age at which he may perhaps have been perfectly capable of talking. All the minor details of my patient's case almost excluded the possibility of shifting the date in this way. Moreover, the fact should be taken into account that these scenes of observing parental intercourse are by no means rarely brought to light in analysis. The condition of their occurrence, however, is precisely that it should be in the earliest period of childhood. The older the child is, the more carefully, with parents above a certain social level, will the child be deprived of the opportunity for this kind of observation.

other doubts; but I can assure the reader that I am no less critically inclined than he towards an acceptance of this observation of the child's, and I will only ask him to join me in adopting a *provisional* belief in the reality of the scene. We will first proceed with the study of the relations between this "primal scene" and the patient's dream, his symptoms, and the history of his life; and we will trace separately the effects that followed from the essential content of the scene and from one of its visual impressions.

By the latter I mean the postures which he saw his parents adopt—the man upright, and the woman bent down like an animal. We have already heard that during his anxiety period his sister used to terrify him with a picture from the fairy-book, in which the wolf was shown standing upright, with one foot forward, with its claws stretched out and its ears pricked. He devoted himself with tireless perseverance during the treatment to the task of hunting in the second-hand bookshops till he found the illustrated fairy-book of his childhood, and had recognized his bogy in an illustration to the story of *The Wolf and the Seven Little Goats.* He thought that the posture of the wolf in this picture might have reminded him of that of his father during the constructed primal scene. At all events the picture became the point of departure for further manifestations of anxiety. Once when he was in his seventh or eighth year he was informed that next day a new tutor was coming for him. That night he dreamt of this tutor in the shape of a lion that came towards his bed roaring loudly and in the posture of the wolf in the picture; and once again he awoke in a state of anxiety. The wolf phobia had been overcome by that time, so he was free to choose himself a new anxiety-animal, and in this late dream he was recognizing the tutor as a father-surrogate. In the later years of his childhood each of his tutors and masters played the part of his father, and was endowed with his father's influence both for good and for evil.

While he was at his secondary school the Fates provided him with a remarkable opportunity for reviving his wolf phobia, and of using the relation which lay behind it as an occasion for severe inhibitions. The master who taught his form Latin was called Wolf. From the very first he felt cowed by him, and he was once taken severely to task by him for having made a stupid mistake in a piece of Latin translation. From that time on he could not get free from a paralysing fear of this master, and it was soon extended to other masters besides. But the occasion on which he made his blunder in the translation was also to the purpose. He had to translate the word *filius,* and he did it with the French word *fils* instead of with the corresponding word from his own language. The wolf, in fact, was still his father.[10]

The first "transitory symptom" [11] which the patient produced during the treatment went back once more to the wolf phobia and to the fairy tale of *The Seven Little Goats.* In the room in which the first sessions were held there was a large grandfather clock opposite the patient, who lay on a sofa facing away from me. I was struck by the fact that from time to time he turned his face towards me, looked at me in a very friendly way as though to propitiate me, and then turned his look away from me to the clock. I thought at the time that he was in this way showing his eagerness for the end of the hour. A long time afterwards the patient reminded me of this piece of dumb show, and gave me an explanation of it; for he recalled that the youngest of the seven little goats hid himself in the case of the grandfather clock while his six brothers were eaten up by the wolf. So what he had meant was: "Be kind to me! Must I be frightened of you? Are you going to eat me up? Shall I hide myself from you in the clock-case like the youngest little goat?"

The wolf that he was afraid of was undoubtedly his father but his fear of the wolf was conditional upon the creature being in an upright

---

[10] After this reprimand from the schoolmaster-wolf he learnt that it was the general opinion of his companions that, to be pacified, the master expected money from him. We shall return to this point later. I can see that it would greatly facilitate a rationalistic view of such a history of a child's development as this if it could be supposed that his whole fear of the wolf had really originated from the Latin master of that name, that it had been projected back into his childhood, and, supported by the illustration to the fairy tale, had caused the phantasy of the primal scene. But this is untenable; the chronological priority of the wolf phobia and its reference to the period of his childhood spent upon the first estate is far too securely attested. And his dream at the age of four?

[11] Ferenczi.

posture. His recollection asserted most definitely that he had not been terrified by pictures of wolves going on all fours or, as in the story of *Little Red Riding-Hood,* lying in bed. The posture which, according to our construction of the primal scene, he had seen the woman assume, was of no less significance; though in this case the significance was limited to the sexual sphere. The most striking phenomenon of his erotic life after maturity was his liability to compulsive attacks of falling physically in love which came on and disappeared again in the most puzzling succession. These attacks released a tremendous energy in him even at times when he was otherwise inhibited, and they were quite beyond his control. I must, for a specially important reason, postpone a full consideration of this compulsive love; but I may mention here that it was subject to a definite condition, which was concealed from his consciousness and was discovered only during the treatment. It was necessary that the woman should have assumed the posture which we have ascribed to his mother in the primal scene. From his puberty he had felt large and conspicuous buttocks as the most powerful attraction in a woman; to copulate except from behind gave him scarcely any enjoyment. At this point a criticism may justly be raised: it may be objected that a sexual preference of this kind for the hind parts of the body is a general characteristic of people who are inclined to an obsessional neurosis, and that its presence does not justify us in referring it back to a special impression in childhood. It is part of the fabric of the anal-erotic disposition and is one of the archaic traits which distinguish that constitution. Indeed, copulation from behind—*more ferarum* (in the fashion of animals) —may, after all, be regarded as phylogenetically the older form. We shall return to this point too in a later discussion, when we have brought forward the supplementary material which showed the basis of the unconscious condition upon which this falling in love depended.

Let us now proceed with our discussion of the relations between his dream and the primal scene. We should so far have expected the dream to present the child (who was rejoicing at Christmas in the prospect of the fulfilment of his wishes) with this picture of sexual satisfaction afforded through his father's agency, just as he had seen it in the primal scene, as a model of the satisfaction that he himself was longing to obtain from his father. Instead of

this picture, however, there appeared the material of the story which he had been told by his grandfather shortly before: the tree, the wolves, and the taillessness (in the over-compensated form of the bushy tails of the putative wolves). At this point some connection is missing, some associative bridge to lead from the content of the primal scene to that of the wolf story. This connection is provided once again by the postures and only by them. In his grandfather's story the tailless wolf asked the others *to climb upon him.* It was this detail that called up the recollection of the picture of the primal scene; and it was in this way that it became possible for the material of the primal scene to be represented by that of the wolf story, and at the same time for the *two* parents to be replaced, as was desirable, by *several* wolves. The content of the dream met with a further transformation, and the material of the wolf story was made to fit in with the content of the fairy tale of *The Seven Little Goats,* by borrowing from it the number seven.[12]

The steps in the transformation of the material, "primal scene—wolf story—fairy tale of *The Seven Little Goats,*" are a reflection of the progress of the dreamer's thoughts during the construction of the dream: "longing for sexual satisfaction from his father—realization that castration is a necessary condition of it—fear of his father." It is only at this point, I think, that we can regard the anxiety-dream of this four-year-old as being exhaustively explained.[13]

---

[12] It says "six or seven" in the dream. Six is the number of the children that were eaten; the seventh escaped into the clock-case. It is always a strict law of dream-interpretation that an explanation must be found for every detail.

[13] Now that we have succeeded in making a synthesis of the dream, I will try to give a comprehensive account of the relations between the manifest content of the dream and the latent dream-thoughts. *It was night, I was lying in my bed.* The latter part of this is the beginning of the reproduction of the primal scene. "It was night" is a distortion of "I had been asleep." The remark, "I know it was winter when I had the dream, and night-time," refers to the patient's recollection of the dream and is not part of its content. It is correct, for it was one of the nights before his birthday, that is, Christmas Day.

Suddenly the window opened of its own accord. That is to be translated: "Suddenly I woke up of my own accord," a recollection of the primal scene. The influence of the wolf story, in which the wolf

Footnote 13 (continued)

leapt in through the window, is making itself felt as a modifying factor and transforms a direct expression into a plastic one. At the same time the introduction of the window serves the purpose of providing a contemporary reference for the subsequent content of the dream. On Christmas Eve the door opens suddenly and one sees before one the tree with the presents. Here, therefore, the influence of the actual expectation of Christmas (which comprises the wish for sexual satisfaction) is making itself felt.

The big walnut-tree. The representative of the Christmas tree, and therefore belonging to the current situation. But also the tree out of the wolf story, on which the tailor took refuge from pursuit, and under which the wolves were on the watch. Moreover, as I have often been able to satisfy myself, a high tree is a symbol of observing, of scopophilia. A person sitting on a tree can see everything that is going on below him and cannot himself be seen. Compare Boccaccio's well-known story, and similar *facetiae.*

The wolves. Their number: *six or seven.* In the wolf story there was a pack, and no number was given. The fixing of the number shows the influence of the fairy tale of *The Seven Little Goats,* six of whom were eaten up. The fact that the number two in the primal scene is replaced by a larger number, which would be absurd in the primal scene, is welcomed by the resistance as a means of distortion. In the illustration to the dream the dreamer brings forward the number five, which is probably meant to correct the statement "It was night."

They were sitting on the tree. In the first place they replace the Christmas presents hanging on the tree. But they are also transposed onto the tree because that can mean that they are looking. In his grandfather's story they were posted underneath the tree. Their relation to the tree has therefore been reversed in the dream; and from this it may be concluded that there are further reversals of the latent material to be found in the content of the dream.

They were looking at him with strained attention. This feature comes entirely from the primal scene, and has got into the dream at the price of being turned completely round.

They were quite white. This feature is unessential in itself, but is strongly emphasized in the dreamer's narrative. It owes its intensity to a copious fusion of elements from all the strata of the material, and it combines unimportant details from the other sources of the dream with a fragment of the primal scene which is more significant. This last part of its determination goes back to the white of his parents' bedclothes and underclothes, and to this is added the white of the flocks of sheep, and of the sheep-dogs, as an allusion to his sexual researches among animals, and the white in the fairy tale of *The Seven Little Goats,* in which the mother is recognized by the white of her hand. Later on we shall see that the white clothes are also an allusion to death. (There does not seem in fact to be any further clear reference to this point. The connection is perhaps with the episode of the winding-sheet.)

They sat there motionless. This contradicts the most striking feature of the observed scene, namely, its agitated movement, which, in virtue of the postures to which it led, constitutes the connection between the primal scene and the wolf story.

They had tails like foxes. This must be the contradiction of a conclusion which was derived from the action of the primal scene on the wolf story, and which must be recognized as the most important result of the dreamer's sexual researches: "So there really is such a thing as castration." The terror with which this conclusion was received finally broke out in the dream and brought it to an end.

The fear of being eaten up by the wolves. It seemed to the dreamer as though the motive force of this fear was not derived from the content of the dream. He said he need not have been afraid, for the wolves looked more like foxes or dogs, and they did not rush at him as though to bite him, but were very still and not at all terrible. We observe that the dream-work tries for some time to make the distressing content harmless by transforming it into its opposite. ("They aren't moving, and, only look, they have the loveliest tails.") Until at last this expedient fails, and the fear breaks out. It expresses itself by the help of the fairy tale, in which the goat-children are eaten up by the wolf-father. This part of the fairy tale may perhaps have acted as a reminder of threats made by the child's father in fun when he was playing with him; so that the fear of being eaten up by the wolf may be a reminiscence as well as a substitute by displacement.

That the wishes act as motive forces in this dream is obvious. First there are the superficial wishes of the day, that Christmas with its presents may already be here (a dream of impatience) and accompanying these is the deeper wish, now permanently present, for sexual satisfaction from the dreamer's father. This is immediately replaced by the wish to see once more what was then so fascinating. The mental process then proceeds on its way. Starting from the fulfilment of this last with the conjuring up of the primal scene, it passes on to what has now become inevitable—the repudiation of that wish and its repression.

The diffuseness and elaboration of this commentary have been forced on me by the effort to present the reader with some sort of equivalent for the convincing power of an analysis carried through by oneself; perhaps they may also serve to discourage him from asking for the publication of analyses which have stretched over several years.

After what has already been said I need only deal shortly with the pathogenic effect of the primal scene and the alteration which its revival produced in his sexual development. We will only trace that one of its effects to which the dream gave expression. Later on we shall have to make it clear that it was not only a single sexual current that started from the primal scene but a whole set of them, that his sexual life was positively splintered up by it. We shall further bear in mind that the activation of this scene (I purposely avoid the word "recollection") had the same effect as though it were a recent experience. The effects of the scene were deferred, but meanwhile it had lost none of its freshness in the interval between the ages of one and a half and four years. We shall perhaps find in what follows reason to suppose that it produced certain effects even at the time of its perception, that is from the age of one and a half onwards.

When the patient entered more deeply into the situation of the primal scene, he brought to light the following pieces of self-observation. He assumed to begin with, he said, that the event of which he was a witness was an act of violence, but the expression of enjoyment which he saw on his mother's face did not fit in with this; he was obliged to recognize that the experience was one of gratification.[14] What was essentially

new for him in his observation of his parents' intercourse was the conviction of the reality of castration—a possibility with which his thoughts had already been occupied previously. (The sight of the two girls micturating, his Nanya's threat, the governess's interpretation of the sugar-sticks, the recollection of his father having beaten a snake to pieces.) For now he saw with his own eyes the wound of which his Nanya had spoken, and understood that its presence was a necessary condition of intercourse with his father. He could no longer confuse it with the bottom, as he had in his observation of the little girls.[15]

The dream ended in a state of anxiety, from which he did not recover until he had his Nanya with him. He fled, therefore, from his father to her. His anxiety was a repudiation of the wish for sexual satisfaction from his father—the trend which had put the dream into his head. The form taken by the anxiety, the fear of "being eaten by the wolf," was only the (as we shall hear, regressive) transposition of the wish to be copulated with by his father, that is, to be given sexual satisfaction in the same way as his mother. His last sexual aim, the passive attitude towards his father, succumbed to repression, and fear of his father appeared in its place in the shape of the wolf phobia.

And the driving force of this repression? The circumstances of the case show that it can only have been his narcissistic genital libido, which, in the form of concern for his male organ, was fighting against a satisfaction whose attainment seemed to involve the renunciation of that organ. And it was from his threatened narcissism that he derived the masculinity with which he defended himself against his passive attitude towards his father.

We now observe that at this point in our narrative we must make an alteration in our termi-

---

[14] We might perhaps best do justice to this statement of the patient's by supposing that the object of his observation was in the first instance a coitus in the normal position, which cannot fail to produce the impression of being a sadistic act, and that only after this was the position altered, so that he had an opportunity for making other observations and judgments. This hypothesis, however, was not confirmed with certainty, and moreover does not seem to me indispensable. We must not forget the actual situation which lies behind the abbreviated description given in the text: the patient under analysis, at an age of over twenty-five years, was putting the impressions and impulses of his fourth year into words which he would never have found at that time. If we fail to notice this, it may easily seem comic and incredible that a child of four should be capable of such technical judgments and learned notions. This is simply another instance of *deferred action*. At the age of one and a half the child receives an impression to which he is unable to react adequately; he is only able to understand it and to be moved by it when the impression is revived in him at the age of four; and only twenty years later, during the analysis, is he able to grasp

with his conscious mental processes what was then going on in him. The patient justifiably disregards the three periods of time, and puts his present ego into the situation which is so long past. And in this we follow him, since with correct self-observation and interpretation the effect must be the same as though the distance between the second and third periods of time could be neglected. Moreover, we have no other means of describing the events of the second period.

[15] We shall learn later on when we come to trace out his anal eroticism, how he further dealt with this portion of the problem.

nology. During the dream he had reached a new phase in his sexual organization. Up to then the sexual opposites had been for him *active* and *passive*. Since his seduction his sexual aim had been a passive one, of being touched on the genitals; it was then transformed, by regression to the earlier stage of the sadistic-anal organization, into the masochistic aim of being beaten or punished. It was a matter of indifference to him whether he reached this aim with a man or with a woman. He had travelled, without considering the difference of sex, from his Nanya to his father; he had longed to have his penis touched by his Nanya, and had tried to provoke a beating from his father. Here his genitals were left out of account; though the connection with them which had been concealed by the regression was still expressed in his phantasy of being beaten *on the penis*. The activation of the primal scene in the dream now brought him back to the genital organization. He discovered the vagina and the biological significance of masculine and feminine. He understood now that active was the same as masculine, while passive was the same as feminine. His passive sexual aim should now have been transformed into a feminine one, and have expressed itself as "being copulated with by his father" instead of "being beaten by him on the genitals or on the bottom." This feminine aim, however, underwent repression and was obliged to let itself be replaced by fear of the wolf.

We must here break off discussion of his sexual development until new light is thrown from the later stages of his history upon these earlier ones. For the proper appreciation of the wolf phobia we will only add that both his father and mother became wolves. His mother took the part of the castrated wolf, which let the others climb upon it, was seized with fear as soon as it was reminded of the fact of its taillessness. It seems, therefore, as though he had identified himself with his castrated mother during the dream, and was now fighting against that fact. "If you want to be sexually satisfied by Father," we may perhaps represent him as saying to himself, "you must allow yourself to be castrated like mother; but I won't have that." In short, a clear protest on the part of his masculinity! Let us, however, plainly understand that the sexual development of the case that we are now examining has a great disadvantage from the point of view of research, for it was by no means undisturbed. It was first decisively influenced by the seduction, and was then diverted by the scene of observation of the coitus, which in its deferred action operated like a second seduction.

4. An empirical investigation of the castration complex in dreams

CALVIN HALL AND ROBERT L. VAN DE CASTLE

ACCORDING TO THE CLASSICAL THEORY OF THE CASTRATION COMPLEX as it was formulated by Freud (1925, 1931, 1933), the male is afraid of losing his penis (castration anxiety) and the female envies the male for having a penis (penis envy). One consequence of this envy is that she wants to deprive the male of his organ (castration wish).

The empirical work investigating this topic has generally produced results consistent with Freud's formulation. Hattendorf (1932) indicated that the second most frequent question asked of mothers by children in the 2- to 5-year-old group concerned the physical differences between the sexes. Horney (1932) reported that when a clinic doctor tried to induce boys and girls to insert a finger in a ball that had developed a split, significantly more boys than girls hesitated or refused to accede to this request. Using a doll play interview Conn (1940) noted that two-thirds of children who reported that they had seen the genitals of the opposite sex could not recall their attitude or feelings about the initial discovery and over one third who could recall their attitude definitely felt something was wrong. On the basis of these results the author concludes (Conn, 1940, p. 754), "It appears that the large majority of boys and girls responded to the first sight of genital differences with tranquil, unperturbed acceptance." This conclusion was criticized by Levy (1940), who carried out repeated doll play interviews with children and concluded (p. 762),

"The typical response of the children in our culture, when they become aware of the primary difference in sex anatomy, confirms the psychoanalyst's finding, namely, that castration anxiety is aroused in boys and a feeling of envy with destructive impulse toward the penis in girls." In a widely quoted review of psychoanalytic studies by Sears (1943) a few years later he summed up the castration studies with the statement (p. 36), "Freud seriously overestimated the frequency of the castration complex." In a study of problem children, Huschka (1944) reported that 73 percent of parents dealt with masturbation problems destructively and that the most common threat was that of genital injury. The normal children used by Friedman (1952) completed stories involving castration situations and the author interpreted his data as offering support for the commonness of castration anxiety, particularly in the case of boys.

The remaining studies used college students as subjects. Blum (1949) found significantly more responses to the Blacky Test indicative of castration anxiety among males than females. A method of scoring castration anxiety from TAT scores was developed by Schwartz (1955) who found (1956) that male homosexuals displayed significantly more castration anxiety than normal males and that males obtained higher castration anxiety scores than females. Using a multiple-choice question about the castration card of the Blacky, Sarnoff and Corwin (1959) reported that males with high castration scores showed significantly greater increase in fear of death than low castration males did after being exposed to sexually arousing stimuli.

The foregoing studies indicate that techniques designed to elicit unconscious material are generally successful in demonstrating the manifestations of the castration complex that

SOURCE. Article by Calvin Hall and Robert L. Van de Castle, "An empirical investigation of the castration complex in dreams" in the *Journal of Personality*, Vol. 33, pp. 20–29, 1965.

This investigation was supported by a USPHS research grant No. MH 06510 from the National Institute of Mental Health, USPHS.

would be predictable from Freudian theory. It should follow then, that since dreams have been characterized as "the royal road to the unconscious," manifestations of the castration complex would be clearly discernible in dreams. The present study was undertaken to investigate whether differences in dream contents, presumably related to castration reactions, would appear between adult male and female dreamers.

The specific hypothesis tested in this investigation is that male dreamers will report more dreams expressive of castration anxiety than they will dreams involving castration wishes and penis envy while the pattern will be reversed for females, i.e., they will report more dreams containing expressions of castration wishes and penis envy than they will dreams containing castration anxiety.

Method

Subjects

A total of 120 college students divided into three groups of 20 males and 20 females each served as Ss. Groups 1 and 2 were students in Hall's undergraduate class in personality at Western Reserve University during 1947 and 1948. The recording of nocturnal dreams was described to the students as a class project for which they would be given extra credit if they participated, but would not be penalized for not doing so. They were given opportunities to earn extra credit in other ways than recording dreams. Dreams were reported on a standard report form. These dreams have been published in *Primary Records in Psychology* (Barker and Kaplan, 1963), and Groups 1 and 2 consist of the first 40 of the 43 female series and the first 40 of the 44 male series reported therein.

Group 3 were students in Van de Castle's class in abnormal psychology at the University of Denver during 1962 and 1963. They were required to hand in an average of two dreams a week. Standard instructions similar to those on Hall's form were given. Students were allowed to turn in daydreams if they could recall no nocturnal dreams, but only nocturnal dreams were scored in this study.

Scoring for Castration Complex Indicators in Dreams

A scoring manual which sets forth the criteria for castration anxiety (CA), castration wish (CW), and penis envy (PE) in reported dreams was devised. These criteria were selected because either they directly reflect concern over castration or they represent displacements from one part of the body, i.e., the genitals, to another part of the body e.g., the hand, or they make use of commonly recognized symbols for the male genitals, e.g., guns, knives, and pens. Copies of a revised version of the original manual (*Institute of Dream Research*, 1964) are available on request to the authors. A summary of the criteria follows.

Criteria for Castration Anxiety

1. Actual or threatened loss, removal, injury to or pain in a specific part of the dreamer's body; actual or threatened cutting, clawing, biting or stabbing of the dreamer's body as a whole or to any part of the dreamer's body; defect of a specified part of the dreamer's body; some part of the dreamer's body is infantile, juvenile, or undersized.

2. Actual or threatened injury or damage to, loss of, or defect in an object or animal belonging to the dreamer or one that is in his possession in the dream.

3. Inability or difficulty of the dreamer in using his penis or an object that has phallic characteristics; inability or difficulty of the dreamer in placing an object in a receptacle.

4. A male dreams that he is a woman or changes into a woman, or has or acquires female secondary sex characteristics, or is wearing woman's clothes or accessories.

Criteria for Castration Wish

1. The criteria for castration wish are the same as those for castration anxiety except that they do not occur to the dreamer but to another person in his dream.

Criteria for Penis Envy

1. Acquisition *within* the dream by the dreamer of an object that has phallic characteristics; acquisition of a better penis or an impressive phallic object.

2. The dreamer envies or admires a man's physical characteristics or performance or possession that has phallic characteristics.

3. A female dreams that she is a man or changes into a man, or has acquired male secondary sex characteristics, or is wearing man's clothing or accessories which are not customarily worn by women.

Each dream was read and scored for each of these criteria. The maximum score was one point for each condition, even if several independent instances of the same condition occurred within the dream. It was possible, however, for the same dream to be scored for more than one condition, e.g., a dream could be given one point for CA and one point for PE.

After the writers had acquired practice in the use of the manual, a reliability study was made. One hundred nineteen dreams of eight males and 123 dreams of eight females were scored independently by the writers. The scores were then compared. An agreement was counted if both judges scored the same condition, e.g., a castration anxiety, in the same dream or if both judges did not score a condition, e.g., penis envy, in the same dream. A disagreement was counted if one judge scored for a condition and the other judge did not score for the same condition in the same dream. The results are presented in Table 1.

Table 1. Percentage of Agreement between Two Scorers

Number Dreamers	Number Dreams	Castration Anxiety	Castration Wish	Penis Envy
8 males	119	87	94	96
8 females	123	89	94	93
16	242	88	94	94

Results

The number of dreams containing scorable elements for the three groups of Ss is shown in Table 2. It will be noted that in every group the number of male dreams exceeds the number of female dreams for castration anxiety, while in every group the number of female dreams is higher than male dreams for both the castration wish and the penis envy categories.

Since the distribution of scores for any cate-

Table 2. Number of Dreams Showing Castration Anxiety (CA), Castration Wish (CW) and Penis Envy (PE) among College Students

| Group[a] | Number of Dreams Analyzed | | Number of Dreams Containing | | | | | |
| | | | Castration Anxiety | | Castration Wish | | Penis Envy | |
	Male	Female	M	F	M	F	M	F
1	308	305	40	7	5	8	2	5
2	327	328	54	15	11	21	5	13
3	318	323	57	35	21	32	9	14
Total	953	956	151	57	37	61	16	32
Range (per dreamer)	7–24	10–21	0–8	0–4	0–4	0–6	0–2	0–3

[a]$N = 20$ male and 20 female dreamers for each group

gory was markedly skewed with zero scores predominating for many individual dreamers, it was felt that the assumptions for any parametric statistic such as t could not be met. Statistical evaluation of the hypothesis was therefore made by use of the Chi-square technique. The unit of analysis was the *individual dreamer*. The analysis consisted of determining the number of male and female dreamers whose CA score exceeded the combined total of their CW and PE scores and the number of male and female dreamers whose combined CW and PE scores exceeded their CA score. Ties (10 male and 19 female) were evenly divided between these two groupings. The resulting 2 x 2 table is shown in Table 3.

Table 3. Number of Male and Female Dreamers with CA Scores Higher and Lower than CW and PE Scores

	CA More Than CW and PE	CW and PE More Than CA	Total
Number of male dreamers	48	12	60
Number of female dreamers	21.5	38.5	60
	69.5	50.5	120

$$\chi^2 = 24$$

The majority of male dreamers had higher CA scores while the majority of female dreamers had higher CW and PE scores. The hypothesis of this study was thus supported at a high level of statistical significance ($p < .001$).

Do each of the conditions, CW and PE, contribute substantially to the obtained difference? Table 2 reveals that each of these conditions appears in approximately twice as many female dreams as male dreams. To make sure that such a differences was not produced by a few atypical dreamers, a count was made of the number of women whose scores for each of these separate conditions exceeded that of their CA score. It was found that 20 women had CW scores higher than CA scores, whereas only 5 males scored in this direction, and that 12 women had PE scores higher than their CA scores whereas the same was true for only 1 male. The answer to the question raised earlier is that both CW and PE contribute substantially to the obtained difference.

To look at the sex differences from another viewpoint let us examine the relative freedom from castration anxiety in male and female dreamers. Exactly 50 percent ($N = 30$) of women in the present sample had zero CA scores whereas only 13 percent ($N = 8$) of males received zero CA scores. These additional analyses concur in supporting the hypothesis of this investigation, namely that manifestations of castration anxiety in dreams are more typical of males and manifestations of both castration wishes and penis envy are more typical of females.

Discussion

Although the differences are clearcut in favor of the hypothesis, nonetheless there are many manifestations of castration wish and penis envy in men's dreams and many manifestations of castration anxiety in women. The male's wish to castrate others and his envy and admiration of another man's physical and sexual equipment are not difficult to understand. In view of the great amount of physical aggression that is expressed in men's dreams (Hall and Domhoff, 1963), and the amount of competition that men engage in during their waking life, perhaps it is not surprising that their dreams should contain castration wishes and penis envy. Moreover, these may be, as psychoanalytic theory claims, an archaic wish in the male to castrate the father which manifests itself in displaced ways in their dreams. But castration anxiety still takes precedence over these other themes in male dreams.

The amount of castration anxiety in female dreams is less easy, perhaps, to comprehend. Why should there be anxiety over losing something they do not have and never have had? The psychoanalytic explanation is that females unconsciously feel they once had the same genital organs as the male, and that they were taken from them. The menses are a constant reminder of this fantasied event. Accordingly, we would expect to find in their dreams expressions of this fantasied castration. Men dream of what might happen whereas women dream of what they think has happened. The fact that anxiety is usually stronger for an anticipated future event than for a realized past one would explain why men have more castration anxiety than women do.

It will be observed (Table 2) that more castration anxiety is expressed in the dreams of males (151 occurrences) than castration wish plus penis envy is in the dreams of females (93 occurrences). The explanation for this may be that the female displaces her penis envy in other ways than that of wishing to castrate others. Freud (1917) mentions two such displacements. He writes: "In girls, the discovery of the penis gives rise to envy for it, which later changes into the wish for a man as the possessor of a penis. Even before this the wish for a penis has changed into a wish for a baby" (p. 132).

This suggested to us another testable hypothesis, namely, that more dreams of babies and of getting married should be reported by women than by men. Accordingly, we went through the 1909 dreams and scored them for the presence of weddings and babies. Females had 60 dreams in which weddings or preparations for weddings occurred: males had only 9 such dreams. Females had 85 dreams in which babies or very young children figured; males had 32 such dreams. These findings appear to confirm the hypothesis, although, of course, other explanations for women dreaming more than men do of weddings and babies may occur to the reader.

The subjects of this investigation were for the most part in their late teens and early twenties. What happens to manifestations of the castration complex in dreams with age? Relative to this question we would like to mention the findings obtained from analyzing 600 dreams collected from a man between the ages of 37 and 54. The 600 dreams were divided into six sets of 100 dreams each. Each dream was scored for castration anxiety, castration wish, and penis envy. The results are presented in Table 4.

Table 4. Manifestations of the Castration Complex in the Dreams of a Middle-Aged Man

	Incidence per 100 Dreams							Average for
	I	II	III	IV	V	VI	Average	College Men
Castration anxiety	14	18	13	15	10	17	14.5	15.8
Castration wish	4	3	2	5	8	5	4.5	3.9
Penis envy	2	1	2	0	1	2	1.3	1.7

The incidence for each of the three categories does not vary to any great extent over the 17 years, nor do the averages differ noticeably from the averages for college men. In this one case, at least, castration anxiety appears to express itself at the same rate in dreams into the fifties.

In an earlier investigation by one of the writers (Hall, 1955), it was concluded that the dream of being attacked is not a manifestation of castration anxiety as suggested by the findings of Harris (1948) but represents the feminine attitudes of weakness, passivity, inferiority, and masochism as formulated by Freud. The findings of the present study do not conflict with the earlier one because the criteria used for scoring castration anxiety were different than the criterion used for identifying the dream of being attacked. The dream of being attacked consists, for the most part, of attacks on or threats to the dreamer's *whole* body. In the present study, attacks upon the whole body are categorically excluded except for a small number of cases where the threat is one of cutting, clawing, biting, or stabbing. The damage or threat must be to a *specific part* of the body in order for it to be scored as castration anxiety. Moreover, the criteria used in the present investigation are much more extensive. They include damage to a possession of the dreamer, his difficulty in using phallic objects, and the feminization of a male.

Although the hypothesis of this investigation was derived from Freudian theory, and its confirmation therefore supports the theory, the results may be accounted for by other theoretical positions. For example, the greater incidence of injuries and accidents in male dreams may merely reflect the nature of the activities in which they engage in waking life as compared with the activities of women. It is believed that men engage in more dangerous activities and take more risks than women do. If this is the case it might be expected that their dreams would be in accord with their waking life experiences. On the other hand, if they do in fact take more chances and risk physical harm, this raises the question of why they do. It does not suffice, we feel, to say that they have adopted the role which "society" has fashioned for them. Why has "society" created such a role and why do boys acquiesce in being shaped to the role? *Ad hoc* explanations of findings, in any event, are not very satisfying.

Summary

This study was undertaken to investigate whether sex differences would be found in the incidence of manifestations of castration anxiety (CA), castration wish (CW), and penis envy (PE) in dreams. Criteria for each of these three components of the castration complex were formulated on the basis of which a scoring manual was written.

It was hypothesized that male dreamers will report more dreams expressive of CA than they will dreams involving CW and PE whereas the pattern will be reversed for females, i.e., they will report more dreams containing expressions of CW and PE than they will dreams containing CA. The hypothesis was supported for 3 different groups of college students evenly divided as to sex, and the combined results for the 120 students were significant beyond the .001 level.

Additional data were also presented to show that many more women than men dream about babies and weddings and that the relative incidence of the various castration components remains quite stable throughout a long dream series spanning 17 years.

Although the results are congruent with Freudian theory, and to that extent add to the construct validity of the castration complex, it was recognized that alternative theoretical positions could be invoked to account for the findings of this investigation.

REFERENCES

Barker, R., and Kaplan, B. (Eds.) *Primary records in psychology.* Publication No. 2. Lawrence, Kansas: University of Kansas Publications, 1963.

Blum, G. S. A study of the psychoanalytic theory of psychosexual development. *Genet. psychol. Monogr.,* 1949, 39, 3–99.

Conn, J. H. Children's reactions to the discovery of genital differences. *Amer. J. Orthopsychiat.,* 1940, 10, 747–754.

Freud, S. (1917) On transformations of instinct as exemplified in anal erotism. In *The Standard Edition,* Vol. XVII, pp. 127–133. London: The Hogarth Press, 1955.

Freud, S. (1925) Some psychical consequences of the anatomical distinction between the sexes. In *The Standard Edition,* Vol. XIX, pp. 248–258. London: The Hogarth Press, 1961.

Freud, S. (1931) Female sexuality. In *The Standard Edition,* Vol. XXI, pp. 225–243. London: The Hogarth Press, 1961.

Freud, S. (1933) *A new series of introductory lectures on psychoanalysis.* Chapter 5, pp. 153–185. New York: Norton, 1933.

Friedman, S. M. An empirical study of the castration and Oedipus complexes. *Genet. psychol. Monogr.,* 1952, 46, 61–130.

Hall, C. S. The significance of the dream of being attacked. *J. Pers.,* 1955, 24, 168–180.

Hall, C. and Domhoff, B. Aggression in dreams. *Internat. J. soc. Psychiat.,* 1963, 9, 259–267.

Harris, I. Observations concerning typical anxiety dreams. *Psychiatry,* 1948, 11, 301–309.

Hattendorf, K. W. A study of the questions of young children concerning sex. *J. soc. Psychol.,* 1932, 3, 37–65.

Horney, Karen. The dread of woman. *Internat. J. Psychoanal.,* 1932, 13, 348–360.

Huschka, Mabel. The incidence and character of masturbation threats in a group of problem children. In S. S. Tomkins (Ed.) *Contemporary psychopathology.* Cambridge: Harvard Univ. Press, 1944.

Institute of Dream Research. A manual for scoring castration anxiety, castration wishes, and penis envy in dreams. 1964.

Levy, D. M. "Control-situation" studies of children's responses to the differences in genitalia. *Amer. J. Orthopsychiat.,* 1940, 10, 755–762.

Sarnoff, I. and Corwin, S. B. Castration anxiety and the fear of death. *J. Pers.,* 1959, 27, 374–385.

Schwartz, B. J. Measurement of castration anxiety and anxiety over loss of love. *J. Pers.,* 1955, 24, 204–219.

Schwartz, B. J. An empirical test of two Freudian hypotheses concerning castration anxiety. *J. Pers.,* 1956, 24, 318–327.

Sears, R. Survey of objective studies of psychoanalytic concepts. *Soc. Sci. Res. Coun.,* 1943, Bulletin 51.

5. Personality differences in the capacity for verbal recall

JOSEPH ADELSON AND JOAN REDMOND

WHEN WE THINK OF THE TOPIC "psychoanalysis and memory" we are likely to bring to mind Freud's theory of repression; and we are also apt to think of that curious scatter of experiments—some of them knowing and clever, some of them innocent of understanding—which have striven to confirm or confute Freud's observations. Many of these studies concentrate on the stimulus: they ask whether a certain type of stimulus—"disturbing," "unpleasant"—can, by evoking anxiety, bring into play the ego's defenses so as to inhibit or distort recall. Other studies center on the experimental subject: by inducing a momentary state of distress, they seek to bring about some disturbance in recall.

Our research approaches psychoanalysis and memory from a somewhat different perspective. It focuses on the problem of individual differences in the *capacity* for recall. The topic is much neglected in an otherwise extensive tradition of research; there have been few studies of differences in recall capacity; and there appear to have been none that look to personality as a source of such differences. At a first glance, psychoanalytic theory seems to offer no explicit statement on the problem, but a closer examination yields this hypothesis: individuals fixated at the late anal phase (the so-called anal retentives) have a greater ability to recall verbal material than those fixated at the early anal phase (anal expulsives).

Surely a far-fetched idea; but it may gain plausibility if we take the retentive–expulsive dimension to specify, not psychosexual fixation points per se, but differing forms of ego organization.[1] To begin with the anal retentive: (a) He has developed fairly stable techniques for coping with aggressive impulses. The dominant defenses are reaction-formation, undoing, and the various forms of isolation (including intellectualization). The isolation defenses are especially relevant here: their use gives a systematic and orderly cast to the thought process; verbal stimuli can be effectively organized and codified; when counter cathexes are directed against affects, ideation proper remains undisturbed. (b) His defensive style is characterized by a peculiar absorption in words and concepts. As Fenichel puts it: "He flees from the macrocosm of things to the microcosm of words" (1, p. 295). Cathexes are directed toward language, ideas, the thinking process itself.

These processes occur among (indeed, partly define) the obsessional neuroses. In the severe obsessional personality, however, we generally find that cognitive functioning is seriously burdened by the strenuous demands of defense; among "normal" retentives, cognitive style is in the obsessional direction—systematic and orderly—yet is spared the brittleness and rigidity, the vulnerability to breakthrough that we see among the clinically obsessional.

Far less is known about "anal expulsive" normals, and so we must offer here a more hesitant formulation. We take it that in this group, too, character structure has developed out of the struggle between parent and child on the issue of aggression. The anal retentive tames his hostile drives by turning against them, or

SOURCE. Article by Joseph Adelson and Joan Redmond, "Personality differences in the capacity for verbal recall" in the *Journal of abnormal and social Psychology*, Vol. 57, pp. 244–248, 1958.

[1] The discussion will follow a line of approach suggested by Fenichel (1, pp. 295–300) and Rapaport (3, pp. 622–625).

by isolation; the expulsive person shows a less thorough, less efficient regulation of these impulses. Aggression continues to be discharged, but in a muted, modified way, the dominant defenses being aim-inhibition and displacement. The original aims—aggression and disorder—are, so to speak, blunted, and find a modulated continuation in messiness, rebelliousness, impulsiveness.

The intrapsychic system, then, shows a *relative* failure to neutralize aggressive drives or to bind them adequately through countercathexes. A persistent imbalance between impulses and defense produces sporadic inefficiencies in certain types of cognitive performances. Leakages of aggression elicit anxiety and so bring about momentary disruptions of attention and concentration.

We are now in a position to turn to the problem of recall. Among retentives, the use of isolation permits a heightening of attention to external stimuli; unwelcome impulses and effects, which would disturb attention, are warded off. Equally important, we find a tendency to hypercathect words, an increased alertness to them. In concert, these processes produce a peculiar efficiency in the apprehension of verbal stimuli. Expulsives, on the other hand, are characterized by defensive processes that lead to a decreased capacity for verbal recall; the manner of handling impulses and affects brings about momentary disturbances of attention and concentration.

Method

Subjects. The sample consisted of 61 college women, all of them first-year students at Bennington College.

The Criterion for Anality. The Blacky Test was used to determine the type of anal fixation. Several weeks prior to the experiment itself, the test had been administered on a group basis to all entering students at the college. An S was designated "Expulsive" if she received a score of $++'$ (very strong) or $+$ (fairly strong) on Anal Expulsion, and a score of 0 on Anal Retention; the reverse was true for the scoring of retentiveness. Ss receiving scores on both dimensions were not included. An S was rated "Neutral" if she received 0 scores on both dimensions. The experimental group was composed of 32 expulsives, 18 retentives, and 11 neutrals.

The Stimuli. Two prose passages were used, one with innocuous, the other with disturbing content. We wanted to determine whether the hypothesized differences in recall would be present only when the material was of a nature to evoke defenses, or whether they would also be found with relatively neutral material.

a. "Disturbing" passage. Here we wanted a passage which would be threatening enough to elicit defenses, yet sufficiently decorous to permit its presentation to young ladies in a classroom setting. So we devised a passage which stated, rather crudely, Freud's theory of psychosexuality. It follows:

Psychoanalysis is the creation of Sigmund Freud, who was born in 1856 and died in 1939. Beginning with the attempt to cure neurotic patients, Freud developed one of the most significant systems for understanding human behavior. His psychology has had widespread influence to the extent that it has completely revised the previous understanding of human nature. At the center of his system is the idea that early childhood experiences influence later personality. This is called the Theory of Psychosexual Development, the major features of which follow:

During the first oral stage, the child receives intense pleasure sucking the mother's breast. There is a desire to eat everything and resistance to being deprived of this pleasure when weaned.

During the second oral stage, intense pleasure is received through using the teeth to bite and devour, desiring to chew and gnaw at the mother, with fear of punishment in return.

During the anal stage, pleasure is obtained through retaining bowel movements and through eliminating them. The child resists being trained to be neat and clean, and would rather smear his feces.

During the oedipal stage, the female child feels sexually attracted to her father, is jealous of her mother for possessing him, and wishes for the death or disappearance of her mother.

Between the third and fifth year, children experience intense pleasure through masturbation, by playing with their sexual organs. Along with this there is a strong fear of being caught and punished.

During this same period, female children become aware that they lack a penis. They feel inferior, believing that its absence is a punishment, and are jealous of the male's sexual organ.

Children sometimes feel intense hostility and jealousy toward a sibling. They feel that they are being neglected in favor of the other child, and wish for the sibling's death or disappearance.

b. "Innocuous passage. Here we wanted didactic, colorless prose, and so chose the following passage:

Undoubtedly the most famous brick house in seventeenth century New England was that built for Peter Sergeant in Boston. Sergeant, who had come to Boston in 1667, became a wealthy merchant and later served as a judge and a member of the Governor's Council. The land he bought on October 21, 1676, a large tract extending halfway from Washington to Tremont Street, included a fine garden and orchard, stable, and coach house. The big house which he built with brick walls about 2 feet thick, was completed in 1697. The Sergeant House was early accustomed to society. Governor and Lady Bellomont visited it for several months in 1697, and Sergeant's third wife, whom he married in 1707, was Lady Phips, widow of the former Governor Sir William Phips. After Sergeant's death in 1714 the mansion was purchased by the province (in 1716) to serve as a residence for the royal governors. It was thenceforth known as the Province House.

c. *Scoring*. Because of differences in the sentence structures of the two passages, we used a separate scoring system for each. The "disturbing" passage had been written so as to permit its being scored by phrases, or thought units; S was given one point for each phrase precisely or substantially correct. In the scoring of the "innocuous" passage, one point was given for each word (except for conjunctions and prepositions) correctly reproduced; dates and numbers accurately recalled were given two points. Since the scoring of the "innocuous" passage was more or less mechanical, requiring only the counting of words, no study of interjudge agreement seemed necessary. For the scoring of the "disturbing" passage, scoring criteria were first established for each phrase; then a sample of the protocols was scored separately by two judges. Agreement between them was nearly complete and formal testing of interjudge agreement was therefore omitted.

Administration. The recall tasks were administered to five classes in freshmen literature which met at the same hour. The experimenter introduced the task in these words: "Read these papers carefully twice. You will be asked questions on them later." Ss were then given the passages to read. The passages were printed on separate sheets of paper. The classes were allowed about ten minutes to read the material. The passages were then collected, writing paper distributed, and Ss told: "Now write down all you can remember about what you have just read." This was a test of immediate recall. We were also interested in learning what differences, if any, would be present in delayed recall. One week later, the experimenters therefore returned to the classes and asked the Ss to reproduce all they could now remember about the passages.

There were 78 Ss in the five classes; all are included in the analysis, except those with Blacky scores on both anality dimensions, and those who were absent from either or both of the class meetings when the recall testings were done.

Results and Discussion
Anal Retention vs. Expulsion and Recall

In Table 1, we find the results for both passages and for immediate and delayed recall. Retentives show a significant superiority in reproduction of both types of material; their advantage persists over time.

We may gain a more graphic impression of the differences if we look at the data from the

Table 1. Differences between Expulsives and Retentives in Verbal Recall
(Expulsives $N = 32$; Retentives $N = 18$)

Tests	Group	M	SD	t	P
Innocuous passage—Immediate recall	Expulsive	19.9	12.84	2.25	.05
	Retentive	28.3	12.08		
Innocuous passage—Delayed recall	Expulsive	9.9	6.00	2.60	.02
	Retentive	15.1	8.66		
Disturbing passage—Immediate recall[a]	Expulsive	21.6	9.59	2.68	.02
	Retentive	28.7	12.29		
Disturbing passage—Delayed recall[a]	Expulsive	11.1	5.92	3.66	.001
	Retentive	19.3	8.94		

[a] The mean scores for the disturbing passages refer to thought units.

point of view of quartile extremes. For example, when we consider the distribution of scores for "disturbing passage—immediate recall," we find that retentives, who make up 36 per cent of the total sample contribute 69 per cent of the scores in the top quartile and only 9 per cent in the bottom quartile. Roughly equivalent distributions are found for the other passage and other testings.

We made no specific hypothesis about the neutral Ss; however, we wanted to determine the recall performance of this group. If we take the Ss to represent average functioning in recall, we would have some basis for judging whether the expulsive-retentive differences are due to the superior recall capacity of retentives, the inferior capacity of expulsives, or both. We found that for all four comparisons the neutral group is located midway between the other two. This finding suggests that both the retentive and expulsive may occupy extreme positions in recall performance.

Other Possible Sources of the Differences

a. *Other psychosexual dimensions.* We next considered whether differences in recall are associated exclusively with anality; could it be that anality is one of several psychosexual dimensions where we would find similar differences? To test this possibility, we looked for recall differences (both passages, both testings) on all of the other Blacky dimensions; that is, we compared the recall scores of high and low groups on Oral Sadism, Oral Eroticism, Oedipal Intensity, and so on; we also compared high and low groups on Total Pregenitality. Of 40 differences tested, only two were significant at the .05 level: the high group on Oedipal Intensity has better recall scores for the "innocuous passage—delayed recall"; the low group on Ego Ideal has higher recall scores on "disturbing passage—immediate recall." These results (two of 40 at the .05 level) are what we would expect by chance alone.[2]

It is interesting to note that no Blacky group receives recall scores (on each of the four passage-testing comparisons) as high as those received by the retentives; and only one Blacky group has a mean recall score as low as those received by the expulsives.

b. *Intellectual capacity.* Another possible ex-planation of the results is that expulsives and retentives are intellectually unequal, and that the differences in recall performance are due to intellectual differences associated with the type of anal fixation. To check this, we compared the SAT scores (V and M) of both groups; these were available for most of our Ss. For both V and M there are no significant differences between the groups; indeed, their means are almost identical.

Partial Replication

An unpublished study by Nahin (2) supports some of these findings. Nahin's research was on a somewhat different topic, but a portion of her study duplicates some elements of the present one. The criterion for anality was the Blacky Test; Ss were Bennington College freshmen. However, she used only a "disturbing" prose passage (basically equivalent to the one reported here) and tested only for immediate recall. She found significant differences between expulsive and retentive Ss.

Nonverbal Recall

What about the recall of nonverbal stimuli? Should we expect to find expulsive-retentive differences here as well? The question is relevant to some parts of the theory underlying this research. The retentive S is presumed to be sensitive to words, at least in some respects: he tends to reduce anxiety inherent in "things" by capturing them verbally, by transposing them into the safer, more tractable realm of language: taming by naming, let us say. There develops, then, a peculiar efficiency in certain (though surely not all) verbal performances, as this study has suggested. Now one might wonder whether this capacity is operative only when the stimuli are verbal (or can be made so by being "named" or "labelled"), or whether we are dealing with a more general disposition.

We cannot, unfortunately, provide a satisfactory answer to the question. Although we carried out a study of the recall of nonverbal stimuli, circumstances did not allow a precise enough duplication of the conditions of the verbal recall research. It is reported here briefly.[3]

A set of 20 abstract line drawings were developed. The pictures were simple enough in design to permit ready reproduction by the ex-

---

[2] The tables which report these and other results described here may be found in Redmond (4).

[3] The authors are grateful to John Hirtzel for carrying out the analysis of the data.

perimental Ss, and were so drawn that they did not resemble common forms or objects; consequently, they could not be "labelled." In the experiment, the drawings were projected on a screen, one at a time, for 15 seconds. Ss were students in a large lecture class at the University of Michigan, all of whom had earlier been tested for expulsion–retention. Except for slight and necessary changes in wording, the instructions were the same as in the verbal recall study. After the drawings had been exposed, the group was asked to reproduce them. The reproductions were scored by a six-category scheme (e.g., perfect reproduction; one slight error, etc.) Male and female Ss were treated separately, since they distribute differently on expulsion–retention; there were 33 female retentives and 22 expulsives, 21 male expulsives and 10 retentives. Expulsion–retention differences, within sex, were tested for each of the six scoring categories and for various combinations of categories. No significant differences were found; in fact, recall scores throughout are highly similar.

But the variations in experimental procedure are too marked to allow us to treat the two recall studies as comparable. In all likelihood, recall performance can be significantly influenced by differences in motivational conditions, experimental set, testing atmosphere, and so on. It seems the most judicious course to take the findings on nonverbal recall as, at best, suggestive.

Discussion

The study has demonstrated that under certain conditions we can obtain personality differences in verbal recall. Yet all of our experience in the area of personality and cognition warns us to caution in generalizing the findings. The results may very well be tied to a particular set of experimental conditions: change the stimuli, in length or content; change the experimental instructions; change the method of testing recall, from reproduction to recognition, as an example; use a different sampling of Ss; make any of these changes and, for all we know, the differences may fail to appear. Our understanding of the expulsion-retention variable and of the influence of personality on recall is still too uncertain to allow us to extrapolate the findings with any sense of confidence.

There are, then, a great many occasions for speculation offered by the research. The sti-

muli, the details of administration, the experimental atmosphere (especially the role of anxiety in producing the results)—each of these gives us an opportunity to reconsider the meaning of the experiment. But perhaps the most critical question to be raised concerns the expulsion–retention variable itself.

In formulating the central hypothesis of the research, we took the position that recall differences are based on capacity differences; equivalent motivation was assumed for both groups of Ss. The assumption, however, is open to challenge: can we explain the findings equally well as arising from motivational differences between expulsives and retentives?

A considerable body of unpublished data makes this a highly credible alternative. Anal retentives, it appears, show a marked disposition towards compliance and conformity, especially so in the presence of authority; anal expulsives are distinguished by an edgy, often sullen independence. Thus we can well imagine the retentives, solemn, *bürgerlich,* eager to do well, bending to the experimental task with dedication and gravity; and it is quite as easy to see the expulsives, skeptical or diffident or rebellious, giving the task only cursory attention.

There is, at this moment, no way of choosing between the motivational and cognitive interpretations of the findings; they are equally plausible. If the nonverbal recall experiment had been comparable to the earlier study, then we would have some reason for believing that motivational differences are not the source of the recall differences. (Even so, it could be argued that nonverbal stimuli do not engage motivation or interest to the same degree that words do.) As it is, the question must remain open, awaiting further research.

The position we take on this issue—motivation vs. capacity—will determine whether we view the recall differences as a function of differences in acquisition, or retention, or performance. If a motivational factor is involved we can regard it as influential at any or all points between stimulus presentation and reproduction. The contrast between eager and indifferent attitudes towards the task might operate in the amount of attention given the stimuli, or in the intention to retain what was learned, or in the degree of interest in reproducing the stimuli.

Our own approach is derived from the cognitive concepts of psychoanalytic theory, and so we interpret the findings as an outcome of variations in cognitive style. From this viewpoint, one is led to stress differences in the capacity for attention and concentration, which would operate with particular force during the process of acquisition. We would then see the experiment as a study of incidental learning, rather than retention or performance.

Summary

It was hypothesized that "anal retentive" individuals have a greater ability to recall verbal material than "anal expulsive" subjects. The hypothesis was derived from an analysis of differences in ego organization between the two groups.

The subjects were 61 first-year college women. The criterion of "anality" was the Blacky Test: there were 32 expulsives, 18 retentives, and 11 neutrals. Subjects were asked to read two prose passages, each of several hundred words. One passage discussed sexual and aggressive themes and was considered "disturbing" in content; the other was an "innocuous" description of colonial architecture. Subjects were asked to reproduce the passages immediately after presentation and again one week later.

Retentives showed a significant superiority over expulsives in the reproduction of both passages immediately and one week later. Neutrals scored midway between the two extreme groups on the four testings. There were no differences in intellectual capacity between retentives and expulsives as measured by the SAT., V and M. None of the other Blacky dimensions is associated with recall differences. The findings have been partially corroborated in another study. A study of the recall of nonverbal stimuli showed no differences between expulsives and retentives; since the research methods of this study differed in some possibly critical respect from the investigation of verbal recall, the findings are offered as suggestive rather than definitive.

REFERENCES

1. Fenichel, O. *The psychoanalytic theory of neurosis.* New York: Norton, 1945.
2. Nahin, Barbara. Psychosexuality and memory. Unpublished thesis, Bennington College, 1953.
3. Rapaport, D. *Organization and pathology of thought.* New York: Columbia Univer. Press, 1951.
4. Redmond, Joan. Anality and memory. Unpublished thesis, Bennington College, 1954.

6. An investigation of the psychoanalytic theory of paranoid delusions

HAROLD S. ZAMANSKY

THE PURPOSE OF THE PRESENT STUDY WAS TO INVESTIGATE, using an objective, partially validated technique, the psychoanalytic hypothesis that people who suffer from paranoid delusions have strong but unacceptable homosexual urges. In addition, an attempt was made to study the nature of these impulses and of the defenses created against them.

The psychoanalytic explanation of the dynamics involved in the development of paranoid delusions is that these delusions serve as defensive measures to enable the patient to handle a strong conflict over powerful but unconscious homosexual strivings. What happens is that the proposition "I (a man) love him" is converted by reaction formation into "I hate him." As further insurance that the homosexual wish will not become conscious, this second proposition is transformed, by means of projection, into "He hates me" (5). One should find, then, that persons with paranoid delusions have strong homosexual wishes, but that these wishes are not permitted existence on a conscious level. Psychoanalysts generally (2, p. 435) have felt that this formulation applies not only to pure paranoia, but also to cases of the paranoid type of schizophrenia.

In the five decades since this formulation by Freud, his views have been supported by many psychoanalysts (3, 15, 16, 17). Other analysts, while agreeing that the paranoid individual is characterized by powerful but unconscious homosexual conflicts, have suggested that homo-

SOURCE. Article by Harold S. Zamansky, "An investigation of the psychoanalytic theory of paranoid delusions" in *Journal of Personality*, Vol. 26, pp. 410–425, 1958.

sexuality itself serves a defensive function in the development of the psychosis and is not the primary etiological factor (7, 9, 14, 18). Knight (9), for example, pointed out that the strong homosexual wish of the male paranoid is, in actuality, a very intense and desperate attempt to neutralize and erotize a tremendous unconscious hate directed toward the father. The very powerful need to keep the homosexual urges from awareness is based not on cultural pressures which prohibit the expression of these urges, but on the fact that the least approach to the object arouses intense anxieties that both the object and the patient will be destroyed by the hostility in the patient and the consequent hostility aroused in the object. These theoretical positions were based on and supported by observations made by psychoanalysts in the usual analytic situation with their patients. The question must be raised, however, as to whether the setting of analytical therapy constitutes an adequate observational situation for the testing of an hypothesis. Psychoanalysts have at times been accused of finding in their patients the material they set out to find. Few attempts, for example, have been made by psychoanalysts to compare their findings with a suitable control group.

On the other hand, other investigators have attempted to test the psychoanalytic hypothesis using techniques other than the usual analytic interview and have varied widely in the degree to which their findings supported Freud's conclusions. The studies of Aronson (1), Gardner (6), Musiker (12), and Norman (13) were generally supportive. On the other hand, investigations such as those of Klein and Horowitz (8) and Miller (10) indicated that an intimate relation between paranoid delusions and homosexuality could be demonstrated for only a relatively small percentage of the cases studied.

Because of the conflicting and sometimes ambiguous results of the studies in this area and because of the lack of proper controls in many of them, it seems that the psychoanalytic hypotheses concerning paranoid delusions have yet to be adequately confirmed.

The Present Study

The necessity for obtaining a measurable expression of a need despite powerful forces which act constantly to inhibit its manifestation presented the most difficult practical problem in this study. In developing the technique employed in the present investgation, we began with the assumption that homosexuality is a function of a greater than usual attraction toward members of one's own sex and/or an active rejection of members of the opposite sex. From this it follows that if an individual with strong homosexual urges is placed in a situation in which there is an equal opportunity for attraction to either a member of his own sex or of the opposite sex, he should manifest by his behavior (if the task is appropriately disguised) a greater attraction to the member of his own sex, and a lesser attraction to the opposite sex, than would the heterosexually oriented person.

More specifically, given an appropriately disguised task, it was expected that if a series of pairs of pictures, each pair consisting of a picture of a man and of a woman, were shown, one pair at a time, to a man with strong homosexual needs, he would spend a larger proportion of the total exposure time looking at the male member of the pairs than would a person with less or none of these needs.

Given the further assumption that paranoid individuals are characterized by strong homosexual needs, the following hypotheses seemed reasonable:

Hypothesis 1: Men with paranoid delusions, when compared to men without these delusions, will manifest a greater attraction to males than to females.

Hypothesis 2: Paranoid men will manifest a greater avoidance of homosexually threatening stimuli than will nonparanoid men.

Hypothesis 3: Paranoid men, when compared with nonparanoid men, will express a greater preference for women and a lesser one for men as this expression becomes more explicit or conscious.

Hypothesis 4: Paranoid men, when compared with nonparanoid men, will manifest a greater attraction to males than to neutral (nonhuman) objects.

Hypothesis 5: Paranoid men will manifest a greater avoidance of women than will nonparanoid men.

The picture-pairs technique employed in the present study to test these propositions is based on the assumption that a person will manifest a preference for (or a rejection of) a particular kind of erotic object by looking more (or less) at it than at another kind of object. An initial attempt to validate this technique (19), using groups of normal and overt-homosexual males, suggested that it may be considered a valid reflector of object choice.

Method

Subjects

In the present study, two groups of Ss, all patients at the Boston State Hospital, were used. The experimental group consisted of 20 males, most of whom were formally diagnosed as either paranoid condition or dementia praecox, paranoid type, in all of whom the dominant clinical symptom consisted of delusions of persecution, of reference, or of grandeur. These Ss (as well as the controls) were selected on the basis of their psychiatrist's recommendation and of a thorough study by the writer of the individual case histories. The experimental Ss ranged in age from 23 to 45 years, with a mean of 30 years. The range of the duration of their present hospitalization was from one month to two years, seven months, and averaged 13 months. Sixteen of the 20 Ss had a formal education consisting of some years of high school or better; 12 were or had been married. Twelve Ss had been engaged in skilled or highly skilled occupations, while eight had been working at relatively nonskilled jobs such as shipper and shoe worker.

The 20 control patients were selected with a view to their being as similar to the experimental Ss as possible, with the exception of the presence of a dominant paranoid picture. All of the control patients were formally diagnosed as belonging to one of the subtypes of dementia praecox other than the paranoid type. Their age ranged from 19 to 42 years and averaged 33 years. They had been hospitalized from two

months to two years, nine months, with a mean
of 18 months. Eighteen Ss had had some high
school education or better; only two had ever
been married. Thirteen had been engaged in
skilled or highly skilled occupations.

Experimental Measure

In the measure of latent homosexuality, 24
pairs of cards, each 9 x 12 inches, were used.
On each card was pasted a picture cut from a
popular magazine. The pictures were exhibited,
a pair at a time, in a specially designed tachisto-
scope-like viewing apparatus, which permitted
the undetected observation of the S's eye movement by an E seated at the other end of the
apparatus. Three push-button-controlled timers,
operated by E, recorded the total exposure time
as well as the S's male-side and female-side
fixation times for each pair of cards. The observation and timing were done for all the Ss by
the writer. To insure against the E's learning the
location of any particular picture, the left-right
order of the cards was randomly changed after
every three or four Ss.

Psychoanalytic theory states that though
strong homosexual impulses are present in people with persecutory delusions, there are also
ego defenses to prevent the emergence of these
impulses into awareness. Thus, it is necessary in
a technique of this sort that the Ss be as unaware as possible of the fact that they are exercising some selection regarding which picture
in each pair they look at for a longer period of
time. For this reason, the instructions to the S
indicated that the experiment was a study of
the perception of differences in size. He was
told that he was to look carefully at each pair
of pictures in the viewing apparatus and tell the
E which member of the pair was larger, that is,
which picture had the greater overall surface
area. In actuality, both pictures in any one pair,
with the exception of three pairs of neutral pictures (i.e., pictures without people, usually
landscapes of some sort), were identical in area,
although their shapes usually differed. The S
was allowed to look at each pair of pictures until
he felt ready to make a judgment of size. Thus,
the exposure time of each pair was left entirely
up to the Ss.

As has been stated, 24 pairs of pictures were
used in the experiment. Of these, six pairs consisted of a picture of a man and of a woman in
ordinary dress and position, and three pairs of
two or more men and two or more women. Since
the task was disguised, it was expected that, if
the psychoanalytic formulation is correct, the
experimental Ss would spend a greater proportion of the exposure time looking at the male
member of each pair of pictures than would the
control Ss (Hypothesis 1).

In addition to testing for a preponderance of
homosexual tendencies in paranoid over nonparanoid persons, an attempt was also made to
obtain a manifestation of the strong defensive
measures which are said to come into play
whenever the emergence of these impulses into
consciousness is threatened. For this purpose,
two measures were used: (a) Included in the
24 pairs of pictures were four pairs of male-
female pictures in which the men were pictured
in poses which would appear threatening to a
person attempting to ward off unconscious
homosexual impulses (e.g., two men kissing,
two men dressed in towels in a locker room
with one man resting his hand upon the other's
thigh). The pictures of the females in these
pairs were in ordinary pose, not intended to be
threatening. In the case of these four pairs of
pictures, it was expected that the experimental
Ss would fixate less on the male and longer on
the female member of each pair in an effort to
avoid the threatening male pictures (Hypothesis 2). (b) After all the pictures had been
presented once, the entire series was shown
again, and this time the S was asked to state
which picture of each pair he found more appealing—which appeared to attract him more.
It was expected in the case of the paranoid S
that, since the matter of preference was now
presented to him on a much more conscious
level, his defenses would manifest themselves in
such a way that he would select significantly
fewer pictures of males than he had favored by
his fixation in the first part of the experiment
(Hypothesis 3).

Besides investigating the presence of homosexual urges and defenses against them in paranoid individuals, some attention was devoted to
the question of whether this homosexuality consists primarily of an attraction to men or a rejection of women. For this purpose, four pairs
were included in the 24 pairs of pictures which
consisted of a picture of a man and a neutral
picture (one without any people), as well as
four pairs which consisted of a picture of a
woman and a neutral picture. It was considered that an attraction to males would be implied if an S fixated longer than did the control
Ss on the male cards of the male-neutral pairs.
Similarly, an avoidance of women would be implied if he looked longer than the control Ss at
the neutral pictures of the female-neutral pairs
(Hypotheses 4 and 5).

Finally, three pairs were included in which
both pictures were neutral ones. These were
used to lessen the chance that the Ss would become suspicious that it was their reactions to
people that E was primarily concerned with.
The order of the five different kinds of pairs

was systematically varied throughout the entire series of 24. Table 1 summarizes the kinds of pictures used.

Table 1. Description of Picture-Pairs

Kinds of Pairs	Number of Such Pairs
Male-female	9
Male-neutral	4
Female-neutral	4
Threatening male-female	4
Neutral-neutral	3
Total	24

All the pictures of people (men, women, and threatening men) used in this study were selected from a group of about 175 photographs. The final selections were made from the ratings of five judges (advanced graduate students in clinical psychology). These judges were asked to rate all the male pictures along a four-point scale, in terms of the amount of threat they would have for a person defending against latent homosexual tendencies if he were shown the pictures in the context of performing an intellectual task. The pictures of women were rated according to the degree of threat they would have for a male S who is severely threatened by women as sexual objects. From these ratings, only those pictures upon which all five judges agreed closely were selected for inclusion in the experiment. The threatening male pictures were selected from those given a high rating on the threat continuum. The ordinary-pose male pictures (used in the male-female and male-neutral pairs) were taken from those rated as low in threat value. All of the female pictures were taken from the low end of the threat scale. The agreement of the five judges with one another on the threat value of the pictures finally selected to be used in the test was better than 90 per cent.

Scoring Procedure

In the case of the nine male-female pairs of pictures, all the scores were expressed as the number of seconds spent looking at the male pictures minus the number of seconds spent looking at the female pictures. Such a score was obtained for each S on each pair of pictures. Then these scores were averaged (divided by nine) for each S across all male-female pairs. Finally, these individual mean scores were averaged (divided by 20) for each group of Ss. Thus the final score (Mean Attraction Score)

expresses in seconds the mean excess amount of time spent looking at the male pictures in the nine male-female pairs by all 20 Ss in any one group. This same general procedure was also followed in arriving at the Mean Attraction Score for the other types of picture pairs. In the four threatening male-female pairs, the four male-neutral pairs, and the four female-neutral pairs, the original scores were expressed as the number of seconds spent looking at the threatening male, ordinary male, and female cards, respectively, minus the time devoted to the female, neutral, and neutral cards respectively.

Comparison of Groups

The performances of the experimental and control groups on any series of picture-pairs (such as male-female or female-neutral) were compared by calculating the significance of the difference between the Mean Attraction Score earned by each group for that particular set of cards. The usual formula for the significance of differences between the means of two independent samples was used. Since the direction of difference was predicted in advance in the hypotheses, all statistical results reported were based on one-tail tests of significance.

Since the individual Attraction Scores for the two groups of Ss were in some cases not normally distributed, the results yielded by the t tests were checked against comparisons of the experimental and control groups by means of the Mann-Whitney test (and, in the case of Hypothesis 3, the Wilcoxon matched pairs test), a nonparametric measure which is independent of assumptions about the shape of the population distribution (**11**, pp. 314–317).

Results

Hypothesis 1: Men with paranoid delusions, when compared to men without these delusions, will manifest a greater attraction to males than to females. The results summarized in Table 2 reveal that the paranoid Ss tended, on the average, to look 1.49 seconds longer at pictures of men in the nine male-female pairs. The score of −.70 for the nonparanoid schizophrenics indicates that these Ss averaged .70 second longer at the pictures of women. The difference between these two scores is significant at beyond the .001 level. The corresponding median scores for experimental and control groups were 1.47 and −1.03 seconds respectively, and the Mann-Whitney test of the difference between the two groups was also significant at less than the .001 level ($z = 4.37$). These results lend strong experimental support to psychoanalytic formulations and to frequent clinical reports that paranoid delusions are usually accompanied by homosexual tendencies.

Table 2. Mean Attraction Scores (MAS) and Significance Levels

	Types of Picture-Pairs				
	Male-Female	Threatening Male-Female	Male-Neutral	Female-Neutral	Neutral-Neutral
MAS:					
Experimental group	1.49	1.41	.56	−2.02	−.28
MAS:					
Control group	−.70	.85	−.90	−.88	−.88
t	5.34*	.98	2.18†	1.46	1.28

*$p < .001$ †$p < .05$

Hypothesis 2: Paranoid men will manifest a greater avoidance of homosexually threatening stimuli than will nonparanoid men. This is one of the two measures by which it was attempted to obtain a manifestation of the defensive mechanisms which are said to prevent the homosexual impulses from entering awareness. It was expected that in the case of the four pairs containing the threatening male pictures, the experimental Ss would look less at the male and longer at the female pictures than would the control Ss. The second column of Table 2 shows that there was no significant difference between the Mean Attraction Scores of the two groups, i.e., the two groups did not differ in the proportion of time spent looking at the threatening male cards; thus, the prediction was not supported. Two possible reasons for this are that, (a) contrary to analytic theory, the paranoid person does not have a strong need to keep homosexually threatening material from awareness and (b) the threatening stimuli used in the experiment were, in fact, not sufficiently threatening to call forth an explicit avoidance reaction. While the data provide no definitive basis for choosing between these hypotheses, it will be seen from the discussion of Hypothesis 3, which follows, that the first of these explanations is highly untenable.

Hypothesis 3: Paranoid men, when compared with nonparanoid men, will express a greater preference for women and a lesser one for men as this expression becomes more explicit or conscious. The second technique employed in attempting to obtain a manifestation of the paranoid's defenses against the awareness of homosexual impulses was to compare his selection of female pictures, as indicated by the amount of time he spent looking at them in preference to male pictures, with his selection when asked explicitly to specify "Which do you prefer?" The evaluation of Hypothesis 3 was based on the nine pairs of male-female pictures. Table 3 reports the results of comparisons for the experimental and control Ss. The figures in the

first two rows of this table are group means and are based on raw scores which indicate the number of female pictures preferred by each S (either by verbal selection or by a longer fixation time than for the corresponding male picture) in the nine male-female pairs. Since each group was compared with itself, the calculation of t was based on the usual formula for the significance of differences between the means of two equated samples.

Table 3. Verbal Preference vs. Preference by Fixation

	Experimental Group	Control Group
Verbal preference	5.75	5.80
Fixation preference	2.80	5.60
t	4.40*	.27

*$p < .001$.

As Table 3 indicates, when the paranoid Ss were asked to state which picture they preferred, they selected a significantly greater number of women (and so, of course, fewer men) than they did when their preference was assessed by determining which picture they tended to look at longer (a much less explicit process). As a matter of fact, the mean of their verbal choices was almost identical with that of the control group. On the other hand, the control Ss displayed no meaningful difference between the number of male and female pictures selected by verbal choice and by fixation preference. A nonparametric analysis of these data, using Wilcoxon's matched pairs test, yielded similar results.

These results support the hypothesis that, when measured by a disguised technique, men suffering from paranoid delusions indicate a higher preference for males than do men without paranoid delusions; however, when the question of their choice is made more explicit, and so more conscious, defensive forces are set into motion which lower the expressed preference for males and cause this preference to approximate that of persons who do not suffer from paranoid delusions.

Hypothesis 4: Paranoid men, when compared with nonparanoid men, will manifest a greater attraction to males than to neutral (non-human) objects.

Hypothesis 5: Paranoid men will manifest a greater avoidance of women than will nonparanoid men. The present study has corroborated the psychoanalytic contention that men with strong paranoid delusions may be characterized by more powerful homosexual urges than those who are relatively free of these delusions. One may ask further, however, whether this homosexuality is characterized by a primary attraction to men as sexual objects or whether it reflects principally a reaction to a rejection of women. As Knight pointed out (9, p. 150), Freud's theory did not attempt to analyze the forerunners of the proposition, "I love him." In the present experiment an attempt was made to explore this question by the inclusion of four pairs of male-neutral and female-neutral pictures in the series of stimulus cards. The third column of Table 2 indicates that the experimental Ss showed a preference for the pictures of males (in the male-neutral pairs) that was significantly greater than that of the control group. On the other hand (fourth column, Table 2), while there was some tendency ($t = 1.46$) for the experimental Ss to reject the female pictures (in the female-neutral pairs) more than did the controls, this difference was not statistically significant. Similar results were obtained from an analysis of these data by means of the Mann-Whitney test: a statistically significant ($z = 1.97$) preference by the experimental Ss for the male pictures and a trend ($z = -1.34$) toward avoidance of the female pictures. While these results fail to support Hypothesis 5 at an adequate level of statistical significance, the trend noted in the data suggests that the null hypothesis should be accepted with caution.

With this caution in mind, the present evidence indicates that the male paranoid is characterized by a strong attraction to men, without necessarily rejecting women as sexual objects.

The Neutral-Neutral Picture Pairs

The last column of Table 2 indicates that the experimental and control groups were not significantly differentiated by the three pairs in which neither picture was of a person. Since these pairs were included only to prevent the Ss' guessing the central focus of the experiment, no significant difference between the two groups was expected here.

Discussion

The present experiment has corroborated the hypothesis that men with paranoid delusions are characterized by stronger homosexual needs than men who do not suffer from these delusions. The results of the attempt to demonstrate the presence of defensive measures that function to prevent these needs from entering the persons' cognitive field have been somewhat more equivocal. A comparison between the experimental and control groups' performance on the threatening male-female pictures yielded nonsignificant differences.

More conclusive evidence comes from the second technique employed to demonstrate defenses against awareness of homosexuality. Here the results indicated that when the purpose of the test was disguised, the paranoid's choice of males was significantly greater than that of the nonparanoid, *but* when the matter of his selection was made more explicit and, presumably, more conscious, his choices of males approximated those of the nonparanoid in the same situation. From these results it appears that when homosexual impulses threaten to approach consciousness, the ego fulfils its protective function by bringing about a reorganization of cognitive forces so that, at least on a superficial level, the paranoid individual functions vis à vis objects of opposite sex in a manner approximating that of the nonparanoid person. It may be that in this suggestion lies one explanation of the discrepant findings of investigators in this area, i.e., it is likely that researchers have varied in the extent to which their techniques have evoked a defensive reaction in their Ss which tended to obscure their results. It is, perhaps, no coincidence that the greatest experimental support of the psychoanalytic hypothesis has come from those studies which made use of projective techniques. These techniques have the advantage of permitting the S to give evidence of certain needs without his being aware that he is doing so.

Though the present experiment has demonstrated a greater degree of homosexuality in men with paranoid delusions than in nonparanoid individuals, these results tell us nothing about the role which homosexuality plays in the development of these delusions. Is it, as Freud believed, the primary etiological factor, or is it merely a link in a chain of psychodynamic factors leading eventually to the development of delusions? The present experiment was not designed to answer this question directly. Nevertheless, it is possible to make a number of inferences from the pattern of the results.

These inferences are based upon a consideration of the nature of the paranoid's homosexual attraction. The results of the present experiment indicate that the experimental Ss displayed a clear-cut preference for male figures (male-neutral pictures). On the other hand, the data did not demonstrate conclusively that the male paranoid tends to avoid female figures. If one assumes, then, that paranoid men are characterized by an attraction to males without necessarily expressing a rejection of women, the following reasoning seems appropriate:

Freud, in his discussion of homosexuality, listed a number of possible etiological factors (4, p. 241 ff.). Most of these suggest that the (male) individual turns to men as sexual objects as the result of severe anxiety incurred at the idea of relations with women. For example, the individual may not be able to tolerate the absence of the penis in his love objects, or he may fear castration by the female sex organ, or he may feel required to reject women because of his father's wrath. In all of these cases a rejection of women as sexual objects precedes the development of an attraction to men.

In this same paper (4), however, Freud went on to mention yet another origin of homosexuality. He pointed out that powerful aggressive impulses that could culminate in death-wishes directed against male siblings might, "under the influence of training," yield to repression and transformation, so that "the rivals of the earlier period became the first homosexual love-objects." Here, then, is an instance in which homosexuality may involve an attraction to men without being based on a prior rejection of women. Freud commented (4, p. 243) that this pattern "led only to homosexual attitudes, which . . . did not involve a horror of women." He was, however, careful to emphasize that this pattern might be typical only of homosexuals; he felt that, " . . . it is a complete contrast to the development of persecutory paranoia, in which the person who has before been loved becomes the hated persecutor, whereas here [in homosexuality] the hated rivals are transformed into love objects" (4, p. 242).

Knight (9), however, suggested that the paranoid's homosexuality is actually a defense against powerful aggressive wishes toward male figures. In this, Knight has, in a sense, applied to the homosexuality of the paranoid one of Freud's explanations of general homosexuality and has thus presented an integrated theory of paranoid dynamics, one that takes into account more recent developments in psychoanalysis. It should be noted, however, that while both writers were dealing with the management of intense hostility toward male figures, Knight's focus was upon the figure of the father, while Freud's was upon male siblings.

If one considers, in the present experiment, that the paranoid patients were characterized by an attraction to males without at the same time manifesting a rejection of women, such a pattern would be consistent with what one would expect if the homosexual attraction were a function of intense hostile feelings directed toward male figures. It is suggested, therefore, that the results of the present experiment support the view of paranoia presented by Knight, namely, that the person with paranoid delusions is indeed characterized by strong homosexual impulses, but that these impulses themselves serve a defensive function, that of helping to neutralize and erotize powerful hostile wishes against male figures.

It is of interest here that in another study by the writer (19) in which the performances of male overt homosexuals and normal controls were compared on the set of picture-pairs employed in the present experiment, the homosexuals manifested *both* an attraction to male figures and a rejection of female figures, although the latter was not so clearly demonstrated as the former. While a comparison of the two experiments is not entirely justifiable because the Ss in the present study were somewhat older and of lower educational and socioeconomic status than the overt homosexuals, it is, nevertheless, tempting to speculate that the homosexuality which is characteristic of the overt homosexual may, in some degree, be of a different psychodynamic origin than that involved in the development of paranoid delusions. In contrast to the paranoid individual, the overt homosexual's choice of male objects appears to be, at least in part, a function of his inability to tolerate the anxiety aroused by erotic relations with women.

This way of accounting for the data is highly speculative and needs testing by further experiments. It does, however, lead to hypotheses that might serve as the basis for these experiments. One would expect, for example, that overt homosexuals would have less unconscious hostility toward men, or would be better able to handle their conscious aggressive feelings toward them, than would people with paranoid delusions. Again, one would expect overt homosexuals to be more sensitive to anxieties of castration by women and to regard them more as threatening figures.

The question of "choice of symptom" has always baffled students of psychopathology. In the area of the present experiment, theorists have been embarrassed by the question of why, given strong homosexual impulses, one person develops paranoid delusions and another becomes an overt homosexual. Perhaps the answer lies in different origins of the homosexual attraction. The person whose homosexuality serves as a defense against strong hostile wishes dares not risk intimate contact with other men. Therefore, there is a great need for him to develop a means of avoiding this, such as projecting his homosexual impulses away from himself or transforming them into another emotional guise. The person, however, in whose homosexuality a hatred for members of the same sex plays a less important role has less of an intrapsychic need to deny it and can afford to give direct expression to his homosexual impulses in his behavior.

Summary

In this study an attempt was made to investigate the psychoanalytic theory that paranoid delusions are developed in an attempt to cope with powerful but unconscious homosexual urges. In addition, some aspects of the nature of these urges and of the defenses erected against them were studied. Two matched groups of Ss were used: a group of 20 hospitalized psychotic males (mostly diagnosed dementia praecox, paranoid type) in whom paranoid delusions were a dominant symptom, and 20 hospitalized schizophrenic males in whom paranoid symptoms were absent. The experimental technique provided for a measure of object choice as the difference in time spent looking at pictures of different kinds of (human) objects. The following hypotheses were tested:

1. Men with paranoid delusions, when compared to men without these delusions, will manifest a greater attraction to males than to females.

2. Paranoid men will manifest a greater avoidance of homosexually threatening stimuli than will nonparanoid men.

3. Paranoid men, when compared with nonparanoid men, will express a greater preference for women and a lesser one for men as this expression becomes more explicit or conscious.

4. Paranoid men, when compared with nonparanoid men, will manifest a greater attraction to males than to neutral (nonhuman) objects.

5. Paranoid men will manifest a greater avoidance of women than will nonparanoid men.

The results of the experiment supported the first, third, and fourth hypotheses at a statistically significant level. The paranoid Ss spent a significantly greater amount of time than did the nonparanoids in looking at the pictures of men in the male-female pairs and in the male-neutral pairs. When asked to express verbally their preference for pictures of men or of women, the paranoid Ss selected significantly fewer men than they had chosen by the less explicit fixation-time technique. A similar difference was not manifested by the control Ss. These findings support the following conclusions:

1. Men with paranoid delusions tend to have stronger homosexual impulses than male psychotics who are relatively free from these delusions.

2. Men with paranoid delusions tend to avoid explicit or direct manifestations of homosexual object preference.

3. The homosexuality of paranoid men tends to be characterized by a primary attraction toward men as sexual objects, and not necessarily by an avoidance of women.

The results of the present experiment also permit the following inferences which are, however, merely speculations at the present stage of investigation:

1. The homosexuality of the male paranoid appears as an intermediary process in the development of his delusions, rather than being the primary etiological agent.

2. One of the defensive functions which the homosexuality of the male paranoid serves is to help neutralize and erotize powerful aggressive wishes directed toward male figures.

REFERENCES

1. Aronson, M. L. A study of the Freudian theory of paranoia by means of the Blacky Pictures. *J. proj. Tech.*, 1953, **17**, 3–19.
2. Fenichel, O. *The psychoanalytic theory of neurosis.* New York: W. W. Norton and Co., 1945.
3. Ferenczi, S. On the part played by homosexuality in the pathogenesis of paranoia. In *Sex in psychoanalysis.* New York: Basic Books, Inc., 1950.
4. Freud, S. Certain neurotic mechanisms in jealousy, paranoia and homosexuality. In *Collected papers*, Vol. II. London: Hogarth Press, 1950.
5. Freud, S. Psychoanalytic notes upon an autobiographical account of a case of paranoia (dementia paranoides). In *Collected papers*, Vol. III. London: Hogarth Press, 1950.
6. Gardner, G. E. Evidences of homosexuality in one hundred and twenty unanalyzed cases with paranoid content. *Psychoanal. Rev.*, 1931, **18**, 57–62.
7. Hendrick, I. The contributions of psychoanalysis to the study of psychoses. *J. Amer. med. Ass.*, 1939, **113**, 918–924.
8. Klein, Henriette R., & Horowitz, W. A. Psychosexual factors in the paranoid phenomena. *Amer. J. Psychiat.*, 1949, **105**, 697–701.
9. Knight, R. P. The relationship of latent homosexuality to the mechanism of paranoid delusions. *Bull. Menninger Clin.*, 1940, **4**, 149–159.
10. Miller, C. W. The paranoid syndrome. *Arch. Neurol. Psychiat.*, 1941, **45**, 953–963.
11. Mosteller, F., & Bush, R. R. Selected quantitative techniques. In G. Lindzey (Ed.), *Handbook of social psychology.* Cambridge, Mass.: Addison-Wesley, 1954, pp. 289–334.
12. Musiker, H. R. Sex identification and other aspects of the personality of the male paranoid schizophrenic. Unpublished doctoral dissertation, Boston Univer., 1952.
13. Norman, J. P. Evidence and clinical significance of homosexuality in 100 unanalyzed cases of dementia praecox. *J. nerv. ment. Dis.*, 1948, **107**, 484–489.
14. Nunberg, H. Homosexuality, magic and aggression. *Int. J. Psychoanal.*, 1938, **19**, 1–16.
15. Payne, C. R. Some Freudian contributions to the paranoia problem. *Psychoanal. Rev.*, 1913–14, **1**, 76–93, 187–202, 308–321, 445–451.
16. Payne, C. R. Some Freudian contributions to the paranoia problem (continued). *Psychoanal. Rev.*, 1915, **2**, 93–101, 200–202.
17. Shockley, F. M. The role of homosexuality in the genesis of paranoid conditions. *Psychoanal. Rev.*, 1913–14, **1**, 431–438.
18. Thorner, H. A. Notes on a case of male homosexuality. *Int. J. Psychoanal.*, 1949, **30**, 31–47.
19. Zamansky, H. S. A technique for assessing homosexual tendencies. *J. Pers.*, 1956, **24**, 436–448.

7. Infantile trauma, genetic factors, and adult temperament

GARDNER LINDZEY, DAVID T. LYKKEN, AND HARVEY D. WINSTON

IN SPITE OF A WELTER OF EMPIRICAL AND THE-
ORETICAL ACTIVITY centering upon the role of
infantile experience as a determinant of adult
personality it is evident that there are few important issues in this area that have been satisfactorily resolved. Prominent among these open
issues is the potential contribution of gene
structure to the relation between infantile experience and adult temperament. Although
King (1958) has identified gene factors as one
of seven major parameters to be considered in
studying the relation between infantile experience and adult effects, there is little in the way
of compelling empirical findings concerning the
role of genetic factors in this setting.

This sparse activity in the world of observation exists in spite of a history of theoretical
interest in this issue. There are few general
theories of behavior that fail to take into consideration, at least implicitly, the potential impact of constitutional or genetic factors upon
early experience and its consequences. Perhaps
the most influential and persistent emphasis
upon the role of heredity in this context has
been provided by Freud (1905) with his discussions of the determinants of fixation, but
his position differs from other personality
theorists on this issue primarily in regard to
explicitness.

The present study was designed to provide
further evidence relevant to this general issue.
Because of traditional difficulties involved in
using human subjects for studies spanning the

life history of the organism and the additional
requirement that genetic variation be controlled, it was necessary to use subjects drawn
from inbred strains of mice.

While the most unusual aspect of this study
inquired into the interaction between gene
factors and the effects of infantile trauma, it
would be a rash investigator indeed who risked
his all on an interaction term. Consistent with
this premise is the fact that our study also
provides information concerning the general
effects of infantile trauma, their situational
generality and duration, as well as further evidence regarding the influence of genetic factors
upon various measures of temperament.

A word should be said concerning previous
results that are relevant to the relation between
infantile trauma and emotionality, for here, as
well as in connection with the interaction effect
we have just discussed, we have made specific
predictions prior to the study. Clear evidence
of an increase in emotionality in mice as a result of infantile trauma has been demonstrated
by Hall and Whiteman (1951), while other investigators working with mice (Stanley & Monkman, 1956) and with rats (Griffiths & Stringer,
1952) have failed to find any significant differences in emotionality between control and traumatized animals. One investigator (Ader, 1957)
actually has reported results indicating that
treated rats were *less* emotional than control
animals. Although these studies have led to
conflicting results, the firmness of the findings
of Hall and Whiteman (1951), coupled with
consistent evidence from human investigations
(Bowlby, 1951) and a boost from psychoanalytic
theory, led us to predict that early traumatic
experience would produce an increase in emotionality (timidity).

SOURCE. Article by Gardner Lindzey, David T.
Lykken, and Harvey D. Winston, "Infantile trauma,
genetic factors, and adult temperament" in *Journal
of abnormal and social Psychology*, Vol. 61, No. 1,
pp. 7–14, 1960.

In summary, this study was designed to provide information concerning:

1. The importance of genetic factors as determinants of emotionality, timidity, and activity.

2. The general effects of infantile trauma, their situational generality, and the duration of these effects through time.

3. The influence of genetic factors upon the relation between infantile trauma and adult temperament.

Method

Subjects

The (Ss) of this investigation were offspring of breeding animals belonging to four different inbred strains of mice. The parent animals were obtained from a colony maintained by John J. Bittner of the Cancer Biology Laboratories of the University of Minnesota and represent the outcome of many generations of brother-sister matings. The conventional labels for these strains and the approximate number of generations of controlled brother-sister matings are as follows: C57BL/1 or B/1 (51 generations); C3H (93 generations); DBA/8 or D/8 (27 generations); JK (71 generations). The first three strains were selected on the basis of prior information (Lindzey, 1951) indicating diversity in emotionality, while the JK strain was selected because observation of them in the colony suggested that their behavior was quite different from the other strains. They were also selected so that all four strains could be identified easily by their distinctive coat color.

Within each strain the successive litters at birth were assigned alternately to either the experimental or the control group with the restriction that when the second litter by a particular mother was born that it would be given a different assignment than the first litter. This shifting procedure was continued through all litters until the desired number of animals in either the control or experimental group was achieved, and all subsequent litters were then assigned to the other group until the necessary number was reached. Because of the impossiblity of predicting survival rates precisely for a period of almost four months, a variable number of animals resulted in the different experimental groups. The smallest number in any single group was 23 while the largest number was 36. The total number of animals included in the study was 259.

Each litter was raised in a separate cage with the mother until 24 days of age, at which time the young were weaned and segregated by sex. Animals were individually identified by an ear punch code, but this operation was not carried out until completion of the first consequent measure in order to avoid the possibility that this relatively traumatic procedure would wipe out the effects of our experimental treatment.

Infantile Trauma

Control and experimental animals were raised under the same conditions except that at four days of age those animals assigned to the experimental group were on four successive days exposed to an extremely loud, high frequency, auditory stimulus. The procedure followed was essentially the same as that described by Hall and Whiteman (1951) and involved placing the mice on a thin cardboard container in a #1 12-gallon wash tub with a doorbell (#504 Eclipse) fixed to the side. After a 2-minute interval the doorbell was rung for 2 minutes, following which the mice were left in the tub for another two minutes before being returned to their cages. On the first three trials all animals were placed together in the tub, but on the fourth trial they were separated. The procedure for the control animals was precisely the same except that the bell was not rung while they were in the tub.

Consequent Measures

30-Day Open Field Test. Beginning at 30 days of age each mouse was placed for 2 minutes in the same type of wash tub in which the auditory trauma had been administered. The tub was brightly lighted by a shielded 150-watt glazed bulb that was placed directly over the tub at a height of approximately 1½ ft. The mouse was left in the tub for 2 minutes at the end of which time the incidence of defecation and urination was recorded and the mouse returned to his living cage. This measure was repeated on 10 successive days. The measure of emotionality was simply presence or absence of defecation and/or urination during each trial.

Stovepipe Test. This instrument was devised by Stone (1929) as a measure of timidity or of the "dominance of hiding tendency over hunger," (p. 36) and was used by Hall and Whiteman (1951) in the study referred to earlier. In this measure the mouse was placed in a starting box connected with a U-shaped stovepipe (each unit approximately 2 ft. in length) that led to a goal box containing a food receptacle holding wet mash. Thus, all that the mouse had to do to reach the food was to enter the stovepipe, follow the passage, and leave the dark pipe for the more brightly illuminated goal box. The mice were again given 10 trials on successive days, commencing at 70 days of age, and they were run under 22½ hrs. of food deprivation. The measure employed was the total time that it took on the 10 trials for the mouse to enter the goal box. The few mice that on particular trials failed to leave the starting box within 5 minutes were on these trials arbitrarily assigned the same time as the mouse that took the longest time in reaching the goal box.

100-Day Open Field Test. Commencing at 100 days of age the open field test was repeated for 10 trials with the measure of emotionality consisting of presence or absence of defecation and/or urination summed across the 10 trials for each S. In addition a measure of motility was secured by dividing the wash tub into 12 spaces of equal area and counting the number of spaces that each mouse moved through during the two minute trial and again summing the results of the individual trials over the 10 days.

Analysis of Data

The obvious method of statistical analysis for our data was a 2 × 4 analysis of variance and this technique was used for all data except those derived from the first open field test. In the latter case the absence of individual identification made it impossible to summate scores over the 10 trials and, in general, made it virtually impossible to devise a sensitive measure of the interaction hypothesis. Demonstration of strain differences and treatment effects was not particularly difficult, in part because they were relatively evident, and here we have relied upon descriptive presentation and the use of such simple devices as the sign test. The best estimate of interaction that could be devised, however, was to adapt the chi square test and then to apply this test separately to the data for each of the 10 days. This is obviously a somewhat unsatisfactory test of the interaction. We have not hesitated to apply one-tailed tests of significance to data related to directional hypotheses stated in advance of the study.

For purposes of analysis of variance we reduced all groups to the size of the smallest group in order to avoid the complexities of disproportionality. Ss were eliminated on a chronological basis beginning with the animals that were last to complete the procedures. In the case of descriptive presentation of results we have included all animals studied with an appropriate indication of the number in each group.

Results and Discussion

Gene Determinants of Temperament. Here we are concerned with strain differences in two open field measures of emotionality, the stovepipe measure of timidity, and an open field measure of motility. The findings are clear and dramatic. No sentient person could observe the data reported in Tables 1–6 and conclude for any one of these attributes that the animals in all the strains could have been drawn from a single common population. In some instances the strains are so different as to show virtually no overlap. In view of the fact that the only known difference between these strains lies in their genetic constitution, it seems a prudent conclusion that genetic factors make a considerable contribution to each of our three measures of temperament.

Our findings are given added weight when coupled with the results of a number of earlier investigations using both rats (Hall, 1938; Broadhurst, 1958) and mice (Lindzey, 1951; Thompson, 1953, 1956; McClearn, 1959), all

Table 1. Percentage of Animals Defecating Daily on 30-Day Open Field Test

| Strain | Treatment | N | Day | | | | | | | | | | Average |
			1	2	3	4	5	6	7	8	9	10	
C57BL/1	Control	28	28.6	28.6	32.1	53.6	35.7	39.3	46.4	32.1	28.6	17.9	34.3
C57BL/1	Experimental	25	32.0	36.0	40.0	40.0	60.0	52.0	36.0	40.0	36.0	32.0	40.4
C3H	Control	34	85.3	88.2	82.3	64.7	73.5	70.6	85.3	73.5	73.5	73.5	77.1
C3H	Experimental	39	92.3	92.3	92.3	79.5	82.0	84.6	92.3	94.9	94.9	100.0	90.5
DBA/8	Control	37	64.9	81.1	73.0	70.3	62.2	64.9	62.2	64.9	59.5	67.6	67.0
DBA/8	Experimental	35	54.3	80.0	82.9	80.0	82.9	82.9	74.3	57.1	77.1	71.4	74.3
JK	Control	29	58.6	79.3	82.8	86.2	100.0	89.6	96.5	72.4	93.1	86.2	84.5
JK	Experimental	32	90.6	87.5	84.4	90.6	93.8	96.9	90.6	87.5	87.5	93.8	90.3

Table 2. Consistency of Emotionality Measure in 1951 Study and Present Study

	C57BL	C3H	DBA
Percent defecation (1951)	37 ($N = 100$)	72 ($N = 100$)	68 ($N = 100$)
Percent defecation (present study)	34 ($N = 28$)	77 ($N = 34$)	67 ($N = 37$)

of which demonstrate wide strain differences on comparable measures. More interesting than this general congruence is a specific examination of the incidence of defecation on the part of the three strains included in both the present study and the previous investigation by Lindzey (1951). In each study, C57, DBA, and C3H strains were employed and in each case an open field test of emotionality was utilized. In Table 2 the percentage of animals defecating in each strain in the earlier study, and the percentage of defecation over 10 trials in each strain in the present study, are compared. The figures are highly constant in spite of the fact that the data were collected with more than a decade of time intervening, with considerable variation in the details of the open field test, with different persons collecting the data, and with animals that are not even known to belong to the same subline within the various strains. Even worse, we *do* know that the two samples were drawn from colonies that have been separated long enough to provide ample opportunity for "genetic drift" as well as spontaneous mutation. Given all of these sources of potential variation it is quite surprising to find the consistency of the strains and the measure so great. Thus, we are afforded the luxury of simultaneously gaining confidence in the stability of the organism we are studying and the reliability of our measure.

In general, these findings serve to emphasize again the pervasive impact upon behavior of genetic factors and thus strongly suggest the inadequacy of attempts to formulate or ac-count for behavior that do not direct careful attention to the role of hereditary factors. It is interesting to note that it is not necessary to inbreed selectively for particular characteristics in order to produce clear evidence for the influence of genic factors upon behavior. Inbreeding of the present animals was uninfluenced by the temperament characteristics of interest in the present study, and, in spite of this, we find the particular genetic patterns that have been isolated are dramatically different in their behavioral consequences.

Influence of Infantile Trauma upon Temperament. What exactly were the effects of the auditory, infantile trauma? The reader will recall our prediction that this experience would lead to an increase of emotionality and timidity. Examination of the data summarized in Table 1 reveals that in spite of the awkwardness resulting from our inability to identify individual animals, there is little doubt that the experimental treatment led to an increase in emotionality as measured by the 30-day test. Inspection of the proportion of experimental and control animals defecating on each of the 10 trials within the four strains reveals that 32 of the 40 comparisons point to the greater emotionality of the traumatized animals. This incidence of "hits" is well beyond the 1% level of significance, even utilizing the relatively insensitive sign test. Actually, the within-strain results for the C3H animals (on all 10 trials the experimental animals showed a greater proportional defecation) are by themselves sig-

Table 3. Analysis of Variance of Stovepipe Test

Source	df	Sum of Squares	Mean Square	F	P
Treatment	1	2,350,782	2,350,782	1.93	<.10*
Strain	3	241,013,412	80,337,804	65.96	<.0001
Interaction	3	10,241,048	3,413,682	2.80	<.05
Within (error)	176	214,356,579	1,217,935		
Total	183	467,961,821			

* One-tailed test.

Table 4. Analysis of Variance of 100-Day Open Field Test: Emotionality

Source	df	Sum of Squares	Mean Square	F	P
Treatment	1	16.5093	16.5093	2.86629	<.05*
Strain	3	679.4458	226.4819	39.3211	<.0001
Interaction	3	2.1082	.7027		
Within (error)	176	1013.7287	5.7598		
Total	183	1711.7920			

* One-tailed test.

nificant at below the 5% level using the sign test, while results for the other strains (7 or 8 trials out of 10 in which experimentals defecate more) approach significance.

The results of the stovepipe test, summarized in Table 3, provide suggestive evidence ($p <$ .10) for a treatment effect indicating greater timidity (slower in getting to reward) on the part of the traumatized mice. Consistently, we find in Table 4 that at the 100-day open field

Table 5. Analysis of Variance of 100-Day Open Field Test: Motility

Source	df	Sum of Squares	Mean Square	F	P
Treatment	1	14,635.2	14,635.2	1.29	<.50
Strain	3	1,421,619.4	473,873.1	41.8	<.0001
Interaction	3	24,268.4	8,089.5	.071	
Within (error)	176	1,994,390.6	11,331.8		
Total	183	3,454,213.6			

test there is also a difference in emotionality indicating that the treated animals were more emotional. Only in the case of motility, as revealed in Table 5, do we find little indication of treatment effects upon behavior.

To summarize, there seems little doubt that subjecting infant mice to a noxious, auditory stimulus of high intensity leads to an increase

in emotionality in adulthood and there is some basis for believing that there is also an increase in timidity. There is no evidence, however, that this experience influences motility in an open field setting.

These findings confirm our prior expectations and fit very neatly with the results reported by Hall and Whiteman (1951) on the basis of

Table 6. Means and SDs for Stovepipe Test and 100-Day Open Field Test

Strain	Treatment	Stovepipe		100-Day Emotionality		100-Day Motility	
		Mean (N = 24)	SD	Mean (N = 23)	SD	Mean (N = 23)	SD
C57BL/1	Control	2301	1339	4.26	3.40	401.2	135.3
C57BL/1	Experimental	2069	882	4.57	3.19	355.0	165.1
C3H	Control	3322	1669	8.43	1.58	198.2	110.7
C3H	Experimental	4312	1039	9.35	1.05	188.1	85.9
DBA/8	Control	773	436	6.39	2.84	272.5	63.3
DBA/8	Experimental	778	407	6.96	2.71	287.7	99.7
JK	Control	1480	1061	8.87	1.51	163.3	67.1
JK	Experimental	1601	1007	9.48	1.02	133.0	53.7

similar experimental operations. However, our results directly contradict the conclusion of Ader (1957), based upon an investigation dealing with rats, and are inconsistent with the findings of Griffiths and Stringer (1952), and Hunt and Otis (1955) based on observation of rats, as well as the findings of Stanley and Monkman (1956) derived from the study of mice. There are so many parametric differences between all of these studies (species of animal, nature of trauma, age at trauma, age at consequent measure) that it is probably useless to attempt a rational analysis of the basis for these experimental differences. It is worth note, however, that there is actually no evidence in any study for infantile trauma *decreasing* emotionality. Although Ader has suggested this possibility, his own data, in the only study in which he employed stimuli that could reasonably be considered noxious or traumatic (Ader, 1959), suggest a heightening of emotionality as a result of infantile trauma. Moreover, Ader's attempts to account for the findings of Hall and Whiteman on the basis of the fact that they used seizure-susceptible mice and an infantile trauma identical to that used in producing audiogenic seizures, is not supportable in view of the fact that the present study led to comparable results with strains such as the C57BL/1 and C3H, which are very low in seizure incidence (Lindzey, 1951).

Duration of traumatic effects. Because of the imprecision of our measures and the differences in the form of our data at age 30 days and age 100 days, it is impossible to make any exact estimate of the extent to which the experimental effects may have diminished with the passage of time. However, it is evident that at 30 days, at 70 days, and at 100 days, the influence of the infantile trauma is clearly observable. Whatever may have been lost in intensity, the main effect is still manifest at the time of the last measure. Actually, a close descriptive inspection of the results of the present study, and the results contained in the Hall and Whiteman paper, suggest that there may have been some diminishing of treatment effects by the time of the 100-day test, but there is no firm evidence to support this contention.

Generality of traumatic effects. One obvious and important question has to do with the narrowness with which the effects of the infantile trauma are linked to situations resembling the original traumatic setting. Obviously, the implications of the trauma for the organism are very different if it leads to a generalized response disposition that is elicited in many settings, rather than leading to effects that can be observed only in situations very similar to the original one. Both Beach and Jaynes (1954) and Ader (1959) attempt to account for the increased emotionality following infantile trauma reported by Hall and Whiteman on the basis of the similarity between the traumatic setting and the setting in which emotionality was measured. The results of the present study are quite specific in refuting this proposal, as we secured consistent empirical findings in connection with both Stone's measure of timidity and Hall's open field measure. The stimulus differences between the stovepipe test and the open field test are so profound that if we are willing to concede the possibility of stimulus generalization from the original setting to the stovepipe test, we have already granted tremendous generality to the effects of the trauma. In brief, then, our findings suggest that the results of the infantile trauma are of a relatively general nature and should be discernible in a wide variety of different settings.

Impact of Genetic Variation upon Effects of Infantile Trauma. We have already seen that our behavioral measures of temperament are heavily influenced by genetic variation and that these same measures covary with traumatic, infantile experience. The essential question remaining is whether these two sets of determinants show any interaction. Are the changes in temperament that can be attributed to early infantile experience in part dependent upon the gene structure of the organism undergoing the experience?

It was impossible to devise a completely satisfactory test of the interaction effect for the 30-day open field test of emotionality because the individual animals were not identified. Consequently, the best we could do was to measure the interaction between strain and treatment effects for each of the 10 trials individually. The resulting x^2 coefficients provide no evidence to support the hypothesis of interaction. It is true that we would have preferred to use a single more sensitive measure of emotionality (incidence of defecation summed over 10 days), and it is possible to speculate that with this increased sensitivity we would have been able to detect an interaction. There is, however, no direct evidence to support this contention.

Our second measure of interaction between

strain and treatment effects deals with the stovepipe measure of timidity and, as the results summarized in Table 3 indicate, we found clear evidence for the existence of an interaction. These results suggest that changes in timidity resulting from the infantile trauma are in part dependent upon the strain (genetic makeup) of the mouse. In particular, the C57BL/1 mice seemed much less influenced by the experimental treatment than the other strains. The third test of the interaction hypothesis is presented in Tables 4 and 5, where we find no evidence for an interaction between strain and treatment in effects upon emotionality or motility at the 100-day test.

The simplest conclusion that can be derived from these findings is that there is an interaction between gene factors and infantile trauma for timidity, as measured by the stovepipe test, but not for emotionality or motility. While this finding may ultimately be substantiated, there are certain unsatisfactory aspects to our test of the interaction of strain and infantile trauma in the case of the two emotionality measures and the measure of motility. The test for the 30-day data had to be carried out upon single observations rather than observations cumulated over 10 days and the test of interaction for the 100-day data may have suffered from a diminishing of treatment effects at this stage. It is known that the analysis of variance measure of interaction is not a powerful test and it is possible that interaction could be demonstrated only with more powerful treatment effects or a larger number of Ss. Our failure to find treatment effects upon motility made our interaction measure in this area relatively meaningless.

So far as our hypothesis is concerned, we have obtained evidence for the existence of interaction between strain and infantile treatment effects as predicted, but this relationship was not so general as we had expected. Our conviction concerning the existence of some degree of interaction is strengthened by the results obtained by King (1959), demonstrating an interaction between the effects of infantile handling and membership in different subspecies, and Valenstein, Riss, and Young (1955), suggesting a relationship between the effects of isolation upon sexual behavior and membership in a particular inbred strain. An additional study by King (1957) also provides evidence suggestive of such an interaction, although the experimental treatment (isolation) did not take place in this case until after weaning. The findings indicate that changes in aggressive behavior that were produced by isolation in one mouse strain were not duplicated in a second strain. There is unfortunately, no direct test of the difference between the two strains in treatment effects. Joint consideration of all of these findings provides a relatively firm basis for concluding that the consequences of infantile trauma are in part dependent upon the genetic structure of the organism experiencing the trauma.

What are the implications of such a finding for psychological theory? One may contend that these results, even secured in connection with mere mice or guinea pigs, provide a type of confirmation of Freud's assertion that any attempt to map early experience into adult behavior must allow for the contribution of genetic factors. While such a statement has a rather hollow sound at the level of human behavior because of the little that is known concerning the gene structure of man, it does have some specific empirical implications. For example, our results would suggest that when an investigator works with Ss of unknown or uncontrolled heredity, it is altogether possible to conduct an otherwise exemplary study of the effects of infantile experience and fail to find evidence for such effects. Or, more generally, we may expect that a variety of different empirical findings might be observed in similar studies as a consequence of investigators dealing with Ss of various genetic backgrounds, rather than as a result of faulty experimental technique. In general, this is a finding that makes life more complex for both investigator and theorist, and in an area where there has never been any shortage of complexity.

Summary

This investigation was concerned with the effects of infantile trauma upon adult temperament, the influence of genetic factors upon temperament, and the possibility of an interaction between early experience and gene structure in their influence upon adult behavior.

Four strains of homozygous mice were used in the study, with the infant offspring assigned by litter to either an experimental or control group. In all, 259 mice were studied. The experimental mice, beginning at four days of age, were exposed on four successive days to a noxious, auditory stimulus while the control animals were treated in an identical manner except that they were not exposed to the traumatic stimulus. At 30 days of age all mice were examined for 10 successive days in an open field test of emotionality and beginning at 70 days of age the mice were again observed for 10 successive days in a stovepipe test of timidity. A final measure of emotionality, and a measure of motility, were secured from 10 days of observation in an open field test beginning at 100 days of age.

The data obtained provide clear and compelling evidence for the importance of genetic factors as determinants of emotionality, timidity, and motility. The four strains displayed marked differences in all three attributes. There was also direct evidence for the influence of infantile trauma upon emotionality and suggestive evidence in regard to timidity, but no evidence for such an influence upon motility. The effects of the infantile trauma were enduring, extending at least to an age of 100 days, and were not limited to stimulus situations closely similar to the original traumatic situation. We found evidence of an interaction between the effects of infantile trauma upon stovepipe timidity and genetic factors, but there was no evidence for such an interaction in the case of emotionality. All of our positive findings are supported by evidence supplied by other investigators.

These findings not only demonstrate the central developmental importance of genetic factors and infantile trauma, they also underline the relative complexity of the relationship between infantile experience and adult behavior. Given an interaction between gene factors and infantile trauma it is readily understandable that inconsistent results might be observed by investigators working with heterozygous Ss of unknown gene structure. Finally, we have pointed to the consistency between the present findings and Freud's formulations concerning the role of constitutional factors in the developmental process.

REFERENCES

Ader, R. Effects of early experience on emotionality. *Amer. Psychologist*, 1957, **12**, 410.

Ader, R. The effects of early experience on subsequent emotionality and resistance to stress. *Psychol. Monogr.*, 1959, **73**(2, Whole No. 472).

Beach, F. A. & Jaynes, J. Effects of early experience upon the behavior of animals. *Psychol. Bull.*, 1954, **51**, 239–264.

Bowlby, J. *Maternal care and mental health.* Geneva: World Health Organization, 1951.

Broadhurst, P. L. Determinants of emotionality in the rat: III. Strain differences. *J. comp. physiol. Psychol.*, 1958, **51**, 55–59.

Freud, S. Three essays on the theory of sexuality. (Originally published 1905.) In *The standard edition of the complete psychological works of Sigmund Freud.* Vol. 7. London: Hogarth, 1953, pp. 125–248.

Griffiths, W. J. Jr., & Stringer, W. F. The effects of intense stimulation experienced during infancy on adult behavior in the rat. *J. comp. Physiol. Psychol.*, 1952, **45**, 301–306.

Hall, C. S. The inheritance of emotionality. *Sigma Xi Quart.*, 1938, **26**, 17–27.

Hall, C. S., & Whiteman, P. H. The effects of infantile stimulation upon later emotional stability in the mouse. *J. comp. physiol. Psychol.*, 1951, **44**, 61–66.

Hunt, H. F., & Otis, L. S. Restricted experience and "timidity" in the rat. *Amer. Psychologist*, 1955, **19**, 432.

King, J. A. Relationships between early social experience and adult aggressive behavior in inbred mice. *J. genet. Psychol.*, 1957, **90**, 151–166.

King, J. A. Parameters relevant to determining the effect of early experience upon the adult behavior of animals. *Psychol. Bull.*, 1958, **55**, 46–58.

King, J. A., & Eleftheriou, B. E. Effects of early handling upon adult behavior in two subspecies of deermice, *Peromyscus maniculates. J. comp. physiol. Psychol.*, 1959, **52**, 82–88.

Lindzey, G. Emotionality and audiogenic seizure susceptibility in five inbred strains of mice. *J. comp. physiol. Psychol.*, 1951, **44**, 389–393.

McClearn, G. E. The genetics of mouse behavior in novel situations. *J. comp. physiol. Psychol.*, 1959, **52**, 62–67.

Stanley, W. C., & Monkman, J. A. A test for specific and general behavioral effects of infantile stimulation with shock in the mouse. *J. abnorm. soc. Psychol.*, 1956, **53**, 19–22.

Stone, C. P. Wildness and savageness in rats of different strains. In K. S. Lashley (Ed.), *Studies in the dynamics of behavior.* Chicago: Univer. Chicago Press, 1932, pp. 3–55.

Thompson, W. R. The inheritance of behavior: Behavior differences in fifteen mouse strains. *Canad. J. Psychol.*, 1953, **7**, 145–155.

Thompson, W. R. The inheritance of behavior: Activity differences in five inbred mouse strains. *J. Hered.*, 1956, **47**, 147–148.

Valenstein, E. S., Riss, W., & Young, W. C. Experiential and genetic factors in the organization of sexual behavior in male guinea pigs. *J. comp. physiol. Psychol.*, 1955, **48**, 397–403.

Jung's Analytic Theory

For Freud, there is an abundance of primary sources and research from which to choose. For Jung, there is only an abundance of primary sources. These primary sources, it is true, contain much that is empirical in nature, for Jung believed that all of his writings were factual rather than speculative. Among his generous and characteristically outspoken comments on the first draft of the chapter on Analytic Theory which was written for *Theories of Personality*, he expostulated in one of them "Why don't you show the facts? *I am always talking of facts.* My concepts are merely names for *facts*. I have no system." (Jung's underlining.) Many psychological readers are not likely to agree with Jung's own appraisal of his writings. Many of his *facts* appear to be speculations. Some of this difference of opinion arises out of contrasting views regarding the nature of research. Jung and many of his followers employ the comparative method. By this they mean a comparison of myths, symbols, and religions in various cultures and during different historical periods. They also include as research the presentation of case material from patients undergoing treatment. To the American psychologist, research demands controls against the operation of bias and chance factors and some measure of quantification, both of which are absent in Jung's research.

Several Jungians were asked to make suggestions of empirical studies to be included in this volume. One replied, "In Jungian psychology today, the research studies that go on are simply within the laboratory of the individual personalities of the analyst and his case."

In view of this situation, it is paradoxical that Jung first attracted the attention of American psychology by quantitative, experimental studies using the word association test, a subject upon which he was asked to lecture at Clark University in 1909. His typology, especially the two major attitudes or orientations of personality, extraversion and introversion, also stimulated a good deal of paper-and-pencil testing in the United States and England. Within the last few years, a new test, the Myers-Briggs Type Indicator, which purports to measure not only the attitudes but also the four basic psychological functions of thinking, feeling, sensation, and intuition, has been published. Although it is being used in a number of contemporary investigations, its validity has not as yet been adequately demonstrated. There have been a few clinical studies that have made use of Jung's method of active imagination, and an experimental paper by Bash noted in *Theories of Personality*.

After making a survey of the research generated by Jung's viewpoint and finding none which was adequate according to the criteria of objectivity, quantitative analysis, and the use of controls, it was decided to restrict the selections to the primary sources; that is, to the eighteen volumes of Jung's writings. These selections display the style and strategy of Jung's thinking about some of his most original concepts: archetype, symbol, and self. The fourth selection shows how Jung interprets a dream. The reader may wish to compare his method of dream interpretation with that of Freud's as presented in the last chapter. These selections also suggest the kind of empirical evidence from which Jung derived his concepts.

1. Patterns of behavior and archetypes

C. G. JUNG

WE HAVE STATED THAT THE LOWER REACHES OF
THE PSYCHE begin where the function emanci-
pates itself from the compulsive force of instinct and becomes amenable to the will, and
we have defined the will as disposable energy.
But that, as said, presupposes a disposing subject, capable of judgment and endowed with
consciousness. In this way we arrived at the
position of proving, as it were, the very thing
that we started by rejecting, namely the identification of psyche with consciousness. This dilemma resolves itself once we realize how very
relative consciousness is, since its contents are
conscious and unconscious at the same time,
i.e., conscious under one aspect and unconscious
under another. As is the way of paradoxes, this
statement is not immediately comprehensible.[1]
We must, however, accustom ourselves to the
thought that conscious and unconscious have
no clear demarcations, the one beginning where
the other leaves off. It is rather the case that

SOURCE. Selection from C. G. Jung, "Patterns of
behavior and archetypes" in "The structure and
dynamics of the psyche," *The Collected Works,* Vol.
8, pp. 200–234. Edited by Sir Herbert Read,
Michael Fordham, Gerhard Adler; translated from
the German by R. F. C. Hull. New York: Pantheon,
1960. Copyright held by Bollingen Foundation, Inc.

---

[1] Freud also arrived at similar paradoxical conclusions. Thus, in his article "The Unconscious" (p.
177): he says: "An instinct can never become an
object of consciousness—only the idea that represents the instinct can. *Even in the unconscious,
moreover, an instinct cannot be represented otherwise than by an idea.*" (My italics.) As in my above
account we were left asking, "Who is the subject of
the unconscious will?" so we must ask here, "Exactly *who* has the idea of the instinct in the unconscious state?" For "unconscious" ideation is a *con-
tradictio in adjecto.*

the psyche is a conscious-unconscious whole. As
to the no man's land which I have called the
"personal unconscious," it is fairly easy to prove
that its contents correspond exactly to our definition of the psychic. But—as we define "psychic"—is there a psychic unconscious that is
not a "fringe of consciousness" and not personal?

I have already mentioned that Freud established the existence of archaic vestiges and
primitive modes of functioning in the unconscious. Subsequent investigations have confirmed this result and brought together a wealth
of observational material. In view of the structure of the body, it would be astonishing if the
psyche were the only biological phenomenon
not to show clear traces of its evolutionary history, and it is altogether probable that these
marks are closely connected with the instinctual
base. Instinct and the archaic mode meet in the
biological conception of the "pattern of behavior." There are, in fact, no amorphous instincts, as every instinct bears in itself the pattern of its situation. Always it fulfils an image,
and the image has fixed qualities. The instinct
of the leaf-cutting ant fulfils the image of ant,
tree, leaf, cutting, transport, and the little ant-
garden of fungi.[2] If any one of these conditions
is lacking, the instinct does not function, because it cannot exist without its total pattern,
without its image. Such an image is an *a priori*
type. It is inborn in the ant prior to any activity, for there can be no activity at all unless
an instinct of corresponding pattern initiates
and makes it possible. This schema holds true of
all instincts and is found in identical form in all
individuals of the same species. The same is
true also of man: he has in him these *a priori*

---

[2] For details see C. Lloyd Morgan, *Habit and
Instinct.*

instinct-types which provide the occasion and the pattern for his activities, in so far as he functions instinctively. As a biological being he has no choice but to act in a specifically human way and fulfil his pattern of behaviour. This sets narrow limits to his possible range of volition, the more narrow the more primitive he is, and the more his consciousness is dependent upon the instinctual sphere. Although from one point of view it is quite correct to speak of the pattern of behaviour as a still-existing archaic vestige, as Nietzsche did in respect of the function of dreams, such an attitude does scant justice to the biological and psychological meaning of these types. They are not just relics or vestiges of earlier modes of functioning; they are the ever-present and biologically necessary regulators of the instinctual sphere, whose range of action covers the whole realm of the psyche and only loses its absoluteness when limited by the relative freedom of the will. We may say that the image represents the *meaning* of the instinct.

Although the existence of an instinctual pattern in human biology is probable, it seems very difficult to prove the existence of distinct types empirically. For the organ with which we might apprehend them—consciousness—is not only itself a transformation of the original instinctual image, but also its transformer. It is therefore not surprising that the human mind finds it impossible to specify precise types for man similar to those we know in the animal kingdom. I must confess that I can see no direct way to solve this problem. And yet I have succeeded, or so I believe, in finding at least an indirect way of approach to the instinctual image.

In what follows, I would like to give a brief description of how this discovery took place. I had often observed patients whose dreams pointed to a rich store of fantasy-material. Equally, from the patients themselves, I got the impression that they were stuffed full of fantasies, without their being able to tell me just where the inner pressure lay. I therefore took up a dream-image or an association of the patient's, and, with this as a point of departure, set him the task of elaborating or developing his theme by giving free rein to his fantasy. This, according to individual taste and talent, could be done in any number of ways, dramatic, dialectic, visual, acoustic, or in the form of dancing, painting, drawing or modelling. The result of this technique was a vast number of complicated designs whose diversity puzzled

me for years, until I was able to recognize that in this method I was witnessing the spontaneous manifestation of an unconscious process which was merely assisted by the technical ability of the patient, and to which I later gave the name "individuation process." But, long before this recognition dawned upon me, I had made the discovery that this method often diminished, to a considerable degree, the frequency and intensity of the dreams, thus reducing the inexplicable pressure exerted by the unconscious. In many cases, this brought a large measure of therapeutic success, which encouraged both myself and the patient to press forward despite the baffling nature of the results.[3] I felt bound to insist that they were baffling, if only to stop myself from framing, on the basis of certain theoretical assumptions, interpretations which I felt were not only inadequate but liable to prejudice the ingenuous productions of the patient. The more I suspected these configurations of harbouring a certain purposefulness, the less inclined I was to risk any theories about them. This reticence was not made easy for me, since in many cases I was dealing with patients who needed an intellectual *point d'appui* if they were not to get totally lost in the darkness. I had to try to give provisional interpretations at least, so far as I was able, interspersing them with innumerable "perhaps" and "ifs" and "buts" and never stepping beyond the bounds of the picture lying before me. I always took good care to let the interpretation of each image tail off into a question whose answer was left to the free fantasy-activity of the patient.

The chaotic assortment of images that at first confronted me reduced itself in the course of the work to certain well-defined themes and formal elements, which repeated themselves in identical or analogous form with the most varied individuals. I mention, as the most salient characteristics, chaotic multiplicity and order; duality; the opposition of light and dark, upper and lower, right and left; the union of opposites in a third; the quaternity (square, cross); rotation (circle, sphere); and finally the centring process and a radial arrangement that usually followed some quaternary system. Triadic formations, apart from the *complexio oppositorum* in a third, were relatively rare and formed

---

[3] Cf. "The Aims of Psychotherapy," pars. 101ff.; and *Two Essays on Analytical Psychology,* pars. 343ff.

notable exceptions which could be explained by special conditions.[4] The centring process is, in my experience, the never-to-be-surpassed climax of the whole development,[5] and is characterized as such by the fact that it brings with it the greatest possible therapeutic effect. The typical features listed above go to the limits of abstraction, yet at the same time they are the simplest expressions of the formative principles here at work. In actual reality, the patterns are infinitely more variegated and far more concrete than this would suggest. Their variety defies description. I can only say that there is probably no motif in any known mythology that does not at some time appear in these configurations. If there was any conscious knowledge of mythological motifs worth mentioning in my patients, it is left far behind by the ingenuities of creative fantasy. In general, my patients had only a minimal knowledge of mythology.

These facts show in an unmistakable manner how fantasies guided by unconscious regulators coincide with the records of man's mental activity as known to us from tradition and ethnological research. All the abstract features I have mentioned are in a certain sense conscious: everyone can count up to four and knows what a circle is and a square; but, as formative principles, they are unconscious, and by the same token their psychological meaning is not conscious either. My most fundamental views and ideas derive from these experiences. First I made the observations, and only then did I hammer out my views. And so it is with the hand that guides the crayon or brush, the foot that executes the dance-step, with the eye and the ear, with the word and the thought: a dark impulse is the ultimate arbiter of the pattern, an unconscious *a priori* precipitates itself into plastic form, and one has no inkling that another person's consciousness is being guided by these same principles at the very point where one feels utterly exposed to the boundless subjective vagaries of chance. Over the whole procedure there seems to reign a dim foreknowledge not only of the pattern but of its meaning.[6] Image and meaning are identical; and as the first takes shape, so the latter becomes clear.

Actually, the pattern needs no interpretation: it portrays its own meaning. There are cases where I can let interpretation go as a therapeutic requirement. Scientific knowledge, of course, is another matter. Here we have to elicit from the sum total of our experience certain concepts of the greatest possible general validity, which are not given *a priori*. This particular work entails a translation of the timeless, ever-present operative archetype into the scientific language of the present.

These experiences and reflections lead me to believe that there are certain collective unconscious conditions which act as regulators and stimulators of creative fantasy-activity and call forth corresponding formations by availing themselves of the existing conscious material. They behave exactly like the motive forces of dreams, for which reason active imagination, as I have called this method, to some extent takes the place of dreams. The existence of these unconscious regulators—I sometimes refer to them as "dominants"[7] because of their mode of functioning—seemed to me so important that I based upon it my hypothesis of an impersonal collective unconscious. The most remarkable thing about this method, I felt, was that it did not involve a *reductio in primam figuram*, but rather a synthesis—supported by an attitude voluntarily adopted, though for the rest wholly natural—of passive conscious material and unconscious influences, hence a kind of spontaneous amplification of the archetypes. The images are not to be thought of as a reduction of conscious contents to their simplest denominator, as this would be the direct road to the primordial images which I said previously was unimaginable; they make their appearance only in the course of amplification.

On this natural amplification process I also base my method of eliciting the meaning of dreams, for dreams behave in exactly the same way as active imagination; only the support of conscious contents is lacking. To the extent that the archetypes intervene in the shaping of conscious contents by regulating, modifying, and motivating them, they act like the instincts. It is therefore very natural to suppose that these factors are connected with the instincts and to inquire whether the typical situational patterns which these collective form-principles appar-

---

[4] The same applies to the pentadic figures.

[5] So far as the development can be ascertained from the objective material.

[6] Cf. *Psychology and Alchemy*, pp. 211f.

[7] Cf. *Two Essays on Analytical Psychology*, par. 151.

ently represent are not in the end identical with the instinctual patterns, namely, with the patterns of behavior. I must admit that up to the present I have not laid hold of any argument that would finally refute this possibility.

Before I pursue my reflections further, I must stress one aspect of the archetypes which will be obvious to anybody who has practical experience of these matters. That is, the archetypes have, when they appear, a distinctly numinous character which can only be described as "spiritual," if "magical" is too strong a word. Consequently this phenomenon is of the utmost significance for the psychology of religion. In its effects it is anything but unambiguous. It can be healing or destructive, but never indifferent, provided of course that it has attained a certain degree of clarity.[8] This aspect deserves the epithet "spiritual" above all else. It not infrequently happens that the archetype appears in the form of a *spirit* in dreams or fantasy-products, or even comports itself like a ghost. There is a mystical ura about its numinosity, and it has a corresponding effect upon the emotions. It mobilizes philosophical and religious convictions in the very people who deemed themselves miles above any such fits of weakness. Often it drives with unexampled passion and remorseless logic towards its goal and draws the subject under its spell, from which despite the most desperate resistance he is unable, and finally no longer even willing, to break free, because the experience brings with it a depth and fulness of meaning that was unthinkable before. I fully appreciate the resistance that all rooted convictions are bound to put up against psychological discoveries of this kind. With more foreboding than real knowledge, most people feel afraid of the men-

acing power that lies fettered in each of us, only waiting for the magic word to release it from the spell. This magic word, which always ends in "ism," works most successfully with those who have the least access to their interior selves and have strayed the furthest from their instinctual roots into the truly chaotic world of *collective consciousness.*

In spite or perhaps because of its affinity with instinct, the archetype represents the authentic element of spirit, but a spirit which is not to be identified with the human intellect, since it is the latter's *spiritus rector.* The essential content of all mythologies and all religions and all isms is archetypal. The archetype is spirit or psuedo-spirit: what it ultimately proves to be depends on the attitude of the human mind. Archetype and instinct are the most polar opposites imaginable, as can easily be seen when one compares a man who is ruled by his instinctual drives with a man who is seized by the spirit. But, just as between all opposites there obtains so close a bond that no position can be established or even thought of without its corresponding negation, so in this case also "les extremes se touchent." They belong together as correspondences, which is not to say that the one is derivable from the other, but that they subsist side by side as reflections in our own minds of the opposition that underlies all psychic energy. Man finds himself simultaneously driven to act and free to reflect. This contrariety in his nature has no moral significance, for instinct is not in itself bad any more than spirit is good. Both can be good. Negative electricity is as good as positive electricity: first and foremost it is electricity. The psychological opposites, too, must be regarded from a scientific standpoint. True opposites are never incommensurables; if they were they could never unite. All contrariety notwithstanding, they do show a constant propensity to union, and Nicholas of Cusa defined God himself as a *complexio oppositorum.*

Opposites are extreme qualities in any state, by virtue of which that state is perceived to be real, for they form a potential. The psyche is made up of processes whose energy springs from the equilibration of all kinds of opposites. The spirit/instinct antithesis is only one of the commonest formulations, but it has the advantage of reducing the greatest number of the most important and most complex psychic processes to a common denominator. So regard-

---

[8] Occasionally it is associated with synchronistic or parapsychic effects. I mean by synchronicity, as I have explained elsewhere, the not uncommonly observed "coincidence" of subjective and objective happenings, which just cannot be explained causally, at least in the present state of our knowledge. On this premise astrology is based on the methods of the *I Ching*. These observations, like the astrological findings, are not generally accepted, though as we know this has never hurt the facts. I mention these special effects solely for the sake of completeness and solely for the benefit of those readers who have had occasion to convince themselves of the reality of parapsychic phenomena. For a detailed discussion, see the final paper in this volume.

ed, psychic processes seem to be balances of energy flowing between spirit and instinct, though the question of whether a process is to be described as spiritual or as instinctual remains shrouded in darkness. Such evaluation or interpretation depends entirely upon the standpoint or state of the conscious mind. A poorly developed consciousness, for instance, which because of massed projections is inordinately impressed by concrete or apparently concrete things and states, will naturally see in the instinctual drives the source of all reality. It remains blissfully unaware of the spirituality of such a philosophical surmise, and is convinced that with this opinion it has established the essential instinctuality of all psychic processes. Conversely, a consciousness that finds itself in opposition to the instincts can, in consequence of the enormous influence then exerted by the archetypes, so subordinate instinct to spirit that the most grotesque "spiritual" complications may arise out of what are undoubtedly biological happenings. Here the instinctuality of the fanaticism needed for such an operation is ignored.

Psychic processes therefore behave like a scale along which consciousness "slides." At one moment it finds itself in the vicinity of instinct, and falls under its influence; at another, it slides along to the other end where spirit predominates and even assimilates the instinctual processes most opposed to it. These counter-positions, so fruitful of illusion, are by no means symptoms of the abnormal; on the contrary, they form the twin poles of that psychic one-sidedness which is typical of the normal man of today. Naturally this does not manifest itself only in the spirit/instinct antithesis; it assumes many other forms, as I have shown in my *Psychological Types*.

This "sliding" consciousness is thoroughly characteristic of modern man. But the one-sidedness it causes can be removed by what I have called the "realization of the shadow." A less "poetic" and more scientific-looking Greco-Latin neologism could easily have been coined for this operation. In psychology, however, one is to be dissuaded from ventures of this sort, at least when dealing with eminently practical problems. Among these is the "realization of the shadow," the growing awareness of the inferior part of the personality, which should not be twisted into an intellectual activity, for it has for more the meaning of a suffering and a

passion that implicate the whole man. The essence of that which has to be realized and assimilated has been expressed so trenchantly and so plastically in poetic language by the word "shadow" that it would be almost presumptuous not to avail oneself of this linguistic heritage. Even the term "inferior part of the personality" is inadequate and misleading whereas "shadow" presumes nothing that would rigidly fix its content. The "man without a shadow" is statistically the commonest human type, one who imagines he actually *is* only what he cares to know about himself. Unfortunately neither the so-called religious man nor the man of scientific pretensions forms any exception to this rule.

Confrontation with an archetype or instinct is an *ethical* problem of the first magnitude, the urgency of which is felt only by people who find themselves faced with the need to assimilate the unconscious and integrate their personalities. This only falls to the lot of the man who realizes that he has a neurosis or that all is not well with this psychic constitution. These are certainly not the majority. The "common man" who is preponderantly a mass man, acts on the principle of realizing nothing, nor does he need to, because for him the only thing that commits mistakes is that vast anonymity conventionally known as "State" or "Society." But once a man knows that he is, or should be, responsible, he feels responsible also for his psychic constitution, the more so the more clearly he sees what he would have to be in order to become healthier, more stable, and more efficient. Once he is on the way to assimilating the unconscious he can be certain that he will escape no difficulty that is an integral part of his nature. The mass man, on the other hand, has the privilege of being at all times "not guilty" of the social and political catastrophes in which the whole world is engulfed. His final calculation is thrown out accordingly; whereas the other at least has the possibility of finding a spiritual point of vantage, a kingdom that "is not of this world."

It would be an unpardonable sin of omission were one to overlook the *feeling-value* of the archetype. This is extremely important both theoretically and therapeutically. As a numinous factor, the archetype determines the nature of the configurational process and the course it will follow, with seeming foreknowledge, or as though it were already in possession of the goal to be circumscribed by the centring process.[9] I would like to make the way in which the archetype functions clear from this simple example. While sojourning in equatorial east Africa, on the southern slopes of Mount Elgon, I found that the natives used to step out of their huts at sunrise, hold their hands before their mouths, and spit or blow into them vigorously. Then they lifted their arms and held their hands with the palms toward the sun. I asked them the meaning of what they did, but nobody could give me an explanation. They had always done it like that, they said, and had learnt it from their parents. The medicine-man, he would know what it meant. So I asked the medicine-man. He knew as little as the others, but assured me that his grandfather had still known. It was just what people did at every sunrise, and at the first phase of the new moon. For these people, as I was able to show, the moment when the sun or the new moon appeared was "mulungu" [10] and is translated by the missionaries as "God." Actually the word *athista* in Elgonyi means sun as well as God, although they deny that the sun is God. Only the moment when it rises is *mungu* or *athista*. Spittle and breath mean soul-substance. Hence they offer their soul to God, but do not know what they are doing and never have known. They do it, motivated by the same preconscious archetype which the ancient Egyptians, on their monuments, also ascribed to the sun-worshipping dog-headed baboon, albeit in full knowledge that this ritual gesture was in honour of God. The behavior of the Elgonyi certainly strikes us as exceedingly primitive, but we forget that the educated Westerner behaves no differently. What the meaning of the Christmas-tree might be our forefathers knew even less than ourselves, and it is only quite recently that we have bothered to find out at all.

The archetype is pure, unvitiated nature,[11] and it is nature that causes man to utter words and perform actions whose meaning is unconscious to him, so unconscious that he no longer gives it a thought. A later, more conscious humanity, faced with such meaningful things whose meaning none could declare, hit upon the idea that these must be the last vestiges of a Golden Age, when there were men who knew all things and taught wisdom to the nations. In the degenerate days that followed, these teachings were forgotten and were now only repeated as mindless mechanical gestures. In view of the findings of modern psychology it cannot be doubted that there are preconscious archetypes which were never conscious and can be established only indirectly through their effects upon the conscious contents. There is in my opinion no tenable argument against the hypothesis that all the psychic functions which today seem conscious to us were once unconscious and yet worked as if they *were* conscious. We could also say that all the psychic phenomena to be found in man were already present in the natural unconscious state. To this it might be objected that it would then be far from clear why there is such a thing as consciousness at all. I would, however, remind the reader that, as we have already seen, all unconscious functioning has the automatic character of an instinct, and that the instincts are always coming into collision or, because of their compulsiveness, pursuing their courses unaltered by any influence even under conditions that may positively endanger the life of the individual. As against this, consciousness enables him to adapt in an orderly way and to check the instincts, and consequently it cannot be dispensed with. Man's capacity for consciousness alone makes him man.

The achievement of a synthesis of conscious and unconscious contents, and the conscious realization of the archetype's effects upon the conscious contents, represents the climax of a concentrated spiritual and psychic effort, in so far as this is undertaken consciously and of set purpose. That is to say, the synthesis can also be prepared in advance and brought to a certain point—James's "bursting point"—unconsciously, whereupon it irrupts into consciousness of its own volition and confronts the latter with the formidable task of assimilating the contents that have burst in upon it, yet without damaging the viability of the two systems, i.e., of ego-consciousness on the one hand and the irrupted complex on the other. Classical examples of this process are Paul's conversion and the Trinity version of Nicholas of Flue.

By means of "active imagination" we are put in a position of advantage, for we can then make the discovery of the archetype without

[9] Cf. *Psychology and Alchemy*, Part II, for evidence of this.

[10] Mulungu = 'spirit, soul, daemonism, magic, prestige': *Two Essays*, par. 108.—Editors.

[11] "Nature" here means simply that which is, and always was, given.

sinking back into the instinctual sphere, which would only lead to blank unconsciousness, or, worse still, to some kind of intellectual substitute for instinct. This means—to employ once more the simile of the spectrum—that the instinctual image is to be located not at the red end but at the violet end of the colour band. The dynamism of instinct is lodged as it were in the infra-red part of the spectrum, whereas the instinctual image lies in the ultra-violet part. If we remember our colour symbolism, then, as I have said, red is not such a bad match for instinct. But for spirit, as might be expected,[12] blue would be a better match than violet. Violet is the "mystic" colour, and it certainly reflects the indubitably "mystic" or paradoxical quality of the archetype in a most satisfactory way. Violet is a compound of blue and red, although in the spectrum it is a colour in its own right. Now, it is, as it happens, rather more than just an edifying thought if we feel bound to emphasize that the archetype is more accurately characterized by violet, for, as well as being an image in its own right, it is at the same time a *dynamism* which makes itself felt in the numinosity and fascinating power of the archetypal image. The realization and assimilation of instinct never takes place at the red end, i.e., by absorption into the instinctual sphere, but only through integration of the image which signifies and at the same time evokes the instinct, although in a form quite different from the one we meet on the biological level. When Faust remarks to Wagner: "You are conscious only of the single urge/O may you never learn to know the other!" this is a saying that could equally well be applied to instinct in general. It has two aspects: on the one hand its multitudinous forms enter into consciousness as images and groups of images, where they develop numinous effects which offer, or appear to offer, the strictest possible contrast to instinct physiologically regarded. For anyone acquainted with religious phenomenology it is an open secret that although physical and spiritual passion are deadly enemies, they are nevertheless brothers-in-arms, for which reason it often needs the merest touch to convert the one into the other. Both are real, and together they form a pair of opposites, which is one of the most fruitful sources of psychic energy. There is no point in deriving one from the other in order to give primacy to one of them. Even if we know only one at first, and do not notice the other until much later, that does not prove that the other was not there all the time. Hot cannot be derived from cold, nor high from low. An opposition either exists in its binary form or it does not exist at all, and a being without opposites is completely unthinkable, as it would be impossible to establish its existence.

Absorption into the instinctual sphere, therefore, does not and cannot lead to conscious realization and assimilation of instinct, because consciousness struggles in a regular panic against being swallowed up in the primitivity and unconsciousness of sheer instinctuality. This fear is the eternal burden of the hero-myth and the theme of countless taboos. The closer one comes to the instinct-world, the more violent is the urge to shy away from it and to rescue the light of consciousness from the murks of the sultry abyss. Psychologically, however, the archetype as an image of instinct is a spiritual goal toward which the whole nature of man strives; it is the sea to which all rivers wend their way, the prize which the hero wrests from the fight with the dragon.

Because the archetype is a formative principle of instinctual power, its blue is contaminated with red: it appears to be violet, or again, we could interpret the simile as an apocatastasis of instinct raised to a higher frequency, just as we could easily derive instinct from a latent (i.e., transcendent) archetype that manifests itself on a longer wavelength.[13] Although it can admittedly be no more than an analogy, I nevertheless feel tempted to recommend this violet image to my reader as an illustrative hint of the archetype's affinity with its own opposite. The creative fantasy of the alchemists sought to express this abstruse secret of nature by means of another, no less concrete, symbol: the Uroboros, or tail-eating serpent.

I do not want to work this simile to death, but, as the reader will understand, one is al-

---

[12] This expectation is based on the experience that blue, the colour of air and sky, is most readily used for depicting spiritual contents, whereas red, the "warm" colour, is used for feelings and emotions.

[13] Sir James Jeans (*Physics and Philosophy,* p. 193) points out that the shadows on the wall of Plato's cave are just as real as the invisible figures that cast them and whose existence can only be inferred mathematically.

ways delighted, when discussing difficult problems, to find support in a helpful analogy. In addition this simile helps to throw light on a question we have not yet asked ourselves, much less answered, the question regarding the *nature* of the archetype. The archetypal representations (images and ideas) mediated to us by the unconscious should not be confused with the archetype as such. They are very varied structures which all point back to one essentially "irrepresentable" basic form. The latter is characterized by certain formal elements and by certain fundamental meanings, although these can be grasped only approximately. The archetype as such is a psychoid factor that belongs, as it were, to the invisible, ultra-violet end of the psychic spectrum. It does not appear, in itself, to be capable of reaching consciousness. I venture this hypothesis because everything archetypal which is perceived by consciousness seems to represent a set of variations on a ground theme. One is most impressed by this act when one studies the endless variations of the mandala motif. This is a relatively simple ground form whose meaning can be said to be "central." But although it looks like the structure of a centre, it is still uncertain whether within that structure the centre or the periphery, division or non-division, is the more accentuated. Since other archetypes give rise to similar doubts, it seems to me probable that the real nature of the archetype is not capable of being made conscious, that it is transcendent, on which account I call it psychoid. Moreover every archetype, when represented to the mind, is already conscious and therefore differs to an indeterminable extent from that which caused the representation. As Theodor Lipps has stressed, the nature of the psychic is unconscious. Anything conscious is part of the phenomenal world which—so modern physics teaches—does not supply explanations of the kind that objective reality requires. Objective reality requires a mathematical model, and experience shows that this is based on invisible and irrepresentable factors. Psychology cannot evade the universal validity of this fact, the less so as the observing psyche is already included in any formulation of objective reality. Nor can psychological theory be formulated mathematically, because we have no measuring rod with which to measure psychic quantities. We have to rely solely upon qualities, that is, upon perceptible phenomena. Consequently psychology

is incapacitated from making any valid statement about unconscious states, or to put it another way, there is no hope that the validity of any statement about unconscious states or processes will ever be verified scientifically. Whatever we say about the archetypes they remain visualizations or concretizations which pertain to the field of consciousness. But—we cannot speak about archetypes in any other way. We must, however, constantly bear in mind that what we mean by "archetype" is in itself irrepresentable, but has effects which make visualizations of it possible, namely, the archetypal images and ideas. We meet with a similar situation in physics: there the smallest particles are themselves irrepresentable but have effects from the nature of which we can build up a model. The archetypal image, the motif or mythologem, is a construction of this kind. When the existence of two or more irrepresentables is assumed, there is always the possibility—which we tend to overlook—that it may not be a question of two or more factors but of one only. The identity or non-identity of two irrepresentable quantities is something that cannot be proved. If on the basis of its observations psychology assumes the existence of certain irrepresentable psychoid factors, it is doing the same thing in principle as physics does when the physicist constructs an atomic model. And it is not only psychology that suffers from the misfortune of having to give its object, the unconscious, a name that has often been criticized because it is merely negative; the same thing happened in physics, since it could not avoid using the ancient term "atom" (meaning "indivisible") for the smallest particle of matter. Just as the atom is not indivisible, so, as we shall see, the unconscious is not merely unconscious. And just as physics in its psychological aspect can do no more than establish the existence of an observer without being able to assert anything about the nature of that observer, so psychology can only indicate the relation of psyche to matter without being able to make out the least thing about its nature.

Since psyche and matter are contained in one and the same world, and moreover are in continuous contact with one another and ultimately rest on irrepresentable, transcendental factors, it is not only possible but fairly probable, even, that psyche and matter are two different aspects of one and the same thing. The synchronicity phenomena point, it seems to me, in this direction, for they show that the nonpsychic can behave like the psychic, and vice versa, without there being any causal connection between them. Our present knowledge does not allow us to do much more than compare the relation of the psychic to the material world with two cones, whose apices, meeting in a point without extension—a real zero-point—touch and do not touch.

In my previous writings I have always treated archetypal phenomena as psychic, because the material to be expounded or investigated was concerned solely with ideas and images. The psychoid nature of the archetype, as put forward here, does not contradict these earlier formulations; it only means a further degree of conceptual differentiation, which became inevitable as soon as I saw myself obliged to undertake a more general analysis of the nature of the psyche and to clarify the empirical concepts concerning it, and their relation to one another.

Just as the "psychic infra-red," the biological instinctual psyche, gradually passes over into the physiology of the organism and thus merges with its chemical and physical conditions, so the "psychic ultra-violet," the archetype, describes a field which exhibits none of the peculiarities of the physiological and yet, in the last analysis, can no longer be regarded as psychic, although it manifests itself psychically. But physiological processes behave in the same way, without on that account being declared psychic. Although there is no form of existence that is not mediated to us psychically and only psychically, it would hardly do to say that everything is merely psychic. We must apply this argument logically to the archetypes as well. Since their essential being is unconscious to us, and still they are experienced as spontaneous agencies, there is probably no alternative now but to describe their nature, in accordance with their chiefest effect, as "spirit," in the sense which I attempted to make plain in my paper "The Phenomenology of the Spirit in Fairytales." If so, the position of the archetype would be located beyond the psychic sphere, analogous to the position of physiological instinct, which is immediately rooted in the stuff of the organism and, with its psychoid nature, forms the bridge to matter in general. In archetypal conceptions and instinctual perceptions, spirit and matter confront one another on the psychic plane. Matter and spirit both appear in the psychic realm as distinctive qualities of conscious contents. The ultimate nature of both is transcendental, that is, irrepresentable, since the psyche and its contents are the only reality which is given to us *without a medium.*

General Considerations and Prospects

The problems of analytical psychology, as I have tried to outline them here, led to conclusions that astonished even me. I fancied I was working along the best scientific lines, establishing facts, observing, classifying, describing causal and functional relations, only to discover in the end that I had involved myself in a net of reflections which extend far beyond natural science and ramify into the fields of philosophy, theology, comparative religion, and the humane sciences in general. This transgression, as inevitable as it was suspect, has caused me no little worry. Quite apart from my personal incompetence in these fields, it seemed to me that my reflections were suspect also in principle, because I am profoundly convinced that the "personal equation" has a telling effect upon the results of psychological observation. The tragic thing is that psychology has no self-consistent mathematics at its disposal, but only a calculus of subjective prejudices. Also, it lacks the immense advantage of an Archimedean point such as physics enjoys. The latter observes the physical world from the psychic standpoint and can translate it into psychic terms. The psyche, on the other hand, observes itself and can only translate the psychic back into the psychic. Were physics in this position, it could do nothing except leave the physical process to its own devices, because in that way it would be most plainly itself. There is no medium for psychology to reflect itself in: it can only portray itself in itself, and describe itself. That, logically, is also the principle of my own method: it is, at bottom, a purely experiential process in which hit and miss, interpretation and error, theory and speculation, doctor and patient, form a *symptosis* or a *symptoma*—a coming together—and at the same time are symptoms of a certain process or run of events. What I am describing, therefore, is basically no more than an outline of psychic happenings, which exhibit a certain statistical frequency. We have not, scientifically speaking, removed ourselves to a plane in any way "above" the psychic process, nor have we translated it into another medium. Physics, on the other hand, is in a position to detonate mathematical formulae—the product of pure psychic activity—and kill seventy-eight thousand persons at one blow.

This literally "devastating" argument is calculated to reduce psychology to silence. But we can, in all modesty, point out that mathematical thinking is also a psychic function, thanks to which matter can be organized in such a way as to burst asunder the mighty forces that bind the atoms together—which it would never occur to them to do in the natural course of things, at least not upon this earth. The psyche is a disturber of the natural laws of the cosmos, and should we ever succeed in doing something to Mars with the aid of atomic fission, this too will have been brought to pass by the psyche.

The psyche is the world's pivot: not only is it the one great condition for the existence of a world at all, it is also an intervention in the existing natural order, and no one can say with certainty where this intervention will finally end. It is hardly necessary to stress the dignity of the psyche as an object of natural science. With all the more urgency, then, we must emphasize that the smallest alteration of the psychic factor, if it be an alteration of principle, is of the utmost significance as regards our knowledge of the world and the picture we make of it. The integration of unconscious contents into consciousness, which is the main endeavour of analytical psychology, is just such an alteration of principle, in that it does away with the sovereignty of the subjective ego-consciousness and confronts it with unconscious collective contents. Accordingly ego-consciousness seems to be dependent on two factors: firstly, on the conditions of the collective, i.e., the social, consciousness; and secondly, on the archetypes, or dominants, of the collective unconscious. The latter fall phenomenologically into two categories: instinctual and archetypal. The first includes the natural impulses, the second the dominants that emerge into consciousness as universal ideas. Between the contents of collective consciousness, which purport to be generally accepted truths, and those of the collective unconscious there is so pronounced a contrast that the latter are rejected as totally irrational,

not to say meaningless, and are most unjustifiably excluded from the scientific purview as though they did not exist, However, psychic phenomena of this kind exist with a vengeance, and if they appear nonsensical to us, that only proves that we do not understand them. Once their existence is recognized they can no longer be banished from our world-picture, even though the prevailing conscious *Weltanschau-**ung* proves to be incapable of grasping the phenomena in question. A conscientious study of these phenomena quickly reveals their uncommon significance, and we can hardly avoid the conclusion that between collective consciousness and the collective unconscious there is an almost unbridgeable gulf over which the subject finds himself suspended.

As a rule, collective consciousness wins hands down with its "reasonable" generalities that cause the average intelligence no difficulty whatever. It still believes in the necessary connection of cause and effect and has scarcely taken note of the fact that causality has become relative. The shortest distance between two points is still, for it, a straight line, although physics has to reckon with innumerable shortest distances, which strikes the educated Philistine of today as exquisitely absurd. Nevertheless the impressive explosion at Hiroshima has induced an awestruck respect for even the most abstruse alembications of modern physics. The explosion which we recently had occasion to witness in Europe, though far more terrible in its repercussions, was recognized as an unmitigated psychic disaster only by the few. Rather than do this, people prefer the most preposterous political and economic theories, which are about as useful as explaining the Hiroshima explosion as the chance hit of a large meteorite.

If the subjective consciousness prefers the ideas and opinions of collective consciousness and identifies with them, then the contents of the collective unconscious are repressed. The repression has typical consequences: the energy-charge of the repressed contents adds itself, in some measure,[14] to that of the repressing

---

[14] It is very probable that the archetypes, as instincts, possess a specific energy which cannot be taken away from them in the long run. The energy peculiar to the archetype is normally not sufficient

factor, whose effectiveness is increased accordingly. The higher its charge mounts, the more the repressive attitude acquires a fanatical character and the nearer it comes to conversion into its opposite, i.e., an enantiodromia. And the more highly charged the collective consciousness, the more the ego forfeits its practical importance. It is, as it were, absorbed by the opinions and tendencies of collective consciousness, and the result of that is the mass man, the ever-ready victim of some wretched "ism." The ego keeps its integrity only if it does not identify with one of the opposites, and if it understands how to hold the balance between them. This is possible only if it remains conscious of both at once. However, the necessary insight is made exceedingly difficult not by one's social and political leaders alone, but also by one's religious mentors. They all want decision in favour of one thing, and therefore the utter identification of the individual with a necessarily one-sided "truth." Even if it were a question of some great truth, identification with it would still be a catastrophe, as it arrests all further spiritual development. Instead of knowledge one then has only belief, and sometimes that is more convenient and therefore more attractive.

If, on the other hand, the content of the collective unconscious is realized, if the existence and efficacy of archetypal representations are acknowledged, then a violent conflict usually breaks out between what Fechner has called the "day-time and the night-time view." Medieval man (and modern man too, in so far as he has kept the attitude of the past) lived fully conscious of the discord between worldliness, which was subject to the *princeps huius mundi* (St. John 12: 31 and 16: 11),[15] and the will of God. For centuries this contradiction was demonstrated before his very eyes by the struggle between imperial and papal power. On the moral plane the conflict swelled to the ever-

lasting cosmic tug of war between good and evil in which man was implicated on account of original sin. The medieval man had not yet fallen such a helpless victim to worldliness as the contemporary mass man, for, to offset the notorious and, so to speak, tangible powers of this world, he still acknowledged the equally influential metaphysical potencies which demanded to be taken into account. Although in one respect he was politically and socially unfree and without rights—e.g., as a serf—and also found himself in the extremely disagreeable situation of being tyrannized over by black superstition, he was at least biologically nearer to that unconscious wholeness which primitive man enjoys in even larger measure, and the wild animal possesses to perfection. Looked at from the standpoint of modern consciousness, the opposition of medieval man seems as deplorable as it is in need of improvement. But the much needed broadening of the mind by science has only replaced medieval one-sidedness—namely, that age-old unconsciousness which once predominated and has gradually become defunct—by a new one-sidedness, the overvaluation of "scientifically" attested views. These each and all relate to knowledge of the external object and in a chronically one-sided way, so that nowadays the backwardness of psychic development in general and of self-knowledge in particular has become one of the most pressing contemporary problems. As a result of the prevailing one-sidedness, and in spite of the terrifying optical demonstration of an unconscious that has become alienated from the conscious, there are still vast numbers of people who are the blind and helpless victims of these conflicts, and who apply their scientific scrupulosity only to external objects, never to their own psychic condition. Yet the psychic facts are as much in need of objective scrutiny and acknowledgement. There are objective psychic factors which are every bit as important as radios and automobiles. Ultimately everything (particularly in the case of the atom bomb) depends on the uses to which these factors are put, and that is always conditioned by one's state of mind. The current "isms" are the most serious threat in this respect, because they are nothing but dangerous identifications of the subjective with the collective consciousness. Such an identity infallibly produces a mass psyche with its irresistible urge to catastrophe. Subjective consciousness must, in order to

---

to raise it into consciousness. For this it needs a definite quantum of energy flowing into the unconscious from consciousness, whether because consciousness is not using this energy or because the archetype attracts it to itself. The archetype can be deprived of its supplementary charge, but not of its specific energy.

[15] Although both passages hint that the devil was cast out during the life-time of Jesus, in the Apocalypse the business of rendering him harmless is deferred until Doomsday (Rev. 20: 2ff.).

escape this doom, avoid identification with collective consciousness by recognizing its shadow as well as the existence and the importance of the archetypes. These latter are an effective defence against the brute force of collective consciousness and the mass psyche that goes with it. In point of effectiveness, the religious outlook of medieval man corresponds roughly to the attitude induced in the ego by the integration of unconscious contents, with the difference that in the latter case susceptibility to environmental influences and unconsciousness are replaced by scientific objectivity and conscious knowledge. But so far as religion, for the contemporary consciousness, still means, if anything, a creed, and hence a collectively accepted system of religious statements neatly codified as dogmatic precepts, it has closer affinities with collective consciousness even though its symbols express the once-operative archetypes. So long as the communal consciousness presided over by the Church is objectively present, the psyche, as said, continues to enjoy a certain equilibrium. At all events, it constitutes a sufficiently effective defence against inflation of the ego. But once Mother Church and her motherly Eros fall into abeyance, the individual is at the mercy of any passing collectivism and the attendant mass psyche. He succumbs to social or national inflation, and the tragedy is that he does so with the same psychic attitude which had once bound him to a church.

But if he is independent enough to recognize the bigotedness of the social "ism," he may then be threatened with subjective inflation, for usually he is not capable of seeing that religious ideas do not, in psychological reality, rest solely upon tradition and faith, but originate with the archetypes, the "careful consideration" of which —religere!—constitutes the essence of religion. The archetypes are continuously present and active; as such they need no believing in, but only an intuition of their meaning and a certain sapient awe, which never loses sight of their import. A consciousness sharpened by experience knows the catastrophic consequences that disregard of this entails for the individual as well as for society. Just as the archetype is partly a spiritual factor, and partly like a hidden meaning imminent in the instincts, so the spirit, as I have shown,[16] is two-faced and paradoxical: a

great help and an equally great danger."[17] It seems as if man were destined to play a decisive role in solving this uncertainty, and to solve it moreover by virtue of his consciousness, which once started up like a light in the murk of the primeval world. Nowhere do we know for sure about these matters, but least of all where "isms" flourish, for they are only a sophisticated substitute for the lost link with psychic reality. The mass psyche that infallibly results destroys the meaning of the individual and of culture generally.

From this it is clear that the psyche not only disturbs its own natural order but, if it loses its balance, actually destroys its own creation. Therefore the careful consideration of psychic factors is of importance in restoring not merely the individual's balance, but society's as well, otherwise the destructive tendencies easily gain the upper hand. In the same way that the atom bomb is an unparalleled means of physical mass destruction, so the misguided development of the soul must lead to psychic mass destruction. The present situation is so sinister that one cannot suppress the suspicion that the Creator is planning another deluge that will finally exterminate the existing race of men. But if anyone imagines that a healthy belief in the existence of archetypes can be inculcated from outside, he is as simple as the people who want to outlaw war or the atom-bomb. Such measures remind one of the bishop who excommunicated the cock-chafers for their unseemly proliferation. Change of consciousness begins at home; it is a secular matter that depends entirely on how far the psyche's capacity for development extends. All we know at present is that there are single individuals who are capable of developing. How great their total number is we do not know, just as we do not know what the suggestive power of an extended consciousness may be, or what influence it may have upon the world at large. Effects of this kind never depend on the reasonableness of an idea, but far more on the question (which can only be answered ex effectu): is the time ripe for change, or not?

*   *   *   *   *   *

---

[16] Cf. "The Phenomenology of the Spirit in Fairytales."

[17] Aptly expressed in the logion cited by Origen (Homiliae in Jeremiam, XX, 3): "He who is near unto me is near unto the fire. He who is far from me is far from the kingdom." This "unclaimed saying of the Master" refers to Isiah 33:14.

As I have said, the psychology of complex phenomena finds itself in an uncomfortable situation compared with the other natural sciences because it lacks a base outside its object. It can only translate itself back into its own language, or fashion itself in its own image. The more it extends its field of research and the more complicated its objects become, the more it feels the lack of a point which is distinct from those objects. And once the complexity has reached that of the empirical man, his psychology inevitably merges with the psychic process itself. It can no longer be distinguished from the latter, and so it turns into it. But the effect of this is that the process attains to consciousness. In this way, psychology actualizes the unconscious urge to consciousness. It is, in fact, the coming to consciousness of the psychic process, but it is not, in the deeper sense, an explanation of this process, for no explanation of the psychic can be anything other than the living process of the psyche itself. Psychology is doomed to cancel itself out as a science and therein precisely it reaches its scientific goal. Every other science has, so to speak, an outside; not so psychology, whose object is the inside subject of all science.

Psychology therefore culminates of necessity in a developmental process which is peculiar to the psyche and consists in integrating the unconscious contents into consciousness. This means that the psychic human being becomes a whole, and becoming whole has remarkable effects on ego-consciousness which are extremely difficult to describe. I doubt my ability to give a proper account of the change that comes over the subject under the influence of the individuation process; it is a relatively rare occurrence, which is experienced only by those who have gone through the wearisome but, if the unconscious is to be integrated, indispensable business of coming to terms with the unconscious components of the personality. Once these unconscious components are made conscious, it results not only in their assimilation to the already existing ego-personality, but in a transformation of the latter. The main difficulty is to describe the manner of this transformation. Generally speaking the ego is a hard-and-fast complex which, because tied to consciousness and its continuity, cannot easily be altered, and should not be altered unless one wants to bring on pathological disturbances. The closest analogies to an alteration of the ego are to be found in the field of psychopathology, where we meet not only with neurotic dissociations but also with the schizophrenic fragmentation, or even dissolution, of the ego. In this field, too, we can observe pathological attempts at integration—if such an expression be permitted. These consist in more or less violent irruptions of unconscious contents into consciousness, the ego proving itself incapable of assimilating the intruders. But if the structure of the ego-complex is strong enough to withstand their assault without having its framework fatally dislocated, then assimilation can take place. In that event there is an alteration of the ego as well as of the unconscious contents. Although it is able to preserve its structure, the ego is ousted from its central and dominating position and thus finds itself in the role of a passive observer who lacks the power to assert his will under all circumstances, not so much because it has been weakened in any way, as because certain considerations give it pause. That is, the ego cannot help discovering that the afflux of unconscious contents has vitalized the personality, enriched it and created a figure that somehow dwarfs the ego in scope and intensity. This experience paralyzes an over-egocentric will and convinces the ego that in spite of all difficulties it is better to be taken down a peg than to get involved in a hopeless struggle in which one is invariably handed the dirty end of the stick. In this way the will, as disposable energy, gradually subordinates itself to the stronger factor, namely to the new totality-figure I call the *self*. Naturally, in these circumstances there is the greatest temptation simply to follow the power-instinct and to identify the ego with the self outright, in order to keep up the illusion of the ego's mastery. In other cases the ego proves too weak to offer the necessary resistance to the influx of unconscious contents and is thereupon assimilated by the unconscious, which produces a blurring or darkening of ego-consciousness and its identification with a pre-conscious wholeness.[18] Both these developments make the realization of the self impossible, and

---

[18] Conscious wholeness consists in a successful union of ego and self, so that both preserve their intrinsic qualities. If, instead of this union, the ego is overpowered by the self, then the self too does not attain the form it ought to have, but remains fixed on a primitive level and can express itself only through archaic symbols.

at the same time are fatal to the maintenance of ego-consciousness. They amount, therefore, to pathological effects. The psychic phenomena recently observable in Germany fall into this category. It is abundantly clear that such an *abaissement du niveau mental*, i.e., the over-powering of the ego by unconscious contents and the consequent identification with a pre-conscious wholeness, possesses a prodigious psychic virulence, or power of contagion, and is capable of the most disastrous results. Developments of this kind should, therefore, be watched very carefully; they require the closest control. I would recommend anyone who feels himself threatened by such tendencies to hang a picture of St. Christopher on the wall and to meditate upon it. For the self has a functional meaning only when it can act compensatorily to ego-consciousness. If the ego is dissolved in identification with the self, it gives rise to a sort of nebulous superman with a puffed-up ego and a deflated self. Such a personage, however saviourlike or baleful his demeanour, lacks the *scintilla*, the soul-spark, the little wisp of divine light that never burns more brightly than when it has to struggle against the invading darkness. What would the rainbow be were it not limned against the lowering cloud?

This simile is intended to remind the reader that pathological analogies of the individuation process are not the only ones. There are spiritual monuments of quite another kind, and they are positive illustrations of our process. Above all, I would mention the *koans* of Zen Buddhism, those sublime paradoxes that light up, as with a flash of lightning, the inscrutable interrelations between ego and self. In very different language, St. John of the Cross has made the same problem more readily accessible to the Westerner in his account of the "dark night of the soul." That we find it needful to draw analogies from psychopathology and from both Eastern and Western mysticism is only to be expected: the individuation process is, psychically, a border-line phenomenon which needs special conditions in order to become conscious. Perhaps it is the first step along a path of development to be trodden by the men of the future—a path which, for the time being, has taken a pathological turn and landed Europe in catastrophe.

To one familiar with our psychology, it may seem a waste of time to keep harping on the long-established difference between becoming conscious and the coming-to-be of the self (individuation). But again and again I note that the individuation process is confused with the coming of the ego into consciousness and that the ego is in consequence identified with the self, which naturally produces a hopeless conceptual muddle. Individuation is then nothing but ego-centredness and auto-eroticism. But the self comprises infinitely more than a mere ego, as the symbolism has shown from of old. It is as much one's self, and all other selves, as the ego. Individuation does not shut one out from the world, but gathers the world to oneself.

With this I would like to bring my exposition to an end. I have tried to sketch out the development and basic problems of our psychology and to communicate the quintessence, the very spirit, of this science. In view of the unusual difficulties of my theme, the reader may pardon the undue demands I have made upon his good-will and attention. Fundamental discussions are among the things that mould a science into shape, but they are seldom entertaining.

Supplement

As the points of view that have to be considered in elucidating the unconscious are often misunderstood, I would like, in connection with the foregoing discussions of principle, to examine at least two of the main prejudices somewhat more closely.

What above all stultifies understanding is the arrant assumption that "archetype" means an inborn idea. No biologist would ever dream of assuming that each individual acquires his general mode of behaviour afresh each time. It is much more probable that the young weaverbird builds his characteristic nest because he is a weaver-bird and not a rabbit. Similarly, it is more probable that man is born with a specifically human mode of behaviour and not with that of a hippopotamus or with none at all. Integral to his characteristic behaviour is his psychic phenomenology, which differs from that of a bird or quadruped. Archetypes are typical forms of behaviour which, once they become conscious, naturally present themselves *as ideas and images*, like everything else that becomes a content of consciousness. Because it is a question of characteristically human modes, it is hardly to be wondered at that we can find psychic forms in the individual which occur not only at the antipodes but also in other epochs with which archaeology provides the only link.

Now if we wish to prove that a certain psychic form is not a unique but a typical occurrence, this can be done only if I myself testify that, having taken the necessary precautions, I have observed the same thing in different individuals. Then other observers, too, must confirm that they have made the same or similar observations. Finally we have to establish that the same or similar phenomena can be shown to occur in the folklore of other peoples and races and in the texts that have come down to us from earlier centuries and epochs. My method and whole outlook, therefore, begin with individual psychic facts which not I alone have established, but other observers as well. The material brought forward—folkloristic, mythological, or historical—serves in the first place to demonstrate the uniformity of psychic events in time and space. But since the meaning and substance of the typical individual forms are of the utmost importance in practice, and knowledge of them plays a considerable role in each individual case, it is inevitable that the mythologem and its content will also be drawn into the limelight. This is not to say that the purpose of the investigation is to interpret the mythologem. But, precisely in this connection, a widespread prejudice reigns that the psychology of unconscious processes is a sort of *philosophy* designed to explain mythologems. This unfortunately rather common prejudice assiduously overlooks the crucial point, namely, that our psychology starts with observable facts and not with philosophical speculations. If, for instance, we study the mandala structures that are always cropping up in dreams and fantasies, ill-considered criticism might raise, and indeed has raised, the objection that we are reading Indian or Chinese philosophy into the psyche. But in reality all we have done is to compare individual psychic occurrences with obviously related collective phenomena. The introspective trend of Eastern philosophy has brought to light material which all introspective attitudes bring to light all over the world, at all times and places. The great snag so far as the critic is concerned is that he has no personal experience of the facts in question, any more than he has of the state of mind of a lama engaged in "constructing" a mandala. These two prejudices render any access to modern psychology impos-

sible for not a few heads with scientific pretensions. There are in addition many other stumbling-blocks that cannot be overcome by reason. We shall therefore refrain from discussing them.

Inability to understand, or the ignorance of the public, cannot, however, prevent the scientist from employing certain calculations of probability of whose treacherous nature he is sufficiently well informed. We are fully aware that we have no more knowledge of the various states and processes of the unconscious as such than the physicist has of the process underlying physical phenomena. Of what lies beyond the phenomenal world we can have absolutely no idea, for there is no idea that could have any other source than the phenomenal world. If we are to engage in fundamental reflections about the nature of the psychic, we need an Archimedean point which alone makes a judgment possible. This can only be the nonpsychic, for, as a living phenomenon, the psychic lies embedded in something that appears to be of a nonpsychic nature. Although we perceive the latter as a psychic datum only, there are sufficient reasons for believing in its objective reality. This reality, so far as it lies outside our body's limits, is mediated to us chiefly by particles of light impinging on the retina of the eye. The organization of these particles produces a picture of the phenomenal world which depends essentially upon the constitution of the apperceiving psyche on the one hand, and upon that of the light medium on the other. The apperceiving consciousness has proved capable of a high degree of development, and constructs instruments with the help of which our range of seeing and hearing has been extended by many octaves. Consequently the postulated reality of the phenomenal world as well as the subjective world of consciousness have undergone an unparalleled expansion. The existence of this remarkable correlation between consciousness and the phenomenal world, between subjective perception and objectively real processes, i.e., their energic effects, requires no further proof.

As the phenomenal world is an aggregate of processes of atomic magnitude, it is naturally of the greatest importance to find out whether, and if so how, the photons (shall we say) enable us to gain a definite knowledge of the reality underlying the mediative energy processes. Experience has shown that light and matter both behave like separate particles and also like waves. This paradoxical conclusion obliged us to abandon, on the plane of atomic magnitudes, a causal description of nature in the ordinary space-time system, and in its place to set up invisible fields of probability in multidimensional spaces, which do in fact represent the state of our knowledge at present. Basic to this abstract scheme of explanation is a conception of reality that takes account of the uncontrollable effects the observer has upon the system observed, the result being that reality forfeits something of its objective character and that a subjective element attaches to the physicist's picture of the world.[19]

The application of statistical laws to processes of atomic magnitude in physics has a noteworthy correspondence in psychology, so far as psychology investigates the bases of consciousness by pursuing the conscious processes until they lose themselves in darkness and unintelligibility, and nothing more can be seen but effects which have an *organizing* influence on the contents of consciousness.[20] Investigation of these effects yields the singular fact that they proceed from an unconscious, i.e., objective, reality which behaves at the same time like a subjective one—in other words, like a consciousness. Hence the reality underlying the unconscious effects includes the observing subject and is therefore constituted in a way that we cannot conceive. It is, at one and the same time, absolute subjectivity and universal truth, for in

principle it can be shown to be present everywhere, which certainly cannot be said of conscious contents of a personalistic nature. The elusiveness, capriciousness, haziness, and uniqueness that the lay mind always associates with the idea of the psyche applies only to consciousness, and not to the absolute unconscious. The qualitatively rather than quantitatively definable units with which the unconscious works, namely the archetypes, therefore have a nature that *cannot with certainty be designated as psychic*.

Although I have been led by purely psychological considerations to doubt the exclusively psychic nature of the archetypes, psychology sees itself obliged to revise its "only psychic" assumptions in the light of the physical findings too. Physics has demonstrated, as plainly as could be wished, that in the realm of atomic magnitudes an observer is postulated in objective reality, and that only on this condition is a satisfactory scheme of explanation possible. This means that a subjective element attaches to the physicist's world picture, and secondly that a connection necessarily exists between the psyche to be explained and the objective space-time continuum. Since the physical continuum is inconceivable it follows that we can form no picture of its psychic aspect either, which also necessarily exists. Nevertheless, the relative or partial identity of psyche and physical continuum is of the greatest importance theoreti-

---

[19] I owe this formulation to the kind help of Professor W. Pauli.

[20] It may interest the reader to hear the opinion of a physicist on this point. Professor Pauli, who was good enough to glance through the manuscript of this supplement, writes: "As a matter of fact the physicist would expect a psychological correspondence at this point, because the epistemological situation with regard to the concepts 'conscious' and 'unconscious' seems to offer a pretty close analogy to the undermentioned 'complementarity' situation in physics. On the one hand the unconscious can only be inferred indirectly from its (organizing) effects on conscious contents. On the other hand every 'observation of the unconscious,' i.e., every conscious realization of unconscious contents, has an uncontrollable reactive effect on these same contents (which as we know precludes in principle the possibility of 'exhausting' the unconscious by making it conscious). Thus the physicist will conclude *per analogiam* that this uncontrollable reactive effect of the observing subject on the unconscious limits the objective character of the latter's reality

and lends it at the same time a certain subjectivity. Although the *position* of the 'cut' between conscious and unconscious is (at least up to a point) left to the free choice of the 'psychological experimenter,' the *existence* of this 'cut' remains an unavoidable necessity. Accordingly, from the standpoint of the psychologist, the 'observed system' would consist not of physical objects only, but would also include the unconscious, while consciousness would be assigned the role of 'observing medium.' It is undeniable that the development of 'microphysics' has brought the way in which nature is described in this science very much closer to that of the newer psychology: but whereas the former, on account of the basic 'complementarity' situation, is faced with the impossibility of eliminating the effects of the observer by determinable correctives, and has therefore to abandon in principle any objective understanding of physical phenomena, the latter can supplement the purely subjective psychology of consciousness by postulating the existence of an unconscious that possesses a large measure of objective reality."

cally, because it brings with it a tremendous simplification by bridging over the seeming incommensurability between the physical world and the psychic, not of course in any concrete way, but from the physical side by means of mathematical equations, and from the psychological side by means of empirically derived postulates—archetypes—whose content, if any, cannot be represented to the mind. Archetypes, so far as we can observe and experience them at all, manifest themselves only through their ability to *organize* images and ideas, and this is always an unconscious process which cannot be detected until afterwards. By assimilating ideational material whose provenance in the phenomenal world is not to be contested, they become visible and *psychic*. Therefore they are recognized at first only as psychic entities and are conceived as such, with the same right with which we base the physical phenomena of immediate perception on Euclidean space. Only when it comes to explaining psychic phenomena of a minimal degree of clarity are we driven to assume that archetypes must have a nonpsychic aspect. Grounds for such a conclusion are supplied by the phenomena of synchronicity, which are associated with the activity of unconscious operators and have hitherto been regarded, or repudiated, as "telepathy," etc.[21] Scepticism should, however, be levelled only at incorrect theories and not at facts which exist in their own right. No unbiased observer can deny them. Resistance to the recognition of such facts rests principally on the repugnance people feel for an allegedly supernatural faculty tacked on to the psyche, like "clairvoyance." The very diverse and confusing aspects of these phenomena are, so far as I can see at present, completely explicable on the assumption of a psychically relative space-time continuum. As soon as a psychic content crosses the threshold of consciousness, the synchronistic marginal phenomena disappear, time and space resume their accustomed sway, and consciousness is once more isolated in its subjectivity. We have here one of those instances which can best be understood in terms of the physicist's idea of "complementarity." When an unconscious content passes over into consciousness its syn-

chronistic manifestation ceases; conversely, synchronistic phenomena can be evoked by putting the subject into an unconscious state (trance). The same relationship of complementarity can be observed just as easily in all those extremely common medical cases in which certain clinical symptoms disappear when the corresponding unconscious contents are made conscious. We also know that a number of psychosomatic phenomena which are otherwise outside the control of the will can be induced by hypnosis, that is, by this same restriction of consciousness. Professor Pauli formulates the physical side of the complementarity relationship here expressed, as follows: "It rests with the free choice of the experimenter (or observer) to decide . . . which insights he will gain and which he will lose; or, to put it in popular language, whether he will measure A and ruin B or ruin A and measure B. It does *not* rest with him, however, to gain only insights and not lose any." This is particularly true of the relation between the physical standpoint and the psychological. Physics determines quantities and their relation to one another; psychology determines qualities without being able to measure quantities. Despite that, both sciences arrive at ideas which come significantly close to one another. The parallelism of psychological and physical explanations has already been pointed out by C. A. Meier in his essay "Moderne Physik—Moderne Psychologie."[22] He says: "Both sciences have, in the course of many years of independent work, amassed observations, and systems of thought to match them. Both sciences have come up against certain barriers which . . . display similar basic characteristics. The object to be investigated, and the human investigator with his organs of sense and knowledge and their extensions (measuring instruments and procedures), are indissolubly bound together. That is, complementarity in physics as well as in psychology." Between physics and psychology there is in fact "a genuine and authentic relationship of complementarity."

Once we can rid ourselves of the highly unscientific pretence that it is merely a question of chance coincidence, we shall see that synchronistic phenomena are not unusual occurrences at all, but are relatively common. This

[21] The physicist Pascual Jordan ("Positivistische Bemerkungen uber die parapsychischen Erscheinungen," 14ff.) has already used the idea of relative space to explain telepathic phenomena.

[22] *Die kulturelle Bedeutung der komplexen Psychologie*, p. 362.

fact is in entire agreement with Rhine's "probability-exceeding" results. The psyche is not a chaos made up of random whims and accidents, but is an objective reality to which the investigator can gain access by the methods of natural science. There are indications that psychic processes stand in some sort of energy relation to the physiological substrate. In so far as they are objective events, they can hardly be interpreted as anything but energy processes,[23] or to put it another way: in spite of the nonmeasurability of psychic processes, the perceptible changes effected by the psyche cannot possibly be understood except as a phenomenon of energy. This places the psychologist in a situation which is highly repugnant to the physicist: The psychologist also talks of energy although he has nothing measurable to manipulate, besides which the concept of energy is a strictly defined mathematical quantity which cannot be applied as such to anything psychic. The formula for kinetic energy, $E = mv^2/2$, contains the factors m (mass) and v (velocity), and these would appear to be incommensurable with the nature of the empirical psyche. If psychology nevertheless insists on employing its own concept of energy for the purpose of expressing the activity of the psyche, it is not of course being used as a mathematical formula, but only as its analogy. But note: the analogy is itself an older intuitive idea from which the concept of physical energy originally developed. The latter rests on earlier applications of an activity not mathematically defined, which can be traced back to the primitive or archaic idea of the "extraordinarily potent." This mana concept is not confined to Melanesia, but can also be found in Indonesia and on the east coast of Africa; and it still echoes in the Latin *numen* and, more faintly, in *genius* (e.g., *genius loci*). The use of the term *libido* in the newer medical psychology has surprising affinities with the primitive mana. This archetypal idea is therefore far from being only primitive, but differs from the physicist's conception of energy by the fact that it is essentially qualitative and not quantitative. In psychology the exact measurement of quantities

is replaced by an approximate determination of intensities, for which purpose, in strictest contrast to physics, we enlist the function of *feeling* (valuation). The latter takes the place, in psychology, of concrete measurement in physics. The psychic intensities and their graduated differences point to quantitative processes which are inaccessible to direct observation and measurement. While psychological data are essentially qualitative, they also have a sort of latent physical energy, since psychic phenomena exhibit a certain quantitative aspect. Could these quantities be measured the psyche would be bound to appear as having motion in space, something to which the energy formula would be applicable. Therefore, since mass and energy are of the same nature, mass and velocity would be adequate concepts for characterizing the psyche so far as it has any observable effects in space: in other words, it must have an aspect under which it would appear as mass in motion. If one is unwilling to postulate a preestablished harmony of physical and psychic events, then they can only be in a state of interaction. But the latter hypothesis requires a psyche that touches matter at some point, and, conversely, a matter with a latent psyche, a postulate not so very far removed from certain formulations of modern physics (Eddington, Jeans, and others). In this connection I would remind the reader of the existence of parapsychic phenomena whose reality value can only be appreciated by those who have had occasion to satisfy themselves by personal observation.

If these reflections are justified, they must have weighty consequences with regard to the nature of the psyche, since as an objective fact it would then be intimately connected not only with physiological and biological phenomena but with physical events too—and, so it would appear, most intimately of all with those that pertain to the realm of atomic physics. As my remarks may have made clear, we are concerned first and foremost to establish certain analogies, and no more than that; the existence of such analogies does not entitle us to conclude that the connection is already proven. We must, in the present state of our physical and psychological knowledge, be content with the mere resemblance to one another of certain basic reflections. The existing analogies, however, are significant enough in themselves to warrant the prominence we have given them.

---

[23] By this I only mean that psychic phenomena have an energic aspect by virtue of which they can be described as "phenomena." I do not mean that the energic aspects embraces or explains the whole of the psyche.

*

2. Symbol formation

C. G. JUNG

THE PSYCHOLOGICAL MECHANISM THAT TRANS-
FORMS ENERGY IS THE SYMBOL. I mean by this
a real symbol and not a sign. The Wachandi's
hole in the earth is not a sign for the genitals
of a woman, but a symbol that stands for the
idea of the earth woman who is to be made
fruitful. To mistake it for a human woman
would be to interpret the symbol semiotically,
and this would fatally disturb the value of the
ceremony. It is for this reason that none of the
dancers may look at a woman. The mechanism
would be destroyed by a semiotic interpretation—would be like smashing the supply-pipe
of a turbine on the ground that it was a very
unnatural waterfall that owed its existence to
the repression of natural conditions. I am far
from suggesting that the semiotic interpretation
is meaningless; it is not only a possible interpretation but also a very true one. Its usefulness
is undisputed in all those cases where nature
is merely thwarted without any effective work
resulting from it. But the semiotic interpretation becomes meaningless when it is applied
exclusively and schematically—when, in short,
it ignores the real nature of the symbol and
debases it to a mere sign.

The first achievement wrested by primitive
man from instinctual energy, through analogy-
building, is magic. A ceremony is magical so
long as it does not result in effective work but
preserves the state of expectancy. In that case
the energy is canalized into a new object and
produces a new dynamism, which in turn remains magical so long as it does not create
effective work. The advantage accruing from a
magical ceremony is that the newly invested
object acquires a working potential in relation
to the psyche. Because of its value it has a determining and stimulating effect on the imagination, so that for a long time the mind is fascinated and possessed by it. This gives rise to
actions that are performed in a half-playful way
on the magical object, most of them rhythmical
in character. A good example is those South
American rock-drawings which consist of furrows deeply engraved in the hard stone. They
were made by the Indians playfully retracing
the furrows again and again with stones, over
hundred of years. The content of the drawings
is difficult to interpret, but the activity bound
up with them is incomparably more significant.[1]

The influence exerted on the mind by the
magically effective object has other possible
consequences. Through a sustained playful interest in the object, a man may make all sorts
of discoveries about it which would otherwise
have escaped him. As we know, many discoveries have actually been made in this way. Not
for nothing is magic called the "mother of science." Until late in the Middle Ages what we today call science was nothing other than magic.
A striking example of this is alchemy, whose
symbolism shows quite unmistakably the principle of transformation of energy described
above, and indeed the later alchemists were
fully-conscious of this fact.[2] But only through
the development of magic into science, that is,
through the advance from the stage of mere

SOURCE. Selection from C. G. Jung, "Symbol
formation" in "The structure and dynamics of the
psyche," The Collected Works, Vol. 8, pp. 45–61.
Edited by Sir Herbert Read, Michael Fordham,
Gerhard Adler; translated from the German by
R. F. C. Hull. New York: Pantheon, 1960. Copyright
held by Bollingen Foundation, Inc.

---

[1] Koch-Grünberg, Südamerikanische Felszeich-
nungen.
[2] Silberer, Problems of Mysticism and Its Symbolism; also Rosencreutz, Chymische Hochzeit
(1616).

expectation to real technical work on the object, have we acquired that mastery over the forces of nature of which the age of magic dreamed. Even the alchemist's dream of the transmutation of the elements has been fulfilled, and magical action at a distance has been realized by the discovery of electricity. So we have every reason to value symbol-formation and to render homage to the symbol as an inestimable means of utilizing the mere instinctual flow of energy for effective work. A waterfall is certainly more beautiful than a power-station, but dire necessity teaches us to value electric light and electrified industry more highly than the superb wastefuless of a waterfall that delights us for a quarter of an hour on a holiday walk.

Just as in physical nature only a very small portion of natural energy can be converted into a usable form, and by far the greater part must be left to work itself out unused in natural phenomena, so in our psychic nature only a small part of the total energy can be diverted from its natural flow. An incomparably greater part cannot be utilized by us, but goes to sustain the regular course of life. Hence the libido is apportioned by nature to the various functional systems, from which it cannot be wholly withdrawn. The libido is invested in these functions as a specific force that cannot be transformed. Only where a symbol offers a steeper gradient than nature is it possible to canalize libido into other forms. The history of civilization has amply demonstrated that man possesses a relative surplus of energy that is capable of application apart from the natural flow. The fact that the symbol makes this deflection possible proves that not all the libido is bound up in a form that enforces the natural flow, but that a certain amount of energy remains over, which could be called excess libido. It is conceivable that this excess may be due to failure of the firmly organized functions to equalize differences in intensity. They might be compared to a system of water-pipes whose diameter is too small to draw off the water that is being steadily supplied. The water would then have to flow off in one way or another. From this excess libido certain psychic processes arise which cannot be explained—or only very inadequately—as the result of merely natural conditions. How are we to explain religious processes, for instance, whose nature is essen-

tially symbolical? In abstract form, symbols are religious ideas; in the form of action, they are rites or ceremonies. They are the manifestation and expression of excess libido. At the same time they are stepping-stones to new activities, which must be called cultural in order to distinguish them from the instinctual functions that run their regular course according to natural law.

I have called a symbol that converts energy a "libido analogue." [3] By this I mean an idea that can give equivalent expression to the libido and canalize it into a form different from the original one. Mythology offers numerous equivalents of this kind, ranging from sacred objects such as *churingas,* fetishes, etc., to the figures of gods. The rites with which the sacred objects are surrounded often reveal very clearly their nature as transformers of energy. Thus the primitive rubs his *churinga* rhythmically and takes the magic power of the fetish into himself, at the same time giving it a fresh "charge." [4] A higher stage of the same line of thought is the idea of the totem, which is closely bound up with the beginnings of tribal life and leads straight up to the idea of the palladium, the tutelary tribal deity, and to the idea of an organized human community in general. The transformation of libido through the symbol is a process that has been going on ever since the beginnings of humanity and continues still. Symbols were never devised consciously, but were always produced out of the unconscious by way of revelation or intuition. [5] In view of the close connection between mythological symbols and dream-symbols, and of the fact that the dream is "le dieu des sauvages," it is more than probable that most of the historical symbols derive directly from dreams or

---

[3] *Symbols of Transformation,* par. 146.

[4] Spencer and Gillen, p. 277.

[5] "Man, of course, has always been trying to understand and to control his environment, but in the early stages this process was unconscious. The matters which are problems for us existed latent in the primitive brain; there, undefined, lay both problem and answer; through many ages of savagery, first one and then another partial answer emerged into consciousness; at the end of the series, hardly completed today, there will be a new synthesis in which riddle and answer are one." Crawley, *The Idea of the Soul,* p. 11.

are at least influenced by them.[6] We know that this is true of the choice of totem, and there is similar evidence regarding the choice of gods. This age-old function of the symbol is still present today, despite the fact that for many centuries the trend of mental development has been towards the suppression of individual symbol-formation. One of the first steps in this direction was the setting up of an official state religion, a further step was the extermination of polytheism, first attempted in the reforms of Amenophis IV. We know the extraordinary part played by Christianity in the suppression of individual symbol-formation. But as the intensity of the Christian idea begins to fade, a recrudescence of individual symbol-formation may be expected. The prodigious increase of Christian sects since the eighteenth century, the century of "enlightenment," bears eloquent witness to this. Christian Science, theosophy, anthroposophy, and "Mazdaznan" are further steps along the same path.

In practical work with our patients we come upon symbol-formations at every turn, the purpose of which is the transformation of libido. At the beginning of treatment we find the symbol-forming process at work, but in an unsuitable form that offers the libido too low a gradient. Instead of being converted into effective work, the libido flows off unconsciously along the old channels, that is, into archaic sexual fantasies and fantasy activities. Accordingly the patient remains at war with himself, in other words, neurotic. In such cases analysis in the strict sense is indicated, i.e., the reductive psychoanalytic method inaugurated by Freud, which breaks down all inappropriate symbol-formations and reduces them to their natural elements. The power-station, situated too high and unsuitably constructed, is dismantled and separated into its original components, so that the natural flow is restored. The unconscious continues to produce symbols which one could obviously go on reducing to their elements *ad infinitum*.

But man can never rest content with the natural course of things, because he always has an excess of libido that can be offered a more

favourable gradient than the merely natural one. For this reason he will inevitably seek it, no matter how often he may be forced back by reduction to the natural gradient. We have therefore reached the conclusion that when the unsuitable structures have been reduced and the natural course of things is restored, so that there is some possibility of the patient living a normal life, the reductive process should not be continued further. Instead, symbol-formation should be reinforced in a synthetic direction until a more favourable gradient for the excess libido is found. Reduction to the natural condition is neither an ideal state nor a panacea. If the natural state were really the ideal one, then the primitive would be leading an enviable existence. But that is by no means so, for aside from all the other sorrows and hardships of human life the primitive is tormented by superstitions, fears, and compulsions to such a degree that, if he lived in our civilization, he could not be described as other than profoundly neurotic, if not mad. What would one say of a European who conducted himself as follows? —A Negro dreamt that he was pursued by his enemies, caught, and burned alive. The next day he got his relatives to make a fire and told them to hold his feet in it, in order, by this apotropaic ceremony, to avert the misfortune of which he had dreamed. He was so badly burned that for many months he was unable to walk.[7]

Mankind was freed from these fears by a continual process of symbol-formation that leads to culture. Reversion to nature must therefore be followed by a synthetic reconstruction of the symbol. Reduction leads down to the primitive natural man and his peculiar mentality. Freud directed his attention mainly to the ruthless desire for pleasure, Adler to the "psychology of prestige." These are certainly two quite essential peculiarities of the primitive psyche, but they are far from being the only ones. For the sake of completeness we would have to mention other characteristics of the primitive, such as his playful, mystical, or "heroic" tendencies, but above all that outstanding quality of the primitive mind, which is its subjection to suprapersonal "powers" be they instincts, affects, superstitions, fantasies, magicians, witches, spirits, demons, or gods. Reduction leads back to the subjection of the primitive,

[6] "Dreams are to the savage man what the Bible is to us—the source of divine revelation." Gatschet, "The Klamath Indians of South-Western Oregon," cited in Lévy-Bruhl, p. 57.

[7] Lévy-Bruhl, p. 57.

which civilized man hopes he had escaped. And just as reduction makes a man aware of his subjection to these "powers" and thus confronts him with a rather dangerous problem, so the synthetic treatment of the symbol brings him to the religious question, not so much to the problem of present-day religious creeds as to the religious problem of primitive man. In the face of the very real powers that dominate him, only an equally real fact can offer help and protection. No intellectual system, but direct experience only, can counterbalance the blind power of the instincts.

Over against the polymorphism of the primitive's instinctual nature there stands the regulating principle of individuation. Multiplicity and inner divisions are opposed by an integrative unity whose power is as great as that of the instincts. Together they form a pair of opposites necessary for self-regulation, often spoken of as nature and spirit. These conceptions are rooted in psychic conditions between which human consciousness fluctuates like the pointer on the scales.

The primitive mentality can be directly experienced by us only in the form of the infantile psyche that still lives in our memories. The peculiarities of this psyche are conceived by Freud, justly enough, as infantile sexuality, for out of this germinal state there develops the later, mature sexual being. Freud, however, derives all sorts of other mental peculiarities from this infantile germinal state, so that it begins to look as if the mind itself came from a preliminary sexual stage and were consequently nothing more than an offshoot of sexuality. Freud overlooks the fact that the infantile, polyvalent germinal state is not just a singularly perverse preliminary stage of normal and mature sexuality; it seems perverse because it is a preliminary stage not only of adult sexuality but also of the whole mental make-up of the individual. Out of the infantile germinal state there develops the complete adult man; hence the germinal state is no more exclusively sexual than is the mind of the grown man. In it are hidden not merely the beginnings of adult life, but also the whole ancestral heritage, which is of unlimited extent. This heritage includes not only instincts from the animal stage, but all those differentiations that have left hereditary traces behind them. Thus every child is born with an immense split in his make-up; on one side he is more or less like an animal, on the other side he is the final embodiment of an age-old and endlessly complicated sum of hereditary factors. This split accounts for the tension of the germinal state and does much to explain the many puzzles of child psychology, which certainly has no lack of them.

If now, by means of a reductive procedure, we uncover the infantile stages of the adult psyche, we find as its ultimate basis germs containing on the one hand the later sexual being *in statu nascendi*, and on the other all those complicated preconditions of the civilized being. This is reflected most beautifully in children's dreams. Many of them are very simple "childish" dreams and are immediately understandable, but others contain possibilities of meaning that almost make one's head spin, and things that reveal their profound significance only in the light of primitive parallels. This other side is the mind *in nuce*. Childhood, therefore, is important not only because various warpings of instinct have their origin there, but because this is the time when, terrifying or encouraging, those far-seeing dreams and images appear before the soul of the child, shaping his whole destiny, as well as those retrospective intuitions which reach back far beyond the range of childhood experience into the life of our ancestors. Thus in the child-psyche the natural condition is already opposed by a "spiritual" one. It is recognized that man living in the state of nature is in no sense merely "natural" like an animal, but sees, believes, fears, worships things whose meaning is not at all discoverable from the conditions of his natural environment. Their underlying meaning leads us in fact far away from all that is natural, obvious, and easily intelligible, and quite often contrasts more sharply with the natural instincts. We have only to think of all those gruesome rites and customs against which every natural feeling rises in revolt, or of all those beliefs and ideas which stand in insuperable contradiction to the evidence of the facts. All this drives us to the assumption that the spiritual principle (whatever that may be) asserts itself against the merely natural conditions with incredible strength. One can say that this too is "natural," and that both have their origin in one and the same "nature." I do not in the least doubt this origin, but must point out that this "natural" something consists of a conflict between two principles, to which you can give this or that name according to taste, and that this opposition is the expression, and perhaps also the basis, of the tension we call psychic energy.

For theoretical reasons as well there must be some such tension of opposites in the child, otherwise no energy would be possible, for, as Heraclitus has said, "war is the father of all things." As I have remarked, this conflict can be understood as an opposition between the profoundly primitive nature of the newborn infant and his highly differentiated inheritance. The natural man is characterized by unmitigated instinctuality, by his being completely at the mercy of his instincts. The inheritance that opposes this condition consists of mnemonic deposits accruing from all the experience of his ancestors. People are inclined to view this hypothesis with scepticism, thinking that "inherited ideas" are meant. There is naturally no question of that. It is rather a question of inherited *possibilities* of ideas, "paths" that have gradually been traced out through the cumulative experience of our ancestors. To deny the inheritance of these paths would be tantamount to denying the inheritance of the brain. To be consistent, such sceptics would have to assert that the child is born with the brain of an ape. But since it is born with a human brain, this must sooner or later begin to function in a human way, and it will necessarily begin at the level of the most recent ancestors. Naturally this functioning remains profoundly unconscious to the child. At first he is conscious only of the instincts and of what opposes these instincts—namely, his parents. For this reason the child has no notion that what stands in his way may be within himself. Rightly or wrongly it is projected on to the parents. This infantile prejudice is so tenacious that we doctors often have the greatest difficulty in persuading our patients that the wicked father who forbade everything is far more inside than outside themselves. Everything that works from the unconscious appears projected on others. Not that these others are wholly without blame, for even the worst projection is at least hung on a hook, perhaps a very small one, but still a hook offered by the other person.

Although our inheritance consists of psychological paths, it was nevertheless mental processes in our ancestors that traced these paths. If they came to consciousness again in the individual, they can do so only in the form of other mental processes; and although these

processes can become conscious only through individual experience and consequently appear as individual acquisitions, they are nevertheless pre-existent traces which are merely "filled out" by individual experience. Probably every "impressive" experience is just such a break-through into an old, previously unconscious river-bed.

These pre-existent paths are hard facts, as indisputable as the historical fact of man having built a city out of his original cave. This development was made possible only by the formation of a community, and the latter only by the curbing of instinct. The curbing of instinct by mental and spiritual processes is carried through with the same force and the same results in the individual as in the history of mankind. It is a normative or, more accurately, a "nomothetical" [8] process, and it derives its power from the unconscious fact of the inherited disposition. The mind, as the active principle in the inheritance, consists of the sum of the ancestral minds, the "unseen fathers" [9] whose authority is born anew with the child.

The philosophical concept of mind as "spirit" has still not been able to free itself, as a term in its own right, from the overpowering bond of identity with the other connotation of spirit, namely "ghost." Religion, on the other hand, has suceeded in getting over the linguistic association with "spirits" by calling the supreme spiritual authority "God." In the course of the centuries this conception came to formulate a spiritual principle which is opposed to mere instinctuality. What is especially significant here is that God is conceived at the same time as the Creator of nature. He is seen as the maker of those imperfect creatures who err and sin, and at the same time he is their judge and taskmaster. Simple logic would say: if I make a creature who falls into error and sin, and is practically worthless because of his blind instinctuality, then I am manifestly a bad creator and have not even completed my apprenticeship. (As we know, this argument played an important role in Gnosticism.) But the religious point of view is not perturbed by this criticism; it asserts that the ways and intentions of God are inscrutable. Actually the Gnostic argument found little favour in history, because the unassailability of the God-concept obvi-

---

[8] ("Ordained by law."—Editors.)
[9] Söderblom, *Das Werden des Gottesglaubens*, pp. 88ff. and 175ff.

ously answers a vital need before which all logic pales. (It should be understood that we are speaking here not of God as a *Ding an sich,* but only of a human conception which as such is a legitimate object of science.)

Although the God-concept is a spiritual principle *par excellence,* the collective metaphysical need nevertheless insists that it is at the same time a conception of the First Cause, from which proceed all those instinctual forces that are opposed to the spiritual principle. God would thus be not only the essence of spiritual light, appearing as the latest flower on the tree of evolution, not only the spiritual goal of salvation in which all creation culminates, not only the end and aim, but also the darkest, nethermost cause of Nature's blackest deeps. This is a tremendous paradox which obviously reflects a profound psychological truth. For it asserts the essential contradictoriness of one and the same being, a being whose innermost nature is a tension of opposites. Science calls this "being" energy, for energy is like a living balance between opposites. For this reason the God-concept, in itself impossibly paradoxical, may be so satisfying to human needs that no logic however justified can stand against it. Indeed the subtlest cogitation could scarcely have found a more suitable formula for this fundamental fact of inner experience.

It is not, I believe, superfluous to have discussed in considerable detail the nature of the opposites that underlie psychic energy.[10] Freudian theory consists in a casual explanation of the psychology of instinct. From this standpoint the spiritual principle is bound to appear only as an appendage, a by-product of the instincts. Since its inhibiting and restrictive power cannot be denied, it is traced back to the influence of education, moral authorities, convention, and tradition. These authorities in their turn derive their power, according to the theory, from repression in the manner of a vicious cycle. The spiritual principle is not recognized as an equivalent counterpart of the instincts.

The spiritual standpoint, on the other hand, is embodied in religious views which I can take as being sufficiently known. Freudian psycho-

logy appears threatening to this standpoint, but it is not more of a threat than materialism in general, whether scientific or practical. The one-sidedness of Freud's sexual theory is significant at least as a symptom. Even if it has no scientific justification, it has a moral one. It is undoubtedly true that instinctuality conflicts with our moral views most frequently and most conspicuously in the realm of sex. The conflict between infantile instinctuality and ethics can never be avoided. It is, it seems to me, the *sine qua non* of psychic energy. While we are all agreed that murder, stealing, and ruthlessness of any kind are obviously inadmissible, there is nevertheless what we call a "sexual question." We hear nothing of a murder question or a rage question; social reform is never invoked against those who wreak their bad tempers on their fellow men. Yet these things are all examples of instinctual behaviour, and the necessity for their suppression seems to us self-evident. Only in regard to sex do we feel the need of a question mark. This points to a doubt—the doubt whether our existing moral concepts and the legal institutions founded on them are really adequate and suited to their purpose. No intelligent person will deny that in this field opinion is sharply divided. Indeed, there would be no problem at all if public opinion were united about it. It is obviously a reaction against a too rigorous morality. It is not simply an outbreak of primitive instinctuality; such outbreaks, as we know, have never yet bothered themselves with moral laws and moral problems. There are, rather, serious misgivings as to whether our existing moral views have dealt fairly with the nature of sex. From this doubt there naturally arises a legitimate interest in any attempt to understand the nature of sex more truly and deeply, and this interest is answered not only by Freudian psychology but by numerous other researches of the kind. The special emphasis, therefore, that Freud has laid on sex could be taken as a more or less conscious answer to the question of the hour, and conversely, the acceptance that Freud has found with the public proves how well-timed his answer was.

An attentive and critical reader of Freud's writings cannot fail to remark how wide and flexible his concept of sexuality is. In fact it covers so much that one often wonders why in certain places the author uses a sexual terminology at all. His concept of sexuality in-

---

[10] I have treated this same problem under other aspects and in another way in *Symbols of Transformation,* pars. 253, 680; and *Psychological Types* (1923 ed., p. 240).

cludes not only the physiological sexual processes but practically every stage, phase, and
kind of feeling or desire. This enormous flexibility makes his concept universally applicable,
though not always to the advantage of the resulting explanations. By means of this inclusive
concept you can explain a work of art or a religious experience in exactly the same terms
as an hysterical symptom. The absolute difference between these three things then drops
right out of the picture. The explanation can
therefore be only an apparent one for at least
two of them. Apart from these inconveniences,
however, it is psychologically correct to tackle
the problem first from the sexual side, for it is
just there that the unprejudiced person will find
something to talk about.

The conflict between ethics and sex today
is not just a collision between instinctuality and
morality, but a struggle to give an instinct its
rightful place in our lives, and to recognize in
the instincts a power which seeks expression
and evidently may not be trifled with, and
therefore cannot be made to fit in with our
well-meaning moral laws. Sexuality is not mere
instinctuality; it is an indisputably creative
power that is not only the basic cause of our
individual lives, but a very serious factor in
our psychic life as well. Today we know only
too well the grave consequences that sexual
disturbances can bring in their train. We could
call sexuality the spokesman of the instincts,
which is why from the spiritual standpoint sex
is the chief antagonist, not because sexual indulgence is in itself more immoral than excessive eating and drinking, avarice, tyranny, and
other extravagances, but because the spirit
senses in sexuality a counterpart equal and indeed akin to itself. For just as the spirit would
press sexuality, like every other instinct, into
its service, so sexuality has an ancient claim
upon the spirit, which it once—in procreation,
pregnancy, birth, and childhood—contained
within itself, and whose passion the spirit can
never dispense with in its creations. Where
would the spirit be if it had no peer among the
instincts to oppose it? It would be nothing but
an empty form. A reasonable regard for the
other instincts has become for us a self-evident
necessity, but with sex it is different. For us
sex is still problematical, which means that on
this point we have not reached a degree of consciousness that would enable us to do full
justice to the instinct without appreciable moral

injury. Freud is not only a scientific investigator
of sexuality, but also its champion; therefore,
having regard to the great importance of the
sexual problem, I recognize the moral justification of his concept of sexuality even though I
cannot accept it scientifically.

This is not the place to discuss the possible
reasons for the present attitude to sex. It is
sufficient to point out that sexuality seems to
us the strongest and most immediate instinct,[11]
standing out as *the* instinct above all others. On
the other hand, I must also emphasize that the
spiritual principle does not, strictly speaking,
conflict with instinct as such but only with blind
instinctuality, which really amounts to an un-
justified preponderance of the instinctual nature
over the spiritual. The spiritual appears in the
psyche also as an instinct, indeed as a real passion, a "consuming fire," as Nietzsche once expressed it. It is not derived from any other
instinct, as the psychologists of instinct would
have us believe, but is a principle *sui generis*, a
specific and necessary form of instinctual power.
I have gone into this problem in a special study,
to which I would refer the reader.[12]

Symbol-formation follows the road offered
by these two possibilities in the human mind.
Reduction breaks down all inappropriate and
useless symbols and leads back to the merely
natural course, and this causes a damming up of
libido. Most the alleged "sublimations" are
compulsory products of this situation, activities
cultivated for the purpose of using up the unbearable surplus of libido. But the really primitive demands are not satisfied by this procedure.
If the psychology of this dammed-up condition
is studied carefully and without prejudice, it is
easy to discover in it the beginnings of a primitive form of religion, a religion of an individual
kind altogether different from a dogmatic, collective religion.

Since the making of a religion or the formation of symbols is just as important an interest
of the primitive mind as the satisfaction of instinct, the way to further development is logically given: escape from the state of reduction
lies in evolving a religion of an individual character. One's true individuality then emerges
from behind the veil of the collective personality, which would be quite impossible in the

---

[11] This is not the case with primitives, for whom
the food question plays a far greater role.

[12] See "Instinct and the Unconscious," infra.

state of reduction since our instinctual nature is essentially collective. The development of individuality is also impossible, or at any rate seriously impeded, if the state of reduction gives rise to forced sublimations in the shape of various cultural activities, since these are in their essence equally collective. But, as human beings are for the most part collective, these forced sublimations are therapeutic products that should not be underestimated, because they help many people to bring a certain amount of useful activity into their lives. Among these cultural activities we must include the practice of a religion within the framework of an existing collective religion. The astonishing range of Catholic symbolism, for instance, has an emotional appeal which for many natures is absolutely satisfying. The immediacy of the relationship to God in Protestantism satisfies the mystic's passion for independence, while theosophy with its unlimited speculative possibilities meets the need for pseudo-Gnostic intuitions and caters to lazy thinking.

These organizations or systems are "symbola" which enable man to set up a spiritual counterpole to his primitive instinctual nature, a cultural attitude as opposed to sheer instinctuality. This has been the function of all religions. For a long time and for the great majority of mankind the symbol of a collective religion will suffice. It is perhaps only temporarily and for relatively few individuals that the existing collective religions have become inadequate. Wherever the cultural process is moving forward, whether in single individuals or in groups, we find a shaking off of collective beliefs. Every advance in culture, is, psychologically, an extension of consciousness, a coming to consciousness that can take place only through discrimination. Therefore an advance always begins with individuation, that is to say with the individual, conscious of his isolation, cutting a new path through hitherto untrodden territory. To do this he must first return to the fundamental facts of his own being, irrespective of all authority and tradition, and allow himself to become conscious of his distinctiveness. If he succeeds in giving collective validity to his widened consciousness, he creates a tension of opposites that provides the stimulation which culture needs for its further progress.

This is not to say that the development of individuality is in all circumstances necessary or even opportune. Yet one may well believe, as Goethe has said, that "the highest joy of man should be the growth of personality." There are large numbers of people for whom the development of individuality is the prime necessity, especially in a cultural epoch like ours, which is literally flattened out by collective norms, and where the newspaper is the real monarch of the earth. In my naturally limited experience there are, among people of maturer age, very many for whom the development of individuality is an indispensable requirement. Hence I am privately of the opinion that it is just the mature person who, in our times, has the greatest need of some further education in individual culture after his youthful education in school or university has moulded him on exclusively collective lines and thoroughly imbued him with the collective mentality. I have often found that people of riper years are in this respect capable of education to a most unexpected degree, although it is just those matured and strengthened by the experience of life who resist most vigorously the purely reductive standpoint.

Obviously it is in the youthful period of life that we have most to gain from a thorough recognition of the instinctual side. A timely recognition of sexuality, for instance, can prevent that neurotic suppression of it which keeps a man unduly withdrawn from life, or else forces him into a wretched and unsuitable way of living with which he is bound to come into conflict. Proper recognition and appreciation of normal instincts leads the young person into life and entangles him with fate, thus involving him in life's necessities and the consequent sacrifices and efforts through which his character is developed and his experience matured. For the mature person, however, the continued expansion of life is obviously not the right principle, because the descent towards life's afternoon demands simplification, limitation, and intensification—in other words, individual culture. A man in the first half of life with its biological orientation can usually, thanks to the youthfulness of his whole organism, afford to expand his life and make something of value out of it. But the man in the second half of life is oriented towards culture, the diminishing powers of his organism allowing him to subordinate his instincts to cultural goals. Not a few are wrecked during the transition from the biological to the cultural sphere. Our collective education makes practically no provision for this transitional period. Concerned solely with the education of the young, we disregard the education of the adult, of whom it is always assumed—on what grounds who can say?—that he needs no more education. There is an almost total lack of guidance for this extraordinarily important transition from the biological to the cultural attitude, for the transformation of energy from the biological form into the cultural form. This transformation process is an individual one and cannot be enforced by general rules and maxims. It is achieved by means of the symbol. Symbol-formation is a fundamental problem that cannot be discussed here. I must refer the reader to Chapter V in my *Psychological Types*, where I have dealt with this question in detail.

3. The symbols of the self

C. G. JUNG

THE VISION OF THE "WORLD CLOCK" is neither the last nor the highest point in the development of the symbols of the objective psyche. But it brings to an end of the first third of the material, consisting in all of some four hundred dreams and visions. This series is noteworthy because it gives an unusually complete description of a psychic fact that I had observed long before in many individual cases. We have to thank not only the completeness of the objective material but the care and discernment of the dreamer for having placed us in a position to follow, step by step, the synthetic work of the unconscious. The troubled course of this synthesis would doubtless have been depicted in even greater completeness had I taken account of the 340 dreams interspersed among the 59 examined here. Unfortunately this was impossible, because the dreams touch to some extent on the intimacies of personal life and must therefore remain unpublished. So I had to confine myself to the impersonal material.

I hope I may have succeeded in throwing some light upon the development of the symbols of the self and in overcoming, partially at least, the serious difficulties inherent in all material drawn from actual experience. At the same time I am fully aware that the comparative material so necessary for a complete elucidation could have been greatly increased. But, so as not to burden the meaning unduly, I have exercised the greatest reserve in this respect. Conse-

SOURCE. Selection from C. G. Jung, "The symbols of the self" in "Psychology and Alchemy," *The Collected Works,* Vol. 12, pp. 206–213. Edited by Sir Herbert Read, Michael Fordham, Gerhard Adler; translated from the German by R. F. C. Hull. New York: Pantheon, 1960. Copyright held by Bollingen Foundation, Inc.

quently there is much that is only hinted at, though this should not be taken as a sign of superficiality. I believe myself to be quite in a position to offer ample evidence for my views, but I do not wish to give the impression that I imagine I have said anything final on this highly complicated subject. It is true that this is not the first time I have dealt with a series of spontaneous manifestations of the unconscious. I did so once before, in my book *Psychology of the Unconscious* (429a), but there it was more a problem of neurosis in puberty, whereas this is the broader problem of individuation. Moreover, there is a very considerable difference between the two personalities in question. The earlier case, which I never saw at first hand, ended in psychic catastrophe—psychosis; but the present case shows a normal development such as I have often observed in highly intelligent persons.

What is particularly noteworthy here is the consistent development of the central symbol. We can hardly help feeling that the unconscious process moves spiral-wise round a centre, gradually getting closer, while the characteristics of the centre grow more and more distinct. Or perhaps we could put it the other way round and say that the centre—itself virtually unknowable, acts like a magnet on the disparate materials and processes of the unconscious and gradually captures them as in a crystal lattice. For this reason the centre is—in other cases—often pictured as a spider in its web, especially when the conscious attitude is still dominated by fear of unconscious processes. But if the process is allowed to take its course, as it was in our case, then the central symbol, constantly renewing itself, will steadily and consistently force its way through the apparent chaos of the personal psyche and its dramatic entanglements, just as the great Bernoulli's epitaph[1] says of the spiral: "Eadem mutata resurgo." Accordingly we often find spiral representations of the centre, as for instance the serpent coiled round the creative point, the egg.

Indeed, it seems as if all the personal entanglements and dramatic changes of fortune that go to make up the intensity of life were nothing but hesitations, timid shrinkings, almost like petty complications and meticulous excuses manufactured to avoid facing the finality of this strange or uncanny process of crystallization. Often one has the impression that the personal psyche is running round this central point like a shy animal, at once fascinated and frightened, always in flight, and yet steadily drawing nearer.

I trust I have given no cause for the misunderstanding that I know anything about the nature of the "centre"—for it is simply unknowable and can only be expressed symbolically through its own phenomenology, as is the case, incidentally, with every object of experience. Among the various characteristics of the centre the one that struck me from the beginning was the phenomenon of the quaternity. That it is not a question of, shall we say, the "four" points of the compass or something of that kind is proved by the fact that there is often a competition between four and three.[2] There is also, but more rarely, a competition between four and five, though five-rayed mandalas must be characterized as abnormal on account of their lack of symmetry.[3] It would seem, therefore, that there is normally a clear insistence on four, or as if there were a greater statistical probability of four. Now it is—as ·I can hardly refrain from remarking—a curious "sport of nature" that the chief chemical constituent of organic bodies is carbon, which is characterized by four valences; also it is well known that the diamond is a carbon crystal. Carbon is black—coal, graphite—but the diamond is "purest water." To draw such an analogy would be a lamentable piece of intellectual bad taste were the phenomenon of four merely a poetic conceit on the part of the conscious mind and not a spontaneous production of the objective psyche. Even if we supposed that dreams could be influenced to any considerable extent by auto-suggestion—in which case it would naturally be more a matter of their meaning than of their form—it would still have to be proved that the conscious mind of the dreamer had made a serious effort to impress the idea of the quaternity on the unconscious. But in this as in many other cases I have observed such a possibility is absolutely out of the question, quite apart from the numerous historical and ethnological parallels.[4] Surveying these facts as a whole we come, at least in my opinion, to the inescapable conclusion that there is some psychic element present which expresses itself through the quaternity. No daring speculation or extravagant fancy is needed for this. If I have called the centre the "self" I did so after mature consideration and a careful appraisal of the empirical and historical data. A materialistic interpretation could easily maintain that the "centre" is "nothing but" the point at which the psyche ceases to be knowable because it there coalesces with the body. And a spiritualistic interpretation might retort that this "self" is nothing but "spirit," which animates both soul and body and irrupts into time and space at that creative point. I purposely refrain from all such physical and metaphysical speculations and content myself with establishing the empirical facts, and this seems to me to be infinitely more important for the advance of human knowledge than running after fashionable intellectual crazes or trumped-up "religious" creeds.

To the best of my experience we are here dealing with important "nuclear processes" in the objective psyche—"images of the goal," as it were, which the psychic process, being "purposive," apparently sets up of its own accord, without any external stimulus.[5] Externally, of course, there is always a certain condition of psychic need, a sort of hunger, but it seeks

---

[1] In the cloisters of Basel Cathedral.

[2] This has been chiefly observed in men, but whether this is an accident or not I am unable to say.

[3] Mainly observed in women. But it occurs so rarely that it is impossible to draw any further conclusions.

[4] I have only mentioned a few of these parallels here.

[5] The image that presents itself in this material as a goal may also serve as the origin when viewed from the historical standpoint. By way of example I would cite the conception of paradise in the Old Testament, and especially the creation of Adam in the Slavonic Book of Enoch.—27 (b); Forster, 384.

for familiar and favourite dishes and never imagines as its goal some outlandish food unknown to consciousness. The goal which beckons to this psychic need, the image which promises to heal, to make whole, is at first strange beyond all measure to the conscious mind, so that it can find entry only with the very greatest difficulty. Of course it is quite different for people who live in a time and environment when such images of the goal have dogmatic validity. These images are then *ipso facto* held up to consciousness, and the unconscious is thus shown a mysterious reflected image in which it recognizes itself and so joins forces with the conscious mind.

As to the question of the origin of the mandala motif, from a superficial point of view it looks as if it had gradually come into being in the course of the dream-series. The fact is, however, that it only *appeared* more and more distinctly and in increasingly differentiated form; in reality it was always present and even occurred in the first dream—as the nymphs say later: "We were always there, only you did not notice us." It is therefore more probable that we are dealing with an *a priori* "type," an archetype which is inherent in the collective unconscious and thus beyond individual birth and death. The archetype is, so to speak, an "eternal" presence, and it is only a question of whether it is perceived by consciousness or not. I think we are forming a more probable hypothesis, and one that better explains the observed facts, if we assume that the increase in the clarity and frequency of the mandala motif is due to a more accurate perception of an already existing "type," rather than that it is generated in the course of the dream-series.[6] The latter assumption is contradicted by the fact, for instance, that such fundamental ideas as the hat which epitomizes the personality, the encircling serpent, and the *perpetuum mobile* appear right at the beginning.

If the motif of the mandala is an archetype it ought to be a collective phenomenon, i.e., theoretically it should appear in everyone. In practice, however, it is only to be met with in distinct form in relatively few cases, though this does not prevent it from functioning as a concealed pole round which everything ultimately revolves. In the last analysis every life is the realization of a whole, that is, of a self, for which reason this realization can also be called "individuation." All life is bound to individual carriers who realize it and is simply inconceivable without them. But every carrier is charged with an individual destiny and destination, and the realization of these alone makes sense of life. True, the "sense" is often something that could just as well be called "nonsense," for there is a certain incommensurability between the mystery of existence and human understanding. "Sense" and "nonsense" are merely man-made labels which serve to give us a reasonably valid sense of direction.

As the historical parallels show, the symbolism of the mandala is not just a unique curiosity; we can well say that it is a regular occurrence. Were it not so there would be no comparative material, and it is precisely the possibility of comparing the spiritual products of all times and from every quarter of the globe that shows us most clearly what immense importance the *consensus gentium* has always attached to the processes of the objective psyche. This is reason enough not to make light of them, and my medical experience has only confirmed this estimate. There are people, of course, who think it unscientific to take anything seriously; they do not want their intellectual playground disturbed by graver considerations. But the doctor who fails to take account of man's feeling for values commits a serious blunder, and if he tries to correct the mysterious and wellnigh inscrutable workings of nature with his so-called scientific attitude, he is merely putting his shallow sophistry in place of nature's healing processes. Let us take the wisdom of the old alchemists to heart: "Naturalissimum et perfectissimum opus est generare tale quale ipsum est." [7]

---

[6] If we divide the four hundred dreams into eight groups of fifty each, we come to the following results:

I	6 mandalas	V	11 mandalas
II	4 mandalas	VI	11 mandalas
III	2 mandalas	VII	11 mandalas
IV	9 mandalas	VIII	17 mandalas

---

[7] "The most natural and perfect work is to produce that which is like to its self."

4.   An interpretation of a dream

C. G. JUNG

FIRST I MUST ACQUAINT THE READER in some measure with the personality of the dreamer, for without this acquaintance he will hardly be able to transport himself into the peculiar atmosphere of the dreams. There are dreams that are pure poems and can therefore only be understood through the mood they convey as a whole. The dreamer is a youth of a little over twenty, still entirely boyish in appearance. There is even a touch of girlishness in his looks and manner of expression. The latter betrays a very good education and upbringing. He is intelligent, with pronounced intellectual and aesthetic interests. His aestheticism is very much in evidence: we are made instantly aware of his good taste and his fine appreciation of all forms of art. His feelings are tender and soft, given to the enthusiasms typical of puberty, but somewhat effeminate. There is no trace of adolescent callowness. Undoubtedly he is too young for his age, a clear case of retarded development. It is quite in keeping with this that he should have come to me on account of his homosexuality. The night preceding his first visit he had the following dream: "*I am in a lofty cathedral filled with mysterious twilight. They tell me that it is the cathedral at Lourdes. In the centre there is a deep dark well, into which I have to descend.*"

The dream is clearly a coherent expression of mood. The dreamer's comments are as follows: "Lourdes is the mystic fount of healing. Naturally I remembered yesterday that I was going

SOURCE. Selection from C. G. Jung, "An interpretation of a dream" in "Two essays on analytical psychology," *The Collected Works*, Vol. 7, pp. 100–109. Edited by Sir Herbert Read, Michael Fordham, Gerhard Adler; translated from the German by R. F. C. Hull. New York: Pantheon, 1953. Copyright held by Bollingen Foundation, Inc.

to you for treatment and was in search of a cure. There is said to be a well like this at Lourdes. It would be rather unpleasant to go down into this water. The well in the church was ever so deep."

Now what does this dream tell us? On the surface it seems clear enough, and we might be content to take it as a kind of poetic formulation of the mood of the day before. But we should never stop there, for experience shows that dreams are much deeper and more significant. One might almost suppose that the dreamer came to the doctor in a highly poetic mood and was entering upon the treatment as though it were a sacred religious act to be performed in the mystical half-light of some awe-inspiring sanctuary. But this does not fit the facts at all. The patient merely came to the doctor to be treated for that unpleasant matter, his homosexuality, which is anything but poetic. At any rate we cannot see from the mood of the preceding day why he should dream so poetically, if we were to accept so direct a causation for the origin of the dream. But we might conjecture, perhaps, that the dream was stimulated precisely by the dreamer's impressions of that highly unpoetical affair which impelled him to come to me for treatment. We might even suppose that he dreamed in such an intensely, poetical manner just because of the unpoeticalness of his mood on the day before, much as a man who has fasted by day dreams of delicious meals at night. It cannot be denied that the thought of treatment, of the cure and its unpleasant procedure, recurs in the dream, but poetically transfigured, in a guise which meets most effectively the lively aesthetic and emotional needs of the dreamer. He will be drawn on irresistibly by this inviting picture, despite the fact that the well is dark, deep, and cold.

Something of the dream-mood will persist after sleep and will even linger on into the morning of the day on which he has to submit to the unpleasant and unpoetical duty of visiting me. Perhaps the drab reality will be touched by the bright, golden after-glow of the dream feeling.

Is this, perhaps, the purpose of the dream? That would not be impossible, for in my experience the vast majority of dreams are compensatory.[1] They always stress the other side in order to maintain the psychic equilibrium. But the compensation of mood is not the only purpose of the dream picture. The dream also provides a *mental corrective*. The patient had of course nothing like an adequate understanding of the treatment to which he was about to submit himself. But the dream gives him a picture which describes in poetic metaphors the nature of the treatment before him. This becomes immediately apparent if we follow up his associations and comments on the image of the cathedral: "Cathedral," he says, "makes me think of Cologne Cathedral. Even as a child I was fascinated by it. I remember my mother telling me of it for the first time, and I also remember how, whenever I saw a village church, I used to ask if that were Cologne Cathedral. I wanted to be a priest in a cathedral like that."

In these associations the patient is describing a very important experience of his childhood. As in nearly all cases of this kind, he had a particularly close tie with his mother. By this we are not to understand a particularly good or intense *conscious* relationship, but something in the nature of a secret, subterranean tie which expresses itself consciously, perhaps, only in the retarded development of character, i.e., in a relative infantilism. The developing personality naturally veers away from such an unconscious infantile bond; for nothing is more obstructive to development than persistence in an unconscious—we could also say, a psychically embryonic—state. For this reason instinct seizes on the first opportunity to replace the mother by another object. If it is to be a real mother-substitute, this object must be, in some sense, an analogy of her. This is entirely the case with our patient. The intensity with which his childish fantasy seized upon the symbol of Cologne Cathedral corresponds to the strength of his unconscious need to find a substitute for the

mother. The unconscious need is heightened still further in a case where the infantile bond threatens injury. Hence the enthusiasm with which his childish imagination took up the idea of the Church; for the Church is, in the fullest sense, a mother. We speak not only of Mother Church, but even of the Church's womb. In the ceremony known as the *benedictio fontis,* the baptismal font is apostrophized as "immaculatus divini fontis uterus"—the immaculate womb of the divine fount. We naturally think that a man must have known this meaning consciously before it could get to work in his fantasy, and that an unknowing child could not possibly be affected by these significations. Such analogies certainly do not work by way of the conscious mind, but in quite another manner.

The Church represents a higher spiritual substitute for the purely natural, or "carnal," tie to the parents. Consequently it frees the individual from an unconscious natural relationship which, strictly speaking, is not a relationship at all but simply a condition of inchoate, unconscious identity. This, just because it is unconscious, possesses a tremendous inertia and offers the utmost resistance to any kind of spiritual development. It would be hard to say what the essential difference is between this state and the soul of an animal. Now, it is by no means the special prerogative of the Christian Church to try to make it possible for the individual to detach himself from his original, animal-like condition; the Church is simply the latest, and specifically Western, form of an instinctive striving that is probably as old as mankind itself. It is a striving that can be found in the most varied forms among all primitive peoples who are in any way developed and have not yet become degenerate: I mean the institution or rite of initiation into manhood. When he has reached puberty the young man is conducted to the "men's house," or some other place of consecration, where he is systematically alienated from his family. At the same time he is initiated into the religious mysteries, and in this way is ushered not only into a wholly new set of relationships, but, as a renewed and changed personality, into a new world, like one reborn (*quasi modo genitus*). The initiation is often attended by all kinds of tortures, sometimes including such things as circumcision and the like. These practices are undoubtedly very old. They have almost become instinctive mechanisms, with the result that they continue to repeat themselves

---

[1] The idea of compensation has already been extensively used by Alfred Adler.

without external compulsion, as in the "baptisms" of German students or the even more wildly extravagant initiations in American students' fraternities. They are engraved in the unconscious as a primordial image.

When his mother told him as a little boy about Cologne Cathedral, this primordial image was stirred and awakened to life. But there was no priestly instructor to develop it further, so the child remained in his mother's hands. Yet the longing for a man's leadership continued to grow in the boy, taking the form of homosexual leanings—a faulty development that might never have come about had a man been there to educate his childish fantasies. The deviation towards homosexuality has, to be sure, numerous historical precedents. In ancient Greece, as also in certain primitive communities, homosexuality and education were practically synonymous. Viewed in this light, the homosexuality of adolescence is only a misunderstanding of the otherwise very appropriate need for masculine guidance. One might also say that the fear of incest which is based on the mother-complex extends to women in general; but in my opinion an immature man is quite right to be afraid of women, because his relations with women are generally disastrous.

According to the dream, then, what the initiation of the treatment signifies for the patient is the fulfilment of the true meaning of his homosexuality, i.e., his entry into the world of the adult man. All that we have been forced to discuss here in such tedious and long-winded detail, in order to understand it properly, the dream has condensed into a few vivid metaphors, thus creating a picture which works far more effectively on the imagination, feeling, and understanding of the dreamer than any learned discourse. Consequently the patient was better and more intelligently prepared for the treatment than if he had been overwhelmed with medical and pedagogical maxims. (For this reason I regard dreams not only as a valuable source of information but as an extraordinarily effective instrument of education.)

We come now to the second dream. I must explain in advance that in the first consultation I did not refer in any way to the dream we have just been discussing. It was not even mentioned. Nor was there a word said that was even remotely connected with the foregoing. This is the second dream: "*I am in a great Gothic cathedral. At the altar stands a priest. I stand before him with my friend, holding in my hand a little Japanese ivory figure, with the feeling that it is going to be baptized. Suddenly an elderly woman appears, takes the fraternity ring from my friend's finger and puts it on her own. My friend is afraid that this may bind him in some way. But at the same moment there is a sound of wonderful organ music.*"

Here I will only bring out briefly those points which continue and supplement the dream of the preceding day. The second dream is unmistakably connected with the first: once more the dreamer is in church, that is, in the state of initiation into manhood. But a new figure has been added: the priest, whose absence in the previous situation we have already noted. The dream therefore confirms that the unconscious meaning of his homosexuality has been fulfilled and that a further development can be started. The actual initiation ceremony, namely the baptism, may now begin. The dream symbolism corroborates what I said before, namely that it is not the prerogative of the Christian Church to bring about such transitions and psychic transformations, but that behind the Church there is a living primordial image which in certain conditions is capable of enforcing them.

What, according to the dream, is to be baptized is a little Japanese ivory figure. The patient says of this: "It was a tiny, grotesque little manikin that reminded me of the male organ. It was certainly odd that this member was to be baptized. But after all, with the Jews circumcision is a sort of baptism. That must be a reference to my homosexuality, because the friend standing with me before the altar is the one with whom I have sexual relations. We belong to the same fraternity. The fraternity ring obviously stands for our relationship."

We know that in common usage the ring is the token of a bond or relationship, as for example the wedding ring. We can therefore safely take the fraternity ring in this case as symbolizing the homosexual relationship, and the fact that the dreamer appears together with his friend points in the same direction.

The complaint to be remedied is homosexuality. The dreamer is to be led out of this relatively childish condition and initiated into the adult state by means of a kind of circumcision ceremony under the supervision of a priest. These ideas correspond exactly to my analysis of the previous dream. Thus far the development has proceeded logically and consistently with the aid of archetypal images. But now a disturbing factor appears to enter. An elderly woman suddenly takes possession of the fraternity ring; in other words, she draws to herself what has hitherto been a homosexual relationship, thus causing the dreamer to fear that he is getting involved in a new relationship with obligations of its own. Since the ring is now on the hand of a woman, a marriage of sorts has been contracted, i.e., the homosexual relationship seems to have passed over into a heterosexual one, but a heterosexual relationship of a peculiar kind since it concerns an elderly woman. "She is a friend of my mother's," says the patient. "I am very fond of her, in fact she is like a mother to me."

From this remark we can see what has happened in the dream: as a result of the initiation the homosexual tie has been cut and a heterosexual relationship substituted for it, a platonic friendship with a motherly type of woman. In spite of her resemblance to his mother, this woman is not his mother any longer, so the relationship with her signifies a step beyond the mother towards masculinity, and hence a partial conquest of his adolescent homosexuality.

The fear of the new tie can easily be understood, firstly as fear which the woman's resemblance to his mother might naturally arouse —it might be that the dissolution of the homosexual tie has led to a complete regression to the mother—and secondly as fear of the new and unknown factors in the adult heterosexual state with its possible obligations, such as marriage, etc. That we are in fact concerned here not with a regression but with a progression seems to be confirmed by the music that now peals forth. The patient is musical and especially susceptible to solemn organ music. Therefore music signifies for him a very positive feeling, so in this case it forms a harmonious conclusion to the dream, which in its turn is well qualified to leave behind a beautiful, holy feeling for the following morning.

If you consider the fact that up to now the patient had seen me for only one consultation, in which little more was discussed than a general anamnesis, you will doubtless agree with me when I say that both dreams make astonishing anticipations. They show the patient's situation in a highly remarkable light, and one that is very strange to the conscious mind, while at the same time lending to the banal medical situation an aspect that is uniquely attuned to

the mental peculiarities of the dreamer, and thus capable of stringing his aesthetic, intellectual, and religious interests to concert pitch. No better conditions for treatment could possibly be imagined. One is almost persuaded, from the meaning of these dreams, that the patient entered upon the treatment with the utmost readiness and hopefulness, quite prepared to cast aside his boyishness and become a man. In reality, however, this was not the case at all. Consciously he was full of hesitation and resistance; moreover, as the treatment progressed, he constantly showed himself antagonistic and difficult, ever ready to slip back into his previous infantilism. Consequently the dreams stand in strict contrast to his conscious behavior. They move along a progressive line and take the part of the educator. They clearly reveal their special function. This function I have called compensation. The unconscious progressiveness and the conscious regressiveness together form a pair of opposites which, as it were, keeps the scales balanced. The influence of the educator tilts the balance in favour of progression.

In the case of this young man the images of the collective unconscious play an entirely positive role, which comes from that fact that he has no really dangerous tendency to fall back on a fantasy-substitute for reality and to entrench himself behind it against life. The effect of these unconscious images has something fateful about it. Perhaps—who knows?—these eternal images are what men mean by fate.

The archetypes are of course always at work everywhere. But practical treatment, especially in the case of young people, does not always require the patient to come to close quarters with them. At the climacteric, on the other hand, it is necessary to give special attention to the images of the collective unconscious, because they are the source from which hints may be drawn for the solution of the problem of opposites. From the conscious elaboration of this material the transcendent function reveals itself as a mode of apprehension mediated by the archetypes and capable of uniting the opposites. By "apprehension" I do not mean simply intellectual understanding, but understanding through experience. An archetype, as we have already said, is a dynamic image, a fragment of the objective psyche, which can be truly understood only if experienced as a living opposite.

A general account of this process, which may extend over a long period of time, would be pointless—even if such a description were possible—because it takes the greatest imaginable variety of forms in different individuals. The only common factor is the emergence of certain definite archetypes. I would mention in particular the shadow, the animal, the wise old man, the anima, the animus, the mother, the child, besides an indefinite number of archetypes representative of situations. A special position must be accorded to those archetypes which stand for the goal of the developmental process. The reader will find the necessary information on this point in my *Psychology and Alchemy,* as well as in *Psychology and Religion* and the volume produced in collaboration with Richard Wilhelm, *The Secret of the Golden Flower.*[2]

The transcendent function does not proceed without aim and purpose, but leads to the revelation of the essential man. It is in the first place a purely natural process, which may in some cases pursue its course without the knowledge or assistance of the individual, and can sometimes forcibly accomplish itself in the face of opposition. The meaning and purpose of the process is the realization, in all its aspects, of the personality originally hidden away in the embryonic germ-plasm; the production and unfolding of the original, potential wholeness. The symbols used by the unconscious to this end are the same as those which mankind has always used to express wholeness, completeness, and perfection: symbols, as a rule, of the quaternity and the circle. For these reasons I have termed this the *individuation process.*

This natural process of individuation served me both as a model and guiding principle for my method of treatment. The unconscious compensation of a neurotic conscious attitude contains all the elements that could effectively and

---

[2] Respectively, in Vols. 11, 12, and (i.e., my commentary) 13 of the *Collected Works.*

healthily correct the one-sidedness of the conscious mind, if these elements were made conscious, i.e., understood and integrated into it as realities. It is only very seldom that a dream achieves such intensity that the shock is enough to throw the conscious mind out of the saddle. As a rule dreams are too feeble and too unintelligible to exercise a radical influence on consciousness. In consequence, the compensation runs underground in the unconscious and has no immediate effect. But it has some effect all the same; only, it is indirect in so far as the unconscious opposition will, if consistently ignored, arrange symptoms and situations which irresistibly thwart our conscious intentions. The aim of the treatment is therefore to understand and to appreciate, so far as practicable, dreams and all other manifestations of the unconscious, firstly in order to prevent the formation of an unconscious opposition which becomes more dangerous as time goes on, and secondly in order to make the fullest possible use of the healing factor of compensation.

These proceedings naturally rest on the assumption that a man is capable of attaining wholeness, in other words, that he has it in him to be healthy. I mention this assumption because there are without doubt individuals who are not at bottom altogether viable and who rapidly perish if, for any reason, they come face to face with their wholeness. Even if this does not happen, they merely lead a miserable existence for the rest of their days as fragments or partial personalities, shored up by social or psychic parasitism. Such people are, very much to the misfortune of others, more often than not inveterate humbugs who cover up their deadly emptiness under a fine outward show. It would be a hopeless undertaking to try to treat them with the method here discussed. The only thing that "helps" here is to keep up the show, for the truth would be unendurable or useless.

Social Psychological Theories: Adler, Fromm, Horney, and Sullivan

Before Alfred Adler, the founder of Individual Psychology, came to the United States to live (1935), he had been asked by Carl Murchison to summarize his viewpoint in a volume entitled *Psychologies of 1930*. This succint piece written for an audience of psychologists is reprinted here because it reveals almost better than any of his longer writings the full range of Adler's thought.

The selection by Mosak develops in a systematic manner the significance which Adler attributed to the first memories of a person as a basis for understanding his style of life.

It was Adler who emphasized order of birth as a determiner of personality. He believed that the oldest, middle, and youngest children in a family will develop different personalities because they have different social experiences. Although this thesis was tested a number of times in the past, it was not until the recent work of Stanley Schachter that impressive positive confirmations of the hypothesis were obtained. Stimulated by Schachter's findings, other psychologists have been investigating the question anew with encouraging results.

Fromm continues to be a prolific and popular writer on many topics relating to his version of psychoanalysis. A selection from one of his earlier writings is reprinted here because it demonstrates as clearly and as eloquently as anything that Fromm has written how society shapes a person so that he gets personal satisfaction from doing those things that are good for society. In this piece, Fromm also spells out his differences with Freud.

Using Fromm's concept of alienated man as a springboard, Kaplan and Singer performed an ingenious experiment to test the hypothesis that a person who is alienated from his own subjective experiences will not make as acute sensory discriminations as a person who is more accepting of his inner feelings.

Horney consistently maintained that neurosis is geared to society, and that different types of societies will produce different types of neurosis. The selection from her writings which is presented here makes this point very clearly.

Sullivan's writings are characterized by being discursive, polemical, and colloquial. These characteristics may be due to the fact that much of what appears in print under his authorship was not written but was spoken. The writings, for the most part, are edited transcriptions of tape recordings of lectures. Almost any selection from Sullivan's "writings" conveys to the reader the style of the man's thought and expression. The chapter which has been reprinted here deals with a critical period in the life of the individual. How he gets through this period of adolescence pretty much determines, in Sullivan's opinion, how he will get along in society the rest of his life.

It will also be noted in this selection that Sullivan assumes the role of social critic. This is a typical role for him. Sullivan was forthright in condemning what he regarded as inhuman in society. Like other social psychological theorists, he believed that an imperfect society breeds imperfect people, *ergo*, in order to improve man's character it is necessary to improve the society in which his character develops.

During the same year that *Theories of Personality* was published (1957), Timothy Leary produced a volume entitled *Interpersonal Diagnosis of Personality*, which was based largely upon Sullivan's formulations. The method of interpersonal diagnosis is illustrated by Romano's use of it in the marriage counseling setting.

1. Individual psychology

ALFRED ADLER

THE POINT OF DEPARTURE UPON THIS LINE OF RESEARCH seems to me to be given in a work entitled Der Aggressionstrieb im Leben und in der Neurose," published in 1908 and included in a collective volume, *Heilen und Bilden* (1). Even at that time I was engaged in a lively controversy with the Freudian school, and in opposition to them, I devoted my attention in that paper to the *relation* of the child and the adult to the demands of the external world. I tried to present, howbeit in a very inadequate fashion, the multifarious forms of attack and defense, of modification of the self and of the environment, effected by the human mind, and launched on the momentous departure of repudiating the sexual aetiology of mental phenomena as fallacious. In a vague way I saw even then that the impulsive life of man suffers variations and contortions, curtailments and exaggerations, *relative to the kind and degree of its aggressive power*. In accordance with the present outlook of individual psychology, I should rather say: relative to the way the power of cooperation has developed in childhood. The Freudian school, which at that time was purely sexual psychology, has accepted this primitive-impulse theory without any reservations, as some of its adherents readily admit.

I myself was too deeply interested in the problem of what determined the various forms of attack upon the outer world. From my own observations, and supported by those of older authors, also perhaps guided by the concept of a *locus minoris resistentiae*, I arrived at the notion that inferior organs might be responsible for the feeling of psychic inferiority, and in the year 1907 recorded my studies concerning this subject in a volume entitled *Studie über Minderwertigkeit der Organe und die seelische Kompensation* (2). The purpose of the work was to show that children born with hereditary organic weaknesses exhibit not only a physical necessity to compensate for the defect, and tend to overcompensate, but that the entire nervous system, too, may take part in this compensation; especially the mind, as a factor of life, may suffer a striking exaggeration in the direction of the defective function (breathing, eating, seeing, hearing, talking, moving, feeling, or even thinking), so that this overemphasized function may become the mainspring of life, in so far as a *"successful compensation"* occurs. This compensatory increase, which, as I showed in the above-mentioned book, has originated and continued the development of a human race blessed with inferior organs, may in favorable cases affect also the endocrine glands, as I have pointed out, and is regularly reflected in the condition of the sexual glands, their inferiority and their compensation—a fact which seemed to me to suggest some connection between individual traits and physical heredity. The link between organic inferiority and psychic effects, which to this day cannot be explained in any other way, but merely assumed, was evident to me in the mind's experience of the inferior organ, by which the former is plunged into a *constant feeling of inferiority*. Thus I could introduce the body and its degree of excellence as a factor in mental development.

Experts will certainly not fail to see that the whole of our psychiatry has tended in this direction, both in part before that time and quite definitely thereafter. The works of Kretschmer,

SOURCE. Chapter by Alfred Adler, "Individual psychology," in *Psychologies of 1930*, Chapter 21. Edited by Carl Murchison. Worcester, Mass.: Clark University Press, 1930. Copyright by Clark University.

Jaensch, and many others rest upon the same basis. But they are content to regard the psychic minus quantities as congenital epiphenomena of the physical organic inferiority, without taking account of the fact that it is the *immediate* experience of physical disability which is the key to the failures of performance, as soon as the demands of the outer world and the creative power of the child lead in into "wrong" alleys and force upon it a one-sided interest. What I treated there as failure appeared to me later as a premature curtailment of the cooperative faculty, the social impulse, and a greatly heightened interest for the self.

This work also furnished a test for organic inferiority. As proofs of inferiority it mentions insufficient development of physical form, of reflexes, of functions, or retardation of the latter. Defective development of the nerves in connection with the organ and of the brain-centers involved was also considered. But the sort of compensation which would under favorable circumstances occur in any one of these parts was always insisted upon as a decisive factor. A valuable by-product of this study, and one which has not yet been sufficiently appreciated, was the discovery of the significance of the birthmark for the fact that the embryonic development at that point or in that segment had not been quite successful. Schmidt, Eppinger, and others have found this insight correct in many respects. I feel confident that in the study of cancer, too, as I suggested in this connection, the segmental naevus will someday furnish a clue to the aetiology of carcinoma.

In trying thus to bridge the chasm between physical and mental developments by a theory that vindicated in some measure the doctrine of heredity, I did not fail to remark explicitly somewhere that the stresses engendered by the relation between the congenitally inferior organ and the demands of the external world, though, of course, they were greater than those which related to approximately normal organs, were none the less mitigated, to some degree, by the variability of the world's demands; so that one really had to regard them as merely relative. I repudiated the notion of the hereditary character of psychological traits, in that I referred their origin to the various intensities of organic functions in each individual. Afterwards I added to this the fact that children, in cases of abnormal development, are without any guidance, so that their activity (aggression) may develop

in unaccountable ways. The inferior organs offer a temptation but by no means a necessity for neuroses or other mental miscarriages. Herewith I established the problem of the education of such children, with prophylaxis as its aim, on a perfectly sound footing. Thus the family history, will all its plus and minus factors, became an index to the serious difficulties which might be expected and combatted in early childhood. As I said at that time, a hostile attitude toward the world might be the result of excessive stresses which must express themselves somehow in specific characteristics.

In this way I was confronted with the problem of character. There had been a good deal of nebulous speculations on this subject. Character was almost universally regarded as a congenital entity. My conviction that the doctrine of congenital mental traits was erroneous helped me considerably. I came to realize that characters were guiding threads, *ready attitudes* for the solution of the problems of life. The idea of an "arrangement" of all psychical activities became more and more convincing. Therewith I had reached the ground which to this day has been the foundation of individual psychology, the belief that *all psychical phenomena originate in the particular creative force of the individual, and are expressions of his personality.*

But who is this driving force behind the personality? And why do we find mostly individuals whose psychological upbuilding was not successful? Might it be that, after all, certain congenitally defective impulses, i.e., congenital weaknesses, decided the fate of our mental development, as almost all psychiatrists supposed? Is it due to a divine origin that an individual, that the human race may progress at all?

But I had realized the fact that children who were born with defective organs or afflicted by injuries early in life go wrong in the misery of their existence, constantly deprecate themselves, and, usually, to make good this deficiency, behave differently all their lives from what might be expected of normal people. I took another step, and discovered that children may be artificially placed in the same straits as if their organs were defective. If we make their work in very early life so hard that even their relatively normal organs are not equal to it, then they are in the same distress as those with defective physique, and from the same unbearable condition of stress they will give wrong answers as soon as life puts their preparation to any test.

Thus I found two further categories of children who are apt to develop an abnormal sense of inferiority—*pampered children and hated children*.

To this period of my complete defection from Freud's point of view, and absolute independence of thought, date such works as *Die seelische Wurzel der Trigeminusneuralgie* (3), in which I attempted to show how, besides cases of organic origin, there were also certain ones in which excessive partial increase of blood-pressure, caused by emotions such as rage, may under the influence of severe inferiority feelings give rise to physical changes. This was followed by a study, decisive for the development of individual psychology, entitled *Das Problem der Distanz* (4), wherein I demonstrated that every individual, by reason of his degree of interiority feeling, hesitated before the solution of one of the three great problems of life, stops or circumvents, and preserves his attitude in a state of exaggerated tension through psychological symptoms. As the three great problems of life, to which everyone must somehow answer by his attitude, I named: (*a*) society, (*b*) vocation, (*c*) love. Next came a work on *Das Unbewusste* (5), wherein I tried to prove that upon deeper inspection there appears no contrast between the conscious and the unconscious, that both cooperate for a higher purpose, that our thoughts and feelings become conscious as soon as we are faced with a difficulty, and unconscious as soon as our personality-value requires it. At the same time I tried to set forth the fact that that which other authors had used for their explanations under the name of *conflict, sense of guilt,* or *ambivalence* was to be regarded as symptomatic of a *hesitant attitude,* for the purpose of evading the solution of one of the problems of life. Ambivalence and polarity of emotional or moral traits present themselves as an attempt at a multiple solution or rejection of a problem.

This and some other works dating from the time of the self-emancipation of individual psychology have been published in a volume bearing the title *Praxis und Theorie der Individualpsychologie* (6). This was also the time when our great Stanley Hall turned away from Freud and ranged himself with the supporters of individual psychology, together with many other American scholars who popularized the "inferiority and superiority complexes" throughout their whole country.

I have never failed to call attention to the fact that the whole human race is blessed with deficient organs, deficient for coping with nature; that consequently the whole race is constrained ever to seek the way which will bring it into some sort of harmony with the exigencies of life; and that we make mistakes along the way, very much like those we can observe in pampered or neglected children. I have quoted one case especially, where the errors of our civilization may influence the development of an individual, and that is the case of the underestimation of women in our society. From the sense of female inferiority, which most people, men and women alike, possess, both sexes have derived an overstrained desire for masculinity, a superiority complex which is often extremely harmful, a will to conquer all difficulties of life in the masculine fashion, which I have called the *masculine protest*.

Now I began to see clearly in every psychical phenomenon the *striving for superiority*. It runs parallel to physical growth. It is an intrinsic necessity of life itself. It lies at the root of all solutions of life's problems, and is manifested in the way in which we meet these problems. All our functions follow its direction; rightly or wrongly they strive for conquest, surety, increase. The impetus from minus to plus is never-ending. The urge from "below" to "above" never ceases. Whatever premises all our philosophers and psychologists dream of—self-preservation, pleasure principle, equalization—all these are but vague representations, attempts to express the great upward drive. The history of the human race points in the same direction. Willing, thinking, talking, seeking after rest, after pleasure, learning, understanding, work and love, betoken the essence of this eternal melody. Whether one thinks or acts more wisely or less, one always moves along the lines of that upward tendency. In our right and wrong conceptions of life and its problems, in the successful or the unsuccessful solution of any question, this striving for perfection is uninterruptedly at work. And even where foolishness and imbecility, inexperience, seem to belie the fact of any striving to conquer some defect, or tend to depreciate it, yet the will to conquer is really operative. From this net-work which in the last analysis is simply given with the relationship "man-cosmos," no one may hope to escape. For even if anyone wanted to escape, yet, even if he *could* escape, he would still find himself in the general system, striving "upward," from "below." This does not only fix a fundamental category of thought, the structure of our reason, but what is more, it yields *the fundamental fact of our life.*

The origin of humanity and the ever repeated beginning of infant life rubs it in with every psychic act: "Achieve! Arise! Conquer!" This feeling is never absent, this longing for the abrogation of every imperfection. In the search for relief, in Faustian wrestling against the forces of nature, rings always the basic chord: "I relinquish thee not, thou bless me withal." The unreluctant search for truth, the ever unsatisfied longing for solution of the problems of life, belongs to this hankering after perfection of some sort.

This, now, appeared to me as the fundamental law of all spiritual expression: that the total melody is to be found again in every one of its parts, as a greatest common measure—in every individual craving for power, for victory over the difficulties of life.

And therewith I recognized a further premise of my scientific proceeding, one which agreed with the formulations of older philosophers, but conflicted with the standpoint of modern psychology: *the unity of the personality.* This, however, was not merely a premise, but could to a certain extent be demonstrated. As Kant has said, we can never understand a person if we do not presuppose his unity. Individual psychology can now add to that: this unity, which we must presuppose, is the work of the individual, which must always continue in the way it once found toward victory.

These were the considerations which led me to the conviction that early in life, in the first four or five years, a *goal* is set for the need and drive of psychical development, a goal toward which all its currents flow. Such a goal has not only the function of determining a direction, of promising security, power, perfection, but it is also of its essence and of the essence of the mind that this portentous goal should awaken feelings and emotions through that which it promises them. Thus the individual mitigates its sense of weakness in the anticipation of its redemption.

Here again we see the meaninglessness of congenital psychic traits. Not that we could deny them. We have no possible way of getting at them. Whoever would draw conclusions from the results is making matters too simple. He overlooks the thousand and one influences after birth, and fails to see the power that lies in the necessity of acquiring a goal.

The staking of a goal compels the unity of the personality in that it draws the stream of all spiritual activity into its definite direction. Itself a product of the common, fundamental sense of inferiority—a sense derived from genuine weakness, not from any comparison with others—the goal of victory in turn forces the direction of all powers and possibilities toward itself. Thus every phase of psychical activity can be seen within one frame, as though it were the end of some earlier phase and the beginning of a succeeding one. This was a further contribution of individual psychology to modern psychology in general—that it insisted absolutely on the indispensability of *finalism* for the understanding of all psychological phenomena. No longer could causes, powers, instincts, impulses, and the like serve as explanatory principles, but the final goal alone. Experiences, traumata, sexual-development mechanisms could not yield us an explanation, but the perspective in which these had been regarded, the individual way of seeing them, which subordinates all life to the ultimate goal.

This final aim, abstract in its purpose of assuring superiority, fictitious in its task of conquering all the difficulties of life, must now appear in concrete form in order to meet its task in actuality. Deity in its widest sense, it is apperceived by the childish imagination, and under the exigencies of hard reality, as victory over men, over difficult enterprises, over social or natural limitations. It appears in one's attitude toward others, toward one's vocation, toward the opposite sex. Thus we find concrete single purposes, such as: to operate as a member of the community or to dominate it, to attain security and triumph in one's chosen career, to approach the other sex or to avoid it. We may always trace in these special purposes *what sort of meaning the individual has found in his existence*, and how he proposes to realize that meaning.

If, then, the final goal established in early childhood exerts such an influence for better or worse upon the development of the given psychical forces, our next question must be: What are the sources of the individuality which we find in final aims? Could we not quite properly introduce another causal factor here? What brings about the differences of individual attitudes, if one and the same aim of superiority actuates everyone?

Speaking of this last question, let me point out that our human language is incapable of rendering all the qualities within a superiority goal and of expressing its innumerable differences. Certainty, power, perfection, deification, superiority, victory, etc., are but poor attempts to illumine its endless variants. Only after we have comprehended the partial expressions which the final goal effects, are we in any position to determine specific differences.

If there is any causal factor in the psychical mechanism, it is the common and often excessive sense of inferiority. But this continuous mood is only activating, a drive, and does not reveal the way to compensation and overcompensation. Under the pressure of the first years of life there is no kind of philosophical reflection. There are only impressions, feelings, and a desire to renew the pleasurable ones and exclude those which are painful. For this purpose all energies are mustered, until motion of some sort results. Here, however, training or motion of any sort forces the establishment of an end. There is no motion without an end. And so, in this way, a final goal becomes fixed which promises satisfaction. Perhaps, if one wanted to produce hypotheses, one might add: Just as the body approximates to an ideal form which is posited with the germ-plasm, so does the mind, as a part of the total life. Certainly it is perfectly obvious that the soul (mind—*das seelische Organ*) exhibits some systematic definite tendency.

From the time of these formulations of individual psychology dates my book, *Ueber den nervösen Charakter* (7), which introduced *finalism* into psychology with especial emphasis. At the same time I continued to trace the connection between organic inferiority and its psychological consequences, in trying to show how in such cases the goal of life is to be found in the type of overcompensation and consequent errors. As one of these errors I mentioned particularly the *masculine protest,* developed under the pressure of a civilization which has not yet freed itself from its overestimation of the masculine principle nor from an abuse of antithetic points of view. The imperfection of childish modes of realizing the fictitious ideal was also mentioned here as the chief cause for the differences in style of living—the unpredictable character of childish expression, which always moves in the uncontrollable *realm of error.*

By this time, the system of individual psychology was well enough established to be applied to certain special problems. *Zum Problem der Homosexualität* (8) exhibited that perversion as a neurotic construct erroneously made out of early childhood impressions, and recorded researches and findings which are published at greater length in the *Handbuch der normalen und pathologischen Physiologie* (9). Uncertainty in the sexual rôle, over-estimation of the opposite sex, fear of the latter, and a craving for easy, irresponsible successes proved to be the inclining but by no means constraining factors. Uncertainty in the solution of the erotic problem and fear of failure in this direction lead to wrong or abnormal functioning.

More and more clearly I now beheld the way in which the varieties of failure could be understood. In all human failure, in the waywardness of children, in neurosis and neuropsychosis, in crime, suicide, alcoholism, morphinism, cocainism, in sexual perversion, in fact in all nervous symptoms, we may read lack of the proper degree of *social feeling.* In all my former work I had employed the idea of the individual's attitude toward society as the main consideration. The demands of society, not as of a stable institution but as of a living, striving, victory-seeking mass, were always present in my thoughts. The total accord of this striving and the influence it must exert on each individual had always been one of my main themes. Now I attained somewhat more clarity in the matter. However we may judge people, whatever we try to understand about them, what we aim at when we educate, heal, improve, condemn—we base it always on the same principle: social feeling! cooperation! Anything that we estimate as valuable, good, right, and normal, we estimate simple in so far as it is "virtue" from the point of view of an ideal society. The individual, ranged in a community which can preserve itself only through cooperation as a human society, becomes a part of this great whole through socially enforced division of labor, through association with a member of the opposite sex, and finds his task prescribed by this society. And not only his task, but also his preparation and ability to perform it.

The unequivocally given fact of our organic inferiority on the face of this earth necessitates social solidarity. The need of protection of women during pregnancy and confinement, the prolonged helplessness of childhood, gains the aid of others. The preparation of the child for a complicated, but protective and therefore necessary civilization and labor requires the cooperation of society. The need of security in our personal existence leads automatically to a cultural modification of our impulses and emotions and of our individual attitude of friendship, social intercourse, and love. The social life of man emanates inevitably from the man-cosmos relation, and makes every person a creature and a creator of society.

It is a gratuitous burden to science to ask whether the social instinct is congenital or acquired, as gratuitous as the question of congenital instincts of any sort. We can see only the results of an evolution. And if we are to be permitted a question at all concerning the beginnings of that evolution, it is only this—whether anything can be evolved at all for which no possibilities are in any way given before birth. This possibility exists, as we may see through the results of development, in the case of human beings. The fact that our sense-organs behave the way they do, that through them we may acquire *impressions* of the outer world, may combine these physically and mentally in ourselves, shows our connection with the cosmos. That trait we have in common with all living creatures. What distinguishes man from other organisms, however, is the fact that he must conceive his superiority goal in the social sense as a part of a total achievement. The reasons for this certainly lie in the greater need of the human individual and in the consequent greater mobility of his body and mind, which forces him to find a firm vantage-point in the chaos of life.

But because of this enforced sociability, our life presents only such problems which require *ability to cooperate* for their solution. To hear, see, or speak "correctly," means to lose one's self completely in another or in a situation, to become *identified* with him or with it. The capacity for identification, which alone makes us capable of friendship, humane love, pity, vocation, and love, is the basis of the social sense and can be practiced and exercised only in conjunction with others. In this intended assimilation of another person or of a situation not immediately given, lies the whole meaning of comprehension. And in the course of this identification we are able to conjure up all sorts of feelings, emotions, and affects, such as we experience not only in dreams but also in waking life, in neurosis and psychosis. It is always the fixed style of life, the ultimate ideals, that dominates and selects. The style of life is what makes our experiences reasons for our attitude, that calls up these feelings and determines conclu-

sions in accordance with its own purposes. Our very identification with the ultimate ideal makes us optimistic, pessimistic, hesitant, bold, selfish, or altruistic.

The tasks which are presented to an individual, as well as the means of their performance, are conceived and formulated within the framework of society. No one, unless he is deprived of his mental capacities, can escape from this frame. *Only within this framework is psychology possible at all.* Even if we add for our own time the aids of civilization and the socially determined pattern of our examples, we still find ourselves confronted with the same unescapable conditions.

From this point of vantage we may look back. As far as we can reasonably determine, it appears that after the fourth or fifth year of life the style of life has been fashioned as a prototype, with its particular way of seizing upon life, its strategy for conquering it, its degree of ability to cooperate. These foundations of every individual development do not alter, unless perchance some harmful errors of construction are recognized by the subject and corrected. Whoever has not acquired in childhood the necessary degree of social sense, will not have it later in life, except under the abovementioned special conditions. No amount of bitter experience can change his style of life, *as long as he has not gained understanding.* The whole work of education, cure, and human progress can be furthered only along lines of better comprehension.

There remains only one question: What influences are harmful and what beneficial in determinging differences in the style of life, i.e., in the capacity for cooperation?

Here, in short, we touch upon the matter of preparation for cooperation. It is evident, of course, that deficiences of the latter become most clearly visible when the individual's capacity to cooperate is put to the test. As I have shown above, life does not spare us these tests and preliminary trials. We are always on trial, in the development of our sense-organs, in our attitude toward others, our understanding of others, in our morals, our philosophy of life, our political position, our attitude toward the welfare of others, toward love and marriage, in our aesthetic judgments, in our whole behavior. As long as one is not put to any test, as long as one is without any trials or problems, one may doubt one's own status as a fellow of the community. But as soon as a person is beset by any problem of existence, which, as I have demonstrated, always involves cooperative ability, then it will unfailingly become apparent—as in a geographical examination—how far his preparation for cooperation extends.

The first social situation that confronts a child is its relation to its mother, from the very first day. By her educational skill the child's interest in another person is first awakened. If she understands how to train this interest in the direction of cooperation, all the congenital and acquired capacities of the child will converge in the direction of social sense. If she binds the child to herself exclusively, life will bear for it the meaning that all other persons are to be excluded as much as possible. Its position in the world is thereby rendered difficult, as difficult as that of defective or neglected children. All these grow up in a hostile world and develop a low degree of cooperative sense. Often in such cases there results utter failure to adjust to the father, brothers and sisters, or more distant persons. If the father fails to penetrate the circle of the child's interest, or if by reason of exaggerated rivalry the brothers and sisters are excluded, or if because of some social short-coming or prejudice the remoter environment is ruled out of its sphere, then the child will encounter serious trouble in acquiring a healthy social sense. In all cases of failure later in life it will be quite observable that they are rooted in this early period of infancy. The question of responsibility will naturally have to be waived there, since the debtor is unable to pay what is required of him.

Our findings in regard to these errors and erroneous deductions of early childhood, which have been gathered from a contemplation of this relation complex which individual psychology reveals, are exceedingly full. They are recorded in many articles in the *Internationalen Zeitschrift für Individualpsychologie*, in my *Understanding Human Nature* (10), in *Individualpsychologie in der Schule* (11), and in *Science of Living* (12). These works deal with problems of waywardness, neurosis and psychosis, criminality, suicide, drunkenness, and sexual perversion. Problems of society, vocation, and love have been included in the scope of these studies. In *Die Technik der Individualpsychologie* (13) I have published a detailed account of a case of fear and compulsion neurosis.

Individual psychology considers the essence of therapy to lie in making the patient aware of his lack of cooperative power, and to convince him of the origin of this lack in early childhood maladjustments. What passes during this process is no small matter; his power of cooperation is enhanced by collaboration with the doctor. His "inferiority complex" is revealed as erroneous. Courage and optimism are awakened. And the "meaning of life" dawns upon him as the fact that proper meaning must be given to life.

This sort of treatment my be begun at any point in the spiritual life. The following three points of departure have recommended themselves to me, among others: (*a*) to infer some of the patient's situation from his place in the order of births, since each successive child usually has a somewhat different position from the others; (*b*) to infer from his earliest childhood recollections some dominant interest of the individual, since the creative tendency of the imagination always produces fragments of the life ideal (*Lebensstyl*); (*c*) to apply the individualistic interpretation to the dream-life of the patient, through which one many discover in what particular way the patient, guided by the style-of-life ideal, conjures up emotions and sensations contrary to common sense, in order to be able to carry out his style of life more successfully.

If one seems to have discovered the guiding thread of the patient's life, it remains to test this discovery through a great number of expressive gestures on his part. Only a perfect coincidence of the whole and all the parts gives one the right to say: I understand. And then the examiner himself will always have the feeling that, if he had grown up under the same misapprehensions, if he had harbored the same ideal, had the same notions concerning the meaning of life, if he had acquired an equally low degree of social sense, he would have acted and lived in an "almost" similar manner.

REFERENCES°

1. Adler, A. Der Aggressionstrieb im Leben und in der Neurose. (The aggression drive in life

---

° The references have been edited and updated by Heinz Ansbacher.

and in neurosis.) *Fortschr. Med.*, 1908, **26**, 577–584. Reprinted in *Heilen und Bilden.* 3rd ed. Munich: Bergmann, 1928. Pp. 33–42. Partial transl. & comments in *The individual psychology of Alfred Adler.* New York: Basic Books, 1956. Pp. 30–39.

2. ———. *Studie über Minderwertigkeit von Organen.* Vienna: Urban & Schwarzenberg, 1907. Transl.: *Study of organ inferiority and its psychical compensation.* New York: Nerv. Ment. Dis. Publ. Co., 1917.

3. ———. Die psychische Behandlung der Trigeminusneuralgie. (The psychic treatment of trigeminal neuralgia.) *Zbl. Psychoanal.*, 1910, **1**, 10–29. Transl. in *The practice and theory of individual psychology.* Paterson, N. J.: Littlefield, Adams & Co., 1963. Pp. 78–99.

4. ———. Das Problem der Distanz. (The problem of distance.) *Z. Indiv. Psychol.*, 1914, **1**, 8–16. Transl. in *The practice and theory of individual psychology.* Paterson, N. J.: Littlefield, Adams & Co., 1963. Pp. 100–108.

5. ———. Zur Rolle des Unbewussten in der Neurose. (On the role of the unconscious in neurosis.) *Zbl. Psychoanal.*, 1913, **3**, 169–174. Transl. in *The practice and theory of individual psychology.* Paterson, N. J.: Littlefield, Adams & Co., 1963. Pp. 227–234.

6. ———. *Praxis und Theorie der Individualpsychologie.* 2nd ed. Munich: Bergmann, 1924. Transl. *The practice and theory of individual psychology.* Paterson, N. J.: Littlefield, Adams & Co., 1963.

7. ———. *Ueber den nervösen Charakter: Grundzüge einer vergleichenden Individual-Psychologie und Psychotherapie.* Wiesbaden: Bergmann, 1912. Transl. *The neurotic constitution: outline of a comparative individualistic psychology and psychotherapy.* New York: Moffat, Yard, 1917.

8. ———. *Das Problem der Homosexualität: erotisches Training und erotischer Rückzug.* (The problem of homosexuality: erotic training and erotic retreat.) 2nd ed. Leipzig: Hirzel, 1930.

9. ———. Various. In A. Bethe *et al.* (Eds.), *Handbuch der normalen und pathologischen Physiologie.* Vol. 14(1). Berlin: Springer, 1926. Pp. 802–807, 808–812, 842–844, 881–886, 887–894, 895–899. These six contributions are included in Item 8 above.

10. ———. *Menschenkenntnis.* Leipzig: Hirzel, 1927. Transl. *Understanding human nature.* New York: Fawcett World Libr., 1965.

11. ———. *Individualpsychologie in der Schule: Vorlesungen für Lehrer und Erzieher.* (Individual psychology in the school: lectures for teachers and educators.) Leipzig: Hirzel, 1929.

12. ———. *The science of living.* New York: Greenberg, 1929.

13. ———. *Die Technik der Individualpsychologie.* Vol. 1. *Die Kunst, eine Lebensund Krankengeschichte zu lesen.* Munich: Bergmann, 1928. Transl. *The case of Miss R.: the interpretation of a life story.* New York: Greenberg, 1929.

14. ———. *Problems of neurosis* (1929). New York: Harper Torchbooks, 1964.

2. Early recollections as a projective technique

HAROLD H. MOSAK

EARLY RECOLLECTIONS HAVE BEEN THE SUBJECT OF PSYCHOLOGICAL interest since G. Stanley Hall (33) published his paper on this topic in 1899. Most of the subsequently published reports have fallen into three categories. The first consists of a group of taxonomic and statistical studies which classify the age of the recollection, the affective character of the memory, and other aspects of the memory content (16, 17, 20, 21, 31, 34, 40, 48, 53). A second group takes as its starting point Freud's views of earliest recollections as screen memories which cover up infantile sexual conflicts or traumata. Freud's early work convinced him that such incidents were repressed but were revealed in disguised form in the patient's early recollections (25, 26, 27). The recollection, then, repressed rather than expressed (10, 13, 14). Investigators in this second group largely restricted themselves to the study of the hedonic tone of the early memories in an attempt to validate the Freudian theory of repression[1]; few attempted to interpret the content dynamically. Rapaport (50) and Zeller (56) have pointed out that most studies in this latter group did not fulfil the conditions for a true test of repression, while Waldfogel (53) indicates that studies which did appear to verify Freudian repression theory contained erroneous interpretations. In the third group are found those students of perception whom Krech (38) labels as the "New Look" psychologists who feel that

SOURCE. Article by Harold H. Mosak, "Early recollections as a projective technique" in *Journal of projective Techniques*, Vol. 22, pp. 302–311, 1958.

perception and memory are both related to the individual's frame of reference or attitudinal set, that is, to his personal values and needs (22, 46, 47, 54).

Many of the historical antecedents of the last viewpoint can be discovered in the writings of Alfred Adler (2, 3, 4, 5, 6, 7, 8, 9). His followers (1, 10, 11, 12, 14, 18, 24, 28, 29, 36, 41, 42, 43, 44, 45, 52, 55) fall in the third group. Adler differed from Freud in holding that early memories were retained because of a selective factor in memory and that this selective factor was not repression but rather consistency with the individual's attitudinal frame of reference, the life style.[2] Of the manifold experiences of childhood one only retained at the level of consciousness those few experiences which expressed one's approach to life. These incidents did not mold the individual's future life and therefore could not be regarded as causal incidents. They were neither necessarily traumatic incidents nor innocuous camouflage for such incidents, neither pleasant nor unpleasant, although both could be present in some individual's reported memories. The recollections merely reflected the person's perceptual framework within which he interpreted life's experiences. Adler wrote, "Thus his memories represent his 'Story of My Life'; a story he repeats to himself to warn him or comfort him, to keep him concentrated on his goal, to prepare him, by means of past experiences, to meet the future with an already tested style of action" (9, p. 73). Although Adler anticipated by almost three decades the current interest in the relationship between frame of reference and

---

[1] Summaries of this body of literature appear in Cason (15), Dudycha and Dudycha (20), Gilbert (30), and Meltzer (39).

[2] For a more extensive discussion of the Adlerian viewpoint the articles by Ansbacher (10) and Dreikurs (18) are especially valuable.

behavior, his work on early recollections has received scant recognition. Yet an experimental study by Purcell concludes with a "special note . . . of the general support for Adler's views on early memories. Exception was taken only to Adler's opinion concerning the fundamental importance of the very earliest incident an individual can recall" (49, p. 440).[3]

Accepting Adler's assumptions, the earliest recollections could be treated as a projective technique. It should be possible to deduce from them some clues as to how the individual perceives himself in his relationship to his perceived environment.

The earliest recollections, in common with the dream and such projective techniques as free drawings and fingerpainting, have the advantage of being completely unstructured. The individual does not respond to some external stimulus as in the Rorschach or TAT, the properties of which may influence his production. With the exception of the possible influence of the examiner or therapist, the production is influenced only by the individual's perceptual framework which selectively focuses upon the particular memories which he produces.

All memories contain omissions and distortions. The individual colors and distorts, emphasizes and omits, exaggerates and minimizes in accordance with his inner needs. The fact of omission or distortion possesses the same significance as in dream interpretation. The following recollection was elicited from a man who had been raised in a Christian Science home where it was imperative to deny the existence of evil, illness, and death.

ER—My family and two neighbors were sitting around the dining room table. It was a festive occasion. Every one smiling, every one pleased. Father was home.

Interpretation—This is a relatively innocuous account of a pleasant episode as the recollection is reported. However, what is the significance of the last sentence? Upon further inquiry the subject recalled that his father had just returned home from the sanitarium. While the subject in adulthood had broken with this childhood faith, the recollection indicated his still present involvement in his religious precepts and the need not to recognize the existence of illness.

_____
[3] This exception is clarified in a note by Ansbacher (12).

Several studies have attempted to verify the accuracy of the incidents which the respondents related. From our experience, whether the recollection is accurate or not is not germane in interpretation. The significance of the recollection lies in the fact that it has been remembered or thought to be so. As Bartlett (13) suggests, remembering is more a process of construction than one of reproduction. Our experience has indicated that recollections range from what are obvious fabrications, although rarely deliberate lies, to rather accurate portrayals of situations.

Adler recounts one of his recollections which he discovered to be completely fictitious but which reflects "my longing to overcome death" and is consistent with his choice of profession.

Shortly after I went to a board school. I remember that the path to the school led over a cemetery. I was frightened every time and was exceedingly put out at beholding the other children pass the cemetery without paying the least attention to it, while every step I took was accompanied by a feeling of fear and horror. Apart from the extreme discomfort occasioned by this fear I was also annoyed at the idea of being less courageous than the others. One day I made up my mind to put an end to this fear of the death. Again (as on my first resolve), _I decided upon a treatment of hardening._ (Proximity of death!) I stayed at some distance behind the others, placed my schoolbag on the ground near the wall of the cemetery and ran across it a dozen times, until I felt that I had mastered the fear (4, pp. 179–180).

In exchanging reminiscences with a schoolmate when he was in his mid-thirties, Adler discovered that such a cemetery had never existed and other acquaintances corroborated this information. Two other fictional memories in which subjects describe their births may be found in Adler (7) and Hadfield (32). "Recollections" which others have told the respondent may not be interpreted as recollections. If the subject can visualize the incident, it is interpretable; if he proves unable to do so, the incident is not treated as a recollection.

Assuming the consistency of the self as a frame of reference, the memories, since they reflect the self concept, should all be consistent with each other. This does not imply that each memory will convey exactly the same meaning as every other memory produced by the subject (12). As with other projective techniques, interpretations from recollections will supplement, complement, and elaborate upon each other. Thus, the early recollections may be regarded, as personality is, as theme and variations. As Plewa says, "It is not always easy to extract the entire content of a recollection. One recollection can have so many facets, and it is only when one is able to study an individual for a long time that one notices in him the tendencies to be seen in the recollections with their multitude of variations. Therefore no matter how many interpretations one recollection lends itself to, each of these substantiates the unity of the personality" (44, p. 97). Later recollections in a series may furnish details and specifications for generalized attitudes expressed in earlier recollections. Where contradictions appear in the recollections, they exist only as surface phenomena which can be reconciled interpretatively. The technique of reconciliation will be illustrated in the section below.

The Interpretation of Early Recollections

The interpretation of early recollections requires a careful distinction between a recollection and a report. Some clinicians ascribe equal significance to memories which report single incidents and to memories which report general occurrences of childhood. For example, the "I remember one time . . . " memory is accorded the same treatment as the "I remember I used to like to read when I was little." For this writer the former would be termed a recollection while the latter would be regarded as a report. A recollection pertains to a single incident which can be reduced to a "one time" format while the report cannot (18). The recollection, therefore, generally contains more specific detail than is possible in the report and is similar to a TAT story. Second, the recollection can be visualized, whereas the report cannot since it involves a collection of incidents whose individuality has been lost. Frequently, in the clinical situation, in order to verify that the subject is producing a recollection rather than a report, we ask him to close his eyes, to visualize the scene, and to report the incident as he visualizes it with all of its details. While reports are clinically significant, we only interpret recollections projectively.

Early recollections may be regarded as a prototype of the individual's fundamental attitudes (6). Consequently, they are first inter-

preted thematically and second with respect to specific details. In the latter instance enlargement upon the incidents may be requested of the patient. The characters incorporated in the recollection are not treated in interpretation as specific individuals but as prototypes. They represent people or women in general or authority figures rather than the specific individuals mentioned. In this respect our interpretation differs from that of Brodsky (14) who uses the memories as a means of reconstructing the subject's interpersonal relationships during his formative years or that of Eisenstein and Ryerson (23) who see the recollections as the "earliest, perhaps clearest, derivative of forgotten infantile conflicts."

ER—We had a cookie jar on the top shelf in the kitchen. I couldn't reach it by myself, so my uncle lifted me up, and I got the cookie jar.

Interpretation—This memory, given by a woman, is suggestive of a feeling of smallness on her part. In order to get the "goodies" of life, she must rely upon the assistance of bigger people. From a diagnostic viewpoint dependency upon the uncle may be significant. However, the recollection expresses a more generalized dependency feeling either toward all people or with respect to men specifically. Subsequent recollections might inform us which of these two alternatives is more valid. Nevertheless, even were the above incident an isolated occurrence in the subject's life history or perhaps even fictitious with no actual dependency upon the uncle possible, the *retention* of the incident would point to an underlying, generalized feeling of dependency.

While the content of the recollection is given primary consideration, a sequential analysis provides a more rounded picture of the individual, adding some nuances of the personality. In any event, the diagnosis of the self-concept from a single recollection is extremely hazardous. Generalization from a single case is as unreliable here as in other logical and scientific endeavors. The second recollection given by the woman who reported the cookie jar incident demonstrates the additions which sequential analysis makes to the personality picture.

ER—I was sitting on top of a fence. Suddenly I lost my balance, fell off, and broke my jaw.

Interpretation—In the first recollection the patient describes her dependency upon others, especially men. In the above she describes what happens if she relies upon herself. Only disaster can ensue; she cannot stay "on top." This woman felt that she could only be elevated, "lifted up," by a man, and she married one who gave her status and material possessions, the "goodies." When her husband left her and deprived her of her status and his strength, she could not bear living alone and made a suicidal attempt.

We have already mentioned that when apparent contradictions occur, they must be understood in their total context. Occasionally the contradiction merely states that under a certain set of conditions, actual or perceived, the individual will respond in one manner and to another set of circumstances in a second way. An illustration of this type of "contradiction" appears in the following recollections of an adult woman.

ER—I remember that I was under three and the lady next door picked me up over the fence to take me home.

ER—My uncle gave my sister ten cents to kiss him. Then he made me the same offer. I ran out the back door and all the way home.

Interpretation—In the first ER people are depicted as supportive while in the second, they appear to be threatening. Actually the contradiction is resolved when one observes that the supportive person is a woman while the threatening person is a man. Thus, this woman only has a place in the woman's world. The masculine world, especially because it involves sexual behavior, is threatening and she must avoid it.

In interpreting early recollections it should be understood that what is elicited are the individual's attitudes and not a mere description of his overt behavior. Although these attitudes are predominantly unconscious perceptions of the environment and the individual's role in the world, the individual nevertheless operates in accordance with this attitudinal frame of preference. The recollections describe a *modus vivendi* rather than a *modus operandi*. The characteristic outlook rather than the characteristic behavior is portrayed. In the following recollections, among other things, the subject characterizes life as dangerous.

ER—Another child was riding on my bike. He fell off on some glass, cut his arm, and had to be taken to the hospital.

ER—A boy fell off the slide in the school yard. They took him into the school and waited for the doctor to come.

Such a person, behaviorally, may see danger where none exists. He may exaggerate the dangers of life. He may retreat from these perceived dangers with anxious or phobic behavior. Or he may call upon certain defense mechanisms to cope with the omni-present threat. In the compulsive individual, for example, one observes reliance upon ritual and feelings of omnipotence and the necessity to control as response to this danger. Many compulsives are preoccupied with death because this is the greatest threat— the one force which cannot be controlled. Hypochondriacs may exaggerate each body symptom as expressing their conviction that life is fraught with danger. Other individuals may develop into towers of strength or become dependent upon or identify with "strong" people or groups in order to minimize the dangers of life. Still others may actually court or provoke personal disaster in order to confirm their basic attitude. Some flirt with danger in order to prove that they possess a charmed life. While these reactions do not exhaust the repertoire available to people who feel that life is dangerous, they do serve to exemplify the variety of reactions which are possible within a single dimension of an individual's perceptual frame of reference.

Frequently behavioral response is elicited as well as basic attitudes.

ER—I saw a street car coming. I lay down on the tracks to stop it. The motorman got out and chased me down the street. I ran home.

Interpretation—The subject makes mischief, provokes the world, and tries to get by with it. He is willing to risk his life to make mischief and to demonstrate his power and right to do as he pleases, to control the others. He hits and runs.

ER—Mother always spanked us with a hair brush. This day she couldn't find it, so she spanked me with the handle of a scissors. I was frightened and screamed, "I'll be good!"

Interpretation—In addition to certain basic attitudes, this recollection also indicates the subject's behavioral response. He will only promise to behave (whether he will actually behave we can only guess) under the threat of punishment.

To fill out the personality picture thematic analysis accompanied by an analysis of the details in the ER. Consider the following recollections given by two women.

ER—My mother was nursing my younger brother, I ran over and bit her breast.

ER—My mother made me mad. I don't know why. I went to the closet and bit a hole in her favorite dress.

Interpretation—Both recollections on the surface are similar, yet the details make them different. One recognizes the sources of her frustrations; the other does not. The first expresses her aggression directly; the second displaces her anger and attacks circuitously.

Applications

Numerous applications of early recollections may be made. Inasmuch as they constitute a quick device for uncovering an individual's unconscious attitudes, they may be used in situations where rapid screening of individuals is desirable. A study by Kadis, Greene, and Freedman (36) indicates that the ER possess validity for this purpose. A second application occurs in the area of educational and vocational guidance (6, 8, 9). One clue with respect to vocational preparation is offered by Adler (7, 9) who noticed that physicians generally produce a recollection concerning death and illness. He is of the opinion that this ER serves as a directive that death must be fought. Several of Adler's own ER fell within this category. At the age of two he recalls being bandaged with rickets. At age four or five he was run over twice by vehicles; at age five he had pneumonia and " . . . the doctor who had been suddenly called in, told my father that there was no hope of my living" (3, p. 10). His daughter also recalls that one of Adler's ER is concerned with the death of his brother (1).

Some sequences of recollections are primarily concerned with observation and others with participation, some with motor activity and others with complete passivity, some with seeing and some with hearing (16, 34, 48) all of which have vocational implications. Take, for instance, the following recollections of a physiologist of the senses.

ER—It was the first time I saw the sea. I don't remember seeing the sea. I only smelled it and heard it; then I saw it.

Orgler (42) cites similar early recollections of a mathematician and of a motion picture director.

The usefulness of ER in psychotherapy is enhanced by their emergence almost as a matter of course in the analytical psychotherapies without interfering with the continuity of the therapy. They permit the therapist to make initial hypotheses in treatment much before all of the significant material has emerged. Predictions of the patient's reaction to treatment and to the therapist may be formulated at a very early stage in treatment. The three recollections which follow serve to illustrate this point.

ER—I was in my baby carriage. People were looking at me. I was just lying on my back being a baby.

ER—The teacher was talking to us. It was the first day of school. I was trying to be good. I wasn't talking to anyone, wasn't doing anything.

ER—I won a prize in first grade, but I don't know for what. Don't remember my feeling. The teacher just called me up in front of the class and gave it to me.

Interpretation—The passivity of the patient is immediately obvious. He will very likely place the onus of responsibility upon the therapist for the progress of the therapy. He will probably try to be a "good" patient and try to gain the therapist's approval. Overt resistance should not be expected. Expression of feeling will rarely occur. Being the center of attention in therapy will be consistent with his needs. His emphasis is upon getting rather than upon doing.

Discussion

Although the ER constitute a relatively simple projective technique, there are still many unsolved problems. Among the theoretical problems is the question as to whether the recollections can be utilized for differential diagnostic purposes. Rephrased, the question may be stated as—"do people of diverse personality types produce characteristic recollections?" Eisenstein and Ryerson (23), and Friedmann (28) and Feichtinger (24) indicate that the

ER may be used for diagnostic purposes although most other writers are silent on this point.

Another question centers about the "dramatic" recollection. This recollection consists of a vivid, dramatic or traumatic incident—death, disaster, an accident, a unique happy experience—which most people, if it had occurred to them, would probably remember. We have in such instances a rule of thumb—the more "dramatic" an incident, the less significance is attached to the interpretation of the incident since the retention of the incident is at least partially dictated externally; the more innocuous an incident, the greater likelihood the recollection is dictated by the individual's needs. That an incident is not merely remembered because it is dramatic or traumatic is well illustrated by Orgler (43). Even in these "dramatic" incidents the individual's basic attitudes determine how the story will be told, the details that will be emphasized and those which will be omitted.

ER (dramatic)—There was a fire in the town we lived in. Three quarters of the town burned down at night. All kinds of homeless people were brought to my house. There was an old man, a Parkinsonian, burned all over. He was treated in my house. I felt sorry for him.

Interpretation—This recollection would probably be retained for its vividness and the impression it must have made on all who experienced the fire. Yet this recollection, given by a physician, still reveals the uniqueness of the subject's perception of the situation.

ER (innocuous)—I was sitting in the alley playing with some boxes. How nice it felt to sit and arrange the boxes.

Interpretation—Why should a person remember an incident which on the surface is so trivial? Many adults have had similar experiences as children and do not remember them. The recollection becomes more comprehensible when we learn that the patient is compulsive.

Until what age is an ER "early"? Why do not later recollections possess the same significance as earlier recollections? The second question is more easily answered than the first. It would appear that later recollections change with the present mood while early recollections reflect the basic attitudes to life. In line with this we have arbitrarily set age eight as the cutoff point for early recollections. An excep-

tion to this procedure is made when the subject's position in the family constellation has changed in childhood. Thus, for example, in a two child family, if the older child should die, the younger would suddenly be catapulted into the position of an only child. In such instances the underlying attitudes may change very radically. From limited clinical observation it appears that the subject "forgets" his early experiences and only retains memories from the period subsequent to his altered life status.

If ER are consonant with the individual's frame of reference, another question is posed. When the individual's attitudes change in psychotherapy, do his ERs also change? Clinical reports (18, 51) indicate that they do. The patient either (a) produces new memories, (b) "forgets" some of the old memories, i.e. they are not spontaneously produced or sometimes even remembered, (c) furnishes the same memory but divested of the original emotional tone, or (d) recasts the original memories with additions and omissions so that while the incident remains the same, the message it provides the patient is different. As an illustration of the last point, below is the same incident as related by the individual at the beginning and end of treatment.

ER (pre-therapy)—We went to visit these friends of my family. I sat on a man's lap and he did something which was not very nice. I dont' know what but I was afraid and wouldn't go back on subsequent family visits.

ER (post-therapy)—My sisters took me to visit a man. I was on his lap, his hand in my bloomers. I didn't think it was right but I didn't do anything about it.

Occasionally the ER may give clues to underlying insidious processes which may not appear clinically. Such signs appeared in the recollections of the following patient who entered treatment in a deep depression. After several months of treatment the depressive symptoms disappeared and the patient on the surface seemed quite well, so well that she discontinued treatment. Yet the ER she gave prior to the termination of treatment indicated she was not as well as she assumed.

ER—I was sick one day. The teacher had all the kids write to me. I felt good.

ER—I had whooping cough. We were waiting for the bus to come to go to the doctor. Each time a bus came I threw up. This happened four times. When we got on the bus, I threw up out of the window.

ER—My parents were having a party. I caught the measles. I looked at myself in the mirror which I shouldn't have done. I looked terrible. Remember lying in bed, a candle in the room, and the party going on in the next room.

Interpretation—One can still detect in these ER the consciousness of sickness of the patient, her feeling of not belonging, and the secondary gains from being ill.

As can be readily seen the numerous possibilities for the application of the ER have just been tapped and subsequent research should add to the fruitfulness of the technique. To illustrate the many types of interpretation to which ER lend themselves, a complete set of recollections given by a hospitalized male patient is here reproduced.

ER 1—In church with my mother standing next to me singing hymns. It was as if her voice were directed toward me, as if she were singing to me only. I felt like something special.

Interpretation—ER 1 reveals, the individual's need to be something special. Cf. Adler's "drive for significance" (9) and Horney's "search for glory" (35). However, the recollection does not indicate that he does anything to be something special. Instead he is the passive recipient of the attention of others. He is probably an egocentric individual who likes to be the center of attention. Observe also his mention of the singing voice. Perhaps he uses his voice vocationally or avocationally.

ER 2—Age 5 when my mother died. She was lying in the coffin. Suddenly she picked herself up and hugged me.

Interpretation—Here is a bizarre recollection giving us a clue that this individual may be psychotic. Although this memory is fabricated, we observe that he is again the center of attention, the passive recipient of the affection of others, and an individual who is so special that even the impossible is not denied him. Since his mother died when he was five years old and he hardly remembers her, why does she appear so significantly in these recollections? Is he merely revealing his passive-dependent needs? Is he attempting to say in essence, "Others could not possibly give me the special attention a mother would"? It seems in any event that one can only be special through passively

receiving the affection of a woman. We might also surmise that this patient holds no fear of death. According to Horney (35), this patient would be revealing how his demands for uniqueness exempt him from the "rules" of life.

ER 3—I remember the first time it snowed in .... It was the first time any of us had seen snow. Mother dressed us and sent us out to play in the snow. We scooped the snow out of a can and made snowballs. It was fun.

Interpretation—If life is special, out of the ordinary, he can enjoy it. He probably cannot accept mediocrity in himself or routineness in life. Both he and life must be out of the ordinary. For the first time he introduces figures other than his mother which would indicate that his dependency needs do not eliminate social interaction.

ER 4—This was in school. The teacher punished me for something by putting me in a dark closet. I guess she forgot about me, so when I got hungry, I ate her lunch. After a while I had to go to the toilet. I was frantic and didnt' know what to do. So I tried the door and it was open, so I went home. On the way I filled my pants and I thought that when I got home, my mother would be angry with the teacher for causing all this. Then three boys appeared and wanted some money from me. I didnt' have any, so they got out a knife and cut three slits in my belt. I went on home but dont' remember what happened when I got there.

Interpretation—This is a rather complex recollection in which the patient commits certain anti-social acts but does not accept responsibility for his mischief making. His teacher is responsible for "causing all this." The mechanism of projection comes to the fore here and affords us a clue to a possible paranoid process when taken together with ER 2. Again he is exempt from the usual rules. He has a special privilege of non-conformity, and if others do not respect this privilege, they are unfair. The masculine world is depicted as hostile and threatening. Hospital records indicate that the patient was actually diagnosed as paranoid schizophrenic. Although he is engaged in overt homosexual activity (contrary to classical Freudian theory), he did not regard himself as a homosexual, but as something special—a "bisexual." Prior to hospitalization he had been employed as a radio announcer (confirming our guess in ER 1) in a city known for its thrilling atmosphere.

Early recollections lend themselves well to other interpretative frameworks than that illustrated above (9, 31, 67). For example, a Freudian might see in ER 4 a recapitulation of the psycho-sexual development of the patient. The boy is put in a dark closet (the womb). Later he eats the teacher's lunch (oral stage), fills his pants (anal stage), goes toward mother (beginning of the oedipal phase), and meets three boys (three is the symbol for the male genitalia and could be representative of the father) who cut slits in his belt (since the belt is a long, pointed object, he is symbolically castrated).

Summary

Although early recollections have received much attention in the literature, most writers have not treated the recollections projectively. A method for such interpretation is presented with a discussion of the problems involved in interpretation. The technique is useful in rapid psychiatric screening, differential diagnosis, vocational guidance, and in the analytic psychotherapies. Further research would undoubtedly uncover many more uses for this rather simple technique.

REFERENCES

1. Adler, Alexandra. Guiding human misfits. New York: Philosoph. Libr., 1948.
2. Adler, A. Erste Kindheitserrinnerungen. Int. Z. Indiv. Psychol., 1933, 11, 81–90.
3. Adler, A. How I chose my career. Indiv. Psychol. Bull., 1947., 6, 9–11.
4. Adler, A. The practice and theory of individual psychology. London: Kegan Paul, 1925.
5. Adler, A. Problems of neurosis. New York: Cosmopolitan, 1930.
6. Adler, A. The science of living. New York: Greenberg, 1929.
7. Adler, A. The significance of early recollections. Int. J. Indiv. Psychol., 1937, 3, 283–287.
8. Adler, A. Social interest. London: Faber and Faber, 1938.
9. Adler, A. What life should mean to you. New York: Grosset and Dunlap, 1931.
10. Ansbacher, H. L. Adler's place today in the psychology of memory. J. Pers., 1947, 3, 197–207.
11. Ansbacher, H. L. and Ansbacher, Rowena. The individual psychology of Alfred Adler. New York: Basic Books, 1956.
12. Ansbacher, H. L. Purcell's "Memory and psychological security" and Adlerian theory. J. abnorm. soc. Psychol., 1953, 48, 596–597.
13. Bartlett, F. C. Remembering: a study in experimental and social psychology. New York: Macmillan 1932.
14. Brodsky, P. The diagnostic importance of early recollections. Amer. J. Psychother., 1952, 6, 484–493.
15. Cason, H. The learning and retention of pleasant and unpleasant activities. Arch. Psychol., 1932, 21, No. 134.
16. Colegrove, F. W. Individual memories. Amer. J. Psychol., 1899, 10, 228–255.
17. Crook, M. N. and Harden, L. A quantitative investigation of early memories. J. soc. Psychol., 1931, 2, 252–255.
18. Dreikurs, R. The psychological interview in medicine. Amer. J. Indiv. Psychol., 1952, 10, 99–122.
19. Dudycha, G. J. and Dudycha, M. M. Adolescents' memories of preschool experiences. J. genet. Psychol., 1933, 42, 468–480.
20. Dudycha, G. J. and Dudycha, M. M. Childhood memories. A review of the literature. Psychol. Bull., 1941, 38, 668–682.
21. Dudycha, G. J. and Dudycha, M. M. Some factors and characteristics in childhood memories. Child Developm., 1933, 4, 265–278.
22. Edwards, A. L. The retention of affective experiences—a criticism and restatement of the problem. Psychol. Rev., 1942, 49, 43–53.
23. Einstein, V. W. and Ryerson, Rowena. Psychodynamic significance of the first conscious memory. Bull. Menninger Clin., 1951, 15, 213–220.
24. Feichtinger, F. Early recollections in neurotic disturbances. Indiv. Psychol. Bull., 1943, 3, 44–49.
25. Freud, S. A general introduction to psychoanalysis. New York: Garden City, 1938.
26. Freud, S. Repression. In Collected papers. Vol. 4. London: Hogarth, 1925.
27. Freud, S. The unconscious. In Collected papers. Vol. 4. London: Hogarth, 1925.
28. Friedmann, Alice. Early childhood memories of mental patients. Indiv. Psychol. Bull., 1950, 8, 111–116.
29. Friedmann, Alice. First recollections of school. Int. J. Indiv. Psychol., 1935, 1, 111–116.
30. Gilbert, G. M. The new status of experimental studies on the relationship of feeling to memory. Psychol. Bull., 1938, 35, 26–35.
31. Gordon, K. A study of early memories. J. Delinqu., 1928, 12, 129–132.
32. Hadfield, J. A. Reliability of infantile memories. Brit. J. med. Psychol., 1928, 8, 87–111.
33. Hall, G. S. Note on early memories. Pedagog. Sem., 1899, 6, 485–512.

34. Henri, B. and Henri, C. Earliest recollections *Pop. Sci. Mon.*, 1898, **53**, 108–115.

35. Horney, Karen. *Neurosis and human growth.* New York: Norton, 1950.

36. Kadis, Asya, Greene, Janet S., and Freedman, N. Early childhood recollections—an integrative technique of personality test data. *Amer. J. Indiv. Psychol.*, 1952, **10**, 31–42.

37. Kahana, R. J., Weiland, I. H., Snyder, B., and Rosenbaum, M. The value of early memories in psychotherapy. *Psychiat. Quart*, 1953, **27**, 73–82.

38. Krech, D. Notes toward a psychological theory. *J. Pers.*, 1949, **18**, 66–87.

39. Meltzer, H. The present status of experimental studies on the relation of feeling to memory. *Psychol. Rev.*, 1930, **37**, 124–139.

40. Miles, C. A study of individual psychology. *Amer. J. Psychol.*, 1893, **6**, 534–558.

41. Opedal, L. E. Analysis of the earliest memory of a delinquent. *Int. J. Indiv. Psychol.*, 1935, **1**, 52–58.

42. Orgler, Hertha. *Alfred Adler. The man and his works.* London: Daniel, 1939.

43. Orgler, Hertha. Comparative study of two first recollections. *Amer. J. Indiv. Psychol.*, 1952, **10**, 27–30.

44. Plewa, F. The meaning of childhood recollections. *Int. J. Indiv. Psychol.*, 1935, **1**, 88–101.

45. Plottke, P. First memories of "normal" and of "delinquent" girls. *Indiv. Psychol. Bull.*, 1949, **7**, 15–20.

46. Postman, L. and Schneider, B. H. Personal values, visual recognition, and recall. *Psychol. Rev.*, 1951, **58**, 271–284.

47. Postman, L. and Murphy, G. The factor of attitude in associative memory. *J. exp. Psychol.*, 1943, **33**, 228–238.

48. Potwin, E. B. Study of early memories. *Psychol. Rev.*, 1901, **8**, 596–601.

49. Purcell, K. Memory and psychological security. *J. abnorm. soc. Psychol.*, 1952, **47**, 433–440.

50. Rapaport, D. *Emotions and memory.* Baltimore: Williams and Wilkins, 1942.

51. Saul, L. J., Snyder, T. R., and Sheppard, Edith. On earliest memories. *Psychoanal. Quart.*, 1956, **25**, 228–237.

52. Thatcher, P. An early recollection in a case of juvenile delinquency. *Indiv. Psychol. Bull.*, 1944, **4**, 59–60.

53. Waldfogel, S. The frequency and affective character of childhood memories. *Psychol. Monogr.*, 1948, **26**, No. 4 (Whole No. 291).

54. Watson, W. S. and Hartmann, G. W. The rigidity of a basic attitudinal frame. *J. abnorm. soc. Psychol.*, 1939, **34**, 314–335.

55. Way, L. *Adler's place in psychology.* London: Allen and Unwin, 1950.

56. Zeller, A. F. An experimental analogue of repression. I. Historical summary. *Psychol. Bull.*, 1950, **47**, 39–51.

3. Ordinal position and fighter pilot effectiveness

STANLEY SCHACHTER

SO FAR, WE HAVE EXAMINED REAL-LIFE ANAL-OGIES to the experimentally demonstrated relationship of birth rank to the affiliative reaction to anxiety. But what about anxiety itself? In the experiments, first-born subjects when faced with a standard anxiety-provoking situation responded with considerably more fright and anxiety than later-born subjects. Does this result have any explanatory power outside of the immediate experimental situation?

Let us consider first the relationship between anxiety or fright and performance. It is fairly well accepted that there is a non-monotonic relationship between these variables, that is, performance improves with small amounts of anxiety and deteriorates with excessive anxiety. It should be anticipated, then, that under really frightening conditions first-born individuals will be less effective than later-born individuals. Combat would seem the ideal locus for testing this expectation; if this line of reasoning is correct, later-born soldiers should make better fighters than early-born soldiers.

The only data available for testing these propositions derives from a study of fighter pilot effectiveness conducted by Paul Torrance. In a way, the situation of the fighter pilot is almost ideal for purposes of this test: first, there is a clear, unambiguous criterion of fighter pilot effectiveness—the number of enemy planes downed; second, the fighter pilot fights alone and his performance is relatively uncontaminated by the multitude of variables affecting performance in group combat. This isolation

of the fighter pilot does, however, raise one new question. When the individual faces an anxiety-provoking situation alone, does ordinal position have a differential effect on anxiety? No data has yet been presented on the question, but in terms of what is already known about the effects of ordinal position on the arousal of affiliative needs under anxiety, it is conceivable that being alone in such a situation magnifies the fears of the first-born far more than the fears of the later-born individual. If this is correct, it would imply that the anxiety differential between first and later-born individuals is even greater in solitary combat than in group combat and, again, it should be anticipated that the later-born will be more effective fighter pilots than the early-born individuals.

The purpose and procedure of Torrance's study are best explained in his own words:

> The major purpose of the larger study was to discover why pilots with backgrounds comparable with those of the more successful pilots were not themselves equally successful in combat with the MIG's over Korea. The 38 Air Force aces (pilots with 5 or more MIG-15 kills) accounted for 38.2 percent of the total claims, although they represented less than 5 percent of the pilots completing fighter interceptor tours in Korea. Furthermore, 53.5 percent made no kills at all. . . . The subjects of the study are 31 of the 38 aces in air-to-air combat over Korea. Of the seven aces not studied, one was killed in action, one is reported to be held in Manchuria, one was killed in an accident after returning to the States, and the other four were unavailable because of release from the Air Force or the like. Their ages ranged from 24 to 39 years and averaged about 30. Six of those studied are colonels; 3, lieutenant colonels; 6, majors; 13, captains; and 3, first lieu-

SOURCE. Stanley Schachter, "Ordinal position and fighter pilot effectiveness" in *The Psychology of Affiliation*. Stanford: Stanford University Press, 1959.

tenants. Similar studies were also made of pilots with one to four kills and pilots with no kills, matched for rank, age, and World War II combat experience.

There are, then, three matched groups which we will call aces (5 or more kills), near-aces (1 to 4 kills), and non-aces (0 kills). The distribution of these categories as they relate to ordinal position is presented in Table 1, where it will be noted that the data conform to expec-

tations. Some 67.7 percent of the aces, 54.6 percent of the near-aces and 41.0 percent of the non-aces are later-borns. It does appear that later-born flyers are more effective fighter pilots. The overall differences in this table are significant at the .08 level of confidence. Comparing the two extreme groups (aces vs. non-aces) yields a chi-square of 4.95, significant with one degree of freedom at the .03 level of confidence.

Table 1. Ordinal Position and Fighter Pilot Effectiveness

	Ace (5+ Kills)	Near-Ace (1–4 Kills)	Non-Ace (0 Kills)
First-Born and Only	10	15	23
Later	21	18	16

Overall $\chi^2 =$	5.12	Aces vs. Non-Aces	$\chi^2 =$	4.95
d.f. $=$	2		d.f. $=$	1
p $=$	.08		p $=$	.03

Table 2. Effects of Ordinal Position and Family Size on Fighter Pilot Effectiveness

a.   Aces

Family size (Number children)

Ordinal Position	1	2	3	4+
1	6	3	0	1
2		6	4	1
3			2	4
4+				4

b.   Near-Aces

Family size (number children)

Ordinal Position	1	2	3	4+
1	3	9	2	1
2		4	1	4
3			3	4
4+				2

c.   Non-Aces

Family size (number children)

Ordinal Position	1	2	3	4+
1	7	7	6	3
2		2	5	1
3			4	2
4+				2

The experimental result which stimulated this particular analysis was the finding that ordinal position affected the degree of anxiety or fear. Since it is known, from previous analyses that family size also affects the magnitude of anxiety, it is obvious that the effects of family size must again be evaluated before any unequivocal conclusions can be drawn. Fortunately, the data are available to permit such an evaluation and they are presented in Table 2, where the cases in each of the three groups are distributed according to ordinal position and family size. Ignoring, momentarily, the data on only children, examination of the sub-table for aces reveals that for each family size the number of first-borns who are aces is below chance expectations. Chance expectancies are simply computed by dividing the total number of cases falling in families of a given size by family size; e.g., there are 6 aces originating from 3-child families, if chance alone were operating these 6 cases should be equally distributed among the three ordinal positions with 2 cases at each position. For all of the sub-tables, the figure 5 may be used as a convenient and close approximation to the average number of children in families in the combined category used for families with 4 or more children. For this group of aces, then, family size does not appear to be a confounding variable; for all family sizes there are fewer first-borns than would be expected by chance. The data in the sub-table for non-aces reveal quite the opposite trend. For all family sizes, first-borns occur with greater than chance frequency. There are good indications, then, that the effects noted are a function of ordinal position independent of family size.

The data on only children are of special interest, for they do seem to deviate somewhat from the pattern for the first-born flyers. Six of the 10 first-born aces are only children, and these 6 constitute 37.5 percent of the total number of only children in these three groups of pilots. Should this be considered contrary to expectations? Perhaps, but the reader will recall from the discussion of differences between only and first-born subjects in the preceding chapter that there are indications that only children are less fearful than first-born children. In the high-anxiety conditions of the experiments 35 percent of all first-born subjects wanted to drop out of the experiment, while none of the only subjects wanted to drop out. In terms of the differential anxiety explanation of the relationship between fighter pilot effectiveness and ordinal position, these two sets of data can be considered consistent.

If this differential anxiety interpretation is an appropriate explanation of these data on fighter pilots, it should be anticipated that there will be further consistencies with the experimental data. Virtually the sole remaining item for which there is sufficient data to allow meaningful comparison is the effect of family size. In previously reported experiments subjects from small families were more frightened than subjects from large families. Consistency demands, then, that there be proportionately fewer pilots from small families among the aces than among non-aces. The reverse trend might be expected to obtain for pilots from large families. And the data do tend to conform to these expectations. Pilots from small families (2–3 children) compose 48.4 percent of the group of aces, 57.6 percent of near-aces, and 61.5 percent of non-aces. Pilots from large families (4+ children) make up 32.3 percent of the aces, 33.3 percent of near-aces, and 20.5 percent of non-aces.

It would be intriguing to compare these data with similar data on bomber pilots. Since the bomber pilot is a member of a crew, such a comparison might permit evaluation of the effect that being a member of a group has on the relationship of ordinal position to pilot effectiveness. If being a member of a group has little or no effect on anxiety level, precisely the same relationships should be expected for bomber pilots as for fighter pilots. If, as earlier speculation suggested, being a member of a group has differential effects on the anxiety levels of first- and later-born individuals, the relationship between ordinal position and pilot effectiveness should be considerably weaker for bomber pilots than for fighter pilots. In any case, the matter must remain unresolved, for discussion with those who have worked extensively on the criterion problem of bomber pilot effectiveness indicates that the highly interdependent nature of bomber crew action has so far made it impossible to hit upon any satisfactory criterion of bomber pilot effectiveness in combat conditions.

4. Character and the social process

ERICH FROMM

THROUGH THIS BOOK WE HAVE DEALT WITH the interrelation of socio-economic, psychological and ideological factors by analyzing certain historical periods like the age of the Reformation and the contemporary era. For those readers who are interested in the theoretical problems involved in such analysis I shall try, in this appendix, to discuss briefly the general theoretical basis on which the concrete analysis is founded.

In studying the psychological reactions of a social group we deal with the character structure of the members of the group, that is, of individual persons; we are interested, however, not in the peculiarities by which these persons differ from each other, but in that part of their character structure that is common to most members of the group. We can call this character the *social character*. The social character necessarily is less specific than the individual character. In describing the latter we deal with the whole of the traits on which in their particular configuration form the personality structure of this or that individual. The social character comprises only a selection of traits, *the essential nucleus of the character structure of most members of a group which has developed as the result of the basic experiences and mode of life common to that group*. Although there will be always "deviants" with a totally different character structure, the character structure of most members of the group are variations of this nucleus, brought about by accidental factors of birth and life experience as they differ from one individual to another. If we want to understand one individual most fully, these differentiating elements are of the greatest importance. However, if we want to understand how human energy is channeled and operates as a productive force in a given social order, then the social character deserves our main interest.

The concept of social character is a key concept for the understanding of the social process. Character in the dynamic sense of analytic psychology is the specific form in which human energy is shaped by the dynamic adaptation of human needs to the particular mode of existence of a given society. Character in its turn determines the thinking, feeling, and acting of individuals. To see this is somewhat difficult with regard to our thoughts, since we all tend to share the conventional belief that thinking is an exclusively intellectual act and independent of the psychological structure of the personality. This is not so, however, and the less so the more our thoughts deal with ethical, philosophical, political, psychological or social problems rather than with the empirical manipulation of concrete objects. Such thoughts, aside from the purely logical elements that are involved in the act of thinking, are greatly determined by the personality structure of the person who thinks. This holds true for the whole of a doctrine or of a theoretical system as well as for a single concept, like love, justice, equality, sacrifice. Each such concept and each doctrine has an emotional matrix and this matrix is rooted in the character structure of the individual.

We have given many illustrations of this in the foregoing chapters. With regard to doctrines we have tried to show the emotional roots of early Protestantism and modern authoritarianism. With regard to single concepts we have shown that for the sado-masochistic character, for example, love means symbiotic

SOURCE. Selection from Erich Fromm, "Character and the social process" Appendix to *Escape from Freedom*, pp. 277–299. New York: Rinehart, 1941.

dependence, not mutual affirmation and union on the basis of equality; sacrifice means the utmost subordination of the individual self to something higher, not assertion of one's mental and moral self; difference means difference in power, not the realization of individuality on the basis of equality; justice means that everybody should get what he deserves, not that the individual has an unconditional claim to the realization of inherent and inalienable rights; courage is the readiness to submit and to endure suffering, not the utmost assertion of individuality against power. Although the word which two people of different personality use when they speak of love, for instance, is the same, the meaning of the word is entirely different according to their character structure. As a matter of fact, much intellectual confusion could be avoided by correct psychological analysis of the meaning of these concepts, since any attempt at a purely logical classification must necessarily fail.

The fact that ideas have an emotional matrix is of the utmost importance because it is the key to the understanding of the spirit of a culture. Different societies or classes within a society have a specific social character, and on its basis different ideas develop and become powerful. Thus, for instance, the idea of work and success as the main aims of life were able to become powerful and appealing to modern man on the basis of his aloneness and doubt; but propaganda for the idea of ceaseless effort and striving for success addressed to the Pueblo Indians or to Mexican peasants would fall completely flat. These people with a different kind of character structure would hardly understand what a person setting forth such aims was talking about even if they understood his language. In the same way, Hitler and that part of the German population which has the same character structure quite sincerely feel that anybody who thinks that wars can be abolished is either a complete fool or a plain liar. On the basis of their social character, to them life without suffering and disaster is a little comprehensible as freedom and equality.

Ideas often are consciously accepted by certain groups, which, on account of the peculiarities of their social character, are not really touched by them; such ideas remain a stock of conscious convictions, but people fail to act according to them in a critical hour. An example of this is shown in the German labor movement at the time of the victory of Nazism. The vast majority of German workers before Hitler's coming into power voted for the Socialist or Communist Parties and believed in the ideas of those parties; that is, the *range* of these ideas among the working class was extremely wide. The *weight* of these ideas, however, was in no proportion to their range. The onslaught of Nazism did not meet with political opponents, the majority of whom were ready to fight for their ideas. Many of the adherents of the leftist parties, although they believed in their party programs as long as the parties had authority, were ready to resign when the hour of crisis arrived. A close analysis of the character structure of German workers can show one reason—certainly not the only one—for this phenomenon. A great number of them were of a personality type that has many of the traits of what we have described as the authoritarian character. They had a deep-seated respect and longing for established authority. The emphasis of socialism on individual independence versus authority, on solidarity versus individualistic seclusion, was not what many of these workers really wanted on the basis of their personality structure. One mistake of the radical leaders was to estimate the strength of their parties only on the basis of the range which these ideas had, and to overlook their lack of weight.

In contrast to this picture, our analysis of Protestant and Calvinist doctrines has shown that those ideas were powerful forces within the adherents of the new religion, because they appealed to needs and anxieties that were present in the character structure of the people to whom they were addressed. In other words, *ideas can become powerful forces, but only to the extent to which they are answers to specific human needs prominent in a given social character.*

Not only thinking and feeling are determined by man's character structure but also his actions. It is Freud's achievement to have shown this, even if his theoretical frame of reference is incorrect. The determinations of activity by the dominant trends of a person's character structure are obvious in the case of neurotics. It is easy to understand that the compulsion to count the windows of houses and the number of stones on the pavement is an activity that is rooted in certain drives of the compulsive character. But the actions of a normal person appear to be determined only by rational considerations and the necessities of reality. However, with the new tools of observation that psychoanalysis offers, we can recognize that so-called rational behavior is largely determined by the character structure. In our discussion of the meaning of work for modern man we have dealt with an illustration of this point. We saw that the intense desire for unceasing activity was rooted in aloneness and anxiety. This compulsion to work differed from the attitude toward work in other cultures, where people worked as much as it was necessary but where they were not driven by additional forces within their own character structure. Since all normal persons today have about the same impulse to work and, furthermore, since this intensity of work is necessary if they want to live at all, one easily overlooks the irrational component in this trait.

We have now to ask what function character serves for the individual and for society. As to the former the answer is not difficult. If an individual's character more or less closely conforms with the social character, the dominant drives in his personality lead him to do what is necessary and desirable under the specific social conditions of his culture. Thus, for instance, if he has a passionate drive to save and an abhorrence of spending money for any luxury, he will be greatly helped by this drive— supposing he is a small shopkeeper who needs to save and to be thrifty if he wants to survive. Besides this economic function, character traits have a purely psychological one which is no less important. The person with whom saving is a desire springing from his personality gains also a profound psychological satisfaction in being able to act accordingly; that is, he is not only benefited practically when he saves, but he also feels satisfied psychologically. One can easily convince oneself of this if one observes, for instance, a woman of the lower middle class shopping in the market and being as happy about two cents saved as another person of a different character may be about the enjoyment of some sensuous pleasure. This psychological satisfaction occurs not only if a person acts in accordance with the demands springing from his character structure but also when he reads or listens to ideas that appeal to him for the same reason. For the authoritarian character an ideology that describes nature as the powerful force to which

we have to submit, or a speech which indulges in sadistic descriptions of political occurrences, has a profound attraction and the act of reading or listening results in psychological satisfaction. To sum up: the subjective function of character for the normal person is to *lead him to act according to what is necessary for him from a practical standpoint and also to give him satisfaction from his activity psychologically.*

If we look at social character from the standpoint of its function in the social process, we have to start with the statement that has been made with regard to its function for the individual: that by adapting himself to social conditions man develops those traits that make him desire to act as he has to act. If the character of the majority of people in a given society—that is, the social character—is thus adapted to the objectve tasks the individual has to perform in this society, the energies of people are molded in ways that make them into productive forces that are indispensable for the functioning of that society. Let us take up once more the example of work. Our modern industrial system requires that most of our energy be channeled in the direction of work. Were it only that people worked because of external necessities, much friction between what they ought to do and what they would like to do would arise and lessen their efficiency. However, by the dynamic adaptation of character to social requirements, human energy instead of causing friction is shaped into such forms as to become an incentive to act according to the particular economic necessities. Thus modern man, instead of having to be forced to work as hard as he does, is driven by the inner compulsion to work which we have attempted to analyze in its psychological significance. Or, instead of obeying overt authorities, he has built up an inner authority—conscience and duty—which operates more effectively in controlling him than any external authority could ever do. In other words, *the social character internalizes external necessities and thus harnesses human energy for the task of a given economic and social system.*

As we have seen, once certain needs have developed in a character structure, any behavior in line with these needs is at the same time satisfactory psychologically and practical from the standpoint of material success. As long as a society offers the individual those two satisfactions simultaneously, we have a situation where the psychological forces are cementing the social structure. Sooner or later, however, a lag arises. The traditional character structure still exists while new economic conditions have arisen, for which the traditional character traits are no longer useful. People tend to act according to their character structure, but either these actions are actual handicaps in their economic pursuits or there is not enough opportunity for them to find positions that allow them to act according to their "nature." An illustration of what we have in mind is the character structure of the old middle classes, particularly in countries with a rigid class stratification like Germany. The old middle class virtues—frugality, thrift, cautiousness, suspiciousness—were of diminishing value in modern business in comparison with new virtues, such as initiative, a readiness to take risks, aggressiveness, and so on. Even inasmuch as these old virtues were still an asset—as with the small shopkeeper—the range of possibilities for such business was so narrowed down that only a minority of the sons of the old middle class could "use" their character traits successfully in their economic pursuits. While by their upbringing they had developed character traits that once were adapted to the social situation of their class, the economic development went faster than the character development. This lag between economic and psychological evolution resulted in a situation in which the psychic needs could no longer be satisfied by the usual economic activities. These needs existed, however, and had to seek for satisfaction in some other way. Narrow egotistical striving for one's own advantage, as it had characterized the lower middle class, was shifted from the individual plane to that of the nation. The sadistic impulses, too, that had been used in the battle of private competition were partly shifted to the social and political scene, and partly intensified by frustration. Then, freed from any restricting factors, they sought satisfaction in acts of political persecution and war. Thus, blended with the resentment caused by the frustrating qualities of the whole situation, the psychological forces instead of cementing the existing social order became dynamite to be used by groups which wanted to destroy the traditional political and economic structure of democratic society.

We have not spoken of the role which the educational process plays with regard to the formation of the social character; but in view of the fact that to many psychologists the methods of early childhood training and the educational techniques employed toward the growing child appear to be the cause of character development, some remarks on this point seem to be warranted. In the first place we should ask ourselves what we mean by education. While education can be defined in various ways, the way to look at it from the angle of the social process seems to be something like this. The social function of education is to qualify the individual to function in the role he is to play later on in society; that is, to mold his character in such a way that it approximates the social character, that his desires coincide with the necessities of his social role. The educational system of any society is determined by this function; therefore we cannot explain the structure of society or the personality of its members by the educational process; but we have to explain the educational system by the necessities resulting from the social and economic structure of a given society. However, the methods of education are extremely important in so far as they are the mechanisms by which the individual is molded into the required shape. They can be considered as the means by which social requirements are transformed into personal qualities. While educational techniques are not the cause of a particular kind of social character, they constitute one of the mechanisms by which character is formed. In this sense, the knowledge and understanding of educational methods is an important part of the total analysis of a functioning society.

What we have just said also holds true for one particular sector of the whole educational process: the *family*. Freud has shown that the early experiences of the child have a decisive influence upon the formation of its character structure. If this is true, how then can we understand that the child, who—at least in our culture—has little contact with the life of society, is molded by it? The answer is not only that the parents—aside from certain individual variations—apply the educational patterns of the society they live in, but also that in their own personalities they represent the social character of their society or class. They transmit to the child what we may call the psychological atmosphere or the spirit of a society just by being as they are—namely representatives of this very spirit. *The family thus may be considered to be the psychological agent of society.*

Having stated that the social character is shaped by the mode of existence of a given society, I want to remind the reader of what has been said in the first chapter on the problem of dynamic adaptation. While it is true that man is molded by the necessities of the economic and social structure of society, he is not infinitely adaptable. Not only are there certain physiological needs that imperatively call for satisfaction, but there are also certain psychological qualities inherent in man that need to be satisfied and that result in certain reactions if they are frustrated. What are these qualities? The most important seems to be the tendency to grow, to develop and realize potentialities which man has developed in the course of history—as, for instance, the faculty of creative and critical thinking and of having differentiated emotional and sensuous experiences. Each of these potentialities has a dynamism of its own. Once they have developed in the process of evolution they tend to be expressed. This tendency can be suppressed and frustrated, but such suppression results in a new reaction, particularly in the formation of destructive and symbiotic impulses. It also seems that this general tendency to grow—which is the psychological equivalent of the identical biological tendency—results in such specific tendencies as the desire for freedom and the hatred against oppression, since freedom is the fundamental condition for any growth. Again, the desire for freedom can be repressed, it can disappear from the awareness of the individual; but even then it does not cease to exist as a potentiality, and indicates its existence by the conscious or unconscious hatred by which such suppression is always accompanied.

We have also reason to assume that, as has been said before, the striving for justice and truth is an inherent trend of human nature, although it can be repressed and perverted like the striving for freedom. In this assumption we are on dangerous ground theoretically. It would be easy if we could fall back on religious and philosophical assumptions which explain the existence of such trends by a belief that man is created in God's likeness or by the assumption of a natural law. However, we cannot support our argument with such explanations. The only way in our opinion to account for this striving for justice and truth is by the analysis of the whole history of man, socially and individually. We find then that for everybody who is powerless, justice and truth are the most important weapons in the fight for his freedom and growth. Aside from the fact that the majority of mankind throughout its history has had to defend itself against more powerful groups which could oppress and exploit it, every individual in childhood goes through a period which is characterized by powerlessness. It seems to us that in this state of powerlessness traits like the sense of justice and truth develop and become potentialities common to man as such. We arrive therefore at the fact that, *although character development is shaped by the basic conditions of life and although there is no biologically fixed human nature, human nature has a dynamism of its own that constitutes an active factor in the evolution of the social process.* Even if we are not yet able to state clearly in psychological terms what the exact nature of this human dynamism is, we must recognize its existence. In trying to avoid the errors of biological and metaphysical concepts we must not succumb to an equally grave error, that of a sociological relativism in which man is nothing but a puppet, directed by the strings of social circumstances. Man's inalienable rights of freedom and happiness are founded in inherent human qualities: his striving to live, to expand and to express the potentialities that have developed in him in the process of historical evolution.

At this point we can restate the most important differences between the psychological approach pursued in this book and that of Freud. The first point of difference has been dealt with in a detailed manner in the first chapter, so that it is only necessary to mention it here briefly: we look upon human nature as essentially historically conditioned, although we do not minimize the significance of biological factors and do not believe that the question can be put correctly in terms of cultural versus biological factors. In the the second place, Freud's essential principle is to look upon man as an entity, a closed system, endowed by nature with certain physiologically conditioned drives, and to interpret the development of his character as a reaction to satisfactions and frustrations of these drives; whereas, in our opinion, the fundamental approach to human personality is the understanding of man's relation to the world, to others, to nature, and to himself. We believe that man is *primarily* a social being, and not, as Freud assumes, primarily self-sufficient and only secondarily in need of others in order to satisfy his instinctual needs. In this sense, we believe that individual psychology is fundamentally social psychology, or, in Sullivan's terms, the psychology of interpersonal relationships; the key problem of psychology is that of the particular kind of relatedness of the individual toward the world, not that of satisfaction or frustration of a single instinctual desire. The problem of what happens to man's instinctual desires has to be understood as one part of the total problem of his relationship toward the world and not as the problem of human personality. Therefore, in our approach, the needs and desires that center about the individual's relations to others, such as love, hatred, tenderness, symbiosis, are the fundamental psychological phenomena, while with Freud they are only secondary results from frustrations or satisfactions of instinctive needs.

The difference between Freud's biological and our own social orientation has special significance with regard to the problems of characterology. Freud—and on the basis of his findings, Abraham, Jones, and others—assumed that the child experiences pleasure at so-called erogenous zones (mouth and anus) in connection with the process of feeding and defecation; and that, either by overstimulation, frustration, or constitutionally intensified sensitivity, these erogenous zones retain their libidinous character in later years when in the course of normal development the genital zone should have become of primary importance. It is assumed that this fixation at the pregenital level leads to sublimations and reaction-formations that become part of the character structure. Thus, for instance, a person may have a drive to save money or other objects, because he sublimates the unconscious desire to retain the stool. Or a person may expect to get everything from somebody else and not as a result of his own effort, because he is driven by an unconscious wish to be fed which is sublimated into the

wish to get help, knowledge, and so forth.

Freud's observations are of great importance, but he gave an erroneous explanation. He saw correctly the passionate and irrational nature of these "oral" and "anal" character traits. He saw also that such desires pervade all spheres of personality, man's sexual, emotional, and intellectual life, and that they color all his activities. But he mistook the causal relation between erogenous zones and character traits for the reverse of what they really are. The desire to receive everything one wants to obtain—love, protection, knowledge, material things—in a passive way from a source outside of oneself, develops in a child's character as a reaction to his experiences with others. If through these experiences the feeling of his own strength is weakened by fear, if his initiative and self-confidence are paralyzed, if hostility develops and is repressed, and if at the same time his father or mother offers affection or care under the condition of surrender, such a constellation leads to an attitude in which active mastery is given up and all his energies are turned in the direction of an outside source from which the fulfillment of all wishes will eventually come. This attitude assumes such a passionate character because it is the only way in which a person can attempt to realize his wishes. That often these persons have dreams or phantasies of being fed, nursed, and so on, is due to the fact that the mouth more than any other organ lends itself to the expression of this receptive attitude. But the oral sensation is not the cause of this attitude; it is the expression of an attitude toward the world in the language of the body.

The same holds true for the "anal" person, who on the basis of his particular experience is more withdrawn from others than the "oral" person, seeks security by making himself an autarchic, self-sufficient system, and feels love or any other outgoing attitude as a threat to his security. It is true that in many instances these attitudes first develop in connection with feeding or defecation, which in the early age of the child are his main activities and also the main sphere in which love or oppression on the part of the parents and friendliness or defiance on the part of the child, are expressed. However, over-stimulation and frustration in connection with the erogenous zones by themselves do not lead to a fixation of such attitudes in a person's character; although certain pleasurable sensations are experienced by the child in connection with feeding and defecation, these pleasures do not assume importance for the character development, unless they represent—on the physical level—attitudes that are rooted in the whole of the character structure.

For an infant who has confidence in the unconditional love of his mother, the sudden interruption of breast-feeding will not have any grave characterological consequences; the infant who experiences a lack of reliability in the mother's love may acquire "oral" traits even though the feeding process went on without any particular disturbances. The "oral" or "anal" phantasies or physical sensations in later years are not important on account of the physical pleasure they imply, or of any mysterious sublimation of this pleasure, but only on account of the specific kind of relatedness toward the world which is underlying them and which they express.

Only from this point of view can Freud's characterological findings become fruitful for social psychology. As long as we assume, for instance, that the anal character, as it is typical of the European lower middle class, is caused by certain early experiences in connection with defecation, we have hardly any data that lead us to understand why a specific class should have an anal social character. However, if we understand it as one form of relatedness to others, rooted in the character structure and resulting from the experiences with the outside world, we have a key for understanding why the whole mode of life of the lower middle class, its narrowness, isolation, and hostility, made for the development of this kind of character structure.

The third important point of difference is closely linked up with the previous ones. Freud, on the basis of his instinctivistic orientation and also of a profound conviction of the wickedness of human nature, is prone to interpret all "ideal" motives in man as the result of something "mean"; a case in point is his explanation of the sense of justice as the outcome of the original envy a child has for anybody who has more than he. As has been pointed out before, we believe that ideals like truth, justice, freedom, although they are frequently mere phrases or rationalizations, can be genuine strivings, and that any analysis which does not deal with these strivings as dynamic factors is fallacious. These ideals have no metaphysical character but are rooted in the conditions of human life and can be analyzed as such. The fear of falling back into metaphysical or idealistic concepts should not stand in the way of such analysis. It is the task of psychology as an empirical science to study motivation by ideals as well as the moral problems connected with them, and thereby to free our thinking on such matters from the unempirical and metaphysical elements that befog the issues in their traditional treatment.

Finally, one other point of difference should be mentioned. It concerns the differentiation between psychological phenomena of want and those of abundance. The primitive level of human existence is that of want. There are imperative needs which have to be satisfied before anything else. Only when man has time and energy left beyond the satisfaction of the primary needs, can culture develop and with it those strivings that attend the phenomena of abundance. Freud's psychology is a psychology of want. He defines pleasure as the satisfaction resulting from the removal of painful tension. Phenomena of abundance, like love or tenderness, actually do not play any role in his system. Not only did he omit such phenomena, but he also had a limited understanding of the phenomenon to which he paid so much attention: sex. According to his whole definition of pleasure Freud saw in sex only the element of physiological compulsion and in sexual satisfaction the relief from painful tensions. The sexual drive as a phenomenon of abundance, and sexual pleasure as spontaneous joy—the essence of which is not negative relief from tension—had no place in his psychology.

What is the principle of interpretation that this book has applied to the understanding of the human basis of culture? Before answering this question it may be useful to recall the main trends of interpretation with which our own differs.

1. The "psychologistic" approach which characterizes Freud's thinking, according to which cultural phenomena are rooted in psychological factors that result from instinctual drives which in themselves are influenced by society only through some measure of suppression. Following this line of interpretation Freudian authors have explained capitalism as the outcome of anal eroticism and the development of early Christianity as the result of the ambivalence toward the father image.

2. The "economistic" approach, as it is presented in the misapplication of Marx's interpretation of history. According to this view, subjective economic interests are the cause of cultural phenomena, such as religion and political ideas. From such a pseudo-Marxian viewpoint, one might try to explain Protestantism as no more than the answer to certain economic needs of the bourgeoisie.

3. Finally there is the "idealistic" position, which is represented by Max Weber's analysis, *The Protestant Ethic and the Spirit of Capitalism*. He holds that new religious ideas are responsible for the development of a new type of economic behavior and a new spirit of culture, although he emphasizes that this behavior is never *exclusively* determined by religious doctrines.

In contrast to these explanations, we have assumed that ideologies and culture in general are rooted in the social character; that the social character itself is molded by the mode of existence of a given society; and that in their turn the dominant character traits become productive forces shaping the social process. With regard to the problem of the spirit of Protestantism and capitalism, I have tried to show that the collapse of medieval society threatened the middle class; that this threat resulted in a feeling of powerless isolation and doubt; that this psychological change was responsible for the appeal of Luther's and Calvin's doctrines; that these doctrines intensified and stabilized the characterological changes; and that the character traits that thus developed then became productive forces in the development of capitalism which in itself resulted from economic and political changes.

With regard to Fascism the same principle of explanation was applied: the lower middle class reacted to certain economic changes, such as the growing power of monopolies and postwar inflation, with an intensification of certain character traits, namely, sadistic and masochistic strivings; the Nazi ideology appealed to and intensified these traits; and new character traits then became effective forces in supporting the expansion of German imperialism. In both instances we see that when a certain class is threatened by new economic tendencies it reacts to this threat psychologically and ideologically; and that the psychological changes brought about by this reaction further the development of economic forces even if those forces contradict the economic interests of that class. We see that economic, psychological, and ideological forces operate in the social process in this way: that man reacts to changing external situations by changes in himself, and that these psychological factors in their turn help in molding the economic and social process. Economic forces are effective, but they must be understood not as psychological motivations but as objective conditions: psychological forces are effective, but they must be understood as historically conditioned themselves; ideas are effective, but they must be understood as being rooted in the whole of the character structure of members of a social group. In spite of this interdependence of economic, psychological and ideological forces, however, each of them has also a certain independence. This is particularly true of the economic development which, being dependent on objective factors, such as the natural productive forces, technique, geographical factors, takes place according to its own laws. As to the psychological forces, we have indicated that the same holds true; they are molded by the external conditions of life, but they also have a dynamism of their own; that is, they are the expression of human needs which, although they can be molded, cannot be uprooted. In the ideological sphere we find a similar autonomy rooted in logical laws and in the tradition of the body of knowledge acquired in the course of history.

We can restate the principle in terms of social character: The social character results from the dynamic adaptation of human nature to the structure of society. Changing social conditions result in changes of the social character, that is, in new needs and anxieties. These new needs give rise to new ideas and, as it were, make men susceptible to them; these new ideas in their turn tend to stabilize and intensify the new social character and to determine man's actions. In other words, social conditions influence ideological phenomena through the medium of character; character, on the other hand, is not the result of passive adaptation to social conditions but of a dynamic adaptation on the basis of elements that either are biologically inherent in human nature or have become inherent as the result of historic evolution.

5. Dogmatism and sensory alienation: an empirical investigation

MARTIN F. KAPLAN AND ERWIN SINGER

This study was designed to investigate certain aspects of the concept of "alienation" as employed by Fromm. Using Fromm's framework and suggestions offered by Schachtel concerning inherent autocentrism and allocentrism in various sensory modalities, it was hypothesized that: (a) dogmatism as measured by Rokeach's scale and adequacy on sensory discrimination tasks would vary negatively with each other and (b) differences between dogmatic and nondogmatic individuals would be more pronounced in their performances utilizing predominantly autocentric modes than on tasks involving essentially allocentric modalities. Sensory discrimination was assessed by requiring Ss to match and/or differentiate between stimuli in 5 areas. 13 dogmatic and 13 nondogmatic Ss (controlling other relevant variables) served as populations. Data obtained supported the hypotheses at least at the 5% level.

Theoretical Background

Since the days of Breuer and Freud (1957) the notion that psychopathology is characterized by the patient's strenuous attempts to remove from consciousness certain stimuli, be they internal or external, has been prominent in most theories which claim some affiliation to what is loosely referred to as "depth psychology." From "repression" and the other "mechanisms of defense" through "dissociation" to the concept of "estrangement" the common denominator is the assumption that humans

SOURCE. Article by Martin F. Kaplan and Erwin Singer, "Dogmatism and sensory alienation: an empirical investigation" in *Journal of consulting Psychology*, Vol. 27, No. 6, pp. 486–491, 1963.

block from awareness what they deem noxious. What has changed in the evolution of psychological theory are the constructs concerning what is blocked, how the blocking takes place, and why humans engage in such a process of reduction of consciousness. Through the years the emphasis has shifted, at least in certain quarters, from postulating man's attempt to defend himself against libidinal incestuous and/or aggressive inner stimuli to the hypothesis that there exists a more or less prominent tendency to remove from awareness the fact of one's very being and the sense of responsibility implicit in the awareness of being or existing. The empirical research to be reported here addresses itself to some aspects of this debate by investigating certain operations presumably underlying the latter position, i.e., the position which suggests that the central problem to be studied is the degree to which some people attempt to minimize the very awareness of themselves and to what extent this minimization is intricately associated with certain character trends.

As is well known, in discussing psychopathology Fromm (1941, 1955) takes his point of departure from the concept of alienation as developed by Marx in his *Economic and Philosophic Manuscripts* (Fromm, 1961). Alienated or estranged man is to Fromm essentially Kafka's Mr. K or Camus' Stranger. The process of estrangement is said to proceed via a diminution or outright elimination of awareness of the self as an active and separate organism, leading to a sense of being which is characterized by passive drivenness and lack of responsibility for action, be that intellectual, emotional, or even physical activity. Alienated man is said to lose his sense of being "subject" and to become more and more "object" in his own eyes. Schachtel (1959), without actually employing the term alienation, deals with the concept indirectly in his discussion of "objectification" and what he calls the "two basic perceptual modes," the allocentric and the autocentric modes. He suggests that the various sensory modalities are more or less capable of functioning in one or both modes. He proposes that the olfactory and gustatory senses operate essentially in the autocentric modes, i.e., are relatively incapable of objectifying the world but rather arouse reactions and feeling tones which bring about some position vis-a-vis the stimulus yet contribute "no clue at all about object structure [p. 88]." On the other hand, sensory modalities such as hearing and vision are much more capable of objectifying. Inner reactivity may but does not necessarily occur within the perceiver when these latter sensory modalities are employed. A person may correctly identify a given visual stimulus as green without assuming a personal position in terms of a pleasure-displeasure continuum to the stimulation. Schachtel points out that this differential functioning of sensory modalities "is not a matter of absolute alternatives, but rather of the relative predominance of objectification [p. 98]."

If the utilization of the predominantly autocentric modes enhances man's immediate self-awareness through attention to personal experience in addition to mere attempts in objectification; and conversely, if rather exclusive focusing upon predominantly allocentric modalities minimizes subjective experience through emphasis upon grasping the nature of the object without attending to subjective reactions, then it would follow that self-alienated man would de-emphasize the former, i.e., autocentric modalities, and in doing so reduce subjective experience and awareness of self. The predominantly allocentric modes, however, should not undergo such a de-emphasis in the self-alienated person.

While employing different terms Fromm's (1961) discussion of idolatry is consistent with this formulation. He states at one point:

This is, incidentally, also the psychology of the fanatic. He is empty, dead, depressed, but in order to compensate for the state of depression and inner deadness, he chooses an idol, be it the state, a party, an idea, the church, or God. He makes this idol into the absolute, and submits to it in an absolute way [pp. 44–45].

If we pursue the implications of Fromm's thinking further it would become reasonable to hypothesize that the fanatic in his "empty, dead, depressed" state would emphasize the allocentric modalities and de-emphasize the autocentric modes or to restate the proposition in more empirically verifiable terms, that increasing fanaticism or dogmatism would be associated with decreasing autocentric perception and experience. If the fanatic is self-estranged then his self-estrangement is likely to proceed primarily via alienation from those sensory modalities which bring in their wake self-awareness or perhaps require some basic readiness for self-awareness, the awareness of self as a separate, living, and immediately reacting unit.

Before discussing the specific experimental procedures employed a theoretical point needs clarification. While fanaticism and dogmatism are not necessarily synonymous, they seem closely related, for the fanatic as well as the dogmatic are essentially individuals who are in the jargon of psychological description "rigid," incapable of tolerating ambiguity and in Rokeach's (1960) terms "closed-minded." [1] But closed-mindedness in its conceptual meaning is not restricted to the "fanatic" or the "dogmatic" but permeates in one form or another all manifestations of psychopathology. For example, when one says that a person is relatively devoid of insight one proposes, in effect, that the individual in question is closed to or unaware of his feelings, tendencies, impulses, or reactions, is in the broadest sense of the word self-alienated so we return to our original theoretical point of departure, i.e., the proposition that pathology is essentially characterized by a type of fanaticism or dogmatism which reflects itself in varying types of closed-

---

[1] Even though Rokeach makes a subtle distinction between rigidity and dogmatism, employing the former in relation to specific behavioral manifestations, the latter in connection with total belief systems or general orientations, this distinction is for our purposes unnecessary. We shall employ the terms dogmatism and rigidity interchangeably, both denoting a schematized and fixed outlook and orientation towards self and the world. Consequently, the term rigidity as employed here comes close to what Rokeach refers to as dogmatism or closed-mindedness.

mindedness and rigidity, these rigidities expressing themselves in different forms, but all of these forms detracting from self-awareness.

Hypotheses

In order to investigate this proposition empirically we hypothesized that the degree to which the tendency towards dogmatism is operant within a given individual to that extent self-awareness should appear reduced, this reduced self-awareness operationally reflecting itself in decreased emphasis upon the autocentric sensory modalities and relatively elevated emphasis upon the allocentric modes of perception. Schachtel's discussion suggests a rather specific hierarchy or continuum along the autocentric-allocentric dimension. In ascending order of allocentric potential he arranges the sensory modalities in approximately the following order: olfactory, gustatory, tactile, auditory, and visual. Thus he suggests that the olfactory modality is hardly capable of bringing about objectification and is closely associated with the autocentric mode of perception, the visual modality is most capable of objectifying and therefore potentially most closely associated with the allocentric mode of perception (1941, 1955).

On the basis of these considerations the following specific hypotheses were developed: 1a. Highly dogmatic individuals should exhibit significantly lowered sensory acuity when compared with individuals who are relatively free of dogmatism; 1b. As a logical corollary of the above hypothesis there should exist a negative correlation between dogmatism and sensory acuity; 2. Finally, this differentiation in sensory acuity should be most prominent in the autocentric sensory modalities and less pronounced in the allocentric modes. Put a bit differently, declining sensory acuity is expected in all human beings on the allocentric-autocentric continuum but this decline will be more pronounced in highly dogmatic than in relatively nondogmatic individuals.

Method

For purposes of this investigation dogmatism was operationally defined as the score achieved by a subject on the Rokeach Dogmatism Scale

(1960, pp. 71–100). Previous researches have established the usefulness of this device by finding satisfactory correlations between scores achieved on the Scale and personality variables serving as criteria measures. By and large it may be considered the best existing objective measure of closed-mindedness and a host of studies support the reliability and construct as well as criterion validity of the instrument (1960, pp. 101–108, 171–274).

The assessment of the sensory acuity or sensitivity to stimuli proved a more complicated matter. Two procedures were employed to assess *olfactory sensitivity*. First five odors from Henning's Odor Prism were selected. These odors were along the dimension of spiciness at known distances from each other. Three spices, one at a time, were placed under the nose of each subject while his eyes were closed and following MacDonald's suggestion (Woodworth, 1958) the subject was asked to compare the second stimulus presented with the first and the third and to judge which of these resembled most closely the second stimulus. Each set of three spice stimuli was presented in systematically rotated order so that each spice became at least once a comparison stimulus. In the second *olfactory* task three toilet waters were employed. Each scent was presented, one at a time and then one of the three was re-presented, the subject being asked to indicate with which of the original stimuli he was now confronted. Systematic rotation of order of presentation was observed and care was taken to make each scent a comparison stimulus.

Three sets of salt, sugar, and vinegar solutions, each set containing a heavy, a medium, and a slight concentration of the respective additives, served as the stimuli for the *gustatory task*. The concentration in the "medium" solution, however, was always closer to one of the extremes rather than exactly in the middle between them. Each set of the three solutions was presented for three trials, presentation varying from trial to trial. The subject was asked to sip each solution without swallowing and after each sip he was to rinse his mouth with warm water. Each trial consisted of the presentation of two of the three stimuli and the subject was then given the third solution and was asked to indicate which of the preceding two the third solution resembled more closely.

Three sets of swatches of cloth, each 6 inches square, each set containing three swatches of similar texture, were employed in testing for *tactile acuity*. The texture of one set was rough, of the other smooth, and of the third silky. Even though the nature of the materials in each set was rather similar they were of different weave. Subjects were asked to avert their eyes and were given one swatch at a time to touch. They were to rub one hand over the material but were not allowed to lift or to pinch it. 10 seconds were allowed for each swatch. A trial consisted of the presentation of all three materials constituting a set and the re-presentation of one of them, the subject being asked to judge which of the three he had received for the re-presentation. Each set was presented employing systematic rotation procedures three times, making for nine trials in all. Care was taken that the test stimulus appeared at varying points in the presentation procedure.

For the *auditory task* a record, "The Measure of Your Phonograph's Performance," manufactured by the Dubbings Company was secured. The record has several bands, each with a different tone of known frequency. These bands were grouped into three sets, each set containing three tones. Again, the frequencies of two tones were closer to each other than to the third tone. Each set was presented three times, varying the order of presentation, and after the subject had listened to two tones he was asked which of the two the third stimulus resembled more closely.

Finally, for the *visual task* sample paint cards (2 × 1.5 inches) were obtained. There were 12 cards, each a different tint of green, pink, or yellow. In each trial two tints of the same color were presented and the subject was then asked to judge (without being shown the original stimuli again) to which of the two the third tint seemed closer. Since the paint company had ranked the tints in order of distance from the primary color, there was an objective basis for judging a response correct or incorrect.

In order to make scores achieved on the various tasks comparable the number of trials were held constant from task to task, allowing one point for each correct identification or judgment. In this fashion the possible range of scores remained the same for each sensory modality.

From a population of 40 randomly selected subjects who had been given the Rokeach Dogmatism Scale, those 13 who had scored highest and those 13 who had scored lowest on the Scale were given all the above-described sensory discrimination tasks. Procedures for both comparison populations, personnel carrying out the testing and similar relevant variables were controlled and kept constant.

Results

It will be recalled that we suggested in Hypothesis 1a that highly dogmatic individuals would exhibit significantly lowered sensory acuity when compared with individuals who are relatively free of dogmatism. Data having bearing upon this assertion are presented in Table 1.

The data speak for themselves. On five of the six measures evaluated the low dogmatic group proved superior to the highly dogmatic individuals to a degree which makes the differences observable rather unattributable to chance. Only on the visual task is the difference observed, although moving in the predicted direction, relatively small and hence likely to have been the result of chance factors and artifacts. The data must therefore be considered as highly suggestive that Hypothesis 1a represents a valid assertion.

In Hypothesis 1b, a logical corollary of Hypothesis 1a, the above findings are simply expressed in different statistical fashion. A Pearson product-moment correlation of $-.61$ was calculated between our measures of sensory acuity and scores achieved on the Rokeach Scale. This value is attributable to chance factors less than 1:1,000 and, as already stated, expresses in different fashion the observation that with increasing dogmatism sensory acuity decreases.

It was also predicted that the differences in sensory acuity between the two groups would not be uniform from modality to modality but much more follow a gradient of differentiation from relatively minor differences in the primarily allocentric modes to marked differences in the primarily autocentric modes (Hypothesis 2).

Once again the results seem rather unequivocal in support of the hypothesis. The gradient of differences is apparent even though neither group exhibited the exact pattern of performance predicted. It will be noticed that both groups did better on the gustatory task than on the tactile task but this is irrelevant for it should be recalled that absolute performance on the tasks is less important than the gradient of differences in performance predicted and in this respect the data are evidently conclusive. The particular order of differences observed is attributable to chance only on a 1:120 basis, or maximal for the present design.[2]

Discussion

At this point we wish to mention certain methodological difficulties. It is well nigh im-

---

[2] We are indebted to Jacob Cohen of New York University for suggesting the appropriate statistical treatment of this datum.

Table 1. Means and Standard Deviations of All Measures Employed for the High Dogmatic Group and the Low Dogmatic Group

Measure		Low Dogmatic N = 13	High Dogmatic N = 13	Difference	t^a
Dogmatism scale	M	127.92	174.62		
	SD	5.99	13.23	−46.72	10.06†
Olfactory task	M	5.31	3.70		
	SD	.98	1.47	1.61	3.18†
Gustatory task	M	6.00	4.46		
	SD	1.36	1.35	1.54	2.79**
Tactile task	M	5.46	4.00		
	SD	1.51	1.11	1.46	2.70**
Auditory task	M	6.61	5.46		
	SD	1.30	1.60	1.15	1.93*
Visual task	M	6.77	6.07		
	SD	1.25	1.49	.70	1.24
Total sensory	M	30.15	23.69		
	SD	3.23	2.55	6.46	5.41†

[a] p values are for one-tailed tests.
* $p < .05$.
** $p < .01$.
† $p < .005$.

possible to construct tasks in varying sensory modalities which may be deemed equal in difficulty. We have no way of telling whether the visual tasks were comparable to the gustatory tasks. Of course, it would be possible to systematically eliminate items here and add items there until a series of tasks is evolved on which a criterion population would exhibit equal competence from task area to task area and having established such a scale, administer it to various preselected populations. But we believe that this would be begging the question, for we still would not know whether the tasks were comparable; we would only know that a given population obtained identical scores on all tasks. We therefore decided not to concentrate so much on the development of items of illusory comparability in difficulty but much more upon the investigation of differences between groups on various types of tasks and the question of whether these differences would vary in accordance with certain theoretical propositions. Our focus of inquiry was in this direction and we conclude that the closed and dogmatic person appears estranged or alienated from his sensory impressions and this estrangement is more significantly observable in the predominantly autocentric modalities than in those modalities which lend themselves more readily to what Schachtel has called "objectification."

Our data suggest two additional observations and comments. First of all they tend to make one doubt the frequently made assertion that there exists an inherent contradiction between the so-called "objective" and "subjective" approaches to experience. On the contrary, our low dogmatic individuals did not only perform in superior fashion on the predominantly allocentric tasks but also on the predominantly autocentric test items, and vice versa, the highly dogmatic, while doing almost as well as the low dogmatic on the allocentric items, did a remarkably inferior job on the autocentric procedures. In other words closed-mindedness and open-mindedness are not phenomena which appear in some areas of an individual's living and not in others, but much more they are pervasive phenomena, the close-minded is not only closed-minded vis-a-vis personal and highly autocentric experience, he is also close-minded vis-a-vis objectifiable stimulation. Conversely, the open-minded person exhibits this orientation vis-a-vis both autocentric experience and objectifiable data. As a matter of fact the idea suggests itself pointedly that the very openness to experience which makes it possible for a person to be *au courant* with his sensations also enables him to adequately objectify such sensory impressions. And this openness to sense impressions apparently runs parallel to openness to ideas, willingness to examine them critically, and careful analysis of thought. This should not be too surprising for the history of man and civilization is replete with incidents and examples in which those who have contributed most significantly in one area have also shown themselves open to the pursuit of other seemingly opposite endeavors. Leading scientists have been remarkably receptive to aesthetic experience, eager to follow fantastic intuitive hunches, and have exhibited genuine interest in humanistic intellectual pursuits; humanistic intellectuals and men prominent in creative artistic endeavors have exhibited astounding interest and insight in matters scientific. The "two cultures" which Snow (1959) is fond of talking about may not be as remote from each other as one might suspect for genuine involvement in either may very well require a personal quality essential for both.

Furthermore, if neurosis is viewed as dogmatism of sorts, i.e., a restriction of horizons and rigidification along certain lines, these particular lines depending upon the theoretical bent of an author, then our results are highly supportive of the hypothesis that estrangement or alienation is markedly associated with such rigidification, be this association causal, concurrent, or resultant. The design of the present study throws little light upon this question of sequence. We can only speculate and suggest that the observation that the autocentric modalities which appear in human development more prominently at early stages do not lend themselves to the type of objectification our culture demands in order to "get along." It is readily conceivable that such cultural demands bring in their wake a more or less dogmatic orientation towards existing, an orientation which, as we have shown, also entails sensory alienation. Further research bearing upon this sequential issue is sorely needed.

REFERENCES

Breuer, J., & Freud, S. *Studies on hysteria.* New York: Basic Books, 1957.

Fromm, E. *Escape from freedom.* New York: Farrar & Rinehart, 1941.

Fromm, E. *The sane society.* New York: Rinehart, 1955.

Fromm, E. *Marx's concept of man.* New York: Frederick Ungar, 1961.

Rokeach, M. *The open and closed mind.* New York: Basic Books, 1960.

Schachtel, E. The dynamic perception of the symbolism of form. *Psychiatry,* 4, 1941, 79–96.

Schachtel, E. *Metamorphosis.* New York: Basic Books, 1959.

Snow, C. P. *The two cultures and the scientific revolution.* New York: Cambridge University Press, 1959.

Woodworth, R. S. *Experimental psychology.* New York: Holt, 1958.

6. Culture and neurosis

KAREN HORNEY

IN THE PSYCHOANALYTIC CONCEPT OF NEUROSES a shift of emphasis has taken place: whereas originally interest was focussed on the dramatic symptomatic picture, it is now being realized more and more that the real source of these psychic disorders lies in character disturbances, that the symptoms are a manifest result of conflicting character traits and that without uncovering and straightening out the neurotic character structure we cannot cure a neurosis. When analyzing these character traits, in a great many cases one is struck by the observation that, in marked contrast to the divergency of the symptomatic pictures, character difficulties invariably center around the same basic conflicts.

These similarities in the content of conflicts present a problem. They suggest to minds open to the importance of cultural implications, the question of whether and to what extent neuroses are moulded by cultural processes in essentially the same way as "normal" character formation is determined by these influences; and, if so, how far such a concept would necessitate certain modifications in Freud's views of the relation between culture and neurosis.

In the following remarks I shall try to outline roughly some characteristics typically recurring in all our neuroses. The limitations of time will allow us to present neither data—good case histories—nor method, but only results. I shall try to select from the extremely complex and diversified observational material the essential points.

There is another difficulty in the presentation. I wish to show how these neurotic persons are

SOURCE. Article by Karen Horney, "Culture and neurosis" in *American sociological Review*, Vol. 1, pp. 221–230, 1936.

trapped in a vicious circle. Unable to present in detail factors leading up to the vicious circle, I must start rather arbitrarily with one of the outstanding features, although this in itself is already a complex product of several interrelated, developed mental factors. I start, therefore, with the problem of competition.

The problem of competition, or rivalry, appears to be a never-failing center of neurotic conflicts. How to deal with competition presents a problem for everyone in our culture; for the neurotic, however, it assumes dimensions which generally surpass actual vicissitudes. It does so in three respects:

(1) There is a constant measuring-up with others, even in situations which do not call for it. While striving to surpass others is essential for all competitive situations, the neurotic measures up even with persons who are in no way potential competitors and have no goal in common with him. The question as to who is the more intelligent, more attractive, more popular, is indiscriminately applied towards everyone.

(2) The content of neurotic ambitions is not only to accomplish something worth while, or to be successful, but to be absolutely best of all. These ambitions, however, exist in fantasy mainly—fantasies which may or may not be conscious. The degree of awareness differs widely in different persons. The ambitions may appear in occasional flashes of fantasy only. There is never a clear realization of the powerful dramatic role these ambitions play in the neurotic's life, or of the great part they have in accounting for his behavior and mental reactions. The challenge of these ambitions is not met by adequate efforts which might lead to realization of the aims. They are in queer contrast to existing inhibitions towards work, towards assuming leadership, towards all means which would ef-

fectually secure success. There are many ways in which these fantastic ambitions influence the emotional lives of the persons concerned: by hypersensitivity to criticism, by depressions or inhibitions following failures, etc. These failures need not necessarily be real. Everything which falls short of the realization of the grandiose ambitions is felt as failure. The success of another person is felt as one's own failure.

This competitive attitude not only exists in reference to the external world, but is also internalized, and appears as a constant measuring-up to an ego-ideal. The fantastic ambitions appear on this score as excessive and rigid demands towards the self, and failure in living up to these demands produces depressions and irritations similar to those produced in competition with others.

(3) The third characteristic is the amount of hostility involved in neurotic ambition. While intense competition implicitly contains elements of hostility—the defeat of a competitor meaning victory for oneself, the reactions of neurotic persons are determined by an insatiable and irrational expectation that no one in the universe other than themselves should be intelligent, influential, attractive, or popular. They become infuriated, or feel their own endeavors condemned to futility, if someone else writes a good play or a scientific paper or plays a prominent role in society. If this attitude is strongly accentuated, one may observe in the analytical situation, for example, that these patients regard any progress made as a victory on the part of the analyst, completely disregarding the fact that progress is of vital concern to their own interests. In such situations they will disparage the analyst, betraying, by the intense hostility displayed, that they feel endangered in a position of paramount importance to themselves. They are as a rule completely unaware of the existence and intensity of this "no one but me" attitude, but one may safely assume and eventually always uncover this attitude from reactions observable in the analytical situation, as indicated above.

This attitude easily leads to a fear of retaliation. It results in a fear of success and also in a fear of failure: "If I want to crush everyone who is successful, then I will automatically assume identical reactions in others, so that the way to success implies exposing me to the hostility of others. Furthermore: if I make any move to-

wards this goal and fail, then I shall be crushed." Success thus becomes a peril and any possible failure becomes a danger which must at all costs be avoided. From the point of view of all these dangers it appears much safer to stay in the corner, be modest and inconspicuous. In other and more positive terms, this fear leads to a definite recoiling from any aim which implies competition. This safety device is assured by a constant, accurately working process of automatic self-checking.

This self-checking process results in inhibitions, particularly inhibitions towards work, but also towards all steps necessary to the pursuit of one's aims, such as seizing opportunities, or revealing to others that one has certain goals or capacities. This eventually results in an incapacity to stand up for one's wishes. The peculiar nature of these inhibitions is best demonstrated by the fact that these persons may be quite capable of fighting for the needs of others or for an impersonal cause. They will, for instance, act like this:

When playing an instrument with a poor partner, they will instinctively play worse than he, although otherwise they may be very competent. When discussing a subject with someone less intelligent than themselves, they will compulsively descend below his level. They will prefer to be in the rank and file, not to be identified with the superiors, not even to get an increase in salary, rationalizing this attitude in some way. Even their dreams will be dictated by this need for reassurance. Instead of utilizing the liberty of a dream to imagine themselves in glorious situations, they will actually see themselves, in their dreams, in humble or even humiliating situations.

This self-checking process does not restrict itself to activities in the pursuit of some aim, but going beyond that, tends to undermine the self-confidence, which is a prerequisite for any accomplishment, by means of self-belittling. The function of self-belittling in this context is to eliminate oneself from any competition. In most cases these persons are not aware of actually disparaging themselves, but are aware of the results only as they feel themselves inferior to others and take for granted their own inadequacy.

The presence of these feelings of inferiority is one of the most common psychic disorders of our time and culture. Let me say a few more words about them. The genesis of inferiority feelings is not always in neurotic competition. They present complex phenomena and may be determined by various conditions. But that they do result from, and stand in the service of, a recoiling from competition, is a basic and ever-present implication. They result from a recoiling inasmuch as they are the expression of a discrepancy between high pitched ideals and real accomplishment. The fact, however, that these painful feelings at the same time fulfill the important function of making secure the recoiling attitude itself, becomes evident through the vigor with which this position is defended when attacked. Not only will no evidence of competence or attractiveness ever convince these persons, but they may actually become scared or angered by any attempt to convince them of their positive qualities.

The surface pictures resulting from this situation may be widely divergent. Some persons appear thoroughly convinced of their unique importance and may be anxious to demonstrate their superiority on every occasion, but betray their insecurity in an excessive sensitivity to every criticism, to every dissenting opinion, or every lack of responsive admiration. Others are just as thoroughly convinced of their incompetence or unworthiness, or of being unwanted or unappreciated; yet they betray their actually great demands in that they react with open or concealed hostility to every frustration of their unacknowledged demands. Still others will waver constantly in their self-estimation between feeling themselves all-important and feeling, for instance, honestly amazed that anyone pays any attention to them.

If you have followed me thus far, I can now proceed to outline the particular vicious circle in which these persons are moving. It is important here, as in every complex neurotic picture, to recognize the vicious circle, because, if we overlook it and simplify the complexity of the processes going on by assuming a simple cause-effect relation, we either fail to get an understanding of the emotions involved, or attribute an undue importance to some one cause. As an example of this error, I might mention regarding a highly emotion-charged rivalry attitude as derived directly from rivalry with the father. Roughly, the vicious circle looks like this:

The failures, in conjunction with a feeling of weakness and defeat, lead to a feeling of envy towards all persons who are more successful, or merely more secure or better contented with life. This envy may be manifest or it may be repressed under the pressure of the same anxiety which led to a repression of, and a recoiling from, rivalry. It may be entirely wiped out of consciousness and represented by the substitution of a blind admiration; it may be kept from awareness by a disparaging attitude towards the person concerned. Its effect, however, is apparent in the incapacity to grant to others what one has been forced to deny himself. At any rate, no matter to what degree the envy is repressed or expressed, it implies an increase in the existing hostility against people and consequently an increase in the anxiety, which now takes the particular form of an irrational fear of the envy of others.

The irrational nature of this fear is shown in two ways: (1) it exists regardless of the presence or absence of envy in the given situation; and (2) its intensity is out of proportion to the dangers menacing from the side of the envious competitors. This irrational side of the fear of envy always remains unconscious, at least in non-psychotic persons, therefore it is never corrected by a reality-testing process, and is all the more effective in the direction of reinforcing the existing tendencies to recoil.

Consequently the feeling of own insignificance grows, the hostility against people grows, and the anxiety grows. We thus return to the beginning, because now the fantasies come up, with about this content: "I wish I were more powerful, more attractive, more intelligent than all the others, then I should be safe, and besides, I could defeat them and step on them." Thus we see an ever-increasing deviation of the ambitions towards the stringent, fantastic, and hostile.

This pyramiding process may come to a standstill under various conditions, usually at an inordinate expense in loss of expansiveness and vitality. There is often some sort of resignation as to personal ambitions, in turn permitting the diminution of anxieties as to competition, with the inferiority feelings and inhibitions continuing.

It is now time, however, to make a reservation. It is in no way self-evident that ambition of the "no-one-but-me" type must necessarily evoke anxieties. There are persons quite capable of brushing aside or crushing everyone in the way of their ruthless pursuit of personal power.

The question then is: Under what special condition is anxiety invoked in neurotically competitive people?

The answer is that they at the same time want to be loved. While most persons who pursue an asocial ambition in life care little for the affection or the opinion of others, the neurotics, although possessed by the same kind of competitiveness, simultaneously have a boundless craving for affection and appreciation. Therefore, as soon as they make any move towards self-assertion, competition, or success, they begin to dread losing the affection of others, and must automatically check their aggressive impulses. This conflict between ambition and affection is one of the gravest and most typical dilemmas of the neurotics of our time.

Why are these two incompatible strivings so frequently present in the same individual? They are related to each other in more than one way. The briefest formulation of this relationship would perhaps be that they both grow out of the same sources, namely, anxieties, and they both serve as a means of reassurance against the anxieties. Power and affection may both be safeguards. They generate each other, check each other, and reinforce each other. These interrelations can be observed most accurately within the analytic situation, but sometimes are obvious from only a casual knowledge of the life history.

In the life history may be found, for instance, an atmosphere in childhood lacking in warmth and reliability, but rife with frightening elements—battles between the parents, injustice, cruelty, over-solicitousness—generation of an increased need for affection—disappointments—development of an outspoken competitiveness—inhibition—attempts to get affection on the basis of weakness, helplessness, or suffering. We sometimes hear that a youngster has suddenly turned to ambition after an acute disappointment in his need for affection, and then given up the ambition on falling in love.

Particularly when the expansive and aggressive desires have been severely curbed in early life by a forbidding atmosphere, the excessive need for reassuring affection will play a major role. As a guiding principle for behavior this implies a yielding to the wishes or opinions of others rather than asserting one's own wishes or opinions; an overvaluation of the significance for one's own life of expressions of fondness

from others, and a dependence on such expressions. And similarly, it implies an overvaluation of signs of rejection and a reacting to such signs with apprehension and defensive hostility. Here again a vicious circle begins easily and reinforces the single elements: In diagram it looks somewhat like this:

Anxiety plus repressed hostility
   Need for reassuring affection
      Anticipation of, sensitivity to, rejection
         Hostile reactions to feeling rejected

These reactions explain why emotional contact with others that is attained on the basis of anxiety can be at best only a very shaky and easily shattered bridge between individuals, and why it always fails to bring them out of their emotional isolation. It may, however, serve to cope with anxieties and even get one through life rather smoothly, but only at the expense of growth and personality development, and only if circumstances are quite favorable.

Let us ask now, which special features in our culture may be responsible for the frequent occurrence of the neurotic structures just described?

We live in a competitive, individualistic culture. Whether the enormous economic and technical achievements of our culture were and are possible only on the basis of the competitive principle is a question for the economist or sociologist to decide. The psychologist, however, can evaluate the personal price we have paid for it.

It must be kept in mind that competition not only is a driving force in economic activities, but that it also pervades our personal life in every respect. The character of all our human relationships is moulded by a more or less outspoken competition. It is effective in the family between siblings, at school, in social relations (keeping up with the Joneses), and in love life.

In love, it may show itself in two ways: the genuine erotic wish is often overshadowed or replaced by the merely competitive goal of being the most popular, having the most dates, love letters, lovers, being seen with the most desirable man or woman. Again, it may pervade the love relationship itself. Marriage partners, for example, may be living in an endless struggle for supremacy, with or without being aware of the nature or even of the existence of this combat.

The influence on human relations of this competitiveness lies in the fact that it creates easily aroused envy towards the stronger ones, contempt for the weaker, distrust towards everyone. In consequence of all these potentially hostile tensions, the satisfaction and reassurance which one can get out of human relations are limited and the individual becomes more or less emotionally isolated. It seems that here, too, mutually reinforcing interactions take place, so far as insecurity and dissatisfaction in human relations in turn compel people to seek gratification and security in ambitious strivings, and vice versa.

Another cultural factor relevant to the structure of our neurosis lies in our attitude towards failure and success. We are inclined to attribute success to good personal qualities and capacities, such as competence, courage, enterprise. In religious terms this attitude was expressed by saying that success was due to God's grace. While these qualities may be effective—and in certain periods, such as the pioneer days, may have represented the only conditions necessary—this ideology omits two essential facts: (1) that the possibility for success is strictly limited; even external conditions and personal qualities being equal, only a comparative few can possibly attain success; and (2) that other factors than those mentioned may play the decisive role, such as, for example, unscrupulousness or fortuitous circumstances. Inasmuch as these factors are overlooked in the general evaluation of success, failures, besides putting the person concerned in a factually disadvantageous position, are bound to reflect on his self-esteem.

The confusion involved in this situation is enhanced by a sort of double moral. Although, in fact, success meets with adoration almost without regard to the means employed in securing it, we are at the same time taught to regard modesty and an undemanding, unselfish attitude as social or religious virtues, and are rewarded for them by praise and affection. The particular difficulties which confront the individual in our culture may be summarized as follows: for the competitive struggle he needs a certain amount of available aggressiveness; at the same time, he is required to be modest, unselfish, even self-sacrificing. While the competitive life situation with the hostile tensions involved in it creates an enhanced need of security, the chances of attaining a feeling of safety in human relations—love, friendship, social contacts—are at the same time diminished. The estimation of one's personal value is all too dependent on the degree of success attained, while at the same time the possibilities for success are limited and the success itself is dependent, to a great extent, on fortuitous circumstances or on personal qualities of an asocial character.

Perhaps these sketchy comments have suggested to you the direction in which to explore the actual relationship of our culture to our personality and its neurotic deviations. Let us now consider the relation of this conception to the views of Freud on culture and neurosis.

The essence of Freud's views on this subject can be summarized, briefly, as follows: Culture is the result of a sublimation of biologically given sexual and aggressive drives—"sexual" in the extended connotation Freud has given the term. Sublimation presupposes unwitting suppression of these instinctual drives. The more complete the suppression of these drives, the higher the cultural development. As the capacity for sublimating is limited, and as the intensive suppression of primitive drives without sublimation may lead to neurosis, the growth of civilization must inevitably imply a growth of neurosis. Neuroses are the price humanity has to pay for cultural development.

The implicit theoretical presupposition underlying this train of thought is the belief in the existence of biologically determined human nature, or, more precisely, the belief that oral, anal, genital, and aggressive drives exist in all human beings in approximately equal quantities.[1] Variations in character formation from individual to individual, as from culture to culture, are due, then, to the varying intensity of the suppression required, with the addition that this suppression can affect the different kinds of drives in varying degrees.

This viewpoint of Freud's seems actually to encounter difficulties with two groups of data. (1) Historical and anthropological findings[2] do not support the assumption that the growth of

---

[1] I pass over Freud's recognition of individual constitutional difference.

[2] Ruth Benedict, *Patterns of Culture;* Margaret Mead, *Sex and Temperament in Three Savage Societies.*

civilization is in a direct ratio to the growth of instinct suppression. (2) Clinical experience of the kind indicated in this paper suggests that neurosis is due not simply to the quantity of suppression of one or the other instinctual drives, but rather to difficulties caused by the conflicting character of the demands which a culture imposes on its individuals. The differences in neuroses typical of different cultures may be understood to be conditioned by the amount and quality of conflicting demands within the particular culture.

In a given culture, those persons are likely to become neurotic who have met these culturally determined difficulties in accentuated form, mostly through the medium of childhood experiences; and who have not been able to solve their difficulties, or have solved them only at great expense to personality.

7. Malevolence, hatred, and isolating techniques

HARRY STACK SULLIVAN

Required Behavior and the Necessity to Conceal and Deceive

I NOW WANT TO DISCUSS FURTHER the very interesting phenomenon of one's becoming malevolent, and we will see if we can approach a consensus. The gross pattern of a great many things that happen in childhood, as compared with the infantile phase of personality, includes two conspicuous elements. One, as has been emphasized, is the acquisition of not only private but communicative language, with the great returns which the learning of this vitally important human tool always carries with it. But the second element, so far as actual development of interpersonal relations goes, is the more significant difference between the two epochs; it can be stated in terms of required behavior. At birth the infant can do practically nothing to assure his own survival. During infancy, he learns only the grossest culture patterns about zonal and general needs. But throughout the era of childhood there is an increasing demand for his cooperation. The child is expected to do things which are brought to his attention or impressed on him as requirements for action, by the authority-carrying environment—the mother, increasingly the father, and perhaps miscellaneous siblings, servants, and what not.

In childhood—in contradistinction to at least the first two-thirds of the infantile period, and, one rather hopes, the whole infantile period—a new educative influence, *fear*, is brought to bear; we touched on this earlier, but we have not given it very much attention, since it has not so far had remarkable significance with respect to personality development. The discrimination between fear and anxiety is a vital one. Very severe fear and very severe anxiety, so far as I know, feel the same—that is, the felt component is identical—but the discrimination between these two powerful disjunctive processes in life is at times vital. Anxiety is something which I believe is acquired by an empathic linkage with the significant older persons, whereas fear is that which appears when the satisfaction of general needs is deferred to the point where these needs become very powerful. And of these general needs, the need which we particularly want to deal with here is the need to be free from painful sensations. Pain is here defined, not figuratively, but in its most obvious central meaning, hurt—that which occurs, for instance, as a result of sufficient pressure on, or incision into, the actual physical organization, or from misadventures in the internal function of some of the vital organs.

In childhood, perhaps not universally nowadays, but still with great frequency in almost all cultures I think, the child, in contradistinction to the infant, is presumed, at certain times, to deserve or require punishment; and the punishment I am talking about is the infliction of pain. Such punishment can be practically free from anxiety, or it can be strongly blended with anxiety. A parent who very methodically feels that a certain breach of the rules calls for a certain more or less specified form and amount of pain can administer it with no particular anxiety, although possibly with some regret, or possibly with singular neutral feelings as one might have in training a pet. Many parents, however, for a variety of reasons subject the child to anxiety as well as pain. But insofar as punishment, the causing of pain, is used in its

SOURCE. Harry Stack Sullivan, "Malevolence, hatred, and isolating techniques" in *The Interpersonal Theory of Psychiatry*. Edited by Helen Swick Perry and Mary Ladd Gawell. New York: Norton, 1953. Copyright held by W. A. White Psychiatric Fund.

own right as an educative influence, this means a new type of learning—namely, learning enforced by a growing discrimination of the connection between certain violations of imposed authority and pain.

Frequently the child is subjected to punishment—pain with or without anxiety, but almost always with anxiety in this case—where he could have foreseen it except that the pressure of a need, zonal or otherwise, made the foresight ineffective in preventing the behavior. In a much more significant, although necessarily quite infrequent, group of circumstances, there comes punishment—pain with, almost invariably in this case, plenty of anxiety—under circumstances which are such that the child could not possibly have foreseen such an outcome from the behavior. This is particularly likely to happen with irritable, ill-tempered parents who are afflicted by many anxiety-producing circumstances in their own lives, and who tend rather strikingly to take it out on the dog or the child or what not.

Thus we see in childhood a new educative influence which shows up very definitely as actual fear of the capacity of the authority-carrying figure to impose pain. It is a peculiarity of the difference between anxiety and fear that, under fortunate circumstances, the factors in the situation in which one was hurt can be observed, analyzed, identified, and incorporated in foresight for the future, while in the case of anxiety that is only relatively true, at best; and if anxiety is very severe, it has, as I have said before, almost the effect of a blow on the head. Thus one has very little data on which to work in the future—we might almost say there is nothing in particular to be elaborated into information and foresight.

In childhood, the increased effort of the parents to teach, to discharge their social responsibility, and—I regret to say—to discharge a good many of the more unfortunate peculiarities of their personality produces, in many cases, a child who is "obedient" or a child who is "rebellious," and this outcome may appear fairly early. Of course the pattern may alternate in the same child, and have a very definite relationship to the existent personifications of good-me and bad-me; in reasonably healthy circumstances, good-me tends fairly definitely to be associated with obedience—but still with a considerable measure of freedom to play and so on

—and rebelliousness tends to be part of the personification of bad-me.

In this stage of development—when the parents are making increasing efforts to teach the child, when his abilities are maturing, and when he is organizing past experiences and exercising his fantasy, his covert processes in play and make-believe—there is invariably, from very early, a beginning discrimination by the child among the authority-carrying figures, and later, but still quite early, a beginning discrimination of authority situations. In other words, almost all children learn certain indices that stand them in reasonably good stead as to when it is extremely unsafe to violate authority and when there is some chance of "getting away with it." This is, I think, a healthy discrimination which provides useful data, although under certain circumstances, of course, when the parental figures are overloaded with inappropriate and inadequate ways of life, it can be very unfortunate in the way of experience for later life. As the presumed relationship of more-or-less complete dependence of the infant on the mothering one is suspended and the father gets more and more significant, this discrimination by the child of different authority figures and authority situations, insofar as it succeeds—that is, gives information that proves reasonably dependable in foreseeing the course of events—contributes definitely to the growth of and importance of foresight in interpersonal relations. But insofar as the authority figures are confusing to the child and insofar as the authority situations are incongruous from time to time so that, according to the measure of the child's maturing abilities and experience, there is no making sense of them—then, even before the end of the thirtieth month, let us say, we see instances in which the child is already beginning to suffer a deterioration of development of high-grade foresight. In such cases it is quite probable that, in later stages of development, conscious exercise of foresight, witting study of how to get to a more-or-less recognized goal, will not be very highly developed.

Among the things that almost always attend the training of the child to take part in living, to "cooperate" with the parent, to carry out instructions, to do chores and so on, is very frequently the imposition on the child of the concepts of duties and responsibilities. That is certainly good preparation for life in a social order; but again in cases where the parents are uninformed or suffering from unfortunate peculiarities of personality, this training in concepts and responsibilities includes as a very important adjunct (adulterant perhaps) a great deal of training—that is, experience which is presumed, erroneously I think in a great many cases, to be educational—in which the idea of *ought* is very conspicuous.

When it comes to putting into words an adequate statement of the cultural prescriptions which are generally required in the socialization of the young, one really is confronted by a task which requires most remarkable genius. Had culture grown as the work of a single person or a small group of greatly gifted people, almost crushed under their responsibilty for their fellow man, then it is quite possible that one could build up a great structure of statements of what principles govern under all sorts of situations, and the result would be a coherent and rationally understandable social system. But that has been nowhere on earth, that I know of, very strikingly the case; possibly the nearest approach to such a social order is to be found in the regimented groups which have characterized various people at various times. For example, there is at least an attempt to embody often subtly contradictory requirements in such things as army regulations; but people who are really diligent students of army regulations frequently discover that it requires only a minor effort to discover a little conflict in authority, and such a conflict provides room for interpreting a situation according to which of the conflicting authoritative statements apply. But, as I was saying, such regulations do provide a rough approximation to this ideal of a rational culture, in that pretty ingenious people, many of them actively interested in maintaining the peculiar social organization of the military, have done their damndest to put plain statements of *ought* and *must* into words which could be understood by the comparatively uninitiated.

But when it comes to imposing the prescriptions of the culture on the child, these prescriptions are often most glaringly contradictory on different occasions, so that they require complex discrimination of authority situations. Moreover the child is incapable for a good many years of comprehending the prescriptions in terms of their possible reasonableness. And more important than anything else, out of the irrational and impulse-driven type of education by anxiety, and by reward and punishment—that is, tenderness and fear—a great many children quite early begin to develop the ability to conceal what is going on in them, what actually they have been doing behind someone's back, and thus to deceive the authoritative figures. Some of this ability to conceal and to deceive is literally taught by the authority-carrying figures, and some of it represents trial-and-error learning from human example—that is, by observing and analyzing the performances, the successes and failures, of siblings, servants, and the like.

Verbalisms and "As If" Performances

Now these growing abilities to conceal and to deceive tend very early to fall into two of the important patterns of inadequate and inappropriate behavior—considered from the broad point of view—which become troublesome in later life and get themselves called mental disorders or processes in mental disorder. I hope that I have communicated by this time a very firm conviction that no pattern of mental disorder which is purely functional, as it is called— that is, which is an inadequate and inappropriate way of living with other people and with one's personifications—includes anything which is at all novel as to human equipment. Everything that we see in the symptomatology of these nonorganic—that is, nondefect—situations has its reflection in kind, if not in degree, in the developmental history of every one of us. And so, when we get to, let us say, mid-childhood, it is not uncommon to discover that the child has become fairly skillful at concealing what might otherwise bring anxiety or punishment—at deceiving the authority-carrying figures as to the degree or nature of his compliance with their more-or-less recognized demands.

The first of these two patterns we touched on previously—namely, verbalisms which are often called rationalizations, in which a plausible series of words is offered, regardless of its actual, remarkable irrelevancy, which has power to spare one anxiety or punishment. The degree to which verbalisms constitute elements in inadequate and inappropriate living which we call mental disorder, whether mild or severe, is truly remarkable. If you think that this is not a very powerful tool, you overlook its amazing significance in the service of the self-system, in the very striking characteristic of the self-system which makes favorable change so difficult—namely, the self-system's tendency to escape from experience not congruent to its current directions.

But the second pattern is even more impressive than verbalisms: it is the unfortunate—in the sense of being concealing and deceptive—learning of the value of *as if* performances. There are two grand divisions of these. One of them, far from being necessarily troublesome in personality development, is an absolutely inevitable part of everybody's maturing through childhood; and this is the group which perhaps may be called *dramatizations*. A great deal of the learning which the child achieves is on the basis of human examples, and these examples are at this phase authority-invested. The child will inevitably learn in this fashion a good deal about the mother, and, as the father personification becomes more conspicuous, about the father; and this trial-and-error learning by human example can be observed in the child's playing at *acting-like* and *sounding-like* the seniors concerned, and, in fact, playing at *being* them. Probably the progression literally is that one tries first to *act like* and one tries then to act *as if one were*.

In the earlier half of childhood, this inevitable part of one's learning to be a human being becomes a rather serious concern—in terms of what may show up later—only when these dramatizations become particularly significant in concealing violations of cooperation and in deceiving the authority-invested figures. In these latter cases, for a variety of reasons, some of which we will touch on briefly, these dramatizations tend to become what I could perhaps safely call sub-personifications. The roles which are acted in this way that succeed in avoiding anxiety and punishment, or that perhaps bring tenderness when there was no performance based on previous experience to get tenderness, are organized to the degree that I think we can properly call them *personae;* they are often multiple, and each one later on will be found equally entitled to be called *1*. To describe this type of deviation from the ideal personality development, I long since set up the conception of me-you patterns, by which I mean often grossly incongruent ways of behaving, or roles that one plays, in interpersonal relations with someone else. And all of them, or most of them,

seem just as near the real thing—the personification of the self—as can be, although there is no more making sense of them from the standpoint of their representing different aspects of durable traits than there is of translating Sanskrit before you understand language. While these dramatizations are very closely related to learning to be human, they can even in these early days begin to introduce a very strikingly irrational element in the personification of the self.

The other group of these *as if* performances to which I wish to refer is perhaps best considered under the rubric of *preoccupations*. I would like to say a few words about one of my cocker spaniels, because it perhaps makes the point better than anything else I can think of now. This particular dog has always been the most diminutive in a litter of six; she has been kept with two others in this litter to the present time. The two others are a rather large male and a very shrewd and, shall I say, domineering female. The little bitch whom I am attempting to discuss was quite often the butt of the unquestionably painful vigor of the male and the unquestionably clever domineering of the female. Probably as a result of this, this little dog very conspicuously indeed took to remaining apart from her brother and sister, and could be observed very diligently digging great holes and trenches in the environment. This was literally quite a complex performance, in that each scoop of dirt that was flung out between her hind legs had to be examined carefully lest it contain something edible or otherwise interesting; the little dog would dig furiously in one of these mammoth excavations, rush around, examine the dirt thrown out, go down and get another shovel full—a tremendous activity for literally hours at a time. Somehow there seemed to be a stipulation that as long as she was so hard at work, the other two would leave her alone most of the time. But time has passed; she has been rescued from her unhappy submersion in the bigger siblings; and nowadays she treats them very roughly when she meets them. Now the trash man is outstanding around our place as a stimulus for provoking fear in the dogs—they are all quite upset when he shows up and to some extent are afraid of the mammoth truck and the din and so on that goes on about it. But when he is around, this little dog, alone out of the whole family, goes out and barks furiously at him. But she stops, after almost every third bark, to dig frantically, and to rush around and examine the dirt again, and then she goes back and roars furiously at him again. It is not, I think, too much to infer that this dog is really very timid, having had excellent reasons for being afraid in the past, but that she became so accustomed to being saved in the past by being preoccupied with her digging that the excess of fear in this situation leads to the reappearance of her preoccupation with digging.

In the human being, preoccupation as a way of dealing with fear-provoking situations or the threat of punishment, and of avoiding or minimizing anxiety appears quite early in life. And quite often the irrational and, shall I say, emotional way in which parental authority is imposed on the child, teaches the child that preoccupation with some particular onetime interesting and probably, as it turns out, profitable activity is very valuable to continue, not because it is any longer needed for the maturation of abilities or for satisfaction in new abilities, but as a preoccupation to ward off punishment and anxiety. Now if these performances are not only successful in avoiding unpleasantness, but also get positive reward by the child's being treated tenderly and approved, that naturally sets him on what will later be a strikingly complex way of life—that to which we refer as the *obsessional*.

Anger and Resentment

I have touched previously on learning by doing certain things in play *like* mother or *like* father, and by playing at *being* mother and father. There is one particular phase of this type of learning which is very evident in our ordinary contact with our fellow being, as well as in the psychiatrist's contact with the patient or vice versa. This is learning, from authority figures, a peculiar way of avoiding or neutralizing a fear-provoking situation. You may remember that earlier we spoke of how behavior that could be called, generically, rage behavior arose even in the extremely young when certain types of physical restraint were imposed which produced terror, particularly restraint that might interfere with the breathing movements. Now in punishment situations where pain is to be inflicted, there is invariably an element of restraint of freedom of movement—a particularly deliberate attempt on the part of the

punishing person to interfere with the child's escaping the actual physically enforced pain. This, I believe, would, in any very young child who had missed disastrous experience up to then, lead to a movement in the general direction of such fear that rage behavior would be called out. But rage behavior doesn't have any particular value in this situation. And so, since the possibility of analysis and discrimination, and the exercise of foresight are already fairly well under way by now, instead of rage itself occurring as a frequent eventuality, what might be described as a version of its felt component —namely, anger—comes to be quite important. Especially in circumstances in which children are punished by an angry parent—but in all cases sooner or later, if only from improving discrimination of the progression of forbidding gestures in the authority-invested adults—everyone learns the peculiar utility of anger; I think that this statement is probably precisely true, although some people also learn that anger itself can bring a great deal of punitive treatment. But children invariably—or so nearly invariably that we don't need to pay a vast deal of attention to the exceptions—in their play are angry with their toys; and later they are angry with their imaginary companions. And the patterns of the child's being angry, the circumstances when it is suitable, and so on, are pretty much profits from his experience with the authority-carrying adults among whom he lives; what the child tends to show, in general, is that his toy, or whatever, has violated his authority in connection with the business of his *being* mother or *being* father. From this beginning, almost everyone—at least almost all the more fortunate of the denizens of our world—come to use anger very facilely, very frequently; and they use it when they would otherwise be anxious. In other words, it comes to be the process called out by mild degrees of anxiety in a truly remarkable number of people. But when one is around the age of thirty months, it may or may not be that one is well trained in the use of anger with the authority-carrying adults; in the more unhappy parental situations, one does not get very much encouragement that way, in partial result of which it comes about that in certain unhappy homes, children well into the school years have tantrums, which are in essence unmodified rage behavior.

In a great many other unfortunate homes children develop a complex modification of this rather simple use of anger. This more complex modification is the classical outcome of a situation in which the child is going on his way perfectly all right, so far as he can see, whereupon punishment, almost always with anxiety, is discharged upon the child for activity the forbidden aspect of which could not have been foreseen by the child—where there is no possibility of his understanding what the punishment is for. Or the punishment may be for activity so attractive that the possibility of punishment, even though foreseen, was ignored. In those circumstances, a great many children learn that anger will aggravate the situation, and they develop what we properly call *resentment*. Thus resentment is the name of the felt aspect of rather complex processes which, if expressed more directly, would have led to the repressive use of authority; in this way resentment tends to have very important covert aspects. In the most awkward type of home situation, these covert processes are complicated by efforts to conceal even the resentment, lest one be further punished; and concealing resentment is, for reasons I can't touch on now, one of our first very remarkable processes of the group underlying the rather barbarously named "psychosomatic" field. In other words, in the concealing of resentment, and in the gradual development of self-system processes which preclude one's knowing one's resentment, one actually has to make use of distribution of tension in a fashion quite different from anything that we have touched on thus far. And these processes, which have nothing to do with activity such as a tantrum or something of that kind, are utilized for getting rid of tension so as to avoid activity which would otherwise be revealing, be noticed, and bring punishment.

The Malevolent Transformation

All these generalities about childhood acculturation are background for the circumstances under which the child develops in the direction, not of being obedient or being rebellious, but of being malevolent. Now the ways that malevolence shows in childhood may be numerous. Thus there are so-called timid children whose malevolence shows by their being so afraid to do anything that they just always fail to do the things that are most urgently de-

sired. The great group is the frankly mischievous, and from there we may progress to the potential bully, who takes it out on some younger member of the family, and on the pets, and so on.

But under what circumstances does so remarkable and, may I say, so ubiquitous a thing as malevolence appear as a major pattern of interpersonal relations in childhood? A great many years of preoccupation with this problem has eventuated in a theory which is calculated to get around the idea that man is essentially evil. One of the great social theories is, you know, that society is the only thing that prevents everybody from tearing everybody to bits; or that man is possessed of something wonderful called sadism. I have not found much support for these theories—that man is essentially a devil, that he has an actual need for being cruel and hurtful to his fellows, and so on—in the study of some of the obscure schizophrenic phenomena. And so as the years passed, my interest in understanding why there is so much deviltry in human living culminated in the observation that if the child had certain kinds of very early experience, this malevolent attitude toward his fellows seemed to be conspicuous. And when the child did not have these particular types of experience, then this malevolent attitude was not a major component.

And the pattern that appeared was approximately this: For a variety of reasons, many children have the experience that when they need tenderness, when they do that which once brought tender cooperation, they are not only denied tenderness, but they are treated in a fashion to provoke anxiety or even, in some cases, pain. A child may discover that manifesting the need for tenderness toward the potent figures around him leads frequently to his being disadvantaged, being made anxious, being made fun of, and so on, so that, according to the locution used, he is hurt, or in some cases he may be literally hurt. Under those circumstances, the developmental course changes to the point that the perceived need for tenderness brings a foresight of anxiety or pain. The child learns, you see, that it is highly disadvantageous to show any need for tender cooperation from the authoritative figures around him, in which case he shows something else; and that something else is the basic malevolent attitude, the attitude that one really lives among enemies—that is about what it amounts to. And on that basis, there come about the remarkable developments which are seen later in life, when the juvenile makes it practically impossible for anyone to feel tenderly toward him or to treat him kindly; he beats them to it, so to speak, by the display of his attitude. And this is the development of the earlier discovery that the manifestation of any need for tenderness, and so on, would bring anxiety or pain. The other elaborations—the malevolence that shows as a basic attitude toward life, you might say, as a profound problem in one's interpersonal relations—are also just an elaboration of this earlier warp.

A start in the direction of malevolent development creates a vicious circle. It is obviously a failure of the parents to discharge their social responsibility to produce a well-behaved, well-socialized person. Therefore, the thing tends to grow more or less geometrically. Quite often the way in which the parents minimize or excuse their failure to socialize the child contributes further to his development of a malevolent attitude toward life—and this is likely to be on the part of the mother, since it is difficult to picture a malevolent transformation's occurring at all if the mother did not play a major part in it. A particularly ugly phase of this is found in cases in which the mother is very hostile toward the father, and has exceedingly little sympathy or satisfaction with him; so from very early in the child's life, she explains the increasingly troublesome character of his behavior, his manifestation of as much malevolence as is safe, by saying that he is just like his father in this particular, or just like his father's younger brother, or something of that kind. While the initial references of this kind communicate very little information, their continuation for long enough does tend to warp the child's personification of himself in the direction of something detestable, to be avoided and so on, thereby making very important contributions to his conviction that he will always be treated thoroughly badly.

And in the long course of development, even more subtly destructive are the instances where malevolence has come about because the mother is malevolent toward the child, in which case quite frequently, from very early, there is a good deal of verbal reference which takes the curious form of saying to aunts, uncles, neighbors, and others, "Yes, he has a bad temper just like me," or, "Yes, he is rebellious just like me." One should keep in mind that the mothering one is bound to be significant in all personality evolutions—she can't be otherwise; now when the child gets so that he doesn't think it safe to live among people because he is just like the person that he has to live with, and he gets punished a lot for it, the situation becomes a bit difficult, to say the least. The question arises: If it is all right for mother, why not for me?

Let me conclude by saying that the general conception of malevolence is of very considerable importance. It is perhaps the greatest disaster that happens in the childhood phase of personality development, because the kind of "ugly"—as it is often called—attitude which it produces is a great handicap to the most profitable experience one could have in subsequent stages of development. It is from the second stage of personality development that a good deal of the foundations of one's attitude toward authoritative figures, superiors, and so on, is laid. So one often learns costly ways of getting around anxiety-provoking and fear-provoking situations—costly in the sense that one never feels exceedingly good or worthy; and these ways of avoiding such situations are not greatly contributory to one's useful information and foresight about living. Thus there can occur this very serious distortion of what might be called the fundamental interpersonal attitude; and this distortion, this malevolence, as it is encountered in life, runs something like this: Once upon a time everything was lovely, but that was before I had to deal with people.

8. The use of the interpersonal system of diagnosis in marital counseling

ROBERT L. ROMANO

MARITAL COUNSELING HAS BEEN DESCRIBED as a special kind of psychotherapy in terms of the aims of the treatment endeavor, and the focus given the marriage interaction during the counseling sessions (Bychowski & Despert, 1952; Gamberg, 1956; Mudd & Kirch, 1957). Most often in practice, both husband and wife are counseled, so that each can be helped to recognize his own perceptual distortions of and inappropriate response to the other. While each marital participant needs to be considered individually from the psychodynamic standpoint, marriage counseling throws special emphasis upon the relationship between husband and wife.

Ailing marriages are most often the result of a mutual failure in "consensual validation." That is to say, husband and wife fail to agree on the interpersonal intent of their own and their spouse's marital behavior. A dependent husband, for example, may seek comfort and support from a wife whom he perceives as nurturant. She, on the other hand, may be in conflict over her own dependency needs and may then view her spouse's request for support as demandingly hostile. She may despise this evidence of his weakness and long for someone whom she, herself, can lean on. However, when the husband attempts to supply her with emotional props and controls, his wife misinterprets his behavior as autocratic and humiliating. A mutual conflict of errors in interpretation ensues.

SOURCE. Article by Robert L. Romano, "The use of the interpersonal system of diagnosis in marital counseling" in *Journal of counseling Psychology*, Vol. 7, No. 1, 1960.

The psychologist who counsels the "neurotic" marital relationship must be able to define the discrepancies that occur in the way each of the partners perceives himself and the other at various levels of awareness as a preliminary to the correction of these interpretive errors. It might be said that a definition of these discrepancies in perception constitutes a diagnosis of the disturbed marriage relationship.

The Interpersonal System of Diagnosis

The interpersonal methodology described at length by Leary (1957) and others (Freedman, Leary, Ossorio & Coffey, 1951; Romano, 1954) provides a theory of interpersonal behavior and a set of methods and tools especially suited to the analysis of an ongoing interaction between human beings. It is impossible to give a full description of the system in this paper, so that only those aspects immediately relevant to the topic will be discussed.

The interpersonal theory of personality, derived from the work of Sullivan (1940), emphasizes the psychological processes occurring between individuals. In this frame of reference, behavior is viewed as functional and purposive, motivated by the need to gratify wishes, perhaps only imperfectly understood, and to avoid anxiety.

The variables of the diagnostic method have systematic interpersonal reference, and permit classification of personality data derived from different sources or "levels." For example, the observed interpersonal *behavior* occurring between individuals may differ widely from the participant's *self-report* of his behavior. These levels of observations are different still from the manner in which a person may define the interpersonal role of a hero in a Thematic Apperception story. This last, the projective test response, is considered to reflect one's *private* or *preconscious* interpersonal perceptions. In each case, however, these data can be classified in terms of the same system of variables.

The schema of classification for these personality data can be conceptualized as a two-dimensional field (See Fig. 1), where the verti-

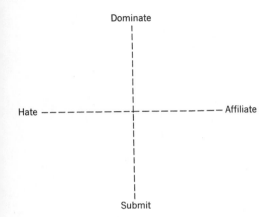

Dominate

Hate — — — — — — — — — — — — — — Affiliate

Submit

Figure 1. The two-dimensional field comprised by the intersection of the status and affect continua. It should be noted that the verbs designating the ends of the continua are sample terms employed for the sake of clarity.

cal axis is a status continuum of dominance and submission, while the horizontal axis is an affect continuum of hostility and affiliation. The field readily divides itself into eight sectors which represent the extreme points of the continua, and four blends of these nodal points. (See the remaining figures.) Techniques for the reliable measurement and rating of behavior and the personality productions of individuals have been devised (Leary, 1957).

The ratings are then classified around this system of variables, yielding distributions of interpersonal data which can be relegated to the three different levels mentioned above (observed behavior which is termed Level I, conscious report which is Level II, and preconscious projection or Level III data).

In this paper Level I data will not be considered. Level II data, conscious *self* and significant *other* descriptions, were obtained by the

use of the Interpersonal Check List.[1] Level III, or private perceptual data, are obtained by rating Thematic Apperception stories in terms of the system of variables.

Scores from the Interpersonal Check List and the TAT can be converted by a trigonometric formula and normative data to a single point on the two-dimensional field or "grid" represented schematically in Figure 1, and in the other figures. This single point represents a summation of the various vectors or "pulls" operating in the interpersonal field (Leary, 1957, pp. 68–69).

The marital partners to be discussed below were chosen to illustrate the diagnostic use of interpersonal data. The case of Mr. and Mrs. George presents for study a conscious view of themselves and each other. In the second case, Mr. and Mrs. Tom, the Level II conscious perceptions are compared with the subjects' projective (private, Level III) perceptions as derived from his characterization of the hero and interacting other in TAT stories. Studying the personality data for the marital partners simultaneously provides insight into the marital interaction and its failure.

The Diagnostic Procedure

Following an initial interview held separately with husband and wife, each partner is given a battery of psychological tests, including the Interpersonal Check List described above, and ten cards of the TAT that are used to obtain the Level III ratings.[2]

Both husband and wife are asked to apply the check list to themselves, and to their spouse, mother, and father or any other significant figure in their life.

---

[1] The Interpersonal Check List is an inventory of descriptive phrases or "traits" which locate themselves in the eight sectors of the two-dimensional field of Figure 1. The subject uses the items to characterize himself and various other people. The construction, reliability, and validity of the check list is discussed at length in Leary (1957, pp. 455–463).

[2] These TAT cards are: 1, 2, 3BM, 4, 6BM, 6GF, 7BM, 12M, 13MF, 18BM for men, and: 1, 2, 3GF, 4, 6BM, 6GF, 7GF, 12M, 13MF, 18GF for women. The reliability and validity of this special use of the TAT is discussed at length in Leary (1957, pp. 464–479).

The special test material is then scored and summarized on the diagnostic grid.

Interpretive Analysis of the Data

The method described briefly above provides a course of clinical information relevant to the personality of the individual in his social role at large, and in particular in relation to his spouse. His self-regard (Level II) can be compared with his conscious views of his parents and his wife, yielding similarities and discrepancies that reflect upon his capacity to understand or sympathize with the "other." Similarity between his self-regard and his view of the other can be termed *identification* while lack of similarity in scores may reflect *disidentification* or antagonism.

The discrepancy between his Level II self score, and his Level III hero score, throws

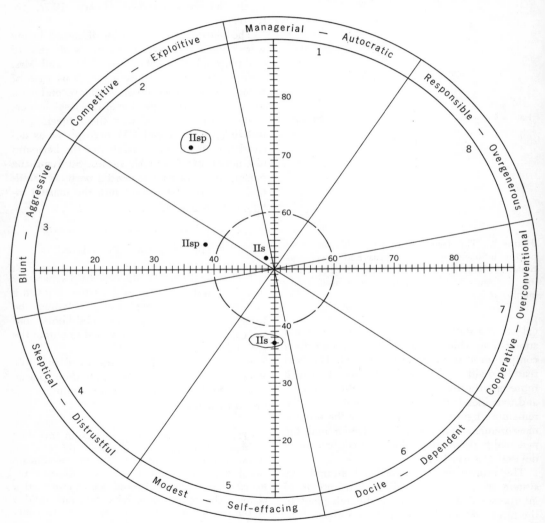

Figure 2. A marriage of mutual frustration and hostility: Mr. and Mrs. George. The two-dimensional field in the form of a circular grid. (From Leary, 1957.) The grid shows how the field is divided into eight sectors. The summary points shown are for Level II ratings. IIs is the summary of the subject's view of himself. IIsp is the summary of the subject's view of his spouse. The circled points are the wife's; the uncircled are the husband's.

light upon the internal processes at work. Level III data may represent warded off impulses that result in self-defeating behavior. Sometimes a marital partner may perceive accurately the warded off Level III characteristics of his spouse, and, in fact respond to the spouse, not on the basis of the spouse's conscious view of himself but more accurately in terms of the spouse's warded off traits which creep into his behavior without his awareness. Sometimes mutual deception is unwittingly played, as in the case of Mr. and Mrs. Tom, the second case discussed.

A Marriage of Mutual Frustration and Hostility: Mr. and Mrs. George. Figure 2 presents the two-dimensional field in the form of a circular grid.[3]

On this circular grid are summarized a husband and wife's Level II ratings of themselves and each other. It will be noted that there is considerable discrepancy between the way each spouse perceives himself and is perceived *by* his spouse. The wife consciously views herself as a strongly submissive and self-effacing person (her scores total and fall more than one sigma from the mean in the submissive "modest self-effacing" sector of the field) while her husband perceives her as a hostile aggressive person.

She, on the other hand, views *him* as an extremely narcissistic exploitive man, demanding, rejecting and selfish, while he views himself as only mildly competitive; (his score for himself falls so close to the mean as to imply that he actually feels himself to be a well-rounded and flexible individual).

It will readily be seen that such a constellation of scores implies considerable frustration and hostility in this marriage, which, in fact, was the main complaint of each partner. In the interviews each partner expressed the feeling of being victimized and despised by the other. Further, each partner felt that he or she had done nothing to provoke such behavior towards him. The wife felt herself to be a passive docile woman while the husband felt himself to be only "normally" ascendant and aggressive as "a man should be."

---

[3] The point of intersection of the two axes is the mean of dominant-submissive and affiliative-hostile scores for the normative population. The inner broken circle is located at one sigma from the mean. (From Leary, 1957.)

The Case of Mr. and Mrs. Tom. This young couple came referred by their family physician who was aware of the marital discord in their lives. Mr. Tom, a 32 year old man presenting a rather hostile and wary facade, complained bitterly against his wife who, he was convinced, had betrayed him with another man. He felt that he was justly hostile since she was by no means a "loving" wife to him.

Mrs. Tom, on the other hand, a somewhat immature 27 year old woman, insisted that she was faithful, although admitting that she had fantasied an escapade with a male acquaintance. She explained that this other man was tender and affectionate in contrast to her harsh punitive husband. Although there was constant marital clash, she denied giving Mr. Tom any provocation for his hostility, stating that her aspect of the marital discord was "self defense" or, at the worst, retaliative.

Mrs. Tom: Interactional Personality Data. Figure 3 presents the interpersonal findings on Mrs. Tom.

Mrs. Tom consciously describes her husband (IIsp) as an extremely competitive and exploitive individual who is selfish and inconsiderate. She describes her own father (IIf) in much the same way, although perceiving him as having these characteristics to a lesser degree. This immediately implies that she tends to identify consciously her husband with her father, and raises the question as to how much she is responding to Mr. Tom on the basis of the father-daughter relationship.

Her mother (IIm) she characterizes as a responsible and giving individual, slightly more dominant then herself (IIs). She tends to perceive herself and her own actions as cooperative and affiliative, and not deviating very far from the mean. There is a fair correspondence between her own scores and those of her mother, implying a moderate conscious identification.

However, the TAT stories Mrs. Tom creates, depict heroes who are aggressive hostile people, reacting violently to their environment and toward those with whom they interact. Mrs. Tom *says* she is kind, cooperative, and affiliative. But her TAT heroes, reflecting tendencies within herself only imperfectly perceived, behave in aggressive violent ways. The discrepancy between these two summary points (Level IIs and Level IIIh) is a measure of the amount and type of "repression" and "denial" going on within her personality.

The hostility ratings for her TAT heroes (IIIh) are all the more significant since her TAT "other" figures are not particularly autocratic people. The score for the "other" figures in the TAT stories (IIIo) deviates less than one sigma from the mean in the dominant sector of the grid.

Mr. Tom: Interactional Personality Data. Consulting the diagnostic grid for Mr. Tom (Figure 3) it will be seen that he consciously ascribes exploitive competitive traits to himself.

He sees himself (consciously) in much the same way that his wife views him. He tells us he is very much like his father, pointing up the strength of his conscious paternal identification.

When we examine the nature of his TAT heroes, we get an inkling of considerable turmoil within him. His TAT heroes are weak, distrustful, wary people who need to be constantly on guard against the powerful dominating environment (IIIo). He is striving to "be like father," competitive, self-seeking, and rivalrous, but he

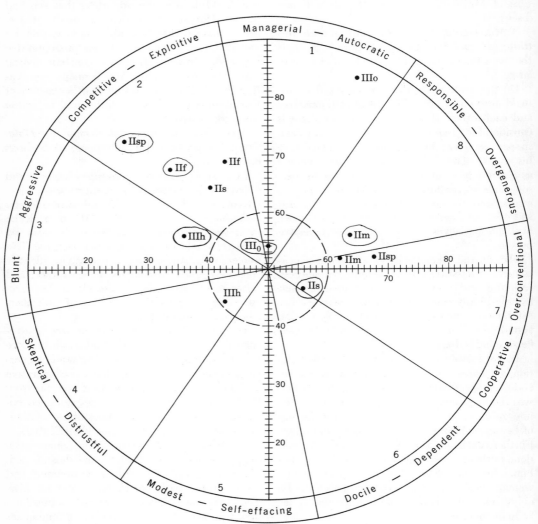

Figure 3. Interpersonal personality data from two levels on Mr. and Mrs. Tom. Key: Circled points are for Mrs. Tom; uncircled points are for Mr. Tom. IIs is the conscious view of self; IIsp is the conscious view of spouse; IIm is the conscious view of mother; IIf is the conscious view of father; IIIh is the preconscious hero (TAT stories); IIIo is the preconscious "other" (TAT stories).

needs to hold in abeyance his private perception of his own weakness. This, of course, has considerable implication in regard to his jealousy and doubt regarding his wife.

In spite of his complaints against Mrs. Tom, he continues to characterize and consciously identify her with his mother, as an affiliative and cooperative woman. Apparently, to him this is "femininity" just as his own behavior is viewed as "masculine." An Oedipal coloring to his jealousy of his wife is suggested by the conscous identifications Mr. Tom makes.

Marital Dynamics. Each partner views himself at Level II in a way very similar to his spouse's view of him. At the same time, each partner wards off (Level III) aspects of himself which are incompatible with his conscious self-picture. In the husband's case, these are submissive and covertly resistive traits; in the wife's case, they are hostile, directly aggressive characteristics.

It seems clear that this self deception is maintained not only intrapsychically, but that the disturbed marriage relationship helps to enhance it. That is, by perceiving her husband as an ascendant competitive person, Mrs. Tom helps him to maintain this attitude toward himself, thereby insuring that his fear of weakness remains warded off. Similarly, Mr. Tom "helps" his wife to maintain the illusion that she is a "feminine" woman without aggressive impulses or needs. This is strong evidence for the interpretation that the "neurotic" marital interaction is, in one sense, needed by each of the marital partners to avoid the collapse of their own intrapsychic defense system.

But, as with all neurotic compromise, full satisfaction is impossible. Mr. Tom expresses to the psychologist dissatisfaction with his wife's depriving attitude which he interprets as a reflection on his manhood (i.e. "she prefers another man!"), thereby obscuring his own dependency needs experienced unconsciously. And Mrs. Tom longs for affection and tenderness from her husband, failing to recognize that she threatens and goads him into punitive action.

Prognosis for Counseling. Mr. Tom's marital behavior accords closely with his conscious view of himself and with his wife's description of him, test wise (Level II) and in the interviews. But Mr. Tom consciously identifies with his father (i.e., "I am like father, and father is manly.") Counseling with him will therefore probably be difficult, since he will be threatened by an attempt to help him understand how he contributes to the marital discord. This will be interpreted as an attempt to intervene in his identification with his father. Further, helping him to revise his definition of his wife will add more threat to his burden. These processes will tend to reactivate and bring into consciousness those aspects of himself and the Level IIIo autocratic world which he must ward off (father).

Mrs. Tom can come to an acceptance of her hostile impulses more readily because, according to her definition of the significant others (husband and father), she has justification. She consciously describes these two men as exploitive people who may take advantage of her if she lets them. Mr. Tom, on the other hand, does not have justification for his feelings of weakness and suspicion unless he is willing to perceive his father as a rival with whom he must compete.

On these grounds, the aims of the counseling process will be modified for Mr. Tom. He will be helped to strengthen his positive perceptions of himself, at the same time encouraged to relax his harsh grip on his wife. Mrs. Tom can tolerate a more uncovering approach to her hidden hostility.

Summary

A theoretical approach emphasizing the interpersonal aspects of personality, and a methodology for the analysis of personality in interactional terms was presented. It is believed that the method has particular relevance in the marriage counseling situation where the focus of the treatment endeavor is on the interaction between husband and wife. Marital dynamics are a function of the psychodynamics of the marital participants, since in the final analysis, any structured human interaction has its psychological origins in the intrapsychic processes of the individuals involved. This does not deny the reality of external considerations but insists that the interpretation of these factors depends upon the person's unique internal organization. The diagnostic methodology described here deals systematically with this *intrapersonal* aspect of the marriage partners also.

It is believed that the methodology will be useful in evaluating the effects of marriage counseling, and further work of this sort is in process.

REFERENCES

Bychowski, G., & Despert, Louise. (Eds.) *Specialized techniques in psychotherapy*. New York: Basic Books, 1952.

Freedman, M., Leary, T., Ossorio, A., & Coffey, H. The interpersonal dimension of personality. *J. Person.*, 1951, **20**, 143.

Gomberg, M. Present status of treatment program. In V. Eisenstein (Ed.), *Neurotic interaction in marriage*. New York: Basic Books, 1956.

Leary, T. *Interpersonal diagnosis of personality*. New York: Ronald Press, 1957.

Mudd, Emily, & Kirch, A. (Eds.) *Man and Wife: A source book of family attitudes, sexual behavior, and marriage counseling*. New York: Norton, 1957.

Romano, R. A quantification of the psychotherapeutic process. Unpublished doctoral dissertation, Washington Univer., 1954.

Sullivan, H. *Conceptions of modern psychiatry*. Washington, D. C.: W. A. White Psychiatric Foundation, 1940.

Murray's Personology

In recent years Henry Murray has continued to reshape and modify his theoretical formulations and at the same time he has pursued his ingenious attempts to uncover central aspects of personality through empirical devices. In addition to the papers reprinted here the interested reader will wish to consult his recent chapter entitled "Preparations for the Scaffold of a Comprehensive System" (Murray, 1959) which contains a wealth of information concerning the origin of his theoretical ideas as well as the introduction of new concepts and formulations.

We have selected the first paper, *In Nomine Diaboli*, for inclusion here in spite of the fact that it has not appeared recently and was discussed at some length in *Theories of Personality*. Our willingness to override these important selection criteria provides a good index of our admiration for this sensitive psychological analysis of a great American novel, *Moby Dick*. The paper reveals clearly Murray's depth of psychological understanding as well as the richness of his general scholarship. In the second paper, *American Icarus*, Murray directs his concepts and clinical sensitivity to the understanding of a flesh and blood individual and the attempt to extract from this case a concept (Icarus Complex) that possesses an important degree of generality. Murray's versatility is nicely revealed in these first two papers—one dealing with a fictional hero and a famous author and the other with an obscure but comprehensively studied adolescent male.

The third and most recent paper, *Studies of Stressful Interpersonal Disputations*, was presented by Murray following his receiving the Distinguished Scientific Award of the American Psychological Association. It provides a glimpse of the research with which he is presently occupied. In this investigation a small number of persons in a social setting are appraised by multiple methods and observers (the multiform method) in an effort to expand our understanding of an important affect—anger. The paper also includes a number of recommendations in regard to how to conduct personological research.

Finally, we have a chapter by a former student (Morris I. Stein) concerned with the application of typological concepts to the study of scientists and Peace Corp volunteers. The author makes clear the direct influence that Murray has had upon him and also reveals the central role that is played in his research by concepts and methods originated by Murray. This paper is taken from a volume (R. W. White, 1963) that was published in honor of Murray and which contains a wide variety of theoretical and empirical contributions by individuals who have been directly influenced at some point in their careers by Henry Murray.

REFERENCES

Murray, H. A. Preparations for the scaffold of a comprehensive system. In S. Koch (Ed.) *Psychology: A study of a science*. Vol. 3. New York: McGraw-Hill, 1959, pp. 7–54.
White, R. W. *The study of lives*. New York: Atherton, 1963.

1. In nomine diaboli

HENRY A. MURRAY

NEXT TO THE SEIZURES AND SHAPINGS OF CREA-
TIVE THOUGHT—the thing itself—no comparable
experience is more thrilling than being witched,
illumined, and transfigured by the magic of
another's art. This is a trance from which one
returns refreshed and quickened, and bubbling
with unenvious praise of the exciting cause,
much as Melville bubbled after his first reading
of Hawthorne's *Mosses*. In describing *his* experience Melville chose a phrase so apt—"the
shock of recognition"—that in the thirties Ed-
mund Wilson took it as the irresistibly perfect
title for his anthology of literary appreciations.
Acknowledging a shock of recognition and paying homage to the delivering genius is singularly
exhilarating, even today—or especially today—
when every waxing enthusiasm must confront
an outgoing tide of culture.

In our time, the capacities for wonder and
reverence, for generous judgments and trustful
affirmations, have largely given way, though
not without cause surely, to their antipathies,
the humors of a waning ethos: disillusionment,
cynicism, disgust, and gnawing envy. These
states have bred in us the inclination to dissect
the subtlest orders of man's wit with ever-
sharper instruments of depreciation, to pour all
values, the best confounded by the worst, into
one mocking-pot, to sneer "realistically," and,
as we say today, "assassinate" character. These
same humors have disposed writers to spend
immortal talent in snickering exhibitions of vul-

garity and spiritual emptiness, or in making delicate picture-puzzles out of the butt-ends of life.

In the face of these current trends and tempers, I, coming out of years of brimming grate-
fulness for the gift of *Moby-Dick*, would like to
praise Herman Melville worthily, not to bury
him in a winding-sheet of scientific terminology.
But the odds are not favorable to my ambition.
A commitment of thirty years to analytic modes
of thought and concepts lethal to emotion has
built such habits in me that were I to be waked
in the night by a cry of "Help!" I fear I would
respond in the lingo of psychology. I am suffering from one of the commonest ailments of our
age—trained disability.

The habit of a psychologist is to break down
the structure of each personality he studies into
elements, and so in a few strokes to bring to
earth whatever merit that structure, as a structure, may possess. Furthermore, for reasons I
need not mention here, the technical terms for
the majority of these elements have derogatory
connotations. Consequently, it is difficult to
open one's professional mouth without disparaging a fellow-being. Were an analyst to be confronted by that much heralded but still missing
specimen of the human race—the normal man—
he would be struck dumb, for once, through lack
of appropriate ideas.

If I am able to surmount to some extent any
impediments of this origin, you may attribute
my good fortune to a providential circumstance.
In the procession of my experiences *Moby-Dick*
anteceded Psychology, that is, I was swept by
Melville's gale and shaken by his appalling sea
dragon before I had acquired the all-leveling
academic oil that is poured on brewed-up waters, and before I possessed the weapons and
tools of science—the conceptual lance, harpoons,
cutting irons, and what-nots—which might have

SOURCE. Article by Henry A. Murray, "In nomine
diaboli" in the *New England Quarterly*, Vol. 24,
pp. 435–452, 1941.

This essay was read at the exercises to commemorate
the centennial of the publication of *Moby-Dick*
(Williams College, September 3, 1951).

reduced the "grand hooded phantom" to mere blubber. Lacking these defenses I was whelmed. Instead of my changing this book, this book changed me.

To me, *Moby-Dick* was Beethoven's *Eroica* in words: first of all, a masterly orchestration of harmonic and melodic language, of resonating images and thoughts in varied metres. Equally compelling were the spacious sea-settings of the story, the cast of characters and their prodigious common target, the sorrow, the fury, and the terror, together with all those frequent touches, those subtle interminglings of unexampled humor, quizzical and, in the American way, extravagant, and finally the fated closure, the crown and tragic consummation of the immense yet firmly-welded whole. But still more extraordinary and portentous were the penetration and scope, the sheer audacity of the author's imagination. Here was a man who did not fly away with his surprising fantasies to some unbelievable dreamland, pale or florid, shunning the stubborn objects and gritty facts, the prosaic routines and practicalities of everyday existence. Here was a man who, on the contrary, chose these very things as vessels for his procreative powers—the whale as a naturalist, a Hunter or a Cuvier, would perceive him, the business of killing whales, the whale-ship running as an oil factory, stowing-down, in fact, every mechanism and technique, each tool and gadget, that was integral to the money-minded industry of whaling. Here was a man who could describe the appearance, the concrete matter-of-factness, and the utility of each one of these natural objects, implements, and tools with the fidelity of a scientist, and, while doing this, explore it as a conceivable repository of some aspect of the human drama; then, by an imaginative tour de force, deliver a vital essence, some humorous or profound idea, coalescing with its embodiment. But still more. Differing from the symbolists of our time, here was a man who offered us essences and meanings which did not level or depreciate the objects of his contemplation. On the contrary, this loving man exalted all creatures—the mariners, renegades, and castaways on board the *Pequod*—by ascribing to them "high qualities, though dark" and weaving round them "tragic graces." Here, in short, was a man with the myth-making powers of a Blake, a hive of significant associations, who was capable of reuniting what science had put asunder—pure perception and relevant emotion—and doing it in an exultant way that was acceptable to skepticism.

Not at first, but later, I perceived the crucial difference between Melville's dramatic animations of nature and those of primitive religionmakers: both were spontaneous and uncalculated projections, but Melville's were in harmony, for the most part, with scientific knowledge, because they had been recognized as projections, checked, and modified. Here, then, was a man who might redeem us from the virtue of an incredible subjective belief, on the one side, and from the virtue of a deadly objective rationality, on the other.

For these and other reasons the reading of *Moby-Dick*—coming before Psychology—left a stupendous reverberating imprint, too lively to be diminished by the long series of relentless analytical operations to which I subsequently subjected it. Today, after twenty-five years of such experiments, *The Whale* is still *the* Whale, more magnificent, if anything, than before.

Before coming to grips with the "mystery" of *Moby-Dick* I should mention another providential circumstance to which all psychologists are, or should be, forever grateful, and literary critics too, since without it no complete understanding of books like *Moby-Dick* would be possible today. Ahead of us were two greatly gifted pioneers, Freud and Jung, who, with others, explored the manifold vagaries of unconscious mental processes and left for our inheritance their finely-written works. The discoveries of these adventurers advantaged me in a special way: they gave, I thought, support to one of Santayana's early convictions, that in the human being imagination is more fundamental than perception. Anyhow, adopting this position, some of us psychologists have been devoting ourselves to the study of dreams, fantasies, creative productions, and projections—all of which are primarily and essentially emotional and dramatic, such stuff as myths are made of. Thus, by chance or otherwise, this branch of the tree of psychology is growing in the direction of Herman Melville.

To be explicit: psychologists have been recognizing in the dream figures and fantasy figures of today's children and adolescents more and more family likenesses of the heroes and heroines of primitive myths, legends, and fables —figures, in other words, who are engaged in comparable heroic strivings and conflicts, and experiencing comparable heroic triumphs or fatalities. Our ancestors, yielding to an inherent propensity of the mind, projected the more relevant of these figures into objects of their environment, into sun, moon, and stars, into the unknown deeps of the sea and of the earth, and into the boundless void of heaven; and they worshipped the most potent of these projected images, whether animal or human, as super-beings, gods, or goddesses. On any clear night one can see scores of the more luminous of such divinities parading up and down the firmament. For example, in Fall and Winter, one looks with admiration on that resplendent hero Perseus and above him the chained beauty, Andromeda, whom he saved from a devouring monster, ferocious as Moby Dick. Now, what psychologists have been learning by degrees is that Perseus is in the unconscious mind of every man and Andromeda in every woman, not, let me hasten to say, as an inherited fixed image, but as a potential set of dispositions which may be constellated in the personality by the occurrence of a certain kind of situation. Herman Melville arrived at this conclusion in his own way a hundred years ago, sooner and, I believe, with more genuine comprehension than any other writer.

An explanation of all this in scientific terms would require all the space permitted me and more. Suffice it to say here that the psychologists who are studying the elementary myth-makings of the mind are dealing with the germy sources of poetry and drama, the fecundities out of which great literature is fashioned. Furthermore, in attempting to formulate and classify these multifarious productions of the imagination, the psychologist uses modes of analysis and synthesis very similar to those that Aristotle used in setting forth the dynamics of Greek tragedy. In these and other trends I find much encouragement for the view that a rapprochement of psychology and literary criticism is in progress, and that it will prove fruitful to both callings. As an ideal meeting ground I would propose Melville's world of "wondrous depths."

To this Columbus of the mind, the great archetypal figures of myth, drama, and epic were not pieces of intellectual Dresden china, heirlooms of a classical education, ornamental bric-a-brac to be put here and there for the pleasure of genteel readers. Many of the more significant of these constellations were inwardly experienced by Melville, one after the other, as each was given vent to blossom and assert itself.

Thus, we are offered a spectacle of spiritual development through passionate identifications. Only by proceeding in this way could Melville have learnt on his pulses what it was to be Narcissus, Orestes, Oedipus, Ishmael, Apollo, Lucifer. "Like a frigate," he said, "I am full with a thousand souls."

This brings me to the problem of interpreting *Moby-Dick*. Some writers have said that there is nothing to interpret: it is a plain sea story marred here and there by irrelevant ruminations. But I shall not cite the abundant proof for the now generally accepted proposition that in *Moby-Dick* Melville "meant" something—something, I should add, which he considered "terrifically true" but which, in the world's judgment, was so harmful "that it were all but madness for any good man, in his own proper character, to utter or even hint of." What seems decisive here is the passage in Melville's celebrated letter to Hawthorne: "A sense of unspeakable security is in me this moment, on account of your having understood the book." From this we can conclude that there *are* meanings to be understood in *Moby-Dick,* and also —may we say for our own encouragement?— that Melville's ghost will feel secure forever if modern critics can find them, and, since Hawthorne remained silent, set them forth in print. Here it might be well to remind ourselves of a crucial statement which follows the just quoted passage from Melville's letter: " I have written a wicked book." The implication is clear: all interpretations which fail to show that *Moby-Dick* is, in some sense, wicked have missed the author's avowed intention.

A few critics have scouted all attempts to fish Melville's own meaning out of *The Whale,* on the ground that an interpretation of a work of art so vast and so complex is bound to be composed in large measure of projections from the mind of the interpreter. It must be granted that preposterous projections often do occur in the course of such an effort. But these are not inevitable. Self-knowledge and discipline may reduce projections to a minimum. Anyhow, in the case of *Moby-Dick,* the facts do not sustain the proposition that a critic can see nothing in this book but his own reflected image. The interpretations which have been published over the last thirty years exhibit an unmistakable trend towards consensus in respect to the drama as a whole as well as many of its subordinate parts. Moreover, so far as I can judge, the critics who, with hints from their predecessors, applied their intuitions most recently to the exegesis of *The Whale*, can be said to have arrived, if taken together, at Melville's essential meaning. Since one or another of these authors has deftly said what I clumsily thought, my prejudices are strongly in favor of their conclusions, and I am whole-hearted in applauding them, Mr. Arvin's[1] most especially, despite their having left me with nothing fresh to say. Since this is how things stand, my version of the main theme of *Moby-Dick* can be presented in a briefer form, and limited to two hypotheses.

The first of them is this: Captain Ahab is an embodiment of that fallen angel or demi-god who in Christendom was variously named Lucifer, Devil, Adversary, Satan. The Church Fathers would have called Captain Ahab "Antichrist" because he was not Satan himself, but a human creature possessed of all Satan's pride and energy, "summing up within himself," as Irenaeus said, "the apostasy of the devil."

That it was Melville's intention to beget Ahab in Satan's image can hardly be doubted. He told Hawthorne that his book had been boiled in hell-fire and secretly baptized not in the name of God but in the name of the Devil. He named his tragic hero after the Old Testament ruler who "did more to provoke the Lord God of Israel to anger than all the Kings of Israel that were before him." King Ahab's accuser, the prophet Elijah, is also resurrected to play his original rôle, though very briefly, in Melville's testament. We are told that Captain Ahab is an "ungodly, god-like" man who is spiritually outside Christendom. He is a well of blasphemy and defiance, of scorn and mockery for the gods—"cricket-players and pugilists" in his eyes. Rumor has it that he once spat in the holy goblet on the altar of the Catholic Church at Santa. "I never saw him kneel," says Stubb. He is associated in the text with scores of references to the Devil. He is an "anaconda of an old man." His self-assertive sadism is the linked antithesis of the masochistic submission preached by Father Mapple.

Captain Ahab-Lucifer is also related to a sungod, like Christ, but in reverse. Instead of being light leaping out of darkness, he is "darkness leaping out of light." The *Pequod* sails on

Christmas Day. *This* new year's sun will be the god of Wrath rather than the god of Love. Ahab does not emerge from his subterranean abode until his ship is "rolling through the bright Quito spring" (Easter-tide, symbolically, when the all-fertilizing sun-god is resurrected). The frenzied ceremony in which Ahab's followers are sworn to the pursuit of the White Whale —"Commend the murderous chalices!"—is suggestive of the Black Mass; the lurid operations at the try-works is a scene out of Hell.

There is some evidence that Melville was re-reading *Paradise Lost* in the summer of 1850, shortly after, let us guess, he got the idea of transforming the captain of his whale-ship into the first of all cardinal sinners who fell by pride. Anyhow, Melville's Satan is the spitting image of Milton's hero, but portrayed with deeper and subtler psychological insight, and placed where he belongs, in the heart of an enraged man.

Melville may have been persuaded by Goethe's Mephistopheles, or even by some of Hawthorne's bloodless abstracts of humanity, to add Fedallah to his cast of characters. Evidently he wanted to make certain that no reader would fail to recognize that Ahab had been possessed by, or had sold his soul to, the Devil. Personally, I think Fedallah's rôle is superfluous and I regret that Melville made room for him and his unbelievable boat-crew on the ship *Pequod*. Still, he is not wholly without interest. He represents the cool, heartless, cunning, calculating, intellectual Devil of the Medieval myth-makers, in contrast, to the stricken, passionate, indignant, and often eloquent rebel angel of *Paradise Lost*, whose rôle is played by Ahab.

The Arabic name "Fedallah" suggests "dev(il) Allah," that is, the Mohammedans' god as he appeared in the mind's eye of a Crusader. But we are told that Fedallah is a Parsee—a Persian fire-worshipper, or Zoroastrian, who lives in India. Thus, Ahab, named after the Semitic apostate who was converted to the orgiastic cult of Baal, or Bel, originally a Babylonian fertility god, has formed a compact with a Zoroastrian whose name reminds us of still another Oriental religion. In addition, Captain Ahab's whale-boat is manned by a crew of unregenerate infidels, as defined by orthodox Christianity, and each of his three harpooners, Queequeg, Tastego, and Daggoo, is a member of a race which believed in other gods than the one god of the Hebraic-Christian Bible.

---

[1] Newton Arvin, *Herman Melville* (New York, 1950.)

Speaking roughly, it might be said that Captain Ahab, incarnation of the Adversary and master of the ship *Pequod* (named after the aggressive Indian tribe that was exterminated by the Puritans of New England), has summoned the various religions of the East to combat the one dominant religion of the West. Or, in other terms, that he and his followers, Starbuck excepted, represent the horde of primitive drives, values, beliefs, and practices which the Hebraic-Christian religionists rejected and excluded, and by threats, punishments, and inquisitions, forced into the unconscious mind of Western man.

Stated in psychological concepts, Ahab is captain of the culturally repressed dispositions of human nature, that part of personality which psychoanalysts have termed the "Id." If this is true, his opponent, the White Whale, can be none other than the internal institution which is responsible for these repressions, namely the Freudian Superego. This then is my second hypothesis: Moby-Dick is a veritable spouting, breaching, sounding whale, a whale who, because of his whiteness, his mightly bulk and beauty, and because of one instinctive act that happened to dismember his assailant, has received the projection of Captain Ahab's Presbyterian conscience, and so may be said to embody the Old Testament Calvinistic conception of an affrighting Deity and his strict commandments, the derivative puritan ethic of nineteenth-century America, and the society that defended this ethic. Also, and most specifically, he symbolizes the zealous parents whose righteous sermonizings and corrections drove the prohibitions in so hard that a serious young man could hardly reach outside the barrier, except possibly far away among some tolerant, gracious Polynesian peoples. The emphasis should be placed on that unconscious (and hence inscrutable) wall of inhibition which imprisoned the puritan's thrusting passions. "How can the prisoner reach outside," cries Ahab, "except by thrusting through the wall? To me, the White Whale is that wall, shoved near to me . . . I see in him outrageous strength, with an inscrutable malice sinewing it." As a symbol of a sounding, breaching, white-dark, unconquerable New England conscience what could be better than a sounding, breaching, white-dark, unconquerable sperm whale?

Who is the psychoanalyst who could resist the immediate inference that the *imago* of the mother as well as the *imago* of the father is contained in the Whale? In the present case there happens to be a host of biographical facts and written passages which support this proposition. Luckily, I need not review them, because Mr. Arvin and others have come to the same conclusion. I shall confine myself to one reference. It exhibits Melville's keen and sympathetic insight into the cultural determinants of his mother's prohibiting dispositions. In *Pierre*, it is the "high-up, and towering and all-forbidding . . . edifice of his mother's immense pride . . . her pride of birth . . . her pride of purity," that is the "wall shoved near," the wall that stands between the hero and the realization of his heart's resolve. But instead of expending the fury of frustration upon his mother, he directs it at Fate, or, more specifically, at his mother's God and the society that shaped her. For he saw "that not his mother had made his mother; but the Infinite Haughtiness had first fashioned her; and then the haughty world had further molded her; nor had a haughty Ritual omitted to finish her."

Given this penetrating apprehension we are in a position to say that Melville's target in *Moby-Dick* was the upper middle-class culture of his time. It was *this* culture which was defended with righteous indignation by what he was apt to call "the world" or "the public," and Melville had very little respect for "the world" or "the public." The "public," or men operating as a social system, was something quite distinct from "the people." In *White Jacket* he wrote: "The public and the people! . . . let us hate the one, and cleave to the other." "The public is a monster," says Lemsford. Still earlier Melville had said: "I fight against the armed and crested lies of Mardi (the world)." "Mardi is a monster whose eyes are fixed in its head, like a whale." Many other writers have used similar imagery. Sir Thomas Browne referred to the multitude as "that numerous piece of monstrosity"; Keats spoke of "the dragon world." But closest of all was Hobbes: "By art is created that great Leviathan, called a commonwealth or state." It was in the laws of this Leviathan, Hobbes made clear, that the sources of right and wrong reside. To summarize: the giant mass of Melville's whale is the same as Melville's man-of-war world, the *Neversink*, in *White Jacket*, which in turn is an epitome of Melville's *Mardi*. The Whale's white forehead and hump should be reserved for the world's heavenly King.

That God is incarnate in the Whale has been perceived by Mr. Stone,[2] and, as far as I know, by every other Catholic critic of Melville's work, as well as by several Protestant critics. In fact, Mr. Chase[3] has marshalled so fair a portion of the large bulk of evidence on this point that any more from me would be superfluous. Of course, what Ahab projects into the Whale is not the image of a loving Father, but the God of the Old Dispensation, the God who brought Jeremiah into darkness, hedged him about, and made his path crooked; the God, adopted by the fire-and-brimstone Puritans, who said: "With fury poured out I will rule over you." "The sword without and the terror within, shall destroy both the young man and the virgin." "I will also send the teeth of beasts upon them." "I will heap mischiefs upon them." "To me belongeth vengeance and recompense."

Since the society's vision of deity, and the society's morality, and the parents and ministers who implant these conceptions, are represented in a fully socialized personality by an establishment that is called the Superego—Conscience as Freud defined it—, and since Ahab has been proclaimed "Captain of the Id," the simplest psychological formula for Melville's dramatic epic is this: an insurgent Id in mortal conflict with an oppressive cultural Superego. Starbuck, the First Mate, stands for the rational realistic Ego which is overpowered by the fanatical compulsiveness of the Id and dispossessed of its normally regulating functions.

If this is approximately correct, it appears that while writing his greatest work Melville abandoned his detached position in the Ego from time to time, hailed "the realm of shades," as his hero Taji had, and, through the mediumship of Ahab, "burst his hot heart's shell" upon the sacrosanct Almighty and the sacrosanct sentiments of Christendom. Since in the world's judgment, 1851, nothing could be more reproachable than this, it would be unjust, if not treacherous, of us to reason *Moby-Dick* into some comforting morality play for which no boldness was required. This would be depriving

Melville of the ground he gained for self-respect by having dared to abide by his own subjective truth and write a "wicked book," the kind of book that Pierre's publishers, Steel, Flint, and Asbestos, would have called "a blasphemous rhapsody filched from the vile Atheists, Lucian and Voltaire."

Some may wonder how it was that Melville, a fundamentally good, affectionate, noble, idealistic, and reverential man, should have felt impelled to write a wicked book. Why did he aggress so furiously against Western orthodoxy, as furiously as Byron and Shelley, or any Satanic writer who preceded him, as furiously as Nietzsche or the most radical of his successors in our day?

In *Civilization and its Discontents* Freud, out of the ripeness of his full experience, wrote that when one finds deep-seated aggression—and by this he meant aggression of the sort that Melville voiced—one can safely attribute it to the frustration of Eros. In my opinion this generalization does not hold for all men of all cultures of all times, but the probability of its being valid is extremely high in the case of an earnest, moralistic, nineteenth-century American, a Presbyterian to boot, whose anger is born of suffering, especially if this man spent an impressionable year of his life in Polynesia and returned to marry the very proper little daughter of the Chief Justice of Massachusetts, and if, in addition, he is a profoundly creative man in whose androgynic personality masculine and feminine components are integrally blended.

If it were concerned with *Moby-Dick*, the book, rather than with its author, I would call *this* my third hypothesis: Ahab-Melville's aggression was directed against the object that once harmed Eros with apparent malice and was still thwarting it with presentiments of further retaliations. The correctness of this inference is indicated by the nature of the injury —a symbolic emasculation—that excited Ahab's ire. Initially, this threatening object was, in all likelihood, the father, later, possibly, the mother. But, as Melville plainly saw, both his parents had been fashioned by the Hebraic-Christian, American Calvinist tradition, the tradition which conceived of a deity in whose eyes Eros was depravity. It was the first Biblical mythmakers who dismissed from heaven and from earth the Great Goddess of the Oriental and primitive religions, and so rejected the feminine

---

[2] Geoffrey Stone, *Melville* (New York, 1949).

[3] Richard Volney Chase, *Herman Melville: A Critical Study* (New York, 1949).

principle as a spiritual force. Ahab, protagonist of these rejected religions, in addressing heaven's fire and lightning, what he calls "the personified impersonal," cries: "But thou art my fiery father; my sweet mother I know not. Oh, cruel! What hast thou done with her?" He calls this god a foundling, a "hermit immemorial," who does not know his own origin. Again, it was the Hebraic authors, sustained later by the Church Fathers, who propagated the legend that a woman was the cause of Adam's exile from Paradise, and that the original sin was concupiscence. Melville says that Ahab, spokesman of all exiled princes, "piled upon the whale's white hump the sum of all the general rage and hate felt by his whole race from Adam down." Remember also that is was the lure of Jezebel that drew King Ahab of Israel outside the orthodoxy of his religion and persuaded him to worship the Phoenician Astarte, goddess of love and fruitful increase. "Jezebel" was the worst tongue-lash a puritan could give a woman. She was Sex, and sex was Sin, spelled with a capital. It was the Church periodicals of Melville's day that denounced *Typee*, called the author a sensualist, and influenced the publishers to delete suggestive passages from the second edition. It was this long heritage of aversion and animosity, so accentuated in this country, which banned sex relations as a topic of discourse and condemned divorce as an unpardonable offense. All this has been changed, for better and for worse, by the moral revolutionaries of our own time who, feeling as Melville felt but finding the currents of sentiment less strongly opposite, spoke out, and with their wit, indignation, and logic, reinforced by the findings of psychoanalysis, disgraced the stern-faced idols of their forebears. One result is this: today an incompatible marriage is not a prison-house, as it was for Melville, "with wall shoved near."

In *Pierre* Melville confessed his own faith when he said that Eros is god of all, and Love "the loftiest religion of this earth." To the romantic Pierre the image of Isabel was "a silent and tyrannical call, challenging him in his deepest moral being, and summoning Truth, Love, Pity, Conscience to the stand." Here he seems to have had in mind the redeeming and inspiring Eros of Courtly Love, a heresy which the Medieval Church has done its utmost to stamp out. *This*, he felt convinced, was *his* "path to God," although in the way of it he saw with horror the implacable conscience and worldly valuations of his revered mother.

If this line of reasoning is as close as I think it is to the known facts, then Melville, in the person of Ahab, assailed Calvinism in the Whale because it blocked the advance of a conscience beneficent to evolutionary love. And so, weighed in the scales of its creator, *Moby-Dick* is not a wicked book but a *good* book, and after finishing it Melville had full reason to feel, as he confessed, "spotless as the lamb."

But then, seen from another point, *Moby-Dick* might be judged a wicked book, not because its hero condemns an entrenched tradition, but because he is completely committed to destruction. Although Captain Ahab manifests the basic stubborn virtues of the archprotestant and the rugged individual carried to their limits, *this* god-defier is no Prometheus, since all thought of benefiting humanity is foreign to him. His purpose is not to make the Pacific safe for whaling, nor, when blasting at the moral order, does he have in mind a more heartening vision for the future. The religion of Eros which might once have been the secret determinant of Ahab's undertaking is never mentioned. At one critical point in *Pierre* the hero-author, favored by a flash of light, exclaims, "I will gospelize the word anew"; but he never does. Out of light comes darkness: the temper of Pierre's book is no different from the temper of *Moby-Dick*. The truth is that Ahab is motivated solely by his private need to avenge a private insult. His governing philosophy is that of nihilism, the doctrine that the existing system must be shattered. Nihilism springs up when the imagination fails to provide the redeeming solution of an unbearable dilemma, when "the creative response," as Toynbee would say, is not forthcoming, and a man reacts out of a hot heart—"to the dogs with the head"—and swings to an instinct—"the same that prompts even a worm to turn under the heel." This is what White Jacket did when arraigned at the mast, and what Pierre did when fortune deserted him, and what Billy Budd did when confronted by his accuser. "Nature has not implanted any power in man," said Melville, "that was not meant to be exercised at times, thought too often our powers have been abused. The privilege, inborn and inalienable, that every man has, of dying himself and inflicting death upon another, was not given to us without a purpose. These are last resources of an insulted and unendurable existence."

If we grant that Ahab is a wicked man, what does this prove? It proves that *Moby-Dick* is a *good* book, a parable in epic form, because Melville makes a great spectacle of Ahab's wickedness and shows through the course of the narrative how such wickedness will drive a man on iron rails to an appointed nemesis. Melville adhered to the classic formula for tragedies. He could feel "spotless as the lamb," because he had seen to it that the huge threat to the social system, imminent in Ahab's two cardinal defects—egotistic self-inflation and unleashed wrath—was, at the end, fatefully exterminated, "and the great shroud of the sea rolled on as it rolled five thousand years ago." The reader has had his catharsis, equilibrium has been restored, sanity is vindicated.

This is true, but is it the whole truth? In point of fact, while writing *Moby-Dick* did Melville maintain aesthetic distance, keeping his own feelings in abeyance? Do we not hear Ahab saying things that the later Pierre will say and that Melville said less vehemently in his own person? Does not the author show marked partiality for the "mighty pageant creature" of his invention, put in *his* mouth the finest, boldest language? Also, have not many interpreters been so influenced by the abused Ahab that they saw nothing in his opponent but the source of all malicious agencies, the very Devil? As Mr. Mumford has said so eloquently, Ahab is at heart a noble being whose tragic wrong is that of battling against evil with "power instead of love," and so becoming "the image of the thing he hates." With this impression imbedded in our minds, how can we come out with any moral except this: evil wins. We admit that Ahab's wickedness has been cancelled. But what survives? It is the much more formidable, compacted wickedness of the group that survives, the world that is "saturated and soaking with lies," and their man-of-war God, who is hardly more admirable than a primitive totem beast, some oral-aggressive, child-devouring Cronos of the sea. Is this an idea that a man of good-will can rest with?

Rest with? Certainly not. Melville's clear intention was to bring not rest, but *unrest* to intrepid minds. All gentle people were warned away from his book "on the risk of a lumbago or sciatica." "A polar wind blows through it,"

he announced. He had not written to soothe, but to kindle, to make men leap fom their seats, as Whitman would say, and fight for their lives. Was it the poet's function to buttress the battlements of complacency, to give comfort to the enemy? There is little doubt about the nature of the enemy in Melville's day. It was the dominant ideology, that peculiar compound of puritanism and materialism, of rationalism and commercialism, of shallow, blatant optimism and technology, which proved so crushing to creative evolutions in religion, art, and life. In such circumstances every "true poet," as Blake said, "is of the Devil's party," whether he knows it or not. Surveying the last hundred and fifty years, how many exceptions to this statement can we find? Melville, anyhow, knew that *he* belonged to the party, and while writing *Moby-Dick* so gloried in his membership that he baptized his work *In Nomine Diaboli*. It was precisely under these auspices that he created his solitary masterpiece, a construction of the same high order as the Constitution of the United States and the scientific treaties of Willard Gibbs, though huge and wild and unruly as the Grand Canyon. And it is for this marvel chiefly that he resides in our hearts now among the greatest in "that small but high-hushed world" of bestowing geniuses.

Here ends this report of my soundings in *Moby-Dick*. The drama is finished. What became of its surviving author?

Moby-Dick may be taken as a comment on the strategic crisis of Melville's allegorical life. In portraying the consequences of Ahab's last suicidal lunge, the hero's umbilical fixation to the Whale and his death by strangling, the author signalized not only his permanent attachment to the *imago* of the mother, but the submission he had foreseen to the binding power of the parent conscience, the Superego of middle-class America. Measured against the standards of *his* day, then, Melville must be accounted a *good* man.

But does this entitle him to a place on the side of the angels? He abdicated to the conscience he condemned and his ship *Pequod*, in sinking, carried down with it the conscience he aspired to, represented by the sky-hawk, the bird of heaven. With his ideal drowned, life from then one was load and time stood still. All he had denied to love he gave throughout a martyrdom of forty years, to death.

But "hark ye yet again—the little lower layer." Melville's capitulation in the face of overwhelming odds was limited to the sphere of action. His embattled soul refused surrender and lived on, breathing back defiance, disputing "to the last gasp" of his "earthquake life" the sovereignty of that inscrutable authority in him. As he wrote in *Pierre,* unless the enthusiast "can find the talismanic secret, to reconcile this world with his own soul, then there is no peace for him, no slightest truce for him in this life." Years later we find him holding the same ground. "Terrible is earth" was his conclusion, but despite all, "no retreat through me." By this dogged stand he bequeathed to succeeding generations the unsolved problem of the talismanic secret.

Only at the very last, instinct spent, earthquake over, did he fall back to a position close to Christian resignation. In his Being, was not this man "a wonder, a grandeur, and a woe?"

2.   American Icarus

HENRY A. MURRAY

IF IT WERE NOT FOR A DREAM of flying through the air on a maid's rump and an impromptu story of a modern Pegasus fertilizing from the sky a poor farmer's barren fields (and his cow to boot)—if it were not for these two exploits of the imagination, a psychologist might never have been goaded to delve in celestial myths and, with a selection of these in mind, to brood over the episodes of Grope's terrestrial career and personality.[1]

Could this short, dark-haired, loose-knit young man be a reincarnation of Tammuz, Attis, or Adonis? A fertility god or sky hero? Such questions would never have occurred to anyone who noticed him approaching on a campus path—collar open at the neck, unshaved most probably, and with a dazed look as if he had just got out of bed. "A typical adolescent," one might have thought in passing. There was little about him to impel a second glance.

As far as we could see, Grope's overt atti-

tudes and behaviors were not far from commonplace. There is nothing unusual, surely, in an apathetic reaction to college courses, lectures, and required reading. Not rare, though less frequent, is withdrawal from competitive extra-curricular activities. The only manifest attitude which seemed incongruent with the prevailing sociological portrait of today's American adolescent was Grope's reluctance to become engaged in any erotic ventures. An embarrassment in this sphere, however, is not so irregular as our magazines—Life and Look, say—might lead us to believe: in our files are numerous case records of college men who are Grope's match on this count. In short, when assessed in terms of overt reactions and proactions, our subject seems to belong to an extraordinary class of college variants.

It is when weighed in the scales of imaginary activities that Grope stands out as an unduplicated wonder. For these he had an abundance of free hours. Having rejected most opportunities to participate in real endeavors, he had little to interfere with his enjoyment of countless private shows of his excelling fitness for irreal endeavors, mostly of heroic scope. So pure, so unmodulated, so archetypal, were the majority of these dramas—exhibited in his dreams, reveries, story constructions, and most highly valued goals—that we could not escape the supposition that they had come all the way from childhood in their present shapes, with but slight revisions by negating or by counteracting tendencies. At our disposal there were no facts that contradicted this hypothesis, a good many that supported it.

The conclusion to be tentatively submitted here is that one highly influential covert part of Grope's current personality consists of a com-

SOURCE. Henry A. Murray, "American Icarus" in *Clinical Studies in Personality*, Vol. 2, pp. 615–641. Edited by A. Burton and R. E. Harris. New York: Harper, 1955.

---

[1] Grope, the hero of this story, was one of an aggregate of college students who volunteered to serve as subjects in a series of experiments and tests conducted at the Psychological Clinic, Department of Social Relations, Harvard University. The enterprise was financed by grants from the Rockefeller Foundation and from the Laboratory of Social Relations. For many of the findings included in this report I am indebted to my colleagues—Gardner Lindzey, Goodhue Livingston, Henry W. Riecken, Mortimer Slaiman, Robert N. Wilson, Esme Brooks, Tamara Dembo, Herbert Goldings, Josephine L. Murray, and Barbara Tuttle.

pound infantile complex, or unity thema, which approximates an ideal type.[2]

Procedures

1. *Autobiography and interviews.* Grope was given a brief outline of important topics to serve as guide in writing his autobiography; and then, after his autobiography had been delivered and read, he was interviewed three times (each for an hour), with items in this document serving as starting points for special lines of interrogation.

2. *Questionnaires and inventories.* Grope filled out the following forms (an asterisk * indicating a form that is not yet published): (a) * Inventory of Overt Behaviors; (b) * Inventory of Abilities; (c) Extraversion-Introversion Questionnaire (Gray after Jung); (d) Four Functions Questionnaire (Gray after Jung); (e) Ascendance-Submission Test (Allport); (f) Study of Values (Allport and Vernon); (g) * Literary Knowledge and Interests (Wilson); (h) Psychosomatic Inventory (McFarland).

3. *Projective procedures.* The unhappily named "projective" tests administered to Grope included: (a) MAPS (Shneidman); (b) Four Pictures (van Lennep); (c) Tri-Dimensional (Twitchell-Allen); (d) Dramatic Productions (Erikson); (e) Standard TAT (Murray); (f) * TAT No. 2 (Murray); (g) Rorschach; (h) * Musical Reveries; (i) Sentence Completion (modified); (j) * Sentence Construction; (k) * Similes; (l) Draw-A-Family; (m) Szondi; (n) * Mind-Reading; (o) * Psychodramatic.

4. *Miscellaneous.* Grope also acted as a subject in three special research projects: (a) Happiness Study (Goldings); (b) Facial Asymmetry Study (Lindzey); and (c) Study of Autonomic Reactions to Film of a Primitive Initiation (Mutilation) Ceremony (Lindzey, Ax, and Aas). Data pertinent to the assessment of Grope's level of mental ability were obtained from the college office: ratings on entrance examinations and course grades.

---

[2] An "ideal" unity thema, or "ideal" integrate of infantile complexes, is a convenient theoretical construct, or fiction, which may be defined as a constellation of clear-cut, interdependent themas (forms of dynamic interaction) coupled with evaluations, which is not adulterated or contaminated by irrelevant, inconsistent or antithetical components.

Since there is no space here to report the results of all these procedures, I shall select from our total collection of findings only those which seem most relevant to the formulation of the historic course of Grope's manifest personality and the formulation of his covert personality, or "unity thema," as expressed in his imagination. Although this circumscription of aim necessitates the exclusion of certain less related aspects of Grope's personality, it may be reassuring to know that it has not entailed the omission of any significant facts reported in his autobiography. The following is a reconstructed transcript of that document written, for the most part, in his own words.

Past History, Autobiography

1. *Family history.* Grope was born near Springfield, Illinois, of a middle-class family in comfortable circumstances. His father graduated from a state university, worked his way from salesman to buyer in the shoe department of a large store, and, in middle age, organized a wholesale shoe distributing company of his own. His mother also had a college education. After graduation she did promotional work for a department store and later engaged in various civic enterprises. She gave birth to three children: Grope, our subject, another son born two years later, and fourteen years after that a daughter. During Grope's youth, the family lived mainly in two suburban homes, with a few summers spent in the country, near one of the Great Lakes.

2. *Infancy and childhood.* Grope was a fat baby with curly hair. He believes that he was breast fed but has no idea at what age he was weaned. Weighing six and a half pounds at birth, he quadrupled his weight in the first year. Despite his rolls of fat, he learned to walk when he was twelve months old.

Grope's earliest memory is of dumping his supper on the floor. Seated in a high chair, he was asked by his mother if he wanted some string beans and, being in a bad mood, repeatedly said no, even though he usually liked string beans. She finally put the plate in front of him, and it was at this point that he upset it and pushed the beans on the floor. This, he writes, "was my feelings of grief that accompany a sort of 'martyr complex' or 'cut off your nose to spite your face complex.' " (In an interview he defined the complex as a willingness to reject or throw away something he wanted or to fail in an enterprise if, by so doing, he could thwart and condemn, and thus aggrieve his parents. It seems that in his mind a suffering remorseful mother was the acme of sweet revenge.)

Grope has always been somewhat finicky about food. During his later grade-school years this finickiness was, in fact, the root of his most tempestuous quarrels with his mother. When he came home for lunch, he would sometimes run out of the house and back to school if he saw that turnips and cauliflower were being served. (Thus in one act did he deprive himself and condemn his mother.)

Several memories between the ages of 2 and 4 are of food: a cookie shop, a cookie given him by a lady, his mother saying, "What do you say?"; noticing a large display of fruit in a railroad station and being told by his mother that they were dates; receiving a "great big beautiful lollypop" at school and having his mother cut away all but a tiny piece of it.

Grope wet his bed and his pants quite frequently until he was 11. It was a daily issue at first which necessitated his carrying an extra pair of pants to nursery school. (He started nursery school at 3.) When he wet he would cry so sorrowfully that the teacher would give him a cookie and then change his clothes. He tells us that his parents now believe that his enuresis persisted because he "didn't have enough affection." There may be some grains of truth in this, because both parents drove to work immediately after breakfast and were likely to be too tired when they returned in the evening to spend much time with their children. To their eldest, playing alone most of the day, the summers seemed "interminable." When night came he would not go to bed without a particular, highly valued knotted bundle of cloth, which he called "my Ewa." Today, he imagines that in a child's life such an object "takes the place of a doll, which in turn takes the place of a Deity or an omnipresent mother."

In his autobiography Grope devoted an unusual amount of space to an account of the toys of his childhood and of the course of his attachment to them. Whenever he was made to wait for something he had asked his parents for, his desire for that particular thing, and hence the value of it, in his mind's eye, would rise. But within a week or two of its arrival, the toy's appeal would begin to wane and before very long it was discarded, broken, or perhaps stolen. His Mechano set, his chemistry set, and his bricklaying set each had lost its luster by the end of the day it was presented to him. Only his painting set, his cap pistol, and his bicycle held his interest for any length of time. He tells of a toy auto he enjoyed until the day he sat his little brother in it and sent it rolling down a hill. Since the little fellow couldn't steer, the descent ended in a collision which bent the front axle. (There is no mention of the sibling's fate.) The auto was useless after that. Only once did Grope "very seriously" want something—a pocket watch, and his father, responsive as usual to his requests, bought him a good one which cost about five dollars. When last seen, it was lying in the snow with both hands broken and the crystal gone. "This sight of utter waste sorely disgusted me and the memory still makes me slightly angry." All of a piece with these experiences is Grope's summary statement: "Throughout my life I have found it very difficult to accept gifts properly. My appreciation is restrained and unenthusiastic." (This avowal was later confirmed by observing Grope's dead-pan response to an "experimental" gift.)

He learned to ride a bicycle when he was 7. His father would run behind him with his hand on the seat while he turned the pedals. One day he went thirty yards in one stretch but, on looking round and seeing that his father had stopped supporting him, fell off. ("Which shows what confidence will do.") He was quite proud that he was able to ride a bicycle when other boys his age could not. One night he left the bicycle outside and it was stolen.

Grope would sometimes "make up" knowledge and say something astonishing for a child of his years. Once, at the age of 6, at his grandfather's house he overheard a discussion about fire. He announced that "Fire is a yellow-orange gas from outer space." This utterance made such a hit that he was asked to repeat it over and over again until he got "sick of it."

Between the ages of 3 and 10 Grope was in the care of a German maid who tried to teach him how to read the clock. Each time he got it wrong she would slap him in the face, which only made him more flustered and her "more frustrated." But the maid appealed to him despite this treatment, or perhaps because of it.

3. *School Experiences.* Since he had gone to nursery school when he was 3, Grope did not have to attend kindergarten. He has few memories of his early years at primary school, except that he showed talent for drawing in second grade, and at home read and reread the Oz books (by L. F. Baum). In the third grade he overheard his teacher telling his mother that he was bright.

He acquired no athletic abilities until he moved to another school, just before entering fifth grade. Near his new home there were real woods which he enjoyed tremendously. He liked to climb birch trees and swing down again to earth, over and over again. He "shinnied up" practically every tree he could find. He developed a lot of strength this way, and one day after school he threw down, one by one, every boy in the class. He states that he soon became the best athlete in the school, the best football player, the best drawer, the smartest (with the highest mark on an achievement test), the first person to be elected president of the sixth-grade class, and the only person to be elected twice. The teacher kept telling him in front of the class that he was most likely to succeed. Besides, he was commander-in-chief of a club he formed, and "half a dozen girls" had a crush on him. He tells us that outwardly he was very modest, but inwardly he was convinced that no one surpassed him in all-around ability.

He enjoyed painting lessons in sixth grade and did quite a bit of this until his sophomore year in high school, when other activities took precedence; but he still had time for his drawing.

His "fall" began in sixth grade with loss of weight and sluggishness. He had many colds during that summer and when he went back to school in the seventh grade found that he hadn't grown an inch. The following winter he was in bed for two straight months. When he got well, his athletic career was "shot." He had lost his muscle and, what was more important to him, his courage. He feels that after this he was never much of an athlete. Today he plays only a fair game of pingpong, tennis, baseball, and basketball. During his illness (seventh grade) he learned to play chess with such expertness that he beat all his relatives. He also learned to play bridge at this time.

Grope's account of his "fall" and subsequent lack of distinction at school is not wholly in accord with his list of high-school accomplish-ments. In his freshman year he won the bantamweight boxing title and in his senior year the middleweight title. Despite illnesses he played varsity tennis and junior varsity football. He was skillful in managing the campaign of the seventh-grade class president and the junior-grade vice-president, both of whom won. He was elected treasurer of his class sophomore year, and a member of the Student Council. Also, he was editor of the yearbook and an excellent comedian and master of ceremonies, talents which his classmates acknowledged by electing him "Biggest Joker" on graduation. In his studies he did well; he received the highest mark on a mathematics achievement test, was the only boy in his class to win a certificate on a nationwide scholastic test, and passed the college board examinations with creditable grades. In his spare time he collected stamps, drew and painted, played chess and bridge. He enjoyed building model airplanes.

His friendships were many but casual, never enduring. When he was a freshman in high school he was very close to a boy who lived on his street until a teacher happened to remark that familiarity breeds contempt. Both boys took this very seriously and their friendship deteriorated. At college he made no real friends until the end of his sophomore year. Currently he is extremely fond of one boy, a former member of his card-playing clique.

From eighth through tenth grade Grope suffered from halitosis, which he believes, made him much less popular and thus gave rise to a distressing inferiority complex. He thought he could make himself less offensive by speaking with a minimal expiration of breath, and now, six years later, his voice is habitually so low that his words are not always audible.

4. *Sexual experiences.* Grope's sexual potentialities were first aroused when he was about 8, the object of his "erotic tendencies" being the maid who was in charge of him. Seeing her breasts on one occasion started a sort of interior excitement which he did not think about or try to define but the nature of which was indicated in a dream in which he rode through the sky on the rump of this maid. He began to get inexplicable erections before urinating and when he was angry or frustrated. One of his more bizarre fantasies was that of flying over a city and urinating on the buildings, all of which were constructed out of women's bodies. A little later, his sex education began informally.

Learning "dirty words and dirty jokes," etc., he began to get a general idea "of what females were for." One of his chief misconceptions was that intercourse was achieved when the male inserted his penis into the female anus. As time went on, however, things became clearer and his curiosity was appeased by reading the more pertinent parts of Clendenning's *The Human Body.*

Outside of parties where Spin the Bottle and Post Office were played, he had nothing that approached an affair until he was 16, when he had a year-long romance with an 18-year-old girl. This affair petered out because he had "never heard or imagined of going beyond the leg-wrestling stage without making it actual intercourse." When he was 17 he "went steady" with a girl his own age, but they never got beyond the mutual masturbation stage and they finally separated, his reason being "too much sex."

He had never seen any reason for masturbating and believed that his friends did it merely to prove to themselves that they were virile. But at a summer camp where he was employed after graduating from high school he had occasion to discuss masturbation with one of the dishwashers. When asked by Grope why he masturbated, the young man replied, "Well, for the *thrill.*" This was news! Grope determined to start that very night. He has been masturbating frequently ever since. He suffers no remorse as he keeps reminding himself that the more sexually active he is now (according to Kinsey's findings), the longer he will retain his potency in later life.

At college this form of sexual outlet has taken the place of dating. He had only a few blind dates in freshman year, none since. He is looking forward to marriage and right now would settle for any girl who is "attractive, intelligent, non-argumentative, has large lips, wide hips, and is willing and able to bear me about half-a-dozen boys."

5. *Family relationships.* Grope thinks that the relationship between his parents has been a "pretty good" one, despite occasional quarrels which are likely to terminate with his mother weeping. As for himself, Grope affirms that he has never loved either his mother or his father, his present attitude being one of confirmed indifference, mixed with a fair amount of "loyalty and respect." While work-

ing for his father's company last summer he gained some appreciation of this parent's business acumen, but his opinion of his mother is no higher than it was ten years ago. He thinks that her deficiences of character outweigh her intellectual gifts. It is she who has disappointed him the most. Notwithstanding this, Grope insists that his parents have always been devoted and generous to him. They often tried to encourage him (with ill success) and were more thrilled than he whenever he was in any way outstanding. He is nonetheless disposed to believe that they must have made a lot of mistakes in rearing him, their first child.

When Grope's sister was born, a few years ago, his parents, "having read books on sibling rivalry," tried to heap an unusual amount of affection upon both him and his brother. This, he feels, was ridiculous, since by that time he had long outgrown any dependence on their love.

During his teens Grope had many fierce quarrels with his parents, ending by his plotting various schemes for revenge, such as six-weeks silent treatment. He often imagined his own death and his parents' subsequent grief, one particularly gratifying fantasy being that of resurrection from the grave as a ghost and then of gloating unseen over his mother's remorseful grief.

Grope's brother was born when he was 3, but, he assures use, there was no sibling rivalry in those early years. In fact, he hardly ever thought of him. His brother was a nonentity until the age of 8, at which time the two boys began playing together and getting into fights. They became good friends in high school, when Grope began to appreciate him a little more. He states that he doesn't fight with his brother now, the latter being an inch taller, ten pounds heavier, and solid muscle.

6. *Ambitions, goals, values.* As a child Grope wanted to be an orange grower. Later, after reading a book on China by Pearl Buck, he "became incensed with the desire" to go there, "an industrially backward land," and build bridges. He also thought of becoming a painter. As his estimation of his own power increased, he became "more and more inspired and confident" about his role in life.

His major recurrent fantasy was one of landing on a desert island in the Pacific with a band of followers, discovering an inexhaustible spring of fresh water and an abundant food supply, and then founding a new civilization with himself as king and lawgiver. He often dreamed and daydreamed of self-propelled flights and of jumping off a high place and floating gracefully and gently to the ground. But he was almost equally hospitable to less extravagant fantasies: he considered becoming a prize fighter, an actor, an army general, a millionaire, an inventor, a psychiatrist, and a teacher. "It would be a lot of fun working with kids, teaching them with a sense of humor, and having them think you are a 'good guy.'" He has imagined himself a famous tap dancer, a singer, and a movie comedian. He is attracted by the stage and has a tentative plan of enrolling in some school of the drama. His more immediate intention, however, is to enlist in the Air Corps and become a pilot. Although in his opinion world wars are preventable evils, he expects another one within fifteen years, which will destroy much or most of civilization. The two worst things that might happen to him are (a) to be maimed in the war and (b) to lose his self-confidence. Finally, he writes: "If I could remodel the world to my heart's content, I would establish a sound World Government and would like to be the dictator, a good dictator." He would be "most proud" of having his name "go down in history as a leader, or as an artist, or as a discoverer or inventor."

He thinks that his insight increased most rapidly during his early teens when he was embattled with his parents. It was then also that he began working out his philosophy, the chief tenet of which is that every person's goal in life is happiness. Another tenet is that happiness is attainable in a number of different ways, depending on the individual. In his own case, the major sources of prospective happiness, and hence the most valued goals, are money, power, glory, and fame. "These are the alternatives of most normal men." He has never been to church and states that he is "sure there is no sort of God or vital force."

At the moment Grope feels that he is spiritually becalmed. In the past, his development has always occurred in "spurts or cycles." "If I did something well, I would be spiritually elevated, that is, my spirits would become gay. In the last few years my spirits have been in equilibrium and my development has more or less stagnated." Today he does not seem to be able to decide anything. He will either try to turn over a new leaf academically or get a job some place, such as opening a snack bar with a friend. Concluding his topic, he writes: "I am just biding my time and waiting for the day when the 'soul' will ignite and this inner fire will send me hurtling (two rungs at a time) up the ladder of success."

7. *Evaluations of self and others.* Grope highly esteems "all other people." Everyone seems to him interesting and exciting (more or less); but he especially admires the personalities and achievements of supremely great men. He has had many heroes—da Vinci and Van Gogh in particular. At times, he tells us, he derives a lot of personal satisfaction from being gregarious, but he gets depressed if he is guilty of a *faux pas:* he "kicks himself mentally" for days.

Grope feels that the world's estimate of him is that he is a "pretty nice guy." As for his own estimate of himself, he used to think he was "pretty hot stuff," but now he "just agrees with the world."

Components of Current Manifest Personality

In unfamiliar social situations Grope is keenly observant but shyly self-suppressed; he speaks little and with a very low voice. He waits for the alter to make the first move. Once his embarrassment has dissolved, however, he becomes relaxed, tensionless, responsive, and quietly jocose. In this phase he strikes one as an easygoing, good-natured fellow—a "good guy"—with a keen, ever present, satirical, though somewhat juvenile, sense of humor.

Grope reports that a few months after his arrival at Harvard he came to the conclusion that he was a "small frog in a big puddle," surrounded by many far superior competitors for athletic, social, and academic honors. No hope for glory. Since then he has made the minimum amount of intellectual effort. He studies very little and cuts many of his lectures, especially if they come before noon. As a result, he is on probation, ranking well below the scholarship level predicted for him—an "under-achiever." He has joined no organizations, has accepted no roles or responsibilites, and dates no girls. This abstinence allows him to devote the maximum amount of time to sleep, relaxation, daydreaming, and playing bridge with a small clique of cronies. Of these the one he most liked has recently been flunked out of college. Except for this boy, he gives no evidence of affectional attachments.

Grope was rated (on a 1–6 point scale) by himself, by two of his acquaintances, and by six members of the Clinic assessment staff on a large number of manifest behavioral variables. Only those variables on which he was almost unanimously rated among the lowest 25 percent of our subjects (1 or 2), or on which he was almost unanimously rated among the highest 25 percent (5 or 6), will be mentioned here.

Grope was judged to be unusually passive (inactive, indolent, apathetic) under current conditions, though not incapable of considerable, though spasmodic, activity under more favorable conditions (need Passivity 5). There were no *objectifications* of ambition (need Achievement 1). These two ratings (high passivity, low achievement) are confluent with our subject's inability to start on his own steam and to keep going without coöperation or without anticipation of a close reward (need Autonomy, Self-Sufficiency 1, and Endurance 1).

All of a piece with these estimates was the high mark Grope received on need Exhibition, Recognition (5), which was clearly a very strong disposition of his personality, though manifested during the current period only when he found himself in a familiar, congenial, and appreciative social group, at which times this need was likely to be fused with Playmirth (6). He gained the attention he enjoyed by comical displays. It might be said that Expression, Exhibition was a part of Grope's overt *private* personality (behaviors manifested in intimate interactions with receptive, reciprocating alters), because in more public or less familiar situations this disposition was checked by his fear of committing a *faux pas* or "making a fool of himself" (need Inavoidance 5, coupled with a persisting Inferiority Complex).

Grope was also rated high (5) on need Excitance (enjoyment of novelty, excitement, thrills, spectacles, etc.) and high (5) relative to other undergraduates on need Sentience (appreciation or composition of artistic forms), despite the fact that his drawings were not "serious art" but more in the nature of satirical cartoons (Playmirth again predominating). Most questionable—in fact definitely wrong in

retrospect—was the rating of 5 on need Affiliation, because, though habitually good-natured, smiling, and responsive, Grope had formed no firm and lasting friendships. He seemed to be existing without links, a free-floater in today's "lonely crowd," a passing acquaintance, with whom one is never seriously involved and on whom one can never seriously depend, a man of superficial contacts who does not attach himself for long to any one person and yet is dependent on everyone he meets. His self was open to friendliness—in no way distant, withdrawn, encased, aloof, resentful, or suspicious (need Rejection 2). He was rated below average on overt sexual behavior (need Sex 2) but rather high (5) on sexual and social curiosity (voyeurism).

Grope's room was always in a "mess"; he did not put his belongings in allotted places, and when he took off his clothes at night, he dropped them on the floor where they remained till morning. His appearance, handwriting, and written papers were all equally disorderly (need Order 1, and need Retention [conservation of possessions] 2). So much for the most striking of Grope's overt (manifest, or objectified) needs.

It was inferred on the basis of these and other evidences that Grope was very low (1) on degree of Ego Structuration and equally low (1) on degree of Superego Integration. He has very seldom, if ever, been concerned with moral questions and has no memory of ever feeling guilty or remorseful. No sociocentric interests or group identifications are apparent. His most valued goals—money, power, glory, fame—are perceived in a purely egocentric fashion. He has no religion. His dominant axis of evaluation is superiority-inferiority (of ability, wealth, social status, authority, and prestige); the ethical axis is absent or repressed, as it is in psychopathic personalities. This notwithstanding, Grope is guilty of nothing more hurtful or illegal than a few minor boyhood thefts. He seems to be free of vicious inclinations.

Grope rated himself high on Artistic Ability (6), Entertaining Ability (5), Social Ability (5), and Intuitive Ability (5), but very low on Self-Directive Ability (1) and Memory Ability (1).

Grope's responses on most of our questionnaires and inventories placed him in the middle range. He came out high (5), however, on Extraversion, and on the Studies of Values indi-

cated more concern with Political issues than
with the other five. On Level of Satisfaction
he was low average and also low average in his
estimates of the satisfaction level of other persons (supplementary self-projection).

Interpretation of Current Manifest Personality

Since Grope showed considerable interest in
athletics and scholarship at high school and
was periodically quite energetic in organizing
and promoting various social enterprises, we
surmise that his current apathy, his lack of enthusiasm and will power, his submission to a
sluggish id, is "situational," rather than un-
changeably constitutional. The current situation
is one of being outclassed in all spheres by
more talented and/or more resolute associates.
Evidently, he is not devoted to any form of athletics for its own sake, to learning for its own
sake, or to any one of the numerous accessible
extracurricular activities for its own sake; nor
is he prompted by a need to learn some skill
and to accomplish something for the sake of
a resulting inner satisfaction or self-respect. It
is glory he is after—praise, prestige, and fame—
and since his present situation offers no prospects of these rewards, why should he exert
himself?

Another significant attribute of Grope's current situation is the absence of parental support. During his school years in Illinois he had
been constantly spurred on and, "whenever in
any way outstanding," applauded by his for-
him-ambitious parents, and among his classmates, furthermore, during at least one glorious
period of his life, he had been the "best" at
everything. But at Harvard unhappily no such
encouragements were at hand, and without encouragement he had no confidence, and without confidence he was nothing. He had to learn
his worth from the lips of others. This conclusion was confirmed by the finding that a few
sentences of "experimental" praise set him
going at his books for a week or more on two
occasions.

Another confirmation comes from the story
Grope composed for Picture 7 of the TAT:

A gray-haired man is looking at a younger man
who is sullenly staring into space.

Here's a serious and intense young man, methodical, who the moment he entered Harvard
knew he was going to be a pure physicist. He
graduated Magna, Phi Beta Kappa, and went
on to graduate school, where he was more or
less a protégé of one of the great, good professors there, because he demonstrated unusual
ability to learn, to grasp complicated theories
as well as experiments in applied physics. Of
course by this time, six years, he'd be in for
a Ph.D. He is wondering if there is more to
life than just studying. He's having his doubts
about whether he can be happy being a physicist, working by himself instead of with others.
This kind professor in the Graduate School sees
the despondency of the last few weeks and decides to have a talk with him. He tries to encourage him at first, by saying, "If you want,
I have a very good job set up for you with one
of the big companies." This guy shrugs and
finally decides to tell the scientist about what's
been bothering him. He does, and this scientist
is very understanding, and says, "Well, when I
was your age I felt the same way." He had a lot
of insight. He told him exactly what he was
thinking about. He said that he felt the same
way when he was his age, and that he must look
for a purpose in life. It was just a psychological
talk, kind of bolstered him. Well, anyway, the
young man goes along with this. He just needed
that extra push.

Among the internal conditions contributing
to Grope's present slump in his weak, unintegrated, and immature ego system (already
mentioned)—the absence of work habits and
the insufficiency of will power, the inability,
when bored or tired, to force himself to finish
something he has undertaken. Another determinant is his low tolerance of failure, his fear
of "falling." This might stem from a childhood
supposition that his ambitious parents would
not respect him if it were proved that he was
not among the best. By not competing, by not
trying, he can avoid the demonstration of this
humiliating probability. But in the sphere of
scholarship it is a different matter: how can he
both abstain from effort and avoid the stigma
of being expelled from college? At this point
another factor begins to operate, Grope's "spite
complex": failure can be used as a weapon of
condemnation. He confessed that by flunking
out of college he could prove that his father
had erred in urging him to go to Harvard
rather than to Illinois or to some smaller college
where he might have been a "big frog."

One final all-important determinant of
Grope's collapse at Harvard is the height, diversity, and inconstancy of his ideal self-con-

ception (a fitful sequence of heterogeneous ego-ideal figures, some of whom—a self-propelled sky flier, the founder of a new civilization, the dictator of a world government, a famous inventor—are far beyond his present reach). With these glorious visions running through his head, how can he bend down to day-by-day pedestrian exertions in order to make for himself a little name at Harvard? He says that, although he used to think he was "pretty hot stuff," he has finally come round to the world's view that he is merely a good guy. This is what his intellect has decided; but the conflict is not thereby settled: to his soul a good guy is not nearly good enough. Hence, it is necessary for him to constantly refight the battle between his ideal self-conception and his real self-conception, as the following TAT story No. 8 makes evident.

An adolescent boy looks straight out of the picture. The barrel of a rifle is visible at one side, and in the background is the dim scene of a surgical operation, like a reverie-image.

This picture seems to show the imaginations of a boy. . . . The kid is a college student, leaning up against one of the pillars of Widener and thinking. He's a little frustrated by things at school—the competition, and the state of affairs, not only in school, but the fact that the world in his day is so much tougher. He feels that if he lived back in the days of, say, Aristotle he would certainly have thought up some of the fundamental concepts of physics or chemistry, or could have become a great doctor. If he wanted to be a pre-med student in this day, it would be very hard to achieve anything, any fame and glory. He takes time out to think back on the old days. Now he thinks he's a doctor on this warship, trying to perform an operation, using the light that comes through one of the portholes and a dim lantern. He thinks how people would look up to him the way he sterilizes everything, a practice not usually done then. . . . The reason he's doing these daydreams is because he doesn't feel he can get much glory in this age, this civilization. He needs to go back to an older one in his thoughts. He finally realizes that perhaps there were geniuses in the old days too. He would not have had any more chance then to achieve glory than he does now. He feels he must be satisfied with his time and position, and must get happiness out of some of the fundamental personal things in life, rather than getting his name in a history book. Anyway, he finally realizes his mediocrity. Before he went to school he thought he was

good and he comes to school and realizes there are many others better than him, who have intellectual intelligence over him. He thinks that due to all this competition he will never get anywhere in a society like this, where there seem to be so few inventions left. He daydreams about a past where he would certainly have made a name for himself, there was so much room for growth. After two more years of study he realizes he isn't such a hot shot and has to be content with an average existence.

Components of Covert Personality

1. *Urethral erotism.* Grope recalls experiencing (during boyhood) erections just previous to urination, as observed by Halverson (1) in babies; and he entertained the idea that babies were made by urinating into a woman's rectum. In short, sex was apperceived in urinary terms. Also he manifested, in high degree, every other concomitant of urethral erotism, as defined by Freud and his followers: cathection of fire, "burning" ambition, exhibitionism, and voyeurism. Remember Grope's bright saying: "Fire is a yellow-orange gas from outer space." Even today he "gets a thrill" by lighting wastepaper in his tin scrap basket and seeing it flare up. There is a high incidence of pertinent fire imagery in his projective protocols. Finally, there is the association of persistent enuresis and urethral erotism (dreams of urination accompanied by ejaculation) which we and others have found in a number of personalities. Thus, the evidence for the presence and continued operation of this rather enigmatic infantile complex is about as complete as one can reasonably demand without a full-length psycho-analysis.

2. *Ascensionism.* This is the name I have given to the wish to overcome gravity, to stand erect, to grow tall, to dance on tiptoe, to walk on water, to leap or swing in the air, to climb, to rise, to fly, or to float down gradually from on high and land without injury, not to speak of rising from the dead and ascending to heaven. There are also emotional and ideational forms of ascensionism—passionate enthusiasm, rapid elevations of confidence, flights of the imagination, exultation, inflation of spirits, ecstatic mystical up-reachings, poetical and religious—which are likely to be expressed in the imagery of physical ascensionism. The upward thrust of desire may also manifest itself in the cathection of tall pillars and towers, of high

peaks and mountains, of birds—high-flying hawks and eagles—and of the heavenly bodies, especially the sun. In its most mundane and secular form, ascensionism consists of a craving for upward social mobility, for a rapid and spectacular rise of prestige.

In Grope's case, ascensionism was fused—at the very start perhaps—with urethral erotism. Recall his dream of flying through the air on the maid's rump (in conjunction with his urinary theory of intercourse) and his fantasies of urinating from the sky on the bodies of women. Then read the following story told to one of the (unpublished) TAT 2 pictures:

Barn surrounded by snow. A winged horse is flying across the sky. The head of a bearded man is in right lower corner. In the snow is the dim outline of a girl's face.

An old hermit went out into the woods and built himself a farm. After thirty years of living all by himself on the crops he produced, he got pretty tired of this humdrum existence, so he decided that he wanted to re-enter the competitive world and try to sell, was planning on selling his crops, planning to build some sort of a fortune. So he worked for a few years, couldn't seem to get very large crops, really good crops. They wouldn't grow. What he needed was more fertilizer, but he couldn't afford fertilizer in any quantity, so he was practically at his wits' end, and one night he decided to turn to religion; and as miracles will happen, the very next day Pegasus flew over and fertilized all his plants. Not only that, but the cow in the born bore him a daughter; something he had always wanted. In the picture here, he is squinting in his happiness; feeling that life has really been rewarding. So the picture is the spirit of happiness.

Grope reported many dreams and daydreams of rising in the air and flying, sometimes in a car or in a horse-drawn chariot, like Apollo's. Other fantasies were of shooting through space and landing on the planet Mars.

In his autobiography he proudly tells us that he learned to walk at 12 months and to ride a bicycle at 7 years; and he devotes a long paragraph to a detailed account of each stage of his baby sister's progress in overcoming the pull of gravity. In addition to these items are Grope's passion for climbing trees, swinging out and down, his fantasy of becoming a tap-dancer, the model airplanes he built, his admiration for Leonardo da Vinci's flying machine, and his intention of enlisting in the Air Corps, and

the twelve or more flying creatures he saw in the Rorschach blots: two butterflies, two flying bats, a flying dog, a horse's head with hoofs emerging from a cloud bank, a pair of vultures being swooped on from above by a pair of eagles and these attacked by a flock of jumping woodpeckers. Asked by a hypothetical fairy godmother to make "seven wishes," he listed Height as his fourth wish.

3. *Cynosural narcism.* This strikes me as a suitable term (more embracing than exhibitionism) to denote a craving for unsolicited attention and admiration, a desire to attract and enchant all eyes, like a star in the firmament. It is first supremely gratified at that *epiphanal* moment of babyhood when the grandparents and relatives arrive at the cradle, with gifts perhaps, to beam with wonder at this new emergence of pure potentiality, pure Being. No memory of this, of course, in Grope; but in line with it is the grandfather's astonishment (at a later date) when the child came out with his cynosural pronouncement about fire. The cynosural ego-ideal which Grope shaped for himself after he entered fifth grade and became the best at everything has remained to this day almost intact. In Draw-A-Family his self-portrait, twice the size of his father's and his mother's, was of a prodigiously strong athlete, corresponding in every way to his description of the image that came to mind when he was handed the blank card (No. 16) of the TAT:

Well, I see a huge, powerful man. He is in the midst of throwing a shot-put. He weighs about 310 pounds and stands 6 feet, 6 inches high. He has no clothing except bathing trunks. There he stands with spectators all around him. He's about to win his third straight decathlon. Not only is he the most perfect physical specimen in all of Greece, but he is a nice guy, unspoiled. Everyone likes him. They practically worship him. He is a sensation; a wonderful box-office draw. . . .

Already we begin to see a close, emotionally logical—indeed, an almost inevitable—connection, if not fusion, between ascensionism and cynosural narcism: the way to attract all eyes is to be very tall, to stand erect above the multitude, and best of all to rise in the air like a god. Remembering that in Grope's personality ascensionism was fused with urethral erotism and that urethral erotism ordinary reaches its peak in the phallic phase of psychosexual development, we may surmise that we are dealing with an imagination in which an ascending cynosural phallus was transmuted into an ascending cynosural body, both being "pretty hot stuff" and possibly on this account associated with fire, to constitute, in any event, the kind of burning ambition which Grope portrays in his concluding sentence: "I am just biding my time and waiting for the day when my 'soul' will ignite and this inner fire will send me hurtling (two rungs at a time) up the ladder of success." Clearly this type of ambition depends on the carrying power of an unpredictable upsurge or excess of psychic energy (spontaneity, creative zest, self-confidence, enthusiasm), an excess which may someday be shown to consist of a quantum of sublimated erotic energy. In any event, little reliance is placed on will power, discipline, industry, conscientiousness.

Furthermore, since the youthful energy—passionnate, romantic, fiery—that serves as motive power for this type of ambition is not likely to continue on a high level for very long without frequent reinforcements, its strategy entails a series of short, spirited, and spectacular achievements, never a long, slow, and methodical, solitary and inconspicuous, course of action.

The association of an ascending cynosural body and ascending fire is illustrated by Grope's story to Card 17 (TAT). The fourth World War ended, he said, when a nation of supermen overran the globe, and now, in each conquered country, the victors are trying by means of strength tests to select other possible supermen with whom to start a new race. He continues as follows:

A naked man is clinging to a rope. He is in the act of climbing up or down.

. . . In this case this person elected to climb a rope; he was quite strong. The bottom of the rope was made of an inflammable—soaked in potassium chloride, I guess. They would set fire to the bottom of it and the flames would go at a certain slightly increasing rate. If the person failed to reach the top before the flames did, of course he was killed. This person starts out like fury and by fifty yards the rope is burned only about five yards from the bottom. . . . About seventy-five yards up his arms are like lead-weight. He doesn't feel that he can go any further. . . . He goes another five or ten yards and suddenly he slips back and barely manages to catch on five yards below. By now the flames are about half way up. Then

he gets panicky, gets another tremendous burst, and goes about ten yards. He hangs on there and watches the flames increasing their momentum. . . . He goes on taking about a foot at a time, the flames getting nearer. He can't rest—very hard to rest hanging on to a rope. He finally gets about ten yards from the top, that's the last thing he remembers.

The end of this story suggests the next component.

4. *Falling, precipitation.* "Falling" denotes an undesired or accidental descension of something (usually a human body or the status [reputation] of a person, but it may be feces, urine, or any cathected object). "Precipitation," on the other hand, means a consciously or unconsciously desired calamitous descension: the S allows himself to fall or leaps from a height (precipitative suicide), or he pushes another person over a cliff, throws something down, or purposely urinates or defecates on the floor. In one or the other of these two categories—it is often difficult to say which—fall a large number of items in Grope's case history: diurnal and nocturnal enuresis (eleven years of it), frequent micturition (checked on the Psychosomatic Inventory), several memories of fecal incontinence, fantasies of urinating and defecating from the air, the episode of throwing down a plate of string beans (his "martyr complex"), of dropping or throwing down his pocket watch, of shoving his little brother down a hill, of throwing stones down from a height on girls, of throwing down, one by one, every kid in his class, and recently, at college, his writing a comedy in which a rich man (father figure) is thrown by a huge gorilla down a water closet.

Finally, there is Grope's memory of falling off a bicycle and his statement that he often fell from trees, a resonance, perhaps, of earlier more traumatic falls during his learning-to-walk stage. The question of falling or not falling is central in the account he gives of his baby sister's efforts.

In all this we may dimly perceive an ascension-descension cycle on different levels: (a) fiery tumescence (ascension) of penis followed by detumescence (descension) with urination (precipitation of water); (b) ascension of desire for cathected toy followed by descension of cathection and precipitation of toy; (c) ascension of body followed by fall or precipitation (as in the story of rope climber and several other stories); and (d) ascension of status (prestige) followed by descension (the "fall" after this phenomenal sixth-grade success and now his "fall" at college). This is an archetypal thematic sequence against which we are warned by the ancient aphorism: "Pride cometh before a fall." Very probably the Adlerian formula is applicable here: Grope's ardent desire to ascend is a counteractive disposition excited by one or more experience of descent—let us say, some unremembered locomotive accidents coupled with recurrent enuresis, intensified by several falls of status, beginning at 2 years with his displacement from the cynosural center by the birth of that "nonentity," his younger brother.

This ascension-descension sequence is also reminiscent of the great cycles of nature, especially the solar cycle, and the myth of the solar hero, his superior origin, humble foster parentage, rise to glory, decline, death, and resurrection. The precocious, importunate, and extravagant character of Grope's ascensionism suggests that he belongs with the adolescent, overreaching, would-be solar heroes, Icarus and Phaëthon—father-superseding enthusiasts with unstructured ego systems.

Grope's early conflict on the physiological level between fire and water (heat and cold, erection and urination) was entertainingly projected into the weatherman on high in the story he told to Card 11 (TAT):

A road skirting a deep chasm between high cliffs. On the road in the distance are obscure figures. Protruding from the rocky wall on one side is a long head and neck of a dragon.

This must be prehistoric times. A crowd of animals (live in this nice fertile valley). They are half baboon and half pig. And each year they have terrible weather. It would either be a drought, or a flood, extreme heat or extreme cold. So they all gather around and decide to send someone up to the weather maker's place. . . . When he got up there he found that the place was a combination of all the weather. It seems there was fire from one side and rain up above. . . . "What do you want?" . . . This representative presented his case and asked why he had to send so many kinds of bad weather down on all this nice peace loving community. So this weather maker said, "Well, look at it this way, I have all weathers up here and I try to keep them all off you. I have not weather, cold weather, wet and dry weather up here all at once. How do you think I feel

about it anyway? Most of the time I keep at least three of these different kinds of weather up here. I only get rid of one of them. If I wanted to be mean I could send them all out." . . .

Limitations of space forbid the printing of more than these few items out of our large collection of to-me-convincing evidences of the dynamic interdependence, in the mind of this young man, of fire (heat, passion) and ascension of body (rising, flying), of ascension and descension (falling, precipitation), of fire and water, and of descension and water (falling water or falling of body into water). One illustration of this last, truly Icarian association (precipitation into water) must suffice. It is the sixth story on Grope's MAPS protocol:

Well, the man in the striped tie, the Harvard tie, majored in physics (smiles). But he is not a good physicist. He doesn't work. He married a woman for the money she was capable of earning. (But the wife's rapid promotion aroused the envy and ire of the assistant buyer, her unsuccessful male rival at the department store. The buyer, armed with a gun, waylaid her one evening on the Cottage Farm Bridge.) He said to the woman: "Either you resign or I'll shoot you." "No, don't," she said and kept backing away, until she tripped and went over the railing into the river hundreds of feet below. (Two policemen arrive on the scene, followed shortly by the drowned woman's husband and son. The husband, realizing that he and his son have lost their one means of support, pushes the boy over the rail into the water, and then pushes one of the policemen after him.) The salesman sees his chance to make amends. So he shoots the husband, and turns to the other policeman and says, "Can't I go free? Have I paid my debt to society?" . . . The policeman shoots the man, but on the way back he is so drunk with delight that he stumbles over the rail. To this day, no one really knows what happened out there. (Six deaths, four by falling into water.)

Evidences of matricidal and patricidal fantasies (or an anal aggressive type), as well as of castration anxiety, are fairly plentiful; but these are common occurrences in the minds of young men and to stress them here would divert attention from the less conventional integrate of themas which constitutes the thesis of this paper.

5. *Craving for immortality.* No doubt the narcistic core in every man yearns for perpetual existence; but of all our subjects Grope is un-exampled in giving Everlasting Life ("I might settle for 500 years") as one of his seven wishes for himself. If everlasting life on earth is impossible, then one can conceive of resurrection of the body or the soul. As illustration we have Grope's fantasy of breaking out of his tomb, digging his way up, and hovering in phantom form over his parents' house. In three of his stories the hero dies and comes to life again. If resurrection (re-ascension) is not to be vouchsafed a man, there is the possibility of *replication*, which may be defined as the process whereby one or more persons are transformed in the image of the subject. It is the complement of identification, or emulation: the implanting of a memorable and impelling image of the self in the minds of others. This is the evolutionary significance of Grope's over-reaching need for attention, worship, fame—glory in the highest. But if this is denied a man, there is still the possibility of immortalizing his likeness through reproduction. Grope was not invited by the idea of an enduring, stable marriage. For himself he prophesied divorce. What he did crave, however, was a number of tall sons with profiles somewhat better than his own. To Card 13 of the TAT he told the following story:

A young man is standing with downcast head buried in his arm. Behind him is the figure of a woman lying in bed.

John, the man pictured here, liked children. When he went away to school, he used to think a lot about children. . . . As he liked them, he wanted to have his own, but he could never find a girl that he really wanted. So after he graduated, he came home, at night, and first he went into the maid's room—that's the room pictured here. He woke the maid up, and *she* said, "Oh, how good to see you again, John." John, who was not one for mincing words, said, "Listen maid, I want children. Children mean a lot to me. How about it?" So the maid said, "No, no, John no, I am already bespoke." So John said, "Well, in that case there is nothing for me to do." Well, I imagine the thought came to him that now that she was dead he couldn't have his children anyway. It suddenly hit him and he was quite peeved.

Other data reveal a profound concern with the possibility of impotence or sterility.

6. *Depreciation and enthrallment of women, bisexuality.* Grope spoke contemptuously of his mother and cynically of women generally. Love was a never felt experience. But, as his projective protocols made plain, women were nonetheless important, if not indispensable, to him as glorifying agents: a female was (a) someone to be "swept of her feet," to be driven "sex-mad" by the mere sight of him; (b) someone to applaud his exploits; (c) someone with "wide hips" to bear him sons; and (d) someone to mourn his death. As one might expect in such a person, there were abundant evidences of a suffusing feminine component coupled with some degree of homosexuality. This is best illustrated by a story he told in the Tri-Dimensional Test. A king announces that he will give half his kingdom to the person who creates the most beautiful thing in the world. The last contestant (hero of the story) comes forward and says, "I have created a replica of myself." Whereupon the king says, "*That* is the most beautiful thing in the world, therefore *you* are the most beautiful thing in the world. Will you be my queen?" The king takes the hero as his male queen and gives this androgynous beauty half his kingdom (cynosural ascension of status).

Interpretation of Covert Personality

1. *Icarus complex.* This integrate might be defined as a compound of (a) cynosural narcism and (b) ascensionism, combined with (c) the prospection of falling. It seems to be derived, in its extreme form, from a fixation at the urethral-phallic stage of development, before object love has been attained. Consequently, it is associated with (d) the cathection of fire, and, if enuresis or incontinence become an issue, with (e) an abundance of water imagery. Furthermore, as offspring of this complex is (f) a craving for immortality (some form of re-ascension) as well as (g) a conception of women as objects to be utilized for narcistic gains.

I am inclined to the tentative opinion that the Icarus complex is the immature (perhaps perpetually adolescent) form of what might be termed the Solar complex, a complex which is characterized by the same genetical components but, in addition, by a relatively strong ego structure supported by tested abilities, which serves to constrain the reckless aspirations of youth within the bounds of realizable achievements, and thus to neutralize the dread of falling.

If tendencies for genital exhibitionism and arsonism are both suppressed, an Icarus or Solar complex might be objectified on the physical and technical levels by such cynosural and ascensionistic enterprises as high jumping, pole vaulting, discus throwing, high diving, fancy skating, circus acrobatics, ballet dancing, tree surgery, reckless mountain climbing, stunt aviating, or parachuting. On the verbal-social level one might think of singing or acting on the stage (becoming a Hollywood star), charismatic oratory and leadership, messianic enthusiasm and prophecy. But for the fullest expression of the complex one must turn to ardent romantic poetry (Byron, Shelley), to mythic philosophy (Socrates in *Phaedrus,* or Nietzsche in *Thus Spake Zarathustra*), or to some form of up-yearning (erotic) mysticism.

2. *Predisposing determinants.* To explain the urethral-phallic fixation in this case, to explain the absence of emotional maturation to the stage of object attachment (oedipal love), one must go back in Grope's history to still earlier experiences and their chief resultant—a revengeful (almost implacable) rejection of the mother, because she (scrupulously following her day's dicta: (a) that children should be fed by the clock and (b) that maternal nurturance should be minimal) let the child cry, with his oral and affectional needs unsatisfied, much longer than is tolerable at his age. According to Sullivan (2) and others, such unrelieved intensity of need, combined with "desertion" by the mother, is likely to result in a kind of self-protecting apathy with rejection of both the giver and her gift when they do ultimately arrive—too late. This hypothesis would explain why Grope can give no reason, can remember no incident, which might account for his never having loved his mother, as well as for his food memories, his finickiness about food, his peculiar attitude toward gifts, and, most particularly, the incident of dumping the plate of string beans on the floor and his "spite complex." The hypothesis is further substantiated by Grope's mother's fairly full communication respecting her trustful adherence to the then-fashionable principles of John B. Watson.

Among Grope's story constructions there is one of a young man whose father shuts him up in total darkness. "No light ever entered the room. He could not perceive himself or anything around him." After thirty years of this, the hero "sort of lost his virility." In another story the boy hero dies in bed but regains life when his father brings him a cup of chicken soup. A somewhat similar story ends differently: The child hero goes to bed and calls for one and then a second glass of water. When he calls for a third, there is no response either from his father or his mother. "He was in bed a long time. He started yelling." But no one comes. Finally, the boy puts on his clothes, leaves the house, and lies down across the railroad track to be run over by an oncoming locomotive.

3. *Unity thema.* The unity thema in this personality, as we have interpreted it, is a compound of the just-mentioned but not elaborated Mother Rejection complex and the less well-known and hence more fully illustrated Icarus complex. Assuredly there were other constituents of Grope's covert personality—particularly those of an anal expulsive derivation—but here again, the prescribed space limits prohibit even the briefest exposition.

The surmise that Grope's overt personality during his college years—marked by apathy and withdrawal—was situationally determined is substantiated by his "conversion" into an enthusiastic, self-involved hard-working and cooperative fellow within a few weeks after leaving college when he found in a summer theatre an admirable channel for his cynosural narcism.

REFERENCES

1. Halverson, H. M. Genital and sphincter behavior of the male infant. *J. genet. Psychol.,* 1940, **56,** 95–136.
2. Sullivan, H. S. *The interpersonal theory of psychiatry.* New York: W. W. Norton & Co., 1953.

3. Studies of stressful interpersonal disputations

HENRY A. MURRAY

BETWEEN ME AND THE SUBSTANCE of all that I can say in the allotted time are several pages of writing, the contents of which may be summarized as follows:

1. A short introduction with a barely discernible thread of humor;

2. A prosaic survey of the seven major components of what some of us have called the "multiform system of assessment" which is old hat to most of you;

3. A passage in which it is pointed out that two of the essential components of this system have been grievously neglected by most psychologists in their investigations of normal personalities, one being the collection by various means of an abundance of experiential, biographical data from each subject, and the other being a serious, systematic attempt to construct a coherent formulation of each personality;

4. The Jeremiad of an aging psychologist who views with sorrow and misgivings the apparent accentuation of certain powerful forces that are keeping a multiplicity of his colleagues dissociated from the nature and experiences of actual people by binding their energies to an enthralling intellectual game played with abstract counters of dubious importance and of spurious relevance to human life.

Integration Plan

Having been led to the belief that this dissociation, if prolonged, would seriously impede

SOURCE. Article by Henry A. Murray, "Studies of stressful interpersonal disputations" in *American Psychologist*, Vol. 18, pp. 28–36, 1963.

the full future development of psychology, I am eager to propose a remedy which could be instituted at numerous centers in this country on a scale that might be just sufficient to make a decisive, vital difference in the evolution of our discipline. The suggested remedy consists of integrating the endeavors of experimental specialists with those of personologists engaged in a multiform assessment program. That is, instead of choosing either to learn a lot about a single area of human activity or to learn a little about a lot of areas, everybody chooses both, and can attain both by a division of interrelated labors.

There are only two rules to this integration plan, as I shall call it, the first being that all experimenters will use the same population of thoroughly assessed subjects, no matter how many other subjects they may need. The enormous advantage of this arrangement is that each experimenter, without any expenditure of his own time, will have at his disposal to help him in interpreting his findings, not only the results of other experiments, but the massive collection of data (several hundred rank orders, for example) obtained by the assessment process. The second rule—with even greater potentialities for a sophisticated science of psychology as well as for broadening the horizon of every student—calls for two series of meetings of experimentalists and personologists: one series to formulate the personality of each subject as a unit, and another series to attempt plausible explanations of the variant individual responses in each experiment taken as a unit. The aim would be to test the most promising of these plausible explanations, and in due course to attain the enviable position of being able to predict the critical reactions of each individual subject with a fair measure of accuracy and precision.

To be a little more specific, let me outline one possible version of the integration plan. First there will be four variously trained and variously experienced personologists (members or research associates of a department of psychology) who are engaged in a three-year program of intensive study of 25 preselected subjects. They will be assisted in the assessment process by second-year graduate students who will administer, as part of their technical training course, some of the simpler tests and questionnaires. Then there will be several graduate students of more advanced standing, seven in number, let us say, each of whom is planning an experiment to be performed for a PhD degree. Their interests may vary all the way from those of a physiological-psychologist in search of more precise knowledge respecting the temporal correlates of marked changes in the heart rate to those of an investigator of higher mental processes who wishes to test certain propositions as to the power of a subject to recall different parts of a dyadic conversation in which he has actively participated.

Now, as it happens, a few of us at Harvard—research fellows for the most part—found that these two experimental aims and five others could be pursued in unison as interdependent parts of a single chain of linked procedures. The topics of the other five studies, each concerned with a different aspect of a stressful, two-person disputation, were as follows: (a) the determinants of variations among judges in estimating degree of anxiety and of anger; (b) personological and situational determinants of degree of anxiety and of anger; (c) personological correlates of variations of mentational and linguistic style under stress; (d) typological differences as manifested in retrospectively experiencing and reporting a stressful, verbal interaction; and (e) apperceptions and evaluations of an alter before and after meeting him and being exposed to his insulting criticisms.

Now, as partial demonstration of how researches such as these can be readily coordinated, let me outline as briefly as possible the series of techniques that was carried out by a number of us at the Annex (as I shall call our workshop in Cambridge, Massachusetts), first in 1957 with the compliance of 23 comprehensively assessed college sophomores, and then, in 1960 with a comparable aggregate of 21 subjects. Imagine that you are one of these volunteer subjects.

Experimental Procedures. First, you are told you have a month in which to write a brief exposition of your personal philosophy of life, an affirmation of the major guiding principles in accord with which you live or hope to live.

Second, when you return to the Annex with your finished composition, you are informed that in a day or two you and a talented young lawyer will be asked to debate the respective merits of your two philosophies. You are given a copy of his philosophy and he is given a copy of your philosophy. You are told that a moving picture will be taken of this debate.

Third, on arriving at the Annex on the appointed day, you are given these directions: The debate will be limited to three 6-minute periods separated by two shorter silent periods, in which to rest or collect your thoughts. The first period will be for mutual orientation, for asking and answering questions, clarifying certain points. In the second period the young lawyer will present his criticisms of your philosophy and your task will be to defend it as logically as possible. In the third and final period it will be your turn to call attention to whatever weaknesses you have noted in the lawyer's philosophy. At this point you are introduced to the young lawyer, and in his company escorted to the brilliantly lighted room where the debate will take place in front of a one-way mirror and a hole in the wall for the lens of a moving picture camera with sound track. Before sitting down next to each other, the leads of a cardiotachometer (which records instantaneous heart rates and respirations) are strapped to your chest and to the lawyer's chest by Paul Gross.

Fourth, a signal is given and the discussion starts, continuing through three differentiated periods as you were told it would. In the second period, however, the lawyer's criticism becomes far more vehement, sweeping, and personally abusive than you were led to expect. The directions given to the lawyer were the same as you received, except that he was told to anger you and, adhering to a rehearsed and more or less standardized mode of attack, he will almost certainly succeed in doing this, having been successful in all the dyads we have witnessed. Dyad is the convenient four-letter word we use to refer to each of these 18-minute two-person interactions, plus four inactive periods amounting to 9 minutes, i.e., about 27 minutes in all.

Fifth, after the termination of the debate, you are taken to a room where you are left alone with the instruction to write down as much as you are able to recall of what was said by the lawyer and by yourself, word for word if possible and in proper sequence.

Sixth, as soon as you have reached the end of your memories of the verbal interactions, you are escorted to the room of an interviewer (Alden Wessman), where you are encouraged to relax, and to say what comes to mind while you relive in your imagination the dyad as you experienced it, chronologically from start to finish. When you are through with this—about 30 minutes later, let us say—you are asked certain questions designed to obtain as valid estimates as you both *can* give and *will* give of the intensity of certain variables, such as felt anxiety, felt anger, involvement in the task, liking or disliking the lawyer, respecting or disrespecting his ability or views. A final short questionnaire covering these and other points completes your set of exercises for that day. The interviewer is left with a tape recording of the whole proceeding.

At four appointed times subsequent to your participation in the stressful dyad, you will be called back to the Annex. On two occasions there will be another verbal memory test similar to the one I have described, the aim of which is to measure the percentage of different classes of speech units in the dyad that are recalled by each subject after 2 weeks and after 8 weeks. In addition to these sessions there will be two interviews, in one of which you will again be asked to relive the experience of the dyad and to report it as you go along. In the other interview, the plan of which was both conceived and executed with extraordinary cleverness by Gerhard Nielsen, you will witness and become involved in two or three showings of the sound film of your own dyad. You will see yourself making numerous grimaces and gestures of which you were unconscious at the time, and you will hear yourself uttering incongruent, disjunctive, and unfinished sentences. You are likely to be somewhat shocked by your performance and will be moved to identify with yourself as you were feeling and thinking during those stressful moments; and when the experimenter, *this* experimenter, stops the film at

critical points, and asks you what you associate with this and that physiognomic movement or with this and that verbal expression, you are likely to become uncommonly communicative and your free associations may lead you back to childhood memories. Counting the other two reliving interviews and the three memory sessions, you will spend about 8 hours all told trying to recapture various aspects of those 18 minutes under stress.

I have devoted more minutes than I can well afford to this account of how we secured reports of your subjective experience of the dyad as a whole and in detail, because nothing more about the phenomenology of it all will be said this morning, and I wanted to assure you that we considered the covert, inner aspect of that event as essential and revealing as its overt, outer aspect.

Raw data. The dyad in which you participated has perished as an event in time and you are through with it and we with you, in a sense and for a while. But we are in no sense through with the imperishable data pertinent to that event which you have left behind with us, the nature of which I have already briefly indicated: (*a*) a cardiotachometric tracing of your heart and respiration rates, (*b*) a sound film portraying your physical expressions and your verbal interactions with the lawyer, (*c*) a typed record of the exchange of words, (*d*) a tape recording of the debate giving both voice and words, and (*e*) a series of typed protocols of everything that you said about the dyad as you retrospectively relived it. So far as I know, these interrelated temporal records of your discussion are more precise and more complete than those of any other dyadic event in human history. But *cui bono?* As they stand they are nothing but raw data, meaningless as such; and the question is what meaning, what intellectual news, can be extracted from them?

Certain Methodological Principles

Besides presenting a plan for coordinating the aims and efforts of experimental specialists and personological generalists, and besides describing a series of procedures as an example of how seven different experimental projects can be coordinated, I had another purpose for this paper to which I shall now attend, namely, to set forth a few of the strategic methodological principles, or aims, which guided the ordination (designing, planning) of our interlocked techniques. These principles will be illustrated by references to what we have learned so far regarding the determinants of variations of the heart rate during a dyadic verbal transaction of varying stressor potency.

1. *Make the experimental conditions as natural as possible.* Although some degree of artificiality is unavoidable in the design of an experiment, we have assumed (without unequivocal evidence) that the wanted range of emotional, conational, and mentational involvement of the subjects (and hence sufficient elevations of the heart rate) is more frequently obtained when the experimental conditions (the directions if any, the setting, the successive stimulus situations, etc.) are naturalistic (i.e., comparable to those that occur, commonly or exceptionally, in everyday life) and, conversely, that the degree of such involvement is generally less when artificiality is conspicuous and a subject has reason to say to himself, "this is nothing but an experiment, an attempt to show that I can be excited by these means." We have also assumed that the reactions of a subject (including changes of his heart rate) will be less natural (less representative of those that occur in everyday life) if his freedom of action is impeded, either, say, by strapping him to an array of instruments and telling him not to move, or by providing him with no opportunity for effective mental action, no problem to solve, or no way of altering the course of events by verbal means; or by limiting each of the subject's responses to a mere choice between two or more predetermined alternatives, instead of expecting him to *compose* adequate responses. It is not unlikely that the change of the heart rate after stimulation varies in direction or degree according to whether a subject is set (*a*) to inhibit or (*b*) to actuate, either all impulses or impulses of a certain class.

As to the naturalness of our experimental conditions, it may be said that heated arguments are common in the ordinary course of social events and dyadic discussions before a camera are daily occurrences on TV programs; but that an unwanted and unnecessary degree of artificiality was introduced in most of the dyads by the suddenness, intensity, and irrationality of the lawyer's criticisms in the second of the active phases of the dyad.

2. *Aim at a temporal, holistic model of the observed event by obtaining synchronized recordings of the occurrence and intensity of each of the most influential participating variables.* "Holistic model" in this sentence means (*a*) a sufficiently complete model *of* the whole (entire) event, one which includes all parts (variables) that are of noteworthy relevance and significance, and (*b*) a model of the event *as a whole*, one which represents the interdependence of the parts (variables) and in so doing exhibits whatever degree of unity or disunity may prevail. Pertinent to this principle is our assumption that variations in the heart rate are determined by the interaction of several different variables. The importance of synchronized temporal records of the occurrence and intensity of each of the relevant variables is obvious, since only in this way can one discover what intrasubject, sequential (cause and effect), or concomitant relationships among the variables recur with dependable regularity. Furthermore, we should not lose sight of the basic tenet that time is an inherent component or attribute of every process and that the history of an event *is* the event.

In charting changes in the intensity of a variable, such as anxiety or anger, or changes in the heart rate or speech rate, a good deal may depend on the duration of the time unit that is represented by a single figure (the average of all measures obtained during that temporal segment). In representing changes in heart rate, for example, the choice of a short micro time unit of 5 seconds (with one point indicating the average interval between six successive beats if the rate is 60 beats per minute) will generally eliminate the effects of respiration (occurring at the rate of roughly 12 a minute); and a choice of a large micro time unit of 30 seconds will generally result in the obliteration of the effects of gross muscular motility if the frequency and magnitude of these movements remain constant; and the choice of a large macro time unit of 6 minutes will obliterate the effects of changes of stimulation during the course of that phase, and so forth. Some of these points will be demonstrated later.

3. *Assume that every psychological variable is a hypothetical (theoretical) construct, the activity of which can be inferred only on the basis of one or more of its subjective and/or objective manifestations.* For centuries every psychological variable was conscious by definition;

but within the last half century most psychologists have come round to Freud's conception of unconscious psychic processes; and a host of psychologists have been persuaded, first of all, by Pavlov and Watson, to study organisms who are unable to report whatever awareness of interior mental experiences they may have. As a result many psychologists are now accustomed to the practice of inferring (on the basis of more or less rigorously defined criteria) the operation of imperceptible central (psychic) variables. In view of the prevalent American bias in favor of "behavioral" psychology I am strongly disposed to stress the understanding to be gained from the development of a sophisticated "experiential" psychology.

4. *Attempt to explain the reactions, especially the variant reactions of every individual subject.* We do not say that every person is unique, but say, instead, that every person is in certain very general respects like *all* other persons, in certain less general respects like *some* other persons (persons of this or that sex, age, culture, status, vocation, type, etc.), and in certain particular respects like no other person. As usual, we take note of whatever is common to all subjects, and then of whatever is common to this and to that aggregate or class of subjects, and, finally, we investigate in great detail whatever eccentric or hitherto unknown particularities are manifested by different individuals. From endeavors to understand these unique features have come the greater portion of our "new ideas." But these endeavors, I believe, would have had little chance of bearing fruit if we had had to deal with subjects whose lives and personalities were unexplored to us. Here, then, is another good reason for adhering to the practice of performing experiments only on thoroughly assessed persons.

Now, to illustrate the application of the third principle (variables as theoretical constructs), I shall present an outline of our conception of anger, and then to illustrate the second principle (synchronized temporal tracings) I shall describe one of our ways of estimating the degree of anger.

Theoretical and Operational Definition of Anger. Anger was defined as an hypothetical state of excitation in certain not-yet-definitely-localized, subcortical regions of the brain (say, in the hypothalamus and limbic systems) which, if sufficiently intense, produces various

manifestations of which the following could be discriminated in our data:

1. Covert manifestations: (a) experienced, or felt, anger, (b) aggressive words or images of aggressive actions invading the stream of consciousness, and (c) certain "emotional" qualities of the temporal structure of mentation; the avowals of all of which by the subject (at various times in the three postdyadic interviews) are ordinarily but not always modulated by some degree of inhibition (suppression).

2. Physiological manifestations: autonomic excitations, including changes of the heart rate and respiration rate as recorded on the polygraph by the cardiotachometer, the nature of which changes seems to depend on the character of the situation.

3. Overt manifestations: (a) physiognomic and motoric phenomena which can be seen in the silent moving picture and analyzed in great detail by means of a perceptoscope projecting one frame at a time; (b) verbal productions of an oppositional, rude, critical, aggressive, or insulting nature which can be read in the typed protocol; (c) vocal qualities, such as louder and more rapid speech which, in conjunction with the verbal productions, can be heard in the playback of the magnetic tape recording of the dyad; and, finally, (d) temporal patterns of these motoric, verbal, and vocal manifestations, which can be synchronously seen and heard in the sound movie in conjunction with the behavior of the alter, or lawyer; all of which manifestations of central processes are modulated to some degree by the subject's efforts to control and to conceal them.

To be complete, this scheme would have to be supplemented by the addition of physical (muscular) endeavors, such as fighting, and by further specifications here and there, for example as to the qualities of voice and flow of speech which may be recorded instrumentally, or discriminated without instruments even when one does not understand the language spoken by the subject. But these supplementations are not pertinent to our data which allows for only four completely independent sources of information (cf. 1, 2, 3a, and 3b) which may be compared in respect to their dependability as indices of central anger.

Here I shall limit myself to estimations of anger based on observations of the sound movie which combines the vocal qualities of speech with two of the independent sources of information (physiognomic movements and verbal productions). These estimates were made from moment to moment independently and simultaneously by six psychologists (Arthur Couch, Paul Gross, Kenneth Keniston, David Ricks, Bernard Rosenthal, and myself), each of whom held a dial whose movements produced tracings on a polygraph, that could be synchronized with the tracings of the heart rate, as well as with the speech units produced by the two debaters.

The overt manifestations of five other, preselected psychological variables (the subject's level of anxiety, gross motility, vocal-verbal intensity, and task involvement, and the potency of the lawyer's criticisms and insults) were estimated, one by one, in a similar fashion, two of these variables by six judges and three by two judges. I shall not discuss, at this time, the question of the determinants of the unreliability of these estimates, but return to the second methodological principle that I mentioned, which calls for a temporal record of each variable, and illustrate the difference in amount of information gained between choosing a macro or a meso time unit for each point that is represented in a graph by showing two records of the heart rate, before, during, between, and after the dyadic interactions.

Figure 1 shows first, the average basal heart rate (74) for all subjects and then seven average dyadic heart rates plotted against time. (The average of about 12 afternoon pulse rates, as counted by each subject on different days under resting conditions, was taken as that subject's basal heart rate.) The three black circles

give the average HR (absolute heart rate) for each of the periods of active verbal interchanges (a 6-minute time segment). The white circles give the average HR for each of the verbally inactive periods: pre-dyadic first, post-dyadic last, and two intradyadic rest periods. Time units of this percentage of toal time (about four to six minutes in this case) are called by us macro units and each cycle is called a macro figure. What can we learn from this macrotemporal chart?

1. Note the relatively great elevation of the heart rate (above the average basal rate of 74) before the start of the dyad, an index of a high degree of anticipatory central excitation, and then note a similar anticipatory rise before Phase 6, the phase in which the subject had been instructed to criticize the lawyer's views.

2. Note the increase of heart rate during the transition from an overtly inactive state to an overtly active state in all three instances. Micro analyses show that this occurred in 18 of our 21 subjects.

3. Note that the average heart rate in the sixth phase, when most of the subjects were criticizing the lawyer, was considerably higher than it was in Phase 4, when they were *being* criticized.

4. Note the surprising and in-this-graph-unexplainable fact that the average heart rate in the fourth phase (when the subjects were insulted) was no higher than it was in the second phase during which the interpersonal atmosphere was friendly.

Figure 2 is a *meso*temporal chart which exhibits 17 successive figures, one for the first, or

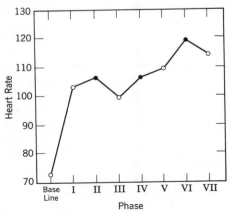

Figure 1. Average heart rate during stressful dyad (with seven points).

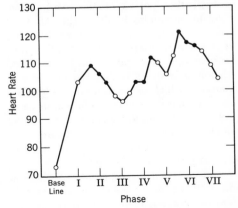

Figure 2. Average heart rate during stressful dyad (with 17 points).

predyadic, phase, then one for each of 15 sub-phases (9 active and 6 inactive) of the dyad proper, and finally one for the seventh, or post-dyadic, phase. Each black circle is the average for a 2-minute time unit (instead of for a 6-minute time unit), a choice of temporal segment which certainly gives you a more intelligible picture of what generally occurred during those stressful proceedings.

1. Take note of some new information: first, the fall of the heart rate during Phase 2 and again during Phase 6, one reasonable explanation of which would be in terms of homeostatic principles, namely that an elevated heart rate always tends to fall as the person becomes habituated to the existing situation, provided the stressor potency of the siuation does not increase. During the first two-thirds of Phase 4 the subjects were confronted by a series of unexpected provocations in the form of personally offensive criticisms from the lawyer, and consequently the existing HR level did not fall, but was sustained during the middle subphase and in the last phase ascended sharply. The low HR level during the first subphase of Phase 4 as compared to the level during the initial but unaggressive subphase of Phase 2 might be partly explained by the low level in the middle of resting Phase 3 (the level from which the heart rate had to rise) as compared to the higher level of Phase 1, the predyadic phase. And the lower HR level during the middle subphase of Phase 4 as compared to the level in the third subphase might be partly explained by the fact that subjects talked far less in the first two subphases of Phase 4 than they did during any other period of the dyad; since, according to our micro findings, the HR level is lower, as a rule, when subjects are listening than it is when they are talking. Another possible explanation that needs to be explored through micro analyses is that the eruption of covert anger (which came suddenly in the first subphase of Phase 4 when conditions more or less prohibited its ample expression) produced momentary increase in blood pressure (the noradrenalin effect) and a consequent decrease in the heart rate in some subjects.

2. Again note that the heart rate was high at the end of Phase 4, by which time most subjects had become engaged in self-defensive refutations and still higher in Phase 6 when they were both most talkative and most offensively aggressive. Taking this covariation of heart rate

and vigorous verbal activity in conjunction with the fall in level during the first two-thirds of each resting period, as well as with the other pertinent facts that I have mentioned (e.g., the rise of the heart rate at the end of each of three inactive periods, and the additional rise beyond this point, in all instances, as the subject went from inaction to interaction), the data exhibited in our graphs all point to a positive correlation of the heart rate with (a) anticipated interactivity of a certain sort and (b) with the first phase of actual interactivity. After that, if the intensity level of the interactivity decreases or remains constant, the heart rate will decline; but if the intensity level increases the heart rate will rise or remain constant. Viewing these facts within a functional frame of reference, we might say that the circulatory system of the majority of our subjects was over-prepared (by nervous excitement) for Phase 2 and for Phase 6 (i.e., the subjects anticipated, consciously or unconsciously, more stressors, more demands for quick, difficult, and effective responses, than they subsequently encountered), and as they came to the realization that the situational demands were not so pressing (less than they were physiologically prepared to meet), their heart rates fell to a level that was appropriate to the apperceived current state of affairs. This well-known habituational, or homeostatic, fall of the heart rate, particularly in Phase 2, was the cause of numerous negative intrasubject correlations between heart rate and anxiety (nervous excitement); because, since the subjects were not filmed during any of the inactive periods, the judges had no grounds for inferring a high level of anxiety at the very start of the interaction. Generally speaking, the judges started Phase 2 (the first phase to be observed in the movie) at zero and moved up as signs of nervousness appeared and reappeared and their confidence in the significance of these signs became less wavering. Therefore, while the judges' tracings for anxiety were mounting ("catching up" to the subject's current emotional state) the subject's heart rate was declining. This was but one of many unexpected complications we encountered.

My first reason for showing the two graphs of average heart rate changes during the dyad was to illustrate the general principle (which applies to data such as ours) that, above an ascertainable low limit, the shorter the time segment which is represented by a single figure, the greater will be the amount of usable information to be gained by mere inspection. My second reason was to point out the suitability of the synchronized mesotemporal graphs of our major variables: They present nine opportunities for intersubject correlations between the rank orders of the average subphase intensities of the variables and eight opportunities for intrasubject correlations of their concurrently changing intensities between subphases. Besides these we have the opportunity afforded by the macrotemporal graphs for three more sets of intersubject intercorrelations and finally a set of intercorrelations based on average variable intensities for the total dyad, yielding in all 13 intersubject correlation coefficients for each pair of variables. Finally, to end this paper with a little meat to chew on, it was my intention to summarize the unexpected results of the execution, by Paul Gross and others, of some of the just-enumerated possible correlations for comparison with the information gained through a close inspection of the mesotemporal graph (Figure 2).

The first surprise, if not distress, was occasioned by the finding that the elevated heart rate, calculated in the manner I described earlier, was correlated to a significant degree with *none* of our major variables, in *contrast* to the absolute heart rate which correlated positively with all our "activity" variables, in two instances at the 5% level of significance. This result, which at first blush runs counter to accepted principles of measurement in physiology, constitutes a riddle for which I have no ready answer, except to report that the correlation of $-.78$ between basal heart rate and elevated heart rate might conceivably be the key to its solution. In any case, the average of 13 rank order correlations were significantly positive between absolute heart rate and both of our two measures of manifest drive, or need achievement, in the dyad (the apparent degree of continuous concentration and emotional-mentational-verbal energy devoted to the accomplishment of the assigned task): (*a*) *vocal-verbal intensity,* aver. $+ .45$ (range from $+ .19$ to $+ .59$, with all but one over $+ .34$); and (*b*) *task-involvement,* aver. $+ .42$ (range from $+ .31$ to $+ .56$). The fact that these correlations are all positive, that they are consonant with all the data presented by the graphs, and that they make functional sense, suggests that individual differences among our subjects in respect to

basal heart rate and degree of sensitivity of the neurocardiac system were not so great or influential as to cancel the possibility of demonstrating a consistent relationship between motivation and heart rate under the stressful conditions that existed in the dyads. The comparably high heart rates of surgeons while performing major operations could likewise be attributed to this functional relationship. Also positive, but to no significant degree, are the correlations between HR and (*c*) *manifest anger,* aver. $+ .30$ (range from $+ .11$ to $+ .49$), and (*d*) *gross muscular motility,* aver. $+ .29$ (range from $+ .16$ to $+ .35$). Most surprising was the absence of any correlation with (*e*) *anxiety,* aver. $- .03$ (range $+ .15$ to $- .28$), and a not-yet-explained, slightly negative correlation with *press* (the alter's *vocal-verbal* intensity and *aggressiveness*), aver. $- .26$ (range $+ .04$ to $- .58$). The averages of the intrasubject correlations were also significantly positive for absolute heart rate and vocal-verbal intensity, gross muscular motility, and task-involvement, in that order, and insignificantly positive for press and anger. The correlation with anxiety was in this slightly negative.

As to anxiety, we might first of all raise the question of whether this is the most appropriate term to apply, say, to a surgeon at the start of a difficult emergency operation. His nervousness is not morbid anxiety in the Freudian sense (fear of conscience), nor is it associated with any tendency to escape, to withdraw, or to avoid, in the usual sense: Surgery is his chosen profession and here is his opportunity to save a life and thus to achieve an all-important result. It might be said, however, that he is bent on avoiding disaster for both his patient and himself. But, regardless of these and other objections, I shall continue to use the term "anxiety" for the duration of this paper to stand for a nervous apprehension of the forthcoming possibility of experiencing some sort of acute pain, distress, failure, exposure, shame, or disgrace. Now, despite the fact that none of our rank order correlations between heart rate and anxiety were positive, it is clear from the graph that the effect of predyadic anxiety (nervous excitement) on the heart rate (elevating it 33 points on the average) is greater than that of any other definable variable, that is to say, heart rate and anxiety *are* in fact positively correlated, as effect and cause, or cause and effect, in all subjects. The contradiction can be explained, in functional terms, by assuming that anxiety (situational fear is a mobilization of energy for emergency action in a situation that is apprehended as perilous. If the anxiety is high and a resulting drive to overt action is correspondingly high, particularly if the drive is combined with anger as well as an increase of gross motility, the heart rate will be in the highest range, and since the signs of anxiety will be largely obscured or inhibited by the vigorous and focused ongoing activity (verbal in our experiments), the subject will be given a rather low rating on anxiety and a very high rating on both vocal-verbal intensity and task involvement (see the curve of Tandy in Figure 3). If, on the other hand, an equally high degree of anxiety results in a form of action which may

be termed "surrender and submission," with extrapunitiveness replaced by a mild intra-punitiveness, the heart rate will fall and remain at a low level, as one can see in the case of Keeper, also represented in Figure 3. Keeper will receive low ratings on vocal-verbal intensity and high ratings on manifest anxiety. This, in brief, is a partial explanation of the absence of positive correlations between heart rate and anxiety.

And now I have come to the end of my allotted time, with only a few seconds in which to show one last figure (Figure 4) in which the average heart rates of seven subjects with the highest drive ratings are compared with the average heart rates of seven subjects with the lowest drive ratings.

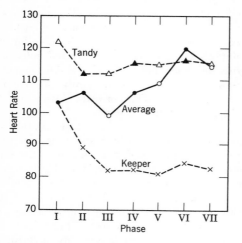

Figure 3. Average heart rate of two deviant cases compared to group average.

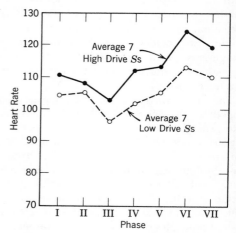

Figure 4. Average heart rate for seven subjects with highest drive and seven subjects with lowest drive.

4. Explorations in typology

MORRIS I. STEIN

IT WAS WHEN I WAS A PSYCHOLOGICAL INTERNE that I first read *Explorations in Personality*.[1] Even before opening the book, two things made immediate and lasting impressions: the book had *Explorations* in the title, and the seal on the jacket with the ever-present whale contained the inscription, "Let not him who seeks cease until he finds, and when he finds he shall be astonished." Then I arrived at the Harvard Psychological Clinic. (Somehow to say "Harvard" alone would be inappropriate, because life centered so much around the yellow house on Plympton Street.) Here at Henry Murray's informal seminars the foundations were laid for my future interests—TAT, assessment, and creativity. But, more important, here was the source of stimulation and inspiration for new explorations and new surprises. Henry Murray is thus responsible not for the results of my explorations, but the direction they have taken.

In Defense of Types

In the spirit of this occasion I would like to present the beginnings of a recent exploration in which Murray's system of needs plays a central role. The venture is concerned with a topic that is currently out of fashion—typologies. Some of the reasons why they are out of fashion relate to the criticism of previously existing typologies. Others relate to the fact that, for the past several decades, psychologists have been trained in emulating the models of the physical

SOURCE. Morris I. Stein, "Exploration in typology" in *The Study of Lives*, pp. 280–303. Edited by R. W. White. New York: Atherton, 1963.

[1] Henry A. Murray *et al.*, *Explorations in Personality*. New York: Oxford University Press, 1938.

sciences and so concern themselves with the relationships between variables. And finally, without attempting to exhaust the list of criticism, typologies are, for some, "undemocratic." Nevertheless, matters of fashion should not be permitted to stand in the way of an exploration.

The stimulus for this exploration came out of the following experiences. After completing several studies in which I was concerned with the variables that might differentiate between two groups, it was apparent that the significance of a variable in the context of one personality was somewhat different or even very different from its significance in another context. For example, let us say that need achievement was the differentiating variable. For one individual it may have an aggressive and forceful quality, whereas for another it lacks any compulsive quality and is indeed associated with playfulness and pleasure. An individual's personality is reflected not in his separate motives but in the organization of his motives. Differences of organization become important, especially if one is interested not only in understanding but in predicting behavior and is concerned with the conditions under which certain behaviors will become manifest. One way of coping with this problem is through the fullness of the case study, but this has the disadvantage of being rather cumbersome when one has to deal with large numbers of individuals. Consequently, it seemed that some compromise had to be effected between nomothetic and idiographic approaches.

Another experience that stimulated this exploration was related to assessment. In assessment, where one is concerned with the differences between groups that vary in the degree to which they achieve a criterion or standard of performance, one frequently finds that there are different ways of achieving the same criterion.

For example, in differentiating between successful and unsuccessful students, one of the things that often stands out is that there are various pathways to success. One student achieves it by memorizing course content, and another learns and integrates the material. There is no single profile of *the* successful student, just as there is no profile for *the* creative individual. It is probably more accurate to say that regardless of the criterion there are several profiles of the individuals capable of achieving it. Once again, what I have said is not too startling since it is consistent with the principle of equipotentiality.

Let me continue with an observation from another area. In an experimental investigation of efficiency in problem solving, it was apparent that subjects would follow different kinds of approaches.[2] One subject would try to "pull the answer" out of the problem; another would "feel" his way through and appear to trust his intuition in making his decisions; and a third appeared to be hoping that through some random movements he might so manipulate the stimuli that the solution would occur to him —as indeed, for some, it would. From these observations it appeared as if one subject followed the principles of reinforcement, while another followed the principles of Gestalt psychology. It was also apparent that their behaviors were congruent with the different types of personalities involved, but these differences would not stand out in the final result, where only separate variables were related to the criterion.

The problem is more pervasive. We also encounter it when we survey the various theories of personality and the conflicts between theorists. Some of the diversity and conflict arises because of differences in the types of individuals studied. Maskin points out that "Freud used hysteria as the model for his therapeutic method, depression as the basis for his later theoretical conjectures. Adler's clinical demonstrations are rivalrous, ineffective, immature character types. Jung's examples were restricted to a weary, worldly, successful, middle-aged group. Rank focused upon the conflicted, frustrated, rebellious artist aspirant. Fromm's model is the man in a white collar searching for his individuality. And Sullivan's example of choice

is the young catatonic schizophrenic."[3] Types, then, are implicit in our theorizing; might it not be worthwhile to make them explicit and, in doing so, might we not be better able to integrate our knowledge?

Types Based on Self-Images

Because of the potential significance a knowledge of types has for both research and theory but with full awareness that types are out of fashion, this exploration was begun. Its aim was to learn whether a typological system based on self-images could satisfy, at least initially, some minimal criteria and whether it could be useful in illuminating some problems that are encountered in applying psychological knowledge. Among the minimal criteria for useful types were the following: they should be internally meaningful and consistent; they should be relatively independent of each other; they should be differentially related to other criteria; and they should have different developmental histories. Assessment methodology was selected to explore the usefulness of types.

The types are based on two different populations. One consists of a group of 116 Ph.D. chemists employed in industrial research organizations. The other is a group of eighty Peace Corps volunteers.

The group of 116 chemists, who were in their mid-thirties and came from three different industrial organizations, participated in a study of creativity. They were divided into three categories. One was a group of men regarded as "more creative" by virtue of the ratings they obtained from their superiors, peers, and subordinates. The second was a group of "less creative" men selected by the same procedure. Both groups represented approximately the upper and lower 20 per cent of the available chemists in their organizations. There was a "middle group" which remained undefined, and this makes up the third subgroup.

The Peace Corps volunteers consist of a group of eighty young men in their mid-twenties who

---

[2] Sidney J. Blatt and Morris I. Stein, "Efficiency in Problem Solving," *Journal of Psychology*, XLVIII (1959), 193–213.

[3] Meyer Maskin, "Adaptations of Psychoanalytic Technique in Specific Disorders," in Jules H. Masserman, ed., *Science and Psychoanalysis*, Vol. III: *Psychoanalysis and Human Values* (New York: Grune and Stratton, 1960), pp. 321–352.

were assessed for assignment to a newly developing country. All but one of them have some college education, and about half completed college. At the time they applied to the Peace Corps, they had no idea whether they would be accepted, where they would be sent, or what they would do. From the large number who had applied, eighty were screened as acceptable for further training and selection for a community development project. At the conclusion of the training program and the second stage of the screening process, sixty-two men were selected for the project. The men rejected included those who had educational difficulties or personality problems, as judged by the training and assessment staffs. After assessment, the sixty-two selected men were assigned in two-man teams to various communities where, together with a local co-worker, they would work with the local populace in building roads, schools, aqueducts. What is probably more critical, they participate in teaching the villagers how they can better their lot by virtue of their own efforts. These volunteers were studied during the training program and after they had been in the field for six months. They will continue to be studied at periodic intervals in the future.

Both populations were used to investigate the value of typology. Our explorations have not proceeded so far as to enable us to investigate all the same issues with both groups. But with both the chemist and the Peace Corps populations we inquired as to the types of individuals that made them up and the degree to which they were independent of each other. With both groups we were also interested in the relationships between the types and some criterion —creativity for the chemists and effectiveness after a six-month period for the Peace Corps volunteers. In these instances, we were especially interested in learning whether the obtained data would be consistent with the principle of equipotentiality—namely, that different types might be able to achieve the same criterion. With the chemists we inquired further into the relationships between the types and one critical antecedent factor; with the Peace Corps volunteers we inquired into some issues that arise in assessment—the problem of risk in selection and the problem of change over time in the field.

The method for obtaining the information on which the types are based is a self-description questionnaire, consisting of twenty paragraphs,

each describing the manifestations of a different need after Murray. It includes the following needs: abasement, achievement, affiliation, aggression, autonomy, blamavoidance, counteraction, defendance, deference, dominance, exhibition, harmavoidance, infavoidance, nurturance, order, play, rejection, sentience, sex, and succorance.[4] The test was initially developed for use with the chemists, and the needs were selected because they were regarded as potential inhibitors or facilitators of creative activity. In responding to the questionnaire, the subject is asked to rank the needs from 1 to 20, from the one which is most descriptive of himself (rank of 1) to the one which is least descriptive (rank of 20).

As I have said in discussing the problems that stimulated this exploration, the functional significance of a need is dependent on the context in which it appears. It is the ranking procedure just described which makes it possible to highlight individual organizational systems. Previously I gave the example of two types of achievements—one with an aggressive and the other with a playful component. These differentiations are possible when, in one ranking, need achievement and aggression appear close together and, in the other, they are not only far apart but play is ranked close to achievement. A ranking procedure is also consistent with Murray's theoretical formulations in which he points out how needs may fuse with each other or may be subsidiary to one another. This condition might not be satisfied with other theoretical frameworks.

The potential significance of the questionnaire is based on the assumption that the picture an individual has of himself will have an effect on how he will behave. It also assumes that the twenty different needs are shared by all individuals to a greater or lesser extent and that the needs may be manifest in a variety of ways. It is further assumed that individuals vary in their need hierarchy. Theoretically, there are many ways of ranking the twenty paragraphs and many patterns are possible, although I shall consider only the nine types found in our data.

---

[4] The descriptive paragraph for need abasement, as an example, is: "I passively submit to external forces. I accept injury, blame, criticism, and punishment. I surrender. I am resigned to fate. I admit my inferiorities, errors, wrong-doings, or defeats. I blame myself.

The questionnaires were administered separately to the two groups. The individual rankings of all subjects were intercorrelated in each group, and separate Q-analyses were computed. The principal components of each of the intercorrelation matrices were extracted and rotated via the Varimax method to yield simple structures. The data for the chemists yielded a five-factor solution, and the data for the Peace Corps population a four-factor solution. To arrive at a picture of the types, subjects who loaded highest on each of the factors were selected as type definers, and their mean ranking of the needs was used in establishing the need hierarchy for the type. In the chemist population 78 out of the 116 men were type-definers (26 for Type A, 16 for Type B, 13 each for Types C and D, and 10 for Type E). Out of the eighty Peace Corps volunteers, forty-six were type-definers

(19 in Type I, 12 in Type II, 10 in Type III, and 5 in Type IV). Since the order in which the needs appear in Tables 1 and 2 are based on the absolute values of the needs within types, one must be cautioned that in comparing types a need may appear in the same ordinal position, although its absolute value may be different in each instance.[5]

In each population, eighteen needs were found to differentiate significantly among the types by analysis of variance. To condense the data and to investigate which of the needs contribute most to the uniqueness of the type, the average ranking of a need in one type was compared with its average ranking in all other types, for a total of thirty-six comparisons. Only those

_____

[5] A more complete presentation of the statistical analysis is reserved for another communication.

Table 1. Need Hierarchies among the Five Types Found in the Chemist Population

Type A	Type B	Type C	Type D	Type E
Achievement	Affiliation	Achievement	Achievement	Achievement
Affiliation	Blamavoidance	Counteraction	Affiliation	Counteraction
Play	Counteraction	Autonomy	Counteraction	Affiliation
Counteraction	Order	Aggression	Order	Autonomy
Sentience	Achievement	Dominance	Nurturance	Nurturance
Dominance	Deference	Defendance	Defendance	Order
Order	Infavoidance	Rejection	Dominance	Sentience
Exhibition	Harmavoidance	Order	Exhibition	Sex
Autonomy	Nurturance	Affiliation	Autonomy	Succorance
Sex	Play	Sex	Deference	Deference
Deference	Defendance	Harmavoidance	Aggression	Dominance
Nurturance	Autonomy	Infavoidance	Play	Deference
Harmavoidance	Abasement	Play	Harmavoidance	Infavoidance
Defendance	Sentience	Exhibition	Succorance	Blamavoidance
⎡Aggression⎤[*] ⎣Infavoidance⎦	Sex	Blamavoidance	Infavoidance	Play
Rejection	Succorance	Sentience	Blamavoidance	Rejection
Blamavoidance	Exhibition	Succorance	Sentience	Aggression
Succorance	Rejection	Deference	Rejection	Abasement
Abasement	Dominance	Nurturance	Abasement	Harmavoidance
	Aggression	Abasement	Sex	Exhibition

* The bracketed needs represent ties.

needs were then retained for which there were differences of one standard deviation or more in twelve or more comparisons. This analysis yielded twelve critical needs: nurturance, deference, autonomy, aggression, blamavoidance, sentience, play, sex, dominance, achievement, exhibition, and succorance. The intercorrelations of the ranks for each of the types were calculated to investigate the degree of resemblance between types both within and between populations. Within populations there is a great deal of independence. The highest intercorrelation among the chemist types was .41, and among the Peace Corps types it was .45. Higher intercorrelations were obtained between populations, and if one selects a correlation of .80 as a criterion of identity, then it might be said that two types (II and E) are subtypes of a larger type.

Types among Industrial Chemists

The type descriptions focus on the dynamic interrelationships between the needs, but they should be regarded with caution, for at the moment they are tentative. Complete and thorough descriptions will be possible only after more intensive study. It should be remembered, furthermore, that the type descriptions are based on self-descriptive data and hence refer to self-images; whether and to what extent these self-images are consistent with other types of personality data is an issue that will not be dealt with here. In writing these descriptions we were, however, aided by some knowledge of several individuals who were type-definers and by experience with the questionnaire administered to persons who had also taken rather complete batteries of clinical tests. To avoid the problem

Table 2. Need Hierarchies among the Four Types Found in the Peace Corps Population

Type I	Type II	Type III	Type IV
Affiliation	Affiliation	Achievement	Nurturance
Nurturance	Achievement	Affiliation	Play
Counteraction	Sentience	Counteraction	Sex
Achievement	Sex	Dominance	Affiliation
Deference	Autonomy	Nurturance	Autonomy
Sex	Counteraction	Order	⌈ Sentience ⌉*
Order	Nurturance	Exhibition	⌊ Succorance ⌋
Succorance	Play	Sex	Exhibition
Blamavoidance	Dominance	Deference	Counteraction
Play	Rejection	Defendance	Order
Dominance	Succorance	Play	Abasement
Harmavoidance	Order	⌈ Aggression ⌉*	Defendance
Infavoidance	Deference	⌊ Autonomy ⌋	Deference
Sentience	Blamavoidance	Sentience	Dominance
Exhibition	⌈ Harmavoidance ⌉*	Rejection	Infavoidance
Defendance	⌊ Defendance ⌋	Succorance	Achievement
Autonomy	Aggression	Harmavoidance	Blamavoidance
Rejection	Infavoidance	Abasement	Harmavoidance
Abasement	Exhibition	Infavoidance	Aggression
Aggression	Abasement	Blamavoidance	Rejection

* The bracketed needs represent ties.

of "freezing" their identities in terms that might become clichés, the types are not named. As has been indicated above, the types found among the chemists are identified by letters, and those among the Peace Corps volunteers by Roman numerals.

Type A. The individuals who compose this type are achievement-oriented. But their ambitions and aspirations are not so intense that they overlook interpersonal relationships. They like to be with others and enjoy cooperating with them. They trust others and in turn are loyal to their friends. Although they may want to please others and win their affection, they are not inclined to be submissive nor are they inclined to avoid situations in which they might lose the love of others. Although their social relationships are obviously not without warmth, they are not likely to become involved with others by showing intense sympathy, nor is it very characteristic of this group to go out of its way to support or comfort others. When the occasion demands, members of this type can be critical of others without feeling that they have to be unduly sensitive to others' feelings. By the same token, members of this type do not look to other people for advice, guidance, and emotional support. Indeed, this type ranks need succorance lower than do any of our eight other types.[6] Although it is uncharacteristic of individuals of this type to submit passively to external forces and to surrender or resign to fate, they are not insistent upon expressing their autonomous strivings. They can accept restrictions and probably effect compromises. Among the other characteristics of persons in this group is the fact that they appear capable of accepting their libidinal strivings, and that their aggressive needs appear to be under integrative control. Unlike our other types of creative individuals but like Type IV among the Peace Corps population, the men of Type A can do things for fun and without purpose. They enjoy play and relaxation. They like to laugh, they are easygoing, and can be lighthearted and merry. These men also seek out and enjoy sensuous impressions and aesthetic feelings. Possibly it is this combination of need play and need sentience which

gives the impression that members of this type may be characterized as open to new experiences. They can selectively filtrate the most important factors from these experiences and so maintain mastery and control of their environments in an orderly and organized fashion which is more flexible than constricting. All this is not to say that members of this type are without anxieties. Although the sources of their anxieties are not clear and although they may not experience very intense anxiety, it is conceivable that they may become anxious when their freedom is interfered with or when they find themselves lacking in resources to solve the problems that confront them.

Type B. The men in this group find it most important to please others and win their affection. Such behavior comes at the cost of their own spontaneity. They are so insecure that they will seek out many relationships and not be discriminating in their choice of friends. They will avoid situations in which they might lose others' love or in which they might be blamed for their actions. They are not likely to be assertive, forceful, or severe with others. Indeed, they have difficulty in dealing with their aggressive feelings. This type ranks blamavoidance higher and aggression and dominance lower than any of the other eight types. They strive to be inoffensive by avoiding hurting other people's feelings and by striving to overcome their own weaknesses. In social relationships they are likely to appear apprehensive and inhibited. Although they try to maintain their self-respect at a high level, they seem to be lacking in internal sources of evaluation. They probably function best in well-structured situations where they can tell what is required of them. These requirements they will try to fulfill in a reasonable but not necessarily outstanding fashion, for their drive to succeed is not very strong. Nor are they likely to stray far from what they know, since doing so might expose their inadequacies and possibly make them vulnerable to attack.

Type C. This type, like Type A, is also achievement-oriented. But, unlike a man in Type A who combines achievement with affiliation and play, a man in Type C is more driven, and his ambition has a more hostile quality about it. He ranks aggression higher than do any of the other eight types. Achievement may be so important to him that, when he fails in an undertaking, he returns to master it and so to demonstrate that he has few, if any, weaknesses

---

[6] In a description of a type, the term "lower" refers to a rank that is closer to the least descriptive end of the continuum (toward a rank of 20) and the term "higher" refers to the most descriptive end of the continuum (toward a rank of 1).

or that he will not allow fears to stand in his way. In this sense, he may be both counteractive and counterphobic. He will be inclined to be defensive, on his guard against criticism, and argumentative in support of his own position. He is likely to perceive others as obstacles to be removed, ignored, or surpassed. He is critical and discriminating in his choice of friends, and he may well be inclined to be snobbish, disgusted, and bored with other people, rather than comforting and supportive. He ranks need nurturance lower than any of the eight types and therefore is likely to reject others whom he regards as inferior. Because his autonomous needs are high, he is not one to bow to custom or conform to tradition. He likes to dominate situations, and he prides himself on being free and acting according to impulse. The impulses he expresses are likely to be aggressive ones. He is prone to conflict with his superiors, for he does not necessarily respect them; and he is unlikely to fulfill their requests unless he believes they foster his own ends. In this regard he is more extreme than our other types, for he ranks need deference lower than all of them. As one studies the hierarchy of needs within this type, one cannot help but gain the impression that men in this type are compensating for inferiorities and weaknesses.

Type D. The first three needs of this type are achievement, affiliation, and counteraction. Unlike Type C, however, the achievement of a man in this type is not colored by intense personal pressures; and unlike Type A, his achievement is not characterized by playfulness or enjoyment. Indeed, this type is not inclined to express his libidinous strivings. He ranks need sentience and need sex lower than do the other eight types. For a man in this group, there seems to be a moral commitment to work. In his work as in his other habits he is likely to be neat and precise, and he enjoys arranging and organizing things. Such emphasis on order protects him from criticism and blame. Members of this type do not see themselves as giving in to external forces easily. Rather, they view themselves as controlling their environments just as they control themselves. Men in this type will work together with others in a cooperative enterprise, taking more satisfaction in the efficient accomplishment of a task, however, than in the sharing of feelings. These men are inclined to help others who need their aid. And, on such occasions, one has the impression that

their aid stems more from an ethical code than from compassionate feeling. One also has the impression that they have incorporated the values of others rather than finding their own, and those which they have accepted they seek to perpetuate. An individual in this type accepts "the tried and the true," and when he does occasionally venture forth on his own, he does not deviate markedly from the *status quo.* Finally, should anyone frustrate this man's style of life, it is likely that his equanimity will be disturbed and the aggression that was previously channeled into work will be provoked.

Type E. A man of this type is achievement-oriented as are the men in Types A, C, and D. However, whereas Type A has a playful attitude in his achievement orientation and desires positions in which he can be dominant, Type E has little need to be the center of things so long as he is free to do what he wants. In contrast to Type C, who is primarily concerned with his own goals and regards others as sources of frustration, Type E is both more affiliative and more nurturant. And, whereas Type D pursues his goals by checking out the tried and the true, Type E is more inclined to accept his own hunches. Type E differs from all types (including those just mentioned) by placing more emphasis on resisting coercion and restrictions. The members of this type avoid relationships in which they might be dominated; rather, they prefer relationships which are marked by cooperation and trust. They are sympathetic persons; they will help others and not dominate them. They regard themselves as independent and free to act according to their impulses. In satisfying their impulses, however, they will not be exhibitionistic. Indeed, they rank need exhibition lower than do any of the other types. Furthermore, in being independent there is something of a serious or stable cast to their activities, for they rank need play lower than do all of the other types. Although a man in Type E is fairly well organized, the order he achieves does not stem from any attempt to impose structure on his environment, but rather from his capacity to "sense" and "feel" his environment. He enjoys these experiences and does not hesitate to follow his impressions.

These, then, are the five types we found among our 116 chemists. If they are meaningful and useful, then we should say that they differ on a variety of characteristics other than those covered by the twenty needs. Such an investigation is currently under way, but I shall limit myself here to several points relating the types to creativity.

It will be recalled that the 116 chemists were made up of three subgroups. One was a group of "more creative" men ($N = 31$), the second was a group of "less creative" men ($N = 34$), and the third or middle group ($N = 51$) was undefined. Judgments of "more" and "less" creativity were based on ratings obtained from the men's superiors, colleagues, and subordinates. Since our type-definers in the chemist population do not include all persons studied, we also find a decrease in the number of "more" and "less" creative individuals among our type-definers. The data indicate that among the type definers there are twenty-three more creative and twenty-five less creative individuals.

The first question we may ask is how are these persons distributed among the types. We find that more and less creative men appear in all types, which is consistent with the principle of equipotentiality. Of the twenty-three more creative men, 48 per cent are of Type A, 9 per cent of Type B, 34 per cent equally divided between Types C and D, and 9 per cent of Type E. Of the less creative men, 16 per cent are of Type A, 36 per cent of Type B, 12 per cent of Type C, 24 per cent of Type D and 12 per cent of Type E. Thus, the largest proportion of more creative men appears in Type A, and the largest proportion of less creative men appears in Type B. Type A also yields a larger ratio of more creative to less creative individuals. In all the other types combined there are almost equal proportions of more and less creative subjects ($x^2 = 7.84$, $p < .02$).

In a further analysis of the data, all 116 chemists were categorized by creativity status ("more," "less," and undefined) as well as by their relative loadings on Factors A and B. Analysis of these data indicated that a significantly larger proportion of "more creative individuals were among those men whose factor loadings were above the median on Factor A and below the median on Factor B, whereas a larger proportion of "less" creative individuals showed the reverse pattern ($x^2 = 18.45$, $p = < .01$). Thus, we find a differential relationship between the types and an important aspect of behavior.

Another criterion of the meaningfulness of types is that they should be related to antecedent data and biographical information. There is much biographical information that we have

on the types, which will be analyzed in the future. At present, we should like to present data on only one aspect of parent-child interaction for the two types, A and B, on which we have most data.

In attempting to understand how "more creative" individuals develop, we investigated the possibility that they were exposed to complexity early in life. One source of early complexity is the extent to which the subject perceived the mother as inconsistent in relation to himself. It was assumed that an inconsistent mother might be frustrating to the child and that the child, to structure his own environment or to satisfy his needs, would be thrown more onto his own resources than a child reared in a consistent environment; and that this experience of using his own resources would stand him in good stead in future creative work. Obviously, one kind of experience alone would be insufficient to develop a "more creative" adult. Other conditions must also exist, but first it would be necessary to establish the importance of inconsistency.

To gather the necessary data, a questionnaire entitled "Interpersonal Relations in Childhood" was utilized. In this questionnaire subjects were asked to rate on a 7-point scale the degree of consistency or inconsistency they recall having perceived in their mother. The item read, "As a child I felt my mother was," and then the rating was to be indicated on a continuum that ranged from "very consistent" to "very inconsistent."

When the data for all the "more" ($N = 31$) and all the "less" ($N = 34$) creative men among the 116 chemists were analyzed, it was found that the former did indeed regard their mothers as less consistent ($H = 5.04$, $p = < .05$). Consequently, if inconsistency of the mother was related to creativity status, it should also differentiate between the Type A and Type B groups. Here we find a trend in the direction of the hypothesis. The Type A group does tend to rate their mothers as less consistent than does the Type B group ($H = 2.65$, $10 > p > .05$).

It was previously indicated that Types A and B differ in their relationships to creativity status. Let us now ask what is there about the A typological vector the enables individuals who load heavily on this factor to be regarded as "more creative" and what is there about the B typological vector that would limit or restrict creative activity? For the discussion of these relationships it must be borne in mind that both "more" and "less" creative groups conduct their activities in industrial research environments where they must fulfill scientific, professional, administrative, employee, and social roles.[7] Placed in this context it soon becomes apparent that the groups are differently disposed to fulfilling their various roles, and in what follows are several suggestions that will be investigated in the future.

A Type A person, oriented to achievement and willing to cooperate with others, appears well suited to carry out his activities within the organized social system of an industrial laboratory. The fact that he trusts others probably aids him in communication. He can accept information from others and at the same time discuss his own ideas and findings with them, so that he might profit from constructive criticism. At the same time, he is not an abasive individual; he does not submit to others and probably does not passively accept others' ideas, for he has internalized criteria for reacting to and evaluating problems. It is this same lack of submissiveness which is probably involved in his capacity to question existing data and theories. In pursuing the unknown and seeking novel accomplishments he is further aided by the fact that need play is rather high. He can engage in activities that have no immediate purpose and so can break down existing *Gestalten* into their component parts, which he studies to see how they can, through some reintegrative process, be developed into new and useful ideas. In this activity, he is also aided by his aesthetic sensitivity, which enables him to differentiate between the unnecessary or irrelevant and so arrive at more elegant solutions to problems. His behavior is goal-directed. He is not oriented to avoiding situations or being blamed for his actions; he is confident in what he does and not bothered by the ambiguity generated when an existing structure is disrupted. The fact that he is capable of impulse acceptance suggests that internal boundaries are relatively flexible, and thus they may be capable of "regression in service of the ego."[8] He is probably motivated in his search for novelty to demonstrate his mastery and control of his environment, and what he generates in this regard he presents to others in a forceful and masterful fashion. Finally, he can assume positions of leadership where he is responsible for the activities of others.

Type A, characterized by striving and internal freedom which appear well organized and purposeful, seems to be capable of fulfilling the scientific, professional, administrative, and social roles in the industrial research organization. Members of this type would probably have difficulty, however, in fulfilling the employee role.

By contrast to Type A, consider Type B and his capacity to fulfill the role requirements. Type B appears to lack the freedom and spontaneity to disrupt existing products, processes, and ideas. Being more oriented to avoidant behavior, he is likely to find his security in what exists and will not deviate markedly from what confronts him. Consequently, he will encounter problems in fulfilling both the scientific and professional roles. In these roles he will be further incapacitated by the emphasis men of this type place on people rather than objects, theories, and ideas. Both in working on his research and in the fulfillment of the administrative role, he will encounter problems because he finds it difficult to be assertive. He might produce creative products if he were a member of a team in which another individual offered many ideas from which he could select one tenable and worthy of testing. Even under such circumstances he would require reassurance, probably frequently, that what he had done was appropriate. After several such experiences a man of this type might be able to go off on his own, provided he still had a supportive environment. In view of his emphasis on affiliation, his low need rejection, his blamavoidant attitude, and his desire to make up for his shortcomings, a man of this type seems to be better suited for the fulfillment of social and employee roles.

There are too few men in Types C, D, and E to allow for much discussion. However, some speculation, which may lead to hypotheses for future test, is in order. Further study of the men in Type C may indicate that they may have difficulty fitting into an organizational framework. Their needs autonomy, aggression, and dominance may handicap them in relating to others. The intensity of their behavoir also suggests that creative members of this type may "burn themselves out before their time." One might also venture the hypothesis that this

---

[7] Morris I. Stein, "The Roles of the Industrial Researcher" (unpublished).

[8] Ernst Kris, *Psychoanalytic Explorations in Art* (New York: International Universities Press, 1952).

group, under periods of stress, may experience psychosomatic ailments. These individuals are likely to be more capable of dealing with ideas and thus are better oriented to fulfilling the scientific role, but they will chafe at the bit when they have to fulfill social and employee roles. They will likely "drive" their subordinates and so have problems with the administrative role. And, finally, they may have difficulty in taking orders from their superiors.

Type D, with its emphasis on achievement, affiliation, order, and nurturance, may find the administrative role most to his liking. In addition, he will probably tolerate and not too grudgingly acquiesce to the employee and social roles. But, because his needs dominance and exhibition are high, he hopes not to stay in the confinement of these two roles for very long but to rise in the organization. He is well organized and probably good at translating scientific data to the company client. He lacks, however, the spontaneous and "creative" spark in the fulfillment of scientific and professional roles that is evident in Type A. It may be hypothesized that those of Type D who are regarded as creative have achieved their novel products and processes through problem solving or a trial-and-error approach.

The men of Type E will be aided in fulfilling the scientific and professional roles by their emphasis on achievement, autonomy, and their aesthetic attitude. They will also be able to fulfill the social role but are likely to get too involved wtih people because their needs affiliation and nurturance are rather high. This consideration would also affect them if they were in administrative positions. However, they may have difficulty in attaining these positions, since they are not very dominant or exhibitionistic. In all likelihood, it may be that they can achieve such positions in research organizations, where their superiors look for people who have valuable ideas but are not likely to push themselves forward.

These, then, are some speculations as to how and why the types may manifest differential effectiveness in fulfilling their roles, and especially why the men of Type A may be better disposed to creative activity in industrial research organizations than are members of other types.

There are several other aspects of the relationship between creativity status and typology that should not be overlooked. As was pointed out previously, the data indicate that there is no single psychological picture of *the* individual who is regarded as more creative; more creative persons appear in all types. Future research may bring to light the different processes these individuals follow in producing novelty. Moreover, being of a type (at least insofar as self-images are concerned) does not guarantee that an individual will produce creative products. The type indicates only that individuals who make it up may possess some of the necessary conditions for creativity. There is much more to be considered about the individual and about the transactions between the individual and his environment before completely accurate predictions can be made.[9]

The data also indicated that *within* a type one finds both "more" and "less" creative individuals. This, again, may be a function of many factors. At the moment, inspection of the similarities and differences between individuals within a type suggests that the less creative individuals may be positive or negative exaggerations of the critical features of the type, or they may be conflicted about the type they represent. With regard to the matter of conflict, one must bear in mind that the types relate to self-images. Thus, it is conceivable that an individual may try to be of a type of self-image but have difficulty in carrying it off. Stating this point differently, it is suggested that in a "pure" type there is internal dynamic equilibrium. Those who are not of a pure type may be under strain. To investigate this point further, it would be critical to have additional clinical data on the types and especially to investigate the behavior of individuals who are congruent or incongruent with regard to typologies based on both clinical data and self-images.

For a typological system to have significance, as we pointed out earlier, it has to satisfy certain criteria. Thus far, utilizing the data of "more" or "less" creative individuals it has been possible to show that the types are independent and meaningfully related to significant aspects of behavior. For at least two of them it was also pointed out that they tend to differ on a critical

---

[9] Morris I. Stein, "A Transactional Approach to Creativity," in C. W. Taylor, ed., *The 1955 University of Utah Research Conference on the Identification of Creative Scientific Talent* (Salt Lake City: University of Utah Press, 1956), pp. 171–181.

developmental variable. Finally, several hypotheses were suggested that require further investigation.

Types among Peace Corps Volunteers

The final criterion for our types is that they must enable us to cope better with certain research problems. The problems on which it is hoped that they will cast light are in the area of assessment.

Assessment may be regarded as composed of two major phases, diagnostic and predictive. In the diagnostic phase one seeks to learn as much as one can about the individual. Using this information and, where possible, knowledge of the situation in which the individual will be placed, the assessor then attempts to predict how well the individual will perform. The prediction is not a probability statement but is first manifest in the individuals accepted and rejected and is later checked by field data. The predictive aspect is actually the risk-taking part of the assessment process. One of the problems in assessment is to know which individuals are the risks and, if they are, whether the risk is worth taking. Another problem in assessment arises after an individual has been selected for an undertaking: to what extent will he change as a result of his new experiences and in what direction will these changes occur?

The assessment of the Peace Corps volunteers provided an opportunity to investigate these problems. It will be recalled that these volunteers were a group of young men who were screened from a much larger group as having the potential for work in a newly developing country. Final decisions as to who would go overseas were made at the end of a training period. Not all those accepted for training were selected for overseas duty, so that it was possible to use acceptance-rejection rates as reflections of risk. Furthermore, since data are available on the men after they had been in the field for six months, it has been possible to inquire whether these risks were worth taking. Finally, some of the field data may also be used to learn something about the changes that have taken place in the men.

It should be pointed out that the self-description questionnaire was administered to the men at the beginning of their training and that it figured very little, if at all, in the assessment proceedings. A Q-analysis of the data yielded four types. The average rankings of these types appear in Table 2 and the description of each of them follows.

Type I The individual in this type appears to be dedicated to other people. He enjoys being with and working with other people. In doing so, he finds greatest satisfaction in assisting helpless individuals and in supporting, comforting, and protecting others. The average rank for need nurturance in this type is higher than for all other types. A man of this type is sympathetic. He avoids hurting others and he will not be critical or severe in his interpersonal relationships. For him, need aggression is his lowest need. Compared to the others we studied, a person of this type is lowest on autonomy and highest on deference. Consequently, he appears to be one who is relatively lacking in independence. He can be dominated by others and is likely to accept restrictions placed on his behavior. Indeed, he will strive to conform to others' wishes; when he knows what they want, he will try to fulfill their requests.

Type II Members of this type also enjoy being with people and working with them. Unlike members of Type I, however, they place greater emphasis on need achievement. In striving to attain their goals, these men are likely to follow internal frames of reference. They believe they know what is best. They want to follow their own inclinations and in so doing would be inclined to come into conflict with authority. They are sensitive, aware of both internal needs and external stimuli. Compared to the other three types, they are more likely to seek out and enjoy sensuous impressions and to enjoy aesthetic feelings. Their average rank for need sentience is higher than for the three other types. But, since need order appears low in their hierarchy of needs, they may find themselves frustrated in utilizing their aesthetic impressions constructively. Left to their own devices, members of this type are likely to leave a situation which is not to their liking, rather than cope with the difficulties they encounter, and to seek a new environment which will give them greater satisfaction. The need hierarchy for this type correlates most highly with Type E in the chemist population. Type II differs from Type E in that he is more likely to give in to impulse expression and is lower on control features than Type E.

Type III An individual of this type aims to get things accomplished. He enjoys working with others, but it is most important to him to be in control of the situation. Compared to the three other types, the average rank for need achievement and need dominance is highest in this type. A man of this type sees himself as confident and likes to influence others, but at the same time he is aware of others' needs and can be quite nurturant and sympathetic. He is inclined to be systematic in what he does and to accept responsibility. He is not likely to avoid situations because he might be blamed for his actions. Compared to the three other types, average rank for need blamavoidance is lowest in this type. A man of this type gives higher priority to fulfilling goals than to satisfying his impulse life. When he does satisfy his impulses, he will do so in a socially acceptable and approved manner, rarely overindulging himself, for he would not like to appear inferior. He gives the impression that he will strive to be upright and sincere in whatever he does by following a code that he has been taught.

Type IV The top ranking need of this type is nurturance. A person in this group enjoys going to the aid of helpless individuals with whom he can be supporting and comforting. Compared to the other types of individuals, the average rank for need achievement in this group is lowest. For a member of this type, need nurturance serves the function of finding other individuals with whom he can share experiences in which impulse needs were frustrated and perhaps also the function of staving off any restriction or punishment that he might encounter for indulging his impulse needs. Need play and need sex are not only ranked high within this type but the average ranks on these needs are higher than for any other type. A man of this type is not very discriminating in his interpersonal relationships, for rejection is his lowest ranked need. Indeed, a member of this group likes to have others around him so that he can be seen and heard, can entertain and amuse. In this he also differs from the other types for, on the average, he ranks need exhibition higher than they do. At the same time, he also needs others to provide him with affection and tenderness. In this too he differs from the other types, for his average rank for need succorance is higher than others. He will seek out others who will provide him with sympathetic understanding and possibly some direction and leadership, but not domination, for this man prides himself in not being abasive or submissive to others. He is not very well organized, for he sees organization as coercive and does not see order as allowing for freedom. Nor is he an achieving person for, compared to the other types, his average rank for need achievement is lowest. He gives the impression that he regards himself as a free soul who would be just as happy to see others go their own way too. Underneath it all he may be thankful that others are more organized, because it is through their presence that he can go off and satisfy his own impulses. Finally, if others are kindly disposed toward him and provided him with leadership in a permissive atmosphere, he will under these conditions be able to develop and achieve goals.

These, then, are the four types we found among the eighty men who were accepted for further training and selection. Let us now turn to the several questions to which we sought answers. The major question of risk is broken down into three subquestions: If an individual is of a type, what are the probabilities that he will be accepted for overseas duty? Do their anticipated problems differ from those actually experienced in the field? How effective are these types in the field? With regard to the second major question of change we inquired whether changes appeared in the men's values—specifically, authoritarian values. Answers to these questions would contribute to a better understanding of assessment procedures and some of the difficulties usually encountered therein.

It will be recalled that the type analysis was based on eighty men, forty-six of whom were type definers. The largest number of type definers (nineteen) were categorized as Type I, and approximately 80 per cent, or fifteen, were accepted. Type II contains the second largest group of type definers (twelve); half of them were accepted and half rejected. Ten men were categorized as Type III, and all were accepted. Finally, Type IV contains five men, three of whom were accepted and two rejected. In other words, if a man was of Type I or III, the probabilities were good that he would be accepted for overseas duty. However, if he was of Types II or IV, the probabilities were about equal that he would be accepted or rejected.

If one assumes a relationship between the self-images of these types and behavior during training and interview, then it is likely that members of Type I impressed the assessment staff with their affiliative and nurturant needs and the likelihood that they would be most congruent with the service orientation of the Peace Corps. Type III may have impressed the assessors with his confidence and assertiveness and the likelihood that he would be action-oriented and capable of implementing the Peace Corps program. Types II and IV may have presented more serious problems. Compared with the other types, Types II and IV rank needs related to impulse-life higher and they appear to be less socialized, less directed, and less likely to fit in with requests for conforming behavior. Since these individuals are more self-directed and given to basic need satisfaction, they do pose serious problems when one has to predict their behavior in situations about which one has relatively little information. The question is, however, was the decision to accept or reject Types II and IV made solely on the basis of whether or not the self-directed aspect of their personalities came through during the interview situation? This question we are unable to answer at the present time.

The type analysis has so far highlighted the question of potential risk for overseas duty. We shall later present data that will tell us whether these risks were worth taking. But let us first inquire into the difficulties the men said they experienced after they had been in the field for six months.

During the training period in the United States the volunteers were presented with a check list on which they could indicate the intensity with which they anticipated problems in the field (lonesomeness, living in a strange surrounding, etc.). After they had been in the field for six months, the group was asked to indicate the degree to which it had actually experienced these same difficulties. On the first administration of the test, Type I anticipates most difficulty, Types III and IV follow, and Type II anticipates least difficulty. On the second administration of the check list, after a six-month period in the field, the data of Types I, III and IV stay relatively the same; there is no appreciable change between the intensity of their anticipated and experienced problems. However, the one type that shows the largest increase in intensity between anticipated and experienced problems is Type II ($t = 3.29$, $p = <.05$). Furthermore, the discrepancy indicates that this type of individual may under-

estimate the problems he might encounter in the field. These data also support the previous point that men of Type II are among the greater risks. However, the fact that a man is a risk may or may not be related to his effectiveness in the field, as we shall see.

To obtain a global measure of effectiveness in the field after a six-month period, ratings were collected from the men's supervisors on a seven-point scale ranging from 0 for "very poor" to 6 for "outstanding." A minimum of three ratings was available for each man. Analysis of the data indicates that the average (median) effectiveness ratings for Types I and III, the "least risk" types, were lower (2.75 and 2.58, respectively) than the effectiveness ratings for Types II and IV (3.25 and 4.00, respectively). Although these differences are not statistically significant, the trend is in favor of the greater risk types. One wonders, therefore, whether the Types II and IV who were rejected might not have been worthy candidates for overseas assignment.[10]

The last question to which we turn is, what kinds of people change while in the field and, if they do change, in what direction. An answer to this question would obviously be of value to areas other than assessment. It would be applicable to studies in therapy and to studies investigating the effects of education. In this exploration we investigated the change in values. Specifically, we inquired into the change of F-scale scores for our population of Peace Corps volunteers over a period of six months. The brief version of the F-scale, developed by Daniel J. Levinson, was administered both during training and in the field to all available Peace Corps volunteers, and the intercorrelation between the two administrations was .82. A regression equation was calculated, and the deviation between a man's actual score on the second administration and his expected score was obtained. Analysis of these data indicated that compared to all other groups Type III changes most from what one would expect. And, unlike the other three types which tend

---

[10] Inspection of other data on the relationships among types, difficulty of assignment, and over-all effectiveness of those volunteers already in the field suggests that, in future research, we may learn more about the overseas conditions under which the rejected Types II and IV might have been effective.

to obtain lower F-scale scores after their field experience, members of Type III tend to obtain higher F-scale scores than one would expect.

It will be recalled from the descriptions of the Peace Corps types that Type III differed from the others in several important respects. Their average ranks for needs achievement and dominance were higher and their average ranks for needs play and sex were lower than those found in other types. In a sense, the men of Type III are more forceful and more action-oriented than the other persons studied. When such individuals confront a situation in which they have to wait patiently for the development of results, is it not possible that they would think how much more they could accomplish if they could have more control and be more authoritarian? Might this not also change their value system? We hope to learn more about these individuals when they are revisited and we shall be especially interested in learning whether their reactions were short-lived or whether the early changes were reinforced.

Summarizing the assessment study, it may be said that the typological analysis has highlighted those men who are potential risks and the reasons why they might be so. It has also suggested that some of these risks might have been worth taking. And, finally, it has been helpful in studying problems of change.

Conclusion

This completes the description of our exploration to date. As in all explorations, one cannot tell where it will finally lead. For the moment, at least, it has been helpful in integrating a body of data and in illuminating some problems. It has been possible to provide tentative descriptions of individuals, based on the dynamic interrelationships between their needs. These descriptions provide a more meaningful basis for differentiating among individuals than is provided when one focuses solely on the discrete variables on which they differ and so loses sight of the persons involved. By bringing to light the varieties of individuals who can achieve the same criterion, our exploration has cautioned us against the errors that arise from being inconsistent with the principle of equipotentiality. Finally, not only has our exploration been helpful in clarifying some problems in assessment procedures, but it has also furthered our understanding of individuals who are involved in two types of cultural change.

There is still much to be done. There is still the need to explore whether the types we found differ in behavioral characteristics other than those we considered; and there is still the need to investigate the relationships between types based on self-images and those based on other personality data. Should our efforts continue to be meaningful and productive, one cannot help wondering if they might not also be useful in other areas. Is it not possible that we could further our understanding of human behavior if we explored how different types of individuals learn, perceive, solve problems, etc.? No doubt there is much reluctance to consider typologies in the light of history, and no doubt it may be impossible to meet all the desirable criteria for a typological system.[11] Avoidance of these problems, however, not only delays the development of a classification system that would foster progress in personality research, as it has in other sciences; but it also delays the integration of available knowledge. As we continue our efforts in understanding man, let us not overlook the varieties of men.[12]

[11] Isidor Chein, "Personality and Typology," *Journal of Social Psychology*, XVIII (1943), 89–109.

[12] Parts of this research were supported by the Carnegie Corporation and by the Peace Corps. I am grateful to John Neulinger, I. Chein, S. Schachter, and J. Colmen for their critical reactions and suggestions.

Lewin's Field Theory

Although many of Lewin's concepts of personality have been incorporated into the mainstream of psychology and continue to stimulate research, the theory itself has not been expanded or modified to any significant extent since Lewin's death. This is in sharp contrast to his other major contribution to modern psychology, namely, the formulation of a theory of group dynamics. Group dynamics both as a theory and as a field of research is one of the most viable areas in present-day psychology.

We have selected from among Lewin's many writings an article that is particularly far-ranging in scope. In it, Lewin relates how his theory developed out of observation and experiment and provides illustrations of this development drawn from the work of Zeigarnik and others on interrupted tasks. He discusses such constructs as tension systems, needs and quasi-needs, and field forces in the context of methodology and research. He sets forth his views on the rate at which formalization and quantification should take place in psychology. And finally he answers some of the criticisms that have been made of his work.

The other empirical papers represent various facets of Lewin's theory of personality. Gordon and Thurlow's study is a sequel to Mary Henle's monograph which was discussed at length in *Theories of Personality*. They found that a completed task of medium valence could serve as a substitute for an incompleted task which was either high or low in valence.

Barthol and Ku's experiment is a clever test of Lewin's formulation of the psychoanalytic concept of regression. It is the human counterpart of a number of animal studies. The reader who has tried to learn to tie a bowline knot will identify sympathetically with the task set for the subjects by Barthol and Ku.

There have been an abundance of level of aspiration studies. The one included here by O'Connell and Lundy was performed in a psychosomatic setting and demonstrates the pervasive utility of one of Lewin's best known concepts. They found that hypertensive cardiac patients showed higher levels of aspiration in response to failure than did nonhypertensive arterio-sclerotic cardiac patients.

1.   Formalization and progress in psychology

KURT LEWIN

1

IN RECENT YEARS there has been a very marked change in the attitude of American psychology. During the 1920's and early 1930's psychologists were, on the whole, rather adverse to theory. Governed by a naive metaphysical belief, they were apt to consider "fact finding" the only task of "scientific" psychology, and were particularly skeptical of the idea of psychological laws in the fields of needs, will, and emotion, that is, in fields other than perception and memory.

Today, a definite interest in psychological theory has emerged, due partly to the efforts of a few psychologists (particularly Tolman and Hull in animal psychology). The need for a closer fusion of the various branches of psychology demands tools which permit better integration. The practical tasks of mental hygiene and education demand conceptual tools which permit prediction. Neither demand can be met without theory.

Now, however, it seems necessary to point to certain dangers of theorizing. Enthusiasm for Theory? Yes! Psychology can use much of it. However, we will produce but an empty formalism, if we forget that mathematization and formalization should be done only to the degree that the maturity of the material under investigation permits at a given time.

Philosophically, there seems to exist only an "either-or": if scientific "facts" and particularly all so-called dynamic facts are not merely "given data," but inseparably interwoven with theoretical assumptions, there seems to be no

SOURCE. Selection from Kurt Lewin, "Formalization and progress in psychology" in *Field Theory in Social Science: Selected Theoretical Papers*, Chapter I. Edited by Darwin Cartwright. New York: Harper, 1951.

choice other than to base every statement in psychology on theoretical assumptions.

For the psychologist, as an empirical scientist, the situation looks rather difficult. He finds himself in the midst of a rich and vast land full of strange happenings: there are men killing themselves; a child playing; a child forming his lips trying to say his first word; a person who having fallen in love and being caught in an unhappy situation is not willing or not able to find a way out; there is the mystical state called hypnosis, where the will of one person seems to govern another person; there is the reaching out for higher, and more difficult goals; loyalty to a group; dreaming; planning; exploring the world; and so on without end. It is an immense continent full of fascination and power and full of stretches of land where no one ever has set foot.

Psychology is out to conquer this continent, to find out where its treasures are hidden, to investigate its danger spots, to master its vast forces, and to utilize its energies.

How can one reach this goal? At first, in what might be called the "speculative epoch," the attempt was made to dig down deep into the ground. A peculiar something was reported to lie underground as the hidden source of energy. One gave it the name "association." New investigators drove their shafts down at somewhat different places. They found something different which they called "instinct." A third group of explorers reported a different entity, "libido." And all claimed to have found *the* foundation on which the land rested. By this time, psychologists had become rather tired of the various claims. It had become clear that the continent was much larger than was suspected at first. Perhaps there was more than one source of energy. The whole depth-sounding process had become rather open to suspicion, particularly since no explorer seemed able to bring his material up to the surface for inspection in broad daylight. How was one ever to prove a real connection between the entities supposedly existing underground and what was going on at the surface? There, open to all eyes, and unquestionable, interesting phenomena presented themselves. The psychologist now turned to extensive traveling over the surface of the continent, eager to find new phenomena, to describe them exactly, to count and to measure them, to register their growth.

This procedure, however, did not prove altogether satisfactory either. After all, what the psychologist observed were human beings. Children needed help and education; delinquent people needed guidance; people in distress wanted cure. Counting, measuring, and classifying their sorrows did not help matters much. Obviously one had to go to the facts "behind," "below the surface." How to accomplish this without the fallacies of the speculative epoch? That is the dominant methodological question of psychology today, at the beginning of its "Galilean period."

The answer is something like this: to make oneself master of the forces of this vast scientific continent one has to fulfill a rather peculiar task. The ultimate goal is to establish a network of highways and superhighways, so that any important point may be linked easily with any other. This network of highways will have to be adapted to the natural topography of the country and will thus itself be a mirror of its structure and of the position of its resources.

The construction of the highway system will have to be based partly upon assumptions which cannot be expected to be fully correct. The test drilling in exploring the deposits will not always lead to reliable results. Besides, there is a peculiar paradox in the conquering of a new continent, and even more so in that of a new scientific field. To make the proper tests, some machinery has to be transported, and such transportation presupposes more or less the same road, the construction of which is contingent upon the outcome of the test. In other words, to find out what one would like to know one should, in some way or other, already know it.

What should science do to resolve this paradox? If it is wise, it follows the same procedure used in a systematic exploration of the resources of a new land: small paths are pushed out

through the unknown; with simple and primitive instruments, measurements are made; much is left to assumption and to lucky intuition. Slowly certain paths are widened; guess and luck are gradually replaced by experience and systematic exploration with more elaborate instruments. Finally highways are built over which the streamlined vehicles of a highly mechanized logic, fast and efficient, can reach every important point on fixed tracks.

By and large, the actual development of a science seems to follow this general pattern. Yet frequently somebody, thinking he knows where an important treasure lies, tries to build a superhighway straight to this point without regard for the natural structure of the country. Much enthusiasm and work are put into such roadbuilding, but after some time it becomes apparent that this superhighway is a dead end leading nowhere.

Formalization and mathematization in psychology, if prematurely done, may lead us to the building of such logical superhighways. Formalization will have to be achieved if psychology is to become an acceptable science, and psychology can and must take definite steps in that direction now. However, the promising beginning and the growing interest for such undertaking will soon turn into disappointment if certain dangers, arising partly from recent trends in philosophy and logic, are not frankly discussed and avoided.

I feel somewhat obliged to take this matter up, because two of my books[1] deal mainly with the conceptual tools of psychology. Some of the critics, who did not realize that these conceptual tools have been used for several years in a great number of investigations in a variety of fields, seem to have concluded that my main interest in psychology is formalization or mathematization. Nothing can be more erroneous. As psychologists we are interested in finding new knowledge about, and deeper insight into, psychological processes. That is, and always has been, the guiding principle. Theory, mathematization, and formalization are tools for this purpose. Their value for psychology exists only in so far as they serve as a means to fruitful pro-

---

[1] *Principles of Topological Psychology* (New York: McGraw-Hill Book Co., 1936); The conceptual representation and the measurement of psychological forces, *Contr. psychol. theor.*, 1938, 1, No. 4, Duke University Press.

gress in its subject matter, and they should be applied, as complex tools always should, only when and where they help and do not hinder progress.

II

Some psychologists interested in "strict logical derivations" have criticized our experimental work for not being written in the form: (*a*) definition, (*b*) assumption, (*c*) conclusion. On the other hand, French[2] writes:

In the course of fifty years [psychoanalysis] has developed an extensive system of scientific concepts but the concepts have grown step by step as a necessary and inevitable product of Freud's attempt to orient himself in a bewildering chaos of psychological facts that no one previously had been able to understand. Due to close contact of these new concepts with the facts, one set of concepts was devised to explain one set of facts and a new problem would give rise to an entirely new set of concepts. . . . Topological psychology on the other hand starts with a self-consistent mathematical discipline and then goes to look for facts to fit it (p. 127).

As an answer I may be permitted to survey the actual historical development. My work in psychology began with experiments on association and the *determinierende Tendenz*.[3] The intention was not to criticize associationism but rather to refine the measurement of the "strength of the will" as developed by Ach. His work at that time, I believe, was the most precise theoretically in the field of will and association. After three years of experimentation with hundreds of series of nonsense syllables, and after thousands of measurements of reaction times (at that time one had to measure in 1/1000 seconds) I became convinced that there was no point in trying to improve the exactness of this measurement. The attempts were all based on the assumption of the classical law of association as stated, e.g., by G. E. Müller. The experiments however seemed to prove conclusively, contrary to my expectation, that this assumption had to be abandoned or decidedly

modified. It was necessary to distinguish two rather different types of habits (associations): "need habits" (like alcoholism) and "execution habits" (like pulling a lever up rather than down). The first types represents a "tension" (source of energy), a need such as hunger, which demands satisfaction either directly or through substitution. The execution habit, on the other hand, is in itself no source of action. It is equivalent to a pattern of restraining forces determining a certain path. Without a need or quasi-need the execution habit does not lead to action.

After an interruption due to the first World War, a systematic attempt was made to test the positive assumption growing out of this criticism of the law of association. The first step was an attempt to achieve a more precise conceptual analysis. Dynamically, an "association" is something like a link in a chain, i.e., a pattern of restraining forces without intrinsic tendency to create a change. On the other hand, the tendency to bring about action is basic to a need. This property of a need or quasi-need can be represented by coordinating it to a "system in tension." By taking this construct seriously and using certain operational definitions, particularly by correlating the "release of tension" to a "satisfaction of the need" (or by the "reaching of the goal") and the "setting up of tension" to an "intention" or to a "need in a state of hunger," a great number of testable conclusions were made possible.

After these basic conclusions had been proved valid, mainly through the experiments of Zeigarnik[4] and Ovsiankina,[5] the theory was expanded to include problems like psychological satiation, substitution on the reality and irreality level and in play situations, the measurement of substitute value, the level of aspiration, its shift after success and failure, the effect of distance from the goal upon the strength of psychological forces; in short, the pattern of goals and needs, their interrelation, and the ways of satisfying them, were studied. Today, a multitude of problems including personality and personality development, cognitive structure, social and

---

[2] Thomas M. French: A review of *A Dynamic Theory of Personality* and *The Principles of Topological Psychology*, by Kurt Lewin. In *Psychoanalytic Quarterly*, 1937, 6, 122–128.

[3] Kurt Lewin. Die psychische Tätigkeit bei der Hemmung von Willensorgängen und das Grundgesetz der Assoziation, *Ztschr. f. Psychol.*, 1917, 77, 212–247.

[4] B. Zeigarnik: Über das behalten von erledigten and unerledigten Handlungen, *Psychol. Forsch.*, 1927, **9**, 1–85.

[5] M. Ovsiankina: Die Wiederaufnahme von unterbrochenen Handlungen, *Psychol. Forsch.*, 1928, **11**, 302–389.

cultural relations are being attacked with a set of related concepts.

If one looks through our publications in the order that they have been published one will, I think, agree that the various theoretical assumptions and constructs have been developed rather slowly step by step. The assumptions were made rather tentatively at first and with a fair amount of hesitation. Only to the degree that more and more empirical facts could be brought together experimentally, the theory gained in firmness and more specific statements emerged.

This gradual elaboration based on empirical facts and a great variety of experiments holds true particularly for the mathematical aspects of the theory. The application of topological and vector concepts was first made in a way which left it open whether we had to deal merely with a pedagogical device or rather with a real scientific representation. Only to the extent that these conceptual tools proved to be valuable in formulating problems, and permitting derivations which could be tested experimentally, did they become essential parts of the theory and of its dynamic constructs.

French's criticisms of the *Principles of Topological Psychology* overlook the fact that this first attempt at a systematic survey of the conceptual tools used in our research was not made till after many years of empirical work with them. What French says about the gradual growth of psychoanalytic concepts out of psychological facts can as well be said in regard to the use of topological and vector concepts in field theory. As a matter of fact, the feeling for the necessity of rather slow and careful theorization was the main reason which restrained us from using strict, so-called formalistic derivations in those early experimental studies. That does not mean that I considered those derivations to be not fully stringent or that I did not esteem the value of a mathematical logical language which I had found very helpful when treating problems of comparative theory of science.[6] However, it would have been premature to present certain ideas "*more geometrico*," i.e., by setting forth so-called formal definitions, assumptions, and deductions with-

out being able to do so in well-defined mathematical symbols, in the form of equations or similar representations of functional dependence. If one uses terms of everyday language such as "frustration," "need," "earning," without being able to coordinate mathematical entities to them, one might as well use the normal form of reasoning. To present statements employing amathematical constructs "*more geometrico*" suggests a degree of exactness of derivation which, I am afraid, cannot generally be reached with those types of constructs. This holds true even when these conceptually rather vague constructs are operationally well defined. We will come back to this point later.

One can go even one step further. The dynamic constructs used for example in the study of Zeigarnik may be said to be already of that type which readily lends itself to a strict mathematical representation. However, we felt that it would be wiser to wait with the formalistic representation until these constructs had proved more thoroughly to be empirically fruitful. A too high degree of formalization is likely to endanger this plasticity.

Psychology cannot try to explain everything with a single construct, such as association, instinct, or gestalt. A variety of constructs has to be used. These should be interrelated, however, in a logically precise manner. Moreover, every theoretical statement brought forth to explain certain empirical data should be carefully examined not only in the light of these data but in the light of the totality of empirical data and theoretical statements of psychology. In other words *ad hoc* theories should be avoided. Bringing together the total field of psychology and doing that in a logically consistent manner might well be viewed as one of the basic purposes of our approach. The demand for a new level of precision in regard to the conceptual properties of the constructs, with a view to an ultimately strictly mathematical representation, is but a means to this end. On the other hand, it has been realized that without such mathematization the development of a consistent scientific psychology is impossible in the long run.

III

Occasionally criticisms have been made that the number of subjects in some of our experiments was not sufficiently large. It is probable that, in one or the other experiment, a greater

[6] Kurt Lewin: *Der Begriff der Genese in Physik, Biologie, und Entwicklungsgeschichte* (Berlin: Springer, 1922).

number of cases would have added to the reliability; and, of course, additional confirmation is always desirable. But, where other investigators have repeated our experiments in a competent manner, our results have stood up very well on the whole. Besides, different types of confirmation are most desirable for different types of questions. For instance, if one wishes to find out how the frequency of resumption depends upon the point at which an activity has been interrupted one will have to use a relatively great number of cases to get reliable results, for the problem involved is how within one situation a gradual quantitative change of one factor changes another factor quantitatively. In such cases the problem of the exactness of measurement is paramount and therefore a great number of cases is important.

Take, on the other hand, such questions as whether the effect of an intention is that of a link (association) or the creation of a quasi-need (equivalent to a tension system). If the latter theory is correct, one should expect a fair number of resumptions after interruption. The study of about one hundred interruptions by Ovsiankina shows indeed 80 per cent of resumption. There is some merit in trying another group of one hundred interruptions. If, however, this group again shows about 80 per cent of resumption, one can follow two lines. Either one tries to determine the actual percentage of resumption as accurately as possible, or one is mainly interested in the question whether the effect of an intention can be adequately understood as the creation of a tension system. For the latter question it is at present of minor importance whether the percentage of resumption is 75, 80, or 85, because any of these figures would be in line with the general assumption. To prove or disprove the theory of tension systems, it seems much more important to find a variety of derivations from this theory which should be as different as possible from each other, and to test as many as possible of these derivations, even if this test should be rather crude quantitatively at the beginning.

IV

It might be well to illustrate this point by reviewing in detail the first experimental study of the above-mentioned series, viz., the experiments of Zeigarnik, which were carried out in the years 1920 to 1928 about the recall of finished and unfinished action. Let us repeat' some of Zeigarnik's derivations making use, however, of the formal apparatus of symbols and equations which has been developed in the meantime.

The Basic Assumptions and the Main Derivation. The critical experiments about association and "the measurement of will power" mentioned above had suggested the theory that the effect of an intention was equivalent to the creation of an inner personal tension. The purpose of Zeigarnik's experiment was to provide a first experimental test of this theory. The theory contains two basic assumptions.

(A1) Assumption 1. The intention to reach a certain goal G (to carry out an action leading to G) corresponds to a tension (t) in a certain system (S^a) within the person so that $t\,(S^a) > 0$. This assumption coordinates a dynamic construct (system in tension) with the observable syndrome popularly called "intention."

(A2) Assumption 2. The tension $t(S^a)$ is released if the goal G is reached.

$$t(S^a) = 0 \text{ if } P \subset G$$

Zeigarnik uses as a symptom for the existence of the tension the tendency to recall activities corresponding to the system in tension. The expectation of the existence of such a system is based on the following:

(A3) Assumption 3. To a need for G corresponds a force $f_{P,\,G}$ acting upon the person and causing a tendency of locomotion toward G.

$$\text{if } T\,(S^a) > 0 \qquad f_{P,\,G} > 0$$

This assumption determines the relation between need and locomotion. In other words it means a construct of tension in the person and the construct of force for locomotion in the environment.

Assumptions $(A1)$, $(A2)$, and $(A3)$ are rather general in nature and have been used as basic assumptions for a great variety of deductions and experimentation. It may be possible to eliminate $(A3)$ to a certain degree and to replace it by a combination of $(A1)$ and $(A2)$. One could say without formally introducing the construct of force for locomotion that if $t(S^a) > 0$ there should result according to $(A2)$ a tendency to change the life space so that $t(S^a) = 0$. We prefer, however, to state $(A3)$ as a separate assumption.

(A3a) Assumption 3a. A need leads not only to a tendency of actual locomotion towards the goal region but also to thinking about this type of activity; in other words the force $f_{P,\,G}$ exists not only on the level of doing (reality) but also on the level of thinking (irreality);

$$\text{if } t(S^G) > 0 \qquad f_{P,\,R} > 0$$

where R means recall.

This last assumption of Zeigarnik is more specific in character. It can be viewed as a specialization of $(A3)$. For the derivations of Zeigarnik this specific form $(A3a)$ rather than $(A3)$ is needed.

From the three assumptions $(A1)$, $(A2)$, and $(A3a)$ follows:

(D1) Derivation 1. The tendency to recall interrupted activities should be greater than the tendency to recall finished ones. This derivation can be made as follows. We indicate the completed task by C, the unfinished one by U, and the corresponding systems by S^c and S^u respectively. We can then state

$$(a)\ t(S^u) > 0 \text{ according to } (A1)$$

$$(b)\ t(S^c) = 0 \text{ according to } (A2)$$

Hence $(c)\ f_{P,\,U} > f_{P,\,C}$ according to $(A3a)$, on the level of thinking. In other words, there is a greater tendency to recall spontaneously unfinished tasks than finished tasks.

Experimental Proof. The first objective of Zeigarnik was to test experimentally this conclusion and it was found to be correct, the

$$\text{quotient } \frac{\text{recalled unfinished tasks}}{\text{recalled completed tasks}} = \frac{RU}{RC} \text{ being}$$

1.9 approximately. Experiments where certain tasks were first interrupted but later on allowed to be finished served to prove that it is not the experiences connected with the interruption itself which are the cause of this result but the reaching or not reaching of the goal. In this experiment the recall was not more frequent than in the case of tasks completed without interruption.

After this main conclusion has been found to be true two procedures are open. One can feel that one has done enough for the proof of the main assumption and can go into more exact quantitative measurements, or one can try to find new independent derivations from the basic assumptions and test these experimentally with

the purpose of corroborating them. Zeigarnik embarked mainly upon the second alternative.

Field Theoretical Implications of the Construct "Tension." Using the construct of a "system in tension" for representing psychological needs definitely presupposes a field theory. Conceptually, tension refers to the state of one system relative to the state of surrounding systems. The essence and the purpose of this construct is to include a tendency for change in the direction of equalization of the state of neighboring systems. The construct, therefore, presupposes a geometric representation of the person and a distinction of functional subparts or "systems" within the person, with a definite position in regard to each other. This is but an elaboration of the conceptual properties already implied in the construct tension. Formalistically, one can express the basic relation between neighboring tension systems in the following way:

(C1) If $t(S^1) \neq t(S^2)$ and $b_{s1} \cdot b_{s2} \neq 0$, a tendency exists to change so that $t(S^1) = t(S^2)$. In this formula b_{s1} and b_{s2} indicate the boundaries of the systems S^1 and S^2, $b_{s1} \cdot b_{s2}$ their common part.

The construct tension furthermore presupposes definite assumptions as to the dynamic character of this field, e.g., if the systems corresponding to different needs or quasi-needs should be able to maintain different amounts of tension during a certain period, one will have to assume that this field is not too fluid. If it should be a very fluid field, any differences between the tension levels of the various systems would be found to disappear in a very short time because of the fact that the tendency of equalization resulting from the local tensions would not meet any resistance; in other words, if a quasi-need is coordinated to a tension system which may show its effect even over a considerable time interval, one has to assume that dynamically the person cannot be considered as entirely fluid. On the other hand, a person cannot be regarded as entirely rigid. Otherwise, the effect which one need has on other needs and on the tension level of the person as a whole could not be accounted for. A person, therefore, has to be conceived of as having a medium degree of fluidity in regard to the intercommunication of his tension systems. It is clear that this degree of fluidity may vary from person to person and from situation to situation for a single person. Assuming the constancy of the structural relations of a given set of systems (and assuming a temporarily impermeable boundary surrounding the set as a whole), one can express this statement in the following way:

(C2) Let us indicate the absolute difference between the tension $t(S^1)$ and the tension $t(S^2)$ of two neighboring systems S^1 and S^2 at the time the tensions are being built up by $t(S)^1 - t(S)^2\,^\circ$, the time since then elapsed by Ti, the tension difference at this time by $\mid t(S^1) - t(S^2) \mid^{Ti}$, and the fluidity by fl. Then we can state

$$\mid t(S^1) - t(S^2)\mid^\circ - \mid t(S^1) - t(S^2)\mid^{Ti} = F(Ti, fl)$$

where F symbolizes a monotonously increasing function.

This means: the change in the tension difference of neighboring systems depends upon the time interval and the fluidity. Of course, this holds true only if the tensions of these systems are not changed by other factors, e.g., release of tension by reaching the goal.

As far as I can see, (C1) and (C2) are necessary conceptual elements of the construct tension. The coordination of needs and quasi-needs to this construct tension, therefore, makes it possible to derive a number of facts which may seem rather remote from the problem primarily investigated. These predictions could hardly be made without this specific dynamic theory, and therefore if they can be proved they are of particular value for the confirmation of the theory.

Derivations in Regard to the Fluidity of the Field and the Communication between Tension Systems

(D2) The difference in tension between systems corresponding to unfinished and finished tasks decreases with the time interval elapsed since the creation of the tension system.

Derivation: Follows immediately from the right side of the equation (C2) by means of (A1) and (A3a).

Experimental Proof. The Zeigarnik quotient decreases from about 1.9 to about 1.2 if the recall test has been postponed one day.

If we are correct in assuming that the maintenance of a tension difference between the partial systems of an individual depends upon a sufficient rigidity of the medium, a quicker decrease of tension could occur if the person is more fluid. To prove this conclusion experimentally, Zeigarnik had to find a state which could reasonably be characterized as increased

fluidity (fl). The general symptoms of fatigue seem to justify

(A4) *Assumption 4.* $fl\ (P\ tired) > fl\ (P\ nontired)$.

(D3) The Zeigarnik quotient $\dfrac{RU}{RC}$ is smaller for tired than for nontired subjects.

Derivation. It follows immediately from the denominator in (C2) by means of (A1), (A3a), and (A4).

Experimental Proof. Subjects who were tired during performance and recall yielded a quotient of .7; those tired during performance but not during recall, a quotient of .6; those not tired during performance but tired during recall, 1.0. This threefold variation was made because a fluid state of a person might prevent the building up of any considerable tension difference. The last variation shows that even if the tension has been built up in a nontired state, the quotient becomes smaller if the subject is tired during recall. (The problem of the quotient being smaller than 1 is accounted for by factors not discussed here; they are discussed by Zeigarnik in her paper.)

Several experimental data and other observations suggest that the levels of greater irreality (levels of wishes and dreams) have to be considered as more fluid than the level of reality (level of action). From this it would follow that needs and quasi-needs related to these more irreal levels should show a quicker diffused discharge of tension.

(A5) *Assumption 5.* $fl = F$ (degree of irreality).

(D4) The rate of decrease of the Zeigarnik quotient, within a given time interval, increases with the degree of irreality of activities involved.

$$\left(\frac{RU}{RC}\right)^\circ - \left(\frac{RU}{RC}\right)^{Ti} = F \text{ (degree of irreality)}.$$

Derivation. (D4) follows immediately from (C2) in connection with (A1), (A3a), and (A5).

Experimental Proof. Brown[7] has shown that the ability to recall interrupted "irreal" activities decreases faster than the ability to recall the more "real" ones. (It is possible that the

[7] J. F. Brown: Über die dynamische Eigenshaften der Realitäts und Irrealitätsschichten, *Psychol. Forsch.*, 1933, 18, 143–190.

experiment of Brown does not deal with differences in the degree of reality but rather with differences between more peripheral activities as against more central ones on approximately the same level of reality. In this case, his experiment would show that the more peripheral region of a person has to be regarded as more fluid.)

One way to destroy the differences of tension in the various systems of the inner personal region seems to be the creation of a high emotional tension or, more specifically, a quick shift up and down of strong emotional tension. The bringing up of the general emotional tension within a person to a magnitude of a different order than that corresponding to the relatively weak quasi-needs created in these experiments would, one might expect, equalize these tensions or at least make their differences practically negligible. A sudden change up and down of such a magnitude might well destroy quite a number of walls between the systems or bring about another process equivalent to their de-differentiation and equalize the tensions in this way. As the constructs of "permeability" and "elasticity" are not elaborate enough at present to warrant a formalistic representation we prefer to give this statement in verbal form:

(A6) *Assumption 6.* Strong waves of emotional tension destroy tension differences corresponding to relatively superficial needs.

(D5) The Zeigarnik quotient $\dfrac{RU}{RC}$ after an emotional excitement and "let down" is smaller than without such a process intervening between performance and recall.

Derivation. It follows from (A6), (A1), and (A3a).

Experimental Proof. After experimentally created emotional waves the Zeigarnik quotient decreases to .6. A similarly low quotient of .75 is shown by those subjects who have been emotionally excited during the experiments as a result of their general life situation.

As a last example in this group of derivations which are based mainly on the spatial relations between the various systems and on their amount of communication, we mention the following: A condition for a difference between the systems corresponding to finished and unfinished tasks is that the systems corresponding to each individual task in the experiment are set up from the beginning as sufficiently separated within the person. For if these various systems are subparts of one comprehensive unit without much separation, no great difference in tension can persist. In this case there may be differences in the tension levels of those greater units but no differences between the various subsystems within the larger units. That sufficiently strong boundaries between the systems are a prerequisite for the persistence of tension is already contained in (C1) and (C2).

(D6) The Zeigarnik quotient RU should be about 1.0 if S^u and S^c are not sufficiently separated.

Derivation. Follows directly from (C1) and (C2) in connection with (A1) and (A3a).

Experimental Proof. A larger unit in which the single tasks, no matter whether finished or unfinished, are not much separated, can be created by the setting up of a cognitive structure at the beginning of the experiment, according to which the single tasks appear as parts of a more highly unified series. In such settings the quotient was found to be about .97.

Derivation in Regard to Intensity of Quasi-Needs. One can elaborate our basic assumption (A1) about the relation between psychological needs and tension systems by correlating the intensity of the tension to the intensity of the need.

(A1a) *Assumption (A1a):* $t(S^g) = F(n^g)$ where n^g means the intensity of the need correlated to the goal G.

Correspondingly, we can elaborate the basic assumption (A3) and (A3a) concerning the relation between tension and force for locomotion and recall into a quantitative relation.

(A3b) *Assumption (A3b):* $|f_{P, G}| = F|t(S^g)|$ where $f_{P, G}$ means the strength of the force in the direction of locomotion or recall.

(D7) $$\frac{RU}{RC} = F(n^u)$$

Derivation. (D7) follows from (A1a), (A3a), and (A3b).

Experimental Proof. It is to be expected that subjects who are particularly ambitious will show quasi-needs of a greater intensity than the average subject, whereas subjects whose involvement in the activities is particularly weak should have particularly weak quasi-needs. Zeigarnik has grouped separately those subjects who according to their general behavior in the experiment could be characterized as "ambitious" (without regard to the Zeigarnik quotient). She found that their quotient showed a value of 2.75 as against 1.9 for the average kind of subject. On the other hand, a group of subjects who merely did "what the experimenter told them" without getting personally involved showed a quotient of 1.03, much less than the average. According to Zeigarnik the most seriously involved group of subjects were children. Indeed, their quotient shows a value of 2.5. It may be that there are other factors which contribute to this result. Marrow[8] has attacked the problem of the relation between the intensity of the need and the Zeigarnik quotient in a particularly careful way. He compares the control group of subjects with another group in a situation of competition. He still further sharpens this competition either by praise or by blame. Although he uses a different type of activity, the Zeigarnik quotient of the control group was again 1.9, whereas in the situation of competition, where the need of the subject is very much intensified, the Zeigarnik quotient went up decidedly, in the case of encouragement to 2.17, in the case of blame to 2.10. Marrow showed that the Zeigarnik quotient was particularly high for those tasks which directly followed after the experience of praise or blame by the experimenter.

Derivations in Regard to Psychological as Against Non-Psychological Characterization of Tasks. It is a general presupposition of psychological field theory that one has to be careful to use psychological rather than "objective" sociological or physical categories. There are cases where an activity might be finished from the subject's point of view although it might be classified as interrupted by the experimenter. On the other hand, there are outwardly finished activities which psychologically are unfinished for the subject.

According to (A2) the release of tension is coordinated to the reaching of the goal and this reaching of the goal has to be understood psychologically. From this follows:

$$(D8) \quad \frac{RU}{RC} = 1 \text{ if } P \supset G \text{ at the time of "in-}$$
terruption."

Derivation. This follows directly from (A2) in connection with (A1) and (A3a).

Experimental Proof. Zeigarnik reports a number of specific cases of outwardly unfinished,

psychologically finished activities where the quotient was about 1. Marrow used a special experimental setup where the subject was told that the experimenter was merely interested in finding out whether or not the subject was able to carry out the task and that he would interrupt as soon as he had received this impression. Thus, the interrupted task here psychologically appears finished. Marrow found indeed that the Zeigarnik quotient in this case was .74.

We might mention here the difference between continuous and end tasks. The end tasks such as making a chair out of plasticine or writing a poem have a rather well-defined end, so that in the case of interruption the subject has definitely not reached the goal, whereas by finishing he has reached it. In this case the Zeigarnik quotient is decidedly greater than 1, viz., 1.8. In the case of a continuous task, however, such as putting beads on a string, the subject does not reach a definite goal after "finishing" nor does he definitely get outside the goal region if "interrupted." Therefore the tension in those cases should not be very much different. Indeed, the Zeigarnik quotient is 1.1. (The low values of both R_c and R_u found by Zeigarnik show that the continuous task, no matter whether outwardly interrupted or finished, is psychologically finished.)

$$(D9) \quad \frac{RU}{RC} = 1 \text{ if } P \supset G \text{ at the time of}$$
"finishing."

Derivation. In this case a tension $t > o$ remains both in the systems S^u and S^e because none of the tasks is psychologically finished. (D9) follows directly from (A2) in connection with (A1) and (A3a).

Experimental Proof. For interesting tasks the Zeigarnik quotient was found to be equal to 1. In the case of an interesting task, there is still a need to go back to this type of activity even if the special example has been solved.

Derivation in Regard to Additional Field Forces. According to general field theory the actual behavior is related to the resulting force acting on the person at that time. It is therefore always important to know which other forces might influence behavior aside from those specifically established in the experiment. In Zeigarnik's experiments the forces in the direction of recall are due to two sources: the instruction to recall given by the experimenter $if_{P, R}$. (The symbol *if* designates an "induced" force

[8] A. J. Marrow: Goal tensions and recall (I & II), *J. gen. Psychol.*, 1938, **19**, 3–35; 37–64.

rather than a force corresponding to one's "own" need.) This is but a further application of $(A1)$ and $(A3)$ in regard to the activity of recalling. In addition, there is a force in the direction of spontaneous recall $Ff_{P, R}$ due to the tension $t(S^u)$ corresponding to the interrupted task according to $(A3a)$.

The recall of a finished task is therefore due to the force $if_{P, R}$ whereas the recall of the unfinished task is due to $if_{P, R} + f_{P, R}$. From this follows:

$(D10)$ The more the recall loses its spontaneity and becomes the result of the experimenter's instruction, the more the Zeigarnik quotient approaches 1:

$$\frac{RU}{RC} \to 1$$

Derivation. One can assume that on the average

$$| if_{P, RU} | = | if_{P, RC} |$$

from $(A1)$, $(A3)$ and $(A3a)$ it follows that

$$f_{P, RU} > 0; f_{P, RC} = 0$$

Although we do not know the general laws governing the addition to forces, it seems safe to deduce from these relations that

$$| if_{P, RU} + f_{P, RU} | > | if_{P, RC} + f_{P, RC} |.$$

Hence we can write

$$\frac{RU}{RC} = F\left(\frac{if_{P, RU} + f_{P, RU}}{if_{P, RC} + f_{P, RC}}\right)$$

and this fraction converges towards 1, if the spontaneous forces remain constant and the induced forces are increased.

Experimental Proof. Zeigarnik found that the quotient of those subjects who experienced the experiment as a memory test and therefore had a relatively high $if_{P, R}$ was 1.5 (as against the average of the whole group of 1.9); whereas those subjects who performed the recall in a spontaneous mood of "telling about" had the very high quotient of 2.8.

V

Psychologists agree that the value of constructs and theories in an empirical science depends in the last analysis on their fruitfulness in "explaining" known facts and predicting unknown ones. Not infrequently it has been stated that theories which merely explain known facts

are of no particular value. I cannot agree with this view. Particularly if the theory combines into one logical system known facts which previously had to be treated by separate theories; it would have a definite advantage as an organizational device. Besides, agreement with the known facts proves the adequacy of this theory at least to a certain degree. It is true, however, that it is a clearer test of the adequacy of the theory if one can make predictions from it and prove these predictions experimentally. The reason for this difference seems to be that empirical data generally allow for quite a range of different interpretations and classifications and that therefore it is usually easy to invent a variety of theories covering them.

Most of the proofs used in the study of Zeigarnik have had the character of predicting unknown facts. These facts are generally not of a nature which one would have expected from everyday experience. As a matter of fact, at the time the experiments were carried out one would have had to predict the opposite results for the main experiment according to the laws of association and emotion accepted at that time. And these predictions are the more significant as they deal with a wide range of psychological data: they link problems of memory with problems of fatigue; with momentary emotional states; with attitudes such as ambition, which are generally considered to belong to the field of personality; with perceptual structurization (seeing the tasks separately or as one series); with problems of development and personality constancy. In what single experimental study do a few constructs and theorems allow for a greater manifold of experimentally testable predictions in different fields of psychology? Zeigarnik's study, to my mind, sufficiently demonstrated the fruitfulness of constructs and theories to warrant continued investigation. There have since been a great number of studies about satiation, level of aspiration, success and failure, substitution, habits, emotion, environmental structure and forces, social power fields, social pressure, feeblemindedness, development and regression—all of which have been based on this field theoretical approach. They have been carried out partly by my co-workers, but to a considerable extent by independent investigators. They have confirmed and elaborated these results and thus indirectly shown the value of the constructs used. Nearly all of this experimentation was quantitative in character in the sense that this is used in psychology today. Of course, difficulties have arisen, and more serious difficulties may still arise later. Until now, however, the contradictions have been minor ones and generally could be clarified quite simply. To hold that all these results could have been predicted without these constructs and theorems might be logically possible; actually, it was these constructs which first led to the predictions. Besides, to my knowledge, there is not yet any other theory formulated which actually would account for the totality of these results.

The attempt to develop a field theory on the basis of mathematically defined constructs and theorems is, however, very much at an early stage. Thus, in spite of what seems to be an astonishingly wide range of consistent applications, one will have to be ready for major changes. As Hull[9] most appropriately points out, it should be the virtue of an empirical theory not to refrain from making definite assumptions which might later turn out to be wrong. That no major change has had to be made until now I mainly attribute to one aspect of our methodological procedure, viz., the method of gradual approximation. We have tried to avoid developing elaborate "models"; instead, we have tried to represent the dynamic relations between the psychological facts by mathematical constructs at a sufficient level of generality. Only gradually, and hand in hand with experimental work, was the specification of the constructs attempted.

To my mind, such a method of gradual approximation, both in regard to the constructs used and the technical measurement in experiments, is by far the most cautious and "empirical." In this way a minimum of assumption is made.

The mathematician too easily forgets that the problem of mathematics in psychology is one of applied mathematics. It cannot be the task of the psychologist to develop new mathematical propositions, nor to look for particularly complicated mathematical laws. Instead, he will have to be interested in using as simple mathematical tools as possible. The mathematician will have to realize, in addition, that to apply a system of mathematical concepts in an empirical field one does not necessarily have to prove directly the adequacy of the basic mathematical axioms of this system one by one. It is as well to prove the fruitfulness of some of the derived propositions of this mathematical system for the representation of the empirical properties of the field in question. If the representation of spatial relations in physics by Euclidean geometry had not been permitted until its axioms (such as the divisibility *ad infinitum* of any part of the space) were proved one by one to hold also for the physical space, physics could never have used Euclidean geometry. All one can say is this: if one coordinates certain physical processes to certain geometrical entities one can make certain physical predictions. Such a fruitfulness of coordinating certain physical processes to entities of one rather than of another kind of geometry is all that one can mean by saying that a certain type of geometry holds or does not hold for the physical space. Exactly the same procedure is followed if certain psychological processes (such as social locomotion) are coordinated to certain entities of topological or hodological geometry (such as path). There can be no other meaning and no other proof of the applicability of these geometries to psychology than the fruitfulness of predictions based on such coordination.

The nonmathematician, on the other hand, has accused us of using highbrow mathematical or physical concepts. In several places it has been explained that using spatial geometrical concepts does not necessarily mean using physical concepts. In regard to logico-mathematical deduction there is no difference in principle between numerical and geometrical concepts. It seems necessary to emphasize two points which should warn us against a too early formalization and may be helpful in describing with greater precision the purpose of mathematization in an empirical science like psychology.

VI

In recent years it has been much emphasized, particularly by Hull and his students, that a psychological theory should be presented in the form of definitions, assumptions, and conclusions. This argumentation should be carried out step by step so that its logical stringency can be easily checked. We, too, have emphasized for quite a while that psychology will have to depend on strictly logical derivations

[9] C. Hull: The problem of intervening variables in molar behavior theory, *Psychol. Rev.,* 1943, **50**, 273–291.

and that a step in this direction is at present one of the most urgent tasks. Hull has attempted to fulfill this task, as far as I can see, mainly by retaining the traditional concepts of conditioned reflex and by elaborating them and presenting them in the order of definitions, assumptions, and conclusions.

One should recognize the value of a presentation of psychological argumentation in the form of such a strict scheme because it might help to discover shortcomings of a less formal reasoning. I feel, however, that we are not dealing here with the most essential aspect of the development of psychology towards a science which uses logical derivations based on well-defined constructs. The terms conditioned reflex, inhibition, excitatory tendency, frustrations, etc., as used in such derivations are operationally more or less well defined. However, little attempt has been made to clarify the conceptual properties of those constructs. One does not ask whether any of these constructs has mathematically the properties of a vector, or a scalar, or a tensor, whether it is a region in a field, a pattern of regions, or a change occurring within a region. No attempt is made to approach what is called in physics the dimension of a construct. In short, the conceptual properties of the constructs, i.e., their logical interdependence as opposed to their empirical interdependence as discovered by experiments, are left entirely vague. An outstanding example is the construct *intelligence* which is very well defined operationally but so poorly defined conceptually that practically no logical derivation seems possible. In the long run, it seems hopeless to approach a satisfactory logical level in psychology and, at the same time, to leave conceptually vague the dynamic constructs which play an outstanding part within the framework of derivation.

The necessary conceptualization of psychology cannot be reached by merely repeating, in a more formalistic manner, the statements of an existing psychological school like that of conditioned reflex or of psychoanalysis. Logical form and content are closely interwoven in any empirical science. Formalization should include the development of constructs every one of which is considered from the start both as a carrier of formal implication and as an adequate representation of empirical data. This implies that the operational and the conceptual definitions are not arbitrarily related but show an internal coherence (e.g., the possibility of co-ordinating psychological force operationally to locomotion and conceptually to a vector is mainly based on their common feature of directedness). It further implies that the various constructs should be built up in such a way as to be parts of one logically consistent and empirically adequate system.

Without the development of such a type of dynamic constructs the mere formalization of the traditional constructs might hamper progress in psychology, in spite of a possible gain in precision. One psychologist believes that association is something real, libido or gestalt but a magic word; another is equally convinced that libido or instinct is something real. Which psychological constructs are accepted and which are repudiated depends mainly upon the system-language in which the individual psychologist has been taught to think. It is clear that the formalization of such a language into an elaborate system is apt to have a freezing effect. Even after conceptually well-defined concepts have been found, it may be well to postpone formalization until their empirical fruitfulness has been well established.

This is the reason why the original presentation of Zeigarnik's derivations and results was not given in a formalistic system. Similar caution is advisable in new psychological fields such as experimental social psychology. The further the conceptual development proceeds in psychology as a whole, the quicker will it be possible to apply formalisitic representation even to new fields.

VII

What is accomplished in regard to representing psychological relations by means of topological and vector concepts, and what should be the next objectives? If I may express my own feeling about this question, which will be answered properly, of course, only by the future development of psychology, I would stress the following points:

1. The possibilities of a field theory in the realm of action, emotion, and personality are firmly established. The basic statements of a field theory are that (a) behavior has to be derived from a totality of coexisting facts, (b) these coexisting facts have the character of a "dynamic field" insofar as the state of any part of this includes the statement that we have to deal in psychology, too, with a manifold, the

interrelations of which cannot be represented without the concept of space. In fact all psychological schools implicitly agree with this statement by using concepts like approach or withdrawal, social position, and so forth in their descriptions. It is more and more recognized, although there are still some exceptions, that the spatial relations of psychological data cannot be adequately represented by means of the physical space, but have to be treated, at least for the time being, as a psychological space. It is everywhere accepted that this "life space" includes the person and the psychological environment.

In regard to proposition (*b*) the situation is similar. Even theories originally based on a coordination of isolated stimuli to isolated reactions have developed in a direction which brings them at least very close to (*b*). A good example of this is the theory of Hull, which does not correlate a reaction to a single stimulus such as an optical one, but to a "pattern of stimuli" which includes goal and drive stimuli. In principle it is everywhere accepted that behavior (*B*) is a function of the person (*P*) and the environment (*E*), $B = F (P,E)$, and that *P* and *E* in this formula are interdependent variables.

2. The first prerequisite for a scientific representation of the psychological field is the finding of a geometry adequate to represent the spatial relations of psychological facts. We know from the history of physics that an empirical space might be represented by different geometries: at first physics used Euclidean, more recently Riemannian geometry. It is to be expected that for psychology, too, more than one geometry might be found useful. Today, one will be more satisfied to find at least one geometry which permits a mathematical interpretation of terms like "approach" and "withdrawal" without being psychologically meaningless. The hodological space[10] is supposed to be such a geometry. The hodological space is a finitely structured space, that is, its parts are not infinitely divisible but are composed of certain units or regions. Direction and distance are defined by "distinguished paths" which can easily be coordinated to psychological locomo-

tion. Such a geometry permits an adequate representation of the step-by-step character of most psychological processes. It permits furthermore an adequate answer to the puzzling necessity to ascribe different psychological directions to locomotions in the same physical direction if the goal of these locomotions is different. This is particularly important for the problem of the roundabout route. The hodological space permits the description of the structural relations within the person as well as in his psychological environment. For instance, the degree of differentiation of the person and the peripheral and central layers can thus be defined. Hodological space is no less useful for describing the structure of groups and their changes. Its greatest value, however, becomes apparent when we deal with problems of dynamics.

3. During the latter part of the last century the development of dynamic concepts in scientific psychology was governed by the fear of slipping into the "metaphysics of teleology." The idea that not the future but the past has to be considered as the "cause" of behavior was one of the major motives in developing associationism. At that time anything connected with the concept of direction was considered to be a teleological approach. The concept of goal was suspect and had to be replaced by something which did not imply the concept of direction. Other aspects of teleology looked upon with no less suspicion were: "foresight," which permits the avoiding of obstacles, and "consciousness," which takes into account the total setting. Associationism tried hard to avoid these allegedly unscientific elements. It tried to develop a concept of association devoid of the logical element of direction. Association should be "blind" and based entirely on the past (that meant that the theory of association had to be based on the concept of repetition).

Of course the facts of goals, needs and will were too important simply to be neglected. With psychology under the spell of the dichotomy "teleology" or "causation by the past," nothing else seemed to be left for those psychologists who were impressed by the importance of goal-seeking and directedness than to resort to a definite teleological theory. McDougall is a classic representative of this approach. The associationists, too, could not entirely neglect goal-directed and meaningful behavior. They tried to take goals, intentions, and

---

[10] Kurt Lewin: The conceptual representation and the measurement of psychological forces, *Contr. Psychol. Theor.*, 1938, **1**, No. 4, Duke University Press.

will into their system, and it is interesting to see how by doing this the character of the associationistic theory was changed. Thorndike's law of effect and Ach's concept of *determinierende Tendenz* ascribe to those types of repetition which are connected with certain aspects of a goal (reaching the goal, or setting up an intention) the creation of particularly strong associations. Hull recognized the importance of goals and needs by including goal- and need-stimuli as important elements into those "stimulus patterns," which are assumed as the cause of a reaction. More and more, the theory of associationism (conditioned reflex) has been influenced by the attempt to derive directed activities without assuming directed dynamic factors.

According to field theory, behavior depends neither on the past nor on the future but on the present field. (This present field has a certain time-depth. It includes the "psychological past," "psychological present," and "psychological future" which constitute one of the dimensions life space existing at a given time.) This is in contrast both to the belief of teleology that the future is the cause of behavior, and that of associationism that the past is the cause of behavior. Furthermore, it is an error to consider the assumption of directed factors as characteristic of teleology. The causal explanations in physics certainly do not avoid such assumptions: physical force is a directed entity, a vector. Psychology, too, becomes in no way metaphysical by resorting to constructs of vectorial character such as psychological forces. This permits a direct attack on the problems of directed action. In addition, by defining direction in terms of hodological space, an adequate representation is possible of what has been meaningful in some of the other claims of teleology. The puzzling relation between knowledge and dynamics which had a mystical character in teleology is made understandable at least in one fundamental point: it becomes clear why lack of knowledge has the effect of a barrier. The mysterious ability of animals to make round-about routes can be rationally related to the fact that equilibria in the hodological space depends upon the totality of relations in the field.

4. A variety of psychological processes, I feel, can be treated with relative adequacy with the conceptual tools at hand.[11] These include

the basic *characteristics of needs* and the various ways of their gratification, including substitution. The *substitute value* of one activity for another can be measured, and the general conditions for substitute value can be derived. Substitution involves the basic problems of *setting up new goals* and of the *level of aspiration*. In this field an important step forward has been made by the derivation of the somewhat paradoxical tendency to prefer difficult goals to easy ones, (a tendency which seems to contradict the "law of parsimony"). We have already mentioned that many problems related to the process of *striving for a given goal* can be attacked, particularly the relation between the *cognitive structure* (learning, insight, roundabout route) and the direction and the strength of the psychological forces. The same holds for many problems connected with *conflict situations*. The treatment of problems of *atmospheres* might be specifically mentioned. It is possible to derive the effect of pressure of different degrees upon the degree of the momentary *personality differentiation*. The predictions concerning the effect of *frustration* upon *productivity* and *regression* have been borne out by experiment. The degree of *rigidity* or dynamic communication between the subparts of the person (one of the basic factors in personality besides its degree of differentiation) has been measured. Finally, one result which seems to me of great consequence: the size of those regions which, at a given time, have the character of undifferentiated *units in the life space* has become measurable, at least in certain cases.[12] A number of predictions about the effect of the size of these units on animal behavior have been verified.[13]

As to the next tasks, it is hoped that the quantitative measurement of psychological forces will be accomplished soon. This will provide the answer for the laws of the composition of forces (resultant forces) and aid in the measurement of tension. One of the fields which most urgently requires improvements is that of social psychology. To my mind, it is possible today to define *groups* and group goals operationally and with the type of constructs referred

---

[11] For a more detailed description of the research mentioned here, See Chapter X.

[12] Dorwin Cartwright: Relation of decision-time to the categories of response, *Am. J. Psychol.*, 1941, **54**, 174–196.

[13] Claude Buxton: Latent learning and the goal gradient hypothesis, *Contr. Psychol. Theor.*, 1940, **2**, No. 2, Duke University Press.

to. With their help predictions have been made, and experimentally confirmed, about the effect of certain *social atmospheres* on group life. However, a number of basic constructs in social psychology, including that of inducing fields (power fields), need refinement.

The progress thus far made in the conceptual development of psychology warrants much optimism. The idea that such phenomena as hope or friendship could ever be represented by geometrical or other mathematical concepts would have seemed beyond any realistic ex-

pectation a few years ago. Today such representation is possible and of great help in dealing with these phenomena. I have no doubt that the concepts of topology and hodological space, or concepts of a similar nature, will prove fruitful for representation and prediction in every field of psychology. On the other hand, one of the most important factors for steady progress in any science is good judgment in deciding which problems are ready for attack and which are better delayed until a more mature state of that science has been reached.

2.　Substitution with interrupted tasks of differing valence

ANITRA GORDON AND WILLARD THURLOW

Introduction

Tendency to complete an interrupted task has been related by Lewin to the operation of a system under tension (3, p. 184). Completion of the interrupted task presumably releases the tension of the system corresponding to it. Completion of a second task may result in a decreased tendency for the subject to complete a prior incomplete task. In this case, *substitution* is said to have taken place. Henle (1, p. 73–81; 2) reported experiments on the influence of valence on substitution, utilizing both objectively similar and dissimilar tasks. In her results it is not completely clear which valence (that of Task 1 or Task 2) was chiefly responsible for the results. The present experiment was designed to overcome these difficulties of interpretation by including suitable control conditions. These experiments, run with children, utilized objectively dissimilar tasks, and aimed to answer the following questions: (*a*) Will substitution occur when a low valence task is followed by an objectively dissimilar medium valence task? (*b*) Will substitution fail to occur when a high valence task is followed by an objectively dissimilar medium valence task?

Procedure

The following general conditions were used: (*a*) *LM* : Low valence task, interrupted, fol-

SOURCE. Article by Anitra Gordon and Willard Thurlow, "Substitution with interrupted tasks of differing valence" in *The Journal of genetic Psychology*, Vol. 93, pp. 303–305, 1958.

lowed by medium valence task, completed. (*b*) *L−* : Low valence task, interrupted, followed by simple questions ("How old are you?" etc.), taking up the same average time as *M* in the *LM* condition. Questions were kept constant for all subjects. (*c*) *HM* : High valence condition corresponding to *LM*. (*d*) *H−* : High valence condition corresponding to *L−*. In all conditions, the main interest was to see whether resumption of the interrupted task would occur. One minute was allowed for resumption. (Preliminary experimentation indicated that resumption—and completion—tended to occur within one minute if it occurred at all.)

The subjects, 32 children (age 4½–6½ years), were each run in all conditions. Conditions *LM* and *L−* (or *HM* and *H−*) were administered first; then after a pause of 15 minutes the other pair of conditions was administered. Order of conditions within pairs, and also tasks used for each valence condition were counterbalanced among subjects. The following six tasks were used: (*a*) cutting out animal, (*b*) putting together puzzle (11 pieces), (*c*) building wall, 12 blocks, (*d*) coloring in picture, (*e*) stringing 12 beads, (*f*) putting together simple form board. The six tasks were first demonstrated to the subject; then his order of preference for the tasks was determined. Tasks ranked 1 and 2 were designated high valence tasks; 3 and 4, medium valence tasks; 5 and 6, low valence tasks. Valences determined from initial rankings were used for the first pair of experimental conditions. Valences were redetermined after the 15-minute pause, and these redetermined valences were used for the second pair of conditions.

Results

Percentage resumption (and completion) for the interrupted task was as follows: $H-$, 100; HM, 78; $L-$, 72; LM, 50. The hypothesis (derived from Henle) that LM should be significantly less than $L-$ was confirmed (beyond .05 level, using test for correlated proportions). The hypothesis (also derived from Henle) that HM should not be significantly different from $H-$ was not confirmed (difference significant beyond .05 level). Thus significant substitution was demonstrated when a medium valence task followed both a high valence and low valence interrupted task.

Discussion

It should be noted that although substitution occurred significantly, a large number of the subjects did not show a substitution effect. This may well be a function of the subjects we used. The difference in subjects used must be remembered in comparing our results to those of Henle, who used college students.

This experiment is considered to be only a first step in the investigation of the influences of valence on substitution. There are a number of further questions to be answered. For instance we need to know to what extent degree of completion of the second task influences substitution.

Summary

"Substitution" is said to have taken place when completion of a second task results in a decreased tendency for a subject to complete a prior incomplete task. The present experiment was designed to determine the degree of substitution obtained when a medium valence task followed a high valence or low valence incompleted task. Tasks used were objectively dissimilar. Subjects were 32 children whose ages ranged from 4½ to 6½ years.

Statistically significant degrees of substitution were found. It is concluded that a medium valence task can provide significant substitution for an incomplete high or low valence task. It has also been pointed out that a large number of the children did not show a substitution effect under the conditions of this experiment.

REFERENCES

1. Henle, M. An experimental investigation of dynamic and structural determinants of substitution. *Contrib. Psychol. Theo.*, 1942, **2**, No.3.
2. ———. The influence of valence on substitution. *J. of Psychol.*, 1944, **17**, 11–19.
3. Lewin, K. A Dynamic Theory of Personality. New York: McGraw-Hill, 1935.

3. Regression under stress to first learned behavior

RICHARD P. BARTHOL AND NANI D. KU

IN A REPORT ON STUDIES OF FRUSTRATION IN young children, Barker, Dembo, and Lewin (1941) and Barker, Dembo, Lewin, and Wright (1947) state that " . . . strong frustration causes tension which leads to emotionality and restlessness, to de-differentiation of the person, and hence to behavioral regression." They described behavior changes in children when faced with a frustrating situation, indicating less "constructiveness of play," a deterioration of social interaction, and "intellectual regression." Other studies (Hamilton & Krechevsky, 1933; Kleemeier, 1942; O'Kelly: 1940a, 1940b) have accumulated evidence showing that there is regression in behavior following stress or frustration.

This paper[1] describes a study[2] designed to test the hypothesis that under stress or frustration the person regresses to the *earliest* learned behavior that is appropriate to the situation. In other words, if a person has learned two or more responses to a stimulus situation, he will respond with the first learned of these when placed under stress. Mowrer (1940), among others, has shown that frustrating a particular learned behavior causes the organism to revert to earlier learned behavior. Maier (1949, p. 66) has

SOURCE. Article by Richard P. Barthol and Nani D. Ku, "Regression under stress to first learned behavior" in *The Journal of abnormal and social Psychology*, Vol. 59, No. 1, July 1959. Copyright held by American Psychological Association.

[1] This paper was reported in part at the 1955 meetings of the American Psychological Association.

[2] The experiment was conducted while the writer was on the faculty of the Pennsylvania State University.

pointed out some of the problems inherent in these earlier studies:

Hamilton and Krechevsky, Everall, Sanders, Martin, O'Kelly, and Mowrer believe that frustration causes a return to a former response (historical regression), but in their studies adequate controls were not present for distinguishing between the return to a former response and the abandoning of the prevailing response for a new one that just happened to correspond to an earlier response. The above authors used punishment for disrupting a prevailing response and demonstrated that some animals persisted in this response whereas others did not. That frustration tends to make animals return to a former response, however, is open to question.

In the view advocated here, the source of stress may be entirely unrelated to the behavior, and the person may have a free choice among behaviors that were learned at various times. The terms "stress" and "frustration" are used interchangeably under the assumption that frustration, fatigue, and conflict are specific cases of the more generalized state of stress.

Method

The tying of a bowline knot was selected for study because there are two quite dissimilar methods of achieving the end result. Eighteen Ss were randomly divided into two groups. Both groups were taught both methods of tying the knots but in different order. In a later stressful situation Ss were asked to "tie a knot." Whether the S used the method learned first or second was then noted.

The details are as follows. The Ss, 4 men and 4 women undergraduates at the Pennsylvania

State University, were told that they were participating in two separate studies. One was an investigation of training methods, and the other was the validation of a new intelligence test. Ostensibly as part of the former study they met with the second author to learn how to tie a bowline. Each S learned both methods of tying the knot. There is a simple straightforward way of tying a bowline, Method A, that includes a story which makes it easy to learn. Method B is more elegant and faster but harder to learn. Most Ss seemed to prefer tying the knot by Method B once they had mastered it. The motions used for the two methods are quite dissimilar; until the final product is achieved there is no apparent relation between the two methods.

Group I learned Method A first; Group II, Method B. The training sessions were conducted informally and there was no evidence of stress or anxiety. The criterion for training was five consecutive perfect trials, each trial under four seconds. After a lapse of time ranging from one to four days, each S was trained in the second method of tying the knot. Time between training periods was determined by the mutual convenience of E and the Ss. All Ss completed training no later than three days prior to the stress situation.

The stress situation consisted of the taking of a difficult intelligence test late at night under restrictive conditions. The first eight Ss, all women, reported to E at 1:00 A.M. on a Sunday morning immediately after returning from a dance. The remaining ten, four men and six women, reported to E immediately after finishing a final examination at 9:00 P.M. on a Thursday evening.[3] The Ss were told that they were to take a simple intelligence test designed for high school students, and that the average college student would be able to answer most of the questions without difficulty. Actually the test used was the Lepley Synonym Vocabulary Test (Lepley, 1955; Lepley & Zeigler, 1956), which is designed to discriminate at the upper levels of intelligence as well as at the normal range. The average college student would find many words in the test that he would not have encountered before. The test has 16 parts, each of which requires the S to match each of 30 words with one of five common words. The test usually requires between 40 minutes and one hour for completion. The Ss were required to spend 12 minutes on each part and were not

allowed to proceed to the next section until the time had elapsed. The total time was thus 3½ hours. The Ss had time after each section during which they had nothing to do. They were not allowed to smoke, talk, leave the room, or direct any overt activity toward anything but the test proper. Notes made by Es indicate that the experience was stressful. Seven of the Ss had to be kept awake by constant reminders. One S burst into tears. In spite of the admonitions for silence many comments were made such as "how many more minutes to go" or "can't I smoke just one cigarette?" At the end of the time the group was extremely irritable and restless. It should be pointed out that the Ss knew that they would be kept up late and that they were to take the test. After the conclusion of the experiment a complete explanation was given, and the Ss departed quite amicably.

At the end of the 3½-hour test, the Ss were called out of the room individually in random order, handed a cord, and told "tie a knot."

As a check on the importance of the stress situation in determining the response, all Ss had been asked to tie a knot under conditions that were considered to be without stress. The results were that nine tied the knot by the method learned first and nine by the method learned second. Method B was slightly preferred, ten to eight. These results indicate that the factor of primacy was not the determining one in a non-stress situation.

Results

Sixteen of the 18 Ss tied a bowline by the method learned first. The remaining two tied a bowline by the method learned second. Using the binomial test (Siegel, 1956, p. 39), the null hypothesis was rejected at the .001 level.

All of the nine Ss in Group I used Method A; seven of the nine in Group II used Method B. One of the two who used Method A volunteered the fact that he had belatedly remembered that he had learned to tie the knot in this way while a Boy Scout. (All volunteers had been screened for this information before the training period; two had been rejected because they had already learned the knot.) The other S in Group II who used Method A started to tie the knot by Method B but stopped midway and used the other, simpler, method.

Discussion and Conclusion

The initial hypothesis was clearly supported for the case of *two* learned responses: if a per-

---

[3] Separate analyses of the results for the first eight and the last ten Ss support the same conclusions as the pooled analysis. Only the latter will therefore be reported in this paper.

son has learned two alternate responses to a stimulus and is placed under stress unrelated to the behavior being observed, he responds to the stimulus with the earlier learned behavior pattern. The more general formulation that regression occurs to the *first* learned behavior appropriate to the situation was not adequately tested, since there were only two responses available to the Ss; a study allowing three or more alternatives would serve to decide whether the response pattern is the first learned or merely an earlier learned response.

The stimulus, "tie a knot," was deliberately chosen to allow the Ss the opportunity of tying a knot that had been learned under different conditions and much earlier than the bowline. The second author, who had trained all of the Ss in the knot tying, and who therefore was presumably identified with the bowline, gave the Ss the stimulus instructions. All of the Ss were familiar with the simple overhand knot, usually learned at a very early age while learning to tie shoes. Not only was this response learned earlier, but it had received much more practice over the years and had the advantage of recency, since the Ss had all tied their shoes subsequent to the training on the bowline. No S tied an overhand knot or any other knot except the bowline. This result was predicted on the grounds that tying the bowline would be seen as the only appropriate behavior under the circumstances.

The concept of specific regression suggests that under stress the person does not simply go back along some time dimension and produce more "primitive" behavior as if he were younger, but instead responds in a way that gave him his first taste of success under similar conditions. Lepley (1954) has stated that variability in behavior is decreased under disturbed and excited states, a statement that fits with the concept of regression under stress. He also indicated that variability has high survival value and is related to intelligence. If regression is not adaptive because it tends to reduce variability of behavior, one might ask why the evolutionary processes have not weeded out this characteristic. Perhaps it is because at times of stress the organism does not have time to consider what it is going to do, but instead must act immediately. Other factors then determine whether the response is adequate to meet the needs of the situation. Thus, even stereotyped or regressive behavior allowed Aesop's cat to escape the hunters, since it was not necessary for him to take the time to select one of several responses. The fox, with many available responses, was caught and killed while making up his anthropomorphic mind.

REFERENCES

Barker, R. G., Dembo, T., & Lewin, K. Frustration and regression: An experiment with young children. *Univ. Ia. Stud. Child Welf.*, 1941, **18**, No. 1.

Barker, G. R., Dembo, T., Lewin, K., & Wright, M. E. Experimental studies of frustration in young children. In T. M. Newcomb & E. L. Hartley (Ed.), *Readings in social psychology.* New York: Holt, 1947, Pp. 283–290.

Hamilton, J. A., & Krechevsky, I. Studies in the effect of shock upon behavior plasticity in the rat. *J. comp. Psychol.*, 1933, **16**, 237–253.

Kleemeier, R. W. Fixation and regression in the rat. *Psychol. Monogr.*, 1942, **54**, No. 4 (Whole No. 246).

Lepley, W. M. Variability as a variable. *J. Psychol.*, 1954, **37**, 19–25.

Lepley, W. M. The rationale, construction, and preliminary try-out of the Synonym Vocabulary Test. *J. Psychol.*, 1955, **39**, 215–225.

Lepley, W. M., & Zeigler, M. L. The Synonym Vocabulary Test: Standardization and validation. *J. Psychol.*, 1956, **41**, 419–425.

Maier, N. R. F. *Frustration: The study of behavior without a goal.* New York: McGraw-Hill, 1949.

Mowrer, O. H. An experimental analogue of "regression" with incidental observations on "reaction formation." *J. abnorm. soc. Psychol.*, 1940, **35**, 56–87.

O'Kelly, L. I. An experimental study of regression. I. Behavioral characteristics of the regressive response. *J. comp. Psychol.*, 1940, **30**, 41–53. (a)

O'Kelly, L. I. An experimental study of regression. II. Some motivational determinants of regression and perseveration. *J. comp. Psychol.*, 1940, **30**, 56–95. (b)

Sears, R. R. Survey of objective studies of psychoanalytic concepts. *Social Sci. Res. Council*, 1943, **51**, 76–104.

Siegel, S. *Nonparametric statistics for the behavioral sciences.* New York: McGraw-Hill, 1956.

4. Level of aspiration in hypertensive cardiac patients compared with nonhypertensive cardiac patients with arteriosclerotic heart disease

DESMOND D. O'CONNELL AND RICHARD M. LUNDY

THE PRESENT STUDY IS CONCERNED with the application of the "level of aspiration" technique to the study of persons with cardiac disease. Since 1930, when Hoppe first described the level of aspiration phenomenon, only six studies cited in *Psychological Abstracts* relate to physical or physiological conditions. Two studies—one reported by Berkeley (1952) and one reported by Gerard and Phillips (1953)—found a reliable relationship between adrenal activity and level of aspiration scores. Little and Cohen (1951) found that asthmatic children showed significantly higher levels of aspiration than nonasthmatic. Hecht (1952) was able to differentiate ulcer patients from colitis patients on level of aspiration scores, the ulcer patients getting significantly higher "D scores." Scodell (1953) also found differences between peptic ulcer patients and a neurotic (non-ulcer) control group on a level of aspiration test as well as on several other measures; the ulcer group had lower level of aspiration scores than the neurotic group. Raifman (1957) found that a group of ulcer patients showed significantly higher levels of aspiration than a group of normals and a group of neurotics. The present study will attempt to determine whether persons with hypertensive heart disease can be differentiated from persons with nonhypertensive arteriosclerotic heart disease on a level of aspiration task.

SOURCE. Article by Desmond D. O'Connell and Richard M. Lundy, "Level of aspiration in hypertensive cardiac patients compared with nonhypertensive cardiac patients with arteriosclerotic heart disease" in *Journal of consulting Psychology*, Vol. 25, No. 4, pp. 353–359, 1961.

Perhaps the best known effort to describe distinctive personality characteristics of persons with cardiac disease is that of Dunbar (1948) who described personality profiles for several types of patient. Alexander (1950) considers that probably the most valid of Dunbar's profiles is that of the "coronary" [1] patient. Yet an objective study of 46 coronary patients performed more recently by Miles, Waldfogel, Barrabee, and Cobb (1954), using psychiatric interview, social history, and psychological tests, disagrees with or fails to confirm most of the specific characteristics attributed to coronary patients by Dunbar. The study did show, however, more strenuous work histories, with more physical and psychological stress and strain than the group of normals; in this respect the study tends to confirm that part of Dunbar's profile which pictures the coronary patient as a consistently striving person who works harder and longer than the average adult (Dunbar, 1948, p. 307). Alexander (1950, p. 72) agrees with Dunbar on this characteristic.

---

[1] It will be noted that the word "coronary" in the introductory section has been used in quotation marks. This is because the term needs clarification; "coronary" and "hypertensive" are not mutually exclusive types of heart disease. Dunbar noted, for example, that 27% of the patients with coronary occlusion in her study also had hypertension (Dunbar, 1948, p. 251). Many hypertensives may eventually have coronary occlusion or coronary insufficiency. Miles, Waldfogel, Barrabee, and Cobb (1954) in their study of coronaries, limited the study to cases in which there had actually been a coronary attack—occlusion of the coronary artery—with an absence of hypertension.

The person with hypertensive cardiac disease is characterized by Dunbar as having in common with coronary patients a constant striving to subdue or surpass competitors, but as being different from coronary patients in that hypertensives have a greater fear of criticism, a greater fear of responsibility, a greater fear of falling short. They are more likely to choose occupations below their ability and are usually less successful than coronaries (Dunbar, 1948, p. 264).

If hypertension is preceded by a history of being unsuccessful, fearful of criticism, or of responsibility, and of falling short, as suggested by Dunbar, it may produce a different pattern of response on a level of aspiration test than would be produced by a more successful, less fearful history. There is some support for this hypothesis in the literature. Sears (1940), for example, has shown that chronically unsuccessful children, as judged by school achievement, show a different pattern of response from successful children on a level of aspiration test. The pattern was not necessarily one of lowered aspirations, however, as might be suggested by Dunbar's assertion that the hypertensive is more likely to choose occupations below his ability. In Sears' study the unsuccessful group produced a bimodal distribution, showing either an unrealistically higher level of aspiration or an unnecessarily low level of aspiration. The successful individual typically sets his goal near but slightly above his last previous performance. Kurt Lewin (Lewin, Dembo, Festinger, & Sears, 1944) in his review of the literature and again in 1948 affirms these as characteristic reactions of the successful and the unsuccessful individual in level of aspiration situations.

In a recent theoretical article concerned with level of aspiration and risk taking behavior, Atkinson (1957) has drawn a distinction between those responses, or persons, whose motivation is to achieve success, and those whose motivation is to avoid failure. Those who seek to achieve success typically chose a task near their achievement level, i.e., where the uncertainty of success or failure is greatest. Those who seek to avoid failure typically set their goals either very high or very low. Thus in a level of aspiration study we might be concerned with two kinds of responses: the achievement oriented and the failure oriented. These types of responses seem comparable to Scodel's "typi-

cal" and "atypical" responses. Similarly, Scodel (1953) divides the atypical responses into atypical high and atypical low responses.

If Dunbar is correct in her assertions about persons with coronary heart disease and those with hypertensive heart disease, the two groups should be similar when achievement oriented behavior is considered. The responses of the two groups in their failure oriented behavior, however, should differ, according to her view that the hypertensives are more fearful of failure. She also states that the direction of this failure oriented reaction is toward choosing atypically low levels of aspiration—in Atkinson and Scodel's terms.

Although the writings of Dunbar have given impetus to this general investigation, the findings of Miles et al. (1954), have cast considerable doubt about her specific hypotheses. The approach of the present investigation, however, is not to test Dunbar's specific hypotheses. Rather, we feel that the status of the theoretical positions is such that only an empirical approach is presently warranted. Thus, the questions asked in the present study are: do hypertensive heart cases differ from nonhypertensive, arteriosclerotic heart cases in (a) the number of achievement oriented, aspiration responses, and (b) the extent and direction of the failure oriented responses?

Method

Subjects

All subjects were adult male veterans between the ages of 32 and 65, hospitalized at Veterans Administration Hospital, Wood, Wisconsin. Patients in this hospital are from Wisconsin, Michigan, and Illinois; the largest percentage of patients are from the Milwaukee metropolitan area.

All new admissions to the hospital were reviewed and a list made of all those showing an admission diagnosis of heart disease or suspected heart disease. After the medical diagnostic procedures had been completed, the cases were discussed with the ward physician. Subjects with an established diagnosis of "Hypertensive Heart Disease" were assigned to one group; subjects with an established diagnosis of "Arteriosclerotic Heart Disease" and an absence of hypertension were assigned to the second group. Subjects with other types of heart disease were eliminated from further consideration as not meeting the criteria of the defined groups. Among those meeting the definitional or categorical requirements no eliminations were made except subjects who were mentally or physically incapable of cooperating in the study (for example, subjects who have had a cardiovascular accident resulting in hemiplegia, or aphasia, or deterioration of mental functioning).

Medically there is always the possibility that a subject in the nonhypertensive arteriosclerotic group has at some time in the past been hypertensive. However, from the standpoint of research design, such a misclassification would not invalidate a positive finding. Thus, if there is a psychological variable associated with the presence of hypertension, and the present study indicates that the nonhypertensive group and the hypertensive group differ significantly on this variable, the significance level would be a minimal value; transfer of the misclassified case to the hypertensive group in which it belongs would only serve to increase the significance level.

Associated diseases found to be present coincident with the primary diagnoses of hypertensive or arteriosclerotic heart disease were of interest, but were not used in selecting the subjects because to do so would change the basis of selection and disturb the research design of the study.

Each subject was given 11 15-second trials on the Placing test of the Minnesota Rate of Manipulation Test. He was asked to set a goal prior to each trial. The test was presented to him as a test of his coordination.

This task was selected after consideration of a number of factors. The literature on the use of the level of aspiration technique reveals that a wide variety of tasks, both verbal and motor, have been used; tasks used, for example, include card sorting, cancellation, addition, pegboards, bowling games, target tests, and the Rotter Aspiration Board. A decision was made in favor of the Minnesota Placing test for the following principal reasons: (a) Hecht (1952) found significant differences between peptic ulcer and ulcerative colitis patients using the Purdue Pegboard; the Minnesota Placing test is a somewhat similar performance-type test of coordination but requires less finger dexterity and less precise placement. (b) Bowling games and other "game"-type tasks in level of aspiration studies have been criticized by Barnett, Handelsman, Stewart, and Super (1952), Stubbins (1950), and others as having too much of a "play" atmosphere and not being closely related to life situations. This has led to the practice in recent level of aspiration studies of introducing penalties or other extraneous motivation. If this criticism has any validity, it

might be that a game-type task would be even less meaningful and challenging to the older individuals with which the present study deals. On the other hand, it was our feeling that the Minnesota Placing test would prove to be a meaningful task when presented as "a test of coordination" to a hospitalized cardiac patient who has just come through a cautiously graded progression in amount of physical activity permitted and who is very much aware of and concerned about his physical limitations.

Test Instructions

Standardization of instructions was considered especially important in this study because it is known from previous studies of level of aspiration technique, such as those of Irwin and Mintzer (1942), of Walder (1951), and of Saji (1951) that the form of the stimulus question affects the results. Thus, "What score do you expect to get?" "What do you hope to get?" or "What will you try to get?" may bring different responses. Using Frank's (1941) definition of level of aspiration as, "the level of future performance in a familiar situation which an individual *explicitly* undertakes to reach," we have used as our stimulus question: "How many blocks will you try to get in on the next trial?" After the initial trial, the stimulus question was shortened to: "How many will you try for this time?"

Age

Age has not been shown to be a significant factor in level of aspiration studies; studies of this factor which have been done, such as those by Adams (1939), Walter (1948; Walter & Marzolf, 1951), and Reissman (1953), have tended to show that level of aspiration behavior is not significantly related to age. However, some of the studies did not examine age as a continuous variable but merely compared "old" groups with "young" groups; other studies which did examine age as a continuous variable have usually considered only a very limited range of ages. Because there has been insufficient research on age as a variable in level of aspiration behavior, and because age is known medically to be related to arteriosclerotic heart disease, it was our feeling that it should be controlled in the present study. The age of each subject was therefore recorded for comparison (see Results section).

Stage of Recovery

Although the effect of stage of recovery on level of aspiration behavior is unknown and uninvestigated, it seemed desirable to control this factor. The experimental task was light sedentary activity involving only 15 seconds of activity at a time and an over-all time of only about 15 minutes; yet it required rapid movement of the arm, and might be either a real or a perceived threat in the early stages of recovery from cardiac disease. Thus no patients were scheduled until they reached the "ambulatory" stage of recovery, and this was approximately the same for all subjects.

Education

The average education for the Hypertensive group is 8.7 with a standard deviation of 2.0, and a range of 5–13 years of formal schooling completed. This compares with an average of 8.8 and a standard deviation of 2.6 for the Arteriosclerotic group, with a range of 4–14 years completed.

Table 1. Difference between the Means of the Hypertensive and Arteriosclerotic Groups using the "A" Scores

Group	N	M	SD	SE_D	t
Hypertensive	24	5.75	2.57		
				0.72	1.83*
Arteriosclerotic	23	4.43	2.34		

* $p < .10$.

Method of Scoring the Aspiration Responses

Although many systems of scoring have been used in various studies in the literature, the most widely used is the D score or the average discrepancy between the subject's performances and his aspirations. The D score, however, fails to take account of what would appear to be an important psychological variable: the effect of success or failure upon the subject's immediately subsequent aspiration. Thus, an average D score of $+1$ for one person may represent a very consistent aspiration to do one better than the last performance no matter whether it was a success or failure experience. For another person a $+1$ score could represent an average of quite different reactions following success or failure.

Guided by the Atkinson (1957) formulation that the achievement oriented individual sets his goal at the point of greatest uncertainty of success or failure, and assuming that this point is slightly above his last previous performance, we have set up the following operational definitions for the present study: achievement oriented aspiration—one point above the last previous performance; failure oriented high aspiration—two or more points above the last previous performance; failure oriented low aspiration—a goal at or below the last previous performance. The performances of the subject are operationally classified as follows: Success —reaching or surpassing one's goal; Partial Failure—a performance one point below the goal set; Failure—a performance two or more points below the goal set.

From the responses, two scores are derived: (a) An achievement oriented score designated as the "A score"; this is the total number of achievement-oriented responses. (b) A failure oriented score designated as the "F score"; this is the algebraic sum of the failure oriented responses weighted in the following manner: a high aspiration response following a Success was given a weight of 1; a high aspiration response following a Partial Failure was given a weight of 2; a high aspiration response following a Failure was given a weight of 3. Similarly, a low aspiration following a Failure was assigned a weight of -1; a low aspiration response following a Partial Failure was assigned a weight of -2, and a low aspiration response following a Success was assigned a weight of -3.

Results

Table 1 presents results of a t test comparing the achievement oriented scores of the Hypertensive group with those of the non-hypertensive Arteriosclerotic group. The difference between the means is not statistically significant, although the direction of the difference shows a higher mean for the Hypertensive group.

Table 2 presents the results of a t test comparing failure oriented scores of the Hypertensive group with those of the non-hypertensive Arteriosclerotic group. The difference between the means was significant beyond the .05 level. A mean of 0.38 was found for the Hypertensive group, indicating that this group gave high aspiration responses about as often as low aspiration responses. A mean of -7.61 was found for the non-hypertensive Arteriosclerotic group, indicating that this group predominantly gave low aspiration responses.

Age has not generally been shown to be significantly related to level of aspiration. However, since it is known medically that it is related to arteriosclerosis, the question was raised as to the possibility that age had affected the results. However, analysis revealed identical means for the groups. The average age of the Arteriosclerotic group was 54.17, with a standard deviation of 8.43; the average age for the Hypertensive group was 54.13, with a standard deviation of 8.94. The ages ranged from 32 to 63 in the Arteriosclerotic group and from 34 to 65 in the Hypertensive group. The age factor, then, is not significant in the present study.

Table 2. Difference between the Means of the Hypertensive and Arteriosclerotic Groups Using the F Scores

Group	N	M	SD	SE_D	t
Hypertensive	24	+0.38	12.45	3.54	2.26†
Arteriosclerotic	23	−7.61	11.79		

† $p < .05$.

Table 3 presents a comparison of the performance scores of the two groups. The mean of the Arteriosclerotic group was 13.91 with a standard deviation of 2.61; the mean of the Hypertensive group was 12.88 with a Standard deviation of 2.04. The difference of 1.03 in the means was not statistically significant.

Table 4 presents a comparison of the degree of improvement of the two groups as measured by the difference between the score on the first trial and the highest score attained on any of the subsequent trials. For the Arteriosclerotic group, the mean improvement was 3.48 with a standard deviation of 1.24. The mean for the Hypertensive group was 3.29 with a standard deviation of 1.28. The slight difference in the mean improvement (.19) was not statistically significant.

Discussion

The intent of this study was to determine whether a group of hypertensive cardiac patients would differ from a group of non-hypertensive arteriosclerotic cardiac patients on a level of aspiration test. The results show that when the level of aspiration is measured in terms of failure oriented responses, the two groups differ significantly with the hypertensives showing a higher level of aspiration response. In Atkinson's (1957) terms there are two ways of responding to fear of failure: choosing a goal in excess of reasonable expectation, or choosing a goal which can be easily attained. Thus, to defend against anxiety, the failure

Table 3. Performance Scores of the Hypertensive and Arteriosclerotic Groups

Group	N	M	SD	SE_D	t
Hypertensive	24	12.88	2.04	0.65	1.57
Arteriosclerotic	23	13.91	2.61		

Table 4. Degree of Improvement of the Hypertensive and Arteriosclerotic Groups

Group	N	M	SD	SE_D	t
Hypertensive	24	3.29	1.28	0.38	0.50
Arteriosclerotic	23	3.48	1.24		

oriented individual either chooses a goal so high that failure to attain the goal is not destructive, or chooses a goal which is low enough so that he can be sure of achieving it. In terms of fear of failure, our data, therefore, suggest that in avoiding failure, the arteriosclerotic is more likely than the hypertensive to utilize the defense of choosing an easily attainable goal.

Analysis of the *frequency* of the achievement oriented responses fails to show a statistically significant difference between the groups. However, the significant finding is that when the failure oriented responses of both groups are analyzed, the hypertensive was more likely than the arteriosclerotic to choose a response which was so high as to assure failure. The difference between the arteriosclerotic and the hypertensive lies in the results of their different approaches to failure. The arteriosclerotic avoids the personal feeling of failure by "arranging" for objective success, i.e., by setting his aspiration low. The hypertensive, by contrast, arranges for objective failure. Thus no matter what the reason, the hypertensive less often reaches his goal—that is, he objectively fails.

The results of this study lead us to speculate about a possible relationship between hypertension and continual self-chosen failure. Reiser, Brust, and Ferris (1951) have discussed the role of "life stress" in the development of hypertension, assuming that the patient's reaction to the stress is elevated blood pressure. But just what, in the life stress of the hypertensive, would lead to the blood pressure elevation? Further, what in the life stress distinguishes the hypertensive from the arteriosclerotic, for the psychosomatic literature (Miles et al., 1954) includes studies which find that all heart patients live under more psychological stress than normals.

Our data would support the hypothesis that continued failure, resulting from too high goals, rather than a general life stress, can lead to hypertensive reactions. In attempting to explain this relationship, we hypothesize that continued failure is in some way associated with a physiological withdrawal of blood from the arteriolar bed. The increased blood pressure of the hypertensive follows from the peripheral resistance in the arteriolar bed. Thus the hypertensive reaction is not the direct result of general psychological stress, but rather, is the direct result of the hypertensive avoidance reaction to the

specific stress of continued failure. Support for the notion that the hypertensive reaction, i.e., constriction of peripheral vessels, is not due to general psychological stress itself comes from a well-controlled study by Baker and Taylor (1954) which found that skin temperature rises, i.e., arterioles dilate, under general psychological stress.

The present results also force some modification of Dunbar's characterization of the hypertensive. Hypertensives may fear falling short, as she suggests, but they react to this fear, not by choosing goals too low, as she suggests, but by choosing goals so high that they cannot possibly be achieved. Thus they insure failure.

Because this is the first study, to our knowledge, to apply level of aspiration techniques to the study of psychological variables in heart disease, the results obtained suggest further study of cardiac patients with this technique.

Summary

Twenty-four hypertensive cardiac patients and 23 nonhypertensive arteriosclerotic cardiac patients hospitalized at a Veterans Administration Hospital were administered a level of aspiration task based on the Minnesota Rate of Manipulation Test. Achievement oriented scores and failure oriented scores were derived from the aspiration responses. An achievement oriented response was operationally defined as an aspiration one point above the last previous performance; a failure oriented response was defined as either "high" (two or more points above last previous performance), or "low" (at or below the last previous performance). No significant difference between the groups was found in the frequency of achievement oriented scores. However, when failure oriented responses were broken down into high and low response patterns, the hypertensive group gave significantly ($p < .05$) less low aspiration responses than the nonhypertensive arteriosclerotic group. Level of performance and degree of improvement were not significantly different for the two groups. The hypertensive group "arranged" for repeated failure by consistently setting excessively high goals. It is hypothesized that the withdrawal of blood from the arteriolar bed, resulting in increased blood pressure, is an avoidance reaction to the repeated and continual failure experiences which the failure oriented hypertensive arranges for himself in a neurotic fashion.

REFERENCES

Adams, D. K. Age, race, and responsiveness of levels of aspiration to success and failure. *Psychol. Bull.*, 1939, 36, 573. (Abstract)

Alexander, F. *Psychosomatic medicine.* New York: Norton, 1950.

Atkinson, J. W. Motivational determinants of risk-taking behavior. *Psychol. Rev.*, 1957, 64, 359–372.

Baker, L. M., & Taylor, W. M. The relationship under stress between changes in skin temperature, electrical skin resistance, and pulse rate. *J. exp. Psychol.*, 1954, 48, 361–366.

Barnett, G. J., Handelsman, I., Stewart, L. H., & Super, D. E. The occupational level scale as a measure of drive. *Psychol. Monogr.*, 1952, 66 (10, Whole No. 342).

Berkeley, A. W. Level of aspiration in relation to adrenal cortical activity and the concept of stress. *J. comp. physiol. Psychol.*, 1952, 45, 443–449.

Dunbar, F. *Psychosomatic diagnosis.* New York: Harper, 1948.

Frank, J. D. Recent studies of the level of aspiration. *Psychol. Bull.*, 1941, 38, 218–225.

Gerard, D. L., & Phillips, L. Relation of social attainment to psychological and adrenocortical reactions to stress. *AMA Arch. Neurol. Psychiat.*, 1953, 69, 350–354.

Hecht, I. The difference in goal striving behavior between peptic ulcer and ulcerative colitis patients as evaluated by psychological techniques. *J. clin. Psychol.*, 1952, 8, 262–265.

Irwin, F. W., & Mintzer, M. G. Effect of differences in instructions and motivation upon measures of the level of aspiration. *Amer. J. Psychol.*, 1942, 55, 400–406.

Lewin, K. *Resolving social conflicts.* New York: Harper, 1948.

Lewin, K., Dembo, Tamara, Festinger, L., & Sears, Pauline. Level of aspiration. In J. McV. Hunt (Ed.), *Personality and the behavior disorders.* Vol. 1. New York: Ronald, 1944. Pp. 333–378.

Little, Sue W., & Cohen, L. D. Goal setting behavior of asthmatic children and of their mothers for them. *J. Pers.*, 1951, 19, 376–389.

Miles, H. H. W., Waldfogel, S., Barrabee, Edna L., & Cobb, S. Psychosomatic study of 46 young men with coronary artery disease. *Psychosom. Med.*, 1954, 16, 455–477.

Raifman, I. Level of aspiration in a group of peptic ulcer patients. *J. consult. Psychol.*, 1957, 21, 229–231.

Reiser, M. F., Brust, A. A., & Ferris, E. B., Jr. Life situations, emotions and the course of patients with arterial hypertension. *Psychosom. Med.*, 1951, 13, 133.

Reissman, L. Levels of aspiration and social class. *Amer. sociol. Rev.*, 1953, 18, 233–242.

Saji, M. The degree of reality in level of aspiration. *Jap. J. Psychol.*, 1951, 21(3–4), 56–69.

Scodell, A. Passivity in a class of peptic ulcer patients. *Psychol. Monogr.*, 1953, 67(10, Whole No. 360).

Sears, P. S. Levels of aspiration in academically successful and unsuccessful children. *J. abnorm. soc. Psychol.*, 1940, 35, 498–536.

Stubbins, J. The relationship between level of vocational aspiration and certain personal data: A study of some traits and influences bearing on the prestige level of vocational choice. *Genet. psychol. Monogr.*, 1950, 41, 327–408.

Walder, L. O. The effects of instructions, order, and sex-ethnic group in level of aspiration situations. Unpublished masters dissertation, University of Hawaii, 1951.

Walter, L. M. The relation of age and sex to levels of aspiration. Unpublished masters dissertation, Illinois State Normal University, 1948.

Walter, L. M., & Marzolf, S. S. The relation of sex, age, and school achievement to levels of aspiration. *J. educ. Psychol.*, 1951, 42, 285–292.

Allport's Psychology of the Individual

The discriminating eclecticism which has characterized Gordon Allport for decades is still a pervasive feature of his theoretical writings. Recently he presented a restatement (Allport, 1961) of his major volume on personality theory that included many significant departures from his earlier writings. Most of these changes have had the effect of expanding the range of events or determinants of behavior to which his systematic position directs specific attention.

The topics dealt with in the papers presented here are a blend of the familiar and the novel—of themes that Allport has dealt with for decades and of approaches that are quite new. In the first paper, *The Open System in Personality Theory*, we find Professor Allport in the familiar role of provocative and historically oriented teacher. He argues that most personality theorists have overlooked tendencies that represent growth or the achievement of a higher stage of development, in favor of tendencies concerned with the maintenance of some pre-existing state. He emphasizes once again the organic or systematic character of the behavior of the individual. He also joins other writers in suggesting that the most appropriate model for representing human behavior is the "open system" which explicitly acknowledges the importance of forces external to the person—for him a relatively novel emphasis.

The second paper, *The General and the Unique in Psychological Science*, was selected as providing the best, and most recent example of Allport's position in regard to the importance of uniqueness or individuality as a key to understanding personality. What he says here is obviously consistent with his past position, but at the same time he employs concepts that were first introduced in his most recent book and he provides an extended discussion of the particular methods of study that are particularly appropriate for the study of individual (morphogenic) traits.

The discussion of "units" clearly reveals Allport's enduring concern with taxonomy or the classification and description of personality. He deals directly with one of psychology's most central problems and while he provides no final resolution of the problem he makes painfully clear how much remains to be accomplished and he furnishes important suggestions in regard to directions that are most likely to lead to advances.

The final paper is an empirical study selected to emphasize the diversity of research areas that Allport has approached during his career. It reports an experimental study of the perception of movement in a cross-cultural perspective and is an outgrowth of a year spent teaching and conducting research in South Africa. It is of particular interest because it reflects clearly Allport's heightened interest in recent years in the role of socio-cultural determinants of behavior.

REFERENCES

Allport, G. W. *Pattern and growth in personality.* New York: Holt, 1961.

1. The open system in personality theory

GORDON W. ALLPORT

OUR ORB OF COMMON INTEREST has two faces—one turned toward social psychology, the other toward personality. As things stand at the moment the first visage seems to me slightly depressed; the second slightly manic. However that may be, I should like to start this discussion by bringing the two faces into confrontation.

My first observation is that as members of Division 8 we are conspicuously the victims of fashion. Although our persona is sedate and seemly, we have our own hula hoops, flying saucers, and our own way of flagpole sitting. The interquartile range of our crazes I estimate to be about 10 years. McDougall's instinct theory held sway from 1908 to approximately 1920. Watsonian behaviorism dominated the scene for the next decade; then habit hierarchies, then field theory; now phenomenology. We never seem to solve our problems or exhaust our concepts; we only grow tired of them. At the moment it is fashionable to investigate response-set, coding, sensory deprivation, person perception, and to talk in terms of system theory—a topic to which we shall soon return. Ten years ago fashion called for group dynamics, Guttman scales, and for research on the centipedal properties of the authoritarian personality. Twenty years ago it was frustration-aggression, Thurstone scales, and national morale. And so it goes. We are fortunate that each surge of fashion leaves a rich residue of grain.

Fashions have their amusing and there serious side. We can smile at the way bearded problems receive tonsorial transformation. Having tired of "suggestibility" we adopt the new

hairdo known as "persuasibility." Modern ethology excites us, and we are not troubled by the recollection that a century ago John Stuart Mill staked down the term to designate the new science of human character. We like the neurological concept of "gating," conveniently forgetting that American functionalism always stood firm for the dominance of general mental sets over specific. Reinforcement appeals to us but not the age-long debate over hedonism. The problem of freedom we brush aside in favor of "choice points." We avoid the body-mind problem but are in fashion when we talk about "brain models." Old wine, we find, tastes better from new bottles.

The serious side of the matter enters when we and our students forget that the wine is indeed old. Picking up a recent number of the *Journal of Abnormal and Social Psychology* I discover that the 21 articles written by American psychologists confine 90% of their references to publications of the past 10 years, although most of the problems they investigate have gray beards. In the same issue of the journal, three European authors locate 50% of their references prior to 1949. What this proves I do not know, excepting that European authors were not born yesterday. Is it any wonder that our graduate students reading our journals conclude that literature more than a decade old has no merit and can be safely disregarded? At a recent doctoral examination the candidate was asked what his thesis on physiological and psychological conditions of stress had to do with the body-mind problem. He confessed he had never heard of the problem. An undergraduate said that all he knew about Thomas Hobbes was that he sank with the *Leviathan* when it hit an iceberg in 1912.

SOURCE. Article by Gordon W. Allport, "The open system in personality theory" in *Journal of abnormal Psychology*, Vol. 61, pp. 301–310, 1960.

A Psycholinguistic Trifle

Our windows are pretty much closed toward the past, but we rightly rejoice in our growth since World War II. Among the many fortunate developments is rejuvenation in the field of psycholinguistics. (Even here, however, I cannot refrain from pointing out that the much discussed Whorfian hypothesis was old stuff in the days of Wundt, Jespersen, and Sapir.) Be that as it may, I shall introduce my discussion of open systems in personality theory by a crude Whorfian analysis of our own vocabulary. My research (aided by the kind assistance of Stanley Plog) is too cursory to warrant detailed report.

What we did, in brief, was to study the frequency of the prefix *re-* and of the prefix *pro-* in psychological language. Our hypothesis was that *re-* compounds, connoting as they do again-ness, passivity, being pushed, or maneuvered, would be far more common than *pro-* compounds connoting futurity, intention, forward thrust. Our sample consisted of the indexes of the *Psychological Abstracts* at 5-year intervals over the past 30 years; also all terms employing these prefixes in the Hinsie and Shatzky *Psychiatric Dictionary* and in the English and English *Psychological Dictionary*. In addition we made a random sampling of pages in five current psychological journals. Combining these sources it turns out that *re-* compounds are nearly five times as numerous as *pro-* compounds.

But, of course, not every compound is relevant to our purpose. Terms like reference, relationship, reticular, report do not have the connotation we seek; nor do terms like probability, process, and propaganda. Our point is more clearly seen when we note that the term reaction or reactive occurs hundreds of times, while the term proaction or proactive occurs only once —and that in English's *Dictionary*, in spite of the fact that Harry Murray has made an effort to introduce the word into psychological usage.

But even if we attempt a more strict coding of this lexical material, accepting only those terms that clearly imply reaction and response on one side and proaction or the progressive programming of behavior on the other, we find the ratio still is approximately 5:1. In other words our vocabulary is five times richer in terms like reaction, response, reinforcement, reflex, respondent, retroaction, recognition, regression, repression, reminiscence than in terms like production, proceeding, proficiency, problem solving, propriate, and programming. So much for the number of different words available. The disproportion is more striking when we note that the four terms reflex, reaction, response, and retention together are used 100 times more frequently than any single *pro-* compound excepting problem solving and projective—and this latter term, I submit, is ordinarily used only in the sense of reactivity.

The weakness of the study is evident. Not all terms connoting spontaneous, future oriented behavior begin with *pro-*. One thinks of expectancy, intention, purpose. But neither do all terms connoting passive responding or backward reference in time begin with *re-*. One thinks of coding, traces, input-output, and the like. But while our analysis leaves much to be desired it prepares the way for our critique of personality theory in terms of systems. The connecting link is the question whether we have the verbal, and therefore the conceptual, tools to build a science of change, growth, futurity, and potential; or whether our available technical lexicon tends to tie us to a science of response, reaction, and regression. Our vocabulary points to personality development from the past up to now more readily than to its development from here-on-out into the future.

The Concept of System

Until a generation or so ago science, including psychology, was preoccupied with what might be called "disorganized complexity." Natural scientists explored this fragment and that fragment of nature; psychologists explored this fragment and that fragment of experience and behavior. The problem of interrelatedness, though recognized, was not made a topic for direct inquiry.

What is called system theory today—at least in psychology—is the outgrowth of the relatively new organismic conception reflected in the work of von Bertalanffy, Goldstein, and in certain aspects of gestalt psychology. It opposes simple reaction theories where a virtual automation is seen to respond discretely to stimuli as though they were pennies-in-the-slot. Interest in system theory is increasing in psychology, though perhaps not so fast as in other sciences.

Now a system—any system—is defined merely as a complex of elements in mutual interaction.

Bridgman (1959), as might be expected of an operationist, includes a hint of method in his definition. He writes, a system is "an isolated enclosure in which all measurements that can be made of what goes on in the system are in some way correlated" (p. 188).

Systems may be classified as closed or open. A closed system is defined as one that admits no matter from outside itself and is therefore subject to entropy according to the second law of thermodynamics. While some outside energies, such as change in temperature and wind may play upon a closed system, it has no restorative properties and no transactions with its environment, so that like a decaying bridge it sinks into thermodynamic equilibrium.

Now some authors, such as von Bertalanffy (1952b), Brunswik (1955), and Pumpian-Mindlin (1959), have said or implied that certain theories of psychology and of personality operate with the conception of closed systems. But in my opinion these critics press their point too far. We had better leave closed systems to the realm of physics where they belong (although even here it is a question whether Einstein's formula for the release of matter into energy does not finally demonstrate the futility of positing a closed cgs system even in physics). In any event it is best to admit that all living organisms partake of the character of open systems. I doubt that we shall find any advocate of a truly closed system in the whole range of personality theory. At the same time current theories do differ widely in the amount of openness they ascribe to the personality system.

If we comb definitions of open systems we can piece together four criteria: there is intake and output of both matter and energy; there is the achievement and maintenance of steady (homeostatic) states, so that the intrusion of outer energy will not seriously disrupt internal form and order; there is generally an increase of order over time, owing to an increase in complexity and differentiation of parts; finally, at least at the human level, there is more than mere intake and output of matter and energy: there is extensive transactional commerce with the environment.[1]

While all of our theories view personality as an open system in some sense, still they can be fairly well classified according to the varying emphasis they place upon each of these criteria, and according to how many of the criteria they admit.

Criterion 1. Consider the first criterion of material and energy exchange. Stimulus-response theory in its purest form concentrates on this criterion to the virtual exclusion of all the others. It says in effect that a stimulus enters and a response is emitted. There is, of course, machinery for summation, storage, and delay, but the output is broadly commensurate with the intake. We need study only the two poles of stimulus and response with a minimum of concern for intervening processes. Methodological positivism goes one step further, saying in effect, that we do not need the concept of personality at all. We focus attention on our own measurable manipulations of input and on the measurable manipulations of output. Personality thus evaporates in a mist of method.

Criterion 2. The requirement of steady state for open systems is so widely admitted in personality theory that it needs little discussion. To satisfy needs, to reduce tension, to maintain equilibrium, comprise, in most theories, the basic formula of personality dynamics. Some authors, such as Stagner (1951) and Mowrer (1959) regard this formula as logically fitting in with Cannon's (1932) account of homeostasis.[2] Man's intricate adjustive behavior is simply an extension of the principle involved in

---

[1] von Bertalanffy's definition explicitly recognizes the first two of these criteria as present in all living organisms. A living organism, he says, is "an open system which continually gives up matter to the outer world and takes in matter from it, but which maintains itself in this continuous exchange in a steady state, or approaches such steady state in its variations in time" (1952a, p. 125). But elsewhere in this author's writing we find recognition of the additional criteria (1952a, p. 145; 1952b, p. 34).

[2] In a recent review Mowrer (1959) strongly defends the homeostatic theory. He is distressed that the dean of American psychologists, Robert Woodworth (1958) has taken a firm stand against the "need-primacy" theory in favor of what he calls the "behavior-primacy" theory. With the detailed merits of the argument we are not here concerned. What concerns us at the moment is that the issue has been sharply joined. Need-primacy which Mowrer calls a "homeostatic" theory does not go beyond our first two criteria for an open system. Woodworth by insisting that contact with, and mastery of, the environment constitute a pervasive principle of motivation, recognizes the additional criteria.

temperature regulation, balance of blood volume, sugar content, and the like, in the face of environmental change. It is true that Toch and Hastorf (1955) warn against over-extending the concept of homeostasis in personality theory. I myself doubt that Cannon would approve the extension, for to him the value of homeostasis lay in its capacity to free man for what he called "the priceless unessentials" of life (1932, p. 323). When biological equilibrium is attained the priceless unessentials take over and constitute the major part of human activity. Be that as it may, most current theories clearly regard personality as a *modus operandi* for restoring a steady state.

Psychoanalytic theories are of this order. According to Freud the ego strives to establish balance among the three "tyrants"—id, superego, and outer environment. Likewise the so-called mechanisms of ego defense are essentially maintainers of a steady state. Even a neurosis has the same basic adjustive function.[3]

To sum up: most current theories of personality take full account of two of the requirements of an open system. They allow interchange of matter and energy, and recognize the tendency of organisms to maintain an orderly arrangement of elements in a steady state. Thus they emphasize stability rather than growth, permanence rather than change, "uncertainty reduction" (information theory), and "coding" (cognitive theory) rather than creativity. In short, they emphasize being rather than becoming. Hence, most personality theories are biologistic in the sense that they ascribe to personality only the two features of an open system that are clearly present in all living organisms.

There are, however, two additional criteria, sometimes mentioned but seldom stressed by biologists themselves, and similarly neglected in much current personality theory.

---

[3] When we speak of the "function" of a neurosis we are reminded of the many theories of "functionalism" current in psychology and social science. Granted that the label, as Merton (1957) has shown, is a wide one, still we may safely say that the emphasis of functionalism is always on the usefulness of an activity in maintaining the "steady state" of a personality or social or cultural system. In short, "functional" theories stress maintenance of present direction allowing little room or none at all for departure and change.

Transatlantic Perspective. Before examining Criterion 3 which calls attention to the tendency of open systems to enhance their degree of order, let us glimpse our present theoretical situation in cross-cultural perspective. In this country our special field of study has come to be called "behavioral science" (a label now firmly stuck to us with the glue of the Ford millions). The very flavor of this term suggests that we are occupied with semiclosed systems. By his very name the "behaviorial scientist" seems committed to study man more in terms of behavior than in terms of experience, more in terms of mathematical space and clock-time than in terms of existential space and time; in terms of response more than in terms of programming; in terms of tension reduction more than tension enhancement; in terms of reaction more than proaction.

Now let us leap our cultural stockade for a moment and listen to a bit of ancient Hindu wisdom. Most men, the Hindus say, have four central desires. To some extent, though only roughly, they correspond to the developmental stages of life. The first desire is for pleasure—a condition fully and extensively recognized in our Western theories of tension reduction, reinforcement, libido, and needs. The second desire is for success—likewise fully recognized and studied in our investigations of power, status, leadership, masculinity, and need-achievement. Now the third desire is to do one's duty and discharge one's responsibility. (It was Bismarck, not a Hindu, who said: "We are not in this world for pleasure but to do our damned duty.") Here our Western work begins to fade out. Excepting for some pale investigations of parental punishment in relation to the development of childhood conscience, we have little to offer on the "duty motive." Conscience we tend to regard as a reactive response to internalized punishment, thus confusing the past "must" of learning with the "ought" involved in programming our future (Allport, 1954, pp. 68–74). Finally, the Hindus tell us that in many people all these three motives pall, and they then seek intensely for a grade of understanding—for a philosophical or religious meaning—that will liberate them from pleasure, success, and duty (Smith, 1958). (Need I point out that most Western personality theories treat the religious aspiration in reactive terms as an escape device, to be classified along with suicide, alcoholism, and neurosis?)

Now we retrace our steps from India to modern Vienna and encounter the existentialist school of logotherapy. Its founder, Viktor Frankl, emphasizes above all the central place of duty and meaning, the same two motives that the Hindus place highest in their hierarchy of desire. Frankl reached his position after a long and agonizing incarceration in Nazi concentration camps. With other prisoners he found himself stripped to naked existence (1959a). In such extremity what does a person need and want? Pleasure and success are out of the question. One wants to know the meaning of his suffering and to learn how as a responsible being he should acquit himself. Should he commit suicide? If so, why; if not, why not? The search for meaning becomes supreme.

Frankl is aware that his painfully achieved theory of motivation departs widely from most American theory, and he points out the implication of this fact for psychotherapy. He specifically criticizes the principle of homeostasis (1959b) as implying that personality is a quasi-closed system. To cater to the internal adjustments of a neurotic, or to assume that he will regain health by reshuffling his memories, defenses, or conditioned reflexes is ordinarily self-defeating. In many cases of neurosis only a total breakthrough to new horizons will turn the trick.

Neither Hindu psychology nor Frankl underestimates the role of pleasure and success in personality. Nor would Frankl abandon the hard won gains reflected in psychoanalytic and need theory. He says merely that in studying or treating a person we often find these essentially homeostatic formulations inadequate. A man normally wants to know the whys and wherefores. No other biological system does so; hence, man stands alone in that he possesses a degree of openness surpassing that of any other living system.

Criterion 3. Returning now to our main argument, we encounter a not inconsiderable array of theories that emphasize the tendency of human personality to go beyond steady states and to strive for an enhancement and elaboration of internal order even at the cost of considerable disequilibrium.

I cannot examine all of these nor name all the relevant authors. One could start with McDougall's proactive sentiment of self-regard which he viewed as organizing all behavior

through a kind of "forward memory" (to use Gooddy's apt term—1959). Not too dissimilar is the stress that Combs and Snygg place on the enhancement of the phenomenal field. We may add Goldstein's conception of self-actualization as tending to enhance order in personality; also Maslow's theory of growth motives that supplement deficiency motives. One thinks of Jung's principle of individuation leading toward the achievement of a self (a goal never actually completed). Some theories, Bartlett and Cantril among them, put primary stress on the "pursuit of meaning." Certain developments in post-Freudian "ego psychology" belong here.[4] So too does existentialism with its recognition of the need for meaning and of the values of commitment. (The brain surgeon, Harvey Cushing, was speaking of open systems when he said: "The only way to endure life is to have a task to complete.")

No doubt we should add Woodworth's recent advocacy of the "behavior primacy" theory as opposed to the "need" theory, Robert White's emphasis on "competence," and Erikson's "search for identity."

Now these theories are by no means identical. The differences between them merit prolonged debate. I lump them here simply because all seem to me to recognize the third criterion of open systems, namely, the tendency of such systems to enhance their degree of order and become something more than at present they are.

We all know the objection to theories of this type. Methodologists with a taste for miniature and fractionated systems complain that they do not lead to "testable propositions" (cf. Roby, 1959). The challenge is valuable in so far as it calls for an expansion of research ingenuity. But the complaint is ill-advised if it demands that we return to quasiclosed systems simply because they are more "researchable" and elegant. Our task is to study what is, and not what is immediately convenient.

Criterion 4. Now for our fourth and last criterion. Virtually all the theories I have mentioned up to now conceive of personality as something integumented, as residing within the

---

[4] Pumpian-Mindlin (1959) writes: "The focus of clinical psychoanalysis on ego psychology is a direct result of the change from a closed system to an open one" (p. 1051).

skin. There are theorists (Kurt Lewin, Martin Buber, Gardner Murphy, and others) who challenge this view, considering it too closed. Murphy says that we overstress the separation of man from the context of his living. Experiments on sensory deprivation Hebb (1955) has interpreted as demonstrations of the constant dependence of inner stability on the flow of environmental stimulation. Why Western thought makes such a razor-sharp distinction between the person and all else is an interesting problem. Probably the personalistic emphasis in Judeo-Christian religion is an initial factor, and as Murphy (1958, p. 297) has pointed out the industrial and commercial revolutions further accentuated the role of individuality. Shinto philosophy, by contrast, regards the individual, society, and nature as forming the tripod of human existence. The individual as such does not stick out like a raw digit. He blends with nature and he blends with society. It is only the merger that can be profitably studied.

As Western theorists most of us, I dare say, hold the integumented view of the personality system. I myself do so. Others rebelling against the setting of self over against the world, have produced theories of personality written in terms of social interaction, role relations, situationism, or some variety of field theory. Still other writers, such as Talcott Parsons (1951) and F. H. Allport (1955), have admitted the validity of both the integumented personality system and systems of social interaction, and have spent much effort in harmonizing the two types of systems thus conceived.

This problem, without doubt, is the knottiest issue in contemporary social science. It is the issue which, up to now, has prevented us from agreeing on the proper way to reconcile psychological and sociocultural science.

In this matter my own position is on the conservative side. It is the duty of psychology, I think, to study the person-system, meaning thereby the attitudes, abilities, traits, trends, motives, and pathology of the individual—his cognitive styles, his sentiments, and individual moral nature and their interrelations. The justification is twofold: (a) there is a persistent though changing person-system in time, clearly delimited by birth and death; (b) we are immediately aware of the functioning of this system; our knowledge of it, though imperfect, is direct, whereas our knowledge of all other out-

side systems, including social systems, is deflected and often distorted by their necessary incorporation into our own apperceptions.

At the same time our work is incomplete unless we admit that each person possesses a *range* of abilities, attitudes, and motives that will be evoked by the different environments and situations he encounters. Hence, we need to understand cultural, class, and family constellations and traditions in order to know the schemata the person has probably interiorized in the course of his learning. But I hasten to warn that the study of cultural, class, family, or any other social system does not automatically illumine the person-system, for we have to know whether the individual has accepted, rejected, or remained uninfluenced by the social system in question. The fact that one plays the role of, say, teacher, salesman, or father is less important for the study of his personality than to know whether he likes or dislikes, and how he defines, the role. And yet at the same time unless we are students of sociocultural systems we shall never know what it is the person is accepting, rejecting, or redefining.

The provisional solution I would offer is the following: the personality theorist should be so well trained in social science that he can view the behavior of an individual as fitting any system of interaction; that is, he should be able to cast this behavior properly in the culture where it occurs, in its situational context, and in terms of role theory and field theory. At the same time he should not lose sight—as some theorists do—of the fact that there is an internal and subjective patterning of all these contextual acts. A traveler who moves from culture to culture, from situation to situation, is none the less a single person; and within him one will find the nexus, the patterning, of the diverse experiences and memberships that constitute his personality.

Thus, I myself would not go so far as to advocate that personality be defined in terms of interaction, culture, or roles. Attempts to do so seem to me to smudge the concept of personality, and to represent a surrender of the psychologist's special assignment as a scientist. Let him be acquainted with all systems of interaction, but let him return always to the point where such systems converge and intersect and are patterned—in the single individual.

Hence, we accept the fourth (transactional) criterion of the open system, but with the firm warning that it must not be applied with so much enthusiasm that we lose the personality system altogether.

General Systems Theory

There are those who see hope for the unification of science in what James Miller (1955) called "general behavior systems theory." This approach seeks formal identities between physical systems, the cell, the organ, the personality, small groups, the species, and society. Now critics (e.g., Buck, 1956) complain that all this is feeble analogizing, that formal identities probably do not exist, and that attempts to express analogies in terms of mathematical models result only in the vaguest generalities. As I see it, the danger in attempting to unify science in this manner lies in the inevitable approach from below, that is, in terms of physical and biological science. Closed systems or systems only partly open become our model, and if we are not careful, human personality in all its fullness is taken captive into some autistic paradise of methodology.

Besides neglecting the criteria of enhanced organization and transaction general systems theory has an added defect. The human person is, after all, the observer and interpreter of systems. This awkward fact has recently been haunting the founder of the operational movement, P. W. Bridgman (1959). Can we as scientists live subjectively within our system and at the same time take a valid objective view thereof?

Some years ago Elkin (1947) published the case of "Harry Holzer," and invited 39 specialists to offer their conceptualizations. As might be expected, many different conceptualizations resulted. No theorist was able entirely to divest the case of his own preconceptions. Each read the objective system in terms of the subjective. In other words, our theories of personality—all of them—reflect the temperament of the author fully as much as the personality of *alter*.

This sad spectre of observer contamination should not, I think, discourage us from the search for objectively valid theory. Truth, as the philosopher Charles Pierce has said, is the opinion which is fated to be ultimately agreed to by all who investigate. My point is that "the

opinion fated to be ultimately agreed to by all who investigate" is not likely to be reached through a premature application of general systems theory, nor through devotion to any one partially closed theory. Theories of open-systems hold more promise, though at present they are not in agreement among themselves. But somewhere, sometime, I hope and believe, we shall establish a theory of the nature of personality which all wise men who investigate, including psychologists, will eventually accept.

Some Examples

In the meantime, I suggest that we regard all sharp controversies in personality theory as probably arising from the two opposed points of view—the quasiclosed and the fully open.

The principle of reinforcement, to take one example, is commonly regarded as the cement that stamps in a response, as the glue that fixes personality at the level of past deeds. Now an open-system interpretation is very different. Feigl (1959, p. 117), for instance, has pointed out that reinforcement works primarily in a prospective sense. It is only from a *recognition* of consequences (not from the consequences themselves) that the human individual binds the past to the future and resolves to avoid punishment and to seek rewards in similar circumstances, provided, of course, that it is consonant with his interests and values to do so. Here we no longer assume that reinforcement stamps in, but that it is one factor among many to be considered in the programming of future action (Allport, 1946). In this example we see what a wide difference it makes whether we regard personality as a quasiclosed or open system.

The issue has its parallels in neurophysiology. How open is the nervous system? We know it is of a complexity so formidable that we have only an inkling as to how complex it may be. Yet one thing is certain, namely, that high level gating often controls and steers lower level processes. While we cannot tell exactly what we mean by "higher levels" they surely involve ideational schemata, intentions, and generic personality trends. They are instruments for programming, not merely for reacting. In the future we may confidently expect that the neurophysiology of programing and the psychology of proaction will draw together. Until they do so it is wise to hold lightly our self-closing metaphors of sowbug, switchboard, giant computor, and hydraulic pump.

Finally, an example from motivation theory. Some years ago I argued that motives may become functionally autonomous of their origins. (And one lives to regret one's brashness.)

Whatever its shortcomings the concept of functional autonomy succeeds in viewing personality as an open and changing system. As might be expected, criticism has come chiefly from those who prefer to view the personality system as quasiclosed. Some critics say that I am dealing only with occasional cases where the extinction of a habit system has failed to occur. This criticism, of course, begs the question, for the point at issue is why do some habit systems fail to extinguish when no longer reinforced? And why do some habit systems that were once instrumental get refashioned into interests and values having a motivational push?

The common counterargument holds that "secondary reinforcement" somehow miraculously sustains all the proactive goal-seeking of a mature person. The scientific ardor of Pasteur, the religio-political zeal of Gandhi, or for that matter, Aunt Sally's devotion to her needlework, are explained by hypothetical cross-conditioning that somehow substitutes for the primary reinforcement of primary drives. What is significant for our purposes is that these critics prefer the concept of secondary reinforcement, not because it is clearer, but because it holds our thinking within the frame of a quasiclosed (reactive) system.

Now is not the time to re-argue the matter, but I have been asked to hint at my present views. I would say first that the concept of functional autonomy has relevance even at the level of quasiclosed system. There are now so many indications concerning feedback mechanisms, cortical self-stimulation, self-organizing systems, and the like (Chang, 1950; Hebb, 1949; Olds & Milner, 1954) that I believe we cannot deny the existence of self-sustaining circuit mechanisms which we lump together under the rubric "perseverative functional autonomy."

But the major significance of the concept lies in a different direction, and presupposes the view that personality is an expanding system seeking progressively new levels of order and transaction. While drive motives remain fairly constant throughout life, existential motives do not. It is the very nature of an open system to achieve progressive levels of order through change in cognitive and motivational structure. Since in this case the causation is systemic we cannot hope to account for functional autonomy in terms of specific reinforcements. This condition I would call "propriate functional autonomy."

Both perseverative and propriate autonomy are, I think, indispensable conceptions. The one applies to the relatively closed part-systems within personality; the other to the continuously evolving structure of the whole.

A last example. It is characteristic of the quasiclosed system outlook that it is heavily nomothetic. It seeks response and homeostatic similarities among all personality systems (or, as in general behavior systems theory, among *all* systems). If, however, we elect the open system view we find ourselves forced in part toward the idiographic outlook. For now the vital question becomes "what makes the system hang together in any one person?" (cf. Taylor, 1958). Let me repeat this question, for it is the one that more than any other has haunted me over the years. *What makes the system cohere in any one person?* That this problem is pivotal, urgent, and relatively neglected, will be recognized by open-system theorists, even while it is downgraded and evaded by those who prefer their systems semiclosed.

Final Word

If my discourse has seemed polemical I can only plead that personality theory lives by controversy. In this country we are fortunate that no single party line shackles our speculations. We are free to pursue any and all assumptions concerning the nature of man. The penalty we pay is that for the present we cannot expect personality *theory* to be cumulative—although, fortunately, to some extent personality *research* can be.

Theories, we know, are ideally derived from axioms, and if axioms are lacking, as in our field they are, from assumptions. But our assumptions regarding the nature of man range from the Adlerian to the Zilborgian, from the Lockean to the Leibnitzian, from the Freudian to the Hullian, and from the cybernetic to the existentialist. Some of us model man after the pigeon; others view his potentialities as many splendored. And there is no agreement in sight.

Nils Bohr's principle of complementarity contains a lesson for us. You recall that he showed that if we study the position of a particle we cannot at the same time study its momentum. Applied to our own work the principle tells us that if we focus on reaction we cannot simultaneously study proaction; if we measure one trait we cannot fix our attention on pattern; if we tackle a subsystem we lose the whole; if we pursue the whole we overlook the part-functioning. For the single investigator there seems to be no escape from this limitation. Our only hope is to overcome it by a complementarity of investigators and of theorists.

While I myself am partisan for the open system, I would shut no doors. (Some of my best friends are quasiclosed systematists.) If I argue for the open system I plead more strongly for the open mind. Our condemnation is reserved for that peculiar slavery to fashion which says that conventionality alone makes for scientific respectability. We still have much to learn from our creative fumblings with the open system. Among our students, I trust, there will be many adventurers. Shall we not teach them that in the pastures of science it is not only the sacred cows that can yield good scientific milk?

REFERENCES

Allport, F. H. *Theories of personality and the concept of structure.* New York: Wiley, 1955.

Allport, G. W. Effect: A secondary principle of learning. *Psychol. Rev.,* 1946, **53,** 335–347.

Allport, G. W. *Becoming: Basic considerations for a psychology of personality.* New Haven: Yale Univer. Press, 1954.

Bridgman, P. W. *The way things are.* Cambridge: Harvard Univer. Press, 1959.

Brunswik, E. The conceptual framework of psychology. In, *International Encyclopedia of Unified Science.* Vol. 1. Chicago: Chicago Univer. Press, 1955.

Buck, R. C. On the logic of general behavior systems theory. In H. Feigl & M. Scriven (Eds.), *Minnesota studies in the philosophy of science.* Vol. 1. Minneapolis: Univer. Minnesota Press, 1956.

Cannon, W. B. *The wisdom of the body.* New York: Norton, 1932.

Chang, H. T. The repetitive discharge of corticothalamic reverberating circuit. *J. Neurophysiol.,* 1950, **13,** 235–257.

Elkin, F. Specialists interpret the case of Harry Holzer. *J. abnorm. soc. Psychol.,* 1947, **42,** 99–111.

Feigl, H. Philosophical embarrassments of psychology. *Amer. Psychologist,* 1959, **14,** 115–128.

Frankl, V. E. *From death camp to existentialism.* Boston: Beacon, 1959. (a)

Frankl, V. E. Das homöostatische Prinzip und die dynamische Psychologie. *Z. Psychother. med. Psychol.,* 1959, **9,** 41–47. (b)

Gooddy, W. Two directions of memory. *J. indiv. Psychol.,* 1959, **15,** 83–88.

Hebb, D. O. *The organization of behavior.* New York: Wiley, 1949.

Hebb, D. O. The mammal and his environment. *Amer. J. Psychiat.,* 1955, **111,** 826–831. (Reprinted: In Eleanor Maccoby, T. M. Newcomb, & E. L. Hartley (Eds.), *Reading in social psychology.* New York: Holt, 1958. Pp. 335–341).

Merton, R. K. *Social theory and social structure.* (Rev. ed.) Glencoe, Ill.: Free Press, 1957.

Miller, J. G. Toward a general theory for the behavioral sciences. *Amer. Psychologist,* 1955, **10,** 513–531.

Mowrer, O. H. A cognitive theory of dynamics. Review of R. S. Woodworth, *Dynamics of behavior. Contemp. Psychol.,* 1959, **4,** 129–133.

Murphy, G. *Human potentialities.* New York: Basic Books, 1958.

Olds, J., & Milner, P. Positive reinforcement produced by electrical stimulation of septal area and other regions of rat brain. *J. comp. physiol. Psychol.,* 1954, **47,** 419–427.

Parsons, T. *The social system.* Glencoe, Ill.: Free Press, 1951.

Pumpian-Mindlin, E. Propositions concerning energetic-economic aspects of libido theory. *Ann. NY Acad. Sci.,* 1959, **76,** 1038–1052.

Roby, T. B. An opinion on the construction of behavior theory. *Amer. Psychologist,* 1959, **14,** 127–134.

Smith, H. *The religions of man.* New York: Harper, 1958. (Mentor Book Ed., 1959).

Stagner, R. Homeostasis as a unifying concept in personality theory. *Psychol. Rev.,* 1951, **58,** 5–17.

Taylor, J. G. Experimental design: A cloak for intellectual sterility. *Brit. J. Psychol.,* 1958, **49,** 106–116.

Toch, H. H., & Hastorf, A. H. Homeostasis in psychology. *Psychiatry,* 1955, **18,** 81–91.

von Bertalanffy, L. *Problems of life.* (Trans. of *Das biologische Weltbild,* 1949) New York: Wiley, 1952. (a)

von Bertalanffy, L. Theoretical models in biology and psychology. In D. Krech & G. S. Klein (Eds.), *Theoretical models and personality theory.* Durham: Duke Univer. Press, 1952. (b)

Woodworth, R. S. *Dynamics of behavior.* New York: Holt, 1958.

2. The general and the unique in psychological science

GORDON W. ALLPORT

LET ME TAKE MY TEXT FROM THE OPENING
SENTENCE of *Ethical Standards of Psychologists*,
the official code set forth by the American Psychological Association (1959). This sentence
defines a psychologist as a person "committed
to increasing man's understanding of man." The
code itself makes it abundantly clear that both
man in general and *man in particular* are the
objects of our concern. Thus the psychologist,
as psychologist, can properly make two sorts
of statement; he can say:
1. the problem of human personality concerns
   me deeply;
2. the problem of Bill's personality concerns
   me deeply.

Although superficially similar the two statements are poles apart. In the second we are
speaking of one and only one person; in the
first we are abstracting elusive properties from
all of the three billion inhabitants of the earth.
Both statements are true; both appropriate;
and both fall squarely within the domain of
psychological science.

Some people, to be sure, object to this broad
coverage. Artists, literati, some psychiatrists,
perhaps a few clinical psychologists, would say
that to generalize about personality is to lose it.
Bill, as an integral datum, we are told, cannot
belong to scientific psychology. He can be represented only by the methods of biography,
drama, or other artistic portraiture. Bill himself
might say to the psychologist, "If you think
those pockmarks on your silly IBM card represent *me*, you have another guess coming."

Among scientific psychologists the objection

takes a somewhat different form. Usually we
repress one half of the APA definiton, and say
that our job is to reach only generalized formulae—propositions that hold across the board for
all mankind, or at least for some identifiable
section of the population. We recognize the
single case as a useful source of hunches—and
that is about all. We pursue our acquaintance
with Bill long enough to derive some hypothesis,
and then spring like a gazelle into the realm of
abstraction, drawing from Bill a "testable proposition" but carrying with us no coordinated
knowledge of him as a structuar unit. We tolerate the single case only as a take-off point. We
forgive Ebbinghaus for performing 163 experiments on himself, since almost immediately
his findings were confirmed on other subjects.
Luckily these subjects, like him, displayed a
logarithmic relationship between the percentage
of material forgotten and the time elapsing after
the original act of learning. We forgive Köhler
and Wallach for intensive work on their own
figural after-effects, for it was soon confirmed
that others too show a displacement of the percept, after long stimulation, away from the
retinal area stimulated.

But imagine the consternation if some deviant
psychologist (perhaps I myself) were to say,
"Can't we linger longer with Ebbinghaus and
discover in his life what relationships might
exist between his memory functions and *his*
motives and *his* cognitive style and *his* aspirations?" The objection would be: "Of what use
is that? Even if we find the relationship we'd
have to generalize to other people or else we'd
have nothing of any scientific value."

Such is the prevailing "response set" of our
specialty. The intricacy of internal structure in
concrete lives seldom challenges or detains us.

SOURCE. Article by Gordon W. Allport, "The general and the unique in psychological science" in
Journal of Personality, Vol. 30, pp. 405–422, 1962.

Our concern is with commonalities and comparabilities across individuals.

This response set is undoubtedly derived from our submissiveness to the goals and procedures of natural science. And this submissiveness is not in itself a bad thing. Up to now it has taught us much. The question is whether we have become so enslaved that we overlook an important half of our particular professional assignment which is "increasing man's understanding of man."

It does no good to argue that every individual system in nature is unique; every rat, every porpoise, every worm; and that it is only the general laws of their functioning that lead to comprehension. No, we can't take this easy way out of the dilemma. The human system, unlike all others, possesses a degree of openness to the world, a degree of foresight and self-awareness, a flexibility and binding of functions and goals that present a unique structural challenge far more insistent than that presented by any other living system. It is because of their essential stereotypy and lack of variation that psychologists like to draw their generalizations from lower animals. But for my part I venture the opinion that all of the infrahuman vertebrates in the world differ less from one another in psychological functioning and in complexity of organization, than one human being does from any other.

And so I wonder whether the time has not come for students of personality to shake themselves loose from a too-rigid response set, and perhaps even to reverse it. Instead of growing impatient with the single case and hastening on to generalization, why should we not grow impatient with our generalizations and hasten to the internal pattern? For one thing we should ask, are our generalizations really relevant to the case we are studying? If so, do they need modification? And in what ways is this individual the asymptote of all our general laws?

Or to state the procedure more simply: Why should we not start with individual behavior as a source of hunches (as we have in the past), and then seek our generalizations (also as we have in the past), but finally come back to the individual—not for the mechanical application of laws (as we do now), but for a fuller, supplementary, and more accurate assessment than we are now able to give? I suspect that the reason our present assessments are now so often feeble and sometimes even ridiculous, is because we do not take this final step. We stop with our wobbly laws of personality and seldom confront them with the concrete person.

The Dimensional and the Morphogenic

The issue before us is not new. More than a hundred years ago John Stuart Mill proposed that we distinguish sharply between psychology, the science of mind-in-general, and ethology, a science of character (having no relation to what is called ethology today). To his mind ethology should trace the operation of psychological laws in specifically individual combinations—such as the pattern of the single person or of a single culture or nation. Somewhat similar was Dilthey's proposal to distinguish between "explanatory" and "understanding" psychology. Said Dilthey, "We explain nature, but we understand human beings," Windelband too would recognize two classes of science: the nomothetic (seeking general laws) and the diographic (dealing with structured pattern).

In confronting this same problem William James almost threw up his hands in despair. It is well known that after writing his textbook, he concluded that general psychological laws are poor stuff. He declared that psychology has not produced "a single law in the sense in which physics shows us laws. . . . This is no science, it is only the hope of a science" (1961 ed., p. 335). Perhaps the ensuing half-century of intensive research would have strengthened his faith in general laws; but I doubt it. At any rate he not only questioned the validity of general laws but, champion of the individual though he was, he seemed to feel that the concrete person must also inevitably elude psychology. In his *Memories and Studies* (1912) he wrote,

. . . in every concrete individual, there is a uniqueness that defies all formulation. We can feel the touch of it and recognize its taste, so to speak, relishing or disliking, as the case may be, but we can give no ultimate account of it, and have in the end simply to admire the Creator (pp. 109 f.).

And so at the end of his career James seems to despair of psychology as a science of either the general or the concrete.

The problem has not yet been solved, but I for one detect signs of progress. For one thing it increasingly haunts us, in our dual roles as

experimenter and clinician, as theorist and practitioner. A decade ago Meehl (1954) wrote
a distinguished treatise on the subject entitled
Clinical vs. Statistical Prediction. His own position he declared to be "ambivalent." Some called
it middle-of-the-road (but only those, I think,
whose own adaptation level was somewhere to
the right of Sarbin and Lundberg).

Meehl's book draws an important distinction.
It points out that in comparing so-called clinical
with so-called statistical procedures we may be
talking about (*a*) the methods we employ and
the type of data we use, or (*b*) about the way
we piece together these data and reach a final
assessment. Thus the data, on the one hand,
may be percentile scores or other quantifiable
dimensional data; or they may be looser types
of information, case records, free associations,
and the like. Further, in reaching a conclusion
from these data we may use statistical procedures with mechanical regularity, or we may
—as Dilthey advises—simply try to "understand"
the pattern. Meehl's chief concern is with the
latter issue. Does one handle the data (whatever they be) more successfully through using
the statistical cookbook, or through global comprehension? While this issue is surely central,
it is not the focus of my interest in the present
paper. Here I am concerned rather more with
Meehl's first problem: the type of data that
should go into our assessments.

More recently a German author (Graumann,
1960) puts the problem this way: shall our units
of analysis in the study of personality be derived
from general psychological concepts, or from
lives as actually lived? Another statement of
the issue is found in the presidential address of
L. S. Hearnshaw (1956) to the British Psychological Society. He first calls attention to the
strain that exists between the demands of conventional scientific method and "the appreciation of the richness of human individuality." He
pleads for "a constant search for concepts which
while capable of scientific definition and em-
ployment, nevertheless possess humanistic implications" and reflect patterned structure accurately.

It would serve no good purpose here to review the long-standing debate between parti-
sans of the nomothetic and idiographic methods, between champions of explanation and
understanding. Indeed, to insure more rapid
progress I think it best to avoid traditional terms
altogether. For the purposes of our present dis-

cussion I shall speak of "dimensional" and "morphogenic" procedures. Let me explain the latter term.

The science of molecular biology shows us
that life-substances are identical across species.
The building blocks of life—vegetable and animal—turn out to be strikingly uniform in terms
of nucleic acids, protein molecules, and enzy-
matic reactions. Yet an antelope differs from an
ash tree, a man from an antelope, and one man
is very unlike another. The challenge of mor-
phogenesis (accounting for pattern) grows more
rather than less acute as we discover the commonalities of life. Yet biologists admit that morphogenic biology lags far behind molecular (or
dimensional) biology. So too does morphogenic psychology lag far behind dimensional
psychology.

The commonalities in personality are the
horizontal dimensions that run through all individuals. We focus our attention chiefly upon
these commonalities: for example, upon the
common traits of achievement, anxiety, extraversion, dominance, creativity; or upon the common processes of learning, repression, identification, aging. We spend scarcely one per cent of
our research time discovering whether these
common dimensions are in reality relevant to
Bill's personality, and if so, how they are patterned together to compose the Billian quality
of Bill. Ideally, research should explore both
horizontal and vertical dimensions.

I have already rejected the easy solution that
assigns the general to science and the unique
to art. I should like also to dispose of another
proposed solution. Some psychologists would
say that Bill, our individual, is known primarily
by his conformity to, or deviation from, universal norms or group norms. His private and
unique qualities are only the residual peculiarities left over when we have accounted for most
of his behavior in terms of general norms. My
colleagues, Professors Kluckhohn, Murray, and
Schneider (1953, p. 53) have expressed the
thought by saying every man is in certain
respects:

a. like all other men (universal norms)
b. like some other men (group norms)
c. like no other men (idiosyncratic norms).

Now it is certainly true that we often wish to
use universal and group norms. We want to
know whether Bill, relative to others, is high or
low in intelligence, in dominance, in affiliative-

ness. But although Bill can be compared profitably on many dimensions with the average human being or with his cultural group, still he himself weaves all these attributes into a unique idiomatic system. His personality does not contain three systems, but only one. Whatever individuality is, it is not the residual ragbag left over after general dimensions have been exhausted. The organization of Bill's life is first, last, and all the time, the primary fact of his human nature.

Since we cannot brush our problem aside we do well to ask how a truly morphogenic psychology (sadly neglected up to now) can become a scientific asset. To become such it will have to learn certain lessons from dimensional empiricism, and from positivism—most of all the lesson of observer reliability. It is not sufficient to "intuit" the pattern of Bill or Betty. All of their friends do this much, with greater or less success. A science, even a morphogenic science, should be made of sterner stuff. The morphogenic interpretations we make should be testable, communicable, and have a high measure of predictive power.

My purpose is to suggest certain procedures that seem to me to be morphogenic in nature, or at least semi-morphogenic, and yet to be at the same time controlled, repeatable, reliable. Before I do so, let us look more closely at the question of successful prediction, which, we are told, is the acid test of a valid science.

Prediction: Dimensional and Morphogenic

Prediction based on general or dimensional information is called actuarial. For many purposes it is surprisingly accurate. One marvels, for example, at the correctness with which insurance companies predict the number of deaths that will occur by highway accidents, from cancer, or from suicide. The chances of a hypothetical average man for survival or death are all the insurance business wants to know. Whether Bill himself will be one of the fatal cases it cannot tell—and that is what Bill wants to know.

The situation is exactly the same in psychology. Actuarial prediction enables us, with fair success, to predict what proportion of boys, having a certain type of physique and family history, will become delinquent; what percentage of engaged couples, having various types of background, will enjoy successful marriage. Actuarial prediction can tell approximately what the average student's university record will be on the basis of his elementary school record or I.Q. It can advise industry concerning crucial cutting points on psychological tests by designating the score below which most applicants would probably fail on the job.

Note please that these actuarial predictions are far more useful to insurance companies, school authorities, police, and industrial management than to Bill himself. As a person he is frozen out, for although statistical generalizations hold with small error for large populations they do not hold for any given individual. And as practitioners we have fully as much responsibility to Bill as to his employers or to the public. Nay, if we follow our own professional code of ethics, we have more.

Suppose we take John, a lad of 12 years, and suppose his family background is poor; his father was a criminal; his mother rejected him; his neighborhood is marginal. Suppose that 70 per cent of the boys having a similar background become criminals. Does this mean that John himself has a 70 per cent chance of delinquency? Not at all. John is a unique being, with a genetic inheritance all his own; his life-experience is his own. His unique world contains influences unknown to the statistician: perhaps an affectionate relation with a certain teacher, or a wise word once spoken by a neighbor. Such factors may be decisive and may offset all average probabilities. There is no 70 per cent chance about John. He either will or will not become delinquent. Only a complete understanding of his personality, of his present and future circumstances, will give us a basis for sure prediction.

It was this line of argument, I believe, that led Meehl (1954) to say, "Let us see what the research evidence is regarding the relative success of dimensional and morphogenic prediction." Surveying such relevant studies as were available, Meehl concludes that morphogenic (what he calls "clinical") prediction seems to be actually inferior. More successful are predictions made mechanically with the aid of a standard formula. Best to keep strictly to our Rorschach diagnostic signs, to our I.Q. measures, to our profile on the Minnesota Multiphasic Personality Inventory, and to other standard predictive indexes. We can, of course, weight the signs, but we must do so according to rule. We may give one sign twice as much weight as another, just as a cook uses two cups of flour but only one of sugar. Meehl appropriately calls the procedure he advocates the "cookbook" method.

The point is that whenever we deal with well-defined variables, possessing a known relation to a pathological type, or to success in occupation or in school, we are usually safer in following the cookbook method of combining scores according to a formula known to have a good average validity. If strictly followed the logical outcome of this procedure would be the early elimination of the clinician or practitioner as assessor or diagnostician. A computing machine could handle the data more accurately than a fallible psychologist. In coming years we shall, no doubt, increasingly encounter IBM diagnoses and IBM predictions in psychological practice. It does no good to shudder at such a *lèse majesté* to human dignity. It will surely come to pass. But already we can sense its limitations.

Limitations of the Cookbook

In the first place, as Meehl (1957) himself has pointed out, the cookbook is usable only under restricted circumstances. The dimensions studied must be objectively defined, reliably measured, validly related to the target of prediction (e.g., to vocational success), clearly normed for a population to which the subject belongs. Most of the dimensions we employ have not attained this level of objective perfection.

The question of weighting signs gives us special difficulty. Suppose John has a good engineering profile, but also scores high in aesthetic interests; suppose he is introverted, but has high ego-strength; and with all this suffers some physical disability—what then does the final pattern signify? Cookbook enthusiasts might say a computer could tell us. But could it? In all the world there are not enough cases of this, or of any other, personal pattern to warrant assured actuarial prediction.

Again, by keeping within a previously established dimensional frame the cookbook procedure rules out insights peculiarly relevant to the individual. True, the computer can tell whether Sam should be diagnosed as schizophrenic. But whether Sam's love for his sister

and her way of dealing with him are such as to effect his recovery, the computer cannot tell. A dimensional frame is a rigid thing. It is like giving to the cook ingredients that will produce only dumplings while imagining that she has the freedom to produce a cake.

Further, the dimensions imposed on the individual are dimensions of interest to the investigator, or to the hospital, school, or firm. For this reason they may not be relevant in guiding John. The most salient features of his life—his aspirations, his sense of duty, his existential pattern, may be left untouched. In every dimensional analysis there are inevitably many "empty cells."

Finally, as for the discovery that clinical or morphogenic predictions are in fact poorer than cookbook predictions, I can only say, "What a pitful reflection on the inventiveness and sensitivity of psychologists!" The findings—which, by the way, are not necessarily the last word on the matter—prove only that we do not yet know how to maximize clinical skill through training. I suspect that our present emphasis on tests and cookbooks may actually be damaging the potential skill of young clinicians and advisers. There are studies that indicate that clinicians grow confused when they have too many data concerning an individual life, and that for this reason their predictions are better when they fall back on a mere formula (Sarbin, Taft, & Bailey, 1960, pp. 262–264). But this finding, too, points chiefly to our neglect in inventing and training in sensitive morphogenic methods.

Recently, Meehl (1959) has shown that under certain circumstances a combined actuarial and clinical—a kind of "configural"—procedure is superior in predictive power to either method used alone. This is progress indeed. But I would raise two objections: (1) the level of success achieved is still to low; (2) the diagnostic instruments employed in the first instance are too one-sided. The original instruments on which the predictions are based are nearly always of a dimensional or horizontal order (extending across people) and seldom of an intensive vertical order (within the person).

My point is that while dimensional diagnostic methods are an indispensable half of the psychologist's tools of trade, the other half of the tool box is, up to now, virtually empty. I recall that a few years before his death I was discussing this matter with the beloved psychologist, Edward Tolman. He said to me with his characteristic twinkle, employing the then-current terminology, "I know I should be more idiographic in my research, but I just don't know how to be." My reply now, as then, is, "Let's learn!"

Morphogenic Methods

To start simply: it is worth asking whether we ought to seek only objective validation for our measuring instruments. Why not demand likewise, where possible, subjective validation by asking our subject what he himself thinks of the dimensional diagnosis we have made? (If the subject is a child, a psychotic, or manifestly defensive, this step, of course, has no point). Too often we fail to consult the richest of all sources of data, namely, the subject's own self-knowledge. During the war psychiatrists were assigned the task of screening candidates for the armed services. While they employed various dimensional tests, it is said that the best predictive question turned out to be, "Do you feel that you are emotionally ready to enter military service?" The men themselves were often the best judges—although, of course, not infallible.

One might think that the existential outlook in psychology (now spreading at considerable speed) could logically be expected to bring a revolution in methods of psychological assessment. Its basic emphasis is upon the individual as a unique being-in-the-world whose system of meanings and value-orientations are not precisely like anyone else's. Hence an existential psychologist, be he conducting research, assessment, or therapy, would seem to need procedures tailored to each separate case. But up to now followers of this school of thought have not been as inventive as their own basic postulate requires. There is a methodological lag.

It is true that psychiatrists and clinical psychologists have long known that they should take the patient's own story as a starting point. But almost immediately they redact this story into general categories, dismembering the complex pattern of the life into standard dimensions (abilities, needs, interest inventories, and the like), and hasten to assign scores on their favorite variables. One notes too that therapists who claim to be existential in their orientation also tend to employ standard procedures in treatment. Their techniques and even their interpretations are sometimes indistinguishable from orthodox psychoanalysis (G. W. Allport, 1961a).

Our conceptual flexibility is greater than our methodological flexibility. Let me illustrate the point by reference to the valuable and extensive bibliography of nearly 500 items prepared by Ruth Wylie (1961). Most of these items deal with empirical studies of the self concept. (The very fact that the self in recent years has been readmitted to good standing in psychology is proof of our conceptual flexibility.) A close inspection, however, shows that virtually all the studies approach the self concept only via general dimensions. We encounter such descriptions as the following: "this test infers self-esteem from scores on an anxiety questionnaire"; or "nine bipolar semantic differential scales are employed"; or "self ratings of 18 trait words on a five-point scale from which self-acceptance is inferred." I am not objecting to these studies but point out that they are methodologically stereotyped.

But let us turn now to what at present lies available in the morphogenic half of our tool box. My inventory will be illustrative rather than exhaustive. I shall be brief in describing each method, hoping that the array as a whole will help to make clear what I mean by morphogenic method, and, best of all, may stimulate further invention.

1. Familiar is the method of matching, used with profit by both German and American investigators (see G. W. Allport, 1961 (b), pp. 387 f. and 446 f.). This method invites us to fit together any record of personal expression, however complex, with any other record. We test our skill in seeing that this case record must fit such-and-such a test profile; or that this handwriting goes with that voice. It is a good way to discover how much of a perceptible form-quality saturates separate performances. Although the method gives us no insight into causal relationships it is, so far as it goes, a good example of a 100 per cent morphogenic procedure.

2. Another wholly morphogenic technique was devised by Baldwin (1942) who made use of a long series of personal letters written by one woman, Jenny by name. Her unique thought-structure, i.e., associative complexes, was the object of interest. If she talked about women, money, or nature, with what feeling-tone did she mention them? If she mentioned her son what

else did she mention in the same context? This technique, called by Baldwin "personal structure analysis," is highly revealing, and is carried through without reference to any general or dimensional norms.

3. Somewhat similar, and wholly morphogenic, is the procedure recommended by Shapiro (1961) for psychiatrists. On the basis of a five-hour intensive interview with a patient he constructs a questionnaire which from that time on is standard for this patient but not directly relevant to any other patient. Administered over intervals of months or years, the instrument will show the course of development, including improvement or deterioration in health.

4. A somewhat more ambitious attempt, still wholly morphogenic, would be to attempt to discover the number and range of all the major structural foci a given life possesses. Many years ago in his *Experiment in Autobiography*, H. G. Wells, asserted that there were only two major themes in his life: interest in world government and in sex. Elsewhere I have explored the possibility that a life may be understood almost completely by tracing only a few major themes or intentions. Probably two is too few for most lives (perhaps especially for H. G. Wells), although it is said that Tolstoy after his conversion had only one major theme: viz., the simplification of life. More typical, I believe, would be the case of William James, who, according to his biographers, R. B. Perry (1936, chaps. 90–91), had eight dominant trends. In some preliminary explorations with my students (G. W. Allport, 1958), I find that they regard it possible to characterize a friend adequately on the average with 7.2 essential characteristics, the range falling for the most part between 3 and 10.

What to call these central motifs I do not exactly know. They are "essential characteristics," for the most part motivational in type although some seem to be stylistic. F. H. Allport (1937) has proposed the term "teleonomic trends" and suggests that we proceed to regard them as life-hypotheses held by the individual, and count carefully how many of his daily acts can accurately be ordered to one or more of these trends. The idea has merit but it has not yet been systematically tried out. One question is whether we can obtain sufficiently high observer-reliability (i.e., reliable judgments of the fit of specific acts to the hypothesized trend).

At present it is only one of the avenues of research needing exploration.

5. Suppose we are interested in an individual's value system. Direct questioning is useful, of course. "What would you rather have than anything else in the world?" "What experiences give you a feeling of completeness, of fully functioning, or of personal identity?" "What," in Maslow's terms, "are your peak experiences of life?" Elsewhere I have argued strongly for the use of such direct questions as these, for in important matters we should grant our client the right to be believed. Projective methods should never be used without direct methods, for we cannot interpret the results of projective testing unless we know whether they confirm or contradict the subject's own self-image (see G. W. Allport, 1960, chap. 6).

But how can we grow more precise in this type of work, benefitting from lessons learned from objective dimensional procedures? One such technique is the "self-anchoring scale," devised by Kilpatrick and Cantril (1960). It consists of a simple diagram of a ladder, having 10 rungs. The subject is asked first to describe in his own terms the "very best or ideal way of life" that he can imagine. Then he is told that rung 10 at the top of the ladder represents this ideal. Similarly he is asked to describe the "worst possible way of life" for himself. This he is told is the bottom of the ladder. Now he is asked to point to the rung on the ladder where he thinks he stands today—somewhere between the bottom and top rungs. He can also be asked, "Where on this scale were you two years ago? Five years ago? Where do you think you will be five years hence?"

This device has considerable value in personal counselling. It is also used by the authors to study rising or falling morale in different countries, e.g., in those having undergone recent revolution as compared with those living in a static condition. In this case, a curious thing happens, a completely morphogenic instrument is adapted for use as a tool for nomothetic research. Ordinarily, of course, the situation is reversed: it is a nomothetic mold that is forced upon the individual.

All these various examples suffice to show that it is possible to examine the internal and unique pattern of personal structure without any dependence whatsoever on universal or group norms. All the methods I have mentioned up to now are completely morphogenic, although they are seldom explicitly recognized as such.

Semi-Morphogenic Methods

Let us turn our attention to certain procedures that are highly useful for exploring individuality even though they are in part also dimensional.

6. First, there is the common dimensional instrument, the rating scale. Many years ago Conrad (1932) asked teachers to rate pupils on 231 common traits. The teachers were thus forced to make the assumption that all children did in fact possess all 231 traits in some degree. Proceeding on this assumption the teachers agreed poorly, as reflected in a median reliability coefficient of .48. After this nomothetic orgy, the same teachers were asked to star *only* those traits that they considered to be of "central or dominating importance in the child's personality." On this part of their task the teachers agreed almost perfectly, their judgment correlating .95. This result shows that low reliability may be due to the essential irrelevance of many of the dimensions we forcibly apply to an individual. On well-configurated prominent dispositions there is likely to be good agreement.

A related method is the simple adjective check list. Here the rater is confronted with perhaps hundreds of common trait-names (which are, of course, common linguistic dimensions). But he is required to use only those that seem to him appropriate to the primary trends in the individual life.

Both the method of starring and the use of the check list have the advantage of permitting us to discard irrelevant dimensions—a feature lacking in most other dimensional procedures.

7. Another half-way method is the Role Construct Repertory Test, devise by Kelly (1955). The method asks the subject to tell in what way two concepts are alike and how they differ from a third. The concepts might, for example, be *mother, sister, wife*. The subject could, for instance, reply that mother and sister are alike because both are comforting; and the wife different because she is demanding. Not only is the particular response revealing of his family attitudes, but over a long series of comparisons it may turn out that the subject has a character-

istic cognitive style in which the polarity of comfortableness vs. demandingness may recur time and time again. This method is not wholly morphogenic since it prescribes for the subject what "significant others" he shall characterize, and in other ways limits his spontaneous choices, but it allows none the less for a certain amount of morphogenic discovery.

8. Certain other devices for approaching cognitive style likewise move in a desirable direction. I have in mind Broverman (1960) who employs standard tests with his subjects, but makes his interpretations entirely in terms of the subject's tendency to do well or poorly on a given type of test relative to his own mean for all tests. By the use of such ipsative scores he is able to determine which responses are strong or weak with respect to other responses within the same individual.

If this line of thought were extended we would be moving toward a psychophysics of one person—a desirable advance indeed. We would at last know, so to speak, the relation between Bill's sensory acuity and his interests, between his cognitive style and his tempo, between his respiration and extraversion. To what extent it is necessary to start, as Broverman does, with standard dimensional measures, is a question for the future. I doubt that we can answer it a priori.

9. Another mixed method is the Allport-Vernon-Lindzey *Study of Values* (1960), devised to measure the relative prominence of each of the six Spranger *Lebensformen* within a particular person. The resulting profile does not tell how high or low a given person stands on the economic, theoretic, or religious value in the population at large, but only which value is relatively most, or next most, or least prominent in his own life. This type of profile is semi-dimensional, semi-morphogenic.

10. Sometimes the Q sort (Stephenson, 1953) is said to be an idiographic technique. Yet it, like other devices we are now considering, goes only part way. It has the merit of making use of self-report, and can be used for measuring changes in the self concept. As ordinarily used, however, only a standard set of propositions is employed, thus creating for the subject little more than a standard rating scale. And if the subject is forced, as he often is, to produce a quasi-normal distribution among his sorts he is further restricted. In short, the method can

be rigidly dimensional. Yet it is a flexible method, and some variants are highly promising, perhaps especially when combined with inverse factor analysis.

11. For example, Nunnally (1955) studied one therapy case over a two-year period, using 60 statements selected for their unique relevance to this person (and this, I think, is a great improvement over the use of uniform lists). The patient made her sorts under many different sets of instructions on many occasions. Using an inverse factor analysis it was possible to find three fairly independent factors that comprised her total self concept. During therapy these factors showed only a moderate change.

It strikes me as curious that out of the thousands and thousands of factor-analytic studies that smother us today, scarcely any are carried through in such a manner as to discover the internal, unique, organizational units that characterize a single life. Even inverse factor analysis does not fully achieve this goal unless the initial information employed is selected for its morphogenic relevance. A good deal of creative work still lies ahead for factor analysis. It has potentiality, I think, for discovering the main foci of organization in a given life, but has not yet moved far enough in this direction.

Final Word

This survey of possible relevant methods is not complete, but may indicate that by a deliberate shift of procedures we can bring the laggard end of our science up to a more flourishing level. To effect the shift we shall have to restrain to some extent our present dimensional debauch.

In this paper I have introduced the term "morphogenic psychology," borrowed from, but not identical with the usage in biology. It is, I think, a good term, better than "idiographic" which so many students of personality misuse and misspell. I hope the concept "morphogenic" catches on, but even more do I hope that the types of research to which I have ventured to apply the label will flourish and spread. Already we know that personality (in general) is an interesting topic for study. But only when morphogenic methods are more highly developed shall we be able to do justice to the fascinating individuality that marks the personalities of Bill, John, and Betty.

REFERENCES

Allport, F. H. Teleonomic description in the study of personality. *Char. & Pers.*, 1937, 6, 202–214.

Allport, G. W. What units shall we employ? Chap. 9 in G. Lindzey, (Ed.), *Assessment of human motives.* New York: Rinehart, 1958. Also chap. 7 in G. W. Allport, *Personality and social encounter.* Boston: Beacon, 1960.

Allport, G. W. The trend in motivational theory. Chap. 6 in *Personality and social encounter.* Boston: Beacon, 1960.

Allport, G. W., Vernon, P. E., Lindzey, G. *A Study of Values.* (3rd ed.) Boston: Houghton Mifflin, 1960.

Allport, G. W. Comment. In R. May, (Ed.), *Existential psychology.* New York: Random House, 1961. Pp. 94–99. (a).

Allport, G. W. *Pattern and growth in personality.* New York: Holt, Rinehart & Winston, 1961. (b).

Allport, G. W. Das Allgemeine und das Eigenartige in der psychologischen Praxis. *Psycholog. Beitr.*, 1962, 6, 630–650. Also: The unique and the general in psychological science. In J. A. Ross, & R. Thompson, (Eds.), *Proceedings of the Summer Conference,* Western Washington State College, 1961, pp. 25–37.

American Psychological Association. Ethical standards of psychologists. *Amer. Psychologist,* 1959, 14, 279–282.

Baldwin, A. L. Personal structure analysis: A statistical method for investigation of the single personality. *J. abnorm. soc. Psychol.*, 1942, 37, 163–183.

Broverman, D. M. Cognitive style and intra-individual variation in abilities. *J. Pres.*, 1960, 28, 240–256.

Conrad, H. H. The validity of personality ratings of preschool children. *J. educ. Psychol.*, 1932, 23, 671–680.

Graumann, C. F. Eigenschaften als Problem der Persönlichkeits-Forschung. Chap. 4 in P. Lersch, and H. Thomae (Eds.), *Persönlichkeitsforschung und Persönlichkeitstheorie.* Gottingen: Hogrefe, 1960.

Hearnshaw, L. S. *Bull. Brit. Psychol. Soc.*, 1956, 1, No. 36. See also, G. W. H. Leytham, Psychology and the individual. *Nature*, 1961, 189, No. 4763, pp. 435–438.

James, W. *Memories and studies.* New York: Longmans, Green, 1912.

James, W. *Psychology: The briefer course.* G. W. Allport, (Ed.) New York: Harper, Torchbooks, 1961.

Kelly, G. A. *The psychology of personal constructs.* Vol. 1. New York: Norton, 1955.

Kilpatrick, F. P., & Cantril, H. Self-anchoring scale: A measure of the individual's unique reality world. *J. indiv. Psychol.*, 1960, **16**, 158–170.

Kluckhorn, C. M., Murray, H. A., & Schneider, D. M. (Eds.), *Personality in nature, society, and culture*. New York: Knopf, 1953.

Meehl, P. E. *Clinical vs. statistical prediction*. Minneapolis: Univ. Minn. Press, 1954.

Meehl, P. E. When shall we use our heads instead of a formula? *J. counsel. Psychol.*, 1957, **4**, 268–273.

Meehl, P. E. A comparison of clinicians with five statistical methods of identifying psychotic MMPI profiles. *J. counsel. Psychol.*, 1959, **6**, 102–109.

Nunnally, J. C. An investigation of some propositions of self-conception: The case of Miss Sun. *J. abnorm. soc. Psychol.*, 1955, **50**, 87–92.

Sarbin, T. R., Taft, R., & Bailey, D. E. *Clinical inference and cognitive theory*. New York: Holt, Rinehart & Winston, 1960.

Shapiro, M. B. The single case in fundamental clinical psychological research. *Brit. J. med. Psychol.*, 1961, **34**, 255–262.

Stephenson, W. *The study of behavior*. Chicago: Univ. Chicago Press, 1953.

Wylie, Ruth C. *The self concept: A critical survey of pertinent research literature*. Lincoln: Univ. Nebraska Press, 1961.

3.   What units shall we employ?

GORDON W. ALLPORT

MAN'S NATURE, LIKE ALL OF NATURE, seems to be composed of relatively stable structures. The success of psychological science, therefore, as of any science, depends in large part upon its ability to identify the major structures, substructures, and microstructures (elements) of which its assigned portion of the cosmos is composed.

Early Inadequate Units

The Humors. From the fourth century B.C. to the seventeenth century A.D. the life sciences —indeed all the sciences—were badly frozen because they had chosen unproductive units of analysis—the Empedoclean elements of earth, air, fire, and water. These units and these alone are the "root of things'—so said Hippocrates and Galen, so said all the sages of the Middle Ages and Renaissance, including both Christian and Islamic scholars (see Sherrington, 1953). Personality theory, such as it was, was written entirely in terms of the four temperaments arising, men said, from the humoral distillations of the four cosmic elements—black bile (*melancholic*), yellow bile (*sanguine*), blood (*choleric*), and phlegm (*phlegmatic*). *Quatuor humores in nostro corpore regnant* sang the thirteenth-century medical poem. This rigidity of analysis endured at least until the time of Harvey, whose discovery of the circulation of the blood in 1628 cast doubt upon the whole humoral doctrine (see Allport, 1937).

The Faculties. Freed at last from this incubus, psychology perversely entered a second ice age by adopting the conception of "faculties"— units scarcely more productive than the humors. The faculties set forth by the Thomists, by Christian Wolff, by the Scottish school, and by the phrenologists have a certain common-sense appeal, but they do not satisfy modern theorists.

Instincts and Drives. Under the influence of Darwin, personality theorists traded faculties for instincts. The ensuing era, lasting approximately sixty years, cannot be called an ice age, for it brought with it McDougall's elegant and consistent defense of instincts and their derivatives, the sentiments. More than anyone else, McDougall fixed our attention upon the possible existence of uniform motivational units. Freud reinforced the search, though unlike McDougall, he himself offered no clear taxonomic scheme. During this era innumerable instincts were discovered, postulated, invented. In 1924 Bernard reported that more than 14,000 different instincts had been proposed, and that no agreement was yet in sight. Sensing disaster in this direction, psychologists started fishing in fresher waters. The doctrine of drives (a limited form of instinct) continued to hold the behaviorist fort, and still to some extent does so, but most psychologists nowadays seem to agree with Hebb (1949) that to equate motivational structure with simple drives or biological needs is a wholly inadequate procedure.

Difficulties and Complexities of Contemporary Search

I mention these fragments of history in the hope that they will give perspective to our contemporary search. It is clear that we have not yet solved the problem of the units of man's

SOURCE. Gordon W. Allport, "What units shall we employ?" in *The Assessment of Human Motives,* pp. 239–260. Edited by G. Lindzey. New York: Rinehart, 1958.

nature, though the problem was posed twenty-three centuries ago. It is equally clear that psychology lags far behind chemistry, which has its periodic table of elements; behind physics with its verifiable if elusive quanta; and even far behind biology with its cell. Psychology does not yet know what its "cell" may be. It is partly for this reason that skeptics question psychology's right to be called a science. Its investigators have not yet reached agreement on what units of analysis to employ.

Some of the trouble lies in the fact that psychology could make little use of a "cell," even if it discovered one. (It has given up the "reflex arc," which for a time seemed to serve the purpose.) Psychology's peculiar problem lies in the existence of many different levels of organization whose number and nature are as yet unascertained. Units of structure may be smaller or larger, depending on our interests. If we happen to be concerned with an elementary behavioral problem, such as the alternate extension and flexion of the leg, we may adopt *spinal innervation* as our unit. If we wish to classify forms of motor activity, then *walking* seems a more acceptable unit. Should we be interested in interpersonal behavior, we can conceivably establish a measurable habit of *walking away from people* (thus approaching Karen Horney's conception). If our concern is with the generalized dispositions of personality, we may consider some such unit as a *trait of withdrawal*. Fine-grained or coarse-grained—units of both orders have their place. Ultimately, of course, our hope is to be able to reduce molar units to molecular and, conversely, to compound molecular units into molar.

But we are far from this goal. Even at the coarser levels of analysis we are not in agreement on the kinds of units we seek. Shall they be habits or habit systems, needs or sentiments, vectors, factors, trends, or traits? Shall they be drives or dimensions, *Anschauungen* or attitudes, regions, syndromes, personal constructs, or ergs? All have been proposed and empirically defended. The most hopeful note in the confused situation is that for the past thirty years there has been boundless zeal for both measurement and theory. By now the measured aspects of personality cannot fall far short of the 14,000 instinctive units reported by Bernard. When psychologists face up to this orgy of units, let us hope they will not fall into the state of collapse that terminated the earlier search for in-

stincts. There seems to be no immediate danger, for one reads in the *American Psychologist* (1957, p. 51):

A Ford Foundation grant of $238,400 will enable a research team of the University of Minnesota to conduct a five year study aimed at developing a more adequate system of descriptive, diagnostic, and dynamic categories. . . . The team will work toward developing terms or systems of terms maximally descriptive of personality.

I have elected to speak on this bewildering topic, not because I have a secret solution for a two-thousand-year-old problem, nor because I am so clairvoyant that I can prevision the final Minnesota results. I do so because I believe that our present research lacks perspective on its own efforts, and I should like to achieve a balanced view of the efforts of assessors to date. Toward the end of this paper I shall venture one somewhat radical proposal for a shift of direction in our research.

Central Propositions for a New Approach

First, a few central propositions on which I hope we can all agree. It seems clear that the units we seek in personality and in motivation are relatively complex structures, not molecular. They lie in the upper reaches of what Hull called the habit hierarchy, and not at the level of specific habits. We do not seek cells or even cell assemblies; we do not seek reflexes, hedons, traces, or quanta of endocrine discharge, or the gating processes of the nervous system. Ultimately, of course, we should like to translate complex structures into microelements and discover their neurohumoral counterparts. But at present, and for some time to come, we must be satisfied to search out the generalized units that define relatively broad forms of organization.

There is a second proposition on which I hope we can reach equally rapid agreement. Methodologists tell us that we can never observe a motive or a trait or any similar unit directly. We agree. They tell us that any unit we discover is only a "hypothetical construct" or an "intervening variable." Here, too, they are right, though for my part I vote for "hypothetical construct," which, in the usage proposed by MacCorquodale and Meehl (1948), implies that the units we seek, though invisible, are factually existing. Methodologists tell us, furthermore, that we must have sound and repeatable operations for establishing the units we fix upon; we may not bring them into being by merely naming them, as did the addicts of instinct a generation or two ago. Again we agree. In fact, we do well to accept all the cautions and safeguards of modern methodology, save only that excess of zeal which holds all units to be fictional and existing only in the manipulations of the investigator.

A third proposition will detain us longer, for it has to do with the greatest stumbling block of all in our search for objectively existing structures. I refer to the unquestioned variability of a person's behavior from situation to situation. Motivational units discovered under laboratory conditions often seem to evaporate when the subject moves from the laboratory to his office, to his home, to his golf club. Indeed, his behavior in these familiar settings may often seem contradictory. Situational variability has led many social scientists to the conviction that any search for a consistent personality with specifiable motives and traits is doomed to failure.

Recently I attended a conference of psychologists working on the problem of the "perception of persons" (see Tagiuri, 1958). At this conference one heard much about perception but little about persons, the object of perception. The reason, I think, is that the participants were keenly aware of the chameleonlike changes that mark a person as he moves from situation to situation. They much preferred to study the perception-of-a-person-in-a-situation, and thus evade the question of what the person is really like. Not only does the individual vary his behavior, but our perception of him is heavily affected by our subjective sets, by our liking for him, by his uncongeniality, or by his degree of similarity to ourselves. The perceiver himself may, therefore, be the principal source of variance; the situation in which the object-person acts may be the second source of variance; and the fixed traits and motives of the object-person may be only a minor factor.

The hope for an accurate assessment of motives and traits is thus badly bedeviled by the person's variability and by the perceiver's bias. It is also badly bedeviled by the uncertainty of criteria. When are we to know that our assessment is accurate and veridical? Not by

comparing our assessment with ratings by others, who may be subject to both common and idiosyncratic errors. Not by the self-report of the subject, who is capable of self-deception. Not by prediction of future behavior, which will depend to a considerable extent on the situation that evokes this behavior. Not by other tests and measurement, for these too are fallible.

Situational Variables

Role Theory. All these objections are sound, and their combined force is today, as I say, leading many investigators away from the assessment of motives and persons. One tempting escape is found in the concept of "role." Emanuel Brown, to use one example, is no longer viewed as a single person: he is a colligation of roles. As a teacher he meets certain expectancies; as a father, others; still others as a citizen, or as a Rotarian. In one of his enthusiastic moments William James (1910) took the same way out. "A man," he says, "has as many selves as there are distinct groups of persons about whose opinion he cares." (p. 179)

The extreme version of this situational doctrine is found in Coutu's book, *Emergent Human Nature* (1949), where the author argues that the search for traits of personality and their assessment is chimerical; that the most we can say of any person is that in a given situation he has a specific tendency to respond to a certain limited way. The only acceptable unit, therefore, according to Coutu, is the "tinsit" or "tendency-in-a-situation."

Unless we can successfully refute the extreme forms of role theory and tinsit theory, and James's statement about the social self, our work should cease here and now. What is the use of assessing motivation or personality if behavior is as dependent on the situation as these theories assert? Let us see what may be said on the other side.

Safeguards against Situational Variability. In the first place, some of our assessment methods have built into them a safeguard against situational variability. They explicitly vary the situation. Thus a person's disposition to be ascendant, or his aesthetic value, or his neurotic tendency is tested by a wide range of items depicting a great variety of situations commonly experienced. While some studies show that a trait measured in this way does vary, say, from the academic to the business situation, or from the athletic to the purely social, it is more common to find that the person carries with him, by and large, his typical level of anxiety, a typical amount of aesthetic interest, of ascendance, or a typical aspiration level, or a fairly constant degree of prejudice.

In the second place, it is obviously not true that a man has as many social selves as there are groups whose opinion he prizes. A man who is deferential, ambitious, or compulsive in the office is not likely to shed these characteristics at home or on the golf course. Their intensity may vary and their mode of expression may alter, but true Jekyll and Hyde cases are exceedingly rare. So far as roles are concerned, is it not a fact that characteristic styles run through a person's conduct even when he is playing diverse roles? Is it not also true that a person *seeks* the roles that are most congenial to his personality, avoiding others that cramp his style or put an undue strain upon his internal motivational structure? That some persons are forced into roles they do not like we must admit, just as we must admit that a range of variation marks anyone's behavior according to the circumstances in which he finds himself.

But though these factors greatly complicate our search for structures, they need not discourage us. There is too much consistency, too much dependability, too much sameness in a person's behavior to warrant the surrender of our task.

Two Suggested Solutions for Simplifying the Situational Problem. There are two steps we can take to meet this problem. We can continue to seek methods of assessment that cross over many situational boundaries. Pencil-and-paper techniques can do so more easily than experimental techniques, since the former can ask the subject about his behavior in many daily contexts. But if a technique is limited to a given experimental situation (as is the Rorschach, for example), we can at least insist that our diagnosis be confirmed by additional evidence drawn from ancillary techniques.

Elsewhere I have deplored our reliance on too limited a battery (1953). Projective tests, for example, need the supplement of direct methods, for otherwise we may obtain a picture of certain latent tendencies without ever knowing whether these are separated from or integrated with conscious interests and self-knowledge. It makes a world of difference whether anxiety, or homosexuality, or aggression are repressed tendencies or whether they are fully accepted and known. Projective devices used alone would never answer this question.

Besides using multiple or wider devices to enlarge the coverage of situations, we may often need frankly to admit the limited range covered by our assessment. We can say, for example, that this college student in a series of tests at college displays such and such characteristics. Just what he will do at home or in business we cannot be sure. Or that this patient, manifestly disturbed, shows such propensities, but that, owing to his condition, no wider generalization is allowable at this time.

What I am saying is that situationism is a serious obstacle to overcome. Diagnosticians should be more aware of the problem and strive for broader coverage in their instruments; at the same time they should safeguard their statements about motivation by making clear the conditions covered by the battery.

Relating Intraindividual Structure to Situational Patterns. But let us not join the camp of skeptics who say that an individual's personality is "a mere construct tied together with a name"—that there is nothing outer and objectively structured to be assessed. No scientist, I think, could survive for long if he heeded this siren song of doubt, for it leads to shipwreck. An astronomer spots a star. Like any good realist he assumes that it has properties, elements that compose it, and structure, all of which it is his scientific duty to search out and to study. When a botanist dissects a plant he does not assume that he is dissecting a construct tied together by a name. It is a plant; and its structure and its functioning interest him. Similarly, the psychologist of personality wants to come as close as he can to the veridical structure of the person he studies, and he does so in spite of the extensive and troublesome situational variability, and in spite of his own errors of observation and measurement, which he tries constantly to reduce.

A theoretical task for the future is to relate the intraindividual structure to the recurrent situational patterns which in themselves may be regarded as complex social or cultural structures. In the terms of F. H. Allport, we have to deal both with *trend structures* in the personality and with *tangential collective struc-*

tures. Between them exists some degree of *interstructurance*. Analytical research, such as that carried out by Tannenbaum and Allport (1956) should help us to determine the differentials of energy in the individual's pattern of behavior that may be ascribed, on the on hand, to internal-trend structures and, on the other, to tangential structures.

Units of Motivation and Units of Personality

We move nearer to the heart of our subject. What is the relation between units of motivation and units of personality? I would suggest that all units of motivation are at the same time units of personality, but that not all units of personality are simultaneously units of motivation. Only a few writers have made this distinction systematically. Murray (1938) does so when he distinguishes motivational needs, or vectors, from the styles or manners of fulfilling needs represented by actones and verbones. Similarly, McClelland (1951, 1956) distinguishes motives from traits and from schemata. *Traits* he limits to recurrent patterns of expressive or stylistic behavior; *schemata*, to attitudinal orientations, cognitive and symbolic habits, and frames of reference. To him *motives* alone are the dynamic or causal forces, and these he finds satisfactorily designated by the term "needs."

We will all agree that some characteristics of personality are of a highly dynamic order, while some are of an instrumental or stylistic order. There is, for example, a distinct difference between a hate-filled complex or a driving ambition, on the one hand, and a style of urbanity or a hesitating manner, on the other. In Lewin's terms, certain regions are capable of greater tension than others. And some regions (the stylistic) are called into play only to guide the individual in the execution of more central motives. Thus a young man who is hungry for friendships goes out in the evening on a quest, but conducts himself according to his own peculiar style of timidity or confidence, reticence or garrulity. His need for affiliation and his style of seeking it are both characteristics of personality, the one being more dynamic (more motivational) than the other.

At the same time, we are not all in agree-

ment about what constitutes a motivational unit. If we were to follow Murray, McClelland, or Freud, we would put on the one side only the inferred forces called needs, instinctual energies, or id impulses. On the other side, we would put the schemata, traits, cathexes, and features of ego structure. The implication here is that there are raw, primary, urgelike forces that alone constitute units of motivation. It is chiefly these, of course, that the projective tests seek to assess. But for my part I cannot believe that motivational units are as abstract as this procedure implies. Let me illustrate my misgiving by reference to a certain man's interests. He is, let us say, profoundly interested in politics. This simple statement tells you a great deal about his motivational structure. Is it helpful, for purposes of assessment, to dissipate this integral structure in some such analysis as follows? He has an aggressive drive, a need for externalization, and a modicum of father fixation—all of which are cathected on politics; he has certain cultural schemata that he has learned, and has a habit of reading the political news in the morning paper, together with a history of reinforcement so far as civic participation is concerned. Or to make the point simpler, shall we say that his need for aggression (which some might hold to be the ultimate motivational unit in his case) is somehow arbitrarily cathected by politics? Or shall we say—I think more accurately—that his aggression and his interest are now all of a piece? His passion for politics is one true structural fact, no matter what his past behavior history may have been. You will recognize that I am here enlisting the principle of functional autonomy.

There is no need to debate this issue now. I want merely to point out that ultimate motivational units may not be only the unconscious urges, ergs, needs, or instinctual energies favored by certain forms of psychodynamic theory; nor are they accessible solely through projective techniques, even though these are certainly legitimate tools to use in a total battery of assessment methods.

Classes of Units in Current Assessment Research. Let us ask now what classes of units we find in current assessment research. No single investigator deals with them all, for each specializes in his own pet dimensions. Our question is what picture emerges if we try to catch a glimpse of all the investigators at work at once.

Tests and scales: The preference of many investigators for multivariate scales makes difficulty at the outset for our attempt at orderly classification. A generation ago we were content with one test for ascendance-submission, with a wholly separate test for extroversion-introversion, and so on. While such single scales are still with us, our hunger for omnibus instruments has grown. Take a field of neuroticism. At first (in 1917), we had the Woodworth Personal Data Sheet, which measured one and only one alleged unit—a neurotic disposition. The Cornell Index developed by Weider in 1945 still yielded a general score for the selection or rejection of armed service personnel, but at the same time differentiated various types of neurotic maladjustment. More widely used today is the MMPI, with its 550 items subdivided into twenty-six unitary tendencies. Most of these relate to pathological trends, but one cannot say that the units sought are conceptually uniform. Thus our multiphasic instruments, our many-faceted inventories, our multiple-factor devices, and our miscellaneous profiles make it hard to sort out the types of units involved. The current vogue is to assess everything all at once, but in the process the possibility of theoretical analysis seems to suffer. I wonder whether this desire is not caused in part by the fact that the Rorschach Test at first claimed to measure "the total personality." Such an intoxicating possibility led us to give up our earlier slingshot scales and adopt the shotgun inventory.

In spite of the shotgun's scatter, let us try to classify the units sought in personality assessment. Without claiming any finality for my listing, I call attention to ten classes of units that seem to me to be widely studied today.

The ten classes of units studied today: 1. INTELLECTUAL CAPACITIES. This area is so large in its own right that we ordinarily segregate it from both motivation and personality assessment. I mention it here only because a complete assessment could not possibly leave it out of account. Some day, I hope, we may be able to relate intellectual functioning more intimately than we now do to motivational and personal functioning.

2. SYNDROMES OF TEMPERAMENT. In this group we note recent progress. One thinks of the work of Sheldon, of Thurstone, Cattell, Guilford, and others. Thanks to their efforts, we can now assess such units as general activity, sense of well-being, restraint, emotional stability, lability, somatotonia. While one could wish for a stricter limitation of the concept of temperament than some of these investigators employ, still they deal constructively with units representing the prevailing "emotional weather" in which personalities develop.

3. UNCONSCIOUS MOTIVES. Without doubt the greatest interest of clinical psychologists is in units of this general class. Sometimes they are called needs (though no one insists that all needs are unconscious); often they involve dimensions with a Freudian flavor, such as anxiety, aggression, oral or anal trends, Oedipal fixation. The theory holds that such deep and buried motives are somehow more real and basic than units tapped by other methods. This contention, as I have already indicated, can never be proved unless both direct methods and projective methods are used for the same variables with the same personalities.

4. SOCIAL ATTITUDES. Here are units of quite a different order. While they have been evolved chiefly in social psychology, they are part and parcel of any complete clinical assessment program. We want to know how our subject views the church, or how he regards Russia. We want to know his liberal or conservative tendencies, likewise his score on scales for authoritarianism, ethnocentrism, dogmatism, traditional family ideology. These last-mentioned units illustrate the inevitable arbitrariness of our classification, for while they deal with social attitudes they likewise pretend to disclose deeper aspects of character structure, and thus overlap with our other categories.

5. IDEATIONAL SCHEMATA. Growing out of the study of social attitudes we find today considerable concern with generalized thought-forms. One may cite Klein's efforts to discover general styles or *Anschauungen* which cut through both motivational and cognitive functions. One may cite Kelly's proposal to study the constructs a person employs in viewing the world around him. Witkin (1954) and others establish the syndromes of "field dependence" and "field independence." Though Witkin's diagnostic method is anchored in perceptual measurement, he finds that the "field dependent" person is characterized also

by anxiety, by fear of his impulses, by poor impulse control, and by a general lack of awareness of his own inner life.

6. INTERESTS AND VALUES. In contrast to unconscious motivational units, we find many dimensions that deal with structured motives rather than with their presumed underlying dynamics. Here we would cite measures of interest in art, farming, or salesmanship. We would cite the six Spranger units as measured by the Allport-Vernon-Lindzey *Study of Values*. Perhaps here, too, we would locate the summary measure of masculinity-femininity based on a potpourri of conscious choices.

7. EXPRESSIVE TRAITS. A number of units seem to fall halfway between motivational and stylistic dimensions. For want of a better term, we may call them expressive. Among them we may include dominance tendencies, extroversion, persistence and empathy, also sociability, self-control, criticalness, accessibility, and meticulous or "just so" trends.

8. STYLISTIC TRAITS. This group receives least attention, probably because psychologists regard stylistic traits as lying on the surface of personality. One might include here politeness, talkativeness, consistency, hesitancy, and the measurable manners of behaving. Ultimately we may expect that these stylistic characteristics will be related to deeper structural units, but they are also measurable in their own right.

9. PATHOLOGICAL TRENDS. Many investigators prefer to analyze motivation and personality in familiar clinical terms. Hysteric, manic, neurotic, schizoid dispositions are the sort of units we find employed in the assessments of both normal and abnormal personalities. We have spoken of the evolution of these measures from the Woodworth PD sheet to the MMPI. One could mention as equally illustrative of this group the Humm-Wadsworth Test and other derivations from the Kraepelin and Kretschmer classifications.

10. FACTORIAL CLUSTERS. As yet I have not referred to factors. Factorial units in part belong in the classes we have already considered. Clearly, Thurstone's "primary mental abilities" are properly classified under Intellectual Capacities, Most of the factors proposed by Guilford and Zimmerman can be located under temperament syndromes or under expressive traits. Most of Cattell's factors can be similarly sorted.

But at the same time many of the factors that result from summarizing mathematically the data from many tests used with many people often defy conceptual analysis in any of the preceding classes. Thus Guilford and Zimmerman (1956) report an "unidentified" factor, called C_2, that represents some baffling blend of impulsiveness, absentmindedness, emotional fluctuation, nervousness, loneliness, ease of emotional expression, and feelings of guilt. When units of this sort appear—and I submit that it happens not infrequently—one wonders what to say about them. To me they resemble sausage meat that has failed to pass the pure food and health inspection.

I am not saying that factorial analysis does not have its place in the search for units. It seems to me that when factor analysts deal with a conceptually defined field to start with, such as extroversion and introversion, they often succeed in improving for us the clarity and accessibility of dimensions. In other words, factors are better when they follow theory than when they create it.

Factors are simply a summary principle of classification of many measures used with (usually) many people. This property does not suddenly endow them with new power. They are not, as some enthusiasts hold, "the cause of all human conduct," nor are they "source" traits as opposed to "surface" traits. Nor are they the "influence" underlying all behavior. They are neither more nor less motivational than other units. Usually they are nothing more than empirically derived descriptions of the average man.

In this respect factors do not differ markedly from the other types of units we have described. All of them presume to offer scalable dimensions; that is to say, they are common units in respect to which all personalities can be compared. None of them corresponds to the cleavages that exist in any single personality unless the single personal structure happens to be like that of the empirically derived average man. Still, scalable dimensions are useful dimensions, and we hope that work will continue until we reach firmer agreement concerning their number and nature.

I cannot claim that the thousands of dimensions proposed to guide our analysis of motivation and personality can all be neatly included in this tenfold scheme; but it may be helpful to our thinking.

As yet investigators have reached little or no agreement; they are not yet able to say, "These are the most useful units to employ." For the guidance of elementary students, Woodworth and Marquis (1947), basing their classification on Cattell (1946), ventured a "List of the most clearly established primary traits":

Easy-going, intelligent, emotionally stable, dominant, placid, sensitive, trained and cultured, conscientious, adventurous, vigorous, hypersensitive, friendly.

But professional psychologists are not yet ready to fix upon this, or any other "primary" list.

Intercorrelation of traits: A word should be said about the intercorrelation of traits. Factor analysis in its earlier years hoped to eliminate this troublesome phenomenon by seeking factors orthogonal to one another. But even factor analysts now admit that this goal is impracticable. A certain tendency to co-exist must be expected among human qualities. Of course, if correlations are very high (as they would certainly be between scales for "dominance" and "ascendance," or for "depression" and "melancholy"), it would be foolish to retain separate scales for synonymous, or nearly synonymous, traits.

One of the most insistent intercorrelations that occur indicates a general soundness, or strength, or dependability of character structure, or the opposite syndrome. Vernon (1953) shows how this pattern—he calls it "dependability"—emerges in factorial studies. The Grant Study at Harvard, working intensively with normal young men, was forced to adopt a general over-all measure of "soundness" (Heath, 1945). In general, it does not seem that a "halo" effect deriving from the bias of raters can account for this finding.

When such persistent intercorrelations occur between any clusters of traits, what shall we call them—types? syndromes? far-reaching dimensions? My own preference would be for "syndrome," since the term clearly indicates co-existence among conceptually distinct variables. The term "type," I fear, would lead us into trouble, since the term has many additional meanings.

Individual Structural Pattern. Now let us turn finally to a somewhat alarming possibility. What shall we do if the cleavages in any single life do not correspond to the empirical cleavages derived from studies of the average man? Can it be that our unending search for common units, now multiplying year by year, is a kind of nomothetic fantasy on our part? Can it be that the structural organization of Joseph Doakes's personality is unique to him alone?

If such a possibility seems too traumatic to face, let us ask the question in a milder way. Suppose we leave our common units unmolested and apply them as seems helpful in our assessment work; what shall we do when a given case seems to be completely by-passed by the common dimensions? A. L. Baldwin (1946), for example, in discussing four nursery school children, writes that the group analysis gave reasonably accurate interpretations of the behavior of three of the four children, but the fourth was not described adequately in terms of the group factors. And he adds, "Even in cases where group factors were approximately accurate, some aspects of the individual's personality were not revealed" (p. 168).

Perhaps what we need is fewer units than we now use, but units more relevant to individual structural patterns.

Pilot exercise: To gain some preliminary insight into this matter I tried a simple pilot exercise with ninety-three students. I asked them "to think of some one individual of your own sex whom you know well"; then "to describe him or her by writing in each space provided, a word, phrase, or a sentence that expresses fairly well what seems to you to be some essential characteristic of this person." The page provided eight spaces, and the students were told to "use as many spaces as you need." The term "essential characteristic" was defined as "any trait, quality, tendency, interest, etc. that you regard as of major importance to a description of the person you select."

After the student had finished with the first page he received a second page that added two additional blank spaces for further characteristics. The question was then asked, "Do you feel the need for more than ten essential characteristics? If so, about how many more do you think you would need?" A further question asked, "Do you feel that some of the characteristics you have named are duplicates (i.e., more or less synonymous), so that really fewer would have sufficed? If so, about how many in all would have been sufficient?"

Faulty though this method may be, the results are not without interest. Only 10 per cent of the subjects felt that they needed more than ten "essential characteristics," and for the most part these were vague regarding the total number that would be required: two said they needed an additional ten, one needed fifty, others did not know.

Ninety per cent of the students, however, found the exercise meaningful and the total of ten spaces provided fully adequate. On the average, they indicated that 7.2 "essential characteristics" would cover their needs, the range being from 3 to 10.

One might object that the method employed had the effect of suggesting a rather small number of "essential characteristics." Perhaps this is so, though I shall in a moment cite independent supporting evidence for the proposition that a relatively small number of structural units covers the major aspects of personality.

From my point of view the weakness of the experiment lies chiefly in the somewhat sketchy definition of "essential characteristic." Many students, though not all, were content with common trait names, such as *friendly, loyal, intelligent,* or *dependable.* I should not expect such terms ordinarily to do justice to the peculiar coherent structure of friendliness, loyalty, intelligence, or dependability that mark the life in question. Here we are confronted with the universal problem in all idiographic research: nouns cut slices *across* people rather than *within* people. It requires more deftness with language than most of us possess to put together a phrase or sentence that will pinpoint *individual* structure. It is precisely here that the gifts of the novelist and biographer exceed those of the psychologist.

In literature: Turning for a moment to the field of biography, we find confirmation of our point in Ralph Barton Perry's (1936) definitive volumes on *The Thought and Character of William James.* Summing up his exhaustive study of this complex and fascinating figure, Perry concludes that in order to understand him one must deal with eight leading "traits" or "ingredients." He first lists four "morbid or "pathological traits—tendencies that taken by themselves would have proved to be severe handicaps. These are (1) hypochondria, (2) preoccupation with "exceptional mental states," (3) marked oscillations of mood, and (4) repugnance to the processes of exact thought. Blended with, and redeeming, these morbid trends are four "benign" traits: (5) sensibility,

(6) vivacity, (7) humanity, (8) sociability. While, like the students in our exercise, Perry uses common trait names, he proceeds immediately to define them in such a way that the peculiar Jamesian flavor of each ingredient is brought to light. Clinical psychologists need some of the biographer's skill in particularizing terms. Standing alone, such terms are only hollow universals.

It seems to me that George Kelly in his *Psychology of Personal Constructs* (1955) is approaching the same goal from a different direction. He holds that the important thing about any person is the major way in which he construes his life-experiences, including his social contacts. Hence, in order to understand a person, we should adopt what Kelly calls the "credulous approach." Through interviewing or by studying self-characterizations, perhaps with the aid of the Role Construct Repertory Test (REP), we arrive at our diagnosis. The method yields constructs that are unique to the individual as well as constructs he has in common with others. Further, it leads to the discovery of the unique pattern of relations, among the several constructs of a given person. Speaking of widely used scaling and factoring procedures; Kelly rightly observes that while such methods provide a quick and sure exploitation of common constructs (applicable to all people) they prevent us from discovering new and unique constructs and fall into the additional error of assuming that the greatest commonality defines the greatest truth.

In a personal communication Professor Kelly tells me that he is not yet prepared to say how many major constructs the average individual uses, but sometimes, he reports, an individual's responses to REP "can be condensed into one or two major dimensions with two or three rows left over as specific constructs." It is true that people with an intellectual bent often seem to produce a variety of constructs, but their large vocabulary does not entirely obscure the relative simplicity of their patterns. Kelly speaks likewise of a useful therapeutic rule of thumb. "The patient may change the topic in the middle of an interview but he rarely changes the theme." Themes are persistent and recurring. While each person may have certain specific and concrete constructs that apply to limited and special areas of experience, Professor Kelly concludes that the clinician does not ordinarily identify more than "four of five major construct dimensions." We hope that work with the REP Test and with other quantitative clinical instruments will continue until we find a firm answer to our question.

A similar promising lead lies in the technique of "personal cluster analysis" set forth by Alfred Baldwin (1942). Analyzing an extensive written correspondence from an elderly woman, he discovers only four or five major ideational and value-laden themes.

Another related proposal was put forward some years ago by F. H. Allport (1937), who suggested measuring the consistency of an individual's acts in relation to his own principal life purposes or "teleonomic trends." The investigator could from previous acquaintance hypothesize the principal themes or trends (or "constructs" or "clusters") he expects to find in a given life. He could then by observation—with due checks for reliability—order the daily acts of the individual to these hypothesized dimensions. If we used this method systematically we might well find, as do Perry, Kelly, and Baldwin, that a handful of major structures covers the life surprisingly well, even though specific and unrelated minor trends may likewise appear.

Individuality in human nature: The proverbial visitor from Mars would, I think, find it incomprehensible that so little sustained work has been done in this promising direction of individuality. He would say to the earthbound psychologist: "Human nature on your planet is infinitely diverse. No two people are alike. While you give lip service to this proposition, you immediately discard it. What is more, people's internal structural organization—individual by individual—may be far simpler and more accessible than you think. Why not take the cleavages nature offers you and follow them through? Even granted that uniformities run through nature at its lower levels of organization—the chemical elements composing the body are identical—still at the higher levels or organization where the psychologist works the units you seek are not uniform at all. A baby, once started on the road of life, will fashion, out of his unique inheritance and special environment, nodes of accretion, foci of learning, directions of growth, that become increasingly unique as the years roll along. And won't you have a good laugh at yourself when you discover this elementary fact? And then perhaps you'll look for your units where you ought to look for them—in each developing life."

I venture to hope we shall heed the admonition of the visitor from Mars. That we have not done so is due, of course, to the prevailing conviction that science cannot deal with individual cases at all, excepting as they exemplify general laws or display uniform structures. The philosophers of the Middle Ages felt the same way, their dogma being *scientia non est individuorum.* But isn't the definition of science at best an arbitrary matter—at worst, an idol of the den?

Summary

In the interest of perspective, let me summarize my principal points. The search for the units that comprise motivation and compose personality is very ancient. Not until the past generation or two has appreciable progress been made. During recent years, however, we have followed a bewildering array of approaches, many of them fresh and imaginative, and resulting in more measured aspects than anyone can conveniently compute. Broadly speaking, these uncounted thousands of nomothetic units fall into ten classes: intellectual capacities, syndromes of temperament, unconscious motives, social attitudes, ideational schemata, interests and values, expressive traits, stylistic traits, pathological trends, and factorial clusters not readily classifiable in the other nine categories. Some investigators, of course, propose units that combine two or more of these classes. While I suspect there may be some overenthusiasm for certain categories (I would name here the overzealous use of projective tests for tapping unconscious motives and overaddiction to factorial units), still I would not discourage research in any of these ten directions.

We have to accept the fact that up to now relatively little agreement has been achieved. It seems that each assessor has his own pet units and uses a pet battery of diagnostic devices. But it is too early to despair. Instead of discouragement, I hope that our present disagreement will lead to continuous and wholesome experimentation. Essential to continued progress is a firm belief in the "outer reality" of personal and motivational systems. The fact that the units we seek are invisible should not deter us. Nor should we yield to the destructive skepticism of certain extreme methodologists who hold that the whole search is chimerical. Finally, while we must admit the variabilities of the structures we seek, which are caused by changing situations without and continual growth and change within, we should take this fact into our design and theory, not surrendering our belief that reasonably stable personal and motivational structures exist.

Such, in brief, is the present state of affairs with nomothetic assessment, as I see it. But I have argued in addition that we will do well to turn to the fresher possibilities that lie in improved idiographic analysis. Nor should we be deterred by preconceived ideas about what science can and cannot with propriety do. The conquerors of Mt. Everest did not allow themselves to be blocked by the sacred cows they encountered in the streets of Darjeeling. Nor should we. But perhaps the goal ahead may not be as formidable as Mt. Everest. It may turn out to be only as high and as wide and as human as the personality of John Citizen, who is after all our old and familiar friend.

REFERENCES

Allport, F. H. Teleonomic description in the study of personality. *Char. & Pers.*, 1937, **6**, 202–214.

Allport, G. W. *Personality: a psychological interpretation.* Chap. 3. New York: Holt, 1937.

———. The trend in motivational theory. *Amer. J. Orthopsychiat.*, 1953, **23**, 107–119.

American Psychologist, 1957, **12**, 51.

Baldwin, A. L. Personal structure analysis: a statistical method for investigating the single personality. *J. abnorm. soc. Psychol.*, 1942, **37**, 163–183.

———. The study of individual personality by means of the intraindividual correlation. *J. Pers.*, 1946, **14**, 151–168.

Bernard, L. L. *Instinct: a study in social psychology.* New York: Holt, 1924. P. 220.

Cattell, R. B. *Description and measurement of personality.* Yonkers, N.Y.: World Book, 1946.

Coutu, W. *Emergent human nature.* New York: Knopf, 1949.

Guilford, J. P., and Zimmerman, W. S. Fourteen dimensions of temperament. *Psychol. Monog.*, 1956, No. 417.

Heath, C. W., *What people are.* Cambridge: Harvard University Press, 1945.

Hebb, D. O. *The organization of behavior.* New York: Wiley, 1949.

James, W. *Psychology: briefer course.* New York: Holt, 1910.

Kelly, G. A. *The psychology of personal constructs.* Vol. I. New York: Norton, 1955. P. 34

McClelland, D. C. *Personality.* New York: Dryden, 1951. See also his Personality: an integrative view. In J. L. McCary (ed.), *Psychology of personality.* New York: Logos, 1956.

MacCorquodale, K., and Meehl, P. E. On a distinction between hypothetical constructs and intervening variables. *Psychol. Rev.*, 1948, **55**, 95–107.

Murray, H. A., *et al. Explorations in personality.* New York: Oxford University Press, 1938.

Perry, R. B. *The thought and character of William James.* Vol. II. Chaps. 90–91. Boston: Little, Brown, 1936.

Sherrington, Charles. *Man on his nature,* 2nd ed. Chap. 1, New York: Doubleday Anchor Books, 1953.

Tagiuri, R., and Petrullo, L. (eds.). *Person perception and interpersonal behavior.* Stanford University Press, 1958.

Tannenbaum, A. S., and Allport, F. H. Personality structure and group structure: an interpretative study of their relationship through an event-structure hypothesis. *J abnorm. & soc. Psychol.*, 1956, **53**, 272–280.

Vernon, P. E. *Personality tests and assessments.* London: Methuen, 1953.

Witkin, H. A., Lewis, H. B., Hertzman, M., Machover, K., Meissner, P., and Wapner, S. *Personality through perception.* New York: Harper, 1954.

Woodworth, R. S., and Marquis, D. G. *Psychology.* New York: Holt, 1947.

4. Cultural influence on the perception of movement: the trapezoidal illusion among Zulus

GORDON W. ALLPORT AND THOMAS F. PETTIGREW

TRADITIONALLY, theories of the visual perception of movement—with which the present study deals—have been divided into two classes: 1. The *nativistic*, i.e., theories emphasizing the role of retinal and cortical functions relatively unaffected by learning, habit, experience, or meaning; and 2. The *empiricistic*,

SOURCE. Article by Gordon W. Allport and Thomas F. Pettigrew, "Cultural influence on the perception of movement: the trapezoidal illusion among zulus" in *Journal of abnormal Psychology*, Vol. 55, pp. 104–113, 1957.

For their services as interpreters we wish to thank Kate Mdlala, Ethan Mayisela, Emmanuel Zuma, and Mr. September. For assistance in conducting the experiments we are indebted to Eric Barnett, Peter Hey, and Ann Pettigrew. In making arrangements for the investigations we received kind cooperation from the Native Affairs Commissioner of the Province of Natal, from Dr. John Bennett of the Polela Health Center, Dr. Wolfgang Bodenstein of the Ceza Medical Mission, Max Marwick of the Institute for Social Research of the University of Natal, Dr. B. Gampel of the Natal Medical School, and Mr. J. Mngadi of the Lamontville Community Center; also from the Paramount Chieftainess, Thoko C. Zulu. For the opportunity to spend several months as members of the Institute for Social Research at the University of Natal, we are grateful to the Principal, Dr. E. G. Malherbe.

The Original suggestion for the experiment grew out of conferences with Hadley Cantril for whose strategic advice we are grateful. We benefited likewise from discussion with F. P. Kilpatrick and E. Engel. The investigation received financial support from a grant from the Rockefeller Foundation to Princeton University for research in perception.

i.e., theories giving primary weight to the role of experience and learning.

For our purposes it is essential to subdivide empiricistic theories into two groups:

Cumulative habit: Stressing the effects of many types of early, remote, and generalized experience which by transfer or cross conditioning become a major determinant of the perception of movement. Toch and Ittelson (22, p. 199) state that "contemporary empiricism" favors this type of approach, offering its explanations of perceived movement in terms of "weighted averages of experiential sediments of all kinds acting inseparably."

Object connotation (meaning): Explaining perceived movement largely in terms of familiar objects. One sees continuous wing motion in an electric sign representing a bird in flight, although the stimulus actually occurs discontinuously in two or in three fixed positions. This theory would hold that our familiarity with birds in flight causes us to fill the gaps with perceived motion. A good statement of this theory of stroboscopic movement may be found in James (9). This author insisted that "perception is of definite and probable things." In explaining illusions, James leaned heavily upon their resemblance to familiar objects. In so doing he was merely rendering more concrete and specific Helmholtz's theory of "unconscious inferences" and Wundt's "assimilation" theory.

At the present time none of these theories can be defended in their exclusive purity. F. H. Allport (1) makes this fact abundantly clear. No empiricist, for example, can deny the native physiological substrate of the perception of movement nor its structural properties as represented by Korte's laws governing the phi-movement (13). Conversely, no nativist can deny the contribution that past experience may make to perceived movement. Wertheimer, for instance, admits that "it is certainly correct that past experience can influence the conditions (Verhältnisse) of stroboscopic vision" (23, p. 79). Von Schiller (21, p. 195) makes the suggestion—especially important for the present research—that attitudinal set and expectancy are particularly effective in determining the perception of movement in ambiguous (*alternative*) situations.

Many authors who have worked with perceived movement, e.g., Neff (17) and Hall and Earle (7), have favored an eclectic view. They have concluded that native and experiential factors both contribute, as do likewise momentary set and the previous level of adaptation. And they allow, among experiential factors, for both *cumulative habit* and *object connotation* (meaning).

While the eclectic position is no doubt correct there is, as Toch and Ittelson insist (22), still a fundamental question concerning "the relative primacy or importance of learning processes and physiological conditions." Theorists do tend to lean in one direction or the other. The distinction between nativists and empiricists still exists. Among the former, one thinks of Wertheimer (23), Koffka (12), Metzger (14), Michotte (15); among the latter, of Helmholtz (8), Piéron (19), Ames (2), Wundt (24), Cantril (4), G. E. Müller (16), Kilpatrick (11), and Toch and Ittelson themselves (22).

The Cross-Cultural Approach

To gain light on this dispute psychologists have often asked, "How about primitive peoples?" If we can find a tribe or a culture where relevant past experience can be ruled out, we could then determine whether the perception resembles that of western peoples. If it does so, then the argument for nativism is presumably stronger. The first extensive attempt to apply this test was made by W. H. R. Rivers during the Torres Strait expedition in 1898 (20). Rivers presented to the island natives a whole array of visual illusions and compared their reports with western norms. For some of the illusions there were no appreciable differences; for others, the natives seemed on the whole less susceptible than westerners. While Rivers himself does not make the point clearly, his results seem to show that illusions involving object connotation (e.g., a European street scene) are far less compelling to the natives than are illusions having no such object connotation (e.g., the rotating spiral) (20, esp. pp. 130 f.).

It is not easy for western psychologists to visit primitive tribes, nor to conduct among them adequately controlled experiments. The present article, however, deals with one such attempt. But before we describe it, the theoretical point at issue should be made entirely clear: *We do not claim to be testing the merits of the nativist or empiricist positions directly.* For reasons that will appear in the course of our discussion, we do not believe that comparative perceptual studies on western and on primitive peoples can solve this particular riddle. *We claim only to have illuminated the part played by object connotation (meaning) in the perception of motion as over and against the part played by either nativistic determinants or cumulative habit.* Our experiment is *not* able to distinguish between the role of these last two factors.

The Rotating Trapezoidal Window. Before the days of Gestalt psychology it was customary to regard visual illusions as oddities, as exceptional experiences to be accounted for either in terms of nativistic or experiential constraints. Today, however, we make little distinction between illusions and veridical perceptions, since no illusion lacks veridical elements and no veridical perception is devoid of subjective shaping. So-called illusions are simply instances of perception where the discrepancy between impression and knowledge (whether the knowledge be the subject's or the experimenter's) is relatively striking. It is in such "looser" conditions of perception that theorists often seek to obtain light on the relative weight of factors entering into the normal perceptual process. The reasoning is not unlike that which leads psychologists to study exaggerated functions in psychopathology in order to obtain light on the same but less exaggerated functions of the normal mind.

Our experiment follows this logic, making use of the rotating trapezoidal window described by Ames (2)—a device that has been called "a dramatic masterpiece of ambiguous stimulation" (1, p. 276). The window (Figure

1) is so proportioned that as it rotates, the length of the longer edge is always longer on the retina than is the shorter edge (even when the shorter edge is nearer). The resulting perception is normally one of oscillation or sway; the observer apparently tending to keep the longer edge nearer to him. Instead of seeming to rotate, as it actually does, the window is seen to sway back and forth in an arc of 90 to 180 degrees.

An appended cube and rod add great interest to the illusion, since the perceived *rotating* of these objects conflicts sharply with the perceived *sway* of the window. In consequence, the cube is usually seen to detach itself and swing without support in a ghostly fashion in front of the window (for that period of time when the shorter edge, to which it is attached, is in fact nearer to the subject). Similarly, the rod bends, twists or "cuts through" the mullions in order to accommodate itself to the phenomenal oscillation. The observer finds the bizarre effect both amusing and inexplicable.

The window used in the present experiment is smaller than the original Ames window; length 13¼ inches, height of the long side 12½ inches, height of the short side 9 inches. Ames demonstrated that within limits the ratio of the sides of the trapezoid to one another cannot affect the illusion. The optimum speed of rotation Ames reports as 3 to 6 r.p.m. Our own motor driven window ran slightly less than 2 r.p.m. The original Ames window had mullions dividing it into 15 frames; ours had 6 frames (probably more normal for a "window"). For certain comparisons, we employed also a true rectangular window, 12″ x 10½″.

The explanation Ames gives for the illusion maintains (*a*) that the observer, owing to familiarity with rectangular windows assumes *this* window to be rectangular; and (*b*) that owing to long experience with doors, windows, and similar objects, the observer has learned to interpret longer retinal stimulations as coming from nearer objects. Hence, the longer edge of the window is interpreted as being nearer, and the window is seen to oscillate rather than to rotate.

Ames (2, p. 14) gives a clearly empiricistic explanation with a leaning toward the object connotation version:

In his past experience the observer, in carrying out his purposes, has on innumerable occasions had to take into account and act with respect to rectangular forms, e.g., going through doors, locating windows, etc. On almost all such occasions, except in the rare case when his line of sight was normal to the door or window, the image of the rectangular configuration formed on his retina was trapezoidal. He learned to interpret the particularly characteristic retinal images that exist when he looks at doors, windows, etc., as rectangular forms. Moreover, he learned to interpret the particular degree of trapezoidal distortion of his retinal images in terms of the positioning of the rectangular form to his particular viewing point. These interpretations do not occur at the conscious level, rather, they are unconscious and may be characterized as *assumptions* as to the probable significance of indications received from the environment.

It should be added that Ames does not insist that object connotation ("windowness") is the sole determinant of the illusion. He himself employed a variety of trapezoidal figures and discovered that even a plane surface of trapezoidal shape arouses the illusion of sway, though to a much less degree than does a "window frame" (2, p. 29).

The Hypothesis. In order to test the "object connotation" theory, we studied various groups of Zulu children (10–14 years old) in Natal whose own culture is virtually devoid not only of windows, but, to a surprising extent, of angles, straight lines, and other experiential cues that would presumably "cause" the illusion if it were wholly a product of experience. Our hypothesis therefore is:

Zulu children, provided they are unacculturated (amabinca) *will report the illusion of sway in the trapezoidal window less often than will urbanized acculturated Zulu children* (amabunguka) *or than white ("European") children.*

The Zulu Culture. Zulu culture is probably the most spherical or circular of all Bantu cultures, possibly the most spherical of all native African cultures (though it would be difficult to prove this contention). The word "zulu" means heavens or firmament, and the aesthetic ideal of round rather than angular styles affects native art, architecture, and speech.

Huts are invariably round (rondavels) or else beehive shaped, whereas in other Bantu tribes they are sometimes square or rectangular. Round huts arranged in a circular form with round stockades to fence in animals, constitutes a typical African homestead (kraal).

Fields follow the irregular contours of the rolling land, and never seem to be laid out in the next rectangular plots so characteristic of western culture.

The typical Zulu hut has no windows, and no word from such an apperture exists. In the more primitive beehive grass huts, doors are merely round entrance holes; in the round mud huts doors are amorphous, seldom if ever neatly rectangular. Cooking pots are round or gourd shaped. In his studies among Zulus, L. Doob (6) finds that the less acculturated natives, relative to westernized natives, show a statistically significant preference for circles over squares when they are asked to choose between designs drawn in these shapes (personal communication to the authors).

It is commonly said in Natal that Zulus fresh from reserves cannot plow a straight furrow and are unable to lay out a rectangular flower bed. Such inability is of course overcome with experience and training, but the initial defect would seem clearly related to the circularity that is characteristic of life on the reserves and to the lack of familiarity with straight layouts.

Linguistically, the same bias towards circularity is seen. While it is possible to say "round" in Zulu, there is no word for "square." There is a word for "circle" but not for "rectangle." To speak of window, of square, or of rectangle at all, a Zulu is forced to borrow these terms from Afrikaans or from English—provided he is able to do so.

The Subjects. The experiment required the use of two contrasting groups of subjects (Ss): those who had lived all or most of their lives in western culture, and those who were unacculturated. Even in the Bantu reserves or in Zululand itself it is not possible to make certain that a resident does not know what a window is like. While schools, churches, and health centers are few and far between, they are nevertheless within the possible range of visitation by most native inhabitants, even children. Our experiments at Polela and Ceza took place in health centers, at Nongoma in a court house. The Ss, to be sure, were brought in from remote parts of the reserves by lorry, or came on foot; but they had at least this one-time acquaintance with a rectangular building and windows.

Still, it is possible to say that the experiment dealt with two widely contrasting groups in respect to the degree of experience they had had with western architecture and ways of life.

Some members of the more primitive groups, for example, may never have seen windows with rectangular panes of glass prior to the actual experimental situation.

By using herd boys as Ss—mostly between 10 and 14 years of age (few of them knew their age exactly)—we were able to make certain that they had never been off the reserves and had never attended school. Boys of the same age comprised our urban control groups: one group of European boys at Greyville Community Center; another group of Bantu boys at the Lamontville Community Center in Durban. Most of these urban boys were attending school.

Our major experiment thus involved the following groups:

Group A   Urban European boys   (20 cases)
Group B   Urban African boys   (20 cases)
Group C   Polela Rural Africans   (20 cases)
Group D   Nongoma Rural Africans   (20 cases)

A rough indication of the cultural differences between the rural and urban groups lies in answers to the question asked at the end of the experiment about the rectangular window, "What does this look like?" The percentage saying "windows" or "window frame" among the urban children was 88; among the rural, 45.

Procedure. The procedure involves four conditions, varying two factors bearing on the perception of the illusion: monocular vs. binocular viewing and distance from the stimulus object. Each S saw first the rectangular, and then the trapezoidal window in at least 3 full revolutions under each of the following conditions.

First trial: 10 ft.   binocular
Second trial: 10 ft.   monocular
Third trial: 20 ft.   binocular
Fourth trial: 20 ft.   monocular

It was thought that this order would impose the "hardest" condition first and therefore minimize the effects of suggestion. One might fear that if at 20 feet with one eye a subject easily perceived the illusion he might become accustomed to expecting oscillation in the trapezoidal window at closer distances and under binocular conditions. Conversely, of course, it might be argued that a subject who cannot perceive the illusion at ten feet binocularly would form an expectation that might prevent his obtaining it under easier conditions. We shall refer later to a control experiment (starting at 20 feet monocularly) designed to check on any suggestive effect that might arise from our order of presentation.

The experimenter (E) required the assistance of a second psychologist who kept records of the Ss' reports, also of an interpreter with all African Ss. Care was taken to prevent Ss who had finished the experiment from communicating with Ss who had not.

After being put at ease, the S gave his age (if he knew it) and his degree of education (if any). The S then sat in a chair placed at the proper distance from the window and was told to watch carefully the movement that he would see. After approximately three revolutions the E asked, "How does it seem to you to be moving?" Often the S spontaneously used his hands to indicate the motion until the E was satisfied whether a full rotation or a fluctuation was intended. The use of hand motion by the S proved to be fully convincing, for when he reversed the hand at precisely the right moment for the illusion to occur there could be no question concerning his experience. This device gave a useful check on the accuracy of the translator's report of the S's verbal statments.

After obtaining a report for the rectangular window in each of the positions, the trapezoidal window was inserted in place of the rectangular, and the same method of report employed. In addition, the S was asked to tell whether the motion of the trapezoidal window was "like" that of the first window. This procedure served as a further check on the verbal description and hand report. In nearly all cases it was possible to record a clear and unequivocal judgment of the S's perception. Less than three per cent of all judgments were listed by the E as "uncertain."

Whenever the illusion was reported for the first condition, the bar was inserted and the S asked, "How does the bar move?" and "Does the bar stay straight?" On occasional trials when the S had reported both the sway of the window and the bending of the bar, the cube was attached and the S asked to describe its motion. In these cases there was usually laugh-

ter (as with American Ss) and considerable confusion and difficulty manifested in decribing so unreal and "spooky" a motion. Because of the difficulty of communicating concerning these complex phenomena we make no further systematic use of the cube and rod in the present study.

At the conclusion of the experiment, the S was asked what the rectangular window "looked like." He also stated his preference for one of two geometrical drawings presented to him in pairs (a circle, square, trapezoid). He then received a slight payment for his services (usually one pound of sugar or a candy bar and sixpence).

Results

General results. Table 1 gives the results for the two unacculturated groups (Nongoma and Polela Reserves) and for the two districts within metropolitan Durban, African (Lamontville), and European (Greyville).

Combining all four conditions, there is a very significant tendency for the urban groups to report the illusion more often than the rural groups (corrected 2×2 $X^2 = 15.34$; $p < .001$). This difference is most marked with the first condition (corrected 2×2 $X^2 = 12.38$; $p < .001$). There is also a significant trend with the second condition (corrected 2×2 $X^2 = 4.80$; $p < .05$) and a slight tendency with the third condition (corrected 2×2 $X^2 = 1.87$; $p < .20$) for the rural children to observe the illusion less often than the urban children. Virtually no difference exists with the fourth, 20 feet and one eye condition.

Table 1. Number Reporting Illusion (Boys 10–14 Yrs. of Age, N = 20 in Each Group)

Condition	Nongoma Rural Yes	No	Uncertain	Polela Rural Yes	No	Uncertain	African Urban Yes	No	Uncertain	European Urban Yes	No	Uncertain
First condition (10', both eyes)	3	17	0	4	14	2	13	7	0	11	9	0
Second condition (10', one eye)	14	6	0	16	4	0	19	1	0	19	1	0
Third condition (20', both eyes)	8	12	0	17	1	2	16	3	1	16	4	0
Fourth condition (20', one eye)	18	2	0	17	2	1	18	2	0	19	0	1
Totals	43	37	0	54	21	5	66	13	1	65	14	1

Table 2 expresses the results in an alternative way. Since four conditions of presentation were used we can determine in how many of these four conditions on the average each of the cultural groups reported the illusion. For the two unacculturated groups combined, the illusion is reported in 2.425 of the four conditions, while for the acculturated groups the average is 3.275. This mean difference has high statistical significance ($t = 3.51$; $p < .001$).

Table 2. Distribution of Scores

Sample	Number of Yes's					Average
	4	3	2	1	0	
Nongoma	2	4	10	3	1	2.15
Polela	4	10	3	2	1	2.70
Urban African	12	4	2	2	0	3.30
Urban European	11	5	3	0	1	3.25
Total ($N = 80$)	29	23	18	7	3	2.85

It is evident from Tables 1 and 2 that city dwellers, whether Zulu or European, find the illusion somewhat more compelling than do rural ("primitive") natives. This tendency is especially pronounced at 10 feet with binocular vision—a condition when binocular cues of true depth (in this case, true rotation) are most plentiful. The reader will also note that the results for Polela (rural) stand somewhat between those for the city children and those from Nongoma (rural). At ten feet binocularly, they resemble those of Nongoma; at twenty feet binocularly, those of the city boys. Polela is, in fact, one hundred miles closer to Durban than is Nongoma which lies in the heart of Zululand. There is no doubt that the children in Polela have somewhat more familiarity with western architecture (specifically with windows) than do the children of Nongoma. The results (Table 2) correspond to a continuum of cultures: city children having a maximum of familiarity with western architecture, Nongoma children the least.

Preference for circles. Following the experiment, all Ss were shown drawings of a square, a trapezoid, and a circle (in pairs), and asked to express a preference. Table 3 indicates that those who expressed a preference for the circle (at least once in the two pairings) tend in the African groups to report the illusion *less* often. This tendency holds for all experimental conditions for all three African groups. The relationship is statistically significant, however, for only the binocular conditions. Circle-preferring Zulu

Table 3. Percentage of Cases Reporting Illusion among Subjects Preferring and Not Preferring Circle

Condition	Combined African Groups $N = 60$		European Group $N = 20$	
	Preferring Circle $N = 39$	Not Preferring Circle $N = 21$	Preferring Circle $N = 12$	Not Preferring Circle $N = 8$
10′ binocular	28	43	58	50
10′ monocular	79	86	100	88
20′ binocular	59	86	83	75
20′ monocular	87	90	100	88
All conditions	63	76	85	75

children report the illusion significantly less often than the angle-preferring Zulus in Conditions 1 and 3 (corrected $2 \times 2 \; X^2 = 3.89$; $p < .05$), but the difference in the monocular, second and fourth, conditions is not significant (corrected $2 \times 2 \; X^2 = 0.18$, n.s.). There are no differences approaching significance between the circle and noncircle-preferring European Ss.

Let us assume that the aesthetic preference for circles may provide an index of the subjective closeness of the individual to Zulu culture (since it is, as we have seen overwhelmingly a circular culture). If we do so we may say that this subjective closeness seems to predispose the S to resist the illusion. Stated in terms of transactional theory, rectangles and trapezoids have less functional significance for him. His preception of the window's rotation is accordingly more frequently veridical.

We have noted that this influence is significant only in the conditions involving *binocular* perception. A reasonable interpretation would be that cultural effects cannot easily change the basic demand character of the illusion monocularly perceived, but may do so when binocular conditions leave more latitude for choice and for interpretation among a greater number of cues.

This result then, so far as it goes, lends some weight to the contention that "cultural significance" is playing an appreciable part in determining the results.

Illusion with rectangle. Before viewing the trapezoidal window, every S in all four conditions first saw the rectangular window rotating. The purpose was to make sure that the sway (oscillation) reported for the trapezoid was judged to be *different* from the motion of the rectangular window. In most cases, indeed, the S was able to make the distinction clearly, indicating by gesture and by words that the rectangular window went "round and round" whereas the trapezoid oscillated.

There were cases, however, where the rectangular window was reported as oscillating. In fact, nearly one-third of the 80 Ss reported such a phenomenon at one or more of the four conditions. The actual percentage reporting sway in the *rectangular* window at each of the four conditions is:

First condition	0
Second condition	8
Third condition	16
Fourth condition	28

It is conceivable that this curious and somewhat unwelcomed finding may be a result of a "suggestive" order of presentation. Thus, no S seeing the rectangle before the trapezoid under the first condition (10 feet binocularly) reported the phenomenon. And, with the exception of 3 cases, no S reported the rectangular illusion in the second, third, or fourth condition *unless* he had previously reported the trapezoidal illusion. Altogether, 81 per cent of our Ss reported the illusion monocularly at 20 feet for the trapezoidal window, but only 28 per cent did so for the rectangular window under the same condition. In virtually all these cases the Ss had grown accustomed to seeing oscillation at some previous stage with the trapezoid.

Pastore (18), however, finds that more than half of his 58 American college Ss reported sway with the rectangle during a three-minute exposure, and at considerable distance from the window (where the retinal angle subtended by the two shapes may be subliminal). He does not tell whether the Ss had grown accustomed to the sway of the trapezoid before they reported sway in the rectangle. We must leave this problem for the time being unsolved.

A Control Experiment

In order to determine whether unwanted suggestive effects, caused by our order of presentation, were influencing the results at the optimal stage for the trapezoidal illusion (viz., 20' monocularly) we simplified our procedure with entirely new Ss. Urban and rural Africans served as before. To secure the latter, we visited the Ceza Medical Mission in Zululand, approximately 20 miles from Nongoma. Both Ceza and Nongoma are in the deepest part of the native reserves, over 200 miles north of Durban. Polela, as we have said, lies about 100 miles west of Durban and has more European influence (e.g., European-style architecture). This fact, we repeat, seems to explain why, as Tables 1 and 2 show, the Polela Ss report the illusion somewhat more frequently than do Ss at Nongoma or Ceza.

In the control experiment, the S was asked to cover one eye. Sitting at twenty feet from the rotating trapezoidal window he then described its motion (both in words and by hand motion). Later he was seated at ten feet from the object and using both eyes described the motion, comparing it with the previous motion. Finally he was, as in the other groups, asked his preference for the circular, square, or trapezoidal figures. None of these herd boys had ever been to school.

For an urban control group we used a fresh population of Lamontville boys of the same age range.

Results. Table 4 gives the results. These data are practically identical with those of the Nongoma and urban African samples cited previously. Again, the rural Zulu group reported the illusion significantly less often than the urban Zulu group in 10′ binocular condition (corrected $2 \times 2\chi^2 = 11.53$; $p < .001$),

but no differences appear at the 20′ monocular condition. This similarity of data proves that the order of presentation is not an important variable.

At the Ceza Mission Hospital we tested also a group of eleven expectant mothers, only one of whom had ever left the reserve. Eight reported the illusion at 20′ monocularly, two did not, and one was uncertain. None of the eleven, however, reported it at 10′ binocularly. These cases confirm the trend in all our tables that "primitives" are less able to perceive the sway in the trapezoidal window illusion under marginal conditions (i.e., at 10′ binocularly) than are city dwellers.

Table 4. Number Reporting Illusion in Control Experiment

Condition	Ceza (Rural) N = 24			Lamontville (Urban) N = 21		
	Yes	No	Uncertain	Yes	No	Uncertain
First condition (20′, monocular)	22	2	0	20	0	1
Second condition (10′, binocular)	2	18	4	14	7	0

Something should be said concerning the qualitative differences reported by Ss who first reported the illusion at 20′ monocularly and then again at 10′ binocularly. Not infrequently their reports at 10′ binocularly were "mixed," that is to say, sometimes they saw the oscillation and sometimes not. In every case, the S was asked to tell the "difference" if any existed between the movement seen at 20′ monocularly and that at 10′ binocularly. Most Ss claimed that there was a difference: sometimes the window at the closer distance seemed to move faster, sometimes in a bigger arc, sometimes even in the reverse direction. And often, as we have said, the reports at 10′ binocularly were "mixed" —the subjects reporting sometimes a full rotation and sometimes a sway. We record "yes" to the illusion at 10′ binocularly if at any point in the experiment the S reports a clear oscillation. Since the same criteria were applied at both Ceza and Lamontville, no source of error is introduced.

If the reader is acquainted with the illusion he will no doubt recognize this ambiguity in the perception at 10′ when binocular cues are powerful evidence for true rotation, and yet the tendency to see illusory sway likewise ex-

ists. Because of this dual tendency we consider 10′ binocularly as a *marginal* condition for the illusion. What is important for our purposes is the finding that under such marginal conditions urban children, who are familiar with western architecture, report the illusion much more frequently than do herd boys on the Zulu reserves.

As in the major experiment our Ss expressed their preference, in three paired comparisons, for a circle, trapezoid, or square. Since only seven cases of the 45 failed to choose the circle at least once, we changed our criterion slightly from that used in Table 3. We determined the occurrence of the illusion among those who chose the circle *twice* as compared with those who chose it only once or not at all. Table 5 shows that in this population likewise, Ss who show a preference for circles tend—particularly in the binocular condition—to report the illusion somewhat less frequently than those who do not. The differences are not statistically significant but are in the same direction as those reported in Table 3. The implication of this finding, we repeat, seems to be that Ss whose aesthetic preference lies with the circularity of their tribal culture are the most resistant to the illusion.

Table 5. Percentage of Cases Reporting Illusion Among Subjects Preferring Two Circles

Combined African Groups (Ceza and Lamontville);
$N = 44$

Condition	Preferring Two Circles N = 15	Preferring Less than Two N = 29
20′ monocular	92	97
10′ binocular	27	38

At the conclusion of the experiment the investigator showed each S the rectangular window and asked, "What is this?" (In order to make certain that the children would have an opportunity to say "window" if they perceived the resemblance, the question was asked in three different ways in the Zulu language.) To one or more of these three questionings 67 per cent of the urban children said "window," but only 26 per cent of the Ceza children gave the same reply. If we combine all cases who said "window" at both Ceza and Lamontville we find an appreciable, though not statistically significant, tendency for them to report the illusion more often than do children who did not recognize the windowness of the stimulus object (corrected $2 \times 2 \ x^2 = 2.81$; $p < .10$ when both conditions are combined). So far as it goes, this finding (Table 6) lends support to the object-connotation theory of the perception of movement, especially under the 10′ binocular condition.

Table 6. Percentage of Subjects Recognizing Stimulus as a "Window" Who Report the Illusion

Condition	Recognizing "Window" N = 20	Not Recognizing "Window" N = 24
20′ monocular	100	88
10′ binocular	55	29

Discussion

Our most striking finding is that under optimal conditions (monocularly at 20 feet) virtu-

ally as many primitive Zulus report the trapezoidal illusion as do urban Zulus or Europeans. Taking this one partial result by itself we can say that the experiment supports either the nativistic or the cumulative habit theory. It does not by itself give us grounds for choosing between them.

Nativists might argue, for example, that whenever a longer and a shorter projection on the retina occur simultaneously the longer will assume a figure character and therewith a frontal position in the perception (other conditions being equal). Thus, some form of isomorphism obtains between retinal-cortical processes and the perception itself.

An empiricist with a "cumulative habit" preference might say that myriad ocular-motor adjustments from infancy have built up a dependable expectancy that longer projections on the retina will betoken nearer objects. One learns through repeated experience that longer retinal images of trees, cattle, people, stand for *nearer* objects (provided, of course, that one assumes such objects to be of equal size whether far or near from the eyes). It is not necessary for the S to have acquaintance with specific objects (in this case a window) in order to make a similar inference. The transfer effect is wide. Even the shadows painted on the rotating window are reminiscent of the S's experience with shadows in nature. Old experiences automatically condition novel experiences even though the latter are only analogous.

One assumption that may play a decisive part in this case is the assumption of "right angularity." From earliest life the child is conditioned to the fact that perpendicular objects best withstand the force of gravity. Circular though his culture is, his basic frame of reference is still one of verticals and horizontals. Seeing an entirely new object (the trapezoidal window) he assumes unconsciously (no less than do people who are familiar with windows) that its shape is rectangular. Just like people in western culture he may make this assumption even if he "knows" that the object is not in reality rectangular. This assumption, together with the assumption that longer objects on the retina are usually nearer objects, would predispose him to perceive that the longer edge of the window is always nearer (thus inducing the perceived oscillation). No less than people in western culture he would fail to "correct" his assumptions of right-angularity and of long-edges-being-near-edges by his "knowledge" of the trape-zoidal shape of the stimulus.

Our major result is clearly not compatible with a narrowly conceived object-connotation theory. It is not necessary for the S consciously to assume that the object is a window in order to experience the illusion. True, as Table 6 suggests, the specific object connotation seems somewhat to favor the illusion, but it is clearly not the decisive determinant. Thus, for example, 88 per cent of those who did not consciously recognize the frame as a "window" nevertheless experienced the illusion at 20′ monocularly.

Yet, at the same time, our results show that object connotation cannot be disregarded. It also plays a part. Let us review the evidence:

1. Under all *suboptimal* conditions, as we see in Tables 1 and 4 (10 feet monocularly, and binocularly at 10 or 20 feet) there is a tendency for unacculturated Ss to report the illusion less frequently than do the acculturated.

2. The Ss who recognize the "windowness" of the stimulus object tend to report the illusion somewhat more frequently especially at 10 feet binocularly (Table 6).

3. African Ss expressing a preference for circles (assumed here to indicate a subjective closeness to the rotund Zulu culture) tend to report the illusion less often than those expressing preference for angular figures (Tables 3 and 5).

We conclude that experience with, and identification with, western culture make it more likely that the illusion will be perceived under marginal (suboptimal) conditions.

One fact reported by Ames, and mentioned above, supports our interpretation. He finds that a plane trapezoidal frame yields appreciable oscillation, but that the addition of mullions, panes, and shadows enhances the illusion. In other words, specific "thingness" contributes to the experience though it does not account for it wholly (6, pp. 28-31). And we may again allude to von Schiller's contention that expectancy is effective in determining perceived movement under marginal (*alternativ*) conditions.

May Brenner (3) likewise makes the point that when marginal conditions obtain, the S is forced to depend on stimulus *meaning*. On the other hand, when optimal stimulus conditions obtain, even brain-damaged cases report apparent movement to much the same degree as do normal cases.

Several other experiments have dealt with the effects of meaning on apparent movement. Thus, Jones and Bruner (10) report that in a stroboscopic experiment the line drawing of a man is seen to be in motion more actively than is a nonsense figure. De Silva (5) had previously established this same fact. Jones and Bruner conclude that "the more probable and practiced the movement, the more adequately will the movement experience maintain itself under suboptimal conditions" (10, p. 165). This conclusion is in agreement with our own.

Toch and Ittelson (22) report an experiment in which drawings of a bomb stroboscopically presented are seen in a downward (falling) motion, whereas drawings of an airplane presented in an identical fashion are seen in an upward (rising) motion. Though this experiment taken by itself favors an object-connotation theory, the authors argue in general for the cumulative-habit theory. They contend, rightly no doubt, that the nativist position cannot be adequately tested short of a longitudinal study of infants from birth. They believe that generalized past experience accounts for our major dispositions to perceive stroboscopic or other illusory movement, but allow that under conditions of ambiguity or equivocation specific meaning connotations will enter to determine the direction and nature of the movement. Here, too, our findings are concordant.

If we leave the field of experimental testing for a moment, we can find many familiar instances of the role of object connotation in resolving perceptual ambiguities. A streak of light in the night sky may be seen as a shooting star, as distant fireworks, or as a jet plane, depending largely on one's expectations. Bartlett tells of the Swazi chieftain who perceived all traffic policemen in London as friendly beings, because in Swazi culture the upraised arm is an amiable greeting. A child in a dentist's chair, more familiar with space-ships than with nitrous oxide, perceives the inhalator as a spaceship toy. Every projective test assumes that ambiguous (multivalent) stimuli will receive subjective structuring on the basis of need, set, expectancy, or habit.

Our experiment does not introduce factors of need or of set, but deals only with the relevance of past experience (meaning) as a determinant of perceived movement. It may, however, be pointed out that among sophisticated observers of the trapezoidal illusion under marginal conditions (e.g., at 10 feet binocularly) a voluntary effort to see or not to see the window as oscillating (or as rotating) can also be effective, especially if the observer picks out some detail of the window to watch during the rotation, thus inhibiting the impression as a whole. Meaning is not the only determinant entering into the resolution of perceptual ambiguity, but it is one of them.

Returning to James's statement that, "Perception is of definite and probable things," we may say that under optimal conditions of stimulation definite structure is conferred by physiological conditions or by deeply ingrained functional habits of spatial adjustment, or by both. But when marginal conditions prevail, an association with the most "probable" object is often called upon to provide the definiteness that is otherwise lacking.

What we have called "marginal" conditions should receive a further word of explanation. We use the term in our experiments to indicate that perceptual conflict is present. Under binocular conditions (especially at 10′) there are many cues that "give away" the true rotation; at the same time there are operating also the assumptions that the window is rectangular and that longer objects are nearer. Under such a condition of conflict our finding is that urban children resolve the conflict with the aid of the supplementary assumption of "windowness." Not being able to draw on this supplementary assumption, the rural children as a rule resolve the conflict in favor of the binocular (or true) evidence. In this particular case, therefore, one might say that the primitive children see things "as they are" more often than do the children of civilization.

Conclusion

The perception of motion as represented in the rotating trapezoidal window is governed, under *optimal* conditions, by nativistic determinants or by the unconscious utilization of residual (but not immediately relevant) experience, or by both. (Our experiment does not enable us to decide this issue.) At the same time, object connotation (meaning) based on closely relevant cultural experience helps to determine the nature of the perceived movement under *marginal* conditions.

An adequate theory of perceived movement

must therefore allow a place for the subject's specific assumptions of meaning even though it cannot be based solely on this foundation.

REFERENCES

1. Allport, F. H. *Theories of perception and the concept of structure.* New York: John Wiley, 1955.
2. Ames, A., Jr. Visual perception and the rotating trapezoidal window. *Psychol. Mongr.*, 1951, **65**, No. 7 (Whole No. 324).
3. Brenner, May W. The effects of brain damage on the perception of apparent movement. *J. Pers.*, 1956, **25**, 202–212.
4. Cantril, H. *The "why" of man's experience.* New York: Macmillan, 1950.
5. DeSilva, H. R. An experimental investigation of the determinants of apparent visual movement. *Amer. J. Psychol.*, 1926, **37**, 469–501.
6. Doob, L. An introduction to the psychology of acculturation. *J. soc. Psychol.*, 1957, in press.
7. Hall, K. R. L., & Earle, A. E. A further study of the pendulum phenomenon. *Quart. J. exp. Psychol.*, 1954, **6**, 112–124.
8. Helmholtz, H. von. *Physiological optics.* Vol. III, Chaps. 26, 78. Transl. by J. P. C. Southall. Optical Society of America, 1925.
9. James, W. *Principles of psychology.* Vol. II, Chap. 19. New York: Henry Holt, 1890.
10. Jones, E. E., & Bruner, J. S. Expectancy in apparent visual movement. *Brit. J. Psychol.*, 1954, **45**, 157–65.
11. Kilpatrick, F. P. Two processes in perceptual learning. *J. exp. Psychol.*, 1954, **47**, 362–370.
12. Koffka, K. *Principles of Gestalt psychology.* New York: Harcourt, Brace, 1935.
13. Korte, A. Kinematoskopische Untersuchungen. *Z. f. Psychol.*, 1915, **72**, 193–206.
14. Metzger, W. *Gesetze des Sehens.* Frankfurt: Kramer, 1936.
15. Michotte, A. *La perception de la causalité.* Paris: Vrin, 1946.
16. Müller, G. E. *Komplextheorie und Gestalttheorie.* Göttingen: Vandenhoeck & Ruprecht, 1923.
17. Neff, W. S. A critical investigation of the visual apprehension of movement. *Amer. J. Psychol.*, 1936, **48**, 1–42.
18. Pastore, N. Some remarks on the Ames oscillatory effect. *Psychol. Rev.*, 1952, **59**, 319–323.
19. Pieron, H. Remarques sur la perception du mouvement apparent. *Année Psychol.*, 1934, **34**, 245–48.
20. Rivers, W. H. R. *Cambridge anthropological expedition to Torres Straits.* Reports, Vol. II,

Pt. 1: Introduction and Vision. Cambridge Univer. Press, 1901.

21. Schiller, P. von. Stroboskopische Alternativversuch. *Psychol. Forsch.*, 1933, **17**, 179–214.

22. Toch, H. H., & Ittelson, W. H. The role of past experience in apparent movement: a revaluation. *Brit. J. Psychol.*, 1956, **47**, 3, 195–207.

23. Wertheimer, M. *Experimentelle Studien uber das Sehen von Bewegung. Drei abhandlungen zur Gestalttheorie*, Erlangen: Verlag d. Phil. Akad., 1925, 1–105.

24. Wundt, W. *Gründzuge de physiologischen Psychologie*, Vol. II, (6th ed.) Leipzig: Engelmann, 1910.

Organismic Theory

An important influence on the thinking of the present generation of psychologists was a book with the simple title, *The Organism*, by Kurt Goldstein. Not himself a psychologist by training—he was trained as a medical doctor—Goldstein's book appeared at a time (1939) when it seemed to many psychologists that the individual had all but disappeared in a fission of reflexes and segmental responses. *The Organism* put Humpty-Dumpty, fragmented by behaviorism, together again, and once more psychologists were asked to view man as a whole. It is, perhaps, ironical that this picture of the whole man emerged out of Goldstein's researches on brain-injured soldiers of the first World War, but irony became insight when Goldstein demonstrated that even in the brain-injured, the drive to maintain the integrity of the organism is a transcendental drive. Coupled with Gestalt psychology which had already made an impact upon American psychology, and firmly rooted in a philosophical tradition which was eloquently reiterated by the South African, Jan Smuts, in *Holism and Evolution, The Organism* provided many psychologists with an antidote for the atomistic analysis of behavior. It is altogether fitting, therefore, that a selection from this influential book should introduce this chapter. It reads with the same freshness and relevance today that it did when it was first published a quarter of a century ago.

Goldstein's viewpoint as stated in his various writings is more of a posture and a program than it is a theory. Although the organismic attitude permeates contemporary research, it is not easy to point to any large area of investigation which has been generated specifically by Goldstein. An exception is the problem of abstract versus concrete behavior which was formulated by Goldstein and which has been widely investigated. One article by Norman Milgram on this topic has been included here.

Since the publication of *Theories of Personality* Andras Angyal has died, leaving as a legacy at least two unpublished works on personality. These are being now edited and are soon to be published. The chapter we have selected from one of these volumes is an updating of Angyal's position regarding the dualistic organization of personality.

The final selection, one from the writings of A. H. Maslow, is a lucid, forthright, and contemporary statement of a humanistic view of man, a view that appears to be steadily gaining in favor.

1. The organism

KURT GOLDSTEIN

AS OUR STARTING POINT, we are taking phenomena exhibited in man when the brain cortex is damaged. This, for two reasons: First, because, with some justification, we attribute a particular, dominating significance to the cortex; and thereby, phenomena appearing during its injury will be especially relevant for our *understanding of the essential nature of man.* Second, because the analysis of these phenomena enables us to demonstrate certain *general laws of the disintegration of function;* and thereby these laws in turn, will be especially relevant for our understanding of the organism's functions.

A study of most of the former publications may convey the impression that cortical injury is usually followed by a loss of circumscribed functions, such as speech, visual perception, or motor performance. Writers on the subject actually assumed this to be so. According to this conception, they distinguished and designated various disease syndromes by such terms as aphasia in its various forms, visual agnosia, apraxia, etc. They assumed also that circumscribed centers controlled those particular functions.

In recent years, however, improved observation has led to a change of this view. It has been found that, even in cases of circumscribed cortical damage, the disturbances are scarcely ever confined to a single field of performance. In such intricate syndromes, we deal not only with a simple combination of disparate disturbances, but also with a more or less unitary, basic change which affects different fields homolously, and expresses itself through different symptoms. It has also become apparent that

SOURCE. Selection from Kurt Goldstein, "The organism" in *The Organism,* Chapter 1, pp. 15–49, 51–52, 55–58, 59, 61. Boston: Beacon Press, 1963.

the relationship between mental performances and definite areas in the brain, constitutes a far more complicated problem than the so-called localization theory has assumed.

This difference in observations should not lead us to believe that the more recent investigators are more competent than the earlier ones. The early investigations were those of experts who were highly esteemed and real masters in their field. Rather, a difference in the methodology was responsible for the emergence of other facts.

The problem of methodology has the greatest significance for psycho-pathology, and for biological research in general. For example, in the descriptions of symptoms given by the so-called "classicists" on the subject of aphasia—we choose these because they demonstrate the general procedure particularly well—we find that their characteristic tendency, their reference to a hypothetical "primary symptom," renders a given symptomatology plausible. In motor-speech disturbance, for instance, an impairment of the "motor-speech images" was regarded as the "primary" symptom. Where this speech defect was found associated with a disturbance of the writing function, the latter was likewise interpreted as a consequence of the impairment of the "motor-speech images." In word deafness, an impairment of the sensory speech images was assumed to be the primary symptom. From this primary symptom, they also attempted to explain the further symptoms found in such cases, for instance, paraphasia.

The fundamental principle of this procedure is, of course, reasonable. We shall see later, that we cannot obtain direct proof of a functional disturbance. To define the latter, we are dependent upon conclusions derived from changes in performances as exhibited in the symptoms. Such procedure can be conclusive, only if we ascertain, by accurate analyses of every disturbed performance, the one functional disturbance which really does account for the appearance of the various changes. This exactness can hardly be expected from pioneer work in an unknown field, where obviously one must begin by examining the most striking features. And this is not dangerous as long as one bears in mind that the phenomena which first attract attention are not necessarily essential, or basic, not necessarily the key to all subsequent phenomena. Such phenomena stand out only by virtue of certain circumstances; and while they may appear to be characteristic, they do not necessarily support a theoretical foundation for understanding the genesis of the whole symptomatological structure. The danger arises only when this discrimination between essential and incidental phenomena is neglected, and when the scientist forgets that he bases his theory upon such a defective foundation. The incidental phenomena may have value only for preliminary orientation, and may, at best, merit the position of a crude working hypothesis. The real crisis arises when, even in the face of new findings, the investigator cannot free himself from the former theory; rather he attempts to preserve it, and by constant emendations, to reconcile it with these new facts, instead of replacing it by a new theory fit to deal with both the old and new facts. This error has not been avoided in the evolution of the classical doctrine.

The Problem of Determination of Symptoms

The basic error in the procedure under consideration was the failure to recognize the complex problem involved in the method of symptoms. We have become so accustomed to regard symptoms as direct expressions of the damage in a part of the nervous system that we tend to assume that, corresponding to some given damage, definite symptoms must inevitably appear. We do so, because we forget that normal as well as abnormal reactions ("symptoms") are only expressions of the organism's attempt to deal with certain demands of the environment. Consideration of this makes it evident that symptoms are by no means certain to become self-apparent. Symptoms are answers, given by the modified organism, to definite demands: They

are attempted solutions to problems derived on the one hand from the demands of the natural environment, and on the other from the special tasks imposed on the organism in the course of the examination. We shall see that in the everyday life of the patient, a certain transformation of the environment goes hand-in-hand with each defect, and tends to prevent certain disturbances from manifesting themselves. It is of primary interest that the *appearance of symptoms depends on the method of examination,* although the significance of this fact has been largely overlooked. By focusing attention only upon certain phenomena, or upon a selected few, the investigator comes to isolate "symptoms." Phenomena, more striking than others, are registered first, and so give the impression of being *the* dominant symptom. Most likely to attract attention, of course, are the atypical reactions to a normal situation, and especially, the *complete* absence of any reaction when one is expected.

In this way, complete loss of a special function tends to be the outstanding symptom, and conceals the real or basic defect. On other occasions, those phenomena appear, more or less accidentally, as outstanding symptoms, which are answers elicited by specific questions presented by the examiner.

Of course, these "questions" are not fortuitous, but are dictated by the investigator's fundamental ideas about the phenomena he is studying. It is true, these ideas themselves may have been suggested by the data; but frequently a theory has been evolved on the basis of symptoms that have gained their apparent pre-eminence purely by chance. This bias has often resulted in delaying the understanding of the symptoms and the advance of research. Of course, if one tried to include *all* symptoms in the construction of a theory, no theory could ever be elaborated. Obviously, such theorizing presumes that one has grouped the symptoms into the more and less relevant—the primary and secondary—and has tried to build only upon the so-called primary symptoms. In making this distinction, the investigator is commonly prejudiced by theoretical viewpoints which have proved useful in other fields of research, and which he judges—usually without testing their qualifications—to be adequate for the material at hand.

Heretofore, psycho-pathological symptoms were explained in the light of concepts borrowed from reflexology and the prevailing association psychology. The theory that the structure of the nervous system is based on a number of separate mechanisms, each functioning independently, led to the supposition that circumscribed injuries would result in disorders specific to the mechanisms involved. Consequently, the investigator looked for the latter and found them, because he noticed only the disorders which best corresponded to the theory, i.e., disorders which could be regarded as changes resulting from the failure of a hypothetically independent and separate function. Just as normal events had been explained as composites of *elementary* processes, so also, symptoms were interpreted as changes of similar mechanisms of mental elements. When the investigator assumed that an impairment of motor speech images was the cause of the motor aphasia, or an impairment of visual images the cause of alexia, he believed that his deductions were genuinely based upon the symptoms. Actually, such explanations were merely the outcome of a theoretical preconception, merely an *interpretation of the phenomena* in terms of a special theory, i.e., association psychology.

The correctness of the basic assumption was accepted so implicitly, that no attempt was made to prove that the images in question really played the part in *normal* speech which it was assumed they did. Neither was any attempt made to ascertain whether these images were actually defective in patients.

Once the basic concept of the importance of specific areas for certain functions was formulated, and seemingly confirmed, it now determined all subsequent investigations, especially because of its applicability to practice. Thereafter, the question was confined to the decision as to whether the supposed individual centers and pathways functioned in a "normal" or "abnormal" manner. Still more serious was the fact that this concept became the criterion for determining whether or not individual phenomena belonged in the given syndrome resulting from injury to a certain area. If, besides the phenomena which had been regarded as essential symptoms, others were found, these were pushed aside as "complications" that disturbed the "purity" of the case, and were considered the result of some injury incurred simultaneously in another area. Or, if this were not done, an attempt was made to explain them as merely secondary effects contingent upon the hypothetically primary disturbance. Yet not even the growing necessity for the most diverse modifications of the basic conception and for the most daring theoretical constructions has deterred theorists from building such auxiliary hypotheses.

Three Methodological Postulates. Clearly such reasoning in circles has necessarily delayed the realization that the basic concept is untenable. Yet this procedure can be regarded as characteristic of the majority of clinical, physiological, and biological research of the older school. In what respect does our procedure differ from that described? Simply, in that we have endeavored to record, in an open-minded fashion, *all* phenomena. Pursuing this aim, there result three methodological postulates equally valid for the examination of patients or animals.

(1) The first methodological postulate is: Consider initially all the phenomena presented by the organism (in this case it may be a patient), *giving no preference, in the description, to any special one.* At this stage no symptom is to be considered of greater or less importance. Only under these conditions is the description correct. It must be left for future investigation to determine how far one symptom, rather than another, is essential for understanding the underlying changes of a function.

Every unbiased and exhaustive examination of a case repeatedly teaches us that alteration of a given performance, even if at first sight it appears to be very prominent, is not necessarily of primary significance for understanding the underlying functional disturbance. On the other hand, a trifle which barely attracts notice may be of the utmost importance. For example, as long as the most prominent symptom of amnesic aphasia, namely, the difficulty in finding words, was allowed to suggest the plantation of this disease, the theory that the basic disturbance consisted in a reduced evocability of speech images, appeared perfectly satisfactory. But as soon as a subtle and formerly neglected alteration in the total behavior of the patient was taken into consideration, there resulted not only an entirely different conception of the underlying functional disturbance, but a new insight into the meaning of the aphasic phenomena was made possible. The difficulty in finding words, formerly regarded as the main symptom, retreated into the background. The theory of the reduced evocability of speech images became obsolete, because it could be sustained only by means of auxiliary hypothese—hypotheses not required in *our* explanation—since the patients are quite capable of using the words under specific circumstances. They have not lost the use of words per se, but the ability of employing words as bearers of *meaning*. Under circumstances where the latter is not demanded, and the words "belong" to an action or concrete situation, the patient "has the words." The inability to find and use words voluntarily is not due to the primary defect of the speech mechanism, but to a change in their total personality which bars them from the situation where meaning is required.

(2) The second methodological postulate concerns the correct description of the observable phenomena themselves. It was a frequent methodological error to accept what amounted to a mere description of the effect; but an effect might be *ambiguous* with respect to its underlying function. Therefore, only a thorough analysis of the causes of such effects, of success or failure in a given task, for example, can provide clarification. The older psychopathological investigations usually confined themselves to the question of whether a patient actually gave, or failed to give, the correct response in a task. This "plus or minus method," however, is inadequate, no matter whether we are dealing with positive or negative results. If we regard a reaction only from the standpoint of the actual solution of a task, we may overlook the deviation from normality, because the individual completes the task by a detour which may not be evident in the solution. Only accurate analysis, through an examination which makes it impossible for the patient to achieve a result in a roundabout way, can disclose the defect. If our capacity to observe were not so imperfect, closer attention would show that the patient has reached the goal in an abnormal manner, for of course, under such conditions the results cannot correspond, in *all* details, to the normal. Once we become alive to this fact, diagnosis is often simplified by noting small and hitherto unobserved deviations. We may use an example to illustrate this.

Patients with loss of "categorical behavior" find it difficult, for instance, to consider an individual color according to a category such as redness, greenness, etc. When we ask patients to select all red color skeins of the Holmgren wool samples, they often place the colors "in a row": the lightest to the darkest red. On the

basis of this we might assume that they have proceeded categorically, since they have apparently selected the shades according to a concept —in this case that of brightness, and therewith have placed them in a row. This assumption, however, is based on an *error of observation*, namely, a disregard for the slight differences which distinguish the patient behavior from a behavior determined by the categorical attitude. It can easily be shown that they have not proceeded and cannot proceed categorically: they are not able to arrange the colors in a row as to their brightness, if *asked* to do so. They also fail in the task of putting together all the reds in a heap—activities which presuppose the categorical attitude.

These observations make it rather doubtful whether the patient originally selected the skeins according to the category of brightness. Actually, if one more carefully examines the manipulations of the patient, one discovers that he has not really laid down a *row* according to brightness. What he did, was to place *one shade beside another, one at a time*. In this way, single pairs of similar shades were formed under the guidance of the concrete sensory cohesion between the *last* skein and the *next* similar one. By this procedure of "successive pairs," he finally came to an arrangement which *in toto looked like* a scale of brightness, but really was not. In selecting a new skein the patient was entirely and solely dependent on the skein which immediately preceded it. This accounts for the pairing of, and the *intervals* between the skeins. That his procedure was determined by this "piece to piece" performance, could be shown by the fact that when the examiner removed the skein the patient had last placed in position, he was unable to continue with his "series." This showed that he depended on the immediately preceding skein for the selection of the new one. We mention this example to show how vital it is, for an accurate interpretation, that description of phenomena be minute and exact. And, in order that the description be correct, how careful must be the attention given to those small matters all too easily overlooked through theoretical bias.

Equally ambiguous are the negative results of a medical examination. The *wrong* response is too often judged to be a simple failure, whereas actually, under careful analysis, it may throw considerable light upon the mental functions of the patient. Only by this means can we discover whether there is really a defect in the ability demanded by the task, or whether the patient has failed only because of special circumstances induced by the task situation. Furthermore, in the wrong response, analysis often uncovers a detour which the patient has used, perhaps because the normal way was not practicable. Such facts may have an important bearing on the explanation of the capacities of the organism.

(3) The third methodological postulate we wish to stress is that no phenomenon should be considered without reference to the organism concerned, and to the situation in which it appears. We shall have to refer to this point so often that it is not worth further elaboration at this time. Little as this requirement has been observed in the past, because of theoretical bias, it should nonetheless become a matter of course in the future. Many an error would have been avoided in psychopathology if this postulate, quite deliberately stated by Hughlings Jackson decades ago, had not been so completely neglected. The same postulate holds to no less a degree for animal behavior observations. Later on we shall deal in detail with the fundamental difficulties following from the application of this precept, since it necessitates taking into account the organism as a whole.

We wish to refute briefly two possible objections to our methodological postulates. The first concerns the charge that, according to our postulates, one can never really determine *at what point an examination can be regarded as completed.* As a matter of fact, it never is. But there is still a great difference between the two forms of procedure: between the usual description and enumeration of separate disturbances, such as those of visual or linguistic performances, etc., and our procedure, which is primarily directed toward the cognition of the whole, and, within this frame of reference, seeks to analyze as many individual performances as possible. This technique will certainly obviate the grossest errors, *even though it may not lead to absolutely incontestable results.* Bearing in mind this aim of completeness, it will be possible to avoid precipitate theoretical conclusions and the rigid maintenance of any hypothesis preventing us from radically revising our theories, on the strength of new experience. In the course of the examination, one comes to a point when one feels that the analysis can be terminated without risk of gross errors in the interpreta-

tion. The examination must be carried far enough at least to insure that (on the basis of facts) a theory can be developed which will *render understandable all observed phenomena in question,* and which will make it possible to predict how the organism will react, even in such tasks hitherto not investigated. Only such an analysis is to be considered adequate.

The procedure of investigating the patient, which Gelb and I have described as a case of visual agnosia, may provide an example. On the basis of our first examinations, which were not sufficiently exhaustive, we had formed a hypothesis which was not quite adequate. Further examinations drove us to the formulation of a new hypothesis which did justice to both old and new facts. The further we advanced with the examinations, the more clearly delineated did the functional disturbance in this case become. Finally, we have progressed so far toward constructing the total picture of the patient that we can predict with relatively great certainty how he will behave in any situation, even in respect to tasks which we have not yet examined. Only cases which have been investigated with such thoroughness should be used in the formation of a theory. *One single extensive analysis of this sort is much more valuable than many examinations involving many patients, but yielding only imperfect conclusions.*

This leads to the second objection to our postulates. Our procedure necessarily enforces *a limit upon the number of cases investigated.* To examine many cases so thoroughly would be patently impossible. It is argued that this may vitiate the conclusiveness of the statements, since we may have encountered a special instance which cannot serve as pattern for the explanation of others. This objection completely misses the point:—

First: The accumulation of even a myriad of imperfectly investigated cases can in no way guide us toward recognition of the true facts. There is no alternative to carrying the examination of each case to the extent we have indicated.

Second: Important though it may be to seek repeated confirmation of our findings through new case material, such *confirmation adds nothing essential to our knowledge.* Those patients must be subjected to investigation who offer a guarantee of unequivocal statements of fact, as well as of theoretical interpretation. Under such conditions, the conclusions drawn from one case will likewise have validity for others. Since the basic laws are the same, the multiplicity encountered in various instances will be readily understood, once these basic laws are recognized. True, a new observation may induce us to modify somewhat our original assumptions; but if the analysis of the first observation was sufficient, this modification can be made without conflict, whereas imperfect analysis of ever so many cases may be very misleading—as the literature bears witness only too clearly.

If patients with cortical injuries are examined according to these methodological principles (I am thinking primarily of patients whose "central" cortical region has been injured), an extraordinarily intricate picture results, a systematic account of which has been given in a number of papers.

Disintegration of Performances and the Hierarchy within the Organism

Before outlining the features which all these cases have in common, we must define the term "performances." We call performance of an organism any kind of behavior, activity, or operation as a whole or in part, which expresses itself overtly, and bears reference to the *environment*. Hence physiological processes, events within the nervous system, mental activities, attitudes, affectivities are *not* performances as long as they do not manifest themselves in some overt action—any *disclosable* outward behavior. More specifically, a performance is a coming to terms of the organism with environmental stimuli by a behavioral act, be this eyelid-closure under stimulation or a total movement like running towards a goal, or hearing, seeing, etc. The aforementioned outline may now be presented:

(1) A single performance or performances in a specific field (e.g., visual, motor)[1] will never drop out alone. Invariably *all* performance fields are affected, although the degree to which the individual field is involved, varies.

(2) *A single performance field will never drop out completely. Some individual performances are always preserved.* Responses to the apparently equal demands of equal tasks do not drop out indiscriminately under all circum-

stances. There is a peculiar and, at first, subtle variation of reaction, even when the demand remains constant. This inconsistency is usually explained as the effect of some disturbances of "general functions," such as fatigue, etc., or it is argued away. Actually, it indicates to us the need for further analysis.

(3) The modification of performances manifested by a patient in different fields is in principle of the same nature. The different symptoms can be regarded as expressions of *one and the same basic disturbance*. In spite of this, we are confronted with various syndromes having to do with the question of localization.

(4) The basic disturbance can be characterized either as a *change of behavior*, or as an *impairment of the functions of the brain matter*. The discussion of the latter, we have to postpone. Here we shall merely confine ourselves to a characterization of the change in behavior. We venture to remark that whenever the patient must transcend concrete (immediate) experience in order to act—whenever he must refer to things in an imaginary way—then he fails. On the other hand, whenever the result can be achieved by manipulation of concrete and tangible material, he performs successfully. Each problem which forces him beyond the sphere of immediate reality to that of the "possible" or to the sphere of representation, insures his failure. This manifests itself in all responses such as action, perception, thinking, volition, feeling, etc. The patient acts, perceives, thinks, has the right impulses of will, feels like others, calculates, pays attention, retains, etc., as long as he is provided with the opportunity to handle objects concretely and directly. He fails when this is impossible. This is the reason why he does not succeed in intelligence tests. This is also the reason why he can grasp a little story as long as it concerns a familiar situation in which he, himself, has participated. But he will not understand a story—certainly no more difficult for the average person—requiring him to place himself, in imagination, in the position of someone else. He does not comprehend metaphors or puzzles. He can manipulate numbers in a practical manner, but has no concept of their value. He can talk if there is some concrete subject matter present for him to depend upon, but he cannot recount material unrelated to him, or report it purely conceptually. He is incapable of representation of direction and localities in objective space, nor can he estimate distances;

---

[1] Hereafter, we shall speak in this context of a "performance field."

but he can find his way about very well, and can execute actions which are dependent upon perception of distance and size.

Depending on which of these manifestations of the basic disturbance has been brought into focus, they have been named respectively: disturbance of *"symbolic expression"* (Head), of the *"representational function"* (Woerkom), of *"categorical behavior"* (Gelb and Goldstein). With regard to the effect of the change, one may, in emphasizing the disturbance of that capacity which is prerequisite for the performance in question, talk of impairment of the capacity to *comprehend the essential features of an event.*

Or we might point to the patient's inability to emancipate and withhold himself from the world, the shrinkage of his freedom, and his greater bondage to the demands of environment. The most general formula to which the change can be reduced is probably: The patient has lost the capacity to deal with *that which is not real—with the* possible.

Inquiring now into the question of how the various performances reveal the impairment, we find that voluntary performances are particularly affected, while activities directly determined by the situation remain relatively intact. Adapting a performance so that it corresponds to the changing demands of the situation requires a voluntary attitude. Therefore, all those performances which require, for their proper execution, such a voluntary shifting, must suffer, e.g., all "choice reactions." *The isolated performances are affected to a greater degree than the so-called total responses.* This shows itself in a greater loss of isolated movements than of integrated movements, as well as in the inability to distinguish the details of a picture (the whole of which may yet be recognized), or in the inability to pronounce a single word or single letters out of context. The disintegration of a familiar function *proceeds from the highly differentiated and articulated state to a more amorphous total behavior.*

The symptoms vary with the severity of impairment, and the degree to which one area or another is affected. The *basic disturbance, however, remains the same.* I cannot produce proof of this assertion here. I might emphasize at the same time, however, that for our particular purposes, the differences of opinion are unimportant. One thing is agreed upon: cortical injury does not result in the loss of isolated performances, but in *systematic disintegration following the principle that certain forms of behavior will be impaired while others remain intact.* Only with this in mind, will it be possible to make a distinct classification of the performances which the patient can and cannot carry out, as well as to provide a meaningful description of the symptoms.

Is our characterization of the change after cortical injury satisfactory? Are we really dealing exclusively with the impairment of certain kinds of behavior? *Have not "contents" also dropped out?* Certainly! Yet it must be admitted that many of these losses are secondary, since it is true that certain contents appear only within certain kinds of behavior. The impairment of the behavior entails the loss of numerous contents. This is perhaps most clearly demonstrable in cases of what are known as "amnesic aphasia." Patients suffering in this way have lost the ability to call objects by their *names. Seemingly, they lack the "content": names.* The analysis, however, indicates that, in such cases, we are dealing with a disturbance of "categorical" behavior, an impairment of the capacity to experience and to handle "meaning," which is requisite for "naming" objects. This explains why the patients cannot find the words in those situations where the words have to function as symbols—as representations for something. The loss of "contents" is therefore secondary.

But contents can also be embedded in other forms of behavior, namely, those which belong to acquired faculties; for example, words memorized in foreign languages. Such contents may be preserved, in spite of a disturbance of the aforementioned behavior. To illustrate: Some individuals, with a good command of language, of superior linguistic knowledge, are able to name certain objects, even when they are afflicted with "amnesic aphasia." Under other conditions, these acquired performances may be lost when the substratum is damaged. Only exact analysis can show whether, in any particular case where "contents" are lacking, we are dealing with a *consequence of behavior disturbance, or of loss of these acquisitions.* Only in the case of these acquired faculties are we entitled to speak of contents. The distinction is of fundamental importance for accurate diagnosis of a disturbance, as well as for any attempt to prescribe therapeutic exercises, because only correct diagnosis of the change can provide the correct procedure. These comments apply equally well to the interpretation of content losses in operated animals, and to all experiments of relearning after injury, etc.

Accurate observation of many cases teaches us that disintegration of function always results in the *same pattern of distribution of the intact and affected modes of behavior*. The behavior we have characterized as categorical behavior always suffers first. We are well justified in crediting the intact organism with a greater performance capacity than the injured one, and in admitting that the "higher" or more complex performances require a more intact substratum than the simpler ones. Therefore, we speak of a hierarchy or descending scale of disintegration, in which the higher performances are more disturbed than the simpler ones. Study of the phenomena in progressive and regressive brain processes most clearly reveals such a hierarchy in the *regular* succession of the onset of the various symptoms, and their abatement in recovery.

We might venture to say that the most complicated performances, those first to be impaired, are probably the ones most essential and most vital to the existence of the organism, and further, with respect to the nature of the organism, they have the highest functional significance. Through the deterioration of those performances, the organism loses its most characteristic properties. We may become particularly conscious of this fact by contrasting an individual suffering from brain injuries with a normal person. Those behavioral forms which are earliest and most markedly affected express the main characteristics of man, and bring to the fore his unique place in nature.

In this way, the order manifested in the disintegration may provide us with the idea of a hierarchy of capacities and performances—a stratified structure of the organism. Of course, it is not hierarchical in the sense that the individual forms of behavior represent performances existing in isolation, side by side, and only linked one to the other. It is not so simple as that.

Characterization of Performances According to Their Functional Significance or Value and Their Survival Importance

Our use of the terms "higher" and "lower" functional significance or "value," requires clarification. If, from one standpoint, we characterize certain forms of behavior as *intrinsically valuable* because of their significance for the nature of the organism, we might, from another standpoint, characterize other performances as *most important* because they resist the effect of injury. Without doubt, the survival of "automatic" performances, in contrast to that which we have characterized as "higher," more conscious, or more voluntary, is of special importance for the organism, inasmuch as they are those which *insure mere existence*. In this sense, we would be justified in speaking of performances which have *greater or less importance for survival*. This is what is implied in the expression "the instinct of self preservation." If this means preservation only in the sense of continued survival, we may ask the questions: Does such an "instinct" exist in the normal organism? More specifically, can it be regarded as belonging to the highest level of functioning or is not the appearance of such a "drive," as the predominant feature in an individual, itself a symptom of abnormality—a pathological phenomenon? As we shall see, the normal organism is characterized as a "Being" in a temporal succession of definite form. For the realization of this "Being," the existence, the "mere being alive," plays, of course, a prominent, but by no means the essential role. Under extreme circumstances, it can be compatible with the "nature" of an organism to renounce life, i.e., to give up its bodily existence, in order to save its most essential characteristics—for example, a man's ethical convictions. *Preservation of material existence becomes "essential" only after defect sets in,* and possibly in certain emergencies. In the latter case, the body achieves the position of supreme importance, since all the other possibilities of self-realization are bound to it. Regarding the defective organism, the scale of performance values is likely to differ from that of the normal. In order to preclude any misunderstanding, we shall differentiate in the future, between *functional significance* or value—by which we shall mean "essential to the nature of the organism,"—and "survival importance" by which we shall mean "paramount in the preservation of its life." In the normal organism, the two usually go hand in hand inasmuch as here preservation also means preservation of the intrinsic nature so far as that is possible. In the pathologically changed organism, the preservation of existing potentialities, the survival importance, comes to the fore. At present we only wish to stress the importance of the principle of hierarchy indicated in the laws of disintegration, and will subsequently return to this question with special reference to the structure of the organism.

Certain General Rules Determining Organismic Life

Normal ("Ordered") Behavior and "Disordered Behavior." Catastrophic Reaction. A description of the mere defects does not give an adequate characterization of the injured condition of the organism. In order to understand the latter completely, we must also pay close attention to the intact performances. Indeed, the question of how the organism can continue to exist in spite of such great impairments, spurs us on to this task. Let us first consider another peculiarity of the injured organism, which will throw considerable light upon the solution of this problem, and which must come to our notice if we follow our first methodological postulate. With this in mind, we find that *each effective performance or each failure is an integrated feature in a definite total behavior pattern.* At first, it may seem as if we were dealing with an obscure, unintelligible, unsystematic alternation between successful performances and failures. No explanation of this alternation which resorts to fluctuation of so-called higher functions or faculties, such as attention, fatigue, etc., reaches the core. It shifts the explanation to an allegedly underlying, but equally unintelligible functional disturbance. We can reach an understanding of this alternation only by considering the total behavior in which the individual performance appears. Total behavior can be divided into *two basic classes, objectively distinguishable;* to one of these classes belong the effectual, to the other, the deficient performances. The first kind of behavior, we call "ordered," the second "disordered" or "catastrophic." We shall encounter these two types repeatedly, but at first we must provide a more accurate phenomenological description of both. In an ordered situation, responses appear to be constant, correct, adequate to the organism to which they belong, adequate to the species and to the individuality of the organism, as well as to the respective circumstances. The individual himself experiences them with a feeling of smooth functioning, unconstraint, well-being, adjustment to the world, and satisfaction, i.e., the course of behavior has a *definite order,* a total pattern in which all involved organismic factors—the mental and the somatic down to the physico-chemical processes—participate in a fashion appropriate to the performance in question. And that, in fact, is the criterion of a normal condition of the organism. Hence, ordered and normal behavior are synonymous inasmuch as the behavior is normal because it is "ordered." The "catastrophic" reactions, on the other hand, are not only "inadequate" but also disordered, inconstant, inconsistent, and embedded in physical and mental *shock.* In these situations, the individual feels himself unfree, buffeted, and vacillating. He experiences a shock affecting not only his own person, but the surrounding world as well. He is in that condition which we usually call *anxiety.* After an *ordered* reaction, he can ordinarily proceed to another, with difficulty or fatigue. Whereas, after a castastrophic reaction, his reactivity is likely to be impeded for a longer or shorter interval. He becomes more or less unresponsive and fails even in those tasks which he could easily meet under other circumstances. The disturbing after-effect of catastrophic reactions is long-enduring. Discrimination between these two types of behavior is fundamental for the correct analysis of the performance of an organism. *The solution of a task will depend upon whether the task itself has arisen during the course of performances which are within the realm of the capabilities of the patient, or transcend the latter.*

Tendency to Ordered Behavior. In time the patient will—despite the persistence of the defect—*return to an ordered condition.* Obviously, this will be especially true of those patients whose disease came to a standstill, leaving a certain defect. The picture, during the acute state, is usually so complicated and varying as to make an unambiguous analysis impossible—which fact, incidentally, is analogous to the situation in animal experiments, immediately after experimental destruction of certain areas. But this does not mean that the acute state can teach us nothing. On the contrary, it can yield valuable information about certain types of behavior in the organism. I am thinking particularly, in this respect, of the significance of the analysis of shock. At any rate, the picture after "recovery" is much better suited for analysis, if for no other reason than its relative consistency. Therefore, for the present, we shall confine ourselves to analyzing phenomena in cases which have been "cured," although still persisting in some defects.

Examination of patients in this re-ordered condition convinces us that the remaining performances show a number of peculiarities which are of interest, not only because of their mere occurrence, but also because they throw light upon the question of how the *disordered organism regains a state of order*. If it is correct to assume that disordered behavior results from the fact that the organism is confronted with tasks with which it cannot cope, then, in a defective organism, disordered behavior necessarily will predominate. In this state, the organism is confronted by its environment with many a task which has become insoluble on account of such a defect. But, in the fact of this condition, how does the organism again achieve a state of order? Let us consider the facts:

Lack of Self-Perception of Defects. Tendency to Exclusion of Defects. We are first struck by the observation that the *disturbing stimuli apparently have no effect on the behavior*. This becomes evident, when we study the subjective experiences of the patients, as well as their objective behavior.

This lack of *self-perception* of a disturbance has been looked upon as a peculiarity resulting from a definite kind of damage to the cortex, and an attempt has been made to explain it, either in terms of localization, or through the assumption of faculty disturbances, such as those of attention, perception, or memory. None of these explanations has proved adequate. Redlich and Bonvicini have already pointed out that we are dealing, in such cases, with general mental disturbances which have nothing to do with abnormalities of memory, imagery, or the like; and Anton had emphasized the great similarity between the behavior of these patients and that of certain hysterics. According to my observations, this resulting ineffectiveness of disturbance is also to be found in cases without any injury of the brain or mental disturbances per se, so for example, where total blindness is produced exclusively by gross damage of the peripheral optic nerve. The study of such cases, and also of a great many variously localized brain injuries, has shown me that the phenomenon which we are discussing is certainly not confined to any specific type or place

of lesion in the brain; and we cannot speak simply of psychotic reactions, even in the sense of hysteria. Rather, we are facing apparently quite normal biological reactions to a very grave defect.

Modification of Preserved Performances and of Milieu in a Defect. Disturbances, of course, can be rendered ineffective only if such demands which would provoke their coming to the fore are not made upon the organism—in other words, if the patient's *milieu is modified in an adequate way*. This modification is partially brought about by the activity of the persons dealing with the defective organism. In experiments with animals, for instance, the experimenter tries to keep his operated animals alive, and arranges the environment in such a way as to prevent any detrimental situation. Similarly, the physician plays a protective role toward the patient. But the organism itself aids in the attainment of a new milieu adequate to his altered condition. In the interest of general biology, it is of course desirable to study this process more closely. The animal seeks situations in which it is not exposed to dangers which may arise, due to its disabilities. For instance, sympathectomized animals show a clear aversion to cold air and draft in the winter time; they prefer to stay near a radiator.

Cortical Lesions. Avoidance of Catastrophic Situations. In man, this modification of milieu manifests itself in very definite changes of behavior. First of all, we find that the patients avoid, as far as possible, all situations which would occasion catastrophic reactions. Of course, this avoidance by no means implies that the patient has consciously recognized the situation and its danger. The nature of his defect usually makes this impossible for him, and actually he remains quite passive in the matter. When an objectively endangering stimulus is on its way, a catastrophic reaction sets in immediately, precluding any adequate response to the situation. The patient then appears completely aloof from the world. It is not so much that the endangering situation has been actively avoided, as that the patient has been passively protected from it. If, however, the patient has had frequent opportunities to observe that certain situations entail catastrophic reactions, and if he can learn to recognize these situations through certain "criteria" which are within his mental grasp, then he can also actively avoid the situation. We find continually that patients obstinately refuse to do certain apparently harmless things, and we can immediately understand their refusal, if we keep this fact in mind.

Substitute Performances. Tendency to Hold to the Preserved Performance Level. The "avoidance" of dangerous situations is brought about especially by the patient's tendency to *maintain a situation with which he can cope.* When we try to force him into a situation which he has identified as catastrophic, he deliberately seeks to escape through some other performance—a "substitute performance." Patients often develop great ingenuity in this respect. The content of this substitute performance may seem quite meaningless, may even be rather irrelevant, or indeed, disagreeable to the patient; but he will be less disturbed by it than if he were compelled to meet the demands of the situation with which he is actually confronted. The significance of these substitute performances rests not so much in their contents, as in the fact that this mode of response lies within the capacities of the patient, and *that, as it takes place, nothing can happen which might lead to catastrophe.* At a certain stage of disintegration, these substitute actions are the last resource, the only means by which existence can be maintained. In this sense, they are meaningful; they enable the organism to come to terms with the environment, at least in some way.

Tendency to Undisturbed State. The aforementioned significance of the fact that the patient has a tendency to perform what he is capable of, makes intelligible why he is practically never idle. So long as patients are neither asleep nor at rest, they are always occupied with something. If a certain action is demanded of them, they must first be aroused—often with difficulty—from some other engrossing activities. The performances which the patient can carry out, and to which he always tends to cling, have the character of stereotypy and exhibit little variation. This gives the impression that the patients have a pronounced disposition to maintain the most uniform and undisturbed condition. But this is not a genuine restful state of a leisurely, contemplative person. Indeed this state is susceptible to disturbance by accidental, extraneous events with which the person may not be fit to cope. Careful observation reveals that this uniformity is "rest" only in appearance, and that the patient is, in fact, never idle. By always "doing something" which

is he is capable of, the patient keeps himself so occupied, so engrossed, so secluded from the outside world, that he remains unaffected by many events of his environment. But anything of significance to him, in the respective situation, is quite well noticed, perceived, and retained. This escape from the environment into a condition which protects him from situations which are dangerous to him, has its analogy in the so-called death feint of animals. Just as this attitude in animals is not to be understood as the result of a volitional act, but as a biological phenomenon occasioned primarily by shock and anxiety, so also is the behavior of the patient to be understood.

Tendency to Orderliness. A characteristic means, by which patients with brain injuries avoid catastrophic situations, is a tendency towards *orderliness.* Such individuals may become veritable fanatics in this respect. The brain-injured patients, whom I had under my observation for many years, kept their closets in model-condition. Everything had its definite place, and was so arranged that the patient could find it and take it out as easily as possible. Everything, in other words, was "in order," from the patient's point of view. When, on a table in front of such a patient, we place various objects in a haphazard arrangement we observe that if he notices them at all he will put them in order, setting side by side those things which seem to him to belong together.

Suppose a patient has just finished writing on a piece of paper. The examination is over. I take the pencil and place it carelessly on the sheet of paper which happens to lie obliquely upon the table. As he gets up, the patient removes the pencil, puts the paper in line with the edge of the table, and then sets the pencil down, as parallel as possible, to the border of the paper. If, without comment, I again set the pencil obliquely on the paper, the patient, provided he has been watching, may once more place it in the same way as before. This game can be repeated several times, until he is either distracted by something else, or is told explicitly that I want it this and this way. In this case, the patient resigns himself to the situation, though usually with an expression of marked discomfort.

"Disorder" is unbearable for him. What does disorder, in this sense, mean? Objective disorder is really just as non-existing as objective order. Disorder means an arrangement which forces upon one, not simply a single, definite criterion such as "availability of objects," but several or many. Complete disorder, as far as this is at all possible, would not force anything upon the individual, but would leave him completely free choice.

There are, of course, several possible arrangements of the same objects, depending on the attitude with which one approaches the things. For example, the appeal of an order to the active attitude will differ from its appeal to the contemplative attitude. Even in action there is a difference in the preference of a certain order. It depends upon whether a simple, habitual activity flows out of the situation, or whether a choice between certain ends is necessitated or the creation of new meaningful arrangements is required.

The more manifold the tasks are which a person can perform, the more his arrangements will appear disorderly to another person who is only capable of fulfilling a few tasks, be it that he can only apprehend either single objects or certain objects in a definite context. For such persons, the position of objects next to each other, or objects together in small heaps, will represent the best order, the "real" order, and everything else will stand for disorder. All patients with brain injury have a tendency towards such "primitive" order. Only by this arrangement are they able to execute, with the least expenditure of energy, performances essential to them. Only in this way can they react adequately. Other arrangements agitate and upset them, by demanding behavior which they can execute, if at all, only with great expenditure of energy, and which, therefore, tend to bring about a catastrophic situation.

The principal demands which "disorder" makes upon them are: choice of alternatives, change of attitude, and rapid transition from one behavior to another. But this is exactly what is difficult or impossible for them to do. If they are confronted with tasks which make this demand, catastrophic reactions, catastrophic shocks, and anxiety inevitably ensue. To avoid this anxiety the patient clings tenaciously to the order which is adequate for him, but which appears abnormally primitive, rigid, and compulsive to normal people. In other words, the "sense of order" in the patient is an expression of his defect, an expression of his impoverishment regarding an essentially human trait: the capacity for adequate shifting of attitude.

Anxiety and Avoidance of "Emptiness." The dread of catastrophic reactions must also be thought of as a reason for another phenomenon frequently observed in patients with brain lesions: the tendency to avoid "emptiness."

It is a common experience to find that patients with aphasia, if asked to write anything on a piece of paper lying in front of them, usually start directly at the top edge and crowd their writing as close as possible, line upon line. Only with the greatest effort, if at all, can they be induced to leave a larger interlinear space, or even to write in the center of a blank sheet of paper. They show analogous behavior in other performances. Attempts to interfere with this procedure disquiet them, and it becomes quite apparent how disagreeable such pressure is to them. One might be tempted to say that the patient is suffering from a phobia of empty space, but this view is derived from the world of the normal, and does not do justice to that which takes place in the patient's mind. This kind of patient is not at all capable of having an idea or subjective experience of emptiness, for to do so would require an abstract attitude which they do not possess. It is characteristic of the change in these patients, that they can experience contents, and objects, only if they are confronted with something concrete, something tangible, something which they can *handle*. In view of this condition, certainly no such object as empty space exists for them. On the other hand, there is no doubt about the anxiety, restlessness, the inner resistance they experience wherever the situation objectively demands experience of emptiness. The dread probably arises from the fact that empty space does not become an adequate stimulus, and therefore leads to an inadequate catastrophic reaction. It is the dread of such reactions which makes the patients cling tenaciously to something "filled," to an object to which he can react, or with which he can establish contact through activity. In the same way as we explained the avoidance of catastrophic situations in general—that is by inference from certain situational criteria—we can explain why the patient avoids situations of empty space, even though for him, the latter has no real existence. Often it only seems as if the patient were avoiding emptiness, when actually he is clinging tenaciously to its concrete contents, knowing that as soon as he gives up this point of reference he will become helpless, ineffective, disturbed, and driven to catastrophic reaction.

Immediately upon deprivation of such points of reference, the patient fails completely, or desperately seeks devices to help him cleave to the concrete. These points of reference may easily escape the notice of a perfunctory observer, but they are extremely characteristic of the behavior of such patients. For instance, one of our patients can write only if he is first allowed to draw a line parallel to the upper margin of the paper. Whether or not he is successful in writing probably depends upon whether he can keep an eye on the upper margin, and hold fast to it, so to speak. Another patient can read only if an individual letter presented to him stands on a line; otherwise he fails. Or he will try to draw a line under the letter; having done that, he reads promptly.

Relative Maintenance of Ordered Behavior by Shrinkage of Milieu According to Defect. These alterations of "preserved performances" imply an extraordinary limitation of the environment in which the patient naturally lives. This statement involves a fact which we are later to recognize as a particularly important law of behavior having general validity: *a defective organism achieves ordered behavior only by a shrinkage of its environment in proportion to the defect.*

These modifications in the behavior patterns of a person with a brain injury should be borne in mind in our observations of injured animals. It is to be expected that such subtle changes in animal behavior will often be overlooked, since they have escaped notice even in human behavior. Exactitude is all the more imperative since analogous modifications may impair the animal's capacities.

Tendency to Optimal Performance. Hemianopsia and Formation of Complete Visual Field. The Adjustmental Shifts. Observation of patients with brain injury also teaches us that there is a tendency for the injured organism to *maintain a performance capacity* on the highest possible level, compared to its former capacity. When one performance field is disturbed, the most important performances of that field survive the longest, and tend to be most readily restored. A particularly instructive example of this fact is furnished by the *vision* of hemianoptic patients. If we examine a patient with total destruction of the calcarine cortex of one hemisphere (the central termination of the optic tract), we find that he suffers from hemianopsia, i.e. *total blindness of corresponding halves of the visual field of both eyes.* Even

though this condition appears consistently, under examination with a perimeter, the behavior of these patients in everyday life fails to indicate that they see nothing in one half—let us say, the right half—of the visual field. At all events, they recognize objects within an area, where stimulation, during perimetrical examination, is ineffective. Subjectively, they are aware of a somewhat impaired vision, but it is by no means true that they see only one half of the object, or even that they see them less distinctly on one side.

Precise exploration shows that the patients are not limited to half a field of vision, but that their field of vision is arranged around a center like in normals, and that, likewise, the region of the clearest vision lies approximately at this center. As we shall demonstrate later, a visual field of such formation is requisite for the most important visual functions, especially for the perception of objects. That the organism manages to preserve this most important performance, in spite of the defect, is particularly characteristic of the way in which the organism functions in general. Therefore, we should discuss, in greater detail, these conditions which have been very carefully studied.

Apparently the patient perceives stimuli originating in that part of the outer world corresponding to the blind half of his retina. That this part of the retina has not become sensitive to stimulation can be demonstrated by use of the perimeter. Therefore, we can only conclude that these stimuli have been registered with the other part, i.e. the intact half of the retina. Careful investigation actually shows this to be the case. If we present the patient with a series of figures next to each other on a blackboard, and ask him to state which he sees most distinctly, he does not designate, like a normal person, that figure which would register on an area corresponding to the macula, but one which lies a little further to the side. Apparently, that point in the outer world seems clearest to him which is reflected not on the border of the intact retina, where the old macula now lies, but on an area *within* the intact retina. The latter could happen only if the eyes shifted their position from the normal. *Such a displacement can actually be observed.* To possess a visual field which is arranged around a center is of extraordinary importance for vision. An object is clearly seen only if it lies in the center of the visual field which surrounds this object. Normally, when we look at a series of objects in sequence, with the intention of seeing each one clearly, we move our eyes in such a way that the objects in question are always focused on the macula, in which position they always occupy the center of the visual field.

This state of affairs is attained by the displacement of the eyes. Thus, the patient regains clear vision despite the defect of his visual apparatus. That this transformation is an expression of a *tendency toward maintaining optimal performance* is clearly shown by the fact that it occurs only when the calcarine cortex is *completely* destroyed—in other words, when this side of the calcarina is really unable to convey impressions which can be used in the perception of objects.

Modification and Preservation of Performances. The Rules of Adjustmental Shift in Defects. We shall later have occasion to point out corresponding examples in other fields. Surveying all the facts in question we are led to a statement of the following general rules:

1. In case of impairment of a performance field, those performances tend to survive which are most important or necessary with regard to the *functioning of the whole organism*.

2. As long as it is possible that *the needs of the total organism*, with reference to a special performance field, *can be fulfilled* in the usual way, so long will the *premorbid modus operandi be maintained*. If this is impossible, an adjustmental shift occurs, conforming in principle to the first rule.

3. The organism tolerates all those disturbances in other fields which must necessarily result from the adjustmental shift in any one field. Here again the principle is valid, that the whole organism is less handicapped by these disturbances than it would be by the original impairment in the field which is now modified in its function.

4. Finally, we must call attention to a particularly important factor. The shift occurs *suddenly. It is not a result of training, and it happens without the knowledge of the patient*.

This last fact confronts us again very clearly in instances of lesion of the calcarine area. It is impossible to determine, with certainty, at what moment the above modification occurs in these cases. We have no definite information as to how, in the initial state of disturbance, the patient really sees things. But from all

indications, the modification is to be found at the time the patient is again using his visual apparatus effectively. In any event *it is not the result of training*, as the fact of its occurrence without the knowledge of the patient proves. As Fuchs has shown, the patient may, in a special test situation, intentionally look past one side of the object (i.e. the mentioned eye dislocation) because he experiences subjectively that he now sees better—without knowing the reason why. We must leave open the question of whether or not this intentional "looking past" occurs only in the experimental situation. In ordinary life, whenever he "looks at an object," the eyes assume the mentioned displacement, without the patient being at all aware of the fact.

Energy and Performance. Finally, there is the question of the *dependency of performance upon the available energy*. Before presenting the facts, let us introduce the problem with a few brief remarks about the source of this energy. It must be remembered that external stimuli not only initiate the process in the nervous system, but also represent sources of energy. This is true, not only of the stimulus which evokes the most prominent reaction, but for the host of manifold stimuli which are continuously impinging upon the organism. Besides the external stimuli, those which affect the nervous system from within, play a considerable part. I should like to point out especially that the connection between the nervous system and the rest of the body is not to be ignored. We must not overlook the fact that the whole organism presents *one* unit, in which the nervous system, if considered by itself, is only an artifically isolated part. Inasmuch as the nervous system *in vivo* is an integral part of the organism, its sources of energy must be the same as those which sustain the activity of the whole organism. In carrying on this function, individual organs (e.g. the ductless glands) have a specific significance. In order to appreciate the range of the nervous system's functions, we must take into account its special relation to the general sources of energy, such as the nutritional factor, the oxygen content of the blood, etc. Only in this way can we hope to understand the characteristics of the symptomatology in a given case. The symptom analysis suggests a few conclusions:

The available energy supply is constant, within certain limits. If one particular performance requires especially great energy expenditure, some other performance suffers thereby.

Relevant to this, I should like to point out certain facts to which I called attention years ago while I was trying to obtain an understanding of hallucinatory phenomena. At that time I remarked upon the antagonistic character of the energy distribution between sensory and thought performances, which manifests itself in the reduced vividness of our sensory experiences and in our inattentiveness to them during the thought process. A similar antagonism exists between motor and sensory phenomena, between verbal and non-verbal performances, and so on. In these, and similar cases, we can assume that one performance is weakened because the available energy is being used to maintain activity in that mechanism upon which the other performance depends. This becomes particularly evident in pathological conditions. It can readily be assumed that a brain lesion will impede the functioning. Expressed in terms of energy, this means that special energies will become necessary to maintain a function. This assumption is founded upon the observed fact that patients fail in those performances, which they otherwise can accomplish, when performances involving an injured area are simultaneously required of them. If we ask an aphasic patient to read aloud, he may not be able to understand what he reads, because of the impediment of the speech activity. The energy is exhausted in coping with this impediment. But if he reads silently, he may be able to read with full understanding. This dependence of performance on the available energy may manifest itself in a phenomenon which is, at first, rather surprising: *frequently, patients who suffer complete destruction of a field essential to a certain performance, may on the whole be less afflicted than those who suffer only partial destruction.* A patient with hemiamblyopia (a less intensive injury of one calcarine area) is, to a certain extent, actually more disturbed in his vision that a patient with a total destruction of this area. In terms of energy this is easily explainable: The organism tends to function in the accustomed manner, as long as an at least moderately effective performance can be achieved in this way. This is true in minor calcarine lesion, where the afflicted area remains in use. Under these conditions, the energy distribution is the same as before. Because

of this damage to the area, poor vision results. If, on the other hand, one of the calcarine areas is completely destroyed the total amount of energy at the disposal of both calcarinae flows into the *one which is intact.* The flow into the destroyed region is, so to speak, blocked. The high energy charge of the intact side effects a shift of the entire brain activity, so that actually a more efficient result is obtained, at least as far as vision is concerned.

Reference of Symptoms and Performances to the Whole of the Organism. Is the Organism a Whole, and If So, How Can We Recognize It As Such? Analysis of the phenomena resulting from cortical lesion has revealed to us a number of general laws governing the life of the organism. Ever and again, the principle of the close relationship of the individual phenomenon to the "whole" of the organism forces itself upon us. Subsequent considerations will show us that this relationship holds equally well for those performances or symptoms due to injuries to other organs of the body. We should like to stress the fact that the relationship is not at all confined to the phenomena resulting from the function of the cerebral cortex.

But what do we really mean by this word "whole," that we were careful to place in quotation marks? As long as we confine ourselves to a statement of general rules regarding the part-whole-relationship, we can leave the question of the essential nature of the whole untouched. But if we wish to understand an individual performance this is no longer permissible. If we say that the organism tends to modify itself, in spite of the defect, in such a way that those performances which are most important for it are made possible, we are positing certain essential characteristics of the organism, without offering any explanation for the way in which this knowledge has been obtained. Thus, for example, we say that a particular form of vision, or some similar activity, *characterizes* the organism concerned. This procedure is appropriate, because only in this way can we attain knowledge of the general rules of holistic and organismic processes. Yet this remains insufficient. The procedure is always exposed to a certain skepticism regarding these rules. Above all, it is inadequate for an understanding of an individual response, primarily because it is doubtful whether the characteristics we have assumed are in fact "genuine" properties of the organism concerned. In fact, each single performance which we observe introduces anew the question of whether we are dealing with a phenomenon which is really equivalent to an essential characteristic of the organism.

In order to answer this question we must truly know the organism. There can be no doubt that this knowledge is attainable only through the scientific or analytic, "anatomizing" method, that only the empirical data obtained thereby can be considered. To be sure, this analysis may take any one of several forms. It may bring into focus the morphological and physiological organization, or the physical and chemical composition, or the so-called somatic and mental phenomena, and so on. Of course, we cannot simply survey this manifold material and see what sort of a picture of the organism will emerge therefrom. We have to deal first with the more fundamental question of whether, and to what extent, the material yielded by analysis is at all suitable to provide a picture of the organism. We are concerned with the question of what light this material throws upon the performances of the organism; whether or not it impels us to regard the organism as a whole, and if so, how we arrive at a conception of the "whole," as represented in this organism. For this purpose it is immaterial which sort of facts we take as our point of departure. We will connect our discussion with that material which is embodied in the theory of the so-called reflexes. And this will be done because such data seem best fitted to deal with the methodological approach leading to an understanding of the organism.

2.   Preference for abstract versus concrete word meanings in schizophrenic and brain-damaged patients

NORMAN ALVIN MILGRAM

IT IS GENERALLY HELD that of the recognized cognitive abilities, vocabulary fund is least susceptible to disturbance and is, therefore, the most stable index of premorbid functioning in disturbed persons (1, 11, 13). It is also generally held that schizophrenic and brain-damaged patients differ from normals in the use and understanding of words (6, 8, 12, 14, 15). There is, however, no necessary contradiction between these statements. Yacorzynski (16), Goldstein (5, pp. 11–12), Rapaport (10, p. 149), and others have suggested that the stability of word usage in clinical populations is more apparent than real. As Yacorzynski stated the issue, "It appears reasonable to assume that the reason why the vocabulary of the deteriorated individual remains relatively unchanged is because easier methods of reaching the same end results are left to the organism even if the more difficult solutions are no longer available" (16, p. 265). Several experimental studies (2, 3, 7) have confirmed "Yacorzynski's hypothesis" and have shown that while gross word definitions are adequately retained, the more subtle, conceptual usages of words are impaired.

The present study enlarges upon an earlier investigation by Flavell (4) who found that in a special test situation in which S is asked to select the one of two choice words which is "closest in meaning" to a given stimulus word,

SOURCE. Article by Norman Alvin Milgram, "Preference for abstract versus concrete word meanings in schizophrenic and brain-damaged patients" in *Journal of clinical Psychology*, Vol. XV, No. 2, pp. 207–212, April 1959.

normals selected words bearing an abstract or essential meaning relationship to the stimulus word more often than schizophrenics. Flavell's investigation, like the majority of others in this area, dealt with the verbal performance of schizophrenics alone. An investigation of the verbal performance of brain-damaged patients and a comparison of their performance with that of schizophrenics appear warranted both from empirical and theoretical points of view.

Method

The present study compares the preferences of schizophrenic, brain-damaged, and normal Ss for abstract or essential versus concrete or nonessential word meaning relationships. Although the three groups will be equated on vocabulary fund, systematic differences in word usage are expected to emerge, *i.e.*, normals will select abstract meaning relationships more often than schizophrenics or brain-damaged patients. In Flavell's study significant differences between schizophrenics and normals were found only for the total abstract score, but not for the separate abstract or concrete categories. Certain changes from Flavell's procedure are being introduced in the present study to accentuate the preferential weight given each of the separate abstract and concrete word meaning categories by the three groups.

Subjects. Three male groups consisting of 32 schizophrenics, 30 brain-damaged patients, and 20 normals were used. The criteria for selection of the schizophrenic group included (*a*) a psychiatric diagnosis of schizophrenia (paranoid, 24; hebephrenic, 2; catatonic, 2; and chronic, undifferentiated, 2) and (*b*) no neurological involvement, no somatic therapy (insulin coma or electric shock) within the past six months, and no history of lobotomy.

The criteria for the selection of the brain-damaged group included (a) a neurological diagnosis of damage to the cerebral cortex (vascular disease, 9; degenerative disease, 12; chronic brain syndrome, 9) and (b) no previous history of severe mental disturbance and no evidence of psychosis at time of testing.

A final criterion for inclusion in any subject group was the willingness and ability of S to attend to instructions and to follow through with the demands of the testing situation (of which the data reported in the present paper are a small portion). Excluded from this study were litigious paranoid patients and mute catatonic patients who refused to cooper-

ate; also excluded were grossly impaired brain-damaged patients, especially patients with severe aphasia.

The two clinical groups were drawn from the psychiatric and neurological wards of two hospitals of the Veterans Administration. The normals were drawn from the medical wards of one hospital and from the general population outside the hospital. The three groups were equated on age and vocabulary fund as measured by the Vocabulary Subtest of the Wechsler-Bellevue; the vocabulary scores are reported as IQ scores. Data on age, years of formal education, and IQ are shown in Table 1. A statistically significant, but small, difference between normals and the two clinical groups in years of formal education was observed.

Table 1. Age, IQ and Years of Formal Education

Group		Age	IQ	Education
N	M	44.6	116.2	12.0
	SD	(15.2)	(10.0)	(2.7)
S	M	43.1	114.9	10.8
	SD	(13.4)	(15.7)	(3.2)
BD	M	45.6	110.5	11.5
	SD	(15.2)	(17.7)	(3.2)

Procedure

This test (Figure 1) was taken from Flavell (4) with some modifications in procedure and new word items, and consisted of 48 items each containing a stimulus word and two choice words. All the stimulus words were nouns; the choice words were nouns, adjectives, or verbs. On a given item, the stimulus word was related to one of the response words in one of three *abstract* ways and to the other response word in one of four *concrete* ways. The seven different types of relationship between stimulus and response words were as follows:

1. *Synonym (Syn)*, e.g., "car" - "auto."
2. *Supraordinate (Supra)*, e.g., "car" - "vehicle."
3. *Subordinate (Sub)* e.g., "car" - "Ford."
4. *Part-Whole (PW)*, e.g., "car" - "fender"
5. *Adjective (A)*, e.g., "car" - "flashy."
6. *Verb (V)*, e.g., "car" - "drive."
7. *Concrete Context (CC)*, e.g., "car" - "garage."

Of the above seven categories, the first three are considered abstract, essential meaning relationships; the last four are concrete, nonessential

meaning relationships. Each of the abstract categories was paired with each of the concrete categories four times, to make a total of 48 items. In a given item, the stimulus word is related abstractly to one choice word and concretely to the other.[1]

Subjects were tested individually and were instructed to read aloud the stimulus word and to select from the two choice words the "one that means most nearly the same" as the stimulus word. The maximum score for any one abstract category was 16; for a concrete

---

[1] This represents a departure from Flavell who paired each of the eight categories (he used a Homonym category which I discarded in the present study) to each of the other seven, e.g., some items were *Syn-Supra* and *PW-CC*. As a result in his study Ss chose between two abstract or two concrete response alternatives on over 40% of the items. In the present study Ss chose only between an abstract and a concrete response alternative on all items. This change was made to maximize the hypothesized deficit of the experimental groups in choosing responses from each of the separate abstract and concrete categories.

Figure 1. Word Meaning Test (The Abstract Responses are Italicized)

1. Tune — *melody*(S) - sing(V)
2. Electricity — dynamo(CC) - *energy* (SP)
3. Parcel — *package*(S) - wrapper (PW)
4. Book — page(PW) - *novel*(SB)
5. Salt — *spice*(SP) - sprinkle (V)
6. Hobby — interesting(A) - *stamps*(SB)
7. Harbor — ships(CC) - *bay*(S)
8. Hour — *time*(SP) - minute (PW)
9. Rabbit — ears(PW) - *bunny*(S)
10. Knife — *dagger*(SB) - blade (PW)
11. Blanket — warm(A) - *cover*(S)
12. Dog — *poodle*(SB) - bark(V)
13. Sickness — hospital(CC) - *illness* (S)
14. Mother — *parent*(SP) - dear(A)
15. Bird — nest(CC) - *robin*(SB)
16. Stairs — *steps*(S) - climb(V)
17. Hat — head(CC) - *clothing* (SP)
18. Dream — *nightmare*(SB) - sleep (CC)
19. Mountain — high(A) - *Rockies*(SB)
20. Shirt — *garment*(SP) - sleeve (PW)
21. Silk — smooth(A) - *material* (SP)
22. Bacon — *meat*(SP) - fry(V)
23. Auto — drive(V) - *ford*(SB)

24. Stove — *oven*(S) - hot(A)
25. Boat — *canoe*(SB) - row(V)
26. Violin — strings(PW) - *fiddle* (S)
27. Flower — garden(CC) - *rose*(SB)
28. Water — *liquid*(SP) - drink(V)
29. Eggs — hen(CC) - *food*(SP)
30. King — crown(CC) - *monarch* (S)
31. Tree — *Pine*(SB) - branch (PW)
32. Camera — *equipment*(SP) - lens (PW)
33. Weight — heavy(A) - *ton*(SB)
34. Winter — *season*(SP) - cold(A)
35. Wagon — wheel(PW) - *cart*(S)
36. Candy — *gumdrop*(SB) - sweet (A)
37. String — tie(V) - *twine*(S)
38. Breakfast — morning(CC) - *meal* (SP)
39. Saloon — *tavern*(S) - noisy(A)
40. River — *Mississippi*(SB) - flow (V)
41. World — *globe*(S) - round(A)
42. Bureau — drawer(PW) - *furniture*(SP)
43. Lake — swim(V) - *pond*(S)
44. Pocketbook — *purse*(S) - money(CC)
45. Moon — shine(V) - *planet*(SP)
46. Container — *box*(SB) - top(PW)
47. Grandmother — old(A) - *relative*(SP)
48. Direction — *north*(SB) - compass (CC)

category, 12. Thus, for example, if a S chose only abstractly related choice words, his abstract score was 48.

Results and Discussion

The results summarized in Table 2 confirm the hypothesis that normals select abstract word meaning relationships more than schizophrenics and brain-damaged patients. It is also observed that schizophrenics are significantly superior to the brain-damaged patients in this regard. The total mean scores for the groups were 42.60, 38.38, and 31.74, respectively. With respect to the separate response categories, normals and schizophrenics chose significantly more abstract and fewer concrete words than did brain-damaged patients; significant differences between normals and schizophrenics were obtained on all but two categories, PW and CC. It is concluded that a person may retain the ability to summon up creditable definitions to words without retaining the ability to discriminate the abstract-concrete or essential-nonessential continuum of word meaning. This conclusion applies to both experimental groups, but more especially to the brain-damaged group. Only five of the 30 brain-damaged patients received scores as high or higher than the lowest score obtained by a normal; the overlap between schizophrenics and normals was considerably greater with 19 of 32 schizophrenics scoring higher than the lowest normal.

Rank-order correlation coefficients were computed for the three groups between age and abstract scores and were significant only for the schizophrenic group (.30, significant at .05 level, one tail test). The explanation for this inverse relationship between verbal age and

Table 2. Means and Standard Deviations of Scores of Abstract and Concrete Categories

Category		Normals	Schiz.	Brain-Dam.	P N > Schiz.	P Schiz. > BD
Total Abstract Score	M	42.60	38.38	31.84	<.01*	<.001
	SD	3.21	7.56	7.07		
Synonym	M	15.35	13.97	11.47	<.001	<.001
	SD	.81	2.28	2.68		
Supraordinate	M	14.50	13.22	11.07	<.05	<.02
	SD	1.50	2.97	3.20		
Subordinate	M	12.75	11.19	9.30	<.05	<.02
	SD	1.86	3.18	2.76		
Part-Whole	M	1.75	2.00	3.30	ns.	<.05
	SD	1.65	1.69	2.44		
Adjective	M	1.60	3.19	4.77	<.01	<.02
	SD	1.47	2.65	2.38		
Verb	M	.55	2.09	3.90	<.001	<.01
	SD	1.00	1.96	2.34		
Concrete Context	M	1.50	2.34	4.30	ns.	<.01
	SD	1.28	2.44	2.04		

* The *t* Test with Snedecor's Correction was used because the assumption of homogeneity was untenable for the eight comparisons made above.

abstractive ability may lie in the fact that chronicity of illness and hospitalization in the schizophrenics are a direct function of age. The older schizophrenics have had lengthy hospitalizations, while the younger schizophrenics have suffered from disturbances of relatively recent onset. Hence, the older, more chronically ill and deteriorated patients failed to do as well in the conceptual use of words as the younger, more acute patients. This explanation is consistent with Flavell's finding of a positive relationship between abstractive ability and adequacy of everyday social interaction. While no measures of social interaction were made in this study, clinical observation showed the older, more chronically ill schizophrenics to be in less adequate social contact and interaction than the younger schizophrenics. Rabin, King, and Ehrmann (9) have also showed that long-term schizophrenics were significantly lower than normals and short-term schizophrenics on three measures of vocabulary performance.

Rank-order correlation coefficients between IQ and abstractive ability were also computed. These correlations were highly significant (.001 level) for the normals and the schizophrenics (.67 and .77 respectively), but were not for the brain-damaged group (.25). These findings further highlight the discrepancy in the brain-damaged group between the ability to retain the approximate definitions to words and the ability to use words conceptually. For the normals and schizophrenics, a high vocabulary score is generally associated with a high abstract score; for the brain-damaged patients a high score in vocabulary may be earned by a person with considerable deficit in cognitive abilities as a result of which he earns a low score on a verbal conceptual task.

When a comparison is made of the response hierarchy of each group, it is noted that *Syn*, *Supra*, and *Sub* were chosen in descending order of frequency by the three groups, except that the difference between *Syn* and *Supra* did not reach significance for the two clinical groups. Whether this represents the hierarchy of meaning relationships in the general population of adult thinkers is unanswered. It should be noted, however, that Flavell observed the same hierarchy with his groups, although his items and scoring procedure[2] differed from those used in the present study.

Turning to the concrete categories, no such hierarchy prevailed. V was chosen least frequently by normals, of the four concrete categories. A was chosen most frequently by the two clinical groups and CC was chosen second in frequency to A by the brain-damaged group. All other differences were not significant. A possible explanation of the preference for A is that adjectives have a strong sensory stimulus value; normal adults are able to inhibit the tendency to respond to this stimulus and are able to follow the logically determined habits of word meaning; schizophrenics and brain-damaged patients are less able to inhibit this tendency, hence they are more likely to choose an adjective over an abstractly related word than they are to choose one of the other types of concretely related word categories.

Summary

The present study compared the preferences of schizophrenics, brain-damaged patients, and normals for abstract or essential versus concrete or nonessential word meaning relationships. Although these three groups were presumably equated in ability for defining words (Vocabulary Subtest scores), both schizophrenic and brain-damaged patients chose fewer abstractly related words than normals. This disturbance in the abstract-concrete continuum of word meaning was greater and more consistently observed in the brain-damaged group than in the schizophrenic group. Results were interpreted as supporting "Yacorzynski's hypothesis."

---

[2] For Flavell, a category score represented the preference of items of that category over items of all other categories, abstract or concrete. In the present study an abstract category score represents the preference of items of that category over items of the four concrete categories only; conversely concrete items were matched only with abstract items.

REFERENCES

1. Babcock, Harriet. An experiment in the measurement of mental deterioration. *Arch. Psychol.*, 1930, No. 117.
2. Chodorkoff, B. and Mussen, P. Qualitative aspects of the vocabulary responses of normals and schizophrenics. *J. consult. Psychol.*, 1952, **16**, 43–48.
3. Feifel, H. Qualitative differences in the vocabulary responses of normals and abnormals. *Genet. Psychol. Monogr.*, 1949, 39, 151–204.
4. Flavell, J. Abstract thinking and social behavior in schizophrena. *J. abn. soc. Psychol.*, 1956, **52**, 208–211.
5. Goldstein, K. and Scheerer, M. Abstract and concrete behavior: an experimental study with special tests. *Psychol. Monogr.*, 1941, **53**, No. 2.
6. Goldstein, K. Methodological approach to the study of schizophrenic thought disorder. In J. S. Kasanin (Ed.) *Language and thought in schizophrenia.* Berkeley, Calif.: Univ. of Calif. Press, 1944, 17–40.
7. Harrington, R. and Ehrmann, J. C. Complexity of response as a factor in the vocabulary performance of schizophrenics, *J. abn. soc. Psychol.*, 1954, 49, 362–364.
8. Moran, L. J. Vocabulary knowledge and usage among normal and schizophrenic subjects. *Psychol. Monogr.*, 1953, **67**, No. 20.
9. Rabin, A. L., King, G. F. and Ehrmann, J. C. Vocabulary performance of short-term and long-term schizophrenics. *J. consult. Psychol.*, 1955, **50**, 255–258.
10. Rapaport, D. *Diagnostic psychological testing.* Chicago: Year Book Publishers, 1945, Vol. I.
11. Schwartz, R. Mental deterioration in dementia praecox. *Amer. J. Psychiat.*, 1932, **12**, 555–560.
12. Vigotsky, L. S. Thought in schizophrenia. *Arch. Neurol. Psychiat.*, 1934, **31**, 1063–1077.
13. Wechsler, D. *The measurement of adult intelligence.* (3rd Ed.) Baltimore: Williams & Wilkins, 1944.
14. Werner, H. *Comparative psychology of mental development.* Chicago: Follett, 1948.
15. White, W. A. The language of schizophrenia. *Arch. Neurol. Psychiat.*, 1926, **16**, 395–413.
16. Yacorzynski, G. K. An evaluation of the postulates underlying the Babcock Deterioration Test. *Psychol. Rev.*, 1941, **48**, 261–267.

3. The theory of universal ambiguity

ANDRAS ANGYAL

IN DISCUSSING INTEGRATION, I have described how richness and range are achieved in personality through a multiple utilization of a relatively small number of components, through their successive reordering into a variety of patterns. Because of this mode of functioning, personality must be viewed as a multivalent, pluralistic organization. Such a description, however, is not sufficient since it side steps the main issue. Man is to be understood not in terms of any specific traits he possesses, or any specific patterns they form, but in terms of the overall pattern that organizes these traits and their multiple interconnections. In the course of my work with neurotic patients I have been searching for a conceptualization of personality adequate for the practical tasks of education and therapy. The most significant general statement I am able to make as a result of this search is that while personality is pluralistic in the detail of its functioning, in its broad outline it is a *dualistic* organization.

There is no life course in which every developmental experience has been traumatic nor one from which all deleterious influences have been absent. There are both healthy and traumatic features in every child's environment and in his relations with it; the early attempts at relating oneself to the world succeed in part, and in part fail. As a result, the personality of the child develops simultaneously around two nuclei, forms two patterns. One of them may be underdeveloped but it is never absent. One pattern is based on isolation and its derivatives:

SOURCE. Andras Angyal, "The theory of universal ambiguity," in *Neurosis and Treatment: A Holistic Theory*, Chapter 8, pp. 99–115. Edited by E. Hanfmann and R. M. Jones. New York: Wiley, 1965.

feelings of helplessness, unlovableness, and doubts about one's prospects. The other is based on the confidence that a modicum of one's autonomous and homonomous strivings may be realized more or less directly. The overall system principle of the human personality, the guiding pattern of life composed of the two basic tendencies, does not change when the neurotic orientation comes into being. Whether in health or in neurosis, our life is guided by the same unalterable superordinate trends, autonomy and homonomy. But when two opposite sets of convictions have been formed about the nature of the world and the self, these trends function in a setting of very different expectations.

One outlook, while not indiscriminate optimism, reflects the confidence that the "supplies" for one's basic needs exist in the world and that one is both adequate and worthy of obtaining these "supplies." The neurotic belief is that these conditions are not available or that they can be made available only by extremely complicated and indirect methods. Thus, in one way of life, the two basic human propensities function in an atmosphere of hope, confidence, trust, or faith, if you like. In the other, the propelling forces are the same, but they function in an atmosphere of diffidence, mistrust, and lack of faith. Phenomenological concepts such as hope, trust, and faith have not yet achieved a clear position in systematic theorizing, but no one can doubt that these states, as well as their opposites, do exist and are extraordinarily potent irrespective of whether or not they can be translated into current psychological concepts. Confidence and diffidence, conviction and doubt that human life is livable in this world, mark the "great divide," the point at which our path bifurcates and our life acquires its dual organization and its basic existential conflict.

The differences between the two ways of life, or the two "worlds" that are elaborated from the two nuclear convictions, have been stated, by implication, in the description of the main features of neurosis. They shall be briefly recapitulated here. The two patterns differ not only in their system principle but also in their integrational features. Although each can be tightly organized, the organization of the neurotic system bears the imprint of its origin in the state of isolation and anxiety; several of its features represent defects or integration along the dimensions of depth, progression, and breadth.

One of the two worlds is real, the other fictitious. This is not, strictly speaking, due to the truth or falsehood of the assumptions governing each system; both of them are expressions of faith and neither can be validly proved. But doubt and anxiety have the effect of making the images developed to elaborate or to disguise the basic neurotic assumptions ever more compelling and indiscriminate, so that reality easily falls victim to fantasy. In the healthy system, the basic assumptions do not call for disguises, and the confidence in one's ability to manage in the world as it is permits a realistic perception of the negative aspects of life.

The world visualized in the healthy pattern feels like one's home; it is rich in opportunities, lawfully ordered, and meaningfully related to the person. The world of neurosis is foreign and threatening, full of obstacles and dangers, lawless, capricious, a chaos rather than a cosmos. The consequences of this difference are many. In the "good" world it is possible and rewarding to pursue positive goals which one desires and enjoys; in the threatening world the main concern and joy must be to escape danger. The difference between working for and working against something is reflected in the fixed predominance of fear and anger in the neurotic as against the more positive feeling tone and the wider range of normal emotions. Communication and the absence of it are crucial for contact both with people and things. Love and community formation are easy in the one pattern, difficult or impossible in the other. In the healthy orientation it is possible to perceive wholes, to see things in a wide perspective,

to receive impressions which point beyond the datum itself; continuity and intentionality make the world meaningful. In the neurotic orientation, the things and events of the world appear as isolated items or fragments. The long view is replaced by short sightedness; the fresh outlook yields to a stereotyped and biased one. Impressions cannot be fully valued and enjoyed, because their pointing quality, their "message character," is lost; the result is a truncated experience.

The person himself is also transformed by the negative fantasies about himself and by assuming poses and characteristics that are not genuine and are meant to disguise his imagined lack of worth. While in the confident orientation the person feels, thinks, and speaks as he is and not as he is "supposed" to be, the neurotic, having settled for appearances, acts for the sake of effect. He is not in touch with his real wishes, and the main function of his thoughts and acts is more often to "prove" than to enjoy. Since the connection between the expression and that which is expressed has been multiply twisted, neurotic behavior has no depth; it is superficial and inexpressive. A vivid example of settling for appearances is one patient's boyhood memory of how frustrated he was when a swimming instructor wanted him to take his feet off the ground. The boy finally cried in exasperation, "But *it looks like* swimming with just my arms, and nobody can see my legs under the water." He was genuinely nonplussed when the instructor did not accept his solution. This patient's adult life was, to all outward appearances, filled with exemplary achievements. It was only in his sex life that he was faced with the insufficiency of merely "looking" successful.

Integration along the dimension of progression is also disturbed in neurosis. In the healthy orientation the means are an organic part of the total activity and are positively valued both as a way to the goal and in their own right as part of a whole. In the neurotic system everything is a means toward some vague end which is secretly believed to be unreachable. Means activities are thereby devalued, and so is the present as such, because everything is merely preliminary. If the neurotic is not dreaming about some value lost in the past, he is constantly hurrying and expecting. The present is related to his future no more organically than the means are related to his goals or his personal trends to expression. Both in experience and in his actions the neurotic leads an impoverished disintegrated existence. Many of his actions conflict with his other impulses and take no account of the surrounding realities; such incongruous, disharmonious actions are necessarily self-defeating.

Personality as an Ambiguous Gestalt

In the psychoanalytic theory of complexes these interfering unconscious forces are not thought of as single repressed impulses; complexes are partial organizations. The hypothesis of duality which I propose extends the use of the organizational principle by assuming the existence, not of discrete complexes, but of more inclusive systems competing for influence on the person's conduct of his life.

We live, all of us, in two worlds, not in one, but we don't live in these worlds simultaneously. Health and neurosis are not segments of personality so that one might be neurotic in some aspects of one's life and healthy in others at the same time. The two patterns which are almost mirror reversals of each other, two alternate ways in which our basic trends can seek expression, are both total organizations. Health and illness are determined by the dominance of one of the two systems. When one system becomes dominant, it tends to organize the total field, the total life of the person, since every Gestalt tends toward a complete realization of its system principle. The healthy aspects do not remain healthy, and the neurotic ones do not remain neurotic when the opposite organization gains dominance. The parts in a system function as such not through their imminent qualities but through their positional values; they change their mode of functioning when they become parts of a different system. Health and neurosis are to be thought of as two organized processes, two dynamic Gestalts organizing the same material, so that each item has a position within two different patterns. There can be shifts between the two, lasting or short lived, in either direction, but at any given moment the person is either healthy or neurotic, depending on which system is dominant.

This mode of coexistence of the two systems cannot be represented by depicting them side by side or by picturing one as enclosed in the other (as complexes or repressed conflicts are sometimes represented). They coexist, as it were, within each other. The dynamic aspect of the relationship, the coexistence of two fields of forces, can be expressed through the following metaphor: If a straight elastic rod is bent to form a loop, it retains its resiliency, a molecular arrangement that will straighten it out again as soon as the constraining force is removed. While it is bent, two organizations are present: the one that keeps it bent and the one that could straighten it out. Depending on which system is stronger the arrangement of the parts will be straight or crooked. This metaphor expresses quite well the simultaneous existence of two competing dynamic factors and the primacy of the ever-present factor of health, but it does justice neither to the complex articulation of the two systems, nor to the all-or-none character of their dominance.

In these respects the dual personality organization is represented much more adequately by being likened to a visual *ambiguous Gestalt* of the kind you find reproduced in treatises on visual perception. In the one most frequently seen the spatial arrangement is such that the picture may be perceived as representing either a black vase on a white background or two white faces in profile, turned toward each other. The basis for both organizations is there, but only one of the two can be perceived at any given moment. When a shift occurs, what was seen as the figure becomes the background, and each item of the spatial arrangement acquires a new meaning as part of a representation of a different object; the two images never mix. Because of its dual organization human life similarly is an ambiguous Gestalt, each part process having a different function and meaning, depending on whether it takes place within the Gestalt of health or the Gestalt of neurosis. Everything in life has a double meaning—hence universal ambiguity.

The theory of universal ambiguity has far-reaching consequences for the theory and therapy of neurosis. It precludes the conception of neurosis as a rotten part of a healthy apple, or a limited segregated growth within the person, a plant that can be pulled out by the roots without disturbing or changing the rest of the personality. The neurotic person is neurotic throughout, in every area of his life, in all the crannies and crevices of his existence.

Conversely, one cannot say that there is in anyone only an element or segment of personality that is healthy. One is healthy throughout and this health extends over one's entire existence, down to the most distorted forms of behavior and the most troublesome symptoms. The so-called "healthy core," the patient's real self, will not be found stuck away in some distant or hidden region of his personality; it is to be found right there, where it is least expected. Health is present potentially in its full power in the most destructive, most baneful, most shameful behavior.

As a boy, one patient felt compelled to drink his own urine. Later he managed, with the aid of a contraption of his own invention, the difficult feat of performing fellatio on himself. The most agonizing paroxysms of shame accompanied these revelations, which demonstrated his isolation, his morbid preoccupation with himself, and the fantastic indirections he felt were necessary to achieve gratification. Yet the same behavior expressed diverse "completion" and "fulfillment" motives: "I could have belonged in the family circle only if I had given up the right to be alone; still the circle had to be completed, so I made my own." These distortions also expressed the tendency to experience sensuality to its fullest and a determined wish to affirm his uniqueness in the face of tempting conventional compromises.

In an ambiguous Gestalt, the parts do not belong independently to one pattern or another. All parts belong to both patterns and have their function assigned to them by the currently dominant system principle. There is therefore no motivational force that the person has to discard in therapy. If the pattern of health becomes dominant, the problematic factors will find their places within it in a system-consistent fashion. I do not mean that, for instance, a neurotic headache as such can find a comfortable niche in a healthy organization. I mean that whatever attitude the headache is expressing will fit constructively into the healthy pattern, filling a vital role and not being merely tolerated, and then this attitude will not be expressed through headaches. One of the frequent obstacles to therapy is that the patient conceives of the process of getting well as getting rid of something within him. This is like tearing away a part of himself, and he cannot wish it wholeheartedly. Alternately he may conceive of the therapeutic goal as becoming reconciled to an irremovable handicap

or defect and learning to live with it, not a very inspiring prospect. Both conceptions are based on the idea of a segmental disturbance which can be removed or kept but not changed. Viewing neurosis as an organization provides a basis for a different conception of therapy, which will be discussed later.

The dual organization of human life, with one or the other pattern predominating, is often obscured from view because it is overlaid with what might be called the surface or social personality. In this stratum some manifestations of the two basic patterns may form a spurious kind of apparent synthesis. This surface patterning of personality, however, can hardly be considered an organization in its own right. Even in many healthy people this phenomenal level is superficial and devoid of personal roots. Since it is determined largely by compliance or compromise with conventions, such patterning is sometimes almost entirely verbal or composed of routine actions. It serves as a front for others and in part for oneself.

For the neurotic, the existence of this superficial structure provides easy proof that his life is no different from that of anyone else and blunts the secret impact of his feelings of futility. He may climb on a streetcar like anyone else and, even though he feels pushed, competitive, and on the alert, he may carry on a "perfectly normal" conversation all the while with another whose outward behavior is no different from his. The blandness of this culturally accepted cover is in strong contrast to the strength and vitality of either of the underlying organizations. In almost all styles of psychotherapy the patient is encouraged to abandon the superficial level; that is why therapy is the situation of choice for observing the workings of the principle of universal ambiguity.

Shifts of Dominance

The dual patterning of personality cannot become clearly visible, even to observation that penetrates beyond the surface, as long as one system maintains a strong dominance. The co-existence of two incompatible all-inclusive structures can be clearly and strikingly demonstrated only when a shift takes place between two patterns both of which are well developed and strongly articulated—much as the visual ambiguous Gestalts are revealed only through shifts. Such dramatic, seemingly sudden shifts are rare, but they do happen. Foremost among them are the phenomena of conversion, such as religious conversions exemplified by the reports collected by W. James, those described in some case histories of Alcoholics Anonymous, and the less well-known, spontaneous radical changes which are not formulated by the person in religious terms. No less clear cut is the evidence provided by sudden sweeping personality changes after an accumulation of traumata or an accumulation of insights in therapy. Similarly, some cases of traumatic neurosis and relapse after successful therapy represent shifts from health to neurosis. Cases of hysterical dual personality, though not founded in the basic dual pattern we have described, also demonstrate the possibility of complex alternate organizations coexisting in the same person. Some people, in whom both the healthy and the neurotic systems are strongly organized, report vivid experiences of periodic change of mood and behavior, each mood incorporating one of the two basic orientations.

Shifts cannot be expected to occur if, or as long as, the nondominant pattern is underdeveloped and has a low degree of organization. Consequently the best opportunity for observation of shifts is afforded the therapist at that time in therapy when, the neurotic pattern having been weakened and the healthy one strengthened, both are approximately equal in strength and give marked indications of competing for the patient's allegiance. The strongest empirical support for the hypothesis of the dual organization of personality comes from the observations made at this stage of the therapeutic process. The dynamic effects exerted by each Gestalt as it struggles toward a complete realization of its system principle by eliminating or refitting system-inconsistent elements can be best observed at this time. The resulting shifts are well exemplified by the experience of a patient who visualized his former way of life as a Roman circus arena where he had become very skillful in avoiding the lions, and in nothing else. He felt that in therapy he had learned to spot and reach the exits from the arena, but once he was outside, the doors looked to him "just as inviting in a devilishly compelling way; from the outside they are not exits, they are entrances—and before I know it, there I am right back dodging the lions."

Universal Ambiguity

The ambiguity created by the dual organization of human life is reflected in the fact that, taken outside of its context, every item of human experience and behavior has a double meaning. Language sometimes assigns different terms to the two meanings and sometimes combines them under one term, but regardless of the verbal formulation and its evaluative connotation, the two discernible meanings of any human trait are commonly evaluated in diametrically opposite ways. In the chapter on homonomy we have discussed how the healthy wish to be needed, to be of help, acquires its neurotic counterpart in a compulsive assumption of obligations and how "love" can mean possessiveness. These examples could be multiplied. Dependence, though the term has taken on a pejorative meaning, actually is one aspect of every community formation, an expression of the homonomous trend. Only the dependence that expresses the neurotic feeling of helplessness, and consequently far exceeds the objective necessity for support, merits negative evaluation. Pride is highly thought of when it expresses self-respect and pleasure in real achievement; in some dialects, "proud" is the equivalent of "glad." Yet "pride goes before a fall," and Horney uses the term "pride system" to designate an essential component of neurosis. Submission and surrender both refer to a state of nonassertion of individuality, of losing oneself in something else, but the difference is momentous. One submits to the alien and becomes diminished through submission; one surrenders one's isolation to enter into a larger unit and enlarges one's life.

These examples do not imply that each personal manifestation has only two psychological meanings, only two fixed contexts. Since personality is a multiple organization, each item of behavior can serve as an expression of a variety of motives and be a part of a multitude of subsystems even within the same person. All these multiple meanings, however, are subsystems of one of the two major patterns. This grouping is not an arbitrary classification in terms of the "good-bad" polarity; rather the fact that a linguistic formulation of any human phenomenon can be given positive and negative connotations reflects the ambiguity created by the dual patterning of personality. This ambiguity often functions as an obstacle to communication in the theoretical discussion of human issues. The participants may disagree because in using identical or similar terms they assign to them not only different but practically opposite meanings.

An instructive example of both the dual and plural meanings of an attitude for which our language has but one name is afforded by the analysis of curiosity as it appears in healthy and in unhealthy contexts. Normal curiosity arises from the person's wish to broaden out, to learn about people and things for the sake of increased mastery and participation. Neurotic curiosity has entirely different goals and an entirely different emotional coloring. In one of its forms it is born of a feeling of helplessness; one feels that one does not know how to live and looks enviously at others who seem to be "successful" at it. The purpose of watching them is to find out "how they do it" in order to copy their methods; one does this without any reference to one's own inclinations and competencies, so that the borrowed methods remain inorganic accretions. Success is viewed as being achieved by some trick, not as growing out of one's total conduct of life. Much of the popular "adjustment" literature capitalizes on this neurotic trait; one reads it not to straighten out one's life but to learn the "techniques." The goal of curiosity in this pattern is the appropriation of something belonging to others; it is a method of stealing and one goes about it stealthily. It may well happen that the patient attempts to "steal" something which he actually possesses without knowing it, but this does not change the meaning of his act.

A more striking form of neurotic curiosity is directed defensively and aggressively against the assumed dangerous world. One seeks to "dig up the dirt" to alleviate one's own assumed worthlessness through comparison with the shortcomings of others but even more to protect oneself by storing up ammunition for an attack. One is gathering information that can be used against others, whether or not one is aware of this goal. Some go about it quite openly and make themselves disliked by asking personal questions that are "none of their business."

More often, however, even publicly available information is gathered stealthily, and the person may engage in fantasies of the type "if he only knew that I know," a kind of secret psychological black mailing. He feels both maliciously triumphant and extremely guilty and fearful for having broken into another's privacy and stolen his secrets. This aggressive pattern is an essential component of voyeurism. Yet, in a perverted form the normal wish for human contact is present even in this aggressive form of curiosity. In all such cases that I have known there was an enormous craving to be loved.

"Amalgamation"

When a healthy motive and a neurotic one, each occupying an important position in the system to which it belongs, are aroused or expressed by an identical or strongly analogous behavior pattern, the two meanings of this pattern may coalesce or amalgamate. The pattern can then no longer function alternately now as a part of one organization and now as a part of the other. When the pattern is being utilized in the service of the dominant organization, it activates the meaning which attaches to it in the latent one and an inhibiting stalemate may result. An example of such a situation is provided by some types of fear of success. This fear can arise from a variety of neurotic motives, such as the boy's fear that his father will punish his attempts to become an active adult male. These motives, however, can amalgamate with others having strong roots in the healthy organization. In certain contexts, individual success may be seen by the person as separating him from his "universal background" of which the parents are representatives, thus condemning him to an isolated lonely existence. If this meaning of success is prominent for the person, the force of the neurotic motives is increased by that of the healthy ones and, in therapy, the fear will not yield until *both* its roots have been laid bare. Amalgamation can also take place between two distinct neurotic meanings of a pattern. However, the strength and persistence of some of the most destructive damaging symptoms—of which fear of success is one—often have their source in the amalgamation of the two meanings that represent health and neurosis.

Such was the case of a brilliant and dedicated young scientist whose career was on the verge of being eclipsed when he developed a circumscribed inability to prepare for his doctoral examination. As a child he had suffered from a deep uncertainty about what was expected of him. His father seemed to wish only to be left alone by his son and punished all attempts to attract his attention. The boy embarked early on various research pursuits, an effective and creative way of cultivating certainty and courting expectations. These activities brought gratification and success, but they skirted the issue of the needs and expectations of the loved ones. As he put it, "It was all for *me*." The examination in which he had to meet the expectations of his teachers in order to obtain the degree, a confirmation of his "right to success," brought the issue to a head. The study block, while neurotically self-destructive, was expressive of healthy impulses as well. It reintroduced an element of uncertainty into a pattern that had become excessively centered on establishing certainty, and it covertly expressed his wish to give up his too willful control which permitted no sharing with others.

Defense Mechanisms as Types of System Action

The theory of universal ambiguity represents a radical departure from the customary ways of viewing neurosis and health. It requires a reappraisal and a reformulation of those major concepts which have previously proved useful in the study of personality dynamics, and it makes some of these concepts appear in a new light.

The point can be best illustrated by a consideration of the defense mechanisms. I see the defense mechanisms as processes taking place not between the conscious and unconscious, or between ego, and superego, and id, but between the two major organizations of personality which struggle for dominance. The conflict of these two incompatible orientations, these two ways of adapting to life, is the basic conflict of human existence. Within this framework the processes referred to as defense mechanisms acquire a new significance. They are organizational devices, specific types of system action, through which each system seeks to complete itself in a manner consistent with its system principle and to maintain this organization, thereby preventing the alternate system from reaching a position of dominance.

This conception has two implications. First, it implies that the "defense mechanisms" have two functions: the internal organization of the system and its defense against the alternate one. Both functions can be fulfilled by means of one process. The organizing function is in the forefront when the given system is in a position of dominance; the defensive function becomes prominent when the two systems are in strong competition. Second, this conception implies an essential symmetry in the organizational-defensive maneuvers of the two systems; they maintain themselves and thereby ward off each other with identical or similar means. This symmetry is not complete, for several reasons. The system based on confidence, when it is securely dominant, can maintain this position with a minimum of special devices. It is a relatively self-consistent stable system. The neurotic system, with its double focus on fear and on hope, is not stable even when it is entrenched. It must continue to use many devices to achieve at least a semblance of consistency. Some of these defense mechanisms—those that result in a crass distortion of facts—are not compatible with the principles governing the system of health. Furthermore, the traditional formulation of some of the defense mechanisms obscures those components that are capable of functioning bilaterally, on behalf of either health or neurosis. Reformulations are required to make these components obvious. In spite of these qualifications the proposition stands that defense mechanisms are part and parcel of the dynamics of systems and as such are utilized both by the system of health and by the system of neurosis. I shall demonstrate this proposition with examples of two dynamic processes for only one of which a traditional formulation is available.

In the original formulation of *repression* certain impulses are considered to be made incompatible with the person's sense of self-esteem by parental reflection of socio-cultural sanctions and are therefore excluded from consciousness. According to my theory, the repressed is that which is inconsistent with the dominant organization, whichever it be. Repression remains a very useful concept, but it takes on new properties. It is no longer a one-way affair but a two-way affair. Not only the neurotic feelings and trends but the healthy ones too may be repressed, in this case by the neurotic organization. Both organizations are repressive, in the general sense of the term, because they are incompatible Gestalts, two total patterns struggling for dominance. If one system gains dominance, the other is *eo ipse* subdued or submerged, and this may take the form of excluding it from consciousness, i.e., of repression in the technical sense of the word. This conception is borne out by numerous observations that one can and does repress feelings and wishes that are in no way socially tabooed and are even considered laudable.

One of the mechanisms that come to light in analysis becomes very prominent at the stage when an intensive struggle takes place between neurosis and health. Like many dynamic devices, it has no traditional name. I would call it perversion if this term did not connote sexual perversions, which are unrelated to the process in question. It would also be described as annexation or *appropriation*.

Let us picture a patient who is considered a very warm-hearted person, and let us say that in analysis he discovers in himself a strong tendency to exploit people. He can then say, "My kindness is phony; when I get a person well buttered up I exploit him. I have no real warmth." He may, however, be wrong. His warmth may not be a pretense but a genuine trait that has developed within the context of the health system but is used at times within a neurotic context, for a neurotic purpose. Figuratively speaking, it is unlawfully appropriated by the competing organization and perverted to its uses. This process can take place in reverse as well. A misgiving about therapy frequently expressed by people who feel that they are creative is that they may lose their originality, that they will become flattened out and turn into ordinary John Does. Usually this does not happen, but such misgivings are not entirely unfounded; the energy of the tension created by the neurosis *can* serve socially valuable purposes. If it does happen, the question may be asked whether such an outcome is healthy or neurotic.

In the psychoanalytic literature this question has been much, and inconclusively, debated in relation to sublimation, a concept which can be made to coincide with *one* of the two directions appropriation can take. In terms of my theory, the neurotic pattern appropriated by the healthy system remains neurotic unless its inner structure is changed. Yet it is used for a good purpose. We do not have to assume that all

philanthropists are sincere lovers of mankind. People do good in this world out of quite unrespectable motives. The neurotic's wish to escape from doubt and turmoil can on occasion facilitate constructive decisions. A striking example of a neurotically founded impulse being made to serve health is a suicidal attempt that turns into a plea for help. The very thought of suicide can serve as protection if the person feels that he can bear his suffering because he knows he can stop it at any moment.

I see appropriation, or "perversion," as a very important mechanism, and, like repression, it is clearly a two-way street. It is used to a different extent by different people; those who use it extensively are extremely confusing to others. When in therapy the submerged healthy pattern comes more and more to the fore and the two systems struggle for dominance, each appropriates features that belong to the other and utilizes them for its own purpose.

Id and Ego in the Light of the Theory of Duality

The hypothesis of dual organization of personality establishes a distinction which I consider more basic than the ones between conscious and unconscious or between id, ego, and superego. It cuts across the other divisions and seems to me to make for greater clarity, especially in ordering one's observations of the therapeutic process. Needless to say, the distinction between the conscious and the unconscious remains important; no adequate description of personality dynamics and of the process of therapy can be given without taking into account the consequences of vital processes reaching consciousness, or remaining unsymbolized. However, as I tried to show in discussing repression, the dynamic factors reside in the two systems qua systems; both of them are organizations of the total personality process and consequently both include conscious and unconscious factors.

With regard to the structural division of personality, though I can see good reasons to justify it, I have found that the more I made use in my thinking of the idea of dual organization, the less I had occasion to think in terms of id, ego, and superego. In therapeutic work it is a great advantage for the therapist to be able to talk to his patients essentially in the language of concepts in which the therapist actually thinks, even though translated into the vernacular. I have found that formulations based on my theory made very good sense to the patients, meeting, as it were, their own concepts. On the other hand, I have found the concepts underlying the traditional structural division to be useless in therapeutic conversation, and sometimes worse than useless.

In trying to see how the psychoanalytic concepts could be meaningfully fitted into the cross-cutting framework of my hypothesis so as to retain their theoretical usefulness, I did not have much success with the concepts of id and ego. Since each of the two systems in terms of which I think organizes the total content of personality, id, ego, and superego would have to be present in each. Such doubling of concepts would make sense only if one could ascribe clear-cut differences to each of these three structures, depending on whether each forms a part of the system organized by the confident or by the pessimistic and uncertain expectations. This cannot be done in the case of id and ego without violating their conceptual properties. But if one does not change its properties, the concept of id is altogether incompatible with the holistic point of view. In thinking about personality in terms of its most general trends, which ramify down to specifics, I do not assign a special position to those functions that are physiologically fixed, and even less do I consider them the basis from which all other functions derive. These functions are dynamically important, particularly because of the absolute necessity of satisfying these vital needs, but still they are only a few of the many manifestations of personality. Consequently I can only think of the id as either this special group of functions, or as a totality of functions in a very primitive early state of organization.

The question of how the concept of ego could be related to my system is the most obscure. Ego seems to be, first, the embodiment of the organizational principle as such, the totality of the organizational aspects of all human functions. In this meaning ego participates equally in the two systems I postulate. Both the system of health and the system of neurosis can be strongly and articulately organized, and in both this organization functions also as a defense against the other system. On the other hand, the function of reality testing, also ascribed to the ego, finds a greater development in the system of health than in that of neurosis. Finally, as a source of motivation ego seems to embody the trend to increased autonomy.

Superego: Duality of Conscience

The concept of superego has a more concrete and coherent content; I can think of this structure as a special subsystem of personality without violating either the concept of superego or that of a system. Within the framework I have outlined, the concept of superego would have to be doubled, and I feel that there is a sound empirical basis for doing just that. There is a healthy conscience without which the person is sick, a psychopathic personality, and there is an unhealthy one which makes the person spend his life worrying whether he has stepped on the cracks in the pavement.

It seems to me that in the classical psychoanalytic formulation of the superego, the problem of the healthy conscience is not touched upon. The superego appears as a central accident, a necessary evil; it is not inherent in human nature as such but is an extraneous result of social development, something required not by the individual but only by society. Actually it boils down to fear of punishment or ostracism. The assumption is that, except for this ever-present fear, everyone would break the Ten Commandments and obey the 11th: Thou shalt not get caught. Even when the commands and the punishment for breaking them have been internalized, the superego still represents an external factor, the society as mediated by the parents; it is not an organic growth. In its extreme forms this kind of conscience which flourishes in neurosis and never is totally absent in health, implies the conception of a power that represents the *mythical enemy*, an alien and arbitrary force, an irrational authority. The "superego rules" that emanate from this power become idols or frightening demons.

There is no doubt that fear of punishment lives in all of us and that many of the "moral principles" we feel to be our own originate in this fear, but that is not all there is to conscience. There is another aspect which does not depend on swallowing something that has been forced down one's throat by society, but expresses certain value attitudes inherent in human nature. I derive this factor from the trend toward homonomy, from the need to belong and to identify with persons, groups, or causes. Guilt generated by this conscience may be termed "real guilt." It is not fear but an emotional re-action to having acted against somebody or something with which one is genuinely identi-fied; such an act of disloyalty is also an offense against one's own integrity. The pattern that underlies the experience of real guilt, in spite of the wide cultural variation of its content, is a universal expression of a universal human trend. When acceptance of the "Superego rules" is founded in the homonomous trend, they function (no matter how nonsensical their con-tent) as expressions of the person's own ethical attitudes, and any offense against them is guilt laden.

A patient told me of a childhood event about which he felt most ashamed and guilty. He was Jewish and lived in a neighborhood where he was exposed to some very painful scenes in the street. There was an old man in the neighbor-hood who made his living by teaching Hebrew and who was apparently intellectually limited or peculiar in some other way. He was the target of non-Jewish children who often made fun of him. Once my patient was caught in a crowd of these children as they were shouting, "Jew, Jew" and throwing stones at the old man, who was running away crying. My patient panicked and in his anxiety started running and shouting with the children. He was closely identified with the Jewish group and with certain features of Judaism, but on this occa-sion his fear got the better of him and he acted against the things he was devoted to.

This anecdote illustrates the central phenome-non of real guilt: the betrayal of somebody or something one loves. This is also a self-betrayal, because one acts not in line with one's genuine values but out of one's weakness, one's fear. Usually hate is also involved—in the case I have described there was not only love but also anger against the community which exposed its members to threat—but the presence of a positive tie is the necessary precondition of real guilt. An act directed against somebody who is an enemy, and nothing but an enemy, would not arouse guilt. But real people rarely live up to the qualifications of the mythical enemy. Even in those whom we hate we can usually see something that represents a pos-sibility for human contact, and we can con-sequently feel a measure of guilt toward them.

Guilt based on love is radically different from guilt based on fear of retaliation, but in many instances the two are so closely interwoven that it is useful to have a term which covers the whole complex. Both kinds of guilt feelings can be called superego functions; the term conscience, however should be reserved for the pattern which underlies the experience of real guilt. To disentangle the different roots of guilt feelings is not simple. In every course of therapy a great deal of effort must be devoted to this task and to working out the problems of con-science and guilt. Even if someone feels guilty because he engages in masturbation, it is not enough to try and reassure him, e.g., by giving him statistics of its incidence or other pertinent information. The correct information should be given, and it does bring relief, but that is not the end of the story. Before getting this in-formation the patient was convinced that he was doing something evil and yet he continued doing it, so there is still the issue of guilt to deal with, the issue of having acted against the wishes and beliefs of those whom one loved.

In therapy it is necessary to disentangle the various aspects of guilt because one cannot treat all guilt indiscriminately by assuaging it, passing it off as unimportant, or citing extenuat-ing circumstances. We have the double task of freeing the patient from pangs of "conscience" which are ultimately based on irrational fears, and of awakening and strengthening his real conscience, making him feel real guilt. This second goal is fully as important as the first, if not more so. The patient's insight, accom-panied by a feeling of guilt, into the nature of his neurosis as a self-betrayal and a betrayal is a necessary step in the development of his mo-tivation for reconstructing his life.

The Dual Source of Anxiety

In conclusion a word about the position of anxiety within the dual organization of person-ality. Anxiety arises not only out of the state of isolation but also out of anticipating such a state. Consequently anxiety will appear when-ever the dominant organization is threatened with dissolution, regardless of whether the threat is directed against the pattern of neurosis or health. This is not as paradoxical as it may sound, if one recalls that both systems aim at fulfilling the basic human trends and are perceived as ways toward that goal. Although only in the healthy pattern are human purposes actually being realized, the entrenched neurotic pattern nurses the dim hope that they may be realized yet. A threat to the position of dominance of either pattern by its underdeveloped or subordinated alter-system is a threat to the only known path away from isolation and toward fulfillment. Hence anxiety, though phenomenologically undistinguishable, can arise from either of the two opposite camps. Freud's hesitancy and change in his formulation of anxiety is significant in this connection: there is good empirical basis for equating anxiety both with the (transformed) repressed content and with the reaction of the repressor to the threat of the repressed.

Anxiety signals the existence of a threat to whichever system is dominant, and leads to the enhancement of its self-protective measures. Thus it serves indiscriminately as a safeguard of the status quo. Those for whom the dominance of the pattern of health has been a hard-won position often find that sensitivity to anxious feelings is the best sentinel against the re-encroachment of the neurosis and an effective reminder that only challenges husband confidence. When the issue is to exchange neurosis for health, little progress can be made if anxiety is quickly allowed to initiate defensive measures which serve to protect and consolidate the old pattern. To collaborate with anxiety in this case means to make our first enemy our last ally.

4. Some basic propositions of a growth and self-actualization psychology

A. H. MASLOW

WHEN THE PHILOSOPHY OF MAN (his nature, his goals, his potentialities, his fulfillment) changes, then everything changes. Not only the philosophy of politics, of economics, of ethics and values, of interpersonal relations and of history itself change, but also the philosophy of education, the theory of how to help men become what they can and deeply need to become.

We are now in the middle of such a change in the conception of man's capacities, potentialities and goals. A new vision is emerging of the possibilities of man and of his destiny, and its implications are many not only for our conceptions of education, but also for science, politics, literature, economics, religion, and even our conceptions of the non-human world.

I think it is finally possible to begin to delineate this view of human nature as a total, single, comprehensive system of psychology even though much of it has arisen as a reaction *against* the limitations (as philosophies of human nature) of the two most comprehensive psychologies now available, behaviorism, or associationism and classical, Freudian psychoanalysis. Finding a single label for it is still a difficult task, perhaps a premature one. I have called it the "holistic-dynamic" psychology to express my conviction about its major roots. Some have called it "organismic," following Goldstein. Sutich and others are calling it the

SOURCE. Article by A. H. Maslow, "Some basic propositions of a growth and self-actualization psychology," in *Perceiving, behaving, becoming: a new focus for education.*" (1962 Yearbook of Association for Supervision and Curriculum Development, Washington, D.C.)

"self-psychology." We shall see. My own guess is that, in a few decades, if it remains suitably eclectic and comprehensive, it will be called simply "psychology."

I think I can be of most service by writing primarily for myself and out of my own work rather than from that of other thinkers, even though I am sure that the areas of agreement among them are very large. A selection of works of this "third force" is listed in the references. Because of space limitation, I will present only some of the major propositions of this point of view, especially those of importance to the educator. In general, I should warn the reader that at many points I am out ahead of the data, sometimes *way* out.

1. We have, each one of us, an essential inner nature which is intrinsic, given, "natural" and, usually, very resistant to change.

It makes sense to speak here of the hereditary, constitutional and very early acquired roots of the *individual* self, even though this biological determination of self is only partial, and far too complex to describe simply. In any case, this is "raw material" rather than finished product, to be reacted to by the person, by his significant others, by his environment, etc.

I include in this essential inner nature instinctoid needs, capacities, talents, anatomical equipment, physiological balances, prenatal and natal injuries, and traumata to the neonatus. Whether defense and coping mechanisms, "style of life," and other characterological traits, all shaped in the first few years of life, should be included, is still a matter for discussion. I would say "yes" and proceed on the assumption that this raw material very quickly starts growing into a self as it meets the world outside and begins to have transactions with it.

2. Each person's inner nature has some characteristics which all other selves have (species-wide) and some which are unique to the person (idiosyncratic). The need for love characterizes every human being that is born (although it can disappear later under certain circumstances). Musical genius, however, is given to very few and these differ markedly from each other in style, e.g., Mozart and Debussy.

3. It is possible to study this inner nature scientifically and objectively (that is, with the right kind of "science") and to discover what it is like (*discover*—not invent or construct). It is also possible to do this subjectively, by inner search and by psychotherapy, and the two enterprises supplement and support each other.

4. Even though weak, this inner nature rarely disappears or dies, in the usual person, in the United States (such disappearance or dying is possible, however). It persists underground, unconsciously, even though denied and repressed. Like the voice of the intellect, it speaks softly, but it *will* be heard, even if in a distorted form. That is, it has a dynamic force of its own, pressing always for open, uninhibited expression. Effort must be used in its suppression or repression, from which fatigue can result. This force is one main aspect of the "will to health," the urge to grow, the pressure to self-actualization, the quest for one's identity. It is this that makes psychotherapy, education and self-improvement possible in principle.

5. However, this inner core, or self, grows into adulthood only partly by (objective or subjective) discovery, uncovering and acceptance of what is "there" beforehand. Partly it is also a creation of the person himself. Life is a continual series of choices for the individual in which a main determinant of choice is the person as he already is (including his goals for himself, his courage or fear, his feeling of responsibility, his ego-strength or "will power," etc.). We can no longer think of the person as "fully determined" where this phrase implies "determined only by forces external to the person." The person, insofar as he *is* a real person, is his own main determinant. Every person is, in part, "his own project," and makes himself.

6. No psychological health is possible unless this essential core of the person is fundamentally accepted, loved and respected by others and by himself (the converse is not necessarily true, i.e., that if the core is respected, etc., then psychological health must result, since other prerequisite conditions must also be satisfied).

The psychological health of the chronologically immature is called healthy growth. The psychological health of the adult is called variously, self-fulfillment, emotional maturity, individuation, productiveness, self-actualization, etc.

Healthy growth is conceptually subordinate, for it is usually defined now as "growth toward self-actualization," etc. Some psychologists speak simply in terms of one overarching goal or end, or tendency of human development, considering all immature growth phenomena to be only steps along the path of self-actualization (5, 11).

Self-actualization is defined in various ways, but a solid core of agreement is perceptible. All definitions accept or imply: (*a*) Acceptance and expression of the inner core or self, i.e., actualization of these latent capacities and potentialities, "full functioning," availability of the human and personal essence, and (*b*) minimal presence of ill health, neurosis, psychosis, of loss or diminution of the basic human and personal capacities.

7. If this essential core (inner nature) of the person is frustrated, denied or suppressed, sickness results, sometimes in obvious forms, sometimes in subtle and devious forms, sometimes immediately, sometimes later. These psychological illnesses include many more than those listed by the American Psychiatric Association. For instance, the character disorders and disturbances are now seen as far more important for the fate of the world than the classical neuroses or even the psychoses. From this new point of view, new kinds of illness are most dangerous, e.g., "the diminished or stunted person," i.e., the loss of any of the defining characteristics of humanness, or personhood, the failure to grow to one's potential; valuelessness (see proposition 19); etc.

That is, general illness of the personality is seen as any falling short of growth, or of self-actualization. And the main source of illness (although not the only one) is seen as frustration of the basic needs, of idiosyncratic potentials, of expression of the self, and of the tendency of the person to grow in his own style, especially in the early years of life.

8. This inner nature, as much as we know of it so far, is definitely not "evil," but is either

what we adults in our culture call "good" or else it is neutral. The most accurate way to express this is to say it is "prior to good and evil." There is little question about this if we speak of the inner nature of the infant and child. The statement is much more complex if we speak of the "infant" as he still exists in the adult.

This conclusion is supported by all the truth-revealing and uncovering techniques that have anything to do with human nature: psychotherapy, objective science, subjective science, education and art. For instance, uncovering therapy lessens hostility, fear, greed, etc., and increases love, courage, creativeness, kindness, ultruism, etc., leading us to the conclusion that the latter are "deeper" more natural, and more basic than the former, i.e., that what we call "bad" behavior is lessened or removed by uncovering, while what we call "good" behavior is strengthened and fostered by uncovering.

9. "Evil" behavior has mostly referred to unwarranted hostility, cruelty, destructiveness, aggressiveness. This we do not know enough about. To the degree that this quality of hostility is instinctoid, mankind has one kind of future. To the degree that it is reactive (a response to bad treatment), mankind has a very different kind of future. My opinion is that the weight of the evidence so far indicates that *destructive* hostility is reactive, because uncovering therapy reduces it and changes its quality into "healthy" self-affirmation, forcefulness, righteous indignation, etc. In any case, the *ability* to be aggressive and angry is found in all self-actualizing people, who are able to let it flow forth freely when the external situation "calls for" it.

The situation in children is far more complex. At the very least, we know that the healthy child is also able to be justifiably angry, self-protecting and self-affirming, i.e., reactive aggression. Presumably, then, a child should learn not only how to control his anger, but also how and when to express it.

10. This inner core, even though it is biologically based and "instinctoid," is weak rather than strong. It is easily overcome, suppressed or repressed. It may even be killed off permanently. Humans no longer have instincts in the animal sense, powerful, unmistakable inner voices which tell them unequivocally what to do, when, where, how and with whom. All that we have left are instinct-remnants. And furthermore, these are weak, subtle and delicate, very

easily drowned out by learning, by cultural expectations, by fear, by disapproval, etc. They are *hard* to know, rather than easy. Authentic selfhood can be defined in part as being able to hear these impulse-voices within oneself, i.e., to know what one really wants or does not want, what one is fit for and what one is *not* fit for, etc.

11. For all these reasons, it is at this time best to bring out and encourage, or, at the very least, to recognize this inner nature, rather than to suppress or repress it. Pure spontaneity consists of free, uninhibited, uncontrolled, trusting, unpremeditated expression of the self, i.e., of the psychic forces, with minimal interference by consciousness. Control, will, caution, self-criticism, measure, deliberateness are the brakes upon this expression made intrinsically necessary by the laws of the social and natural worlds outside this psychic world, and, secondarily, made necessary by fear of the psyche itself. Speaking in a very broad way, controls upon the psyche which come from *fear of the psyche*, are largely neurotic or *psychotic*, or not intrinsically or theoretically necessary. (The healthy psyche is not terrible or horrible and therefore does not have to be feared, as it has been for thousands of years. Of course, the *un-healthy* psyche is another story). This kind of control is usually lessened by psychological health, by deep psychotherapy, or by any *deeper* self-knowledge and self-acceptance. There are also, however, controls upon the psyche which do not come out of fear, but out of the necessities for keeping it integrated, organized and unified. And there are also "controls," probably in another sense, which are necessary as capacities are actualized, and as higher forms of expression are sought for, e.g., acquisition of skills by the artist, the intellectual, the athlete. But these controls are eventually transcended and become aspects of spontaneity, as they become self.

The balance between spontaneity and control varies, then, as the health of the psyche and the health of the world vary. Pure spontaneity is not long possible because we live in a world which runs by its own, nonpsychic laws. It *is* possible in dreams, fantasies, love, imagination, the first stages of creativity, artistic work, intellectual play, free association, etc. Pure control is not permanently possible, for then the psyche dies. Education must be directed then *both* toward cultivation of controls and cultivation of spontaneity and expression. In our culture and at this point in history, it is necessary to redress the balance in favor of spontaneity, the ability to be expressive, passive, unwilled, trusting in processes other than will and control, unpremeditated, creative, etc. But it must be recognized that there have been and will be other cultures and other eras in which the balance was or will be in the other direction.

12. Coordinate with this "acceptance" of the self, of fate, of one's call, is the conclusion that the main path to health and self-fulfillment is via basic need gratification rather than via frustration. This contrasts with the suppressive regime, the mistrust, the control, the policing that is necessarily implied by basic evil in the human depths. Intrauterine life is completely gratifying and nonfrustrating and it is now generally accepted that the first year or so of life had better also be primarily gratifying and nonfrustrating. Asceticism, self-denial, deliberate rejection of the demands of the organism, at least in the West, tend to produce a diminished, stunted or crippled organism, and even in the East, bring self-actualization to very few, exceptionally strong individuals.

13. In the normal development of the normal child, it is now known that *most* of the time, if he is given a really free choice, he will choose what is good for his growth. This he does because it tastes good, feels good, gives pleasure or *delight*. This implies that *he* "knows" better than anyone else what is good for him. A permissive regime means not that adults gratify his needs directly, but make it possible for *him* to gratify his needs and to make his own choices, i.e., let him *be*. It is necessary, in order for children to grow well, that adults have enough trust in them and in the natural processes of growth, i.e., not interfere too much, not *make* them grow, or force them into predetermined designs, but rather *let* them grow and *help* them grow in a Taoistic rather than an authoritarian way.

14. But we know also that the *complete absence* of frustration is dangerous. To be strong, a person must acquire frustration-tolerance, the ability to perceive physical reality as essentially indifferent to human wishes, the ability to love others and to enjoy their need-gratification as well as one's own (not to use other people only as means). The child with a good basis of safety, love and respect-need-gratification is able to profit from nicely graded frustrations and become stronger thereby. If they are more

than he can bear, if they overwhelm him, we call them traumatic, and consider them dangerous rather than profitable.

It is via the frustrating unyieldingness of physical reality and of animals and of other people that we learn about *their* nature, and thereby learn to differentiate wishes from facts (which things wishing makes come true, and which things proceed in complete disregard of our wishes), and are thereby enabled to live in the world and adapt to it as necessary.

We learn also about our own strengths and limits by overcoming difficulties, by straining ourselves to the utmost, by meeting challenge, even by failing. There can be great enjoyment in a great struggle, and this can displace fear.

15. To make growth and self-actualization possible, it is necessary to understand that capacities, organs and organ systems press to function and express themselves and to be used and exercised, and that such use is satisfying and disuse irritating. The muscular person likes to use his muscles, indeed *has* to use them in order to "feel good" and to achieve the subjective feeling of harmonious, successful, uninhibited functioning (spontaneity) which is so important an aspect of good growth and psychological health. So also for intelligence, for the uterus, the eyes, the capacity to love. Capacities clamor to be used, and cease their clamor only when they *are* well used. That is, capacities are also needs. Not only is it fun to use our capacities, but it is also necessary. The unused capacity or organ can become a disease center or else atrophy, thus diminishing the person.

16. The psychologist proceeds on the assumption that for his purposes there are two kinds of worlds, two kinds of reality, the natural world and the psychic world, the world of unyielding facts and the world of wishes, hopes, fears, emotions, the world which runs by nonpsychic rules and the world which runs by psychic laws. This differentiation is not very clear except at its extremes, where there is no doubt that delusions, dreams and free associations are lawful and yet utterly different from the lawfulness of logic and from the lawfulness of the world which would remain if the human species died out. This assumption does not deny that these worlds are related and may even fuse.

I may say that this assumption is acted upon by *many* or *most* psychologists, even though they are perfectly willing to admit that it is an insoluble philosophical problem. Any therapist *must* assume it or give up his functioning. This is typical of the way in which psychologists by-pass philosophical difficulties and act "as if" certain assumptions were true even though unprovable, e.g., the universal assumption of "responsibilty," "will power," etc.

17. Immaturity can be contrasted with maturity from the motivational point of view, as the process of gratifying the deficiency-needs in their proper order. Maturity, or self-actualization, from this point of view, means to transcend the deficiency-needs. This state can be described then as meta-motivated, or unmotivated (if deficiencies are seen as the only motivations). It can also be described as self-actualizing, Being, expressing, rather than coping. This state of Being, rather than of striving, is suspected to be synonymous with selfhood, with being "authentic," with being a person, with being fully human. The process of growth is the process of *becoming* a person. *Being* a person is different.

18. Immaturity can also be differentiated from maturity in terms of the cognitive capacities (and also in terms of the emotional capacities). Immature and mature cognition have been best described by Werner and Piaget. I wish to add another differentiation, that between D-cognition and B-cognition (D=Deficiency; B=Being). D-cognition can be defined as the cognitions which are organized from the point of view of basic needs or deficiency-needs and their gratification and frustration. That is, D-cognition could be called selfish cognition, in which the world is organized into gratifiers and frustrators of our own needs, with other characteristics being ignored or slurred. The cognition of the object, in its own right and its own Being, without reference to its need-gratifying or need-frustrating qualities, that is, without primary reference to its value for the observer or its effects upon him, can be called B-cognition (or self-transcending, or unselfish, or objective cognition). The parallel with maturity is by no means perfect (children can also cognize in a selfless way), but in general, it is mostly true that with increasing selfhood or firmness of personal identity (or acceptance of one's own inner nature) B-cognition becomes easier and more frequent. (This is true even though D-cognition remains for *all* human beings, including the mature ones, the main tool for living-in-the-world.)

To the extent that perception is desire-less and fear-less, to that extent is it more veridical, in the sense of perceiving the true, or essential or intrinsic whole nature of the object (without splitting it up by abstraction). Thus the goal of objective and true description of any reality is fostered by psychological health. Neurosis, psychosis, stunting of growth, all are, from this point of view, cognitive diseases as well, contaminating perception, learning, remembering, attending and thinking.

19. A by-product of this aspect of cognition is a better understanding of the higher and lower levels of love. D-love can be differentiated from B-love on approximately the same basis as D-cognition and B-cognition, or D-motivation and B-motivation. No ideally good relation to another human being, especially a child, is possible without B-love. Especially is it necessary for teaching, along with the Taoistic, trusting attitude that it implies. This is also true for our relations with the natural world, i.e., we can treat it in its own right or we can treat it as if it were there only for our purposes.

20. Though, in principle, growth toward self-actualization is easy, in practice it rarely happens (by my criteria, certainly in less than one percent of the adult population). For this, there are many, many reasons at various levels of discourse, including all the determinants of psychopathology that we now know. We have already mentioned one main cultural reason, i.e., the conviction that man's intrinsic nature is evil or dangerous, and one biological determinant for the difficulty of achieving a mature self, namely that humans no longer have strong instincts.

There is a subtle but extremely important difference between regarding psychopathology as blocking or evasion or fear of growth toward self-actualization and thinking of it in a medical fashion, as akin to invasion from without by tumors, poisons or bacteria, which have no relationship to the personality being invaded.

21. Growth has not only rewards and pleasures but also many intrinsic pains, and always will have. Each step forward is a step into the unfamiliar and is possibly dangerous. It also means giving up something familiar and good and satisfying. It frequently means a parting and a separation, with consequent nostalgia, loneliness and mourning. It also often means giving up a simpler and easier and less effortful life, in exchange for a more demanding, more

difficult life. Growth forward *is in spite of* these losses and therefore requires courage and strength in the individual, as well as protection, permission and encouragement from the environment, especially for the child.

22. It is therefore useful to think of growth or lack of it as the resultant of a dialectic between growth-fostering forces and growth-discouraging forces (regression, fear, pains of growth, ignorance, etc.). Growth has both advantages and disadvantages. Non-growing has not only disadvantages, but also advantages. The future pulls, but so also does the past. There is not only courage but also fear. The total ideal way of growing healthily, is, in principle, to enhance all the advantages of forward growth and all the disadvantages of notgrowing, and to diminish all the disadvantages of growth forward and all the advantages of not-growing.

Homeostatic tendencies, "need-reduction" tendencies, and Freudian defense mechanisms are not growth-tendencies but defensive, painreducing postures of the organism. But they are quite necessary and normal (not pathological, necessarily) and are generally prepotent over growth-tendencies.

23. All this implies a naturalistic system of values, a by-product of the empirical description of the deepest tendencies of the human species and of specific individuals (8). The study of the human being by science or by self-search can discover where he is heading, what is his purpose in life, what is good for him and what is bad for him, what will make him feel virtuous and what will make him feel guilty, why choosing the good is often difficult for him, what the attractions of evil are. (Observe that the word "ought" need not be used. Also such knowledge of man is relative to man only and does not purport to be "absolute".)

24. The state of being without a system of values is psychopathogenic, we are learning. The human being needs a framework of values, a philosophy of life, a religion or religion-surrogate to live by and understand by, in about the same sense that he needs sunlight, calcium or love. This I have called the "cognitive need to understand." The value-illnesses which result from valuelessness are called variously anhedonia, anomie, apathy, amorality, hopelessness, cynicism, etc., and can become somatic illness as well. Historically, we are in a value interregnum in which all externally given value

systems have proven to be failures (political, economic, religious, etc.), e.g., nothing is worth dying for. What man needs but does not have, he seeks for unceasingly, and he becomes dangerously ready to jump at *any* hope, good or bad. The cure for this disease is obvious. We need a validated, usable system of human values that we can believe in and devote ourselves to (be willing to die for), because they are true rather than because we are exhorted to "believe and have faith." Such an empirically based *Weltanschauung* seems now to be a real possibility, at least in theoretical outline.

Much disturbance in children and adolescents can be understood as a consequence of the uncertainty of adults about their values. As a consequence, many youngsters in the United States live not by adult values but by adolescent values, which of course are immature, ignorant and heavily determined by confused adolescent needs. An excellent projection of these adolescent values is the cowboy, or "Western," movie.

25. At the level of self-actualizing, many dichotomies become resolved, opposites are seen to be unities and the whole dichotomous way of thinking is recognized to be immature. For self-actualizing people, there is a strong tendency for selfishness and unselfishness to fuse into a higher, superordinate unity. Work tends to be the same as play; vocation and avocation become the same thing. When duty is pleasant and pleasure is fulfillment of duty, then they lose their separateness and oppositeness. The highest maturity is discovered to include a childlike quality, and we discover healthy children to have some of the qualities of mature self-actualization. The inner-outer split, between self and all else, gets fuzzy and much less sharp, and they are seen to be permeable to each other at the highest levels of personality development.

26. One especially important finding in selfactualizing people is that they tend to integrate the Freudian dichotomies and trichotomies, i.e., the conscious, preconscious and the unconscious (as well as id, ego, superego). The Freudian "instincts" and the defenses are less sharply set off against each other. The impulses are more expressed and less controlled; the controls are less rigid, inflexible, anxiety-determined. The superego is less harsh and punishing and less set off against the ego. The primary and secondary cognitive processes are more equally available and more equally valued (in-

stead of the primary processes being stigmatized as pathological). Indeed in the "peak-experience" the walls between them tend to fall altogether.

This is in sharp contrast with the classical Freudian position in which these various forces were sharply dichotomized as (a) mutually exclusive, (b) with antagonistic interests, i.e., as antagonistic forces rather than as complimentary or collaborating ones.

27. Healthy people are more integrated in another way. In them the conative, the cognitive, the affective and the motor are less separated from each other, and are more synergic, i.e., working collaboratively without conflict to the same ends. The conclusions of rational, careful thinking are apt to come to the same conclusions as those of the blind appetites. What such a person wants and enjoys is apt to be just what is good for him. His spontaneous reactions are as capable, efficient and right as if they had been thought out in advance. His sensory and motor reactions are more closely correlated. His sensory modalities are more connected with each other (physiognomical perception). Furthermore, we have learned the difficulties and dangers of those age-old rationalistic systems in which the capacities were thought to be arranged hierarchically, with rationality at the top.

28. This development toward the concept of a healthy unconscious, and of a healthy irrationality, sharpens our awareness of the limitations of purely abstract thinking, of verbal thinking and of analytic thinking. If our hope is to describe the world fully, a place is necessary for preverbal, ineffable, metaphorical, primary process, concrete-experience, intuitive and esthetic types of cognition, for there are certain aspects of reality which can be cognized in no other way. Even in science this is true, now that we know (a) that creativity has its roots in the nonrational, (b) that language is and must always be inadequate to describe total reality, (c) that any abstract concept leaves out much of reality, and (d) that what we call "knowledge" (which is usually highly abstract and verbal and sharply defined) often serves to blind us to those portions of reality not covered by the abstraction. That is, it makes us more able to see some things, but less able to see other things. Abstract knowledge has its dangers as well as its uses.

Science and education, being too exclusively abstract, verbal and bookish, do not have enough place for raw, concrete, esthetic experience, especially of the subjective happenings inside oneself. For instance, organismic psychologists would certainly agree on the desirability of more creative education in perceiving and creating art, in dancing in (Greek style) athletics and in phenomenological observation.

The ultimate of abstract, analytical thinking is the greatest simplification possible, i.e., the formula, the diagram, the map, the blueprint, certain types of abstract paintings. Our mastery of the world is enhanced thereby, but its richness may be lost as a forfeit, *unless* we learn to value B-cognition, perception-with-love-and-care, free floating attention—all of which enrich the experience instead of impoverishing it.

29. This ability of healthier people to dip into the unconscious and preconscious, to use and value their primary processes instead of fearing them, to accept their impulses instead of always controlling them, to be able to regress voluntarily without fear, turns out to be one of the main conditions of creativity. We can then understand why psychological health is so closely tied up with certain universal forms of creativeness (aside from special talent) as to lead some writers to make them almost synonymous.

This same tie between health and integration of rational and irrational forces (conscious and unconscious, primary and secondary processes) also permits us to understand why psychologically healthy people are more able to enjoy, to love, to laugh, to have fun, to be humorous, to be silly, to be whimsical and fantastic, to be pleasantly "crazy," and in general to permit and value and enjoy emotional experiences in general and peak experiences in particular and to have them more often. And it leads us to the strong suspicion that learning *ad hoc* to be able to do all these things may help the child move toward health.

30. Esthetic perceiving and creating and esthetic peak experiences are seen to be a central aspect of human life and of psychology and education rather than a peripheral one. This is true for several reasons: (a) All the peak experiences are (among other characteristics) integrative of the splits within the person, between persons, within the world, and between the person and the world. Since one aspect of health is integration, the peak experiences are moves toward health and are themselves momentary healths. (b) These ex-

periences are life-validating, i.e., they make life worthwhile. These are certainly an important part of the answer to the question, "Why don't we all commit suicide?"

31. Self-actualization does not mean a transcendance of all human problems. Conflict, anxiety, frustration, sadness, hurt, and guilt can all be found in healthy human beings. In general, the movement, with increasing maturity, is from neurotic pseudo-problems to the real, unavoidable, existential problems inherent in the nature of man (even at his best) living in a particular kind of world. Even though he is not neurotic he may be troubled by real, desirable, and necessary guilt rather than neurotic guilt (which is not desirable or necessary), by an intrinsic conscience (rather than the Freudian superego). Even though he has transcended the problems of Becoming, there remain the problems of Being. To be untroubled when one *should* be troubled can be a sign of sickness. Sometimes, smug people have to be scared *"into* their wits."

32. Self-actualization is not altogether general. It takes place via femaleness *or* maleness, which are prepotent to general-humanness. That is, one must first be a healthy, femaleness-fulfilled woman before general-human self-actualization becomes possible.

There is also a little evidence that different constitutional types actualize themselves in somewhat different ways (because they have different inner selves to actualize).

33. Another crucial aspect of healthy growth to selfhood is dropping away the techniques used by the child, in his weakness and smallness for adapting himself to the strong, large, all-powerful, omniscient, godlike adults. He must replace these with the techniques of being strong and independent and of being a parent himself. This involves especially giving up the child's desperate wish for the exclusive, total love of his parents while learning to love others. He must learn to gratify his own needs and wishes, rather than the needs of his parents, and he must learn to gratify them himself, rather than depending upon the parents to do this for him. He must give up being good out of fear and in order to keep their love, and must be good because *he* wishes to be. He must discover his own conscience and give up his internalized parents as a sole ethical guide. All these techniques by which weakness adapts itself to strength are necessary for the child, but immature and stunting in the adult.

34. From this point of view, a society or a culture can be either growth-fostering or growth-inhibiting. The sources of growth and of humanness are essentially within the human person and are not created or invented by society, which can only help or hinder the development of humanness, just as a gardener can help or hinder the growth of a rosebush, but cannot determine that it shall be an oak tree. This is true even though we know that a culture is a *sine qua non* for the actualization of humanness itself, e.g., language, abstract thought, ability to love; but these exist as potentialities in human germ plasm prior to culture.

This makes theoretically possible a comparative sociology, transcending and including cultural relativity. The "better" culture gratifies all basic human needs and permits self-actualization. The "poorer" cultures do not. The same is true for education. To the extent that it fosters growth toward self-actualization, it is "good" education.

As soon as we speak of "good" or "bad" cultures, and take them as means rather than as ends, the concept of "adjustment" comes into question. We must ask, "What kind of culture or subculture is the 'well adjusted' person well adjusted *to?"* Adjustment is, very definitely, *not* necessarily synonymous with psychological health.

35. The achievement of self-actualization (in the sense of autonomy) parodoxically makes *more* possible the transcendance of self, and of self-consciousness and of selfishness. It makes it *easier* for the the person to be homonomous, i.e., to merge himself as a part in a larger whole than himself. The condition of the fullest homonomy is full autonomy, and, to some extent, vice versa, one can attain to autonomy only via successful homonomous experiences (child dependence, B-love, care for others, etc.). It is necessary to speak of levels of homonomy (more and more mature), and to differentiate a "low homonomy" (of fear, weakness and regression) from a "high homonomy" (of courage and full, self-confident autonomy).

36. An important existential problem is posed by the fact that self-actualized persons (and *all* people in their peak experiences) occasionally live out-of-time and out-of-the-world, (atem-

poral and aspatial) even though mostly they *must* live in the outer world. Living in the inner psychic world (which is ruled by psychic laws and not by the laws of outer-reality), i.e., the world of experience, of emotion, of wishes and fears and hopes, of love, of poetry, art and fantasy, is different from living in and adapting to the nonpsychic reality which runs by laws the person never made and which are not essential to his nature even though he has to live by them. The person who is not afraid of this inner, psychic world can enjoy it to such an extent that it may be called "heaven" by contrast with the more effortful, fatiguing, externally responsible, world of "reality," of striving and coping, of right and wrong, of truth and falsehood. This is true even though the healthier person can adapt more easily and enjoyably to the "real" world, and has better "reality testing," i.e., does not confuse it with his inner, psychic world.

It seems quite clear now that confusing these inner and outer realities, or having either closed off from experience, is highly pathological. The healthy person is able to integrate them both into his life and therefore has to give up neither, being able to go back and forth voluntarily. The difference is the same as the one between the person who can *visit* the slums and the one who is forced to live there always. (*Either* world is a slum if one can not leave it.) Then paradoxically that which was sick and pathological and the "lowest" becomes part of the healthiest and "highest" aspect of human nature. Slipping into "craziness" is frightening only for those who are not fully confident of their sanity. Education must help the person to live in both worlds.

37. The foregoing propositions generate a different understanding of the role of action in psychology. Goal-directed, motivated, coping, striving, purposeful action is an aspect or by-product of the necessary transactions between a psyche and a nonpsychic world.

A. The D-need gratifications come from the world outside the person, not from within. Therefore adaptation to this world is made necessary, e.g., reality-testing, knowing the nature of this world, learning to differentiate this world from the inner world, learning the nature of people and of society, learning to delay gratification, learning to conceal what would be dangerous, learning which portions of the world are gratifying and which dangerous or useless for need-gratification, learning the approved and permitted cultural paths to gratification and techniques of gratification.

b. The world is in itself interesting, beautiful and fascinating. Exploring it, manipulating it, playing with it, contemplating it, enjoying it are all motivated kinds of action (cognitive, motor and esthetic needs).

But there is also action which has little or nothing to do with the world, at any rate at first. Sheer expression of the nature or state or powers (*Funktionslust*) of the organism is an expression of Being rather than of striving. And the contemplation and enjoyment of the inner life not only is a kind of "action" in itself but is also antithetical to action in the world, i.e., it produces stillness and cessation of muscular activity. The ability to wait is a special case of being able to suspend action.

38. From Freud we learned that the past exists *now* in the person. Now we must learn, from growth theory and self-actualization theory that the future also *now* exists in the person in the form of ideals, hopes, goals, unrealized potentials, mission, fate, destiny, etc. One for whom no future exists is reduced to the concrete, to hopelessness, to emptiness. For him, time must be endlessly "filled." Striving, the usual organizer of most activity, when lost, leaves the person unorganized and unintegrated.

Of course, being in a state of Being needs no future, because it is already *there*. Then Becoming ceases for the moment and its promissory notes are cashed in the form of the ultimate rewards, i.e., the peak experiences, in which time disappears.

REFERENCES

1. Gordon W. Allport. *Becoming: Basic Considerations for a Psychology of Personality.* New Haven, Conn.: Yale University Press, 1955. 106 p.

2. Andras Angyal. *Foundations for a Science of Personality.* New York Commonwealth Fund. 1941. 398 p.

3. C. Bühler. *Values in Psychotherapy.* Glencoe, Ill.: Free Press, 1962.

4. Erich Fromm. *Man for Himself; An Inquiry into the Psychology of Ethics.* New York: Holt, Rinehart, and Winston, 1947. 254 p.

5. Kurt Goldstein. *Organism; a Holistic Approach to Biology Derived from Pathological Data in Man.* New York: American Book Co., 1939, 533 p.

6. Karen Horney. *Neurosis and Human Growth; The Struggle Toward Self-Realization.* New York: W. W. Norton & Co., 1950. 391 p.

7. Abraham H. Maslow. *Motivation and Personality.* New York: Harper & Brothers, 1954. 411 p.

8. Abraham H. Maslow, editor. *New Knowledge in Human Values.* New York: Harper & Brothers, 1959. 268 p.

9. Rollo May and others, editors. *Existence; A New Dimension in Psychiatry and Psychology.* New York: Basic Books, 1958. 445 p.

10. Clark Moustakas, editor. *The Self; Explorations in Personal Growth.* New York: Harper & Brothers, 1956. 284 p.

11. Carl R. Rogers and Rosalind F. Dymond. *Psychotherapy and Personality Change.* Chicago: University of Chicago Press, 1954.

Sheldon's Constitutional Psychology

In spite of the fact that William Sheldon has continued to conduct research relevant to his earlier investigations and also has modified and made more objective his method of somatotyping, he has produced no major publications in recent years. However, there has been a reasonable incidence of significant investigations—a number of which have provided strong confirmation of some of Sheldon's most interesting results.

The first paper in this section reports an investigation by Child of the relation between somatotype variables and self-ratings of personality. The study is primarily of interest because virtually all possibility of experimenter bias has been removed. Thus, whatever association is observed between body build and behavior is largely independent of contamination of data of the sort that might have operated in the case of Sheldon's major study of physique and temperament.

The study by Walker resembles Child's investigation but employs children as subjects and involves observer ratings rather than self-ratings. Again the likelihood of important bias, such as may have been present in Sheldon's study, is very much reduced here. The study by Kline and Tenny relates somatotype ratings to personality but this time the focus is on abnormal personality. Here we find suggestive evidence for associations between somatotype dimensions on the one hand and psychosis and recovery from psychosis on the other which are generally consistent with Sheldon's formulations and findings.

The study by Glueck and Glueck examines the relation between physique and delinquency under conditions that are much more adequately controlled than in Sheldon's study of delinquency. In spite of the superior protections against experimenter bias the investigators find a powerful confirmation of Sheldon's earlier findings concerning physique and delinquency.

The final paper is an attempt by one of the editors (G.L.) to examine the position of morphological or structural variables in modern psychology and to evaluate their potential contribution to certain selected areas of psychological investigation. One of the principal reasons for its inclusion is that it provides brief discussion of some of the most recent and interesting work that has been done in this area.

1. The relation of somatotype to self-ratings on Sheldon's temperamental traits*

IRVIN L. CHILD

SHELDON (4) HAS REPORTED an extremely close relationship between somatotype and three sets of temperamental characteristics which he has defined. Sheldon's findings are based upon ratings made by him after intensive personal study of each of his subjects. This method, like clinical procedures in general, may be admirably suited to the discovery of new relationships. But it is not adequate for determining which of the relationships which seem to be discovered are genuine or how close any of them are. The method provides no control over the possibility that the investigator's bias, through influencing his ratings, may have produced some considerable part, or even all, of each relationship found between physique and supposed psychological characteristics.

In the attempt to determine the objective validity of Sheldon's conclusions, other psychologists have tended at first to rely on objective measuring instruments which they already had available. Whether laboratory techniques or paper-and-pencil tests have been chosen, the general outcome has been to find evidence of, at most, only a very slight relationship between these measures and somatotype. It has always remained possible, however, that the reason for this outcome is simply that the measuring instruments, having been devised for other purposes, are not particularly representative of certain really significant aspects of behavior which are related fairly closely to somatotype. These studies, then, are valuable in definitely identifying certain aspects of behavior as not appreciably related to somatype, but may not contribute much to solving the problem of the validity of Sheldon's findings.[1]

The present paper reports a study in which the possibility that the investigator's bias may influence the personality measures is eliminated, but in which the personality measures used appear to be more relevant to Sheldon's hypotheses than do the objective measures used in previous studies.

Subjects and Procedure

The potential subjects drawn on for this study consisted of 532 male students at Yale University who were somatotyped during their freshman year (1946–47) by Dr. W. H. Sheldon and who were still attending the University during the following academic year. The photographing of these students, for purposes of somatotyping, was done at the university's gymnasium. The students who were somatotyped comprised approximately one third of the freshman class, and were selected primarily on the basis of their being engaged in particular activity groups at the time at which these groups were called

SOURCE. Article by Irvin L. Child, "The relation of somatotype to self-ratings on Sheldon's temperamental traits" in *Journal of Personality*. Vol. 18, pp. 440–453, 1950.

*Grateful acknowledgment is made to Dr. Sheldon for his generous help in supplying the somatotypes and criticizing the questionnaire which was used, and to Mr. Robert J. H. Kiphuth and Dr. T. E. Blesh of the Department of Physical Education at Yale for their cooperation in the study.

[1] A study which uses standard psychological tests yet is relevant to more of Sheldon's work than are other similar studies is the recent one by Smith (5). Smith's article also reviews those earlier studies which have had somewhat positive results.

on to be photographed. All freshmen are required to participate in gymnasium activities. The purpose of the somatotyping was to add to the data on varieties of physique which Dr. Sheldon had available for the preparation of an atlas of physique. It must be recognized that there is some possibility that the initial procedure of selecting students for somatotyping could have selected a group of people in whom correlations between physique and behavior would be markedly different from what would be found in the entire freshman class. This possibility seemed sufficiently remote, however, to justify a study of the relation of certain personality measures to somatotype in this group of potential subjects, taking advantage of the accurate somatotyping which had already been done.

Out of the 532 potential subjects, 60 were in a course given by the author in their sophomore year and, as an exercise in this course, filled out the questionnaire which will be described below. The questionnaire was sent by mail to the other 472 potential subjects with a request that they fill it out and return it for scientific purposes. It was returned by 354 of these students, making a total of 414 actual subjects. In both procedures used in obtaining subjects' cooperation, careful measures were taken to insure anonymity in the handling of the data and knowledge of these measures on the part of the subjects.

At the end of the questionnaire, the subjects were asked to indicate what they guessed the purpose of the questionnaire to be. Only 1 per cent of the subjects guessed anything which at all resembled the true purpose. The aim of insuring that the ratings used in this study should be made under conditions such that they would not be influenced by the rater's preconceptions about physique and personality appears to have been achieved.[2]

The questionnaire was constructed especially for this study. It consisted of multiple-choice questions asking the subject to rate or characterize himself with respect to various kinds of variation in behavior, attitudes, and feelings. The questions were based on Sheldon's account (4, pp. 24–94) of 60 temperamental traits which he reports to be correlated with the three main dimensions of physique recognized in his system of somatotyping (20 traits are reported to be positively related to each of the three dimensions of physique). Each of the 60 traits was represented by at least one question. Some of the questions were designed to ask about the trait as a whole as described by Sheldon; more of them, however, asked about some one aspect or exemplification of the trait, on the ground that self-ratings would probably be more reliable and valid the more definite and specific the aspect of behavior to be rated. Examples of the content of the questions will be given later in connection with the presentation of results.

Results

The Consistency of Relationships between Physique and Behavior. In advance of collecting the data, the author wrote down a set of predictions about the correlations between dimensions of physique and responses to items in the questionnaire. These predictions were those which followed from two simple assumptions: (1) that the self-ratings by the subjects on each item would be positively related to their objective status with respect to the item; (2) that the objective status of the subjects with respect to each item would be related to somatotype in the way asserted by Sheldon for the temperamental trait which the item was intended to sample or represent. The predictions were based only on Sheldon's assertion of a positive correlation between a given dimension of physique and a particular set of 20 temperamental traits. They did not make use of Sheldon's assertion of a negative correlation between the dimension of physique and the two other sets of 20 temperamental traits (except in so far as some of this latter relationship is definitely implied by the former).

Because some traits as described by Sheldon were represented by more than one item in the questionnaire, the number of predictions for

---

[2] Of course a person's estimates of his own characteristics, as they are built up through his lifetime, may be influenced by generally current notions about the relation between physique and personality. What we can feel confident of is that the question of physique and its relation to personality was not in general an immediate stimulus at the time of making these ratings.

each dimension of physique exceeded 20; it was 31 for endomorphy, 30 for mesomorphy, and 35 for ectomorphy.[3]

Each prediction was then tested by dichotomizing the two variables involved—a dimension of physique and answers to a questionnaire item—and tabulating the results in a two-by-twofold frequency distribution. The dichotomizing was done in the following ways:

1. Each dimension of physique was dichotomized at the point which gave as nearly as possible a 50-50 division of the subjects. (For endomorphy this was between 3 and 3½, for mesomorphy between 4 and 4½, and for ectomorphy between 3½ and 4, on a scale running from 1 to 7 by half unit steps.)

2. The majority of questionnaire items, for which the possible answers fell along a continuum, were likewise dichotomized at the point which gave as nearly as possible a 50-50 division of the subjects.

3. A few questionnaire items, based on the tripolar traits in Sheldon's system, had three possible answers, each one predicted to be related to one of the three dimensions of physique. For these items the dichotomy was made between the one answer for which a particular

[3] This does not mean that 94 items were involved. There were actually 66 items. In the case if bipolar or tripolar traits in Sheldon's system, a relation to a single questionnaire item was predicted for two or for all three of the dimensions of physique.

relation was predicted, and the other two answers.

Each frequency distribution was inspected, first, for whether the direction of the relationship agreed with the prediction and, second, for the level of statistical significance of the relationship, as determined through the use of x^2. The results obtained are summarized in Table 1.

The results give a marked confirmation of the existence in these data of a set of relationships which are consistent with Sheldon's generalizations about physique and temperament. Of 96 predictions based on Sheldon's views, 77 per cent are confirmed by the direction of relationship found in these data. Of the 74 correlations which are in the predicted direction, 20 reach significance at the 5 per cent level, whereas only one of the 21 correlations contrary to prediction is significant at the 5 per cent level. The most marked contrast between the results which conform to prediction and those which do not is found in the number of instances of results significant at the 1 per cent level, where the contrast is between 10 and none.

The three dimensions of physique differ in the confirmation of predictions. The major difference is that many fewer predictions are confirmed at acceptable levels of statistical significance for endomorphy than for the other two dimensions of physique. There is no very appreciable difference among the dimensions in the proportion of predictions confirmed by direction of relationship alone.

Table 1. Outcome of Predictions of Relationships between Dimensions of Physique and Self-Ratings on Particular Questionnaire Items

	Dimension of Physique		
	Endomorphy	Mesomorphy	Ectomorphy
Number of predictions confirmed at 1 per cent level	1	6	3
Number of predictions confirmed at 5 per cent level only	2	3	5
Number of predictions confirmed in direction, but not significant	21	13	20
Number of predictions disconfirmed in direction, but not significant	6	8	7
Number of predictions disconfirmed at 5 per cent level only	1	0	0
Number of predictions disconfirmed at 1 per cent level	0	0	0

The test of each prediction is based on approximately 400 subjects. To a person with a strong faith in the importance of somatotype as a determinant of behavior, it might therefore be surprising that so few predictions are confirmed at acceptable levels of statistical significance. The next question then is, What evidence can be obtained from this study about the magnitude of the relationships which appear to exist?

The Magnitude of Relationships between Physique and Behavior. To determine the magnitude of the relationships between physique and behavior, it seems desirable to deal with a score derived from a number of questionnaire items rather than with single items. Sheldon's terms *viscerotonia, somatotonia,* and *cerebrotonia* will be used here as convenient labels, referring to whatever set of behavioral tendencies may be found correlated with endomorphy, mesomorphy, and ectomorphy, repectively.

The method of determining a score for each of these behavioral tendencies—viscerotonia, somatotonia, and cerebrotonia—was influenced by the following considerations:

1. Only those items were used in which the possible answers fell along a continuum. This type of item lends itself to deriving an over-all score better than the tripolar items in which one of three types of extreme was to be chosen.

2. The selection of items cannot be based on information from the same sample of subjects as those to whom the scoring will be applied, or else the correlations between behavioral tendencies and somatotype will be inflated by random errors of sampling and measurement. Hence the subjects were divided at random into two equal-sized groups of approximately 200 each.

3. There seemed no reason to restrict the items here to those for which specific positive predictions follow from Sheldon's system. The items were extended to include those for which a fairly definite negative prediction seemed to follow from Sheldon's system. The procedure used was as follows:

1. For one half of the subjects, the relation between each item (of the appropriate kind) and each dimension of physique was tabulated in the way described in the preceding section. For each dimension of physique, the seven items were chosen, the relations of which to the dimension of physique were most significant

as determined by the use of χ^2. (The number *seven* was chosen arbitrarily.) One set of seven items thus selected defined *viscerotonia* for purposes of this study, one set *somatotonia,* and one set *cerebrotonia.* The items in the three sets are given in abbreviated form below:

Viscerotonia

Gets to sleep easily.

Is not easily awakened in the middle of the night.

Is inclined to eat more than is really needed to maintain weight and growth.

Tends not to be apprehensive, insecure, or worried.

Tends to be complacent about himself and his relations with the world.

Tends to conform to the ceremonies of social interaction.

Is characterized by amiability or good will towards everybody he knows or meets.

Somatotonia

Withstands pain easily and willingly.

In talking with another person, looks at him right in the eyes.

Has real desire for strenuous physical exercise.

Likes cold showers.

Likes to swim nude.

Likes to participate in strenuous or dangerous physical adventure.

Likes to have collar and shirt front open.

Cerebrotonia

Does not withstand pain easily and willingly.

Is not characterized by amiability and good will towards everybody he knows or meets.

Does not find sheer enjoyment of other people's companionship to be of the greatest importance.

Lacks real desire for strenuous physical exercise.

Does not like to swim nude.

Prefers a few very intimate friends to having many friends.

Does not like to participate in strenuous or dangerous physical adventure.

It will be noted that four items, scored in opposite directions, are shared by somatotonia and cerebrotonia; one item, scored in opposite directions, is shared by viscerotonia and somatotonia.

2. For the other half of the subjects, the answers to each set of seven items were used to obtain a score for viscerotonia, etc.

Table 2. Correlations between Dimensions of Physique and Sets of Self-Ratings Described in Text

Self-Ratings	Dimension of Physique		
	Endomorphy	Mesomorphy	Ectomorphy
Viscerotonia	+.13	+.13	−.15
Somatotonia	+.03	+.38	−.37
Cerebrotonia	−.03	−.38	+.27

3. The three scores so obtained, for each subject in this group, were then plotted against each of the three dimensions of physique, and correlation coefficients were calculated. The results are presented in Table 2.

The correlations between each dimension of physique and the corresponding psychological measure based on the questionnaire are all positive, and vary from .13 to .38.[4] The 1 per cent confidence intervals for these correlations are: for endomorphy, from −.05 to +.30; for mesomorphy, from +.22 to +.52; for ectomorphy, from +.10 to +.43. It is thus possible, but not certain, that appropriate measures based on self-ratings such as were used here have a quite sizable relationship with dimensions of physique. It is reasonably certain that this relationship does not at all approach the magnitude of the relationships reported by Sheldon between dimensions of physique and his measures of temperament.

In view of the fact that self-ratings of the sort used here probably do not have high validity, it seems fair to conclude that these results suggest (though they do not prove) that somatotype has an important influence on personality. Exactly how important that influence is, however, we are not yet in a position to judge.

Discussion

The Significance of the Present Results. The results reported here appear to establish on an entirely objective basis that the relationships reported by Sheldon between somatotype and various aspects of personality hold true with considerable consistency, and to suggest that their magnitude is sufficient to warrant considering somatotype as an important determinant of personality. With respect to the first of these two outcomes, the study fails to be definitive only because of the possibility that the original selection of potential subjects may somehow have introduced correlations which would not be found in an unselected group.

These general implications of the present study appear to emerge also from studies by Morris of philosophical and aesthetic preferences in relation to somatotype (2). Unfortunately, Morris's studies have not yet been reported in sufficient detail to permit evaluation.[5]

The results reported here also seem to show that self-ratings can be a useful technique in studying the relation between physique and personality. This fact, and the similar outcome of Morris's studies which have used subjects' expressions of preference, should be encouraging to those who wish to explore this problem further with techniques which permit a guarantee of objectivity. On the other hand, it must be noted that results obtained with self-ratings may be difficult to interpret. If people high in endomorphy say that they eat more than is really needed, for example, what does this mean? That they really eat more than they need? That they eat only what they need, but that they notice they eat more than other people? That they eat just as much as others, but because of weight-consciousness or delight in food are more aware of their eating and imagine they eat more? That they accept unquestioningly a popular stereotype about people of their physique? Complete freedom from possible bias of the investigator cannot be the sole criterion for selection of methods for all studies in a field

---

[4] These correlations would not be greatly affected by correction of attenuation. The three psychological measures have reliability coefficients of .71, .89, and .92, as determined from test-retest data on about 50 subjects.

[5] The results of one other study which appears to establish the same point, that by Coffin (1), seem to the present author too likely to be due either entirely or in part to an artifact, as noted by Smith (5).

in which the methods thus chosen may prevent getting the answer to some of the important questions.

The General Problem of Physique and Personality. Reasearch on physique and personality has tended to have as its intellectual setting the controversy as to the relative importance of heredity and environment in influencing behavior. Since it is generally plausible that differences in physique are an outcome preponderantly of genetic differences, the hereditarian is eager to show that personality is closely related to physique. For the same reason, the environmentalist is pleased to be able to show that personality is not closely related to physique, because his general bias then gives him confidence that personality differences arise from environmental influences.

This setting of controversy has hampered the integration of this problem into the general body of psychological research and theory. Even the psychologist who sees the possible integration is likely to be influenced in his estimation of its significance by his bias on the underlying controversy about heredity vs. environment. On the one hand Shaffer says:

Perhaps all that is of value in the theories of physical habitus is adequately summarized in the old humorous statement that a fat boy has to be good-natured because he can't fight and he can't run. (3, p. 342)

On the other hand, Sheldon, despite a great deal of specific recognition of the role of physique as a condition for adjustment, seems rather to lean on the general kind of interpretation indicated in his statement that "morphology and temperament, as we measure them, may constitute expressions at their respective levels of essentially common components" (4, p. 401). And in another passage he remarks:

Academic psychology offers training in the methodological techniques of rigorous and systematic quantification. That is about all it offers to constitutional psychology at the present time. (4, p. 430)

The conceptual tools that Sheldon has developed—concepts of dimensions of physique and of corresponding dimensions of temperament—are ones that seem especially consistent with the hereditarian position. They are consistent with an interpretation of each kind of dimension in terms of simple hypothetical genetic variables; if there are indeed complexities arising through a degree of independence among the specific physical attributes and among the specific aspects of behavior, these complexities might be concealed under the averaging implied by dealing with gross dimensions. Sheldon's concepts have had an obvious heuristic value in the development and exposition of his work. To the extent that his findings are valid, his concepts have descriptive and interpretative value in understanding individual personalities. It is likely, however, that for the advancement of knowledge and the eventual improvement of clinical understanding, those concepts need to be supplemented or replaced by more specific ones.

From the point of view of general psychology the specific concepts that would seem to be needed are: specific concepts about variations in physique that either directly determine behavior or influence behavior through modifying the conditions for learning, and specific concepts about the kinds of variations in behavior that are influenced by these variations in physique. Such specific concepts should lead to the asking of significant questions that would not be raised in connection with an over-all scheme of dimensions of physique and of temperament. Let us look at some examples in connection with each of Sheldon's three dimensions of physique.

In Sheldon's account of high endomorphy and its temperamental accompaniments, there appear two aspects of physique which seem most likely candidates for consideration as possible basic variations in physique which have behavioral consequences. One is the excess of weight in relation to musculature. The other is a presumed bodily condition making for strong hunger drive and high reward value of eating. Most of the 20 temperamental traits defining *viscerotonia* may be viewed as possible outgrowths, through learning, of these basic characteristics. If these two characteristics are basic but vary to some extent independently, then certain of the temperamental traits should be to that extent independent of each other. Variations in cultural norms about eating and other oral activities, moreover, should influence the consequences of the high hunger drive but not the consequences of the excess of weight in relation to musculature. Variations in cultural norms about the performance of physical labor, about means of locomotion, and about athletic games, should have the opposite pattern of effects. If these two presumed basic conditions vary in the age at which they operate (e.g., the great increase in weight in some physiques in middle adulthood), then certain behavioral effects will be most pronounced at certain ages.

In the case of high mesomorphy, some of the possible basic aspects of physique which can be extracted from Sheldon's work are: a physique which permits very forceful responses, a physique which provides a high drive for physical activity, an appearance of looking older than one is, a relative insensitivity to pain. Again, the relative independence of such possibly basic characteristics, or of the social treatment accorded to them, may lead to different consequences of a single degree of mesomorphy. For example, ruthlessness might be correlated with mesomorphy in a society, or in a class, where there were weak sanctions against physical aggression; in a society, or class, with strong sanctions against physical aggression the person high in mesomorphy may be especially severely punished and become less ruthless than the person low in mesomorphy. The effects of overmaturity of appearance would be expected to differ according to the culturally determined importance, and the rigidity, of age grading.

High ectomorphy appears to have as basic characteristics, with obvious behavioral implications, the following: an easily damageable physique, a physique that allows rapid but not forceful response, a tendency to appear younger than one is, and possibly a greater sensitivity to stimulation. The psychological effects of damageableness should depend somewhat on the prevalence of hazards in the life situation. The effects of the greater capacity for speed than for force should depend on the prestige value of various physical achievements, and on the extent to which the outcome of physical aggression (or the threat of it) is allowed to influence interpersonal relationships.

It may ultimately be possible and useful to distinguish three levels of effect of physique on personality: (1) the direct implications of the physique alone (e.g., the capacity for making forceful responses, possible differences in primary drive strength); (2) certain learned consequences which result from the conditions which the physique sets for the person's learning, and which result so uniformly under all

circumstances of human life that they may be thought of as nearly inevitable consequences of physique; (3) other learned consequences which also result from the conditions which the physique sets for the person's learning, where the meaning of these conditions varies so much with life circumstances that the effects of physique are not uniform in various segments of mankind. Sheldon appears to assume that the first two levels of effect play a larger role than many other psychologists would suppose; who is right in this matter cannot be settled by controversy but only by some rather laborious research. But the needed research does not seem likely to be done except under the influence of an attempt at an integration of this problem into general scientific knowledge of human behavior, and an analytic approach which will ask specific questions about the exact psychological processes involved. As Sheldon's concepts of dimensions of physique and of temperament tend to assume an answer that is not yet known to be true, rather than raising questions, it is doubtful that they are the most useful concepts to guide the needed research, however great their other merits.

Summary

A questionnaire was constructed to obtain self-ratings on a variety of personal characteristics asserted by Sheldon to be related to somatotype. The questionnaire was answered by about 400 male college sophomores who had been accurately somatotyped. The following conclusions are drawn:

1. Sheldon's findings as to the existence and direction of correlations between somatotype and a variety of personal characteristics, when tested with this more objective technique, were on the whole confirmed.

2. The results obtained are consistent with, but do not establish, the view that the magnitude of these correlations is large enough to warrant considering somatotype as a really important determinant of personality.

3. The only apparent source of possible error which might prevent these conclusions from being taken as certain lies in the fact that the initial selection of subjects was not entirely a random one.

The relation of research on physique and personality to general psychology is briefly discussed.

REFERENCES

1. Coffin, T. E. A three-component theory of leadership. *J. abnorm. soc. Psychol.*, 1944, **39**, 63–83.

2. Morris, C. Individual differences and cultural patterns. In Kluckhohn, C., and Murray, H. A. (eds.), *Personality in nature, society and culture*. New York: Knopf, 1949, Pp. 131–143.

3. Shaffer, L. F. *The psychology of adjustment*. Boston: Houghton Mifflin, 1936.

4. Sheldon, W. H. (with the collaboration of S. S. Stevens). *The varieties of temperament*. New York: Harper, 1942.

5. Smith, H. C. Psychometric checks on hypotheses derived from Sheldon's work on physique and temperament. *J. Personal.*, 1949, **17**, 310–320.

2. Constitutional factors in the prognosis of schizophrenia

NATHAN S. KLINE AND ASHTON M. TENNY

THE MAJORITY OF PSYCHIATRISTS today believe that there exists an organic disturbance in schizophrenic patients. Attempts to discover the nature of the organic pathology have been largely based on comparing the results of a specific test in schizophrenia (or its subtypes) with normal or psychoneurotic controls. In general, this approach has not been too productive of clear-cut or meaningful data.

There exists, however, a different approach; namely, to utilize a testing method that divides patients or controls into various groupings on the basis of its own criteria, and to investigate secondarily whether these groupings bear any relationship to psychiatric diagnoses. This method has yielded more provocative results but the positive findings show little intercorrelation. If some method of dividing individuals into significant groups could be found that also showed a high correlation with other positive test results from apparently unrelated fields, a key might be provided that would ultimately unlock some of the organic puzzles.

In our own approach to this problem, we had done extensive testing and obtained detailed information on several thousand patients. We have tried various "keys" and feel that the somatotype as conceived by Sheldon may provide the crude beginnings of such a systematizing principle.

SOURCE. Article by Nathan S. Kline and Ashton M. Tenney, "Constitutional factors in the prognosis of schizophrenia" in *American Journal of Psychiatry*, Vol. 107, pp. 432–441, 1950.

Purpose

The intent of the present study is to determine whether a significant correlation exists between the prognosis of schizophrenics and the somatotypes of these patients.

Method

An attempt was made to somatotype 2,100 consecutive admissions to the Veterans Administration Hospital at Lyons, N. J. Various factors made it impossible to obtain a somatotype rating on all of these admissions. Some were too ill or uncooperative to be photographed; some died or were discharged before adequate photographs could be obtained. In some cases, the photography itself was unsatisfactory. In addition, no special effort was made to obtain nonneuropsychiatric admissions, which constitute some 15% of the total. It was possible, however, to obtain over 70% of the consecutive schizophrenic admissions and this is believed to constitute a good sample. Although an additional 15% of these patients is still hospitalized, they have not been included in the present series, since it is felt that this would give an undue weight to the patients with a poorer prognosis. Only those patients whose somatotype photographs were obtained within 10 days of admission in the routine manner are, therefore, included. The records of all of the 2,100 admissions were at least partially reviewed. During the period of the study, some of the patients were admitted and discharged, only to be readmitted during this same period. In some of the cases there were 2, 3, and even 4 readmissions. For the purpose of study, regardless of how many readmissions, the patient is counted only once. Among the 2,100 total admissions, 123 of these were duplications of this sort. The term "readmission" refers specifically to readmissions within the series, and does not refer to whether these patients had been hospitalized at a time prior to the beginning of the series.

Of the first 1,000 admissions on whom adequate photographs were obtained (designated by LA, Lyons Admission Series), 455 were schizophrenics. Table 1 illustrates the per-

Table 1. Percentage Breakdown by Diagnosis

	Percentage Breakdown of 2,100 Consecutive Admissions	Number of Patients Admitted	Number of Patients Readmitted	Times Readmitted 1, 2, 3, 4	Number of Patients Obtained For LA Series	% of Total Admissions Included in LA Series
1. Schizophrenic	32.49	643	18	17, 1	455	70.76
a. Paranoid	14.20	281	10	9,1	204	72.60
b. Unclassified	8.44	167	5	....	116	69.46
c. Hebephrenic	4.14	82	3	....	64	78.05
d. Catatonic	2.58	51	0	....	31	60.78
e. Mixed	1.57	31	0	....	24	77.42
f. Simple	1.52	30	0	....	16	53.33
g. Latent	0.05	1	0	....	0	....
2. Psychoneurotic	21.63	427	37	28, 6, 2, 1	276	64.49
a. Anxiety	14.0	277	30	23, 5, 1, 1	187	67.51
b. Conversion	2.22	43	3	....	25	56.82
c. Depression	1.52	30	..	....	14	46.67
d. Hypochondriac	0.45	9	1	....	9	100.0
e. Obsessive-compulsive	0.56	11	..	....	8	72.73
f. Asthenia	0.45	9	..	....	5	55.56
g. Situational maladjustment	0.20	4	..	....	2	50.0
h. G. I. and cardiovascular	0.20	4	..	....	2	50.0
i. Passive-dependence	0.61	12	..	....	8	66.67
j. Passive-aggressive	0.15	3	..	....	2	66.67
k. Dissociative	0.40	8	..	....	5	62.50
l. Somatization	0.35	7	..	....	5	71.43
m. Mixed	0.51	10	3	1, 1, 1	4	40.0
3. Organic	11.67	232	29	24, 4, 1	103	44.59
a. Alcoholic	3.69	73	11	8, 2, 1	38	52.05
b. Luetic	0.81	16	..	....	7	43.75
c. Epileptic	4.04	80	17	15, 2	39	48.75
d. Arteriosclerotic	1.77	35	1	....	8	22.86
e. Post-traumatic	1.11	22	..	....	8	36.36
f. Mental deficiency	0.30	6	..	....	3	50.0
4. Psychopathic	3.39	67	7	6, 1	41	61.19
5. Involutional	0.40	8	..	....	4	50.0
6. Paranoid state	0.30	6	..	....	4	66.67
7. Manic-depressive	1.36	27	2	....	20	74.07
8. Undiagnosed psychosis	0.35	7	..	....	3	42.86
9. Psychotic depression	0.15	3	1	....	2	66.67
10. Miscellaneous	0.25	5	..	....	2	40.0
11. Neurologic	8.59	169	8	....	45	26.47
12. Ruptured disc	1.72	34	1	....	14	41.18
13. Nonneuropsychiatric	14.50	287	17	16,1	27	9.41
14. Insufficient observation	2.58	51	2	....	4	7.84
15. Dental	0.61	12	..	....	0	....

centage breakdown by diagnosis of the 2,100 admissions and the proportion of each of these diagnoses that constitute our first 1,000 cases.

The somatotype photographs were obtained under conditions that met Sheldon's own exacting demands for completely satisfactory posing. One of the co-authors had been associated with Sheldon for a number of years and was thoroughly familiar with Sheldon's technique.

To forestall any question as to the adequacy of the somatotype rating, one print of each of the thousand cases was sent to Sheldon, who made the somatotype rating. An illustration of such a print for each of the extremes of somatotype is illustrated in Figures 1, 2, and 3. The genital and face regions were not blocked out, however, as they are in the present illustrations. It should be strongly emphasized that these were all the data that Sheldon ever received about any of these patients. There was no indication whatsoever as to diagnosis, or even whether the patient was a neuropsychiatric or a medical admission.

The 3 germinal embryonic layers develop in varying degrees. In Figure 1 is pictured the endomorph, in whom endodermal elements predominate. The dominance of muscular and bony tissue is illustrated by the mesomorph in Figure 2. The individual in whom the ecto-

dermal layers are most fully developed is shown by the photograph of the ectomorph in Figure 3.

The clinical folders of the thousand cases included in this first series were studied. Seven pages of outlined information were abstracted from each of the 1,000 patients' records and included biosocial histories, symptoms, official staff diagnosis, etc. In addition, the military service records of the 455 schizophrenics were obtained from the Army, Navy, Coast Guard, and Marines, and were also reviewed in great detail. Approximately two-thirds of the total 1,000 patients in the series had had electrocardiograms and half of these had had cardiac consultations. Many of these patients also received a battery of neurophysiological tests and these, as well as all other pertinent data, have been recorded and will constitute the main body of the completed report.

The first patient in the series entered the hospital October 1, 1947, and the thousand admissions had been completed by April of 1949. These patients followed their normal hospital course, and in October of 1949 (2 years after the first admission and 6 months after the last admission) a survey was made of which patients were still hospitalized, which had been discharged with maximum hospital benefit, which had died, eloped, etc. Sheldon's somatotype

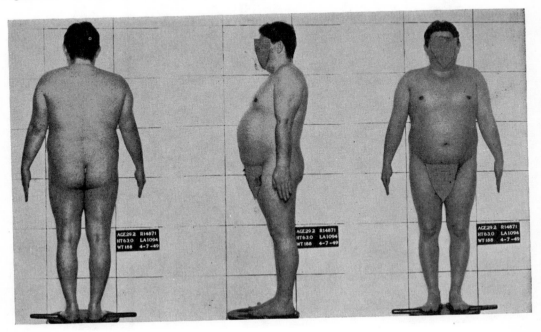

Figure 1.   Endomorph.

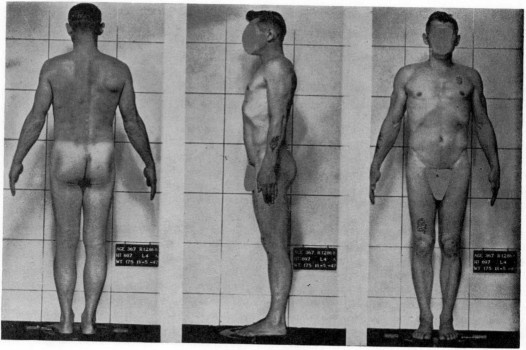

Figure 2.   Mesomorph.

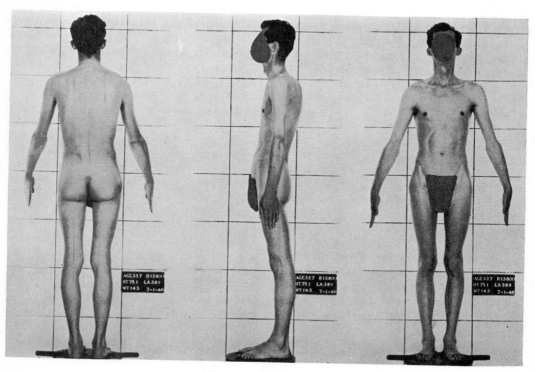

Figure 3.   Ectomorph.

ratings were then correlated with (1) diagnosis, and (2) disposition of the patient by the end of this period. Since Sheldon knew nothing of the patients' diagnosis, or disposition, and the hospital staff knew nothing of Sheldon's ratings, it is unlikely that any bias could have been introduced that would contaminate the results.

Results

In graphically presenting the results, a deviation has been made from Sheldon's graphic method.

Figures 4 and 5 present a tripolar figure, with endomorphy at the lower left, mesomorphy above, and ectomorphy at the lower right. In Sheldon's method of presentation, the absolute somatotype rating forms the basis of the scale:

thus a 7 in mesomorphy would appear at the very top of the figure. In our method of presen-

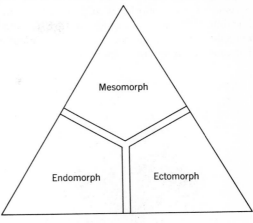

Figure 4.

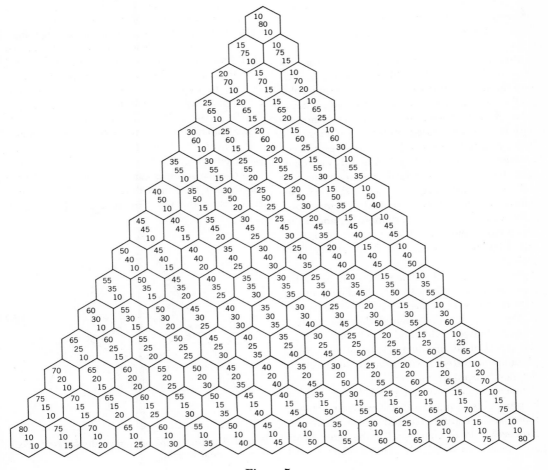

Figure 5.

tation, a percentage breakdown is used instead, since it presents a simpler method of graphing. The rating of an individual at the extreme of mesomorphy would be 10% endomorphic, 80% mesomorphic, and 10% ectomorphic, since no person can be completely deficient in any of the 3 embryonic layers.

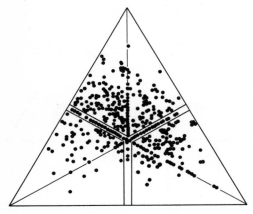

Figure 6. Total schizophrenics.

Figure 6 illustrates the distribution of somatotype of the total 455 schizophrenics admitted into the series. Of these, 45.7% are mesomorphs, 23.5% with a secondary endomorphic component, 8.1% balanced, with equal endomorphy and ectomorphy as secondary characteristics, and 14.7% with a secondary ectomorphic characteristic. Among the 13.0% eminently endomorphic 10.1% were secondarily mesomorphic and 1.3% secondarily ectomorphic, with 1.5% balanced. In the 25.9% dominantly ectomorphs, 3.3% were secondarily endomorphic and 17.6% secondarily mesomorphic, with 5.1% having equal balance between the 2 secondary components.

At the time of the first review, 45.3% of the patients were still hospitalized. The somatotype distribution of these patients is presented in Figure 7. It will be noted that the greatest contrast between this and the figure showing the distribution of somatotypes of all schizophrenics admitted is the relative reduction in the mesomorphic area.

Since patients are not rated "recovered," it is impossible to make a direct contrast between those still hospitalized and those recovered. However, the discharge with the most favorable prognosis is "MHB." This discharge, with

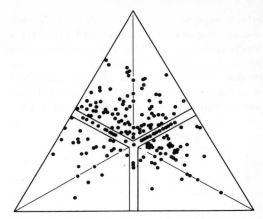

Figure 7. Total schizophrenics still hospitalized.

"maximum hospital benefit," means that the patient has received the greatest possible benefits that the hospital could offer, and most patients who would fall within the "recovered" group are encompassed by this designation. A certain number of these patients, however, remain actively schizophrenic although they may be able to adjust outside the hospital and are therefore discharged with maximum hospital benefit, since the hospital cannot be of further benefit to them. Only about 5% of the total schizophrenics admitted had been discharged MHB at the end of this first review period. Their somatotype distribution presents a striking contrast to that of the patients still hospitalized. (Fig. 8)

A comparison was made between the patients discharged MHB and those remaining hospitalized, using the Chi Square method. None of

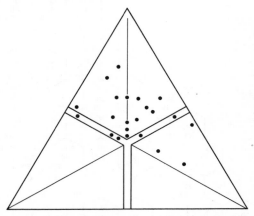

Figure 8. Total schizophrenics discharged maximum hospital benefit.

the endomorphs and none of the endomorphic ectomorphs were discharged MHB, so that the probability of a significant negative relationship between lack of endomorphy or endomorphic ectomorphy and discharge MHB is extremely high. There was also a positive correlation between mesomorphy and MHB discharge (Chi Square equalling 4.6, which means that there were less than 4 possibilities in a hundred of this distribution occurring by chance. Corrections for small numbers were used in obtaining Chi Square).

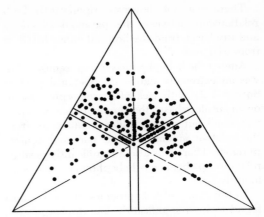

Figure 10.   Total paranoid schizophrenics.

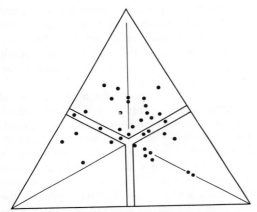

Figure 9.   Total schizophrenics discharged from trial visit.

Figure 9 presents the distribution of those patients discharged from trial visits. Patients placed on trial visit are considered potential candidates for readmission and are actually kept on the hospital rolls. Usually at the end of the year, those patients who have not found it necessary to return to the hospital are discharged from their trial visit status. This by no means indicates that the patient is "cured" but merely that he has been able to make some kind of adjustment outside the hospital, even though it may be in the custodial care of his family. If the patients with equally dominant mesomorphy and endomorphy and equally dominant mesomorphy and ectomorphy are included with those clearly mesomorphic, a statistically significant positive relationship is found between mesomorphy and discharge from trial visit, or MHB benefit (at the 5% confidence level).

An immediate objection that may be raised to these findings is that perhaps one diagnostic subcategory, e.g., paranoid schizophrenics, may

be dominantly of one somatotype and therefore prognosis is primarily related to diagnosis of subcategory rather than somatotype. To clarify this point, it was necessary to determine whether any positive relationship existed between diagnoses and somatotype. The somatotype distributions of the paranoid schizophrenics is presented in Figure 10. Compared with the other schizophrenics, the paranoids were found to have a significantly high amount of mesomorphy (only 5 possibilities in a hundred of chance occurrence), and an even higher negative correlation with ectomorphy; i.e., there was only about once chance in 500 that the relationship paranoia and low ectomorphy could occur by chance. The endomorphy was relatively low in both paranoids and hebephrenics, but the difference between these two groups was significant.

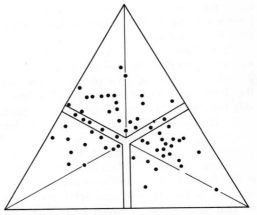

Figure 11.   Total hebephrenic schizophrenics.

There was not, however, significantly high relationship between the paranoid diagnosis and discharge from the hospital either MHB or from trial visit.

Among the hebephrenic schizophrenics, there was an extremely significant relationship (Chi Square 7.2) with lack of mesomorphy. Again on an absolute basis, the amount of endomorphy was small but did not differ significantly from the relative amount in the paranoid schizophrenics. There was also a significantly positive relationship between hebephrenia and ectomorphy.

In this group of hebephrenics, there was also found to be a significantly low discharge rate, either maximum hospital benefit, or from trial visit.

None of the mixed schizophrenics were discharged MHB, and even when combined with those discharged from trial visit, there is no significant relationship.

The simple schizophrenics showed no definite relationship between body type and diagnosis but showed a significantly high discharge rate, both MHB and from trial visit.

The positive findings may be summarized as follows:

1. The paranoid schizophrenics tended to be mesomorphs, with very few ectomorphs. The hebephrenics, on the other hand, were primarily ectomorphs with extremely few mesomorphs, compared to what might have been expected with a chance distribution. No other significant relationships between dominant body type and diagnosis were found.

2. The simple schizophrenics had a relatively good prognosis and the hebephrenics a relatively poor one. Aside from these, relationship between diagnosis and prognosis does not appear to be significant.

These figures immediately raise the conjecture as to whether the hebephrenics with very low mesomorphy and poor prognosis were not the determining factor in the over-all relationship between high mesomorphy and good prognosis. It was therefore necessary to correlate relationship between MHB discharges and somatotype, excluding the hebephrenics entirely from the series. When this is done, there is still found to be a significant correlation between high mesomorphy and MHB discharges so that relationship between body type and prognosis is evidently more basic than relationship between diagnosis and prognosis. It was similarly found that the relationship between high mesomorphy and MHB discharges (as well as when discharges from trial visit are combined with MHB discharges) existed whether the paranoid schizophrenics were included in the series or were not.

The strong relationship between high mesomorphy and a good prognosis was even more greatly emphasized when it was noted that patients with a mesomorhpy of 5½ or more on Sheldon's 7-point scale had a better prognosis than those with lower mesomorphy (at the 1% confidence level). On the other hand, patients with an endomorphy of 4 or more had a very significantly poorer prognosis for MHB discharges than those with less endomorphy. (Only one possibility in a thousand of chance occurrence of this finding.)

The absolute maximum for total endowment using Sheldon's ratings is 12½. Total endowment is obtained by adding the somatotype ratings for each of the 3 components, e.g., an individual with endomorphy 3, mesomorphy 5, ectomorphy 2, would have a total endowment of 3 plus 5 plus 2, which equals 10. In the present series, it was found that schizophrenic patients with a total endowment of 11½ or more and those with a total endowment of only 9 or less showed a significantly low discharge rate.

Discussion

In one sense, the present series does not constitute a typical mental hospital population since the patients were all males and had all been accepted for military service. This means that those who broke down early in life, or appeared extremely unstable, are not included in the series since they were not accepted for military service. It appears highly probable that this resulted in the elimination from the group of a considerable number of ectomorphs and endomorphs, who were excluded from military service by reason of being "over" or "under" weight. The findings obtained are therefore very likely much more significant than they would be under other circumstances, since the range of somatotype distribution was curtailed in the endomorphic and ectomorphic categories.

That mesomorphy is high in paranoia and low in hebephrenia has long been suspected.

Similarly, that ectomorphy is high in hebephrenia and mesomorphy is low has also been surmised. That there was virtually no chance of unconscious bias by reason of the fact that the somatotype rater knew nothing of the diagnosis and the diagnoser had no knowledge of somatotype rating has resulted in a clear-cut statistically valid demonstration of these relationships. Considering the nature of the group with its elimination of endomorphic and ectomorphic extremes, the reliability of the findings is augmented. The relationship between hebephrenia and poor prognosis merely serves as a check since the fact has already been well demonstrated. The finding of a statistically valid relationship between high mesomorphy and good prognosis has not previously been emphasized. The implication of this in selecting patients for insulin and electric shock will be discussed in a future paper where the correlation between response to these somatic therapies and somatotype is being investigated. The apparent poor prognosis of endomorphic schizophrenics needs further validation. Another finding that may be of considerable value is that individuals who are overendowed or underendowed, as far as total constitution is concerned, tend to have a poor prognosis.

Implications

It is well to emphasize that we do not feel that somatotype is the final determining factor in the type or prognosis of schizophrenia. The ultimate answers probably lie in the biochemical and biophysical fields. Direct approach to the problem through biochemistry and biophysics has, however, only resulted in a welter of data that are consistent only in the fact that they are extremely variable. We have already obtained considerable information from other patients of the larger study, which leads us to believe that many physiological responses—and ultimately the biochemical and biophysical relations upon which they rest—vary in direct relationship with somatotype. On the basis of the present study, it appears indisputable that a relationship does exist between the subtypes of schizophrenia and somatotype, as well as between prognosis and somatotype. The introduction of somatotyping as an "organizing principle" may quite possibly make order out of what is now chaos because of individual differences.

Summary

1. In a series of 2,100 consecutive admissions to the Veterans Administration Hospital, Lyons, N. J., 72% of the schizophrenics were photographed in the standardized somatotype position shortly after admission.

2. These somatotype photographs were rated by Dr. William H. Sheldon, who had no knowledge as to the diagnosis, disposition, or any other pertinent information about the patients. Since these patients were included in a much larger series made up of psychoneurotics, neurological cases, and nonneuropsychiatric patients, in addition to the schizophrenics, the rater had no way of knowing even that they were schizophrenics.

3. The patients were allowed to follow their normal course in the hospital without awareness on the part of the staff as to their somatotype rating. The staff had no particular training in possible relationships between somatotype and psychiatric factors.

4. In all, 1,000 relatively consecutive admissions were somatotyped in the present series and an extremely detailed review made of all pertinent material, including records while in service, laboratory data, cardiac and ECG consultations, symptomatology, etc.

5. Two years after the first patient in the series was admitted (and 6 months after the last series admission), the disposition of the patients was reviewed.

6. There was found to be a significantly positive correlation between mesomorphy and good prognosis and a suggestively poor one with high endomorphy.

7. This correlation between prognosis and somatotype proved to be independent of correlations between somatotype and diagnosis. In other words, relationship between prognosis and somatotype is more basic than relationship between prognosis and diagnostic subcategory.

8. Significant correlations were found to exist between somatotype and diagnosis: Mesomorphs tended to be paranoid and not hebe-

phrenic, whereas, ectomorphs tended to be hebephrenic and not paranoid.

9. It was also found that those who were overendowed, or underendowed from an absolute point of view, had a poor prognosis.

10. On the basis of other parts of the study, it is suggested that with the somatotype as a frame of reference a much-needed factor will be introduced into the organic approach to schizophrenia, making comprehensible much of the data that are now characterized only by their great variability.

3. Body build and behavior in young children: body build and nursery school teacher's ratings

RICHARD N. WALKER

THIS STUDY, part of a larger research project, investigates some relations between children's physique and their behavior in a nursery school setting. It tests the adequacy of certain predictions based on the work of William Sheldon and explores additional areas of possible physique-behavior interrelations.

Sample

The main subjects were 73 boys and 52 girls, all the children attending the Gesell Institute Nursery School during one or both of two consecutive years, with the exception of (a) children having physical handicaps, (b) children falling clearly outside the intelligence distribution of the rest of the group, (ac) children of nonwhite racial background, (d) children whose stay in school was too short to permit teacher ratings, and (e) children who refused to be photographed. At the time of photographing, the children ranged in age from 2-6 to 2-11, 3-6 to 3-11, or 4-6 to 4-11. Socioeconomic status of the sample was biased upward and along academic lines: 95 per cent of the children's fathers held college degrees and over half held a degree at the doctoral level. As judged from the PARI scores of a subgroup, the children's mothers were relatively homogeneous

SOURCE. Selection from Monograph by Richard N. Walker, "Body build and behavior in young children: body build and nursery school teacher's ratings" in *Child Development Monograph*, pp. 75–79, 1962.

in disagreeing with statements endorsing punitiveness and authoritarian control. The children formed a sample of well cared for, well nourished, healthy, bright subjects.

Procedure

Each child was photographed in the nude in standard pose in front, side, and back position. The physique evaluations were made from these photographs by three judges, two of whom never saw the subjects and one of whom was acquainted with the children. Each judge rated each child for manifest level of three physique dimensions: endomorphy (roughly speaking, fatness), mesomorphy (muscle and bone development), and ectomorphy (slenderness).

A set of 63 rating scales was asembled for appraising the children's nursery school behavior. Before any ratings were made, a set of predictions was drawn up concerning the probable direction of correlation of each behavior item with each physique variable. These predictions were based on Sheldon's report of physique-behavior relations in college men.

The children were then rated on the behavior scales. Each was rated independently by four or five teachers. Of the 15 teachers who contributed ratings, three knew that these were to be used for physique-behavior comparisons. At least three naive judges' ratings were averaged with each rating by an informed judge. From the 63 individual items of the inventory, nine more general scales were developed, each composed of two to six intercorrelated items.

The Measuring Instruments

Physique Ratings

Along with the 125 photographs of children whose behavior was rated, the judges evaluated an additional 249 photographs of children in the same age range who had attended the nursery school in previous years. Standard scores were computed for endomorphy, mesomorphy, and ectomorphy for each judge's ratings at each age. and these were averaged for the three judges. These mean scores were transformed into somatotype-like scores with a mean of 3.5, a standard deviation of 1.0, and an interval of .5. Each physique component at each age then ranged by half steps from 1 or 1½ to 6½ or 7, with a mean of 3½. Coefficients of reliability for the average of the standard scores of the three judges fell near .90 for endomorphy and ectomorphy at each age. Interjudge agreement in rating mesomorphy was lower, represented by coefficients of around .85 for the boys and around .70 for the girls. For a subsample of children rated at more than one age (two judges did not know which were repeats), all retest correlations for a one-year-interval reached or exceeded .90, when corrected for attenuation. The small group of children rated at 2 and 4 years showed lower values, though all exceeded .70.

Behavior Ratings

A rating of the child's compliance-resistance in the photographing situation was made by the photographer and, during the second year of the study, by the teacher assisting. Correlations between the two were .93 for the 31 boys rated by both, .80 for the 32 girls.

For the individual items of the nursery school behavior scale, Horst's index of reliability of the average of scores of multiple judges was computed for the first year's ratings. Median reliability indices for the different age groups ranged from .71 to .81. Reliability coefficients for the cluster scores for the total sample were higher, ranging from .75 to .92 and with two thirds of the coefficients exceeding .85.

Results

Reaction to the Photographing Situation

While no age differences appeared in compliance ratings, marked differences appeared between the sexes, boys being the more resistant. Children of endomorphic physique tended to be resistant to the situation, while mesomorphs and ectomorphs tended to be compliant, in the case of both boys and girls. (Three of the six coefficients were significant.) Multiple correlations between the three physique variables and compliance reached .42 for boys, .67 for girls.

Outcome of the Predictions

Of the total of 292 predictions made for boys and girls for the three physique variables, 73 per cent were confirmed in direction and 21 per cent were confirmed beyond the .05 level while 3 per cent were disconfirmed beyond the .05 level. Sex differences in success of prediction were clear: over a third of predictions made for boys were significantly confirmed, less than 10 per cent for girls. The three physique components also showed differences in success ratios. Relations with mesomorphy were best predicted; for boys close to half the predictions made were confirmed at a significant level. Relations with ectomorphy were intermediate in success, though nearly as many predictions were confirmed significantly for boys. Relations with endomorphy were predicted with little better than chance success for the girls and slightly less than chance success for the boys.

Nursery School Behavior and Individual Physique Components

Endomorphy. For boys, only one cluster score, aggressiveness, correlated significantly with endomorphy, and this evidently by virtue of the correlation of both with mesomorphy. Ten individual behavior items were associated with endomorphy, six of them in a direction opposite to that which had been predicted. Together with nine items significant only at the .10 level, these give a picture of assertive aggressiveness (self-assertive, revengeful, easily angered, inconsiderate, quarrelsome, etc.), high energy level (ambitious, daring, noisy, boyish), extraversion (does not daydream, social in play), and low sensitivity (insensitive to pain, feelings not easily hurt, few nervous habits). For girls also one cluster score, cooperativeness, correlated significantly with endomorphy. Only a single individual rating item was significantly associated with endomorphy, though together with the four items significant at the .10 level it contributed to a consistent picture of good personal-social adjustment (recovers quickly from upsets, not tense, does not daydream, direct in solving social problems, social in play).

Mesomorphy. For boys, all but one of the nine cluster scores showed significant relation with mesomorphy, as did 24 of the individual rating items. The girls showed just three significant correlations between mesomorphy and the cluster scores, eight between mesomorphy and the individual rating items. Characteristic of both boys and girls high in mesomorphy is a dominating assertiveness (leader in play, competitive, self-assertive, easily angered, attacks others, etc.), high energy output, openness of expression, and fearlessness. The girls combine this assertiveness with socialness, cheerfulness, and warmth. The boys' items give more suggestion of hostility (quarrelsome, revengeful, inconsiderate) and of an impulsive, headlong quality to their activity (daring, noisy, quick, accident prone, self-confident, etc.).

Ectomorphy. Boys and girls each showed two cluster scores which correlated with ectomorphy, but 27 individual items showed significant association with ectomorphy for the boys, just eight for the girls. In common for both sexes are items suggesting a certain aloofness (not social in play, does not attack others, daydreams, indirect in solving problems). Different items for boys and girls suggest an emotional restraint in both (boys: not easily angered, not expressive in movements, not talkative, etc.; girls: not dramatic, not open in expressing feelings, low verbal interests). For boys, the items in general define a cautious, quiet child, not self-assertive, hesitant to give offence, looking to adults rather than to children for approval, sensitive, slow to recover from upsets. He appears lacking in energy reserves (not energetic, dislikes gross motor play, enjoys hand activities, has few accidents). For girls, the composite picture is similar but tends more to indicate a somberness of outlook—unfriendly, tense, not gay or cheerful, irritable.

Total physique pattern. Combination of the three physique components in multiple regression correlation with the cluster scores gave little increase over the highest single-component coefficients for the boys, somewhat greater increase for the girls. The multiple correlations ranged from .20 to .52.

A graphic technique of analysis suggests higher relations, particularly for the boys. In this method, the physique rating of each individual is plotted on a somatotype distribution chart, the plotted point indicating whether the subject is below or above average on the cluster score in question. A single, straight cutting line is then drawn which separates the total distribution of subjects into (approximately) equal halves and which gives a maximum of above-average subjects in one half. For this dichotomy a tetrachoric correlation can be computed. For a majority of the nine traits, the cutting lines chosen by inspection closely approximated a single, common cutting line. For boys, a dichotomy contrasting mesomorphs and mesomorphic endomorphs with ectomorphs and ectomorphic endomorphs produced differences in rates of aggressiveness, energy level, and sensitivity corresponding to tetrachoric correlations in the .60's. The traits

of fearfulness, cheerfulness, and cooperativeness showed less striking separation by this common cutting line. Two other cutting lines showed some suggestion of association with behavior differences in boys, though the evidence was weaker. A line separating endomorphs and ectomorphs appears to separate boys more oriented to peer approval from boys more oriented to adult approval. And a line separating endomorphs from mesomorphs separates boys resistant in the photographing situation from boys compliant in that setting.

For girls, only a single cutting line was found which appeared associated with behavior differences. Girls plotted in the mesomorphic area of the chart differ from other girls in showing greater aggressiveness, cheerfulness, socialness, and energy, as well as less fearfulness and less sensitivity.

Conclusions

It is concluded that in this group of preschool children important associations do exist between individuals' physiques and particular behavior characteristics. Further, these associations show considerable similarity to those described by Sheldon for college-aged men, though the strength of association is not as strong as he reports. It is suggested that the relations are multiply determined, arising from primary bodily conditions (e.g., strength, energy, sensory thresholds), from direct learnings concerning the efficacy of different modes of behavior and adjustment techniques, and from less direct learnings regarding expectations and evaluations accorded to different physiques by others. Other factors, possibly innate, as well as opportunity for and encouragement of particular behaviors, appear important in directing the physique-associated behavior. This is suggested by the mesomorphic girls' channeling of their energies more into social activities, the mesomorphic boys' more into physical, gross-motor activity. The young ages of the subjects would seem to give some weight to constitutional and direct-learning factors as contrasted with reputation variables, which others have pointed out as important at later ages. In particular, variations in physical energy, in bodily effectiveness for assertive or dominating behavior, and in bodily sensitivity appear as important mediating links between physique structure and general behavior.

4.   Unraveling juvenile delinquency

SHELDON GLUECK AND ELEANOR GLUECK

Somatotypes

Two complementary methods were used by Seltzer in analyzing the delinquents and non-delinquents from the point of view of bodily types: (1) On the basis of trained inspection of the photographs of each boy, a somatotype rating was made by an assistant, dependent upon the physique components clearly apparent at the time the pictures were taken. (2) A matched-pair comparison was made between the delinquent series and the non-delinquent series to discover differences between the delinquent and non-delinquent in each pair compared. One method could thus serve as a check against the other.

In the first method, the two sets of photographs having first been commingled, each was scrutinized and judged with respect to the predominance of each of the three major physique components: endomorphy, mesomorphy, ectomorphy. After the photographs were assembled into three classes on the basis of this primary examination, they were re-examined to select those that represented extreme incidence of a component. This resulted in three polar groups: extreme endomorphs, extreme mesomorphs, and extreme ectomorphs. A third scrutiny of the pictures remaining from the original sortings yielded a three-fold classification under each component of physique, to take account of the participation of the other components. Thus, the group deemed endomorphic was subdivided into mesomorphic endomorphs, endomorphs, and ectomorphic endomorphs; the mesomorphs

fell into endomorphic mesomorphs, mesomorphs, ectomorphic mesomorphs; the ectomorphic group was sorted into mesomorphic ectomorphs, ectomorphs, endomorphic ectomorphs. The photographs were thereby sorted into twelve classes; and a thirteenth was reserved for subjects "regarded as displaying midrange physical endowment in which none of the three traits assumes dominance over the other two in any marked degree."

The following table compares the incidence of each of the somatotype classes arrived at by this careful inspectional method applied by trained anthropologists.

The predominance of the mesomorphic type among delinquents, previously indicated by the anthropometric analyses, is abundantly clear from Table 1. The table shows that twice as many of the delinquents (60.1% : 30.7%) were found to have a predominance of the mesomorphic component. The non-delinquents, on the other hand, are primarily characterized by ectomorphy, nearly thrice as many of them (39.6%, as contrasted with 14.5% of the delinquents) having this component dominance. Moreover, the non-delinquent group shows itself to be less homogeneous than the delinquent group. Unlike the delinquents, none of the somatotype classes among the non-delinquents amounts to as much as 60%; and while, as noted, the ectomorphic-dominant group among the controls consists of four-tenths (39.6%) of the total, the mesomorphic is close behind with three-tenths (30.7%). In both the endomorphic-dominant type (11.8%: 15%) and the balanced type (13.5% : 14.7%), the delinquents and non-delinquents are not markedly different.

However, a more minute analysis of these categories shows significant variations. Thus,

SOURCE. Selection from Sheldon Glueck and Eleanor Glueck, *Unraveling Juvenile Delinquency*, New York, The Commonwealth Fund, 1950, pp. 192–197.

Table 1. Somatotypes

	Delinquents		Non-Delinquents				
Endomorphic Component Dominance	Number	Per Cent	Number	Per Cent	Percentile Ratio	C.R.	P*
Extreme endomorphs	6	1.2	24	5.0	1 to 4.2	3.4	<.05
Endomorphs	14	2.8	23	4.8	1 to 1.7	1.6	<.11
Mesomorphic endomorphs	16	3.2	7	1.5	2.1 to 1	1.8	<.08
Ectomorphic endomorphs	23	4.6	18	3.7	1.2 to 1	0.8	<.08
Subtotal	59	11.8	72	15.0			
Mesomorphic Component Dominance							
Extreme Mesomorphs	115	23.2	34	7.1	3.3 to 1	7.2	<.05
Mesomorphs	84	16.9	59	12.2	1.4 to 1	2.1	<.05
Endomorphic mesomorphs	66	13.3	15	3.1	4.3 to 1	6.0	<.05
Ectomorphic mesomorphs	33	6.7	40	8.3	1 to 1.2	0.6	<.55
Subtotal	298	60.1	148	30.7			
Ectomorphic Component Dominance							
Extreme ectomorphs	9	1.8	70	14.5	1 to 8.1	7.4	<.05
Ectomorphs	25	5.0	71	14.7	1 to 2.9	5.1	<.05
Endomorphic ectomorphs	21	4.2	15	3.1	1.4 to 1	0.9	<.37
Mesomorphic ectomorphs	17	3.4	35	7.3	1 to 2.1	2.7	<.05
Subtotal	72	14.4	191	39.6			
No Component Dominance							
Balanced Types	67	13.5	71	14.7	1 to 1.1	0.5	<.62
Total	496	99.8	482	100.0			

* It should be recalled that a P of <.05 indicates statistical significance in the physique study.

extreme endomorphs—very few in number—occur less frequently among the delinquents than among the non-delinquents (1.2% : 5%); extreme mesomorphs are thrice as frequent among the former as the latter (23.2% : 7.1%); but extreme ectomorphs are only an eighth as frequent (1.8% : 14.5%). It should also be noted that while the non-delinquents predominate in extreme endomorphy, the proportion of endomorphic mesomorphs among the delinquents is four times that of the non-delinquents (13.3% : 3.1%).

Thus, although mesomorphy definitely constitutes the major basis of differentiation between the delinquents and non-delinquents,

and ectomorphy predominates among the latter, the existence of subtypes in the two groups, in which the participation of other constitutional elements is evident, should not be overlooked.

The second method used for classification into somatotypes was to take each matched pair and, by comparing the delinquent with the non-delinquent, to arrive at the relative difference between the two in respect to the degree of strength of the various components. These judgments of relative difference were recorded as *same, slight, moderate, marked*. For example, comparing a delinquent mesomorph with his non-delinquent mate, who happened to be an ectomorph, the following judgment might be recorded:

Endomorphy : Delinquent slightly stronger than non-delinquent.
Mesomorphy : Delinquent markedly stronger than non-delinquent.
Ectomorphy : Delinquent markedly weaker than non-delinquent.

"Differences were recorded only when they were clear-cut and readily observable; other-wise the component was designated as being in the *same* strength in both subjects." The matched-pair comparison was made by Selt-zer; the inspectional somatotyping by Ash-ton Tenney. This complementary approach strengthens the reliability of the findings.

The following table shows the outcome of the comparison of 482 matched pairs of delin-quents and non-delinquents.

It is clear from Table 2 that the matched-pair comparisons of relative strength of the

Table 2. Comparison of Strength of Endomorphic, Mesomorphic, and Ectomorphic Components among 482 Matched Pairs of Delinquents and Non-Delinquents

	482 Matched Pairs	
Endomorphic Component	Number	Per Cent
Delinquent *markedly stronger* than non-delinquent	20	4.1
Delinquent *moderately stronger* than non-delinquent	70	14.5
Delinquent *slightly stronger* than non-delinquent	167	34.6
Delinquent *same* as non-delinquent	93	19.3
Non-delinquent *slightly stronger* than delinquent	70	14.5
Non-delinquent *moderately stronger* than delinquent	35	7.3
Non-delinquent *markedly stronger* than delinquent	27	5.6
Total	482	99.9
Mesomorphic Component		
Delinquent *markedly stronger* than non-delinquent	68	14.1
Delinquent *moderately stronger* than non-delinquent	96	19.9
Delinquent *slightly stronger* than non-delinquent	135	28.0
Delinquent *same* as non-delinquent	68	14.1
Non-delinquent *slightly stronger* than delinquent	85	17.6
Non-delinquent *moderately stronger* than delinquent	24	5.0
Non-delinquent *markedly stronger* than delinquent	6	1.2
Total	482	99.9
Ectomorphic Component		
Delinquent *markedly stronger* than non-delinquent	24	5.0
Delinquent *moderately stronger* than non-delinquent	42	8.7
Delinquent *slightly stronger* than non-delinquent	83	17.2
Delinquent *same* as non-delinquent	79	16.4
Non-delinquent *slightly stronger* than delinquent	114	23.7
Non-delinquent *moderately stronger* than delinquent	76	15.8
Non-delinquent *markedly stronger* than delinquent	64	13.3
Total	482	100.1

various components result in a consistently greater mesomorphic dominance among the delinquents than the non-delinquents, while the reverse is true in respect to ectomorphic dominance. The endomorphic participation is more ambiguous. While cases of markedly stronger endomorphy are somewhat more frequent among the non-delinquents, slightly and moderately stronger endomorphic differentiation predominate among the delinquents. (See Table 1.)

Thus, both by inspection of the individual photographs and through a comparison of matched pairs of cases by independent observers, the striking finding emerges that among the delinquents mesomorphy is unquestionably the most dominant component, the other types being represented in about equal proportions but in relatively small numbers. Among the non-delinquents, on the other hand, the ectomorphic component predominates, although not to the extent that mesomorphy characterizes the delinquents. Mesomorphy is also appreciably represented among the non-delinquents, while endomorphy and the balanced type are far less frequent. Detailed analysis reveals that the delinquents have an excess of extreme mesomorphs, mesomorphs, and endomorphic mesomorphs, and a deficiency of extreme endomorphs, extreme and ordinary ectomorphs, and mesomorphic ectomorphs.

Summary

The anthropologic analysis has demonstrated that the following significant differences exist between the delinquents and the non-delinquents with whom they were matched:

In gross bodily size the delinquents are superior to the non-delinquents, this superiority being expressed especially in the shoulders, chest, waist, and upper extremities, and outlining the picture of the masculine physical type with tapering torso, heavy arms, small face, strong neck, and wide shoulders.

The delinquents evidence a lag in physical growth until about the fourteenth year, when they spurt forward to a superiority over the non-delinquents.

Indices of bodily proportions bring out more strikingly the differences between the two groups, especially the greater laterality of the body build of the delinquents, with a corresponding deficiency in the linear element, and the comparative strength of this linear component among the non-delinquents.

The delinquents are relatively more homogeneous in physique than the non-delinquents.

Bodily disproportions are less frequent among the delinquents than among the non-delinquents.

Although the great majority of both groups have a strong masculine component in their physiques, weakness here is only a fourth as frequent among the delinquents as among the controls.

Two independent methods of classification into physique types reveal that, absolutely and relatively, the delinquents are mesomorphic in constitution (muscular), containing a much higher proportion of all mesomorphic types than the non-delinquents and a far lower proportion of ectomorphs (linear, thin). Ectomorphs, endomorphs (round, plump), and balanced types are decidedly subordinate among the delinquents. The control group of non-delinquents contains no extreme predominance of any somatotype, but it does have substantial numbers of both ectomorphs and mesomorphs, with the former in excess; endomorphs and balanced types do not appear often among the non-delinquents.

Considering that these findings were arrived at by various avenues of independent analysis, the results take on particular significance. When tracing the development of character and conduct, we must examine constitutional endowment along with the early influences surrounding the child in his home, school, and neigborhood.

5. Morphology and behavior*

GARDNER LINDZEY

The theme of this sermon is that human structure and function are significantly intertwined. In the lines to follow I propose to assert the relative neglect by American students of behavior of the physical person and its components, to suggest some possible determinants of this persistent myopia, to examine some arguments and evidence for the importance of such constitutional parameters for the psychologist, and, finally, to mention a few illustrative areas of potential research interest. Initially I should make clear that I am using the term morphology quite broadly to refer not only to the physical, structural aspects of the organism but also to any externally observable and objectively measurable attribute of the person, thus embracing such variables as hirsuteness, symmetry, color and even esthetic attractiveness.

American Resistance to Constitutional Psychology

It is a commonplace observation that American psychologists have been reluctant to give serious consideration to the study of morphology and behavior (cf. MacKinnon & Maslow, 1951; Hall & Lindzey 1957) and some of the determinants of this enduring resistance are quite

clear. First, it is undeniable that our attention has been devoted primarily to the study of social and behavioral *change*. The modal emphasis among psychologists in America has been upon learning, acquisition, shaping, or the modification of behavior, and not upon those aspects of the person and behavior that appear relatively fixed and unchanging. As has been said elsewhere, "One important by-product of American democracy, the Protestant ethic, and the dogma of the self-made man has been the rejection of formulations implying that behavior may be innately conditioned, immutable, a 'given.' Because it is commonly accepted that physical characteristics are linked closely to genetic factors, the suggestion that physical and psychological characteristics are intimately related seems to imply a championing of genetic determinism. It is not surprising that such a conception has been unable to muster much support in the face of the buoyant environmentalism of American psychology." (Hall & Lindzey, 1957, p. 337)

A second significant deterrent has been the spectacular failure of the influential formulations of Gall and Spurzheim (1809) concerning body and behavior, coupled with the popularity of morphological variables among such diagnostic charlatans as palmists and physiognomists. These two conditions provide a ready-made cloak of naivete, ignorance or dishonesty for the person interested in working in this area.

Third is the fact that constitutional psychology has in recent decades become so

SOURCE. Chapter by G. Lindzey "Morphology and behavior" in *Behavioral Consequences of Genetic Differences in Man.* Edited by J. N. Spuhler, Viking Fund Publications (in press).

* A modified version of this paper was presented as the presidential address of Division 8 (Personality and Social Psychology) of the American Psychological Association, September 5, 1964. The manuscript was written while in residence at the Center for Advanced Study in the Behavioral Sciences and its preparation was facilitated by a grant from the Ford Foundation and a Special Fellowship from the National Institute of Mental Health. I am grateful to Edward E. Jones for his helpful comments.

closely associated with the name and work of William Sheldon that attitudes toward the one are scarcely separable from attitudes toward the other. In his research and writing Sheldon is much more the sensitive naturalist, observer and categorizer and much less the hard, quantitative and objective scientist than would be optimal to assure a good press from our colleagues. Moreover, in his writings he has proven to be singularly adept at ridiculing or parodying just those aspects of the scientific posture of psychologists that are most sensitively, rigidly and humorlessly maintained. One might argue convincingly that if Sheldon had conducted the same research but had reported it in an appropriately dull, constricted and affectless manner (consistent, let us say, with *Journal of Experimental Psychology* standards) its impact upon the discipline of psychology might have been much greater. What I am suggesting is that acceptance of Sheldon's work was impaired by a general resistance on the part of American psychologists to the study of behavior in relation to fixed characteristics and, conversely, that his irreverent and unconventional style provided further support for the belief that the study of morphology and behavior was an unsanitary practice. Whatever the determinants, it seems clear that American psychology in the past and present has maintained a suspicious hostility toward formulation and investigation concerned with body and behavior. Perhaps only the study of behavior in relation to the soul has been equally unpopular among psychologists.

Morphological Dimensions

A word should be said concerning available variables and methods for describing the physical person. It is obvious that we do not yet have agreement concerning those components or dimensions that can be employed most fruitfully to represent morphological variation, although there are three sets of variables and attendant measures that have had a reasonable range of modern application. First, and best known, are Sheldon's (1940, 1954) components of endomorphy, mesomorphy and ectomorphy; with ratings for each dimension derived from a standardized set of photographs by means of a complex rating procedure or through the actuarial use of a small number of relatively

objective indices. The full details of the latter procedure have not yet been fully published, but the indices are age, height, ponderal index, and trunk index. Parnell (1958) has devised an alternative method of measuring comparable variables which he labels fat, muscularity and linearity. His ratings are based upon a small number of anthropometric measures of subcutaneous fat, bone length, and girth of arm and calf. Third is Lindegård's (1953; Lindegård & Nyman, 1956) scheme which includes four variables—length, sturdiness, muscularity and fat. His dimensions were identified with the aid of factor analysis and they are rated by means of a combination of anthropometric measurements and performance (strength) tests.

It is clear that much important research remains to be done in further identifying alternative or additional dimensions to represent the body and that the existing dimensions and measures are far from ideal. Indeed there have been a number of publications (e.g., Hammond, 1957a, 1957b; Hunt, 1952) that have been sharply critical of the best known measurement systems. Still the deficiencies that inhere in these particular schemes and measurement operations must be expected to attenuate or obscure attempts to relate these variables to behavior. Thus, whatever well-controlled associations we now observe between morphology and behavior may be considered to represent minimum estimates rather than an upper limit. It is important to note that in spite of diversity in the particular measures or indices investigators have commenced with, and differences in the methods of analysis they have employed, there is a high degree of congruence among the three sets of variables that are currently popular. Finally, and perhaps most important, we do possess a set of existing tools with which one readily can initiate research in this area.

Mechanisms Mediating a Hypothetical Relationship Between Morphology and Behavior

Ultimately, justification for increased interest in morphology and behavior must rest upon the provision of compelling empirical evidence for important associations between these two sectors of the person. Before turning to even a glimpse at empirical evidence, however, it seems reasonable to examine the rational and theoretical basis that can be provided to motivate an interest in such relationships. In brief, what we are concerned with here is a specification of the reasonable pathways or mechanisms whereby an important association between physical and behavioral components might be achieved. A crude classification suggests that there are five discriminable means that might lead one to predict such associations.

First is the possibility that a *common experiential* or environmental class of *events* has a characteristic *influence* upon personality or *behavior and,* at the same time, has a regular and detectable effect upon *morphology.* For example, if we accept certain psychoanalytic formulations (Bruch, 1947) concerning the relation between obesity and a particular type of parent-child relation—maternal overprotectiveness—and assume, moreover, that physical components are influenced by weight and diet factors, we would confidently expect some degree of association between the endomorphic or fat factor and those behavioral consequences that are believed to be associated with maternal overprotectiveness. Or, if we accept the report of Landauer and Whiting (1965) that in societies where noxious and traumatic experiences are a regular part of the socialization practice, "the mean adult male stature was over two inches greater than in societies where these customs were not practiced" and assume, moreover, that such early experiences also have an influence upon behavior, we would once again expect physique and behavior to be importantly linked. There is, of course, a good deal of lower animal evidence (e.g., Denenberg, 1962; Lindzey, Winston & Manosevitz, 1963) to support this same point of view—that early experience influences both morphology and behavior. In brief, this position makes the reasonable assumption (with some supporting evidence) that there are certain important events that serve to determine, both physical and behavioral development in a manner that produces significant associations between outcomes in these two spheres.

Second is the inevitable observation that *behavior is directly limited or facilitated* to some degree *by the physical person.* Even the most dedicated and competitive 145 pound athlete cannot aspire realistically to play first string tackle for a Big Ten university, nor is it likely that the 260 pound tackle could ever compete successfully in a marathon race or as an effective jockey. A male whose maximum height is 5'4" cannot reasonably expect to compete with John Thomas or Valeri Brumel. The frail ectomorph cannot expect to employ physical or aggressive responses with the same effect as the robust mesomorph. Height, strength, weight and comparable dimensions place direct and unmistakable limits upon what responses the individual can hope to make adaptively in a given environmental setting.

A third factor, which is closely related to the second, concerns the *indirect consequences of* a particular set of *physical attributes.* For example, within our society, if an individual's biological makeup places him well above most others in size and strength, it is very likely that he will be recruited early in his life into competitive athletics and that this experience will play an important role in his life. Those who have undergone or studied the impact of four to ten years of varsity athletics upon behavior would scarcely question the profound implications of this experience for many important aspects of the individual's values, dispositions and overt behavior. To take a widely divergent example, it is now carefully documented for women that linearity (ectomorphy) is negatively associated with rate of physical and biological maturation. A study by McNeil & Livson (1963), the only published research with which I am familiar that employs Sheldon's new and presumably more actuarial method of somatotyping, provides compelling evidence for a significant association between a process of great psychological importance and one morphological component. No observer of the adolescent female, or student of the socialization process, would be likely to deny that the age at which a girl becomes, in some sense, a woman, has significance for her psychological development; and here we have clear evidence that the more linear her physique, the slower she will be in undergoing and completing this developmental stage.

The two examples that have been cited could be multipled endlessly by listing the implications of particular kinds of bodies for particular kinds of environmental events and experiences. Surely there is some degree of regular behavioral impact attendant upon being a handsome man as opposed to an ugly man; a "stacked" girl as opposed to a fragile, linear girl; a large, powerful man in comparison to a small, weak man.

Fourth is a special case of the indirect implications of physique, and relates to *role specification* or the social stimulus-value of particular variations in the physical person. Insofar as a given society includes a number of individuals who hold common expectations in regard to the "fat man," the "lean and hungry person," "the red head," "the receding chin," etc., it is clear that the individuals who fit these physical prescriptions will be exposed to a somewhat different set of learning experiences or environmental events than the person of more modal body or whose physique is extreme in a different manner. Whether the behavior that is expected of the particular physique is grounded in firm empirical observation, casual superstition, or magical thinking, if the expectation is maintained by a sizeable number of persons it creates a different social reality for those who fit the prescription. Whether they conform to social expectation or vigorously oppose it, they are influenced by a common set of experiential determinants that set them off from those of a different morphology and, consequently, we might expect to find some uniformities in their behavior not shared by persons of very different physique.

Finally, we come to the mechanism which is probably most objectionable to the majority of American psychologists—*joint biological determinants of both behavior and physique*. This type of association could be produced by a known set of physiological processes that demonstrably influence both behavior and physique. (in the abstract it is easy to cite endocrine function) or the link might be produced by a common set of genetic determinants, with or without information concerning the process whereby genetic variation is translated into morphological and behavioral variation. To take a simple case, for both man and lower animal it is well known that a large proportion of the morphological variables that have been studied are importantly influenced by genetic variation. For example, the two major twin studies that have examined physical attributes (Newman, Freeman & Holzinger, 1937; Osborne & DeGeorge, 1959) report heritability coefficients for specific morphological attributes that for the most part are above .70.

Sheldon's physique components are reported by Osborne & DeGeorge to display appreciably lower heritability coefficients (Total Somatotype: Males = .36; Females = .61) but it remains clear that genetic variation makes a significant contribution to morphological variation.

Given this observation, it seems altogether reasonable to anticipate that the chromosomal loci that influence variation in morphology may have multiple or pleitropic effects, some of which are behavioral. To use an illustration made somewhat remote by phylogenetic regression, my colleague Harvey Winston and I (Winston & Lindzey, 1964), working with mice, have produced tentative evidence suggesting that albinism (which is determined by a recessive gene cc in linkage group 1) is associated with a relative deficiency in escape learning. Whether this particular finding is sustained or not, there is every reason to expect that comparable pleitropic effects linking physical and behavioral components will be found in a variety of behavioral and physical areas. Even at the human level we may expect comparable, although perhaps more complex, examples. Indeed, if we are willing to include the realm of pathology in our discussion, it is clear that there are numerous examples of conditions which, under the normal range of environmental variation, are controlled by genetic variation and include both behavioral and physical deviations. An evident example of this is Down's Syndrome (Mongolism) which as a result of modern cytological advances we now know to be produced by a genetic anomoly, typically involving either trisomy or translocation associated with the 21st chromosome (Jarvik, Falek & Pierson, 1964), and which leads to a variety of dramatic behavioral and physical consequences. Here, then, is a particular kind of genetic variation (objectively identifiable) which leads to profound and undeniable effects in both the physical and behavioral sphere. Numerous other examples could be discussed including Huntingdon's Chorea, Phenlyketonuria, and Infantile Amaurotic Idiocy.

The main generalization I wish to extract from what has just been said is that working within the assumptions that are common to most psychologists (whether learning, developmental, physiological, social, or what not) it appears altogether reasonable for one to expect to observe important associations between morphology and behavior. Or, stated in the ritual terminology of modern psychology, given appropriate information concerning morphology we may expect with reasonable confidence to have some degree of predictive control over the variance of behavior.

Some Illustrative Findings

This is obviously not the place to attempt a serious literature survey, but what I can do is select several areas where there has been a reasonable amount of investigative activity and examine the trend and implications of the data. The two active areas I will discuss are concerned with (1) estimating the direct relation between observer ratings of personality and morphological variables; and (2) relating morphology to a complex achievement variable, in this case criminal behavior.

Personality Ratings. Almost every introductory psychology student has learned to recognize and distrust the striking findings that Sheldon (1942) has reported between dimensions of physique and temperament. Studying 200 male college students individually over a considerable period of time, he assigned ratings to each subject for his three somatotype components and also, on the basis of extensive interviewing and observing, he made ratings for three temperament variables that were intended to represent aspects of behavior associated with each of the dimensions of physique. When the temperament ratings were correlated with ratings for the associated physique component the correlations ranged from +.79 to +.83. There are a number of factors that would have to be considered in a full discussion of why so much co-variation was observed, but for most psychologists the explanation has seemed to lie in the fact that Sheldon himself executed both sets of ratings. Consequently, one may reason that implicitly Sheldon's prior convictions or expectations in this area led him to rate both physique and temperament in a consistent manner, whatever may have existed in reality.

There have been many other studies relating morphological variation to ratings of personality and most of them have produced at least some evidence for association between these two domains. Let us here direct our attention upon two studies that have minimized, more suc-

cessfully than most, the possibility of contamination of data or experimenter bias.

The first investigation was executed by Irvin Child (1950) utilizing 414 male, undergraduate students who were routinely somatotyped as freshmen and who, as sophomores, completed a questionnaire that consisted of multiple-choice questions concerning the subjects' own behavior and feelings. Each item was designed to measure some aspect of behavior that, on the basis of Sheldon's study of temperament, was believed to be related to one or more dimensions of physique. In advance of any analysis of the data a total of 94 predictions were made concerning associations between self ratings and somatotype ratings—these predictions were simple reflections of what Sheldon had already reported. The somatotype ratings were assigned by Sheldon on the basis of the standard photographs and without any knowledge of the questionnaire results. More than three quarters (77%) of the predictions were confirmed in regard to the direction of the relationship between physical component and self rating, and more than one fifth of the predictions were confirmed at the five per cent level; while only one of the findings that reversed the prediction was significant at the five per cent level. When Child combined certain of the items into scales for each of the temperament variables so that they could be correlated with the physique dimensions, he observed positive correlations between the comparable physique and temperament dimensions, the highest of which was +.38.

The most important observation here is that even when we eliminate the major design and inference shortcomings of Sheldon's study, we still observe a pattern of relations between physique and behavior that resembles in direction, if not degree, the findings reported by Sheldon. The magnitude of association between self ratings and morphology is obviously much less than that reported by Sheldon, but it is difficult to know what proportion of this change is attributable to elimination of experimenter bias and what proportion is due to the relative insensitivity of self ratings.

A similar study was carried out by Walker (1962) working with 125 male and female nursery school children. The somatotype measures were based upon ratings made independently by three different judges which were then combined by an averaging method. Two of these judges never saw the children while the third was acquainted with them. Each of the children was also rated on a one to seven scale for 64 specific behavioral items by two to five judges, none of whom were involved in the morphological ratings and at least two of whom were ignorant of the purpose of the study. Again, the individual score for each item was determined by averaging the judges' ratings. These items also had been selected for their pertinence to Sheldon's findings and a total of 292 specific predictions were made in advance and tested separately for the male and female subjects. Altogether, 73% of the predictions were confirmed in direction and 21% were confirmed at or below the 5% level of significance while only 3% were disconfirmed at the 5% level.

Once again we observe significant and appreciable relations between morphological variation and behavior which are consistent with Sheldon's findings, even though the major opportunities for systematic bias have been removed. Again, the degree of association is less than that reported by Sheldon but the fact that these observer ratings of behavior might be considered less sensitive than those used by Sheldon, in addition to the use of young children as subjects, makes it difficult to consider these findings as clearly contradictory on this score.

The principal generalization I wish to derive from these findings is that the most firmly based evidence we now possess suggests the existence of important associations between morphology and behavior (just as reason would assert), while the magnitude of this relation, or rather its varying magnitude depending upon the conditions of study, remains to be determined precisely. If, as the climate of current opinion urges, the magnitude of association reported by Sheldon represents in large measure co-variance attributable to experimental error, this fact remains to be demonstrated unequivocally. Moreover, in view of the extensive criticism of his study, it does seem odd that there has not been one single effort at a careful replication eliminating the major defects in Sheldon's study, while at the same time attempting to preserve other relevant conditions as exactly as possible. What we have witnessed, instead, has been the complacent dismissal of a potentially important set of results without any serious attempt at an empirical resolution.

Criminal Behavior. We turn now to a morphological correlate that is far removed from specific ratings of items or components of personality. Here we are concerned with a complex outcome variable, criminal behavior, that includes a wide variety of topographically different forms of behavior and is undoubtedly related to many different antecedent events. Again I will limit my discussion to the initial findings reported by Sheldon and a small number of subsequent investigations involving similar questions and methods.

Over an eight-year period Sheldon and his collaborators (Sheldon, 1949) conducted a study of physique and behavior with the residents of a rehabilitation home for boys in Boston. The findings of this study are largely clinical or descriptive but he does present a graphic comparison of college youths and his delinquent subjects which makes clear that while the college distribution shows a clustering about the mid-range physique (4-4-4), the delinquent youths show a tendency to cluster in the "northwest region." In brief, mesomorphs, particularly endomorphic mesomorphs, are over represented among the delinquents. This generalization, although initially supported by little in the way of convincing empirical data, has been re-examined subsequently in four separate studies that have involved better controls and more objective analysis of data.

The best known of these subsequent studies was conducted by Glueck and Glueck (1950, 1956) and involved the study of 500 persistent delinquents and 500 proven non-delinquents; matched in age, intelligence, ethnic background and place of residence. Independently of any knowledge of the classification of the individual subjects, their physiques were rated in terms of the relative dominance of Sheldon's three components. An examination of the somatotype distributions for the two groups provides a powerful confirmation of Sheldon's findings—approximately 60% of the delinquent youths were classified as mesomorphic while only about 30% of the non-delinquent subjects were so classified. Moreover, less than 15% of the delinquents were categorized as ectomorphic and almost 40% of the normal subjects were placed in this category. A final item of confirmation was found in the incidence of endomorphic mesomorphs in the delinquent (13%) and non-delinquent (3%) subjects. All in all, under what appear to be very well controlled circumstances, a quantitative analysis of the relation between criminal behavior and morphological variation provides a highly significant and impressive confirmation of Sheldon's rather impressionistic findings.

A study by Epps and Parnell (1952) is of particular interest because it involved both a change in society (England) and in sex (girls) and yet also led to the observation that when female delinquents were compared with female college students they were "shorter and heavier in build, more muscular and fat." (Epps and Parnell, 1952, p. 254.) A more recent study by Gibbons (1963) also employed English subjects, in this case male, and again found a substantial confirmation of the finding that delinquent youth are predominantly of "northwest physique."

Another recent study (Cortes, 1961), involved the use of Parnell's techniques of measurement and the comparison of 100 adolescent boys who had been convicted by courts of violations of the criminal law with a group matched in age but with no record of delinquent behavior. When the subjects were classified according to their dominant physique component, Cortes found 57% of the delinquents to be mesomorphic while only 19% of the normal subjects were so classified. On the other hand, 33% of the normal subjects were dominantly ectomorphic in comparison to 16% of the delinquents. In spite of the different somatotyping method, and other variations in procedure, these results almost exactly parallel the findings of the Gluecks' and provide further confirmation for the original association reported by Sheldon.

Thus, four separate studies involving different methods, different sexes and different societies, some of them employing excellent controls against experimenter bias, have produced findings that are consistent among themselves and congruent with Sheldon's initial report. No one is likely to argue seriously that mesomorphy directly causes (or is caused by) criminal behavior but an association as consistently and strongly observed, and involving as complex and socially important a variable as criminal behavior, obviously warrants further systematic study.

It is even possible to see hints of an interesting association between these findings and those that have been reported in connection with psychopathic or sociopathic traits. Lykken (1957), in an ingenious study, has reported a deficiency in capacity for avoidance learning on the part of the "constitutional psychopath." More recently, Schachter (in press) has replicated this finding and introduced the fascinating additional observation that sociopaths show considerable improvement in avoidance learning when injected with adrenaline, while normal subjects demonstrate no such change in performance. It is interesting to note that Sheldon's (1942) early description of the somatotonic temperament (corresponding to mesomorphy) placed considerable emphasis upon indifference to pain and low anxiety. If it should eventually be shown unequivocally that low anxiety, deficient avoidance learning and an atypical effect of adrenaline upon avoidance learning are all associated with extremes of mesomorphy, there would be the possibility of integrating a variety of discrete and individually important results bearing upon criminal behavior. Such results obviously would have implications extending far beyond study of the psychopath or criminal.

Areas of Potential Research Interest

I have just mentioned several areas of investigation that seem to me to promise significant returns. Before closing, permit me to briefly allude to a few additional topics that may offer similar rewards. It should be clear that these selections are quite arbitrary and in no sense intended to represent the entire range of investigative possibilities.

Effects of Early Experience. A recent consequence of Freud's seminal observations and the findings of ethologists and comparative psychologists has been an intense contemporary interest in the effects of early experience. Numerous studies with both human and lower animal subjects exploring this problem (Beach & Jaynes, 1954; Bowlby, 1951; Denenberg, 1962) have left most observers convinced that variation in early experience has important implications for adult behavior or personality. Unfortunately there are many disagreements concerning the exact nature of the function linking infantile experience and adult behavior. Even in connection with such a seemingly simple question as whether traumatic or strong noxious stimulation in infancy has adaptive or maladaptive effects, or increases or decreases emotionality, the answer seems by no means clear (e.g., Denenberg, 1961; Levine, 1961; Hall & Whiteman, 1951; Lindzey, Lykken & Winston, 1960a, 1961a, 1961b). One significant question here is whether there may not be important differences in the nature (and perhaps even the direction) of effects from the same noxious stimulus when administered to different classes of organisms; whether the same stimulus may not have a quite different impact upon different bodies, with different sensitivities and varying response capacities. It is at least possible that certain kinds of stimulation will have divergent effects upon the fragile, linear, hyper-reactive infant and the heavy, spherical and sluggish infant. Indeed, one might argue that evidence from a variety of lower animal sources (King & Eleftheriou, 1959; Valenstein, Riss & Young, 1955), including our own research (Lindzey, Lykken & Winston, 1960; Lindzey, Winston & Manosevitz, 1963; Winston, 1963), indicates that the effects of early experience are influenced by genotype or biological variation, thus providing presumptive support for just such a formulation. All of this implies that introduction of morphological variation as a parameter or variable to be studied when examining the effects of early experience might shed considerable light upon the complexities of this important area.

Psychopharmacology. To select still another fashionable area of research, there is the largely unexamined interaction between morphological variation and effects of psychoactive drugs. One of the major puzzles that plagues research in psychopharmacology is the observation of very large individual differences in reaction to the same doses of the same drug under the same environmental conditions. Undoubtedly there are many factors contributing to this variation but one such class may consist of morphological variables. Indeed, beginning with Sheldon's (1942) temperament descriptions of his polar physical varieties we find a number of hints that observers have believed this to be the case. In fact, the gross morphological variable of weight has always been considered an important parameter in predicting the effects of any drug—psychoactive or not.

Moreover, there is considerable evidence from lower animals for the influence of biological determinants, including genotype, upon response to particular drugs, including alcohol (McClearn & Rodgers, 1951, 1961). All in all, whether concerned with alcohol, narcotic agents, or the more recent hallucinogenic and tranquilizing drugs, there seems every reason to expect morphological variation to play a meaningful role in determining the psychological effects of the drug.

Social Interaction and Morphology. As a final illustrative item it may be appropriate to mention a topic that appears to have little fit with current psychological interest. Modern social psychology has shown very little interest in the physical structure of the persons who are studied in temporary or enduring interaction. Indeed an examination of the index of the *Handbook of Social Psychology* (Lindzey, 1954) reveals no entries for "physique" or "somatotype" and only a single entry for "physical factors."

In spite of this systematic neglect, few, if any, would deny that the physical attractiveness of a person, whether male or female, has a marked influence upon the way in which he is responded to by others. It would come as a shock to most of us if we found that social status, popularity and such had no relation to esthetic appeal. Likewise the question of how big, how strong, how quick, how well coordinated have obvious implications for the way in which the person is perceived by others, as well as the way in which he participates in group functioning.

Many years ago Freud (1914) pointed to a fascinating area of investigation in his remarks concerning the social significance of the narcissism encountered prototypically in the big cats and beautiful women. For a complex of reasons we seem to have shown little professional interest in lions, tigers, or stunning women. Perhaps now is the time to restore beauty and other morphological variables to the study of social phenomena.

REFERENCES

Bowlby, J. *Maternal care and mental health.* Geneva: World Health Organization, 1951.

Bruch, Hilde. Psychological aspects of obesity. *Psychiatry*, 1947, **10,** 373–381.

Child, I. The relation of somatotype to self-ratings on Sheldon's temperamental traits. *J. Pers.*, 1950, **18**, 440-453.

Cortes, J. B. *Physique, need for achievement, and delinquency.* Doctoral dissertation, Harvard Univ., 1961.

Denenberg, V. H. Comment on "Infantile trauma, genetic factors, and adult temperament." *Psychol. Rep.*, 1961, **8**, 459-462.

Denenberg, V. H. The effects of early experience. In E. S. E. Hafez (Ed.) *The behaviour of domestic animals.* Baltimore: Williams & Wilkins, 1962, pp. 109-138.

Epps, P. & Parnell, R. W. Physique and temperament of women delinquents compared with women undergraduates. *Brit. J. med. Psychol.*, 1942, **25**, 249-255.

Freud, S. On narcissism. In *Standard Edition Vol. XIV*. London: Hogarth Press, 1957. (Originally published in 1914)

Gall, F. J. & Spurzheim, J. G. *Recherches sur le Systeme nerveux.* Paris: Schoell, 1809.

Gibbens, T. C. N. *Psychiatric studies of Borstal lads.* London: Oxford, 1963.

Glueck, S. & Glueck, Eleanor. *Unraveling juvenile delinquency.* New York: Harper, 1950.

Glueck, S. & Glueck, Eleanor. *Physique and delinquency.* New York: Harper, 1956.

Hall, C. S. & Lindzey, G. *Theories of personality.* New York: Wiley, 1957.

Hall, C. S. & Whiteman, P. H. The effects of infantile stimulation upon later emotional stability in the mouse. *J. comp. physiol. Psychol.*, 1951, **44**, 61-66.

Hammond, W. H. The constancy of physical types as determined by factorial analysis. *Human Biol.*, 1957a, **29**, 40-61.

Hammond, W. H. The status of physical types. *Human Biol.*, 1957b, **29**, 223-241.

Hunt, E. A. Human Constitution: an appraisal. *Amer. J. phys. Anthrop.*, 1952, **10**, 55-73.

Jarvik, Lissy F., Falek, A. & Pierson, W. P. Down's Syndrome (Mongolism): the heritable aspects. *Psychol. Bull.*, 1964, **61**, 388-398.

King, J. A. & Eleftheriou, B. E. Effects of early handling upon adult behavior in two subspecies of deermice, *Peromyscus maniculatus. J. comp. physiol. Psychol.*, 1959, **52**, 82-88.

Landauer, T. K. & Whiting, J. W. M. Some effects of infant stress upon human stature. *Amer. Anthrop.* (in press).

Levine, S. Discomforting thoughts on "infantile trauma, genetic factors, and adult temperament." *J. abnorm. soc. Psychol.*, 1961, **63**, 219-220.

Lindegård, B. Variations in human body-build. *Acta Psychiatrica et Neurologica. Supplementum* **86**, 1953, 1-163.

Lindegård, B. & Nyman, G. E. Interrelations between psychologic, somatologic, and endocrine dimensions. *Lunds Universitets Årsskrift*, 1956, **52**, (No. 8), pp. 1-54.

Lindzey, G. *Handbook of social psychology.* Vols. I & II. Reading, Mass.: Addison-Wesley, 1954.

Lindzey, G., Lykken, D. T. & Winston, H. D. Infantile trauma, genetic factors, and adult temperament. *J. abnorm. soc. Psychol.*, 1960, **61**, 7-14.

Lindzey, G., Lykken, D. T. & Winston, H. D. Confusion, conviction, and control groups. *J. abnorm. soc. Psychol.*, 1961a, **63**, 221-222.

Lindzey, G., Lykken, D. T. & Winston, H. D. Trauma, emotionality, and scientific sin. *Psychol. Rep.*, 1961b, **9**, 199-206.

Lindzey, G., Winston, H. D. & Manosevitz, M. Early experience, genotype and temperament in *Mus musculus. J. comp. physiol. Psychol.*, 1963, **56**, 622-629.

Lykken, D. T. A study of anxiety in the sociopathic personality. *J. abnorm. soc. Psychol.*, 1957, **55**, 6-10.

MacKinnon, D. W. & Maslow, A. H. Personality. In H. Helson (Ed.) *Theoretical foundations of psychology.* New York: Van Nostrand, 1951, pp. 602-655.

McClearn, G. E. & Rodgers, D. A. Differences in alcohol preference among inbred strains of mice. *Quart. J. Stud. Alcohol.*, 1959, **20**, 691-695.

McClearn, G. E. & Rodgers, D. A. Genetic factors in alcohol preference of laboratory mice. *J. comp. physiol. Psychol.*, 1961., **54**, 116-119.

McNeil, D. & Levison, N. Maturation rate and body build in women. *Child Develpm.*, 1963, **34**, 25-32.

Newman, N. H., Freeman, F. N. & Holzinger, K. J. *Twins: a study of heredity and environment.* Chicago: Univ. Chicago Press, 1937.

Osborne, R. H. & De George, F. V. *Genetic basis of morphological variation.* Cambridge: Harvard Univ. Press, 1959.

Parnell, R. W. *Behavior and physique: an introducton to practical and applied somatometry.* London: Arnold, 1958.

Schachter, S. Crime, cognition and the automatic nervous system. *Nebraska Symposium on Motivation.* Lincoln, Neb.: Univ. Nebraska Press (in press).

Sheldon, W. H. (with the collaboration of S. S. Stevens & W. B. Tucker). *The varieties of human physique: an introduction to constitutional psychology.* New York: Harper, 1940.

Sheldon, W. H. (with the collaboration of S. S. Stevens). *The varieties of temperament: a psychology of constitutional differences.* New York: Harper, 1942.

Sheldon, W. H. (with the collaboration of E. M. Hartl & E. McDermott). *Varieties of delinquent youth: an introduction to constitutional psychiatry*. New York: Harper, 1949.

Sheldon, W. H. (with the collaboration of C. W. Dupertius & E. McDermott). *Atlas of men: a guide for somatotyping the male at all ages*. New York: Harper, 1954.

Valenstein, E. S., Riss, W. & Young, W. C. Experimental and genetic factors in the organization of sexual behavior in male guinea pigs. *J. comp. physiol. Psychol.*, 1955, **48**, 397–403.

Walker, R. N. Body build and behavior in young children: I. Body build and nursery school teachers' ratings. *Monogr. Soc. Res. Child Develpm.*, 1962, **27**, No. 3 (Serial No. 84).

Winston, H. D. Influence of genotype and infantile trauma on adult learning in the mouse. *J. comp. physiol. Psychol.*, 1963, **56**, 630–635.

Winston, H. D. & Lindzey, G. Albinism and water escape performance in the mouse. *Science*, 1964, **144**, 189–191.

SECTION
IX

Factor Theories

The characteristic and impressive productivity of R. B. Cattell and H. J. Eysenck has continued unabated during recent years. Together with their students they have published such an amazing array of books and articles that it is difficult to provide adequate representation of their writings within the limited space available here.

The recent writings of Raymond B. Cattell provide a significant and logical extension of his previous work. The technique of factor analysis has remained at the core of his studies and he has continued to be concerned with fundamental problems of classification or taxonomy. Moreover he has made serious efforts to introduce elements of unity or consistency into the extensive research literature concerned with factor analysis. The first paper included here, *The Nature and Measurement of Anxiety*, provides a simple discussion of factor analysis and illustrates the application of this technique to the study of anxiety. The paper clearly reveals the diversity of subjects and measures with which Cattell is at home and also suggests the potential merit of factor analysis as an aid to taxonomy, concept formation and the clarification of personality variables.

The paper written with Warburton illustrates the application of factor analysis in a comparison of the personality structure of American and British students. The focus of the study is upon the variables of extraversion and anxiety as measured by the *Sixteen Personality Factor Questionnaire*—an instrument which itself represents the outcome of many years of factor analytic research. The third paper, written with Shotwell and Hurley, demonstrates the possibility of applying factor analysis to the study of the individual case, in this instance a mentally retarded patient. The full range of Cattell's research interests is nicely illuminated by these two papers, which range from a large scale study of normal personality structure in different countries to the detailed appraisal of a single hospitalized patient.

Although Eysenck's recent writings are linked with his earlier work, they also provide unmistakeable evidence of important changes in his orientation.

For example, it seems clear that his research and theorizing are less closely tied to the method of factor analysis today than they were a decade or two ago. Moreover, his theoretical writings, as well as many of his empirical studies, show an increasing impact from Pavlov and modern S-R theory. This general state of affairs is nicely illustrated by the first paper reproduced here, *Biological Basis of Personality*. The article emphasizes Eysenck's long-time belief in the importance of biological determinants of personality, it utilizes variables that have been identified principally through the use of factor analysis and it employs the concepts of learning theory to provide an interpretation of the findings under discussion. His emphasis upon the importance of genetic determinants of behavior is not only consistent with his own formulations and research in the past, it also provides a clear instance of congruence with the theoretical statements and empirical research of Cattell.

The paper written with Claridge was selected as providing an excellent example of Eysenck's interest in substituting objective techniques of measurement for traditional psychiatric classification. In this study, which involves the comparison of hysteric, dysthymic and normal subjects on a number of diverse measures, we encounter many of the personality variables that have been employed frequently by Eysenck and observe the familiar method of factor analysis. In addition, we find Eysenck employing the statistical technique of multiple discriminant analysis and using the *Maudsley Personality Inventory* which is the rough equivalent for him of Cattell's *Sixteen Personality Factor Questionnaire*.

The final selection, *Learning Theory and Behaviour Therapy*, is principally of interest because it demonstrates the increased involvement that Eysenck and his associates have manifested in psychotherapy. He has been known for some time as an ardent critic of conventional practices in this area—particularly as exemplified by psychoanalysis—and in recent years he has become increasingly active in the study and promotion of "behavior therapy." Proponents of behavior therapy present their approach as based upon modern learning theory and thus more scientific and rational than alternative procedures. This group has now reached a point in volume and vigor where they have assumed many of the properties of a school—comparable to client-centered counselling or psychoanalysis—and H. J. Eysenck has clearly served as one of the major rallying points in the emergence of this set of ideas and practices.

1. The nature and measurement of anxiety

RAYMOND B. CATTELL

OURS IS SAID TO BE THE AGE of anxiety, but what exactly is anxiety and how can it be measured? What are its manifestations and how does it affect the functioning of human beings? The initial difficulty in answering such questions—as in so many problems of psychology—is one of definition. A generation has passed since Edward Lee Thorndike replied to critics of psychological measurement with the dictum: Everything that exists, exists in some degree and can be measured. Since then psychometry—the branch of psychology concerned with measurement—has done rather better at inventing scaling systems, units and tests than at defining the entities to be scaled. In Thorndike's

SOURCE: Article by Raymond B. Cattell, "The nature and measurement of anxiety" in *Scientific American*, Vol. 208, pp. 96–104, 1963.

own field the proliferation of empirical definitions of intelligence finally reduced many psychologists to the desperate statement: "Intelligence is what intelligence tests measure." What led to a way out of this morass was the development of the technique of factor analysis by Charles E. Spearman, Louis L. Thurstone, Sir Cyril Burt, and other psychologists. In my laboratory at the University of Illinois we have been applying factor analysis to the problem of defining and learning how to measure anxiety.

To seek to define anxiety is to attempt to tie down something recognized by everyone in two distinct ways: as an inner experience known from introspection and as a pattern of behavior observable in ourselves and in others as restlessness, irritability, tremor and so on. Sigmund Freud wrote much about anxiety but

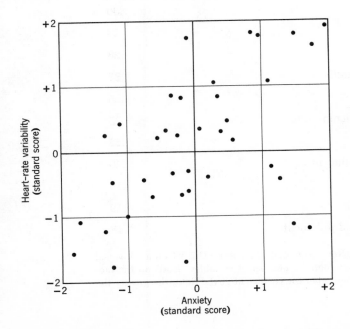

Figure 1. Correlation between a patient's heart-rate variability and his anxiety as rated by psychiatrists is shown by this "scatter plot." The physiological and psychological measurements are reduced to "standard scores," in which the mean is taken to be zero and the deviation from the mean is independent of the raw scores. When the observations are plotted, their elliptical pattern indicates that the variables correlate positively but moderately.

was content to fall back largely on introspection and semantics for its definition. He pointed to the solid distinction in his native language between *Furcht* (fear) and *Angst* (anxiety), and most psychologists have followed him in considering anxiety to be quite different from fear. At the very least anxiety is viewed as being a fear triggered by cues or symbols for some remote and uncertain danger rather than one physically or immediately present.

Other definitions go further afield. One U.S. school of learning theorists would have us consider anxiety as being the main drive to action. Almost in polar opposition to this view of anxiety as the effective mover is the clinical view expressed by Frank M. Berger (who discovered the chemical that led to the tranquilizer meprobamate) that anxiety is a disorganizer of effective action. Related to this disorganization concept is the psychoanalytic view that anxiety is the central problem in neurosis. In looser thinking this often degenerates into the notion that anxiety and neurosis are synonymous, with the result that people with a high anxiety level are treated as neurotics. Clearly the various theorists are talking about different things when they mention anxiety, and a heavy preliminary investment of research in simply isolating and measuring anxiety is strongly indicated.

The technique we have worked with, factor analysis, is in principle quite simple, although it does involve some complicated matrix algebra and usually requires the aid of electronic computers. In essence it involves the intercorrelation of a large number of observations to find out what factor or factors control them. The factor—"anxiety," for example—can then be defined and measured in terms of the variables that are its clearest manifestations.

When one looks at a mass of social or biological variables so richly interrelated that one cannot tell which are important and which are incidental, which are dependent on others and which are independent, it is useful to watch their mode of variation under the impact of changing circumstances and see what goes with what and to what extent. So might a hunter peer into a jungle swamp and wait for some telltale movement to show that what looked like two logs is actually one crocodile. The factor analyst uses the correlation coefficient to calculate the precise extent to which two measured

Variable	Loading
High susceptibility to annoyance	.56
High willingness to admit common faults	.47
High tendency to agree	.38
High heart rate	.30
Slow reaction time	.28
Low writing pressure	.28
Low total physical strength	.27
High critical severity	.25
High autonomic conditioning rate	.25
Low hand-steadiness	.22
High emotionality of comment	.20
High self-criticism	.19
Less alkaline saliva	.19
Slow speed of perceptual judgment	.18

"Loading Pattern" for a factor designated as anxiety (U.I. 24 on a Universal Index of factors) shows how highly a number of variables "load" on the factor, or correlate with it. The higher the coefficient at the right, the greater the association with anxiety.

variables covary, or move together. The coefficient can range from $+1.0$ through 0 to -1.0, indicating, respectively, a complete positive correlation, no relation at all and a complete negative, or inverse, correlation. A correlation can be demonstrated visually by a "scatter plot" of the kind illustrated in Figure 1. Each dot on the chart represents an observation of a patient at one session during which psychiatrists rated his anxiety level and a record was made of the degree to which his heart rate was varying. When these dissimilar measurements are reduced to "standard scores" and plotted on two coordinates, their pattern indicates the degree of correlation between "anxiety" and heart-rate variability. The fact that most of the dots fall into a rough ellipse (the closest approach to a straight line one can expect when many influences are at work) shows that there is a positive correlation between the two variables. The computation of a correlation coefficient from the actual anxiety ratings and heart-rate measurements gives a value of $+.49$,

which is a fairly marked relation as psychological variables go.

Even when such a relation is obtained it can be interpreted as indicating that variable a influences b, that b influences a or that some as yet unmeasured entity influences both of them. The investigator usually seeks to fix such causal dependencies by observing in time sequences or by forcibly isolating and manipulating one of the variables. The factor analyst, partly because he often deals with unmanipulable things such as the private lives of clinical patients, takes a different approach. Instead of observing a and b alone, he may observe a large number of variables in a group of subjects. With values for, say, 100 variables taken on a large number of subjects, he can work out a square correlation matrix containing coefficients for all the possible 4,950 relations among the variables. By applying factor-analysis computations to this matrix he can discover the number of independent variables, or factors, that must be at work to account for the com-

	Variable	Loading
Objective Tests	Raised cholinesterase	.78
	High hippuric acid	.74
	High willingness to admit common faults	.58
	High susceptibility to annoyance	.46
	High rate of respiration	.45
	High steroid hormone level	.43
	High heart rate	.30
	High systolic pulse pressure	.29
	Less alkaline saliva	.23
	Fast reversible perspective	.19
	High saliva volume	.13
Questionnaire Primaries	Low ego-strength (C—)	.77
	Low will-control (Q$_3$—)	.51
	High ergic tension (Q$_4$)	.48
	High guilt proneness (O)	.37
	High nonconformity (M)	.31

Anxiety can be measured in an individual over a period of time. This is the loading pattern for anxiety as a fluctuating state rather than as the personality trait U.I. 24.

plex interrelations represented by the coefficients. And he can learn a good deal about the nature of these factors in terms of their pattern of effects on the dependent variables.

In the undisciplined infancy of psychology theorists often fell into the trap, originally pointed out by Francis Bacon, of assuming that because there is one word there must be one thing. An open-minded investigator must begin by questioning that assumption—by asking, in this field, if there is one thing called anxiety or several distinct and possibly unrelated forms of anxiety response.

At various times a variety of introspective, behavioral and physiological manifestations have been alleged to be signs of underlying anxiety. They include low hand-steadiness, inability to look someone in the eye, sinking feeling in the stomach, dry mouth, high irritability, raised muscle tension, decreased power of concentration, high emotionality in word choice, lack of readiness to try new tasks, tendency to jump at noises, high galvanic skin response, more rapid conditioning and a tendency to see threatening objects in blots or unstructured drawings. Between 1948 and 1960 we measured such objective-test variables as these in groups of from 100 to 500 people—young and

old, mentally healthy and mentally ill—and then intercorrelated the hypothesized anxiety manifestations. The correlations turned out to be generally positive and significant. And through factor analysis they pointed to the existence of a single, pervasive factor of anxiety.

Up to this stage the assumption that there is a single entity that can be called anxiety was vindicated. In major respects the factor agreed with what is covered by the semantic concept of "anxiety." But not every popularly alleged manifestation of anxiety was confirmed. For example, in anxiety salivary output turned out to increase rather than to decrease. General muscle tension did not correlate in the way a tense person might expect from introspection. What correlated with the anxiety factor was tension in the trapezius, the large muscle that runs from the shoulder to the back of the head; handwriting pressure was actually significantly lower in persons of high anxiety.

Once a factor has been checked in several samples of people and across several ranges of measurement, it provides a "loading pattern" (see illustration on page 358) that shows the degree of influence of the underlying independent variable on each of the main manifestations in terms of correlation coefficients be-

Variable	Loading
Inability to do simple addition and subtraction mentally	.57
Stuttering and upset of speech with delayed auditory feedback	.57
Slow and erratic recognition of upside-down forms	.57
Aspiration-level high relative to performance	.55
Poor ability to co-ordinate simultaneous spatial cues	.55
Low metabolic rate change in response to stimuli	.50
Low readiness to tackle unpleasant activities	.47
Numerous "indecisive" responses in questionnaires	.44
Errors in reciting alphabet with prescribed skipping	.42
Rapid increase of errors when made to hurry	.31
High motor-perceptual rigidity	.29
Affected more by color than form in artistic preferences	.25
High body sway in suggestibility sway test	.20

"Regression" is one of the factors that distinguish neurotics from other people, and is indexed as U.I. 23. This is the loading pattern for some variables influenced by U.I. 23.

tween the factor—anxiety in this case—and the variable. The loading pattern provides a means of recognizing and identifying the factor and a basis for more developed hypotheses about its nature. It also tells one how to test for the factor. Although anyone is free to affix such names as "anxiety" or "intelligence" to whatever he pleases, there is now an objectively discovered, repeatable response pattern to which one can refer when the label is used. In this case it dictates a particular battery of tests—usually the composite of measurements from the 10 or so most highly loaded manifestations—for anxiety experiments. To avoid merely semantic disputes factors are sometimes indexed simply by number. In a proposed Universal Index of factors that psychologists interested in such matters have been compiling, I have indexed anxiety as U.I. 24. When expert psychiatric diagnosticians rate patients for anxiety level, their estimates correlate more consistently and more highly with the U.I. 24 battery than with any other factor. Although the correlations shown in the U.I. 24 table (which is based on the work of John Hundleby of the University of Illinois and Kurt Pawlik of the University of Vienna) are not high, they are mean values across five experiments, and they have since risen to higher values in longer tests developed after the exploratory research phase.

Although a psychologist feels on firmest ground when he has located anxiety as a behavioral pattern in U.I. 24, he is also interested to see how anxiety emerges in the introspective account the subject gives of himself in responding to a questionnaire. The factoring of questionnaire items is an established branch of psychometrics. Among 16 major factors established by David R. Saunders, Glen F. Stice, Richard Coan, Bien Tsujioka, Rutherford B. Porter, and me there were a number that appeared to have "anxiety content." One, which I called "ergic tension" or "drive tension" and labeled as factor Q_4, came out of such questions as are listed in the illustration on page 364. Another, indexed as O, had items indicating guilt proneness. Still another was the reciprocal of ego strength, or "ego weakness" (C −).

Could the existence of only one functional unity of response in behavior—U.I. 24—be reconciled with several factors in the area of introspection? It is possible in factor analysis to correlate factors themselves and then to factor-analyze their correlation matrix just as one did the original variables. What comes out of this is a "second order" factor. (General intelligence is a second-order factor among such primary abilities as verbal ability, spatial ability, numerical ability and so on.) When we factored some 20 of the personality factors based on data from questionnaires, precisely those six factors that a psychiatrist would consider to have anxiety content—and no others—fell into a single second-order factor. At that point, therefore, we had one factor in behavioral response and one in introspection, but the possibility remained that they would prove to be not the same thing—that people who measured high on the "mental interior" factor might not show identical scores on the behavioral "exterior" factor. A crucial test with more than 500 Air Force men proved that these two ways of measuring were operating on the same entity: the correlation between them was close to + 1.0. This close correspondence can be shown in visual terms (see illustration on page 362) by a technique that will be discussed later in this article.

Why should a first-order factor in one medium turn up as a second-order factor in another? Finding six partially distinct influences in introspection corresponding to one in behavior must mean, in the first place, that introspection is more sensitive. It could also mean that a causal mechanism is being revealed in terms of six different sources of one common pool of anxiety. As usual with purely correlational evidence, one cannot say for sure in which direction the causality acts. But if the anxiety factor represents, as it were, a common reservoir of anxiety to which ego weakness, guilt proneness, frustrated drive and other primary factors contribute, our results would offer striking experimental vindication of some of Freud's theories as to the origin of anxiety in neurotics. At the same time, this experimental approach introduces several concepts beyond any in classical psychoanalysis, because factor analysis, like the microscope, opens up relations that cannot be seen by the unaided eye of the clinician.

The concept of U.I. 24 with which I have dealt so far has rested solely on observations of the individual differences among people, that is, on anxiety as a trait of personality. But anxiety also varies in level in the same person from time to time. The psychologist wants to

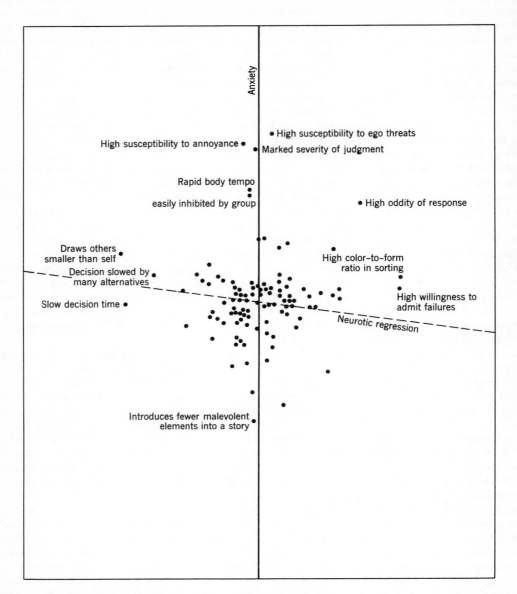

Figure 2. Independence of the anxiety and regression factors, U.I. 24 and U.I. 23, is shown here in geometric terms. Each dot is the end point of a vector representing a measured variable, its direction and distance from the origin determined by factor-analysis computations. There are as many dimensions in the solid "graph" so produced (from which this is a two-dimensional projection) as there are factors at work on the variables. Tests points tend to coagulate in "hyperplanes," or multi-dimensional galaxies, which indicate the positions in which to place various factors; these factors emerge as axes of the "graph" placed as perpendiculars to the galaxies. Projected in two-dimensional space, a hyperplane should ideally appear as a line, but it is usually (as in this diagram) a lens-shaped swarm of points. A test like "Marked severity of judgment," lying in the hyperplane of neurotic regression, has zero-projection, or "zero-loading," on it; that is, it does not correlate with regression. On the other hand it loads highly on anxiety; it is, in other words, closely associated with anxiety. The greater the angle between two tests or factor axes, the more independent they are of each other. In this case the anxiety and regression axes are nearly perpendicular to each other; they are independent.

discover the pattern of anxiety as a fluctuating state and to find out if it is the same as that of the personality trait. This question can be explored through single-person factor analysis, in which one person is measured every day, for perhaps 100 or 200 days, on the various alleged measures of anxiety. When these time series are correlated, a significant positive correlation should exist among variables affected by the same underlying source. For example, if higher systolic blood pressure, irritability, tremor and "Yes" answers to certain questionnaire items are all signs of anxiety, they should vary together as the onslaught of daily events

raises and lowers the anxiety level. Investigation showed that the pattern for anxiety as a state is unmistakably the same species of response as that for the trait (see lower illustration on page 359). It differs in some tendency of the physiological variables to load more highly on the state factor. By working with the same subject one could eliminate individual differences resulting from extraneous influences on the variables.

Experiments with individuals have been particularly valuable in locating the physiological concomitants of anxiety and in distinguishing the anxiety pattern from other states, such

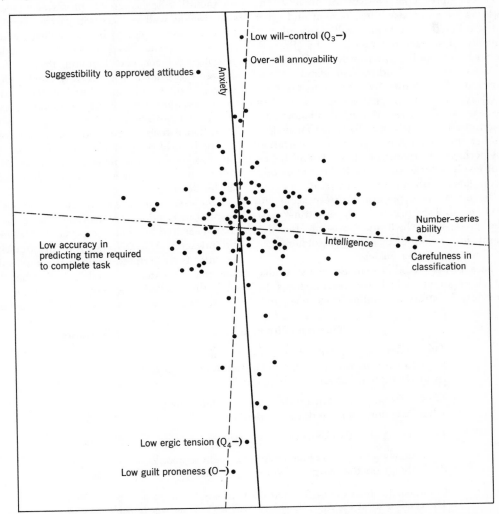

Figure 3. Close correlation between anxiety as defined by objective tests (U.I. 24) and anxiety as a second-order factor derived from questionnaire data is shown by this diagram: the questionnaire axis (broken black line) is nearly aligned with the U.I. 24 behavioral axis (solid black line). But the axis for intelligence performance (white line) is almost perpendicular to the anxiety axis.

as stress, fatigue and excitement, with which it has often been confused experimentally and conceptually. Harold Persky and Roy R. Grinker of Michael Reese Hospital in Chicago, working with paratroopers in training, found that during what appeared to be anxiety periods the level of hippuric acid in the urine and of adrenal cortical steroids in the blood rose, the white-cell count and electrical skin resistance decreased and breathing speeded up. Ivan H. Scheier of my laboratory, together with Grinker, Sheldon Korchin and others at Michael Reese, studied patients undergoing various stresses and located a specific pattern of physiological upset characteristic of anxiety; the patterns for effort stress, excitement and other states differed both behaviorally and physiologically. Further investigations by Roy B. Mefferd and Louis J. Moran at the University of Texas and by Hudson Hoagland at the Worcester Foundation for Experimental Biology leave little doubt that anxiety and effort stress are two different things. Psychologically the effort-stress pattern usually shows no anxiety or other emotionality, only strong concentration and perhaps awareness of effort. High cholesterol levels, which we found to be completely uncorrelated with anxiety, may really belong to the effort-stress pattern. Anxiety seems to affect metabolism primarily by upsetting anabolic processes, which may account for the weight loss suffered by combat soldiers exposed to unremitting anxiety.

There is even evidence in Scheier's results that effort stress (which has resemblances to Hans Selye's "stress adaptation stage one" and

arises from physical as well as mental causes) may have some inverse relation to anxiety. When a person grapples with a difficulty, he shows the stress response; when he retreats and attempts escapist solutions, he shows anxiety. The so-called psychosomatic neurotic, who develops a physical symptom from his encounter with a problem, is in this sense the opposite of a neurotic.

Whether or not anxiety originates as a response to prolonged and remote fear signals, it is quite different from fear as an actual response pattern. Fear is associated with the release of adrenalin; anxiety is not. Fear dries the mouth, whereas anxiety produces increased salivation as well as increased gastric secretion. Fear is sometimes described as realistic, whereas anxiety is considered unrealistic and indeed neurotic. Scheier and I found that students showed raised anxiety levels three weeks before an important examination but lowered anxiety and raised effort stress at the examination itself. The raised anxiety may be "neurotic" in the sense that it does no good, but it is a response to a real-world danger. If such anxiety is neurotic, so also is fear neurotic when it arises from a present danger about which nothing can be done.

Some years ago Hans J. Eysenck of Maudsley Hospital in London demonstrated that a factor I had measured by objective psychological tests and indexed as U.I. 23 powerfully distinguishes neurotics from normals. Some of the manifestations that consistently correlate with what Eysenck then called the neuroticism factor but that we conceive of as "regression" (only one

Questionnaire item	Loading
Do you find yourself with strong moods of anxiety, amusement, sorrow, etc., which you cannot account for by anything that has recently happened?	.60
Do you frequently get in a state of tension and turmoil when thinking over the day's happenings?	.57
Do quite small setbacks irritate you unduly?	.56
Do you, when forced to remain inactive, begin to doodle, draw things on the margin of your paper, etc.?	.55

Questionnaire items can be factored like behavioral or physiological variables. The coefficients at the right show how well a "Yes" answer to each question correlates with a factor designated as "ergic tension." When this factor and others based on questionnaires are factored in turn, anxiety emerges as a "second order" factor influencing them. Questions are from anxiety scale published by Institute for Personality and Ability Testing.

of the components in neuroticism) are set out in the illustration on page 360.

The factor-analysis evidence for the independence of the influences defined as anxiety and regression can be presented visually. The variables are drawn as vectors from a common origin; the more closely correlated the variables are, the closer together they will lie, so that a group of mutually highly correlated variables will look like a sheaf of arrows. The number of dimensions in the space common to these vectors reflects the number of factors required to explain them. Since any set of variables usually involves a number of factors, a plot of the vectors would not be a conventional two-dimensional graph but an imaginary construct in a "hyperspace" of many dimensions. The nature of the experimental results identifies certain variables as factors; these can be treated as the axes of a co-ordinate system. When the end points of the vectors representing variables are projected on these axes in two dimensions, their location represents their loading on the axes.

Because the angles representing the relations among variables are implicit in the correlation results, the whole vector system is rigid. It can, however, be rotated with respect to the axes. The analyst wants to find the one position in which the factors and variables lie in their true relation. For this purpose he depends on the principle of "simple structure," which assumes that in an experiment involving a broad and well-sampled set of variables it is improbable that any single influence will affect all of them. In other words, it is more "simple" to expect that any one variable will be accounted for by less than the full complexity of all the factors acting together. This implies that there should be dense groups, like astro-

nomical galaxies, constituted by variables unaffected by any one factor. In multidimensional space each such galaxy would lie in a "hyperplane"; in three dimensions it would be a disk lying in a plane. Projected in two-dimensional space it should reveal itself as a row of variables lining up with "zero loading"—that is, with no correlation or projection—on some factor axis moved to the correct position.

Such dense disks are indeed found in real data. By placing each chosen axis perpendicularly to a well-defined disk, the analyst rotates his results finally to a unique explanatory position. He thereby establishes the factor to which any set of variables is least related and the one with which it correlates most highly. The illustration on page 362 is a plot, in the plane set by the anxiety and regression factors, of data from a study of 111 variables, covering 18 factors, made by Richard Coan of the University of Arizona on a group of 164 seven-year-old children. The variables fall into two hyperplanes seen as rough ellipses (one rarely gets the galaxies exactly on edge in a row) lying along the axes and intersecting at the origin. The fact that these axes are almost at right angles to each other, with very different kinds of variables projecting close to each of them, shows that they are almost completely independent influences, with very different characteristics.

A similar plot makes clear the close relation, reported earlier in this article, of the behavior-based to the questionnaire-based data on anxiety (see illustration on page 363). The axis of the second-order questionnaire factor aligns itself, within the limits of experimental error, with that of the U.I. 24, or behavioral, factor. This diagram is also of interest in that it shows

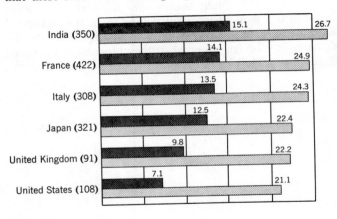

India (350) 15.1 26.7
France (422) 14.1 24.9
Italy (308) 13.5 24.3
Japan (321) 12.5 22.4
United Kingdom (91) 9.8 22.2
United States (108) 7.1 21.1

Figure 4. Intercultural differences in anxiety and neuroticism were revealed by questionnaire data. The anxiety score is shown by the dark bars (possible range, 6 to 30) and the neuroticism score by the light bars (possible range, 6 to 54). The differences between countries were statistically significant except, in anxiety, for the U.K. and U.S. and, in neuroticism, for France and Italy. Numbers at left show size of the group tested in each country.

the psychological and statistical independence of anxiety and intelligence. The direction of the anxiety factor is fixed by the hyperplane oriented largely in intelligence-performance results. The axis representing the intelligence factor is approximately perpendicular to the anxiety axes. In this group of airmen anxiety and intelligence were almost completely independent of each other, and this has proved to be the case in most other experiments.

Factor analysis, then, succeeds in sorting out anxiety from two things with which it is constantly confused: the stress reaction and the neurotic-personality maladjustment. The more precise measurements of anxiety that are now possible also clarify the relation between anxiety and a factor such as intelligence and should help to answer many similar questions about the relation between anxiety and various situations and performances.

During the past decade, for example, almost every theoretically possible relation between anxiety and learning has been reported as being experimentally supported. Our results make it seem probable that those who found better school achievement with higher anxiety were mixing a state measure with a trait measure a few weeks before an examination, and that workers who correlated better achievement with lower anxiety were using an anxiety measurement tainted with neuroticism components. The issue was confused by the inclination of many learning theorists to assume that all learning is conditioning. Our experiments do show more rapid conditioning of autonomic, or involuntary, responses with higher anxiety. On the other hand, learning as reflected by grades is slightly but significantly inversely related to anxiety. It still remains to be seen which is cause and which is effect.

New objective and questionnaire-based anxiety batteries developed by Scheier have already yielded verifiable results showing differences in anxiety level with age, occupation, clinical syndromes and national culture. Anxiety fluctuates in early childhood, rises most consistently in adolescence and declines considerably through adulthood until it rises again after 60 or 65. Among occupations, newspaper editors, artists and air cadets in training have been found to have high anxiety; policemen, clerical workers and engineers have lower levels. Probably both personnel selection and the nature of the jobs are responsible for these differences. Among patients in mental health clinics those diagnosed as anxiety hysterics have the highest scores and alcoholics are also far above average. But the average scores for psychotics, whether schizophrenic or manic-depressive, are not very different from those of the general population.

Some surprising results have come from comparisons across cultures. To obtain data the questionnaire items were translated carefully (often back and forth twice) and checked by working out the factor structure until it was practically identical in each of the nations under study. When the scores were compared, some major differences appeared. Indians and Frenchmen, for example, showed substantially higher anxiety and neuroticism levels than Americans did (see illustration on page 365). This hardly fits the American's treasured view of himself as the most harassed of mortals, or the notion that anxiety is tied up with the pace and complexity of industrialized society. National comparisons are invidious and notoriously tricky, but these results may possibly fit a theory that low anxiety is associated with better economic level and closer political integration. This fits recent data showing still higher anxiety levels in countries that are split culturally and politically and that are low in economic status. Perhaps—and this is a subject for research—the U.S. might head the list in effort stress rather than anxiety. But if the U.S. is the archetypal 20th-century culture, literary psychologists may be far astray when they project their personal feelings to call this the age of anxiety.

2.   A cross-cultural comparison
of patterns of extroversion and anxiety

RAYMOND B. CATTELL AND FRANK W. WARBURTON

The Present Experimental Status of the Anxiety Factor

THE CONCEPT OF EXTRAVERSION is at least as old as the writings of Jung (1923), while that of anxiety, apart from its special Freudian theoretical implications is much older. On the other hand, the tying down of these concepts in factors statistically uniquely determined (Cattell, 1952; Cattell, 1957c; Cattell & Scheier, 1958a; Cattell & Scheier, 1960; Eysenck, 1952), and in standardized tests (Cattell, 1946; Cattell, Saunders, & Stice, 1957; Cattell & Scheier; 1961) for such factors is very recent.

The question of whether the many behavioural and introspective manifestations which are semantically labelled as 'anxious' arise, in our culture, from a single functional influence or from several, was studied by Cattell & Scheier (1958a) in an investigation which showed that *a single, underlying, simple-structure factor can be isolated,* accounting for a substantial part of the variance in some 814 diverse introspective, behavioural and physiological measures. This functionally unitary character was found to hold not only in terms of measurement of individual differences, among normals and patients, but also in terms of a common pattern of mood fluctuation from day to day.

The technique for revealing mood fluctuation, which has been defined as P-technique (Cattell, 1952; Cattell 1957c), shows that al-

most exactly the same variables fluctuate together from day to day, (Cattell & Scheier, 1961). The only noticeable difference is that certain physiological measures, such as systolic blood pressure, 17-OH cortico-steroid secretion, etc., are more highly loaded on the state (mood) pattern than on the more stable characterological factor (Cattell & Scheier, 1961).

When a very wide range of objective personality measures are used, i.e. measures in which the subject is not consciously evaluating himself, but simply having his behaviour recorded, it has been shown that the anxiety factor is distinct from any previously known factor. It clearly distinguishes itself from such established patterns as that of general intelligence, or the general neuroticism factor isolated by Cattell (1946) and Eysenck (1952) and refined by Cattell & Scheier (1961). Nor can it be confused with extraversion-introversion factor (Cattell, 1957c; Eysenck, 1952; Jung, 1923). The factor which Eysenck called neuroticism, and which he and his co-workers have clearly established by criterion rotation as strongly differentiating neurotics and normals, is one which Cattell and his co-workers have established, with even more the replications (1957a), on the other side of the Atlantic. It has been called by the latter 'regression' (Cattell & Scheier, 1961), rather than 'neuroticism', because it seems to have the character of a regressive loss of interest and capacity to mobilize, rather than the actual dynamic conflict, commonly thought of as the neurosis itself. Moreover, to call this *the* neuroticism factor seems undesirable because Cattell & Scheier (1961) have shown the neurotics differ significantly from normals not only on this regression factor, but

SOURCE. Article by Raymond B. Cattell and Frank W. Warburton, "A cross-cultural comparison of patterns of extroversion and anxiety" in *British Journal of Psychology*, Vol. 52, pp. 3–15, 1961.

also by having high anxiety scores on the anxiety factor battery, higher introversion, and significantly higher scores on several other factors, with which we need not here be concerned.

Neurotics, defined and experimented upon as a medically distinct subgroup, differ from the rest of the population not on a single dimension but almost equally on half a dozen dimensions. The importance of anxiety and of introversion for the medical psychologist reside in the fact that they significantly distinguish neurotics, though the former is much more strongly involved than the latter. Comparative cultural studies of neuroticism eventually require attention to all distinguishing factors, but we are here concentrating upon anxiety and introversion because they have been most clearly shown, by their simultaneous appearance in replicated factor analyses covering a wide range of variables, to be independent of each other, and of other factors in neurosis.

Patterns of Anxiety and Extraversion

Some years ago (Cattell & Scheier, 1958a), a systematic research was begun, starting with all the self-descriptive terms in the dictionary aiming to develop a 'personality sphere' of questionnaire items which would cover, in a representative way, the whole area of introspectible and self-evaluative response. Ultimately repeated factor analyses of over 500 varied items of this kind led to the *Sixteen Personality Factor Questionnaire* (Cattell, Saunders & Stice, 1957) which differed from most questionnaires in utilizing this representative design, instead of concentrating upon one *a priori* subjectively defined area of behaviour (Cattell, 1957c) of idiosyncratic interest to the investigator. The factors in the sixteen P.F. test are not the artificial, orthogonal abstractions of the pure statistician, but have the functional relations to one another which examination of the data in the general population by the criterion of simple structure, shows to exist. This relation, as one might expect is that they are slightly correlated or 'oblique.' One would indeed suspect that we are dealing with unreal abstractions if it were found, for example, that general intelligence is absolutely uncorrelated with ego strength, since the possession of higher general ability may to some slight degree assist in the cognitive aspects of emotional integration. And

so on in terms of other relationships between factors which will occur to the observant clinician.

Now since the factors are somewhat correlated it is possible to form a correlation matrix among them when the factors have been measured upon a sufficient sample of the general population. This matrix expressing correlations among the factors, can itself be factored, leading to what have been called 'second-order factors.' The reader may remember that Thurstone's dozen primary ability factors were soon shown thus to yield second-order factors, one of which is Spearman's 'g' or general intelligence. On factoring the principal dimensions of personality, as represented by these sixteen primary factors, one does not obtain a single large factor, but five or six second-order factors, of which only two, however, have persisted in different experiments with high consistency of pattern. From their content there is no doubt that most psychologists would want to call these two largest second-order factors extraversion versus introversion and anxiety versus lack of anxiety (or 'adjustment') as we have stated above. But let us examine the evidence for this conclusion more closely.

There have now been no fewer than seven second-order factorings or questionnaire measurements (Cattell & Scheier, 1960). In all these seven previous studies another second-order factor has stood out with about the same magnitude as anxiety and with equally good consistency from research to research. This we have interpreted as the extraversion-introversion dimension. The highest loaded factor in this pattern is most commonly the primary called cyclothymia versus schizothymia, or factor A. The next largest is the surgency versus desurgency factor, and after that the factor which has been called 'parmia.' This label is for 'parasympathetic resistance to stimulation,' since this H factor shows evidence of substantial autonomic involvement and is also highly hereditarily determined, whereas surgency-desurgency is largely environmentally determined (Cattell, Blewett, & Beloff, 1955). In the second-order anxiety factor the largest loading is usually on Q 4 which has been called id pressure or undischarged instinctual energy, the next highest is on O, or guilt proneness, while in both the state (mood) factor and the trait factor a high position is occupied by C—, ego weakness. In fact this second-order factor embraces those, and *only* those, factors among primaries which have reference to anxiety in their content or which one would expect, on dynamic grounds, to be associated with anxiety.

Personality Patterns within Cultures

It is the contention of the multivariate experimenter (in agreement with the clinician, and with a critical eye on the concepts of the univariate, 'brass instrument' experimentalist) that the concepts employed by the clinician, if true, would always be verifiable by factor analytic investigations. For if the verbal classifications of the clinician are correct, implying, for example, that a particular dynamic temperamental tendency is a unitary one, then it should be possible to demonstrate this by showing that its manifestations correlate in the manner required by the hypothesis. Within the two areas, America and the British Commonwealth, in which the great bulk of the experimental, factor analytic study of psychological structure has taken place, there has indeed been excellent agreement on the functional unity of at least half a dozen concepts, notably, general intelligence, the presently discussed concepts of anxiety and extraversion, cyclothymia, ego strength, and a few others (Cattell, 1946; Cattell, 1956). It next becomes important that agreement be tested between these psychometric concepts on the one hand, and on the other the insightful concepts of practising clinicians. Where this has been tried, as when Cattell and Scheier compared their factor measurements of anxiety with psychiatrists' ratings, it has, in fact, been found (Cattell & Scheier, 1958*b*) that the consensus of opinion shown by the psychiatrists agrees with the factor pattern, though the ratings of individual psychiatrists may show features which extend beyond the common factor pattern. For example, when one psychiatrist was asked to rate eighty-six people in the consulting room situation for their level of anxiety, it was found that his ratings correlated largely with the anxiety factor measures (Cattell & Scheier, 1958*b*) and also, to some extent, with measures of a quite distinct factor of inhibition. Apart from such errors in the use of terms, however, it would seem that we have now in this area considerable agreement between different experimental approaches and the clinical approach, regarding the nature of the major concepts with which clinical psychology deals.

Admittedly, much research still remains to be done, particularly in bringing out the more remote expressions of these factor patterns. But we would no longer regard it as premature to turn to the question of how far these factors might vary from culture to culture, and what inferences might be drawn from any discovered differences of pattern. We know in extraversion-introversion, for example, that factors A (cyclothymia-schizothymia) and H (reactivity to threat) seem to express largely inborn temperamental tendencies, whereas F or surgency-desurgency more definitely represents the extent to which the person has become inhibited. Possibly, in a culture such as that of America, where more extravert behaviour is generally approved, it might happen that surgency-desurgency differences would be found to contribute less to the total extraversion pattern than in Britain. For in America everyone is presumably at a low level of inhibition, with little range. (In fact, surgency comes out as would then be expected in the present investigation, the factor loadings being $+0.48$ for the U.S. and $+0.70$ for Britain.) Or again, in the second-order anxiety factor, if guilt-proneness, as a result of more emphasis on super ego development in a culture, should contribute more to the total anxiety factor in culture X than in culture Y, then this might be shown by an exchange in positions between factor O, guilt-proneness, and factor C—, ego weakness, in terms of their rank order in contribution to the total anxiety. (There is actually no marked difference with the present samples, C loading -41 and -53, and the O factor $+69$ and $+62$ in the two groups.)

Nature of Second-Order Factors

We must first ask whether the British and American patterns are of the same genus before we ask whether they differ as species. In other words, let us first examine what *constancy* of the factor patterns exists between the two cultures so that we may begin by discussing the interpretation of whatever is *common* in form.

We shall discuss extraversion-introversion first, as being a more cut-and-dried concept. Of the five principal primary components of

Table 1. The Extraversion-Introversion and Anxiety Patterns in British and American Samples

		I Anxiety		II Introversion	
		British	American	British	American
A	Cyclothymia	−01	+07	−35	−46
C	Ego-strength	−41	−53	−03	−10
E	Dominance	−00	+02	−49	+01
F	Surgency	+14	+17	−70	−48
G	Super-ego strength	−24	−09	+28	+01
H	Parmia (Adventurousness)	−18	−66	−62	−33
I	Premsia (Sensitivity)	−08	+03	+11	−01
L	Paranoid tendency	+50	+56	−23	+13
M	Autia (or Bohemianism)	+40	+07	−21	+51
N	Shrewdness	+02	−08	+03	+09
O	Guilt proneness	+69	+62	−02	+07
Q1	Radicalism	+25	−12	+12	+42
Q2	Self-sufficiency	+20	−06	+35	+38
Q3	Self-sentiment	−40	−66	+14	+01
Q4	Id pressure	+62	+62	−18	+09

Those underlined may be considered out of the hyperspace, i.e. significantly loaded, in terms of the *joint* British and American evidence.

extraversion-introversion A and H have already had their nature briefly indicated. We have also discussed the nature of surgency-desurgency as a form of behaviour depending upon the degree of inhibition, or punishment, and of seriousness of demand to which the individual has been exposed in his early life. The nature of the primary factor Q 2, called, in its introvert direction, self-sufficiency, is not yet understood, though descriptively, it is quite clear, from the items loading highly in the factor, that it refers to an individual who prefers to make decisions by himself, who has independent views, and who is self-sufficient in relation to society generally. The nature of M, called Autia, is also under investigation, but its general nature descriptively is also clear, namely, that it is a tendency to have a vivid inner life, to be rather subjective in one's judgements, and to be Bohemian and unconcerned about practical matters in life generally. It has been shown to be associated with artistic and general creativity, i.e. it distinguishes creative from non-creative people of the same intelligence level. There is considerable difference in the manner in which the primaries M and H(−) operate in the resultant second-order factor of introversion. The H(−), Threctia factor, defined as autonomic susceptibility to threat, shows

itself outwardly as shyness. The person high in M, Autia, on the other hand, is introverted (in the United States; we shall discuss the British result later) not by reason of withdrawal from external stimulation but because he has a rich inner life which he finds sufficiently entertaining. Thus the total introvert pattern is accounted for by a combination of innate and acquired patterns, very different in their mode of operation. This is one reason why the designation of an individual as an introvert needs to be qualified by reference to the primary factors which bring introversion about; for the quality of introversion will be different according to which primaries are prominent.

Looking now at the anxiety factor pattern (factor I, Table 1), one can see that the contributing primaries fit very well the classical psychoanalytic description of the origins of anxiety. Anxiety is high, in the first place, whenever id pressure (Q4) (Cattell *et al.* 1957) is high. That is to say whenever there is a failure successfully to discharge libido, (if we follow the libido concept as *total* instinctual energy, of all kinds) then there is a predisposition to anxiety. Secondly, the O factor of guilt proneness (Cattell *et al.* 1957) fits the psychoanalytic view of the super ego as one of the prime creators of anxiety. Next we observe the large role of C−, i.e. ego weakness (Cattell, 1957c; Cattell et al. 1957) which indicate that the individual with the weaker ego will experience the greater anxiety. Presumably, whatever the instinctual tensions, they will be experienced as a greater threat if the ego is weak. Factor Q3 is at present interpreted (Cattell, 1957c; Cattell et al. 1957) as self sentiment, in McDougall's sense of a set of attitudes centered on maintaining good self repute and self control. As an examination of the actual questionnaire items will show, this factor shows itself principally in the individual having high standards of self control, calmness and integration. Thus the person who has not cultivated such standards tends to show greater anxiety.

The two principal factors which do not immediately fit into any previous theory are H and L. As we have already seen in connexion with introversion, H is a constitutional shyness or susceptibility to threat. It is surely rather remarkable that psychoanalysis, in its preoccupation with dynamic factors as such, appears to have overlooked the rather obvious fact that, other things being equal, the person of greater dispositional timidity will show greater anxiety in relation to whatever inner and outer threats he experiences. On the other hand, the role of the paranoid factor I, remains obscure. It could be interpreted either by saying that the paranoid individual tends to become so isolated from society that anxiety is created, or, alternatively, that prolonged high anxiety may, perhaps through some impairment of cognitive function, bring about paranoid ideas. This case reminds us that, theoretically, each and every one of the correlations between a first-order and a second-order factor could be interpreted causally in either direction. That is to say, we could view these personality factors as contributors to anxiety, which, in the main, we have done, or alternatively, we could view anxiety as productive of these personality structures and conditions.

Procedure

Our experiment to investigate cultural constancy took two groups of undergraduate students of corresponding socio-economic status. There were both men and women students in each country's sample, the totals being in the case of the British group 112 graduate students in the Department of Education, University of Manchester, and 90 students in the Department of Industrial Administration in the College of Advanced Technology, Birmingham. The pattern for the American group is based on a broader foundation than for the British, consisting of three separate factor analyses covering 604 men and women undergraduates. The values in Table 1 are the mean loadings for these three studies, while the British pattern comes from a single factor analysis of raw data pooled from the two groups.

The scores were correlated by product-moment correlation and factor analyzed by the centroid method, eight factors being extracted. The rotation for simple structure then proceeded in this eight dimensional space, together with fourteen additional variables orthogonal to most of the 16 P.F. factors, thus constituting good "hyperspace stuff" (Cattell, 1952).

Actually, our attainment of simple structure began by using an analytical oblimax approach and then rotating by single space plots until the number of variables in the ±10 hyperspace reached a plateau and stayed at the plateau (Cattell, 1952). This required six overall rotations. The resulting rotated factor matrices for the first two factors are shown in Table 1.

Differences in the Form and Level of the Anxiety Pattern

Although the similarity of the British and American patterns in Table 1 is evident to the eye, those who wish to express it statistically may at present do so in two ways: (1) by the correlation coefficient, which has an r of +0.880 for anxiety, and +0.606 for extroversion; and (2) by the Cattell-Baggaley salient variable similarity index, m, which has significance values of $P = 0.001$ and $P = 0.01$, respectively, for the anxiety and extroversion patterns.

We shall now concern ourselves with the differences instead of similarities in manifestation in the two cultures, beginning in this section with the anxiety pattern. These differences can express themselves in two ways: (1) as a difference of pattern, and (2) as a difference in level. Differences of level can be subjected to a common, simple test of statistical significance, but evaluating differences of pattern requires the development of new statistical significance tests for which we have no space in the present article. There is no essential connexion between pattern and level, for a first-order primary personality factor may have a higher loading in the factor analytic pattern in a given culture, and yet be represented by a lower mean score. We have to distinguish between *relative* weight in the culture (factor loading) and *absolute* level of mean score.

Only two differences in pattern will be discussed, the tendency of M, Autia (Bohemianism) to be more strongly loaded in the British than the American pattern, and of H, Threctia to be more loaded in the American than the British (Table 1). With American populations the loading in M, Autia, is typically quite insignificant, although postive; Autia, as at present understood (Cattell, 1957c; Cattell *et al.* 1957), is a partly constitutional tendency to think autistically and to have an inner productivity and tenacity of phantasy that has little relation to external realities. The higher factor loading in the British sample could mean either that anxiety is more frequently expressed in this way in America than in Britain, or, accepting the opposite possible causation of correlation, that this autonomy of behaviour is more anxiety provoking in Britain than America. Even at the statistical level there are reasons (simple structure) for accepting the former as more probable, and it makes better psychological sense. Contingently, we shall hypothesize that anxiety is more prone to express itself in British than American culture in the form of phantasy activity, as a result of the greater inhibition imposed by the culture and the lesser opportunities for 'acting out.'

The greater role of dispositional timidity $(H(-)$, Threctia) in the American culture in determining the individual's level of anxiety needs to be compared with our finding that it also plays a larger role in the anxiety of children. The most likely hypothesis is that the British culture is more inhibited and introvert, so that anxieties arise more from conflicts in the complex mazes of the culture, and less from realistic threats of the environment. It seems reasonable to suppose that dispositional timidity would play a greater role in magnifying anxieties in an extravert culture.

Turning next to the comparison of the *levels* of total anxiety score, we have the alternatives of computing the anxiety by weighting the primary factor scores on the American, the British or a compromise of these loadings. The differences are trivial. For this exploratory study, we used the British beta weights. These beta weights have been applied to the primary factor scores for the British and American subjects (Table 3). Table 2, shows that the American students are at a higher anxiety level, to a very significant degree $(P < 0.001)$. Parenthetically, this finding that the American student operates at a higher level of anxiety (with implications in relation to competitiveness and readiness radically to re-adapt) agrees with impressions of both authors in some years of experience with both groups of students.

Differences in the Form and Level of the Extraversion-Introversion Pattern

Noteworthy differences can be seen on the right-hand side of Table 1. Dominance (E factor), Surgency (F factor) and Parmia (H factor) play a greater role of extraversion in Britain, while Practical Concernedness (the op-

Table 2. Mean Scores in Second-Order Factors (Standard Deviations in Brackets)

	I. Anxiety	II. Introversion
British University $(N = 112)$	4.5(1.9)	6.2(1.8)
American University $(N = 604)$	5.5(1.8)	5.5(1.8)
British College of Technology $(N = 92)$	3.8(1.9)	5.3(1.9)
Significance of differences between American University and British University	0.001	0.001
Significance of differences between American University and British College of Advanced Technology	0.001	N.S.
Significance of differences between British University and British College of Advanced Technology	0.001	0.001

posite of Autia, M factor) and Radicalism (Q1 factor) enter more strongly into the American pattern. As to the main difference, which is in dominance, our hypothesis will again hinge on the prior hypothesis that the British culture is more inhibiting, complex and authoritarian in structure. We know that among children the dominance factor is responsible for much disobedient behaviour (Cattell, 1957 c), and Maslow has shown that breaking conventions is as strongly correlated with the dominance dimension in adults (Maslow, 1954). Dominance may load extraversion not because of any intrinsic connexion with extraversion (indeed, the evidence is rather that the dominant male approaches in pattern the novelist's 'strong, silent man' (Cattell, 1957 c)); but because at important developmental stages it leads the individual to reject the approved introvert standard, just as he tends to question *any* cultural standard.

A somewhat similar hypothesis looks most probable in explaining the greater connexion with parmia-threctia (H factor) in Britain. This factor has been shown to be substantially constitutional (Cattell *et al.* 1955), and a number of physiological connexions have been found for it (Cattell, 1957 c). Clinically it might be confused with dominance, but factor analysis shows the boldness versus shyness involved in H springs from a quite different cause, which can be summarized as a thick-skinned attitude versus a sensitive reaction to punishment. Where the general weight of inhibiting influences, especially in childhood, is greater, one would expect individuals to be more 'spread out,' i.e. for H to contribute greater variance, with respect to overt, extravert behaviour.

There is a close relationship of surgency-desurgency to parmia-threctia, such that some, like Meeland (1952) have had difficulty in separating them, while others have questioned the separation, or proceeded like Eysenck (1952), as if only a single "extraversion" component were involved. Their separation requires much skill because they are "co-operative" (Cattell, 1952), acting on the same variables, in that the H factor defines individual differences in *susceptibility* to inhibition, while F defines differences in *exposure* to inhibition. There is accumulating evidence that the score on surgency-desurgency is a function of the severity of the individual's life struggle and of cultural demands upon him, e.g. there is a

tendency for the upper social class to be significantly more surgent than the lower middle class (Cattell, 1957c), and for hardworking scientists to be more desurgent than the general population or well-to-do playboys (Cattell & Drevdahl, 1955). The greater loading of surgency-desurgency (F factor) in the British extraversion-introversion pattern is therefore to be interpreted as expressing a greater environmental range—possibly the effect of a greater class range—in the British population.

The remaining differences, on primary factors Q 1 and M, are difficult to integrate into basic psychological concepts. The greater tie-up of introversion with radicalism in America possibly expresses a purely sociological law, namely, that in a wave of transition, which has passed in Britain but is current in America, introverts are more likely to hold the new developing views, since social solidarity is a need of the extravert. On the other hand, the association of autia with introversion in America, which disappears or is slightly reversed in the British group, seems to require a more complex psychological explanation. From its nature, one would certainly expect autia, with its phantasy activity and neglect of environmental demands, to belong to the introvert aggregate, which it consistently does in the American samples. But in the present British sample it is a function more of anxiety. This will deserve more thought when others have checked our experimental finding.

As to the level on the total extraversion-introversion dimension, the procedure for calculation was precisely the same as for anxiety, with the result shown in Table 2. That the American university student should score significantly more extravert than his British counterpart should surprise no social anthropologist or observant traveller. It is noteworthy that the British technology student is more extraverted than his university coeval.

Some Differences in the Organization of the Self

Although our primary concern is with the massive second-order factors of anxiety and extraversion, we have set out in Table 3 the differences separately analyzed for the sixteen separate primary personality dimensions. Again we have set out the British group in two

Table 3. Mean Score on Sixteen Primary Personality Factors (Standard Deviations in Brackets)

Second-order factors	Anxiety					
Primary Personality Factors	C— Ego weakness	O Guilt proneness	M Bohemi- anism	Q3— Low self sentiment	Q4 Id pressure	L Paranoid tendency
American University ($N =604$)	5.5(2.0)	5.5(2.0)	5.5(2.0)	5.5(2.0)	5.5(2.0)	5.5(2.0)
British University ($N = 112$)	4.9(1.8)	4.5(2.8)	5.1(2.2)	4.9(2.6)	4.4(1.9)	5.8(1.7)
British College of Advanced Technology ($N = 92$)	4.0(1.3)	3.6(1.8)	4.6(1.7)	4.7(1.2)	4.7(2.0)	3.9(1.6)
Significance of differences between British University and American University	0.01	0.001	N.S.	0.05	0.001	N.S.
Significance of differences between American University and British College of Advanced Technology	0.001	0.001	0.001	0.001	0.001	0.001
Significance of differences between British University and British College of Advanced Technology	0.001	0.01	N.S.	N.S.	N.S.	0.001

Second-order factors	Extraversion				
Primary Personality Factors	A Cyclo- thymic tendency	F Surgency	H Extraversion	E Dominance	Q2— Dependence
American University ($N =604$)	5.5(2.0)	5.5(2.0)	5.5(2.0)	5.5(2.0)	5.5(2.0)
British University ($N = 112$)	5.1(2.1)	5.0(2.3)	6.3(2.5)	3.5(2.2)	4.3(1.9)
British College of Advanced Technology ($N = 92$)	4.8(1.4)	4.8(2.0)	6.3(2.2)	6.6(2.2)	6.5(1.3)
Significance of differences between British University and American University	N.S.	0.05	0.01	0.001	0.001
Significance of differences between American University and British College of Advanced Technology	0.001	0.01	0.01	0.001	0.001
Significance of differences between British University and British College of Advanced Technology	N.S.	N.S.	N.S.	0.001	0.001

Second-order factors	Radicalism		Tender-Tough Mindedness		
Primary Personality Factors	Q Radical- ism	G— Low super ego	I Emotional Sensitivity	N Tender- minded- ness	B Intelligence
American University ($N =604$)	5.5(2.0)	5.5(2.0)	5.5(2.0)	5.5(2.0)	5.5(2.0)
British University ($N = 112$)	5.9(2.1)	5.9(1.9)	6.4(1.8)	5.7(1.8)	8.4(1.2)
British College of Advanced Technology ($N = 92$)	5.6(1.2)	7.1(1.5)	4.9(1.9)	6.0(1.9)	5.3(1.3)
Significance of differences between British University and American University	N.S.	0.05	0.001	N.S.	0.001
Significance of differences between American University and British College of Advanced Technology	N.S.	0.001	0.01	0.05	N.S.
Significance of differences between British University and British College of Advanced Technology	N.S.	0.001	0.001	N.S.	0.001

samples, so that some idea can be gained of what is likely to belong to the culture pattern as a whole, and what may merely be due to an educational-occupational subgroup. Indeed, we propose to comment only on dimensions in which both British groups show significant divergence in the same direction from the American.

The difference in primary factor B, general intelligence (Spearman's 'g') may be briefly dismissed as being precisely what is to be expected when, in the university age group, about 1 in 70 goes to a university in Britain and 1 in 7 in America. In this respect, and perhaps in others too, the best equivalent for the American university undergraduate would be obtained in Britain by putting university and technical college students together, in a mixture of roughly 1 to 10.

The biggest personality differences, as it happens, are on primaries already covered in anxiety and introversion. However, it is noteworthy that the biggest contribution to the higher anxiety of the Americans comes from id pressure (Q 4) and guilt proneness (O), (Cattell, 1957a). The former indicates a higher general level of instinctual stimulation, and is the only factor we have found which substantiates the Freudian concept of level of undischarged libido.

The difference in guilt proneness is of the same order. The American group, relative to either British sample, has a higher mean score for factor G (Super Ego Strength). It must be pointed out, in passing, that the factor analytic and the psychoanalytic approaches show a clear disagreement on super ego concepts, in that the latter speaks always of a single super ego, whereas multivariate experiment has consistently yielded three factors, namely O, guilt proneness, G, super ego strength, and Q 3, self sentiment; G and O seem analogous to F and H in extraversion, in that O has constitutional variance and may be 'the capacity to acquire ego,' while G may represent more precisely the actual learning experience.

Whether this interpretation is confirmed or not, there is evidently a very interesting difference of structure, with respect to these factors, between the British and American cultures. The Americans score higher on both aspects of super ego strength, but lower on the more rational control through the self sentiment, the differences being significant in one case beyond

$P = 0.05$, and in five beyond $P = 0.001$. This may be associated with the well-known observation of a greater development of a rationalist moral outlook in Britain and a more fundamentalist moral outlook in America.

The only remaining factor deserving comment is the ego strength factor C, which is significantly higher in both British samples. It is reasonable to hypothesize that we are dealing here, in the lower ego strength of the American, with a secondary effect of that same childhood education which produces a stronger super ego, at the expense of the ego. As suggested above, the results here point to an intriguing cultural difference of development in the area of the self. Possibly some greater stability in the British upbringing gives greater ego strength, aided by the lesser emphasis, in an increasingly secular-rationalist atmosphere, on early super ego development. Compensation for a lesser degree of super ego control, then, possibly comes about in the British educational experience through the stronger and more conscious development of the self sentiment, aiming at the polish of the gentleman rather than the rigid convictions which the society of saints planted in New England.

Summary

1. A comparison has been made between 604 Americans and 204 British subjects, the former largely University undergraduate students, the latter university students in one sample (112) and College of Advanced Technology students in the other (92). They were measured on the first-order and second-order personality dimensions of the Sixteen Personality Factor Questionnaire.

2. The form of the anxiety and the extraversion-introversion patterns (both second-order) were so similar in the two national subcultures that there is confirmation of the correctness of using the same concepts—anxiety and introversion—in both groups.

3. However, there are considerable species differences within the common genus. For example, dominance is more instrumental in extraversion in Britain, and dispositional timidity differences play a larger role in the pattern of anxiety in America.

4. In terms of second-order factors, the American students are found to be at a signifi-

cantly higher level of anxiety than either British group, and are more extravert than the British university group.

5. When differences are examined in terms of primary personality dimensions it is hypothesized that the higher American anxiety arises from greater ergic tension (excess of stimulation over satisfaction) and greater guilt proneness. Higher surgency more consistently contributes to the greater American extraversion.

6. Apart from the differences in the two concepts we were most concerned to study, we also found a rather striking difference in the structure of the self, in that the British group showed significantly higher ego strength (C factor) and self sentiment development (Q 3 factor), while the American group showed higher super ego development, both in terms of guilt proneness (O factor) and strength of the learned socio-moral pattern (G factor). These differences may be related to differences in the prominence of fundamentalist religious education as contrasted with rationalist, humanistic approaches to moral questions.

7. There are also some indications that British University students are, in terms of second-order factors, more emotionally sensitive and more radical than American students. Thus, on the whole, the British students are less anxious, more introverted, more sensitive and more radical; the American students are more anxious, more extraverted, less sensitive and more conservative.

REFERENCES

Cattell, R. B. (1946). *The Description and Measurement of Personality*. New York: World Book Co.

Cattell, R. B. (1952). *Factor Analysis*. New York: Harper and Bros.

Cattell, R. B. (1956). Second-order factors in the questionnaire realm. *J. Consult. Psychol.* **20**, 411–18.

Cattell, R. B. (1957a). *The Objective Analytic Personality Factor Battery*. Champaign, Ill.: Instit. Pers. and Abil. Testing, 1602–4 Coronado Dr.

Cattell, R. B. (1957b). A universal index for psychological factors. *Psychologia*, **1**, 74–85.

Cattell, R. B. (1957c). *Personality and Motivation Structure and Measurement*. New York: World Book Co.

Cattell, R. B., Blewett, C. B. & Beloff, J. R. (1955). The inheritance of personality. A multiple variance analysis determination of approximate nature-nurture ratios for primary personality factors in Q data. *Amer. J. Hum. Genet.* **7**, 122–46.

Cattell, R. B. & Drevdahl, J. C. (1955). A comparison of the personality profiles of eminent researchers with those of eminent teachers and administrators. *Brit. J. Psychol.* **46**, 248–61.

Cattell, R. B. Saunders, D. R. & Stice, C. (1957). *Handbook for the Sixteen Personality Factor Questionnaire*. Champaign. Ill.: Instit. Pers. and Abil. Testing.

Cattell R. B. & Scheier, I. H. (1958a). The nature of anxiety: a review of thirteen multivariate analyses comprising 816 variables. *Psychol. Rep.* **4**, 351–88.

Cattell, R. B. & Scheier, I. H. (1958b). Clinical validities by analysing the psychiatrist exemplified in relation to anxiety diagnoses. *Amer. J. Orthopsychiat.* **28**, 699–713.

Cattell, R. B. & Scheier. I. H. (1961). *The Meaning and Measurement of Neuroticism and Anxiety*. New York: The Ronald Press. (In the Press.)

Eysenck, H. J. (1952). *The Scientific Study of Personality*. London: Routledge and Kegan Paul.

Jung, C. J. (1923). *Psychological Types*. New York: Harcourt, Brace.

Maslow, A. H. (1954). *Motivation and Personality*. New York: Harper and Bros.

Meeland, F. (1952). *An investigation of hypothesis for distinguishing personality factors A, F and H*. Ph.D. thesis. Univ. Ill. Library.

3. Motivational structure of an hospitalized mental defective

ANNA M. SHOTWELL, JOHN R. HURLEY,
AND RAYMOND B. CATTELL

FREUD, MC DOUGALL, MURRAY, AND OTHERS, in attempting to isolate basic dimensions of motivation, did not have the benefit of the factor analytic methods which have enabled Cattell and his co-workers to substantiate the concepts of drive, ego structure, and sentiment. On the assumption that factor analysis of many scores obtained on objective attitude measuring devices would reveal a limited number of motivational components which could account for the multitude of phenomena observed in dynamic behavior, Cattell pioneered three researches: an R-technique study to isolate and identify the basic motivational determinants (Cattell, 1950), another R-technique study to confirm the findings of the first and to develop alternative objective measuring methods (Cattell & Miller, 1952), and a P-technique study to confirm further and to clarify the ideas elicited by the other two studies as well as to investigate the applicability of these ideas to an individual (Cattell & Cross, 1952). The present case study continues this line of research.

The objective here was to discover the motivational dimensions of an institutionalized mental defective by objective P-technique factor analysis and to ascertain whether the findings were congruent with clinical understanding of the case and with earlier factor analytic results on nondefectives.

SOURCE. Article by Anna M. Shotwell, John R. Hurley, and Raymond B. Cattell, "Motivational structure of an hospitalized mental defective" in *Journal of abnormal and social psychology*, Vol. 62, pp. 422–426, 1961.

Method

The subject, a female patient at Pacific State Hospital in California, was a heavy-set 15-year-old Negro mental defective of mild degree who had come from an unfit home. Her mother was sexually promiscuous and probably of retarded intelligence. After the subject's father molested her sexually, her mother killed him with the subject a witness to the killing. The subject was described by the hospital staff as quiet, somewhat withdrawn, and undemonstrative, but usually cooperative. For a period of 100 days (5 days per week for 20 weeks), she was given a series of tests and was rated on various traits by her school teachers, by the technician in charge of her ward, and by herself. The test instruments, constructed on the assumption that drives and sentiments are revealed as patterns among attitudes, were designed to measure attitudes in an objective manner by means of ratings, questions about activities, word association, and paired comparisons. Each previously known dynamic factor in the literature was represented by at least two marker variables, i.e., variables which were strongly loaded in the previously known factor were carried over in some form and used in this investigation.

To distinguish each type of evaluative variable from all other variables in the factor matrix, a letter prefix was assigned as follows: RT, ratings by school teacher; RW, ratings by ward technicians; RS, self-ratings; QA, questions regarding activities; WA, word association; and PC, paired comparisons.

The subject was rated by herself and two others on 14 traits. The best possible score was 10; the worst possible was 0. Of the 42 trait ratings, only 9 proved variant enough to be retained for analysis.

Most of the original 22 questions regarding the subject's daily activities required only a ysis, the remainder being eliminated because tion, "How many cigarettes have you smoked?" required a quantitative answer. Of the original group of 22, 9 questions were retained for analysis, the remainder being eliminated because they displayed little or no variance.

Thirty-four word association items were presented to the subject in the format:

top. . . . . . lid_____ winner_____

The second and third words of the series were assumed to represent one of several hypothesized drives and sentiments. From these two words, the subject was to choose the one which she first associated with the first word of the series. It was assumed that the choice of one word over another would be determined by her attitudes. The subject's choices were then pooled to obtain a score for each of the hypothesized drives and sentiments. Since the sequence of items was changed from day to day, there was no chance for the subject to mechanize her responses.

Paired comparisons consisted of having the subject indicate which of a pair of statements, each printed on a separate slip of paper, most strongly represented her present desires. Sixteen statements were constructed so as to define each attitude by inclusion of its parts: the stimulus situation, an organism, a need, a course of action, and an object concerned in that course of action. One of the statements was, "I want a good looking boy to make love to me." Since each statement was paired against every other statement, the subject made 120 choices each day for 100 days. Again the sequence of presentation was altered daily to obviate the possibility of the subject repeating responses mechanically. The 16 statements as well as the Word Association test were markers for seven drives and one sentiment. The seven drives were sex-mating, gregariousness, appeal-dependence, escape-fear, self-assertion, parental-protective, and narcissistic play. The eighth motivational component hypothesized was the self-sentiment.

Analysis of data. As a result of the above procedure, each of the original 98 variables was represented by measures on 100 items. Means, standard deviations, and all possible intercorrelations were computed for each of the 98 variables. Upon inspection of the results, the decision was made to eliminate 56 of the original 98 variables. The major reason for this was that the data displayed little or no variance for these measures. The intercorrelations of the remaining 42 variables were then factor analyzed by the complete simple centroid method (Thurstone, 1947). The diagonal values were

set at unity. The resulting factor matrix was then rotated to orthogonal simple structure by the method of quartimax (Neuhaus & Wrigley, 1954). Quartimax failed to disperse fully the main centroid. Consequently, the unrotated factor matrix was again rotated, this time to oblique simple structure. The method used was a combination of oblimax (Pinzka & Saunders, 1954) and Hurley's analytical method.[1] A decent oblique simple structure was finally obtained, with a total of 11 rotated factors remaining for interpretation.[2]

Discussion

Of the 11 factors found, 7 corresponded to factors found by previous researchers. Of 2 new factors, 1 did not lend itself to precise interpretation, and 1 was a subfactor. The factors are shown below in estimated order of variance accounted for.

Factor I—The Sex Erg

		Loading
PC 10	I want a good-looking boy to make love to me	.70
PC 11	I want to go to a good movie every week	.64
RT 1	Lack of shyness	.57
PC 25	I don't want to keep good control of my temper	.53
PC 13	I want to watch games like baseball	.51
PC 20	I don't want to help people in trouble	.50
PC 12	I want to take an active part in recreation	.49
PC 21	I don't want my parents always to have what they need	.39
WA 35	Sex-mating (word association)	.12

---

[1] The unrotated factor matrix was first rotated by the method of oblimax to give an idea of the oblique structure. Then a rotated matrix V_{ij} was postulated on the basis of the oblimax solution. V_{ij} was constructed to display simple structure. The matrix equation $F_o t = V_{ij}$ was then solved for t, the transformation matrix. All statistical computations were performed on the University of Illinois digital computer, ILLIAC.

[2] Tables containing the unrotated factor matrix, the transformation matrix, the rotated factor matrix, and the cosine matrix have been deposited with the American Documentation Institute. Order Document No. 6742 from ADI Auxiliary Publications Project, Photoduplication Service, Library of Congress; Washington 25, D. C., remitting in advance $1.25 for microfilm or $1.25 for photocopies. Make checks payable to: Chief, Photoduplication Service, Library of Congress.

This component is one which has accounted for the most variance in all of the studies in which it has appeared. Variables PC and PC 11 label this as a sex component. The other variables, in general, contribute to the picture of an uninhibited, amoral drive which has already found expression in sports and recreation. Variable WA 35 is included even though the loading is low, in order to show that its direction lines up with the sense of the factor as illustrated by the other variables.

Factor II—Fear-Anxiety Erg

		Loading
PC 17	I want there to be fewer deaths	.54
RT 1	Shyness	.40
PC 16	I want the U. S. to have better protection against the A-bomb	.39
RS 8	Amount of worry (high)	.35
RS 5	Cooperation (low)	.34
PC 23	I don't want time to enjoy my own company	.33
QA 30	Did you watch TV yesterday? (Yes)	.21
WA 38	Escape-fear (word association)	.08

The general sense here is of a motivational component akin to anxiety. Variable RT 1 indicates withdrawal, whereas Variable PC 23 would seem to leave the subject no alternative but extraversion. Thus, the central problem of almost any anxiety syndrome is seen. This factor also removes any doubt as to one of the most useful functions of the television set, the poor man's Miltown.

Factor III—Self-Regard Sentiment

		Loading
RW 3	Evenness of temper	.73
RW 4	Daydreaming	.71
PC 24	I want to do things to make people respect me	.37
PC 13	I don't want to watch games like baseball	.33
PC 11	I don't want to go to a good movie every week	.31
RS 7	Loneliness	.31
PC 25	I want to keep good control of my temper	.24
WA 42	Self-sentiment (word association)	.22

We have here a pensive, self-regarding quality, coupled with a resolve to perform in a socially acceptable fashion in one's activities. It is thought of as a sentiment rather than the drive of self-assertion (Cattell, 1957) because its pattern more closely fits that of the pre-

viously defined sentiment (Cattell, 1950; Cattell & Cross, 1952; Cattell & Miller, 1952). This sentiment is somewhat analogous to what Horney (1950) means in speaking of the "tyranny of the should."

Factor IV—Gregarious Erg

		Loading
WA 42	Self-sentiment (word association)	.52
WA 36	Gregarious drive (word association)	.49
WA 41	Narcissistic-play drive (word association)	.49
PC 12	I want to take an active part in recreation	.37
PC 13	I want to watch games like baseball	.36
PC 11	I want to go to a good movie every week	.27

"Man is a social animal . . ." is here again restated in factor analytic terms. A drive to be part of the crowd is manifested by the desire for participation in essentially social activities such as baseball and movies. The gregarious erg is not as clear here as in previous research. It seems here to be mixed in with goodly helpings of self-regard and self-love or desire for self-enhancement. Variables WA 36, PC 12, and PC 13 are markers from previous research. This factor demonstrates superb simple structure and has no significantly high correlations with any other factors. Perhaps further research will be able to rotate the confusing Variables WA 42 and WA 41 out of the picture.

Factor V—Appeal-Dependence Erg

		Loading
WA 39	Lack of self-assertion (word association)	.62
WA 38	Lack of escape-fear (word association)	.54
RS 9	Poor state of health	.39
PC 14	I want to feel close to God	.35
PC 15	I want to have the advice of my parents	.34
WA 37	Appeal-dependence drive (word association)	.32

The strong appearance here of Variables PC 14, PC 15, and WA 37 leads to the conclusion that this factor represents the dependency drive. It is the "Mama's boy," the homesick child at camp, and the confused neurotic's plea for help. A lack of self-assertion and escape-fear is entirely consistent with this interpretation, as is a poor state of health. Picture the person who has been "down on his luck" for a relatively long period of time.

Factor VI—Menstruation-Depression

		Loading
PC 10	I don't want a good-looking boy to make love to me	.43
PC 23	I want time to enjoy my own company	.41
RS 9	Poor state of health	.29
QA 34	Are you menstruating? (Yes)	.25

A more solid, impressive display of the efficacy of factor analysis could hardly be found outside the textbooks of Thurstone and Burt. It naturally follows that a girl who is menstruating considers herself in a poor state of health, wants to be alone, and especially wants no amorous entanglements at this delicate time. This type of factor has not appeared before in factor analytic research.

Factor VII—Self-Assertion

		Loading
PC 18	I want to earn more money	.52
PC 15	I don't want to have the advice of my parents	.48
QA 27	Did you get a letter from home yesterday?	.40
WA 40	Parental-protective drive (word association)	.38
QA 28	Did you write a letter home yesterday?	.28
PC 23	I don't want time to enjoy my own company	.27
RT 2	Reduced quantity of work	.26
RS 7	Loneliness	.25
PC 19	I want to succeed in my life's work	.25
PC 22	I don't want to spend more time on smoking or drinking	.24
RS 6	Happiness	.24
WA 39	Self-assertion drive (word association)	.07

This factor has the poorest simple structure in the rotated reference vector matrix. The variance of the factor is spread thin over many seemingly unrelated variables. The presence of Variables PC 18, PC 15, PC 19, and PC 22 lead strongly to the interpretation that this represents a motivational component of self-assertion even though the factor is generally muddy. Perhaps further research will provide the answer to the unsatisfactory pattern found here.

Factor VIII—Sub-Factor: "Good Time Yesterday"

		Loading
QA 29	Did you spend any money yesterday?	.54

QA 31	Did you read any books on the ward yesterday? (Yes)	.49
QA 32	Did you eat between meals yesterday? (Yes)	.46
QA 33	Did you play any games on the ward yesterday? (Yes)	.46
PC 22	I want to spend more time on smoking and drinking	.26
PC 15	I don't want to have the advice of my parents	.22

This factor correlates highly with Factor IX, Narcissism (.51), and has no real substance in itself. Therefore, it is interpreted as a subfactor of Factor IX. This interpretation means that in another experiment, with possibly a larger number of measurements being taken, this "factor" would resolve itself into Factor IX.

Factor IX—Narcissism Erg

		Loading
QA 31	Did you read any books on the ward yesterday? (Yes)	.68
QA 33	Did you play any games on the ward yesterday? (Yes)	.58
PC 22	I want to spend more time on smoking or drinking	.38
QA 27	Did you get a letter from home yesterday? (No)	.32
RS 8	Low amount of worry	.32
PC 23	I want time to enjoy my own company	.28
QA 26	Did you dream about your boyfriend last night? (Yes)	.28
WA 41	Narcissistic-play drive (word association)	.14

As previously mentioned, most of the variables of Subfactor VII are included here as a subset. This component is interpreted as an erg of narcissism, a self-love or desire to make oneself feel better, etc. In Freudian terms, it represents one of the paths along which the self-worshipping libidinal energy may flow. It compels its possessor to have interest investments in sex, drinking, and other "fun" activities. In the realm of clinical diagnosis, the clinician would suspect conflict if this factor and Factor III, the self-regard sentiment, were simultaneously running at relatively high levels in the same person.

Factor X

		Loading
RS 7	Low amount of loneliness	.45
PC 22	I want to spend more time on smoking or drinking	.36
RS 6	Unhappiness	.34
RS 8	I don't want to succeed in my life's work	.32
PC 14	Low amount of worry	.31

PC 19 I don't want to feel close to God   .30

PC 20 I want to help people in trouble   .30

There is seemingly no plausible interpretation which can be made of Factor X. It is reproduced here as much as an indication of the writers' bewilderment as for the reader's amusement. An awkward, tentative hypothesis is that this is a component somehow connected with philanthropy, a sentiment possessed by one with much money (no worry) and many friends (no loneliness) but with an urge to help others. Variables RS 8 and PC 19 may indicate guilt feelings.

Factor XI—Repressed Sex Component

Loading

WA 35 Sex-mating (word association)   .39

WA 40 Parental-protective drive (word association) (negative)   .35

PC 23 I want time to enjoy my own company   .34

QA 26 Did you dream about your boyfriend last night? (Yes)   .31

QA 27 Did you get a letter from home yesterday? (No)   .31

This is the last factor to be retained from the factor matrix. As such, the variance which it accounts for is necessarily lower than that accounted for by the other 10 factors. It is here interpreted as a component of repressed sex energy. The clash of feelings for one's parents and feelings for oneself comes into sharp focus in this pattern. The rise of this factor in intensity from day to day could be a signal of dammed-up sex energy looking for release. The sense of this factor, even though it correlates .37 with the Sex Erg, is not one of a constant flow of sexual vitality. Rather, it suggests the accumulation of sex vitality which has not yet gained expression.

Summary

Objective tests whose motif was structured after that of devices employed by previous researchers were administered to a maladjusted mental defective who was a patient in a mental institution. The scores on the tests were correlated and factor analyzed. On interpretations of the factors after appropriate rotation to oblique positions, the factors so discovered appeared to be essentially congruent with previous research. Further, the factor pattern that emerged was capable of being interpreted as the motivational structure of the subject.

The possibility that not all ergs (drives) and metanergs (sentiments) were found does not detract from the basic fact that with suitable instruments one can measure and reveal the fundamental dynamic structures of a maladjusted mental defective. The implications of this for clinical practice are promising. Further confirmatory research is needed to furnish a valid, reliable instrument which can be successfully and economically used as both a diagnostic and a predictive tool. The hope that such a tool can be produced depends on the degree to which clinicians and psychometrists can work together.

REFERENCES

Cattell, R. B. The discovery of ergic structure in man in terms of common attitudes. *J. aborm. soc. Psychol.*, 1950, **45**, 598–618.

Cattell, R. B. *Personality and motivation structure and measurement.* New York: World Book, 1957.

Cattell, R. B., & Cross, K. P. Comparison of the ergic and self-sentiment structures found in dynamic traits by R- and P-techniques. *J. Pers.*, 1962, **21**, 250–271.

Cattell, R. B., & Miller, A. A confirmation of the ergic and self-sentiment patterns among dynamic traits by R-technique. *Brit. J. Psychol.*, 1952, **43**, 280–294.

Horney, Karen. *Neurosis and human growth.* New York: Norton, 1950.

Neuhaus, J. O., & Wrigley, C. The quartimax method. *Brit. J. statist. Psychol.*, 1954, **7**, 81–92.

Pinzka, C., & Saunders, D. R. Analytic rotation to simple structure: II. Extension to an oblique solution. (RB-54-31) Educational Testing Service Bulletin, 1954. (Multilithed)

Thurstone, L. L. *Multiple-factor analysis.* Chicago: Univer. Chicago Press, 1947.

4. Biological basis of personality

H. J. EYSENCK

LIKE OTHER SCIENCES, psychology has the dual task of: (*a*) describing accurately, and preferably quantitatively, the material which forms its subject-matter, that is, behaviour; (*b*) of producing a causal theory which deduces the observed behaviour patterns from more fundamental causes. As human beings are biological organisms, it seems reasonable to expect that ultimately these causes should be looked for in the constitutional endowment of the person, that is, in certain physiological, neurological, biochemical and endocrinological properties of his body. Genotypic variations along these lines will, of course, interact with the environmental influences to produce the phenotypic behaviour patterns which we can observe and describe, and it is not part of our thesis to deny the importance of environmental differences. However, social psychologists, clinical psychologists and others have, in recent years, stressed environmental influences to the almost complete exclusion of biological factors, and it seemed desirable to redress the balance to some extent by stressing certain facts supporting the view that biological factors were of considerable importance in the genesis of individual differences and personality.

Descriptively, there is now considerable agreement among experts that a large part of personality can be reduced to the interplay of two dimensions, one of which is usually labelled extroversion–introversion, the other emotionality, neuroticism, or instability as opposed to stability. This theory goes back at least as far as the great medieval physician Galen, and his doctrine of the four temperaments, and the rela-

tion between these temperaments and our two dimensions is shown in Fig. 1; the outer ring of this figure shows the results of large numbers of factor analytic studies of ratings and self-ratings, carried out by such workers as Cattell, Guilford and myself. There is considerable agreement at this descriptive level between medieval theory and modern discovery (1).

My main reason for assuming that these personality dimensions do in fact have a constitutional basis lies in the results from large numbers of experimental investigations carried out on identical and fraternal twins, showing that with respect to both extroversion and neuroticism, identical twins are very much more alike than are fraternal twins. This, of course, is also true with respect to intelligence, and in line with modern genetic theories it is commonly interpreted as providing strong evidence for the hereditary nature of these traits and abilities. The criticism has sometimes been made that possibly identical twins, being so alike, are also treated more alike by parents, teachers, etc, than are fraternal twins who resemble each other less closely. If this were true then the general argument would be weakened, and one would be forced to put a great deal of weight on an interaction effect between heredity and environment. The recent work of Shields (2), however, suggests that this criticism is not, in fact, valid. In addition to fraternal twins, he examined identical twins brought up separately, as well as identical twins brought up together, and with respect to intelligence, extroversion and neuroticism, he found that identical twins brought up separately were, if anything, more alike than identical twins brought up together. The actual figures of the inter-class correlations were as follows, listing first the value for the twins brought up sepa-

SOURCE. Article by H. J. Eysenck, "Biological basis of personality" in *Nature*, Vol. 199, pp. 1031–1034, 1963.

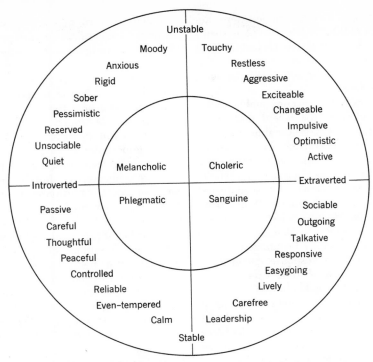

Figure 1. Diagram showing medieval typology (inner circle) and modern personality description in terms of correlational analysis of trait measurements (outer circle). (Reference 7.)

rately, and secondly, the value for the twins brought up together: intelligence, 0·77 and 0·76; extroversion, 0·61 and 0·42; neuroticism, 0·53 and 0·38; for fraternal twins the values were: 0·51, −0·17 and 0·11. These results leave very little doubt about the importance of the part which heredity plays in the genesis of these personality dimensions.

The genetic argument can be extended in various ways. Recent work in Germany, for example, has shown that investigations of familial similarity with respect to extroversion and neuroticism show a degree of relationship to consanguinity, which also strongly supports the hypothesis of inheritance. Another line of argument is derived from the fact that criminals, psychopaths and children suffering from behaviour disorders tend to lie in the 'choleric' quarter so far as personality is concerned; in other words, they tend to be extroverted and unstable. Following the work of Lange in Germany on "Crime as Destiny" much effort has gone into the task of locating criminals with twins and checking whether these twins were concordant or discordant with respect to crimi-

nality. So far as adults are concerned, out of 225 twin pairs 71 per cent were concordant among identical twins, but only 34 per cent among fraternal twins. So far as childhood behaviour disorders are concerned, the proportions are 87 per cent and 43 per cent, respectively. For juvenile delinquents the proportions are 85 per cent and 75 per cent. Altogether these figures again strongly support the hypothesis that genetic factors are of considerable importance in the genesis of these particular behaviour patterns.

When we come to look for a biological basis for our two dimensions of personality, we find relatively little difficulty in relation to neuroticism, emotionality or instability. Persons high on this dimension are characterized by very strong emotional reactions to all classes of stimuli, and there is a well-recognized relationship between emotional reaction and the activity of the autonomic nervous system, particularly its sympathetic branch. There is also evidence, again relating largely to twin studies, strongly reinforced by breeding experiments in animals, that the lability of the autonomic nervous system is, to a considerable extent, determined by hereditary factors. There seems little reason to doubt that the biological basis of individual differences in emotionality is closely connected with the activity of the autonomic nervous system (1).

This conclusion needs certain qualifications, particularly in view of the recent findings in the United States of considerable response specificity in the reaction of the autonomic nervous system. Thus it is found that the autonomic nervous system does not act as a whole, but that certain sub-systems may be activated much more strongly than others. It has been found that this specific innovation is characteristic of a given person even though many different types of stimuli may be utilized, and it has been found that this response specificity is preserved over periods of time extending to several years at least. It is likely that this specificity itself is inherited; it represents, as it were, specific areas of strength and weakness of the autonomic nervous system, with the latter acting as a kind of fuse which may be blown in the case of a neurotic breakdown.

When we turn to extroversion–introversion no obvious identification with any structure in the nervous system can be made, but we hope to show that even so it is not impossible to formulate certain hypotheses which have some limited support in the experimental evidence. The beginning of a theory resulting in such a link-up may be found in the postulation by modern learning theories, following Pavlov, of the importance of excitatory and inhibitory potentials in accounting for a large number of laboratory phenomena. In relation to inhibition, for example, it is postulated that massed practice on any task produces inhibitory potentials which depress the quality of the performance which is being practised, so that subjects working under conditions of spaced practice will show superior performance. It is also maintained that this inhibition, being a kind of cortical fatigue state, will dissipate during rest, thus giving rise to the so-called "reminiscence" phenomenon, that is, an improvement of performance during rest, as indexed by subtracting performance at the end of the pre-rest period from that at the beginning of the post-rest pe-

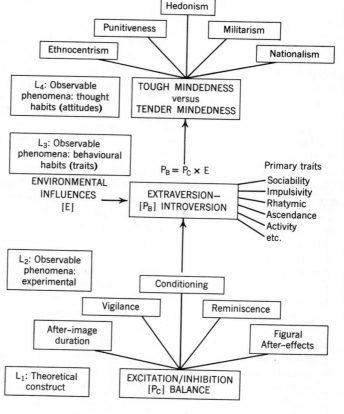

Figure 2. Diagram illustrating relationship between genotype and phenotype in the personality field. (Reference 8.)

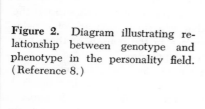

riod. Thirdly, it is deduced from the theory that the growth of inhibition should ultimately lead to the cessation of activity, that is, the occurrence of certain blocks or involuntary rest pauses. All these consequences have frequently been observed, as have others more in the perceptual field such as the so-called "figural after-effect."

I have suggested a link between personality and the theory of excitation and inhibition by postulating that extroverts are characterized by the particularly rapid rise of cortical inhibition, its slow dissipation, and its relatively high level. Conversely, introverts are characterized by the slow growth, rapid dissipation and generally low level of cortical inhibition. The opposite prediction is made with respect to excitation, that is, introverts show a high degree of excitation, extroverts a low degree. (It will, of course, be realized that we are talking about cortical inhibition and excitation, not about inhibited or excited behaviour. Cortical inhibition, by depressing the activity of the highest centres, may give rise to uninhibited behaviour (3)).

Proof for a theory of this kind would, of course, be sought in examining the behaviour of behaviourally extroverted and introverted subjects on laboratory tests of massed and spaced practice, reminiscence, amount of "blocking," length of figural after-effects, etc. Much evidence has been accumulated in recent years to show that the predicted effects do, indeed, differentiate extroverts and introverts in the predicted direction. Technically much of this work is quite complex, as it is often difficult to rule out irrelevant factors which interfere with the pure measurement of the effects in question. Nevertheless, there seems to be little doubt at the moment that in its broad outlines the theory is supported by the experimental facts amassed so far.

Figure 2 gives a systematic picture of the hypothetical relations between the genotypic level we have been discussing hitherto, and the phenotypic level of extroverted and introverted behaviour. It will be seen that we postulate several different levels, going from the hypothetical excitation–inhibition balance at the bottom which we considered to be the physiological basis of our constitutional personality (P_C), to the higher levels of behavioural personality (P_B), which is a product of constitution and environment, and which manifests itself in the form of behavioural habits or traits such as sociability, impulsivity, ascendance, etc., or in terms of thought habits or attitudes. (There is an empirical relationship between tough-minded attitudes and extroverted behaviour patterns.)

The relationship between levels 2 and 3, that is, observable, experimental phenomena, and the observable, behavioural phenomena, is a very complex one which will undoubtedly repay intensive study. We can only discuss here very briefly one particular link as an illustration of the type of argument and empirical demonstration which requires to be adduced. It will be noted that among the laboratory phenomena at the second level I have listed Pavlovian conditioning; the hypothesis states that the process

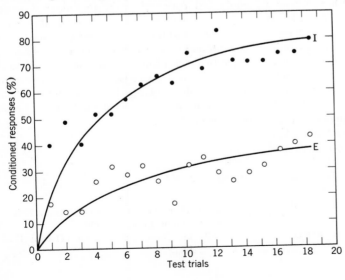

Figure 3. Rate of eyeblink conditioning in groups of introverted and extroverted subjects. (Reference 9.)

of conditioning produces inhibitory potentials, that it does so more strongly in the extrovert than in the introvert, and that consequently introverts should condition better than extroverts. Figure 3 shows the results of some experiments in which introverted and extroverted subjects were given the eyeblink conditioning test in which a sound delivered over earphones constitutes the conditioned stimulus and a puff of air to the cornea of the eye the unconditioned stimulus, producing closure of the eyelid. It will be seen that the hypothesis is supported by the data, introverts showing about twice as high a level of conditioning as do extroverts.

Modern learning theorists have hypothesized that neurotic symptoms, such as phobias, anxieties, obsessional and compulsive behaviour patterns, etc., are nothing more than conditioned autonomic and skeletal responses, and that they can be extinguished according to the rules which govern the extinction of such conditioned responses in the laboratory; there is much empirical support for such a contention. Now it will be clear that such conditioned responses are more likely to occur in individuals predisposed to the development of conditioned responses by the possession of a central nervous system which conditions easily. Thus we would expect, on the basis of these theories, that neurotics of this type would be introverted from the descriptive point of view, and would also condition extremely well. There is much impressive evidence to support both these deductions (4, 5).

It has also been argued that the process of socialization, by means of which the young child learns the mores of his society, is mediated by Pavlovian conditioning, and it would seem to follow that psychopaths ("moral imbeciles"), and criminals generally, should be found largely among persons who are extroverted and who condition poorly. (The argument is, of course, exactly the opposite to that which applies to the neurotics discussed in the previous paragraph.) The evidence is indeed very strong that persons in these groups are extroverted and there are several investigations which show that they condition very poorly, if at all. Pavlovian conditioning, therefore, seems to provide an efficient bridge between our level 1, that of the theoretical construct of the excitation–inhibition balance, and level 3, that of observable behavioural phenomena.

Is it possible to locate any structure within the nervous system which may be responsible for individual differences in these mysterious processes of excitation and inhibition? I would suggest that the ascending reticular formation may fit this prescription reasonably well. This formation, which is located on the spinal cord from the brain stem through the mid-brain to the diencephalon, provides an alternative pathway for ascending impulses proceeding from the periphery to the cortex, impulses travelling along the classical afferent pathways entering the reticular formation via collaterals from the afferent, and giving rise to impulses that are not only directed to the primary cortical projection area but may also be projected profusely over a wide area of the cerebral cortex. Parts of the formation (the so-called ascending reticular activating system) are known to be involved in cortical facilitation; they thus fit in with the psychological concept of "excitatory potential," while the so-called "recruiting system" acts as a suppressor and thus has affinities with the psychological concept, "inhibitory potential."

Evidence for this identification is largely indirect, the strongest argument in favour being perhaps that deriving from the action of stimulant and depressant drugs. These are known to shift a person's position on the extroversion–introversion dimension in the direction of greater introversion (stimulant drugs) or in that of greater extroversion (depressant drugs), and it is known that these drugs on the whole tend to act through the ascending reticular formation (6). This hypothesis linking psychological concepts with physiological structures is offered only very hesitantly; it will undoubtedly require much modification before being found acceptable. However, it does serve to unify several quite distinct lines of research and may, in turn, give rise to experimental studies likely to clarify the issue and to reveal to us more directly some of the biological roots of personality.

REFERENCES

1. Eysenck, H. J., *The Structure of Human Personality* (Methuen, London, 1960).
2. Shields, J., *Monozygotic Twins* (Oxford Univ. Press, 1962).

3. Eysenck, H. J., *The Dynamics of Anxiety and Hysteria* (Routledge and Kegan Paul, London, 1957).

4. Eysenck, H. J. (edit. by), *Experiments in Personality* (Routledge and Kegan Paul, London, 1960).

5. Eysenck, H. J. (edit. by), *Behaviour Therapy and the Neuroses* (Pergamon Press, Oxford, 1960).

6. Eysenck, H. J. (edit. by), *Experiments with Drugs* (Pergamon Press, Oxford, 1963).

7. Eysenck, S. B. G., and Eysenck, H. J., *Brit. J. Psychol.*, **54**, 51 (1963).

8. Eysenck, H. J., *Intern. J. Soc. Psychiat.*, **6**, 12 (1960).

9. Eysenck, H. J., *Brit. J. Psychol.*, **53**, 299 (1962).

5. The position of hysterics and dysthymics in a two-dimensional framework of personality description

H. J. EYSENCK AND G. CLARIDGE

THE PRESENT AUTHORS have always maintained that psychiatric classification in terms of diagnostic labels is not an adequate method of description (Claridge, 1960; Eysenck, 1947, 1952) and that much of the well known unreliability of diagnosis in psychiatry derives from the acceptance in this field of medical practices which are not well suited to the problems at issue (Eysenck, 1960b). Instead, Eysenck has proposed a description in terms of a dimensional framework derived from empirical studies, by means of appropriate statistical techniques—factor analysis and multiple discrimination analysis (Eysenck, 1957). He has also suggested that it was to be expected that groups of psychiatric subjects bearing the same diagnostic label would be found relatively close together in the n-dimensional framework resulting from the execution of such a scheme as that proposed; the degree of correspondence between categorical-diagnostic and continuous-dimensional framework would of course depend largely on (*a*) the reliability of psychiatric diagnosis (which could be increased by only choosing subjects where there was considerable agreement among psychiatrists as to diagnosis), and (*b*) the adequacy of the objective tests chosen to measure the subjects position in the dimensional framework.

In the field of neurotic disorders, the evidence seemed to suggest (*a*) that two main

factors at least were required to account for the personality differences between subjects belonging to different psychiatric categories viz., those of *neuroticism* and *extraversion–introversion;* (*b*) that subjects labeled "hysterics" and "psychopaths" had high scores on neuroticism and extraversion, while subjects labeled "anxiety states," "reactive depressions," or phobic, compulsive, and obsessional patients had high scores on introversion and neuroticism. (This introverted neurotic group was called "dysthymics.") Mixed neurotics were supposed to be intermediate with respect to extraversion–introversion, but of course also high on neuroticism. This theory goes back to Janet and Jung in its main form, although the precise connotation given to the terms has almost certainly changed to some extent in the intervenin years (cf. Eysenck, 1960d, for a historical survey of the development of the concept of extraversion-introversion, and for a review of the experimental literature).

Lately, a questionnaire has been published, called the Maudsley Personality Inventory or MPI (Eysenck, 1959), which purports to measure neuroticism and extraversion–introversion with sufficient reliability (both split-half and repeat are between .8 and .9) to serve as criterion scores when the more laborious measurement of these dimensions of personality by means of a battery of objective tests is not feasible. In normal populations these two scales are independent, or very nearly so, and much evidence has accumulated to show that predictions made on the basis of Eysenck's (1957) dynamic theory of personality can often be verified by having recourse to this questionnaire

SOURCE. Article by H. J. Eysenck and G. Claridge, "The position of hysterics and dysthymics in a two-dimensional framework of personality description" in *Journal of abnormal and social Psychology,* Vol. 64, pp. 46–55, 1962.

(Eysenck, 1960a). Use with neurotic groups, however, has been less successful. It has usually been found (Eysenck, 1959; Sigal, Star, & Franks, 1958) that the two scales do not retain orthogonality but correlate together to an appreciable extent ($r_{EN} = -.45$ approximately); that hysterics have lower neuroticism scores than do dysthymics; and that hysterics not only fail to be more extraverted than normals but may actually have slightly more introverted scores. (Psychopaths tend to behave as predicted, having high neuroticism and extraversion scores.) The results perturbed Sigal et al. (1958) to such an extent that they concluded: "The results suggest that either hysterics and dysthymics cannot be used in the described manner [i.e., as criterion groups for extraversion-introversion], or that the E and N scales do not measure introversion-extraversion and neuroticism, or that both statements are true" (p. 147). In a reply, Eysenck (1958) pointed out some errors in the arguments presented, but there is no doubt that the facts as given have been duplicated in several successive investigations (Eysenck, 1959) and that we are faced with a choice between two possibilities. Either we must give up the notion that hysterics are more extraverted than normals, as well as being more neurotic, or we must seek for some distorting factors in the MPI which account for the anomalous results in comparing normal and neurotic groups (Eysenck, 1958, p. 251). Clearly a recourse to experiment rather than to argument is called for.

The type of experiment required is one in which the three groups in question (normals, dysthymics, hysterics) are administered a battery of objective tests, differentiating between these three groups. The results could then be treated along either or both of the following lines:

A factor analysis could be performed which should give two factors identifiable as neuroticism and extraversion–introversion; factor scores would then be estimated for each subject, and these should discriminate the members of the three groups in such a way that hysterics should have the highest extraversion scores, dysthymics the lowest, while both groups should have higher neuroticism scores than the normals.

A multiple discriminant function (canonical variate) type of analysis could be performed which should give rise to two significant latent roots, identifiable as neuroticism and extraversion–introversion; canonical variate scores could then be obtained by using the latent vectors as weights and multiplying them by the scores on the tests. These scores should then discriminate the members of the three groups in the same way as the factor scores.

A study fulfilling some of these requirements has been reported by Eysenck, Eysenck, and Claridge (1960), except that they concentrated on tests of extraversion almost exclusively, and did not obtain significant discrimination between neurotic and normal groups. Both a factorial analysis and an analysis of discriminance was performed, and on both hysterics emerged as the most extraverted and dysthymics as the most introverted group (the scores derived from the two analyses correlated to the extent of .81). The present study was carried out to give a more extensive and definite answer to the problem by attempting to use tests which would measure neuroticism as well as extraversion-introversion.

Method

Subjects

Neurotic subjects at the Royal Victoria Hospital were selected on admission where the psychiatrists in charge of the case could make a definite diagnosis of anxiety state or hysteria. One psychiatrist's diagnosis was sufficient to admit the patient to the experimental group. The subjects selected were not extreme or "pure" cases, but were chosen by the psychiatrist on the assumption that there would be a good consensus of opinion among psychiatrists regarding the diagnosis. Of the available cases not excluded for reasons given below, less than a third were excluded as presenting too mixed or complex a psychopathology to attempt a ready classification. Cases of immaturity were not included, and patients with evidence of brain damage, psychotic involvement, or drug addiction of any kind (including alcohol) were rejected. In each group there were 14 male and 2 female patients. The normal control group consisted of 16 volunteers, of whom 15 were male and 1 female. All were engaged on various duties in the hospital, including that of nursing orderly, clerk, storeman, and laboratory technician. The mean ages of the three groups were: dysthymics = 27.91, normals = 23.67, and hysterics = 23.78. The dysthymics were significantly older than the other two groups, with an F of 3.239. On weight and intelligence, as measured on Progressive Matrices, there were no significant differences.

Tests

Sedation threshold. This was assessed in terms of the effect of sodium amytal on a simple task, consisting of doubling the digits read out to the subject at intervals of 2 seconds from a tape recording of random digits over earphones, while he was receiving a continuous intravenous infusion of the drug at the rate of 0.1 g/min. Errors were recorded in blocks of five trials, and the threshold was taken as the point midway between the last two blocks with less than 50% errors and the first two blocks in which errors exceeded 50%. In the majority of cases these blocks were consecutive. The amount of drug administered at this point was determined from a chart relating blocks of trials to drug received, and this dosage was then corrected for the weight of the patient, giving the threshold in terms of mgm/Kg.[1]

Maudsley Personality Inventory. The two scales of the MPI were included in the experiment because their inclusion would, if anything, work against the hypothesis under investigation; furthermore, it was considered worth while discovering whether the neurotic groups in this study behaved similarly to those in previous ones.

Five-choice serial reaction task. The subject was required to press one of five keys set in front of five lights, according to which of the lights went on; his response extinguished the light and switched on another one. The order of the lights was random over a series of 50, except that no light appeared twice in succession. The score taken was the number of responses for each minute of the work period. The minutes of continuous performance was followed by a rest of 5 minutes and a further period of practice of 1 minute.

The usual pattern of performance shown by most subjects on this test (Venables, 1959) is a gradual decline in performance level during the first 5 minutes, then an increase in speed during the second 5 minutes of practice. Following the rest the usual reminiscence effect appears, in the form of an abrupt rise in performance level. The measures here taken are starting level and total number of errors.

Spiral aftereffects. The subject is asked to fixate a rotating single-throw 180-degree spiral, and to indicate the duration of the aftereffect. Four trials were given, the spiral being rotated

for one minute each time; trials were alternately clockwise and counterclockwise, with a rest of one minute between trials. The means of the four scores thus obtained were taken as a measure of the subject's performance on this task.

Predictions

The predictions made follow from Eysenck's (1957, 1960a) theory, according to which cortical inhibition is hypothesized to be generated more quickly and more strongly, and dissipated more slowly in extraverts than in introverts; they are, in brief, that extraverts would have *low* sedation thresholds, *high* scores on the E scale of the MPI, *low* starting level and *high* number of errors on the reaction time task, and *short* spiral aftereffects. Predictions with respect to neuroticism are much less obvious, except with regard to the N scale of the MPI; in view of the repeated observation that in neurotic groups N correlates negatively with E we might also expect E to have a negative loading with neuroticism *in this population.* Poor performance on sensory-motor tasks appears to characterize neurotics (Easterbrook, 1958; Eysenck, 1952; Eysenck, Granger, & Brengelmann, 1957) so we might expect the error score to load positively and the starting level score to load negatively on neuroticism. Predictions with respect to the sedation threshold cannot be made with any confidence. Shagass and his colleagues (as quoted by Claridge & Herrington, 1961, in their discussion of this problem) report high thresholds as characteristic of "anxiety," but this is a two-valued concept having loadings on both introversion and neuroticism. We have predicted high thresholds in introverts; this leaves the loading of the threshold on neuroticism indeterminate.

Results

These six sets of scores had been decided upon from the beginning as constituting the material for analysis. In addition, the Manifest Anxiety (MA) scale was administered, but not included in the analysis. Mean scores for the six tests and the MA scale are given in Table 1, together with SDs and F ratios. It will be seen that with the exception of the Five Choice Test Error Score all tests discriminate significantly; it will also be seen that scores on the E scale put the hysterics well to the introverted side of the normals, thus exaggerating the fault found by Sigal et al. (1958). Scores on the sedation threshold level, the spiral aftereffect, and the Error and Starting Level of the five choice test, however, put the hysterics on the

---

[1] For a detailed discussion of the rationale and method of use of the sedation threshold and five-choice serial reaction task, cf. Claridge and Herrington (1961), Claridge (1961), and Venables (1959).

extraverted side of the normal group. We find here the first signs that no single test can be relied upon to decide upon the correct position of groups such as these relative to each other, but that multiple determination is required. The *MA* scale, as expected, shows highest scores for the dysthymic group, and lowest scores for the normals; this was predicted (Eysenck, 1957) on the basis that the *MA* scale is essentially a measure of neuroticism with an admixture of introversion, i.e., that it is specifically aimed at the dysthymic group.

Table 1. Mean Scores of Dysthymics, Normals, and Hysterics

Test	Dysthymics	Normals	Hysterics	F
Sedation threshold	10.18 ± 1.608	7.86 ± 1.313	6.43 ± 1.774	21.837†
E scale	18.31 ± 8.169	31.50 ± 7.575	24.62 ± 8.366	10.120†
N scale	36.62 ± 7.631	19.12 ± 8.392	31.19 ± 11.092	14.354†
Spiral aftereffect	18.79 ± 5.093	11.41 ± 4.125	8.85 ± 3.167	22.576†
Five choice test, starting level	90.14 ± 15.412	82.34 ± 11.331	77.51 ± 12.499	3.530*
Errors	11.12 ± 10.705	8.63 ± 8.748	19.88 ± 20.524	2.563[a]
MA scale	17.00 ± 3.774	6.25 ± 3.699	13.69 ± 5.860	21.903†

[a] ns = not significant at the $p = .05$ level.
* Significant at the $p = .05$ level.
† Significant at the $p = .001$ level.

Multiple discriminant function analysis. Table 2 shows the latent vectors and the latent roots extracted from our set of six tests; both latent roots are fully significant at the .001 level of p. The first variate accounts for 60.99% of the variance, the second one for 39.02%. Mean variate scores are given in Table 3, and the actual positions of the 16 subjects in each of the three groups plotted against the two variates are shown in Figure 1. Lines drawn in the body of the figure at values of 22 for Variate 1 and 12.2 for Variate 2 show that Variate 1 completely and without overlap discriminates between hysterics and dysthymics; this variate may therefore be identified with extraversion-introversion. Variate 2 discriminates slightly less well between normals and neurotics; three members of each group are misclassified. It must of course be remembered that the criterion here is less satisfactory than in the case of the hysteric-dysthymic dichotomy, where psychiatric diagnosis of a clear-cut kind was obtained. The normal subjects in this experiment were normal only in the sense of not, at the time, being under psychiatric care; as Fraser (1947) and Shepherd, Fisher, Stein, and Kessel (1959) have shown, such groups nevertheless contain some 10% of fairly definite neurotics. In spite of our failure to obtain perfect discrimination, therefore, we may perhaps be justified in identifying Variate 2 with neuroticism.

The mean positions of the three groups are shown in Figure 1 in addition to the position of the individual subjects, and it will be seen

Table 2. Latent Factors and Latent Roots

	λ_1	λ_2
Sedation threshold	1.0000000	1.000000
E score	−.0519939	.261961
N score	.0429769	−.354949
Spiral aftereffect	.505898	.158374
Starting level	.0657491	−.073380
Errors	.0156142	.0496781

$\lambda_1 = .732548$ $p < .001$.
$\lambda_2 = .468676$ $p < .001$.

that hysterics lie on the opposite (extraverted) side of the normals, as compared with the dysthymics who lie on the introverted side. Furthermore, the hysterics appear if anything more neurotic than do the dysthymics. These results support the original theory regarding the respective positions of the three groups. It should be noted in this connection that our normal sample was conspicuously more extraverted than would be likely to be found in an unselected group; these Army volunteers had an E score of 31.50, as compared with the population norms of 24.91 given by Eysenck

Table 3. Mean Variate Scores

	λ_1	λ_2
Dysthymics	26.60	8.67
Normals	18.37	14.59
Hysterics	16.50	5.69
	(Extraversion)	(Neuroticism)

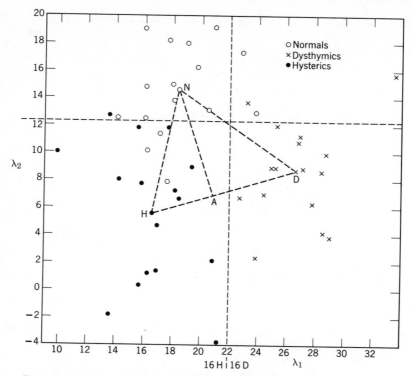

Figure 1. Position of 16 normals, 16 dysthymics, and 16 hysterics in two-dimensional space as determined by analysis of discriminance.

(1959). A similar tendency for Army volunteers to have exceptionally high extraversion scores had been noted in connection with a previous study (Eysenck, 1960a; Hildebrand, 1958). It is possible that this high degree of extraversion was due to the fact that the experimental subjects were volunteers; there is some evidence to suggest that extraverts are more likely to volunteer for experiments of this type. This might account for the fact that while the hysterics are more extraverted than the normals, the difference on this dimension between hysterics and normals is in fact much less than between normals and dysthymics.

An alternative hypothesis to account for this fact, as well as the rather curious finding that the hysterics emerged as more neurotic even than the dysthymics, may be derived from the fact that the canonical variates as extracted from the data depend to some extent on the precise tests used, and are not likely to be collinear with the "true" variates which would be extracted from an infinite series of relevant tests. It is thus possible that the line H–D drawn in Figure 1 might be a better approximation to the "true" extraversion-introversion dimension, while the line N–A would then be an improved approximation to the "true" neu-

roticism dimension. The change would be minimal, and the number of misplacements would not be affected; yet hysterics and dysthymics would be equidistant from the normals, in opposite direction, along the extra-introversion dimension, and also equidistant from the normals, in the same direction along the neuroticism dimension. Further research along these lines, with a better selection of normals, and a greater number of tests, would be required to decide between these hypotheses. Whatever the final verdict, the fact remains that as predicted two highly significant latent roots have emerged from our analysis, thus indicating that two dimensions are required to account for the differences between the three groups studied, and that in this two-dimensional space the three groups are disposed in the form of an (almost exactly) equilateral triangle. The hypothesis that hysterics and dysthymics are, respectively, extraverted and introverted neurotics has thus been confirmed by this analysis.

Factor analysis. Product-moment correlations were calculated between the six scores for the 48 subjects, and a Hotelling principal components factor analysis performed; all six factors were extracted, and the analysis was carried out with three digits retained after the

Table 4. Factor Loadings

	1	2	3	2′	3′
Sedation threshold	.81	−.27	.29	+.39	+.05
E	−.63	−.36	.33	+.48	+.11
N	.61	.19	−.40	−.44	+.07
Starting level	.37	.54	.73	+.29	−.86
Error	−.27	.86	−.15	−.62	−.62
Spiral	.72	−.13	−.14	−.04	+.19

decimal point.[2] Table 4 shows the unrotated factor loadings of the first three factors. Inspection of the plot of Factors 2 and 3 indicated clearly that a rotation in line with Thurstone's principle of simple structure would sort out Factor 3 as a doublet loading on nothing but the two scores derived from the reaction time test, and therefore probably simply an artifact. Accordingly the rotation was performed, and Factors 2′ and 3′ are shown in the table. Following a policy of minimum rotation, which seemed advisable as it gives least room for sub-

jective judgment or arbitrary statistical rules, no further rotations were carried out, and Factors 1 and 2′ are shown in Figure 2. Factor 1 can clearly be identified as introversion-extraversion, all the tests having the predicted loadings on it (sedation threshold, starting level, and spiral aftereffect are positive, E and errors negative). Factor 2 can be identified with neuroticism provided we are willing to accept the very tentative predictions made above.

The validity of both these interpretations can be tested by calculating factor scores for the members of our three groups; if the identification is correct, then these should fall into a pattern identical with that shown in Figure 1. Figure 3 shows the result of such an analysis, and the similarity with Figure 1 will be apparent. Such inspection is instructive, but a more quantitative estimate may be preferred. Factor 1 and Canonical Variate 1 correlate to the extent of .94; Factor 2 and Canonical Variate 2 correlate to the extent of .88. These correlations are high enough to give us some confidence in the identity of the two analyses, and in the accuracy of our factor identification. The cross-correlations, i.e., Factor 1 with Variat 2, and Factor 2 with Variate 1, are statistically insignificant.

As in Figure 1, so here also the baseline of the triangle produced by joining the mean positions of the three groups is not parallel with the horizontal axis, but inclined down towards the left; it follows that a slightly better discrimination might have been achieved by some further rotations. With the small number of cases employed there seemed to be no point

---

[2] There must be some doubt about the advisability of calculating product-moment correlations on a combined set of scores derived from three groups hypothetically situated at different points of a two-dimensional space. Strictly speaking this is not permissible if the hypothesis is in fact true, but the distributions are sufficiently normal, and the overlap sufficiently large, to make it not completely out of the question that the results might have a modicum of meaning.

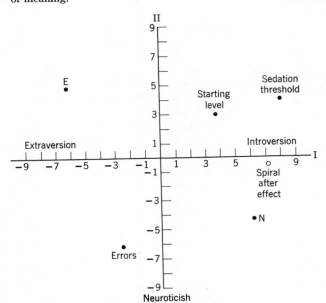

Figure 2. Position of six tests in two-dimensional factor space.

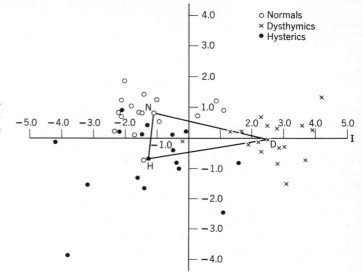

Figure 3. Position of 16 normals, 16 dysthymics, and 16 hysterics in two-dimensional space as determined by factor analysis.

in further analysis, but it should be noted that here also, as before, the hysterics have higher scores on neuroticism than the dysthymics. As in the previous analysis, the hysterics are more extraverted than the normals, but only very slightly so; rotation to make the line linking the mean positions of dysthymics and hysterics collinear with the horizontal axis would increase this separation.

It might appear a task of supererogation to compare the results of these two methods of analysis (factor analysis and multiple discriminant function analysis) when it might be thought on a priori grounds that similarity would be the expected outcome. A mathematical and empirical investigation of the matter by Slater (1960) shows that this is not so, "Very little theoretical justification has been found here for expecting the vectors defined by a factor analysis to coincide with those defined by a discriminatory analysis of the same data; and the evidence examined has shown that they do not converge closely even under particularly favourable conditions." The data examined by Slater were those gathered by Hildebrand (1958) in one of the earliest factorial studies of the two-dimensional hypothesis under discussion (the data were collected in 1952); nothing can illustrate the improvement in the choice of tests for the measurement of introversion-extraversion since those days better than the almost perfect congruence achieved in the present study, as compared with the failure to do so in the previous one. This improvement is likely to be due to the general theory advanced recently and purporting to give a ra-

tional basis to this dimension of personality (Eysenck, 1957), and conversely this success of the tests selected on the basis of the theory must give some support to the postulates of this theory.

Discussion

The results of this analysis make it clear that hysterics and dysthymics, respectively, may indeed with advantage be used as criterion groups of the personality dimension of extraversion-introversion. It remains doubtful whether the hysteric group is as much more extraverted than the normal group, as is the dysthymic group more introverted than the normal group. It is likely that the proper counterpart of the dysthymic group is a combination of hysterics and psychopaths, with the psychopaths somewhat more extraverted than the hysterics; their omission from the group of supposedly extraverted neurotics may be responsible for the appearance of this doubt. No doubt remains about the degree of neuroticism of the hysteric group; in both analyses they had the highest scores on this dimension.

With respect to the MPI, the results leave little doubt, as had indeed been pointed out in the manual (Eysenck, 1959), that the E and N scales do not retain their independence when neurotic samples are being tested, or even normal samples with high neuroticism scores.

Even under these conditions, dysthymics still obtain scores which put them at a much more introverted part of the continuum than the hysterics, and the scales, therefore, retain some of their usefulness even when the level of neuroticism is high. However, comparisons involving both normal and neurotic groups become hazardous, and wrong conclusions may be drawn unless these essential cautions are borne in mind. Furthermore, in spite of their high degree of neuroticism as established by objective tests, hysterics have lower scores on the N scale than do dysthymics; this point also requires caution in interpretation.

If these considerations only affected the MPI, it might be possible to brush the findings aside by refusing to use the test in question; this can hardly be said to resolve the problem, however, in view of the fact that in factorial studies considerable correlations have been found between the MPI on the one hand, and on the other, Cattell's second-order factors of extraversion and neuroticism, Guilford's various primary factor scales, the Taylor *MA* scale, and also some of the MMPI scales, notably the Hysteria, Psychopathy, and Psychasthenia scales (Eysenck, 1960a). What is true of the MPI, therefore, is *eo ipso* likely to be true of these other scales too, and the Hildebrand (1958) study, which used a large number of different types of questionnaires, may be interpreted to support this position. Refusal to use the MPI, therefore, should entail logically the refusal to use any questionnaire, at least until this problem had been thoroughly investigated. Until this has been done, it would appear more reasonable to use these scales as before but bear in mind in the interpretation of results the nonlinearity of regression lines as the region of high neuroticism and high introversion is approached.

Several hypotheses suggest themselves for experimental examination.

The hypothesis of response sets being responsible for the phenomenon cannot be ruled out, although some preliminary data speak against it (Eysenck, 1962). It is difficult to put such an hypothesis in a rigorous form, but this general field of investigation would almost certainly repay study.

The hypothesis of genuine interaction effects between introversion and neuroticism should not be disregarded. There may be a point in the conditionability, which according to theory

characterizes the introvert, where fear responses are acquired at a rate and at a strength which exceeds the strength of the normal extinction processes; this point may delimit a region of positive feedback which could be responsible for the interaction. (Something of this kind is actually postulated by Wolpe, 1958, pp. 63–64, as an explanation of the effectiveness of mild shock in learning neurotic responses.)

There may be a concentration on dysthymic symptoms in the construction of the N scale, and similar questionnaires, which leads to the omission of the main hysterical and psychopathic symptoms—possibly because these are difficult to elicit in a questionnaire (Eysenck, 1947). Milder forms of hysterical and psychopathic disorder might be more similar to those of dysthymics, thus making this problem urgent only at high levels of neuroticism. The *Hy* and *Pd* scales of the MMPI have not succeeded in overcoming this difficulty; in administering them to groups of hysterics, psychopaths, and dysthymics we have found no significant or even suggestive relationship with diagnosis, even when the E scale did show reasonable discrimination (Eysenck, 1962). With normals these scales also tend to work rather better (Eysenck, 1960a).

It has been shown that there is no unitary trait of *sociability,* but that of the items collected into that factor by Guilford (Factor S) approximately half correlate with extraversion, but not with neuroticism, while the others correlate with neuroticism (negatively), but not with extraversion (Eysenck, 1956). Thus there are two sorts of social shyness: introverted ("don't like being with people, but don't mind if I have to") and neurotic ("would like to be with people, but am afraid"). In view of the large part questions on sociability play in the E scale, it is possible that at high levels of introversion this distinction breaks down to some extent, thus causing the sudden break in linearity.

Perhaps the most likely reason for the correlation between introversion and neuroticism among high scoring subjects is one which can be deduced from the general theory of extraversion, according to which cortical inhibition is stronger in extraverts than in introverts. This principle applies to all sensory inputs, proprioceptive as well as exteroceptive; it seems likely therefore that the perception of the autonomic activity characteristic of emotion is equally subject to such inhibition. Now strong and lasting autonomic reactions are of course characteristic of neurotics (and quite generally of individuals with high scores on the N scale). We would expect therefore that in comparing introverted and extraverted neurotics the autonomic reactions of the latter, while equally strong to begin with, would soon be subject to strong inhibitory forces and thus go down to a much lower level as compared with the reactions of introverts. Now the questionnaire items relating to neuroticism tend to refer in the main to long continued autonomic reactions or their consequences, and these in terms of our theory would be expected to be more marked in introverts than in extraverts. This hypothesis, like the others mentioned, is of course susceptible to experimental proof; it seems to involve no *ad hoc* assumptions which cannot be deduced from our general theory and it seems capable of resolving the problem raised by Sigal et al. (1958).

From a more fundamental point of view, it might be argued that the terms "extraversion" and "introversion" have been used rather misleadingly in two different senses. According to Eysenck's (1957) theory, certain innate physiological properties of the central nervous system (the excitation-inhibition balance) lie at the basis of observable extraverted and introverted behavior patterns. The term "extravert" may be applied (*a*) to a person in whom the excitation-inhibition balance is tilted in the direction of high inhibition and low excitation (the *constitutional* extravert), or (*b*) it may be used to refer to the person who is behaving in an extraverted manner (a *behavioral* extravert). As explained in detail elsewhere (Eysenck, 1960c) the theory posits a positive relationship between constitution and behavior, but this relationship is not likely to be perfect. Environmental differences clearly will play an important role in determining the way in which constitutional factors express themselves. Thus it is possible, although unlikely, that a *constitutional* extravert may turn out to be a *behavioral* introvert, or a dysthymic neurotic (Foulds, 1959; Foulds & Caine, 1958).

Certain factors may have contradictory effects on these two variables; thus old age probably alters the *constitutional* balance in the direction of greater *extraversion* and the *behavioral* balance in the direction of greater *introversion*. It is not impossible that neurosis,

whilst leaving the constitutional basis unaffected, shifts the behavioral basis in the direction of greater introversion. To take but one example, normal extraverts are more sociable than normal introverts. It is not inconceivable that the presence of severe neurotic symptoms (whether of a hysterical or dysthymic type) may interfere with social intercourse, thus shifting the behavioral balance towards greater introversion in both extraverts and introverts. Questionnaires such as the MPI are sensitive measures of *behavioral* extraversion; objective tests such as those used in this experiment are probably sensitive measures of *constitutional* extraversion. Factorial studies such as those of Claridge (1960), and the one reported here, show that constitutional and behavioral measures are not unrelated, but it would be a mistake not to distinguish in principle between them. The interesting question arises therefore whether hysteria and dysthymia are more closely related to constitutional or behavioral extraversion; the present results suggest the former. If true, this would mean that from the point of view of testing some of the experimental predictions from Eysenck's inhibition-satiation theory of personality, hysterics and dysthymics as criterion groups would be preferable to normal criterion groups selected on the basis of the MPI, although the latter test would come into its own in the testing of predictions relating the constitutional and behavioral aspects of personality to each other.

Summary

The results are reported of testing 16 normals, 16 hysterics, and 16 dysthymics by means of objective laboratory tests and questionnaires, and analysing the scores by means of multiple discriminant analysis and factor analysis. Both methods give rise to two main principles of classification, or dimensions of personality, which can be identified as extraversion-introversion and neuroticism, respectively; high correlations are found between the respective methods of ordering the 48 subjects along the two continua. Hysterics were found to be extraverted and neurotic, dysthymics were found to be introverted and neurotic; perfect discrimination was achieved between hysterics and dysthymics, and reasonable discrimination between neurotics and normals. Analysis of the questionnaire scores verified previous results in showing a departure from linearity of regression at high levels of introversion and neuroticism scores. The implications of these findings are discussed in relation to the use of hysterics and dysthymics as criterion groups for the study of personality dimensions.

REFERENCES

Claridge, G. The excitation-inhibition balance in neurotics. In H. J. Eysenck (Ed.), *Experiments in personality*. Vol. 2. London: Routledge & Kegan Paul, 1960. Pp. 107–154.

Claridge, G. The effects of meprobamate on the performance of a five-choice serial reaction time task. 1961, in press.

Claridge, G., & Herrington, R. N. Sedation threshold, personality, and the theory of neurosis. *J. ment. Sci.*, 1961, in press.

Easterbrook, J. A. The effect of emotion on cue utilization and the organization of behavior. *Psychol. Rev.*, 1958, 66, 183–201.

Eysenck, H. J. *Dimensions of personality*. London: Routledge & Kegan Paul, 1947.

Eysenck, H. J. *The scientific study of personality*. London: Routledge & Kegan Paul, 1952.

Eysenck, H. J. The questionnaire measurement of neuroticism and extraversion. *Riv. Psicol.*, 1956, 50, 113–140.

Eysenck, H. J. *The dynamics of anxiety and hysteria*. London: Routledge & Kegan Paul, 1957.

Eysenck, H. J. Hysterics and dysthymics as criterion groups in the study of introversion-extraversion: A reply. *J. abnorm soc. Psychol.*, 1958, 57, 250–252.

Eysenck, H. J. *Manual of the Maudsley Personality Inventory*. London: Univer. London Press, 1959.

Eysenck, H. J. *Experiments in personality*. London: Routledge & Kegan Paul, 1960. (a)

Eysenck, H. J. (Ed.) *Handbook of abnormal psychology*. London: Pitman, 1960. (b)

Eysenck, H. J. Levels of personality, constitutional factors, and social influences: An experimental approach. *Int. J. soc. Psychiat.*, 1960, 6, 12–24. (c)

Eysenck, H. J. *The structure of human personality*. London: Methuen, 1960. (d)

Eysenck, H. J. Response set, authoritarianism and personality questionnaires. *Brit. J. soc. abnorm. Psychol.*, 1962, in press.

Eysenck, H. J., Granger, G., & Brengelmann, H. *Perceptual processes and mental illness*. London: Chapman & Hall, 1957.

Eysenck, S. B. G., Eysenck, H. J. & Claridge, G. Dimension of personality, psychiatric syndromes, and mathematical models. *J. ment. Sci.*, 1960, 106, 581–589.

Foulds, G. A. The relative stability of personality measures compared with diagnostic measures. *J. ment. Sci.*, 1959, 105, 783–787.

Foulds, G. A., & Caine, T. M. Psychoneurotic symptom clusters, trait clusters and psychological tests. *J. ment. Sci.*, 1958, 104, 722–731.

Fraser, R. *The incidence of neurosis among factory workers*. London: HM Stationery Office, 1947.

Hildebrand, H. P. A factorial study of introversion-extraversion. *Brit. J. Psychol.*, 1958, 49, 1–12.

Shepherd, M., Fisher, M., Stein, L., & Kessel, W. I. N. Psychiatric morbidity in an urban group practice. *Proc. Roy. Soc. Med.*, 1959, 52, 269–274.

Sigal, J. J., Star, K. H., & Franks, C. M. Hysterics and dysthymics as criterion groups in the study of introversion-extraversion. *J. abnorm. soc. Psychol.*, 1958, 57, 143–148.

Slater, P. Experiments in psychometrics. In H. J. Eysenck (Ed.), *Experiments in personality*. Vol. 2. London: Routledge & Kegan Paul, 1960. Pp. 247–299.

Venables, P. H. Factors in the motor behavior of functional psychotics. *J. abnorm. soc. Psychol.*, 1959, 58, 153–156.

Wolpe, J. *Psychotherapy by reciprocal inhibition*. Palo Alto: Stanford Univer. Press, 1958.

6.   Learning theory and behaviour therapy *

H. J. EYSENCK

IT WOULD PROBABLY BE TRUE to say that the present position in the psychiatric treatment of neurotic disorders is characterized by the following features. (1) With the exception of electroshock, the only method of treatment at all widely used is psychotherapy. (2) In practically all its manifestations, psychotherapy is based on Freudian theories. (3) With the exception of intelligence testing, psychological contributions consist almost entirely in the administration and interpretation of projective tests, usually along psycho-analytic lines. I have argued in the past, and quoted numerous experiments in support of these arguments, that (1) there is little evidence for the practical efficacy of psychotherapy,[1] whether strictly

SOURCE. Article by H. J. Eysenck, "Learning theory and behavior therapy" in *Journal of mental Science*, Vol. 105, pp. 61–75, 1959.

---

* This paper was delivered on 3 July, 1958 to a meeting of the R.M.P.A., and its style inevitably bears traces of the fact that is was originally prepared for verbal presentation. It was followed by another paper, delivered by Mr. Gwynne Jones, giving concrete examples of the application of behaviour therapy from our own experience. Some of these are discussed in his article published in this Journal (29), and it is suggested that readers interested in the theories here advanced may like to consult this article in order to obtain some notion of the practical methods emanating from these theories. A more detailed discussion of many theoretical points that arise may be found in "Dynamics of Anxiety and Hysteria" (15), as well as several of my previous books (7, 9, 11).

[1] When I first suggested that the literature did not contain any kind of unequivocal proof of the efficacy of psychotherapeutic treatment, this conclusion was widely criticized. Since then, however, Dr. Weinstock, Chairman of the Fact-Finding Com-

Freudian or "eclectic" (8, 17); (2) that Freudian theories are outside the realm of science because of their failure to be consistent, or to generate testable deductions (10); and (3), that projective tests are so unreliable and lacking in validity that their use, except in research, cannot be defended (16).[2] I shall not here argue these points again; the evidence on which these views are based is quite strong, and is growing in strength every year. I shall instead try to make a somewhat more constructive contribution by discussing an alternative theory of neurosis, an alternative method of treatment, and an alternative way of using the knowledge and competence of psychologists in the attempted cure of neurotic disorders. It need hardly be emphasized that the brief time at my disposal will make it inevitable that what I have to say will sound much more dogmatic than I would like it to be; I have to ask your indulgence in this respect, and request you to bear in mind all the obvious qualifying clauses which, if included in this paper, would swell it to three times its present size.

Few psychiatrists are likely to deny that all behaviour ultimately rests on an inherited basis,

---

mittee of the American Psychoanalytical Association, has explicitly stated in a lecture delivered at the Maudsley Hospital that his Association made *no claims of therapeutic usefulness for psychoanalytic methods,* and in this country Glover (21) has equally explicitly disavowed such claims. On this point, therefore, leading psychoanalysts appear to share my views to a considerable extent.

[2] This fact is also beginning to be more widely realized, and it is symptomatic that such well-known departments as that belonging to the New York Psychiatric Hospital have followed the lead of the Institute of Psychiatry and discontinued the routine use of projective techniques like the Rorschach.

but even fewer would be prepared to assert that environmental influences played no part in the genesis and modification of behaviour. Once we are agreed that learning and conditioning are instrumental in determining the different kinds of reaction we may make to environmental stimulation, we will find it very difficult to deny that neurotic reactions, like all others, are *learned* reactions, and must obey the laws of learning. Thus, I would like to make my first claim by saying that modern learning theory (24), and the experimental studies of learning and conditioning carried out by psychologists in their laboratories (38) are extremely relevant to the problems raised by neurotic disorders (41). If the laws which have been formulated are, not necessarily true, but at least partially correct, then it must follow that we can make deductions from them to cover the type of behaviour represented by neurotic patients, construct a model which will duplicate the important and relevant features of the patient, and suggest new and possibly helpful methods of treatment along lines laid down by learning theory. Whether these methods are in fact an improvement over existing methods is, of course, an empirical problem; a few facts are available in this connection and will be mentioned later. It is unfortunate that insistence on empirical proof has not always accompanied the production of theories in the psychiatric field—much needless work, and many heart-breaking failures, could have been avoided if the simple medical practice of clinical trials with proper controls had always been followed in the consideration of such claims.

How, then, does modern learning theory look upon neurosis? In the first place, it would claim that neurotic symptoms are *learned patterns of behaviour* which for some reason or other are *unadaptive*. The paradigm of neurotic symptom formation would be Watson's famous experiment with little Albert, a nine months old boy who was fond of white rats (44). By a simple process of classical Pavlovian conditioning Watson created a phobia for white rats in this boy by standing behind him and making a very loud noise by banging an iron bar with a hammer whenever Albert reached for the animal. The animal was the conditioned stimulus in the experiment, the loud fear-producing noise was the unconditioned stimulus. As predicted, the unconditioned response (fear) became conditioned to the C.S. (the rat), and Albert developed a phobia for rats, and indeed for all furry animals. This latter feature of the conditioning process is of course familiar to all students as the generalization gradient (38); an animal or a person conditioned to one stimulus also responds, although less and less strongly, to other stimuli further and further removed from the original one along some continuum.

The fear of the rat thus conditioned is unadaptive (because white rats are not in fact dangerous) and hence is considered to be a neurotic symptom; a similarly conditioned fear of snakes would be regarded as adaptive, and hence not as neurotic. Yet the mechanism of acquisition is identical in both cases. This suggests that chance and environmental hazards are likely to play an important part in the acquisition of neurotic responses. If a rat happens to be present when the child hears a loud noise, a phobia results; when it is a snake that is present, a useful habit is built up!

The second claim which modern learning theory would make is this. People and animals differ in the speed and firmness with which conditioned responses are built up (39). Those in whom they are built up particularly quickly and strongly are more likely to develop phobias and other anxiety and fear reactions than are people who are relatively difficult to condition (15). Watson was lucky in his choice of subject; others have banged away with hammers on metal bars in an attempt to condition infants, but not always with the same success. Individual differences must be taken into account in considering the consequences of any course of attempted conditioning. Nor is the degree of conditionability the only kind of individual variability with which we are concerned. Learning theory tells us that the amount of reinforcement following any action determines in part the amount of conditioning that takes place (43). Thus the louder the noise, the greater the fright of the infant, and the greater the fright, the stronger the phobia. But different children have different types of autonomic system, and the same amount of noise produces quite unequal amounts of autonomic upheaval in different children. Consequently, autonomic reactivity must also be considered; the more labile or reactive the child, the more likely he is to produce strongly conditioned fear reactions, anxieties, and phobias. The individual differences in autonomic reactivity and in condition-ability have been conceptualized as giving rise to two dimensions of personality, namely neu-roticism and introversion respectively (11). The more autonomically reactive, the more prone will the individual be to neurotic disorders. The more easily he forms conditioned responses, the more introverted will his behaviour be. Combine introversion and neuroticism, and you get the dysthymic individual, the person almost pre-destined to suffer from anxieties, conditioned fears and phobias, compulsions and obsessions, reactive depressions and so forth.

But this is only part of the story. Many con-ditioned responses are unadaptive, and con-sequently may embarrass the individual and even drive him into a mental hospital if suffici-ently intense. Yet other conditioned responses are obviously necessary and desirable; indeed, many of them are indispensable for survival. It has been argued very strongly that the whole process of socialization is built up on the prin-ciple of conditioning (35); the overt display of aggressive and sexual tendencies is severely punished in the child, thus producing condi-tioned fear and pain responses (anxiety) to situations in which the individual is likely to display such tendencies. He consequently re-frains from acting in the forbidden manner, not because of some conscious calculus of hedonic pleasure which attempts to equate the immediate pleasure to be gained from indul-gence with the remote probability of later pun-ishment, but because only by not indulging, and by physically removing himself can he re-lieve the very painful conditioned anxiety re-sponses to the whole situation. Anxiety thus acts as a mediating drive, a drive which may be exceedingly powerful by virtue of its com-bination of central, autonomic, skeletal, and hormonal reactions. This mediating role of anx-iety, and its capacity to function as an acquired drive, have been subjected to many well con-ceived experimental studies, and the consensus of opinion appears to leave little doubt about the great value and predictive capacity of this conception (34).

Let us now consider an individual who is deficient in his capacity to form quick and strong conditioned responses. He will be all the less likely to be subject to phobias and other anxieties, but he will also be less likely to form useful conditioned responses, or to be-

come a thoroughly socialized individual. When this lack of socialization is combined with strong autonomic drive reactions (high neuroticism), such an individual is likely to show the neurotic symptomatology of the psychopath or the hys-teric, and indeed, in our experimental work we have found that, as predicted, dysthymic patients and normal introverts are characterized by the quick and strong formation of condi-tioned responses, while psychopaths and nor-mal extraverts are characterized by the weak and slow formation of conditioned responses (12, 14, 15). Thus the deviation from the av-erage in either direction may prove disastrous—too strong conditioning easily leads to dysthy-mic reactions, too weak conditioning easily leads to psychopathic and hysterical reactions. The logic of this whole approach leads me to postulate two great classes of neurotic symp-toms which between them exhaust in principle all the possible abnormal reactions with which you are all familiar. On the one hand we have *surplus conditioned reactions*, i.e. reactions ac-quired along the lines I have adumbrated, and where the reaction is unadaptive, even though originally it may have been well suited to cir-cumstances. On the other hand we have *de-ficient conditioned reactions*, i.e. reactions nor-mally acquired by most individuals in society, which are adaptive, but which because of de-fective conditioning powers have not been ac-quired by a particular person. It is necessary to emphasize that surplus conditioned reactions and deficient conditioned reactions are due to an interplay between such individual factors as conditionability and autonomic lability, on the one hand, and environmental conditions on the other. There will be no socialization for an individual who cannot form conditioned re-sponses at all, but conversely, there will be no socialization for a person growing up on a desert island, however powerful his conditioning mechanism may happen to be. In this paper I have no time to deal with differences in the conditioning forces of the environment, and their relation to such factors as social class, but they should certainly not be forgotten.

Many other testable deductions, apart from the differential conditionability of dysthymics and hysterics, follow from such a formulation. Some of these deductions can be tested in the laboratory, and examples have been given in my book, *The Dynamics of Anxiety and Hys-*

teria. But others can be tested clinically, and for the sake of an example I shall give just one of these. I have shown how psychopathic reactions originate because of the inability of the psychopath, due to his low level of conditionability, to acquire the proper socialized responses. But this failure is not absolute; he conditions much less quickly and strongly than others, but he does condition. Thus where the normal person may need 50 pairings of the conditioned and the unconditioned stimulus, and where the dysthymic may need 10, the psychopath may require 100. But presumably in due course the 100 pairings will be forthcoming, although probably much later in life than the 10 of the dysthymic, or the 50 of the normal person, and then he will finally achieve a reasonable level of socialization. If this chain of reasoning is correct, it would lead us to expect that the diagnosis "psychopath" would by and large be confined to relatively young people, say under thirty years of age; after thirty the course of life should have brought forth the required 100 pairings and thus produced the needed amount of socialization. As far as I can ascertain, clinical psychiatric opinion is in agreement with this prediction.

How does our theory compare with the psychoanalytic one? In the formation of neurotic symptoms, Freud emphasizes the traumatic nature of the events leading up to the neurosis, as well as their roots in early childhood. Learning theory can accommodate with equal ease traumatic single-trial learning, for which there is good experimental evidence (26), but it can also deal with repeated sub-traumatic pain and fear responses which build up the conditioned reaction rather more gradually (42). As regards the importance of childhood, the Freudian stress appears to be rather misplaced in allocating the origins of *all* neuroses to this period. It is possible that many neurotic symptoms find their origin in this period, but there is no reason at all to assume that neurotic symptoms cannot equally easily be generated at a later period provided conditions are arranged so as to favour their emergence.

The point, however, on which the theory here advocated breaks decisively with psychoanalytic thought of any description is in this. Freudian theory regards neurotic symptoms as adaptive mechanisms which are evidence of repression; they are "the visible upshot of unconscious causes" (37). Learning theory does not postulate any such "unconscious causes," but regards neurotic symptoms as simple learned habits; there is no neurosis underlying the symptom, but merely the symptom itself. *Get rid of the symptom and you have eliminated the neurosis.* This notion of purely symptomatic treatment is so alien to psychoanalysis that it may be considered the crucial part of the theory here proposed. I would like to explore its implications a little further later on.

From the point of view of learning theory, treatment is in essence a very simple process. In the case of surplus conditioned responses, treatment should consist in the extinction of these responses; in the case of deficient conditioned responses, treatment should consist in the building up of the missing stimulus-response connections. Yet this apparent simplicity should not mislead us into thinking that the treatment of neurotic disorders offers no further problems. It is often found in scientific research that the solution of the problems posed by applied science is as complex and difficult as is the solution of the problems posed by pure science; even after Faraday and Maxwell had successfully laid the foundations of modern theories of electricity it needed fifty years and the genius of Edison to make possible the actual application of these advances to the solution of practical problems. Similarly here; a solution in principle, even if correct, still needs much concentrated and high-powered research in the field of application before it can be used practically in the fields of cure, amelioration, and prophylaxis.

What are the methods of cure suggested by learning theory? I shall give two brief examples only, to illustrate certain principles; others have been given by G. Jones (29). One method of extinguishing the neurotic response X to a given stimulus S is to condition another response R to S, provided that R and X are mutually incompatible. This method, called "reciprocal inhibition" by Wolpe (45, 46), harks back to Sherrington (40) of course, and may be illustrated by returning to our rat phobic little boy. Essentially what Watson had done was to condition a strong sympathetic reaction to the sight of the rat. If we could now succeed in establishing a strong parasympathetic reaction to the sight of the animal, this might succeed in overcoming and eliminating the sympathetic response. The practical difficulty arises that, to begin with at least, the already established conditioned response is of necessity stronger than the to-be-conditioned parasympathetic response. To overcome this difficulty, we make use of the concept of stimulus gradient already mentioned. The rat close by produces a strong conditioned fear reaction; the rat way out in the distance produces a much weaker reaction. If we now feed the infant chocolate while the rat is being introduced in the far distance the strong parasympathetic response produced by the chocolate-munching extinguishes the weak sympathetic response produced by the rat. As the conditioned parasympathetic response grows in strength, so we can bring the rat nearer and nearer, until finally even close proximity does not produce sympathetic reactions. The sympathetic reaction has been extinguished; the phobia has been cured. This is in fact the method which was used experimentally to get rid of the experimentally induced fear (27), and it has been used successfully by several workers in the field of child psychiatry. More recently Herzberg (23) in his system of active psychotherapy, and more particularly, Wolpe (46) in his psychotherapy by reciprocal inhibition, have shown that these principles can be applied with equal success to the severe neuroses of adult men and women—substituting other methods, of course, for the chocolate-munching, which is more effective with children than with adults!

As an example of the cure of deficient conditioned responses, let me merely mention *enuresis nocturna*, where clearly the usual conditioned response of waking to the conditioned stimulus of bladder extension has not been properly built up. A simple course of training, in which a bell rings loudly whenever the child begins to urinate, thus activating an electric circuit embedded in his bedclothes, soon establishes the previously missing connection, and the extremely impressive list of successes achieved with this method, as compared with the very modest success of psychotherapeutic methods, speaks strongly for the correctness of the theoretical point of view which gave rise to this conception (36).

We thus have here, I would suggest, an alternative theory to the Freudian, a theory which claims to account for the facts at least as satisfactorily as does psychoanalysis, and which in addition puts forward quite specific

suggestions about methods of treatment. I have called these methods "behaviour therapy" to contrast them with methods of psychotherapy.[3] This contrast of terms is meant to indicate two things. According to psychoanalytic doctrine, there is a psychological complex, situated in the unconscious mind, underlying all the manifest symptoms of neurotic disorder. Hence the necessity of therapy for the psyche. According to learning theory, we are dealing with unadaptive behaviour conditioned to certain classes of stimuli; no reference is made to any underlying disorders or complexes in the psyche. Following on this analysis, it is not surprising that psychoanalysts show a preoccupation with psychological methods involving mainly *speech*, while behaviour therapy concentrates on actual *behaviour* as most likely to lead to the extinction of the unadaptive conditioned responses. The two terms express rather concisely the opposing viewpoints of the two schools. Table 1 presents, in summary form, a tabulation of the most important differences between Freudian psychotherapy and behaviour therapy.

What kind of answer would we expect from the Freudians? I think their main points would be these. They would claim, in the first place,

---

[3] The growth of the theoretical concepts and practical methods of treatment subsumed in the term "behavior therapy" owes much to a large number of people. Apart from Pavlov and Hull, who originated the main tenets of modern learning theory, most credit is probably due to Watson, who was among the first to see the usefulness of the conditioned paradigm for the explanation of neurotic disorders; to Miller and Mowrer, who have done so much to bring together learning theory and abnormal human behavior; to Spence, whose important contributions include the detailed analysis of the relation between anxiety and learning; and to Wolpe, who was the first to apply explicitly some of the laws of learning theory to the large scale treatment of severe neurotics. If there is any novelty in my own treatment of these issues it lies primarily: (1) in the pulling together of numerous original contributions into a general theory and (2) in the introduction into this system of the concepts of neuroticism and extraversion/introversion as essential parameters in the description and prediction of behaviour. I would like to emphasize, however, that this contribution could not have been made had the ground work not been well and truly laid by the writers quoted above and by many more, only some of whom are quoted in the bibliography.

that conditioning therapy has frequently been tried, but with very poor results; aversion therapies of alcoholism are often mentioned in this connection. They would go on to say that even where symptomatic treatments of this kind are apparently successful, as in enuresis, the symptom is likely to return, or be supplanted by some other symptom, or by an increase in anxiety. And, in the third place, they would claim that even if in some cases the therapies suggested might be successful, yet in the great majority of cases psychoanalysis would be the only method to produce lasting cures. Let me deal with these points one by one.

Table 1

Freudian Psychotherapy	Behaviour Therapy
1. Based on inconsistent theory never properly formulated in postulate form.	Based on consistent, properly formulated theory leading to testable deductions.
2. Derived from clinical observations made without necessary control observation or experiments.	Derived from experimental studies specifically designed to test basic theory and deductions made therefrom.
3. Considers symptoms the visible upshot of unconscious causes ("complexes").	Considers symptoms as unadaptive conditioned responses.
4. Regards symptoms as evidence of *repression*.	Regards symptoms as evidence of faulty learning.
5. Believes that symptomatology is determined by defence mechanism.	Believes that symptomatology is determined by individual differences in conditionability and autonomic lability, as well as accidental environmental circumstances.
6. All treatment of neurotic disorders must be *historically* based.	All treatment of neurotic disorders is concerned with habits existing at *present*; their historical development is largely irrelevant.
7. Cures are achieved by handling the underlying (unconscious) dynamics, not by treating the symptom itself.	Cures are achieved by treating the symptom itself, i.e. by extinguishing unadaptive C.R.s and establishing desirable C.R.s
8. Interpretation of symptoms, dreams, acts, etc. is an important element of treatment.	Interpretation, even if not completely subjective and erroneous, is irrelevant.
9. Symptomatic treatment leads to the elaboration of new symptoms.	Symptomatic treatment leads to permanent recovery provided autonomic as well as skeletal surplus C.R.s are extinguished.
10. Transference relations are essential for cures of neurotic disorders.	Personal relations are not essential for cures of neurotic disorder, although they may be useful in certain circumstances.

There is no doubt that conditioning treatment of alcoholism has often been tried, and that it has often failed. I have no wish to take refuge in a *tu quoque* argument by pointing out that alcoholism has been particularly difficult to treat by any method whatever, and that psychoanalytic methods also have been largely unsuccessful. I would rather point out that learning theory is an exact science, which has elaborated quite definite rules about the establishment of conditioned reflexes; it is only when these rules are properly applied by psychologists with knowledge and experience in this field that the question of success or failure arises. Thus it is quite elementary knowledge that the conditioned stimulus must precede the unconditioned stimulus if conditioning is to take place; backward conditioning, if it occurs at all, is at best very weak. Yet some workers in the field of alcoholism have used a method in which the unconditioned stimulus regularly preceded the conditioned stimulus; under these conditions learning theory would in fact predict the complete failure of the experiment actually reported! Again, the time relation between the application of the conditioned stimulus and the unconditioned stimulus is a very important one; it is controlled to very fine limits of hundredths of a second in psychological experimentation, and it has been universally reported that conditioning in which any but the optimal time relation is chosen is relatively ineffective. Taking eye-blink conditioning as an example, it is found that a time interval of about ½ second is optimal, and that with intervals of 2½ seconds no conditioning at all takes place (31, 32). No attention seems to have been paid to these points by most workers on alcoholism, who apply the conditioned and unconditioned stimuli in such a vague way that it is often impossible to find out what the actual time relations were. This lack of rigour makes it quite impossible to adduce these so-called experiments as evidence either in favour or against conditioning therapy (19).

How about the return of symptoms? I have made a thorough search of the literature dealing with behaviour therapy with this particular point in view. Many psycho-analytically trained therapists using these methods have been specially on the lookout for the return of symptoms, or the emergence of alternative ones; yet neither they nor any of the other practitioners have found anything of this kind to happen except in the most rare and unusual cases (35). Enuresis, once cured by conditioning therapy, remains cured as a general rule; relapses occur, as indeed one would expect in terms of learning theory under certain circumstances, but they quickly yield to repeat treatment. So certain of success are the commercial operators of this method that they work on a "money back if unsuccessful" policy; their financial solvency is an adequate answer to the psychoanalytic claim. Nor would it be true that alternative symptoms emerge; quite the contrary happens. The disappearance of the very annoying symptom promotes peace in the home, allays anxieties, and leads to an all-round improvement in character and behaviour. Similar results are reported in the case of major applications of behaviour therapy to adults suffering from severe neurotic disorders; abolition of the symptom does not leave behind some mysterious complex seeking outlet in alternative symptoms (35). Once the symptom is removed, the patient is cured; when there are multiple symptoms, as there usually are, removal of one symptom facilitates removal of the others, and removal of all the symptoms completes the cure (46).

There is one apparent exception to this rule which should be carefully noted because it may be responsible for some of the beliefs so widely held. Surplus conditioned reactions may themselves be divided into two kinds, autonomic and motor. Anxiety reactions are typical of the autonomic type of surplus conditioned reactions, whereas tics, compulsive movements, etc., are typical of motor conditioned reactions. What has been said about the complete disappearance of the symptom producing a complete disappearance of the neurosis is true only as far as the autonomic conditioned reactions are concerned. Motor reactions are frequently activated by their drive-reducing properties vis-à-vis the historically earlier conditioned autonomic responses (35); the extinction of the motor response without the simultaneous extinction of the conditioned autonomic response would only be a very partial cure and could not be recommended as being sufficient. As pointed out at the end of the previous paragraph, "removal of all the symptoms completes the cure," and clearly removal of the motor conditioned response by itself, without the removal of the autonomic conditioned response is only a very partial kind of treatment. Behaviour therapy requires the extinction of all non-adaptive conditioned responses complained of by the patient, or causally related to these symptoms.

But how frequently does this type of treatment result in cures? Again I have made a thorough search of the literature, with the following outcome. G. P. treatment, not making use of psychotherapy in any of its usual forms, results in a recovery of about two seriously ill neurotics out of three (4). Eclectic psychotherapy results in a recovery of about two seriously ill neurotics out of three (8). Psychotherapy by means of psychoanalysis fares slightly worse. but results are at a comparable level (17). Results of behaviour therapy of seriously ill neurotics, as reported by Wolpe, are distinctly superior to this, over 90 per cent recovering (46). This difference is highly significant statistically, and it should be borne in mind that the number of sessions required by behaviour therapy is distinctly smaller than that required by psychotherapy, whether eclectic or psychoanalytic. (Wolpe reports an average of about 30 sittings for his cases.)

These results are encouraging, but of course, they must not be taken too seriously. Actuarial comparisons of this kind suffer severely from the difficulty of equating the seriousness of disorders treated by different practitioners, the equally obvious difficulty of arriving at an agreed scale for the measurement of "recovery," and the impossibility of excluding the myriad chance factors which may effect gross behaviour changes of the kind we are here considering. I would not like to be understood as saying that behaviour therapy has been *proved* superior to psychotherapy; nothing could be further from my intention. What I am claiming is simply that as far as they go—which is not very far—available data do not support in any sense the Freudian belief that behaviour therapy is doomed to failure, and that only psychoanalysis or some kindred type of treatment is adequate to relieve neurotic disorders. This Freudian belief is precisely this—a belief; it has no empirical or rational foundation. I have no wish to set up a counter-belief, equally unsupported, to the effect that psychotherapy is doomed to failure, and that only behaviour therapy is adequate to relieve neurotic disorders. What I would like to suggest is simply that a good case can be made out, both on the theoretical and the empirical level, for the proposition that behaviour therapy is an effective, relatively quick, and probably lasting method of cure of some neurotic disorders. This case is so strong that clinical trials would appear to be in order now to establish the relative value of this method as compared with other available methods, such as psychoanalysis, or electroshock treatment. Even more important, I think the evidence would justify psychiatrists in experimenting with the method, or rather set of methods, involved, in order to come to some preliminary estimate of their efficiency. I have noted with some surprise that many psychotherapists have refused to use such methods as conditioning therapy in enuresis, not on empirical grounds; but on *a priori* grounds, claiming that such mechanical methods simply could not work, and disregarding the large body of evidence available. Even in long-established sciences *a priori* considerations carry little weight; in such a young discipline as psychology they are quite out of place. Only actual use can show the value of one method of treatment as opposed to another.

There is one point I would like to emphasize. Freud developed his psychological theories on the basis of his study of neurotic disorders, and their treatment. Behaviour therapy, on the contrary, began with the thorough experimental study of the laws of learning and conditioning in normal people, and in animals; these well-established principles were then applied to neurotic disorders. It seems to me that this latter method is in principle superior to the former; scientific advance has nearly always taken the form of making fundamental discoveries and then applying these in practice, and I can see no valid reason why this process should be inverted in connection with neurosis. It may be objected that learning theorists are not always in agreement with each other (24), and that it is difficult to apply principles about which there is still so much argument. This is only very partially true; those points about which argument rages are usually of academic interest rather than of practical importance. Thus reinforcement theorists and contiguity theorists have strong differences of view about the necessity of reinforcement during learning, and different reinforcement theorists have different theories about the nature of reinforcement. Yet there would be general agreement in any particular case about the optimum methods of achieving a quick rate of conditioning, or extinction; these are questions of fact, and it is only with the interpretation of some of these facts that disagreements arise. Even when the disputes about the corpuscular or wavular nature of light were at their height, there was sufficient common ground between contestants regarding the facts of the case to make possible the practical application of available knowledge; the same is true of learning theory. The 10 per cent which is in dispute should not blind us to the 90 per cent which is not—disagreements and disputes naturally attract more attention, but agreements on facts and principles are actually much more common. Greater familiarity with the large and rapidly growing literature will quickly substantiate this statement (38).

It is sometimes said that the model offered here differs from the psychoanalytic model only in the terminology used, and that in fact the two models are very similar. Such a statement would be both true and untrue. There undoubtedly are certain similarities, as Mowrer (35) and Miller and Dollard (5) have been at pains to point out. The motivating role of anxiety in the Freudian system is obviously very similar in conception to the drive-producing conditioned autonomic responses of learning theory, and the relief from anxiety produced by hysterical and obsessional symptoms in Freudian terminology is very similar to the conditioned drive-reducing properties of motor movements. Similarly, a case could be made out in favour of regarding the undersocialized, non-conditionable psychopathic individual as being Id-dominated, and the dysthymic, over-conditionable individual as being Super-Ego dominated. Many other similarities will occur to the reader in going through these pages, and indeed the writer would be the first to acknowledge the tremendous service that Freud has done in elucidating for the first time some of these dynamic relationships, and in particular in stressing the motivating role of anxiety.

Nevertheless, there are two main reasons for not regarding the present formulation as simply an alternative differing from the psychoanalytic one only in the terminology used. In the first place, the formulation here given differs from the Freudian in several essential features, as can be seen most clearly by studying Table 1. Perhaps these differences are most apparent with respect to the deductions made from the two theories as to treatment. Psychoanalytic theory distrusts purely symptomatic treatment and insists on the removal of the underlying complexes. Behaviour theory on the other hand stresses the purely symptomatological sides of treatment and is unconvinced of the very existence of "complexes." It might, of course, be suggested that there is some similarity between the Freudian "complex" and the "conditioned surplus autonomic reaction" posited by behaviour theory. That there is some similarity cannot be denied, but no one familiar with psychoanalytic writings would agree that the Freudian complex was not in essence a very different conception from the conditioned autonomic response, both from the point of view of its origins, as well as from the point of view of the appropriate method of extinction.

This brings me to the second great difference between the two models. What the Freudian model lacks above all is an intelligible objectively testable *modus operandi* which can be

experimentally studied in the laboratory, which can be precisely quantified, and which can then be subjected to the formulation of strict scientific laws. The stress on such a mechanism, namely that of conditioning, is the most noteworthy feature of the model here advocated. It is entirely due to the great body of research which has been done in connection with the elaboration of laws of modern learning theory that we are enabled to make fairly precise deductions resulting in different methods of treatment for patients suffering from neurotic disorders, and it is with respect to this feature of the model that the relevant case histories and accounts of treatment should be read (28, 33, 47).

It has sometimes been suggested that the criticisms which I have levelled against the psychotherapeutic schools because of their failure to provide adequate control groups to validate their claims regarding the curative properties of their methods, could justifiably be levelled against the accounts given by those who have used behaviour therapy and reported upon the effects achieved. Such a criticism would not be justified for two reasons. In the first place the cases quoted are *illustrative of methods*, not *proofs of psychotherapeutic efficacy*; the only case in which claims regarding relative efficacy have been made contains a statistical comparison with the effects of psychoanalytic treatment of similar cases (46). In the second place the concept of "control" in scientific experiments is somewhat more than simply the provision of a control *group;* the control in an experiment may be *internal*. As an example, consider the experiment reported by Yates (47) on the extinction of four tics in a female patient by means of a rather novel and unusual method, namely that of repeated voluntary repetition of the tic by massed practice. Precise predictions were made as to the effects that should follow, and these predictions were studied by using the fate of some of the tics as compared to the fate of other tics submitted to dissimilar treatment. Thus, practice for two tics might be discontinued for a fortnight, while practice on the other two would go on. By showing that the predictions made could thus be verified, and the *rate of extinction* of the tics varied at will in accordance with the experimental manipulation for such variables as massing of practice, a degree of control was achieved far superior to the simple assessment of significance produced in the comparison of two random groups submitted to different treatments. It is by its insistence on such experimental precision and the incorporation of experimental tests of the hypotheses employed, even during the treatment, that behaviour theory differs from psychotherapy.

There is one further method of pointing up the differences between the two theories and of deciding between them; I mention this matter with some hesitation because too many psychiatrists it seems almost sacrilegious to use animal experimentation in the consideration of human neurosis. However, Fenichel himself (18, p. 19) has quoted "experimental neuroses" as support for the Freudian conception of neurotic disorders, and it is with respect to these experiments that the contrast between the psychoanalytic and our own model may be worked out most explicitly. Fenichel maintains that the model of psychoneurosis "is represented by the artificial neuroses that have been inflicted upon animals by experimental psychologists. Some stimulus which had represented pleasant instinctual experiences or which had served as a signal that some action would now procure gratification is suddenly connected by the experimenter with frustrating or threatening experiences, or the experimenter decreases the difference between stimuli which the animal had been trained to associate with instinct gratification and threat respectively; the animal then gets into a state of irritation which is very similar to that of a traumatic neurosis. He feels contradictory impulses; the conflict makes it impossible for him to give in to the impulses in the accustomed way; the discharge is blocked, and this decrease in discharge works in the same way as an increase in influx; it brings the organism into a state of tension and calls for emergency discharges.

"In psychoneuroses some impulses have been blocked; the consequence is a state of tension and eventually some 'emergency discharges.' These consist partly in unspecific restlessness and its elaborations and partly in much more specific phenomena which represent the distorted involuntary discharges of those very instinctual drives for which a normal discharge has been interdicted. Thus we have in psychoneuroses, first a defense of the ego against an instinct, then a conflict between the instinct striving for discharge and the defensive forces of the ego, then a state of damming up and finally the neurotic symptoms which are distorted discharges as a consequence of the state of damming up—a compromise between the opposing forces. The symptom is the only step in this development that becomes manifest; the conflict, its history, and the significance of the symptoms are unconscious."

Hebb (22) has laid down certain requirements for attempting to demonstrate that experimental neurosis occurs in animals and Broadhurst (2, 3) has examined the literature, and particularly that referred to by Fenichel, from this point of view. Here is his summary.

How does the large body of American work stand up to such an assessment? For the purposes of a recent review (3), the available literature was examined in the light of Hebb's criteria. Noteworthy among this is the work of the group headed by Liddell (1), one of the pioneers of conditioning methodology in the United States, who has used principally the sheep as his experimental subject; of Gantt (20), whose long term study of the dog 'Nick' is well known; and of Masserman (30), who has done extensive work using cats. This is not the place to enter into the details of this evaluation, which is reported elsewhere (3), but the overall conclusion which was reached was that there are few instances in all this work of any cases of experimentally induced abnormalities of animal behaviour which meet all of Hebb's criteria. Let us take, for example, the work of Masserman, whose theoretical interpretation of abnormal behaviour need not concern us here except to note that it was the basis upon which he designed his experiments to produce "conflict" between one drive and another. What he did was this. He trained hungry cats to respond to a sensory signal by opening a food box to obtain food. Then he subjected them to a noxious stimulus, a blast of air, or electric shock, just at the moment of feeding. The resulting changes in behaviour—the animals showed fear of the situation and of the experimenter, and refused to feed further—he identified as experimental neurosis. But the behaviour observed fails to fulfill more than one or two of Hebb's criteria, and, moreover, certain deficiencies in the design of his experiments make it impossible to draw any satisfactory conclusions from them. Thus Wolpe (45) repeated part of Masserman's work using the essential control group which Masserman had omitted—that is, he gave the cats the noxious stimulus alone, without any "conflict" between the fear motivation thus induced, and the hunger which, in Masserman's animals, operated as well—and found that the same behaviour occurred. It hardly needs to be said that a fear response to a threatening stimulus is not abnormal and cannot be regarded as an experimental neurosis.

It is clear from the studies cited that Fenichel is quite wrong in claiming that "experimental neurosis" is in any way analogous to the Freudian model of human neurosis. It appears, therefore, that insofar as these studies are relevant at all they can be regarded as demonstrating nothing but simple conditioned fear responses of the kind called for by our theory. It is perhaps worthy of note that the failure of psychoanalysis to use control groups in the human field has extended to their work with animals, as in the case of Masserman quoted above. Fenichel's easy acceptance of data congruent with his hypothesis is paralleled by his failure to mention data contrary to the psychoanalytic viewpoint. By taking into account all the data it seems more likely that a correct conclusion will be reached.

I would now like to return to some of the points which I raised at the beginning of this paper. I argued then that the special knowledge and competence of psychologists in mental hospitals was largely wasted because of concentration on, and preoccupation with, Freudian theories and projective types of test. I would now like to make a more positive suggestion and maintain that by virtue of their training and experience psychologists are (or should be) experts in the fields of conditioning and learning theory, laboratory procedures, and research design. In suitable cases, surely their help would be invaluable in diagnostic problems, such as ascertaining a given patient's speed of conditioning, in the theoretical problem of constructing a model of his personality dynamics, and in the practical problem of designing a suitable course of behaviour therapy which would take into account all the available information about the case.[4] I am not suggesting that psychologists should themselves necessarily carry out this

course of treatment; it would appear relatively immaterial whether the therapy is carried out by one person or another, by psychologist or psychiatrist. Both types of procedure have been experimented with, and both have shown equally promising results. Indeed, certain aspects of the therapy can obviously be carried out by less senior and experienced personnel, provided the course of treatment is reviewed periodically by the person in charge. Psychoanalysis lays much stress on what is sometimes called "transference," a devil conjured up only to be sent back to his usual habitat with much expenditure of time and energy (18). Behaviour therapy has no need of this adjunct, nor does it admit that the evidence for its existence is remotely adequate at the present time. However that may be, relinquishing the personal relationship supposed to be indispensable for the "transference" relation allows us to use relatively unqualified help in many of the more time-consuming and routine parts of behaviour therapy. In certain cases, of course, personal relationships may be required in order to provide a necessary step on the generalization gradient; but this is not always true.[5]

From a limited experience with this kind of work, carried out by various members of my department, I can say with confidence two things. The direct application of psychological theories to the practical problem of effecting a cure in a particular person, here and now, acts as a very powerful challenge to the psychologist concerned, and makes him more aware than al-

_____

[4] It will be clear that the function here sketched out for the psychologist demands that he be furnished with the necessary tools of his trade, such as sound-proof rooms, conditioning apparatus, and all the other techniques for delivering stimuli and measuring responses on a strictly quantified basis (13). It is equally clear that such facilities do not exist in the majority of our mental hospitals. Until they do, the handicaps under which the clinical psychologist works at such institutions will be all but insurmountable, and no reasonable estimate of their potential usefulness can be formed. One might just as well employ an electroencephalographer and refuse to pay for the machine which he has been trained to use! It would be better to have a few, properly equipped departments than a large number of small, ill-equipped ones as at present. Even in the United States the position is bad; in this country it is worse. A relatively small capital investment would be likely to bear considerable fruit.

[5] As an example of this we may quote a case reported by Graham White. This concerns a child who became anorexic after the death of her father. The therapist adopted the father's role in a variety of circumstances, ranging in order from play with dolls' tea sets to the actual eating situation, and reinforced those reactions which were considered desirable. The theoretical rationale was that the father had become a conditioned stimulus on which eating depended.

most anything else of the strengths and weaknesses of the formulations of modern learning theory. And the successful discharge of this self-chosen duty serves more than almost anything else to convince his psychiatric colleagues that psychology can successfully emerge from its academic retreat and take a hand in the day-to-day struggle with the hundred-and-one problems facting the psychiatrist. It seems to me that the tragic fratricidal struggle between psychiatrists and psychologists which has so exacerbated relations between them in the United States, could easily be avoided here by recognizing the special competence of the psychologist in this particular corner of the field, while acknowledging the necessity of keeping the general medical care of the patient in the hands of the psychiatrist. I believe that most psychiatrists are too well aware of the precarious state of our knowledge in the field of the neurotic disorders to do anything but welcome the help which the application of learning theory in the hands of a competent psychologist may be able to bring.

REFERENCES

1. Anderson, O. P., and Paramenter, A., "A long-term study of the experimental neurosis in the sheep and dog," *Psychosom. Med. Monogr.*, 1941, **2**, Nos. 3 and 4, 1–150.

2. Broadhurst, P.L., "The contribution of animal psychology to the concept of psychological normality-abnormality." *Proc. XIII Internal. Congr. Appl. Psychol.*, 1958.

3. *Idem*, "Abnormal animal behavior." In H. J. Eysenck (Ed.). *Handbook of Abnormal Psychology*, 1959. London: Pitman.

4. Denker, P. G., "Results of treatment of psychoneuroses by the general practitioner. A follow-up study of 500 cases," *New York State J. Med.*, 1946, **46**, 2164–2166.

5. Dollard, J. and Miller, N. E., *Personality and Psychotherapy*, 1950. New York: McGraw-Hill.

6. Estes. W. K. *et al.*, *Modern Learning Theory*, 1954. Appleton-Century.

7. Eysenck, H. J., *Dimensions of Personality*, 1947. London: Routledge & Kegan Paul.

8. *Idem*, "The effects of psychotherapy: an evaluation," *J. Consult. Psychol.*, 1952, **16**, 319–324.

9. *Idem, The Scientific Study of Personality*, 1952. London: Routledge & Kegan Paul.

10. *Idem, Uses and Abuses of Psychology*, 1953. London: Pelican.

11. *Idem, The Structure of Human Personality*, 1953. London: Methuen.

12. *Idem*, "Zur Theorie der Persönlichkeitsmessung," *Ztchr. f. diag. Psychol. u. Personlichkeitsforschung*, 1954, **2**, 87–101, 171–187.

13. *Idem, Psychology and the Foundation of Psychiatry*, 1955. London: H. K. Lewis.

14. *Idem*, "Los principios del condicionamiento y la teoria de la personalidad." *Riv. de Psycologica*, 1957, **12**, 655–667.

15. *Idem, Dynamics of Anxiety and Hysteria*, 1957. London: Routledge & Kegan Paul.

16. *Idem*, Personality tests: 1950–1955. In *Recent Progress in Psychiatry*, G. W. T. H. Fleming (Ed.), 1959. London: J. and A. Churchill.

17. *Idem*, The effects of psychotherapy. In H. J. Eysenck (Ed.), *Handbook of Abnormal Psychology*, 1959. London: Pitman.

18. Fenichel, O., *The Psychoanalytic Theory of Neurosis*, 1945. London: Kegan Paul.

19. Franks, C. M., "Alcohol, alcoholics and conditioning: a review of the literature and some theoretical considerations," *J. ment. Sci.*, 1958, **104**, 14–33.

20. Gantt, W. H., "Experimental basis for neurotic behavior," *Psychosom. Med. Monogr.*, 1944, **3**, 1–211.

21. Glover, E., *The Technique of Psychoanalysis*, 1955. London: Baillière.

22. Hebb, D. O., "Spontaneous neurosis in chimpanzees: theoretical relations with clinical and experimental phenomena," *Psychosom. Med.*, 1947, **9**, 3–16.

23. Herzberg, A., "Short treatment of neuroses by graduated tasks," *Brit. J. Med. Psychol.*, 1941, **19**, 36–51.

24. Hilgard, E. R., *Theories of Learning*, 1956. New York: Appleton-Century.

25. Hilgard, E. R. and Marquis, D. G., *Conditioning and Learning*, 1940. New York: Appleton-Century.

26. Hudson, B. B., "One-trial learning in the domestic rat," *Genet. Psychol. Monogr.*, 1950, **41**, 94–146.

27. Jersild, A. T. and Holmes, F. B., "Methods of overcoming children's fears," *J. Psychol.*, 1935, **1**, 25–83.

28. Jones, H. G., "The application of conditioning and learning techniques to the treatment of a psychiatric patient," *J. abn. soc. Psychol.*, 1956, **52**, 414–420.

29. *Idem*, "Neurosis and experimental psychology," *J. ment. Sci.*, 1958, **104**, 55–62.

30. Masserman, J. K., *Behaviour and Neurosis*, 1943. Chicago: Univ. Press.

31. McAllister, W. R., "Eyelid conditioning as a function of the CS-UCS interval," *J. exper. Psychol.*, 1953, **45**, 412–422.

32. *Idem*, "The effect on eyelid conditioning of shifting the CS-UCS interval," *J. exper. Psychol.*, 1953, **45**, 423–428.

33. Meyer, V., "The treatment of two phobic patients on the basis of learning principles," *J. abn. soc. Psychol.*, 1957 **55**, 261–266.

34. Miller, N. E., "Learnable drives and rewards," S. S. Stevens (Ed.), *Handbook of Experimental Psychology*, 1951. New York: Wiley, 435–472.

35. Mowrer, O. H., *Learning Theory and Personality Dynamics*, 1950. New York: Ronald Press.

36. Mowrer, O. H. and Mowrer, W. A., "Enuresis. A method for its study and treatment," *Amer. J. Orth. Psychiatry*, 1938, **8**, 436–447.

37. Munroe, R. L., *Schools of Psychoanalytic Thought*, 1955. New York: Dryden Press.

38. Osgood, C. E., *Method and Theory in Experimental Psychology*, 1953. London: Oxford Univ. Press.

39. Pavlov, I. P., *Conditioned Reflexes*, 1927. London: Oxford Univ. Press.

40. Sherrington, C. S., *The Integrative Action of the Central Nervous System*, 1926. Oxford: Univ. Press.

41. Shoben, E. J., "Psychotherapy as a problem in learning theory," *Psychol. Bull.*, 1949, **46**, 366–392.

42. Solomon, R. L., Kamin, L. J. and Wynne, L. C., "Traumatic avoidance learning," *J. abnorm. soc. Psychol.*, 1953, **48**, 291–302.

43. Spence, K.W., Haggard, P. F. and Ross, L. G., "UCS intensity and the associated (habit) strength of the eyelid CR," *J. exp. Psychol.*, 1958, **95**, 404–411.

44. Watson, J. B. and Raynor, R., "Conditioned emotional reaction," *J exper. Psychol.*, 1920, **3**, 1–4.

45. Wolpe, J., "Experimental neurosis as learned behavior," *Brit. J. Psychol.*, 1952, **43**, 243–268.

46. *Idem, Psychotherapy by Reciprocal Inhibition*, 1958. Stanford: Univ. Press.

47. Yates, A., "The application of learning theory to the treatment of tics," *J. abnorm. soc. Psychol.*, 1958, **56**, 175–182.

Stimulus-Response Theory

There has been an enormous amount of conceptual and empirical activity relevant to S-R theory in recent years. Literally hundreds of papers have appeared that on theoretical or substantive grounds are well qualified for inclusion in this section. Faced with this profusion of excellent material we have selected first, *Some Implications of Modern Behavior Theory for Personality Change and Psychotherapy*, a paper which may be considered a primary source inasmuch as it was written by Neal Miller, one of the two S-R theorists whose work we focused upon in *Theories of Personality*. This chapter, in addition to providing an elegant statement of Miller's conflict model, summarizes a considerable amount of diverse research all holding direct relevance for S-R theory.

In the second paper, *A Framework for the Study of Personality as a Behavioral Science*, I. E. Farber presents a coherent and insightful perspective on the domain of personality as viewed from the vantage of S-R theory. His treatment is of particular interest because he deals explicitly with so many issues that serve to distinguish or characterize individual personality theorists. Whether discussing the definition of personality, considering problems involved in generalizing from lower animal to man, or weighing the merits of studying the individual rather than the general case, his position represents a distillation from a self-conscious and relatively continuous intellectual tradition beginning with J. B. Watson and descending through Clark L. Hull and Kenneth W. Spence. His discussion of "The Nature and Function of Theories" provides a lucid and scholarly account of the dominant attitude of American psychologists toward theory in psychological science.

The paper by Epstein and Fenz develops a logical extension of Miller's conflict model and applies the revised theory to the prediction of behavior in an anxiety arousing situation—parachute jumping. The study is of unusual interest because it demonstrates the potential flexibility or generality of the theory and at the same time suggests that in the hands of the sophisticated proponent it is possible to make theoretical derivations with considerable rigor.

Perhaps the most dramatic and hotly disputed contemporary approach to psychotherapy is John Rosen's method of "direct analysis." In the fourth paper in this section we find a careful and ingenious use of S-R concepts to provide an understanding of what transpires during the complex interactions between Rosen and his patients. Edward J. Murray, formerly a student of Neal Miller, uses the method of content analysis of therapy protocols to provide the basic data and then utilizes S-R assumptions and concepts to provide an account of what has occurred. Each of the last two studies illustrates the fact that in spite of the origins of S-R theory in the laboratory and its relative conceptual parsimony, it can be applied to highly complex behavioral phenomena with significant outcomes.

1. Some implications of modern behavior theory for personality change and psychotherapy

N. E. MILLER

IN THIS CHAPTER A VARIETY OF TOPICS relevant to personality change and resistance to such change will be covered. Since psychotherapy is an attempt to change personality, it will be shown how the conflict model and the type of analysis put forward in collaboration with John Dollard can be applied to a variety of quite different types of therapy—Freudian and non-Freudian; the use of behavior theory will be urged as a basis for radical innovations which are badly needed in the treatment of mental disease. We will discuss the interactions of organic factors with learning and the importance of changes produced by early experience. We will analyze some of the factors responsible for resistance to change, or, in other words, for the remarkable psychological homeostasis which many individuals show. We will contrast factors producing functional effects analogous to negative feedback, and hence leading to stable equilibrium resisting change, with those producing effects analogous to positive feedback, and hence producing unstable equilibrium susceptible to change. We will try to point out the relevance of some of the more recent results of laboratory studies of learning—especially those on schedules of correlated reinforcement.

SOURCE. Selection by Neal E. Miller, "Some implications of modern behavior theory for personality change and psychotherapy" in *Personality Change*, pp. 149–175. Edited by P. Worchel and D. Byrne. New York: Wiley, 1964.

Work on this paper and some of the studies in it was supported by Grant MY2949 and Grant M647 from the National Institutes of Health, Department of Health, Education and Welfare, Public Health Service, Bethesda, Maryland.

We will deal with an extension of the type of cybernetic analysis originally evolved to deal with copying behavior, and a few words will be said about the problem of unity or disunity of personality.

Applications of Behavior Theory to Radically Divergent Types of Psychotherapy

Although certain successful cases can be enormously convincing—especially to the therapist who is exposed at first hand to the detailed observations—the fact remains that some are baffling and tragically unsuccessful. Furthermore, there is distressingly little rigorous proof that the average improvement of treated patients is better than the spontaneous improvement of untreated ones. Although part of this lack of proof may be due to difficulties inherent in the complex social situations involved, techniques that regularly produce better outcomes would surmount such difficulties. Finally, the social needs for psychotherapy far exceed our ability to provide it with the present laborious and costly techniques. For all these reasons there is an urgent need to improve our techniques. We need to try a number of quite different innovations in our methods of helping these people to change for the better. I believe that modern learning theory can be a useful guide to such innovations in remedial personality education, or, in other words, psychotherapy.

A Variety of Implications of the Conflict Model. Conflict seems to play a central role in many forms of mental disturbance. Let us ex-

theoretical model which is supported by a considerable body of experimental data and which seems to fit many clinical facts.[1] The chief relationships are summarized in the first three figures. These involve the following assumptions which have been studied one at a time in separate simple experiments and verified; a number of the deductions from the joint action of these assumptions in more complex situations have also been verified (Miller, 1944; 1959). The main assumptions are: (*a*) the tendency to approach a goal is stronger the nearer the subject is to it (gradient of approach); (*b*) the tendency to avoid a feared stimulus is stronger the nearer the subject is to it (gradient of avoidance); (*c*) the strength of avoidance increases more rapidly with nearness than that of approach (greater steepness of avoidance gradient); (*d*) the strength of the tendencies to approach or avoid varies directly as the strength of drive upon which they are based (increased drive raises height of entire gradient).

Let us look first at the weak approach and avoidance in Figure 1. When the subject is to the left of the point at which the gradients

intersect, approach will be stronger, so that he will move nearer. But if he moves beyond the point of intersection, avoidance will be stronger so that he will retreat. Therefore, the free-moving subject will tend to remain in the region of the point of intersection. You can see that, when the avoidance is relatively weak, the subject will approach near to the goal even under weak motivation to approach. Then a slight increase of the strength of approach (from weak to moderate) will cause the subject to reach the goal.

The amount of avoidance, and presumably also of fear, actually elicited will depend upon where the subject is, which will be the point at which the two gradients intersect. The fear elicited is represented by the vertical, double-headed arrows. It can be seen that the increase from weak to moderate approach that causes the subject to go the short additional distance forward in order to reach the goal will be expected to produce only a moderate increase (from N to G) in fear.

After the subject reaches the goal, further increases in the strength of approach will not be expected to produce any further increases in fear, since the subject is already at the dangerous goal and cannot move any nearer. Indeed it is conceivable that by increasing the effectiveness of the reward, and making the consummatory responses at the goal more

---

[1] For more details see Miller (1944; 1951; 1961) and Dollard and Miller (1950). The reader who is already familiar with these materials can skip directly to *New Implications for Various Tactics* in this chapter.

Figure 1. When the subject is farther from the goal than the point at which the grandients intersect, approach is stronger than avoidance so that he should continue to approach until he passes intersection, at which point the greater strength of avoidance should stop him.

When the avoidance is weak, so that the subject is able to approach near to the goal, a small increase in the strength of approach (from weak to moderate) causes him to reach the goal and produces only a small increase (from N to G) in the amount of fear elicited.

Throughout, linear gradients are used for clarity, but similar deductions could be made for any curves with a continuous slope steeper for avoidance than approach at each point above the abscissa.

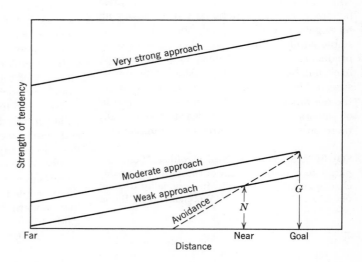

clearly dominant over those involved in fear, the further increase in approach drive might help to eliminate fear by counterconditioning, but this is a problem on which further research is needed.

In the case of a relatively weak conflict based on unrealistic fears, it presumably is relatively easy to produce therapeutic changes by moderate increases in the strength of the drive to approach, so that the subject reaches the goal, extinguishing and counterconditioning his fears. Even in the case of realistic fears based on mild punishment, the subject may tolerate the punishment in order to achieve the goal. Such

therapy can come about readily by natural increases in the drive to approach, or be facilitated by associates who use various means to enhance the attractiveness of the goal, encourage the subject, or even add motivation to escape mild ridicule to the other factors motivating approach. Presumably most subjects whose avoidance is weak enough so that they can be induced to change in this way do not reach a psychotherapist.

The situation that we have been describing may be contrasted with the one represented in Figure 2 in which strong avoidance is motivated by strong fear, so that the subject with

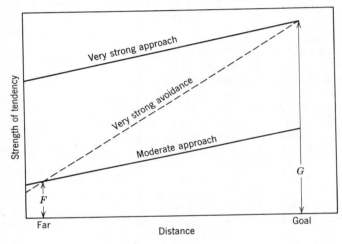

Figure 2. When strong avoidance keeps the subject with moderate motivation far from the goal, very strong motiavtion is required to cause him to reach it, and going considerably nearer to the goal will produce a great increase (from F to G) in the amount of fear elicited.

moderate motivation to approach remains far from the goal. In this case it can be seen that it will take very strong approach motivation to bring him to the goal and that inducing such motivation will produce a great increase (from F to G) in fear. If strong enough motivation to approach is not available, the subject may never reach the goal where he would have the most effective opportunity for extinguishing fear, but may be near enough to it so that he suffers intolerable fear and conflict. Thus, psychotherapists have found that trying to force severe neurotics nearer to the goal that is the source of their fear is not an effective way of producing a favorable change. But as we have just seen, this finding should not be generalized to subjects who are in a weaker conflict so that they are nearer to achieving the goal.

In the same case of a strong conflict, Figure 3 shows what happens when the same amount of advance to the goal is produced by lowering the gradient of avoidance. One can see that,

as the subject considers the goal to be less dangerous and moves nearer to it, we would expect a paradoxical increase (from F to G) in the strength of fear actually elicited. Such increases have been observed by clinicians and are called a negative therapeutic effect. You can also see, however, that the increase produced in this way is much less than the one to be expected when exactly the same advance toward the goal is produced by increasing the strength of motivation to approach. This difference apparently supplies the rationale for concentrating therapeutic efforts on lowering unrealistic fears, or in other words, analyzing the resistance first. After such fears have been reduced enough so that the subject is quite near to achieving the goal, he is in a situation represented by Figure 1 so that it may be all right to move him the additional distance by trying to increase the strength of approach.

New Implications for Various Tactics. This much of the analysis has been presented in

Figure 3. While very strong avoidance keeps the subject far from the goal, decreasing the strength of avoidance so that he comes very near to the dangerous goal will increase the strength of fear. The increase produced in this way, however, is not as great as that produced when, as in Figure 2, the same distance of approach is elicited by increasing the strength of motivation to approach.

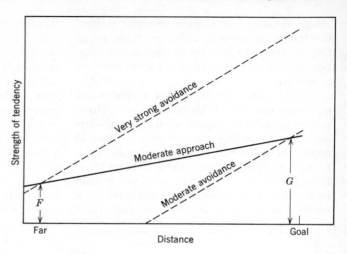

detail before. Now let me draw some further implications which are readily apparent, but apparently have been relatively overlooked. Suppose the fears are realistic, so that the subjects will get severely punished for achieving the goal. In that case the subject will either suffer punishment if he achieves the goal, or strong fear and conflict if the punishment just barely keeps him away from the goal. In such cases, attempting to decrease fear and avoidance will indeed produce a negative therapeutic effect, while conversely, a positive therapeutic effect may be produced by increasing the strength of fear and avoidance to the point where the subject remains far enough away from the forbidden goal so that he is no longer strongly punished or even tempted enough to be in any conflict. Some psychopaths should be helped in this way, which may explain such benefits

as occur in the type of therapy recommended by Mowrer (1953).

What happens if the dangers are realistic, but most of the punishment occurs only some time after the goal has been achieved? This situation is represented diagrammatically in Figure 4. The subject is free to advance toward or retreat from the goal along the dimension of distance represented by the left-hand part of the diagram, but once he achieves the goal, he is inexorably carried forward on the irreversible dimension of time, represented to the right, until he reaches the point at which punishment occurs. The subject might be expected to experience moderate fear before he achieves the goal, but strong fear (commonly called guilt) afterwards. In such a case it can be seen that increasing the height of avoidance might produce great therapeutic changes.

Figure 4. When delayed punishment is given (at time *P*) after achieving the goal, fear should mount rapidly during this delay. The strongest fear actually encountered should be greatly reduced (from *P* to Far, respectively) when the strength of avoidance is increased, so that the subject is prevented from reaching the goal or kept far from it.

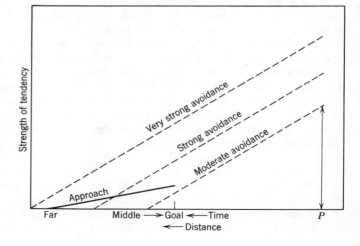

In order to bring out most clearly the essential dynamics, we have greatly oversimplified the foregoing examples. The experienced clinician or student of personality can readily supply his own details and can work out further extensions. We have time here to mention only a few such adaptations.

For example, the intense fear (guilt) elicited after achieving the forbidden goal may motivate various symptoms. In some cases one of the symptoms may be an approach to the same forbidden goal which will initiate a vicious spiral, as in the case of the alcoholic who drinks to relieve his fears and thereby produces a realistic basis for additional fears and guilt.

To take another approach, one may assume that the gradient of approach can vary in steepness, being steeper the more the drive motivating the approach is subject to arousal by external cues, as for example, seems to occur with sex (Miller, 1959). From Figure 5 it can be seen that the paradoxical decrease in fear with increase in height of the gradient of avoidance is greater when the gradient of approach is steeper. This leads to a prediction concerning the circumstances under which a greater negative therapeutic effect should occur from attempting to reduce unrealistic dangers, or similarly a greater paradoxical positive therapeutic effect from increasing the fear of real dangers.

To follow yet other implications, it is apparent that therapeutic changes from increasing the height of avoidance are more feasible in situations in which either the drive responsible for approach does not continue to mount to great heights in the absence of the goal response, or alternative means of satiating the drive are available. Often alternative means

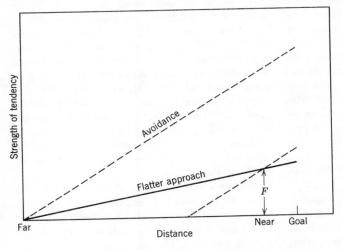

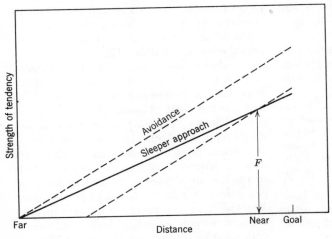

Figure 5. If the gradient of approach is steeper, the positive and negative therapeutic effects become greater; there is more difference in the amount of fear (F) elicited at the near and far points, and less of a change in the strength of avoidance is required to cause the subject to move from one of these points to the other.

are available. In some cases these are blocked by neurotic or unrealistic fears so that the subjects are motivated to approach realistically dangerous, tabooed goals. For example, certain individuals are driven by fears of sexual enjoyment with the spouse to seek extramarital affairs. In such cases the theory suggests increasing the avoidance of the realistically dangerous goal while at the same time decreasing that of the unrealistically feared one. But one might have to work also on the generalization of fear from one situation to the other by using labeling and other techniques to increase the ability to discriminate between the two types of goals.

Discrimination versus Counterconditioning of Fear. In *Personality and Psychotherapy* (Dollard and Miller, 1950) we worked out the details of a learning-theory analysis of repression. We showed how the inhibition of cue-producing responses, or what Pavlov (1957) called "the second signal system," would be expected to interfere with social control and the individual's ability to use the higher forms of problem solving to adapt to changes in his environmental conditions. On the one hand, restoring the cue-producing response, largely verbal, indicates that a certain amount of extinction of fear already has occurred; on the other hand, it provides a basis for better discrimination between realistic and unrealistic fears. Thus restoring the ability to think is an important part of therapy.[2]

Conversely, if the neurotic subject is responding to safe situations with sentences or images which elicit strong fear, teaching the subject not to respond with these inappropriate mediating responses should eliminate the unrealistic fears. This latter process appears to be the goal of the therapy described by Ellis (1962).

Another part of the process, which we certainly included, but perhaps did not emphasize enough, is the experimental extinction and counterconditioning of unrealistic fears. As we pointed out, the extinction of fear can be helped by drugs, provided the extinction of fear will transfer from the drugged to the normal state. Considerable work is now being done along this line; a great deal more is needed. We need laboratory work to develop and screen more effective fear-reducing drugs and determine the principles involved in the best ways of using them (Miller and Barry, 1960; Miller, 1961). We also need clinical work to translate these principles into the most effective techniques of using drugs in both traditional and radically new types of psychotherapy.

Similarly, we need additional research on the principles involved in the extinction and counterconditioning of fear. We need to try radically new means of applying these principles to the therapeutic situation. Wolpe (1958) seems to have made an interesting beginning, but a great deal remains to be done, especially in using the behavior of a social group, instead of that of only a single therapist, in extinguishing and counterconditioning fear. Finally we need more work on the problem of learning to resist pain and fear (Miller, 1960). We also need more ingenious attempts to reward positive tendencies and to train subjects in missing social skills—a task for which the resources of a therapeutic group or community should be more adequate than those of a single therapist working alone.

We also need additional research on the basic mechanism of reinforcement and on whether or not glandular and visceral responses and general levels of activation or depression can be modified, like instrumental somatic responses can, by rewards as well as by classical conditioning. Such problems, and a new hypothesis concerning reinforcement, are discussed elsewhere (Miller, 1963).

Freedom to Innovate. In order to free clinical workers to try the radical innovations that may lead to the improvements that are needed, we first must get rid of some of the unrealistic fears that are inhibiting innovations in psychotherapy. Psychotherapy, as it presently is conducted, often is an extremely difficult and delicate process. Thus one can understand the therapist's unwillingness to deviate from any procedures that he has found to be successful. But the very conditions of current psychotherapy, namely, a rather high incidence of unpredictable successes and failures, with strong

---

[2] But the removal of repression should not be confused with license to be immoral. We cannot be well adjusted if our behavior deviates too widely from the standards of our society. Thus in describing psychotherapy, Dollard and Miller (1950, p. 221) say: "The result is not an escape from the mores of his group. To attempt this escape would almost certainly be maladaptive. In fact the foresight that comes with the removal of repression may help the patient to be on his guard and to exercise socially useful restraint."

rewards for success and strong punishments for failure, are those which are most likely to produce stereotyped superstitious behavior that is strongly resistant to extinction.

One of the superstitions of the past has been that the recording of therapeutic interviews, which is essential for superior research and training, would be extremely difficult and dangerous to the therapeutic relationship, and perhaps even highly unethical. When the therapist overcomes his own fears and merely says something like, "Instead of taking notes I use the modern method of tape recording," many of the anticipated difficulties fail to appear.

Another of the superstitions is that the therapist must learn about the social conditions of the patient's life and his social behavior only through what he can decode from the patient's behavior toward the therapist and his free associations during the therapeutic hours. This rule of the game sometimes can lead to absurd situations in which a patient gives even an experienced therapist an entirely misleading impression of his social behavior and real problems. I believe we need to experiment more extensively with other ways of learning about the patient's social conditions, his behavior, and the actual changes that are, or are not, occurring.

If the therapist is in better touch with the conditions of the patient's life and his actual social behavior in these conditions, he may be in a better position to guide him in securing the rewards which will hasten and consolidate the process of change. But from the point of view of learning theory, one of the things that often makes therapy so difficult is the fact that the therapist does not have direct control over the important rewards and punishments in the patient's environment. Ingenious and courageous attempts to deal with this problem should be fruitful. Perhaps responsibility for a therapeutic regime could be divided between two people: one who is responsible for manipulating the reality conditions of the patient's life, and another who is in the more conventional therapeutic role of trying to help the patient to adjust to these conditions. We have not yet explored all of the possible combinations of individual and group therapy, therapeutic communities and clubs or associations, drug therapy, and re-education that can be suggested by a thorough analysis in terms of the principles and the conditions of social learning. Research along

such lines will be expensive but much less so than manned exploration of the moon or than the enormous personal and social burdens of mental disease.

Interaction of Organic Factors with Learning

The capacity to learn, which plays such an important role in personality change, is of course itself an innate capacity dependent upon the organic nature of the human species. Thus the principles of learning must have an organic basis which in most cases is not yet understood. Organic factors also influence the course of learning. To take a very simple example, physiological experiments show that the suitable stimulation of the isolated spinal cord of the cat can elicit well-coordinated locomotor reflexes of different types—stepping, hopping, trotting. Such reflexes in the spinal cord presumably are a part of the innate wiring diagram and enormously facilitate the learning of various forms of locomotor behavior by making adaptive responses infinitely more likely to occur than they would be if the cat had to learn by sheer trial and error to time correctly the proper combinations of muscular contraction. By facilitating the learning of certain characteristic types of locomotor behavior, such innate patterns also shape the course of learning so that certain gaits are characteristic of certain species. But the learning that occurs in acquiring habits of approaching or avoiding specific objects and learning how to cope with unusual obstacles or terrains tends to disguise the original innate patterns which have so greatly facilitated and shaped that learning.

Similarly, electric stimulation by a chronically implanted electrode of specific points in the unanesthetized cat's lower brain centers can elicit complex patterns. Stimulation in one location regularly elicits coordinated rage responses including dilation of the pupils, hissing, flattening back of the ears, and striking viciously with the unsheathed claws. Such attack is flexibly directed at specific objects such as a stick or a gloved hand inserted into the cage. Stimulation at another point regularly elicits a quite different pattern of cowering and slinking. The uniform localization and patterns of these complex reactions must be innately organized. The normal rage or fear behavior of the cat shows many of the same components, but under specific circumstances, the pattern is considerably modified, and hence disguised, by learning.[3]

These are but a few of the examples that emerge from a careful study of mammalian behavior. It seems highly probable that far more complicated innate patterns exist, that they play an important role in the development of human social behavior, and that these instinctual patterns are modifiable enough so that they tend to be disguised by learning although they may play crucial roles in motivating, facilitating, and shaping socially learned behavior.

Specifically, it is possible that some of the social learnable drives, which I used to think were based on more primary drives, actually have an organic basis of their own, but are subject to channeling, and possibly also to potentiation, by learning which tends to disguise this innate basis. But I have discussed elsewhere (Miller, 1959, pp. 262–272) this possibility and other new trails for research on motivation.

For producing change, the practical importance of a particular class of factors is determined by the range through which it is varied. This range may change with various circumstances, such as the development of new techniques. For example, the organic defect of congenital deafness used to be a catastrophic handicap because it removed the victim from social communication. It was widely thought to include a general deficit in both intellect and personality. With the development of psychological and educational techniques for teaching deaf people sign language, lip reading, and speech, deafness became much less important. The invention of these new psychological techniques dramatically altered the prognosis for this organic defect. Conversely, new operations on the ear can cure certain types of deafness. The importance of manipulating the organic factor in these cases is increased by these operative techniques.

Critical Sensitive Periods. A dramatic example of the care that must be used in unravel-

ing the roles of organic and experiential factors is presented by some of the recent work of Fuller (1962) and his associates in the Jackson Memorial Laboratory at Bar Harbor. Rearing puppies in isolation from the ages of three to twelve weeks is known to produce relatively long-lasting deficits in their social and manipulative responses. Using a series of carefully standardized tests, Fuller and his colleagues studied these effects. A natural conclusion from these results would be that there is a sensitive period for the learning of the types of behavior in which the deprived dogs were deficient, and that the dog loses his capacity for the type of learning required after the sensitive period is over. However, Fuller found that, if puppies reared in isolation were given a tranquilizer, chlorpromazine, during their first test session, their behavior was much more normal. After three days the drug was withdrawn with no regression of behavior.

These observations indicate that the rich normal environment was not necessary for the gradual learning of the items of behavior in question, which probably were developing primarily by maturation, and/or were learned very quickly during the test sessions under drug. Thus, it was not the deprivation per se which did the lasting damage, but the sudden emergence elicited traumatic fears which were learned and which interfered with the performance (and/or very rapid learning) of behavior of which the animal was perfectly capable. The trauma was avoided by the temporary use of the tranquilizer at this crucial juncture.

The factors supposedly involved are summarized in Figure 6. In this case, the capacity for the desired behavior develops in spite of isolation, but as the animal matures his capacity to perceive the complexity and strangeness of the normal situation, so that traumatic fear is elicited by a sudden introduction to it, also begins to develop. These interfering tendencies develop at an increasing rate so that, after the critical period, they are dominant and prevent the normal behavior. When animals are reared in the normal situation, the gradual development of their ability to perceive its complexities prevents them from being overwhelmed by any sudden change.

Hinde (1955) and Moltz (1960) already have applied a similar type of analysis to another example of a "critical period," that for

---

[3] A somewhat similar role is played on the sensory side by innate mechanisms at various levels in the nervous system that process sensory information in ways which help to provide various stable cues related to selected attributes of stimulus objects (Miller, 1959, p. 251; Ratliff, 1961; Hubel and Wiesel, 1962).

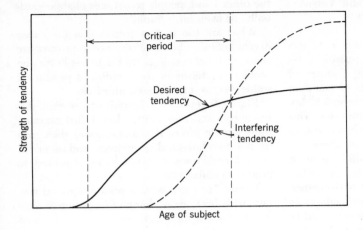

Figure 6. During the critical period the desired tendency is stronger than the interfering one, so that desired responses can be elicited and reinforced. Before the critical period, the desired tendencies have not matured; afterwards, they are inhibited by the interfering ones.

imprinting with certain birds. Hess (1957) found that chlorpromazine would prolong the critical period during which Mallard ducklings could be imprinted to follow a moving object. In this case the interfering tendency might be thought of as something like "fear of strangers" which becomes strong enough after a certain age to prevent the occurrence of following. It can be seen that a critical period may be explained by the acquisition of a habit, or maturation of an instinctual tendency, interfering with the learning or performance of the desired behavior, rather than by a loss of the capacity to learn or perform it, although the latter cannot be ruled out in all cases.

What I have just said should not be taken as a definitive answer to the problem of critical periods, but rather as an example of the type of experimental and theoretical analysis that is needed before we can understand the roles which such periods seem to play in certain types of personality change.

Various Other Bases for Importance of Early Experience. We have been discussing how maturational processes might contribute to critical periods, but there are other factors which also may contribute to the importance of early experience. As Dollard and I (1950) have emphasized, the human infant is unusually dependent and hence highly motivated for certain types of learning, and susceptible to severe traumas that are less likely to occur in later life. Thus it seems easier to acquire neuroses during certain periods of childhood, but when soldiers are subjected to similar extreme situations during combat, they acquire neuroses even though they are adult. Similarly, those trying to produce the drastic changes decribed as "brainwashing" take care to subject the victims to extreme conditions of dependency, helplessness, isolation, and other conditions that create strong motivations in many respects paralleling those occurring in infancy.

The same conditions that determine the earliest learning are likely to persist into later life. The kind of parents who allow an unusually traumatic experience to occur in early childhood may continue, for a considerable span of years, to reinforce maladaptive learning or to fail to reward certain adaptive habits. Thus the importance of the single dramatic incident may be overestimated. Indeed, in some cases the importance of earlier experiences may be overestimated because the infant does not yet possess the capacity to learn from them, and hence is not affected as much as an older child would be.

Society sets up an age-graded program for shaping many important kinds of social behavior. Once an individual gets far enough out of step, he may not be likely to encounter the types of shaping situations that will elicit and reward the missing habits. There is a need for special therapeutic training sequences to restore such individuals to their appropriate level.

Another quite different reason for the importance of early experience is that responses being learned then do not have to compete with habits already established by previous experience. This aspect of early experience leads us on to the discussion of conditions of unstable equilibrium.

Psychological Homeostasis—Stable Versus Unstable Equilibrium

Let us now consider some additional factors determining susceptibility to, or resistance to, change. One of the most striking features of the human personality is its ability to maintain what might be described as psychological homeostasis in the face of many vicissitudes. This capacity is especially impressive when one tries to perform experiments on fatigue, stress, or distraction. The experimental subjects often show great ability to compensate for rather extreme conditions, so that their performance is affected relatively little. And such effects as do occur are often in the form of sudden rather major breaks, which, however may be only momentary. Similar abilities to compensate, sometimes followed by sudden breaks, are observed in the natural social environment. On

the other hand, people sometimes change gradually, or even fairly rapidly.

What are the factors responsible for either psychological homeostasis or progressive change? I believe it is useful to rephrase the problem in terms of the conditions producing stable versus unstable equilibrium.

Figure 7 represents graphically several different dynamic possibilities. Let us first examine these simple physical analogies, and then turn to the psychological principles and environmental conditions that would be expected to produce similar effects.

Figure 7(a) is a weight on a horizontal surface with friction. A change in position is produced when a force acts; there are no marked discontinuities.

Figure 7(b) represents a ball on top of a dome in a situation of unstable equilibrium. A relatively small force in either direction will

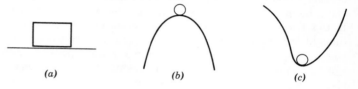

(a)   (b)   (c)

Figure 7. Graphic illustrations of different types of equilibrium discussed in the text.

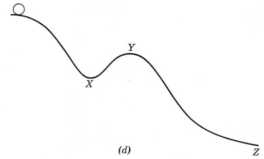

(d)

produce a relatively big effect which is difficult to reverse. The dynamics are analogous to those of positive feedback. We have this situation when two or more quite different weak responses are initially of approximately equal strength and each likely to be rewarded. Whichever one occurs will be strengthened, thus be more likely to occur again and be still further strengthened, so that a progressive change toward that response pattern continues to gain momentum and becomes increasingly difficult to reverse. In such cases, the conditions determining which response occurs first may be crucial. This may be the basis for the old

adage, "as the twig is bent, so the tree will grow." It is one of the reasons for the importance of early experience.

Figure 7(c) is representative of the situation of stable equilibrium—the further the ball is moved off center, the stronger the forces to return it toward center. We shall examine situations of this kind which tend to produce psychological homeostasis, or the equivalent of negative feedback. To the right we have illustrated the situation in which, once a certain amount of change is produced (i.e., getting the ball over the top), there is a sudden break. On the left side we have represented a situation with the dotted line in which there is a limit on lateral movement; the solid line illustrates a situation that has a point beyond which resistance decreases but does not stop.

In 7(d) we have represented the interesting situation in which a change started in a given direction is likely to be maintained for a distance, but then encounters a region of stable equilibrium—the valley at X—where the ball is likely to remain trapped. As we shall see, there are a number of conditions of this kind which tend to limit personality and social development.

Effects of Correlated Reinforcement. In the past, most experiments on learning have studied extremely simple relationships between response and reward. For example, a correct response is rewarded 100 per cent of the time with a fixed amount of reward and an incorrect response is never rewarded. Skinner (1938; Skinner and Ferster, 1957) and his students have made the valuable innovation of studying more complicated schedules of reinforcement and the effects of rewarding specific rates of response. Logan (1960) has extended this work with his program of investigating correlated reinforcement, a topic which is particularly relevant to problems of human personality development.

Under conditions of correlated reinforcement the amount, or the promptness, of reward depends on the speed, amplitude, or some other dimension of performance. It can readily be seen that the situation in which a particular type of behavior is maximally rewarded, and deviations from this optimum receive progressively less reward, will produce effects like those diagrammed in 7(c), if one thinks of the maximum rewards occurring at the lowest point in the U-shaped valley. The sharper the correlation (producing a V instead of a U), the more the variability should be reduced after thorough learning. This greatly reduced variability should also produce resistance to change, because different responses are unlikely to occur and thus cannot be learned, even when conditions have changed so that they might now be more strongly rewarded.

Logan's (1960) experimental results confirm the predictions of greatly reduced variability and also show that correlations of this kind can produce extreme resistance to extinction. The response is likely to remain almost exactly the same for many non-rewarded trials; when

change does finally occur, it comes as a sudden rather complete breakdown of performance. In short, we have seen how appropriate conditions of correlated reinforcement can produce the characteristics of stable equilibrium, or, in other words, psychological homeostasis.

To date only some of the simplest conditions of correlated reinforcement have been studied experimentally, but it is a relatively short step to deduce the effect of certain other patterns of reinforcement, and to test these deductions by experiment. I believe that the effects of certain discontinuities in correlated reinforcement have especially interesting implications for problems of personality change.

Let us consider a situation analogous to that represented in Figure 7(d). The greater amounts of reward should be thought of as occurring at lower levels on the ordinate of the diagram, so that the valley in which a ball would tend to be trapped represents a region of greater reward. It can be seen that, although the subject would receive greater rewards for changing his behavior further towards Z, he is likely to remain "trapped" at X because he has to pass through the zone of diminishing reward at Y in order to get to Z.

To take a simple example, a tennis player who has learned to hit the ball only with a good chop may have to go through a period of losing more points if he wants to practice and develop a good drive. Or a child, who has learned to get his way by highly developed skills of aggression on the playground, may be less rewarded if he changes and tries to be pleasant, because half-way aggression may not work, and he may not be very skillful at getting his way by being pleasant even though this might be more rewarding in the long run.

Often a worker promoted to foreman may lose the reward of equal association with his old friends before gaining the potentially greater rewards from his new position and thus have to go through a difficult period of readjustment analogous to the region Y in Figure 7 (d). Some workers recently promoted to foremen actually ask to be demoted and others do not work for, or even turn down, the opportunity to be promoted. During a transition period of social mobility a person's old friends may punish him for deserting them, while his new associates may resent his intrusion.

In dealing with the general problem of social mobility, yet other factors may contribute to the type of equilibrium we have been discussing. The parents who realize the American dream of giving their children better opportunities than they had, who send their children to a better school for more education and expect them to do better than they did, may suddenly discover that, as their children are moving up and ahead, they are also moving farther away. They want their children to change for the better, but are unhappy when they find them becoming different. Personality changes may frustrate others, conflict with their habits, including perceptual expectancies, and force them to learn new habits. Therefore one's associates may punish change and reward constancy. Even in psychotherapy, the spouse or family may not like the neurotic person's progress toward becoming more self-assertive, and may try to force him back into his former role. Similar factors opposing change sometimes appear when a talent-mobile man is married to a very young, pretty, but intellectually and socially limited, girl. As the man moves into new and more stimulating environments, his personality changes while the girl does not change, so that a formerly happy marriage becomes unhappy.

This brief discussion has been able to illustrate only a few of the factors which can oppose changes in the habits that constitute personality. A far more detailed theoretical and empirical analysis of the conditions producing stable equilibrium, and hence resistance to change, is needed and should be highly profitable.

Factors Favoring Unstable Equilibrium, and Hence Change. We have just been discussing factors favoring stable equilibrium, or resistance to change. But there are other factors which tend to produce positive feedback, unstable equilibrium and hence to facilitate change. For example, there is what might be called "the lucky spiral up." In the academic field which I know best, there is the bright, energetic student who has the good fortune to hit on a topic for a Ph.D. dissertation which comes out strikingly well and is timely. He is likely to get a position at a leading university which gives him a reasonable teaching load and good research space. It is easy for him to get a sizeable research grant which gives him the chance to do enough additional studies so that, with reasonable luck, he is on his way to becoming a productive well-known scholar, moving in a stimulating and supportive environment which

will favor continued success. As the saying goes: "Nothing succeeds like success."

The foregoing case may be contrasted with the student who has the bad luck to run into a string of unexpected difficulties on his dissertation. He may get a position at a poorer university with a heavier teaching load, fewer research opportunities, less chance to get a good research grant, and less stimulation to continue with research. Especially if his next problem should happen to turn out badly, it will be extremely difficult for him to get established. Now, I realize that a talented man is more likely to select a good problem, or to drop a bad one soon, but I also am impressed with the fact that the process of groping forward into the unknown inevitably involves a considerable element of chance.

I would theoretically expect the chance success or failure that has been described to have a general effect on the personality—with success generating optimism, confidence, pride, ambition, and other favorable social traits which will help to contribute to further success. Similarly, failure can lead to frustration, bitterness, insecurity, resignation, or a shift toward different goals in life. While other factors than professional success or failure certainly can play important roles in personality development, I believe that the role of success deserves considerable study and will be found to be a significant factor in cases in which the direction of causality can be determined clearly—for example, brothers settling on arid farms, but with one happening to contain oil.

Effects of Changing Social Groups

As the source of a great many of the rewards and punishments in life, the social group has a great effect on shaping personality. One could devote an entire lecture to the effects of culture, nationality, region, social class, and occupation. Thus, when an individual makes a radical change in his membership in any of these social groups, it is likely to produce eventually a considerable change in his personality. Considerable research has been done on the roles of such social factors, but much much more remains to be done. For example, there is considerable evidence that psychiatric disturbances are related to group factors, and that they are especially likely to occur in disorganized communities.[4] But the factors of cause and effect are difficult to disentangle in such cases; we need studies that are much more extensive, penetrating and analytical.

A Human Research Decade

Since it is impossible deliberately to set up conditions that will produce severe mental disorder in human subjects, and difficult to set up those that will produce other forms of drastic personality change, much of the research has to take advantage of natural experiments. The differences among the various cultures of the world are, therefore, an invaluable source of information about the effects of social conditions on human development. The study of the effects of large differences in the social conditions of these cultures affords a unique opportunity, not only to learn more about the basic principles involved in personality development and in mental disease but also to study medical and biological problems, such as the effects of diet on the cardiovascular system and of various environmental conditions on cancer.

Furthermore, the rapid changes that are occurring in such cultures with the explosive spread of western technology afford unusual opportunities to study the effects of changes in social conditions on personality. However, these opportunities are fleeting. The introduction of technology is homogenizing old cultures at an ever-increasing rate, and enormously reducing the range of differences in relevant variables. If the effects of these cultural differences, and the rapid changes in them, are not studied soon, it will be too late. A human research decade should be organized to take advantage of this unique opportunity before it is lost forever (Miller et al., 1962).

Copying and Cybernetic Behavior

Let us now turn to a theoretical formulation that is relevant to a number of topics—flexible cybernetic behavior, reactions to dissonance, self-images, and psychological homeostasis. We shall start with the original example of a subject learning to match a model by singing the same note (Miller and Dollard, 1941). The subject learns to make a relative response, tensing the vocal cords, to the cue of the direction of a difference, namely, too low a pitch. He stops correcting when the cue of the difference disappears. Had the term been coined then, this type of responding would have been called "cybernetic" (Weiner, 1948). As in a servo system, the behavior is controlled by feedback with stable equilibrium at the closest match.

Another simple example is reaching for a pencil. The subject learns to respond to the discrepancy of being too far to the left by the correction of moving to the right, and to make similar corrections for being too far to the right, and too high or too low. Thus he "homes in" on the pencil.

Making the plausible assumptions which, however, need additional experimental study, that there is a great deal of similarity between the cue of a given difference (such as being too far to the right) in many absolute contexts, and much similarity among the responses of moving more to the left from a variety of postures, it can be seen that it will be easy to generalize such a skill so that it produces a very flexible type of behavior. Thus this type of formulation is a solution to one of the fundamental dilemmas—namely, explaining the flexibility and goal orientation of behavior—that has plagued S-R theories since their inception.

Further steps in refining the skillful performance of cybernetic behavior are learning to respond to larger differences with larger corrections, and also learning to respond to a discrepancy with the arousal of a learned drive and to the reduction in a discrepancy with a learned reward. With this step, the subject automatically motivates himself to match, and rewards himself for closer matches. The relevance of this mechanism to goal-directed, learned drives has been discussed elsewhere (Miller, 1959; 1963).[5]

At the same time that the child is practicing his own crying responses, he is learning to respond to the voices of others. Adults who are feeding, fondling, and otherwise caring for infants usually

---

[4] Some of the studies on this topic are: Hollingshead and Redlich (1958); Leighton (1959); Myers and Roberts (1959); Sarason and Gladwin (1959); Srole et al. (1962).

[5] A somewhat similar mechanism was proposed by Miller and Dollard (1941, p. 68) for some of the unconscious copying involved in shaping the infant's first learning of speech, as follows:

talk to them; thus certain tones of the human voice acquire a reward value and may later be used to soothe the fretful child. It seems possible that this acquired reward value of the sounds in the language generalizes to sounds which the child makes while he is babbling and helps to reinforce the babbling behavior. . . .

It would be interesting to compare the babbling behavior of different children after an attempt had been made to give different phonemes a special acquired reward value. One child would be talked to with a certain phoneme while being fed and with a different but equally pronounceable phoneme while being dressed or having some other routine performed which seems to annoy him. A second child would be talked to with the first phoneme while being dressed and the second while being fed. The babbling behavior of the two children would then be compared. The prediction would be that the child would learn to babble with the phoneme which had been given an acquired reward value more than with the other.

Subsequently this hypothesis has been discussed by Mowrer (1950) at greater length, but he is wrong in concluding that our consideration of a second and additional mechanism means that we must have discarded the first one.

It is obvious that this type of analysis is in many respects similar to one later elaborated upon by Mowrer (1960a). But there are some important differences. First, it is not assumed that all responses are necessarily of this kind; allowances are made for rapid, ballistic responses that are not guided all the way to the goal by proprioceptive feedback (Miller, 1959)[6] Secondly, it is assumed that learning can connect a response (either peripheral movement or central image) to the cue of a specific discrepancy (or to other cues), while Mowrer assumes that learning modifies only the motivational values of cues. On the basis of his assumption, it is difficult to see how a response could be selected rapidly from among a large number of alternatives without many of them having to occur incipiently, so that they may be automatically rejected or selected according

---

[6] This conclusion would seem to be supported by the fact that workers in Konorski's laboratory (e.g., Gorska and Jankowska, 1960) have found that learned responses can be established in completely deafferented limbs, although it is possible that the motor neurons in the cortex that are responsible for these responses have connections, the firing of which can serve as cues so that a certain amount of central feedback may be involved.

to the motivation that has been conditioned to cues of feedback from them. It is obvious that this difficulty becomes progressively worse, when there are a larger number of alternatives—as in choosing the appropriate word out of the many thousands in the subject's vocabulary—or when the behavior must be extremely rapid as in making the correct finger movement in a fast cadenza on the piano. Mowrer (1960b, 286–288) is aware of this difficulty, but does not solve it.

Discrepancy and Dissonance. The idea that a difference can serve as a cue to arouse motivation obviously is relevant also to some of the phenomena which have been described recently as dissonance (Festinger, 1957). But again, there are important differences. While it is conceivable that some motivation may be produced innately by conflict, such as that between anticipatory goal responses and the responses elicited by the absence of the goal object (Miller and Stevenson, 1936; Miller, 1959), it is clear that the motivational reactions to many differences are learned. In the example of learning to match the pitch of a note sung by a model there does not seem to be any innate motivational value to the difference. The same is true of an individual's reactions to a discrepancy in balancing a checkbook.

To take somewhat more complex examples, whether we react with reward, aversion, or indifference to the dissonances of ultramodern music depends on our previous learning. As I have pointed out before (Dollard and Miller, 1950, p. 120; Miller, 1944, p. 457), children do not necessarily react with distress to logical inconsistencies, but after considerable social training, they may come to do so. Many forms of incompatibility are learned; I have speculated elsewhere about some of the mechanisms that could be involved (Miller, 1944; Dollard and Miller, 1950, p. 209).

I believe that it would be profitable to carry the brilliant analyses by some of the proponents of dissonance theory one step further by analyzing some of the different reactions of dissonance in terms of previous learning. In certain cases, this might help to get this type of theory out of the dilemma of being able to give a highly satisfying explanation of what has occurred, but often being able to explain equally easily also the exact opposite.

Reaction to Discrepancies and Psychological Homeostasis. Responding to the cue for a difference with motivation which is proportional to the size of that difference can be a very economical mechanism for supplying motivation only when it is needed (Miller, 1959). For example, a professor may have an approximate schedule of times to be at different places in driving to meet an eight o'clock class or to catch a plane. As long as he is on schedule, little motivation is apparent; we might think that the responses are being performed solely because they have been associated by contiguity. But if a series of unusual conditions in traffic puts him far behind schedule, he starts to respond to the increasing discrepancy between the time on his watch and the time of the schedule with increasingly obvious motivation, and he will attempt to drive faster or take alternate routes to get there on time. Responding to the cue of the difference provides an automatic mechanism for bringing in additional motivation, exactly when it is needed to keep the behavior on schedule. This might be described as a simple example of psychological homeostasis.

A similar mechanism may be involved in compensating for the effects of fatigue or distraction, and in overcoming other difficulties. With sufficient practice, of course, some of the motivation to pull ourselves together and compensate for difficulties can become attached to the cues of the difficulties encountered, so that we react before any signs of poorer performance are apparent.

The same mechanism, analogous to that outlined for copying, can apply to the matching of a variety of internal standards involving either images or verbal cue-producing responses. Thus, the student who has a "gentleman's C" as a standard for academic accomplishment may be expected to relax when his grades are above this, and to try harder when they fall too low. Other examples of what might be called ideals, self-images, or standards will readily occur to you—being able to take it like a man, being a gentleman, being honest, fair, or scientific. The definition of these standards and the attachment of motivational value to them, involves a great deal of social learning. Often the first step is to copy other individuals, and then to copy one's own concept of the standards. We have already pointed out how some of this copying can be unconscious (Miller and Dollard, 1941). What I want to emphasize here is that this cybernetic mechanism can play an important role in the phenomena of psychological homeostasis. With

strong motivation to maintain well-defined standards, the person resists changes that would otherwise be elicited by fluctuations in the environment, but if the standards change, the personality changes.

Some Problems of Equilibrium in Responding to Discrepancies. The foregoing type of analysis is obviously sketchy; many problems need more detailed investigation, such as the nature of the central images or verbalized principles involved, and the details of how the mechanism develops during socialization. An experimental program is needed to determine exactly the types of differences that can serve as cues, widely the responses to such differences will generalize, and the detailed laws of perceptual learning that may be involved. I believe that the study of such problems will be very fruitful.

Yet, other problems will suggest themselves. I have time to sketch only a few. Let us consider how the response might be expected to vary with the size of the discrepancy. At one limit, when the discrepancy is too small to be discriminated, there will be no response, as we have already pointed out. In many situations, a subject will have learned to make a larger response to large discrepancies. But will this tendency continue indefinitely? Are some discrepancies so large that they are not likely to be perceived as on the same continuum?

We would expect that the responses to increasingly larger discrepancies would depend on the way that such responses have been correlated with reinforcement under particular conditions of learning. As long as the subject has been more strongly rewarded (e.g., by escaping stronger punishments) for correcting larger discrepancies, we may expect him to try harder the further he is off, and hence show increasingly stronger resistance to more drastic changes. If he has never experienced discrepancies of the test magnitude, his reaction should depend upon principles of stimulus generalization, which have not yet been, but easily could be, experimentally studied with the direction of a difference as a cue. Will the relationship "the greater, the more" be extrapolated, at least for a distance, or will a gradient of stimulus-generalization decrement begin to be encountered with the first novel size of difference?

In some situations, the subject will have routinely experienced failures for trying to copy models that are too different, and may even have been specifically punished for being presumptuous. In yet other cases, there may be a sharp discontinuity in the conditions of reinforcement at a specific point, such as going bankrupt, being sent to prison, or committed to an institution. We might expect such conditions to favor increased struggle up to a certain point, and then a relatively sudden break as illustrated on the right-hand side of Figure 7(c). We need a great deal more theoretical and empirical analysis of such problems.

Unity and Disunity in Personality

Some aspects of social behavior and motivation are relatively easy to change; others are extremely resistant to change. In the latter case serious alterations often occur throughout the whole personality before the specific item in question will change. We need to know much more about what is responsible for such differences (Miller, 1951).

An attempt should be made to apply to this problem the principles that have already been studied as describing the persistence of simple habits under various schedules of reinforcement and strengths of motivation. The roles of stimulus (and response) generalization in producing unity should be investigated. The relationship of the particular item of behavior to various standards or models of the types we have just been discussing and the conditions of reinforcement for these standards should also be relevant. It can be seen that these standards, or certain general rules such as "honesty is the best policy" provide a basis for learned generalization (Dollard and Miller, 1950, p. 106).

The social conditions of learning are also important. The principle of stimulus generalization operating in other people tends to lead them to generalize with respect to the subject, so that they expect him to respond more consistently, or are frustrated by departures from their simplified stereotype of him, and exert a variety of pressures for conformity to this stereotype. Operating over generations, these forces toward consistency in individuals and cultures can snowball, especially under conditions where certain constellations function better than others, as so convincingly documented by Murdoch (1949). These constellations of interrelated cultural conditions tend to turn out individuals with certain types of personalities. In fact, people in certain social-class cliques all show remarkable similarities. To the extent that the social conditions are unified, the personality will be unified.

On the other hand, from a distance, it is easy to overestimate the similarities in a given culture or social class, and also to overestimate the unity of the different aspects of an individual personality. It is easy to make the error of the Chinese visitor, who says: "All you Americans look alike!" We should not overestimate the unity of personality.

Where patterns of reinforcement are different in different contexts, we will expect discriminations to be learned, so that behavior will be different in these contexts. For example, Asratyan (1961) has trained a dog in one room to salivate to a bell signaling food, and withdraw his paw to a light signaling shock; and in another room to do exactly the opposite, show the approach and salivary responses to the light and the defense reponses to the bell. Many analogous social conditions are encountered and produce analogous inconsistencies. The parents who teach the child always to tell the truth may be embarrassed when he does so in certain social situations and teach him to tell "white lies." Thus, it is not surprising that Hartshorne and May's (1928) classical studies showed that honesty is not a unitary personality trait.

Similarly, the student who shows the most courage on the football field may not be the most courageous when asked to make a short speech before a large group. Children may behave differently at home or when visiting a friend's home. The person who displays such a gracious and cooperative personality to the big boss may display quite a different personality to his subordinates. Generally kind people can be cruel in certain situations, and vicious criminals can be kind to a child, so that as Gilbert and Sullivan have said: "A policeman's lot is not a happy one."

Membership in groups which reward different patterns of behavior should be especially likely to produce disunity of personality, and in fact, it appears to do so. In some cases this disunity produces conflicts, but in other cases the individual does not seem to sense any incompatibility. Has the latter person merely learned to discriminate different contexts? We need a great deal more research on the social conditions and psychological principles of learning that produce unity or disunity in the personality and that cause people either to compartmentalize effectively or to display conflict over "incompatible" personality traits.

REFERENCES

Asratyan, E. A. The initiation and localization of cortical inhibition in the conditioned reflex arc. *Ann. N. Y. Acad. Sci.*, 1961, **92**, 1141–1159.

Dollard, J. & Miller, N. E. *Personality and psychotherapy*. New York: McGraw-Hill, 1950.

Festinger, L. *A theory of cognitive dissonance*. Stanford, Calif.: Stanford University Press, 1957.

Fuller, J. Personal communication, 1962.

Gorska, T., & Jankowska, E. The effect of differentiation on the instrumental conditioned reflexes established in dogs by reinforcing passive movements. *Bulletin de L'Academie Polonaise des Sciences*, CI. II. 1960, **8**.

Hartshorne, H., & May, M. A. *Studies in deceit*, Book I in *Studies in the nature of character*. New York: Macmillan, 1928.

Hess, E. H. Effects of meprobamate on imprinting in waterfowl. *Ann. N. Y. Acad. Sci.*, 1957, **67**, 724–732.

Hinde, R. A. The modifiability of instinctive behavior. *Advanc. Sci. Lond.*, 1955, **12**, 19–24.

Hollingshead, A. B., & Redlich, F. C. *Social class and mental illness*. New York: Wiley, 1958.

Hubel, D. H., & Wiesel, T. N. Receptive fields, binocular interaction and functional architecture in the cat's visual cortex. *J. Physiol.*, 1962, **160**, 106–154.

Leighton, A. H. *My name is legion*. New York: Basic Books, 1959.

Logan, F. A. *Incentive*. New Haven: Yale University Press, 1960.

Miller, N. E. Experimental studies of conflict behavior. In J. McV. Hunt (Ed.), Personality and behavior disorders. New York: Ronald, 1944. Pp. 431–465.

Miller, N. E. Learnable drives and rewards. In S. Stevens (Ed.), *Handbook of experimental psychology*. New York: Wiley, 1951. Pp. 435–472.

Miller, N. E. Liberalization of basic S-R concepts: Extensions to conflict behavior, motivation, and social learning. In S. Koch (Ed.), Vol. 2. *Psychology: A study of a science*. New York: McGraw-Hill, 1959. Pp. 196–292.

Miller, N. E. Learning resistance to pain and fear: Effects of overlearning, exposure, and rewarded exposure in context. *J. exp. Psychol.*, 1960, **60**, 137–145.

Miller, N. E. Some recent studies of conflict behavior and drugs. *Amer. Psychologist*, 1961, **16**, 12–24.

Miller, N. E. Some reflections on the law of effect produce a new alternative to drive reduction. In M. R. Jones (Ed.), *Nebraska symposium on motivation*. Lincoln, Neb.: University of Nebraska Press, 1963. Pp. 65–112.

Miller, N. E., & Barry, H. Motivational effects of drugs: Methods which illustrate some general problems in psychopharmacology. *Psychopharmacologia*, 1960, **1**, 169–199.

Miller, N. E., & Dollard, J. *Social learning and imitation*. New Haven: Yale University Press, 1941.

Miller, N. E. et al. Strengthening the behavioral sciences, Statement by the Behavioral Sciences Subpanel of the Life Sciences Panel, President's Science Advisory Committee, The White House, Washington, D. C. *Science*, 1962, **136**, 233–241.

Miller, N. E., & Stevenson, S. S. Agitated behavior of rats during experimental extinction and a curve of spontaneous recovery. *J. comp. Psychol.*, 1936, **21**, 205–231.

Moltz, H. Imprinting: Empirical basis and theoretical significance. *Psychol. Bull.*, 1960, **57**, 291–314.

Mowrer, O. H. *Learning theory and personality dynamics*. New York: Ronald Press Co., 1950.

Mowrer, O. H. Neurosis, psychotherapy, and two-factor learning theory. In O. H. Mowrer (Ed.), *Psychotherapy: Theory and research*. New York: Ronald, 1953. (a)

Mowrer, O. H. *Psychotherapy: Theory and research*. New York: Ronald, 1953. (b)

Mowrer, O. H. *Learning theory and behavior*. New York: Wiley, 1960. (a)

Mowrer, O. H. *Learning theory and the symbolic processes*. New York: Wiley, 1960. (b)

Murdock, G. P. *Social structure*. New York: Macmillan, 1949.

Myers, J. K., & Roberts, B. H. *Family and class dynamics in mental illness*. New York: Wiley, 1959.

Pavlov, I. P. *Experimental psychology and other essays*. New York: Philosophical Library, 1957.

Ratliff, F. Inhibitory interaction and the detection and enhancement of contours. In W. A. Rosenblith (Ed.), *Sensory communication*. New York: Wiley, 1961. Pp. 183–203.

Sarason, S. B., & Gladwin, T. *Psychological problems in mental deficiency: Part II*. New York: Harper & Bros., 1959.

Skinner, B. F. *The behavior of organisms*. New York: Appleton-Century, 1938.

Skinner, B. F., & Ferster, C. B. *Schedules of reinforcement*. New York: Appleton-Century-Crofts, 1957.

Srole, L., et al. *Mental health in the metropolis: Midtown Manhattan study*. New York: McGraw-Hall, 1962.

Wiener, N. *Cybernetics*. New York: Wiley, 1948.

Wolpe, J. *Psychotherapy by reciprocal inhibition*. Stanford, Calif.: Stanford University Press, 1958.

2.   A framework for the study of personality as a behavioral science

I. E. FARBER

ALMOST HALF A CENTURY AGO, Watson (1919) had, among other things, this to say about personality:

> Let us mean by the term personality an individual's total assets (actual and potential) and liabilities (actual and potential) on the reaction side. By assets we mean first the total mass of organized habits; the socialized and regulated instincts; the socialized and tempered emotions; and the combinations and interrelations among these; and secondly, high coefficients both of plasticity (capability of new habit formation or altering of old) and of retention (readiness of implanted habits to function after disuse). Looked at in another way, assets are that part of the individual's equipment which make for his adjustment and balance in his present environment and for readjustment if the environment changes.
>
> By liabilities we mean similarly that part of the individual's equipment which does not work in the present environment and the potential or possible factors which would prevent his rising to meet a changed environment (p. 397).

And, again:

> During the whole process of human development from infancy to old age, . . . there goes on not only the process of acquisition of habit and the modification of hereditary reaction but also and equally important that of the elimina-

tion of reaction systems which work only up to a certain age. Old situations give way to new and as the situation changes old ways of reacting should be cast off and new ones formed (p. 415).

In my opinion the point of view expressed in these passages is neither tendentious nor antiquated. Among other things, it emphasizes the importance of two aspects of the study of personality: personality as product or structure, the state at any given moment of the ceaseless stream of processes and activities that constitute behavior; and personality as process, change, development. Personality can be fully understood in its cross-sectional aspects only if we know the nature of the events and circumstances of which it is the result, and in its developmental aspects, only if we know the particular behaviors or processes that are modified.

But this view does more than assert the importance of specifying the nature both of reaction systems and their modulators. It treats the probability or degree of susceptibility of the various systems to change in particular ways and degrees under given conditions as fundamental descriptive characteristics of personality. Insofar as personality is described in these terms, it may be unnecessary and even misleading to distinguish between the concept of personality and that of personality change.

The foregoing portrayal of personality differs from others, of course, as other current approaches differ among themselves, in respect to the conceptualizations of the systems or processes that are subject to change, and of the dimensions whereby change may be described. At the same time, divested of metaphysical implications and of commitment to any particular hypotheses concerning the determinants of

SOURCE. Selection by I. E. Farber, "A framework for the study of personality as a behavioral science" in *Personality Change*, pp. 3–5, 20–37. Edited by P. Worchel and D. Byrne. New York: Wiley, 1964.

Work on this paper was supported by a PHS research grant, M-2296, from the National Institute of Mental Health, Public Health Service.

behavior, this formulation appears quite consonant with a good many others frequently characterized as "dynamic," in at least one sense of this much-abused term. With this salute to good company, one may classify it a little more definitely, because of its evident concern with behavior and the learning process, as a behavior- or learning-theoretical view. Though I should be comfortable with these designations, the label "behavioral science" or "behavioral approach" may be preferred by those who consider the adjective "theoretical" gratuitous. None of these terms is altogether unobjectionable, but insofar as they refer to attempts at systematic formulations of the determinants of the acquisition, maintenance, and elimination of particular kinds of behavior or behavior tendencies, they will serve to identify the perspective of the present paper.

Theories of Behavior Versus Theories of Personality

Whether any behavior system or theory can be at once comprehensive enough and detailed enough to encompass the mysteries of personality and personality change is still an open question. One reason why some psychologists are skeptical is that such formulations do not seem to refer at all to a special class of concepts or phenomena called "personality," but rather to behavior in general, or to predispositions inferred from behavior in general. I believe this observation to be quite accurate. Behavior theorists ordinarily do not distinguish between the task of explaining or predicting personality and that of explaining or predicting behavior. To be sure, in discussing personality they are likely to stress certain processes or concepts such as learning and motivation, but this is characteristic of their general approach to psychology. In their typical view, the study of personality is essentially coterminous with the study of behavior.

I must confess to a certain puzzlement concerning some other views of personality, especially in regard to the distinctions between those behaviors or processes that are supposed to comprise or reflect personality and those that are not. Statements such as "Personality is what a man really is" are simply not helpful, since any kind of behavior or hypothetical variable that might reasonably be used to account for

behavior, e.g., habit, libido, press, or positive self-regard, seems equally realistic. Nor does the following amplification seem more satisfying: "Personality is the dynamic organization within the individual of those psychophysical systems that determine his unique adjustments to his environment" (Allport, 1937, p. 48). Except for the term "unique," which is better calculated to reassure people than enlighten them (cf. Eysenck, 1952; Meehl, 1954), this statement does not appear to exclude from consideration any aspect of behavior or a single variable of which behavior in general may be considered a function. Indeed, at the risk of offending both sides, one might point out that the two definitions, the one by Watson and the other by Allport, seem more remarkable for their similarities than their differences.

Still, discussions of personality do not, as a rule, cover every aspect of behavior, though some, even of a non-behavioral sort (e.g., Murphy, 1947), come close. Most frequently, as Hall and Lindzey (1957) observe in their excellent text, they concentrate on motivational variables, i.e., those used to account for the apparently purposive, striving, goal-directed aspects of behavior. Thus, performance on an intelligence test may not be regarded as an index of personality unless there is reason to suppose it is affected by such variables as boredom, achievement needs, anxiety, or hostility toward the tester. Since any kind of behavior, including that involved in taking an intelligence test, running the hundred-yard dash, or whatever, might conceivably be affected by such variables, there seems no clear basis for excluding any kind of behavior from consideration.

I would maintain, therefore, that any relatively comprehensive theory of behavior, especially if it includes variables of a motivational sort, qualifies as a theory of personality. The relative adequacy of the various behavioral approaches in accounting for the complexities of human behavior is, of course, another question.

Now, nothing is more certain than the fact that relations found in such simple instances will sometimes, perhaps usually, fail to hold in more complex instances. No one would deny that changes in the combinations of variables may affect behavior. But unless one has fairly precise notions about the conditions under which a given kind of behavior occurs, it seems exceedingly unlikely that one can decide with any certainty what particular aspects of different or more complex conditions are responsible for a change in that behavior.

Generalizing from the Laboratory to Real Life. Those who argue that the observation of behavior under the artificial and highly controlled conditions of the laboratory has no predictive value for behavior under "real life" conditions sometimes appear to fail to understand the necessity for doing more than simply pointing to the change. What we wish to know is the nature of the variables of which that change is a function. In any event, there is universal agreement on one point: before one generalizes from observations of behavior in the laboratory to real-life situations, one had better consider very carefully the differences between the laboratory conditions and those in real life.

In the light of this recognition of the necessity for considering the variables involved, it is puzzling why anyone who objects to generalizations from laboratory findings should consider it safe to generalize from behavior in one complex, uncontrolled situation to behavior in another. Obviously, circumstances change from one uncontrolled situation to another. When one does not know what variables have changed, generalizations from one real-life situation to another are at least as uncertain as those from controlled situations to real-life situations. An added disadvantage lies in the relatively greater difficulty of disentangling the particular variables that have changed. This is not easy, whether one deals with either controlled or uncontrolled conditions, but under any circumstances the lack of control or information concerning the effects of specific variables can hardly be regarded as a positive aid to understanding and prediction.

Generalizing from Animals to People. In view of the well-known differences between rats, which are non-social and non-verbal, and human beings, who are exceedingly social and verbal, it is not surprising to find a good deal of skepticism concerning the applicability of rat laws to human behavior. Occasionally, there is an autistic element in such criticisms. Some people consider it degrading to be compared with rats, just as some consider it insulting to be compared with infants, as in psychoanalytic theory. But most criticisms of this sort are based on the objective fact that rats and people differ in many and possibly crucial respects. Koch (1956) has expressed in eloquent detail his dis-

belief in the probability of generating the essential laws of human behavior from rat data. He points out that one may not even be able to generate decent laws concerning rats by observing rats, especially if they inhabit different laboratories.

In regard to the latter observation, that one cannot generalize from rats to rats without risk, one can only agree that animal experimenters ought perhaps to describe their experimental conditions more adequately, or to try harder to discover those conditions whose variation is responsible for the reported inconsistencies. I do not believe animal psychologists are generally regarded as unusually deficient in their specification of the variables they know about or in their zeal to discover the ones they do not know about. But perhaps they ought to be doing a more careful job. It is important to note that this calls for more analytic precision, not less.

In regard to the former observation, that one cannot generalize from rats to human beings, it seems fair to repeat that frequently one also cannot generalize from human beings to human beings. Koch (1956) for instance, in describing his own "B states," i.e., his experiences while deeply engrossed in work, maintains that despite the importance of such states, despite their exemplification of behavior in its most organized, energized, and motivated form, current psychological theories are inadequate to the recognition of such states, let alone their explanation. "Subtle and organized descriptive phenomenologies of B states are badly needed by science—but not from individuals whose B-state products are 'creative' only by extravagant metaphor" (p. 68). Whatever one thinks of this pronouncement, it is certain that B-states cannot be observed in rats, and unlikely that they could be even partially accounted for in terms of principles based on rat behavior. But, as Koch himself suggests in the foregoing quotation, it would be rash to suppose that all human beings share these experiences. And in view of the restriction imposed, even among those who might have such experiences, very few could claim the privilege of attempting to communicate them. This is not to say that B-states do not exist, nor that they are unimportant. It does suggest the uncertainties of attempting to generalize from what may be discovered about Koch's B-states to the experiential states of people whose phenomenological descriptions may be limited to a phrase such as "Man, it's the most!" There is grave risk in generalizing from both rats and human beings when important variables differ.

Despite these cautionary notes, I think it possible to point to some instances of successful generalizations from animal as well as other human behavior, i.e., to hypotheses that have turned out to be fruitful. Instead, I should like to tell of an "Aha!" experience I recently had while listening to Frank A. Logan describe some of his animal experiments at Yale, in which delay of reward was balanced against amount of reward in simple choice situations. The experimental results showed that, within limits, rats will choose a longer delay, if the reward is large enough, in preference to shorter delays with lesser rewards. Probably because of obtuseness, it had never before occurred to me in quite the same way that the morality of human beings in giving up the pleasures of this world for the sake of eternal salvation may have something in common with the morality of rats in giving up an immediate reinforcement for the sake of a bigger piece of Purina dog chow. Now, this is undoubtedly a specious analogy at best. It ignores the many disanalogies in the two instances, and may be utterly foolish. But until this has been demonstrated, it suggests some, not by any means all, of the variables of which even sublime sentiments may be a function. Of course, it goes without saying that no matter how intriguing this notion may appear in the context of discovery, it must make its scientific way in the context of justification.

The distaste of some psychologists for animal studies frequently extends to conditioning studies as well, in part because the conditioned reflex appears characteristic of subhuman or subnormal behavior. Again, we might attempt to show how the laws of conditioning have been used as a basis for predicting some relatively complex human activities, such as verbal learning. Instead, we can point to a curious inconsistency in our treatments of such concepts. According to the earlier Gestalt psychologists, insight, or perception of relations, is also a primitive process, altogether characteristic of animals. Yet we seldom hear the argument that this concept is, therefore, useless for the understanding of human behavior. Unfortunately, judgments of what is scientifically useful are all-too-frequently confounded with judgments of what is good or bad. Thus, the successful

efforts of Communists to modify beliefs and actions are likely to be attributed to the use of Pavlovian conditioning techniques, which work only if men are reduced to the level of witless automatons (cf. Farber, Harlow, and West, 1957); our own successful efforts, on the other hand, are likely to be attributed to methods engaging the higher mental processes. It seems just possible, does it not, that many of the same determinants may be operative in both instances?

Proponents of a behavioral approach are likely to answer this question affirmatively because, for the most part, they distrust the doctrines of emergentism. While the variables influencing animal behavior are certainly different and less complex than those influencing human behavior, most behavioral scientists, nevertheless, prefer to look for continuity in the explanatory principles involved. Similarly, they look for continuity between the laws of child and adult behavior, between social and nonsocial behavior, and between normal and abnormal behavior. Whether this sort of search is useful may be open to question. At this stage of the game there appears to be no way of deciding this to everyone's satisfaction.

General Laws and the Individual Case. The foregoing discussion has dwelt on two apparently contradictory principles. The one stresses the necessity for caution in generalizing from one circumstance to another, in the face of inevitable changes in the variables represented. The second holds to the optimistic belief that generalization is frequently possible, even in the face of changes in some of the variables affecting behavior. Behavioral scientists, like others, differ in their relative emphases on these two principles, depending in part on the relative strengths of their empiricist or theoretical predilections; but they are likely to agree that the question whether one can successfully predict from one context to another can be answered only by empirical test.

Some personality theorists, however, appear to consider this a methodological rather than an empirical issue. They may deny, for instance, even the possibility of applying general laws to the prediction of individual behavior. Since, they argue, the variables influencing a given individual's behavior are not exactly duplicated for any other person, and since these variables interact in complicated ways, it is simply not possible to predict anything about one person from laws based on the observation of others. Since each individual is unique, the only legitimate predictions concerning any given person must be based on what is known about that person. Curiously enough this reasoning is ordinarily not extended to the intra-individual case. If it were, we would have to deny the possibility of predicting an individual's behavior even on the basis of what is known about that person, since the variables influencing his behavior at one time can never be exactly duplicated at any other time. At the very least, the ordinal positions of the two occasions differ.

Most behavioral scientists believe that general laws can be reasonably and usefully applied to individuals (Eysenck, 1952; Meehl, 1954). At the same time, they can readily agree that predictions about a given individual will frequently be more precise if they are based on the observation of his own past behavior. Perhaps the main reason for this is that many of the important determinants of his past behavior are likely to persist as determinants of his future behavior. Individuals carry such determinants around with them, so to speak, in the form of their inherited and learned predispositions. Nevertheless, if there is reason to suppose that present conditions are quite different from those in the individual's past, predictions are likely to be more successful if they are based on the behavior of others for whom we know these conditions have obtained. It is gratuitous to say so, but this merely means it may be more useful, in predicting the effects of aging on a given person, to look at old people than at that person at age two; or it may be more useful, in predicting the effects of a certain drug on a person's behavior, to observe other people drunk than that person sober. Of course, the more nearly alike the reference group and the individual in question, the more accurate the prediction. This simply means that the probability of successful prediction from one instance to another is some positive function of the communality of their behavioral determinants (cf. Meehl, 1954).

We should note that this formulation of the issue does not dispose of the empirical question whether general laws can at present be usefully applied to a particular individual in any given instance. The hard job of ascertaining just what the important variables are in any given context, and when a change in one variable changes the significance of another, must still be done.

We may hypothesize to our hearts' content about such matters. But we should not mistake the hypothesis, no matter how firmly held, for empirical proof.

Personality Variables and Behavioral Laws

The preceding section has barely touched on the exceedingly complicated problem of general versus individual prediction. One aspect of this problem relates to the interaction between situational or environmental variables and individual differences variables. Early in this discussion it was stated that behavioral scientists ordinarily find no clear-cut basis for distinguishing between the study of personality and the study of behavior in general. What view does this imply concerning the role of individual differences, especially those customarily classified under the heading of personality? According to many personality theorists, the existence of individual differences constitutes the most significant datum of psychology, yet the general psychologist persists in regarding them as mere annoyances, sources of error variance, to be eliminated or disregarded.

It is a matter of historical fact that, traditionally, experimental psychologists have been primarily interested in variables whose main effects or interactions are more or less independent of the kinds of subconditions known as individual differences. They have never denied the existence or even the importance of individual differences. After all, the classical Structuralists did not restrict their investigations to normal, adult, human observers because they supposed the observations would be unaffected by such variables as psychopathology, age, or species membership. They simply were not interested in the interactive effects of such variables. Many experimental psychologists still are not very interested in these kinds of variables, though this picture has been changing somewhat.

Many personality theorists, on the other hand, are frequently interested only in the kinds of variables that do interact with individual differences. They, in turn, do not usually deny that there may be important situational variables whose main effects override individual differences of one sort or another, but they are simply not so interested in them. We may find intransigents in both camps who absolutely deny the importance of any kinds of variables except the ones they happen to be interested in, but such persons are fortunately not numerous.

Environmental Events, Intervening Variables, and the Individual. Psychologists who deplore the traditional emphasis by experimental psychologists on manipulable environmental variables, to the denigration, as they suppose, of the role of the behaving organism, frequently state their position in a characteristic way, by pointing to the necessity for considering not only the external event, but also its meaning to the individual, or how the individual perceives it.

In a commonsensical way, there is no doubt they are correct. If a physicalistically defined stimulus is presented to an organism, our estimate of the probability of a given response is always contingent on certain assumptions, usually implicit, concerning some characteristics of that organism, e.g., adequate sensory and motor equipment, a relatively intact nervous system, and so on. Woodworth's well-known suggestion that the S-R formula ought to be modified to read "S-O-R" was designed to take account of such contributions by the organism to its own behavior, though he undoubtedly intended the "O" to include more than physiological structures and processes.

Behavioral scientists differ, as we have noted, in their estimates of the usefulness of attributing to organisms such hypothetical, non-observable characteristics as habits, intentions, cognitions, etc. Though all would agree with Skinner that one must beware of the dangers of hypostatization and reification, many are convinced that empiricism is quite compatible with the use of abstract concepts and theories. The construction of intervening variables, for instance, represents one sort of attempt by behavior theorists to delineate the kinds of organismic characteristics that might be useful in accounting for behavior (cf. Spence, 1952). Thus, intervening variables are inferred characteristics of organisms, calculated, among other things, to explain why different individuals, or the same individual at different times, may sometimes behave differently under the same environmental conditions, and sometimes similarly under different environmental conditions. This portrayal may remind some of Allport's definition of a trait as a "neuropsychic system . . . with the capacity to render many stimuli functionally equivalent, and to initiate and guide consistent (equivalent) forms of . . . behavior"

(1937, p. 295). According to a behavioral view, of course, the usefulness of the concept of a trait, as of that of any other intervening variable, is not assured by the simple expedient of tacking on a reference to unspecified neuropsychic events.

In light of the foregoing analysis, it might be startling, but not altogether beside the mark, to maintain that a theory such as Hull's is the exemplar of personality theories, on the assumption that some of his intervening variables, or some of the constants defining their growth or decline, differ from person to person in a relatively consistent way. One may not like the particular intervening variables Hull has proposed, because they may not appear to bridge the gap between stimulus and response in a satisfactory manner, or because there is reason to suppose that different characteristics or classifications of characteristics would do a better job. It is apparent to everyone, including those who have been influenced by Hull, that more precise and comprehensive conceptualizations are needed to account for behavior. It is simply suggested that the construction of such systems will, as a matter of course, increase our understanding of the individual.

In brief, whatever their particular nature and interrelations, the states and processes conceptualized as intervening variables are indisputably the properties of the individuals from whose behavior they are inferred. Of course, abstract properties do not literally occupy a place in space, but this does not imply that such concepts as drive level, self-regard, or cathexes are not attributes of "real" flesh-and-blood people (cf. Bergmann, 1953).

Despite this happy unanimity of concern for the nature of the behaving organism, it does not necessarily follow that stimuli ought to be *defined* in terms of their meaning to the organism. Rather, the meaning itself must be accounted for in terms of objective factors in the past and present states of the organism and its environment (cf. Bergmann, 1943). From a behavioral standpoint, meanings are certainly important, and conceptualized as mediating processes, play a prominent role in current theoretical formulations. Thus, it is useful, in a variety of situations, to suppose that external events elicit some sort of implicit response whose stimulus components in one way or another modify the overt response to the external event. Familiar examples of such mediating processes are the fractional anticipatory goal response (r_g-s_g), emotional states (r_e-s_e), and anticipatory frustration (r_F-s_F) discussed by such theorists as Spence (e.g., 1956) and Amsel (e.g., 1962).

Another sort of mediating mechanism is the one discussed by Kendler and Kendler (1962), among others, representing a symbolic response to external cues. This implicit response and its accompanying stimulus components can be used to explain a wide variety of phenomena, including, as we have noted, stimulus equivalence and distinctiveness. Since the hypothetical implicit stimulus may serve to explain why ostensibly different environmental events may elicit the same response, and apparently similar environmental events may lead to different responses, one may be tempted to regard the "real" stimulus as consisting of both the external event *and* its accompanying mediator, or even to consider the external event inconsequential, the only relevant factor being the nature of the mediational process, i.e., the "meaning" of the external event. I must leave the question of what can reasonably be meant by "reality" to those more competent to discuss the philosophical issues, but it seems to me that if one insists that stimuli be defined in terms of one sort of inferred process, i.e., symbolic mediation, one could with equal justification insist that they be defined in terms of any or all the others, e.g., motives, expectancies, inhibitory states, and so on. This sort of equating of observable events with inferred events, i.e., intervening variables, seems a dubious basis for clarifying theoretical problems.

Although I believe it necessary to distinguish between stimuli as observables and inferred characteristics of the organism as non-observables, it seems reasonable to consider behavior as the invariable function of both. If we think the stimulus is unimportant, we might try substituting a very different stimulus, to see whether the response does not change; and if we think the organism is unimportant, let us substitute a bag of potatoes in place of the usual psychological subject (Bergmann, 1951).

To say that every response is a function of both stimulus conditions and the organism is to say it is not possible to attribute any behavior exclusively to either the one or the other. There is something puzzling, for instance, about the supposition that the effects of length of a word list or the degree of similarity of the items in the list are attributable to extraorganismic factors, whereas the arousal of disgust by the same items is due to an intraorganismic factor. Why should variations in motivation or inhibitory tendency due to massing of practice be considered the result of extraorganismic variables exclusively, but variations in the same states due to anticipation of failure because of the same antecedents be considered the result of intraorganismic variables exclusively?

A case in point is Gill's (1959) recent classification of ego-functions, including perception, thought, memory, and concept formation as intrapsychic, but interpersonal and social factors as extraorganismic. We wonder how interpersonal and social factors are to have any effect on the organism independently of the processes of perception, thought, and memory. Perhaps all that is meant in this instance is that environmental events and hypothetical organismic processes or states can, and ought to be, independently defined. If so, this and similar formulations are in good accord with the behavior theoretical view that stimuli ought not be defined in terms of "what they mean" to the individual.

A consideration of the historical roots of the widespread tendency to classify behaviors according to inner or outer determinants would take us far afield. It may be of interest, however, to observe that one historical basis for this dichotomy appears to be the conventional distinction between associative and non-associative determinants of behavior. In the old days of classical associationism, ideas were endowed with their own adhesive qualities. They came together, stuck, or were separated in accordance with certain principles; but though their locus was presumably somewhere inside the organism, the power of association resided, not in the organism, but rather, in some sense, in the ideas themselves. Some psychologists may suppose that behavior theorists, particularly since they typically use an S-R terminology, still conceive of the association between environmental events and behavior according to this old associationistic formula. It must be admitted that they often speak as though associative strength is a characteristic of stimuli. But this is merely a verbal shorthand, perhaps an unfortunate one, if it is so liable to misunderstanding. Let it be noted that it is the organism, not the stimulus impinging on his receptors that does the associating. The term $_sH_R$ refers to an intraorganismic process, just as much as do the terms relating to motivation or emotion.

After all this, it may be salutary to recall the reservations held by behavioral scientists, in common with Skinner, respecting explanations of behavior in terms of inferred characteristics of the organism. Such inferences must be made on the basis of observations that are independent of the particular instance of behavior the characteristic is supposed to explain. There is no use saying a person runs away because he is afraid, if the fear is inferred wholly from his running away. If we observe that a given person habitually behaves in an inconsiderate, selfish, and malicious way, whereas in the same situations another habitually behaves in a kind and considerate way, it may be useful to characterize these behaviors, or for that matter, the persons, as respectively "mean" and "generous." But saying that these people behave in their respective ways *because* the one is mean and the other generous is to appeal to the kind of empty explanatory fiction Skinner and many others warn against. When we know the objectives conditions under which a given behavior or behavioral characteristic occurs, we can explain any relevant behavior in terms of those conditions. We need not appeal to some hypothetical characteristic to which they supposedly give rise. This caveat applies as well to intervening variables. If they do no more than account for the particular behavior from which they are adduced, they are fatuous.

Traditionally, the kinds of objective conditions to which behavior theorists have given most attention have been temporally antecedent events, i.e., they have relied more on historical than on ahistorical laws. This does not imply that anyone supposes that the variables affecting behavior can be anything but contemporaneous. Events in the past history of organisms can influence current behavior only insofar as they are represented in their current traces. Anyone who thinks otherwise believes in ghosts. Historical laws are used, *faute de mieux*, in the absence either of satisfactory measures of these traces that are independent of the observable behaviors they occasion, or of techniques for manipulating them directly.

This strategy involves no basic theoretical issue. Thus, behavioral scientists fully appreciate the current advances in our understanding of the physiological processes and anatomical structures mediating behavior, recognizing that this knowledge is indispensible to the bridging of the gap between past events and current behavior. From their view, the import of the breakthrough in physiological psychology lies precisely in its departure from the dismal tradition of inferring physiological processes solely on the basis of the behaviors they are intended to explain. It is the definitional independence of the variables in a law that is important, not their reference to historical rather than ahistorical events.

Response-Defined Concepts. Behavioral scientists differ, as we have indicated, in their evaluation of the usefulness of attempts to explain behavior in terms of hypothetical states or processes of the organism. And they are particularly skeptical when the inferred characteristic are defined in terms of behavior rather than environmental conditions. Even apart from the dangers referred to, the difficulties in attempting to decide on the basis of behavior alone whether variations in a given performance are more probably due to variations in one class of hypothetical determinants than another are formidable (vid., Brown and Farber, 1951). Everyone, so far as I know, takes it for granted that every kind of behavior is multiply determined, and that the determinants may interact. To use an obvious example, at any given moment two people may perform in the same way because one has high drive and low habit strength and the other high habit strength and weak drive. It is not easy to devise techniques that permit the disentangling of these different strands.

A related difficulty to which experimentalists are likely to point is the fact that many behavioral measures may be intrinsically interrelated. For instance, to use only one of innumerable possible examples, it is known that the correlation between Manifest Anxiety Scale scores and those on the psychasthenia (Pt) scale of the MMPI is about $+.70$ to $+.80$ for college sophomores, even after the common items are removed. Pt scores are sometimes considered a measure of emotional expressiveness, as contrasted with repressiveness. The correlation of the MAS scores with the K-Scale of the MMPI is frequently found to be about $-.70$. K is supposedly a measure of defensiveness. And Edwards (1957) reports a correlation of $-.84$ between the MAS and his Social Desirability Scale, which is supposed to measure strength of desire to make a good impression. In the face of these impressive relations, how can one say whether the MAS measures drive level, emotional expressiveness, lack of defensiveness, or disinterest in making a good impression, or any, or all of these? And what about all the other tests, present and future, whose relations with the MAS, though not yet computed, will undoubtedly reach comparable orders of magnitude? What, then, does the test measure?

In one sense, this is a trivial question, and requires but a trivial answer, though, unfortunately, one that constructors and users of tests sometimes fail to see, namely, that giving tests different names does not guarantee that they reflect different characteristics, and giving them the same names does not necessarily mean they reflect the same determinants. If all these highly interrelated measures are related to all other kinds of behaviors in the same way, they measure the same thing, regardless of their labels.

Occasionally, however, this confusion among the characteristics inferred from behavior is not merely nominal. For instance, height and weight are highly correlated in the general population, yet no one supposes they are merely different names for the same thing. What if defensiveness and desire to make a favorable impression are independent, but nevertheless empirically related in a given population? How, then, could we decide whether they reflect different organismic states or processes? Or better, if the one measure is related to some other mode of behavior, which hypothetical variable is responsible for the relation?

These are not trivial questions, and their answers are not easily come by. One kind of answer is simply the observation that there is never any guarantee in science against the inaccurate indentification of determinants. And this holds as well for experimental variables, i.e., those that are directly manipulable, as for differential variables, whose values must be selected wherever and whenever they occur. Suppose, for instance, the number of food responses in a free association test or, for that matter, speed of running in a straight alley, is shown to be a function of length of food deprivation. How do we know these results are not due to variations in blood-sugar level, or changes in bodily weight, or any number of other variables associated with food deprivation? As Miller (1959) points out, in attempting to specify behavioral antecedents, "It is possible to proceed down the scale to an almost infinite number of possible empirical independent variables; even the most detailed operational description of procedure involves assumptions about the general applicability of the terms used. It is impossible for a theorist to be completely certain in advance whether or not these assumptions are justifiable. It is equally impossible for a person who believes himself to be a pure empiricist to avoid such assumptions" (p. 215).

It is usually possible, given skill and patience, to tease out ever-finer specifications of the variables entering into behavioral laws. So too with response-defined variables; by careful selection of cases, statistical correction, or the elimination of errors of measurement, we can frequently decide which of several variables, even though they be highly correlated, determine the form of the relation under consideration. If it turns out, as it frequently does, that a given behavior is a joint function of several response variables, the circumstance is one quite familiar to experimentalists. For instance, no one is unduly disturbed by the finding that the probability of drinking is a function of both dryness of the mucous membranes and general water deficit. The additional fact that these two variables are themselves frequently related under many conditions is a complication, to be sure, but not an insuperable one.

All we can reasonably ask in regard to either experimental or differential variables is that they be specified as precisely as possible. We should then be prepared to discover, soon enough, that more precise and detailed specifications are necessary.

The Nature and Function of Theories

Thus far, relatively little of our discussion has been directly concerned with the nature or role of theory in psychology, at least as this term is typically used by personality theorists. It has been mainly concerned, instead, with some fundamental propositions: that behavior is lawful; its antecedents are discoverable by naturalistic methods; guesses as to the antecedents of behavior are best verified by the method of prediction; the laws relating behavior to its antecedents are initially most easily discovered by observing simple behavior in simple situations; at least some of the variables and laws identified in simple situations are likely to be useful, in interaction with new factors, in explaining more complex behavior in more complex situations; it may sometimes be useful to infer or guess at certain characteristics or properties of organisms that might account for variations in behavior under ostensibly similar environmental conditions; and finally, these hypothetical properties, whether defined in terms of behavioral antecedents or some aspects of behavior itself, might reasonably be considered as personality variables. Clearly, only the last two points bear very closely on the question of theory.

Behavior Theories and S-R Language. It will be recalled that this entire discussion started with the question: "What do behavioral approaches to personality have in common, and how do they differ from other views?" A partial answer, with some elaborations and digressions, has been given in terms of the foregoing propositions. What they come to, in a word, is an emphasis on the formulation of empirical laws and the analysis of the variables comprising them. As we have noted, the assumption that it is the business of behavioral science to explicate the relations between objectively defined environmental and behavioral events is in itself no theory, but rather a metatheoretical or pretheoretical preference. Those who adopt this approach, especially if they have an interest in the phenomena of learning, are likely to use the terms "S" and "R" to refer, respectively, to the environmental and behavioral events, and the familiar formula "S-R" to indicate a relation between these two classes of variables. In addition, those who use this terminology are perhaps more than others committed to the view that complex behavior can be understood, at least in part, in terms of concepts and relations adumbrated in the observation of simpler sorts of behavior. Not all theorists, not even all behavior theorists, entirely share the belief that S-R concepts are adequate to this task (cf. Koch, 1959). Kendler and Kendler (1962) have commented on one reason for such misgivings:

Much of the objection to S-R language stems from the apparent discrepancy between active, flowing behavior and the inert, static, single S-R association. Using S-R language does not mean complex behavior *actually* consists of S-R connections. After analyzing the concept of light, Toulmin (1953) concludes: "We do not *find* light atomized into individual rays: we *represent* it as consisting of such rays" (p. 29). Applying the same idea to the concept of the

S-R associations: we *represent* it as consisting of such S-R associations." The concept of S-R association, therefore, must be judged not in terms of its ability to provide a clear image of behavior, but rather in its capacity to represent the facts of behavior (p. 3).

Although S-R formulations share a certain strategy, as the foregoing quotation indicates, the notion of S-R is not a theory either, but rather a pretheoretical model. Thus, its adoption does not imply a single level or kind of conceptualization of either "stimulus" or "response" (Brown, 1961; Miller, 1959). It does not imply that S-R laws are the only ones of importance in psychology (Spence, 1948). It does not imply any particular stand with respect to the necessity or desirability of introducing hypothetical constructs in accounting for behavior. And it certainly does not imply any substantial agreement concerning either the specific observable variables or hypothetical variables of which particular responses or response classes are a function. In brief, "S-R" is simply a type of terminology employed by some empirically-minded psychologists, including some who are also theoretically inclined.

What, then, is meant by a "behavioral theory"? In physics, the term "theory" refers to a system of interrelations among highly abstract concepts which serves to organize a very large number of laws that were previously unrelated (Spence, 1956, 1957). Comprehensive theories, i.e., those serving to organize a considerable number of laws, depend on the state of knowledge in a given area. If many empirical relations are known, then the theories may unify a large area. In psychology, at least according to the view of behavior theorists such as Spence, the development of a body of empirical laws is still in its early stages, so the possible unifying power of theory is relatively small.

This rather modest conception of theory is a far cry from the grandiose conceptualizations of some personality theorists. One reason for this is the insistence that every term in the system, no matter how abstract, be referable in some way to observable events. This requirement, sometimes referred to, not altogether correctly, as that of "operational definition," simply states the necessity for indicating more or less unambiguously the nature of the circumstances under which the term is to be used. Furthermore, these circumstances ought to be of a sort concerning which there is a high degree of intersubjective agreement. Theories that achieve apparent comprehensiveness by the use of concepts that have no clear-cut referents of this sort may have a certain suggestive value in the context of discovery, but in the context of justification their ambiguity precludes any rigorous test of their purported relations. It is apparently possible, however, for behavior theorists to take somewhat different stands in respect to the methodological implications of this requirement, as the recent discussions of the notion of construct validity amply demonstrate (e.g., Bechtoldt, 1959; Campbell, 1960; Cronbach and Meehl, 1955).

The Economic Function of Theories. Theories, even of such limited scope as those now existing in psychology, seem to serve two functions, the one economic and the other integrative. The economic function appears to have been the one emphasized by Tolman (1936) when he introduced the concept of the "intervening variable." He noted that the function relating any kind of behavior to its many determinants is likely to be exceedingly complex, and also, that these functions differ for different sets of antecedent conditions and for different kinds of behaviors. Therefore, he proposed that certain hypothetical notions be introduced to decrease the number of statements necessary to indicate all these relations. Feigl (1945), observing that the concept "electric current" has precisely this status of an intervening variable between numerous causal conditions and numerous effects has clearly indicated the nature of this stratagem:

If there are m causal conditions and n possible effects we would need mn statements in order to formulate all possible observable relations. If, however, we introduce our auxiliary concepts the number of statements required shrinks to $m + n$. For large numbers m and n the conceptual economy is accordingly quite considerable (p. 257).

Miller (1959) has recently suggested how one might design experiments to test the hypothesis that various kinds of behavioral indexes in various experimental contexts might actually be accounted for in terms of a single construct of this sort.

There is some reason to believe that the economic function of such theorizing is served in part by Skinner's procedure of classifying antecedents of various kinds under the same rubric, e.g., "motivation," because they bear the same kinds of functional relations to a given aspect of behavior. As he says of the concept of "drive":

The term is simply a convenient way of referring to the effects of deprivation and satiation and of other operations which alter the probability of behavior in more or less the same way. It is convenient because it enables us to deal with many cases at once. There are many ways of changing the probability that an organism will eat; at the same time, a single kind of deprivation strengthens many kinds of behavior. The concept of hunger as a drive brings these various relations together in a single term (1953, p. 144).

Thus, despite his renunciation of theory, Skinner's procedure, and even its rationale, appears to bear a certain resemblance to those followed by self-acknowledged behavior theorists. Perhaps, as Miller (1959) has suggested, Skinner has not been too impressed with the theoretical significance of this procedure, because he tends to deal with only one index of behavior, rate of bar-pressing. Obviously, even if the number of m causal variables is very large, if the number n of response variables is only one, mn will always be less than $m + n$. Consequently, no simplification can ensue from the use of intervening variables.

The Integrative Function of Theories. The second function of a theoretical structure is to integrate various empirical laws within a given domain, by linking the constructs used to account for one set of laws with those used to account for other sets. In this way, one may establish a "network of connected concepts" (Feigl, 1945). In a theoretical structure detailed enough to include statements of relations among several hypothetical variables, the deductive consequences of the supposition that an empirical variable is related to one or another of these intervening variables may be quite far-reaching, and in some cases may lead to unexpected conclusions.

Since such abstract statements about the merits of theory are rather unconvincing, we might consider an example of such guessed-at interrelations and their empirical implications, even at the risk of getting finally to some substantive issues. This example is from the theoretical structure formulated by Hull and Spence —only because it is the one I am most familiar with. There is no implication that different formulations would not yield equally pertinent instances.

Consider the consequences of the supposition that a given variable Y is related to general drive level (D). If it is further assumed that the strength of responses is some function of habit strength (H) multiplied by drive level $(R = H \times D)$, one can make a rather large number of predictions concerning the effects on behavior of variations in Y. For instance, increases in the value of Y should lead to the following consequences: improved performance in situations in which the strongest habit is correct, but poorer performance when the strongest habit is incorrect; greater responsiveness to generalized stimuli, but better discrimination between the training and generalized stimuli when presented simultaneously; steepened slopes of psychophysical functions relating to sensory thresholds, but no change in the absolute threshold. All these, and a substantial number of other consequences may be deduced from the Hull-Spence theory, on the hypothesis that Y is a drive factor (e.g., Brown, 1961; Spence, 1956). These consequences depend, of course, on the assumed relations between empirical variables and intervening variables as well as those among the intervening variables.

In the case of any particular variable Y, of course, the predicted consequences may not appear. In this eventuality, one must conclude either that Y is not a drive variable, or some of the assumptions relating drive to other constructs and to behavior are incorrect, or both. The point is, unless one has a theory in which these relations are made explicit, there would be no reason even to look for these possible effects on behavior.

In an earlier section, note was taken of the wide variety of tests that have yielded scores highly correlated with those of the Manifest Anxiety Scale. A few years ago, Davids (1955) asked a question that has probably occurred to many psychologists: in view of these high relations between MAS scores and those on other, well-established instruments, some of which may be even more valid measures of anxiety, why has there been so much emphasis on the MAS? In my opinion, the answer is obvious: because of the supposition that these scores might be related to one of the intervening variables in the Hull-Spence theory and, consequently, to variations in all the kinds of be-

haviors theoretically affected by this variable. In other words, the popularity of the MAS resulted, not necessarily from any intrinsic value of the test itself, and certainly not from its title, which is in some respects misleading, but from its presumptive relation to constructs within a comparatively highly integrated theory.

Since, as Spence (1958) has stated, the primary function of the sort of theoretical scheme he employs " . . . is to provide for the unification of what, without the theory, would be a multiplicity of isolated or unconnected facts and laws" (p. 140), assigning any variable to a place in the theory permits the deduction of a variety of behaviors which would otherwise not be suspected. For example, it is quite probable that MAS scores represent, in part, the strength of the desire to make a good impression (Edwards, 1957). But I wonder whether anyone seriously believes that this conceptualization would have led to studies of eyelid conditioning, or psychophysical functions, or the steepness of stimulus generalization gradients, or paired-associates learning, or for that matter Davids' own investigation of productivity in a word association test (Davids and Eriksen, 1955).

It may be of some interest to note that many of the predictions based on the assumption that the MAS measures drive level have been borne out; in other instances, the predictions have met with but indifferent success. Indeed, if the Hull-Spence theory is correct, then some of these findings demonstrate that the MAS also measures characteristics other than D. Since no one, to the best of my knowledge, ever doubted this (Farber, 1954, 1955), these demonstrations are not too surprising. Whether the evidence indicates that it measures D at all is perhaps still a moot question. Indeed, in a larger context, it may be questioned whether it is necessary or useful for theoretical purposes to posit a non-associative concept of D at all (e.g., Brown, 1961; Estes, 1958; Postman, 1953).

These questions are of the utmost importance. Nevertheless, in considering the metatheoretical nature and functions of theory, they are in a sense quite irrelevant. If the MAS does not measure D, perhaps some other indexes, such as certain kinds of autonomic or cortical activity will do so. Perhaps no kind of behavior indexes will prove useful for this purpose. Perhaps the kinds of behavioral phenomena accounted for in terms of the Hull-Spence theoretical formulation will be better integrated within new theoretical systems, which may not contain the construct of drive level at all. Theories are not sacrosanct. They are formulated for only one purpose—to account for the behavioral data. If they fail to do so, they must be modified or discarded.

I believe a number of behavior theories have proved useful in providing a basis for predicting behavioral phenomena of interest even to those who consider such approaches too simplistic to account for the complexities of personality. Miller's studies of fear and conflict, Skinner's studies of operant conditioning, and the extension of both to the area of psychotherapy are cases in point. New theories are being constructed and older ones revised, the better to incorporate and account for new findings. It is in the very nature of behavior theoretical formulations that they be modified on the basis of empirical facts. Since the empirical facts of psychology include those relating to individual differences, one may anticipate that as behavior theories become more precise and more comprehensive they will encompass more and more phenomena now referred to under the rubric of "personality." I, for one, look forward to the day, which I do not expect to see myself, when personality theories are regarded as historical curiosities.

REFERENCES

Allport, G. W. *Personality*. New York: Henry Holt, 1937.

Amsel, A. Frustrative nonreward in partial reinforcement and discrimination learning: Some recent history and a theoretical extension. *Psychol. Rev.*, 1962, 69, 306–328.

Bechtoldt, H. P. Construct validity: A critique. *Amer. Psychologist*, 1959, 14, 619–629.

Bergmann, G. Psychoanalysis and experimental psychology: A review from the standpoint of scientific empiricism. *Mind*, 1943, 52, 122–140.

Bergmann, G. The logic of psychological concepts. *Phil. Sci.*, 1951, 18, 93–110.

Bergmann, G. Theoretical psychology. In C. P. Stone (Ed.), *Annual review of psychology.* Stanford, Calif.: Annual Reviews, 1953. Pp. 435–458.

Brown, J. S. *The motivation of behavior.* New York: McGraw-Hill, 1961.

Brown, J. S. & Farber, I. E. Emotions conceptualized as intervening variables—with suggestions toward a theory of frustration. *Psychol. Bull.*, 1951, 48, 465–495.

Campbell, D. T. Recommendations for APA test standards regarding construct, trait, or discriminant validity. *Amer. Psychologist*, 1960, 15, 546–553.

Cronbach, L. J., & Meehl, P. E. Construct validity in psychological tests. *Psychol. Bull.*, 1955, 52, 281–302.

Davids, A. Relations among several objective measures of anxiety under different conditions of motivation. *J. consult. Psychol.*, 1955, 19, 275–279.

Davids, A., & Eriksen, C. W. The relation of manifest anxiety to association productivity and intellectual attainment. *J. consult. Psychol.*, 1955, 19, 219–222.

Edwards, A. L. *The social desirability variable in personality assessment and research.* New York: Dryden, 1957.

Estes, W. K. Stimulus-response theory of drive. In M. R. Jones (Ed.), *Nebraska symposium on motivation.* Lincoln, Neb.: University of Nebraska Press, 1958, Pp. 35–69.

Eysenck, H. J. *The scientific study of personality.* London: Routledge & Kegan Paul, 1952.

Farber, I. E. Anxiety as a drive state. In M. R. Jones (Ed.), *Nebraska symposium on motivation.* Lincoln, Neb.: University of Nebraska Press, 1954. Pp. 1–46.

Farber, I. E. The role of motivation in verbal learning and performance. *Psychol. Bull.*, 1955, 52, 311–327.

Farber, I. E., Harlow, H. F., & West, L. J. Brainwashing, conditioning and DDD (debility, dependency, and dread). *Sociometry*, 1957, 20, 271–285.

Feigl, H. Operationism and scientific method. *Psychol. Rev.*, 1945, 52, 250–259.

Gill, M. M. The present state of psychoanalytic theory. *J. abnorm. soc. Psychol.*, 1959, 58, 1–8.

Kendler, H. H., & Kendler, Tracy S. Vertical and horizontal processes in problem solving. *Psychol. Rev.*, 1962, 69, 1–16.

Koch, S. Behavior as "intrinsically" regulated: Work notes towards a pretheory of phenomena called "motivational." in M. R. Jones (Ed.), *Nebraska symposium on motivation.* Lincoln, Neb.: University of Nebraska Press, 1956. Pp. 42–86.

Koch, S. Epilogue. In S. Koch (Ed.), *Psychology: A study of a science.* Vol. 3. *Formulations of the person and the social context.* New York: McGraw-Hill, 1959. Pp. 729–788.

Meehl, P. E. *Clinical vs. statistical prediction.* Minneapolis: University of Minnesota Press, 1954.

Miller, N. E. Liberalization of basic S-R concepts: Extensions to conflict behavior, motivation, and social learning. In S. Koch (Ed.), Vol. 2. *Psychology: A study of a science.* New York: McGraw-Mill, 1959. Pp. 196–292.

Murphy, G. *Personality*. New York: Harper & Bros., 1947.

Skinner, B. F. *Science and human behavior*. New York: Macmillan, 1953.

Skinner, B. F. The design of cultures. *Daedalus*, 1961, **90**, 534–546.

Spence, K. W. The postulates and methods of behaviorism. *Psychol. Rev.*, 1948, **55**, 67–78.

Spence, K. W. *Behavior theory and conditioning*. New Haven: Yale University Press, 1956.

Spence, K. W. The empirical basis and theoretical structure of psychology. *Philos. Sci.*, 1957, **24**, 97–108.

Spence, K. W. A theory of emotionally based drive (D) and its relation to performance in simple learning situations. *Amer. Psychologist*, 1958, **13**, 131–141.

Tolman, E. C. Operational behaviorism and current trends in psychology. *Proc. 25th Anniv. Celebration Inaug. Grad. Stud.* Los Angeles: University of Southern California, 1936. Pp. 89–103.

Toulmin, S. *The philosophy of science*. London: Hutchinson University Library, 1953.

Watson, J. B. *Psychology from the standpoint of a behaviorist*. Philadelphia: Lippincott, 1919.

3.   Theory and experiment on the measurement of approach-avoidance conflict

SEYMOUR EPSTEIN AND WALTER D. FENZ

A NUMBER OF YEARS AGO, Luria (1932) introduced a technique for the measurement of conflict and reaction to stress. Among other procedures, he verified his approach by testing students before an unusually critical examination and by testing prisoners facing the death penalty and other serious sentences. The present study follows in the tradition of Luria's work in that an acute real life event is investigated, an attempt is made to measure affect selectively related to the event rather than the general affective state alone, and a specially devised word association test is used. The approach differs from Luria's in some of the measures investigated, in the substitution of a stimulus dimension for a dichotomous classification of the stimulus, and in the overall theoretical orientation. The critical event is a parachute jump for an inexperienced parachutist.

There is little question but that the first few jumps for a novice parachutist represent an acute approach-avoidance conflict between need for adventure, excitement, or prestige on the one hand, and fear of death and injury on the other. Expressions such as, "It was the most frightening experience of my life," or "For a while I thought I would not be able to go through with it," are commonly heard. Parachuting would seem to be comparable in momentary intensity to the events studied by Luria (1932), and clearly fulfills the conditions of an approach-avoidance conflict. In addition, parachuting has a unique advantage in that, unlike a murder or a critical examina-

tion, it can be repeated within short intervals, thereby allowing for the use of subjects as their own controls and for the investigation of experience and mastery. Finally, the frequency and timing of a parachute jump can be controlled according to the experimental plans of the investigator. In the present study, novice sport-parachutists were tested on the day of an anticipated jump and at a time 2 weeks from a jump. The general influence of parachuting and of time of testing upon responses to a stimulus dimension are investigated in relation to a theoretical model.

A Model for the Measurement of Conflict with Projective Techniques

The model required is one which represents approach as stronger at the goal than avoidance, since subjects by their own choice advance to the goal. Such a model adapted from Miller (1948), is presented in Figure 1. It is

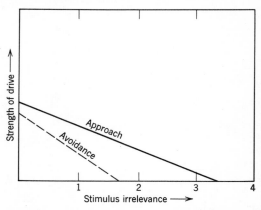

Figure 1. Strength of approach and avoidance drive as a function of a stimulus dimension.

SOURCE. Article by Seymour Epstein and Walter D. Fenz, "Theory and experiment on the measurement of approach-avoidance conflict" in *Journal of abnormal and social Psychology,* Vol. 64, pp. 97–112, 1962.

assumed that there is an approach drive and an avoidance drive associated with parachute jumping, and that the approach drive can be represented by a less steep gradient as a function of an increasing dimension of stimulus relevance than the avoidance drive. It is assumed that drives have activating and directing properties which can be separately represented. It is assumed that the magnitude of drive produced increment in approach response can be represented by the algebraic difference of the approach and avoidance drives (see Figure 2). It is assumed that approach can

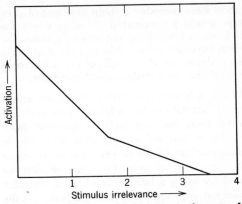

Figure 3. Activation as a function of a stimulus dimension.

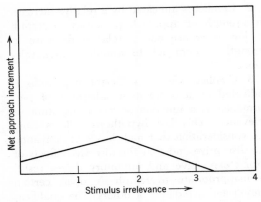

Figure 2. Net approach increment as a function of a stimulus dimension.

be measured by goal relevant verbal responses and avoidance by the failure to produce such responses when they are normally elicited by the stimulus. It should be noted that the model permits the direct prediction of drive produced *increment* in approach response only and not overall drive relevance of the response, which is predominantly a function of the stimulus.

In regard to activation, it is assumed that the magnitude of conflict produced activation can be represented by the sum of the magnitudes of the approach and avoidance drives disregarding algebraic sign (see Figure 3). It is assumed that activation can be measured by the GSR (Woodworth & Schlosberg, 1954), or by some other measure of autonomic activity, or a measure of somatic tension.

One advantage in having the gradients represent drives rather than responses or response tendencies, as in Miller's (1948, 1951) model, is that it immediately suggests the gradients be added if activation is to be considered, and

allows for the prediction of two types of event from one basic model. A further reason for assuming a central concept of drive with activating and directive components is that naturalistic observation reveals that a person or animal brought into increasingly close contact (as measured by distance, goal relevant cues, or perceived availability) to a goal object exhibits increasing activation as well as stronger approach (or avoidance) responses. It is the unusual child who does not become perceptibly more excited (activated) as a wished-for event (e.g., Christmas morning) approaches, in addition to making approach responses (looking for and questioning about presents). Finally, not only is a central concept of drive helpful in referring to simultaneous changes in activation and goal direction brought about by the presence of a goal object, but, more important, the two aspects of drive are often reducible to each other. In the absence of experimentation it will be necessary once more to turn to observation and example.

A dog belonging to one of the authors provides an excellent illustration. The animal makes intense approach responses in the form of running and leaping toward a ball, and clearly exhibits a gradient of approach by reacting more vigorously when the ball is near than when it is far. However, if he is commanded to sit still, and the ball made to approach the dog, a gradient of activation is observed in place of a gradient of approach. As the ball is brought closer, the dog becomes perceptibly more tense, his muscles appear to bulge through his skin, and a general tremor appears. We have no doubt but that if physiological measures of activation were recorded a steep gradient of activation would be indicated. Finally, when the ball is almost touching the animal's nose, the tension becomes unbearable and the dog barks vigorously, snaps at the ball, or entirely breaks the inhibition and dashes about the room.

While it is true that Miller allows for gradients of activation by relating avoidance to learned fear, his approach is different from our own in that we assume that activation is a characteristic of all drives. We hypothesize that a gradient of activation can be demonstrated by using a barrier or physical restraint to prevent approach, but that gradients resulting from inhibition of approach responses are steeper, since they are determined by activation from two drives.

In adapting Miller's model to projective techniques, it is necessary to substitute verbal expression for approach and verbal inhibition for avoidance.[1] This raises the question of whether the principles of conflict that have been worked out by Miller and his colleagues in simple situations can, in fact, be translated into this different and more complex situation. The most critical assumption in the conflict and displacement models is that the gradient of avoidance is steeper than the gradient of approach. Miller (1948, 1951) indicates that this is not always the case but is contingent upon approach being more dependent than avoidance upon a physiological state. He indicates that the conditions are satisfied when approach is based upon hunger, and avoidance upon

learned fear. If this is true, it would follow that inhibitory reactions should produce steeper gradients than the drives they inhibit, as the former are contingent upon the latter, and therefore more removed from any primary drive.

Assuming that the gradient of inhibition is steeper than the gradient of expression, the following hypotheses are indicated for the measurement of conflict with stimulus dimensions built into projective techniques:

1. Conflict is indicated by a sharp rise in activation as a function of increasing stimulus relevance.

2. Conflict is indicated by a relative increase in strength of approach responses to stimuli of low relevance and a relative decrease in strength of approach to stimuli of high relevance.

3. Conflict, when of sufficient magnitude, is indicated by a decrease in adequacy of performance as a function of increasing stimulus relevance. This last hypothesis follows from the consideration that high levels of activation are disruptive and that the directive effects of strong expressive and inhibitory drives result in inappropriate overemphasis upon certain stimuli and avoidance of others. The qualification that the conflict must be "of sufficient magnitude" is added to take into consideration that the curve of performance as a function of activation is probably inverted U shaped (Malmo, 1959).

---

[1] It has come to our attention, after writing this paper, that Miller (1959), in his more recent work, has also related his model to projective techniques. However, he neither recommends the construction of stimulus dimensions nor the use of measures of activation. He believes that a projective response can be viewed as a displaced response, but that the relationship is complicated by additional considerations. (For an earlier discussion of the construction of stimulus dimensions in projective techniques to measure drive and conflict, see Epstein & Smith, 1956). We agree with Miller on the complexity of the projective response, and, as will be seen later, find that predicting net approach increment as a function of conflict is theoretically complex in itself, apart form the consideration of other factors. Nevertheless, we believe that the difficulties may not be insurmountable, and even if they are for net approach increment, they will not be for measures of activation.

Model Applied to the Present Study

In the present study, parachutists were tested on the day of a jump and at a time 2 weeks removed from the jump. The model must, therefore, take into account time to a critical event. As a first step, models corresponding to Figures 1, 2, and 3, but with a time dimension substituted for a stimulus dimension, can be considered. If anticipated time to an event is taken as a measure of distance from the event, the proposed model corresponds to Miller's model for conflict. As the study simultaneously investigates the effects of two dimensions, it is necessary to consider a three-dimensional model. Such a model, which is analogous to combining Miller's models for conflict and displacement, is illustrated in Figure 4.[2] The curve for activation as a function of the stimulus dimension is taken from Figure 3 and reproduced on the axis. A corresponding curve for activation as a function of a time dimension is represented on the x axis. Four points are selected along the time dimension, and the relationship of level of activation to the stimulus dimension for these points in time is indicated along the surface of the figure. The four resultant curves are extracted and repre-

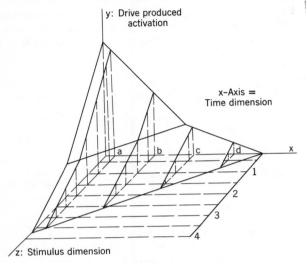

Figure 4. Activation as a function of a stimulus and a time dimension.

sented to scale in Figure 5, which presents a family of curves for different time intervals to the jump. It is apparent that the gradients become higher and steeper as time to the jump increases.[3]

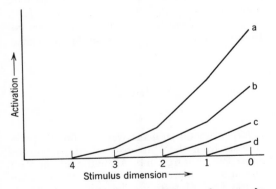

Figure 5. Activation as a function of a stimulus dimension with time treated as a parameter. (The letters correspond to the letters in Figure 4, with a representing the shortest, and d the longest time interval.)

From Figure 5 and assumptions already made, the following predictions are indicated for the present experiment:

1. Parachutists at both times of testing will produce positive gradients as a function of an increasing stimulus dimension on the following measures: GSR, reaction time, and appropriateness of response. The prediction for reaction time follows from the consideration that for the word association test, response latency is an index of adequacy of response.

2. Parachutists tested on the day of an anticipated jump will produce higher and steeper gradients on each of the above measures than parachutists tested 2 weeks from a jump.

In order to predict the increment in approach response as a simultaneous function of a stimulus and time dimension, it is again necessary to consider a three-dimensional model. The curve for net approach increment from Figure 2 is reproduced on the x and z axes of Figure

---

[2] See Murray and Berkun (1955) for an ingenious study in which a three-dimensional model of conflict and displacement is used to predict performance of rats in a runway with displacement alleys.

[3] It should be noted that the change in steepness of the slopes is a consequence of adding the two gradients. If either gradient alone were represented, a series of parallel curves differing only in height would be obtained. This may be observed in Curves c and d, which do not contain a component of the avoidance drive.

6, with the x axis representing the time dimension and the z axis the stimulus dimension. The solid figure produced differs from the one for activation in that instead of a change in steepness there is a change in direction of slope. The surface can be described as a triangle leaning into a corner with the apex bent down to meet the intersection of the vertical walls at a point below the point of inflection. Four

planes parallel to the yz plane represent the same four time intervals as in the figure for activation (see Figure 4). The intersection of these planes with the surface of the figure represents the relationship of net approach increment to the stimulus dimension for the time interval in question. The curves are extracted from Figure 6 and presented as a family of curves in Figure 7. Referring to Figures 6 and

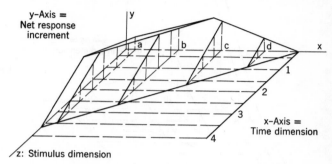

Figure 6. Net approach increment as a function of a stimulus and a time dimension.

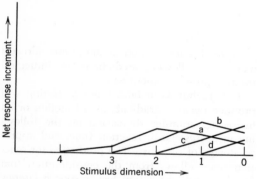

Figure 7. Net approach increment as a function of a stimulus dimension with time treated as a parameter. (The letters correspond to the letters in Figure 6, with a representing the shortest, and d the longest time interval.)

7, it can be observed that the change in direction of the slope for both the time dimension and the stimulus dimension makes the prediction of net approach increment much more complex than was the case for activation. Depending upon the point along the time dimension selected, an increase along the stimulus dimension can result in an increase or a decrease in net approach increment. On either side of the point of inflection the same values occur, so that a lack of precision in locating the point of inflection is more critical than was the case for activation. Despite these difficulties, which prevent more specific predictions, the follow-

ing would seem to be indicated for the present study: (a) Parachutists at both times of testing will produce more parachute relevant responses than nonparachutists to words at the lower end of the stimulus dimension. (b) Parachutists on the day of an anticipated jump will produce more parachute relevant responses to stimuli of low parachute relevance and less parachute relevant responses to stimuli of high parachute relevance than parachutists tested 2 weeks from a jump, i.e., there is a significant interaction between time to a jump and stimulus relevance.

Method

Subjects

Experimental subjects were 16 novice parachutists from the University of Massachusetts Sport Parachuting Club. All had made at least one and not more than three parachute jumps at the time of testing. The subjects were recruited at the regular meeting of the parachute club and were asked to take part in the experiment for the payment of the costs of one parachute jump. The experimental group was matched with a comparable group of control subjects selected from students in an elementary course in psychology at the University of Massachusetts who volunteered to take part in experiments. Three additional subjects who had considerable experience with parachuting, were also tested.

Materials

Parallel forms of word association tests were constructed containing words with four levels of relevance to parachuting. The words were selected from a larger group rated on a four-point scale of parachute relevance by three experienced parachutists. Only words on which full agreement was reached were retained. The words were presented in increasing order of relevance to prevent highly relevant words from influencing responses to words of lower relevance. Three anxiety words were added to each list mainly out of curiosity, and were placed at the end of the list in order not to interfere with the dimension. One or more neutral words was presented between parachute relevant words and between anxiety words, and 10 neutral words were presented at the beginning of the list to reduce practice effects. Following are the word lists, with level of parachute relevance designated by figures, except for neutral words which were treated as the lowest level of relevance, and with anxiety words designated by the letter a:

Word List A: SALT, QUIET, RED, JOY, FOOT-BALL, CITIZEN, MUSIC, CHAIR, SWISS CHEESE, HUNGRY, SKY_1, RHINOCEROS, $LAND_1$, BOOK, $MOUNTAIN_1$, MOON, WHITE, $FALL_2$, LOUD, DOG, $FLOAT_2$, SCISSORS, $ALTITUDE_2$, LION, SWIFT, $BAIL\text{-}OUT_3$, STOVE, RADIATOR, $CANOPY_3$, TAXI, GREEN, $TARGET_3$, SOUR, $FEAR_a$, BEAUTIFUL, $BLACKOUT_a$, MAN, $INJURY_a$, CARPET, HAPPY.

Word List B: MONKEY, MOON, RED, ELEPHANT, KEY, KING, COMFORT, SLEEP, SCREWDRIVER, CHICKEN, WIND, GREEN, $SAND_1$, PAPER, PENCIL, $HILL_1$, BLACK, STAR, $DESCEND_2$, HEAVY, FOOTBALL, $OPENED_2$, HAMMER, $HARNESS_2$, CAT, HARD, $JUMP_3$, LAMP, EAT, $PARACHUTE_3$, TOWN, PINK, $RIPCORD_3$, BITTER, $ANXIETY_a$, SOFT, $KILLED_a$, BOY, $HURT_a$, TABLE, FUN.

Words were presented by a tape recorder at 30-second intervals after having been screened by four judges for clarity of pronunciation. Subjects were instructed to respond as quickly as possible with the first word that occurred to them. Response words were recorded by the experimenter. Recordings of skin resistance were obtained from a direct current Hunter GSR apparatus, operating on the principle of a Wheatstone bridge. The apparatus was adapted for finger electrodes, and resistance was registered by an automatic recording pen. Time from end of stimulus to beginning of response was recorded by a pen-marker controlled by the experimenter.

Procedure

Eight experimental subjects were tested on the day of a jump, and again 2 weeks after the jump; eight others were tested 2 weeks before a scheduled jump, and again on the day of the jump. Subjects were required to refrain from jumping for 2 weeks preceding the "before jump" testing and for 2 weeks following the "after jump" testing, and to make no additional jumps between the testing sessions. Testing on the day of a jump took place 1-3 hours preceding the jump. Sixteen control subjects were tested twice with a 2-week interval between testing. In all cases, List A was presented in the first session, List B in the second session.

Upon entering the experimental room and being seated facing the examiner, a brief explanation was given about the word association test, during which the subject was told that the purpose of the test was to measure emotions related to parachuting. Electrodes were then attached to the right hand index and middle fingers. After about 3 minutes, to permit the electrodes to polarize and the subject to become accustomed to them, the tape recorded list of words was introduced with the comment:

Now we will begin a test of speed of association to words. After you have heard a word—and not before you have heard the whole word—say the first word that occurs to you as quickly as possible. If you are not sure of a word, respond to what you think it was. Please do not make comments or ask questions between words, but save them for the end of the test. Any Question?

Where distributions permitted, the data were evaluated by analyses of variance. In one analysis, experimental subjects were used as their own controls, and nonparachutists were omitted. This permitted an orthogonal arrangement of experimental condition and order. In a second analysis, control subjects were compared on first and second testing.

Results

Galvanic Skin Response

Response to the stimulus dimension. Galvanic skin response was measured by change in conductance immediately following presentation of a stimulus word. In order to make the results independent of selective perception, which in itself was found to be a significant variable, GSR was analyzed only for words which had not received a score for misperception. In addition, GSR scores were eliminated for words in the stimulus dimension when it was clear that the subject interpreted a word in a sense other than the one on which it had been dimensionalized, e.g., the response "winter" to FALL. Finally, GSRs to neutral words which elicited parachute relevant responses were discarded, as their neutral status had become questionable. By eliminating the complicating effects of perception, we could reasonably assume a meaningful stimulus dimension for each of the experimental subjects, instead of a dimension of the probability that the word is related to parachuting. Luria (1932) follows the latter procedure when he categorizes his stimuli as critical, doubtful, or indifferent. In order to correct for the resultant unequal number of responses in a category scores were represented by average GSR per category. Actually, very few words were discarded, never more than one word in any of the categories other than neutral, for which two was the maximum. The results would be essentially the same, but more difficult to interpret, had all words in a category been used. In representing the neutral words, the first 10 "practice" words were not counted.

Sixteen out of 16 experimental subjects produced a gradient of increasing GSR as a function of increasing stimulus relevance. One control subject also produced a gradient, but on questioning it turned out that he had been a paratrooper in the Army. His data were replaced by that of another control subject. For every experimental subject the gradient on the day of a jump was higher and steeper than on a control day. Although statistical analysis might appear to be superfluous, analyses of variance were carried out to investigate the effects of sequence, order, individual differences, and to allow for a comparison with the analyses of reaction time and of anxiety words. In addition, since the findings on the gradients were unequivocal, an opportunity was afforded for testing the relative validity of three commonly used indices of GSR[4]

---

[4] The three measures were change in resistance as measured in ohms, change in conductance as measured in mhos, and change conductance as measured in log mhos. Results obtained from each measure were plotted for each experimental subject. On all three measures 16 of the 16 subjects showed a gradient of response corresponding to the dimension of stimulus relevance, and for each subject the gradient on the day of the jump was steeper than on the day remote from the jump.

Analysis of variance for each separate transformation yielded parallel results. A comparison of the three measures indicated that F values for log conductance change were less pronounced than for resistance change and conductance change. This discrepancy may be attributed to the fact that the logarithmic measure reduced the distance between highly divergent scores. Logarithmic transformation is commonly used to reduce the relationship

It is apparent that the control group produces no gradient (see Figure 8). The mean GSR in micromhos is 1.04 for neutral words and .95 for words of high relevance. The parachutists produce a gradient on the control day and a higher and steeper gradient on the day of a jump, all of which is in accordance with prediction.[5] The mean GSR in micromhos for

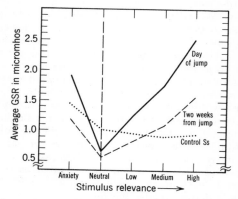

Figure 8. GSR of parachutists and controls to a stimulus dimension and to anxiety words.

---

between conductance change and prestimulus level. Inspection of the data indicated a positive relationship between prestimulus conductance level and magnitude of the deflection. In order to determine whether the results on GSR for the transformed measures of conductance could be attributed to differences in prestimulus level, the same analyses of variance were run on average prestimulus level as on GSR. The analysis of variance for prestimulus levels of experimental subjects on the day of the jump against prestimulus levels on the day remote from the jump did not yield a difference approaching significance. When experimental subjects under both conditions were compared to control subjects the analysis of prestimulus conductance measures also failed to yield significant values. The results for conductance change therefore could not be attributed to absolute conductance levels. That findings which were conclusively present by inspection were measured with least reliability by log conductance units throws some doubt on the advisability of this transformation for GSR data.

[5] The differential steepness of the gradients for the three groups cannot be attributed to the unequal heights of the gradients. The curves for the parachutists intersect the curve for the controls, and maintain their differential slopes with respect to each other within the same range on the ordinate. If anything, the difference in the heights of the gradients can be attributed to the difference in slopes, rather than the reverse, as the parachutists on the day of a jump and a control day do not differ significantly on neutral words.

neutral and high relevant words, respectively, is .56 and 1.57 on a control day, and .65 and 2.59 on the day of a jump.

Only the analysis of variance for parachutists serving as their own controls is presented, as no source of variance approached significance for the analysis of control subjects. In Table 1 it can be seen that there are significant differences for experimental condition, for stimulus dimension, and for the interaction of experimental condition and stimulus dimension. Significance is also indicated for the main effect of individual differences and for the interaction of individual differences with experimental condition. Apparently, not only do individuals differ reliably in the overall magnitude of their GSRs, but they also differ in the effect an approaching critical event has upon their GSRs. Perhaps this indicates an interesting personality variable that should be followed up in further work.

An additional finding of interest is that the parachutists have a smaller mean GSR than the control subjects to neutral words on both the day of a jump and the control day (see Figure 8). When tested by a separate analysis of variance for neutral words only, the difference is found to be significant at the .01 level.

Reaction to anxiety words. A comparison of mean GSR to neutral and anxiety words (see Figure 8) indicates that both experimental and control subjects react more strongly to anxiety words than to neutral words. This difference is greatest for experimental subjects on the day of a jump, with a mean difference in micromhos of 1.28, next for experimental subjects on the day remote from a jump, with a mean difference of .64, and least for control subjects, with a mean difference of .41. As with neutral words the parachute group on a control day has a lower GSR to anxiety words than the control group. The analysis of the parachutists as their own controls is presented in Table 2, where it can be seen that not only do parachutists react significantly differently to anxiety and neutral words (C, .001 level) and that their differential reaction varies as a function of proximity to the jump (G × C, .001 level), but there are also significant individual differences in GSR across conditions (subjects), in change in GSR from control day to jump-day (Subjects × G), and in difference in GSR between neutral and anxiety words (Subjects × C). In the analysis of control subjects by themselves the difference between anxiety and neutral words is significant at the .05 level.

It is noteworthy that the parachutists on both the day of a jump and a control day produce larger GSRs to high relevant words than to anxiety words, which is consistent with the assumption that the gradients represent activation rather than fear alone.

Reaction Time

Response to the stimulus dimension. Reaction time produced similar results to GSR. In

Table 1. Analysis of Variance of GSR to a Stimulus Dimension for Parachutists on the Day of a Jump and a Control Day

Source of Variance	df	MS	F
Between-subjects	15		
Sequence (Q)	1	129.41	1.15
Subjects	14	111.70[a]	11.67†
Within-subjects	112		
Group (G)	1	795.51	17.07**
Q × G	1	46.92	1.00
Subjects × G	14	46.58[a]	4.87†
Dimension (D)	3	1309.91	95.12†
Q × D	3	11.01	.79
Subjects × D	42	13.77[a]	1.44
G × D	3	143.71	15.02†
Q × G × D	3	5.43	.56
Subjects × G × D	42	9.57[a]	
Total	127		

[a] Error term for mean squares above it up to the next error term. The Subjects × G × D interaction was used to evaluate all other error terms.

** Significant at .01 level.

† Significant at .001 level.

Table 2. Analysis of Variance of GSR to Neutral and Anxiety Words for Parachutists on the Day of a Jump and a Control Day

Source of Variance	df	MS	F
Between-subjects	15		
Sequence (Q)	1	133.58	2.26
Subjects	14	59.00[a]	6.88†
Within-subjects	48		
Group (G)	1	267.62	4.46
Q × G	1	50.70	.84
Subjects × G	14	59.94[a]	6.97†
Category (C)	1	1483.10	29.17†
Q × C	1	72.58	1.42
Subjects × C	14	50.85[a]	5.91**
G × C	1	165.53	19.27†
Q × G × C	1	9.61	1.12
Subjects × G × C	14	8.59[a]	
Total	63		

[a] Error term for mean squares above it up to the next error term. The Subjects × G × C interaction was used to evaluate all other error terms.

** Significant at .01 level.

† Significant at .001 level.

Figure 9 it can be seen that at both times of testing the parachute group produces a positive gradient of reaction time as a function of the stimulus dimension, and that the gradient is higher and steeper on the day of a jump than on a control day. On the control day, mean reaction time is 1.41″ for neutral words and 2.32″ for words of high parachute relevance. On the day of a jump the corresponding values are 1.45″ and 3.40″. The control subjects produce no gradient. Analysis of variance for the parachutists reveals that the difference associated with experimental condition (G), with the stimulus dimension (D), and with the interaction of experimental condition and stimulus dimension (G × D) are all significant (see Table 3). No source of variance is significant in the analysis of variance for the control group.

Of additional interest, and parallel to the findings in GSR, is the indication in Figure 9 that mean reaction time of parachutists to neutral words on a control day ($M = 1.41″$) is less than for control subjects ($M = 1.69″$), although in this case the analysis of variance of neutral words alone fails to reach significance.

Reaction to anxiety words. A comparison of mean reaction time to neutral and anxiety words that it took all groups longer to respond to anxiety than to neutral words (see Figure 9). The difference is greatest for parachutists on the day of a jump (1.12″), next for parachutists on a control day (0.84″), and least for control subjects (0.37″). The results are similar to those obtained for GSR (compare Figures 8 and 9). The findings are confirmed by analysis of variance. The analysis of parachutists on the day of a jump and a control day yields significance at the .01 level for experimental condition and for stimulus category, and significance at

Table 3. Analysis of Variance of Reaction Time to a Stimulus Dimension for Parachutists on the Day of a Jump and a Control Day

Source of Variance	df	MS	F
Between-subjects	14		
Sequence (Q)	1	1.34	.42
Subjects	13	3.12	8.66†
Within-subjects	112		
Group (G)	1	10.88	15.32**
Q × G	1	2.13	3.00
Subjects × G	13	.71ᵃ	1.97*
Dimension (D)	3	12.62	22.53†
Q × D	3	.18	.32
Subjects × D	39	.56ᵃ	1.55
G × D	3	1.62	4.50**
Q × G × D	3	.48	1.33
Subjects × G × D	39	.36ᵃ	
Total	119		

ᵃ Error term for mean squares above it up to the next error term. The Subjects × G × D interaction was used to evaluate all other error terms.

  * Significant at .05 level.
 ** Significant at .01 level.
 † Significant at .001 level.

the .05 level for the interaction of experimental condition with stimulus category (see Table 4). The analysis of control subjects by themselves yields significance at the .05 level for the difference between neutral and anxiety words

Failures in Perception

Perception of stimulus dimension and anxiety. words. Inspection of the data made it apparent that a considerable number of misperceptions and very few other obviously poor responses occurred. Failures in perception were scored when the subject reported that he had

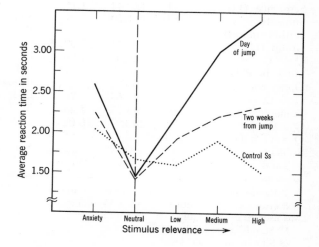

Figure 9. Reaction time of parachutists and controls to a stimulus dimension and to anxiety words.

Table 4. Analysis of Variance of Reaction Time to Neutral and Anxiety Words for Parachutists on the Day of a Jump and a Control Day

Source of Variance	df	MS	F
Between-subjects	14		
Sequence (Q)	1	.14	.07
Subjects	13	2.07[a]	2.46
Within-subjects	45		
Group (G)	1	13.20	9.49**
Q × G	1	.73	.86
Subjects × G	13	1.39[a]	1.65
Category (C)	1	8.48	9.31**
Q × C	1	.64	.76
Subjects × C	13	.91[a]	1.08
G × C	1	4.08	4.85*
Q × G × C	1	.31	.36
Subjects × G × C	13	.84[a]	
Total	59		

[a] Error term for mean squares above it up to the next error term. The Subjects × G × C interaction was used to evaluate all other error terms.

* Significant at .05 level.

** Significant at .01 level.

not heard a word, or when a response was given that was more appropriate to a word that sounded like the stimulus word than to the stimulus itself, such as the response "person" to SKY, where later questioning confirmed that the subject had heard SKY as "guy." Almost all inferred misperceptions were ones that occurred several times, and had been confirmed at least once by later questioning.

Figure 10 presents number of words missed over total words in a category, expressed as a percentage. Low and moderate parachute

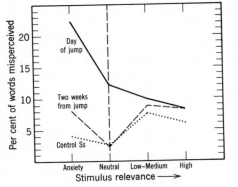

Figure 10. Percentage of misperceptions by parachutists and control subjects of words on a stimulus dimension and anxiety words.

relevant words were combined to increase reliability. Neutral words were restricted to the first 10 practice words because inspection (later verified) suggested that misperception of neutral words was influenced by the preceding parachute relevant word. It is evident in Figure 10 that parachutists on the day of a jump manifest a general perceptual deficit, as indicated by misperception of neutral words. There appears to be a specific deficit for anxiety words, and a relative sensitization[6] to parachute relevant words in relation to degree of relevance.

The high number of cases with zero misperceptions produced highly skewed distributions and accordingly chi square analysis of frequency data was used. A comparison between parachutists on the day of a jump and a control day revealed that there were 10 parachutists who produced an unequal number of misperceptions of the first 10 neutral words on the day of a jump and a control day and 6 who produced an equal number of misperceptions. All of the former produced more misperceptions on the day of a jump (significant at the .01 level). Of 11 parachutists who produced an unequal difference between misperception of neutral and high parachute relevant words on the day of a jump and a control day, 9 made relatively fewer misperceptions of parachute words on the day of a jump, which is significant at the .05 level. In addition, 12 out of 16 control subjects as compared to 6 out of 16 parachutists on the day of a jump produced a higher number of misperceptions of high parachute than neutral words, which is significant at the .05 level. Of 10 parachutists who misperceived an unequal number of anxiety words on the day of a jump and a control day, 9 made more misperceptions on the day of a jump, which is significant at the .02 level. Moreover, of 14 parachutists who produced an unequal difference in misperception of neutral and anxiety words on the day of a jump and a control day, 11 misperceived relatively more anxiety words on the day of a jump, which is significant at the .05 level. When comparison was with control subjects, 2 out of 16 controls and 11 out of 16 parachutists on the day of a jump misperceived more anxiety than neutral words, which is significant at the .01 level. Thus, on the basis of statistical analysis it may be concluded that parachutists on the day of a jump manifest a general perceptual deficit, as indicated in their misperception of neutral words, a specific defi-

[6] Perceptual deficit and sensitization are used here descriptively only, and are not meant to imply a reason for the phenomenon.

cit for anxiety words, and relative perceptual sensitization for parachute words.[7]

Perception of neutral words following relevant words. It has been noted that although parachutists on the day of a jump had no difficulty in perceiving parachute related words they tended to misperceive the words that immediately followed. Accordingly, perception of neutral words was investigated as a function of the words preceding them. Figure 11 presents percentage of failures in perception for each of the categories of neutral words. It is evident that parachutists on the day of a jump produce a positive gradient of failures in perception as a function of an increasing stimulus dimension.

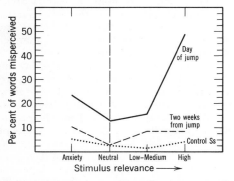

Figure 11. Percentage of misperceptions of parachutists and control subjects.

---

[7] The findings cannot be explained away by interor intralist set effects. For one thing, if there were such set effects, they should influence the control subjects, yet there is no evidence of any perceptual effect for the control subjects. Second, parachutists served as their own controls, with half tested first on the day of a jump, and half tested first on a control day, and a careful analysis indicated that both subgroups behaved similarly. So far as intraserial set effects are concerned, the neutral words were presented before the parachute words, so that influence on the former was not possible. It might be argued that intraserial set effects could account for the sensitization to parachute words and the relative deficit for anxiety words, which appeared last. However, this would influence control subjects as well as parachutists on a control day, and cannot be a factor unless one is willing to postulate differential sets to pick up sets on the day of a jump, which is not too far off from selective perception. To determine whether such was the case, we examined the responses to successive words in the same category. There was no evidence for differential group performance as a functon of an emerging set. It may be concluded that the data cannot be accounted for, directly or indirectly, by intra- or inter-list set effects.

There is also a tendency for parachutists on the day of a jump to misperceive neutral words following anxiety words.

Of 12 subjects who misperceived an unequal number of neutral words following words of high parachute relevance on the day of a jump and a control day, 10 had more misperceptions on the day of a jump, which is significant at the .05 level. When comparison is between control subjects and parachutists, 4 out of 16 controls and 10 out of 16 parachutists on the day of a jump misperceive at least one neutral word following a word of high parachute relevance, which is again significant at the .05 level. A comparison of misperception of neutral words following words of high relevance, relative to misperception of first 10 neutral words, reveals that of 15 parachutists who produced an unequal difference on the day of a jump and a control day, 12 made relatively more misperceptions of neutral words following parachute words on the day of a jump, which is significant at the .05 level. When the comparison is between parachutists and control subjects, 2 out of 16 controls and 9 out of 16 parachutists on the day of a jump misperceive relatively more neutral words following words of high parachute relevance than words among the first 10 neutral words, which is significant at the .01 level. It may be concluded that on the day of a jump there is a significant increase in the misperception of neutral words following words of high parachute relevance.[8]

Analysis of neutral words following anxiety words revealed that of eight parachutists who misperceived an unequal number of these words on the day of a jump and a control day, seven made more misperceptions on the day of a jump, which is significant at the .05 level. A comparison of misperception of neutral words following anxiety words relative to misperception of first 10 neutral words for parachutists on the day of a jump and either parachutists on a control day or control subjects approached, but did not reach significance ($p = .05 - .10$). It may be concluded that there is an unreliable tendency for parachutists on the day of a jump to manifest perceptual deficit for neutral words following anxiety words.

Content of Associations

It was predicted that parachutists on the day of a jump relative to a control day would dem-

---

[8] The possibility of intra- and interlist set effects producing the results was considered in the same manner as for the words in the dimension. Again, the results were negative. Luria (1932) also reports cognitive disturbance on neutral words following critical words.

onstrate an increase in parachute relevant responses to stimuli of low relevance and a decrease in parachute relevant responses to stimuli of high relevance. Unfortunately, the prediction could not be tested at the high end of the dimension as stimuli of high relevance almost always elicited responses that were relevant to parachuting, and we were unable to devise a reliable scoring system for determining degree of approach within this range. As for the rest of the dimension, there was no evidence that responses to neutral words and to words of low and moderate parachute relevance were functionally dissimilar. Accordingly, responses to all stimuli were combined into one overall score.

Analysis of variance of the responses of parachutists on the day of a jump and a control day revealed a significant difference between the groups at the .01 level. Parachutists on the day of a jump produced an average of 8.3 parachute relevant words as contrasted with 5.8 on a control day. Control subjects produced the least number of parachute relevant words, with a mean of 3.2.

Three Records of Experienced Parachutists

Although the reliability of results based on a sample as small as three is necessarily low, the results were so striking that we decided they were worth reporting. For both mean GSR and mean reaction time, the gradients for the experienced and inexperienced parachutists were alike on the control day. However, while the inexperienced jumpers produced a monotonic curve on the day of a jump, the experienced jumpers produced a curve similar to it up to an intermediate point on the stimulus dimension, after which it drooped off so sharply that the mean reaction at the upper end of the dimension was no different from what it was at the lower end of the dimension. All 3 experienced jumpers and none of the 16 inexperienced jumpers or 16 controls produced this curve.[9]

Discussion

Measures of Activation

It had been assumed that GSR is a direct measure of activation and that reaction time in a word association test is a measure of adequacy of performance, and therefore, indirectly of activation. Accordingly it was predicted that

[9] We have now, as part of another study, confirmed the results with three more experienced parachutists.

parachutists would produce similar gradients for both measures on a control day, and that the gradients would be higher and steeper on the day of a jump. Apart from supporting the model, the high reliability of the findings with these two measures indicates that they are completely adequate for measuring individual differences. Considering that reaction time and particularly GSR are indirect measures of conflict and not normally under conscious control of the individual, they are particularly promising measures of unconscious conflict. The results are striking enough to warrant testing of known clinical groups with specially devised stimulus dimensions used in conjunction with measures of GSR and reaction time. As an example, ulcer patients might be tested with stimulus dimensions of hostility and dependency built into a word association test or a TAT, and schizophrenics might be tested with stimulus dimensions of nurturance and rejection. A study along the latter lines is presently under way. The approach need not be confined to broad motive states, but specific sources of conflict can be explored as well.

The finding that reaction time produced results almost identical to GSR is consistent with Lanier's (1941) conclusion that the affective change brought about by words representing a conflict influences length of reaction time in the same direction and to about the same extent as GSR. However, it is evident that the relationship between GSR and reaction time is not a direct and simple one. Hathaway (1929) reported a correlation of .60 between GSR and reaction time, while Hunt and Landis (1935) found no relationship. Peterson and Jung (1907) reported that only in certain cases is there a clear relationship. What is probably the case is that GSR and reaction time measure different aspects of conflict. Following the model presented, GSR is a measure of activation, while reaction time, at least in a word association test, is a measure of adequacy of performance, which is a frequent but not necessary concomitant of activation. Assuming that the curve of level of performance as a function of increasing activation is inverted U shaped, the relationship between reaction time and activation would depend in part upon the nature of the task, and in part upon the degree and range of activation sampled. Moreover, in a test where the subject was not required to respond rapidly, reaction time would not be a measure of adequacy of performance. Finally, although increases in activation within the above limitations should increase reaction time, the reverse need not hold and reaction time could be affected by many sources that have no bearing on GSR. To the extent that both measures in a word association test are more highly correlated with conflict than with each other, they should provide useful supplementary measures of conflict.

Measures of Approach and Avoidance

Perceptual sensitization and defense. It had been predicted that positive gradients would be produced by measures of misperception and reaction time on the assumption that both were measures of adequacy of response. Although the prediction was substantiated for reaction time, a significant opposite relationship was found for misperception. Yet, the basic assumptions from which the prediction for misperceptions was made were supported, i.e., the finding on GSR provided evidence of an increase in activation along the stimulus dimension, and the misperception of neutral words following words on the dimension provided evidence that activation interferes with perception. What had not been taken into account is that perception of words along a dimension is a measure of selective content in much the same manner that content of association is. In the present study approach was greater than avoidance, so that net approach increment could be expected to compensate for interference effects from activation. It is as if the subject, despite a general state of high tension and further increases in tension brought about by thoughts of parachuting, nevertheless forces himself to concentrate on parachuting. The effect is to overcome anxiety induced perceptual deficit for parachute relevant stimuli. The adaptive significance of such a reaction is apparent. It is not possible to explain away the findings by word frequencies, familiarity with words, or inter- or intraserial set effects. Thus, the evidence would appear to support unequivocally the phenomenon of perceptual sensitization. The findings on anxiety words equally well support selective perceptual deficit, which in light of the experimental controls and negative findings on set effects, is strongly suggestive of perceptual defense, i.e., an anxiety reducing defense mechanism. On the day of a jump novice parachutists are in a state of acute anxiety, with which they must

come to grips if it is not to interfere with their performance and endanger their lives (Walk, 1959 unpublished). Thinking about and being oriented toward anxiety producing stimuli, i.e., worrying, would only increase level of anxiety, so that there is a strong basis for an avoidance reaction to such thoughts and perceptions. In order to check the anxiety reducing effects of misperception further, we examined the GSRs to anxiety words that were misperceived. Where an innocuous word was perceived in place of an anxiety word, the GSR was reduced. Thus, the overall evidence suggests that perceptual defense did occur for the anxiety words. Although originally unanticipated, perceptual sensitization and defense may well provide effective measures of approach and avoidance. Of course, in situations where unconscious conflict was involved, avoidance would be stronger than approach, and net approach tendency would work in the same direction as activation, so that enhanced perceptual defense might be the only phenomenon that would be found.

It is noteworthy that failures in perception were far more common than all other inadequate responses combined. Luria (1932) noted failures in perception for emotionally disturbing words, but these were no more common than were other inadequate responses, such as perservation, repeating a stimulus word, making an incidental comment, or blocking. The larger number of misperceptions in the present study undoubtedly is a result of the tape recorded presentation, despite the screening of the lists for clarity of pronunciation. Tape recordings obviously provide reduced cues because of the absence of lip movements. It is possible that tape recorded lists containing specially selected categories of words would provide an excellent projective technique for general usage, particularly if fidelity or loudness were varied to provide an optimum level of ambiguity or a measure of perceptual threshold.

Content of association. The results on content of association corresponded to those on perceptual sensitization, i.e., parachutists on the day of a jump produced an increased number of parachute related responses. Unfortunately, the critical prediction so far as the model is concerned, that conflict would be indicated by an increment in parachute relevant responses at the low end of the parachute dimension and a decrement at the high end, could not be adequately tested because all associa tions to the high end of the dimension were uniformly high in relevance. To test the hypothesis it will be necessary to use words at the upper end of the stimulus dimension which facilitate avoidance reactions to a greater extent than the ones used in the present study. Nevertheless, the reduced number of misperceptions at the high end of the dimension leads one to suspect that the hypothesis would not be substantiated. Moreover, there was no evidence within the range of the dimension that could be adequately tested indicating that responses to different levels of the dimension were functionally dissimilar.

The measures of perception and of content of association clearly illustrate the manner in which conflict serves to focus attention in the area of conflict and to produce insensitivity in other areas. The implications for psychopathology are evident, particularly in reference to symptoms involving preoccupation, such as obsessive thinking, and to symptoms of inefficiency and inability to concentrate.

Effect of Experience on the Shape of Gradients

The findings on three experienced parachutists are particularly interesting. A reasonable prediction would have been that experienced jumpers would produce gradients that were lower and less steep than inexperienced jumpers, particularly on the day of a jump, i.e., their gradients would be somewhere between an inexperienced jumper's and a nonparachutists'. However, it was found for both GSR and reaction time that on the day of a jump, experienced jumpers produced similar gardients to inexperienced jumpers up to a midway point along the dimension, after which their gradients reserved direction, so that their GSRs to high relevant parachute words were no different than to neutral words. The resulting GSR and reaction time curves for the experienced jumpers resembled the predicted curve for net approach increment, which was based on the assumption that inhibitory tendencies are in conflict with expressive tendencies. This may indicate that associated with experience and mastery of conflict there is an inhibition of anxiety producing responses. Another possibility, not incompatible with the first, is that the gradient of activation is steeper for cues that are consciously associated with the conflict than for cues that are indirectly conditioned to the conflict, and that with successful experience, the anxiety associ-

ated with the labeled cues is extinguished at a faster rate than the anxiety conditioned to the unlabeled cues. Parachutists, in general, are more apt to consciously relate conflict produced by parachuting to high relevant words, such as PARACHUTE and RIPCORD, than to low relevant words, such as LAND and HILL. It would then follow that with successful experience conflict produced fear should be extinguished faster to the high relevant words than to the low relevant words. If the argument here is correct, it offers an explanation of why anxiety is often elicited by apparently innocuous or unrecognized stimuli, and why it is therapeutic to label stimuli associated with a conflict. In reference to this latter point, an ex-paratrooper colleague told us of how he had experienced an anxiety attack while standing on the platform of a train, until it occurred to him that the perception of the terrain moving by was similar to his perceptions when preparing to jump from an airplane.

Anxiety Reducing Effects of Parachuting

Parachutists obtained lower GSRs and shorter reaction times to neutral stimuli than did control subjects. Possibly, this indicates a personality characteristic which leads people to choose parachuting as a sport. Short reaction times and small GSRs suggest a person who is relatively impulsive and expressive. A second possibility is that parachuting serves to reduce tensions, and that the focusing of conflict and its momentary mastery in one area temporarily reduces conflict and disturbance in other areas, i.e., parachuting is a way of mastering fear. A few records of parachutists tested immediately after a jump revealed an astonishing absence of GSRs. The father of one of the parachutists reported that his son, who is a chronic stutterer, experienced an alleviation of symptoms on the afternoon following his first jump. Another subject, in a letter to the examiner, volunteered information about his increased frustration tolerance following a parachute jump. Reference is here made to the letter, which provides a description of a first jump:

Well, my first static line jump was an experience that left some definite impressions on me. . . . Yes, fear of the unknown was there. I had prepared for this a long time. It was a real challenge to me. I had fears of chickening out, fear that the chute might not open, or that my landing would be hard. I was very anxious to get it over with. The most immediate sequence that is constantly on my mind is the time interval of standing on the wheel and holding on to the struts, being hit by the jumpmaster, and falling backwards till my chute caught. What happened after that is only slightly in my mind. After landing I was happy, emotionally released, and proud of myself in that I had accomplished something I set out to do. This was a good morale booster and reduced my insecurity. . . . While driving back we tried to pick up two girls on the road. They refused, but this did not shatter my ego. I had an "I don't care" attitude. While on the road I did not speed, or at least there was no desire to speed. Another change I noticed was that when I put on the taperecorder to hear some music, I did not want to hear it loud. That night I finished reading a book, but while reading, the experience of jumping was constantly on my mind. . . .

Summary

A theoretical model for the measurement of approach-avoidance conflict was described, and predictions from it were evaluated by examining inexperienced parachutists at two time intervals from a jump. The model is a modification of Miller's model for approach-avoidance conflict. Gradients of drive were represented as a function of a stimulus and a time dimension. From the basic model of drive strength, models of activation and net approach increment were derived. It was assumed that the former could be measured by GSR and by performance deficit, and the latter by verbal content in response to a word association test with a built-in stimulus dimension. It was predicted that parachutists would produce gradients for GSR and for measures of performance deficit, and that the gradients would be higher and steeper on the day of a jump than at a time 2 weeks from a jump. It was further predicted that parachutists on the day of a jump would produce an increased number of goal relevant responses to the lower end of the stimulus dimension and a decreased number of such responses to the upper end of the dimension relative to their performance 2 weeks from a jump.

Eight novice sport-parachutists were tested first on the day of a jump and again 2 weeks later; eight others were tested first 2 weeks before a jump and again on the day of a jump. Sixteen nonparachutists served as controls. The tests consisted of parallel forms of a word association test with four levels of relevance to parachuting and with a group of words related to anxiety.

The major findings were as follows:

1. All 16 parachutists on both the day of a jump and the control day, and no control subjects, produced gradients of GSR as a function of the stimulus dimension. For all 16 parachutists, the gradients were higher and steeper on the day of a jump than on a control day.

2. Anxiety words elicited an increase in GSR from controls as well as parachutists. The increase was greatest for parachutists on the day of a jump, next for parachutists 2 weeks from a jump, and least for controls.

3. Parachutists produced smaller GSRs than nonparachutists to neutral words.

4. The results on reaction time, a measure of performance deficit, were similar to those for GSR.

5. Parachutists on the day of a jump exhibited a general perceptual deficit for neutral words, a greater deficit for anxiety words, and a relative sensitivity for parachute related words. The same results were obtained when parachutists were used as their own controls as when they were compared to nonparachutists. The findings can neither be accounted for by general frequency of or familiarity with words, or by inter- or intraserial set effects.

6. Parachutists on the day of a jump produced more parachute related responses than parachutists on a control day, who in turn produced more such responses than nonparachutists.

7. Three experienced jumpers on the day of a jump all produced a different form of curve for GSR and reaction time than inexperienced jumpers. The curve was similar up to a midpoint in the dimension, after which there was a sharp drop for the experienced jumpers and a continuous increase for the inexperienced jumpers.

It was concluded that the following three effects appear to be useful indicators of conflict: an increase in activation along a stimulus dimension, as indicated by a physiological measure, such as GSR; an increase in performance deficit along a stimulus dimension, as indicated by a formal (noncontent) measure, such as reaction time; and selective approach and avoidance, as indicated by perceptual sensitization and perceptual deficit, or by content of verbal response.

REFERENCES

Epstein, S., & Smith, R. Thematic apperception as a measure of the hunger drive. *J. proj. Tech.*, 1956, **20**, 372–384.

Hathaway, S. R. A comparative study of the psychogalvanic and association time measures: A new psychogalvanic apparatus. *J. appl. Psychol.*, 1929, **13**, 632–646.

Hunt, W. A., & Landis, C. Word association, reaction time, and the magnitude of the GSR. *Amer. J. Psychol.*, 1935, **47**, 143–145.

Lanier, L. H. An experimental study of "affective conflict." *J. Psychol.*, 1941, **11**, 199–217.

Luria, R. *The nature of human conflicts.* New York: Liverright, 1932.

Malmo, R. B. Activation: A neuropsychological dimension. *Psychol. Rev.*, 1959, **66**, 367–386.

Miller, N. E. Theory and experiment relating psychoanalytic displacement to stimulus response generalization. *J. abnorm. soc. Psychol.*, 1948, **43**, 155–178.

Miller, N. E. Comments on theoretical models illustrated by the development of a theory of conflict behavior. *J. Pers.*, 1951, **20**, 82–100.

Miller, N. E. Liberalization of basic S-R concepts: Extensions to conflict behavior, motivation, and social learning. In S. Koch (Ed.), *Psychology: A study of a science.* New York: McGraw-Hill, 1959. Pp. 196–292.

Murray, E. J., & Berkun, M. M. Displacement as a function of conflict. *J. abnorm. soc. Psychol.*, 1955, **51**, 47–56.

Peterson, F., & Jung, C. G. Psychological investigations with the galvanometer and pnuemograph in normal and insane individuals. *Brain*, 1907, **30**, 211.

Woodworth, R. S., & Schlosberg, H. *Experimental psychology.* New York: Holt, 1954.

4. Direct analysis from the viewpoint of learning theory

EDWARD J. MURRAY

ONE APPROACH TO PSYCHOTHERAPY with psychotics which has produced widespread interest, and not a little controversy, is John N. Rosen's method of direct analysis (Rosen, 1953). A number of invited commentaries on direct analysis have appeared (Brody, 1959; Devereaux, 1959; and Scheflen, 1961). The author was asked to make an analysis in terms of learning theory (see Dollard & Miller, 1950).

A visit to the Institute for Direct Analysis at Temple University Medical Center was made. The author observed the therapy at first hand, participated in conferences, and examined a good deal of case material. Rosen's writings and the various commentaries on his method were read. In addition, the typescripts of two cases treated by Rosen were studied clinically and with a content analysis technique.

Direct Analysis Approach

Rosen makes the assumption that psychosis is a dream-like state resulting from a basic rejection of the patient by the mother. The first goal of direct analysis is to "wake up" the patient through the use of direct interpretations, usually in oral terms, of the unconscious feelings expressed symbolically in the symptoms and speech of the psychotic (e.g., "your mother's milk was no good"). Second, the therapist establishes himself as a parent substitute using a variety of techniques. Third, there is a strong attempt to "distance" the

SOURCE. Article by Edward J. Murray, "Direct analysis from the viewpoint of learning theory" in *Journal of consulting Psychology*, Vol. 26, pp. 226–231, 1962.

patient from the psychosis and re-educate him in more adaptive modes of behavior.

The milieu aspects of direct analysis have not received the emphasis they should (see Brody, 1959). A single patient lives in a treatment unit located in an ordinary row house in the city. Two or three aides (recovered patients, college students, etc.), also live with the patient and create a kind of family atmosphere. The irregularly occurring therapy sessions are conducted by Rosen in the living room with the aides, staff members, and professional guests seated about. Rosen may sit with the patient on the couch, hold a hand, or offer a shoulder to cry on. He may also shout at a patient or even wrestle with the patient. The aides pick up Rosen's interpretations and attitudes, and reiterate them during his absence. There is a strong group pressure for the patient to give up his psychosis, admit ordinarily forbidden incestuous desires, murderous wishes, etc., and to get well.

Initially, Rosen believed that this quite short, albeit intensive, therapy was sufficient to achieve a permanent cure for psychosis, but many patients seem to suffer relapses (see Horwitz, Polatin, Kolb, & Hoch, 1958). He concluded that direct analysis has to be followed up by a conventional psychoanalysis in order to secure a patient against a recurrence. Direct analysis, itself, he now thinks of as a way of resolving the psychotic state (see Rosen, 1953, p. 5). In this paper, we will not be concerned with the efficacy of direct analysis but rather with understanding the process. A real cure for schizophrenia is probably a long way off and most likely requires a much better scientific understanding of the very fabric of social existence than we have at the present time.

Content Analysis Method

The method of content analysis developed by the author (Murray, 1956) was modified and applied to the two psychotic cases treated by John Rosen. Unfortunately, it was not possible to obtain more transcribed cases. Motion pictures had been taken of the treatment of these cases and a typescript made from the sound track. The length of the individual treatment sessions varied from about 1 to 3 hours, as is typical in direct analysis. Typescripts were numbered by movie reel and therapy sessions. The reels, lasting approximately an hour, were used as the basic division because of the more uniform length.

The patient's flow of speech was divided into a unit called the "meaning phrase" or "statement." In its simplest form this is merely a simple English sentence (e.g., "I am afraid of losing my mind") with one major thought. In the present study, all of the protocols of the two patients were unit scored by an experienced person. The unit for the therapists remarks is simply everything he says in between two patient statements. Previous studies have shown that these units are highly reliable.

Each of the meaning phrases of the patient's speech was placed in one of four major categories: psychotic symptoms, family conflicts, transference, and irrelevant. These patient statements were scored in context and prefatory statements were included in the relevant category. Psychotic symptoms included disturbed thinking as well as hallucinatory, delusional, bizarre, and anxious material. Family conflicts included all positive, inhibitory, and hostile feelings connected with affectional, sexual, dependence, and independence needs related to the family. Family included parents, siblings, spouse, children, fiancé, and other relatives of importance. The transference category included the same feelings and needs which were expressed toward Rosen.

All of the content scoring for both cases was done by a capable graduate student in clinical psychology who was trained with the content analysis system but was given little information about direct analysis or the particular cases. In order to check on his reliability, two additional clinical psychology graduate students were trained. One scored a reel from Case A and the other a reel from Case B. The total unit by unit agreement was 72% ($p < .0001$).

A simplified scoring system for the therapist remarks was used in this study based on a distinction found useful in studying therapist behavior previously. The remarks were judged as active or passive. The active remarks included: introduction of new topics, interpretations, evaluations, strong opinions, expressions of approval and disapproval, declarations of love and demands for love, and all other remarks containing a good deal of information and feeling. Passive remarks included: simple agreement, mild probes, "Mm," and other low pressure devices used by most therapists to keep the patient talking. A reliability study on a randomly selected hour from Case A showed an 80% agreement between two scores ($p < .001$).

Case A. The first patient, a 19-year-old girl from a poor immigrant family, was sent to the institute and seen for eight interviews of varying length over a period of several weeks. She came from a disturbed family in which several members had been hospitalized. She had been going with a fellow for about 5 years prior to her breakdown. During an Army furlough their sex play became more intense. She avoided intercourse but began to think of herself as a saint for controlling herself so well. Her thinking became increasingly confused, she had fears of death for herself and her boyfriend, and she began to think that her mother was not telling her when the boy was in town.

At the beginning of therapy, the patient was extremely anxious and manifested many psychotic symptoms including peculiar physical sensations, ideas of reference, and hallucinations. Rosen reacted to this by, first of all, clearly labeling the girl as "insane." He also actively elicited hostile and sexual material about the family and about himself. He made many efforts to establish himself in a parental role. The patient showed considerable improvement but had one serious relapse after a home visit between Sessions 5 and 6. Near the end there was a good deal of didactic explanation to the patient. The patient was seen after this in a less formal way and was employed as an aide in the treatment of other patients.

The relationship between psychotic symptoms and family conflicts in Case A is shown in Figure 1. In this figure, as well as subsequent ones, the categories are shown as a percentage of the total number of statements in a reel in order to control for differences in

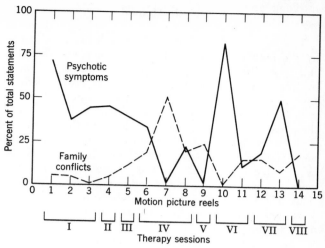

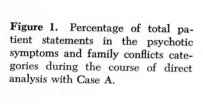

Figure 1. Percentage of total patient statements in the psychotic symptoms and family conflicts categories during the course of direct analysis with Case A.

the reel totals. It can be seen that the psychotic symptoms category is initially high and then decreases until Reel 10 when there is a dramatic upsurge. This was probably related to a disturbing home visit which took place between Sessions 5 and 6. On the other hand, family conflicts, initially low, shows a tendency to increase and, more important, to fluctuate reciprocally with psychotic symptoms. The correlation between the two categories is negative and highly significant ($r = -72, p < .01$). Patient statements about the therapist tend to increase during analysis. The transference material in Case A increased, with some fluctuations, to as high as 50% of the statements in the hour.

Case B. The second patient was a 30-year-old married man from a native lower-class family who was sent to the institute for a period of several weeks during which time he was seen for three intensive interviews by Rosen. While

there was no record of mental illness in the family background, the early environment of the patient was somewhat unstable. After a period of military service he became preoccupied with religion and extremely jealous and suspicious of his wife. His wife left him and his behavior became even more bizarre. He was picked up by the police on the street speaking an unknown tongue which he said was the Holy Ghost talking through him. He also had periods of rolling in the street in a religious frenzy.

In the therapy the patient was initially hostile and preoccupied with religion. Again Rosen clearly labeled the patient as "insane." He elicited hostile and sexual material about the family and wife. The transference relationship did not develop as much in this case as in Case A. The patient showed some alleviation of symptoms.

The content analysis results, shown in Figure 2, are similar to the first case but not quite

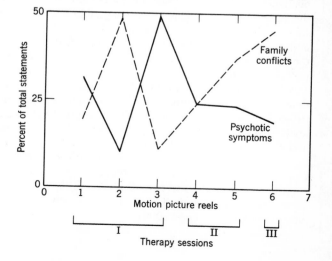

Figure 2. Percentage of total patient statements in the psychotic symptoms and family conflicts categories during the course of direct analysis with Case B.

as striking. There is an over-all downward trend in psychotic symptoms and an increase in family conflicts. The reciprocity between the two categories is rather clear in the graph and is statistically significant ($r = .91$, $p < .02$). The statements about the therapist also increased in Case B but only to a maximum of about 7%.

Incidentally, it is unlikely that these results are due to an artifact introduced by presenting the findings in percentage form. The relationships are essentially the same when frequency comparisons are made. The correlations are not forced by a low ceiling as is shown by the fact that the three categories together, psychotic symptoms, family conflicts, and transference, account for an average of less than 65% of the statements per reel in Case A and less than 60% in Case B. Thus, there is considerable room left for variation.

Therapist's Behavior

The most striking thing about Rosen's behavior during treatment is the punitive attitude about psychotic symptoms beginning with his heavy-handed labeling of the patient as "crazy" and continuing with his angry, ridiculing, and rejecting reactions to the symptomatology. The aides pick up and reiterate Rosen's attitudes. Yet much of this would not appear in a simple content analysis breakdown into approval or disapproval because it gets quite involved. Mockery is often used. Sometimes Rosen will lead on a delusional system and then topple it.

On the other hand there is not only permissiveness but active encouragement for the expression of hostile, sexual, and usually forbidden intimate topics, particularly concerned with family figures. It is with this material that Rosen shows his warm and accepting side.

But there is something Rosen stresses even more than symptoms or family conflict—the patient's relationship to him. Rosen literally forces himself on the patient in the role of an authoritarian but loving parent. He then tries to elicit the murderous, incestual, and dependent feelings originating in the family towards himself. When such feelings are expressed he is very permissive. He will use the parental role, if gained, for didactic instruction in everyday problems of living.

The emphasis Rosen places on the transference relationship is illustrated by the results from the content analysis. Table 1 shows, first of all, the percentage of patient statements in the three categories to which the therapist responded in any way. The differences between the 37% in the transference category and the other two percentages are statistically significant ($p < .001$). Case B shows the same pattern but, because of fewer statements, the differences only approach statistical significance.

Furthermore, this differential responding by the therapist is more clearly seen where the activity and passivity of the therapist's remarks are taken into account. As can also be seen in Table 1, the proportion of active, interpretive, and evaluative remarks is greater when the therapist is responding to transference material than to psychotic symptoms or family conflicts. In Case A both comparisons are statistically significant ($p < .02$) and in Case B both comparisons are highly significant ($p < .001$). In short, the therapist responds more frequently and more actively to transference material.

It is of interest to compare the reaction of the therapist to the two cases. As Table 1 shows, the therapist reacted a greater proportion of the time to material in all categories with Case B probably because he was considerably less verbal than Case A. It is the impression of the writer that the relationship was weaker, both on the part of the therapist and the patient, in Case B. As a rough check on this, the writer counted the frequency of Rosen's famous ex-

Table 1. Therapist Reaction to Patient Content Categories

Patient Content Categories	Percentage of Patient Statements to Which Therapist Reacted		Percentage Active Therapist Remarks	
	Case A	Case B	Case A	Case B
Psychotic symptoms	19	34	33	39
Family conflicts	16	44	33	27
Transference material	37	62	42	100

pressions of "love" in the two cases and found 30 in Case A but none in Case B. On the patient side, recall the low frequency of transference statements. Whether the reason for this is the sex difference, personality differences, or some other factor, remains unknown. It does show, however, that important aspects of direct analysis vary with the patient.

A Learning Theory Interpretation

The psychotic patients can be described as being in an intense conflict between affectionate, hostile, and sexual drives and anxiety dating from the early family relationships but triggered off by the threat to the current relationships with fiancé and wife. The psychotic symptoms are motivated by the anxiety and function as a defense against the family conflicts. The reciprocal relationship between the psychotic symptoms and family conflicts supports this. It is also of great significance to this explanation that in Case A, when the patient was upset by a home visit, the following hour was filled not with discussion of family problems but rather with psychotic material.

When it is working at its best, direct analysis appears to reduce anxiety and psychotic symptoms. To some extent this may be due to an extinction of anxiety. In order to accomplish this, Rosen, with the aid of the therapeutic milieu group, appears to be teaching the patient a new discrimination in which culturally prohibited family feelings are encouraged and psychotic symptoms forbidden.

But the real core of the therapy is the relationship between the patient and therapist. By adopting a parental role and eliciting anxiety laden feelings, Rosen may be permitting a much greater extinction of anxiety than would be possible in the merely verbal descriptions of feelings about people not present. It should be pointed out that the transference relationship in direct analysis does not simply consist in Rosen's "giving love" to the patient—a popular misconception not only of direct analysis but of other types of psychotherapy with schizophrenics. Devereux (1959) is the one who has most clearly stated that, on the basis of his observations, Rosen's aim was to get the patient to *express* affection. Thus, the extinction of anxiety is possible.

Of particular importance in this process is the therapist's reaction to this material. If the therapist becomes anxious this will surely be communicated to the patient in some way. Then, instead of extinction of anxiety, the feelings may become further inhibited. Apparently, Rosen does not get anxious. Eisenbud has pointed to Rosen's lack of fear and hostility toward the patient as the critical factor in the treatment (see Rosen, 1953, p. 85).

If, indeed, the extinction of anxiety is an important part of direct analysis one might ask is this the most efficient method of extinction. The use of punitive techniques for the initial reduction of psychotic symptoms may slow down learning to distinguish reality from fantasy. For example, Garmezy (1952) found that schizophrenics had more difficulty learning a discrimination when the wrong choice was punished in addition to the correct choice being rewarded. Another thing to consider is that direct analysis is a short, intensive therapy. While the experimental evidence is not conclusive, it seems that massed extinction will produce a greater immediate reduction in fear but the effects of distributed trials would be expected to be more permanent (Dollard & Miller, 1950, p. 73). This may be why Rosen gets rapid, dramatic effects which do not seem to be long-lasting without additional psychoanalysis. In contrast, Fromm-Reichmann's (1950) approach avoids the use of punitive techniques and extends treatment over a longer time period, suggesting better conditions for the permanency of extinction. It would be interesting to have comparative data.

Toward the end of direct analysis the therapist introduces didactic discussion and direct instruction. Unfortunately, we have little material on this. But, apparently, Rosen attempts to supply some simple responses for the patient who has not learned them because of anxiety and social withdrawal. He may give an inhibited girl information about sex or even demonstrate how she should move during intercourse. On the other hand, he may become angry at a girl who is promiscuous.

Summary

Direct analysis is an intensive form of psychotherapy for psychotics conducted in a special milieu. An attempt seems to be made to extinguish anxiety about family conflicts while maintaining a punitive attitude towards psychotic symptoms. The approach is highly interpretive and aggressive. The greatest emphasis is placed on a parent-child sort of therapeutic relationship through which anxiety extinction is continued. More adaptive social responses by the patient are encouraged.

REFERENCES

Brody, M. W. *Observations on direct analysis.* New York: Vantage, 1959.

Devereux, G. A. psychoanalytic scrutiny of certain techniques of direct analysis. *Psychoanal. psychonal. Rev.,* 1959, **46**(2), 45–65.

Dollard, J., & Miller, N. E. *Personality and psychotherapy: An analysis in terms of learning, thinking and culture.* New York: McGraw-Hill, 1950.

Fromm-Reichmann, Frieda. *Principles of intensive psychotherapy.* Chicago: Univer. Chicago Press, 1950.

Garmezy, N. Stimulus differentiation by schizophrenic and normal subjects under conditions of reward and punishment. *J. Pers.,* 1952, **21**, 253–276.

Horwitz, W. A., Polatin, P., Kolb, L. C., & Hoch, P. H. A study of cases of schizophrenia treated by "direct analysis." *Amer. J. Psychiat.,* 1958, **114**, 780–783.

Murray, E. J. A content-analysis method for studying psychotherapy. *Psychol. Monogr.,* 1956, **70**(13, Whole No. 420).

Rosen, J. N. *Direct analysis.* New York: Grune & Stratton, 1953.

Scheflen, A. E. *A psychotherapy of schizophrenia: Direct analysis.* Springfield, Ill.: Charles C Thomas, 1961.

Rogers' Self Theory

Carl Rogers has not been content to rest on the laurels he has received for his substantial contributions to psychology. He is constantly redefining, sharpening, elaborating, modifying, and interpreting his position. He writes and speaks to many different audiences because he believes with passion that psychology has much to contribute toward understanding and hopefully toward solving many of the problems that vex people today. The selection made for this book was one written at the request of psychologists to be read by psychologists. It is not, however, couched in professional argot. Rogers states simply and effectively his position, and some of the influences in his life that helped to shape his viewpoint.

The initial empirical selection shows Rogers' and his colleagues' concern for devising objective and quantifiable methods of evaluating the progress and results of psychotherapy. In this area, Rogers has been a pioneer. His research on the process of psychotherapy, an enterprise in which he has been joined by a number of co-workers, was virtually unique when it was initiated.

One criticism that has been voiced by psychologists of Rogers' method of client-centered therapy is that while it may work for those who have mild emotional disturbances, it would be ineffective with patients suffering from more serious mental disorders. Gendlin's paper recounts how the method is being used in the treatment of psychotic patients.

A hallmark of self theory is the significance it attributes to conscious—one might even say—self-conscious reports by the experiencing person. In this respect, it constitutes a third force between psychoanalysis, on the one hand, which seeks out the mind in all of its subterranean hideaways, and behaviorism, on the other hand, which concerns itself largely with overt behavior. It would be hard to imagine self theorists pursuing their empirical activities in an animal laboratory. The consequences for research of the position taken by this third force are far-reaching. It is considerably easier to secure self-reports from conscious human beings than it is to explore the unconscious or to contrive controlled conditions for eliciting overt behavior. Consequently, recent psychological literature is replete with investigations of hypotheses derived from self theory. Most of this literature consists of short articles; many of the investigators make use of Stephenson's Q technique. For a critique of this literature the reader is referred to Ruth Wylie's book, *The Self Concept.*

We have selected a group of research papers which reflect various facets of self theory. Akeret's research shows that the self-concept is not unitary, that it is made up of many kinds of self-feelings which are not necessarily consistent with one another. Turner and Vanderlippe's well controlled study on a college student population confirms the hypothesis that the more congruence there is between what a person thinks he is and what he would like to be, the better adjusted the person is. Suinn, who is represented by two articles, finds in the first study that the more one accepts oneself the more likely he is to accept others, and explains this finding in terms of learning theory. The second article by Suinn, Osborne, and Winfree demonstrates that memory material which is inconsistent with one's self concept is more poorly remembered than memory material which is consistent with one's self concept. In the last paper, Medinnus and Curtis present positive evidence for the hypothesis that mothers who accept themselves are more likely to accept their children.

1. A theory of therapy, personality, and interpersonal relationships, as developed in the client-centered framework

CARL R. ROGERS

Introduction

BEING ONE WHO HAS DEPRECATED the use of compulsion as a means of altering personality and behavior, it is no doubt singularly appropriate that I should be forced to acknowledge the value of the gentle compulsion of a formal request. For some time I had recognized the need of a more adequate and more up-to-date statement of the theories which have been developing in the group associated with client-centered therapy. This might well have remained in the realm of good intentions, had it not been for the formal request from the American Psychological Association, in connection with its Study of the Status and Development of Psychology in the United States, to prepare a systematic statement of this developing theory. To join with others who were endeavoring to formulate their own theories and to use, so far as possible, a common outline—this seemed to be both an obligation and an opportunity which could not be refused. It is this softly voiced but insistent pressure from my colleagues which has caused me to write the following pages now, rather than at some later date. For this pressure I am grateful.

The soil of the theory. No theory can be adequately understood without some knowledge of the cultural and personal soil from which it

SOURCE. Selection from Carl R. Rogers, "A theory of therapy, personality, and interpersonal relationships, as developed in the client-centered framework" in *Psychology: A Theory of Science*, Vol. 3. Edited by Sigmund Koch. New York: McGraw-Hill, 1959.

springs. Consequently I am pleased that the first item of the suggested outline requests a thorough discussion of background factors. This means, I fear, that I must take the reader through some autobiographical material since, although the client-centered orientation has become very much of a group enterprise in every respect, I, as an individual, carry a considerable responsibility for its initiation and for the beginning formulation of its theories. I shall, therefore, mention briefly some cultural influences which may or may not have relevance to the theory itself. I shall not attempt to evaluate these influences, since I am probably a poor judge of the part they have played.

I lived my childhood as a middle child in a large, close-knit family, where hard work and a highly conservative (almost fundamentalist) Protestant Christianity were about equally revered. When the family moved to a farm at the time I was twelve, I became deeply interested and involved in scientific agriculture. The heavy research volumes I read on my own initiative in the next few years regarding feeds and feeding, soils, animal husbandry, and the like, instilled in me a deep and abiding respect for the scientific method as a means of solving problems and creating new advances in knowledge. This respect was reinforced by my first years in college, where I was fond of the physical and biological sciences. In my work in history I also realized something of the satisfactions of scholarly work.

Having rejected the family views of religion, I became interested in a more modern religious viewpoint and spent two profitable years in Union Theological Seminary, which at that time was deeply committed to a freedom of philosophical thought which respected any honest attempt to resolve significant problems, whether this led into or away from the church. My own thinking lead me in the latter direction, and I moved "across the street" to Teachers College, Columbia University. Here I was exposed to the views of John Dewey, not directly, but through William H. Kilpatrick. I also had my first introduction to clinical psychology in the warmly human and common-sense approach of Leta Hollingworth. There followed a year of internship at the Institute for Child Guidance, then in its chaotic but dynamic first year of existence. Here I gained much from the highly Freudian orientation of most of its psychiatric staff, which included David Levy and Lawson Lowrey. My first attempts at therapy were carried on at the Institute. Because I was still completing my doctorate at Teachers College, the sharp incompatibility of the highly speculative Freudian thinking of the Institute with the highly statistical and Thorndikean views at Teachers College was keenly felt.

There followed twelve years in what was essentially a community child guidance clinic in Rochester, New York. This was a period of comparative isolation from the thinking of others. The psychology department of the University of Rochester was uninterested in what we were doing because our work was not, in its opinion, in the field of psychology. Our colleagues in the social agencies, schools, and courts knew little and cared less about psychological ideologies. The only element which carried weight with them was the ability to get results in working with maladjusted individuals. The staff was eclectic, of diverse background, and our frequent and continuing discussion of treatment methods was based on our practical everyday working experience with the children, adolescents, and adults who were our clients. It was the beginning of an effort, which has had meaning for me ever since, to discover the order which exists in our experience of working with people. The volume on the *Clinical Treatment of the Problem Child* was one outcome of this effort.

During the second half of this period there were several individuals who brought into our group the controversial therapeutic views of Otto Rank and the Philadelphia group of social workers and psychiatrists whom he had influenced. Personal contact with Rank was limited

to a three-day institute we arranged; nevertheless his thinking had a very decided impact on our staff and helped me to crystallize some of the therapeutic methods we were groping toward. For by this time I was becoming more competent as a therapist, and beginning to sense a discoverable orderliness in this experience, an orderliness which was inherent *in* the experience, and (unlike some of the Freudian theories which had grown so far from their original soil) did not have to be imposed *on* the experience.

Though I had carried on some part-time university teaching throughout the Rochester years, the shift to a faculty position at Ohio State University was a sharp one. I found that the emerging principles of therapy, which I had experienced largely on an implicit basis, were by no means clear to well-trained, critically minded graduate students. I began to sense that what I was doing and thinking in the clinical field was perhaps more of a new pathway than I had recognized. The paper I presented to the Minnesota chapter of Psi Chi in December, 1940, (later chapter 2 of *Counseling and Psychotherapy*) was the first conscious attempt to develop a relatively new line of thought. Up to that time I had felt that my writings were essentially attempts to distill out more clearly the principles which "all clinicians" were using.

The new influence at Ohio State, which continued to be felt in my years at Chicago, was the impact of young men and women—intellectually curious, often theoretically oriented, eager to learn from experience and to contribute through research and theory to the development of a field of knowledge. Through their mistakes as well as their successes in therapy, through their research studies, their critical contributions, and through our shared thinking, have come many of the recent developments in this orientation.

In the past decade at the University of Chicago the new elements which stand out most sharply are the opportunity for and the encouragement of research, the inclusion of graduate students from education, theology, human development, sociology, industrial relations, as well as psychology, in the ramified activities of the Counseling Center, and the creative thinking of my faculty colleagues, especially those connected with the Center.

The persistent influence which might not be fully recognized, because it is largely implicit in the preceding paragraphs, is the continuing clinical experience with individuals who perceive themselves, or are perceived by others to be, in need of personal help. Since 1928, for a period now approaching thirty years, I have spent probably an average of 15 to 20 hours per week, except during vacation periods, in endeavoring to understand and be of therapeutic help to these individuals. To me, they seem to be the major stimulus to my psychological thinking. From these hours, and from my relationships with these people, I have drawn most of whatever insight I possess into the meaning of therapy, the dynamics of interpersonal relationships, and the structure and functioning of personality.

Some Basic Attitudes. Out of this cultural and personal soil have grown certain basic convictions and attitudes which have undoubtedly influenced the theoretical formulation which will be presented. I will endeavor to list some of these views which seem to me relevant:

1. I have come to see both research and theory as being aimed toward the inward ordering of significant experience. Thus research is not something esoteric, nor an activity in which one engages to gain professional kudos. It is the persistent, disciplined effort to make sense and order out of the phenomena of subjective experience. Such effort is justified because it is satisfying to perceive the world as having order and because rewarding results often ensue when one understands the orderly relationships which appear to exist in nature. One of these rewarding results is that the ordering of one segment of experience in a theory immediately opens up new vistas of inquiry, research, and thought, thus leading one continually forward.

Thus the primary reason for research and systematic theory in the field of therapy is that it is personally dissatisfying to permit the cumulating experiences of therapeutic hours to remain as a conglomeration of more or less isolated events. It feels as though there is an order in these events. What could it be? And of any hunch regarding the inherent order, it is necessary to ask the question, is this really true, or am I deceiving myself? Thus slowly there is assembled a body of facts, and systematic constructs to explain those facts, which have as their basic function the satisfaction of a need for order which exists in me.

(I have, at times, carried on research for purposes other than the above to satisfy others, to convince opponents and sceptics, to gain prestige, and for other unsavory reasons. These errors in judgment and activity have only deepened the above positive conviction.)

2. It is my opinion that the type of understanding which we call science can begin anywhere, at any level of sophistication. To observe acutely, to think carefully and creatively —these activities, not the accumulation of laboratory instruments, are the beginnings of science. To observe that a given crop grows better on the rocky hill than in the lush bottom land, and to think about this observation, is the start of science. To notice that most sailors get scurvy but not those who have stopped at islands to pick up fresh fruit is a similar start. To recognize that, when a person's views of himself change, his behavior changes accordingly, and to puzzle over this, is again the beginning of both theory and science. I voice this conviction in protest against the attitude, which seems too common in American psychology, that science starts in the laboratory or at the calculating machines.

3. A closely related belief is that there is a natural history of science—that science, in any given field, goes through a patterned course of growth and development. For example, it seems to me right and natural that in any new field of scientific endeavor the observations are gross, the hypotheses speculative and full of errors, the measurements crude. More important, I hold the opinion that this is just as truly science as the use of the most refined hypotheses and measurements in a more fully developed field of study. The crucial question in either case is not the degree of refinement but the direction of movement. If in either instance the movement is toward more exact measurement, toward more clear-cut and rigorous theory and hypotheses, toward findings which have greater validity and generality, then this is a healthy and growing science. If not, then it is a sterile pseudo science, no matter how exact its methods. Science is a *developing* mode of inquiry, or it is of no particular importance.

4. In the invitation to participate in the APA study, I have been asked to cast our theoretical thinking in the terminology of the independent-intervening-dependent variable, in so far as this is feasible. I regret that I find this terminology somehow uncongenial. I cannot justify my negative reaction very adequately, and perhaps it is an irrational one, for the logic behind these

terms seems unassailable. But to me the terms seem static—they seem to deny the restless, dynamic, searching, changing aspects of scientific movement. There is a tendency to suppose that a variable thus labeled, remains so, which is certainly not true. The terms also seem to me to smack too much of the laboratory, where one undertakes an experiment *de novo*, with everything under control, rather than of a science which is endeavoring to wrest from the phenomena of experience the inherent order which they contain. Such terms seem to be more applicable to the advanced stages of scientific endeavor than to the beginning stages.

Please do not misunderstand. I quite realize that *after the fact,* any research investigation, or any theory constructed to relate the discovered facts, should be translatable into the language of independent and dependent variables or there is something wrong with the research or theory. But the terms seem to me better adapted to such autopsies than to the living physiology of scientific work in a new field.

5. It should be quite clear from the foregoing that the model of science which I find most helpful is not taken from the advanced stages of theoretical physics. In a field such as psychotherapy or personality the model which seems more congenial to me would be taken from the much earlier stages of the physical sciences. I like to think of the discovery of radioactivity by the Curies. They had left some pitchblende ore, which they were using for some purpose or other, in a room where they stored photographic plates. They discovered that the plates had been spoiled. In other words, first was the observation of a dynamic event. This event might have been due to a multitude of causes. It might have been a flaw in the manufacture of the plates. It might have been the humidity, the temperature, or any one of a dozen other things. But acute observation and creative thinking fastened on a hunch regarding the pitchblende, and this became a tentative hypothesis. Crude experiments began to confirm the hypothesis. Only slowly was it discovered that it was *not* pitchblende, but a strange element *in* the pitchblende which was related to the observed effect. Meanwhile a theory had to be constructed to bring this strange phenomenon into orderly relationship with other knowledge. And although the theory in its most modest form had to do with the effect of radium on photographic plates, in its wider and more speculative reaches it was concerned with the nature of matter and the composition of the universe. By present-day standards in the physical sciences, this is an example of a primitive stage of investigation and theory construction. But in the fields in which I am most deeply interested I can only hope that we are approaching such a stage. I feel sure that we are not beyond it.

6. Another deep-seated opinion has to do with theory. I believe that there is only one statement which can accurately apply to all theories—from the phlogiston theory to the theory of relativity, from the theory I will present to the one which I hope will replace it in a decade—and that is that at the time of its formulation every theory contains an unknown (and perhaps at that point an unknowable) amount of error and mistaken inference. The degree of error may be very great, as in the phlogiston theory, or small, as I imagine it may be in the theory of relativity, but unless we regard the discovery of truth as a closed and finished book, then there will be new discoveries which will contradict the best theories which we can now construct.

To me this attitude is very important, for I am distressed at the manner in which small-caliber minds immediately accept a theory—almost any theory—as a dogma of truth. If theory could be seen for what it is—a fallible, changing attempt to construct a network of gossamer threads which will contain the solid facts—then a theory would serve at it should, as a stimulus to further creative thinking.

I am sure that the stress I place on this grows in part out of my regret at the history of Freudian theory. For Freud, it seems quite clear that his highly creative theories were never more than that. He kept changing, altering, revising, giving new meaning to old terms—always with more respect for the facts he observed than for the theories he had built. But at the hands of insecure disciples (so it seems to me), the gossamer threads became iron chains of dogma from which dynamic psychology is only recently beginning to free itself. I feel that every formulation of a theory contains this same risk and that, at the time a theory is constructed, some precautions should be taken to prevent it from becoming dogma.

7. I share with many others the belief that truth is unitary, even though we will never be able to know this unity. Hence any theory, de-

rived from almost any segment of experience, if it were complete and completely accurate, could be extended indefinitely to provide meaning for other very remote areas of experience. Tennyson expressed this in sentimental fashion in his "Flower in the Crannied Wall." I too believe that a complete theory of the individual plant would show us "what God and man is."

The corollary, however, is of equal importance and is not so often stated. A slight error in a theory may make little difference in providing an explanation of the observed facts out of which the theory grew. But when the theory is projected to explain more remote phenomena, the error may be magnified, and the inferences from the theory may be completely false. A very slight error in the understanding of Tennyson's flower may give a grossly false understanding of man. Thus every theory deserves the greatest respect in the area from which it was drawn from the facts and a decreasing degree of respect as it make predictions in areas more and more remote from its origin. This is true of the theories developed by our own group.

8. There is one other attitude which I hold, which I believe has relevance for the proper evaluation of any theory I might present. It is my belief in the fundamental predominance of the subjective. Man lives essentially in his own personal and subjective world, and even his most objective functioning, in science, mathematics, and the like, is the result of subjective purpose and subjective choice. In relation to research and theory, for example, it is my subjective perception that the machinery of science as we know it—operational definitions, experimental method, mathematical proof —is the best way of avoiding self-deception. But I cannot escape the fact that this is the way it appears to me, and that had I lived two centuries ago, or if I were to live two centuries in the future, some other pathway to truth might seem equally or more valid. To put it more briefly, it appears to me that though there may be such a thing as objective truth, I can never know it; all I can know is that some statements appear to me subjectively to have the qualifications of objective truth. Thus there is no such thing as Scientific Knowledge; there are only individual perceptions of what appears to each person to be such knowledge.

Since this is a large and philosophical issue, not too closely related to what follows, I shall not endeavor to state it more fully here but refer any who are interested to an article in which I have tried to expound this view somewhat more fully (1954). I mention it here only because it is a part of the context in which my theoretical thinking has developed.

A Digression on the Case History of a Construct. Since the abstraction which we term the self is one of the central constructs in our theory, it may be helpful to interpose a somewhat lengthy digression at this point in our list of definitions in order to relate something of the development of this construct. In so doing we will also be illustrating the manner in which most of these defined constructs have come into being in our theory.

Speaking personally, I began my work with the settled notion that the "self" was a vague, ambiguous, scientifically meaningless term which had gone out of the psychologist's vocabulary with the departure of the introspectionists. Consequently I was slow in recognizing that when clients were given the opportunity to express their problems and their attitudes in their own terms, without any guidance or interpretation, they tended to talk in terms of the self. Characteristic expressions were attitudes such as these: "I feel I'm not being my real self." "I wonder who I am, really." "I wouldn't want anyone to know the real me." "I never had a chance to be myself." "It feels good to let myself go and just *be* myself here." "I think if I chip off all the plaster facade I've got a pretty solid self—a good substantial brick building, underneath." It seemed clear from such expressions that the self was an important element in the experience of the client, and that in some odd sense his goal was to become his "real self."

Raimy (1943) produced a careful and searching definition of the self-concept which was helpful in our thinking. There seemed to be no operational way of defining it at that point. Attitudes toward the self could be measured, however, and Raimy and a number of others began such research. Self-attitudes were determined, operationally, by the categorizing of all self-referent terms in interviews preserved in verbatim form by electrical recording. The categories used had a satisfactory degree of interjudge reliability, thus making them suitable scientific constructs for our work. We were encouraged to find that these self-referent attitudes altered significantly in therapy as we had hypothesized they would.

As we focused more upon the concept of the self, clinical experience again gave us further clues as to its nature. For example, in the process of change which appeared to occur in therapy, it was not at all uncommon to find violent fluctuation in the concept of the self. A client, during a given interview, would come to experience himself quite positively. He felt he was worthwhile, that he could meet life with the capacities he possessed, and that he was experiencing a quiet confidence. Three days later he might return with a completely reversed conception of himself. The same evidence now proved an opposite point. The positive new choice he had made now was an instance of silly immaturity; the valid feelings courageously expressed to his colleagues now were clearly inadequate. Often such a client could date, to the moment, the point at which, following some very minor incident, the balance was upset, and his picture of himself had undergone a complete flip-flop. During the interview it might as suddenly reverse itself again.

Consideration of this phenomenon made it clear that we were not dealing with an entity of slow accretion, of step-by-step learning, of thousands of unidirectional conditionings. These might all be involved, but the product was clearly a gestalt, a configuration in which the alteration of one minor aspect could completely alter the whole pattern. One was forcibly reminded of the favorite textbook illustration of a gestalt, the double picture of the old hag and the young woman. Looked at with one mind set, the picture is clearly that of an ugly old woman. The slightest change, and the whole becomes a portrait of an attractive girl. So with our clients. The self-concept was clearly configurational in nature.

Our clinical experience gave us another clue to the manner in which the self functioned. The conventional concept of repression as having to do with forbidden or socially taboo impulses had been recognized as inadequate to fit the facts. Often the most deeply denied impulses and feelings were positive feelings of love, or tenderness, or confidence in self. How could one explain the puzzling conglomeration of experience which seemingly could not be permitted in awareness? Gradually it was recognized that the important principle was one of consistency with the self. Experiences which were incongruent with the individual's concept of himself tended to be denied to awareness, whatever their social character. We began to see the self as a criterion by which the organism screened out experiences which could not comfortably be permitted in consciousness. Lecky's little posthumous book (1945) reinforced this line of thought. We also began to understand other functions of the self in its regulatory influence on behavior, and the like.

At about this juncture Stephenson's Q technique (1953) opened up the possibility of an operational definition of the self-concept. Immediately, research burgeoned. Though we feel it has barely made a start in exploiting the possible testing of hypotheses, there have already been measurements and predictions regarding the self as of this moment, the self in the past, "myself as I am with my mother," "the self I would like to be," etc. Probably the most sophisticated and significant of these studies is that completed by Chodorkoff (1954) in which his hypothesis, stated informally, is as follows: that the greater the agreement between the individual's self-description and an objective description of him, the less perceptual defensiveness he will show, and the more adequate will be his personal adjustment. This hypothesis is upheld and tends to confirm some important aspects of our theory. In general the various investigations have agreed in indicating that the self-concept is an important variable in personality dynamics and that change in the self is one of the most marked and significant changes occurring in therapy.

It should be recognized that any construct is a more or less arbitrary abstraction from experience. Thus the self could be defined in many different ways. Hilgard, for example (1949) has proposed that it be defined in such a way as to include unconscious material, not available to awareness, as well as conscious material. Although we recognize that this is certainly a legitimate way of abstracting from the phenomena, we believe it is not a useful way because it produces a concept which cannot at this point be given operational definition. One cannot obtain sufficient agreement as to the content of the individual's unconscious to make research possible. Hence we believe that it is more fruitful to define the self-concept as a gestalt which is available to awareness. This has permitted and encouraged a flood of important research.

At all times, however, we endeavor to keep in the forefront of our thinking the fact that each definition is no more than an abstraction and that the same phenomena might be abstracted in a different fashion. One of our group is working on a definition of self which would give more emphasis to its process nature. Others have felt that a plural definition, indicating many specific selves in each of various life contexts, would be more fruitful, and this way of thinking has been embodied in, for example, Nunnally's (1955) research. So the search continues for a more adequate conceptualization of this area of our therapeutic experience and for more adequate technical means of providing operational definitions for the concepts which are formulated.

This concludes our interruption of the list of definitions. It is hoped that this one example will give an indication of the way in which many of our basic constructs have developed—not only the self-concept but the constructs of congruence, incongruence, defensiveness, unconditional positive regard, locus of evaluation, and the like. Although the process has been irregular, it has tended to include clinical observation, initial conceptualization, initial crude research to test some of the hypotheses involved, further clinical observation, more rigorous formulation of the construct and its functional relationships, more refined operational definitions of the construct, more conclusive research.

A Continuing program of Theory and Research. The theoretical system and the research program which are connected with client-centered therapy have grown from within themselves. This point can hardly be overemphasized. The thought that we were making a start on a theoretical system would for me have been a most distasteful notion even as little as a dozen years ago. I was a practical clinician and held (*horrible dictu!*) an open scorn of all psychological theory, as my early students at Ohio State can testify. This was true even at the same time that I was beginning to discern the orderliness which existed in the therapeutic process. I like to think that the theoretical system and far-reaching web of research which have developed, have grown in an organic fashion. Each plodding step has simply been a desire to find out this, a desire to find out that, a need for perceiving whatever consistencies, or invariances, or order exists in the material thus far unearthed.

Consequently when I am asked, as I am in the outline suggested for this paper, "the extent to which the systematic program has been realized," I feel it is the wrong question for this system. I have no idea what will be the ultimate realization of the living program which has developed. I can see some of the likely next steps, or the current directions, but have no assurance that these will be taken. We have continued to move in the directions which are *experienced* as rewarding, not necessarily in those directions which logic points out. I believe this has been the strength of the program, and I trust it will continue.

Thus I believe that we are likely to see progress in the following directions, but I am not sure of any of them. It seems likely that further moves will be made toward theory and research in the field of perception, enriching that field by the insights gained in therapy, and being enriched by the wealth of research data and theory in perception which can be brought to bear in the refinement of the theories we are developing. One such study now in progress, for example, is attempting to investigate perceptual changes which occur during therapy. The measures range from those entirely concerned with social perception—of people, of relationships—to those entirely concerned with the physical perception of form, color, and line. Does therapy change only social perception, or does it alter even the most basic perceptual processes? It not, where on this continuum does change cease to occur?

I visualize the same type of *rapprochement* with learning theory, where in my judgment we have much to offer in the way of new directions in that field, as well as being able to use much of the material available there. It also seems likely that a number of the hypotheses we are formulating may be tested in the laboratory, some on human and some on animal subjects, thus linking the field of personality and therapy with so-called experimental psychology. There seems no reason, for example, why research on the establishment and consequences of conditions of worth, as spelled out in this theory, might not be carried out on higher animals, with a wider range of experimental conditions and more adequate controls than could be achieved with human subjects.

I regard it as possible that there may be a closer linking of our theory with the developing interest in creativity in the humanities and social sciences generally, and I trust that this theory may provide a number of relevant hypotheses for testing. I regard it as very likely that the implications of this body of theory for industrial production will be developed much more fully—the beginnings, as described by Richard in Gordon's book (1955), seem very exciting. I believe it is possible that the near future may see a clear linking with the psychiatric group and a testing of the theory in a wider variety of human disorders, with a reduction in the professional parochialism which has thus far kept the medical group largely ignorant of the research in this field.

One direction which appears only theoretically possible is the exploitation in governmental affairs and international relations of some of the implications of this theory. I do not regard this as likely in the near future.

I suspect that the discovery and development of a contextual basis for this theory in some form of existential philosophy will continue. The general orientation of philosophical phenomenology is also likely to continue to have its influence in this respect. These are some of the potentialities for future development—rather grandiose, to be sure—which I see. The extent to which any of them will organically grow is a matter which demands a gift of prophecy I do not have.

Immediate strategy of development. To return, in closing, to the much more immediate issues facing us in the systematic development of the theory, I see several problems which have very high priority if our general systematic thinking is to have a healthy development. I will list these problems and tasks, but the order of listing has no significance, since I cannot determine the priority.

1. We are urgently in need of new and more ingenious tools of measurement. Stephenson's Q technique (1953) has been most helpful and Osgood's method for quantifying semantic space (1954) also seems promising. But most urgently needed of all is a method whereby we might give operational definition to the construct *experience* in our theory, so that discrepancies between self-concept and experience, awareness and experience, etc., might be measured. This would permit the testing of some of the most crucial hypotheses of the theoretical system. To be sure, some attempts have been made to approach such an operational definition, but the instrumentation is exceedingly cumbersome and admittedly inadequate.

2. An increased amount of experience with individuals classed as psychotic, and the testing of a variety of the theoretical hypotheses in therapeutic work with this group and in research with psychotics as subjects, would round out and enrich our systematic thinking in an area in which it is at present inadequate. It would provide the type of extreme reality test which is most helpful in the confirmation, modification, or disproof of a theoretical system. There would seem to be no barriers except practical ones to such a development.

3. An increased amount of experience and careful studies of hypotheses developed from the theory are needed in the area of group relationships. Hypotheses regarding leadership, facilitation of learning, and reduction of social conflict seem particularly fruitful to study. Here again, the test of the theory at one of its deduced extremes would be most helpful in confirming or revising its core.

4. Still another urgent need—no doubt quite evident to readers of this presentation—is the translation of the present theory into terms which meet the rigorous requirements of the logic of science. Although progress in this direction has been made there is still a woefully long distance to go. Such a development, carried through by competent persons, would greatly sharpen the deductive hypotheses which might be drawn from the system, and hence provide more crucial tests of it.

5. The final need I wish to mention may seem to some very contradictory to the one just voiced. Personally I see it as a possible evolutionary step, not as a contradictory one. I see a great need for creative thinking and theorizing in regard to the methods of social science. There is a rather widespread feeling in our group that the logical positivism in which we were professionally reared is not necessarily the final philosophical word in an area in which the phenomenon of subjectivity plays such a vital and central part. Have we evolved the optimal method for approximating the truth in this area? Is there some view, possibly developing out of an existentialist orientation, which might preserve the values of logical positivism and the scientific advances which it has helped to foster and yet find more room for the existing subjective person who is at the heart and base even of our system of science? This is a highly speculative dream of an intangible goal, but

I believe that many of us have a readiness to respond to the persons who can evolve a tentative answer to the riddle.

REFERENCES

Chodorkoff, B. Self-perception, perceptual defense, and adjustment. *J. abnorm. soc. Psychol.*, 1954, **49**, 508–512.

Gordon, T. *Group-centered leadership.* Boston: Houghton Mifflin, 1955.

Hilgard, E. R. Human motives and the concept of self. *Amer. Psychologist,* 1949, **4**, 374–382.

Lecky, P. *Self-consistency: a theory of personality.* New York: Island Press, 1945.

Nunnally, J. C. An investigation of some propositions of self-conception: the case of Miss Sun. *J. abnorm. soc. Psychol.*, 1955, **50**, 87–92.

Osgood, C. E. The nature and measurement of meaning. *Psychol. Bull.*, 1954, **49**, 197–237.

Raimy, V. C. The self-concept as a factor in counseling and personality organization. Unpublished doctoral dissertation, Ohio State Univer., 1943.

Rogers, C. R. & Dymond, R. F. (Eds.) *Psychotherapy and personality change.* Chicago: Univer. Chicago Press, 1954.

Stephenson, W. *The study of behavior: Q-technique and its methodology.* Chicago: Univer. Chicago Press, 1953.

2. Development of a scale to measure process changes in psychotherapy

ALAN M. WALKER, RICHARD A. RABLEN,
AND CARL R. ROGERS

Introduction

THIS PAPER DESCRIBES the application of a scale
for the objective assessment of process or movement in psychotherapy and reports the degree
of reliability and validity found in a preliminary
investigation. Before proceeding to the study
itself, some indication of the way in which it
developed is necessary. The scale in its original form was proposed by Rogers (7) after he
had undertaken an extended study of recorded
interviews for the purpose of discovering commonalities in the process of personality change.
He proposed that clients who feel received in
therapy tend to move away from a general fixity
of functioning and rigidity of structure toward
greater openness, fluidity, and changingness,
along a continuum from stasis to process. As
first presented, the scale was organized into
several stages along the general continuum.
Short interview excerpts and descriptive comments were provided to illustrate the salient
characteristics of each stage.

The present scale represents a refinement of
the original scale based upon further analysis
and study of additional therapy protocols. A
number of separate elements or "strands" were
isolated and identified within the more general
framework of the stage conception of process.
The seven strands constituting the form of
the scale used in this study are briefly described

SOURCE. Article by Alan M. Walker, Richard A.
Rablen, and Carl R. Rogers, "Development of a
scale to measure process changes in psychotherapy"
in *Journal of clinical Psychology*, Vol. XVI, No. 1,
pp. 79–85, January 1960.

below and are presented schematically in Table
1. Fuller descriptions of the characteristics of
each strand at each level are available elsewhere (10). The descriptions presented here
follow closely those of Rogers' (8) paper to
the 1958 APA conference on research, which
also included a preliminary report on the
present research.

EDITORIAL NOTE: Every editor has the duty
to simplify presentations as much as possible,
to hold to a minimum new theoretical constructs
where older ones are still valid, and to relate
new developments to existing theory. In particular, we question the value in this article
of the introduction of the concept of "strand"
as opposed to the older concept of "factor," and
the resulting speculative concept of the
"strands" converging to form a "stream."

Historically, Adolf Meyers' concept of the
stream of life attempted to depict the viscis-
situdes of component processes in the ongoing
process of mental status. It is desirable to attempt to visualize the genetic development of
personality factors over the time dimension.
The fact that a "factor" may make varying contributions to mental status over a period of time
would seem not to necessitate the coining of
the new concept of "strand."

An alternative explanation is offered by
modern integration theory. As a result of
therapy resulting in more self-awareness and
insight, it is assumed that behavior becomes
"integrated" on higher levels which may be
objectively identified. The discrete (separable
and distinct) nature of the factors at the "fixity"
end of the process actually may be an expression of lack of integration, inconsistency or
conflict. In therapy the client becomes able to
organize discrete behaviors into unified integra-

Table 1. A Schematic Presentation of the General Process Continuum (For Simplicity, the Salient Characteristics of Each Strand are Presented at Low, Medium, and High Points Only on the General Process Continuum. In the Study Proper, Seven Stages were Discriminated.)

Strands	Low (I-II)	Process Stages Medium (III-V)	High (VI-VII)
Feelings and personal meanings	Unrecognized Unexpressed	Increasing ownership Increasing expression	Living in flow Fully experienced
Experiencing	Remote from experiencing Unaware	Decreasing remoteness Increasing awareness	Lives in process of experiencing Uses as major referent
Incongruence	Unrecognized	Increasing recognition Increasing direct experiencing	Temporary only
Communication of self	Lacking	Increasing self-communication	Rich self-awareness communication when desired
Construing of experience	Rigid constructions Construction seen as fact	Decreasing rigidity Increasing recognition of own contribution	Tentative constructions Meaning held loosely to be checked against experiencing
Relationship to problems	Unrecognized No desire to change	Increasing responsibility assumed Change often feared	Problems not seen as external object Living in some aspect of problem
Manner of relating	Close relationships avoided as dangerous	Decreasing danger felt	Relates openly and freely on basis of immediate experiencing

tions. Simply the process of bringing together formerly discrete or unperceived factors in consciousness is an integrative process which raises the level of functional integration.

The Law of Parsimony requires that every effort should be made to relate the factors measured by the author's scale with known personality factors, and not to introduce speculative new concepts until the possibility of identifying them with established factors is exhausted.

Sets of four single pages of interview material were chosen systematically from each of the six transcribed cases and recopied without identifying information. The method of sampling provided two pages of material from early interviews and two pages of material from late

interviews for each case. Typically, the interviews chosen for the early sets were the second and third and for the late sets, the two immediately preceding the last interview. Thus there were in all 24 pages of interview material, each identified only by a code number. The pages were placed in random order for presentation to the judges.

Two judges, who differed in theoretical orientation and amount of experience in clinical psychology, worked together for a number of hours training themselves on interview material from other cases in order to learn to make the discriminations called for in the scale. After this training, the judges turned to the data of this study, considering each page as a unit for their purpose. At all times, the judges attempted to assume a "listening attitude" toward the data, trying to understand the significance of the client's remarks for him rather than to evaluate his comments diagnostically.

Several sortings of the data were made following a pre-planned order designed to avoid contamination or confounding within the sequence of discriminations. Since it was possible that time cues might appear in the materials and provide a basis for judging the relative position in therapy of some protocols, the material was sorted for objective evidence of chronology in therapy. Only one segment was positively identified as to time by the two judges. It was therefore concluded that there were no time cues operating in the sample of interviews which would bias the raters' judgment of the stage of therapy.

The most difficult discrimination attempted was to assign an absolute global stage rating to each of the twenty-four unidentified segments using the seven-stage scale of process. For this purpose, the judges introduced decimals between stages for greater precision, resulting essentially in a seventy-point scale. The segments were also independently rank ordered as to process, and as a third task were independently divided into equal groups of eight segments judged to be high, medium, and low on the process continuum.

Strands of the Process Continuum

The Relationship to Feelings and Personal Meanings. This strand refers to the relationship of the individual to the feelings and personal meanings which exist within himself. The phrase "feeling and personal meaning" refers to an emotionally tinged experience together with its significance to the individual. At the lower end of the continuum feelings and personal meanings are unrecognized by the individual and unexpressed, though feelings are perhaps exhibited. Near the midpoint of the scale they are expressed as owned feelings in the present. At the upper end of the continuum, living in the process of experiencing a continually changing flow of feelings becomes characteristic of the individual.

The Manner of Experiencing. Experiencing is regarded as the directly given, felt datum which is implicitly meaningful. (1) It refers to

the individual's sense of *having* experience, which is given in the phenomenal field of every person. When the individual asks himself, "What kind of an experiencing is this?" there is always an implicit answer even though no explicit answer has as yet been conceptualized. The manner of experiencing refers to the extent to which the individual finds himself in this subjective experiencing or very remote from it. At one end of the scale the individual may be quite unaware of the process of experiencing which he is undergoing and keeps himself distant from its implicit meanings. Gradually the individual moves toward a greater awareness of his inner experiencing. Finally, he becomes able to live freely and acceptantly in a fluid process of experiencing, using it comfortably as the major referent for his behavior.

The Degree of Incongruence. Incongruence has been defined (9) as the discrepancy which exists between what the individual is now experiencing and the representation of this in his awareness or in his communication. Such discrepancy cannot be directly known to the individual himself but may be observed. Its opposite is a congruence between the experiencing of the individual and the symbolization or conceptualization of this in his awareness. The continuum runs from a maximum of incongruence which is quite unknown to the individual, through stages where there is an increasingly sharp recognition of the contradictions and discrepancies existing within himself, to the experiencing of incongruence in the immediate present in a way which dissolves it. At the upper end of the continuum there would never be more than temporary incongruence between experiencing and awareness since the individual would not need to defend himself against the threatening aspects of his experience.

The Communication of Self. This continuum deals with the extent to which and the manner in which the individual is able and willing to communicate himself in a receptive climate. The continuum runs from a complete unwillingness to communicate self to a stage where the self involves a rich and changing awareness of internal experiencing which is readily communicated when the individual desires to do so.

The Manner in which Experience is Construed. This and the two following strands are not as sharply differentiated as the four preceding. Nevertheless, their end points and some of their mid points are recognizable. Experience at one end of the continuum is construed rigidly. These constructions are unrecognized as creations of the individual but are thought of as fixed facts. At the other end of the continuum experience is never given more than a tentative meaning or construction. This meaning is always held loosely to be checked and rechecked against further experiencing.

The Relationship to Problems. This is a strand which endeavors to describe the individual's changing relationship to the problem elements of himself. At one end of the scale, the problems are unrecognized and there is no desire to change. Gradually there is increasing recognition that the individual has contributed to these problems. At the upper end there is a living or experiencing of some aspect of the problem. The individual is responsibly in it subjectively rather than seeing it as a kind of external object.

The Manner of Relating. At one end of the continuum, the individual avoids close relationships which are perceived as being dangerous. At the other end of the continuum, he lives openly and freely in relation to the therapist and to others, guiding his behavior in the relationship on the basis of his immediate experiencing.

Method

Six completely transcribed cases from the University of Chicago Counseling Center provided the source of materials for the initial application of the process scale. It was assumed in all cases that the therapist fulfilled, to an adequate degree, the set of conditions thought (5) to be optimal for facilitating the process of change. These cases were mostly brief ones for which research data on outcomes were available. They were chosen to represent a considerable range of outcome, with three representing marked progress and three minimal progress. The cases and the order in which they were ranked by the third author as to progress in therapy, using all the available evidence, are shown in Table 2.

Results

Reliability. On the seventy-point scale, the two judges' independent ratings of the twenty-four segments correlated (Pearson r) .83, significant at the .01 level. On the rank ordering of the segments, a correlation (rho) of .84 was obtained, significant at the .01 level. When judgments as to the eight high, eight medium, and eight low segments were compared, there was 75% exact agreement, 25% one-step disagreement, and 0% two-step disagreement.

Table 2. Ranking of Progress in Therapy of Cases Included in the Study of Process

Rank	Code	Total number of interviews	Sample Interviews	Explanation of ranking
1	Vib	9	2, 3, 7, 8	Rated first in 1949 study (2) on objective evidence
2	Oak	48	2, 3, 46, 47	Showed marked objective progress in 1954 study (4).
3	Sar	4	1, 2, 3, 4	Showed dramatic improvement in four interviews. Judged as a very successful brief case by observers.
4	Bebb	9	2, 3, 7, 8	Showed objective progress in therapy, but decrement during followup period in 1954 study (3).
5	Sim	7	2, 3, 5, 6	Ranked 7.5 out of 10 in progress in 1949 study (2).
6	Sketch	3	1, 2, 2, 3	Ranked 9 out of 10 in progress in 1949 study (2).

Validity. The six cases had been ranked on external criteria as noted above. These rankings were not disclosed to the judges until they had completed their work. An index of change for each case was derived from each rater's judgments by adding together the process ratings for the two late interviews of each case and subtracting from this value the sum of ratings for the two early interviews. Using this index, it was found that the two judges had given identical rankings to the six cases, the order being (1) Vib, (2) Sar, (3) Oak, (4) Bebb, (5) Sketch, (6) Sim. Comparing this order or ranking to that obtained using the external criteria data (Table 2) yielded a rho of .89, significant at the .02 level.

Another way of considering the validity of the ratings is to compare the change on the process scale of the three cases selected as representing marked progress with the change in the three cases selected as representing minimal progress. For the marked progress group the mean changes (based on a process change index derived from pooling the ratings of both judges) were 2.3, 2.0, and 1.5. The overall mean change for the group was 1.93. In the minimal progress group, the changes were 1.2, 0.3, and −0.6. The overall mean for this group was 0.30. It will be noted that there is no overlap between the two groups.

Discussion

It seems apparent that satisfactory interjudge reliability can be obtained in using the process scale in its present form, and that ratings derived from it bear a meaningful relationship to other measures of successful change in therapy. These results were found despite the use of quite small samples of transcribed material, implying that higher reliability should be obtained with increased sampling and perhaps use of auditory cues as well as verbal ones.

Relationship between Continuum and Strands of Process. In our experience with the strand approach to a continuum of process change, it has seemed to us that the usual model of discrete and parallel continua which can be summed or averaged to obtain an overall stage rating does not fit our data. Rather, the strands seem more separable and distinct at the fixity end of the process continuum, where they can be more independently evaluated and rated. Whether the individual is exhibiting a rigid personal construct, or expressing himself on non-self topics, or describing feelings in a way which shows no direct ownership of them, these are rather clearly discriminable elements. But in the later stages of the process, the individual may be experiencing feelings with immediacy—knowing them and experiencing them being synonymous. These feelings are his expression of himself at the moment. They may represent an immediately experienced change in a personal construct. Here all the previously identifiable strands are fused into one moment, and to separate them is artificial. It therefore appears that the most adequate diagrammatic model is one of converging lines, separable at first, but becoming less and less clearly distinguishable. Rogers (8) has suggested the analogy of a stream, originating in separate frozen rivulets, which under the impact of psychological warmth, gradually begin to trickle. The beginning flow may be frozen or dammed at some further point. If the psychological climate continues to be favorable then these individual rivulets increasingly flow into one another. At the optimal point of flow, they form a unified stream of change in which the contribution of the separate tributaries can no longer be accurately distinguished, although all are present. Evaluation of the adequacy of such an assumed model must await further pattern analysis of the strands.

Implications for Change. A prediction is implicit in the development of this conception of the process of personality change. It hints at the possibility that a brief sample of an individual's expressive behavior, taken in a situation in which he feels fully received, can be analyzed to yield knowledge of where he stands on the continuum of personality development and flow; and that this analysis may be possible without knowledge of the individual's genetic history, social and personal background, personality type, psychological diagnosis, or length of time in therapy. If this implicit prediction is even partly fulfilled, it means that the interaction process in therapy is moving into the realm of objective research.

When a reliable operational meaning can be given to this theory of the process of therapy, it will be feasible to test a variety of hypotheses as to the quality and nature of personality change as it occurs in psychotherapy. For example, with an adequate scale of process in therapy, more precise answers than before should be found to such questions as where an individual starts in therapy, how far he progresses, and the amount of difficulty involved in moving from different stages. It may be necessary to reach certain stages in process for lasting change to occur. If the latter is true, it may help explain the puzzle of apparent progress in therapy which is not evident in a later follow-up.

When we turn to implications for the more general area of personality development and for all helping relationships (6, 9) the process concept suggests several lines of thought. If personality development proceeds in the direction of full experiencing and living in an integrated flow of implicit meaning, then the fully functioning person is one who is a stream of process himself, who has become the process of experiencing through which his development has been moving. The difference between this concept and the more usual one of movement toward a new fixity is great and its meaning needs to be explored. The potential applications of the process concept to all helping relationships—not only therapy but teacher-student relationships, parent-child relationships, industrial consultation, and community development —deserve consideration as well.

Summary

A conception of process change in psychotherapy has been elaborated into an overall scale manifest in various partially separable elements or strands of process. The general direction of change is conceived to be from stasis and fixity to changingness and flow in such areas as one's relations to feelings and personal meanings, his manner of experiencing, degree of incongruence, communication of self, construing of experience, relationship to problems, and manner of relating to others. The strands are thought to be more distinct at the fixity end of the continuum and more unitary at the flow end.

The scale was applied to twenty-four unidentified samples, selected without bias from early and late interviews of six cases, judged to vary in amount of change by external criteria. Two judges, working independently, achieved a high degree of reliability in all comparisons. Two different methods of estimating process change from application of the scale showed high agreement with estimates of progress in therapy as derived from objective evidence and counselor ratings.

These results are interpreted to imply that a significant dimension of personality change is being tapped and that further development of the process concept and scale promises to have important implications for our knowledge of therapy, personality change, and perhaps social change as well.

REFERENCES

1. Gendlin, E. The function of experiencing in symbolization. Unpublished doctoral dissertation, Univer. of Chicago, 1958.
2. Raskin, N. J. An analysis of six parallel studies of therapeutic process. *J. consult. Psychol.*, 1949, 13, 206–220.
3. Rogers, C. R. The case of Mr. Bebb; the analysis of a failure case. In C. R. Rogers and Rosalind F. Dymond (Eds.), *Psychotherapy and personality change.* Chicago: Univer. of Chicago Press, 1954, pp. 349–412.
4. Rogers, C. R. The cases of Mrs. Oak: a research analysis. In C. R. Rogers and Rosalind F. Dymond (Eds.). *Psychotherapy and personality change.* Chicago: Univer. of Chicago Press, 1954, pp. 259–348.
5. Rogers, C. R. The necessary and sufficient conditions of therapeutic personality change. *J. consult. Psychol.*, 1957, 21, 95–103.
6. Rogers, C. R. The characteristics of a helping relationship, *Personnel and Guidance Journal,* 1958, 37, 6–16.
7. Rogers, C. R. A process conception of psychotherapy. *Amer. Psychologist,* 1958, 13, 142–149. Also available from the author in an unpublished amplification.
8. Rogers, C. R. A tentative scale for the measurement of process in psychotherapy. In E. A. Rubinstein and M. B. Parlof (Eds.), *Research in psychotherapy.* Washington, D. C.: American Psychological Association, 1959. Pp. 96–108.
9. Rogers, C. R. A theory of therapy, personality, and interpersonal relationship, as developed in the client-centered framework. In Koch, S. (Ed.) *Psychology: A study of a science. Vol. 3. Formulations of the person and the social context.* New York: McGraw-Hill, 1959.
10. Rogers, C. R. and Rablen, R. A. A scale of process in psychotherapy. Unpublished manual, Univer. of Wisconsin, 1958.

3. Client-centered developments and work with schizophrenics

EUGENE T. GENDLIN

THIS PAPER is an early descriptive report on psychotherapy with schizophrenics in a research project sponsored by Carl R. Rogers. The project employs many psychometric and interview measures, a matched control group, and complete tape recordings of the therapy interviews. The project is not yet completed and hence it is not yet established that effective psychotherapy is taking place. Meanwhile much is being clinically observed and learned. Therapists are modifying the client-centered way of doing therapy.

The paper will trace these developments in terms of the trends and theories of the client-centered orientation, but clearly, what is occurring is related to a wider context of present trends in the field of psychotherapy generally. I will therefore begin by quoting some writers outside the client-centered orientation, whose descriptions of their practice indicate at least three trends which are shared by several orientations: increasing emphasis on (1) the personal relationship; (2) the therapist's spontaneity and genuine expressiveness; (3) the subverbal, affective, preconceptual nature of the basic therapeutic communication. Fromm-Reichmann (1959) writes:

The doctor should offer his presence to lonely patients, first in the spirit of expecting nothing but to be tolerated, then to be accepted simply as some person who is there. The possibility that psychotherapy may be able to do something about the patient's loneliness should, of course, not be verbalized at this point. To offer any such suggestion in the beginning of one's contact with an essentially lonely patient could lend itself only to one of two interpretations in the patient's mind: Either the psychotherapist does not know anything about the inextricable, uncanny quality of his loneliness, or he himself is afraid of it.

Whitehorn writes:

B physicians (unsuccessful with schizophrenics) had a tendency either to be passively permissive or to point out to a patient his mistakes and misunderstandings . . . whereas the A physicians (successful with schizophrenics) did little interpretation or instruction, but did express personal attitudes fairly freely on problems that were being talked about by the patient, and did set limits on the kind and degree of obnoxious behavior permitted.

Whitaker, Warkentin and Malone (1959) write:

Nonverbal communication is of primary importance. The patient must avoid intellectual verbiage, lest it be a barrier to the unconscious-to-unconscious affective relationship between therapist and patient.
Silence as such can be a valuable medium for the conduct of the communication between therapist and patient.
The therapist is not simply a projective screen but an active participant in a person-to-person relationship in which he participates with as few technical maneuvers as possible. The therapist's effort is to communicate as fully as possible his feeling responses to the presence of the patient, and his experiences in this relationship.

The trends of current client-centered therapy to some extent resemble the observations of the above-quoted authors and of others. Thus, this paper will report much that is not new. On the contrary, the very recurrence of similar ex-

SOURCE. Article by Eugene T. Gendlin, "Client-centered developments and work with schizophrenics," in *Journal of counseling Psychology*, Vol. 9, pp. 205–211, 1962.

periences and methods in different orientations would seem to point toward phenomena that deserve attention. In the observations of these authors, and, as I shall report, in our own observations, effective psychotherapy with schizophrenics appears to be a largely *personal, expressive,* and concretely experiential or *subverbal* process.

Changes in the Client-Centered Approach Prior to its Application with Schizophrenics

Before I can report the most recent developments in client-centered therapy, I must report the trends and changes in method which were already occurring a few years ago, before the research with schizophrenics began. At that time, along with most other orientations, client-centered therapy was becoming less sectarian, less formal, more personal, more concerned with feeling and immediacy than with verbal content or verbal reflection.

Three lines of modification, especially, were already being made at that time:

1. Seeman (1956) and a number of others found fault with the description of the client-centered response as a "reflection of feeling." In various ways the range of therapist response behavior was being widened. Rogers (1957, 1959), especially, widened the scope to include as therapeutic all modes of responding which could manifest three basic therapeutic attitudes: "empathic understanding," "unconditional positive regard," and "genuineness." An unlimited range of therapist *behavior* might implement and communicate these *attitudes.* Rogers hypothesized that therapy would take place if these attitudes were present and communicated to the client. Thus basic therapist attitudes, rather than any specific "client-centered" behaviors, were thought to be the essential therapeutic factors.

2. In a second line of modification during the last few years, Butler (1958) and others held that therapist spontaneity is related to success in therapy. Rogers formulated as one of the three basic therapeutic attitudes that "the therapist is congruent (genuine) in the relationship." Of course, genuine expressiveness does not mean that the therapist spends most of the hour verbalizing each of his own feelings (most often he would be genuinely experiencing the client's expressive behavior). However,

there has been a striving for undefensive transparency and genuineness of the therapist as the person he is, free of professional or personal artificiality.

3. A third modification was the increasing tendency (Gendlin and Zimring, 1955; Hart, 1961; Rogers, 1959) to view therapy in the client as consisting of feeling events, rather than conceptual insights. The theory of "experiencing" (Gendlin, 1961a; 1962) emphasized that one moment's concrete feeling process could implicitly contain many psychological contents. It might be impossible to conceptualize all of these, yet the client can feel them all as a directly sensed referent within himself. Therapeutic responses aid the client to refer directly to his present feeling process, and to maximize and intensify this process (Rogers, 1959). The interactive conditions of the therapy situations were seen as constituting new experiencing of a fuller, more immediate manner (Gendlin, et al., 1960).

As I shall now show, these three earlier lines of modification in the client-centered approach have grown to be the major characteristics of therapy with schizophrenics.

Client-Centered Therapy in Its Application with Schizophrenics

Characteristic Client Reactions. What is it, in the schizophrenic individual's response to psychotherapy, that has so accelerated just these already incipient lines of development? I will mention four well-known characteristics of the way in which many schizophrenic individuals respond to psychotherapy.

Nonmotivation. Clients were selected according to criteria of the experimental design—age, sex, social class, length of hospitalization, degree of disturbance—as crosscutting variables. When two individuals who matched each other on all these variables were found, a coin was flipped to determine which was a no-therapy control, and which would receive therapy. This method obviated the more usual selection for therapy. Usually individuals who are responsive to staff and become known to them are assigned to psychotherapy. In this way motivated people most often select themselves. We expected and desired a group of clients whose prognosis would not be biased favorably by such self-selection. We more than accomplished this aim!

The majority of the clients who were selected for therapy did not desire it, resisted it, often refused to meet the therapist, and made it difficult for therapy to begin or to continue (Gendlin, 1961b).

Silence. The second characteristic reaction, encountered with the majority of these clients, was silence. This was not the occasional periods of silence which we associate with deep therapy, but continuing silence, interview after interview, often for the whole interview, with the exception of a few sentences.

Nonexploration. A third characteristic concerns the nonexploratory, often non-inward character of what is said. The verbal therapeutic process often seems absent. Often there is a refusal to own feelings explicitly, even though they are just then being implied. There is a high degree of externalization. Problems and interests are located in others and in external circumstances.[1]

Even when there are brief periods of seeming self-exploration, or of deep verbal communication, these do not go to make up a continuing process. The next meetings may again be barren of deep verbal communication, as if nothing had happened. The person does not seem to be engaged in an exploration of his own to approach his subjective problems. Verbally, there is irregular and nonexplorative emotional expression.

Intense subverbal interaction. A fourth characteristic is the intensity of subverbal interaction. It often seems that the individual has given up the niceties of civilized society, and of verbal or consensual checking. Subverbal impressions

---

[1] In this respect these schizophrenic clients resemble the clients who usually fail in client-centered therapy according to the accurate predictions of the studies with the Kirtner Scale of first interview ratings (Kirtner & Cartwright, 1958). The failure-predicting end of the scale indicates external location of problems and lack of inward exploration.

Another group of individuals who usually pose difficulty for client-centered therapy are the parents described by Ellinwood (1959), who bring their children to play therapy and seek help for themselves also, but do not want or expect this help to be psychotherapy.

If the developments in psychotherapy with schizophrenics, described here, are successful, they may apply also to these groups of clients and to many others.

guide him. If it is his impression that the therapist's face reflects a dislike, a disturbance, a rejection, his response is instantaneous and likely to be total. For example, when I hesitate for a moment in the midst of saying something, my client waves me away. It is as if all in an instant my ambivalent, semiunconscious difficulty in formulating my message is sufficient for him to back away from it. Slight movements on either of our parts constitute an intense subverbal conversation. Early in therapy my interest and curiosity in him is often visibly hard for him to bear. More verbal later on, he can say: "Your ears are too big," or less dramatically, "I don't know if I should say anything or not. You're too curious." In many interactions I cannot know whether what I subjectively live with the client is anything like what he feels, but I know that we are engaged in an eventful and deeply felt subverbal interaction.

Therapist Attitudes. As I mentioned earlier, the client-centered method is no longer defined in terms of specific techniques or modes of response, but rather in terms of certain basic attitudes (Rogers, 1957, 1959). Many different orientations, techniques, and modes of therapist response could manifest these attitudes. Therefore, the attitudes I will now describe are not limited to client-centered therapy, yet they alone define "client-centered therapy."

The therapist who endeavors to share the psychotic client's perceptions and feelings sees little therapeutic value in explanatory concepts. These do not help him reach the individual's own experiencing. Because the hospitalized person is so often "administered," his case "disposed" in some way, without much reference to his own experiencing, there is a tendency to discuss him in terms of diagnostic explanatory concepts. In terms of such concepts we have generalized knowledge. In contrast, the therapist who endeavors to be "empathic" focuses his attention on the individual's own experiencing, in so far as the therapist can sense it.

2. Often in a hospital setting the behaviors, aggressions, manifest symptoms, and act-outs become all-important foci of attention. The hospitalized client is often punished or corrected. The therapist, on the contrary, seeks to perceive with the client on the client's side (becomes his "lawyer," as Betz and Whitehorn, 1956 suggest), and has a warm "regard" for him as a person. It is just as true of psychotics as of oth-

ers that as one gets to know the person more deeply one likes him very personally, if concerns with outside factors do not interfere.

3. In a hospital setting there is a remarkable isolation of the client. Not only are his interpersonal contacts narrowed physically, but his contacts are also qualitatively limited, since often he is not responded to at face value. His words are often not taken as a serious message from a person. Similarly, it is common for professional people to withhold their own actual responses and to substitute some professionally appropriate stock response. In contrast, if the therapist attempts to be "genuinely" himself, and self-expressive, then he is foremost a human being capable of shattering the schizophrenic's isolation; he brings a direct human contact. And, although the schizophrenic may not be able to meet this human approach, he has nevertheless in the therapy situation an equally human role. He may fill this role or leave it empty, but it is constantly present as a fully human role.

How These "Therapist Attitudes" Initially Make the Characteristic Client Reactions More Especially Noticeable

The hurt and isolation of schizophrenics generally, and the nonvoluntary way in which these clients were assigned to psychotherapy, would account for their characteristic refusals, silences, and absence of verbal exploration. Yet I think the attitudes of these therapists also tended to bring out more strongly just such reactions, and thus led to modifications in the mode of psychotherapy.

A therapist who is accustomed to initiating therapy by responding to the client's motivations and feelings is sure to be strongly affected by the client's unwillingness to meet with him. Such a therapist is sure to feel temporarily deprived of the basis upon which he works.

Similarly, a therapist whose main focus is to share the client's actual subjective experiencing —a therapist who cares little for external explanations and behavioral corrections—is most likely to note, as a striking characteristic, the client's lack of subjective focus.

The therapist who is accustomed to aiding self-exploration by empathic response will also be especially struck, and put at a loss, by the great amount of subverbal communication. This

is just the sort of communication with which he is trained to empathize, yet the psychotic individual often does not intend to explore—or verbally formulate—these communications. As the therapist attempts to understand verbally, the client withdraws the more.

The therapist who is accustomed to value the client's frequent private search within himself is not likely to interrupt silences. Naturally, he finds that silences stretch into the whole hour and sequences of hours.

I believe that therapists with other methods also encounter the client reactions I described, but perhaps they would not seem as striking as they do when viewed in terms of the client-centered approach.

The Need for Modification of Therapist Behavior

It might be simplest to describe our experiences by saying that when therapy did not seem to be going well, the therapists felt a need to alter their modes of approach. First there are the conflicts that occur in the therapist because of these characteristic patient reactions, conflicts which make it impossible for the therapist to retain his customary attitudes. He comes to feel quite nontherapeutic and seeks ways to alter the situation so as to restore within himself his more familiar therapeutic attitudes. He must find *different* behaviors so as to regain the *same* attitudes which he is accustomed to as therapist. But the obvious alternative ways of behaving also do not restore his own old attitudes. The result is a process (still going on here) of sensitively evolving quite new alternatives of therapeutic respondings where there previously appeared to be no good alternatives. There are three stages in this process.

Awareness of conflict. The client is silent, or talks of trivia. Attempts to verbalize his implicit communications make him angry, fearful, or withdrawing; or, as we try to respond to a deeper level of feeling, we find that the client simply has not meant to look at himself more deeply—and misunderstands us. We have all sorts of impressions and images of what the client feels, since subverbally he does communicate. We wonder what to do with all this richness of events which occurs in our own moment-to-moment experiencing, as we sit quietly or converse superficially. We feel much empathy but can show little. As we go along on a casual level, or in silence, we wonder if we aren't allowing ourselves to be just as helpless as this fearful person. We are in conflict, not knowing whether to push harder or to attempt being even safer. We blame ourselves for too much helpless waiting, then, minutes later, for too much interruption, pressure, and demand. We wonder whether the client is doing anything significant with us, whether we are failing him. We become impatient and angry at giving so much inward receptivity while so little of it seems communicated. We value deeply what little or trivial communication he gives us, and we do not want to push that away. Yet we feel dishonest when we seemingly assent to silence or to this trivial level of communication. Obviously, in such a condition, we feel quite unfamiliar to ourselves as therapists. In order to attempt to restore the inward condition we are *familiar* with as being therapy, we come to behave in *unfamiliar* ways.

The Try-Out of Ready Alternatives. The client refuses to meet with the therapist. Shall he be coerced, or should the relationship be allowed to end before it has really begun? Neither alternative is acceptable. The therapist goes to meet the individual on the ward (coercion of a sort), but leaves him free to walk away. Now the client's participation does not commit him, nor does his walking away constitute a committed refusal. The therapist will visit again later in the week, and will do so explicitly because *he* wants to. This leaves the client's end of the relationship indeterminate until he determines it. The therapist states his own desire to meet with the client, his interests and feelings in this regard, in spite of negative reaction or lack of reaction. Certainly, the therapist in these ways takes more of the initiative than he usually would. Yet he attempts to find modes of taking initiative which are based on his own feelings, and which do not take the place of those initiatives which might later arise in the client. It is a peculiar and subtle resolution of the dilemma. In certain respects the therapist takes more initiative (for himself), yet in other respects he takes less initiative than ever (for the client). Not even the client's commitment to try to form a relationship is assumed, or demanded.

New Modes of Behavior. The same trend of more expressiveness with less imposition applies not only to our mode of *initiating* psychotherapy, but also to our whole way of working *during* psychotherapy. We find that even when we cannot know what the client is thinking and feeling, we can respond to him. If he is silent, I, as therapist, may be quite in the dark as to what he is thinking and feeling. I only know what I am thinking and feeling, and how I imagine him. As I express my present feeling and my vague images of what may be happening between us now, a very personal quality enters into my expressions. I am giving words to my ongoing experiencing with him. There is a quality of personal risk and openness in my saying these things. There is a quality of gentle closeness in giving directly of my imaginings and feelings. In expressions I often state also my intention in saying what I say, and my unsureness concerning what is happening in him. I clearly say: "This is what is happening *in me* now," or "This is what *I imagine* is happening in you (or between us), but I can't be sure." The client lives in a responsive context made up of my person and my openly expressive interaction with him. Yet, his side of the interaction may be quite tentative, implicit, until he wishes to make it explicit as his.

Similarly, the externalizing, event-reporting client stirs in me many feelings for him, and images of him. I desire to hear from him more deeply, welcome him more personally. I can say this, and say it at every juncture at which I particularly feel it. In his descriptions of incidents, I sense him involved in many ways. I can express these (as imaginings of my own). I come to have more, and more often, a sense of the person he is which he omits from his reports of events. I become the one who expresses the feelings, who complains, cries, justifies, understands the private side of things which is misunderstood. I gently express my bafflement or surprise at the dilemma he is in. But these are *my* expressions as an open and expressive person.

I express myself in a fashion (*and this takes a few steps of self-attention each time*) which clearly states *my* feeling (not some judgment or deduction) and is based on my feelings *for* him and my desire to be close to him. As with the silent person, so also with the event reporter, I give voice to what I experience or imagine in him or in the events he reports. I voice it *as my* momentary inward process as we interact. One might say that these therapists frequently establish and continue relationships *by means of* expressing themselves openly and genuinely. This procedure seems to leave the inarticulate and fearful person free, yet gives him a relationship at a time when he still cannot do much to form or maintain one.

Theory. The relatively subtle changes in emphasis which constituted modifications in the client-centered approach prior to its application with psychotics have become major observable developments. To conclude this report, I want to draw them together. The three directions of modification I mentioned were: (1) attitudes, rather than client-centered behavior, as therapeutic factors; (2) genuine expressiveness of the therapist; (3) experiencing (the preconceptual feeling process) constitutes therapy, rather than verbal self-exploration. In a theoretical formulation just brief enough to suit this early stage of observation, I might formulate these three directions in one formula: The therapeutic attitudes (1 above) manifest themselves in interactive behaviors through genuine therapist self-expression (2 above), and this open interaction itself affects the nature of the client's present experiencing process (3 above) so that in spite of threat and withdrawal he may find his experiencing occurring more optimally and in interaction.

Some Open Questions

Complete research results must be awaited for the experimental and matched control groups, before we can know whether *effective* psychotherapy with schizophrenics is taking place. The present paper is therefore a report of current practice. The evaluation of its effectiveness is still an open question.

Psychotherapy generally, with any type of population, seems to involve not only verbalization, but more fundamentally, the client's inward reference to, and struggle with, his directly felt experiencing. The individual's inward data, concretely felt, seem to be the actual staff of psychotherapy, not the words. It may be especially true for the schizophrenic, but it seems true for everyone, that felt experiencing is meaningful in a preconceptual rather than only a conceptual way. Felt experiencing can be endlessly differentiated and conceptualized, yet it is concrete and never really consists of words and concepts.

The schizophrenic may show this especially, since he is so often lost and selfless, and the preconceptual meanings of his experiencing at first seem to him so removed from other persons and so incommunicable that silence or a few nonlogical words are the only possible expression. Very often one can see that his few statements arise from a very eventful, concretely felt process—and that the interactions with the therapist are affecting or enabling this process. In principle, psychotherapy generally, and not only with schizophrenics, may be considered fundamentally as a process of felt experiencing in the context of interpersonal responses. If that is correct, the client and therapist process described in this report would be in the most basic sense the same as that which occurs in any psychotherapy.

REFERENCES

Betz, B., & Whitehorn, J. C. The relationship of the therapist to the outcome of therapy in schizophrenia. *Psychiatric research reports of the American Psychiatric Association,* 1956, **5,** 89–106.

Butler, J. M. Client-centered counseling and psychotherapy. In D. Brower and L. E. Abt (Eds.), *Progress in clinical psychology,* Vol. III. *Changing conceptions in psychotherapy.* New York: Grune & Stratton, 1958.

Ellinwood, Charlotte. Some observations from work with parents in a child therapy program. *Counseling Center Discussion Papers,* Vol. 5, 18, Univer. of Chicago Library, 1959.

Fromm-Reichman, Frieda. *Psychoanalysis and psychotherapy. Selected papers of Frieda Fromm-Reichman.* D. M. Bullard (Ed.), Univer. of Chicago Press, 1959.

Gendlin, E. T. Experiencing: A variable in the process of therapeutic change. *Amer. J. Psychother.,* 1961, **15,** pp. 233–245. (a)

Gendlin, E. T. *Experiencing and the Creation of Meaning.* New York: The Free Press of Glencoe, 1962.

Gendlin, E. T. Initiating psychotherapy with "unmotivated" patients. *Psychiatric Quart.,* 1961, **35,** pp. 134–139. (b)

Gendlin, E. T., Jenney, R. H., & Shlien, J. M. Counselor ratings of process and outcome in client-centered therapy. *J. clin. Psychol.,* 1960, **16,** pp. 210–213.

Gendlin, E. T., & Zimring, F. M. The qualities or dimensions of experiencing and their change. *Counseling Center Discussion Papers,* Vol. 1, 3. Univer. of Chicago Library, 1955.

Hart, J. The evolution of client-centered therapy. *The Psychiatric Inst. Bull.*, Wisconsin Psychiatric Institute, Vol. 1, No. 2. Univer. of Wisconsin, 1961.

Kirtner, W. & Cartwright, D. Success and failure in client-centered therapy as a function of initial in-therapy behavior. *J. consult. Psychol.*, 1958, **22**, pp. 329–333.

Rogers, C. R. The necessary and sufficient conditions of therapeutic personality change. *J. consult. Psychol.*, 1957, **21**, pp. 95–103.

Rogers, C. R. A theory of therapy, personality, and interpersonal relationships as developed in the client-centered framework. In S. Koch (Ed.), *Psychology: A study of a science*, Vol. III. *Formulations of the person and the social context*. New York: McGraw-Hill, 1959, pp. 184–256.

Rogers, C. R. A tentative scale for the measurement of process in psychotherapy. In E. A. Rubinstein, and M. B. Parloff (Eds.), *Research in Psychotherapy*. Washington, D. C.: American Psychological Assn., 1959.

Seeman, J. Client-centered therapy. In D. Brower, and L. E. Abt (Eds), *Progress in clinical psychology*, Vol. II. New York: Grune & Stratton, 1956, pp. 98–113.

Whitaker, C. A., Warkentin, J., & Malone, T. P. The involvement of the professional therapist. In A. Burton (Ed.), *Case studies in counseling and psychotherapy*. Englewood Cliffs, New Jersey: Prentice Hall, 1959.

Whitehorn, J. C. Studies of the doctor as a crucial factor for the prognosis of schizophrenic patients. Paper from the Henry Phipps Psychiatric Clinic of the Johns Hopkins Hospital.

4. Interrelationships among various dimensions of the self concept

ROBERT U. AKERET

DESPITE THE CONTINUED EMPHASIS in the literature on the self concept as an important factor in the study of human behavior and experience, there has been astonishingly little experimental work reported. A probable reason for the dearth of studies is the difficulty in developing effective measurement techniques that can give rich and objective information about the individual's self concept. One approach to an evaluation of the self concept might be through the evaluation of the individual's self acceptance. Such an evaluation of the self concept might clarify whether an individual accepts or rejects himself totally, or whether he may be self accepting in some areas of self and self rejecting in orders. Rogers (1951) believed that it was possible to "study separately the perception of self-characteristics, of self-in-relationship-to-others, of values around which the self is organized, and of goals and ideals." Dividing the perception of self characteristics into different content areas seemed like a functional method for investigating the individual's self concept. This study attempts to demonstrate experimentally whether the individual accepts or rejects himself totally, or whether the individual accepts or rejects himself in some areas and not in others. This study attempts also to demonstrate the degree to which each presumed area of the self concept contributed to the total of the other self-concept areas.

SOURCE. Article by Robert U. Akeret, "Interrelationships among various dimensions of the self concept" in *Journal of counseling Psychology*, Vol. 6, No. 3, 1959.

Procedure

The subjects, Columbia College freshmen, were enrolled in the required Personal Living Course which attempts to promote better understanding of human behavior, and were considered to be a representative sample of the total freshman class. They had been placed arbitrarily into four sections meeting at different times. Thus the experimental group was more representative of a total college population than most other college groups reported on in the literature of self-concept theory. The students were asked to participate voluntarily in the project. The instructor emphasized that code numbers would be used throughout the experiment to insure anonymity, thus making it easier for some students to participate. From a group of 84 subjects, only two students refused to participate, and one student did not complete the tests.

The Q technique, developed by Stephenson (1953) and used by Rogers and others (1954), seemed well suited to measuring self acceptance both totally and in various dimensions of the self concept. The Q technique provides a systematic way to handle a subject's reflections about himself. Briefly, the subject can be requested to sort a number of self-descriptive statements into a number of piles. The experimenter establishes an approximately normal distribution by controlling the number of statements placed in each pile.

1. The subjects were first requested to describe themselves anonymously in the following general areas in order to develop items

which would sample various dimensions of the self concept:

A. *Academic Values.* Feelings about intelligence, motivation, study habits, reading skills, pressure from home, competition, vocational choice.

I. *Interpersonal relations.* Feelings about relating with others, ability to make and keep friends, social sensitivity.

S. *Sexual adjustment.* Feelings about sexual practices, dating, courtship, masturbation, sexual adequacy.

E. *Emotional adjustment.* Feelings, of depression, anxiety, happiness, moodiness, tenseness, disturbance, apathy, tiredness.

These were based upon a "critical incident" study by Malfetti (1951) of the adjustment problems of Columbia College freshmen. The dimensions used were neither exhaustive nor necessarily uncorrelated.

The subjects thus produced a large population of items which were compared, and ambiguous and duplicating items were discarded. Three judges, all fourth-year graduate students in psychology and instructors in the Personal Living Course, were asked to sort individually the statements into the given dimensions of self perception. The three judges had to agree on the placement of an item before it was accepted in a particular scale. Final acceptance of an item was based on clarity and representativeness. No attempt was made to develop an equal number of negative and positive self-descriptive items.

2. The subjects were then given the following instructions:

Sort these statements to describe yourself from those that are least like you to those that are most like you. Make sure you have the same number of statements in each pile as indicated by the required distribution. Be as honest with yourself as possible.

	"Least Like Me"						"Most Like Me"		
Pile	A	B	C	D	E	F	G	H	I
No. of cards	1	4	11	21	26	21	11	4	1

3. The same items and required distribution were used in the next class period, when the subjects were instructed as follows:

Sort these statements to describe your ideal self from those that are least like the ideal to those that are most like the ideal. Make sure that you have the same number of statements

in each pile as indicated by the required distribution. Be as honest with yourself as possible.

The subjects were allowed as much time as needed to complete the self and ideal sort. The two sorts which each subject made were compared and scored in the following way: if an item was placed in pile A on self sorts and pile E on ideal sorts, the discrepancy score was 4 (four piles away from the initial self sort). All items were compared, and the total discrepancy score was used as the measure of self acceptance. No consideration was given to the direction of displacement of an item. Individual discrepancy scores in the various dimensions of self perception were also obtained. Low discrepancy scores indicated greater self acceptance than high discrepancy scores.

Results and Discussion

The self acceptance scores of the 81 subjects were used to intercorrelate different areas of the self concept. Before reporting the correlations obtained, a summary of the split-half reliabilities on the scales seemed appropriate. These appear in Table 1.

Table 1. Split-Half Reliability Summary

	A	I	S	E	Total
Obtained	.617	.436	.634	.703	.752
Corrected*	.763	.607	.776	.826	.858

* Spearman-Brown prophecy formula.

Code: (A) Academic values; (I) Interpersonal relations; (S) Sexual adjustment; (E) Emotional adjustment; and (T) Total self acceptance.

Although the reliabilities reported in Table 1 were not high enough for individual diagnosis, they seemed adequate for an analysis based on intercorrelations. The correlations in Table 2 are significant at the .01 level by a one-tailed test when $r = .260$.

All self-concept areas correlated significantly and positively with the *total* of the other self-concept areas. However, not all of the areas of self intercorrelated at a significant positive level. The results in Table 2 suggest that an individual does not accept or reject himself totally; he may be self accepting in some areas of self and self rejecting in other areas. Thus the individual's self concept does not seem to be a unified gestalt but rather consists of characteristics or dimensions which he values differentially. The individual does not think of himself as being, for example, totally good or bad, but rather evaluates various areas of the self in different ways.

Table 2. Correlation Summary

	A	I	S	E	Total
A		.173	.250	.296	.325*
I			.337	.603	.565*
S				.480	.535*
E					.609*

* Corrected for part-whole inflation (McNemar, 1949).
Code: (A) Academic values; (I) Interpersonal relations; (S) Sexual adjustment; (E) Emotional adjustment; and (T) Total self acceptance.

Judging the individual's degree of psychological adjustment on the basis of the score of the total discrepancy between the self concept and the ideal concept would therefore appear to have serious limitations.

As might be expected, academic self acceptance when compared with interpersonal self acceptance and sexual self acceptance did not correlate at the .01 level of significance, since academic problems are not necessarily related to interpersonal relations or sexual adjustment. All other self-concept area intercorrelations were positive and significant at the .01 level.

Summary and Implications

The purpose of the present investigation is to study experimentally whether the individual accepts or rejects himself totally, or whether the individual accepts or rejects himself in some areas and not in others.

All self-concept dimensions correlated positively and significantly with total self acceptance. Some of the self-concept areas did not themselves intercorrelate at a significant level. This may mean that the individual does not reject or accept himself in a total sense; that is, he may accept or reject himself in some areas and not in others. The individual's self concept does not seem to be a unified gestalt but rather

consists of characteristics or dimensions which he values differentially. Most of the cluster area intercorrelations were significant, but not at a high enough level for interchangeable use. The theoretical and practical advantages of developing a standardized Q technique test in which the self concept is divided into various areas were also discussed.

The study suggests that a standardized test could be developed using the Q technique in which the self concept is divided into various areas. The information derived from an individual's sort would be most helpful diagnostically in counseling and psychotherapy. Problems could be identified and ordered according to the degree of self acceptance. Research could also be carried out to investigate various concepts in personality theory and change. For example, the test could be used to test the hypothesis that help in one given area of personal problems has a beneficial effect on other areas. The test could also be used to investigate the degree to which personality change takes place in various areas of the self concept—during and after counseling or psychotherapy.

REFERENCES

Akeret, R. U. The relationship between self-acceptance and the ability to understand others. Unpublished doctoral dissertation. Advanced School of Education, Teachers College, Columbia Univer., 1956.

Hilgard, E. R. Human motives and the concept of self. *Amer. Psychologist*, 1949, 4, 374–382.

Malfetti, J. L. College hygiene as personal living; a study in general education. Unpublished doctoral dissertation. Advanced School of Education, Teachers College, Columbia Univer., 1951.

McNemar, Q. *Psychological statistics*. New York: Wiley, 1949.

Rogers, C. R. *Client-centered therapy*. Boston: Houghton Mifflin, 1951.

Rogers, C. R., & Dymond, Rosalind F. *Psychotherapy and personality change*. Chicago: Univer. of Chicago Press, 1954.

Stephenson, W. *The study of behavior; Q technique and its methodology*. Chicago: Univer. of Chicago Press, 1953.

5. Self-ideal congruence as an index of adjustment

RALPH H. TURNER AND RICHARD H. VANDERLIPPE

UNDERLYING THE USE OF the Q-sort technique is the theoretical assumption that the satisfaction or concern of an individual with his phenomenal self is an operationally definable datum of great importance in the area of adjustment. The discrepancy between the placements of a given characteristic on the self scale and the ideal scales has been taken as indicating not only the way in which an individual perceives himself as possessing this characteristic but the degree to which he values this trait. Given these assumptions, then successful therapy should be accompanied by a reduction in the magnitude of self-ideal discrepancies. Further, self concepts should change more as a result of therapy than ideal concepts since the latter are firmly anchored as general societal concepts, whereas the former may be more idiosyncratic. These expectations have been confirmed by Butler and Haigh (3).

Nevertheless, the confirmation of these expectations is not itself a sufficient reason for assuming the adequacy of the basic theoretical framework within which the hypotheses were developed. Dymond (4) has pointed out that the therapist's attitude of satisfaction with a case may be communicated to the individual, who then reflects these attitudes in his self-description. Even if this possible source of contamination did not exist, it would still be necessary to test the assumption that a change of the phenomenal self in the direction of the ideal

self may be taken as an indication of better adjustment. Because this is difficult to demonstrate on a before-and-after basis with the same Ss, an alternative is to select two groups who presently represent the before-and-after conditions as defined by self-referent statements and to obtain behavioral criteria of adjustment for each. The need for such an approach has become even more pressing since Taylor (7) has shown that successive Q sorts, without benefit of therapy, reflect changes of the kind reported for successful counseling. Brownfain's study (2) was a step in this direction, but the relationship between his instrument and the conventional Q sort requires exploration.

Method

Measurement of Self and Ideal Self

One hundred and seventy-five upper-class students enrolled in introductory psychology at Oberlin College served as subjects (Ss) on a volunteer basis. The 100 items and general methodology of the SIO Q sort developed by Butler and Haigh (3) were selected because of their frequent and systematic use in current research. Each of the items of self-reference was placed on a 3 x 5 card to facilitate manipulation. The Ss were seen in groups of 20, each S having a set of 100 items, an instruction sheet, and sufficient table space for privacy and easy manipulation of the items. The following instructions were read to the Ss:

> You are about to take part in a preliminary test in connection with a research project in the department of psychology. It is very important that you follow directions as carefully as possible. You have before you a pile of 100 cards. Each card has a

SOURCE. Article by Ralph H. Turner and Richard H. Vanderlippe, "Self-ideal congruence as an index of adjustment" in The *Journal of abnormal and social psychology*, Vol. 57, No. 2, September 1958. Copyrighted 1958 by American Psychological Association.

single sentence written upon it. After I have finished reading these instructions, you are to take the cards and sort them into nine piles in such a way as to describe yourself as you see yourself today. The nine piles will range from those statements that are least like you (Pile 1) to those statements that are most like you (Pile 9). There is a specific number of cards to be placed in each pile. This number is shown on page 2 of these instructions. You can interpret the meaning of each statement in any way you think is correct. I will answer no questions concerning meaning during the sorting. It is very important that you sort these cards as honestly as you can. It is not necessary to attempt arranging the cards within each pile. After you have finished sorting the cards, check to make sure you have the correct number of cards in each pile.

When this self sort was concluded, the items were shuffled and directions given for the ideal sort. These were similar to the instructions given previously except for the substitution of the phrase "sort the cards to describe your ideal self—the kind of person you would most like to be."

Following the mode of analysis adopted by Brownfain (2) and by Hanlon, Hofstaetter, and O'Connor (6), the Ss were divided into two groups, the high comprising the 25 Ss having the highest correlations between self and ideal sorts and the low comprising the 25 having the lowest correlations. This division permitted an approximation to the differences that have been reported for groups seeking therapy as opposed to groups not seeking therapy. No evidence was found that men and women college students differ significantly in the extent of their self-ideal correspondence. This finding is in agreement with that of Block and Thomas (1), who combined the data for their Ss. Similar practice was followed here, yielding a high group of 11 men and 14 women and a low group of 10 men and 15 women. It is in terms of the significance of differences between each of these two groups of 25 Ss on various criteria of adjustment that the validity of the Q sort and the theoretical assumptions upon which it rests were tested. For this purpose, Fisher's t for small samples was utilized. All values are based upon one-tailed tests of significance since a directional hypothesis governed the original design of the experiment.

The Q-Adjustment Score Criterion

Dymond's (4) procedure was followed in utilizing the 37 items of the SIO Q sort that trained clinical psychologists believed a well-adjusted person would say were unlike him (Piles 1-4) and the 37 items they believed a well-adjusted person would say were like him (Piles 6–9). The Q-adjustment score for any S was the number of these 74 items that were sorted into the "correct" side of the distribution in the course of making a Q sort of the self.

Behavioral Criteria of Adjustment

The behavioral criteria against which the Q-sort scores were tested were health, extracurricular participation, sociometric indices, and scholastic adjustment. From the files of the student health service, three indices of health were computed: (a) mean number of days per college year spent in the hospital, (b) mean number of times per college year that assistance for any reason was requested, (c) the total number of negative health items mentioned in the pre-entrance health history as ascertained by a form on which both the student and the family physician had entered appropriate data.

The extracurricular participation score for all Ss in the high and low groups calculated by first compiling a list of 94 extracurricular organizations. Through interviews with officials of each organization, every position within the organizations was given three ratings on five-point scales for the amount of time involved, the status of the position within the particular group, and the status of the position on the campus as a whole. The sum of these three ratings constituted the weight given that position. The number of years a position was held was multiplied by its appropriate weight, and all such products for each activity summed to yield a total score for each S. This was divided by the number of years S had been on the campus to obtain the final participation score.

The sociometric indices involved getting from dormitory housemothers the names of the nine students whose rooms were closest to each S in the high and low groups. Each of the ten students in these living units received a ranking form with the names of the other nine written as column headings to facilitate marking. By entering numbers in the appropriate name column, each student ranked the other nine on each of the following questions: (a) With which person do you spend the most time when you are in a mood to relax? (b) Which person would be best at organizing a group of about 12 people for a particular purpose (such as a clean-up campaign)? (c) If you wanted to talk about a personal problem with a trusted and helpful person, with whom would you be most apt to talk? (d) Which person is the quietest? (e) Which person do you feel has had the most favorable influence upon you? (*f*) Which person makes friends with others most quickly? (*g*) Who would most fairly evaluate the circumstances under which an important college regulation had been broken and decide what punishment, if any, should be given? (*h*) Who is the most cooperative teamworker, working well with a group and doing his/her share? (*i*) Who is most apt to handle wisely any situation which calls for quick, clear thinking? (*j*) Which person is most apt to initiate spontaneous group recreational activities? (*k*) With whom do you (or would you) especially want to be in a dormitory living group again? The mean rank each *S* received from other members of his living group was then computed for each of these items.

The comparative scholastic achievement of the two groups was obtained by comparing the mean cumulative academic grades of those in the high and low groups. Because such a comparison might reflect a difference in initial scholastic potential rather than a difference in adjustment, the mean of the raw scores on the American Council Test (8) was computed for each group. This test, taken by all students during the first week of the freshman year, was found to yield a product-moment correlation of .51 with cumulative grades for the students on this campus. It thus fulfills the function of providing a moderately valid index of scholastic aptitude. To the extent that the two groups do not differ significantly with respect to scholastic aptitude, any significant difference in scholastic achievement may be interpreted as an indication of a difference in scholastic adjustment.

Standard Tests as Criteria

Although not an original part of the study design, 50 of the original Ss were given the Guilford-Zimmerman Temperament Survey (5) as part of another project. Under standard administration and scoring procedures, scores were obtained for the 10 traits measured. Product-moment correlations were run between raw scores for each of these traits, on the one hand, and the correlations between self and ideal *Q* sorts, on the other, the latter being first transformed into corresponding *z* scores.

Results

Table 1 presents the range of the self-ideal correlations in order to facilitate a comparison between the high and the low groups. By use of the *z* transformation, the mean correlations for each group were calculated. The correlation

of .79 indicates reasonably high correspondence between self and ideal ratings for the high group. The corresponding *r* of .11 for the low group does not permit rejection of the hypothesis that the population correlation is zero.

Table 1. Correlation Between Self Sort and Ideal Self Sort

Group	N	Range	Mean z	Equivalent r
All Ss	175	−.08 to .91	.63	.56
High	25	.75 to .91	.08	.79
Low	25	−.08 to .25	.11	.11

Table 2. Mean Group Differences in Health Indices

Health Index	High Group	Low Group	Diff.	t Value	$p <$
Days in hospital	1.14	.93	.21	.458	.35
Reports to clinic	3.99	2.71	1.28	.977	.20
Health history items	1.24	1.84	.60	.470	.35

The Q-adjustment scores for the high group yielded a range of 44–59 with a mean of 52.04. The low group yielded a range of 13–43 with a mean of 29.68. This latter mean corresponds closely to that of 28.80 reported by Dymond (4) for a group that had sought therapy. The mean for the high group is somewhat above the 44.96 she reported for her control group. The range of adjustment represented by the present high and low groups, as measured by this criterion, is certainly no smaller than that found between those seeking therapy and those not seeking therapy. Since the distribution of Q-adjustment scores for the high and low groups did not overlap, there is a significant relationship between self-ideal Q-sort scores and this external criterion of adjustment.

Table 2 indicates that no evidence was found that the high and low groups differed significantly with respect to the number of days spent in the hospital, the number of times the student sought assistance at the health service, or the number of health items mentioned in the preentrance health history.

The mean social participation score for the high group was 20.24, while that for the low group was 13.84. A test of the significance of the difference yielded a *t* of 2.12, significant beyond the .05 level. It appears that those with substantial correlations between self and ideal ratings on the Q sort are significantly more active as measured by this index of social participation than are those whose correlations do not differ significantly from zero.

Table 3. Mean Ranks in Sociometric Items[a]

	High group	Low Group			
Item	$(N - 24)$	$(N - 18)$	Diff.	t Value	$p <$
All	4.2	5.2	1.0	2.38	.03
a	4.6	5.1	0.5	1.34	.10
b	3.7	5.1	1.4	2.50	.01
c	4.4	5.1	0.7	1.75	.05
d	4.9	4.6	0.3	.51	.35
e	4.2	5.3	1.1	2.46	.01
f	4.4	5.3	0.9	1.67	.10
g	4.0	5.0	1.0	1.82	.05
h	4.0	4.7	0.7	1.39	.10
i	4.1	5.3	1.2	2.17	.03
j	4.1	5.8	1.7	3.06	.01
k	4.5	5.3	0.8	1.80	.05

[a] A low rank is considered an indication of better adjustment except in the case of item d.

Table 3 summarizes the data from the sociometric study. The original two groups of 25 each suffered some attrition because of lack of cooperation on the part of some members of the living group. The mean rank received by Ss from those in the living group is indicated for each of the questions and for all items combined. With the combined rank taken as a score for the instrument as a whole, those in the high group achieve a significantly better rating than those in the low group. Examination of the individual items indicates that those in the high group are given preferential ranks without a single exception. Eight of the 11 individual items yielded an acceptable level of significance.

The cumulative academic grade, based upon a point system currently in effect, yielded a mean of 1.78 points for the high group and 1.52 for the low group. This difference, which favors the high group, was found to reach the criterion of significance $(p < .05)$ with a t of 1.81. The mean raw scores of the high and low groups on the American Council Test were 134.6 and 133.1 respectively. This difference was not significant $(p < .40$ with a t of .31). The scholastic superiority of the high group thus does not appear to rest primarily upon an initial difference in scholastic potential and suggests somewhat better scholastic adjustment on the part of those whose self-ideal congruence is high.

Table 4 indicates the correlation between self-ideal congruence expressed as z values and the traits measured by the Guilford-Zimmerman

Temperament Survey (5). Five of these yielded correlations sufficiently large that the hypothesis of zero correlation could be rejected at the .01 level. Those high in self-ideal congruence tended to have high scores in general activity (strong drive, much energy, enthusiasm), ascendance (strong self-defense, leadership, ease in speaking and persuading), sociability (at ease with others, readily established rapport), emotional stability (optimism and freedom from neurotic tendencies), and thoughtfulness (mental poise, observation of behavior in others. capability as supervisor of others, reflectiveness). In each instance, the scores for those high in self-ideal congruence are indicative of better adjustment than are those for Ss low in self-ideal correspondence.

Table 4. Correlations Between Self-Ideal Congruence Expressed as z Values and Traits Measured by the Guilford-Zimmerman Temperament Survey

Trait	Correlation with Self-Ideal Congruence
1. General Activity	.50*
2. Restraint	−.10
3. Ascendance	.58*
4. Sociability	.36*
5. Emotional Stability	.36*
6. Objectivity	−.03
7. Friendliness	−.16
8. Thoughtfulness	.41*
9. Personal Relations	−.25
10. Masculinity	.10

* Significant at the .01 level.

Discussion

Of the criteria of adjustment utilized, a number of significant differences were found between the group high in self-ideal congruence and the group low in this respect. In no instance was a significant difference found in a direction contradictory to the hypothesis. The failure of certain criteria to show a significant difference between the two groups may reflect the inadequacy of these criteria or may indicate that self-ideal congruence is not equally valid as an index of adjustment when applied to all dimensions of adjustment. The possibility of an approach in terms of dimensions of adjustment is suggested by noting that the Q-adjustment score was found to be the external criterion of adjustment most closely related to self-ideal congruence. Since this instrument was the only one in the enviable position of having all its items drawn from the same statements used in the Q sort, it preserved a close relationship with it in terms of the dimensions tapped.

Health-related behavior can occasionally be shown to reflect personal conflict. It may be questioned that it is an appropriate index of adjustment within the adjustment range of the student population sampled. The overlay of genuine organic complaints constitute determiners of behavior that may effectively mask adjustment-motivated behavior in this area.

Block and Thomas (1), contending that self-satisfaction is not linearly related to the social dimension of adjustment, quite properly suggested that it may, as a consequence, have only very limited relevance as an index of the outcome of psychotherapy. It nevertheless appears that in the context of adjustment defined by the criteria utilized here, the theoretical assumptions upon which the conventional Q sort are based received substantial support.

Summary

A test of the theoretical assumptions and the methods upon which the conventional Q sort rests was made using several criteria of adjustment. The results tended to support the theoretical assumptions underlying the Q sort as currently utilized. Although certain criticisms of the procedures involved are not thereby completely invalidated, it would appear that they are not sufficiently serious to justify abandoning either the method or the assumptions supporting the method.

The emergent composite picture of the college student high in self-ideal congruence (as contrasted with the student low in self-ideal congruence) is that of one who participates more in extracurricular activities, has a higher scholastic average, is given higher sociometric ratings by his fellow students, and receives higher adjustment ratings on both the Q-adjustment score and certain traits measured by the Guilford-Zimmerman Temperament Survey.

REFERENCES

1. Block, J., & Thomas, H. Is satisfaction with self a measure of adjustment? *J. abnorm. soc. Psychol.*, 1955, **51**, 254–259.
2. Brownfain, J. Stability of the self-concept as a dimension of personality. *J. abnorm. soc. Psychol.*, 1952, **47**, 597–606.
3. Butler, J. M., & Haigh, G. V. Changes in the relation between self concepts and ideal concepts consequent upon client centered counseling. In C. R. Rogers & Rosalind Dymond (Eds.), *Psychotherapy and personality change.* Chicago: Univer. of Chicago Press, 1954. Pp. 55–75.
4. Dymond, Rosalind. Adjustment changes over therapy from self-sorts. In C. R. Rogers & Rosalind Dymond (Eds.), *Psychotherapy and personality change.* Chicago: Univer. of Chicago Press, 1954, Pp. 76–84.
5. Guilford, J. P., & Zimmerman, W. S. *The Guilford-Zimmerman Temperament Survey: Manual of instructions and interpretations.* Beverly Hills, Calif.: Sheridan Supply Co., 1949.
6. Hanlon, T. E., Hofstaetter, P. R., & O'Connor, J. P. Congruence of Self and ideal self in relation to personality adjustment. *J. consult. Psychol.*, 1954, **18**, 215–218.
7. Taylor, D. M. Changes in the self concept without psychotherapy. *J. consult. Psychol.*, 1955, **19**, 205–209.
8. Thurstone, L. L., & Thurstone, Thelma G. *Psychological examination for college freshmen: 1947 norms.* Washington, D. C.: American Council on Education, 1948.

6. The relationship between self-acceptance and acceptance of others: a learning theory analysis

RICHARD M. SUINN

FOR MANY THEORISTS who have proposed systematic points of view on the nature of personality, the concept of the self has often played an important central role. Once the self-concept is formed and stabilized, it is said to influence later behavior strongly. Special attention has been directed towards the influence that self-attitudes have on attitudes towards others. Adler (1926), Fromm (1947), Horney (1939), and Murphy (1947) have all suggested that the self is an anchorage point, influencing perceptions of and attitudes towards others. This notion of the self as a reference point affecting interpersonal relations is most evident in Sullivanian and Rogerian theory. Sullivan comments that "one can find in others only that which is in the self . . . if the self dynamism . . . be chiefly derogatory (then) it will facilitate hostile, disparaging appraisals of other people" (1947, p. 10). Further: "When one respects oneself . . . so one can respect others . . . as you judge yourself, so shall you judge others" (1940, p. 87). Similarly, Rogers (1951) asserts that "when an individual . . . accepts (himself) . . . then he is necessarily . . . more understanding . . . and accepting of others as separate individuals" (p. 520).

Much research has been conducted to determine whether such a theoretically proposed relationship between self-acceptance and acceptance of others can be demonstrated empirically. Berger (1952), Omwake (1954), Phillips (1951), Sheerer (1949), and Stock (1949)

SOURCE. Article by Richard M. Suinn, "The relationship between self-acceptance and acceptance of others: a learning theory analysis" in *Journal of abnormal and social psychology,* Vol. 63, No. 1, pp. 37–42, 1961.

have all obtained significant results on samples ranging from patients in treatment to prisoners, high school students, college students, and adult education enrollees. Correlations ranged from .36 to .74. Zelen (1954), testing sixth grade children, found that self-acceptance was significantly correlated with acceptance *by* peers, but not with acceptance *of* others. This contrary finding might be explainable on the basis of age differences between the subjects of Zelen's study and other researches. Inspection indicates that, in general, the lower the age group, the lower the correlations found.

Despite these numerous studies, little attempt has been made to specify the variables leading to such correlations. Levy (1956) indicates that self-acceptance can be demonstrated to influence even acceptance of home town. He therefore questions the adequacy of the experimental design and proffered interpretations of previous researches. He further appears to be asking for two departures from previous studies: Offer the subjects a series of *specific* objects to describe rather than the usual, nondefinitive "average-other person," and offer a theoretical formulation that will predict the nature of these new correlations.

The present work extends previous studies in the directions suggested by Levy (1956). Thus, subjects were asked to describe themselves and two specific people, their fathers and their teachers. Predictions regarding the nature of the correlation between self- and other-appraisal and definitive statements of the variables influencing such relationship were derived from a learning theory analysis of the self-concept.

Following a learning theory analysis, several stimulus objects were defined along with certain responses. The self, the father, and the teacher were considered stimulus objects. Test answers were considered responses elicited by these stimulus objects. In research of this type, the responses are designated as reflecting acceptance or nonacceptance. Studies of stimulus response associations indicate that responses originally elicited by a specific stimulus should also tend to be elicited by other stimuli that are similar to the original. The greater the similarity between the new stimuli and the original stimulus, the greater is the tendency towards generalization. It seemed logical to consider the correlation between self-acceptance and acceptance of others as an example of stimulus generalization. Thus, self-acceptance responses originally elicited by the self-as-object are generalized to others-as-objects. It was therefore predicted that there would be a significant positive correlation between self-acceptance and acceptance of others (Prediction 1). Furthermore, since degree of generalization is a function of degree of similarity, it was predicted that the greater the perceived similarity between the self and the other, the greater would be the generalization of self-responses towards the other stimulus object (Prediction 2).

Two assumptions were implied by these predictions. First, that the self is the central or reference stimulus, not the other stimulus object (i.e., the father or the teacher). It was therefore assumed that acceptance responses are first associated with the self and then are generalized towards others. The second assumption was that the self-concept for an adolescent subject is stable and distinct enough to be considered a reference stimulus.[1] If the self-concept is not a distinct stimulus, then it would be difficult for generalization to occur. If the original stimulus' characteristics are vague, changing, or varying, then comparison with the second stimulus may be difficult or impossible.

The third and fourth predictions were de-

rived from findings which indicate that anxiety increases the degree of stimulus generalization (Hilgard, 1951; Mednick, 1957; Rosenbaum, 1953; Wenar, 1954). Prediction 3 was as follows: Self-acceptance generalizes towards acceptance of others as a function of degree of self-acceptance, the greater the self-dissatisfaction (lack of acceptance), the greater the generalization. Similarly, Prediction 4 was stated in this way: Self-acceptance generalizes towards acceptance of others as a function of degree of involvement with the other person; the greater the involvement, the greater the generalization. Subjects have a need to relate to and be accepted by others. This need begins during the long dependency period of infancy and childhood and is manifested in adulthood as need Affiliation (Murray 1938). Further, Zelen's (1954) and Smith's (1958) data suggest that a person who does not accept himself is also rejected by others. Therefore, the greater a subject's self-dissatisfaction, the more likely it is that his Affiliation need will be frustrated. This actual or expected frustration in turn may be hypothesized to lead to an increase in anxiety. And anxiety increases level of stimulus generalization. Hence the prediction that generalization increases with increased self-dissatisfaction.

Involvement was also hypothesized as a significant variable because subject's need to relate to and be accepted by a person increases with greater involvement with him. With this increase in strength of need, frustration of the need should lead to greater anxiety. Thus, it was predicted that there would be greater generalization of self-responses towards fathers than teachers, assuming that the subjects were more involved with parents than with teachers.

Method

Subjects

The subjects were 82 male high school seniors, all of whom were in contact with a male teacher. They were selected from the senior class on the basis of availability of time to participate.

Instrument

Four Q sort decks were developed for use. Each deck was composed of 20 adjectives selected from the 300-item Adjective Check List (Gough, 1955a) in an earlier standardization study. Criteria for selection were as follows:

---

[1] The restriction of the term "stimulus" to mean only "external energy changes impinging on a receptor" is not implied here. It is felt that this strict definition cannot explain adequately the influence of such cognitive and affective variables as thoughts, memories, attitudes, or the self-concept. Consequently, stimulus is considered here as conceptually similar to Dollard and Miller's (1950) terms "cue-producing responses" (p. 98) and "verbal mediation cues" (p. 101, 310).

1. All adjectives were equated for social desirability. Only those adjectives checked by the standardization subjects as highly desirable or desirable and which were judged as favorable in Gough's (1955b, pp. 33–34) own study of his Check List were used.

2. One deck, called the Common Adjective Sort (CAS), included only those adjectives checked by standardization subjects as applicable for describing themselves, their fathers, *and* their male teachers. This deck was developed for use as an independent measure of perceived similarity between these stimulus objects.

3. The remaining three decks, called the Unique Adjective Self-Sort (UASS), the Unique Adjective Father Sort (UAFS), and the Unique Adjective Teacher Sort (UATS), included only those adjectives checked as relevant primarily for description of the self (UASS), the father (UAFS), *or* the male teacher (UATS). The UASS was used by each experimental subject to describe only his perceived self and his ideal self. The UAFS was used for similar descriptions of the subject's father, and the UATS was used only for description of the subject's male teacher.

The purposes of establishing these criteria were to control for social desirability influences while still using adjectives appropriate for description of the named social objects. Kenny (1956; personal communication, 1959) and Kogan and Quinn (1957) report that social desirability factors tend distinctly to influence Q sort behavior. Among various approaches offered by Kenny (personal communication, 1959) as a means of holding constant the effects of social desirability, the method of selecting only desirable traits was used. This procedure is similar to the forced-choice technique used in some personality and interest inventories where the subject is forced to choose from items which are equally desirable. It eliminates the spurious correlation between perceived and ideal sorts which occur because of a specific response set, i.e., that of placing all desirable traits in the "most like (me)" category and all the undesirable traits in the "least like (me)" pile.

Measurement of Acceptance and Similarity

Each subject's perceived self-sort was correlated with his ideal self-sort, giving a Self-Acceptance (SA) score for every subject. Only UASS decks were used. Similarly, each subject's perceived father sort was correlated with his ideal father sort, giving a Father Acceptance (FA) score for every subject. Only UAFS decks were used. Finally, each subject's perceived teacher sort was correlated with his ideal teacher sort, giving a Teacher Acceptance (TA) score for every subject. Only UATS decks were used.

Each subject's perceived self-sort was correlated with his perceived father sort, giving a Self-Father Similarity (S-F sim.) score for every subject. Only sorts from the CAS deck were used. In the same fashion, each subject's perceived self-sort was correlated with his perceived teacher sort, giving a Self-Teacher Similarity (S-T sim.) score for every subject. Only sorts from the CAS deck were used.

Procedure

Experimental subjects, in groups of 10, were asked to describe several designated stimulus objects using the decks provided. Sorting was on a five-point forced rectangular distribution. Subjects sorted in the following order: description of a male teacher was UATS, then with CAS; description of father with UAFS, then with CAS; description of self with UASS, then with CAS; description of ideal teacher with UATS, ideal father with UAFS, and, finally, ideal self with UASS. All decks were collected immediately after each sorting was completed and before directions for the next sorting were given.

Results

Prediction 1. Subjects should generalize self-acceptance responses towards fathers and male teachers. Pearson product-moment correlations between the SA scores and FA scores were .32 ($p < .005$) and .25 ($p < .02$) for the SA scores and TA scores.

Prediction 2. Degree of perceived similarity between the self and the other stimulus affects the size of the generalization effect. This prediction was restated as: As the perceived similarity between self and other increases, the discrepancy between SA scores and Other-Acceptance scores (FA or TA scores) decreases. Discrepancy scores were obtained by taking the absolute difference between each subject's SA score and his Other-Acceptance score (FA or TA). These discrepancy scores were then correlated with perceived similarity scores (S-F sim. or S-T sim.). According to the restated prediction, a significant negative correlation was expected.

The correlation based on the SA-FA discrepancy scores and the S-F sim. scores was $- .24$ ($p = .05$). The correlation based on the SA-TA discrepancy scores and the S-T sim. scores was $- .34$ ($p = .002$).

Prediction 3. The greater the self-dissatisfaction, the greater the generalization. The variance of the FA scores for the 15 subjects with the lowest SA scores was compared with the variance for the 15 subjects with the highest scores. Similarly, the variance of the TA scores for the 15 subjects with the lowest SA scores was compared with the variance for the 15 subjects with the highest SA scores. The *F* ratios, thus computed were not significant.

Prediction 4. Degree of involvement influences generalization; the greater the involvement, the greater the generalization. It was assumed that all subjects were more involved with their fathers than with their teachers. It was therefore expected that the correlation between the SA scores and the FA scores would be greater than the correlation between the SA scores and the TA scores. A *t* test of the differences between these two correlations was not statistically significant.

Discussion

General Implications for Research

The first implication involves experimental design. There is little doubt now that self-acceptance is correlated with acceptance of others. Future research must direct itself towards contributing more detailed information concerning such a relationship. For this reason, it is believed that the most meaningful experimental approach lies in greater specificity. This study has shown that specifically designated stimulus objects can be examined instead of the formerly used, vaguely defined, "average-other person." This new technique does away with the ambiguity of interpreting findings involving the average-other. Furthermore, it allows a more straightforward conclusion: that self-acceptance influences acceptance of others —specifically, of fathers and even teachers.

A second implication applied to theory. Given that the relationship exists, the full value of such a finding is attained only as the *variables* influencing the relationship are better understood. However, as Levy (1956) pointed out, theoretical formulations, thus far, have not provided hypotheses as to what variables are important. In this study, a learning theory orientation was found to be a fruitful source for deriving such hypotheses. It was shown that the self could be assumed to be a stimulus object and that self-acceptance could be viewed as responses elicited by the self. Further, it was found quite feasible and informative to apply knowledge about stimulus generalization to study of self-acceptance and acceptance of others.

A third implication concerns the interpretation of the finding that one variable, perceived similarity, significantly influences the generalization of self-acceptance responses. The interpretation maintained in this report is that perceived similarity is an independent variable influencing the dependent variable, generalization. Another way of interpreting the data is to consider acceptance as one factor used by a person when he rates another on similarity. For example, a subject may judge his father as *similar* to himself on the basis of whether he *accepts* his father as much as he (the subject) accepts himself. The reasoning runs like this: I accept myself; I also accept my father; therefore, my father and I must be similar. Q sort techniques tend to minimize this type of problem inasmuch as the subject is asked simply to describe several people and is unaware of the purpose of such description. However, research is needed to clarify the issue further.

Finally, several further predictions may be derived from the results of this study. As a first example, it is feasible to attempt a prediction of the degree of generalization of self-acceptance to still other people. Thus, it might be predicted that a wife would express dissatisfaction with her husband or children if she were already dissatisfied with herself. The degree of this generalization of self-dissatisfaction would depend upon the degree to which the wife perceived her family as similar to herself. This type of behavior might be called "scapegoating" in social psychology, "projection" in abnormal psychology, or, as suggested here, generalization of self-attitudes toward other similar social objects. Such generalization is quite possibly the explanation for the Sears, Maccoby, and Levin (1957) finding of a significant correlation between a mother's "acceptance for the self (and her acceptance of) the husband, the current situation, the pregnancy, the infant and the child" (p. 59).

Another prediction involves the possibility of adjustive behavior being facilitated by generalization. It is suggested that the variable of perceived similarity be explicitly added to Rogerian and Sullivanian expositions of the way acceptance of self facilitates *realistic* acceptance of others. A self-accepting person is presumably better able to see others as separate social objects from himself (Rogers, 1951, p. 520); he may then also be better able to determine realistically how similar the self is to others; the greater the similarity, then, the greater the acceptance of the other person. Thus, the self-concept can serve as a mediating stimulus, aiding in eliciting adjustive responses. An example of a prediction from this reasoning is that empathic behavior is facilitated where there is some perception of similarity of the other to the self. Nimitz (1956) reflected this idea in the comment, "An individual may exaggerate similarities between himself and others . . . (and this) need be in no way pathological (i.e., it can occur without defensive needs being served)" (p. 279). A therapist may therefore more readily empathize and accept his client by such a process.

Summary

This study was an attempt to provide a theoretical orientation from which the variables influencing the relationship between self-acceptance and acceptance of others could be derived. A learning theory approach was used, whereby the self was considered as a stimulus object and self-acceptance statements were considered responses. The general hypothesis was that these responses associated with the self would be subject to the effects of stimulus generalization.

Eighty-two male high school seniors were asked to describe themselves and two other designated stimulus objects, their fathers and their male teachers. Special Q sort decks, developed in a standardization study, were used for these descriptions. It was predicted that self-acceptance responses would generalize towards the father and teacher as a function of the following variables: degree of perceived similarity between the self and the other stimulus object, degree of self-dissatisfaction, and degree of involvement with the other stimulus object. Results indicate that self-acceptance is significantly correlated with acceptance of father and with acceptance of teacher and perceived similarity is a significant variable influencing this generalization of self-acceptance. There is no support for the proposed influence of degree of self-dissatisfaction or of involvement for adolescent subjects.

The contributions of this study towards better understanding, experimental design, and prediction in studies of this type were discussed.

REFERENCES

Adler, A. *The neurotic constitution.* New York: Dodd, Mead, 1926.

Berger, E. The relationship between expressed acceptance of self and expressed acceptance of others, *J. abnorm. soc. Psychol.*, 1952, **47**, 778–782.

Dollard, J., & Miller, N. *Personality and psychotherapy.* New York: McGraw-Hill, 1950.

Fromm, E. *Man for himself.* New York: Rinehart, 1947.

Gough, H. *Adjective Check List.* Berkeley, Calif.: Institute for Personality Assessment and Research, 1955. (a)

Gough, H. *Reference handbook for the Gough Adjective Check List.* Berkeley. Calif.: Institute for Personality Assessment and Research, 1955. (b)

Hilgard, E., Jones, L., & Kaplan, S. Conditioned discrimination as related to anxiety. *J. exp. Psycho.*, 1951, **42**, 94–99.

Horney, K. *New ways in psychoanalysis.* New York: Norton, 1939.

Kenny, D. The influence of social desirability on discrepancy measures between real self and ideal self. *J. consult. Psychol.*, 1956, **20**, 315–18.

Kogan, W., & Quinn, R. Some methodological problems in the quantification of clinical assessment by Q array. *J. consult. Psychol.*, 1957, **21**, 57–62.

Levy, L. The meaning and generality of perceived actual-ideal discrepancy. *J. consult. Psychol.*, 1956, **20**, 396–398.

Mednick, S. Generalization as a function of manifest anxiety and adaptation to psychological experiments. *J. consult. Psychol*, 1957, **21**, 491–494.

Murphy, G. *Personality: A biosocial approach to origins and structure.* New York: Harper, 1947.

Murray, H. *Explorations in personality.* New York: Oxford, 1938.

Nimitz, E. An example of assimilative projection. *J. abnorm. soc. Psychol.*, 1956, **52**, 279.

Omwake, K. T. The relationship between acceptance of self and acceptance of others shown by three peronality inventories. *J. consult. Psychol.*, 1954, **18**, 443–446.

Phillips, E. L. Attitudes toward self and others: A brief questionnaire report. *J. consult. Psychol.*, 1951, **15**, 79–81.

Rogers, C. *Client-centered therapy: Its current practices, implications and theory.* Boston: Houghton Mifflin, 1951.

Rosenbaum, G. Stimulus generalization as a function of level of experimentally induced anxiety. *J. exp. Psychol.,* 1953, **45**, 35–43.

Sears, R., Maccoby, E., & Levin, H. *Patterns of child rearing.* New York: Row, Peterson, 1957.

Sheerer, E. T. An analysis of the relationship between acceptance of and respect for self and acceptance of and respect for others in 10 counseling cases. *J. consult. Psychol.,* 1949, **13**, 169–175.

Smith, G. Six measures of self-concept discrepancy and instability: Their interrelations, reliability, and relations to other personality measures.

J. consult. Psychol., 1958, **22**, 101–112.

Stock, D. An investigation into the interrelations between the self concept and feelings directed toward other persons and groups. *J. consult. Psychol.,* 1949, **13**, 176–180.

Sullivan, H. S. Conceptions of modern psychiatry. *Psychiatry,* 1940, **3**, 1–117.

Sullivan, H. S. *Conceptions of modern psychiatry.* Washington, D. C.: William Alanson White Psychiatric Foundation, 1947.

Wenar, C. Reaction time as a function of manifest anxiety and stimulus intensity. *J. abnorm. soc. Psychol.,* 1954, **49**, 335–340.

Zelen, S. Acceptance and acceptability: An examination of social reciprocity. *J. consult. Psychol.,* 1954, **18**, 316.

7. The self-concept and accuracy of recall of inconsistent self-related information

RICHARD M. SUINN, DORENE OSBORNE, AND PAGE WINFREE

Problem

ROGERS (4, P. 503) HYPOTHESIZES that "As experiences occur in the life of the individual, they are denied symbolization . . . (if) the experience is inconsistent with the structure of the self." Interpreting "denied symbolization" as "denied immediate recall," Cartwright (1, p. 212) showed that mean recall scores for inconsistent items were lower than scores for consistent items. This study investigated the extended hypothesis that degree of accuracy of recall is related to *degree* of inconsistency between the self-concept and the new material.

Procedure

Thirty Introductory Psychology Freshmen described themselves on 100 adjectives (Adjective Rating Scale) derived from the Gough Adjective Check List (2). All adjectives were socially desirable by Gough's criteria (3, p. 33) as a control for this variable. All items were adjectives well within the common vocabulary of the Ss as indicated by the Thorndike-Lorge frequency counts (5). This criterion provided a control for word-frequency effects on memory. Each S rated each adjective on a scale from 1 (most like me) to 6 (least like me). Directions were then given such that every person was rated by two others in the class. Five days later, each S was presented a completed ARS

SOURCE. Article by Richard M. Suinn, Dorene Osborne, and Page Winfree, "The self-concept and accuracy of recall of inconsistent self-related information" in *Journal of clinical Psychology*, Vol. 18, p. 473–474, 1962.

said to represent the composite of the ratings by others of him. This actually involved faked ratings designed to present each S with a set of self-related items discrepant from the S's own self-concept. Each faked ARS contained 50 adjective-ratings zero degrees discrepant from the S's own previous self-rating (Group 0), 25 one degree discrepant (Group I), and 25 two degrees discrepant (Group II). Thus Group 0 adjective-ratings were consistent with, while Group I and II ratings were to varying degrees inconsistent with the S's self-concept. The method of obtaining the discrepancies is best explained by illustration: If the S described himself on the adjective 'calm' with a rating of 6 (least like me), a zero discrepancy would be a composite rating also of 6, a one degree discrepancy would be a rating of 5, a two degree would be a rating of 4. The direction of the discrepancy was randomly chosen as were the adjectives to form each group. Two days later, Ss again filled out the ARS, this time as they remembered the composite ratings to be.

Accuracy scores were computed for each S for each of the 3 groups of adjectives. If the S recalled the composite rating exactly, he was given a score of 0 for that adjective; if he missed by one degree (e.g., by checking a rating of 3 where the composite rating was 2), he was given a score of 1, and so forth up to a maximum possible score of 3. High scores thus represented low accuracy of recall. These scores were summed across all Ss and divided by the sample size to provide a mean accuracy score for Group 0 adjectives, a mean for Group I and a mean for Group II. Mean Group 0 was the degree of accuracy of recall when adjectives were zero degrees discrepant, Mean Group I was the degree of accuracy for one degree discrepant adjectives, and Mean Group II was the accuracy for the two degrees discrepant items.

Results and Summary

Results indicate that accuracy decreased with increase in degree of discrepancy of the adjectives to be recalled. Thus, Mean Group 0 was .53, Mean Group I was .68, and Mean Group II involved the highest inaccuracy of recall at 1.09. All differences between means were significant beyond the .001 levels of significance.

It is concluded that degree of accuracy of recall of self-related items is a function of the degree to which the items are inconsistent with the self-concept.

REFERENCES

1. Cartwright, D. Self-consistency as a factor affecting immediate recall. *J. abnorm. soc. Psychol.*, 1956, **52**, 212–219.
2. Gough, H. *Adjective check list.* U. of Calif.: IPAR, 1955.
3. Gough, H. *Reference handbook for the Gough Adjective Check List.* U. of Calif., Berkeley: IPAR, 1955.
4. Rogers, Carl. *Client-centered therapy.* Boston: Houghton-Mifflin, 1951.
5. Thorndike, E. L. and Lorge, I. *The teacher's book of 30,000 words.* New York: Columbia Univ., 1944.

8. The relation between maternal self-acceptance and child acceptance

GENE R. MEDINNUS AND FLOYD J. CURTIS

TWO MEASURES OF SELF-ACCEPTANCE and one measure of child acceptance were administered to 56 mothers of children enrolled in a parent-participating cooperative nursery school in order to test the hypothesis of a significant positive relation between maternal self-acceptance and child acceptance. The hypothesis was confirmed. The semantic differential technique for assessing child acceptance holds promise for further research in this area.

Assessment of parental attitudes has received a tremendous amount of attention in research concerned with factors influencing the child's personality development. While the content of most current parent attitude tests focuses on the parent's attitude toward a number of aspects of child rearing, of at least equal importance is the parent's attitude toward the individual child in terms of an acceptance-rejection dimension. In case studies of emotionally disturbed children, the inference frequently is made that one or both of the parents reject the child. Support for the emphasis on the importance of parental acceptance comes also from factor analyses of parent behavior ratings (Schaefer, 1959) and of parent attitude scales (Zuckerman, Ribback, Monashkin, & Norton, 1958). In both analyses, an acceptance-rejection factor appeared in addition to an authoritarian-democratic one.

SOURCE. Article by Gene R. Medinnus and Floyd J. Curtis, "The relation between maternal self-acceptance and child acceptance" in *Journal of counseling psychology*, Vol. 27, No. 6, pp. 542–544, 1963.

A number of personality theorists have suggested that the attitudes held toward the self are reflected in the attitudes held toward others. Fromm (1939), for example, maintains that self-love and the love of others go hand in hand. He notes that a failure to love the self is accompanied by a basic hostility toward others. Horney (1950) feels that the person who does not love himself is incapable of loving others. Rogers (1951) argues that when a client enters therapy he typically holds a negative self-concept; he is unable to accept himself. However, once the client becomes more accepting of himself, he begins to be more accepting of others.

The attitudes which a child holds toward himself, especially those dealing with self-esteem and self-worth, play an important role in his personality development. The extent to which a child develops a positive self-concept depends crucially upon the extent to which he is accepted by the "significant others" (typically his parents) in the early years.

While numerous studies could be cited showing a relation between self-acceptance and acceptance of others, a majority of these have used as subjects college students or individuals receiving counseling or therapy. There is almost no research evidence for the relation between parental self-acceptance and acceptance of the child, though several investigations have described the effects on the child's personality development of parental nonacceptance. Most of this research has dealt with clinic populations, however, and the research involving normal parents and children is meager and less confirmatory.

Hypothesis

The purpose of the present investigation was to test the hypothesis that there is a significant positive relation between self-acceptance and child acceptance in a nonclinical group of mothers of young children.

Method

Subjects

Fifty-six mothers of children enrolled in a parent-participating cooperative nursery school served as subjects. The mothers ranged in age from 25 to 45 years with a mean of 32; years of education ranged from 11 to 18 with a mean of 14. The children in the nursery school on whom the mothers made the ratings ranged in age from 3 to 5 with a mean of 4 years.

Procedure

Two measures of self-acceptance and one measure of child acceptance were administered during two consecutive meetings of the mother group. The self-acceptance measures were the Bills Index of Adjustment and Values (Bills, Vance, & McLean, 1951) and a semantic differential scale of 20 bipolar adjectives in which the distance (D) between the mothers' ratings of "Me (as I am)" and "Me (as I would most like to be)" was defined operationally as the extent of self-acceptance. The child acceptance measure consisted of the same set of bipolar adjectives with the distance between the mothers' ratings of "My child (as he is)" and "My child (as I would most like him to be)" defined as the extent of maternal acceptance of the child.

Results and Discussion

The intercorrelations among the three self-regard scores and the child acceptance measure are provided in Table 1. All of the coefficients are in the expected direction; the negative correlations are due to the method of scoring the tests. On the Bills self-acceptance measure, the

Table 1. Correlations among Maternal Self-Acceptance and Child Acceptance Measures

Measures	Bills self-acceptance	Bills adjustment	Semantic differential child acceptance
Semantic differential self-acceptance	−.57**	.53**	.33*
Bills self-acceptance		−.57**	−.48*
Bills adjustment			.28

* $p < .05.$
** $p < .01.$

higher scores indicate greater self-acceptance while the Bills adjustment scores and the semantic differential self-acceptance scores are discrepancy scores with the higher scores denoting less favorable self-attitudes. The findings strongly support the hypothesis of a significant positive relation between maternal self-acceptance and child acceptance.

It is likely that the present sample of mothers was restricted in terms of the child acceptance dimension. The mothers were concerned and interested enough in their children to spend the considerable time and effort which is involved in participation in the cooperative nursery school. Since moderate correlations were obtained in this rather restricted range of subjects, one might expect higher correlations to emerge in a study of mothers randomly selected from the general population.

The validity of the measure employed to assess child acceptance remains to be established. Subsequent research may show that factors in the parent-child relationship other than acceptance are reflected in this instrument. However, the fact that positive results were obtained in the present study suggests that the semantic differential approach holds promise as an instrument for assessing the dimension of parental acceptance of the child. The technique is easy to administer and score, and its purpose in assessing child acceptance appears to be somewhat disguised.

REFERENCES

Bills, R. E., Vance, E. L., & McLean, O. S. An index of adjustment and values. *J. consult. Psychol.*, 1951, **15**, 257–261.

Fromm, E. Selfishness and self-love. *Psychiatry*, 1939, **2**, 507–523.

Horney, Karen. *Neurosis and human growth.* New York: Norton, 1950.

Rogers, C. *Client-centered therapy.* Boston: Houghton Mifflin, 1951.

Schaefer, E. S. A circumplex model for maternal behavior. *J. abnorm. soc. Psychol.*, 1959, **59**, 226–235.

Zuckerman, M., Barrett-Ribback, Beatrice, Monashkin, I., & Norton, J. Normative data and factor analysis on the parental attitude research instrument. *J. consult. Pychol.*, 1958, **22**, 165–171.

Murphy's Biosocial Theory

Gardner Murphy, like so many other major personality theorists, is still very active in elaborating and expanding his biosocial theory, and in applying it to a number of critical human problems. Nor has he been inactive in pursuing empirical support for his theory. The Menninger Foundation program of studies on perceptual learning, which Murphy heads, is well known to psychologists.

From Murphy's recent writings, we have selected an excerpt from *Human Potentialities*. In this paper, Murphy discourses on the pleasures to be derived from sensory and motor activities, and how these pleasures may be enhanced by cultivating our sense organs and muscles. Murphy is no believer in one, two, or a few basic drives. He believes that the body has many needs, not the least of them being needs for sensory and motor stimulation.

The next article by Santos and Murphy gives an overview of the Menninger Foundation studies of perceptual learning. This is followed by two articles detailing the actual procedures used in studying perceptual learning.

The term "canalization", although introduced by Janet, has become familiar to psychologists through Murphy's writings. Canalization, it will be recalled, describes the process by which a drive or motive obtains a specific object or objects on which to discharge its energy. The study by Hartley and Perelman, which shows how hungry persons subject to strange foods come to like them better, is one of the few investigations of the canalization process.

Murphy's interest in and his substantial contribution to the field that is called parapsychology is of long standing. These contributions, he feels, are an integral part of his theory of personality. It is altogether fitting, therefore, that we include a selection from one of his recent books, *The Challenge of Psychical Research*, and that we follow that selection with one from a research monograph by Gertrude Schmeidler. Schmeidler has stated that her research "and the thinking behind that research, derive almost entirely from Gardner Murphy. It was Murphy who, in his seminar at Harvard, transformed my vague curiosity about psychic research into a serious interest; it was he who initiated the first of these experiments by offering both funds and a basic hypothesis ('ESP arises in an unconscious, highly motivated state, free from conscious censorship')—a hypothesis incisive enough to be stimulating and yet general enough to leave the experimenter the pleasure of working out the details." (Quoted from the introduction to *ESP and Personality Patterns* by Gertrude R. Schmeidler and R. A. McConnell.) Schmeidler's research is highly original inasmuch as it shows that ESP is interwoven with personality, thereby bearing out Murphy's view that the paranormal dimensions of personality obey the same laws as the normal dimensions do. In fact, one may conclude from Schmeidler's findings that the word 'paranormal' is a misnomer; that extra sensory perception (clairvoyance and mental telepathy, for instance) is as normal as any other psychological process. It may well be, as we stated in *Theories of Personality*, that Murphy's work in this area and his stimulation of such research as that performed by Gertrude Schmeidler will turn out to be the most significant contribution that he has made to psychology.

1.   Human potentialities

GARDNER MURPHY

The Nature of the Impulse toward Discovery

THE WORLD TO WHICH OUR EXTENDED SENSE INTRODUCES US is potentially exciting; it is a come-on to discovery. We reach out toward new experiences, lovingly gloat over them, turn an eagle eye toward fine differentiation among them, modes of grouping and ordering them; put them into hierarchies and systems; look always for new experiences, and new modes of organization. Let us now attempt to understand the basis for this craving for new experience. It is tempting to use the label "curiosity drive." But to speak of "curiosity" is too little and too much; too little because an idle glance at the sports page is also "curiosity"; too much because it simply slaps a name upon what has not been analyzed or understood.

To begin with, this craving certainly seems related to some of our visceral needs. Mankind's interests are not dependent on his viscera in any simple and clear way. In contrast to his animal brethren, he is potentially in love with the sky, the earth, and the sea, and all that flies, runs, or crawls upon or within them. He loves to dissect, to analyze, to reconstruct, to create, to fathom, to understand, to grasp both sensory values and abstract relationships[1] in virtually everything that exists or can be imagined to exist. Although we recognized a visceral component, we seemed to find a place for the (Platonic) view that we find universal or abstract or general law or order in what our senses apprehend and that we are carried beyond the realm of the senses to the realm of beauty in which generalization, or capacity for the universal, is expressed. But there is also a place for still a third factor, a nonspecific definition of human interests which makes the human constitution capable of almost unlimited resonance, beating in tune with much which acts upon it. This will give us a threefold basis for the craving to know and understand: (1) the visceral drives; (2) the love of order; (3) resonance to the nature and structure of that which surrounds us. All of these components appear in the first human nature, but they are reworked and enriched by culture until in their turn, as we shall see, they begin to transform both the first and the second human natures.

Pointing to the visceral components is the fact that clinical data, notably the data of psychoanalysis and ethnology, underscore the reality of veiled instinctual satisfactions from the rhythms of wind and water; man finds in the things about him apt reminders of his own primitive needs and action tendencies. The second view, which emphasizes man's quest for order and form, finds no great quarrel with this first view, but instead of emphasizing the instinctual tendencies rooted in the viscera emphasizes especially the goodness of form which arises from the rhythms of action and, as in the magnificent synthesis by Rudolf Arnheim,[2] finds the balance, symmetry, and rhythm of the neuro-muscular activity in which the

SOURCE: Selection from Gardner Murphy, *Human Potentialities*, pp. 178–194. New York: Basic Books, 1958.

[1] D. E. Berlyne has made vivid the distinction between the need for *perceptive contact* and the need for *understanding*—"epistemic" curiosity ("A Theory of Human Curiosity," *Brit. J. Psychol.*, Vol. 45, 1954, pp. 180–191). This restatement of a well known traditional distinction may also be useful, in some degree, in differentiating art and science: Both art and science utilize both of these kinds of curiosity, art emphasizing the perceptual, science the epistemic. But both contain many other ingredients as well (cf. Arnheim, p. 180 and p. 291).

[2] *Art and Visual Experience: A Psychology of the Creative Eye*, University of California Press, 1954.

whole body is involved a primary cue to the goodness and order to which all the arts aspire.

The last of these views, the *nonspecific* doctrine, can claim no such lofty interpretations. Like an Epicurean at the Stoics' meeting, it begs only to be allowed to utter very simple and pedestrian realities. It points empirically to the fact that the more complex the central nervous system, as we go from simpler to higher animals, the more there is of the response to anything and everything as exciting and interesting—the more sharply the world of spatial and temporal relationships stand out, as contrasted with simple physical satisfactions, and the greater the fascination with movement and order, whether what is sought is perfection or simply the earthly things which act upon the body. For, from this third point of view, there is a potential excitement about sheer reality in itself and about our capacity to respond to it; human potentialities are realized wherever sense organs, muscle, and brain are at work, and wherever the impact of a real thing upon these sensitive and hungry tissues of ours can make itself felt, engendering a hunger which often demands more of the stuff which gave it birth. As Walt Whitman had it, poetry belongs "to real things, and to real things only." One wants more and more of the world itself, not because it is the best of all possible worlds but because it is there; not because it is ideal but because it is real; not because it contains unlimited hidden meanings—though, indeed, as we shall see, it does contain them—but because in its own right it is exciting, moving, satisfying, yet always prompting to new modes of contact, always giving birth to new hungers. If so, our urge to new experience must be a tremendously potent, though largely latent, component in human nature.

From the position to which we have now come, all three of the doctrines just stated seem relevant and useful. It may turn out that there are contradictions between them and therefore that refinements and choices must be made. It may also turn out that the three doctrines are all directly to be derived from the evolutionary view of human beings and from empirical materials on the development of infants and children, and that the problem is one of integration of empirical findings in such a way as to give full scope to the reasonable applications of all three conceptions.

Let us ask, for example, what part a scientific understanding of rhythmic movement would play in our enjoyment of a fine ballet, of a graceful woman's walk? There is not the slightest doubt that there are, both in the broad and in the more narrowly defined sense, erotic components in response to bodily grace. Indeed in the beautiful rhythms of courtship behavior of birds and insects, as in nature's direct and primitive use of color in arousing strong feeling, it is hardly possible to doubt that the esthetic has an intimate relation to the erotic. Nor can there be the slightest doubt that deformity, old age, imperfect sexual differentiation, strained and awkward modes of movement, can all interfere with the broadly sensuous and, more specifically, erotic components in the response to the ballet and to the graceful walk. There is, then, clearly some reason for saying that the response to grace in posture and movement is to some degree directly erotic and to some degree a "sublimated" response; and if so, it seems likely that a scientific quest of rhythm, the delight in orderly temporal patterns, contains such elements.

At the same time, there is a huge difference between what might be called a direct or gross erotic appeal and a more complex one involved in the art form of the ballet or the rhythmic pattern of walking to which the term "grace" could be applied. As the Platonists have pointed out, there are simplicities, balances, principles of order or form, which to some degree can be generalized. They can be found not only in the woman's walk but in the fanning movements of a butterfly's wings, or indeed in the movements of the walking beam of a ship, or the path of a baseball into the bleachers. Here there is a mathematical pattern to which even the Pythagoreans had access—the sort of thing to which they pointed in their insistence that number was the key to beauty. It is the realization of numerically ordered line, surface, and temporal units that expresses the Pythagorean view of beauty as form. To some degree the erotic may be viewed not as the *source* but as a *subtype* of the human need for form. As always, human nature is both general and specific.

But the story is not yet fully told. What can the *nonspecific* theory offer that is as good as this? What can it set side by side with Homer's Helen of Troy or Goethe's Faustian dream of the eternal feminine? It can offer only a very simple thing—the conception supported by humble, daily, empirical observations that there is almost nothing at all that does not appeal to eye or ear or nose or sense of balance or need to understand or an impulse to get more of. Babies are interested in virtually everything and only through burns, bumps, or dire consequences learn to give up some of their imperious demands upon the world. Despite this early interest, many things lose their appeal in childhood, as by regimentation and the removal of intrinsic satisfactions in favor of so-called extrinsic rewards, one makes the school world boring. In childhood virtually everything for which our senses and understanding are ready is exciting. Watch children as they respond, for example, to nature-study *before* they learn that it's sissified to be interested in birds and bugs. Or watch their interest in the world of creative activity, social disapproval or the rules which define taboo on such activities, or a sense that these things belong to another kind of people, that they are ego-alien, outside of us, out of bounds to us.[3]

To the argument that most of the early interests to which we have pointed arise from association with something pleasant, the best answer is that many of these things in the world around us patently *lose* their primal interest, year by year, and this despite the role of canalization working in the opposite direction. For many people there have to be more and more sauces and spices added to everyday foods to make them interesting, and in the same way, there must often be a liberal dose of excitement or slapstick or the bizarre or the savagely sadistic to give interest to jaded tastes. Frequently, we contrive to deprive human nature of many pristine delights that come from sensory and conceptual grasp of the world.

Considering how much delight in discovery there can be in human life—in people, in hobbies, in leisure, in the decorative arts, in reading, in thinking and looking—one can only wonder why many human beings settle down to a narrow area of satisfactions in which in-

stinctual gratifications with a prominent representation of narcissistic or self-love activities, keeping up with the Joneses, and primitive power satisfactions, embellish the competitive industrial scene. Often there seems hardly enough gratifications to balance the vague apprehensions regarding the encroachments of others upon one's privileged position, and the normal fears of illness and accident, losing a job, growing old, and, of course, destruction through war.

Despite such defeats, it seems to me that the interests of mankind *can* flow outward into everything that exists or could exist, unless and until a rebuff of some sort is encountered. It may be through social disapproval, or through the fact that the social situation causes preoccupation with this area to lead to poor results. Or the individual may discover that he has found all there is to be discovered at his level of operation and with the opportunities for study available to him and hence simply settles down to boredom. The limit is set, then, not by the subject matter or by his mind but by a complex socio-cultural totality which says, for example, that he must accept a narrow repetitive task and work within it. The third human nature, the craving for sensory and motor contact and for understanding and manipulating the world emerges wherever it is not nailed down or hemmed in. And health does not consist in the absence of these—or other—normal human cravings. As Florence Clothier[4] says, man needs the capacity to be *disturbed*.

A homely illustration will serve. A child discovers sooner or later the delights of manipulating words in the manner which we call poetry. But after a few years he becomes ashamed as a result of ridicule and hides his poetic efforts at the time when greatest creativeness might well be available—namely, in the pre-adolescent and early adolescent years. Or, if it is the manipulation of tones or colors that gives him greatest satisfaction, he goes on until some teacher tells him that in comparison with others he has no talent, and again the intrinsic satisfaction of the materials of this world are bypassed in favor of the secondary rewards of any social approbation which can be found. Human potentialities can be released only within a specific life space which expresses the world of a given

---

[3] This conception that human wants are directly related to the positive outgoing nature of man, and not only to his visceral tensions has grown with me for so many years that I cannot properly acknowledge my indebtedness. Among biologists I have learned much from L. von Bertalanffy; among psychiatrists, from Lawrence S. Kubie and Karl A. Menninger; among psychologists, from Solomon Diamond, Lois Barclay Murphy, and Robert S. Woodworth.

[4] At the meetings of the American Psychoanalytic Association, 1957.

individual at a given time, and the world can be and usually is ordered in such fashion that negative feelings are powerfuly aligned against the positive feelings which most simple things at first possess.

It is easy then, to put together the three conceptions that have been defined and to say that man naturally and primitively finds everywhere in nature that which is relevant to his instinctual needs; that which is relevant to the order, rhythm, and motion potential of his own body, as the Platonists made clear long ago; and finally, in the interstices between these two great realms of activity, that which is a ceaseless flow of sheer outward response to, and joy in, the world of things and the world of relationships among things. Since this last world is not anchored to the body in any narrow and specific way, it offers almost unlimited potentials. Instead of trying to explain man's love of the smell of the sea, we might do well to think of the humanness of responding to the sheer impact of the world itself. Far indeed from indicating that this would make all objects equally interesting, it would provide that those which had a Platonic formal stimulus value would have some advantage over those which had a sensory appeal and nothing more; and it would make clear that when all three factors are involved, the instinctual, the formal, and the sensory—as exemplified, for example, in the moving tide of great music or poetry, where instinct, form, and sense are all blended—we would have the most stirring, the most enduring, the most dependable sources of profound arousal.

Pythagoras' Number-Theory and Human Rhythms

From this vantage point one might well ask whether the three interpretations of human delight in the stuff of which life is made are really so fundamentally different. We have already noted that a major clue is offered by ideas that were formulated by the Pythagoreans and developed by the Platonists; and we can now develop this more systematically. The Pythagoreans taught that *number* is the key to order and rhythm and ultimately to all beauty, as in music and poetry. The rhythms of a dance or the contours of a vase seem to be made of essentially the same basic stuff as are the rhythms of life which are evident in our deepest physio-

logical and instinctual cravings and fulfillments. Even the humblest manifestations of life, as in amoeba or our own red blood cells, are expressions of ordered rhythmic cycles of activity, as is true also of the larger cosmic trends, quaintly conceived by the ancients as the "harmony of the spheres." [5]

As we pass, moreover, to the broad dispositions which we have called "nonspecific," it is clear that they are similarly rooted in profound physiological rhythms—of a different sort—to which recent biological research has offered an extraordinary key. It has become evident that the patterned and rhythmic activities of the central nervous system are often responses to the patterned and rhythmic activities of the environment; extraordinary things happen when one is "in beat with" the world. Biology has been learning in the last few decades that many rhythms of physical and chemical structure become rhythms within the living system; e.g., waves of depolarization, action currents in the nerve cells, such as those picked up by the electroencephalogram. The rhythmic beating of nerve cells and other tissues in resonance to forms of wave activity impressed upon them give us not only the feeling that man is, so to speak, numerically or numberwise made of the stuff of which his environment is made, but that he is extraordinarily sensitive to modulations of these numbers. If, for example, a subject submits himself to "photic driving," sitting near an instrument which emits flashes at intervals, he may reveal his own breaking point, the point at which the rhythm induces a convulsion. If, for example, the number is 16, he may rapidly lose consciousness as this number of flashes is presented in the standard time interval. Seventeen and 15, however, are safe numbers for him. It is not until we get to 32, or other multiples of 16, that he breaks. This might remind you of the bridge tempo, or the piano wire or even the glass tumbler that is thrown into a frenzy of sympathetic vibration by a tone which "has its number." There are general human rhythms and individuality in rhythms; both are selectively responsive to *outer* rhythms.

The human nervous system possesses, then,

---

[5] There's not the smallest orb which thou behold'st
But in his motion like an angel sings,
Still quiring to the young-eyed cherubins—
    The Merchant of Venice

curious and profound hungers for many objects which are neither meat nor drink, neither satisfiers of oxygen need, nor of sex need, nor or maternal need, nor any other more obvious visceral demand. The extraordinary power of music suddenly makes more sense than ever before when one realizes that, as has become clear in the last few years, the basic rhythms of music are to a very large degree basic rhythms of the vital system itself. A considerable part undoubtedly is directly dependent upon the visceral rhythms, such as those of the heart and respiratory system, but a great deal more, apparently, depends upon the way in which nerve, muscle, and other tissues are made, the resonances inherent in their construction. In a physical and physiological analysis of music, De Quenetain[6] reminds us of the old struggle to define the response to music in terms of some very fundamental capacities for rhythmic response and the interaction of different rhythms within the living system. There is provision for a kind of affective language, a language of resonances, which is very much deeper than the language of words.

As Susanne Langer[7] has beautifully expressed the matter (though not emphasizing these matters of number), the fundamental human capacity for response to ordered sound represents a kind of universal human communication system, of which language is a refinement and an elaboration but of which it can never be a complete expression. Language remains a refined and specialized aspect of a very much broader and deeper general capacity for "emotional" resonance. One can even say that music "means" something that cannot be "symbolized" in words, if one is willing to give up the sharp denotation and the "deictic" or *pointing* role of speech and can recognize a capacity to feel deeply *one with* the substance of the world or with that special class of material substance of which one's neighbors happen to be made. The "pure" music which, in contrast to "program" music, speaks to us deeply of unnamable things is not, from this point of view, talking meaninglessly. Quite above and beyond its capacity to arouse our martial or tender or lonely or despairing or ecstatic moods, it has

a capacity to bring us into touch with certain resonances, certain rhythmic structures, which are inherent in the world. These resonances are as deeply in the world as are the electromagnetic waves that pass through our rooms or through our bodies all the time, of which we are ordinarily not aware until special instruments are devised that enable our bodies to tune in on them.

It is through the sensory mechanisms of the ear, of course, as well as the skin and muscles, that rhythm is conveyed, and it is often necessary for the wide range of environmental rhythms to be stepped down or converted into rhythms which our bodies can pick up through these various senses. The fundamental issue, however, is the fact that, in addition to these, we are discovering peculiar properties (as in the case of "photic driving") which represent basic rhythms of the body and are not ordinarily triggered into action by such waves. It remains to be seen how far we may go in catching and trapping wave forms which will convey moving or illuminating or broadening experiences—whatever you wish to call them—new ways of responding meaningfully as well as affectively to the world. It would appear, however, that there are vastly more rhythms about us than we have guessed; that we respond potentially to a far greater number of them than we had realized; and that we can be enabled through scientific discovery to respond to still more and more of them.

We have, then, discovered a few of the environmental rhythms (light, sound, etc.) to which we are by nature biologically resonant; a few to which we are nonresponsive (e.g., X-ray); a few more to which our bodies are at present sensitive without our knowing it (e.g., action of cosmic rays on germ-cells); a few to which we become sensitive when special equipment is used ("photic driving"). We are on the threshold of discovering an unguessable number of new rhythms, extensions of the experience capacity and the activity capacity of human nature.

All these kinds of responses, like the extensions of the sensory system, are ways of realizing more fully the human potentialities which have lain dormant since man became man. From this point of view, music is not simply the exploitation of a simple auditory sensitivity long useful from an evolutionary point of view; it is the deepening and enrichment of a basic capacity for rhythm and resonance, the end of

[6] Tanneguy de Quenetain, "Origines et aboutissements du pouvoir de la musique," *Realities*, No. 141, 1957, pp. 86–117.

[7] *Philosophy in a New Key*, Harvard University Press, 1951.

which we cannot begin to guess. It proves, as so many other instances of human liberation have proved, to be at the same time a discovery of how man can be more fully man as he is and the creation of much that is equally human, but never was human before, simply because it never could exist before. New ways of acting upon man result in new kinds of humanness. Cycles of new humanness are laid bare by probing more deeply into the latent structure which was never suspected before.

In all these matters of rhythm, moreover, we find huge individual differences. The love of things conceptual may (as in the case of Gauss in his attic, working on the theory of probability) dominate the instinctual and the sensory. For some people in some situations the sheer love of the sea, or even the love of the smell of the sea, may be so great as to overpower any contribution from the instinctual or conceptual components. Human nature is multiple and composite; but whereas we are hardly likely to forget the instinctual or the conceptual components in man's demands upon the world, it is the raw universal sensory response, together with the raw love of grasping, understanding, and immersing oneself in this world, that is in the greatest danger of being forgotten.

This implies that the internal rhythms are subject to the command of the external rhythms. As the biophysicist Selig Hecht would say, "The organism does not adapt itself to the environment; the environment adapts the organism to itself." This is, however, an incomplete rendering of the story. Every organ of the body is part of the "environment" of every other organ. The rich reciprocities of the inner environment involve mutual tuning and adjustment. It has become evident from recent work that one group of cells modulates or controls the rhythms of another. Indeed, what L. K. Frank has called "organic integration" consists of this type of inner attunement. The inner attunement goes with the attunement by the outer environment, and we have a "harmony of the spheres" in miniature.

But this inner attunement means much more than attunement of the living system to its world, and of the various parts to one another. It likewise provides basic protection from destruction. The reason lies in the fact that there are countless rhythms, countless forms of energy

modulations, existing at large in the environment, some of which are benign, some destructive. We are like little fortresses which by their own internal rhythm prevent disruption by outer rhythms. We are like gyroscopes, able to withstand a push which is incompatible with our own basic postures and rhythms. The problems of the adaptability of man to changing social, biological, and physical environments is partly the problem of the capacity to protect the essential inner rhythms while assimilating those outer rhythms which sustain life and permit new regions of existence and experience. Just as each individual is especially vulnerable to certain rhythms, so each individual may be able to maintain counter-rhythms which constitute defense against disruption.

It is apparent, of course, that those most vulnerable are sometimes those who possess the greatest strength in the very respect in which vulnerability appears; for example, that those most sensitive to the rhythms of tone may, like Sidney Lanier, find it too beautiful to bear. Fortunately, the converse of this statement is likewise probably valid: the discovery of regions of special vulnerability may well help us to discover regions of special sensitivity. Of one thing we may be sure: the life rhythms recently discovered by physical analysis of the senses and physical analysis of the rhythms of the central nervous system, notably by the electroencephalogram, point to an extraordinary range of interesting human variations in response to environmental impact. We have an extraordinary range of internal forms of control by which the various portions of the living system can, in attunement with one another, thwart the disrupting influence of alien rhythms and move in the direction of assimilation and utilization of those which are in basic harmony with inner potentials.

From all this it follows that sensory extrapolation of human interests goes hand in hand with extension of the human sense organs, already considered. Indeed, it is to a large degree because of man's potential for rich sensory experience that he has craved the sensory extensions. Economic gain can always help the process along, but it was not the economic factor that led to the sensory extensions, and it is not the economic factor that makes modern men—and, in particular, children—eager for new experience.

Motor Experience and the Extension of Human Nature

Side by side with all the *sensory* extensions go *motor* extensions. Tools are the first such extensions. In our study of paleolithic, neolithic, Bronze Age, and Iron Age men, we recognize that it is not only men that made the tools but tools that made the men. Our own tools are remaking us. Ordinarily, however, we limit our attention to the things that we make rather than to the thought forms that the new objects impose upon us (in particular the retroflex effect of the sheer making process upon the maker).

We assume now that almost anything can be made. It is a maker's world. We no longer find blasphemy but simple realism in the comment of the little Dutch boy who, very skeptical about God, was asked to look through the microscope and see what wonderfully delicate snowflakes God had made. His comment was, "That's not so hard in the winter." Men and children too, learn constantly how things are made and they make things with less and less primeval wonder, until the very making process itself is no longer wonderful but built into their souls. The aboriginal population which, as Margaret Mead tells us, a few decades ago found ghosts and spirits inside the machines which the white man brought, today repairs and builds the machines with the same gusto as that which the white man himself shows. And the making process can become either boring when simplified to the point where it is too fully understood (as in the assembly line), or it can, through a sense of progressive mastery (as in a dramatic workshop), provide a constant renewal of delight in each day's discoveries.

The cultural anthropologists, the historians, the historical sociologists have given us wonderful ideas to work and play with as they have taught us the endless variety of human institutions and the almost limitless malleability, flexibility, adaptability of the human young when encountering the footbinding or mindbinding, the skill-inspiring or philosophy inculcating habits of varied human groups or of classes and guilds within the groups.

They have, however, made the molding of the mind somewhat too easy. They have often suggested that there is no special bent in one direction or another; that mankind is equally ready for almost *any* kind of contortionist adaptation. This has gone too far; has denied the instinctual readinesses and what we have called the platonic dispositions to move more massively in some directions than in others. It has, however, been valuable in reminding us that there is much to be discovered in *any* social order; that there is much which, just because it is a real thing somewhere to be encountered, can have its human appeal. *To discover,* whether the process be sensory, motor, or intellectual, is fulfilling, and it is this fulfillment which the emerging third human nature everywhere craves. It tends toward richer and richer satisfaction, as we understand more fully through "cognitive mastery" and as we control more fully through action.

We may well push beyond this point and ask ourselves the question: What are the biological and cultural biases which limit our capacity for imagining *new societies?* Working against such capacities to conceive the new, what are the old thought forms? What are the special conditions governing the "sociology of knowledge" which guide mankind into the presumption that societies *must* take certain forms rather than others? What, on the other hand, are the kinds of societies that men *might discover;* what are the sensory and conceptual—or, indeed, instinctual—satisfactions in inventing (as in the game of chess) new rules, new orders, new potential deployments of men with reference to one another, with reference to their physical and their cultural environment, with reference to the cosmic totality which they face? Certainly we shall recognize the deeply ingrained cultural assumptions, the unconscious and axiomatic assumptions which even the most radical of men like to make regarding the longevity of the existing kinds of human societies. They led even a Buddha to assume that there will always be unsatisfiable wants, that there will always be temptations which must be renounced, that there will always be a way of light to be followed in contrast to a way of darkness. Karl Marx assumed that, no matter how changed a society might be, there would always be certain invariant attributes of hand, brain, or heart constituting the raw human nature (cf. Lenin's belief that competitiveness would remain, and even increase, in a classless society). Most prophets assume that even in a new social order, the fundamental human traits will persist; the relations of man and woman, the relations of adult and child, the relations of brothers in blood and brothers in function will remain intact; will remain essentially the familiar relations which prehistoric men knew, which Chinese, Indian, Incan, and Mediterranean men have always known. After all, the time perspectives have been such that it would have been preposterous to expect otherwise. The science fiction which looks ahead fifty million years still represents the relations of human beings as essentially the same as they are today, in that kind of unconscious extrapolation of the self-evident which it is the task of books such as this to challenge.

From the present point of view, man, who extends his sensory equipment to see the infinitely small or the infinitely great and who extends his motor equipment to manipulate, through shafts of light or guided missiles, that which moves far beyond his grasp, is only in limited degree the same man that will cast the social orders of the future and extend his control techniques to mold them more to the heart's desire. If mankind can invent, in the manner of Luther Burbank, new citrus fruits and leafy greens for the table of tomorrow, he can likewise invent social orders which presuppose *not* the human nature that we know but the human nature which both biological and social evolution may *create;* can lay down, as it were, in the

manner of the mathematician, the poet, or the prophet, potential relationships of human beings, potential schemata of human relationships which realize the latent potentials that never have been realized and never could be realized within the thought forms of the past or the present. He can literally imagine into existence unknown relations of man and men. It is indeed true that these schemata can depart in no detail from what is *fixed* as human nature; but the theme of our story has been the *meagerness* of what is known to be intrinsically and necessarily fixed. We deal always with a world of intangibles and shadows which strangely mold themselves somehow into solid realities and pass away into shadows again. There is no fixed human nature, no fixed social order, except within the short time span and the local conditions of the neolithic and postneolithic societies that we happen to know, superimposed upon which is the martial technique of the West, followed by the commercial, industrial, and technological skills which this martial society hit upon in the great Mediterranean era. And the danger that we shall stick too closely to the pattern that we happen to know, in our attempt to extrapolate into the future, is far greater than the risk that we shall wildly imagine impossible human beings and impossible relations among them.

2.   An odyssey in perceptual learning

JOHN F. SANTOS AND GARDNER MURPHY

IT WOULD BE PLEASANT IF OUR MEANDERINGS IN THE VAST UNKNOWN of perceptual learning could follow a course indicated by a comprehensive and well-developed theory, so that experimental evidence might be obtained which would confirm or negate inferences from such an elegant system. Unfortunately, this is not the case. We have no well-formulated theory, but only the hope of achieving one. The evidence is so tenuous and contradictory that more spade work seems to be necessary before we can even hope to formulate a comprehensive theory. This state of affairs is not surprising in view of the fact that perceptual learning has been a highly controversial no-man's land for a long time, having been shunned by those interested in the psychology of learning on the one hand and those working with the classical psychology of perception on the other. As Hochberg (5) phrased it, "The problem of perceptual learning remains very poorly understood or formulated, and yet it is an extremely critical area."

The "new look" movement in perception some ten years ago, brought a flood of experiments which related to the problem: By what process can *needs* influence *perception?* In this work one may detect an *implied* interest in perceptual learning, but unfortunately there have been too few attempts to demonstrate the course of such learning. In many instances, as the Gibsons (3) have pointed out, "The learning process is assumed to have occurred in the *past life* of the experimental subject; it is seldom controlled by the experimenter. These are there-fore not true learning experiments, insofar as they do not control practice or take measures before and after training."

Our experiments have been directed by an interest in the perceptual learning process *per se* and the role that reward and punishment may play in its development. In formulating problems and in planning research we have regarded perception as a process intervening between stimulation and overt response; a process which can be inferred from measurable activity of the organism. We assume that this process has some properties which are similar to those of motor activity and, like motor activity, it can be modifed by learning. Perception should therefore obey the principles relevant to response learning. To quote Berlyne (1), "There may be special laws of learning and innate tendencies governing perceptual responses, but there is abundant evidence that many principles found to underlie learning in general, such as those of conditioning and reinforcement, apply also to perception."

Whether rewards and punishments may influence percepts was studied at City College in New York in the 1940's. These studies were based on the proposition that rewards and punishments altered the probability of perceptual response occurrence under similar conditions in the future and that perception should move toward rewarded aspects and away from punished aspects of a perceptual field. Subsequent results have indicated that the original notions were somewhat naïve. For instance, withholding a reward may be punishing and withholding a punishment may be rewarding. Furthermore, a punished aspect may be quickly learned because of its cue or alerting value in avoiding, escaping or minimizing punishment. The experi-

SOURCE. Article by John F. Santos and Gardner Murphy, "An odyssey in perceptual learning" in *Bulletin, Menninger Clinic*, Vol. 24, pp. 6–17, 1960.

ments at City College in New York did indicate, however, that reinforcement could influence the perception of ambiguous figures such as reversible faces, and structured stimuli such as lines whose length was to be judged.

The Menninger Foundation Program

Our early studies at The Menninger Foundation explored some procedures which enabled reinforcement to influence perception. For instance, Jackson (6) confirmed the "Schafer-Murphy effect," the shift in figure-ground organization of the perceptual field under the influence of reward and punishment. The basic idea of the reversible figure experiments, namely that perception moved in the direction of reward and away from punishment, was also extended into the auditory modality by Fred and Charles Snyder (13) and into the tactual modality by Sommer and Ayllon (17) and McNamara, Solley, and Long (9). Their data generally substantiated the original results. When taped prose passages were first differentially associated with monetary rewards and punishments, then presented simultaneously on another tape, the "rewarded" passages were more frequently perceived by a significant majority of the subjects (13). When one tactual profile was presented simultaneously with shock and no opportunity for escape, and another without shock, the subsequent tracing of an "ambiguous" line which was the identical contour for both profiles produced most frequent reports of perceiving the non-shocked profile. When, however, the training procedure allowed escape-from-shock, the previously shocked profiles

were reported most often. These latter results were explained in terms of "alerting and "repressing" mechanisms (9).

After the original experiments were thoroughly checked and scrutinized and some of the conditions under which they could and could not be obtained were established, our attention shifted from establishing the reliability of the original results to concern with the characteristics of the perceptual learning process itself. We wanted to determine whether something approximating a learning function could be obtained if we sampled the process at successive stages in its development. Further, we were curious as to how certain variables would affect the perceptual learning curve: whether perceptual learning is possible with simultaneous presentation of stimuli but without reward or punishment; the permanence of perceptual learning; and whether it is possible by means of conditioning techniques to alter the dominance relations between perceptual possibilities.

Some of these questions were considered in a group of studies involving the conditioning of perception of a Necker Cube. Solley and Santos (16) were able to produce rigid perception of a "balanced" cube by giving verbal rewards (uh-huh, good, you're doing fine, etc.) in connection with "improved" cube presentations. In this procedure 101 exposures of a left-to-right "improved" cube and 101 exposures of a right-to-left "improved" cube were randomly ordered along with 54 exposures of the balanced cube (see Figure 1). One "improved" cube was rewarded on approximately 70 per cent of its presentations and the other "improved" cube was rewarded on approximately 30 per cent of its presentations. Subjects were asked to identi-

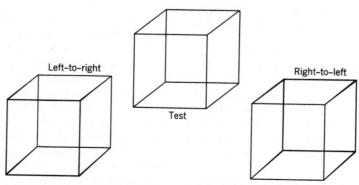

Figure 1. Illustration of improved and test cubes as seen by the Subject (face of cube is 2" × 2").

fy verbally the direction of all cubes during a two-second presentation. Specifically, they were told:

"I am going to show you some cubes which will appear to have either a right-to-left or a left-to-right perspective. That is, the front of the cube will appear to be slightly to the right or to the left. As I show these to you, I want you to tell me which way they appear to you. Some will be more difficult to identify than others."

Not only was it possible to condition perception against initial preference and to countercondition it, but we also demonstrated post-training rigidity in the direction of reward when the balanced cube was exposed continuously *after* training. This work is now being extended. We would like to know more about these rigidity effects, if and how they might be related to personality and situational variables, the extent to which they generalize to other perceptual and performance tasks, and whether frequency of presentation alone is sufficient for obtaining these results. The data thus far indicate that personality variables as measured by simple multiple-choice personality test items are unrelated to conditionability; that generalization of conditionability to other perceptual tasks occurs; and that presentation of the cubes without verbal reward (*i.e.*, sheer practice in looking at the cubes) is not sufficient to alter perception of the balanced cube.

After demonstrating the development of a perceptual learning function, we then turned to a closer inspection of our reward conditions *per se*. We were both intrigued and disturbed by the influence which seemingly unimportant variables had on our results, and began systematically to investigate some of these. Solley and Long (15) have recently published an article which deals with the question "When is uh-huh reinforcing?" That is, what are the necessary

and sufficient conditions for such reinforcements to work? Their observations and data definitely indicate that the experimenter must establish "good rapport" with the subject, or his verbal reinforcements will be ineffective. Of course, this is common clinical knowledge, but we feel the point is important and the operations necessary to establish such rapport must be specified or a basic ingredient for obtaining the results will be lost.

We next considered this question: Given a set of effective reinforcement conditions which *can* influence the course of perceptual learning, is it possible to produce both non-veridical and veridical perceptions (perceptions corresponding to reality)? This consideration is part of the general question as to whether perception necessarily moves toward veridicality or whether the direction of movement is to be understood largely in terms of reward and punishment contingencies. McNamara (8) conducted a series of experiments in which he established that non-veridical perceptions may be produced by differential reinforcement of faulty estimates of length of lines. Different groups of subjects were rewarded or punished for *over* or *under* estimating, respectively, the distances between pairs of parallel lines. They were then tested for transfer effects on a bisected-line illusion and by having them classify "stickmen" as "narrower" (A in Figure 2) or "wider" (B in Figure 2) than a standard (see Figure 2) without being aware that they were judging the standard.

McNamara's data on the bisected-line illusion and the stickmen indicated that prior reward and punishment affected performance on these tasks. Subjects rewarded for overestimating or punished for underestimating on the parallel lines, overestimated on the bisected-line illusion and reported more "wide" stickmen in response to the standard. On the other hand, subjects rewarded for underestimating or punished for

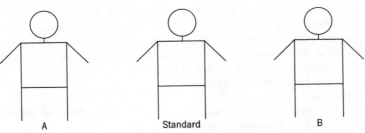

Figure 2. Illustrations of stickmen where horizontal < vertical (Figure A), horizontal > vertical (Figure B) and the "standard" figure.

overestimating on the parallel lines, underestimated on the bisected-line illusion and reported more "narrow" stickmen in response to the standard.

We have not been content to stop with empirical demonstrations which show that rewards and punishments may affect perception or produce misperceptions. We have speculated about the intervening processes or variables which might be influenced by rewards and punishments in a perceptual learning situation. Several studies have been designed to test hypotheses based upon inferences as to how certain of these intervening processes *should* influence perceptual learning. One such study attempted to assess the importance of the "expectancy," "readiness," or "set," of the subjects

in determining subsequent perceptions. In this experiment, Solley and Long (14) presented Schafer-Murphy contour faces (see Figure 3) in conjunction with monetary rewards or punishments during training, then on test trials single faces were combined into an ambiguous figure and subjects were asked to guess which face would be shown. The test figure was then presented and the subject reported which face *was* perceived. While subjects tended to guess the rewarded face in a reward-punishment group (one face rewarded, the other punished) or the non-punished face in a punishment-neutral group (one face punished, the other not), there was no significant correlation between the guesses given in advance and perceptual reports given later.

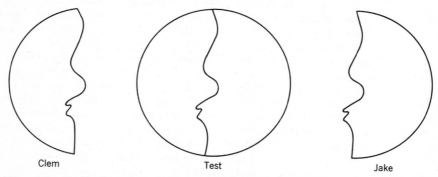

    Clem   Test   Jake

Figure 3. Profile drawings of two single faces and an ambiguous test face used in the Solley-Long experiment. Mirror images of these faces were also employed but are not shown here.

These results are surprising, and we are presently conducting further studies to examine the possibility that "expectancy" may *either* play a lesser role than we had anticipated *or* that its effects may be more obvious very early in the sequence of events and processs that eventuate in a percept. Under continued stimulus impact, "expectancies" may be greatly altered or modified in keeping with veridical demands of the environment. Yet, where "expectancies" are abnormally strong, this may not be the case, and complex selection or distortion may occur. Investigation of such selection and distortion is vastly important for a full understanding of perception and cognition.

It is possible that "expectancy" must be scrutinized with more refined techniques gauged to sample and enhance early, fleeting stages in perception. Procedures are being sought which will produce stronger "expectancies" and have greater effects on perception than were

obtained in the Solley and Long (14) experiment. The guessing behavior which they required of the subject might be regarded as an extinction phase which weakened the strength of "expectancies" so that their influence was not adequately demonstrated. Finally, "expectancies" should be most influential in situations which allow maximal structuring of the perceptual field by internal states. Where there is relatively great structuring of the external field, "expectancies" may operate primarily by selecting aspects most in keeping with internal states.

The Role of Attention

Another variable which we regard as immensely important in influencing the efficiency and clarity of perception is that of attention. The importance of attention has been emphasized in varying degrees since 1924 when Titchener (18) pronounced it to be one of the three fundamental issues upon which any system of psychology must be based. Since then it has been ignored, assumed, or rejected to a large extent. Hebb (4) has criticized modern psychological theories for ignoring and underemphasizing attention. More recently Berlyne (1) has discussed it in behavioristic terms and has made it a cornerstone of his theorizing about perceptual learning.

There are obviously important relationships between expectancy prior to stimulation and the direction of attention after stimulation. The direction of attention is undoubtedly influenced by a multitude of factors, including previous experience, motivation, stimulus characteristics, inhibitory factors, and oscillation phenomena.

In one attempt to manipulate the attention variable and note its effects on perception we have utilized a four-window display panel to show plastic animal figurines to young subjects who were asked to identify the figures as quickly as possible. The windows were lighted singly in random order and remained on for two seconds, with a one-second interlight interval. The combination of "bouncing light" and instructions to "name the animal as fast as you can" kept the children interested and engrossed in the task. They were differentially encouraged (with verbalization such as uh-huh, good, fine, etc.) while in the act of attending, perceiving, and identifying the four figures. One figure was verbally rewarded on approximately 80 per cent of its presentations and the other three on approximately 20 per cent of their presentations. The figure that was predominantly rewarded and the position of presentation were counter-balanced over subjects in such a way as to separate these factors from the reward effects. Following the training series of 120 trials (30 presentations per figure), the child was asked to locate each of the animal figures one at a time among 40 varied figures hung on a peg-board search panel.

Our observations and data revealed a number of interesting facts. During the one-second inter-light intervals of the training phase with the display panel, the eyes of the subject returned more and more often, as if drawn by a magnet, to the locus of the predominantly rewarded figure. These effects were obvious regardless of the figure locus involved, and testify to the efficacy of the verbal reward in shaping overt adjustmental behavior. It should be men-

tioned, however, that certain figures and certain positions had stronger initial potentialities than others (camel because of its distinctive features, and upper left because of reading habits).

Data from the test trials with the search panel indicate that we not only conditioned head and eye movements but, in fact, influenced the perceptual process by differential reward during the act of attending and perceiving. This is substantiated by the ability of the children to locate and identify the most frequently reinforced figure more rapidly than the others. We believe that we may be able to demonstrate even more striking effects with certain equipment and procedural modifications. We have installed one-way vision screen in front of the figures so that they cannot be seen during the inter-trial intervals, thus eliminating any possibility of explaining the results on the basis of more or less familiarity with the different figures. The test situation has also been modified because the original search panel seemed to induce object-by-object search and scanning behavior which may have masked and attenuated the reward effects.

In future studies the four training figures will be projected onto a special screen for a brief interval and the accuracy with which subjects can locate the positions after the exposure will be measured. We are predicting a tighter clustering of placements about the veridical position for the most frequently rewarded figure and more dispersion about the veridical positions for the others. If we have enhanced figural properties or lowered recognition thresholds through differential rewarding of attention, this procedure should provide a more favorable opportunity for the transfer of the effects without undue contamination by extraneous and uncontrolled sources of variation such as point of search origination, position preferences, and head and eye movements.

Closely related to our research on the conditioning of attention are various kinds of perceptual insensitivities and distortions, which were discussed in the previous report (10) under the heading of "scotoma." We have continued to note examples of this process in the course of numerous studies and hope to attack these problems experimentally during the coming year. This work will be based on the notion that we perceive certain things at the cost of excluding others and that perceptual response competition exists just as does motor response competition.

There are numerous possible explanations based upon learning principles which might account for perceptual insensitivities of varying degrees. It is conceivable that because intense reward value has been conditioned to certain stimuli they are more likely to be perceived than other stimuli. This is obviously an "attractive," "selective" process which should result in differential attention deployment and perceptual threshold. Where there are intensely rewarding objects available to occupy the perceptual process, other objects should be neglected and overlooked, if not actively rejected. Another possibility is that punishment value may be conditioned to stimuli, thereby making it difficult if not impossible to achieve clear and undistorted perception of these objects. Here we might speculate that perceptual thresholds have been raised and the result might be a "distractive" process.

The foregoing do not exhaust the range of possibilities, however, because in the latter case the punishment-associated stimulus might have cue value for escape or avoidance behavior which would remove the object or the individual from the punishment. In this case the object may acquire high potency in the perceptual field and have "alerting" value. Where such escape or avoidance behavior is not possible, the punishment associated stimulus may be ignored or rejected in favor of other stimuli in the perceptual field and we might then refer to a "repressive" effect.

The role which affect or emotion might play in producing or supplementing "scotoma" effects is intriguing. The introduction of affect during the process of perceiving could have organizing or disorganizing effects at a number of stages from stimulus presentation to the achievement of a clear percept. Space, however, does not allow a full consideration or discussion of these possibilities. Nevertheless, there are important clinical and theoretical implications involved in investigations which deal with the extent to which perceptual sensitivities and insensitivities may be produced and eliminated and the extent to which they persist, generalize and consolidate.

Feedback

Turning to other problems of interest to us, we have speculated about the importance of autonomic, proprioceptive and other sources of internal stimulation ("feedback") in determining the course of perceptual events. In some fascinating pilot studies Charles Snyder has secured data indicating that autonomic activity (as measured in terms of Galvanic Skin Reflex) may produce distortions in the visual perception of a square. Charles Snyder and Arnold Gerall are presently inaugurating a series of experiments in which they hope to assess the role that proprioceptive stimulation may play in a perceptual learning situation. Their procedure arranges for a given perception (right or left "improved" Necker taneously with certain proprioceptive activity Cube as illustrated in Figure 1) to occur simul- (forearm muscle flexion) and for the sequence of events to be verbally rewarded (uh-huh, good, that's fine, etc.). Subsequent reinstatement of the proprioceptive stimulation in the presence of an ambiguous perceptual stimulus (a "balanced" Necker Cube as illustrated in Figure 1) should produce greater than chance occurrence of the proprioception-associated percept (right or left cube perception).

Implied here is the assumption that proprioceptive stimulation may become an adequate stimulus for the occurrence or modification of aperceptual response. Our interest in this line of investigation was reinforced by the intriguing observations of Braatøy (2). He noted that on many occasions patients in the course of physiotherapy, which included a relaxing massage of arm muscles, were overwhelmed by painful memories which seemingly had been held in check by heightened muscular tension. We wonder whether proprioceptive factors may influence perceptual as well as memoric events.

Behind these exploratory proprioceptive and autonomic investigations is an interest in whether our body and its muscles can supply us with a useful source of information for *overcoming* perceptual and other types of autisms. We might achieve greater understanding of ourselves by critically scanning autonomic and proprioceptive cues available within us.

Other lines of research are being pursued which have not been mentioned in this brief survey. We are investigating some of the similarities and differences between the perception of stimuli above the level of awareness and those a shade below that fascinating and elusive line. Other work is also being done on the relationship between the individual's semantic and perceptual characteristics. Along somewhat different lines we are beginning an intensive investigation of how individual and social variables may affect the perception of a number of three-dimensional illusions.

These then have been the more important developments in our program in the past few years and these are some of the recent problems that have been of great interest to us. To recapitulate: We feel that we have demonstrated the reality of perceptual learning, how it may account for veridical and non-veridical perceptions, its generality in several sense modalities, and its similarity to other learning functions. We have not solved the problems of perceptual learning but have merely identified problems *to be solved*. Nevertheless, this is inevitable in the early stages of research. Perhaps our own biases or "austisms" are too strong, but the work which has been mentioned seems likely to increase our understanding of the ways in which we learn to perceive accurately or inaccurately.

REFERENCES

1. Berlyne, D. E.: Attention, Perception and Behavior Theory. *Psychol. Rev.* 58:137–146, 1951.
2. Braatøy, Trygve: *Fundamentals of Psychoanalytic Technique.* New York: Wiley, 1954.
3. Gibson, J. J. and Gibson, E. J.: Perceptual Learning: Differentiation or Enrichments? *Psychol. Rev.* 62:32–41, 1955.
4. Hebb, D. O.: *The Organization of Behavior.* New York: Wiley, 1949.
5. Hochberg, Julian: Effects of the Gestalt Revolution: The Cornell Symposium on Perception. *Psychol. Rev.* 64:73–84, 1957.
6. Jackson, D. N.: A Further Examination of the Role of Autism in a Visual Figure-Ground Relationship. *J. Psychol.* 38:339–357, 1954.
7. Levine, Robert, Chein, Isidor and Murphy, Gardner: The Relation of the Intensity of a Need to the Amount of Perceptual Distortion: A Preliminary Report. *J. Psychol.* 13:283–293, 1942.
8. McNamara, H. J.: Non-Veridical Perception as a Function of Rewards and Punishments. *Percept. Mot. Skills* 9:67–80, 1959. (Monograph Supplement No. 2.)
9. McNamara, H. J., Solley, C. M. and Long, John: The Effects of Punishment (Electric Shock) on Perceptual Learning. *J. Abnorm. Soc. Psychol.* 57:91–98, 1958.
10. Murphy, Gardner and Solley, C. M.: Learning to Perceive as We Wish to Perceive. *Bull. Menninger Clin.* 21:225–237, 1957.
11. Proshansky, H. M. and Murphy, Gardner: The Effects of Reward and Punishment on Perception. *J. Psychol.* 13:295–305, 1942.
12. Schafer, Roy and Murphy, Gardner: The Role of Autism in a Visual Figure-Ground Relationship. *J. Exp. Psychol.* 32:335–343, 1943.
13. Snyder, F. W. and Snyder, C. W.: The Effects of Monetary Reward and Punishment on Auditory Perception. *J. Psychol.* 41:177–184, 1956.
14. Solley, C. M. and Long, John: Perceptual Learning Versus Response Set Learning. *Percept. Mot. Skills* 8:235–240, 1958.
15. ———: When is "Uh-Huh" Reinforcing? *Percept. Mot. Skills* 8:277, 1958.
16. Solley, C. M. and Santos, J. F.: Perceptual Learning with Partial Verbal Reinforcement. *Percept. Mot. Skills* 8:183–193, 1958.
17. Sommer, Robert and Ayllon, Teodoro: Perception and Monetary Reinforcement: I. The Effects of Reward in the Tactual Modality. *J. Psychol.* 42:137–141, 1956.
18. Titchener, E. B.: *The Psychology of Feeling and Attention.* New York: Macmillan, 1924.

3. The effects of monetary reward and punishment on auditory perception

FRED W. SNYDER AND CHARLES W. SNYDER

Problem

PREVIOUS STUDIES OF THE EFFECTS OF ARBITRARY REWARD and punishment upon response to ambiguous figure-ground situations have been limited to the visual modality. Schafer and Murphy (3) consistently rewarded one half-moon face and punished another by means of giving and taking money from S. In the test series the two faces were combined into a reversible figure-ground pattern. The Ss reported predominantly the "rewarded" face. A repetition, with modifications, by Rock and Fleck (2) did not confirm these results. However, Jackson (1) repeated both the Rock-Fleck and Schafer-Murphy experiments. When he followed the procedure of Rock and Fleck, results were similar to their findings. When the Schafer and Murphy procedure was followed, results similar to theirs were found. A further test by Smith and Hochberg (4), using electric shock for punishment, also tended to confirm the Schafer and Murphy results.

The hypothesis of the present study was that perception of an auditory figure-ground situation can be modified by reward and punishment. More specifically, we predicted that a significant number of Ss would give a greater number of verbal responses for the "rewarded" voice than for the "punished" voice.

Method

Design. The Schafer-Murphy (3) design was modified for the auditory modality. The S was presented two voices speaking at the same time

SOURCE. Article by Fred W. Snyder and Charles W. Snyder, "The effects of monetary reward and punishment on auditory perception" in *The Journal of Psychology*, Vol. 41, pp. 177–184, 1956.

and reported at the end of each trial as much of the content as possible. This test was preceded by a training series of the same voices speaking separately in which S's winning or losing of nickels was paired with particular voices. No overt response was required of S during the training.

Scores for S were obtained from the words reported of each voice. Whether S had reported predominantly words of the rewarded or punished voice was then determined by comparison of his test scores. A sign test was employed to determine the significance of the number of Ss supporting the hypothesis. A *t*-test of difference scores was used to determine if the combined scores for the rewarded voice were significantly greater than for the punished voice.

Apparatus. The material to be read was selected qualitatively for its ease in comprehension, interest to S, and relative neutrality with respect to pleasantness-unpleasantness. Eighteen sentences from Rachel Carson's *The Sea Around Us* were randomly selected for the training. A different random order of the same sentences was used in the test.

For the training, a Magnecorder tape was made of two adult males, "D" and "J," speaking separately. Assignment of voices to the training sentences was random with a voice restricted to not more than two consecutive sentences. For the test period a similar recording was made of both "D" and "J" speaking into the microphone at the same time without regard for each other's voices. An approximate balance in the speech qualities of the two voices was obtained. The test tape was cut into six trials of approximately 10 seconds each.

Subjects. The 41 Ss (17 males, 24 females) of this experiment were obtained from a local business school in two samples of 20 and 21 Ss. An interval of three months elapsed between use of the two samples. The mean age of the combined sample was 19.8 years with a range of 17 to 26 years. In addition to the money he won during the training series, each S was paid one dollar per hour. The Ss were randomly assigned to one of the two reward conditions: Reward Voice "D"—Punish Voice "J," or Reward Voice "J"—Punish Voice "D."

Procedure. The Ss were brought individually to the experimental room and seated at a table. The tape recorder on the table was set to reproduce the voices at an average sound level of 62 decibels I (measured with General Radio Sound-Level Meter, Type 1551-A). Each S was then given the following instructions:

This is a procedure in which I'm going to play the tape recorder; also I have some money here. I'm going to stack some up and that's going to be yours. I'll put some money here and that will be mine. We're going to play with the money. You may get all of the money or you may wind up with none of it, or something in between. What's in your pile you may take with you when you go. You don't have to say anything, but you do have two jobs to do. You have to listen to what's on the tape and you also have to watch whether you're getting money or if it's taken away. Do you have any questions before we start?

The training was begun with two piles each of 10 nickels, one for E and one for S. During the playing of each voice, E transferred nickels between his pile and S's, the direction of the exchange being dependent upon which voice was to be rewarded for the particular S. In order for S to complete the training series with more money than when he had begun, the transfer of nickels had to be unequal. The training series was played through twice. During the first playing, from one to three nickels were exchanged in each transaction in such a manner that S appeared to be losing, although by the end of the run he appeared to be breaking even. During the second playing the transfer of coins now favored S and he was 80 cents ahead by the end. This procedure was adopted in order to sustain the interest of S. To minimize the possibility that S would discover that the voices were the cue for the exchange, E waited a variable time after the beginning of each trial before transferring money and completed the transfer before the voice ceased. At the completion of the training, which took four and one-half minutes, S was told that this was the end of the first part of the procedure and reminded that the money in his pile belonged to him and was to be taken when he left.

Then E said:

I'm going to play a short portion of the tape. Listen and try to get as much as you can out of it. When I stop the tape, repeat word for word, as much as possible, what you heard. Do you have any questions?

The same two voices, speaking the same material as in the training, were then presented together in competition. Although there were normal speech pauses during which only one or neither voice was speaking, most of the time the voices were intermixed. At the end of each trial, S's reproduction of the taped presentation was recorded on a Dictaphone. After the first trial, E said, "All right, did you hear?" When S had responded E said, "Fine," regardless of the voice that was repeated. After the other trials he said merely, "All right."

After the last trial, S was asked whether he listened during the test to both voices, or to one more than the other and was asked to identify the voice. Information regarding S's relative preference for the voices was obtained as well as other bases for discrimination between the two. He was asked if he knew why he was receiving and losing money and if he were aware of the purpose of the experiment. He was also asked if anyone had told him about the experiment before coming, and was cautioned not to discuss the procedure with other Ss.

Results

Each S's responses were scored on the basis of the following criteria: *4 points*—Three or more words in succession in one sentence repeated exactly (counting all words, including articles, conjunctions, etc.). *3 points*—Three or more words in succession in one sentence repeated but allowing synonyms to count. *2 points*—Three or more words in one sentence or their synonyms but words not in proper sequence. *1 point*—One or two words or their synonyms in one sentence repeated but words not necessarily in proper sequence.

The scoring unit was one sentence in a particular voice regardless of shifts to the other voice and back again. These scoring criteria were used in place of a simple word count in order to retain the characteristic of grouping of words into meaningful units. Thus, more weight was given to meaningful groups and less weight to isolated words. In addition, there was a cut-off point at the maximum possible score for each sentence. This minimized the factor of differential ability in recall among Ss.

The scoring technique yielded two scores for each S, one for the "rewarded" and one for the "punished" voice in each trial. For the analysis, the scores for the six trials in the test were totaled. If more of the response units were those associated with the rewarded voice, the S was said to add support to the hypothesis.

The central finding was that 31 out of 41 Ss responded predominately to the previously rewarded voice, the sign test yielding $X^2 = 9.76$; 1 df; $p < .01$. An additional statistic, one which tested the effects of the two training conditions (Table 1) yielded $X^2 = 9.47$; 1 df; $p < .01$. A sign test of the difference between voices (Table 2) resulted in $X^2 = 3.64$; 1 df; $p = .06$. To test further the difference between reward conditions, an analysis of variance (Table 3) was made, using as measures the differences between test scores for the "rewarded" and "punished" voices. Because of the lapse of time between the first 20 and the last 21 Ss, a test of the difference between these samples was included in the analysis of variance.

Results of all Ss were combined since the difference between voices, between samples, and the interaction of voices and samples were not significant. A t-test of the difference scores was made, resulting in $t = 2.61$; 40 df; $p < .02$.

Table 1. Distribution of Subjects in Relation to Voice Predominantly Reported in Test and to Training Condition

Voice Predominant in Test Result	Training Condition		Total
	"D" Rewarded "J" Punished	"J" Rewarded "D" Punished	
"D"	12	2	14
"J"	8	19	27
Total	20	21	41

Table 2. Differences Between Training Conditions in Terms of the Number of Subjects Supporting and Not Supporting the Hypothesis

Test Result	Training Condition		Total
	"D" Rewarded "J" Punished	"J" Rewarded "D" Punished	
+	12	19	31
−	8	2	10
Total	20	21	41

Table 3. Analysis of Variance on Voice Dominance Scores

Source	df	Mean Square	F	P
Voices	1	127.6	1.83	N.S.
Samples	1	155.1	2.23	N.S.
Voice × Samples	1	44.9	.65	N.S.
Within	37	69.6		
	40			

A point biserial correlation between relative scores and sex yielded $r_{pb} = .10$; $p > .10$. A test of the difference between the means of relative scores of males and females resulted in $t = 1.18$; 39 df; $p > .10$. The relative scores employed in these tests had a possible range of −1 to +1 and were computed by subtracting the test score for the "punished" voice from that for the "rewarded" voice and dividing the difference by the sum of these scores.

No relationship was found between test scores and interview responses to questions regarding which voice was preferred or which voice was listened to most. The same was true of a similar analysis of Ss who both identified and preferred the same voice. Of the 41 Ss, seven discovered to some degree why money was being given, although none of the Ss discovered the purpose of the experiment to the extent of knowing which voice was connected with reward or that the test was a measure of the effect of training. Of the seven Ss mentioned, relative scores were correlated with an independent ranking of when S discovered why money was given, resulting in rho = .75; $p = .05$. The discovery of the connection between voices and money was not significantly related to the over-all results ($X^2 = .04$; 1 df; $p > .90$). A total of 16 Ss believed that the experiment was an attempt to test their ability to concentrate. One S specifically said that E was trying to confuse him by distracting him from the real task of listening to the voices by moving the money.

Discussion

The original prediction, that a significant number of Ss would give a greater number of verbal responses for the rewarded than for the punished voice in terms of content, is supported by the data. The results for 41 Ss ($p < .01$) indicate that there is a degree of relationship among the variables of reward-punishment and test scores. The result of a t-test of the difference scores of the test data shows that, with this more sensitive measure, there is an over-all significance ($p < .02$). Although the effect of rewarding voice "D" was not as pronounced as that of rewarding voice "J," results from both conditions are in the predicted direction (Table 2) and are not significantly different (Table 3).

Qualitative observations suggested that the money did, indeed, serve as "reward" for these Ss. Contrary to what happened in some pilot work with more sophisticated Ss, no S in the present experiment hesitated to take his pile of nickels. In fact, many pocketed the nickels after the training before E instructed them to do so. There were occasional remarks at the end of the experiment such as "I'll have cokes for a long time with these," or "I save nickels in my piggy bank." These kinds of reactions were usually followed by refusal to obtain larger denominations for their nickels although this was freely offered. The Ss occasionally remarked that they were "broke" and "could sure use the money." That Ss were interested in the money was further supported by the observation that the Ss compared their winnings after the experiment.

The instructions and reward-punishment technique of the training were planned to

lessen the possibility that S would discover the design. Only seven of the 41 Ss reported in the interview that they had discovered why money was being given and taken away, but no S was able to indicate which voice had been rewarded or punished. No S discovered the purpose of the experiment. If S were aware of the connection between the reward-punishment and the voices during the training, it appears to have been a low level of awareness.

There was a nearly significant correlation between the test effect and the time during the training that S discovered why money was being given. The Ss who made the discovery early during the training gave more positive results than Ss who made the discovery later. However, the over-all results were not dependent upon mere discovery of this connection. Therefore, it is difficult to generalize about any relationship between awareness of the connection and the reward-punishment effect on the basis of this experiment.

The evidence suggests that the results are not predominantly due to the intrinsic attentional factors of the auditory stimuli. Although the effect of rewarding one voice was not as great as rewarding the other voice, the over-all effect is more than can be attributed only to the difference between voices. An analysis of responses to words spoken by one voice during a pause of the other voice indicates that these responses were infrequent and favored neither voice.

One may attempt to explain the results by supposing that the punishment had a greater distractive effect than the reward. If punishment had been used alone, this explanation would be quite tenable. However, in our training procedure the movement of coins for punishment was balanced with that for reward. The balance of distraction was furthered through the use of different modalities for the reward-punishment and ambiguous stimuli.

Summary

As a test of the effects of monetary reward and punishment on responses to an ambiguous auditory pattern a total of 41 Ss were individually presented a training series of recorded sentences spoken alternately by two announcers. While one of these voices was presented, S was given a small amount of money and while the other voice was presented, money was taken away. This was followed by a test in which S was presented the two voices together in competition. The S reported at the end of each trial as much of the content as possible. As predicted, a significantly greater number of Ss produced larger scores for the previously "rewarded" voice than for the previously "punished" voice. A test of the difference scores for the responses to the reward and punishment conditions was also significant. These results cannot be attributed to differences between the intrinsic factors of the auditory stimuli.

REFERENCES

1. Jackson, D. N. A further examination of the role of autism in a visual figure-ground relationship. *J. of Psychol.*, 1954, 38, 339–357.
2. Rock, I., & Fleck, F. S. A re-examination of the effect of monetary reward and punishment in figure-ground perception. *J. Exper. Psychol.*, 1950, 40, 766–776.
3. Schafer, R., & Murphy, G. The role of autism in a visual figure-ground relationship. *J. Exper. Psychol.*, 1943, 32, 335–343.
4. Smith, D. E. P. & Hochberg, J. E. The effect of "punishment" (electric shock) on figure-ground perception. *J. of Psychol.*, 1954, 38, 83–87.

4. Deprivation and the canalization of responses to food

EUGENE L. HARTLEY AND MARVIN A. PERELMAN

SUMMARY—THE PRESENT STUDY, under somewhat more rigorous conditions, has confirmed Lukomnik's original testing of the canalization hypothesis. Within the limits of the procedure employed, sheer familiarization had relatively little effect in modifying S's liking for esoteric foods; but, when S came to the training session hungry, statistically significant changes in the later ratings of the foods then tested were induced. Clearly, Murphy's canalization hypothesis with respect to the increase in liking for one among several potential ways of satisfying a need is supported. It should be noted (as Murphy has commented in a personal communication) that in both the Lukomnik and the present studies, the relation between the amount of food taken to taste and the amount needed for satisfying the hunger has not been established. Whether there has been true need-satisfaction or drive-reduction is as yet an unsolved question, the answer to which seems crucial to the clarification of the basic mechanisms involved in the phenomenon demonstrated.

English and English (1958, p. 75) provide a definition of canalization as "establishing and progressively strengthening a preference for one among several potential ways of satisfying a drive." Over a period of about 25 yr., Gardner Murphy has found it helpful to develop and employ the concept of learning by canalization to supplement the more traditional learning paradigms in accounting for the complex phenomena of personality and social behavior (Murphy, Murphy, & Newcomb, 1937;

SOURCE. Article by Eugene L. Hartley and Marvin A. Perelman, "Deprivation and the canalization of responses to food" in *Psychological Reports*, Vol. 13, pp. 647–650, 1963. Copyrighted by Southern Universities Press, 1963.

Murphy, 1947, 1958). Although Murphy has attempted to clarify the concept and differentiate it from the use of the same term by Janet and by Holt, and from cathexis (Freud), the formation of sentiments (McDougall), mechanisms-may-become-drives (Woodworth), and functional autonomy (G. W. Allport), the fuller elaboration of the canalization hypothesis seems to be awaiting the availability of additional empirical data to provide a proper base for the inductive development of the theory.

An important experimental foundation for the canalization hypothesis, perhaps the most important using *human* Ss, are the studies by Lukomnik (1940) in which were investigated the ratings of the degree of pleasantness of relatively unfamiliar foods by college students before and after a series of familiarization tastings. In the simple familiarization series, the shift in ratings for the selected experimental (E) foods was toward the "pleasant" end of a graphic rating scale but not significantly greater than the shifts for the control (C) foods. However, in one part of the study, three Ss came to two experimental sessions each, after abstaining from eating for 24 hr. In these deprivation series, the rating shifts were clearly significant. The E foods moved 18.44 mm. toward the pleasant end of the 15 cm. graphic rating scale used, while the C foods moved 11.50 mm. toward the unpleasant end. The significance of the difference was evaluated by t test, which yielded $p < .01$. These data led to the conclusion that increase in the strength of the drive being satisfied facilitates the canalization. The importance of this finding for canalization theory calls for independent confirmation with a larger number of Ss and better control of the familiarization factor. To this end the present study was designed.

533

Procedure

The general design involved two groups of Ss, an experimental (D) and a control (F) group, with provision for heightened motivation through food *deprivation* of the D Ss and control for *familiarization* among the F Ss. Each S came individually to three sessions in 1 wk. (scheduled on Mondays, Wednesdays, and Thursdays). All Ss, in the first and third sessions, tasted and rated 10 foods for degree of like-dislike. On the basis of the ratings in the first session, five foods were selected for exposure during the second session; these were the experimental (E) foods. The remaining five foods were the control (C) foods for each S. The five foods were thus tasted three times during the experiment, while the C foods were only tasted twice. The D Ss appeared for their second session after instructions not to take any food prior to the experiment on that day, consequently they may be presumed to represent (approximately) a 10-hr. food deprivation status, from rising to about 5 P.M. The C Ss had no special instructions and followed their customary routines.

For each S, comparison of the E and C foods would include the familiarization feature of 3 vs 2 exposures. For the D Ss the extra exposure was under conditions of deprivation, a condition which did not obtain for the F Ss.

The 10 *foods* used were selected to provide stimuli with which Ss were relatively unfamiliar. The foods were: arrowroot hearts, smoked oysters, blackstrap molasses, sesame butter, Italian pignolia nuts, mussel cocktail in tomato sauce, soya bean granules, game pate, and St. John's bread, also wheat germ (for the F group) and cherry blossoms (for the D group).

Foods were placed in containers which differed in size and shape, numbered 1 to 10, but bore no other identifying symbol or name. On the basis of the ratings in the first session, the E foods were selected for each S so as to provide representation of all parts of the subjective scale: pleasant, indifferent, and unpleasant. The E foods were therefore different for different Ss. Ss were instructed to taste each food, to take as much or as little of each as he felt was necessary for him to be able to rate it fairly.

The *rating scale* involved use of a prepared 9.5-in. ruled line with numerical values at the extremes assigned as 0 and 100. At the appropriate intermediate points, the following values were indicated and defined: 20, Dislike very much; 40, Dislike moderately; 60, Like moderately; 80, Like very much. Ss were instructed orally to consider 0 "as bad as the worst thing you ever tasted," and to interpret 100 "as good as the best thing you ever tasted."

During the first session Ss started rating the foods by pointing along the scale to the appropriate position and were then encouraged to shift to announcing the numerical equivalent of their evaluation. E recorded the judgments as given by Ss either by pointing or, as all soon did, by oral announcement. The recorded ratings were kept concealed from S throughout each session.

Ss were 27 undergraduate students at The City College of New York: 14 in the D group, 13 in the F group. No information was given concerning the purpose or design of the study. The participants were those who responded to an announcement calling for Ss in a "tasting" study and offering a token remuneration for cooperation.

Results

In Table 1 are presented summaries of the ratings for the E and C foods in the first and third sessions, for both the Familiarization (F) and the Deprivation (D) Ss.

Table 1. Ratings of Experimental (E) and Control (C) Foods in Sessions 1 and 3 by the Familiarization (F) and Deprivation (D) Ss

	Session 1		Session 3	
	C	E	C	E
F mean	53.67	51.54	53.85	52.00
σ	7.33	5.82	8.52	8.64
D mean	52.07	48.53	50.43	59.44
σ	9.99	6.69	10.84	8.96

The first question we may ask is: were the foods chosen as E and C actually equivalent in the original ratings? For the F and D groups separately, the mean of the differences between the combined E and C ratings for each S was computed and tested for significant deviation from zero. The differences were not significant ($.10 > p > .05$ in the F and $.60 > p > .50$ in the D group). At the end of the experiment, however, the results were different. When the C and E foods were compared in the third session, the differences in the F group were not significant ($.50 > p > .40$) but were significant in the D group ($.001 > p > .01$).

The evaluation of the five C foods by Ss in both the F and D groups did *not* shift significantly ($.90 > p > .80$, $.50 > p > .40$), however, the E foods did show a significant change among the D ($p = < .001$) but not among the F Ss ($.80 > p > .70$).

To this point the results have been analyzed within the two groups, the D and the F, comparing the E and C foods in the first and third sessions, and comparing the shifts of the E and C foods from the first to the third session. Now we may assay the two conditions, the Deprivation and the Familiarization, by comparison of the responses of the two groups of Ss. With respect to the C foods, there was no significant difference in either the first or the third session ($.70 > p > .60$, $.40 > p > .30$). With the E foods, however, although there was no significant difference in the first session ($.30 > p > .20$); in the third session, the t test yielded $.05 > p > .02$.

Finally, when the mean shift from the first to the third session was studied, comparison of the ratings of the D and F subjects for the C foods showed no significant difference ($.60 > p > .50$); while for the E foods, the difference was significant ($.02 > p > .01$).

REFERENCES

English, H. B., & English, A. C. *A comprehensive dictionary of psychological and psychoanalytical terms: a guide to usage.* New York: Longmans, Green, 1958.

Lukomnik, M. An experiment to test the canalization hypothesis. Unpublished master's thesis, Columbia Univer., 1940.

Murphy, G. *Personality; a biosocial approach to origins and structure.* New York: Harper, 1947.

Murphy, G. *Human potentialities.* New York: Basic Books, 1958.

Murphy, G., Murphy, L. B., & Newcomb, T. M. *Experimental social psychology.* (Rev. ed.) New York: Harper, 1937.

5. Selection from the challenge of psychical research

GARDNER MURPHY

HALF OF THE PROBLEM of achieving a "world perspective" is the problem of integration. How may the eager, restless gropings into many odd corners be induced to yield a coherent and unitary view of our world? How may synthesis, co-ordination, insight, meaning be achieved?

There is, however, another task of equal importance. This is the response to new voices, undeciphered symbols, odd discoveries for which no place can at present be found; the investigation of that which defies today's order and rationality; the resolute and unfrightened recognition of what appears out of place, irrational, meaningless, an affront to reason. In the history of discovery, there have always been the blur and the horror of that which refuses to be assimilated; observations which, however carefully repeated and checked, fall into no predetermined place in the jigsaw puzzle which we conceive to be nature.

Psychical research, or parapsychology, consists of observations recorded in a form which aims at order and intelligibility, but which cannot by any stretch of the imagination be subsumed under the science of today.

Not only are the present data (of parapsychology) difficult to accept, but when the problems of authentication are met, there are problems of conscious and unconscious self-deception on the part of those who experience or witness the phenomena and on the part of the investigators that study them, and perhaps still more on the part of those who read what they have not themselves encountered. Then comes a formidable scientific block, if we accept some

SOURCE. Selection from Gardner Murphy, *Challenge of Psychical Research*, pp. 1, 274–277, 282–285. New York: Harper, 1961.

of them as "facts": the difficulty of obtaining information as to the precise conditions—physiological, psychological, sociocultural—in which these events occur. Finally, hand in hand with this last point, comes the difficulty of duplicating the conditions so that a repeatable experiment can be devised, or conditions specified in which fresh spontaneous phenomena are likely to occur. What we have in the meantime are large masses of more or less authenticated materials, and a rather considerable body of psychological and philosophical speculations as to the conditions, the dynamics, the explanatory principles which will bind these diverse classes of phenomena together.

There is indeed a very considerable theoretical literature, and, as is always true in science, there is a continuum from the hypotheses evoked to throw light upon one *specific* event to the broadening areas of philosophical interpretation in which "models" or systematic philosophical systems are sketched out to explain wider and wider reaches of phenomena. This is clearly no place for the more comprehensive theoretical systems. It is, however, a place in which there may be some obligation on the author's part to sketch a few of the simpler hypotheses from which models are beginning to be devised and in the light of which theoretical systems are today being mapped out.

First, a very general principle which has already been noted above is that psi phenomena are often expressions of unconscious or deep-level dynamic principles reflecting the relation of the person to his physical environment or more commonly to his personal-social environment. When two or more persons are involved, the assumption is that there is deep-level interaction between them. Secondly, hand in hand with this principle goes the assumption that the phenomena are expressions of need, impulse, drive, or purpose; that in harmony with the modern trend to see stress-reduction or goal-seeking as expressions of all life, psi phenomena may well be regarded as directed expressions of conscious or unconscious needs. From this point of view, the act of clairvoyance makes a contact to round out the cognitive grasp of a situation, while a telepathic process may convey and receive information, thus linking two minds together, or might represent empathy, a *feeling with*, a groping toward other individuals psychologically close to the receiver.

Hand in hand with these two principles—the assumption of unconscious dynamics and the assumption of need fulfillment or purpose—comes the assumption of some kind of fundamental dualism, some basic difference, between normal and paranormal processes. One way of stating the situation is that paranormal processes do not represent a part of the time-space-event system which the physical sciences describe. As we have suggested above, there is a certain timeless, spaceless, or we might say transtemporal and transpatial character at the very heart of the paranormal. This is indeed one of the major reasons why the phenomena do not belong to and are rejected by official science. It is at the same time a distinguishing criterion which marks off situations with which a psychology allied to physics can deal and those calling for a somewhat different kind of psychology.

From the foregoing it follows that there is a state of mutual exclusion, or even opposition, between the conditions under which ordinary contact with the environment is made and those in which the rules are suspended and the paranormal supervenes. This may appear at first sight to be in contradiction to the principle of potentiation described below. We must choose our words carefully. Let us say that the evidence tends to suggest that the normal and the paranormal are as a rule found under somewhat different conditions; the paranormal does not appear if the normal is doing its work well. There seem nevertheless to be special cases in which the normal may call upon the paranormal for aid and the two kinds of functions may be blended.

Now if all this is so, it would appear to follow the ideal conditions for the study of the paranormal would involve a certain blunting or limitation of the possibility of normal function.[1] We have studies of semisleeping and sleeping conditions, which together with half-wakeful conditions, drowsiness and hypnosis, as well as various drug states and deliria and toxic states, all seem to offer more than their share of paranormal output. It would appear then to be literally true that the paranormal emerges "when the coast is clear" and the "impediments"[2] to its appearance are removed. One of the paradoxes confronting the experimental parapsychologist is evident: he must use all the psychology he knows with reference to getting motivation and a favourable attitude toward the task and the experimenter. He must structure his task so that it can be paranormally perceived and the results evaluated; he must be alert for incline effects, decline effects, grouping of hits, and other expressions of normal perceptual activity. And at the same time he must keep in mind constantly that he is dealing with a process which probably would not be there at all if conditions were favorable for normal perception, exemplifying the normal range of psychological laws relevant to its occurrence. Parapsychologists must, as it were, create all the conditions under which cognition in general (or perception in particular) would be expected to occur, but then blunt, inhibit, or block the special conditions which favor normal perception! He must use opaque envelopes, screens, or long-distance conditions, so that when once he has aroused the urge to perceive he can prevent all perception of a normal sort from occurring. It is in fact this very paradox which has made the clear formulation of a model for repeatable experiments so difficult to achieve.

Before the curtain falls, however, I wish to deal now explicitly with the question: what can be *believed* in a field in which the data appear to conflict with the basic assumptions of science?

Many thoughtful readers will certainly reach the view that we cannot accuse large numbers of scholars and scientists of fabricating data, bribing confederates, or grossly distorting evidence. In connection with the modern skep-

---

[1] Jan Ehrenwald, *Telepathy and Medical Psychology*, New York, W. W. Norton and Co., 1948.

[2] Gardner Murphy, "Removal of impediments to the paranormal," *Journal of the American Society for Psychical Research*, 1944, Vol. 38, 2–23.

ticism about the positive findings of psychical research, we often find ourselves confronted with the statement: either the data are genuine, or you are accusing a group of scholars of collusion and fraud.

Yet in point of fact, this black-white mode of thinking does not work very well whether in orthodox science or in parapsychology. There is an extraordinary number of instances in ordinary science in which unconscious bias causes people to "see" events that were not really capable of being seen but only inferred; subtle errors arise from assumptions made or oversights regarding unexpected or unpalatable evidence; and almost as common are those forms of self-deception in which one gives the positive evidence the benefit of the doubt. Indeed in my years in ordinary normal research in fields like social psychology, attitude measurement, clinical psychology, psychology of personality, I have seen literally dozens of shaky conclusions follow from shaky assumptions and have myself often been deceived. Even an independent repetition of a good experiment is no guarantee of the soundness of the original conclusions. Some of the faulty assumptions of the original study may have been built into the replication. I have known a considerable number of cases of refusal to publish evidence unfavourable to a position which had once been taken by a person dominant in the field. Psychologists working as I have done through many years with the subtle in-

fluence of wishes upon perception would be in a very foolhardy position in asserting that as a rule, a psychological experiment can easily be repeated and the truth quickly confirmed. This is very far indeed from reality. Truth is come by only after an enormous amount of labor, anxiety, and discipline.

We are dealing with the first steps that lead *up to* the gateway of science; not with a single step within the hall *beyond* those gateways. We have no science of parapsychology; no theoretical system tightly and beautifully organized in the manner of the architect; no solid beams of repeatedly confirmed findings, reproducible by a careful experimenter who can exactly follow the specifications, sure of the general trend of the results that he will get.

Parapsychology is important as a challenge. If it prematurely achieves the position of a closed, massive, monolithic body of data, all thoughtful men will be the losers. There is often a *presumptive* case and the reader will discover this as he moves through the data. This presumptive case will stand out for thoughtful readers, at least this has always been the case in psychical research. It has not been the thoughtful readers, but those who will not read at all but who "know in advance" what can and what cannot happen, that make the most serious problem. A jury of those who will thoughtfully read is the only kind of jury that we have any intention of invoking in the present task.

6.   ESP in relation to Rorschach test evaluation

GERTRUDE SCHMEIDLER

Preliminary Considerations and Statement of Sheep-Goat Hypothesis

THE DATA TO BE REPORTED here were gathered as part of a larger investigation of ESP and personality dynamics. My working hypothesis was that everyone or almost everyone has some ESP ability. The fact that confronted this hypothesis was that some of my subjects made high ESP scores, some middling and some low; their average was near mean chance expectation. My problem, then, was to find whether some psychological factors were associated with the different kinds of scores: whether, in Boring's phrase (1941), these statistical frequencies represented dynamic equilibria. If so, it would be the near-random sampling of psychological traits or attitudes that resulted in the near-random distribution of ESP totals. Other major findings from this larger investigation have already been described in considerable detail (Schmeidler and McConnell, 1958) but will be summarized here because they constitute the background of the present report.

Preliminary tests had indicated that subjects who are friendly to the ESP research made higher ESP scores than subjects who disapproved of it. This is, of course, only what many previous workers have reported. But in my intellectually oriented preliminary group, consisting entirely of psychologists at Harvard, it was striking that friendliness was expressed as acceptance of the possibility of ESP and disapproval as rejection of this possibility. Formal investigations were therefore begun to fol-

SOURCE. Article by Gertrude Schmeidler, "ESP in relation to Rorschach test evaluation" in *Parapsychological Monograph*, No. 2, pp. 3–7, 9, 13–14, 16–17, 22–23, 1960.

low up this lead. Subjects were asked about their attitude toward the possibility of paranormal success in the experimental situation. Their answers "separated the sheep from the goats." To avoid repetition of the cumbersome accurate designations of the two groups, the term "sheep" has been used to designate subjects who state that they accept the possibility of paranormal success in the given experimental situation (even if they think it a very unlikely possibility and even if they think that they themselves cannot succeed) and the term "goats" to designate subjects who state that they believe there is no possibility of paranormal success in the given experimental situation (even if they believe that under other conditions paranormal success might occur). The hypothesis was stated that sheep would tend to have higher ESP scores than goats.

ESP Procedure

The experimental procedure will be sketched only briefly here. (See Schmeidler and McConnell, 1958 and Schmeidler, 1959 for a fuller account.) Stimulus material consisted of concealed lists of randomized targets. There were five possible targets for each response; thus the probability of chance success in any response was 1/5. Each list consisted of 25 items, and the sequence of 25 responses was called a run; thus the mean chance expectation for each run was 5 correct responses or "hits." Subjects' responses were written. All responses received at least two independent checks against the target. Subjects responded to the questions which determined whether they could be classed as sheep or goats before they knew their ESP scores.

Seven series with individually tested subjects gave over-all results in conformity with the sheep-goat hypothesis, although the distribution of scores always showed considerable overlap between sheep and goats, and in many of the series the mean differences between groups was small. The later group experiments also supported the hypothesis, though here there were occasional reversals within a class or within a semester, and the average scores of both sheep and goats were nearer chance than in the individual series. The data are summarized in Table 1. Other investigators, using the same or similar methods, have tended on the whole to obtain somewhat similar results. The hypothesis that sheep will on the average score higher than goats seems therefore to be rather well supported for the samples (consisting almost entirely of college students) that have been tested.

Table 1. Mean ESP Scores of Subjects Who Accepted the Possibility of Paranormal Success under the Conditions of the Experiment (Sheep) and of Subjects Who Rejected This Possibility (Goats)

Subjects	Number of Subjects	Number of Runs (25 Guesses)	Deviation from Chance Expectation	Mean Hits per Run	P
Sheep tested individually	111	1055	+242	5.23	.00019
Sheep tested in groups	692	5985	+614	5.10	.00007
Total sheep	803	7040	+856	5.12	.0000006
Goats tested individually	40	853	−116	4.86	.047
Goats tested in groups	465	4050	−301	4.93	.018
Total goats	505	4903	−417	4.91	.004

Difference between mean scores of sheep and goats tested individually is .37; P = .00006.
Difference between mean scores of sheep and goats tested in groups is .17; P = .00003.

An affirmative conclusion suggested by these data is that ESP success, like success in other activities, is affected by the subject's motivation. Sheep, who in general were interested, friendly and cooperative, could be expected to be motivated toward high scores. Goats, who in general rejected the basic plan of the research ("This is ridiculous!" was a not infrequent comment) could be expected to be motivated against high scores, since failure to hit the targets seemed, to many of them, to prove their thesis that the assigned task was an impossible one.

But here an apparent paradox arises. Almost all goats who discussed the procedure with me reported that while they were making their responses they were consciously trying to succeed, though they knew they could not. But even with this conscious attitude of cooperation on the part of most, the over-all average of the goats was significantly below chance expectation. The paradox can of course be resolved by the inference that the goats' tendency to reject the task was associated with an *unconscious negativism.* Thus our first conclusion should be read as a statement that unconscious motivation as well as consciously held attitudes may influence ESP scoring.

A second, more negative conclusion must also be stated. It is that the sheep-goat division of subjects is not in itself an important factor in ESP success. A large minority of the sheep had ESP scores below mean chance expectation; and a large minority of the goats had ESP scores above this level. Further, there was no indication that the sheep who most completely accepted the possibility of ESP success had the highest ESP scores nor was there evidence from introspective reports that the goats who were most vehement in their rejection of the research had the lowest scores. There is evidence from other work (see Schmeidler and McConnell, 1958) that *qualitative* differences in the reasons for adopting the sheep or goat attitude toward the ESP task are meaningful. The implication is that here a yes-no, all or none division is useful, though finer quantitative gradations are not.

What should be our interpretations of this second conclusion? One surely is that the responses are determined in part by such non-ESP factors as card preferences and sequence patterns, which will show only a chance relation to the targets. Like static in radio reception, this cuts randomly across what is of interest to us. It may well be that the sheep-goat question, which asks only about intellectual attitudes, taps only a minor or fringe part of the motivational pattern. A sheep may fear ESP, or may resent taking part in a task which is tedious to him; and a subject may give lip service to the materialist credo by calling himself a goat but retain delight in childhood fantasies of omniscience because of his secret ESP ability.

In one sense this latter interpretation is a corollary of the first of our conclusions. Both converge on the same research directive: to learn more about the subjects' attitudes and motives, including unconscious motives. The simplest way to attempt this is to ask the subject directly. But preliminary questions along these lines indicated that even with subjects who liked to talk about themselves, the answer had little or no clear relation to ESP scores. And indeed if unconscious motives are important, no other result could be expected. Direct answers to straightforward questions, taken literally, will describe only conscious factors.

What indirect questions could be put to the subjects? There are many questionnaire-type psychological tests which could be employed; and one of these, the Allport-Vernon Study of Values, indicated that it was the subjects most keenly concerned with theoretical, intellectual values who gave the clearest sheep-goat separation (see Schmeidler and McConnell, 1958). But the techniques on which I depended most heavily were projective tests. In these tests the subject must respond to a task in which there is no single "correct" answer. He may be shown a picture and asked to tell an imaginative story about it (Thematic Apperception Test); he may be asked to complete a sentence which begins as vaguely as "John likes . . ." (Sentence Completion Test); he may be shown a mean-ingless ink blot and asked to say what it looks like or what it might be (Rorschach Test). His answers can be influenced only to a small extent by the stimuli, when the stimuli are so vague; to some extent they must be influenced by what he himself brings to the task—by his past experience and his response tendencies, including the unconscious tendencies.

Several such projective methods were explored. One, a study of responses to frustration, gave results which were marginally significant and seemed meaningful: a low positive correlation between ESP scores and the tendency to respond to frustration without aggression, and a low negative correlation between ESP scores and the tendency to respond to frustration with outwardly directed aggression. But my greatest emphasis has been placed on the Rorschach test, where more than one thousand protocols were obtained.

A useful method for quick interpretation of the major adjustment patterns in the Rorschach was proposed by Munroe (1945). It consists essentially of listing twenty-odd scoring categories and defining the normal or "safe" limits for each. When a subject's responses fall outside of those limits he is assigned one, two or three entries on the check list, the number of entries being dependent on the extent of his deviation from the previously stated limits. The total number of checks is his final score and represents an approximation of his general social adjustment. With this measure, then, the higher scores should correspond to less adequate social adjustment. Scoring of a protocol can be completed in ten minutes to half an hour.

In the spring of 1945, group ESP tests were first used in my research project, and I continued to use group tests until 1951. All these group tests were held in college classrooms.

At the same time that the group ESP tests were begun, I began to administer the Rorschach to all subjects who were willing to take it. With the exception of a few who reported that they were color blind, and who therefore could not have their records scored in the conventional way, all ESP subjects tested in college classes by me, or tested for me by a colleague, between 1945 and 1951, for whom Rorschachs were available, are described in the following tables.

The total number of such subjects is 1,062. Of these the first 58 constitute the preliminary group from whom the hypothesis about adjustment was derived; the remaining 1,004 constitute the test group for the hypothesis about adjustment.

For the first 58 subjects, ESP scores were known to me when the Rorschachs were scored. For all later subjects, I performed the Rorschach scoring and made the entries on the Munroe check list before I knew the subjects' ESP scores. In the later years of the research, ESP tests were not administered until after all Rorschach scores had been completed.

After gathering the first 58 Rorschachs I examined the results in the hope of finding Rorschach patterns that related to ESP scores. One lead seemed promising. The sheep with relatively few check list entries (better social adjustment) tended to have higher ESP scores than other sheep; and the goats with relatively few check list entries tended to have lower ESP scores than other goats. This makes good sense in terms of our concept of social adjustment; and since there was the happy combination of a marked trend of the data and a good rationale, it was decided to perform formal investigations of whether the trend would persist in later series.

With this reasoning, no assumption is made about the relation between social adjustment and ESP *ability*. The only expectation is that, whatever the level of ESP ability, its effective *utilization* will tend to be related to adjustment patterns, as is the utilization of other abilities.

To return to a chronological description of the procedure: in preparation for stating the formal hypothesis about adjustment in terms of two distinct groups, I reexamined the available data to find where the line of separation should be drawn. The normative population was the 348 Sarah Lawrence students described by Munroe; and I assumed that the distribution of adjustment there would be approximately the same as in the college groups I tested. In Munroe's sample 53% of the subjects were classed as well adjusted. In my sample of 58 subjects, drawing the dividing line at 10 checks or less for good adjustment gave the separation closest to 53%. This was therefore adopted as the criterion. The same criterion was used throughout the period gathering and scoring data; and at final count about 54% of my subjects had 10 check list entries or fewer and were therefore classed as well adjusted.

The data of the preliminary group are summarized in Table 2.

The formal statement of the hypothesis about adjustment was first published in the following words (Schmeidler, 1947); "Sheep who are well-adjusted will, on the average, make higher ESP scores than sheep who are not; and goats who are well-adjusted will have lower ESP scores than the other goats." Good adjustment was operationally defined as ten or fewer entries on the Munroe check list; poor adjustment was operationally defined as eleven or more entries.

The first examination of the data on ESP scores and social adjustment took the form

Table 2. Preliminary Study of ESP Scores of Sheep and Goats with Good or Poor Adjustment (Subjects Tested Spring, 1945)

| Subjects | Number of Subjects | | | | | |
| | ESP Scores in Relation to Chance Expectation | | | | | |
	Above	At	Below	Number of Runs	Deviation from Chance Expectation	Mean Hits per Run
Well adjusted (0–10 check list entries)						
Sheep	13	0	5	162	+95	5.59
Goats	4	0	11	137	−39	4.72
Poorly adjusted (11 + check list entries)						
Sheep	7	0	7	129	−26	4.80
Goats	6	1	4	99	+ 8	5.08

Table 3. Interim Summary of ESP Scores Collected to Test the Hypothesis that Well Adjusted Sheep Will Have Higher ESP Scores than Other Sheep and that Well Adjusted Goats Will Have Lower ESP Scores than other Goats (Subjects Tested Fall, 1945–1951)

Subjects	Number of Subjects ESP Scores in Relation to Chance Expectation			Number of Runs	Deviation from Chance Expectation	Mean Hits per Run
	Above	At	Below			
Well adjusted (0–10 check list entries)						
Sheep	213	27	130	3189	+610	5.19
Goats	85	13	126	1962	−312	4.84
Poorly adjusted (11 + check list entries)						
Sheep	101	16	128	2112	− 66	4.97
Goats	89	4	72	1421	+114	5.08

Number of well vs. poorly adjusted subjects scoring above vs. at or below chance:

Sheep—Chi Square = 15.77, 1 df; P .001.
Goats—Chi Square = 9.84, 1 df; P .01.

Difference between mean scores of well and poorly adjusted sheep is .22; P .001.
Difference between mean scores of well and poorly adjusted goats is .24; P .001.
Interaction between sheep-goat and adjustment by analysis of variance: F = 25.75; d.f. = 1:10000; P .001.

prescribed by the original hypothesis. The results are summarized in Table 3, and are consistent with the prediction that sheep who are adjudged well adjusted socially (that is, who were assigned 10 check list entries or fewer) will tend to have higher ESP scores than sheep who are adjudged poorly adjusted socially (that is, who were assigned 11 check list entries or more) and that goats who are adjudged well adjusted socially will tend to have lower ESP scores than goats who are adjudged poorly adjusted socially. Analysis by chi square and by t indicate that the hypothesis as it was stated has been confirmed at a high level of statistical significance.

REFERENCES

Boring, E. G. Statistical frequencies as dynamic equilibria. *Psychol. Rev.*, 1941, **48**, 279–301.

Munroe, R. L. Prediction of the adjustment and academic performance of college students by a modification of the Rorschach method. *Appl. Psychol. Monog.*, 1945, No. 7.

Schmeidler, G. R. Rorschach variables in relation to ESP scores. *Journ. Amer. Soc. psychic. Res.*, 1947, **41**, 35–64.

Schmeidler, G. R., Nelson, M. J. and Bristol, M. Freshman Rorschachs and college performance. *Genet. Psychol. Monog.*, 1959, **59**, 3–43.

Schmeidler, G. R. and McConnell, R. A. *ESP and Personality Patterns*. New Haven: Yale University Press, 1958.

Author Index